REGESTA REGUM SCOTTORUM

VOLUME II

The Acts of William I

KING OF SCOTS
1165-1214

edited by

G. W. S. BARROW

with the collaboration of

W. W. SCOTT

at the University Press
EDINBURGH

The series
REGESTA REGUM SCOTTORUM, 1153–1424
will comprise

I. ACTS OF MALCOLM IV, 1153–65
edited by G. W. S. Barrow (1960)

II. ACTS OF WILLIAM I, 1165–1214
edited by G. W. S. Barrow with the collaboration of W. W. Scott (1971)

III. ACTS OF ALEXANDER II, 1214–49
edited by Keith J. Stringer

IV. ACTS OF ALEXANDER III, THE GUARDIANS AND JOHN, 1249–1306
edited by Grant G. Simpson

V. ACTS OF ROBERT I, 1306–29
edited by Archibald A. M. Duncan

VI. ACTS OF DAVID II, 1329–71
edited by Bruce Webster

VII. ACTS OF ROBERT II, ROBERT III, AND THE DUKES OF ALBANY GOVERNORS, 1371–1424
edited by Athol L. Murray

VIII. FACSIMILES OF SCOTTISH ROYAL ACTS, 1153–1424

VOLUME II

EDINBURGH UNIVERSITY PRESS
22 George Square, Edinburgh
ISBN 0 85224 142 9
North America
Aldine Publishing Company
529 South Wabash Avenue, Chicago
Library of Congress
Catalog Card Number 74–106476
Printed in Great Britain by
T. & A. Constable Ltd, Edinburgh

PREFACE

As originally planned, this volume was to have been edited jointly by Mr Scott and myself. Accordingly, we set about the preliminary task of listing, identifying and locating texts, dividing our responsibility chronologically at 1189. We had progressed far enough by 1958 to produce a *Handlist* of the acts, published by the *Regesta* editorial committee in cyclostyled typescript. As we had hoped and intended that it should, publication of the *Handlist* prompted a number of knowledgeable and interested scholars to provide us with information about acts we had overlooked, suggest more precise dating, and correct many of our mistakes. Unfortunately, pressure of work forced Mr Scott in 1965 to give up his position as joint editor. He has, however, continued to take an active interest in the progress of the volume. Besides providing many notes on individual charters, witnesses etc., he has been largely responsible for establishing the chronology of the acts from *c.*1190 to 1214 and for compiling the index of personal names. Moreover, it was owing to his initiative that the important information from Dutch sources relating to Florence of Holland could be incorporated in the introduction and critical apparatus. A special interest in the work from its earliest stages was taken by the late James A. Wright, of Tayport, whose death in 1966 deprived Scottish medieval studies of a scholar whose learning was as profound as it was unassuming. Among many notes and communications sent to me by Mr Wright, mention must be made of an invaluable list of royal clerks and chaplains prepared in 1962. To these two scholars I owe a very special debt of gratitude.

The fact that the whole work of editing has been carried out with the support of the *Regesta* Committee has immensely lightened the editor's labours. The location of texts in private or out-of-the-way archives, the visiting of these archives for description and measurement of documents and the all-important building up of a collection of photographs of originals and other sources was undertaken by the Committee as a whole. While acknowledging the value of this collective support, I am none the less happy to thank the other individual members of the Committee, namely Dr Grant Simpson, Dr Athol Murray, Professor A. A. M. Duncan and Mr Bruce Webster, for the help they have unstintingly afforded over a long period and in a variety of ways. I wish also to record my sincerest gratitude to a number of other scholars: to Mr and Mrs R. W. Munro, who by their unfailing hospitality no less than by their wide-ranging knowledge of Scottish historical matters made many of my numerous visits to the libraries and archives in Edinburgh a source both of pleasure and enlightenment; and, for all their ready assistance and co-operation, to Mrs Marjorie Anderson, Mr B. W. Beckingsale, Mrs Daphne Brooke, Mr

Ronald Cant, Dr Ian Cowan, Professor H. A. Cronne, Professor R. H. C. Davis, Dr John Durkan, Dr Alan Harding, the late Mr W. Percy Hedley, the late Dr Angus Macdonald, Professor Kathleen Major, Dr T. I. Rae, Professor G. O. Sayles, Mr Norman Shead, Professor Peter Stein, Mr Keith Stringer, Mr Ian Stewart, Professor E. L. G. Stones, Mr John Todd and Dr D. E. R. Watt.

I am indebted to many owners of manuscripts for granting me and other members of the *Regesta* Committee access to their muniments and permission to publish them. In particular, I would like to thank the Town Clerks of Aberdeen, Ayr, Inverness, Kirkintilloch, Perth and Rutherglen, the City Archivists of Edinburgh and Glasgow and the County Archivist of Northumberland, as well as the corporations of these burghs and the Northumberland County Council. Crown copyright material in the Scottish Record Office and the Public Record Office is published by permission of the Controller of H. M. Stationery Office. The staffs of these two record offices have rendered much courteous assistance, as have also the staffs of the British Museum, the National Library of Scotland, the university libraries of Aberdeen, Edinburgh and Glasgow, Lincolns Inn Library, the Bodleian Library, the Lincolnshire Archives Committee, the Spalding Gentlemen's Society and the library of the Institute of Historical Research, London. I am grateful to the Deans and Chapters of Carlisle, Durham, Lincoln and Westminster and to their archivists, and to the Roman Catholic Hierarchy in Scotland and the archivist of the Blairs Archives for access to, and leave to publish, manuscript material in their possession. As was true when I collected material for Volume I, I have found private owners of original charters and manuscript copies extremely kind and helpful. Many of these private collections, especially in Scotland, are now in public custody; but a sizeable proportion still remain in private hands, often in the possession of a direct descendant of the original beneficiary. I gladly acknowledge my thanks to the Earl of Ancaster, the Duke of Atholl, Mr J. C. Blackett-Ord, the Duke of Buccleuch and Queensberry, the Marquis of Bute, Messrs Condie, Mackenzie and Company, the Earl of Dalhousie, Sir Alec Douglas-Home, Messrs Dundas and Wilson, W.S., the Countess of Erroll, Captain R. Fergusson-Cuninghame of Caprington, the Earl of Haddington, Mr George Howard, Mr William Mackay junior, the Duke of Montrose, the Earl of Moray, the Earl of Northesk, Messrs Strathern and Blair, W.S., the Earl of Strathmore and Kinghorne, the Countess of Sutherland, Brigadier Alan Swinton of Kimmerghame and the late Marquis of Tweeddale for giving access to the muniments in their possession or custody, and for granting permission to publish documents required for this edition.

The publication of this volume was made possible by an extremely generous grant from the Carnegie Trust for the Universities of Scotland, who have also provided financial assistance without which the *Regesta* Committee could not have undertaken their preliminary programme of visits, photography etc. The British Academy has also provided welcome financial support. The University of Newcastle upon Tyne kindly granted me a term's leave of absence in 1966, which allowed me to make a start on the final phase of turning a somewhat shapeless mass of material into a book. Finally, I should like to thank Miss Joyce Perkins for the meticulous care with which she typed the summaries and comments for each document, the whole of the introduction, and much of the index.

G.W.S.B.
Newcastle upon Tyne, 1970.

CONTENTS

LIST OF ABBREVIATIONS

Abbreviations conform to the *List of Abbreviated Titles of the Printed Sources of Scottish History to* 1560, published as a supplement to the *Scottish Historical Review* of October, 1963. Abbreviations not included in that list conform in general to the principles upon which the list was constructed, explained, ibid., pp. iii-v. The adoption of this system of abbreviation means that many forms of abbreviation used in *RRS*, i, have been changed.

Abbreviatio Placitorum *Placitorum in domo capitulari Westmonasteriensi asservatorum abbreviatio, temporibus regum Ric. I, Johann., Henr. III, Edw. I, Edw. II* (Rec. Comm., 1811).

Aberdeen-Banff Coll. *Collections for a History of the Shires of Aberdeen and Banff* (Spalding Club, 1843).

Aberdeen-Banff Illustrations *Illustrations of the Topography and Antiquities of the Shires of Aberdeen and Banff* (Spalding Club, 1847–69).

Aberdeen Burgh Chrs. *Charters and other Writs illustrating the History of the Royal Burgh of Aberdeen*, ed. P. J. Anderson (Aberdeen, 1890).

Aberdeen Registrum *Registrum Episcopatus Aberdonensis* (Spalding and Maitland Clubs, 1845).

Anderson, *Diplomata* *Selectus Diplomatum et Numismatum Scotiae Thesaurus* (Half title: *Diplomata Scotiae*), ed. J. Anderson (Edinburgh, 1739).

Anderson, *Early Sources* *Early Sources of Scottish History*, 500–1286, ed. A. O. Anderson (Edinburgh, 1922).

Anderson, *Oliphants* J. Anderson, *The Oliphants in Scotland* (Edinburgh, 1879).

Anderson, *Scottish Annals* *Scottish Annals from English Chroniclers*, 500–1286, ed. A. O. Anderson (London, 1908).

APS *The Acts of the Parliaments of Scotland*, edd. T. Thomson and C. Innes (Edinburgh, 1814–75).

Arbroath Liber *Liber S. Thome de Aberbrothoc* (Bannatyne Club, 1848–56).

Arch. Aeliana *Archaeologia Aeliana, or Miscellaneous Tracts, relating to Antiquity*, published by the Society of Antiquaries of Newcastle upon Tyne (1822–).

Ayr Burgh Chrs. *Charters of the Royal Burgh of Ayr* (Archaeological and Historical Collections relating / to Ayrshire and Galloway / to the counties of Ayr and Wigton, 1883).

Balmerino Liber *Liber S. Marie de Balmorinach* (Abbotsford Club, 1841).

Beauly Chrs. *The Charters of the Priory of Beauly* (ed. E. Chisholm Batten, Grampian Club, 1877).

Berwickshire Hist. *History of the Berwickshire Naturalists' Club* (1831–).

BHRS Bedfordshire Historical Record Society (Publications).

Bishop, *Scriptores Regis* T. A. M. Bishop, *Scriptores Regis. Facsimiles to identify and illustrate the hands of royal scribes in original charters of Henry I, Stephen and Henry II* (Oxford, 1961).

BM British Museum.

Brechin Registrum *Registrum Episcopatus Brechinensis* (Bannatyne Club, 1856).

Brinkburn Chartulary *The Chartulary of Brinkburn Priory*, ed. W. Page (Surtees Soc., vol. xc, 1893).

Burns, *Coinage of Scotland* E. Burns, *The Coinage of Scotland* (3 vols., Edinburgh, 1887).

Cal. Chart. *Calendar of the Charter Rolls preserved in the Public Record Office* (6 vols., 1903–27).

Cal. Docs. Scot. *Calendar of Documents relating to Scotland*, ed. J. Bain (4 vols., Edinburgh, 1881–8).

Cal. Papal Letters *Calendar of entries in the Papal Registers relating to Great Britain and Ireland: Papal Letters*, edd. W. H. Bliss and others (London, 1893–).

Cal. Pat. R. *Calendar of the Patent Rolls preserved in the Public Record Office. Henry III* (6 vols., 1901–13).

Cambuskenneth Registrum *Registrum Monasterii S. Marie de Cambuskenneth* (ed. W. Fraser, Grampian Club, 1872).

Chron. Bower *Joannis de Fordun Scotichronicon cum Supplementis et Continuatione Walteri Boweri*, ed. W. Goodall (2 vols., Edinburgh, 1759).

Chron. Fantosme (Becker) 'La Guerre d'Escoce par Jordan Fantosme', ed. P. A. Becker, *Zeitschrift für Romanische Philologie*, lxiv (1944), 478–556.

Chron. Fantosme (Michel) *Chronicle of the War between the English and the Scots in* 1173 *and* 1174, by Jordan Fantosme, ed. Francisque Michel (Surtees Society, xi, 1840).

Chron. Fordun *Johannis de Fordun, Chronica Gentis Scotorum*, ed. W. F. Skene (Historians of Scotland, vols. i and iv, Edinburgh, 1871–2).

Chron. Holyrood *A Scottish Chronicle known as the Chronicle of Holyrood*, ed. M. O. Anderson (SHS, 1938).

Chron. Howden *Chronica Magistri Rogeri de Houedene*, ed. W. Stubbs (Rolls Series, 4 vols., 1868–71).

Chron. Lanercost *Chronicon de Lanercost*, ed. J. Stevenson (Maitland Club, 1839).

Chron. Melrose *The Chronicle of Melrose* (Facsimile Edition), edd. A. O. and M. O. Anderson, with an index by W. C. Dickinson (London, 1936).

Chron. Picts-Scots *Chronicles of the Picts; Chronicles of the Scots*, ed. W. F. Skene (Edinburgh, 1867).

Chron. Stephen *Chronicles of the reigns of Stephen, Henry II and Richard I*, ed. R. Howlett (Rolls Series, 4 vols., 1884–9).

Chron. Wyntoun (Laing) Androw of Wyntoun, *The Orygynale Cronykil of Scotland*, ed. D. Laing (Historians of Scotland, vols. ii, iii and ix, Edinburgh, 1872–9).

Coldstream Chartulary *Chartulary of the Cistercian Priory of Coldstream* (ed. C. Rogers, Grampian Club, 1879).

Coupar Angus Chrs. *Charters of the Abbey of Coupar Angus*, ed. D. E. Easson (SHS, 2 vols., 1947).

Coupar Angus Rental *Rental Book of the Cistercian Abbey of Cupar Angus* (ed. C. Rogers, Grampian Club, 2 vols., 1879–80).

CWAAS (Trans.) Cumberland and Westmorland Antiquarian and Archaeological Society (*Transactions*).

D. & C. Dean and Chapter.

Davis G. R. C. Davis, *Medieval Cartularies of Great Britain* (London, 1958).

Delisle-Berger, *Recueil* *Recueil des actes de Henri II . . . concernant les provinces françaises et les affaires de France*, edd. L. Delisle and E. Berger (3 vols., 1916–1927).

Dowden, *Bishops* J. Dowden, *The Bishops of Scotland* (Glasgow, 1912).

Dryburgh Liber *Liber S. Marie de Dryburgh* (Bannatyne Club, 1847).

Dugdale, *Mon. Angl.* *Monasticon Anglicanum*, etc., edd. R. Dodsworth and W. Dugdale (Vol. i, 1655; vol. ii, 1661; vol. iii, 1673).

Dugdale, *Mon. Angl.* (New) *Monasticon Anglicanum*, etc. A new edition, by J. Caley, H. Ellis and B. Bandinel (6 vols., 1817–18).

Dumfriesshire Trans. *Transactions of the Dumfriesshire and Galloway Natural History and Antiquarian Society* (1862–).

Dunbar, *Scot. Kings* A. H. Dunbar, *Scottish Kings; a revised chronology of Scottish History*, 1005–1625 (2nd edn, Edinburgh, 1906).

Dunfermline Court Book *Regality of Dunfermline Court Book*, 1531–1538, edd. J.M. Webster and A.A.M. Duncan (Dunfermline, 1953).

Dunfermline Registrum. *Registrum de Dunfermelyn* (Bannatyne Club, 1842).

East Lothian Trans. *Transactions of the East Lothian Antiquarian and Field Naturalists' Society* (1924–).

EHR *English Historical Review.*

EPNS English Place-Name Society.

ESC See Lawrie, *Charters.*

Exch. Rolls *The Exchequer Rolls of Scotland*, edd. J. Stuart and G. Burnett (Edinburgh, 1878–1908).

EYC *Early Yorkshire Charters*, vols. i-iii, ed. W. Farrer (1914–16, with index by C.T. and E.M. Clay, 1942); vols. iv-xii, ed. C.T. Clay (1935–65).

Eyton, *Itinerary* R.W. Eyton, *Court, Household and Itinerary of King Henry II*, etc. (London, 1878).

Family of Seton *A History of the Family of Seton during eight centuries*, ed. G. Seton (Edinburgh, 1896).

Family of Skene *Memorials of the Family of Skene of Skene* (New Spalding Club, 1887).

Ferrerius, *Historia* *Ferrerii Historia Abbatum de Kynlos* (Bannatyne Club, 1839).

Fife Court Book *The Sheriff Court Book of Fife*, 1515–22, ed. W.C. Dickinson (SHS, 1928).

Foedera *Foedera, Conventiones, Litterae et Cuiuscunque Generis Acta Publica*, ed. T. Rymer (Rec. Comm. edn, London, 1816–69).

Fraser, *Annandale* W. Fraser, *The Annandale Family Book* (Edinburgh, 1894).

Fraser, *Buccleuch* W. Fraser, *The Scots of Buccleuch* (Edinburgh, 1878).

Fraser, *Carlaverock* W. Fraser, *The Book of Carlaverock* (Edinburgh, 1873).

Fraser, *Douglas* W. Fraser, *The Douglas Book* (Edinburgh, 1885).

Fraser Facsimiles *Facsimiles of Scottish Charters and Letters prepared by Sir William Fraser* (Edinburgh, 1903).

Fraser, *Grant* W. Fraser, *The Chiefs of Grant* (Edinburgh, 1883).

Fraser, *Melville* W. Fraser, *The Melvilles earls of Melville and the Leslies earls of Leven* (Edinburgh, 1890).

Fraser, *Menteith* W. Fraser, *The Red Book of Menteith* (Edinburgh, 1880).

Fraser, *Pollok* W. Fraser, *Memoirs of the Maxwells of Pollok* (Edinburgh, 1863).

Fraser, *Pollok Cartulary* W. Fraser, *The Cartulary of Pollok-Maxwell* (Edinburgh, 1875).

Fraser, *Southesk* W. Fraser, *History of the Carnegies, earls of Southesk, and of their kindred* (Edinburgh, 1867).

Fraser, *Sutherland* W. Fraser, *The Sutherland Book* (Edinburgh, 1892).

Fraser, *Wemyss* W. Fraser, *Memorials of the Family of Wemyss of Wemyss* (Edinburgh 1888).

Gesta Henrici *Gesta Regis Henrici Secundi Benedicti Abbatis*, ed. W. Stubbs (Rolls Series, 2 vols., 1867).

Glasgow Registrum *Registrum Episcopatus Glasguensis* (Bannatyne and Maitland Clubs, 1843).

Guisborough Cartularium *Cartularium Prioratus de Gyseburne*, etc., ed. W. Brown (Surtees Soc., 2 vols., 1889, 1894).

Hailes, *Annals* Sir David Dalrymple, Lord Hailes, *Annals of Scotland from the accession of Malcolm III to the accession of the house of Stewart* (3rd edn, Edinburgh, 1819).

Harl. Harleian, Harley.

Hawick Trans. *Transactions of the Hawick Archaeological Society* (1863–).

HMC Royal Commission on Historical Manuscripts (Reports).

Holm Cultram Recs. *The register and records of Holm Cultram*, edd. F. Grainger and W. G. Collingwood (CWAAS Record Series, 1929).

Holyrood Liber *Liber Cartarum Sancte Crucis* (Bannatyne Club, 1840).

Inchaffray Chrs. *Charters, Bulls and other documents relating to the Abbey of Inchaffray* (SHS, 1908).

Inchaffray Liber *Liber Insule Missarum* (Bannatyne Club, 1847).

Inchcolm Chrs. *Charters of the Abbey of Inchcolm*, edd. D. E. Easson and A. Macdonald (SHS, 1938).

Instrumenta Publica *Instrumenta Publica sive processus super fidelitatibus et homagiis Scotorum Domino Regi Angliae factis*, 1291–96 (Bannatyne Club, 1834).

Itinerary of King John *Itinerary of King John &c.*, in *Rotuli Litterarum Patentium*, i, pt. I, ed. T. D. Hardy (Rec. Com., 1835), following Introduction.

Jaffé, *Reg. Pont. Rom.* *Regesta Pontificum Romanorum ab condita ecclesia ad annum post Christum natum MCXCVIII*, ed. P. Jaffé, 2nd edn by W. Wattenbach, S. Loewenfeld, F. Kaltenbrunner and P. Ewald (2 vols., Leipzig, 1885–8).

Kelso Liber *Liber S. Marie de Calchou* (Bannatyne Club, 1846).

Kennett, *Parochial Antiquities* W. Kennett, *Parochial antiquities attempted in the history of Ambrosden, Burcester, etc.* New edn, by B. Bandinel (2 vols., Oxford, 1818).

Kinloss Recs. *Records of the Monastery of Kinloss*, ed. J. Stuart (Society of Antiquaries of Scotland, 1872).

Laing Chrs. *Calendar of the Laing Charters*, ed. J. Anderson (Edinburgh, 1899).

Laing, *Seals*, i H. Laing, *Descriptive Catalogue of impressions from ancient Scottish Seals* (Bannatyne and Maitland Clubs, 1850).

Laing, *Seals*, ii H. Laing, *Supplemental Descriptive Catalogue of Ancient Scottish Seals* (Edinburgh, 1866).

Landon, *Itinerary* *The Itinerary of King Richard I* (Pipe Roll Soc., New Ser., xiii, 1935).

Lawrie, *Annals* *Annals of the reigns of Malcolm and William, kings of Scotland*, ed. A. C. Lawrie (Glasgow, 1910).

Lawrie, *Charters* *Early Scottish Charters prior to* 1153, ed. A. C. Lawrie (Glasgow, 1905). (Also abbreviated to *ESC.*)

Lennox Cartularium *Cartularium Comitatus de Levenax* (Maitland Club, 1833).

Lindores Chartulary *Chartulary of the Abbey of Lindores*, ed. J. Dowden (SHS, 1903).

Macfarlane, *Genealogical Coll.* *Genealogical Collections concerning families in Scotland, made by Walter Macfarlane* (SHS, 1900).

Macfarlane, *Geographical Coll.* *Geographical Collections relating to Scotland, made by Walter Macfarlane* (SHS, 1906–8).

Mackenzie, *Writers* G. Mackenzie, *The Lives and Characters of the most eminent Writers of the Scots Nation* (Edinburgh, 1708–22).

Macphail, *Pluscardyn* S. R. Macphail, *History of the Religious House of Pluscardyn* (Edinburgh, 1881).

May Recs. *Records of the Priory of the Isle of May*, ed. J. Stuart (Society of Antiquaries of Scotland, 1868).

Melrose Liber *Liber S. Marie de Melros* (Bannatyne Club, 1837).

MGH *Monumenta Germaniae Historica.*

Midlothian Chrs. *Charters of the Hospital of Soltre, of Trinity College, Edinburgh, and other Collegiate Churches in Midlothian* (Bannatyne Club, 1861).

Migne, *PL* *Patrologiae Cursus Completus, Series Latina*, ed. J.-P. Migne (Paris, 1844–64).

MLWL *Revised Medieval Latin Word-List from British and Irish Sources*, prepared by R. E. Latham (British Academy, 1965).

Moray Registrum *Registrum Episcopatus Moraviensis* (Bannatyne Club, 1837).

Morton Registrum *Registrum Honoris de Morton* (Bannatyne Club, 1853).

Nat. MSS. Scot. *Facsimiles of the National Manuscripts of Scotland* (London, 1867–71).

Newbattle Registrum *Registrum S. Marie de Neubotle* (Bannatyne Club, 1849).

Newminster Chartularium *Chartularium abbathiae de Novo Monasterio, etc.*, ed. J. T. Fowler (Surtees Soc., vol. lxvi, 1878).

NLS National Library of Scotland.

North Berwick Carte *Carte Monialium de Northberwic* (Bannatyne Club, 1847).

OPS *Origines Parochiales Scotiae* (Bannatyne Club, 1851–5).

Paisley Registrum *Registrum Monasterii de Passelet* (Maitland Club, 1832; New Club, 1877).

Palgrave, *Docs. Hist. Scot.* *Documents and Records illustrating the History of Scotland*, ed. F. Palgrave (London, 1837).

Panmure Registrum *Registrum de Panmure*, ed. J. Stuart (Edinburgh, 1874).

Percy Chartulary *The Percy Chartulary*, ed. M. T. Martin (Surtees Soc., vol. cxvii, 1911).

Pitfirrane Writs *Inventory of Pitfirrane Writs* 1230–1794, ed. W. Angus (Scottish Record Society, 1932).

PRO Public Record Office, London.

PSAS *Proceedings of the Society of Antiquaries of Scotland* (1851–).

Raine, *North Durham* Appendix to J. Raine, *The History and Antiquities of North Durham* (London, 1852).

RAL *Registrum Antiquissimum of the Cathedral Church of Lincoln*, vols. i-iii, ed. C. W. Foster; vol. iv, edd. C. W. Foster and Kathleen Major; vols. v-ix, ed. K. Major (Lincoln Record Society, 1931–68).

Rec. Com. Record Commission (1800–31).

Reg. Brieves *The Register of Brieves*, ed. Lord Cooper (Stair Society, 1946).

Retours *Inquisitionum ad capellam domini regis retornatarum . . . abbreviatio* (Rec. Com., 3 vols., 1811–16).

RMS *Registrum Magni Sigilli Regum Scotorum*, edd. J. M. Thomson and others (Edinburgh, 9 vols., 1882–97 and 1912).

Rot. Chart. *Rotuli Chartarum in Turri Londinensi asservati* (Rec. Com., 1 volume only published, 1837).

Rot. Litt. Claus. *Rotuli Litterarum Clausarum in turri Londinensi asservati*, ed. T. D. Hardy (Record Commission, 2 vols., 1833–4).

Rot. Scot. *Rotuli Scotiae in Turri Londinensi et in Domo Capitulari Westmonasteriensi asservati*, edd. D. Macpherson and others (Rec. Com., 2 vols., 1814–19).

RRAN *Regesta Regum Anglo-Normannorum*, vol. i, ed. H. W. C. Davis, with the assistance of R. J. Whitwell (1913); vol. ii, edd. C. Johnson and H. A. Cronne (1956); vol. iii, edd. H. A. Cronne and R. H. C. Davis (1968); vol. iv, edd. Cronne and Davis (1969).

RRS *Regesta Regum Scottorum* (vol. i, *Acts of Malcolm IV King of Scots* 1153–65, ed. G. W. S. Barrow, Edinburgh, 1960).

St Andrews Liber *Liber Cartarum Prioratus S. Andree in Scotia* (Bannatyne Club, 1841).

St Bees Register *The Register of the Priory of St Bees*, ed. J. Wilson (Surtees Society, vol. cxxvi, 1915).

Scone Liber *Liber Ecclesie de Scon* (Bannatyne and Maitland Clubs, 1843).

Scot. Stud. *Scottish Studies* (1957–).

SHR *Scottish Historical Review*.

SHS Scottish History Society.

SHS Misc. *The Miscellany of the Scottish History Society* (SHS, 1893–).

SP *The Scots Peerage*, ed. J. Balfour Paul (Edinburgh, 1904–14).

Spalding Misc. *Miscellany of the Spalding Club* (Spalding Club, 1841–52).

SRO Scottish Record Office, Edinburgh.

Stapleton, *Rot. Scacc. Norm.* *Magni Rotuli Scaccarii Normanniae sub regibus Angliae*, ed. T. Stapleton (Society of Antiquaries, 2 vols., 1840–4).

Stevenson, *Documents* *Documents illustrative of the History of Scotland*, 1286–1306, ed. J. Stevenson (Edinburgh, 1870).

Stevenson, *Illustrations* *Illustrations of Scottish History from the Twelfth to the Sixteenth Century*, ed. J. Stevenson (Maitland Club, 1834).

Stevenson, *Wallace Docs.* *Documents illustrative of Sir William Wallace, his Life and Times*, ed. J. Stevenson (Maitland Club, 1841).

Stevenson and Wood, *Seals* J. H. Stevenson and M. Wood, *Scottish Heraldic Seals* (Glasgow, 1940).

Stewart, *Scottish Coinage* I. H. Stewart, *The Scottish Coinage* (2nd edn, 1969).

Stones, *Documents* *Anglo-Scottish Relations, 1174–1328: some selected documents*, ed. E. L. G. Stones (1965).

TRHS *Transactions of the Royal Historical Society.*

VCH *Victoria County History.*

Watson, *CPNS* *The History of the Celtic Place-Names of Scotland* (Edinburgh, 1926).

Wetherhal Register *The Register of the Priory of Wetherhal* (ed. J. Prescott, 1897).

Yester Writs *Calendar of Writs preserved at Yester House, 1166–1503*, edd. C. C. H. Harvey and J. Macleod (Scottish Record Society, 1930).

INTRODUCTION

I. THE LIFE AND REIGN OF WILLIAM I

Unlike his elder brother Malcolm IV, William I—William the Lion as he is usually known—is one of the best remembered kings of Scotland. He is renowned for his military exploits, although these were sometimes unsuccessful and on one occasion disastrous; for his law making, although its scope and extent are much less clearly defined than would be gathered from the confident 'Assise Regis Willelmi' published in the *Acts of the Parliaments of Scotland*; for his founding and patronage of burghs and merchants; for his noble red sandstone abbey of Arbroath, where he lies buried; finally for his sheer endurance, for he was born a few years after the death of Henry I of England and died within two years of the accession of Henry III. So much more is, or can be, known about the detailed course of his reign than we know about his brother's that it would be impossible as well as inappropriate to give an adequate account in the introduction to an edition of his written acts. What follows is therefore a brief notice of the main features of his life and of the political events of his reign, with less emphasis on its better-known aspects such as relations with the Church and with the English crown, and more emphasis on relatively less well known domestic affairs, such as the king's struggle to subdue and control Galloway, the north-western highlands and the far north, his feudal settlement of the eastern lowlands, and his founding or encouragement of urban communities. In the two following sections of the introduction an account will be given of some aspects of Scottish royal government under King William, and the diplomatic—the external appearance and internal structure—of his written acts will be studied and analysed.

William I was born probably in 1143, the second son of Henry earl of Northumberland and Ada de Warenne.[1] One of his earliest appearances in surviving record is as a witness, with his elder brother, to a charter of Bernard de Balliol granting the Tweed fishing of Woodhornstell (on the Northumberland side of the river) to Kelso Abbey.[2] Its date may be 1152–3, after the death of Earl Henry; but already, evidently before his father's death, William had issued a charter of his own (no. 1) in favour of Nostell Priory in the West Riding of Yorkshire (1147–50). Soon after Earl Henry's death in the summer of 1152, King David I made his second grandson earl of Northumberland in succession to his father.[3] William retained this dignity for the next four years, when Henry II of England, going back on his promise to King David in 1149, deprived him of it. It is arguable that this was one of the biggest mistakes that Henry II ever made, for William never outgrew his bitter resentment at being ejected from his patrimony, and Anglo-Scottish relations were bedevilled by the question of Northumberland—or 'the

Northern Counties'—for the next eighty years. It is true that soon after his deprivation William received from King Henry the lordship of Tynedale, a very large tract of upper Northumberland, including the valleys of both North and South Tyne.[4] His brother Malcolm IV probably made some provision for him also within the Scottish kingdom (no.5). All this was never to console William for his loss of the earldom. William seems to have accompanied his brother on Henry II's expedition to Toulouse in 1159,[5] and very probably he took part in Malcolm's Galloway campaigns of the following year. He is named as witness to some thirteen surviving acts of King Malcolm, evenly spaced throughout the twelve years of the reign. It seems clear that he was on hand when, on 9 December, 1165, the death of his invalid brother, surely long expected, occurred at Jedburgh. Malcolm was buried beside his ancestors at Dunfermline, and William's inauguration at Scone followed soon afterwards, on Christmas Eve, 1165. Thus the first main characteristic of William's life to strike us is that he entered upon public affairs at an early age, and gained direct control of the government of Scotland when he was 22. He died in December, 1214, in his 72nd year, having ruled indefatigably, although with much illness in his old age, for only a few days less than forty-nine years. His was by far the longest active reign of any pre-Union Scottish sovereign, for unlike David II or James VI he knew no minority. Moreover, William I lived longer than any of the Capetians or Angevins who were his contemporaries, so long indeed that King John's chancery, not greatly given to rhetorical embellishment, once styled William 'venerable'.[6]

This long reign may be conveniently divided into four parts of rather unequal length, 1165–74, 1174–89, 1189–1209 and 1209–14. For his first seven years William enjoyed the peace at home and with the king of England which his brother's strenuous efforts—and weakness—had bequeathed to him. He tried, almost at once, to regain his lost earldom of Northumberland (probably with Cumberland and North Westmorland also). He crossed to Normandy either in the spring or summer of 1166, meeting Henry II at Le Mont St Michel in August or September and evidently requesting their restoration.[7] The English king's refusal led to William's diplomatic approach to Louis VII at Chartres in July, 1168.[8] This obscure event may have led to an agreement foreshadowing the later alliance of 1173–4, but our evidence is too slight to tell us precisely what was involved. Whatever it was, it could not seriously have worsened relations between William and Henry II, since the king of Scots was at the English court at Windsor in the spring of 1170, and in June of that year attended the coronation of Henry the 'Young King', to whom William did homage on 15 June.[9] During these years 1165–71 William not only found time to cross to the continent, make at least two sojourns at the English court, and visit some at least of the estates which comprised the Honour of Huntingdon (restored to the Scottish king in 1157). The record of his written acts shews that in addition to these visits he spent time at Perth, Stirling and Edinburgh and at a good many places in Angus, Fife, Lothian, Teviotdale and Tweeddale, that he paid at least one visit to the south-west, including

Lanark and Lochmaben, and at least one visit to Moray. Indeed, the pattern of royal journeying which becomes more clearly discernible later in the reign already seems to shew itself in these first few years and may well have gone back into Malcolm IV's time or even David I's. According to this pattern, most of the king's time when in Scotland was passed in Fife, Stirling, the lower Tay valley, Angus and Mearns, Lothian, Tweeddale and Teviotdale. The king's hunting, when he was south of the Forth, was based chiefly on Selkirk and Traquair (with early sojourns at St Mary's Loch). Benorth Forth the king seems to have hunted most often from Clunie in Stormont and his castles of Alyth and Kincardine. Less frequent visits were paid to Berwick upon Tweed in the east, to Lanark and (after *c.* 1185) Dumfries in the west, and to Aberdeen and the Moray Firth burghs, notably Elgin, in the north. Where King William's itinerary differs most markedly from what we know of his brother's or grandfather's is in the shift in the centre of gravity from Edinburgh and the Border valleys to Perth and Forfar: for William, Gowrie, Angus and Mearns seem almost to have formed a miniature kingdom within a kingdom.

Admittedly the chance survival of recorded acts is part of the explanation of this north-eastern emphasis in royal activity, but it can hardly explain it altogether. The king travelled partly to demonstrate his authority and power, partly to use up physical resources from the royal demesne. The conspicuous infrequency of his presence north of the Moray Firth and in Buchan, Mar, Atholl, Strathearn, Menteith, Lennox and Argyll was due to the lack of royal demesne in those regions. But it is noteworthy that no surviving act of King William was issued west of the line Rutherglen-Lanark-Dumfries, despite the importance of King's Kyle and the lower Clyde.

The tide of foreign, chiefly 'Anglo-Norman', influence was still flowing strongly in William I's Scotland. The Frankish character of the king himself, son of Ada de Warenne, grandson of Maud de Senlis, descended from the kings of France and dukes of Normandy, cannot be denied. It was of William and Malcolm that the anonymous Barnwell writer remarked in the early thirteenth century—with palpable exaggeration, yet with undoubted truth—'the modern kings of Scotland count themselves as Frenchmen in race, manners, language and culture; they keep only Frenchmen in their household and following and have reduced the Scots to utter servitude'.[10] The pattern of council and counsel already visible under Malcolm IV, with its powerful 'Anglo-Norman' element and its appreciably smaller native element, was continued at the court of the young William and was not much modified for the rest of his reign. The king's mother Countess Ada lived till 1178,[11] staying mostly at Crail and Haddington, her two dower towns. It is not possible to say what influence she exercised over her son, but there may be truth in the later story that she had no use for Malcolm's yearning for celibacy and a life of religious devotion.[12] At all events, William shewed no such tendencies in the earlier years of his life; it was not until he was approaching his deathbed that he began to be revered as a devout or even saintly figure.

William retained Malcolm's chancellor, Nicholas of Roxburgh, until his death in 1171, and even then did not appoint a 'new' man but re-appointed Walter de Bidun who had been chancellor under David I and (to 1162) under Malcolm IV.[13] Other counsellors of long experience included Andrew bishop of Caithness, a native Scotsman who was to live until 1184 and was regularly at court; David Olifard, who was King David's godson and served as justiciar in the first years of the reign; the Steward Walter son of Alan; the Constable Richard de Moreville; and four major barons who are known to have acted as justices in this early period, Geoffrey I de Melville, Robert Avenel, Richard Cumin and Robert de Quinci. Just as King Malcolm had been closely attended by only two of the native earls, Duncan II of Fife and Cospatric III of Dunbar, so William was closely attended by the same Earl Duncan II (who must surely have been an old man when he died in 1204) and by Earl Waltheof, Cospatric's son. Most of this small group had served Malcolm IV, but William evidently brought in a few younger men of his own choice—Bernard, son of Brien (of whose origins nothing is known), Philip de Valognes (appointed chamberlain early in the reign), and the brothers Robert and Walter of Berkeley, an important but mysterious pair who may have belonged to a group of lords and knights from West Wessex (especially Somerset), associated with the Flemish feudatory Robert of Bampton and with the Lovels of Castle Cary.[14] Both brothers were given good marriages in Scotland, Robert to Cecily daughter of Liulf lord of Maxton (no.342) and Walter to a lady who seems to have been the heiress of, among other lands, Ardoyne in Aberdeenshire (no.344). Walter of Berkeley succeeded Philip de Valognes as chamberlain and held office till his death about 1193, when Philip resumed the office and held it until his death in 1215.[15]

Apart from Bishop Andrew, the king's constant ecclesiastical counsellors in the early part of the reign numbered only four or five, including three bishops whose careers had begun in the royal household: Richard of St Andrews, consecrated in 1165, Ingram of Glasgow (1164–74), whom Jordan Fantôme called 'the best of William's clergy',[16] and Richard of Dunkeld (1170–8). A fourth ecclesiastic who was frequently at court was the obviously influential archdeacon of St Andrews, Matthew, who belonged to a family which had included Robert, bishop of St Andrews (died 1159) and which still included Bishop Robert's nephew, Master John 'the Scot' (who was also Archdeacon Matthew's nephew), the dean of Christianity of Lothian, Aiulf, and various laymen of less individual importance, among them Matthew's brother Odo, steward of the cathedral priory and ancestor of the Kinninmonths of that ilk.[17] Archdeacon Matthew, not a true *curialis*, was in 1172 given the important see of Aberdeen, a short while after the other important northern see of Moray had been given to a Cistercian monk who was also the king's kinsman, Simon de Toeni, sometime abbot of Coggeshall in Essex.[18]

The year 1173, when William was thirty, marks an obvious turning-point into the second and most humiliating period of the reign, the fifteen years of English overlordship. Disregarding the advice of his native earls of Fife and Dunbar, and apparently contrary to the judgement of Bishop Ingram of Glasgow,[19] King William allowed his passionate desire to recover the English northern counties, and the rash clamour of the younger Anglo-Norman hotheads at his court,[19a] to push him into a foolish alliance with Louis VII, Queen Eleanor and the Young King against Henry Plantagenet. The depth of William's feelings may be judged from his offer, reported by Jordan Fantôme, to have his claim settled by a trial of battle between two good knights.[20] If it had been a mistake on Henry's part to deprive William of Northumberland, it was surely an even bigger mistake for William to embark upon a war for which his resources were inadequate and in which his allies were fickle, self-seeking and above all ridiculously ill-organized. The Scots made three incursions across the Border, the first in the late summer of 1173 (when the army mustered at Caddonlee on the Tweed, as its successor was to do 123 years later)[21], the second after the winter truce, in March, 1174,[22] and the third in June and July, 1174,[23] in the course of which the king himself and many barons and knights in his immediate following were surprised and captured at Alnwick (13 July) by a resolute body of English royal officers and northern barons loyal to the elder Henry, capably led by the justiciar Ranulf de Glanvill. Even if William had escaped capture, his campaigning would hardly have brought him much gain. Since he lacked adequate siege machinery and transport, and, perhaps more important, adequate food supplies to allow his forces time to starve out the enemy garrisons, he was unable to take any of the principal strongholds of northern England, such as Carlisle, Newcastle or even Wark on Tweed, just across the Border. It is a more difficult question whether William would really have benefited if the great revolt of 1173–4 had succeeded, if the Young King had come to power in England and Normandy and the 'Angevin Empire' had been divided among his brothers and their hangers-on. It was, admittedly, the Young King's promise to restore the northern counties that finally brought the king of Scots into the war;[24] but whether, or for how long, young Henry or his successors would have kept these promises is another matter.

The complete collapse of William's policy brought about by his capture in 1174 had several serious consequences. In the first place, it led at once to the formal submission of Falaise, confirmed soon afterwards at Valognes (1 and 8 December),[25] and finally confirmed at York on 10 August, 1175, in every circumstance of publicity.[26] The submission was, and was meant to be, humiliating. King William's prolonged captivity and the terms of the 'treaty' itself point unmistakably to the deliberate humbling of the king of Scots by his masterful overlord Henry of Anjou.[27] The chronicle of Melrose Abbey, which down to the end of the reign represents a strongly 'Anglo-Norman' as opposed to a native Scottish point of view, nevertheless writes in or soon after 1189 of the 'heavy yoke of domination and servitude' laid by Henry II upon the Scottish kingdom.[28] A second consequence of William's defeat was a threat to his authority, indeed to his very survival, at home. Galloway had acknowledged Scottish royal authority in David I's time on a friendly basis; it had been brought under direct Scottish overlordship by Malcolm IV only after strenuous campaigning, and was being held within the Scottish kingdom only by means of incoming feudal settlement. As soon as William had been taken prisoner at Alnwick, the two brothers Uhtred and Gilbert, uneasily sharing the lordship of Galloway previously held by their father Fergus, threw off Scottish suzerainty and fought each other for the sole dominion over their unruly province.[29] As a first step they slew or ejected the 'French' and 'English' feudatories who had settled in Galloway in the motte-and-bailey castles which they had built beside its rivers and lochs. Then Gilbert had Uhtred murdered and set himself up as sole lord of Galloway; only the extreme barbarity with which he had treated his brother prevented him from successfully playing Henry II off against William. Even more serious than the Gallovidian problem was the beginning, soon after William's defeat, of the long series of uprisings and incursions in the north and north-west instigated and led by members of the family of MacWilliam, the descendants of David I's cousin William, son of Duncan II king of Scots. It seems clear that the head of this family, in more than one generation, put forward a claim to the Scottish Crown.[30] Their claim by descent from Malcolm Canmore is clear enough, but it would carry more weight if William son of Duncan had ever been known to press it on his own behalf. It may be that the MacWilliams inherited a second claim on the maternal side. The problem of their claim to the throne and its origins cannot be dissociated from the fact that their risings always seem to have begun in the north-western highlands, in Moray west of the Great Glen and in Ross.

A final serious consequence for King William of the submission of Falaise was the stationing of English garrisons in the castles of Berwick, Roxburgh and Edinburgh.[31] Although in theory the occupation was of the castles only, it seems clear that William regarded these three burghs, the largest and richest in his kingdom, as outwith his power for as long as they were dominated by Angevin garrisons. There is a note of annoyance in the king's charter (no.199) granting to the canons of Holyrood Abbey some demesne rents in the environs of Edinburgh 'in exchange for the alms they lost through the *castellani*' (the phrase is repeated), until the king can restore these alms; the *castellani* were of course the English garrison in Edinburgh castle. There is more than annoyance in the king's seizure into his own hands (no.288) of a hall which the monks of Melrose had built in Berwick 'at the time Geoffrey de Neville had custody of my castle of Berwick', Geoffrey and William de Neville being among the agents employed by Henry II to control Lothian and the Border between 1177 and 1189.[32] And there is further evidence of the king's frustration in the arrangements he made to provide Kelso Abbey with alternative income after its normal revenues from Roxburgh were cut off (nos.118, 317).

The decade 1178 to 1188 was possibly the busiest and most strenuous of the entire reign. By its close, or certainly by 1190, William had emerged at the height of his power, at the head of a Scottish kingdom which, though not so large in area as that over which the great King

David had ruled (or claimed to rule), was certainly more homogeneous and more firmly knit together. In these years the king of Scots still shewed stubbornness and lack of judgement, but he also shewed a capacity for dogged persistence and sheer hard work.

The first crisis of the decade arose after the death, in the summer of 1178, of Richard bishop of St Andrews.[33] The Augustinian canons of the cathedral priory, surely knowing that the king would have his own candidate for the see but no doubt inspired by the dissemination of Gregorian ideas favouring free canonical election of prelates, held an election without obtaining the king's leave and chose as Richard's successor Master John 'the Scot', nephew of the former bishop, Robert. Matthew, bishop of Aberdeen, was also an uncle of Master John, and he may well have supported this rash move, in which no doubt the prior, Walter, was especially involved. It seems less likely that the canons had the backing of the archdeacon of St Andrews, Master Walter of Roxburgh.[34] The king, who at this very time was in the midst of his plans to found a splendid abbey at Arbroath in honour of his friend Thomas Becket, was outraged by this affront to his royal dignity. He at once bestowed the see on one of his chaplains, Hugh, and had him consecrated in the cathedral church of St Andrews by certain of the bishops (unfortunately not named). Even before Hugh's consecration, an appeal was made to the papal court on Master John's behalf; and eventually, in 1180, John returned to Scotland with the pope's legate, the sub-deacon Alexius (or Alexis), who first held an enquiry which found that John was the rightful bishop and then excommunicated Hugh for contumacy. With much difficulty, Alexius convened a meeting of four bishops at Holyrood Abbey (15 June), in whose presence Master John was duly consecrated by his uncle Bishop Matthew.

This event marked a clear breach between a 'St Andrews' party, an obviously ecclesiastical group dominated by the kinsmen of old Bishop Robert, and a 'curialist' party enjoying the full support of the king. The extent to which this second party was composed of royal servants may be gauged from the fact that Bishop Hugh, himself a royal chaplain, was accused by Alexius of giving the parish kirk of Dairsie (in the collation of the bishop of St Andrews) to one Jocelin who, in return, would use his influence with the king on Hugh's behalf.[35] This Jocelin can have been no other than Master Jocelin, archdeacon of Dunkeld from *c.*1178 and a clerk in the king's household.[36] We know in any event that in 1180 Alexius excommunicated 'certain clerks of the king' for aiding and abetting Hugh,[37] while in the following year Bishop John the Scot excommunicated Richard de Moreville the Constable and Richard clerk of the provend, *familiares regis Scotiae*, as leaders of the opposing party.[38]

While Hugh went off to plead his cause at Rome, the king drove furth of Scotland not only the newly-consecrated Bishop John but also his uncle Bishop Matthew of Aberdeen and a good many of their relations, allowing their lands and goods to be plundered. The two bishops sought the protection of Henry II in Normandy; some of the canons of St Andrews seem to have taken refuge at the Augustinian priory of Guisborough in the North Riding of Yorkshire;[39] others forced to flee included Aiulf, dean of Lothian, Odo of Kinninmonth the priory's steward (who was either Bishop John's father or else yet another of his uncles), and Roger of Feddinch, a tenant of the priory—described as 'clerks, kinsmen and friends' of John the Scot.[40] The king and his brother David crossed to Normandy in the early summer of 1181 at the summons of Henry II and agreed to a compromise put forward by the English king under which John would give up St Andrews and take any other vacant Scottish see of his own choice, together with the vacant chancellorship. (This office and the see of Dunkeld were then both vacant through the death in 1178 of Walter de Bidun.) Henry's plan was vetoed by Pope Alexander III who, although he had shewn himself a consistent friend of the Scottish church and monarchy, found his patience severely tried by King William's obstinacy. Indeed, the pope went so far as to appoint Archbishop Roger de Pont l'Evêque of York legate in Scotland, assisted by Hugh du Puiset, bishop of Durham, with discretion to impose sentence of personal excommunication upon King William and an interdict upon his realm if he did not receive John the Scot in peace as bishop of St Andrews.

William landed in England on 26 July, 1181, and made a leisurely journey north by way of Canterbury and Nottingham. At Redden,[41] on the Border, he was met by the bishop of Durham and Bishop John the Scot, but the encounter produced only fresh persecutions by the king and the publication of the pope's sentence by Archbishop Roger. Only the death of the pope in August and of the archbishop in November saved the situation for the king of Scots. He sent a mission to the new pope, Lucius III, who was persuaded to lift the sentence, quash the claim of John the Scot to St Andrews, and appoint a special commission to settle the dispute. The pope also sent William the Golden Rose as a token of his reconciliation with the papacy.[42]

The settlement proposed by the commission seems sensible, but it was only put into effect partially. Both bishops were to give up St Andrews and John was to get Dunkeld, the chancellorship and financial compensation. Neither would accept these terms, and in 1183 both went to the *curia* to plead their respective cases. Each resigned St Andrews, whereupon Pope Lucius restored the see to Hugh and gave John the Scot Dunkeld and the other things suggested by the commission. In the event, the dispute outlasted the short-reigning popes Lucius III, Urban III and Gregory VIII, and it was only after Bishop Hugh had died of malaria at Rome in 1188, before he could return from a final hearing of his case by Clement III, that King William and John the Scot were at last reconciled. John, who understandably never got the chancellorship, remained in undisturbed possession of the important bishopric of Dunkeld (surviving until 1203); the king's cousin Roger ('de Beaumont'), who had for a very brief spell enjoyed the chancellorship, was elected bishop of St Andrews in February, 1189, Bishop John being present and raising no objection.[43]

We see in this tiresome story a situation highly typical of western Europe in the twelfth century: on the one hand, an ancient and distinguished church which has come under the dominance of a single ecclesiastical family, who devote themselves to its interests and are confident that they can provide it with bishops, archdeacons and lesser dignitaries, land stewards and even humble free tenants; on the other, an ambitious and energetic secular ruler, determined to vindicate his royal authority, determined to keep the leading bishopric of his realm in his own gift, so that he may bestow it upon a servant of proven trust and loyalty. The remarkable feature of this particular story is that in the end, in spite of the hostility of immensely powerful authorities, Pope Alexander III, King Henry II and the archbishop of York, it was King William and the Scottish crown that emerged victorious. Even allowing that Hugh can have had only a troubled episcopate, and that his successor was not consecrated for nine years, the fact remains that all four men who held the see of St Andrews in William I's reign—Richard, Hugh, Roger and William Malvoisin—were royal servants, appointed by the king's choice. There is no reason to doubt the sincerity of William I's devotion to Thomas Becket, but for all that Gregorian notions of church freedom made little or no headway in Scotland as long as he was king.

While the St Andrews dispute dragged its slow length along, the king was occupied with the problems of Galloway and the north. In 1179, probably in the spring or summer, he and his brother David took a large force to the Moray Firth, presumably to overawe actual or potential opposition.[44] To strengthen the scheme of defence which since King David's days had depended upon a string of royal burghs, Elgin, Forres, Auldearn and Inverness, all on the south side of the Moray Firth, William built two new castles further north and west, one at 'Etherdouer' (now Redcastle) in the west of the Black Isle, the other at Dunskeath, immediately north of the narrows at Cromarty.[45] Two years later, while the king and his brother were at Henry II's court in Normandy discussing the St Andrews dispute, 'some powerful men of the kingdom' (the words are Roger Howden's but he does not identify the men)[46] incited Donald MacWilliam to land in Scotland at the head of an armed multitude bent on plunder and slaughter. Howden alone seems to record information about this rising, and since he ignores the 1179 expedition it may be that he has misplaced under 1181 an event of 1179. In any case, there is no reason to question the truth of three essential elements in Howden's account, first, that Donald MacWilliam had often claimed the throne; secondly, that he had made a number of earlier incursions; thirdly, that he and his army, or most of it, came from outwith the Scottish kingdom, though they could clearly count on support within it.

The events of 1179 and 1181 (if they were indeed distinct) seem to have been inconclusive. The MacWilliams were still at large. In 1186 a band some sixty strong, led apparently by a son of Donald, the son of Malcolm MacHeth, named Adam or Aed (Heth), described as the king's outlaw, were pursued by Earl Malcolm of Atholl into the abbey of Coupar Angus and slain there in defiance of sanctuary.[47] This obscure event should probably be associated with the MacWilliam rebellion. Next summer (1187) the king led a large force to Moray to hunt down MacWilliam. The only contemporary sources for this expedition are the 'Chronicle of Holyrood' (then probably written at Coupar Angus), the Melrose Abbey chronicle and Roger Howden.[48] The last two agree that the king stayed in the castle of Inverness while the earls and their men explored the hinterland in search of food and plunder. The Melrose chronicle says that the earls discovered MacWilliam on a moor 'near Moray' (*prope Muref*) called Mam Garvia, where they defeated his army and slew Donald himself, giving the date as Friday, 31 July. The Holyrood-Coupar chronicle gives the same date for the battle, saying that it was fought 'in Ross' (*apud Ros*). This should mean that Mam Garvia was north, but not very far north, of the Inverness-Beauly Firths and the rivers Beauly and Orrin. Howden, who does not say where the battle was fought, gives a significantly more detailed account than the Melrose chronicle, saying that after the earls had set out to search for MacWilliam they quarrelled among themselves, those who had little love for the king hanging back and obstructing his loyal supporters. In the end, it was a body of three thousand fierce young warriors led by Roland, son of the murdered Uhtred lord of Galloway, who found and defeated the king's enemies and brought back Donald's head in triumph to the king.

The battle of Mam Garvia secured almost unbroken peace for Moray and the north-western highlands for nearly a quarter of a century. One immediate result, it seems, was that the old burgh of Auldearn, whose castle had been betrayed to the rebels by one of the king's servants, Gillecolm the marischal (no.258), was abandoned in favour of a completely new castle, with its accompanying burgh, at the mouth of the River Nairn, from which there was an easy crossing to Cromarty and the far north. A larger consequence was the vigorous development of Moray through the opening up of forest and waste, the settlement of many new incoming families, the growth and prosperity of urban communities and the rapid advance of ecclesiastical organization. The establishment within the diocese of Moray of a settled episcopal administration (and eventually of a bishop's see and cathedral church fixed permanently at Elgin) did not begin until the time of Bishop Simon de Toeni (1172–84), and made no real progress until the episcopate of Simon's successor, the king's trusted clerk Richard of Lincoln, who was consecrated bishop of Moray less than five months before Donald MacWilliam was killed.

Why Donald MacWilliam pressed a claim to the Scots throne which (as far as his father alone is concerned) had lain dormant for over sixty years is one of the larger unsolved mysteries of twelfth-century Scottish politics. One solution, perhaps no more than plausible (see the accompanying table), might run on these lines. Donald, son of William son of Duncan, was clearly not also the son of William's known wife Alice de Rumelli. In a genealogy compiled during the thirteenth century, to illustrate the descent of the lordships of Allerdale and Coupland, William son of Duncan is called 'earl of Moray'.[49] This must be regarded as a significant statement. If William had made a previous marriage with a cousin or sister of Angus earl of Moray, a claimant to the Scots throne in 1130, this would give Donald MacWilliam a mother from whom he would inherit a claim to the throne probably more cogent than that derived from his father. Moreover, Donald would have had an obvious claim to the earldom of Moray, which was held by the Crown in the time of Malcolm IV and William I and was not granted out again until the fourteenth century. We have also to take account of the persistent alliance between the MacWilliams and the MacHeths. Both families can scarcely have been competing for the throne, and it seems probable that while the MacWilliams sought the throne and the earldom of Moray the MacHeths sought restoration of the earldom of Ross.[50] Malcolm MacHeth, probably son of an earl (of Ross?) named Heth who witnessed acts of Alexander I and David I,[51] had a daughter who bigamously married Harold earl of Caithness and Orkney and is said to have stirred up her husband to rebel against King William.[52] Malcolm also had more than one son, the eldest, Donald, being alive in 1156.[53] When Malcolm himself died in 1168, after being earl of Ross for at least six years,[54] the earldom fell into abeyance or reverted to the Crown. It is suggested that Malcolm's son Donald had a son called Aed (Heth) or Adam, named after his great-grandfather Earl Heth. Aed, Donald's son, was killed at Coupar Angus in 1186;[55] and it is suggested that his son would have been the Kenneth MacAht ('son of Aed') killed in Ross in 1215 while rebelling with Donald Bán, a younger son of Donald MacWilliam.[56]

The attraction of this hypothetical solution is that it not only explains the appearance of a MacWilliam claim to the throne after *c.*1165, despite the fact that neither William son of Duncan nor his son William of Egremont is ever known to have put forward any claim, but it also explains the close connexions which the MacWilliam risings seem to have had with Moray and the earldom of Ross. Castles were built in Ross in 1179, presumably against MacWilliam; Donald himself was killed in Ross; it was said to have been on the advice of the nobles of Ross that Donald's son Guthred brought a force from Ireland to Ross in 1211 to lead a revolt against King William,[57] and finally the MacWilliam-MacHeth rising of 1215 was directed against Moray and was successfully beaten off by [Farquhar] Machentagar (Fearchar Mac an t'Sacairt), lay abbot of Applecross, who shortly afterwards was rewarded by the king with the earldom of Ross.[58]

During this busy decade the king's efforts to keep Galloway within his kingdom seem to have dovetailed with his efforts to pacify Moray. After he had done homage and sworn fealty to Henry II and his son at York in 1175, the king of Scots was given leave to take an army to western Galloway to bring the murderer Gilbert to heel.[59] A year later, William escorted Gilbert to the English court at the Worcestershire village of Feckenham, so that he could make his peace for his deed of fratricide. But from 1176 until his death in 1185 Gilbert proved entirely recalcitrant. It became the object of Uhtred's son Roland (*alias* Lachlan) to avenge his father's murder. On Gilbert's death Roland overran western Galloway (Wigtownshire and Carrick) with fire and sword, putting to death many Gallovidian chiefs.[60] This alarmed Henry II, who came to Carlisle in 1186 to punish Roland for overreaching himself. But Roland, surely with King William's connivance, was pardoned and confirmed in his possession of eastern Galloway (Kirkcudbrightshire) of which his father had been lord.[61] It was Scottish royal policy to build up Roland as a strong power in the south-west, and in the 1190s he held the office of justiciar, forerunner of a line of justiciars of Galloway who administered this difficult province until the fourteenth century. The timely death of the lord of Nithsdale (Strathnith), Ralph son of Dunegal, about 1185, enabled the king to seize this strategically important valley as an escheat and to retain for the crown the river-crossing and strong point of Dumfries, where William evidently founded a castle-burgh settlement as an exact parallel to Nairn, about two, and Ayr, about twenty, years later.

The third period of William's reign opened with the death of Henry II in 1189 and consisted of twenty years of independence and prosperity. Already before Henry's death there had been some relaxation of the severest forms of Angevin overlordship.[62] In 1185 the Honour of Huntingdon, of which William had been summarily deprived ten years before, was restored, to be at once given to the king's brother David. In 1186, Henry II found a bride for William, now aged about forty-three. Failing to get papal permission for his granddaughter, a daughter of Henry the Lion duke of Saxony, to marry William, Henry II chose Ermengarde, daughter of Richard *vicomte* of Beaumont, well-born it is true, but of a family much less distinguished and powerful than the Welfs. They were married on 5 September in the royal chapel in Woodstock Park, Archbishop Baldwin of Canterbury celebrating the nuptial mass. King Henry's wedding present was Edinburgh castle, restored on condition that William gave it to his bride as dower together with 100 merks' worth of land and forty knights' fees. Despite the good will engendered by the wedding, Henry kept Berwick and Roxburgh in his own hands. Ermengarde was the first queen of Scots for fifty-five years. She bore her husband at least four children, including one son, Alexander, born at Haddington on 24 August, 1198. Presumably much younger than William, Queen Ermengarde outlived him by nineteen years.

Early in 1188, Henry II undertook to raise a 10 per cent income and property tax throughout his dominions to help to pay for the recovery of Jerusalem (the famous 'Saladin Tithe'). He sent north the bishop of Durham and others to command William to make a contribution to the tithe proportional to the wealth of his kingdom.[63] William gathered together nearly all his bishops and earls and a vast concourse of nobles and their retainers, and confronted the English embassy on the Tweed between Birgham and Wark. Howden retails two slightly different versions of what took place.[64] Either William offered 4,000 merks to have Berwick and Roxburgh, to be told that he must contribute to the tithe as well, or he offered 5,000 merks to redeem the castles and pay the tithe. The magnates of Scotland declared bluntly that even if both kings had taken an oath to pay the tithe they would in no circumstance contribute a single penny. It is hard to believe that William regretted this refusal; his rejection of Henry's demand was the first clear assertion of his independence since 1174.

In 1189 the Scottish king, too poor to pay for the freedom of Jerusalem, was prepared to pay 10,000 merks for his own freedom.[65] Richard I was anxious to have the cash and was well disposed towards William. The obnoxious Treaty of Falaise was cancelled and relations between the English and Scottish crowns were restored to what they had been in Malcolm IV's time. Berwick and Roxburgh were handed back to the Scots. The ransom money was raised, partly at least, by a tax agreed upon at a great council held at Musselburgh at the end of 1189 or early in 1190—possibly the first time that anything like a national tax had been voted in Scotland.[66]

Once again, this time with a friendly and greedy Plantagenet on the English throne, William wasted his energies and would have wasted his money trying to recover the northern counties. In 1193 William personally subscribed 2,000 merks towards Richard I's ransom;[67] in 1194 he bid 15,000 merks to have the counties restored, only to be offered Northumberland without the royal castles.[68] In 1195 William put forward an over-ingenious proposal[69]: his daughter Margaret should marry King Richard's nephew Otto of Brunswick (the future Emperor Otto IV), on condition that Margaret should succeed to the Scottish throne. In the meantime, the young couple would be given Northumberland, Cumberland and Lothian, while the two kings would have reciprocal control over the castles north and south of the Border. This plan, which might have produced some strange results, was vetoed by the Scots nobles, who (says Howden) could not stomach the prospect of a woman married to a foreigner taking the throne of Scotland while the king had a brother (David) and he a son (Henry). William continued to press his claims during the first ten years of John's reign (1199–1209), gaining nothing more than an assurance in 1205 that his possession of Tynedale was not in doubt.[70] It seems likely that the question of the northern counties entered into the 'lost treaties' of 1209 and 1212. Unfortunately the treaties have been destroyed, while after 1201 we no longer have the well-informed Roger Howden to guide us. With the benefit of hindsight which it would be quite unrealistic to expect William to have possessed, we can see that the critical period in determining what share of the British island would be taken by the English, what by the Scottish, crown had already elapsed by 1157. In attempting to put the clock back, albeit for reasons which doubtless seemed compelling at the time, William and his son Alexander II treated the far west and the north with relative neglect and made it harder than it need have been for themselves and their successors to consolidate a balanced and unified *regnum Scotie*.

The pacification of Moray led logically to the extension of royal authority over the rest of the northern mainland. Harold, earl of Caithness and Orkney, having repudiated his first wife, Africa sister of Duncan II earl of Fife, had married a daughter of the pretender

Malcolm MacHeth, who is said to have incited her husband to revolt against the king.[71] An invasion of Moray by the earl's son and one Roderic was repulsed at Inverness by the king's troops, either in 1196 or 1197.[72] Unfortunately the contemporary sources, although circumstantial, are too much in conflict to enable a firm chronology to be established for the events which followed.[73] It seems certain that King William made at least two, and possible that he made three, expeditions to the north in the years 1196 and 1197. As a result of the first, in which King William advanced as far as Caithness and sent his forces to destroy Thurso castle, Earl Harold promised to bring hostages to the king when he was next in Moray. In the autumn (1196?) William came to his new castle at Nairn, and Harold sailed into the nearby harbour of Lochloy (now silted up) bringing only two nephews as hostages, having deceitfully sent away the hostages the king had demanded and having left at home his son and heir Thorfinn. The king therefore put Earl Harold in chains in Edinburgh or Roxburgh castle, only releasing him after his son had been handed over. At this point, Harold's rival for the earldom, Harold the young, grandson of Earl Ronald Kali, fought him for possession and in a battle at Wick was defeated and killed. The bishops of St Andrews and Ross brought Earl Harold to King William, and the earl offered much gold and silver to have Caithness confirmed to him. The king would only allow him to have the earldom if he took back his first wife; this the earl refused, whereupon the king assigned the earldom to the king of Man,[74] Reginald (Ronald) son of Guthred for a premium and an annual rent. Nevertheless, Harold seems to have recovered Caithness, in the course of struggles in which the bishop of Caithness, John, was blinded and had his tongue cut out. Eventually, in 1201 or 1202, the earl made his peace with King William for two thousand pounds of silver; a heavy penance was imposed by Pope Innocent III on the man who had mutilated the bishop.[75]

During these relatively peaceful years, the Scottish crown wielded appreciable military power and enjoyed a measure of wealth and prestige. All this rested mainly on the strength of the king's burghs and on the effectiveness of the feudal settlement by which the king transformed the royal demesne, especially in Gowrie, Angus and Mearns. The creation of knights' fees or feus and the development of burghs were both on a large scale. A considerable number of acts in this collection have to do with the founding, the customs and privileges, the trade and the regulation of the king's burghs (as well as of a few burghs not under the king's immediate lordship). These surviving acts can be only a fraction of the total of acts anent burghs issued in William I's reign. How large a fraction is impossible to judge, but it is enough to point out that only one charter survives which was given directly to the burgesses of Perth, and that no charters at all survive for the major burghs of Berwick on Tweed, Roxburgh, Edinburgh, Stirling, Lanark, Forfar, Montrose or Elgin. Nevertheless, if the documentary record of the period down to 1214 is studied carefully the ubiquity and importance of burghs and burghal trading emerge very clearly. The links between the crown and the burghs were close. A large majority of the king's surviving acts were issued at one or other of a group of leading burghs, and in four of these, Berwick, Roxburgh, Edinburgh and Perth, the king is known to have had mints.[76] Down to 1174 the king's moneyers seem to have acted mainly at the first two; after 1174, during the English occupation of the Lothian castles, the king seems to have moved his moneyer Folpold (Folbald) from Roxburgh to Perth. Edinburgh probably revived its minting activity after 1186; the moneyer Adam who worked there (and at Berwick) may perhaps have been Adam son of Serlo, an Edinburgh burgess of some note.[77] In 1195—the year when his chapel introduced dating by day of the month into the king's written acts—the king 'renewed his coinage'. This means that in place of the older Scottish sterlings which had borne on the reverse a cross with short single arms, his moneyers now substituted a penny whose cross had short 'double' or 'voided' arms. Henry II had made the same change in 1180; the time-lag of fifteen years may have been partly due to the Angevin occupation of leading mint towns, although one would also expect this to have brought the new sterlings to Scotland and thus stimulated an early change. Probably a major factor in determining the renewal of 1195 was the great strain which the raising of the 'ransom' of 1189 would have put on Scotland's sterling resources, despite the probability that much of this sum of 10,000 merks would not have been paid in coin.[78]

Alongside, and to some extent as a complement to, his encouragement of burghs, King William created what was little short of a new landed aristocracy in Scotland. In many parts of the country north of the Forth, and especially north of the Tay, we have evidence of crown lands being granted out to newcomers in return for military service. In this collection there is record of some forty-one acts of fresh infeftment for knights' or sergeands' service, and of these twenty-nine relate wholly or mainly to land north of the Forth, twelve to the south. The process seems to have gone on throughout the reign, and in any case was only an expansion and intensification of what David I and Malcolm IV had done earlier; by 1209, the end of our third sub-division of the reign, the process was far advanced. Families newly settled in Scotland by this means (or settled in regions further north than they had previously been) included Hay, Mortemer, Ruffus (Kinnaird), Montfiquet (Muschet), Valognes, Maule, Berkeley (Barclay), Lovel, Frivill, Montfort, Sibbald, Falconer, Olifard (Oliphant), Addeville, de la Carneille (Guthrie), Benholm of that ilk, Allardyce of that ilk,[79] Hastings, Landells, Freskin (de Moravia or Murray), Seton, Graham, Giffard, Melville, Prat, Revel and many others. If we merely consider the king's work of infeftment in Mearns alone, the thoroughness of his feudalizing policy is impressive. The individuals whom we know from authentic record to have been infeft in land in the Mearns in the time of William I include Earl David, William Giffard, Agatha of Berkeley and her husband Humphrey, Ranulf the falconer, Hugh brother of Elias the clerk, William de Montfort, Robert son of Werenbald (brought in from south-west Scotland), Geoffrey de Melville, Walter Scott of Allardyce, Osbert Olifard, Walter son of Sibbald, Richard de Frivill, and William son of Bernard; to these we should probably add John of Hastings. By no means all those granted military fiefs were incoming 'Normans': knight-service charters were issued to Merleswain of Kennoway, Malise son of Earl Ferteth, Gilbert son of the earl of Angus, and the earls of Fife and Strathearn. By this inexorable process the lower stratum of the older aristocracy benorth Forth, the thanes, whose tenurial position seems to have been much less strong than that enjoyed by the infeft knights and barons, were either totally supplanted or at best, in a few districts, reduced to a rare minority. The result was to give the crown a new aristocracy, confident in its castles and knight-service, capable of offsetting the relative independence of the earls, and able to furnish the king not only with a respectable cavalry arm but also with the justices and sheriffs by means of whom the kingdom was firmly governed.

The last six years of the reign form its distinct fourth period because of three factors whose interplay could no longer be postponed or avoided. The first was the king's advancing age and more frequent illnesses. In these years William had lost the initiative, and his poor health must have played a part in this. Secondly, in a sense complementary, we see King John's growing power and ruthlessness. Lastly, the king of Scots' only son Alexander had now survived to an age at which his future career seemed assured but nevertheless required careful planning. In these years King John came near to dominating a Scottish kingdom whose king was too old and whose heir-apparent was too young to lead it with vigour and confidence.

Ill feeling between William and John was an old story, going back at least to Richard I's accession and exacerbated by the secret agreement which William Longchamp had made with the king of Scots to ensure the succession to the English throne of Arthur of Brittany.[80] In 1209 relations, already strained, reached breaking point over the building of a new castle at Tweedmouth. This was apparently the direct work of King John, into whose hands Tweedmouth had fallen on the death in 1208 of Philip of Poitou bishop of Durham.[81] A story preserved in the chronicle of Walter of Guisborough,[82] which cannot be true as it stands but which may contain an element of truth, suggests that John was prompted by annoyance because William was planning a marriage between one of his daughters and the 'count of Flanders' (Holland?). At all events, the Scots destroyed Tweedmouth castle which they saw, naturally enough, as an unnecessarily provocative threat to their important town of Berwick. John summoned William to meet him at Newcastle in April, but in fact the two kings seem to have met at Bolton near Alnwick, and then to have adjourned their serious discussion to a conference at Norham on Tweed. Here they parted in disagreement about 25 April, and both countries prepared for war. After much hostile manœuvring, on John's side clearly with a formidable army,[83] the kings met again at Norham about 25 July. Their agreement—it would be truer to speak of William's submission—was expressed in a formal treaty whose text is lost. We may accept from the contemporary Melrose chronicle,[84] and from the description of a letter of King John still extant in 1282,[85] that one English concession was the demolition of Tweedmouth castle. The treaty also provided that William's two daughters, Margaret and Isabel, were to be handed over to John for marriage. A bond by William dated at Norham on 7 August (no.488) survives in an English exchequer copy, probably authentic. It obliged the king of Scots to pay no less than 15,000 merks in four annual instalments, 'to have King John's goodwill and in earnest of the agreement into which the two kings had just entered'. Half of this sum seems to have been paid, the remainder remitted.[86] The later Scottish historian John Fordun correctly reports the details of this obligation and also the razing of Tweedmouth.[87] He further says that after nine years Margaret and Isabel of Scotland were to be married in such a way that one of them, presumably the elder or survivor, would wed whichever of John's sons would succeed to the English throne. Some such agreement seems probable, especially in view of the large size of the sum demanded from the Scottish king, a payment hard to explain otherwise. And Fordun's account is supported by two English sources much nearer in point of time to the event. Gervase of Canterbury writes of a marriage agreement,[88] while the charges against Hubert de Burgh, the deposed Justiciar who had had custody of the Scottish princesses and disgracefully married the elder himself, point unmistakably to an English undertaking that the princesses should make royal marriages.[89] Moreover, Chapter 59 of Magna Carta (1215) promised that right should be done to King Alexander II of Scotland 'in the matter of his sisters'.[90] As a final condition of the Norham agreement, King William consented to hand over to the English king the sons of some thirteen or more nobles as hostages, 'against the will of the Scots', says the Melrose chronicle.[91] It may be suggested, but there is no contemporary evidence on the point, that the agreement also included some provision regarding the future of the English northern counties.

Norham was a grave setback for the Scottish monarchy. Not only had William failed to recover Northumberland and Cumberland; he had been forced to pay 7,500 merks, and he had lost, without guarantees for their proper treatment, two of his daughters, neither of whom was ever to marry into the Angevin house. Worse was to come. In the summer of 1211 Guthred, a son of Donald MacWilliam, urged on it is said by the nobles of Ross, put himself at the head of a rising in the north more formidable than those of 1179 and 1187.[92] For a time the king was able to keep the rebellion in check, shewing a vigour astonishing in a man of his age and medical history. Several acts issued in the north, evidently in 1211, bear out Fordun's statement that the king led the campaign against Guthred in person.[93] The summer was followed by an exceptionally long and hard winter, which gave a respite to the rebels as well as to royal troops. Early in February, 1212, possibly after a bout of illness, King William came to Durham to meet King John.[94] It may have been then agreed that John would furnish Brabantine mercenaries for a new summer offensive against MacWilliam. It is certain that the king of Scots, for his part, provided some sort of renewal or confirmation of the lost treaty of 1209. The text of this renewal has also been destroyed. The undated letter, probably of February, 1212, in which William grants to John the marriage without disparagement of his son and heir Alexander and declares that he and Alexander have sworn to support John's son Henry and, if John should die, to maintain him on the English throne 'against all mortal men', survives only in an English exchequer copy of *c.*1230–40, and appears suspect (no.505). A matter so important as Alexander's marriage would surely have been put before a council of the Scottish earls and barons and not given away, almost in secret, by a document whose diplomatic credentials are dubious. But whatever its precise terms, we may be sure that the lost treaty of 1212 brought William no emancipation from Plantagenet domination.

Early in March, 1212, Alexander went south to receive the belt of knighthood from King John, at St Bride's, Clerkenwell.[95] Thus fortified, he returned to Scotland to take a hand in the operations which led eventually to Guthred MacWilliam's capture and execution. John paid his last visit to William of Scotland at the end of June, when the two kings rode across England together from Carlisle to Durham by way of Hexham.[96] The Brabanters were perhaps fighting in Scotland this summer, and in any case a major role seems to have been played at this time by the earl of Winchester, Saer de Quinci, a leading tenant-in-chief in Scotland, evidently trusted by King William, who was also a baron of some importance south of the Border, although hardly enjoying much of King John's trust. Within three years, Earl Saer was to be a principal negotiator for the Great Charter;[97] and the young Alexander, by then king of Scots, was to have obtained from Louis of France and the barons in revolt against John promises and actual charters of all that his father had struggled for in vain during nearly fifty years.[98]

After a prolonged illness and convalescence, which seems to have kept him at Selkirk, Haddington and Edinburgh for much of the year 1213, King William recovered sufficiently to journey north again in the following summer and on 1 August make an effective peace with John earl of Caithness, the only surviving son of the recalcitrant Earl Harold.[99] A month later the king was back at Stirling, where he succumbed to his final illness. He died on Thursday, 4 December, 1214, and was buried six days later in front of the high altar in the magnificent abbey church of St Thomas the Martyr at Arbroath.[100] Two days before the funeral, the king's son Alexander was inaugurated as king of Scots at Scone.

The reputation which William left was of the *vir justus et pius* (no.525), who kept the peace and dispensed justice to all his subjects. His earlier lack of judgement and obstinacy and his earlier sexual licentiousness were alike forgiven. In his later years, indeed, he enjoyed the reverence due to a man of exceptional goodness, almost of saintliness, and even King John's chancery was moved on at least one occasion to style him *venerabilis*.[101] The image of William as above all the upholder of justice led Fordun to use of him the well-known phrase *leo justitiae*;[102] it was perhaps from this that later generations coined the name 'William the Lion' as a renaissance-gothic fancy; however this may be, the name has stuck. No popular epithet ever seems to have become firmly fixed to King William in his own life-time, although one contemporary calls him William 'the ruddy', while the annalist of Loch Cé in Ireland calls him Uilleam Garm, presumably for *garbh*, 'rough' or 'harsh'.[103] This may have been his reputation in the Gaedhealtachd, which already, before the end of his reign, had begun its retreat into the highlands. But although William repressed the revolts of native Gaelic-speaking Scots and others, and although he was unquestionably the most effective 'normaniser' of any of the Scottish kings, it cannot be said that he discriminated against his native subjects, whether of Scottish, Anglian, Cumbrian or Gallovidian stock, in matters of fundamental importance such as law and landholding, or even in military service. Paternalistic and autocratic, conservative in ecclesiastical affairs, William upheld for nearly half a century the proposition that there was such a thing as the kingdom of Scotland and that he was in charge of it.

NOTES TO SECTION I

1. Anderson, *Early Sources*, ii, 205 and n.
2. Lawrie, *Charters*, no.258.
3. Anderson, *Scottish Annals*, 228–9.
4. The grant does not seem to have taken effect until after Michaelmas, 1158; *Pipe Roll*, 4 *Hen. II* (ed. Hunter), 177, 179; *Pipe Roll*, 5 *Hen. II* (Pipe Roll Soc.).
5. *Chron. Fantosme* (Becker), 513, l.1252; (Michel), 58, l.1259.
6. Lawrie, *Annals*, 396; cp. *Chron. Melrose*, 54 (s.a. 1209). Admittedly, John himself could be addressed as 'venerable' in a letter from one of his military supporters at the end of his reign (PRO, DL 36/1, fo.55, fifth document).
7. Lawrie, *Annals*, 114–5.
8. Ibid., 116–7.
9. Ibid., 119.
10. Ibid., 387; Anderson, *Scottish Annals*, 330, n.6.
11. Anderson, *Early Sources*, ii, 299.
12. Lawrie, *Annals*, 78, 102–3.
13. *RRS*, i, 28–9.
14. This group is touched on in *Annales de Normandie* (xve année, 1965), 505–6, 511–12; but the subject still requires detailed investigation.
15. See nos.292–6, 347 below; Anderson, *Early Sources*, ii, 405.
16. *Chron. Fantosme* (Becker), 489, l.383; (Michel), 18, l.385.
17. See my paper on 'The early charters of the family of Kinninmonth of that ilk' in *Essays presented to Kathleen Major* (forthcoming).
18. Anderson, *Early Sources*, ii, 275–6; *Annales de Normandie* (1965), 509.
19. *Chron. Fantosme* (Becker), 487, lines 299ff.; 489, lines 382ff.; (Michel), 16, lines 301ff.; 18, lines 384ff.

19a. Fantôme does not identify the 'wild young men' who incited King William to attack England, but in later passages he refers to Roger de Mowbray and Adam de Port aiding the king of Scots with many knights, and he writes of Adam's 'borderers' (*marchiz*) (*Chron. Fantosme* (Becker), 515, lines 1319–24, 516, lines 1340, 1353; 529, lines 1837, 1841; (Michel), 60, lines 1326–31; 62, lines 1347, 1360; 84, lines 1846, 1850). Roger de Mowbray fled to Scotland from the engagement at Alnwick in July, 1174 (*Chron. Stephen*, i, 185; *Chron. Fantosme* (Becker), 529, l.1832; (Michel), 84, l.1841). The mention of Adam de Port is one of several instances of Fantôme's credibility in detail. Adam, lord of the barony of Kington in south-east Herefordshire, was accused of treason after Henry II's return from Ireland in 1172 and was banished for refusing to stand to justice in the king's court (*Gesta Henrici*, i, 35). After this nothing is heard of him until Fantôme's report of his activities with the Scots in 1173–4; but his presence in Scotland and obligation to the Scottish king are shewn by his grant to Kelso Abbey, probably made at Roxburgh, of the church of 'Wibaldingtun' (*Kelso Liber*, no.357). 'Wiboldingtune' was the Domesday name of a village in the south-eastern corner of Herefordshire, in Brooms Ash hundred (*Domesday Book*, f.182a), identified by A. T. Bannister with Whittington, near Ganarew (*Place-Names of Herefordshire* (1916), 210; cf. I. J. Sanders, *English Baronies* (1960), 57).

20. Fantôme says that William I was prepared to submit his claim to a trial of battle: 'ferai derainement par un sul chevalier': (Becker), 488, l.344; (Michel), 16, l.336.

21. *Chron. Lanercost*, 169. With the phrase used there, *monstratis armis* = 'wapinschaw', compare *armorum ostensionem* used in a quittance issued to Melrose Abbey by James the Stewart of Scotland, referring to the situation after the death of Alexander III in 1286 (*Melrose Liber*, no.396). The host was mustered at Caddonlee in 1244 (*Chron. Bower*, ii, 74).
22. *Chron. Holyrood*, 154 and nn.; Lawrie, *Annals*, 147–8; *Chron. Fantosme* (Becker), 509, l.1099, 'in the month of April' (Lincoln MS.); (Michel), 50, lines 1106ff., 'in May after April' (Durham MS.); shewing that the king of Scots held a council in Scotland in or before May, 1174; probably at Perth, where the monk Jocelin was elected bishop of Glasgow on 23 May, 1174 (Dowden, *Bishops*, 298).
23. *Chron. Holyrood*, 154. *Chron. Fantosme* (Becker), 520ff., shews that Richard de Lucy was not appealed to for help until shortly before he sent Richard of Ilchester to Henry II in Normandy, 24 June, 1174 (cf. Ralph de Diceto, *Historical Works*, ed. Stubbs, Rolls Series, 1876, i, 381).
24. *Chron. Fantosme* (Becker), 485–6, lines 253ff.; (Michel), 12–14, lines 255ff.
25. Anderson, *Scottish Annals*, 258; Stones, *Documents*, 1, n.1.
26. Lawrie, *Annals*, 201–4.
27. The treaty carefully distinguishes between King Henry II, always called 'the lord king' (*dominus rex*), the 'Young King' called 'Henry the king, his (i.e. Henry II's) son', and King William, always called 'king of Scots' (*rex Scottorum*). Under the treaty, felons fleeing from Scotland to England might either be sent back or tried and punished in the English king's court; felons fleeing from England to Scotland had to be restored to England.
28. *Chron. Melrose*, 47.
29. Anderson, *Scottish Annals*, 256–8 and nn.
30. Lawrie, *Annals*, 241: 'Donald son of William son of Duncan, who had often claimed the kingdom of Scotland'; ibid., 387, 'he (i.e., Guthred son of Donald MacWilliam) was of the ancient stock of the kings of Scots'; Anderson, *Early Sources*, ii, 471, the MacWilliams 'wished to obtain the kingdom by force'.
31. The treaty stipulated for the English occupation of Jedburgh and Stirling castles as well, but there is no evidence that these were ever occupied and good evidence that they were not. See also D.W. Hunter Marshall, 'Two early English occupations in Scotland', *SHR*, xxv (1927), 20–3.
32. No.288 below; *Chron. Howden*, ii, 133; *Gesta Henrici*, i, 160. Alan son of Roald, constable of Richmond, seems to have been placed in charge of Edinburgh castle; *SHR*, xxv, 21 and n.
33. *Chron. Melrose*, 42; cf. *Chron. Holyrood*, 164 and n. For the St Andrews election dispute, see ibid., 164–9; Lawrie, *Annals*, 224–78 *passim*; R. Foreville, *L'église et la royauté en Angleterre sous Henri II Plantagenet* (1943), 511–13. For the identification of Master John 'the Scot' with Master John nephew of Bishop Robert, cf. *St Andrews Liber*, 124–5, 138–41, 259–60; *Dunfermline Registrum*, nos.91, 92, 94, 97; *Holyrood Liber*, nos.19, 32; Raine, *North Durham*, no.453; *Kelso Liber*, nos.420, 448. Master John, Bishop Robert's nephew, obviously one of the most prominent of the St Andrews clergy, vanishes from record at the death of Bishop Richard. Moreover, among Master John 'the Scot's' relatives was Aiulf, dean of Christianity of Lothian, first found under Bishop Robert and probably that bishop's chaplain named Aiulf who witnessed Raine, *North Durham*, no.447; cf. *Chron. Howden*, ii, 312.
34. Master Walter (for whom see my unpublished Oxford B.Litt. thesis, 'Scottish royal ecclesiastical policy' (1950), was a regular witness to the *acta* of Bishop Hugh (e.g., *Dunfermline Registrum*, no.98; *Kelso Liber*, no.438, *Scone Liber*, nos.41, 49, 50), and also witnessed with Hugh, between his election and consecration, a charter of Alexander of St Martin (*St Andrews Liber*, 333–4).
35. Ibid., 82–3 (the original letter of Alexis is BM, Cotton Chr., xviii, 35).
36. Master Jocelin archdeacon of Dunkeld appears as a king's clerk along with

Richard de prebenda in *Holyrood Liber*, no.42 = no.292 below; and for his attendance on the king, see nos.273 and 362 (*Moray Registrum*, pp.7, 11).

37. *Chron. Melrose*, 43 (= Lawrie, *Annals*, 230).
38. Ibid., 240.
39. *Guisborough Cartularium*, ii, 48–9, no.684, an agreement between Archbishop Roger of York and Guisborough priory, at the instance and in the presence of the legate Alexius (1180–1), was witnessed by, i.a., Master Vacarius the famous lawyer and Thomas canon of St Andrews (cf. BM, MS.Cott. Cleopatra D ii, fo.238), perhaps the Thomas who became prior of St Andrews before 6 June, 1199 (Raine, *North Durham*, no.467).
40. *Chron. Howden*, ii, 312, 313. For Roger of Feddinch, cf. *St. Andrews Liber*, p.xxv, nos.2, 3.
41. Lawrie, *Annals*, 239 (the form Ravendala, for Redden, is like the form Revedala used in *Gesta Henrici*, i, 64 for the better Revedene of *Chron. Howden*, ii, 57. Cf. *Kelso Liber*, index locorum, s.v. 'Rauedene').
42. Lawrie, *Annals*, 242–5. The Scottish mission to Pope Lucius in March, 1182, included Jocelin bishop of Glasgow, Osbert abbot of Kelso, Arnold abbot of Melrose and Walter prior of Inchcolm. It seems very probable that it also included Archibald abbot of Dunfermline since (1) there is some reason to believe that Abbot Archibald was at Henry II's court at Marlborough in January, 1182 (*SHR*, xxxvi, 139–40, 143); (2) Pope Lucius issued a solemn privilege to Abbot Archibald and the monks of Dunfermline while at Velletri, 30 April, 1182 (*Dunfermline Registrum*, no.238). No.156 below, a protection for an unnamed abbot of Dunfermline going to England with the king seems to belong to 1176 (council at Northampton), rather than 1182.
43. Lawrie, *Annals*, 277–8.
44. *Chron. Melrose*, 42.
45. Ibid. Cf. Anderson, *Early Sources*, ii, 301–2.
46. Lawrie, *Annals*, 241–2. The authority is *Gesta Henrici*, i, 277, 281; and *Chron. Howden*, ii, 263. It is possible that there has been a two-year displacement of Scottish information here in Howden's material, corresponding to that seen in his report under 1180 of the death of Richard bishop of St Andrews.
47. *Chron. Holyrood*, 170–1 (in a passage probably composed at Coupar Angus). Mrs Anderson most kindly let me see a photostat of the Karlsruhe MS. 345 (MS. 'K') of the chronicle. The word after *cognomento*, printed *et* in *Chron. Holyrood*, is written as a most unusual form of ampersand, all the more striking since elsewhere the scribe uses 7 for *et*. It is similar to, but not identical with the Æ diphthong of *Ætholie* in the previous line. Mrs Anderson's note reads 'In K, *et* is written with a large &– sign, a form unusual to the scribe; he may have taken it for a proper name'. I suggest that the scribe has mistaken the personal name Aed, in the form Æt, for an ampersand; and that Adam was an alternative (scriptural) name for one Aed son of Donald. If in addition the phrase *scilicet nepos eius* has been misplaced and rightly relates Aed to Malcolm earl of Atholl, this would fit with the suggestion made here that Aed was the son of Donald son of Malcolm MacHeth, since Malcolm MacHeth's daughter was the sister-in-law of Malcolm earl of Atholl. See table facing p. 12. I have had valuable help from Professor A. A. M. Duncan in attempting a solution of this problem.
48. *Chron. Holyrood*, 171; *Chron. Melrose*, 46; *Gesta Henrici*, ii, 7–9 (very briefly, in *Chron. Howden*, ii, 318).
49. *St Bees Register*, 532 (also *Cal. Docs. Scot.*, ii, no.64); cf. *Wetherhal Register*, 387, where for 'Murres' read 'Murref'.
50. Malcolm MacHeth had been given the earldom of Ross by 1162 (*RRS*, i, 8). I can no longer accept the view put forward there that Malcolm MacHeth was a bastard son of Alexander I. After Kenneth MacAht (perhaps great-grandson of Malcolm MacHeth) was killed in 1215, his slayer, Fearchar Mac an t'Sacairt, was knighted and made earl of Ross by Alexander II (*Chron. Melrose*, 59–60, 84; *RMS*, i, 509; *Moray Registrum*, nos.258, 259).

51. Lawrie, *Charters*, nos.49 ('Beth'), 74 ('Ed'), and 94 ('Head'); if these names stand for the same person.
52. Lawrie, *Annals*, 306; Anderson, *Early Sources*, ii, 348.
53. *RRS*, i, 8.
54. Ibid.; *Chron. Holyrood*, 151.
55. See above, n.47.
56. *Chron. Melrose*, 59; Anderson, *Early Sources*, ii, 404. Dr Anderson considered that Kenneth 'was probably a relative, possibly a son, of Malcolm MacHeth'; but in view of the time gap, great-grandson seems more likely.
57. Lawrie, *Annals*, 377, quoting Fordun: 'de consilio, prout dicebatur, thanorum de Ross'.
58. Above, n.50.
59. Lawrie, *Annals*, 205.
60. Ibid., 256.
61. Ibid., 262–4.
62. For what follows, see ibid., 255, 265–7.
63. Ibid., 271–3. The silence of the Melrose chronicle on this event is remarkable.
64. The two versions are hardly 'materially different', as Stubbs thought (*Chron. Howden*, ii, 338n.), for the thousand merks difference was presumably intended to represent the tithe. This would fit in well with the 'ransom' of 10,000 merks actually paid in 1189–90, which may be seen as the revenues of the Scottish crown and baronage for one year.
65. Lawrie, *Annals*, 281–4.
66. *RRS*, i, 54 and nn.
67. Lawrie, *Annals*, 291.
68. Ibid., 297.
69. Ibid., 301 (Howden begins the year at Christmas, hence for 1196 read 1195 according to modern reckoning).
70. Ibid., 347–8.
71. Ibid., 306; Anderson, *Early Sources*, ii, 348n. According to Flateyiarbok, Earl Harold's second wife was called Hvarflö ð (*Icelandic Sagas*, Rolls Series, i, 221), a name identified by the editor with the Gaelic Gormflaith.
72. *Chron. Melrose*, 49, s.a. 1197; *Chron. Howden*, iv, 10, s.a. 1196.
73. Nos.388, 391–5 below illustrate the king's presence in Moray in this period, but unfortunately they do not shew in which of the two years 1196 or 1197 the king went north, nor do they disprove the suggestion that he may have gone north in both years, as well as twice in one year. *Scone Liber*, no.58, a grant of one Scottish silver merk annually to Scone Abbey by Earl Harold and his son Thorfinn, was presumably issued after reconciliation with King William, but the charter cannot be dated precisely and it may be as late as 1202 (Anderson, *Early Sources*, ii, 356n.).
74. *Chron. Howden*, iv. 12, says 'Reginald son of Somerled, king of Man'. Probably 'king of Man' is correct, and the beneficiary was King Reginald son of Guthred. Flateyiarbok says that King William sought help from Reginald son of Guthred 'the greatest warrior in the western lands' (*Icelandic Sagas*, i, 225; iii, 228; Anderson, *Early Sources*, ii, 350).
75. Lawrie, *Annals*, 338–41.
76. Burns, *Coinage*, i, 47ff. What follows is based on this standard work and on the recent work of Mr I. H. Stewart. I have benefited greatly from Mr Stewart's kindness in sending me the typescript of a paper on early Scottish sterlings and mints, and also from correspondence with him on various matters concerning the Scots coinage.
77. *SHR*, xxx (1951), 47–8.
78. *Chron. Melrose*, 47, speaks of 10,000 merks 'of gold and silver,' but how much was in coined money is impossible to judge. In 1216, King Alexander II's aid was paid at least partly in hides (*Arbroath Liber*, i, no.110).
79. The lairds of Allardyce, who used the Norman personal name Walter, had the cognomen 'Scottus', but this does not necessarily mean that they were native Scots.

80. Lawrie, *Annals*, 287–8 (quoting William of Newburgh).
81. *Chron. Fordun*, i, 277. *Pipe Roll*, 13 *John*, 38, shews that in the period from Midsummer, 1208 to 11 November, 1211, £372 13s. 11d. was spent by the king on the castles and houses of the bishopric at Norham and Tweedmouth.
82. *Chron. Guisborough*, 149.
83. Gervase of Canterbury, *Historical Works* (ed. Stubbs, Rolls Series, 1879–80), ii, 102 speaks of John's *exercitus copiosus*. Other contemporaries call the army *grandis* and *infinitus* (Bury St Edmunds Annals in F. Liebermann, *Ungedruckte Anglo-Normannische Geschichtsquellen* (1879), 147; Annals of Waverley in *Annales Monastici* (ed. Luard, Rolls Series, 1864–9), ii, 262). *Chron. Bower*, i, 525 speaks of 13,000 foot together with 1,500 English knights and almost 7,000 crossbowmen and Brabanters (*branchiorum*). Bower's account of the events of 1209 is full and circumstantial, but it is not known what his sources of information were, although here and there his details can be corroborated. The statement that King William was keeping his court at Traquair while his army was assembled would square well with a muster at Caddonlee (above, n.21).
84. *Chron. Melrose*, 54.
85. *APS*, i, 108, *Negocia tangencia Angliam*: 'Littera regis Johannis quod non possit castrum firmari super portum de Twedmuth'.
86. Ibid.: 'Littera regis Johannis ad recipiendum . vij^{m} et . D . marcas ad opus regis Anglie pro quodam fine et de residuo remittendo.' *Chron. Melrose*, 54, inexplicably has 13,000 merks.
87. Lawrie, *Annals*, 367–8 (= *Chron. Fordun*, i, 277).
88. Gervase of Canterbury, *Hist. Works*, ii, 102: 'one daughter to be given in lawful wedlock to his son, the other to one of the nobles of England'.
89. Matthew Paris, *Chronica Majora* (ed. Luard, Rolls Series, 1872–83), vi, 70–1: the king of Scots, it was said, had handed over his two daughters, the elder of whom was to marry (King) Henry, or if he died his brother Richard of Cornwall. In return for this, King William was to pay 15,000 merks and surrender his claim to the northern counties. See also the terms of the Treaty of York (1237), in Stones, *Documents*, no.7, p.20.
90. Stubbs, *Select Charters* (9th edn), 300.
91. Lawrie, *Annals*, 369; *Chron. Melrose*, 54.
92. Lawrie, *Annals*, 377; Bury Annals, in Liebermann, *Ungedruckte Anglo-Normannische Geschichtsquellen*, 150–1: 'et hoc, ut dicitur, de assensu quorundam magnatum Scotie.'
93. *Chron. Fordun*, i, 278–9; *Chron. Bower*, ii, 531–2; nos.499–502 below. Probably Saer de Quinci and a mercenary force sent by King John took part in this campaign; see n.96 below.
94. Lawrie, *Annals*, 379; *Pipe Roll*, 14 *John*, p.xii.
95. Lawrie, *Annals*, 381–2.
96. *Pipe Roll*, 14 *John*, p.xiii. It seems probable that the passage in the Bury St Edmunds annals printed by Liebermann, op. cit., 150–1, refers to 1211 as well as 1212. Saer de Quinci was in Scotland in 1211 with 100 knights and 100 serjeants (*Rotuli de liberate* (1844), 240; *Curia Regis Rolls*, vi, 290), and he was perhaps the 'certain English noble' mentioned in the Bury annals as in charge of the many Brabanters whom King John sent to King William.
97. J. C. Holt, *Magna Carta* (1965), 144, 153–5, 196.
98. *APS*, i, 108–9. See also Anderson, *Early Sources*, ii, 411–12, where, on p.412, Lothian (*Loonois*) is almost certainly to be understood in the sense of 'Northumberland', a Norman usage employed wrongly by Robert de Torigni (*Chron. Stephen*, iv, 173, 192).
99. Lawrie, *Annals*, 397.
100. Ibid., 398–400.
101. Ibid., 396.

102. *Chron. Fordun*, i, 259.

103. Anderson, *Early Sources*, i, p.cxv; ii, 398 (cf. *Annals of Loch Cé*, ed. W.A. Hennessy, Rolls Series, 1871, i, 250; *Annals of Ulster*, ed. B. MacCarthy, Rolls Series, 1887, ii, 256). For a brief essay on the reign as a whole, see G.W.S. Barrow, 'The reign of William the Lion, king of Scotland', in *Historical Studies*, vii (1969), 21–44.

2. SCOTTISH ROYAL GOVERNMENT
1165–1214

In its broad outlines, the picture of Scottish royal government presented in the introduction to the *Acts of Malcolm IV* holds good for the reign of his brother. But the sources upon which we can draw for knowledge of William I's government are very much fuller than those for the earlier period, and, in addition, the half-century of William's rule saw a steady development in the field of government, not only in matters of detail but also in some fundamentals such as the change from payments in kind to payments in money. The account given here, which is in no sense exhaustive, will follow in its main lines the account in the preceding volume but will try to avoid going over too much of the same ground.

The tendency for Edinburgh to be regarded as the headquarters of government, which seemed to be discernible in the time of David I and Malcolm IV, received a notable setback under King William. No doubt this was chiefly due to the Angevin occupation of Edinburgh castle from 1175 to 1186, a period during which it is noticeable that the king's sojourns at Haddington and Linlithgow seem to take the place of visits he might otherwise have paid to Edinburgh. Discounting spurious items, some 437 acts survive with Scottish place-dates. Of these, forty-five were issued at Perth (forty-six if Scone be added), forty-five at Forfar and forty-four at Stirling. Edinburgh takes only fourth place, with thirty-four acts, to be followed by Selkirk (27), Kinghorn (21), Montrose (20), Haddington (18), Jedburgh (17), Elgin, Lanark, Roxburgh and Traquair (14 each), Dunfermline (12) and Clackmannan (10).[1] These figures give point to what has already been said of the king's tendency to spend much time in Gowrie and Angus, but they must be used with caution. It would need only a handful of Haddington and Linlithgow (8) sojourns to bring the Edinburgh figure within reach of those for Perth and Forfar, just as some of the Jedburgh total represents sojourns which the king would have made at Roxburgh but for the long English occupation. Moreover, the surprisingly large total for Forfar, coupled with the large total for Montrose, reflect at least in part the king's interest after 1178 in his great new abbey at Arbroath. A high proportion of his many acts issued for the Tironensian monks of Arbroath were dated at Forfar or Montrose. At the same time, we must recognize that the decision to found this abbey at a royal thanage on the Angus coast was itself a sign of William's readiness, in contrast with his brother or grandfather, to push northward the area in which royal demesne was most frequented and exploited. This is again emphasized by the fact that whereas very few of David I's or Malcolm IV's acts were issued north of the Tay, some 116 of William I's acts have place-dates benorth Tay, including, besides Forfar, Montrose and Elgin, Alyth (8), Aberdeen (6), Clunie in Stormont and Kincardine (5 each), Charleton, Forres and Kintore (2 each) and Arbroath, Auldearn, Brechin, Longforgan (?), Fyvie, Inverness and Nairn (1 each). From this evidence, supported as it is by chronicle sources, we may be sure that the king was spending more time and transacting more public business in the northern regions of his kingdom than his immediate predecessors had done.

There is a notable contrast if we turn to the south-west, where so few of the king's surviving acts were issued. Just as the founding of Arbroath accounts for a good many of the northern acts, so the absence in the south-west of any religious house to which the king was particularly devoted must explain part of the discrepancy. The *Assise Regis Willelmi* shew us the king holding his courts at Lanark,[2] and the written acts support this by yielding a respectable total of fourteen dated at this burgh. Otherwise, however, we have only two acts at Dumfries, and one each at Lochmaben, Gretna and Rutherglen to bear witness to the king's personal presence in this large and important region.

Not only was there a general shift in the centre of gravity, there were some significant changes in detail. Thus, Berwick on Tweed, which figures prominently as a royal centre under David I and Malcolm IV, drops to a relatively minor position under William. The late act given at 'Invernairn' (no.500) and the earlier act given at Auldearn (no.213) doubtless reflect the founding of the former and abandonment of the latter burgh about 1187. Dunfermline also declined as a royal centre, for nearly all the acts issued there belong to the opening years of the reign; this bears out the view that as a royal burgh Dunfermline 'probably decayed early',[3] being displaced by the abbey's burgh on the opposite bank of the Tower Burn, where the king would not normally stay or issue official acts. For this collection makes it abundantly clear that the king was normally expected to 'lodge at his own' just as he was expected to 'live of his own'. The overwhelming majority of acts were issued at places which are known to have been royal centres or strong-points, either king's burghs, royal castles (such as Alyth, no.410), royal hunting lodges (such as Yarrow and Clunie) or at least royal country houses, such as (probably) Traquair and Fyvie.

THE KING'S HOUSEHOLD

King William had six chancellors in the course of his reign. The first, Nicholas, brother of Adam of Roxburgh, continued in office from the previous reign and died in 1171. His chancellorship is marked by the issue of acts which are formally succinct and simple, and use the royal style without *Dei gratia*. The Breton, Walter de Bidun, who had been chancellor to David I and Malcolm IV, came back to office after Nicholas's death and served until 1178, in which year he was elected bishop of Dunkeld, but died unconsecrated, probably after 14 October.[4] During Walter de Bidun's term of office *Dei gratia* was added to the royal style. There was evidently a vacancy of several years, for as late as 1183 the papacy proposed that the chancellorship should be given to John the Scot, and the office was presumably then vacant. The king did not appoint John, but towards the end of the decade, perhaps as late as 1188, he gave the chancellorship to his cousin Roger, younger son of Robert III 'ès Blanchesmains', earl of Leicester.[5] Roger can hardly have been in office long, for in April, 1189, he was elected to the see of St Andrews, and at the same time the king transferred the chancellor's office to a senior clerk, Hugh of Roxburgh, whose earliest appearance in royal service went back to the opening years of the reign.[6] On the death of Jocelin bishop of Glasgow on 17 March, 1199, Hugh was elected to succeed, perhaps retaining the chancellorship in the meantime; but he died before consecration, on 10 July, 1199.[7] Hugh of Roxburgh's outstanding qualities as chancellor inspired an anonymous admirer, perhaps a colleague, to write a verse eulogy, in which Hugh appears as 'the adornment of the kingdom, jewel of the clergy', a man 'just, prudent and moderate'. 'You are worthy to be remembered,' concludes the eulogist, 'and Scotland rightly rejoices to revere your name, pour out your praises and embrace your feet.'[8] On the following 8 September the office was given to another royal clerk, prominent in royal service since the 1180s, William Malvoisin.[9] Like his predecessor, Malvoisin was elected to Glasgow (October, 1199), and continued to serve as chancellor not only after his election but even after his consecration. Malvoisin cannot have returned to Scotland from his consecration (which took place at Lyons) before February, 1201, soon after which we find him witnessing a royal act as both bishop and chancellor (no.427). On his translation to St Andrews in the following year (20 September) he seems to have resigned the chancellorship, and we hear of no chancellor until November, 1203 (no.434). Even then it seems clear that the holder, Florence or Floris of Holland, was an absentee. He was the son of Count Florence III and Ada, King William's sister, and provost of Utrecht cathedral.[10] There is evidence to suggest that Florence of Holland, elected to Glasgow in 1202, cannot in fact have set foot in Scotland until 1205.[11] Before May, 1207, he had resigned his see,[12] to which he had not yet been consecrated. Florence may have continued as absentee chancellor until his death on 30 November, 1210,[13] for no successor was appointed until 28 June, 1211, when the office went to an experienced royal clerk, William del Bois (de Boscho),[14] who was a clerk in the king's chapel as early as 1193.[15] William del Bois was still chancellor when the king died, played a prominent part in the inauguration of the young Alexander II, and remained in office under the new king for over eleven years. It is noteworthy that of these six chancellors, four were elected, and two consecrated, to bishoprics, and three held the important archdeaconries of St Andrews (Hugh of Roxburgh) and Lothian (Malvoisin and del Bois). We cannot help also noticing an association between the office of chancellor and the bishopric of Glasgow, second in wealth and importance among the Scottish sees. Of the eight different men who served as chancellor between 1153 and 1214, no fewer than four, Ingram, Hugh of Roxburgh, Malvoisin and Florence of Holland, were appointed to the see of

Glasgow, although the total time which all four of them devoted to the see as consecrated bishops amounted to no more than eleven years.

The surviving evidence provides a picture of the composition of the *capella regis*, the king's chapel (including his writing-office), which, although imprecise, may be fairly complete.[16] Under the chancellor, the personnel of the chapel were classified as *clerici regis* and *capellani regis*, and as in Malcolm IV's reign a firm distinction seems to have been drawn between clerks and chaplains, the former being presumably concerned with administrative, secretarial and scribal work, the latter with the spiritual life of the royal household and with celebrating the daily mass for the king to hear. We have record of at least twenty-three different king's clerks in William's reign, but by no means all of these can be assigned to the chapel; several obviously belonged to other household departments which will be looked at in due course. Those whose place in the chapel seems certain were Richard of St Albans (a clerk under Malcolm IV),[17] Richard of Lincoln, Hugh of Roxburgh, Hugh *de sigillo* (otherwise known as 'the other Hugh'),[18] William Malvoisin, William del Bois, Gervase, Thomas of Stirling and Gilbert of Stirling. Hugh of Roxburgh appears as 'chancellor's clerk' as early as Nicholas of Roxburgh's time.[19] A Richard, perhaps Richard of Lincoln, appears as 'chancellor's clerk' in Walter de Bidun's time.[20] One act issued under Walter the chancellor gives us a glimpse of the 'establishment' of the chapel, being witnessed by Hugh (of Roxburgh?), king's clerk, and Hugh (*de sigillo*?) and John, clerks of the chancellor.[21] During the chancellorship of Hugh of Roxburgh four clerks, Hugh (not necessarily identical with Hugh *de sigillo*) and Masters Martin, Nigel and Nicholas are called 'clerks of the chancellor'.[22] It seems clear that clerks so described were not necessarily members of the writing-office or 'secretariat', since Master Martin and Master Nicholas were two of the king's physicians, and it was apparently normal usage to call the royal doctors *clerici regis*.[23] But we seem to be on safer ground with Hugh *de sigillo* himself, whose byname clearly indicates a place in the writing department, and may mean that Hugh had responsibility for the actual day-to-day keeping and use of the seal.[24] His position is underlined by a document of 1193 in which he is called a clerk of the lord king's chapel.[25] Hugh of the Seal remains a somewhat dim figure, despite his many years of loyal service; but he was senior and respected enough to receive the highest award a civil servant might expect, a bishopric. Appointed to Dunkeld in 1214, he died fifteen years later, remembered at Dunkeld as 'the poor people's bishop'.[26] In the 1193 document two other clerks are given the same description as Hugh, Gervase, of whom little else is discoverable, and William del Bois, who seems to have risen rapidly. It is probably not a coincidence that one of the earliest written acts to bear a day-of-month date, belonging to the summer of 1195 (no.379), is written in the same graceful hand as one of November, 1203, which bears the unique subscription 'datum per manum Willelmi de Boscho', in the time of the probably absent chancellor Florence (no.434). Six years of Hugh of Roxburgh's chancellorship had gone by without any reform of the dating apparatus;

yet within two years of the first appearance of William del Bois charters and brieves begin to go out with the day-of-month dating, and one of the first is apparently in William's own handwriting. As we have seen, William del Bois got the chancellorship in 1211. He resigned in 1226 because of ill health,[27] and was never promoted to a bishopric.

Evidence which is tabulated below[28] in the analysis of the hand-writing of surviving originals suggests strongly that the king's clerks were the men who actually wrote (as, no doubt, they also composed) the king's charters and brieves, etc., and that this task was one of high responsibility and skill. Royal scribes, in short, were far from humble nonentities. It is probably not rash to identify five of these scribes by name: Richard of Lincoln, William del Bois, Gervase (formerly a clerk of Bishop Jocelin of Glasgow), Hugh *de sigillo* and Gilbert of Stirling. Of these, del Bois became chancellor, Gilbert of Stirling became bishop of Aberdeen,[29] Hugh *de sigillo* became bishop of Dunkeld, and the probability seems very strong that Richard of Lincoln was 'Richard the king's clerk' who in 1187 was made bishop of Moray.[30] Richard ruled the see for sixteen years, and if this was indeed Richard of Lincoln it might help to explain why the constitution of Lincoln cathedral church was adopted by the church of Moray in the episcopate of Bishop Brice, Richard's immediate successor.[31] It would be tempting, but too speculative, to attach the hand-writing of other well-recorded royal scribes to well-recorded individuals. It is sufficient to say here that truly 'professional' scribes in the king's employment seem to have numbered about a dozen.[32] Enough original acts have survived from every decade of the reign to make it certain that no professional royal scribe who worked for any length of time has gone unrepresented.

We have evidence of some eleven different royal chaplains in the course of the reign, and the pattern of their appearances in record suggests that the court normally had two chaplains serving together. Naturally there might be breaks in this pattern, but the following 'pairs' of chaplains are discernible: 1165–*c.*1168, Richard (previously one of Malcolm IV's chaplains) and Dolfin; *c.*1168–70, Richard (appointed bishop of Dunkeld, 1170) and William; *c.*1170–8, William, Robert and Hugh; after 1178, when Hugh was made bishop of St Andrews, the same William, with Robert and another Hugh (evidently called Hugh 'the little')[33] are recorded until the later 1180s, by which time William has dropped out or is on the point of disappearance, while Hugh appears so fleetingly as to suggest that he was not itinerant with the court.[34] Robert the chaplain appears alone for some time around 1189–90, before being joined by Ralph, but his new colleague may have been the 'Rannulph, the lord king's chaplain' who on 15 June, 1184, granted a tenement in the burgh of Forfar to Coupar Angus Abbey.[35] By 1195, Robert had evidently obtained the archdeaconry of Glasgow and had resigned his place in the king's chapel.[36] His place was taken, as Ralph's junior colleague, by Walter of St Albans. Ralph disappears *c.*1196, at precisely the time that a certain Ralph was made bishop of Brechin,[37] and a chaplain named William, presumably not the earlier William, takes Ralph's place. Walter of St Albans and

William then appear to have had a fairly long spell of office together, probably only broken when, in December, 1207, Walter of St Albans was elected to the see of Glasgow in more effective succession to Florence of Holland.[38] William now became senior chaplain, his junior being named Oliver; and it may be noted that Master Marchisius de Aubeney, one of the chaplains of Roger bishop of St Andrews and (by 1215) a canon of Lincoln, had a brother named Oliver.[39] William and Oliver seem to have remained in office until the end of the reign, but by February, 1213, they had been joined by a chaplain named Robert, who, before the king died, had been elected to the bishopric of Ross.[40]

In the absence of surviving chamberlains' accounts, our knowledge of the day-to-day activity of the *camera regis* is hardly greater for William I's reign than for his brother's. Nevertheless, the chamber does seem to emerge more clearly as an institution, and we are able to form some picture of its personnel. Under William I, the chief chamberlain's office, that of *camerarius regis Scottorum*, was treated as a lay baron's office, but was evidently not made hereditary. The king was served in the office by only two different men, Philip de Valognes (1165–*c.*1171 and *c.*1193–1214) and Walter of Berkeley (*c.*1171–*c.*1193). There is no suggestion in the evidence that the Philip de Valognes who died, as king's chamberlain, in 1215 and was 'honourably buried' in the chapter house of Melrose Abbey was not the same man who appears in King William's service at the very beginning of his reign, and is soon found giving a charter to Melrose of the land of Ringwood, near Hawick, which in King Malcolm's time had been owned by Osulf son of Uhtred.[41] Although both Philip de Valognes and Walter of Berkeley appear many times in the witness lists, and were both required to be hostages under the Treaty of Falaise, there is little to shew of their activity as chamberlains. The frequency of their attestation shews that they were constantly at court, but it is only rarely that we have evidence, as in no.219, of one of the two carrying out a task which may have been appropriate for a chamberlain.

The *camera regis* seems to become more of a reality when we look at the men of lower rank than the two prominent barons who held the chamberlainship. Setting aside lesser *camerarii* such as Edmund and Godfrey, who seem to have served William only before his accession,[42] or Stephen, who was perhaps not a royal servant,[43] we have evidence of a small group of permanent chamber officials, one or two of whom were already in office in the previous reign. The group may have included Peter the clerk of Stirling at the start of the reign,[44] and Richard Revel towards its close,[45] but four men in particular seem to have had undoubted connexions with the chamber, and are not called *clerici*. Ralph *de camera* witnessed four acts of King Malcolm, at Stirling, Edinburgh, Roxburgh and Traquair,[46] and six acts of King William, all at Stirling.[47] His last appearance is *c.*1204 (no.433). His son (unnamed) held the churches of Campsie and Antermony before 1174 (no.120, comment). Herbert *de camera* (not to be confused with Herbert, the baronial chamberlain of David I and Malcolm IV, and father-in-law of the baron Hugh Giffard of Yester) does not appear before 1165, but he witnessed no fewer than twenty-eight of William I's acts, nine of them at either Stirling or Clackmannan. Herbert's son Adam witnessed six acts, all towards the close of the reign. Richard son of Hugh of the chamber, whose wife owned land in Fordell, Fife, and between Dalgety and Leuchat on the shores of the Forth, also witnessed twenty-eight of William I's acts, thirteen of them at Stirling and three at Clackmannan. Richard's father was evidently the Hugh *de camera* who witnessed an act of David I at Clackmannan,[48] and two acts of Malcolm IV, at Stirling and Edinburgh.[49] It seems reasonable to suppose that these long-serving laymen were the men who carried out the permanent routine work of the *camera regis*. The treatise on 'The Scottish king's Household',[50] published by Mary Bateson from Corpus Christi College, Cambridge, MS.37, shews the importance in the household of the *usshiers de office* or *usshiers del us*, the ushers or doorwards of office or of the door, 'who hold office directly of the king' (*qi sont au Roi en chief*), and the so-called 'Laws of Malcolm Mackenneth' specify what appear to be these doorwards, or *hostiarii*, as being of kitchen, hall and chamber respectively.[51] We may guess that some if not all of these cameral personnel under William I held the office of doorward or usher of the chamber. The fact that of the seventy-five recorded appearances of Hugh, Richard, Ralph, Herbert and Adam of the chamber, from the reign of David I to 1214, thirty-five occur at Stirling or Clackmannan, while no other locality approaches this frequency, suggests that the king's chamber, in the sense of a physical repository of coin, treasure and other valuables, may have been located in Stirling castle. At least this must be set beside the evidence that Edinburgh or Roxburgh castles were preferred as the king's most secure receptacles. In 1134, 1196 or 1197 and 1210 Roxburgh and Edinburgh castles were used to house state prisoners;[52] but Roxburgh was not available from 1175 to 1189 nor Edinburgh from 1175 to 1186; and it may be no coincidence that our longest run of references to cameral personnel in the Stirling-Clackmannan area begins about 1175.

Walter son of Alan, who had been Steward to David I and Malcolm IV, continued to serve William I until his death in 1177, although there are signs that towards the end of his life he may not have been so assiduous in attendance at court as in the 1150s and 1160s. It is remarkable that nothing is heard of him during the war of 1173–4, nor was he among the hostages demanded under the peace terms of 1174–5. His son and heir Alan began to witness royal acts in his father's lifetime, but he never seems to have equalled his father's record of constant attendance in the court. He may still have been a relatively young man when he died in 1204. Four years earlier, while King William was at Lincoln doing homage to King John, Alan, without consulting the king, arranged a marriage between his daughter Aveline and the powerful 'earl' or lord of Carrick, Duncan son of Gilbert (Roland of Galloway's first cousin).[53] This action made the king angry, and he took twenty-four pledges from Alan as surety for his good behaviour. Alan's eldest son and heir, Walter II, was perhaps under age when he succeeded his father as Steward. It is noteworthy that he is not named as a witness of the king's important charter founding the burgh of Ayr, probably issued in May, 1205, and there is no evidence that he took any active part in the royal household or in government until the reign of Alexander II.

In the day-to-day management of the household, however, and especially in the administration of its supplies, it is clear that King William had already an embryonic department more or less independent of the Steward. The importance of the royal *prebenda* has already been shewn.[54] Within the first few years of the reign (perhaps at its very outset), Richard *clericus regis de prebenda*, the king's clerk of the provend, witnessed the great confirmation of privileges for St Andrews (no.28). The inference must be that the victualling and provisioning work of the household had been brought under the supervision of a single official. Presumably he was subordinate to the Steward, but in ordinary day-to-day management he must surely have been largely independent. Richard of the provend was a relation of the king, but there is no evidence to shew what the relationship was.[55] He witnessed fifty of the king's surviving acts (most frequently from 1189 to 1203), played a prominent part as the king's loyal supporter in the St Andrews election dispute (1178–88),[56] and in 1203 was made bishop of Dunkeld, dying seven years later at the episcopal manor-house of Cramond and being buried at Inchcolm Abbey.[57]

In the treatise on 'The Scottish King's Household', possibly composed for the benefit of John Balliol and referring to the state of affairs *c.*1286, the clerk of the Provend is described as the senior colleague of a clerk of the Liverance or Livery.[58] There were also clerks of the Wardrobe and the Kitchen, but it is clear that the general business of supply for the household was the responsibility of the clerks of the Provend and of the Liverance, with the former in ultimate control.

Now, it is a striking fact that although we have abundant references to King William's clerks of the provend—Richard until 1203, and Hugh and Adam (parson of Kinghorn) in his later years[59]—we have almost no mention throughout the reign of any clerk of the liverance, nor indeed of the liverance itself. No.161 (1173 × 78) is witnessed by Simon 'of the liverance'. He may not have been a clerk, but merely a sergeand comparable with Adam of the liverance who held Pettinain by sergeandry in the mid-thirteenth century for the service of providing two archers and one man and horse to supply provisions in the king's household to 'gillies and hounds'[60]. No.134 (1172 × 78) is the only act in the collection to refer specifically to a royal clerk of the liverance, Richard, at that time parson of St Cyrus in Mearns. It is notorious that King William employed more than one clerk named Richard, but it will not help to multiply the king's Richards beyond necessity. It is probable that this Richard *clericus de liberatione* and parson of St Cyrus was identical with one of the Richards otherwise known to have been in the king's service. The possible candidates are Richard of St Albans (who served Malcolm IV), Richard of Lincoln, Richard of Arbroath,[61] Richard of Scotia[62] and Richard *de prebenda*. These were not necessarily five different persons; Richard of Arbroath and Richard of Scotia were probably the same. It was normal practice, apt to confuse the modern student, for clerks to be known not only by their place of origin but also by the name of one of the benefices they held. It looks rather as though we had record of four different royal clerks named Richard; that Richard of St Albans died or retired about 1172; that Richard of Lincoln was too closely associated with secretarial work to be concerned with the supply department; and that the king's clerk of the liverance was either Richard 'of Arbroath' *alias* 'of Scotia' or else he was no other than Richard *de prebenda*. The attraction of the latter identification is that the absence of further references to the liverance could be explained by the inference that, at least until 1203, provend and liverance were treated as one, under the control of the king's highly responsible clerk Richard *de prebenda*. A lost charter by William I to his 'kinsman' (no.581), preserved by the laird of Lauriston in St Cyrus in the seventeenth century, might conceivably have been a charter of the church or of land in St Cyrus given to Richard *de prebenda* by the king. At the very end of the reign we find mention of Richard son of Michael, called *expensarius* (no.515).[63] The *expensa* was the victuals and other commodities consumed within the household, and presumably Richard was a member of the supply staff, whether of the king or of the queen is not certain. In no.270 (1187) the word *expensa* seems to be used of an actual sub-department of the household, the 'spence', associated closely with the *coquina*, kitchen. The treatise on the Scottish king's household already referred to makes no mention of the spence, but it devotes a passage to the clerk of the kitchen (subordinate to the clerk of the provend).[64] The list of household officers in the Laws of Malcolm Mackenneth similarly includes the clerk of the kitchen and says nothing of an *expensarius* or of the spence as a department.[65] Both tracts refer to a pantler and a lardiner, of whom we find no mention in the acts of William I, and also to a butler (for whom see below) and a baker. The Laws of Malcolm Mackenneth assign the same salary (half that of the clerk of the kitchen, butler and pantler) to the baker, brewer, master cook and lardiner.[66] Surviving acts of William I and his son provide evidence for what are clearly dynasties of royal bakers and master cooks (nos.174, 510),[67] and for a royal brewer (no.209), who, from his name, seems, suitably enough, to have been a Fleming.[68] Of a clerk of the kitchen, however, there appears to be no trace in this collection.

In earlier reigns, as has been seen, the task of ensuring that each member of the household received his proper rations was carried out by an officer who bore the Gaelic title *rannaire*, 'divider (of food)'.[69] No.164, given at Stirling as late as 1173–8, was witnessed by Gillecrist the *rannaire*. What relationship, if any, he bore to his predecessors, Gillandres and his father Alfwin mac Archill, is unknown. But his name proves that a household office of Gaelic type, held evidently by a native Scot bearing a Gaelic personal name, was still recognized in

King William's court in the 1170s. Gillecrist the *rannaire* should be considered alongside a group of Scottish witnesses who appear in a few acts mostly issued at Perth. Their presence reminds us, in the midst of so much innovation and introduction of English and continental ways, of the traditional flavour and quality of the older royal household establishment, at least in Strathearn, Gowrie and Angus. The group included Gillecolm the marischal, who betrayed Auldearn castle to the MacWilliams in or before 1187; Gillemichel mac Dunecan; and Malcolm mac Gillise (MacLeish), who appears at Stirling with King Malcolm[70] and at Perth with King William.[71] Gillecrist of Forteviot (perhaps the thane of Forteviot) witnessed no.28, at Dunfermline. The member of the group who appears most frequently was Gillecrist son of Samuel's daughter, who witnessed four or five acts, mostly at Perth, and who at the king's command perambulated land in the Mearns along with Geoffrey II de Melville (nos.344, 345). The position of most of these men is obscure. They can scarcely be regarded as important landowners, still less barons, and the likelihood is that they were all royal servants in various capacities, holding their offices by hereditary right.[72]

The office of butler does not seem to have been accorded any special prominence or dignity under William I, though it was never held by a man of less than knightly rank. Ranulf de Soules, lord of Liddesdale and ancestor of a family renowned in later Scottish history and legend, was *pincerna regis Scottorum* at the beginning of the reign, and his nephew William de la Hay, who had already been styled butler under King Malcolm, used the title *pincerna regis Scocie* in a twenty-year tack he granted *c.*1172.[73] William de la Hay was one of the king's most prominent and favoured barons, but no more is heard of his holding the butler's office. One of his younger sons was named Malcolm,[74] and it seems safe to identify this Malcolm de la Hay with Malcolm 'the lord king's butler' who owned property in Perth and an estate in the adjacent parish of Rhynd.[75] Malcolm the butler, who had the rank of knight, witnessed only one act of the king in this collection (no.498), but he is to be found, chiefly in Perthshire and Angus, from the late 1190s to the third or fourth decade of the thirteenth century. Nothing has been discovered about Henry the butler, whose son and grandson were infeft in a small estate in east Fife (nos.286, 402).

The importance and dignity of the constableship did not diminish in William I's reign. Richard de Moreville held the office, and was evidently much about the court, until his death in 1189 or 1190.[76] He was succeeded by his son William, who seems to have been equally assiduous in attending on the king but who died, still probably a fairly young man, in 1196.[77] The office then passed to the king's *protégé* Roland of Galloway, in right of his wife Helen, daughter and only surviving heir of Richard de Moreville; and a report preserved by John Fordun says that Roland paid the king of Scots a relief of 700 merks to have William de Moreville's lands and the constableship.[78] Roland died at Northampton on 19 December, 1200,[79] and was succeeded by his elder son Alan, a powerful and ambitious man who outlived King

William by many years. Contemporary evidence does not shew us the constable in action, and it is only by inference that we may judge that he had general charge of the king's knight-service and feudal forces. It would be rash to assume that he took precedence of the earls in general command of the whole army under the king; it seems more probable that the earls were responsible for their own territorial contingents, which would consist overwhelmingly of men on foot. According to Roger Howden, when King William in July, 1174, divided his army into three parts, keeping one division by him to besiege Alnwick castle, he sent out the other two divisions under the command of Earl Duncan of Fife, the earl of Angus (Gillebrigde) and Richard de Moreville.[80] In this account the earls seem to take precedence of the constable.

A further problem is whether the constable had charge of the various and numerous marischals recorded throughout the reign as serving the king. We have already seen Gillecolm the marischal, whose betrayal of Auldearn points to military duties. Besides him, we find marischals called Simon and Hervey, and (far more frequently) Richard, Philip, Herbert and David.[81] Henry of Braid, sheriff of Edinburgh *c.*1200, is also called a marischal *c.*1193.[82] It hardly seems possible to judge from surviving record whether all or any of these marischals had reached the position of the hereditary marischal described in the treatise on the Scottish King's Household. There the marischal is accorded some dignity as a distinct and hereditary household officer, but he was clearly subordinate to the constable and the steward.[83] He was assisted by two 'valet marischals', and it may be that under William I the multiplicity of marischals is to be explained partly on the hypothesis that certain marischals functioned locally, partly on the hypothesis that some were subordinates, serving simultaneously with a chief or senior marischal.

A related and equally difficult problem is to define the role and relative importance of the king's doorward. In this matter the treatise is informative but surprisingly unhelpful.[84] It draws a picture of a royal household almost swarming with doorwards (*usshiers del us*, *usshiers de office*), one at least for every office and department. Furthermore, the treatise applies the name 'durwardes' (its use of English here is striking) to the twenty-four sergeands who formed the king's personal bodyguard directly under the constable. It seems confusing that these men should be called doorwards, but the explanation lies in the fact that whenever the king was 'in residence' there were always twelve to guard the door 'along with the *hostiarii*' in the daytime, while all twenty-four guarded the king's chamber at night. It may be that Jocelin, King William's doorward who held a toft in Montrose *c.*1189–95 (no.351), was an officer of this sort. It is not possible to discern in the treatise the king's doorward *par excellence* such as apparently served William I. Admittedly, the acts contain only very scanty references to doorwards, the first 400 and more yielding only one mention. But no.427 (1201–2) was witnessed by Thomas the doorward, and this man—Thomas, son of Malcolm of Lundie—was obviously of baronial rank, lord of Lundie in Angus and of a large tract of the earldom of Mar, with a castle at the

Peel of Lumphanan and possibly another at Coull.[85] His younger son and eventual successor Alan Durward rose to great prominence under the next two kings. To judge from the infrequency of Thomas Durward's attestations of royal acts, he was not often at court. It may be suggested that his was in fact an ancient and honourable office which had come in practice to be performed by various deputies. Alan Durward's ambition may have made it once more momentarily significant, but after his death, without sons, in 1275 the office, as a single post of distinction, was allowed to lapse. But the 'Laws of Malcolm Mackenneth' list three doorwards, and of these the *hostiarius aule* may represent the principal doorward of earlier times.[86]

JUSTICE AND ADMINISTRATION

Discussion of these topics must be focused, as it was for the reigns of David I and Malcolm IV, on the dispensing of justice by the king, and on the part played by justices or justiciars, sheriffs, thanes, barons and *judices*. The relative abundance of surviving record allows us to make a more confident appraisal of the working of royal justice and of administrative machinery under William I than was possible for the earlier reigns. The geographical divisions already discernible before 1165 underwent little or no change in William's time, but in the course of his reign we hear of certain additional districts for the first time, and find mention of centres not previously recorded in connexion with royal government. We see the king pushing his jurisdiction more effectively into Moray, Ross, Caithness and Galloway. We see an extension and consolidation of the system of sheriffdoms, so that by the time of the king's death in 1214 there is evidence for the existence of some nineteen (probably twenty-three) sheriffdoms, in contrast with the twelve (perhaps seventeen) sheriffdoms for whose existence there is either clear or circumstantial evidence prior to 1165.[87]

It will be as well to begin with the sheriffs and sheriffdoms, since they held a crucial place in the growth of royal government during the century which followed the accession of King David in 1124. At first sight this may seem an unjustifiably large claim, for the acts themselves provide surprisingly few references to either sheriffs or sheriffdoms by name. Surviving brieves are addressed to the sheriffs of Berwick, Roxburgh and Haddington[88] and, more generally, to the sheriffs of Lothian, the Merse, Galloway, Carrick, Lennox and Moray.[89] No more than ten different sheriffdoms appear in the acts with named sheriffs attached to them: in order of appearance in this collection, these are Dunfermline, Lanark, Roxburgh, Haddington, Traquair (Peebles), Edinburgh, Stirling, Clackmannan, Perth and Forfar. Occasionally, an act will refer to the sheriff of a particular sheriffdom (e.g., Crail, no.490, Inverness, no.500), without the sheriff's name being mentioned. When evidence from other contemporary sources is added to what may be derived from the acts themselves, we reach a certain total of nineteen sheriffdoms (adding to those already listed Ayr (= Carrick?), Berwick, Crail, Inverness, Kincardine (Mearns), Linlithgow, Nairn, Scone

(Gowrie) and Selkirk). The total is probably nearer twenty-three, adding Aberdeen, Dumfries, Elgin and Forres, and assuming, perhaps wrongly, that Carrick (no.374) was an early variant of Ayr. Altogether, it seems possible to produce a total of some thirty-seven different men who held sheriff's office under William I.[90] A close study of the witness-lists moreover, shews that it was quite common for a sheriff to witness a royal act issued within his sheriffdom and yet not be given the title of sheriff. Indeed, only a few sheriffs (the most notable being Alexander, sheriff of Stirling), seem to have been given their title as a matter of course. Others might only occasionally be styled sheriff, but we can be reasonably sure that they were holding office on at least some of the occasions when they witness acts without any title. Such are Henry of Graham sheriff of Edinburgh (witnessing as such no.296, but without title nos.297, 308, 364, 368, all at Edinburgh); Alexander of St Martin (sheriff of Haddington, no.252; no title, nos.100, 235, 242, at Haddington); Simon son of Malbeth (sheriff of Traquair, no.252; no title, nos.221, 306); Roger de Mortemer (sheriff of Perth in 1209 (Lawrie, *Annals*, 364) and in no.523; no title, nos.334, 339, 410, 415, 435, 472); Alexander son of Thor (sheriff of Clackmannan, nos.452, 486; no title, nos.375, 451, 469); David de la Hay (sheriff of Forfar, no.503; no title, nos.419, 434, 454, 458, 474). We should also note that William Cumin is called sheriff of Forfar in no.513, in a retrospective reference. He is a frequent witness in Angus, and was probably sheriff earlier than David Hay.

There are yet again others who, though known from non-royal sources to have been sheriffs, are not so styled in the king's acts, but who appear in these at places and times so appropriate as to suggest that they were then holding sheriff's office. Examples of these 'hidden' sheriffs are Robert de Burneville[91] sheriff of Berwick (no.386); Richard de Melville[92] sheriff of Linlithgow (no.407); Henry of Braid[93] sheriff of Edinburgh (no.492); William son of Thor (or Thorald)[94] sheriff of Stirling (nos.160, 161, 164, 226, 322); Robert son of Werenbald[95] sheriff of Lanark (nos.260, 309, 311); Alexander of Synton[96] sheriff of Selkirk (nos.382, 447, 450, 483); and Reginald of Crawford[97] sheriff of Lanark (no.462). There are of course a few sheriffs mentioned in reputable contemporary sources who do not seem to figure in the acts at all. And there are finally a number of men occurring in the acts, usually in the witness-lists, to whom it is tempting to assign sheriffdoms, however tentatively: such would include William Freskin I (any one, or indeed all, of the sheriffdoms of Moray); Henry of Carmunnock (Lanark); Simon Fraser (Traquair); and Walter of Auchterless (Aberdeen). John of Hastings and Humphrey of Berkeley pose a special problem. Both are known to have served as sheriff of Mearns,[98] but neither witnesses any royal act issued in this sheriffdom during the known period of his tenure of office. On the other hand, both men witness quite frequently in Angus, and it does not seem too rash to suggest that they may have served as sheriffs of Forfar for part at least of the long period from *c.*1164 to the 1190s during which we have no explicit record of any holders of this office.

If we ask from what social class the sheriffs were drawn, it is not easy to give an adequate answer. When a sheriff appears with a Celtic name (Gillebride of Dunfermline, Macbeth of Scone or Gowrie) he is to be compared with those native Scots who served David I and Malcolm IV as sheriffs, but we cannot tell whether such men were substantial local magnates or essentially royal servants. The great majority of William I's sheriffs were evidently incomers of continental stock or origin, but this does not mean that they were all of baronial or even knightly status. There is no denying baronial status to many of the sheriffs, whether native or immigrant, e.g., John son Orm and Walter Corbet (Roxburgh), Alexander of St Martin (Haddington), Simon son of Malbeth or Macbeth (Peebles-Traquair), William Cumin (Forfar) or William Freskin II (Nairn). The records, moreover, shew that there was a marked tendency for a qualified hereditary principle to be recognized by the crown. Although only a very few sheriffdoms (e.g. Selkirk) seem to have been hereditary offices in the strict sense, many sheriffdoms were held by some member of one or other of a group of powerful local families. Thus the Grahams in Lothian, the Frasers in Peebles, the Melvilles in Aberdeen and Mearns and the Freskins (*de Moravia*) in Moray all seem to have established some sort of 'claim' to their sheriffdoms, although this may mean no more than that they were well-placed to influence the king's appointments. Perhaps the most striking example in the period before 1214 is provided by Stirling. It seems likely that Thor or Thorald, Swain's son, lord of Tranent, functioned as sheriff of Lothian under David I.[99] William son of Thor or Thorald was for some years sheriff of Stirling, and was succeeded by his son Alexander. Only in the 1220s was this succession broken with the appointment of Maurice earl of Menteith.[100] At the same time, Alexander son of Thor (evidently William's brother), held the neighbouring sheriffdom of Clackmannan.

Abuse of power by a semi-hereditary sheriff who was also a local baron is a commonplace of Scottish no less than of English history. A Kincardineshire jury of the late twelfth century swore to make a true perambulation between Walter son of Sibbald and Humphrey of Berkeley and not to be swayed 'by any gift or through fear of Humphrey who was then sheriff'.[101] Not all of William I's sheriffs, however, were barons. Michael Fleming and Henry of Braid the marischal (Edinburgh), Geoffrey, son of Richard the steward of Kinglassie (Crail or Fife), and Ralph the clerk (Perth) were surely royal servants rather than local magnates, although Henry of Braid was a knight and both he and Geoffrey son of Richard were landowners.[102] One of the themes of administrative development in the thirteenth century may be the progressive capture of the sheriffdoms by the nobility. Under King William the nobles clearly held no monopoly of this crucial office.

As for the work carried out by the sheriffs, the acts yield little precise information, although they leave no doubt of the ubiquitous activity and indispensability of the sheriffs as the crown's secondary administrative officers. Perambulation and the giving of sasine (*traditio*), enforcement of the obligation to pay teind, responsibility for regular payments from burgh fermes and other crown revenues, enforcement of royal protections and prohibitions, taking poinds and hearing statements by 'warrands' (warrantors)—such seem to have formed the staple of a sheriff's duties.

There is evidence that at least an embryonic sheriff court existed as early as the reign of William I. Chapter XIX of the *Assise Regis Willelmi*, which provides for each sheriff to hold a court in his sheriffdom every forty days, reads like the composition of a period appreciably later than 1214.[103] Chapter XII, however, may be an authentic law of King William.[104] It stipulates for the presence of the sheriff or his sergeand at every session of a lord's court, where their duty will be to see that the court is properly conducted and that law and justice are done. Four crown pleas—murder, rape, plunder and arson—were to be withheld from a lord's jurisdiction, the implication being that the sheriff would have all such cases transmitted to a royal court. This assize seems to be in line with no.80 (1166 × 1172), which allows Robert de Brus a court for Annandale but expressly requires six crown pleas (adding treasure-trove and premeditated assault) to be reserved. Such pleas will be passed, through the agency of a vassal of de Brus nominated by the king, to the court of the king's justices within a named (but illegible) *comitatus* which is probably to be identified as Roxburgh. Here, *comitatus* is surely to be taken to mean 'sheriffdom', as it seems to in Chapter III of the *Assise* dealing with warrandice in cases of stolen cattle. The provision for one of de Brus's vassals to report and present the reserved cases looks like an exceptional favour to a privileged tenant-in-chief.

The nearest that any of the acts seems to come to speaking of a sheriff's judicial powers is in no.39 (*c*.1166). If the abbot of Holyrood should fail to do justice upon one of his men accused or challenged for any reason (save theft or bloodshed) on the open highway, then the sheriff and the justice are to do right to the injured party in accordance with the truth of his cause. But even here the sheriff is associated with the justice or justiciar. The most acceptable interpretation of the surviving evidence is that down to 1214, if not later, royal justice was administered and dispensed in two forms (1) in the *curia regis* proper, before, or in the presence of, the king in person; (2) at a session held by one or more of the royal justices. That such a session would normally have been held at the chief burgh of a sheriffdom is more than likely; and it may have been the sheriff's duty to convene the suitors of the sheriffdom. The sheriffdom court of Lanark is mentioned explicitly in a series of documents of the year 1200 anent the resignation of the lands of Grangehall in Pettinain.[105] The series concludes with this declaration: 'I Peter [son of William de Asseby] have caused this writing to be read out in the sheriffdom court (*comitatu*) of Lanark, in the presence of William de Somerville, Simon Lockhart, Thomas of Covington [and other barons of Clydesdale], on Thursday, 15 June [1200].'[106] An earlier part of the record makes it clear that the business was transacted in the presence of the king's sheriff and bailies of Lanark.[107] But as far as royal justice is concerned, we have no warrant for believing that this was dispensed save immediately, by the king in his *curia*, or by means of the king's authority delegated to men who bore the title of *justitia* or *justitiarius*.

We have record during William I's reign of some fifteen such men, explicitly given this title. The probability is that two or three others, who are found carrying out work characteristic of the justice's office, were serving in this capacity for a time, or *ad hoc*, although not given the title in surviving record.[108] The pattern in which the occurrences of the named justices are distributed throughout the acts is of the greatest interest and significance. It must be emphasized that in the list which follows, the occurrences are only those in which the title justice (justiciar) is given to the man named. David Olifard occurs 10 times, between nos.14 and 108; Robert Avenel twice (nos.129, 130); Earl Duncan II of Fife 45, between nos.134 and 429; Walter Olifard the elder 8, between nos.162 and 248; Richard Cumin twice (nos.174, 175); Robert de Quinci 3 (nos.180, 182, 184); Geoffrey de Melville (the elder?) once (no.192); Roland son of Uhtred 3 (nos.309, 401, 406); William of Lindsay 5 (nos.316, 317, 366, 401, 406); Gervase Avenel 2 (nos.481, 483); Earl Gilbert of Strathearn 2 (nos.337, 433); Earl Patrick of Dunbar 3 (nos.381, 400, 460); David of Lindsay 3 (nos.481, 483, 493); and William Cumin—later earl of Buchan—12, between nos.465 and 522. In addition to these fourteen, Matthew bishop of Aberdeen is said on good authority to have functioned as a royal justiciar probably in the late 1180s or in the 1190s.[109] Understandably, Bishop Matthew would not have been given the title 'justice' in a document, but we should note that he collaborated with Earl Duncan and others in Moray in a perambulation of land for Kinloss Abbey, possibly while he was serving as justiciar (no.543).

If we were dealing only with the men named as justice once, twice or three times, we might suppose that they held office very briefly, and that the absence of title in surviving record necessarily means that they were not then holding office. But this argument cannot be used of David Olifard, Earl Duncan, Walter Olifard the elder and William Cumin. The first three in particular occur often without title in record of the period within which they are known to have acted as justice. It seems out of the question that during these periods they were bobbing back and forth, now in, now out, of office. On the contrary, it is more reasonable to suppose that during the reign of Malcolm IV and the earlier years of William I's reign charter clerks might fail to give the title of justice to a man even when he was actually holding this office. It follows that even in the case of the nine or ten men to whom the title is not given in more than three surviving acts we should not infer that they functioned as justices only very briefly or on an *ad hoc* footing.

The distribution pattern allows us to go further. In the first hundred acts, down to *c.*1172, only David Olifard is named as justice. Earl Duncan's long run of occurrences with title begins *c.*1172, and more or less simultaneously we find Robert Avenel (of Eskdale), Walter Olifard (of Bothwell and Smailholm) and Richard Cumin (of Bedrule and West Linton) making their appearance. We might be tempted to argue from this that David Olifard was sole justice for the first few years of the reign, filling the place of *supprema justicia* referred to under Malcolm IV.[110] After his death, the office would have been shared among two or more men simultaneously. But there is an alternative explanation which seems to fit the evidence better. Under King Malcolm there already existed a justice of Scotia. It seems likely that this position was held by Earl Duncan—who may also, indeed, have been the 'justice of Fife' addressed in a brieve of 1161 × 1164.[111] In view of the pre-1165 practice of not adding the title 'justice' to a man's name in a written document, it would not be surprising if for the first few years of William's reign the earl of Fife—who witnesses often enough—had in fact been justice without being so styled. A new practice, however, was slowly coming in, and was applied (though sporadically) to David Olifard, doubtless because unlike Earl Duncan he had no other mark of distinction.

If this were the case, we could suggest that there was already a regional division of the justiciarship. Earl Duncan could be seen as already justiciar of Scotia, although he is explicitly styled thus only in nos.275 and 388. This would accord closely with the geographical area with which the acts styling the earl 'justice' are concerned, and with the admittedly scanty record of his activity as justice.[112] Earl Duncan died in 1204 and was succeeded, perhaps in the following year,[113] by William Cumin, who is styled *justicia(rius) Scott(orum)* or *justicia Scocie* in five royal acts. There is no question that these men were the direct forerunners of the later Lord Justice-General of Scotland.

David Olifard could be seen as an early (although arguably not the first)[114] figure in a long line of justiciars of Lothian. Our interpretation of the position held by some of those who are styled 'justice' very infrequently is bound to remain inconclusive. But it hardly seems rash to suggest that Walter Olifard the elder was, like his father, justiciar of Lothian, and that he was succeeded in turn by William of Lindsay, Earl Patrick of Dunbar and David Lindsay I.[115] David Lindsay was himself succeeded in the 1220s (perhaps not immediately) by Walter Olifard II, whose tenure as justiciar of Lothian is well established; and he in turn was succeeded by David Lindsay II. The evidence strongly supports the view that Scotia and Lothian each had a justiciar simultaneously (e.g., no.200), and is compatible with the view that within Scotia and Lothian there could be more than one justiciar at a time, although presumably one always held a senior or principal position. Thus, Bishop Matthew of Aberdeen and Earl Gilbert of Strathearn were justices in Scotland benorth Forth contemporaneously with Earl Duncan,[116] while Gervase Avenel appears as a justice in the south contemporaneously with David Lindsay.[117] Roger Howden, a knowledgeable reporter of Scottish events, tells an interesting story of the big spate in the River Tweed in 1199, which carried away the border bridge at Berwick.[118] Its replacement would have to be undertaken jointly by the Scots and the bishop of Durham, as lord of Tweedmouth; and the king of Scotland commanded Earl Patrick of Dunbar to take charge of the Scottish side of the affair. Howden calls the earl 'warden of Berwick, and at that time chief justiciar of the whole kingdom of the Scots'. Howden's words deserve respect, but they must be set against the improbability that Earl Duncan of Fife would have accepted second place, as justiciar of Scotland, towards the end of his life. It seems more likely that Earl Patrick was holding the office of justiciar of Lothian, with which the custody of Berwick would naturally be held. But if this was so, we must note the difficulty that Earl Patrick seems to have been justiciar in July, 1195 (no.381), while it looks as though William of Lindsay was still justiciar as late as August, 1198 (no.400).

It may be suggested further that in addition to the justice of Scotia and the justice of Lothian, there was already before the end of William I's reign a third regional justice, appointed by the king to administer the fiercely independent and separatist south-west: a justiciar of Galloway. In three acts probably belonging to the last decade of the twelfth century, Roland (Lachlan) son of Uhtred, lord of Galloway, is styled 'justice';[119] in two of them he appears with William of Lindsay, also styled 'justice', no doubt of Lothian. Of these, no.406 seems especially significant, for it seeks to enforce what the king calls 'my assize of Galloway' anent the pursuit of thieves. Chapter XXIII of the *Assise Regis Willelmi*,[120] which is surely to be accepted as a genuine product of William I's reign, records a provision anent levying royal cain from Galloway made in the *curia regis* at Lanark on 1 May (year unstated), 'by the *judices* of Galloway . . . before Roland son of Uhtred and other responsible men'. It therefore looks as if Roland had been appointed justiciar of Galloway, perhaps the first of his line, by King William. There does not seem to be any record of a justiciar of Galloway between 1200, when Roland died, and *c.*1258, when John Comyn, lord of Badenoch, held the office.[121] His predecessor may have been his uncle Walter Comyn, earl of Menteith (died 1258),[122] but even if Earl Walter had been justiciar of Galloway in the 1240s this would leave a lengthy gap in the evidence. In view of the paucity of record relating to Galloway this gap would hardly disprove the suggestion put forward here that there were three permanent justiciarships in the Scottish kingdom before 1200, the premier one for Scotia (Scotland north of Forth), another for Lothian, and a third for Galloway.

If this suggestion is correct, a particular interest would attach to the witness list of no.308, granting an annual fair at the beginning of July to the bishop of Glasgow—the foundation of Glasgow Fair. This charter was issued at Edinburgh at some date between 1189 and 1195. It was witnessed by the bishop of Dunkeld and the chancellor, Hugh of Roxburgh. Next come the names of Archibald abbot of Dunfermline, who seems to have acted as a justiciar or at any rate a principal administrative officer for several years before his death in 1198, and of Osbert abbot of Kelso. Immediately after the abbots come Earl Duncan of Fife, Roland son of Uhtred and William of Lindsay. None is accorded an official title, but on the hypothesis put forward here they were respectively justiciars of Scotia, Galloway and Lothian. The six remaining names contain only one man entitled sheriff—Alexander (son of

William) of Stirling—but four others, Walter Corbet (Roxburgh), William Cumin (Forfar), Robert son of Werenbald (Lanark) and Henry of Graham (Edinburgh), are all known to have served as sheriffs. The silence of the king's clerks must not make us ignore the possibility that witnesses to royal acts contained a far higher proportion of officials than a first glance would suggest. Moreover, the evidence from witness-lists seems to be borne out by that provided by the lists of addressees in surviving acts. In this collection there are seventeen brieves addressed specifically to the king's justices and sheriffs, sometimes with the addition of the king's 'officers' or 'bailies'. Four other brieves are addressed simply to sheriffs, with or without other officers. The prevalence of this form of address for legal and administrative brieves points unmistakably to a settled system of administering the law in which royal justices were expected to play a permanent role.

At this point we turn to the treatise on the Scottish king's household, which, as has been suggested above, may belong to *c.*1292. The passage which it devotes to the justices or justiciars is worth giving in full.[123]

> 'Justices. Furthermore, as regards the officers outwith the household, there ought first of all to be suitable Justices (apart from those who hold by inheritance), to be chosen by the afore-named magnates. These Justices shall know how, and be able, to provide law and justice to poor as well as rich, and to preserve and control the rights of the king in all matters which pertain to his crown. They shall do this in such a way that no plaints should be presented to the king save only those which, because the Justices or sheriffs have failed to deal with them, cannot be remedied without the presence of the king himself.
>
> And there shall be in Scotland three Justices, that is to say a Justice of Lothian, a Justice of (Scotland) north of Forth, and a Justice of Galloway. They shall hold their sessions of the justice-ayre twice a year, once at the season of grass and a second time at the season of winter (corn); and they shall appoint coroners for whom they are wont to be responsible. And the Justices ought to enquire on their ayre into the conduct and administration of the sheriffs and sergeands of fee and challenge them at the bar and present their misdemeanours to the king personally, and at other times when they have defaulted.'

Save for the provision anent coroners (who, however, are referred to in Chapter XXX of the *Assise Regis Willelmi*),[124] there is nothing in this important passage which would not apply to William I's reign. On the two central points, we may say with some confidence that the treatise describes a situation which already obtained before 1200: namely, that the role of the justices was to dispense justice evenly to all the king's subjects and to determine all crown pleas save the most solemn or difficult ones; and that there were three justices, for Scotia, Lothian and Galloway respectively. A further point is worth making, in view of the prevailing opinion that Scotland in the thirteenth century relied on ecclesiastical courts for much if not all of its ordinary civil law. As it has been put recently, 'Royal justice was just not sufficiently competent and active, so litigants sought ecclesiastical justice instead'.[125] This thesis could not be sustained for William I's reign, and it may be suspected that it would be difficult to sustain for the thirteenth century save by straining the argument from silence. Against it, at least, we should put the treatise's clear statement, that the justices should 'provide law and justice for poor and rich'. Nevertheless, we cannot fail to notice a striking contrast with contemporary developments in Angevin England. In the first place, the English kings, after *c.*1166, set their faces firmly against regional or locally-based justices. Until justices of the peace began to be appointed nearly two hundred years later, in the middle of the fourteenth century, local royal justices were unknown in England. Secondly, English judicial development, from Henry II's reign onwards, was characterized by the prevalence, eventually the exclusive monopoly, of professionals, who had undergone a lengthy apprenticeship and legal training. This suited—indeed, was essential for—the complexity of the system by which law and justice were administered south of the Border, and the much larger corpus of substantive law. The volume of substantive law in Scotland was obviously much less, and the system of administration was correspondingly much simpler. For whatever reasons, no *cadre* of trained, professional judges grew up in Scotland. The justices under William I were, and under his two successors remained, leading noblemen, drawn from a remarkably restricted range of baronial families. They served as the crown's chief administrative officers in the three principal regions of the kingdom. They cannot be called professional, but that does not mean that they lacked skill or experience, still less that professional skill and advice were not available to them.

Behind the justice-ayres in the sheriffdoms and behind the sheriffdom court itself there presumably lay some tradition of local justice and provincial courts. The *judices* who, in the twelfth and thirteenth centuries, are found attached to provinces everywhere in Scotland north of Forth and also in the south-west, evidently represented a survival of this tradition, and must, indeed, be seen as its professionals, unable fully to adapt to the new substantive law, whether feudal or Roman.[126] We seem to catch a glimpse of this tradition in the famous Kirkness case of *c.*1128,[127] when we are told that King David I 'moved by pity sent his messengers through the province of Fife and Fothrif and called together a multitude of men in one place'. But we can recover almost nothing of these earlier courts, and do not even know whether their sessions depended on royal or comital summons, or were held independently at periods fixed by custom.

Apart from the church courts, which are outwith the scope of this work, the record of William I's reign shews us only (i) the *curia regis*; (ii) the court of the justiciar;[128] (iii) an embryonic sheriff court; and (iv) justice mediated by an express grant of the king to certain tenants-in-chief. This is not the place to discuss the large and still obscure question of the origins of baronial jurisdiction in Scotland, for which one indespensable starting-point is still Rachel Reid's important paper in Volume XXXV of the *English Historical Review* on 'Barony and Thanage'.[129] But attention should be drawn to the evidence for mediated or 'private' justice contained in the acts of King William.

From the time of the 'earliest Scottish charter' (1093–4), a tenant-in-chief might be granted sake and soke by the king.[130] King Duncan II gave this to the monks of St Cuthbert at Durham in respect of the lands of Tyninghame, Auldhame, Scoughall, 'Cnolle' and Hedderwick, all in East Lothian. Though this grant was abortive, King David I, *c.*1126, confirmed St Cuthbert's other lands in Scotland to be held 'with sake and soke, toll, team and infangthief'.[131] Thereafter, this phrase becomes conspicuously rare in royal grants until *c.*1170. Jurisdiction, however, was certainly mediated during the intervening half-century. Scone priory had a court with the right to hold trial by combat and the ordeals of iron and water (*fossa*).[132] Dunfermline abbey had a court, 'royal justice' alone being excluded,[133] while St Andrews priory had a court 'with liberties and quittances of pleas and disputes'.[134] Holyrood abbey likewise had the privilege of holding the *examen duelli, aque et ferri calidi*, and the abbot of Holyrood's court was made equal to the courts of the bishop of St Andrews and the abbots of Dunfermline and Kelso.[135] Acts in this collection (nos.197, 363) shew similar courts being granted to the Tironensians of Arbroath (1178) and Lindores (*c.*1190).

Surviving record is notably less explicit with regard to jurisdiction granted to lay tenants-in-chief. Sometimes a man who has been granted land to hold by knight-service is not assigned any jurisdiction by his charter. More often, the charter will specify liberties and customs, which presumably may include jurisdiction, only by comparison. Thus, Robert de Brus I was to hold Annandale 'with all the customs Ranulf Meschin had in Carlisle',[136] and Ernulf the knight was given Swinton 'with the customs with which Liulf and Udard held it'.[137] By the close of David I's reign a formula of comparison was being used: 'as well and freely as one of my barons, who are his neighbours and hold their fiefs freely, best and most freely holds'.[138] This formula remained in use through Malcolm IV's reign[139] and is typical of the earliest knight-service charters of William I: 'as my other barons most freely and honourably hold their lands of me' (no.9), or 'as my other knights most freely and independently hold their fiefs of me' (nos.42, 43). In Malcolm IV's stewardship charter, however (1161), the formula 'as any one of my barons most freely and independently holds his fief of me' forms the coda to a list of liberties and easements which begins with the familiar jingle 'with sake and soke, toll, team and infangthief'.[140] This ancient compendium was apparently revived by the clerks of King William's chapel within a few years of his accession. Whereas the very important Annandale charter (no.80, 1166 × 1172), which obviously concedes all justice to Robert de Brus II save for six named crown pleas, does not use it, the rather later confirmation for William Freskin I (no.116) grants land in West Lothian and Moray 'with soke and sake, toll, team and infangthief and all the liberties which my other barons have'. Thenceforward there is a steady stream of royal infeftments for knight-service, the majority of which grant sake, soke, toll, team and infangthief. Whatever this jurisdiction comprised, it was not limited to land held for military service. For example, both Orm son of Hugh and William Giffard had charters giving them sake and soke, etc. for estates which were held for money rents (nos.152, 340), while Arbroath abbey was given sake and soke, etc. at its foundation in 1178 (no.197). Taking actual grants or infeftments of land for military service as more significant than charters (some of which are only repetitions or confirmations), we find for William I's reign a total of twenty-eight, of which seven are wholly or predominantly of land south of Forth and twenty-one of land to the north.[141] Disregarding William de Vieuxpont's charter (no.84), because so much of its land was in England, only four of the seven southern infeftments grant sake and soke, etc. (nos.125, 171, 200, 459). By contrast, eighteen of the twenty-two northern infeftments specify sake and soke.[142] There is a similar contrast when we consider the sole addition to the sake and soke jingle which the king's clerks permitted themselves as the reign advanced, the words *cum furca et fossa* ('with gallows and pit'). We may suspect that these words had more practical significance than alliterative phrases borrowed from the extraneous traditions of Anglo-Saxon diplomatic. One actual infeftment out of the seven from south of Forth (nos.200, 390) and no fewer than twelve out of the twenty-one northern infeftments specify *furca et fossa*.[143] In later times, 'pit and gallows' became almost synonymous with baronial jurisdiction, the distinguishing mark and test of a barony. Evidently this usage went far back into Scottish history. It is difficult to explain the apparently special importance of 'pit and gallows' benorth Forth, save on the grounds that the sake and soke jingle by itself had possibly even less precise meaning in this predominantly Celtic-speaking region than in Scottish Northumbria. This seems to be suggested by the careful wording of the Arbroath abbey foundation charter (no.197), where the jingle is immediately followed by the words 'and iron and battle and pit and gallows'.

It hardly seems possible to deduce from surviving record the principle according to which one man (or corporate body) was given jurisdiction and another not. In twelfth-century England it was by no means uncommon for quite small grants of land to carry rights of sake and soke, the inference being that in some cases this privilege had been reduced to little more than a form of words. This does not seem to have been true of contemporary Scottish practice. Small-scale infeftments, including sergeandries (serjeanties) for the service of an archer or light horse-soldier or foot soldier, did not include sake, soke, etc. There may even have been a general rule that infeftments for only half a knight's service did not carry the right to pit and gallows. If so, there were exceptions,[144] and in any event the number of surviving examples is too small to allow firm conclusions to be drawn. The confirmation of pit and gallows to Orm son of Hugh, a member of the old native aristocracy, in respect of his lordship of Inverarity in Angus and of the old abbey of Abernethy on the Tay (no.152) surely proves that this jurisdiction was not a foreign importation tied to tenure by military service.

Provisionally we may say that pit and gallows went with the lordship of estates of a size and importance recognized as sufficient to justify it. On the royal demesne, such estates had anciently been held and administered by thanes, but we can hardly argue that apart from the king himself and the earls no one save thanes could exercise a criminal jurisdiction. We must find room for some stratum of nobility intermediate between the typical thane, attached to his single shire-thanage and possessing ministerial or even serviential characteristics, and the earl wielding authority over a wide region. Such men as Orm lord of Abernethy, Swain son of Thor, lord of Ruthven and Ness son of William, lord of Leuchars seem to belong to this stratum. Where the thane exercised criminal jurisdiction, he did so, presumably, because such jurisdiction was inherent in the lordship enjoyed by the king (or earl), and thanages constituted the channel through which royal and comital lordship had come to be delegated before the twelfth century. Thus we find that the thane of Arbuthnott in Mearns took half the merchets and bloodshed fines from the tenants of the church of St Andrews in Arbuthnott, even although he was not their lord.[145]

There are a number of instances, especially in Gowrie, Angus and Mearns, of new men acquiring from King William known or probable thanages as fiefs for knight-service, to be held with sake and soke and normally with pit and gallows. These include the grant of Inverkeilor to Walter of Berkeley (no.185), Fowlis Easter to Roger de Mortemer (no.302), Kinneff to William de Montfort (no.335), Benholm to Hugh of Benholm (no.350), Benvie and Panmure to Philip de Valognes (no.405), Tealing to William Giffard (no.418), and Guthrie to Walter de la Carneille (no.473), all with sake, soke, toll, team, infangthief and pit and gallows. Conveth in Mearns was certainly a thanage, and when the king conveyed four ploughgates there to Humphrey and Agatha of Berkeley (nos.344, 345) he conveyed the thane's rights with the land; but oddly enough the charters do not specify pit and gallows but limit themselves to sake and soke, etc. Nevertheless, it looks as though this jingle, together with pit and gallows, expressed the jurisdiction which a king's thane was expected to possess, and the incoming barons and knights succeeded to it almost as a matter of course. It was presumably such men whom the king had in mind when, in nos.467 and 475, he permitted ale houses only in villages with resident lords of knightly rank.

There can be no doubt of the social reality behind the legal phraseology of the documents, whether or not this was already somewhat archaic in the twelfth century. Infangthief was no mere formality at Annan in 1148, when Saint Malachy, on his last journey from Ireland to Clairvaux, pronounced a solemn curse upon Robert de Brus II for promising deceitfully to pardon a hand-having thief whom the saint saw the next day hanging from gallows by the roadside.[146] The ordeal of water is brought momentarily to life among the arid verbiage of formularies, when King William commands that Orm of Abernethy shall have no more than two ordeal pits, one at Abernethy for his tenants of Gowrie and Fife, one at Inverarity for his tenants of Angus (no.152). By a royal privilege confirmed in 1215, anyone who consigned a tenant of the knights of the Temple to the ordeal pit (*fovea judicii*) when the Templars were ready to stand pledge for him would incur the king's forfeiture, unless the accused man were a convicted and hand-having thief.[147] An agreement between Coupar Angus abbey and Fergus, younger son of Earl Gilbert of Strathearn, which dates from some ten years after King William's death,[148] provides that the abbey's tenants dwelling on a single oxgang at Meikleour in Perthshire shall owe suit to Fergus's court, there 'to answer and do justice according to the laws of the land'. Any fines they incur, or fees they may pay for making agreements with one another, shall go to the abbot. And then Fergus concludes, quite casually it seems, with these words: 'If, however, it should be necessary for any of these tenants to undergo the judgement of water or of iron or mutilation or beheading or some other death, the execution of all these (judgements) upon the offenders will be carried out by my own men.' Fergus of Strathearn did not rank among the great magnates of Scotland, and the inhabitants of a mere bovate of land can scarcely have been either numerous or of much social consequence. The document is a striking illustration, where so much is obscure, of the matter-of-fact working of baronial justice at the level of the ordinary men and women of the Scottish countryside.

REVENUE AND MILITARY SERVICE

In the introduction to the *Acts of Malcolm IV* nine distinct types of royal revenue were listed and described. The same classification holds good for William I's revenues, but the evidence allows us to add a tenth type, namely borrowing from a money-lender. Eight types of revenue were represented in Malcolm IV's acts, of which seven (i.e., all save the regular feudal incidents and revenue from escheats) can be exemplified in this collection. Beyond noting some instances of each, it is necessary only to draw attention to certain additional information obtainable from record of William I's reign, or from somewhat later record where this appears, in a few cases, to throw light on the pre-1214 situation. A complete list of the various types of revenue will be found in the index of subjects.

(1) Illustrations of the royal demesne being set at ferme are so numerous that it seems probable that most of the king's demesne lands were treated thus. In the earlier years of the reign many fermes were payable in kind; later it seems to have become normal to convert rents into money. Thus in the 1170s and 1180s the king speaks of his revenues in Moray solely in terms of kind (nos.139, 273); in 1199 he adds: 'whether the rents be paid in money or in another way by some alteration' (no.421). Commutation of the teind of the king's rents from Fettykil (Leslie) to 23s. 4d. suggests that the king's whole ferme from that thanage had been changed from malt and oats to an annual payment of seventeen and a half merks (no.166). The confirmation to Roxburgh castle chapel after 1189 of teinds from orchards (?) and seasonal slaughtering seems rather old-fashioned (no.315). No.407 gives a good conspectus of the various sorts of revenue due from a

typical small sheriffdom: in addition to the *firma burgi* from the sheriffdom's sole burgh, there are fermes from estates outwith the burgh, rents from mills (these were normally rendered in cereals, measured in chalders), rents in money, wheat, flour, malt and oats, and finally other revenues of an unspecified nature. The shires of Kinghorn and Kellie rendered fermes in wheat, malt and oats (no.107), the shire of Longforgan rendered wheat (no.16), but fermes did not necessarily stay fixed for long periods. Donald, the fermor of Forthar in Fife (perhaps the thane of Forthar, if this estate ranked as a thanage), rendered a ferme in eels between 1165 and 1171; the crown had earlier received a rent in cheese from this estate and anticipated the possibility of varying the ferme again (no.108).

(2) In contrast with the surviving acts of David I and Malcolm IV, those of William I contain numerous references to the *firma burgi*, all expressed in money terms.

(3) Cain due to the king figures in many of the acts. Normally it appears as a revenue in kind, often in cattle, swine and cheese. This is not the place in which to discuss cain as the great universal tribute of Scotland, corresponding to cornage in the northernmost counties of England and to the *commorth* paid to the princes of Wales. There is abundant evidence to shew that the king received cain from the south-west (e.g., nos.189, 367; Chapter XXIII of the *Assise Regis Willelmi*)[149] and generally from Scotland benorth Forth. In view of the apparent identity of this tribute with the cornage or noutgeld of northern England, it is puzzling to find no explicit record of royal cain in Lothian and the Merse, especially since the cain due to the bishop of St Andrews in this region is well attested. The most likely explanation is that surviving record does refer to cain here, although not by that name nor (save dubiously) by the name of 'cornage'. Thus, the royal kitchen revenues in cows, oxen, hides, woolfells, tallow and fat, which the king received from north and south of Lammermuir, and his cheese rents from Tweeddale, can reasonably be taken as corresponding to his cain from other provinces.[150]

Conveth, or waiting, should perhaps have been classified separately in the introduction to Volume I. Like cain, it was a tribute due to the king (as to others) in respect of his lordship. Conveth, however, was specifically hospitality, entertainment and accommodation, or some payment in lieu of these. Its character is brought out in the obligation by which Henry of Ilderton, a Northumbrian dreng, held Ilderton of Earl Patrick I of Dunbar, 'for thirty shillings and one annual feast'.[151] The most detailed and circumstantial evidence for the realities of conveth in twelfth-century Scotland is contained in the depositions of witnesses called before an ecclesiastical court held at Perth on 10 April, 1206.[152] The case concerned a long-standing dispute between the church of St Andrews, represented by the bishop, and the baronial tenants-in-chief—successors to the earlier thanes—of Arbuthnott in Mearns. Some fourteen men, the longest of whose memories went back for more than forty-seven years, testified that the bishops of St Andrews had always been acknowledged as the direct lords of the church lands, or

Kirkton, of Arbuthnott. Many declared that they had seen two, three or four different bishops given hospitality at the Kirkton by their tenants. The parson of Neudosk and one Gillipedes (Gillepeder?) affirmed that Bishops Robert, Arnold, Richard and Hugh had received their conveth from their own men of Arbuthnott, while Somerled (thane?) of Fetteresso added the significant information that Bishop Roger, while on his progress, had declined to take his conveth at Arbuthnott because of the tenants' poverty.

It seems unlikely that the twelfth-century kings of Scots still enjoyed their conveth in this simple, uncommuted fashion. The fact that no fewer than three portions of royal demesne in the north and east bore the name Conveth[153] suggests that the obligation to entertain the king may once have been organized on a provincial basis, and concentrated into resources payable at, or obtainable from, certain estates. In this collection, no.154 shews that Campsie on the Tay paid an annual sum to the king for waiting, while no.514 provides evidence that the waiting due to the king from the well-endowed priory of Coldingham amounted to twenty merks a year. King William's falconers had been given yearly waiting by the Cistercians of Coupar Angus because of the monks' tenure of a certain piece of land, a burden remitted by Alexander II before 1222.[154] The conveths of Moray mentioned in no.395 were due to the bishop of Moray, and similar conveth due to the bishop of St Andrews from churches in Berwickshire is dealt with in nos.368 and 460. A roll dating from before 1198 and inventoried in 1296 gave particulars of 'old money rents and old waitings' due to the crown.[155]

(4) Cain on ships and imports is referred to mainly in confirmations of acts of previous kings (e.g., nos.26, 28, 60, 63). An interesting import duty which the king allowed the monks of May to levy in the little east Fife havens of Anstruther and Pittenweem consisted of fourpence from the four nets of every ship fishing out of these havens or selling their catches there, as well as from every boat big enough to have a fixed rudder (no.207). The monks and their men were exempted from cain and toll on their own goods and on purchases for their own use. The king kept in his own hand the cain of the two ports, presumably useful appendages of his larger port of Crail, but he commanded his officers who had the duty of collecting this cain to pay the monks a tenth of it. The cain of fish at Crail itself was valuable enough to be the subject of a legal wrangle between persons of high rank at the turn of the thirteenth and fourteenth centuries.[156]

(5) Extraordinary taxation or 'aid' (*auxilium*, *commune auxilium*, or, as in no.169, *geldum regium*) is not mentioned often, save in formulas of exemption or its refusal (e.g., nos.434, 438). No.326 (*c.*1190) refers to the aid which had been 'assized' at Musselburgh. No doubt this aid was raised to enable the king to pay 10,000 merks to Richard I of England to free him and his kingdom from the treaty of Falaise. In 1188, William I had refused to levy a Scottish contribution to the Saladin Tithe: in 1193, however, he managed to raise 2,000 merks (we are not told how) to contribute to Richard I's ransom, and a year later he was ready to pay 15,000 merks for the English northern counties,

but the offer was rejected. Before Michaelmas, 1211, the Scottish *camera regis* was evidently able to pay the 7,500 merks actually insisted upon by King John of England out of the 15,000 stipulated in the treaty of Norham.[157] Again, we have no information on how this sum was raised.

(6) There are hardly any explicit references to the regular feudal incidents, wardship, marriage, relief and escheat. Nevertheless, it seems unlikely that the Scottish crown could not avail itself of these fundamental rights. Fordun's report that Roland son of Uhtred paid a relief of 700 merks for the lands and the constableship held by William de Moreville may be accepted as authentic.[158] It might not be rash to infer that whenever a charter of infeftment used the verb *reddere* in its dispositive clause this meant that the proper relief had been paid. In no.125 (1165 × 1174), the king concedes 'that the mother of Ralph of Graham may be in Ralph's gift', from which we may infer that otherwise the lady's marriage would have been at the king's own disposal. And chronicle sources do indeed shew us King William arranging marriages for his tenants-in-chief in the customary manner.[159] The most striking proof that a Scottish feudal magnate of the later years of William I's reign took the feudal incidents for granted in his dealings with his own vassals is contained in a charter, dating before 1210 and confirmed by no.484, by which Walter Olifard the younger undertook to demand no aids from Alan of Swinton for the lands of Colzie 'save for ransoming me from prison if needful, for the knighting of my eldest son and for the marriage of my eldest daughter'.[160]

(7) There do not seem to be any instances in this collection of revenue obtained from subordinate lordships held by the king, although we must remember that outwith Scotland William I held the lordship of Tynedale for the whole of his reign (save for a brief deprivation in the war of 1173–4), and the Honour of Huntingdon from his accession down to 1173. When the Honour was restored in 1185, it was given immediately to William's brother David. We have no means of telling what the real revenue from Tynedale amounted to, but the somewhat notional figure of £10 a year was what the English exchequer reckoned to lose because Tynedale was in Scottish hands.[161] The lordship rendered no military service to the English crown, and paid cornage at the yearly rate of only 33s. 4d.[162]

(8) The profits of justice and comparable revenues—*placita et lucra*—occur fairly frequently (e.g., nos.30, 39, 60, 189, 363). The king compensated Cambuskenneth abbey for taking back into his own hand (before 1177) the teind of his pleas and profits from Stirling, Stirlingshire and Callendar, originally given by David I (no.161). Forfeitures are at much the same rates as under Malcolm IV, and it may be noted that the figure of £10 for 'full forfeiture' (nos.46, 128, 154, 244, 340) and also the penalty of eight cows (no.281) correspond to the maximum fines which according to the 'Laws of Malcolm Mackenneth', c.8, might be imposed by the justiciar of Lothian and the justiciar north of Forth respectively.[163]

(9) *Military service.* The military power which the crown could

summon to its service, and the relationship between this power and the crown's financial resources, form a large topic, to do justice to which would require a sizeable monograph. Here it is possible only to take a little further the account, admittedly sketchy, given in the introduction to Volume I, indicating the evidence available from acts in this collection, and in any case drawing almost entirely on evidence from before 1214. The distinction between knight-service and common army service emerges more clearly under William I than in the period before 1165. There is no evidence that knight-service was ever laid upon lands held by the church. There is no good evidence that scutage was ever levied in Scotland. On the other hand, church lands were liable for common army service equally with lay estates, and it appears that, at least in certain circumstances or places, this common service might be discharged by payments in kind.

In this collection there is record of some thirty-seven distinct infeftments by the crown for the service of knights, eleven of which relate wholly or chiefly to land south of the Forth and the Antonine Wall, the remainder to land north of this line.[164] Some of this evidence is contained in 'lost acts', but even so, thirty-seven knight-service charters survive from William I's reign, and a surprisingly high proportion of these are originals. In their content and formulas they follow a well-defined pattern, although it cannot be said that they are completely stereotyped. Of the total of thirty-seven distinct infeftments, one confers land assessed at twenty knights' feus,[165] two demand ten knights' service, one is for four knights' service (including much land in England), two are for two knights' service, one for one and a half, eighteen for the service of a single knight, and the remainder for various fractions of a knight's service, of which a half is by far the commonest. In royal grants fractions of one-third and one-fifth do occur, but it is only in sub-infeudations that fractions as small as one-twentieth are found. Thirteenth-century evidence suggests that half and quarter knights' feus in the twelfth century might on occasion represent serjeanty holdings.[166] Garrison duty, or ward, at the king's castles was demanded of military tenants, but we know this almost exclusively through clauses of exemption, as in no.80 and no.582. It is impossible to form an adequate picture of the organization of castle ward under William I. Yet it does not seem unreasonable to guess that in each sheriffdom, at least in the south and east, the recognized baronies had already been made responsible for performing ward at the principal royal castles, there being normally no more than one such castle in each sheriffdom. There seems to be something of a garrison quality about the personnel of a charter by which Malcolm, King William's esquire or armour-bearer, granted to Holyrood abbey land by the gate of Linlithgow, which he had had perambulated by the witnesses to his grant, who included three (perhaps seven) of the king's serjeants or sergeands.[167] The acts reveal occasional glimpses of castle officers. The constable of Roxburgh castle was obviously a baron of the first rank.[168] Of lower rank, but nonetheless men of importance, were the janitors or porters of royal castles. Robert and Reginald, janitors of

Edinburgh castle, appear in nos.28 and 174, Roger janitor of Roxburgh in no.65 and Crane janitor of Montrose in no.556. One of the royal marischals, Gillecolm, had charge of Auldearn castle, but whether as constable, janitor or temporary custodian is not clear. Not every royal castle is likely to have had its own constable, and it seems more probable that in most sheriffdoms the sheriff had this responsibility. The castle janitor remained a kenspeckle figure for many generations. Contemporaries relate that on Thursday, 14 June, 1296, Edward I and his army reached Stirling castle to find that the doors were open with their keys hanging above them, and there remained only the porter to yield up the castle to the invaders.[169]

Serjeanty service was well-established by William I's reign. Seven or eight infeftments for this type of service are recorded among the acts,[170] usually of estates which are clearly smaller than knights' feus, although the equation of a serjeanty with a quarter-knight's feu can be only approximate. It seems to have been usual to require a horsed soldier from a serjeanty tenure, variously described as a 'serjeant' (*serviens*), or an archer, with a haubergel. Such equipment was far in advance of what could be afforded by the poorer men, the husbandmen and neyfs turned soldier, who made up the bulk of the *exercitus Scoticanus*. Yet there are suggestive indications that at the humblest levels of serjeanty feudal military service might coalesce with the ancient pre-feudal common army. No.131, unique among twelfth-century infeftments, grants Cambo in Fife for the service of one foot soldier in the army. No.587 records an infeftment of one Yothre Mac Gilhys, apparently thane of the small thanage of 'Rothenec' (now lost), on the left bank of the lower Spey.[171] This obscure representative of the old order was to hold Meft, in Urquhart 'for the service of a serjeant in the army'. These grants suggest a tentative feudalization of 'common army' or 'Scottish army'.

The common army service of the Scottish kingdom does not form the subject matter of royal charters, but there is good evidence in the acts of William I and in other contemporary sources of its importance and universality. The most graphic introduction to the subject is unquestionably provided by Jordan Fantôme's lines describing the Scots invasion of northern England in the summer of 1173:

> Now the king of Scotland has got his host ready;
> They were assembled at Caddonlea.
> They loved then the very trumpets
> Which afterwards would drive them from the land by force.
> They have gathered a great host from Ross and from Moray;
> For certain, Earl Colban [of Buchan] has not forgotten to bring his service.
>
> Lords, the earl of Angus came with such great support,
> He had more than three thousand Scots under his command.
> There were more naked men than I can well say,
> Such an army has not come out of Scotland since the days of Elijah.[172]

Fantôme's lively verse provides a remarkably early statement of what later sources prove decisively, that the common army of Scotland was based on the earldoms and led by the earls. The nature of its organization is actually emphasized by Fantôme's mention of Ross and Moray, since these provinces had no earls in 1173 and their men must have been summoned by the king directly through his own officers. In no.158 King William confirmed to the monks of May exemption from common army service originally granted by Malcolm IV but significantly confirmed also by the earl of Fife. Within the earldoms, common army seems to have been assessed on the ploughgate or on the davoch and organized and led by the thanes. In the ecclesiastical court case of 1206 already mentioned it was said that the thane of Arbuthnott had the right to enforce 'army service in the lord king's expedition' on the tenants of the bishop of St Andrews along with his own men of the thanage (*viatico in expeditione Domini Regis cum hominibus suis*).[173] Because of the active part which Archibald abbot of Dunfermline took in royal government between 1178 and 1198, a special interest attaches to the terms in which he speaks of common army service in a confirmation to William son of Ingram of the estate of Pinkie in Midlothian,[174] to be held by the best marches by which William's grandfather, Edmund son of Forn, had held it in the time of King David I: 'We grant also to him and his heirs the liberty of staying away from the armies of the lord king unless the army be so universal that the men of Inveresk and Monkton cannot stay at home; in which case he shall find only one man to go'. It is clear that there were degrees of universality or urgency in the general summons for army service, and this is in harmony with evidence from a century or so later. Thus, between 1283 and 1289, the earl of Fife, granting Inchyra to Sir Nicholas Hay, freed the land from all service and custom due to him, 'especially from army service, unless there be a proclamation that every man should go forth to defend his head',[175] while in 1302 the earl of Carrick promised not to demand army service from the tenants of Melrose abbey 'unless the common army of the whole realm is raised for its defence, when all inhabitants are bound to serve'.[176]

No.499 refers to military service of a special kind: the duty of the tenant of the lands of Forglen in Banffshire to serve in the army by bringing the famous 'Bracbennoch', now the Monymusk Reliquary, in which some relic of Columba of Iona was apparently preserved.

(10) *Loans*. No.552 seems to be the sole direct evidence of King William borrowing sizeable sums of money, in this case from the well-known lender Aaron of Lincoln, who died in 1185.

RECORD KEEPING

We should expect the advances made in administrative procedures and machinery under William I to have been reflected in an improved method of keeping records of governmental activity. Such seems to have been the case, although the few central records for which we have some evidence have been lost since the end of the thirteenth century, and we have only indirect evidence for the existence of others. The *curia regis* seems to have been very slow to preserve any record of its proceedings or decisions. For such record we depend on the documents preserved by the par ies to a lawsuit, especially by the winning party. On one occasion, the case of Dunfermline Abbey *versus* Philip and Galiena de Moubray anent the patronage and teinds of Inverkeithing church (1212),[177] we have Dunfermline's copies of the record of what appears to have been a special court in which the *curia regis* was mingled with an ecclesiastical tribunal. It met at Edinburgh on 31 May [1212] in the presence of Queen Ermengarde and the bishop of St Andrews (William Malvoisin), and reached a decision to which were affixed the seals of the queen and the bishop together with those of the bishops of Glasgow and Brechin, the abbots and convents of Arbroath, Lindores, Holyrood and Jedburgh, the convent of Kelso and the prior and convent of St Andrews. Decisions of the justiciars' courts have likewise survived only in copies kept by the parties. Not until 1219 and 1228 do we have explicit evidence that perambulations resulting from court proceedings were written on the lord king's rolls.[178] But indirect evidence suggests that William I's chapel did keep rolls at least of charters and brieves. Apparently in the spring of 1195, the date of time, in the form of the day of the month only, began to be added to such acts.[179] It seems impossible to explain this practice save on the assumption that from this point in the reign onwards the clerks of the chapel began to copy acts on rolls which were made up, or freshly headed, for each regnal year. This hypothesis finds some support from the undeniable advance towards greater uniformity and regularity in the handwriting and form of royal acts during the last two decades of the reign. We have evidence for other sorts of rolls dating from this decade—the same decade, of course, in which the chanceries of England, France and the papacy began to keep a wider variety of rolls or registers than hitherto, organized on more systematic lines. Among the records handed over to Hugh Cressingham in 1296 were rolls of accounts of sheriffs and other officers, some not beginning until 1218, but one at least, said to contain 'seven pieces' (membranes?), dating apparently from 1202 and finishing in 1215.[180] This was headed '*vicesimum compotum* [sic] *Philippi* . . .'. Since Philip de Valognes the chamberlain died in 1215, it is possible that he was the Philip whose surname is lost. Another roll of twenty pieces dealt with divers rents of cows, swine and other things, and was headed 'Rents of cows of Aberdeen'. Its contents point to an early date, and the same may be suggested of 'One great ancient roll of the accounts of the burghs of Scotland', 'One roll of the accounts of the bishoprics of Scotland' and 'Divers rolls and little memoranda of the ancient rents of Stirling and divers fermes'. One roll of three pieces dealt with 'ancient rents in corn and other things' and was headed '*Comp*[*otus*] *Willelmi Comyn com*[*itis*] *de Buchan*', i.e. William Cumin, sometime sheriff of Forfar, who became earl of Buchan *c.*1212. There was one roll of the accounts of William Freskin II as sheriff of Nairn for 1204. Another roll, presumably dating from before 1198, and containing three pieces, was called 'the roll of Abbot Archibald', and dealt with 'ancient rents in money and ancient waitings'.

Archibald abbot of Dunfermline, who died in 1198, was active in the royal service during the 1180s and 1190s, especially associated with the king's clerk Jocelin, whom the king made archdeacon of Dunkeld about the time of the St Andrews election dispute (1178). The abbot perambulated and gave sasine of land 'by the king's command' on a number of occasions of which record happens to survive (nos.286, 291, 317, 402), and acted in the *curia regis* on the king's behalf (no.353). His exact position is not elucidated by any title, and it seems immaterial whether we regard him as an assistant justiciar, assistant chamberlain or general administrator. In some ways the most tantalizing entry on the list of 1296 is 'One roll of knights' feus containing three pieces'. There seems no means of telling whether this went back to King William's time, or even what its purpose was, although one might guess that this was fiscal and concerned with feudal incidents.

We cannot tell how far back sheriffs' accounts go. The neat way in which in no.199 the annual sum of nine merks is made up by adding to a rent of four merks four different items of 33s., 20s., 8s. and 5s. 8d. from four different portions of royal demesne in the environs of Edinburgh strongly suggests the keeping of sheriffdom accounts, presumably in the chamber. The seal tag of no.137 (*c.*1172–3) was cut from a piece of parchment which seems to have had account entries written on it. It is clear that an appreciably greater quantity of coin circulated in Scotland at the end of the twelfth century than at any previous period, much of it struck for King William, who had brought his sterlings into line with those of England in 1195. Yet we must not exaggerate the advances made in royal revenue collection or bookkeeping. We know that Alexander II took an aid in hides in 1216, and King William's aid of 1189–90 was probably also levied partly in cattle or hides.[181] When the bishops of Salisbury and Rochester took refuge at Kelso and Roxburgh about Martinmas, 1209, 'the venerable king of Scotland' (as the Melrose chronicle calls him) made them a courtesy grant not of money but of eighty chalders of wheat, sixty-six of malt and eighty of oats.[182]

NOTES TO SECTION 2

1. See table on p. 81 below.
2. *APS*, i, 378. King William spent Christmas, 1200 at Lanark (*Chron. Howden*, iv, 156).
3. G. S. Pryde, *The Burghs of Scotland* (1965), 43.
4. *Chron. Melrose*, 42, after noting the death of Geoffrey II abbot of Dunfermline, who died 14 October, 1178 (*SHR*, xxxi (1952), 27, n.10).
5. Lawrie, *Annals*, 277–8. Roger of Leicester is often called Roger 'de Beaumont' by modern historians. However convenient, this surname has no contemporary authority, and will not be used here.
6. If he is one of the two Hughs who witness *Melrose Liber*, no.127 (1165 × 74).
7. Lawrie, *Annals*, 314, 319; Anderson, *Early Sources*, ii, 351.
8. *Dialogi Laurentii Dunelmensis monachi ac prioris* ('Lawrence of Durham'), ed. J. Raine (Surtees Soc., lxx, 1880), 86–8.
9. Lawrie, *Annals*, 319.
10. Count Florence III died at Antioch in 1190 while on the Third Crusade, survived by his widow Ada of Scotland and succeeded by their eldest son Theodericus (Dirk or Thierry). For Florence, one of Count Dirk VII's younger brothers, and, by 1198, provost of Utrecht cathedral, cf. P. Molhuysen and P. J. Blok, *Nieuw Nederlandsch Biografisch Woordenboek* (Leiden, 1912), ii, 447; K. Heeringa (ed.), *Oorkondenboek van het sticht Utrecht tot* 1301, ii, (1940), no.540; *Die Register Innocenz' III*, ed. O. Hageneder and A. Haidacher, i (1964), no.70.
11. For Florence's election to Glasgow see *Chron. Melrose*, 51. Florence was evidently at Leiden on 20 February, A.D. 1201 (= 1202), where he witnessed an act of Count Dirk VII (Louis-Philippe C. van den Bergh (ed.), *Oorkondenboek van Holland en Zeeland*, i (1866), no.188). He may have paid a brief visit to Scotland thereafter, but he was evidently in Holland at the date of his brother Count Dirk's death, 4 November, 1203. In the succession struggle which followed, Florence helped his elder brother William count of East Friesland, to seize the county of Holland in opposition to the late count's widow and the count of Loon in Brabant, to whom she had, with unseemly haste, given her daughter and only child in marriage. In 1204 Florence held certain lands by the River Rhine on behalf of Count William, until he was captured by the bishop of Utrecht through the desertion of his own followers, and imprisoned in the castle of 'Hurst' (Hulst?). Later in 1204, however, Count William gained the upper hand; Florence was released, received land forfeited by opponents, and in the autumn led an expedition to Zeeland to attack the castle of Hugh Scarpenes. This must have lasted until late in the year, for the freezing of the waterways made the siege easier. The source for this is the Annals of Egmond, in *Fontes Egmundenses*, ed. O. Oppermann (Historisch Genootschap, 3rd series, no.61, Utrecht, 1933), pp.195ff., especially pp.200–1, 205. Florence was still in Holland within the year 25 March, 1205–24 March, 1206 (Van den Bergh, *Oorkondenboek van Holland en Zeeland*, i, no.203), probably in the earlier part of the year 1205. But Florence's name does not appear in the document recording the final settlement between Count William and Louis, count of Loon, October, 1206 (ibid., no.206).
12. *Paisley Registrum*, 428; Dowden, *Bishops*, 301.
13. *Beka's Egmondsch Necrologium tot* 1205, in *Fontes Egmundenses*, 110:

'Florencius filius Florencii et Ade in Middelburch obiit monachus pridie Kal. Dec. anno 1210'. It is remarkable that no Dutch source gives any hint of Florence's position in Scotland, nor any Scottish source a hint of his position in Holland. Bishop Dowden wrote 'We are ignorant why Florence remained unconsecrated for five years, and why he resigned' (Dowden, *Bishops*, 301); but it might be that Innocent III found Florence's warlike activities in 1204 incompatible with the status of a bishop-elect.

14. *Chron. Melrose*, 55.
15. *Melrose Liber*, no.121.
16. I have been much helped here by discussion and correspondence with Mr Scott; and by an invaluable list of royal clerks and chaplains prepared by the late James A. Wright of Newport on Tay. Here and there I have, perhaps wrongly, come to conclusions different from those reached by these two scholars.
17. *RRS*, i, nos.200, 201; cf. *Melrose Liber*, i, no.127.
18. Ibid. Mr Scott's view is that two Hughs (i.e., Hugh of Roxburgh and Hugh later bishop of Dunkeld) might have been given the by-name *de sigillo* in succession. My own view is that once this name had been applied to a particular royal clerk it would remain his until his death or at least until his promotion to a more exalted position. Thus I believe that the Hugh *de sigillo* appointed bishop of Dunkeld in 1214 was the only royal clerk called Hugh in William I's reign to have had the by-name *de sigillo*. Arguments in favour of Mr Scott's view are that the handwriting (Dd) which I have tentatively identified as that of Hugh *de sigillo* does not appear before *c.*1190, and that there is an interval of some years between Hugh of Roxburgh's promotion to the chancellorship (1189) and the next occurrence of Hugh *de sigillo* (1193); *Melrose Liber*, no.121.
19. *Cambuskenneth Registrum*, nos.216, 218 (1166 × 1171), shewing that Hugh of Roxburgh, chancellor's clerk, held the church of Tullibody.
20. No.72 below.
21. No.141 below (= *Holyrood Liber*, no.51).
22. No.329 below (= *St Andrews Liber*, 228); cf. *Arbroath Liber*, i, no.80, where Master Martin, another witness, was perhaps included among clerks of the chancellor.
23. E.g., *Arbroath Liber*, i, nos.56, 57.
24. Compare the position and title of Robert *de sigillo* in the household of Henry I of England (*Dialogue of the Exchequer*, ed. C. Johnson, 1950, 129).
25. *Melrose Liber*, no.121 (whose date is taken to be 1193 because *Chron. Melrose*, 48, reports Bishop Jocelin's grant and charter of Hassendean church under this year).
26. *Chron. Bower*, ii, 58.
27. Ibid., 57. He died in 1231 (ibid., 59).
28. Pp. 85–91.
29. Dowden, *Bishops*, 103. The statement there that Bishop Gilbert had a brother Richard de Warwich' seems borne out by the charter cited (*St Andrews Liber*, 302), but it might be better to take the words 'fratre nostro' as applicable to the next witness, Simon of Stirling.
30. Dowden, *Bishops*, 146. The late J. A. Wright considered that the royal clerk made bishop of Moray in 1187 was Richard of Lincoln, whose latest occurrences in record belong to the decade following 1178.
31. *Moray Registrum*, nos.45–49; Anderson, *Early Sources*, ii, 368n.; J. Dowden, *The Mediaeval Church in Scotland*, 65.
32. Those listed as Aa, Ai, Aj (Richard of Lincoln), Al, Ba, Bb, Ca, Da (Gervase?), Db (perhaps identical with Da), Dc, Dd (Hugh de sigillo?), De (William del Bois), Df (Gilbert of Stirling).
33. Mr Scott and I are agreed that Hugh 'the little' (*parvus*), who witnessed *Melrose Liber*, no.39 and Raine, *North Durham*, no.466, is to be identified with Hugh the king's chaplain who witnessed another version of the charter last cited (Raine, *North Durham*, no.462).

34. Hugh's name occurs in numerous private deeds of the later twelfth century, almost always relating to Roxburgh and the Tweed valley (e.g., *Brinkburn Chartulary*, nos.157, 158; *Kelso Liber*, nos.140, 141, 248–50, 254–6 and elsewhere; *Melrose Liber*, nos.69, 92). The probability is that he held the important royal chaplaincy attached to Roxburgh castle. He is sometimes called 'Hugh the chaplain, clerk of the king', and is thus an exception to the rule already enunciated that royal clerks and royal chaplains were kept distinct (*Kelso Liber*, nos.368, 384, 413; *Melrose Liber*, no.92). A royal clerk named Hugh (of Roxburgh? *de sigillo*?) witnessed *acta* of Hugh bishop of St Andrews (*St Andrews Liber*, 147, 149, 1178 × 84).
35. *Coupar Angus Rental*, i, 336 (no.43) is a note of a charter granting a burghal tenement in Forfar issued by 'Rannulph the lord king's chaplain', dated Friday after St Barnabas (i.e. 15 June), A.D. 1184. Conceivably, the donor was Ralph; otherwise nothing is known of Rannulph.
36. Simon was still archdeacon at a date not earlier than 10 September, 1195 (*Melrose Liber*, no.122, witnessed by Reginald bishop of Ross), but Robert had succeeded before 2 February, 1196 (ibid., no.90), since he witnesses in company with Master John of Roxburgh, treasurer of Glasgow (a witness to no.72 below), who died on that date, already a novice at Melrose (*Chron. Melrose*, 49). *Melrose Liber*, no.169, a supposed original, is now lost; it is suspicious, and I discount it as evidence for any 'R'. being archdeacon of Glasgow as early as 1191.
37. Ralph's latest occurrence as chaplain seems to belong to 1195 or early 1196 (no.383 below; Dowden *Bishops*, 174).
38. Ibid., 301. For his surname, see no.387 below (= *Kelso Liber*, no.402).
39. *Registrum Antiquissimum of Lincoln*, iii, nos.872, 912; *Records of the Borough of Leicester*, ed. M. Bateson, revised by W. H. Stevenson and J. E. Stocks, no.xiv; *Calendar of Documents preserved in France*, ed. J. H. Round, no.408.
40. No.513; Dowden, *Bishops*, 211.
41. *RRS*, i, no.105; *Melrose Liber*, no.150. It is not clear what claim Philip de Valognes had to Ringwood, and his charter was endorsed 'que non ostendatur sine consilio'.
42. Nos. 3, 5. For Edmund the chamberlain, cf. *RRS*, i, 31 and n., and no.199.
43. No.236.
44. No.130; cp. *RRS*, i, nos.129, 228, 241.
45. The frequency with which Richard Revel witnesses acts after *c.*1200 suggests that he held some post in the household, but whether this was connected with the chamber is not certain.
46. *RRS*, i, nos.221, 226, 228, 241.
47. Nos.161, 226, 373, 427, 431, 433. Occurrences of other cameral personnel in William I's acts are mostly too numerous to be listed here; they may be found in the index.

47a. *Inchcolm Chrs.*, no.12. Note that Richard son of Hugh, with Ralph *de Camera*, witnessed a charter of Alexander son of William son of Thor, as lord of Ochiltree, probably dated at Stirling (*St Andrews Liber*, 321).

48. Lawrie, *Charters*, no.267.
49. *RRS*, i, nos.228, 241.
50. *SHS*, *Misc.*, ii, 35, 36.
51. *APS*, i, 710, c.5.
52. Anderson, *Early Sources*, ii, 183, 348, 383.
53. Lawrie, *Annals*, 326–7.
54. *RRS*, i, 33.
55. *Chron. Melrose*, 51: 'clericus et cognatus domini regis'.
56. Lawrie, *Annals*, 240.
57. Dowden, *Bishops*, 52.
58. *SHS*, *Misc.*, ii, 35–6.
59. Hugh *de prebenda* witnesses *Arbroath Liber*, i, nos.47, 52, 99, 204; *Cambuskenneth Registrum*, no.70; *Melrose Liber*, no.101; *Holyrood Liber*, no.37; *Newbattle Registrum*, no.130. Adam parson of Kinghorn, otherwise Adam of

Kinghorn, clerk witnesses nos.475, 483, 498; cf. *Moray Registrum*, no.52 (afterwards canon and then dean of Dunkeld; *Inchaffray Chrs.*, nos.48, 49, 65). Adam clerk 'de la Provande' witnesses *Midlothian Chrs.*, Reg. de Soltre, no.20 (dating *c.*1216–19), along with 'Gilbert' (probably Geoffrey) clerk 'de la liveresun', i.e. of the liverance.

60. *APS*, i, 98.

61. *Arbroath Liber*, i, nos.2, 91, 173; no.227 below. He was not the same as Richard de prebenda and does not occur together with Richard of Scotia.

62. *Arbroath Liber*, i, no.9 (= no.228 below). He was not the same as Richard de prebenda.

63. Richard the *expensarius* held Peaston (in Ormiston, E. Lothian) and was a benefactor to Soutra hospital (*Midlothian Chrs.*, Registrum domus de Soltre, nos.4, 8).

64. *SHS, Misc.*, ii, 36.

65. *APS*, i, 710, c.5.

66. Ibid.

67. For the king's bakers see nos.174, 510 below, and for his cooks, see *RRS*, i, no.101.

68. No.209 below.

69. *RRS*, i, 32.

70. Ibid., no.243.

71. No.149 below.

72. The surnames McGilchrist and MacLeish have long been established in central Perthshire and may be seen, e.g., in the old kirkyard burial ground of Lagganallachy in Strathbraan.

73. *St Andrews Liber*, 313.

74. *Coupar Angus Chrs.*, i, 23, 100; *Lindores Chartulary*, nos.76, 77, 79.

75. *Coupar Angus Chrs.*, i, 123–4, and references there cited; *May Recs.*, no.41; *Scone Liber*, no.106.

76. *Chron. Melrose*, 47, records Richard de Moreville's death at the end of its annal for 1189, but along with the death of the Emperor Frederick Barbarossa, who died in June, 1190. It is likely that Richard de Moreville did not die before the end of 1189; he was still alive after 23 March, 1189 (*Coucher Book of Furness Abbey*, ed. J. Brownbill (Chetham Soc.), ii, Pt. II (1916), 334–5).

77. *Chron. Melrose*, 49 (after an obit dated 2 February).

78. Lawrie, *Annals*, 303.

79. Ibid., 325.

80. *Gesta Henrici*, i, 66; *Chron. Howden*, ii, 60.

81. Simon (no.186); Hervey (no.264); for others, see entries in index. A David *Marescallus* conceded land at Whitchester (in Longformacus, Berwickshire) to the nuns of Coldstream, *c.*1200 (*Coldstream Cartulary*, no.27).

82. No.325 below.

83. *SHS, Misc.*, ii, 34.

84. Ibid., 33–6.

85. W. Douglas Simpson, *The Province of Mar* (1944), 115–6; *RRS*, i, 31, n.9; *Scone Liber*, no.106; *Arbroath Liber*, i, nos.59, 65. *Chron. Bower*, i, 532 says that in 1211 the king appointed the earls of Atholl and Buchan, Thomas 'of Londy' the king's doorward and Malcolm Morigrond to be captains of a picked force to hunt down Guthred MacWilliam. Malcolm was the son of Morgrund, earl of Mar (*Aberdeen-Banff Illustrations*, ii, 17; *Aberdeen Registrum*, i, 11), and in this context he and Thomas the Doorward together look like a synthetic earl of Mar, while the succession to the earldom was in dispute. See also no.414.

86. *APS*, i, 710, c.5.

87. Sheriffdoms existing by 1165: Berwick, Roxburgh (= Teviotdale), (Lothian), Edinburgh, Linlithgow, Stirling, Lanark, Clackmannan, Dunfermline, Crail, Scone, Perth, Forfar; add (probably) Peebles/Traquair, Haddington, Elgin, Forres, Inverness. For William's sheriffdoms see below.

88. Nos.64, 67, 97, 98, 304.

89. Nos.132, 312, 374, 380.

90. AYR: William, *c.*1200 (*Melrose Liber*, no.36; cf. *Dryburgh Liber*, nos.221–223).
BERWICK: Robert de Burneville (Raine, *North Durham*, nos.216, 264, 388); Adam of Bunkle, × 1203 (ibid., no.265); Walter of Lindsay, 1212 × 1232 (ibid., no.122; *Kelso Liber*, no.303).
CLACKMANNAN: Alexander son of Thor(e) (no.452 below).
EDINBURGH: Henry of Graham (*Newbattle Registrum*, no.85); Henry of Braid (*Holyrood Liber*, no.33); Michael Fleming (ibid., Appendix II, no.7); John of Graham, 1211 × 1215 (*Dunfermline Registrum*, no.189).
FIFE (CRAIL): William (*St Andrews Liber*, 249); Geoffrey son of Richard (ibid., 275, 316; *Cambuskenneth Registrum*, no.37; Balcaskie Charters *penes* Sir Ralph Anstruther, Bt.).
FIFE (DUNFERMLINE): Gillebride, 1165–6 (*St Andrews Liber*, 216).
FORFAR: William Cumin (*Arbroath Liber*, i, p.5); David de la Hay (ibid., no.64); Hugh de Cambrun (BM, MS.Add.33245, fo.152).
HADDINGTON: Alexander of St Martin (no.252 below).
KINCARDINE: John Hastings (*Spalding Misc.*, v, 209–210); Humphrey of Berkeley (*SHR*, xlv, 26).
LANARK: Baldwin of Biggar, 1165 × 1171 (no.43 below); Robert son of Werenbald (*Dryburgh Liber*, no.47); Reginald of Crawford, *c.*1200 (ibid., nos.221–3).
LINLITHGOW: Richard de Melville (*Holyrood Liber*, no.33).
NAIRN: William Freskin II, 1204 (*APS*, i, 118).
PEEBLES/TRAQUAIR: Simon son of Melbet, 1184 (no. 252 below).
PERTH: Ralph the clerk, 1200 × (*Scone Liber*, nos.88–9); Roger de Mortemer, 1209–1212 × (no.523 below; Lawrie, *Annals*, 364).
ROXBURGH: John son of Orm, 1165 × 1171 (no.66 below); Walter Corbet, 1177 × 1189 (*Paisley Registrum*, 89, 254); Herbert of Maxwell, 1194 × 1207 (*Kelso Liber*, nos.166, 207); John of Maxwell, 1207 (ibid., no.207); Bernard of Hadden, 1212 × 1214 (no.515 below).
SCONE/GOWRIE: Macbeth (*Arbroath Liber*, i, no.35; *PSAS*, lxxxvii, 61).
SELKIRK: Andrew of Synton (no.582 below).
STIRLING: Ralph (no.130 below); William son of Thor or Thorald (*Cambuskenneth Registrum*, no.132); Alexander son of William son of Thor (frequently below, e.g. no.432; and cp. *Arbroath Liber*, i, nos.59, 60). Alexander was lord of Ochiltree, in Linlithgow (*St Andrews Liber*, 321).

91. Raine, *North Durham*, no.388.

92. *Holyrood Liber*, no.33.

93. Ibid.

94. *Cambuskenneth Registrum*, no.132.

95. *Dryburgh Liber*, no.47.

96. Not included in the list given above because never found explicitly styled sheriff; but the sheriffdom was granted heritably by King William.

97. *Dryburgh Liber*, nos.221–223.

98. *Spalding Misc.*, v, 209–210; *SHR*, xlv, 26.

99. *RRS*, i, 46. I would now identify 'Durandus' the sheriff with Thorald, taking the name as a latinized French equivalent. Confirmation of this is to be found in *St Andrews Liber*, 180, where William of Lindsay (tenant and heir at Crawford of Swain son of Thor son of Swain) speaks of his *antecessor* Durandus at Binny in W. Lothian (*c.*1180). William of Lindsay gave land at Binny to Cambuskenneth Abbey, of which William son of Thor was a notable benefactor (*Cambuskenneth Registrum*, pp.44, 111). William son of Thor's son Alexander was lord of Ochiltree, close to Binny (*St Andrews Liber*, 321).

100. *Cambuskenneth Registrum*, no.133.

101. *SHR*, xlv, 26.

102. *Holyrood Liber*, no.57; nos.451, 470, 471 below. Cf. *Coupar Angus Chrs.*,

i, no.44 (dated too late by the editor), where Geoffrey says, perhaps speaking with a sheriff's experience, 'as often as God shall increase my worldly wealth, I shall use it to cause the house of Coupar to grow too'.

103. *APS*, i, 377.

104. Ibid., 374–5.

105. *Dryburgh Liber*, nos.221–223.

106. Ibid., no.223 (p.163).

107. Ibid., p.162.

108. E.g., Uhtred son of Fergus and Roger of Minto were commanded by the king to carry out a perambulation of Kirkgunzeon, 1165 × 1175, by means of the older men of the district (BM, MS. Harl. 3891, fos.87^{v}–88^{r}; *Holm Cultram Recs.*, 49). Archibald abbot of Dunfermline, for whose career see above, pp.58–59, seems to have acted as a royal justice.

109. *SHR*, xlv, 25.

110. *RRS*, i, no.220.

111. Ibid., nos.223, 214; and cf. the discussion, ibid., 49–50.

112. Earl Duncan headed a commission appointed to give the monks of Coupar sasine of the marsh of Blairgowrie (*Coupar Angus Rental*, i, 325). Among his colleagues were Roger de Mortemer, who by 1209 was sheriff of Perth, and Macbeth, judex of Gowrie, who may have been identical with Macbeth sheriff of Scone or Gowrie (*PSAS*, lxxxvii, 61). No.590 below was probably transacted in the justiciar's court under Earl Duncan's presidency.

113. No.465 may date as early as 1205.

114. It is conceivable that William of Graham was acting as justiciar of Lothian under David I (Lawrie, *Charters*, nos.72, 121, 143, 230; but especially no.134; *RRS*, i, no.35). But occasionally William witnesses lower down than a known sheriff.

115. Nos.162 (probably placed too early in the series), 195, 197, 199, 200 (Walter Olifard); nos.316, 317, 366, 401, 406 (William of Lindsay); nos.381, 400, 460 (Earl Patrick); nos.481, 483, 493 (David Lindsay I).

116. *SHR*, xlv, 25–6.

117. Nos.381, 400, 481, 483.

118. Lawrie, *Annals*, 320. Earl Patrick is described as 'tunc temporis summus justiciarius totius regni Scottorum'.

119. Nos.309, 401, 406. For 'Lochlan', which may have been the 'true' or native form of Roland's name, see *Holyrood Liber*, no.24. For the equation of 'Roland' with 'Lachlan', etymologically quite distinct, see *Cal. Docs. Scot.*, ii, 209–210, where 'Rouland fiz Aleyn' = Lachlan son of Alan and 'Gilascope fiz Rouland' = Gillespie MacLachlan.

120. *APS*, i, 378.

121. *Cal. Docs. Scot.*, i, no.2155. *Littere Wallie*, ed. J. G. Edwards, 184–6, provides the best text of this document which despite the form of the date must belong to 1258.

122. Earl Walter was put in charge of Galloway after the revolt of 1235, and in 1244 was said to have fortified a castle in Galloway (Anderson, *Early Sources*, ii, 497; Anderson, *Scottish Annals*, 353).

123. *SHS, Misc.*, ii, 36–7.

124. *APS*, i, 380; cf no.80.

125. P. Stein, 'Roman Law in Scotland', in *Ius Romanum Medii Aevi*, pars v, 13b (Milan, 1968), 23. Professor Stein's view follows that adumbrated by the late Lord Cooper of Culross (T. M. Cooper, *Select Scottish Cases of the thirteenth century*, Edinburgh, 1944, Introduction).

126. *SHR*, xlv, 16–26.

127. Lawrie, *Charters*, no.80.

128. No.590 below probably records the settlement of a dispute heard before the justiciar's court.

129. *EHR*, xxxv (1920), 161–99.

130. *SHR*, xxxvii (1958), 119.

131. Lawrie, *Charters*, no.65.

132. Ibid., no.49; *RRS*, i, no.247.
133. Lawrie, *Charters*, nos.74, 209; *RRS*, i, no.118 (p.183).
134. Lawrie, *Charters*, no.163; *RRS*, i, no.174 (p.219).
135. Lawrie, *Charters*, no.143 (p.119); no.39 below.
136. Lawrie, *Charters*, no.54.
137. Ibid., no.100.
138. Ibid., no.222 (= *RRS*, i, no.42).
139. Ibid., nos.255, 256.
140. Ibid., no.184.
141. Nos.80, 85, 116, 125, 171, 200, 459 (south); nos.9, 42, 43, 116, 135, 136, 137, 140, 147, 185, 204, 205, 302, 334, 335, 344, 345, 350, 405, 418, 473, 524 (north).
142. All the preceding save nos.9, 42, 43 and 140.
143. Nos.136, 185, 200, 302, 334, 335, 350, 383, 405, 418, 473, 524.
144. E.g., nos.350, 405.
145. *Spalding Misc.*, v, 211.
146. *Chron. Lanercost*, 160.
147. *RRS*, i, no.287.
148. *Coupar Angus Chrs.*, i, no.35.
149. *APS*, i, 378.
150. *RRS*, i, 36, 39.
151. *Newminster Cartulary*, 268; cf. *Pipe Roll*, 3 *John*, 248, tenure of Middleton and Roddam by Liulf son of Liulf for 30s. per annum and four waitings.
152. *Spalding Misc.*, v, 209–13.
153. (1) Conveth, formerly the name of Laurencekirk parish, Mearns, now restricted to an estate within it; (2) Conveth, now Inverkeithny, Banffshire (I wrongly identified this with Culvie in Marnoch, *Scottish Studies*, vi, Pt.2 (1962), 143, n.74); (3) Conveth now Convinth, Inverness-shire.
154. *Coupar Angus Rental*, i, 329, no.22 (where for *Airimam* read *Annuam*).
155. *APS*, i, 118.
156. *Cal. Docs. Scot.*, ii, nos.880, 1670.
157. *Pipe Roll*, 13 *John*, 40.
158. Lawrie, *Annals*, 303.
159. Ibid., 288, 290.
160. *SHR*, ii (1905), 175.
161. See *Pipe Roll*, 4 *Henry II*, 177, and thereafter in the Pipe Rolls under 'Northumberland' to John's reign.
162. *Pipe Rolls*, 10, 11, 17 *John*, under 'Northumberland'.
163. *APS*, i, 711.
164. To those listed in n.141 above add nos.84, 468 (Tynedale), 472, 554, 557, 559, 564, 573, 576.
165. No.552 (*xx milites feoffatos*). It may be noted that at his marriage in 1186 William I endowed his wife with Edinburgh castle together with 100 merks of revenues and 40 infeft knights (*quadraginta milites feudatos*); Lawrie, *Annals*, 267.
166. *BIHR*, xxix (1956), 19–20.
167. *Holyrood Liber*, no.40.
168. Several acts of King William were witnessed by Gervase Avenel as constable of Roxburgh.
169. Stevenson, *Documents*, ii, 28; *Chron. Lanercost*, 179.
170. Nos.45, 131, 286 (= 394), 469, 497, 560, 589.
171. *APS*, i, 101. For this thanage, see Stevenson, *Documents*, ii, 29 (where for Rapenache read Rathenache); *Moray Registrum*, nos.40, 264 and p.461; *Cal. Docs. Scot.*, ii, 209, 211 (homages of William and Angus of Rothenec). Had the name survived, it would have become Rannoch.
172. *Chron. Fantosme* (Becker), 491–2 (Jeremiah for Elijah); *Chron. Fantosme* (Michel) 22, lines 468–77.
173. *Spalding Misc.*, v, 210.
174. *Dunfermline Registrum*, no.301.

175. Earl of Moray, Darnaway Castle: Gray of Kinfauns Muniments, bdle.84, no.2 (box 5).
176. *Melrose Liber*, no.351.
177. *Dunfermline Registrum*, nos.166, 211; cf. ibid., no.102.
178. *Arbroath Liber*, i, nos.228, 229.
179. See below, p.82.
180. *APS*, i, 117; 'de anno cicli xix[l] (read xix[li] for decennovenali) iii', which was apparently A.D. 1202 (N. H. Nicolas, *Chronology of History* (2nd edn, 1843), 26 and n., 49).
181. *Chron. Melrose*, 47, speaks only of gold and silver.
182. Ibid., 54.

3. ANALYSIS OF THE ACTS OF WILLIAM I

THE ACTS AND THEIR SURVIVAL

Some 521 acts of William I, together with five issued by him before his accession, survive in full texts or (in a few cases) in incomplete texts which are nevertheless sufficient to justify their inclusion in the main corpus. Two of the full texts (nos. 194, 497) are extant only in the form of vernacular translations, but are clearly authentic. A number are either manifestly spurious or at best tampered with or inflated. Four putative acts, the 'rhyming charter' of Polmood[1] and the obvious forgeries whereby King William infefts David of Graham in Charleton and Kinnaber[2] and Walter Comyn earl of Menteith in Lauriston (Mearns),[3] and terminates a dispute between 'Henry de Lambart' and 'Alexander de Olifard'[4] are not included or dealt with here. No fewer than 150—nearly as many as the entire total of full texts for Malcolm IV—survive as originals. A further nine are in the form of originals, although they must belong to various dates in the century or so following King William's death. Of these nine, at least five and perhaps seven seem to be based on authentic acts. Conversely, six acts of which the originals survived down to the nineteenth century, and were published either in facsimile or in reliable editions (or both), may for most purposes be counted in with the total of 150 originals. In addition to the 526 full texts, there is a calendar of seventy 'lost acts', most of which may be accepted as referring to actual charters, brieves, etc., now missing, although a small number have credentials which are, in varying degrees, dubious.

Much the same arguments which were put forward in *RRS*, i, pp. 57–9, to shew that the survivors represent only a small fraction of the total output of written acts, may be used of this collection, but some important qualifications should be made. Uniformity of style and formulas is more marked than under Malcolm IV; yet the total of 521 full texts represents an average output of no more than 10·6 acts *per annum*. It is unrealistic to suppose that the royal clerks achieved their professional quality of workmanship on such poor figures. Under William I the proportion of acts in favour of (or at least anent) laymen and single individuals rises sharply as compared with earlier reigns: over 23 per cent of full texts, and actually 71 per cent of lost acts. These facts reinforce the view expressed in *RRS*, i, that while we can be sure that there have been some losses among acts for ecclesiastical institutions and burghs, we must allow for very considerable losses of acts concerning private individuals. Unfortunately, there seems no way of arriving at even an approximate estimate of losses in this sector.

Among the acts for religious houses, cathedral foundations and so forth, we may feel reasonably certain that the totals for Arbroath (58), Coldingham (24), Dunfermline (23), Kelso (37), Melrose (36) and St Andrews (34) are not far short of the totals of acts actually issued. But in the ecclesiastical sector there have undoubtedly been losses, in some cases complete. Of the cathedral churches, e.g., only Glasgow and Moray seem adequately represented. Of the abbeys and priories, Kilwinning and the Gallovidian houses (Dundrennan, Glenluce, Soulseat) do not appear at all; Dryburgh and Lindores are represented by a mere handful of acts; while, most strikingly, two royal foundations, Jedburgh (with dependencies at Canonbie and Restenneth) and Kinloss in Moray, can muster only two or three acts each. Losses among burgh charters have been relatively even more severe, and some of the loss seems to have taken place in comparatively modern times. No acts survive for Edinburgh, Stirling, Roxburgh, Berwick upon Tweed, Lanark, Elgin and Forfar. There is only a single charter each for Perth and Rutherglen; nothing survives for Haddington, Crail, Linlithgow or Montrose, all royal burghs. It seems unlikely that Dundee, founded by the king's brother in the period *c.*1180–1200, received no charters from the royal chapel: oddly enough, its earliest surviving charter is one of King John of England.[5] Aberdeen and Inverness are the best-represented burghs, yet even here Inverness, which apparently possessed four charters and brieves of William I in the early nineteenth century, has only one original today.

Finally, there is the problem of legislative acts committed to writing and promulgated under William I. This is a subject which cannot be treated adequately until the early law texts have been critically re-examined and edited. Here it is only necessary to point to the existence of at least four 'assizes' promulgated or maintained by William I (nos.71, 124, 281, 406, 442, 475) which do not appear at all in the supposed *Assise Regis Willelmi* or *Assise Regis David*. It seems likely that as far as the genuine legislation of King William is concerned, we have at best an imperfectly preserved record. What proportion of the whole is represented by the fragments which do survive we have, for the present at least, no means of judging.

CLASSIFICATION AND SUBJECT MATTER

All the acts save one (no.30, a diploma of Anglo-Norman type) are in the form of the writ-charter. They shew the same general flexibility as the acts of David I and Malcom IV, but as the reign progresses there is a tendency for forms to become more stereotyped. The great majority of acts in this collection may be classified under the following primary headings. (1) Charters recording an original grant of property by the king, usually of land or rights or a mixture of both. Property and rights thus granted might range from an earldom or a bishopric at one end of the scale (nos.558, 465) to a backyard in a burgh at the other (nos.570–572). The dispositive clause for this class consisted of the formula *do* (or *reddo*), *concedo et confirmo*, usually in the perfect infinitive in an accusative and infinitive construction. (2) Charters confirming original grants by one or more of the king's predecessors. (3) Charters confirming original grants or other transactions by the king's lieges. These form a very large class. The dispositive formula for these two classes was *concedo et confirmo*, again usually in the perfect infinitive. (4) Charters, understandably commonest at the start of the reign, and typically issued in favour of well-endowed religious houses, in which the king combines the elements of (1), (2) and (3). (5) Charters of the same general character as class (1), which specifically record decisions of the *curia regis*, usually in favour of the party in whose archives the document has been preserved. (6) Administrative brieves, sometimes of an ephemeral nature but sometimes quasi-legislative and intended to have permanent validity. (7) Legal brieves. (Examples of both these classes may be found embodied in acts of classes (1) to (5), especially class (4). (8) Letters and diplomatic instruments.

It was normal to give acts of classes (1) to (5) the general address, either in the long or the short form. Classes (6) and (7) may carry the general address, but more often they are addressed to particular officials, by title or name or both. In class (8) no authentic letter of King William survives, but at least two letters to popes (nos.532, 535) and one to a king (no.585) are recorded; no doubt there have been heavy losses in this class. Nos.488 and 505 are addressed generally, but unfortunately neither address is in the normal form and some suspicion must attach to the credentials of no.505.

In the earlier decades of the reign, it was clearly not uncommon for documents in classes (1) to (5) to be produced by the beneficiaries themselves, and we find a corresponding variation in handwriting, size and quality of parchment, and in sealing methods. There is less variety in style and formulas, but even here it is noticeable that in the later decades of the reign, as the proportion of acts produced in the royal chapel rises steeply, the phrases and formulas become markedly more standardized, and this is accompanied by a standardization of such details as sealing methods, size and quality of parchment, and the way in which the text is set out on the available space.

Acts in classes (6) and (7), administrative and legal brieves, may usefully be subjected to a more detailed analysis. The largest section among the legal brieves, those granting the king's protection, has recently been the subject of a profound and wide-ranging comparative study by Dr Alan Harding in the *Juridical Review* (1966).[6] Dr Harding has demonstrated the descent of the later procedures of 'trespass' (in England), or 'wrang and unlauch' (in Scotland), leading in the two kingdoms respectively to the law of tort and the law of delict, from the same original source, namely the king's grant of protection to his subjects and their property. This in turn originated in the concept of the king's peace, whether given by 'hand' or by written instrument. Among the royal brieves of protection of the twelfth century, Dr Harding has listed ten elements,[7] some of which may be found singly but most of which appear in various combinations. If for the purposes of this edition Dr Harding's classification is followed only in part, this is not in any sense to underestimate or ignore the value of his analysis.

On the contrary, it must be seen as the key without which the student will not be able to achieve an understanding or further elucidation of the question. Here, however, we are concerned essentially with those brieves of King William which have actually survived, and it will be convenient to follow and slightly extend the classification adopted in *RRS*, i. To avoid the risk of confusion with Dr Harding's ten numbered elements, sub-divisions of the brieve of protection will here be classified by letters.

Legal Brieves

(i) The brieve *de nativis*. There are twelve surviving examples of brieves ordering the restoration and forbidding the unjust detention of fugitive neyfs. The three earliest (nos.25, 30, 31, relating to Scotia) use the old and evidently obsolescent words *cum(er)lache* and *cumherba*; otherwise the words used are *nativi* and *fugitivi*. In three examples later in the reign (nos.163, 387, 481) the clause 'outwith the royal demesne' is added, implying that neyfs who fled into the king's lands, if not exempted from the process of recovery, were nevertheless in a special category and would be dealt with presumably by the king's own consideration or even at his will. No.326, although perhaps more administrative than legal in character, is closely comparable with the standard brieve *de nativis*: it commands the restoration of tenants who have absconded in order to evade tax.

(ii) The brieve of protection. In Dr Harding's analysis the royal command to restore fugitive neyfs is included among brieves of protection as element ten; it seems, nevertheless, convenient to treat that command separately here, since the surviving brieves seem to shew that, at least from the standpoint of royal administration, it was regularly treated as separate in the twelfth century. Most of Dr Harding's remaining nine elements appear in the examples of royal protections which follow. It should be noted that *RRS*, i, nos.222 and 287 (= nos. 509 and 550 here) contain most of the essential elements of a brieve of protection.

(a) A grant of the king's firm (in one case 'full') peace was common; there are seventeen examples,[8] and in most instances the grant is linked with certain other common elements of the protection. Closely comparable with this is the grant of freedom from secular exactions (e.g., nos.11, 53, 513), and the prohibition of interference (nos.142, *sine vexatione teneat*; 370, *ne quis eos disturbare presumat*). No.67, forbidding royal sergeands to impose special levies or payments on Coldingham priory in respect of pleas and lawsuits, is also to be compared with these more general grants of peace. These sergeands, incidentally, were perhaps the Lothian counterpart of the northern English serjeant of the peace. A further brieve which should probably be considered under the heading of grants of peace and prohibitions of interference is no.38, which seeks to protect the established marches of the beneficiary's estates save where land may have been granted away, sold or exchanged.

(b) Exemptions from the common burdens of defence and taxation were sometimes granted in terms so specific as to suggest that freedom 'from all secular exactions and demands' may not have been strong enough to override the most fundamental obligations of 'aids', army and labour service. Thus, no.30 grants freedom from work on bridges, castles, etc., while no.500 certifies that castle-work has been done voluntarily. Nos.92, 438 and 513 grant freedom from 'aids and works', no.158 freedom from 'army and expedition'. No.152, on the other hand, expressly denies freedom from 'aids, army and works' while granting a layman other privileges.

(c) A central element in the extension of the concept of the king's peace, so that it became some kind of enforceable protection which resulted in the permanent intervention of the king's court in disputes among subjects, was the prohibition of poinding. The king might be persuaded to forbid poinds (*namum, pandum*) to be taken either against anyone save the person actually owing the debt or committing the offence, or else against the holders of courts unless they had failed to do justice. Examples of the first type may be found in nos.28, 30, 155, 176, 303, 513; of the second in nos.39 and 95. The taking of poinds from debtors or opponents to enforce repayment or some other form of justice was connected with the questions of the competence of a particular court to claim jurisdiction and of a competent court's failure to do justice. These questions in turn were connected with the process of replegiation. Very little is known about the working of replegiation under William I, and it is therefore all the more valuable to have the evidence of the Arbuthnott case (no.547) that the bishop of St Andrews could fend off attempts by the local sheriff and forester to trouble his tenants in Arbuthnott anent any matter which came within sheriffdom or forest jurisdiction by obtaining a royal brieve of replegiation. The bishop's bailies, we are told, used to come to the sheriff in such cases *cum brevi Domini Regis*, and give surety (*fidejubebant*) that the men involved would be dealt with in the bishop's court.

(d) No example has been found of a brieve specifically granting the privilege of girth or sanctuary, although good precedents might be found in King Malcolm's grant to Innerleithen or King David's grant of his firm peace to anyone fleeing from danger to life or limb who reached the cell of Lesmahagow or at least the area within the four crosses standing round it.[9] No.68 orders the keepers of the girth of St Mary of Wedale (Stow in Midlothian) not to prevent the abbot of Kelso recovering his tenants if they had fled to Wedale for sanctuary, provided that the abbot was ready to do justice to them.

(e) Brieves for the recovery of debts and for the enforcement of testamentary bequests. Nos.24, 28, 259, 298 and 395 shew that a more or less standard form of brieve was available to help those who found difficulty in recovering debts owed to them, and nos.24, 28, and 354 shew that a comparable brieve existed to compel the executors of a deceased person's will to carry out the terms of a bequest.

(f) Maintenance, which got a bad name in later centuries, was still regarded in the twelfth as a necessary aspect of good lordship. It meant the support which a superior might give to a dependent, most commonly in a legal dispute, either by helping him to present his case in court or by discouraging his opponent from any attempt at bullying. Many examples may be found of kings and other lords promising in writing to maintain their vassals or other dependents (especially religious houses). In this collection, nos.50 and 70 are commands to the king's officers to maintain the beneficiary, while no.294 shews the other side of the coin, since it is a prohibition of any maintenance exercised *against* the interests of the beneficiary.

(iii) Brieves to enforce the payment of teind. There is little to add to the discussion of this type of brieve in *RRS*, i, 65–6, which took the evidence of William I's reign into account. This collection has some eighteen examples of commands to pay teind,[10] several of them in the standard form which would be of special use to a bishop and his officers. In this connexion, we may note no.312, a unique example of what must surely have been a not uncommon brieve, commanding a sheriff to enforce the attendance of parties in the bishop's court and to support with royal authority any sentence of excommunication which the bishop may pronounce.

(iv) No.395 is an example of a royal command closely related to teind enforcement. The king orders all tenants of the bishopric of Moray to render to the bishop his lawful dues, cains and conveths, as freely as they had been rendered in the time of David I and Malcolm IV. This is to be compared with *RRS*, i, no.242, of which the equivalents in this collection are nos.189 and 374. This last can scarcely be called a 'standard' brieve, and is noteworthy for its opening statement: 'Know that I have heard the charters of King David my grandfather and King Malcolm my brother anent the liberties granted to the bishops of Glasgow in respect of the lawful dues and teinds belonging to them throughout their diocese.'

(v) There are nineteen examples of grants of freedom from toll or (rarely) cain.[11] Sometimes the grant is associated with common elements of the protection. In no.285 it is particularized as exemption from toll on salt, and in no.255 the freedom is given to monks only when not acting as merchants; but normally the grant is general and of wide application. Typically, the beneficiary is freed from toll on his own goods throughout all the king's land. The grant of freedom to buy and sell (nos.6, 87, 94, 207, 467, 513), or of a special privilege of buying and selling (no.213) is closely related. A corollary was the enforcement of toll payments in favour of the beneficiary, e.g., nos.244, 250, 462.

Along with these grants of freedom from toll and freedom to buy and sell, we may conveniently notice charters or brieves by which the king records his permission to hold a market (nos.3, 64, 115, 190, 197, 462, 475, 501), a fair (no.308), and a 'hanse' or gild (nos.153, 467).

(vi) It seems to have been uncommon for the king to state explicitly that he has granted his warrandice to a beneficiary, but a clause of warrandice appears in nos.74, 214 and 265, while in no.91 the king requires warrandice from the original donor.

(vii) Although the king's prohibition or his full forfeiture, references to which are very numerous, did not constitute the subject-matter of a special brieve, it is probably appropriate to conclude this section with a brief mention of this penalty clause. Normally the amount of the full forfeiture, where it is stated at all, was £10, although once it appears as £5 (no.248). The larger figure conforms to the rule laid down in the 'Laws of Malcolm MacKenneth', c.8,[12] as does the northern penalty of eight cows specified in no.281.

Administrative and other Brieves

It must be admitted that the boundary between legal and administrative brieves is ill defined. Most if not all legal brieves would have originated in a particular intervention by the king to meet a casual need; although, in twelfth-century Scotland, there is the complication that many legal brieves were borrowed, with little or no change, from the English chancery. This borrowing would tend to reduce the significance of the extempore element. In any case, it may not have been easy, or even necessary, for King William's clerks to decide whether any particular brieve which they drafted was to become the model or type of a brieve which would in future be used to initiate a settled legal procedure. Here attention is drawn to a few miscellaneous brieves and royal commands, some of which may be regarded as at least quasi-legal.

No.398 is a brieve granting the right of free election of a prior by the canons of an Augustinian house. It may be compared with two grants of election made by David I (*RRS*, i, no.8; Lawrie, *Charters*, no.255), both for the Benedictines of Dunfermline.

One group of brieves is linked by an interest in the obligations and rights of a lord's tenants. E.g., no.380 grants permission to move tenants in order to increase the population of Coldingham (a transfer contrasting, yet comparable, with the king's own removal of his tenants of 'Elrehope' to his waste land of Selkirk, no.367). No.436 enforces thirlage to a mill. Nos.60, 62, 77, 226, 352, 437 shew some approach to standardization in their provision that tenants shall have common pasture with those of neighbouring estates.

No.128 is an order to the king's foresters of Banchory to allow the canons of St Andrews to take timber for building their church; forbidding obstruction on pain of the £10 forfeiture. No.234 commands the king's foresters throughout Scotia—here, as usually in texts produced within the Scottish kingdom, meaning the country north of Forth—to allow the Tironensians of Arbroath to take whatever they need for their own use from the royal forests. This brieve evidently arose from a royal grant similar to those made to Coupar Angus by Malcolm IV (*RRS*, i, no.226) and to Holyrood by King David (Lawrie, *Charters*, no.153). We know very little about the organization of royal forests in the twelfth century, but it is clear that a king's forester might be an officer of high rank—John of Hastings, forester of Mearns, was also sheriff. The granting of land to be held 'in forest' (rarely, 'in free forest') followed the pattern established under David I, with the usual penalty of £10 for any unlicensed hunting or cutting of wood (nos.314, 340, 346, 463, 565). No.46 combines with a grant of warren a fairly elaborate provision anent the possession of 'woods and waste'. Twelfth-century grants of warren are rare, but no.335, giving the grantee leave to hunt with four greyhounds, may be seen as a variant. The use of grants of this type implies a fairly advanced degree of control by the crown over forest land and rights, of which there is fuller evidence in the thirteenth century. But there is nothing to suggest the existence of a 'forest law' in Scotland to compare with Norman and Angevin England.

Nos.12 (fragmentary) and 406 are brieves ordering assistance to be given to the beneficiary when engaged in the pursuit of thieves; we may compare *RRS*, i, no.222, evidently re-issued under William I (no.509), which provides for the restoration of stolen goods by the bailies in whose territories they may be discovered.

Nos.289 and 305 are orders respectively to the provosts of Berwick and to the sheriff and provosts of Haddington to make annual payments out of the burgh fermes.

In conclusion, it may be reiterated here that grants of privileges to existing or intended burghs survive in relatively large numbers from William I's reign, even although the losses in this class have probably been considerable.

DIPLOMATIC ANALYSIS OF THE ACTS

The Royal Style. In view of the much larger numbers of originals which have survived there seems less need for caution in arguing for an accepted style for William I than was the case with Malcolm IV. It seems clear that down to *c.*1173–4 the style adhered to by the royal clerks was *Willelmus rex Scottorum*, almost invariably written in the form *W'. rex Scott'*. This was in conformity with the style used for David I and with the style more commonly used for Malcolm IV; and, of course, it was exactly parallel to the *H.* (*H'.*) *rex Angl'* and *S.* (*S'.*) *rex Angl'* of the chanceries of Henry I, Stephen and Henry II, down to 1172–3. The occasional use of *Dei gratia* in King William's style before *c.*1173 is typical of the solemn privileges issued for the major religious houses, documents which for the most part were probably written and indeed composed by the beneficiaries' own clerks. This again is comparable with the usage of previous reigns. Otherwise, the presence of *Dei gratia* may with some confidence be ascribed to force of habit—or even deliberate 'correction'—on the part of later copyists. Taken together, the originals and copies from nos.6 to 144, or thereabouts, are sufficient to establish an official royal style of *W'. rex Scott'*.

At some date between the summer of 1173 (no.144) and the end of 1174 (no.146) *Dei gratia* was added to the official style. No.145, an original which has the *Dei gratia* and was witnessed by Bishop Ingram of Glasgow, who died on 2 February, 1174, might seem to put it beyond doubt that the change had taken place by the first month of that year. But unfortunately no.145 was written by a scribe who cannot be safely classed among the *scriptores regis*; he shews some unusual features, and cannot even be confidently identified with any other writer of royal acts. We have to set against the evidence of no.145 that provided by no.120, admittedly a copy, which can hardly have been issued until the king's brother David had been given the earldom of Lennox. If this grant was made, as seems likely, at Perth in May, 1174, we could argue that the change was not introduced until about that time at the earliest, for no.120 has no *Dei gratia*, and these words were much more likely to be included than omitted by a copyist. If we could establish the reason for the change it might help to determine its date. But it hardly seems possible to do more than guess that it was introduced in deliberate imitation of the new Angevin practice, and that its timing was prompted by the king of Scots' desire to demonstrate that he was as much a true king as Henry fitz Empress. Obviously the new style was not adopted in Scotland until after the Angevin chancery had added *Dei gratia* (between May, 1172, and February, 1173).[13] But it might have been added in Scottish royal acts at almost any time after the outbreak of war in August, 1173 (no.144); and possibly not until after the treaty of Falaise at the end of 1174. It seems clear, however, that the addition was not made later than that year; and from then until the end of the reign the official style was *W'. Dei gratia rex Scott'*. In writing originals, *Dei* was not usually given a capital initial; *gratia* was always contracted, and the contraction might often stand for *gracia*; while *rex* might have a capital initial and *Scott'* a minuscule.

The Address. Both the long and the short forms of the general address appear frequently, there being 185 examples of the former and 256 of the latter. The two types are not distributed at random chronologically. From no.6 to no.132 (i.e., until the earlier 1170s) the short form predominates, despite the relative frequency of large charters of confirmation which normally use the long form. From no.133 to no.347 (approximately) the longer form predominates. Thereafter, and very markedly from no.393 (1196 or 1197), the short form holds the field. This form was typically *omnibus probis hominibus suis totius terre sue*. Occasionally in the earlier years of the reign *totius regni sui* is used (nos.36, 39, 60). There are other very rare variants, almost all confined to the earliest years, e.g., *universis* instead of *omnibus* in no.102. *Clericis et laicis* was a common addition to the shorter address in the earlier acts and had clearly become the rule by about the middle of the reign. Other additions which were occasionally made were *futuris et presentibus* or *modernis et posteris* and the like. The racial address might be added to the short form (no.48, French, English, Scots and Gallovidians; no.78, French, English and Scots), but it was more usual with the longer form and will be discussed below. An alternative to the racial address is found in nos.25, 92, 115 and 437, where *totius Scotie* replaces *totius terre*. This approaches closely to the various special regional or provincial addresses dealt with below, for it may be regarded as certain that Scotia in the address of a royal act did not mean the whole Scottish kingdom, and it is even a question whether it included Moray.

The longer form of the general address remained what it had been under Malcolm IV: *episcopis, abbatibus, comitibus, baronibus, justiciis, vicecomitibus, prepositis, ministris et omnibus probis hominibus suis totius terre sue*. (As already mentioned, *regni sui* (nos.39, 60) is a rare variant of *terre sue*.) *Prioribus* appears after *abbatibus* only in no.62, issued probably very early in the reign. In the first half of the reign it was not uncommon to omit *prepositis* from the longer form. Additional phrases were much the same as with the shorter form; *clericis et laicis* being at first normal and eventually invariable, and such a phrase as *tam presentibus quam futuris* being found now and then (nos.46, 60; cp. no.190, *modernis et posteris*). A few of the earlier acts have distinctly unusual addresses, such as no.28 which prefers *fidelibus* to the standard *probis hominibus*; no.34, which concludes with *ceterisque probis hominibus suis universis*; and, understandably, no.30, in diploma form, which does not have an address in the strict sense but opens with an invocation followed by a pronouncement that the king makes his grants, etc., with the consent of the bishops, earls and barons of his realm. The racial address is confined to the earlier decades of the reign, save that a document such as no.507, which was obviously a slavish reproduction of an earlier model (no.179), might retain the racial address as late as *c.*1212. It appears in nos.27, 39, 46, 48 (short), 61, 74, 75, 78 (short), 80, 81–3 (short), 96, 106, 116, 140, 144, 179 (repeated in 507) and 218. Most of these belong to the earliest years of the reign, but no.218 cannot be earlier than 1179. Moreover, the majority relate to transactions in the country south of Forth. French, English and Scots, in that order, are most commonly addressed; once or twice French and English only (relating to Lothian); and not uncommonly, especially in acts relating to the south-west, French, English, Scots and Gallovidians. The rare 'Welsh' of Malcolm IV's acts have been dropped. Perhaps the most interesting use of the full racial address is in no.144, a protection to Furness Abbey probably issued at the outset of the war of 1173.

The particular or special address is not found very frequently, no doubt because it was normally used in ephemeral acts which have not survived. Individuals might be addressed by name (nos.16, 38), and those following a certain occupation (no.26, 'to all merchants of England'), but most commonly the particular address is used for the officers or merely the inhabitants or 'responsible men' (*probi homines*) of a burgh, sheriffdom or province. Ten examples are among the acts for the Honour of Huntingdon (nos.41, 49–55, 57–8). Apart from these, the following provinces, sheriffdoms, burghs, districts or other geographical entities figure among the addresses: Scotia, Moray, Lothian and the Merse, Galloway, Carrick, Lennox, Fife, Fothrif, Berwick, Roxburgh, Haddington, Banchory and the shires of Arbroath and Ethie. The tendency to address brieves to royal justices and sheriffs has already been noticed. There are four brieves addressed to sheriffs (nos.6, 71, 94, 176), and seventeen to justices and sheriffs, with or without 'officers' or 'bailies' (nos.44, 70, 87, 95, 101A, 131, 156, 160, 177, 178, 182, 189, 207, 250, 259, 294, 354). No.68 addresses the keepers of the sanctuary of Wedale; no.93 the fishermen working around the May Isle; and no.124 the men dwelling on the moors in Borthwick parish.

The addresses of nos.157, 287 (both spurious), 488 and 505 (suspect) are all in different ways unusual. No.157 purports to be a letter to Pope Alexander III, and is no doubt correctly addressed. No.287 has an opening which embodies a fairly normal long general address, *episcopis, comitibus etc.*, but prefixes to this the quite exceptional *omnibus fidelibus sancte matris ecclesie filiis, maxime suis etc.* No.488 may be entirely authentic and is addressed *omnibus ad quos presens carta peruenerit.* No.505 is in the form of English letters patent, quite unparalleled in the usage of the Scottish royal chapel, and is addressed *omnibus fidelibus has litteras uisuris uel audituris.*

The Salutation. With the exception of the spurious no.157, which in any case is a letter, William I's acts invariably use simply *salutem* as the salutation.

The Notification. The two commonest forms of notification were (1) *Sciatis* followed by an accusative and infinitive construction, usually *me (dedisse), concessisse et hac carta mea confirmasse*; (2) *Sciant presentes et futuri,* similarly taking an accusative and infinitive. Of these two forms, not only was the second by far the commoner (328 examples), it also supplanted the first (82 examples) at approximately the same period as that in which the short general address was first overtaken by the longer form, i.e. in the earlier 1170s. The ratio of (1) to (2) in each group of fifty acts from nos.1 to 500 is as follows:

1–50	15:12
51–100	18:13
101–150	20:19
151–200	5:35
201–250	9:33
251–300	3:31
301–350	3:42
351–400	4:38
401–450	3:42
451–500	2:42

Of the last twenty-four acts, all save the suspect no.505 use the second form. It seems clear that in the first five or six years, approximately, the *sciatis* form was preferred, and that thereafter it was virtually superseded by the *sciant* form.

Other forms of the notification are as follows: (3) *Sciatis quod* with the indicative (nos.35, 46, 105, 165, 253 (spurious), 488, 491, 500, 505); (4) *Sciant tam presentes quam futuri* (nos.14, 29, 56, 65, 78, 81–3, 98, 321); (5) *Sciant clerici et laici presentes et posteri* (once *futuri*: nos.834, 106, 111); (6) *Sciant presentes et posteri* (nos.42, 75, 211, 214, 223, 225, 230, 231, 235, 240, 254, 255, 264); (7) *Sciant omnes tam posteri quam presentes* (no.74); (8) *Sciant tam posteri quam presentes* (no.263); (9) *Nouerint omnes tam presentes quam futuri* (no.63); (10) *Nouerint omnes tam posteri quam presentes* (nos.101, 317); (11) *Nouerint presentes et futuri quod* (no.188); (12) *Notum sit uobis quod* (no.287).

The Corroboration. Phrases indicating corroboration are rare. No.94 has the unique wording *Sciatis me dedisse et sigillo meo confirmasse.* No.236 announces an elaborate corroboration with the seals of the king himself, his brother David and the bishop of Glasgow, in addition to those of the parties. No.505 also announces multiple sealing, this time by the king and seven other persons. No.28, with *sigilli mei impressione consigno*, follows earlier precedents (*RRS*, i, no.174; Lawrie, *Charters*, no.163). It also speaks of confirmation by 'royal authority', a term used in nos.30, 39, 63 and elsewhere.

The Harangue. This is relatively even rarer among the acts of William I than in those of Malcolm IV. Two examples, indeed, are merely repetitions of harangues from King Malcolm's or King David's acts (nos.28, 179, 507; cf. *RRS*, i, nos.174, 258). No.39, for Holyrood, has:

> Ex officio suscepte a Deo regni administrationis incumbit nobis non solum ecclesiam et ecclesiasticas personas diligere et honorare, verumetiam elemosinas et beneficia ad eorum sustentationem impendere et ea que ab antecessoribus nostris et ab aliis Dei fidelibus eis collate sunt tueri concedere et confirmare. Unde et dignum duxi etc.

No.62, for Jedburgh, has:

> Ex suscepto regimine Regni incumbit nobis ecclesiam et ecclesiasticas diligere personas et non solum de nostris eis benefacere sed et beneficia ab aliis Dei fidelibus eis collata auctoritate regia confirmare et cum sua eis integritate conservare. Inde est quod etc.

These two harangues in acts for Augustinian houses are verbally so close that one has clearly been the model for the other, or else they both had a common model. No.316 is couched in an altogether unusually rhetorical style and could almost be said to constitute one long harangue; but there are no grounds for suspecting its authenticity. The occasion for its issue was itself unusual, and the act was in the nature of a public charity appeal.

The Text. Very much the same remarks as were made about the text of Malcolm IV's acts apply to those of his brother. It is noticeable that the royal clerks achieved a greater degree of uniformity in the text as the reign progressed. As far as documents of standard type were concerned, original grants, confirmations and common brieves, the clerks worked from a stock of more or less stereotyped formulas, within which they seem to have allowed themselves fewer and fewer variations. An instance of this is seen in their use of the phrase *salvo servitio meo* required in confirmations of grants of land by a tenant in chief to some beneficiary. The phrase is very common indeed, especially in the later part of the reign; but now and again in lengthy confirmations one may find a fuller version, as in no.333 (*salvo servitio de terris hac inscriptis de quibus servitium habere debeo*), no.367 (*salvo servitio meo de illis de quibus servitium de jure habere debeo*). The phrase is also somewhat elaborated in no.434, written by William del Bois, the future chancellor. A similar progress towards common form may be seen in the use of the words *volo itaque et firmiter precipio, quare volo et firmiter precipio, quare prohibeo*, etc.

The Attestation. No.30, modelled closely on its two predecessors of diploma form, nevertheless has the witnesses in the normal manner of a writ-charter, in the ablative case following the words *Testibus hiis*. No.46

also has *Testibus his*, but, significantly, not in the royal scribe version. This phrase, or *His* (*hiis*) *testibus*, is not uncommon in the earlier acts, but the vast majority introduce the testing clause simply with *Teste*, *Testibus* or an ambiguous *T*'. The absence of a normal testing clause in no.505 is only one of several suspicious features in this act. No.193, more obviously spurious, likewise has no attestation. In the early years of the reign acts seem often to have had only two or three witnesses, but although there can hardly have been any standard practice in later years, it was clearly normal for an act to have more witnesses than this named—anything from four or five to ten or a dozen being usual. Naturally, some of the great solemn charters had very long witness-lists. No.28 had thirty-five, no.39 nineteen, no.62 fourteen, no.80 twenty, no.197 twenty-two and no.367 twenty-one. The fact that no. 513, a long solemn confirmation of property and privileges to Arbroath, has only twelve witnesses, may mean that such lengthy arrays were going out of fashion towards the end of the reign. Only at the start of the reign, and in an act probably produced by the beneficiary, might one find the witnesses' names in the nominative case, introduced by the words *Huius autem concessionis et confirmationis mee testes hi sunt* (no.62).

The evidence favours the view that the witnesses named were personally present either when the written act was passed or at least when the decision recorded by it was taken or the dispositive act done. Occasionally it was thought desirable to record the explicit agreement and presence of the king's heir, e.g., in nos.106 and 204. The probability has already been mentioned that in general the witness-lists of the king's acts had a markedly official quality; that is to say, more of the witnesses held some official position in the king's service than might appear at first glance.

The Valediction. No valediction is used in any authentic royal act which survives. No.157, a letter, concludes *Valeat semper sanctitas vestra.* Although this text is spurious, it may be assumed that some phrase of valediction was normal in genuine letters of this type. No.2, an act of William as earl of Northumberland, has the simple *Valete*, placed before the witness-list (and misrendered or omitted in previous printed editions).

The Date

(i) The Date of Place. Some 437 authentic acts survive with place-dates within the Scottish kingdom, and in addition there are ten authentic acts with English place-dates. Each of these English acts was issued at a different place; in Scotland forty-eight different places are represented. The following table gives the order of frequency. (Non-authentic acts are placed in square brackets.)

The omission of the place-date is even more uncommon among William I's acts than among Malcolm IV's. Nos.40 and 41, both originals, have no place-date, although it is clear that they were issued on the same occasion and highly probable that the place of issue was Edinburgh. The absence of a place-date here is all the more remarkable because they were written by the scribe of nos.25 and 27 (and *RRS*, i, no.166),

SCOTLAND

No.	Place	No.	Place
[1] 45	Forfar	3	St Mary's Loch
[1] 45	Perth	2	Auchtermuchty
44	Stirling	2	Charleton
[1] 34	Edinburgh	2	Dumfries
27	Selkirk	2	Forres
21	Kinghorn	2	Kintore
20	Montrose	2	Peebles
18	Haddington	2	Stow (Wedale)
17	Jedburgh	[1] 1	Restalrig
14	Elgin	1	Arbroath
14	Lanark	1	Auldearn
14	Roxburgh	1	Brechin
14	Traquair	1	Bunkle
12	Dunfermline	1	'Forgrund'
10	Clackmannan	1	Forteviot
8	Alyth	1	Fyvie
8	Crail	1	Gretna
8	Linlithgow	[1]	Hyndhopeburnmouth
8	St Andrews	1	Inverness
6	Aberdeen	1	Kinross
5	Berwick upon Tweed	1	Lochmaben
5	Clunie in Stormont	1	Nairn
5	Kincardine (Mearns)	1	Rutherglen
3	Melrose	1	Scone

ENGLAND

No.	Place	No.	Place
1	Carlisle	1	Kingscliffe
1	Donkley Haugh	1	Mitford
1	Durham	1	Norham on Tweed
1	Huntingdon	1	Northampton
1	Kempston	1	Reading

all of which have place-dates. Inferior cartulary copies may well omit the date of place; no.435, without a place-date, comes from a good cartulary but is written in a later hand than the main body of charters and more carelessly. The argument from silence cannot be used in respect of copies, and the evidence of the originals is overwhelmingly strong that the date of place, introduced by *apud*, with the name normally in the vernacular, was regarded as essential.

(ii) The Date of Time. From the start of William's reign until some period in the 1190s, which seems to have been the spring of 1195, the date of time was not normally used in royal acts. Exceptions in authentic acts (e.g., nos.215, 252) go far to prove the rule, for in these, strictly speaking, the dates do not refer to the acts themselves but form part of a narrative connected with the grant or judicial decision which the king has made—a boundary was marked out on the day the charter was made, 21 October, in the year King Louis VII visited Canterbury (1179); or a perambulation was carried out on the Feast of the Exaltation of Holy Cross, A.D.1184. Exceptions in which the time-dates are given at the end of the act, referring strictly to the document itself, appear invariably in forgeries or acts whose text has been tampered with.

In the last two decades of the reign, royal acts bear a date of time in the form of the day of the month, without any year number, whether regnal or of the Christian era. This time-date follows the place-date, and is normally written in the form *.v. die Maii*, *.iiij. die Julii* etc. In copies this occasionally undergoes some change, but in originals scribal usage remains remarkably consistent, and it is rare for an original, such as no.410, to have the numeral written in full. No.405 is an original which cannot be earlier than 1198, yet it omits the time-date altogether. This must be put down to scribal oversight. The administrative significance of the addition of the time-date is discussed above; the form in which it was added is exasperatingly brief for the historical student, and must have been slightly inadequate even for contemporary clerks. Yet this form was adhered to until the seventh year of Alexander II, when the year of grace was used for a short while; and it was not until the eighth year (December, 1221–2) that the regnal began to be used regularly.

What appear to be the earliest acts in the dated series are printed in this collection as nos.376 *et seq*. A few of these belong to April and May and were issued at Clackmannan or Stirling. The year seems to have been 1195, and Roger Howden reports that King William fell ill, presumably seriously ill, at Clackmannan in this year. A further feature of interest is that among the small handful of originals at the start of the dated series three (nos.377, 383, 386) are in the hand of no.434, which is subscribed 'datum per manum Willelmi de Boscho'. This might suggest that it was William del Bois, a clerk of notable assiduity and responsibility, eventually chancellor from 1211 to 1226, who first introduced the practice of dating acts by the day of the month. By implication, whoever was responsible for this change was also responsible for beginning to keep rolls of acts issued under the king's seal.

Other notes on Diplomatic. Among several matters which lie outwith the foregoing classification two have been selected for brief mention, the use of singular and plural and the practice of issuing more than one version by 'duplication' or 'innovation'.

As a rule, throughout William I's reign his acts convey his will in the first person singular. As in previous reigns, one may find the plural used in harangues forming the preamble to an act otherwise keeping to the singular. The resemblance between no.316 and contemporary harangues has been remarked upon, and it is not surprising that this act uses the plural throughout. Certain of the legislative acts anent teind were also framed in the first person plural (nos.179, 507). No.388, unfortunately only a copy of uncertain provenance, but not obviously suspicious, uses the plural in the opening dispositive clause but the singular thereafter. Undoubtedly the most interesting example of the use of the plural is provided by no.493, an original in the hand of a well-known scribe (Gilbert of Stirling?). Its date is Stirling, 22 June, probably in 1210, and it uses the plural consistently in such a way as to suggest that the royal chapel had made a firm decision to change from the older singular usage to the newer plural usage, presumably to bring Scottish practice into line with the chanceries of England and other powers. If this was the case, the decision must have been quickly rescinded, for the only further trace of it in the remaining thirty-one acts comes in no.505, whose credentials are suspect, and in no.507, where the plural usage must be attributed merely to reproducing the wording of a much older text (no.179). Even such important acts as no.513, the solemn confirmation for Arbroath Abbey, and no.519, a *curia regis* judgement anent an earldom, keep to the first person singular.

Something approaching the later practice of issuing duplicates could be seen in *RRS*, i, nos.132, 133, which are almost identical textually although one omits an important place-name which the other includes. Under William I, the issuing of more than one sealed 'original' version of a single act was evidently not uncommon. Occasionally, as with no.175 (*A*) and (*B*), both versions are in the same hand and might be strictly contemporaneous. More often, however, the two versions are in the hands of different scribes one of whom can be shewn to have been at work considerably later than the other (e.g., nos.46, 67, 85), or can at least be shewn to have used a different style of handwriting (e.g., nos.66, 105). In these cases, one version may well be written in an upright charter hand, close to a book hand, while the other is in the hand of a known royal scribe. It is difficult to be sure of the precise purpose of this practice, but its advantage is obvious in the case of brieves which might often need to be shewn to royal officers. Even in the case of the big general confirmations, there would probably be some advantage in having more than one sealed version, provided they were not stored in the same place. Some such duplication seems to underlie the textual discrepancies between the 'original' of no.28 and the cartulary copy; but if so, the clerks responsible were evidently not very accurate. It is unfortunate that we have no evidence for the cost of obtaining charters and brieves from the Scottish royal chapel in the twelfth century. Presumably the fee payable for a large solemn privilege was higher than that for a special brieve, and this in turn may have been higher than that for a stereotyped brieve, e.g., *de nativis*; but this is no more than a guess based on common sense.

PHYSICAL APPEARANCE

Material. With regard to the parchment on which they were written, the same remarks apply to William I's acts as were made in *RRS*, i, p.84. Acts produced, probably, by the beneficiary—especially large confirmation charters—tended to be written on a thick, sometimes rather coarse skin. The shorter acts were for the most part (although not invariably) written on thinner, smoother skins, often still remarkably white (e.g., no.516) and occasionally almost transparent. There seems to have been a tendency for the parchment used to be finer and smoother towards the end of the reign than in its earlier decades. The whole question of what types of skin were used and how they were prepared deserves intensive study which the present editor is incompetent to undertake.

Size. Only two of the acts (nos.43, 133) are less than 5 in. wide, and only thirteen are more than 10 in. wide. Between these extremes some 59 acts are from 5 in. to 7 in. wide, while 78 are between 7 in. and 10 in. There is less variation in average depth. Only six acts (nos.28, 39, 62, 175 (*A*), 236, 367) are more than 10 in. deep; seven are from 7 in. to 10 in., twenty-seven from 5 in. to 7 in., and the rest (108) have a depth of less than 5 in., although not usually less than about 2 in. Left-hand and right-hand margins tend to be narrow or almost non-existent. Top and bottom margins may be somewhat wider, but in general the writing block of William I's acts fills the available parchment almost to the edges.

Handwriting. The problem of discussing the handwriting of Malcolm IV's acts lay in the scarcity of originals. These numbered twenty-seven, of which seven or eight were written by the same hand, 'Scribe A', while other three—not two, as originally considered—were in the hand of one other scribe (*RRS*, i, nos.127, 149, 155). With William I's acts the problem is one of relative abundance. Including a handful of spurious and purported originals and 'renovations' of a period later than 1214, there are 159 originals whose handwriting can be examined. As in the case of Malcolm IV's acts, two chief types of hand may be distinguished, upright charter hands, sometimes verging on true book hands, and cursive, often highly abbreviated, business or court hands. In contrast with Malcolm's short reign the long reign of his brother, and the survival of originals which may be very closely dated from every decade of the reign, enable us to see clearly that the great majority of examples of the former type of hand come from the earlier years of the reign, while every act from the last two decades of the reign, of whose credentials we may feel reasonably confident, was written in one of the cursive 'chancery' or 'chapel' hands. Not counting hands belonging to periods later than 1214, some twenty-six or twenty-seven distinct hands are found in surviving contemporary originals. Eleven are charter hands and sixteen are court hands. Of these sixteen, it seems reasonable to classify twelve or thirteen as belonging to scribes who worked professionally in the royal chapel. It is hard to judge to what extent a royal charter scribe followed a full-time occupation. The fact that in the earlier decades of the reign several scribes are found working simultaneously, while at its close every single surviving original is in the hand of one scribe, suggests that the scribe's office was made more specialized and more of a full-time occupation as the reign progressed. But it is hard to be sure of this because we know neither the total output of William I's charters, brieves, etc., nor, except approximately, the difference in rate of output between different periods of the reign. Business may have been slacker at the close of the reign, though there is no obvious reason why this should have been so. Fewer acts of permanent value as title deeds, etc., may have been produced, but on the other hand there may have been a greater output of ephemeral material.

The different handwritings are listed and described below. The grounds for identifying five of the 'professional' scribes with Richard of Lincoln (Aj), Gervase (Da, also Db?), Hugh de sigillo (Dd), William del Bois (De) and Gilbert of Stirling (Df) are given after the description of their respective hands. Hands are grouped according to the chancellorship in which they are first found for certain. Each chancellorship has been assigned a capital letter as follows: A (Nicholas, 1165–71); B (Walter de Bidun, 1171–8); C (Roger, *c.*1188–9, including preceding vacancy); D (Hugh of Roxburgh, 1189–99); E (William Malvoisin, 1199–1202); F (Florence of Holland, 1203 (?)–10(?); and G (William del Bois or de Boscho, 1211–14). In fact, no hands have been found which can definitely be assigned to the last three chancellorships. Unassigned hands, chiefly of scribes working later than 1214 who have written forgeries, purported originals or 'renovations', have been grouped at the end under the class UD. Within each group, each scribe has been identified by a lower-case letter following the capital. It is convenient, and for most purposes adequate, to equate 'scribe' with 'hand', but it should be noted that strictly speaking the list which follows is a list of hands, not of scribes. It is conceivable that one scribe might have used a 'charter' hand for some documents and a 'court' hand for others. It is probable that some scribes had two styles, one formal, the other more cursive; and it is quite possible that the hands classified below as Da and Db belonged to the same scribe. The numbers in bold type following the code-letters for each scribe refer to acts in this collection. Examples of a scribe's work which are not acts of William I are listed in brackets. The place-dates of each scribe's acts are given, followed by the extreme limits of date between which his work is found.

Aa. **76**
Yarrow Meres (St Mary's Loch) 1166 × 1171.
Small, modest court hand with fine pen; upright, much abbreviated, rather crowded. To be compared with hand of *RRS*, i, no.147 (1157 × 1162).

Ab. **81, 82, 83, 175** (*A* and *B*), **214, 236**. (SRO, GD 55/1, 55/2, 55/6; Yorks. Arch. Soc., MS. Grantley B 20 = Lawrie, *Charters*, no.141; *RRS*, i, no.41; *Melrose Liber*, no.6; *RRS*, i, no.133*A*. *c.*1147 × 1159).
Lanark, (?) Melrose, Perth, Roxburgh. 1166 × 1177 (also 1180?).
Melrose charter hand of considerable longevity, with features of book hand. Upright, usually a broad pen. Note forms for A, M, S, g and Ꝥ (Th ligature).

Ac. **10**
Perth. 1166 × 1171.
Charter hand, comparable with Ab and, more closely, with Bc. Ruled. Possibly a Melrose hand, since Coupar Angus was a daughter-house of Melrose.

Ad. **39**. (BM, Harl. Chrs. III.B 14= *Holyrood Liber*, App. II, no.4, instrument of Richard bishop of St Andrews, self-dated Berwick on Tweed 1166).
Edinburgh. 1165 × 1171.
Careful upright charter hand of book-hand type, but with long ascenders. Ruled. Note especially mark of suspension often placed high above the word, and the forms for E, Æ and ÐÐ.

Ae. **28**
Dunfermline. 1165 × 1171.
Charter hand, upright, with thin pen. Letters blotted here and there. Note E, C, tironian et, use of very large ampersand, and ligature of final '-an'.

Af. **46, 62, 66** (*A*), **105** (*B*)
Berwick, Peebles, Perth, Roxburgh. 1165 × 1171.
Upright charter hand with broad pen. Ruled. Note form of initial W in royal style in 62 and 66(*A*); and T and ÞÐ.

Ag. **26**
Dunfermline. 1165 × 1171.
Idiosyncratic upright charter hand, certain ascenders decorated. Note tironian et and g.

Ah. **25, 27, 40** (*A*), **41**
(SRO, St Andrews chrs. 1 = *RRS*, i, no.166; Lincoln, D. & C. Muniments, Dij/90/3/19= *Reg. Ant. Lincoln*, iii, no.805, facsimile facing p.156. SRO, GD 90/3= 40 (*B*) is a late copy of 40 (*A*), not an example of the same hand).
Dunfermline, (?) Edinburgh. 1165 × 1171.
Careful precise book hand, with sharply cut quill. Ruled. Note splaying of the top of the ascender in b, h.

Ai. **45, 47, 48, 66** (*B*), **67** (*A*), **75, 85** (*A*), **86, 113, 135, 136, 146**
Berwick, Durham, Forfar, Lanark, Mitford, Northampton, Perth, Roxburgh, Selkirk, Yarrow Meres (St Mary's Loch). 1166 × 1185.
Markedly pointed court hand, with tall ascenders, characterized by certain horizontal strokes (e.g., marks of suspension and top stroke of F) being extended in a wavy line. Note also G. A royal scribe.

Aj. **42, 43, 44, 73, 79, 80, 101A, 105** (*A*), **114, 125, 133, 137, 144, 152, 204**
Berwick, Carlisle, Clunie in Stormont, Donkleyhaugh, Edinburgh, Forfar, Linlithgow, Lochmaben, Perth, Selkirk, Stirling. 1165 × 1182.
Plain cursive court hand shewing marked professional competence in its consistent and even quality. Note extremely simple tironian et, and forms for ÐÐ and g.
This scribe may be identified with the king's clerk Richard of Lincoln,

and Richard of Lincoln was probably the royal clerk named Richard who was made bishop of Moray in 1187. As Richard the (or 'my') clerk of Lincoln, he witnesses nos.133 and 137; as Richard the clerk he witnesses nos.42, 44, 73, 78, 80, and 125. Almost invariably his name is found in the final or penultimate position in the witness-list. Similarly he witnesses the following non-originals: nos.143, 226, 230, 231, 232 (as Richard of Lincoln; and cf. *Arbroath Liber*, i, no.54); and also nos.22(?), 72(?), 116, 120, 130, 132, 134, 139, 140, 142, 161; and cf. *Scone Liber*, no.50.

Ak. **14, 145**
Perth, Traquair. 1165 × 1174.
Small undistinctive court hand. It is not certain that these examples are in the same hand (e.g., W and S are different), but similarities seem to outweigh differences. Note d, A, Ric' de Moru' (Morev') and tironian et.

Al. **59, 176, 206**
Bunkle, Linlithgow, (?) Perth. 1165 × 1189.
Court hand verging on charter hand, with tendency to sprawl. Note G and g, and form for pro. Probably a royal scribe.

Ba. **153, 165, 171, 200, 213, 263**
Auldearn, Crail, Kinghorn, Kingscliffe, Perth, Stirling. 1173 × 1185.
Highly idiosyncratic, almost eccentric court hand, uneven in appearance, with marked contrast between broad and narrow strokes. Downward strokes tend to be thickened. Some fussy and unpleasing decoration. Note D, g, N, T and R with its right-hand stroke carried leftward through the ascender. A royal scribe. In general style, and in several points of detail, this hand compares closely with Scribe no.xli of Bishop, *Scriptores Regis*, working *c.*1168 (see Plate XXXIV b).

Bb. **46 (*B*), 167, 178, 181, 266, 267, 294, 302, 338**
(Berwick), Edinburgh, Haddington, Jedburgh, Kinghorn, Perth, Selkirk. 1173 × 1196.
46 (*B*) is a renovation of a charter issued 1165 × 1171, in hand Af.
Pointed angular court hand with exaggeratedly tall ascenders and narrow capitals. Note tironian et. A royal scribe.

Bc. **78, 199**
Haddington, Jedburgh. 1165 × 1186.
Upright charter hand, comparable with Cc, with which this might conceivably be identical. The first example has no *Dei gratia* and is witnessed by Bishop Ingram of Glasgow who died in 1174. Note W, M, G, and prolongation of tail of f and long s.

Ca. **252, 268, 269, 367, 368**
Edinburgh, Haddington, Kinghorn, Roxburgh. 1184 × 1194.
Distinctive court hand in which curves predominate, with exaggerated

ascenders and descenders. Note C, E, G, and T. No.367 is an exceptionally large and ornate piece of calligraphy (inspired by, but falling far short of, *RRS*, i, no.131); but its scribe uses the same R as in the other examples; compare especially the T of Test' in this and no.368.

Cb. **264, 265**
No place-date. 8 March, 1185.
Narrow upright charter hand with affinities to book-hand, and to other Melrose hands. French spelling forms are used in the testing clause. Note contrast between tall narrow capitals and squat minuscules.

Cc. **195, 293, 301, 364**
Edinburgh, Lanark, Traquair. 1177 × 1196.
The identity of these hands is uncertain. Upright charter hand verging on book hand. Note g, S, W. No.293 shews greatest variations from the rest, and is comparable with Bc and even Ak.

Cd. **211**
Forfar. 1179 × 1188.
Small court hand with sharply cut quill. Note small capitals C, H and O.

Ce. **235**
Haddington. 1179 × 1188.
Distinctive court hand using two form of tironian et. Ascender of d is carried leftward through ascender of large minuscule A in the word Ad.

Cf. **322**
Stirling. 1187 × 1190.
Charter hand seemingly in advance of its time. Note tironian et, one crossed, others not.

Da. **286, 303, 309, 313, 340, 341, 343, 350, 365, 380, 414, 422**
Haddington, Forfar, Kinghorn, Lanark, Melrose, Selkirk. 1177 × 1199.
Highly fluent cursive court hand of thoroughly professional quality. No.365 apes a papal privilege with some skill. Tittle used occasionally. Note H, Q, S, T, diphthong Æ, long-tailed g, looped r, tironian et and especially the compendium for Forfar. Perhaps same scribe as Db; in any case a royal scribe. It may be suggested that this scribe was Gervase the clerk, who served for a time as clerk to Jocelin bishop of Glasgow. As 'Gervase our clerk' he witnessed *Paisley Registrum*, 109, an act of Bishop Jocelin dating 1179 × ; he also witnessed as bishop's clerk, along with his other clerks John and Walter, *North Berwick Carte*, no.2, dating 18/19 September, 1194 × 1195. This charter is in the hand of Scribe Da, as is no.365 below, dating 1193 × 1195. No.365 confirms an episcopal charter also dating 1193 × 1195 (*Melrose Liber*, no.121), which though not

written in the hand of Da is witnessed by Gervase as the third of three clerks of the lord king's chapel. It seems that Gervase transferred from the bishop's to the king's service *c.*1194–5; and it may be that all the royal acts in his hand date from 1194 or later. I owe this identification to the unpublished B.Litt. thesis (University of Glasgow, 1965) of Mr N. F. Shead, who has collected a valuable appendix of episcopal *acta* with facsimiles.

Db. **67** (*B*), **314, 320, 342, 369, 410, 418, 429**
Aberdeen, Alyth, Forfar, Linlithgow, Montrose, Roxburgh, Selkirk. 1189 × 1203.
No.67 (*B*), is a renovation of a brieve issued 1165 × 1171, in hand Ai.
Extremely cursive fluent court hand, with distinctive forms for dj in the royal style, tironian et and ligature de. Perhaps this is the same hand as Da, the examples under Da shewing his stiffer, more formal style and the examples under Db his more rapid style. Compare the name Forfar in nos.340 and 342. But the Da examples have dei or di, whereas the Db examples have dj; the capital S in Da differs slightly from that in Db; and the tironian et is more fluent in Db than in Da. A royal scribe, possibly Gervase the clerk, for whom see under Da.

Dc. **85** (*B*), **295, 402, 403**. (SRO, GD 90/10 is a late copy of no.295).
Edinburgh, (Lanark), Scone, Stirling. 1189 × 1200.
No.85 (*B*) is a renovation of a charter issued 1166 × 1182, in hand Ai.
Stylized court hand with fine pen. Ascenders tend to be curved. Note embellishment of left-hand side of f, h, i and l. Probably a royal scribe.

Dd. **375, 401, 405, 427, 428, 429, 432, 439, 444, 446, 451**
Aberdeen, Clackmannan, Haddington, Jedburgh, Kincardine, Stirling. 1189 × 1211.
Court hand of rather angular appearance. Note g, *punctus elevatus*, variety of forms of tironian et. The mark of suspension, resembling a staple used for stapling sheets of paper together, is almost a signature of this scribe's hand. It is suggested that this scribe was the king's clerk Hugh *de sigillo*, first mentioned by that name *c.*1178 and promoted to the see of Dunkeld in 1214. No.444 was evidently issued on the same day as no.445 (Df); whereas no.445, in the hand taken to be that of Gilbert of Stirling, was witnessed by William del Bois and *Gilbert*, clerks, no.444 was witnessed by William del Bois and *Hugh*, clerks, the context indicating that this was Hugh *de sigillo*.

De. **358, 377, 383, 386, (404?), 434**
Berwick, Forfar, Jedburgh, Kincardine, Stirling. 1189 × 1203.
Pleasing rounded cursive hand of practised appearance. Note the mannered sign for -us (e.g., in tocius). No.434 is subscribed 'datum per manum Willelmi de Boscho tempore Florentii Cancellarii, anno ab incarnatione domini m.cciij°', and this hand may be taken to be

that of William del Bois. It seems significant that it first appears in acts belonging to 1195 and early 1196, when the practice of dating by day-of-month was introduced.

Df. **389, 445, 459, 460, 461, 462, 463, 464, 469, 470, 471, 474, 479, 483, 484, 485, 486, 489, 493, (495?), 496, 504, 508, 514, 516, 517, 520, 521, 524**
Auchtermuchty, Clackmannan, Edinburgh, Forfar, 'Forgrund', Haddington, Jedburgh, Kin (cardine?), Lanark, Selkirk, Stirling, Stow, Traquair. 1196 × 1214 (and later).
The most consistent and professional-looking of the hands used in William I's acts. Elegant and mannered but with none of the fussiness characteristic of some court hands of the period. Note A, g and tironian et; and the consistency with which the royal style and address are written, both in the formation of the letters and in the punctuation. This may be taken to be the hand of the king's clerk Gilbert of Stirling. Not only is the scribe's work found under Alexander II, until *c.*1225 (*Inchaffray Chrs.*, no.53), but we should note the occasional witnessing of Df charters by Gilbert of Stirling, and especially the fact that no.445, by Df, was given on the same day as no.444, by Dd; the former is witnessed by William del Bois and Gilbert, clerks of the king, the latter by William del Bois and Hugh, clerks of the king.

UNASSIGNED HANDS

UDa. **509**
(Jedburgh).
Renovation of *RRS*, i, no.222.
Fine-looking, rather mannered hand, which could be as early as 1214 and might, in theory, be a product of William I's chapel. Hand upright, with marked thickening of certain horizontals, e.g., in the mark of suspension. Top of ascender in b, h and l is forked. Ductus of g is large and pronounced. Tittle is used, especially in first line.

UDb. **154**
Charleton.
Renovation or purported original, with provision for sealing through slit in fold, but no trace of tag or seal.
Careful upright charter hand of the first half of the thirteenth century; possibly earlier than 1214, but several decades later than the purported date of issue. Closely comparable with, but rather simpler than, a hand appearing *c.*1240–50 in a charter of John son of Adam son of Odo (of Kinninmonth), SRO, RH 6/27.

UDc. **143, 424**
Edinburgh, Stirling.
Purported originals, with tag and trace of seal (143), with both tag and seal (424).

Plain business or charter hand of the third quarter of the thirteenth century.

UDd. **505**
No place-date.
Purported original, without trace of sealing.
English chancery hand of *c*.1230–40.

UDe. **253**
No place-date.
Purported original, with discrepancy in witness-list. Tag, but no seal remains.
Upright charter-hand of mid- or later thirteenth century, with features of book-hand. Similar to, but hardly identical with, hand of older Melrose cartulary (NLS, MS. Adv. 34.4.11), dating from reign of Alexander III.

UDf. **119**
(Hindhope Burn mouth.)
Purported original, or copy; no trace of sealing. Business hand of fourth quarter of thirteenth century.

UDg. **467**
Stirling.
Purported original, or renovation, with provision for seal on tag; top of tag left but no seal.
Small business hand of earlier fourteenth century.

UDh. **279**
(Perth.)
Purported original, with tag for seal.
Hand difficult to date, since scribe seems to have attempted to simulate an archaic hand, possibly taking Moray Muniments, 32/1/1 as his model. Probably fourteenth century.

The Seal. Despite the great length of his reign, King William seems to have used only one seal, or at least only one design of seal. Whether, or how often, the actual metal matrix had to be replaced during the reign has not been determined. It is noteworthy that although the design of the English great seal was changed between Richard I's first seal and his second, so that thereafter the figure of the king on his throne would hang upright when the seal was placed on the tag, such a change was not made in Scotland until the time of Alexander II.[14] This suggests that the seal used by King William in the latter part of his reign was identical with that used earlier, for the change in English usage would surely have been copied in Scotland soon after it was noticed, given a suitable opportunity.

Fortunately, many more examples of William I's seal survive than of the seals of David I or Malcolm IV. Even so, there have been heavy casualties, and by no means all the surviving examples are in conditions of reasonable security. There are some eighty-four authentic originals which possess either their seals more or less intact or at least enough fragments or traces to deduce their colour or the way in which they were placed on the document. The seal has been described in J. Stevenson and M. Wood, *Scottish Heraldic Seals*, p. 3, in W. de G. Birch's *History of Scottish Seals* (1905), i, pp. 22–4 (with facsimile) and elsewhere.[15] In fact, Birch's photograph gives but a poor impression of the fine quality and liveliness of design of William's seal, the cutting of whose dies was obviously of a very high standard. The seal was appreciably larger than Malcolm IV's, being 3·3 in. in diameter, and bearing the legend, without any abbreviations, on a generous border: + WILLELMVS DEO RECTORE REX SCOTTORVM (obverse and reverse). On the obverse, the king is shewn facing, enthroned in majesty, holding a sword in the right hand (whose point penetrates the border) and an orb and cross in his left. On the reverse, the king is mounted on a finely-cut horse, riding towards the right. The animal's spirited mettle is emphasized by the way in which fore and hind legs penetrate the border (after DEO and REX respectively), the feet reaching almost to the outside edge. The king holds a shield, without heraldic device, on his left arm, across the front of his body, and in his right hand he holds a lance surmounted by a pennon of three streamers.

At least three, and possibly four, different colours of wax were used for the seal: 'natural', ranging in practice from an 'off white' through a very pale brown to a deeper shade, where discoloration may have been produced by the use of a brown varnish; dark green; pink or red; and brown, unless this is not a true 'colour' in the wax, but only the effect of accidental or deliberate discoloration. As with the seal colours under Malcolm IV, it seems impossible to discover any principle governing the use of the different colours. Among the surviving examples, which must be a relatively random sample of the whole, there are sixteen where an unambiguously green wax has been used;[16] eleven have red or pink wax;[17] and forty-eight (including all but one of the Durham-Coldingham originals) have natural wax, usually of a brownish shade, but sometimes pinkish and occasionally a greenish brown. The seals of nos. 81 and 410 have, most oddly, their obverse in one colour and their reverse in another. The reverse is green in both cases, while no. 81 has a red obverse, no. 410 an obverse in natural wax stained brown. It must be admitted that the latter seal has undergone repair, but the two-colour usage may be original. It may be concluded that natural wax (which was probably cheaper) was the type normally used, both for acts of permanent value and for more ephemeral documents; while, a good deal less frequently, red or green wax was chosen, for reasons which are still not at all clear.

The seal was affixed by one of the same three different methods found among Malcolm IV originals: by a parchment tag passing through slits in the folded foot of the document (*sur double queue*); by cords or ribbons passing through holes made in the folded foot; or by a tongue cut from the foot of the document by making an incision at the right-hand side and carrying it to within an inch or so of the left-hand side (*sur simple queue*). Among the originals whose method of seal attachment is still discoverable, 122 have or had their seals attached on a tag passing through single or double slits in the folded foot, fifteen have or had their seals attached on a tongue,[18] while nine employ silk cords or ribbons, usually in more than one colour.[19] The tongue method clearly became much less common in the later part of the reign, for only three examples survive after no.144. Part of the explanation for this disappearance may be that the tongue came to be reserved for purely ephemeral acts, of which very few examples have survived in the original, or indeed at all. On the other hand, the supersession of tongue by tag can hardly be denied over a wider field of material than merely grants of perpetuities and comparably solemn, permanent acts. A very high proportion of surviving originals belong to the last two decades of the reign, and every one of these from no.386 onwards, save for no.427 (cords), has its seal on a tag. Tags might of course vary in width, commonly between about a third of an inch and an inch, but half an inch was a width so common as hardly to be accidental. Length again varied, but it was not uncommon to cut a tag of some sixteen to twenty-two inches, which when doubled and passed through the slits would produce a length of some eight to eleven inches, on which the seal would normally be placed so as to leave about one or two inches of tag protruding from its foot.

The silk cords and ribbons would repay a closer study than can be attempted here. A detailed study of the beautiful woven silk seal ribbon of no.383 and of the less elaborate ribbon of no.80 has been made by Miss Audrey Henshall,[20] to whom I am indebted for permission to give a most inadequately brief summary here. The ribbon of no.383 is made of silk yarn, 2-ply twisted S; the main part is bright apple green and white, the border rose pink and green. The braid is hardly soiled and the colours remarkably bright. The colour pattern consists of horizontal rows of broken chevrons, achieved by the order in which the different coloured yarns were threaded through the tablets. The weave is extremely fine and regular and displays a remarkable skill in the handling of the finer part of the colour pattern. The principal motifs are as follows: (1) An animal resembling a hunting hound, green on a white ground, with long open snout, an eye, ears and feet with three claws; the body is thick at the shoulders and very thin at the loins; the tail is thin and curled (overall length, 1·3 in = 3·4 cm); (2) Peacock, white on green ground, with long closed beak, small head with crest, two short legs and a long elaborate tail; (3) An animal, white on green ground, with small head and open mouth like a beak, long neck with mane, and a plumed tail. The feet appear to be cloven. None of the other ribbons approach this in artistry, but no.80 has a well worked chequer pattern in green and white, apparently silk and linen.[21] It is remarkable that a very high proportion of the surviving silken ribbons or cords belong to charters for prominent lay barons, Bruce, Hay, Graham, etc.

Folding and Endorsement. Where a tag or cords were used, the foot was folded to give sufficient strength to take the weight of the seal. It is doubtful if the royal clerks made any further folds in the acts as they were issued. Nevertheless, the frequency with which early endorsements are found on the central panel of a folded original suggests that it was common practice for the recipient to fold his document at the time it was issued or soon afterwards. In view of the abundant evidence for the handwriting of William I's acts, the absence from the endorsements of any hand which can be safely identified with that of any known royal scribe amounts to proof that the scribes did not attempt any endorsement themselves but left this for the recipient to do if he chose. The practice of endorsing documents is closely connected to the practice of archive-keeping, which is outwith the scope of this work; but it may be remarked here that an extraordinarily high proportion of endorsed originals bear repetitions of the earliest note of contents which scarcely ever seem to convey any fresh information or to have any obvious value. They might almost have been written merely to give the archivist something to do. Now and again, as with no.79 (or *RRS*, i, no.149), the archivist tells us in his endorsement that the document is of no use but has then, fortunately, continued to preserve it.

NOTES TO SECTION 3

1. *RRS*, i, 83–4.
2. *HMC*, II, Appendix, 166; cf. *RMS*, ii, no.2833.
3. SRO, Register of Deeds, vol.viii, fo.220.
4. *SHR*, iv (1907), 481–2; *Archaeologia Aeliana*, ii (1832), 103–4. (This forgery has been based on Raine, *North Durham*, no.642.)
5. Lawrie, *Annals*, 321.
6. A. Harding, 'The medieval brieves of protection and the development of the common law', *Juridical Review* (1966), 115–49.
7. Art. cit., 117–21.
8. Nos.24, 26, 28, 60, 76, 87, 103, 127, 144, 156, 239, 313, 316, 442, 462, 467, 550.
9. Lawrie, *Charters*, no.172; *RRS*, i, no.219.
10. Nos.16, 71, 93, 108, 124, 132, 139, 179, 189, 259, 273, 281, 374, 394, 407, 421, 478, 507.
11. Nos.6, 30, 47, 60, 65, 94, 101A, 177, 207, 213, 255, 283, 285, 313, 388, 429, 462, 513, 550.
12. *APS*, i, 711.
13. R.L. Poole, *Studies in Chronology and History* (1934), 304.
14. *RRS*, i, 87, and n.6.
15. E.g., W. Greenwell and C. Hunter Blair, 'Durham Seals', Part VI, *Archaeologia Aeliana*, 3rd ser., xiii (1916), p.150; Laing, *Seals*, i, 3.
16. Nos.39, 78, 125, 171, 200, 204, 210, 216, 252, 427, 429 (*A*), 429 (*B*), 432, 439, 514, 516.
17. Nos.40, 75, 79, 152, 175 (*A*), 214, 365, 375, 459, 470, 479, 485.
18. Nos.43, 47, 48, 59, 66 (*B*), 73, 76, 101A, 113, 114, 136, 144, 211, 303, 380.
19. Nos.79, 80, 125, 135, 174, 175 (*A*), 264, 383, 427. No.178 has the seal attached by leather thongs.
20. *Archaeological Journal*, cxxi (1965), 157–9.
21. Ibid., Plate XXIII (A).

4. SKELETON ITINERARY OF WILLIAM I

Entries within parentheses are approximations or based on surmise

1165 (December; Dunfermline
Malcolm IV's funeral). Lawrie, *Annals*, 101

1165 December 24; (Scone)
Inauguration. Ibid., 107–8

1166 (March and after; Normandy, Maine, Anjou)
Ibid., 114

1166 July 12–31; Fougères, Brittany
Siege (?). Ibid.

1166 August or September; Genêts, dép. Manche (near Le Mont St Michel)
Meeting with Henry II. Ibid., 114–15

1166 (By October; Scotland)
Ibid., 115

1170 April 5; Windsor
Court of Henry II. Ibid., 117

1170 May 31; Windsor
Ibid., 118

1170 June 14–15; Westminster
Coronation of Henry the 'young king'. Ibid., 118–19

1172 (Before April 2; Stirling
No.133)

1173 (About August 20); Caddonlea, Selkirkshire
Muster of the army. Lawrie, *Annals*, 132–3; *Chron. Holyrood*, 153

1173 During August time was spent at Wark on Tweed and Carlisle engaged on castle sieges.

1174 (March 31 or after); Wark on Tweed
Second siege. Lawrie, *Annals*, 156ff

1174 May 23; Perth
Election of Jocelin bishop of Glasgow. Dowden, *Bishops*, 298

1174 (About the beginning of June?); Carlisle
Siege. *Chron. Fantosme* Michel, 51, 61ff; *Chron. Holyrood*, 154–5

1174 During the period June to July, time was spent at Carlisle, Brough, Appleby, Prudhoe and Alnwick.
Lawrie, *Annals*, 161–81

1174 July 13; Alnwick
Capture of King William by Ranulf de Glanvill and others.
Ibid., 181–4

1174 July 26; Northampton
Ibid., 185

1174 Thereafter King William was taken to Barfleur from Portsmouth, thence to Caen.
Ibid., 187

1174 (After December 1); Falaise
Imprisonment. Ibid., 187, 196

1174 December 8; Valognes
Stones, *Documents*, 1–5; Anderson, *Scottish Annals*, 258

1174 December 11; Leaves Normandy for England
Ibid.

1175 (Before February 2); Scotland
Lawrie, *Annals*, 197

1175 August 10; York
Homage to Henry II and the 'young king'. Ibid., 201

1175 (After August 10); Galloway
Ibid., 205–6

1176 January 23; Northampton
Henry II's council. Ibid., 206–11

1176 October 9; Feckenham, Worcs.
Henry II's council. Ibid., 217–8

1177 July 1; Winchester, thence to Normandy
Military summons. Anderson, *Scottish Annals*, 268–9

1178 (Between February 22 and April 1?); Aberdeen
APS, i, 374; Lawrie, *Annals*, 218

1179 During this year, the king made an expedition to Ross
Ibid., 227

1179 October 21; Selkirk
No.215

1179 December 25; Nottingham
Henry II's council. Lawrie, *Annals*, 227

1180 March 30; Haddington
No.236; Lawrie, *Annals*, 236

1180 July 14; Stirling
Ibid.

1181 (April or May); Normandy
Conference with Henry II anent the St Andrews election dispute. Ibid., 238

1181 During the summer, time was spent in Normandy in company with Henry II, including a visit to Gisors in July.
Ibid., 239

1181 July 26; Cherbourg-Portsmouth
Ibid.

1181 During the period July, August and possibly September, the king accompanied Henry II to Canterbury and went with him to a council held at Nottingham.
Ibid.

1181 (September?); Redden on Tweed
Ibid., 239–41

1182 During this year the king held a three-day council to deal with the St Andrews election dispute. Its location is not known.
Chron. Holyrood, 168–9

1184 During the summer, perhaps in late June, July or August, the king attended Henry II's court in the south of England to discuss his request to marry Maud of Saxony, daughter of Henry the Lion and Maud of England. Both Mauds were in England at this time.
Lawrie, *Annals*, 253; Eyton, *Itinerary*, 256–7

1184 September 14; Haddington
No.252

1184 October 18; Crosslee (in Caddonfoot, Selkirkshire)
No.253

1184 October 30; Perth
APS, i, 376; Lawrie, *Annals*, 252

1185 March 18 (less probably, 10); London, Clerkenwell
Henry II's council. Honour of Huntingdon restored. Lawrie, *Annals*, 254–5; Eyton, *Itinerary*, 261

1185 (About March?); Kingscliffe, Northants
No.263

1186 (End of May); Oxford
Henry II's council. Eyton, *Itinerary*, 268

1186 During the earlier summer the king met Henry II at Carlisle to discuss the problem of Galloway.
Lawrie, *Annals*, 262–5; Eyton, *Itinerary*, 269

1186 September 5; Woodstock
Marriage with Ermengarde de Beaumont. Lawrie, *Annals*, 265–7

1186 September 9; Marlborough
Ibid.

1187 March (1–15); Crail
Election of Richard (of Lincoln?) bishop of Moray. Ibid., 268; Dowden, *Bishops*, 146; no.270

1187 July; Inverness
Expedition against Donald MacWilliam. Lawrie, *Annals*, 269–71

1188 (Probably early in the period February 11–July 10); Birgham on Tweed
Conference with Henry II's envoys to discuss the Saladin Tithe. Ibid., 271–3

1189 April 13; Perth
Election of Roger bishop of St Andrews. Ibid., 277

1189 December 2; Canterbury
Richard I's court. Ibid., 281

1189 About the end of 1189 or early in 1190, the king held a council at Musselburgh and enforced a levy of 10,000 merks of gold

and silver to recover his liberty and his castles from Richard I.
Ibid., 281, 284; no.326

1191 During this year, the king, at Haddington, gave his natural daughter Isabel, widow of Robert de Brus, in marriage to Robert de Ros, lord of Wark on Tweed.
Lawrie, *Annals*, 288

1193 During this year, the king, at Roxburgh, gave his natural daughter Margaret, whose mother was the daughter of Adam of Whitsome (Berwickshire), in marriage to Eustace de Vesci, lord of Alnwick.
Ibid., 290

1194 February 2; Edinburgh
No.368

1194 April 2; Clipstone

1194 April 3; Worksop

1194 April 4; Southwell

1194 April 5; Melton Mowbray

1194 April 6; house of Peter the forester of Rutland

1194 April 7; Geddington

1194 April 9; Northampton

1194 April 12; Silverstone, Brackley, Silverstone

1194 April 17; Winchester

1194 April 22; departs Winchester for Scotland
See diary from Roger Howden, Lawrie, *Annals*, 291–3, 296–8

1195 February 27; Dunfermline
Election of Reginald bishop of Ross. Ibid., 299

1195 During this year the king renewed his coinage and lay ill at Clackmannan.
Ibid., 301

1195 (April 17; Clackmannan
No.376)

1195 (May 5; Stirling
No.377)

1195 (May 25; Clackmannan
No.378)

1195 (July 4; Jedburgh
No.379)

1195 July 17; Selkirk
No.380)

1195 (July 29; Selkirk
No.381)

1195 (August 31; Selkirk
No.382)

1195 (September 17; Jedburgh
No.383)

1196 (February 16; Kinghorn
No.385)

1196 (April 16; Berwick
No.386)

1196 (May 2; Elgin
No.388)

1196 (June 16; Forfar
No.390)

1196 (July 31; Elgin
Nos.391, 392)

1196 (September 25; Aberdeen
No.393)

1196 (October 10, 11; Elgin
Nos.394, 395)

1196 During this year, according to Roger Howden, the king made two expeditions to northern Scotland, the second including a stay at Nairn in the autumn; after which he went to Edinburgh.
Lawrie, *Annals*, 304–6

1197 (June 1; Perth
No.389?)

1197 (August 20; Perth
No.396)

1197 (August 28; Perth
APS, i, 377; Lawrie, *Annals*, 311. The date is Saint Augustine's Day; if of Hippo, to be linked with no.396; if of Canterbury, to be linked with no.389?)

1197 During this year, according to the Melrose Chronicle, the king made an expedition to Moray and remoter parts. Whether this account and Howden's (above) refer to the same year, and if so, which year, or refer to royal expeditions in both years, remains unanswered. Among other factors involved in attempting to answer the question, it may be noted that William de Moreville, who witnessed nos.390, 391, 392, died in 1196, while Earl David the king's brother, who witnessed no.388, was in Normandy on 1 September, 1197; Landon, *Itinerary*, 121.

1198 February 15; (St Andrews)
Consecration of Roger bishop of St Andrews. Lawrie, *Annals*, 310

1198 May 29; Forfar
Election of Reinbald abbot of Scone. *Chron. Bower*, i, 513; No.398

1198 (August 5; Haddington
No.400)

1198 (August 19; Haddington
No.401)

1198 August 24; Haddington
Birth of the king's son and heir Alexander. Lawrie, *Annals*, 313

1198 (August 28; Stirling
No.402)

1198 (September 5; Scone
No.403)

1198 October 16; Stirling
No.404

1199 (March 16; Forfar
No.413)

1199 (April 3; Forfar
No.414)

1199 December 26; Forfar
No.421

1199 December 29; Forfar
No.422

1199 During this year, according to Roger Howden, the king spent a night keeping vigil at the shrine of Saint (Queen) Margaret at Dunfermline Abbey; her feast was 8 July.
Lawrie, *Annals*, 320

1200 (February 5; Stirling
No.424)

1200 November 21; Lincoln
Homage to John king of England. Lawrie, *Annals*, 323–5

1200 November 23; Departs Lincoln for Scotland
Ibid.

1200 December 25; Lanark
Ibid., 338 (for 1201 read 1200)

1201 (April 1; Edinburgh
No.426)

1201 (April 5; Stirling
No.427)

1201 (August 20; Kincardine
No.428)

1201 (August 28; Aberdeen
No.429)

1201 October 12; Musselburgh
Lawrie, *Annals*, 330–331

1202 (March 1; Roxburgh
No.430)

1203 (November 4; Forfar
No.434)

1204 (April 24; Haddington
No.439)

1204 May 9; Selkirk
No.440

1204 (July 8; Haddington
Nos.444, 445)
1204 (August 2; Jedburgh
No.446)
1204 (September 22, 25; Selkirk
Nos.447, 448)
1205 (January 2; Forfar
No.453)
1205 (February 1; Forfar
No.454)
1205 (March 26; Alyth
Nos.455, 456)
1205 (April 11, 17; Forfar
Nos.457, 458)
1205 (May 7; Traquair
No.459)
1205 (May 16; Stow
Nos.460, 461)
1205 (May 21; Lanark
No.462)
1205 (July 8; Stirling
No.463)
1205 (July 19; Stirling
No.464)
1205 (August 24; Alyth
No.465)
1205 (September 7; Forfar
No.466)
1205 (October 10, 11; Stirling
Nos.467, 468)
1205 (October 13; Clackmannan
No.469)
1205 During this year, according to the Melrose Chronicle, Earl David did homage to Alexander of Scotland; probably in the period October–December.
Lawrie, *Annals*, 348–9; *Rot. Chart.*, 159
1206 (January 8; Auchtermuchty
Nos. 470, 471)
1206 February 9–12; York
meeting with King John
1206 (March 22; Clunie in Stormont
No.472)
1206 (April 16; Forfar
No.474)
1206 (August 18; Kintore
No.475)

1206 (August 25; Elgin
No.476)

1206 (September 18; Kintore
No.477)

1206 (November 12; Aberdeen
No.478)

1207 May 26–28; York
meeting with King John (Lawrie, *Annals*, 357; *Itinerary of King John*; *Pipe Roll*, 9 *John*, 78)

1207 The king had a safe-conduct to visit King John at York on 11 November, but this meeting does not seem to have taken place; Lawrie, *Annals*, 357.

1208 (March 17; Forfar
No.479)

1208 (July 6; Traquair, Selkirk
Nos.481, 483)

1208 August 13–17, King John travelled from Newcastle upon Tyne to Carlisle via Hexham and Haltwhistle; *Pipe Roll*, 10 *John*, p.xxii.

1208 (November 6; Selkirk
No.483)

1208 (November 8; Edinburgh
No.484)

1209 Before April, the king was detained at Traquair by serious illness.
Lawrie, *Annals*, 362

1209 (April 18; Jedburgh
No.485)

1209 Before April 23; Bolton near Alnwick
Conference with King John. Ibid., 361–2

1209 April 23–26; Norham on Tweed
Conference with King John. Ibid.

1209 May 24; Stirling
Great Council. Ibid., 363

1209 (May 28; Clackmannan
No.486)

1209 Between the end of May and the end of July, the king's itinerary included stays at Forfar, Edinburgh, Traquair, Melrose and Roxburgh.
Lawrie, *Annals*, 363–7

1209 (July 5; Alyth
No.487)

1209 About July 25–August 7 or after; Norham on Tweed
Peace made with King John; daughters given up to king of England to be married, on terms now lost; 15,000 merks promised to be paid to King John. Ibid., 365–71; no.488

1210 (January 7; Stirling
No.489)

1210 (January 14; Crail
No.490)

1210 (May 20; Stirling
No.491)

1210 (May 23; Edinburgh
No.492)

1210 (June 22; Stirling
No.493)

1210 According to *Chron. Bower*, i, 528–9, the king was at Perth about Michaelmas (29 September), with his brother Earl David, and had to escape by boat when the town was flooded by the Tay and Almond. Soon afterwards, the king held a great council at Stirling to raise an aid to pay the money promised to King John.

1210 (December 7; Kincardine
No.494)

1210 According to *Chron. Bower*, i, 529, the king was seriously ill at Kintore after spending Christmas in Moray; his illness lasted until 'the feast of Saint Matthew'. If we emend this to Saint Matthias, the king's sojourn at Kintore would have ended on February 24.

1211 (February 29; Forfar
No.495)

1211 (May 6; Kincardine
No.496)

1211 (June 2; Montrose
No.497)

1211 (June 11; Forfar
No.498)

1211 (June 28; Aberdeen
No.499)

1211 (August 18; Nairn
No.500)

1211 (October 2; Forres
No.501)

1211 (October 9; Fyvie
No.502)

1211 (October 15; Forfar
No.503)

1211 (December 3; 'Forgrund'
No.504)

1211 During this year, the king led an expedition to Moray and Ross against Guthred MacWilliam.
Lawrie, *Annals*, 377–8.

1212 February 2; Durham
meeting with King John. Ibid., 379; *Pipe Roll*, 14 *John*, p.xii

1212 February?; Norham
Lawrie, *Annals*, 379; No.505 (?)

1212 (May 20; Stirling
No.506)

1212 June 25–28; Carlisle, Hexham, Durham
In company with King John. *Pipe Roll*, 14 *John*, p.xiii

1212 (July 6; Stirling
No.507)

1212 (July 9; Clackmannan
No.508)

1213 (January 14; Traquair
No.510)

1213 (January 19; Traquair
No.511)

1213 (February 23, 25, 28; Selkirk
Nos.512–514)

1213 (March 13; Haddington
No.515)

1213 (April 21–22; Edinburgh
Nos.516, 517)

1213 (August 10; Edinburgh
No.518)

1213 December 7; Edinburgh
No.519

1214 (April 29; Selkirk
No.520)

1214 (May 16; Jedburgh
No.521)

1214 August 1 and after; Moray
Peace made with John earl of Caithness and Orkney. Lawrie, *Annals*, 397

1214 (August 17; Elgin
No.522)

1214 (September 8; Stirling
No.523)

1214 (November 25; Stirling
No.524)

1214 December 4; Stirling
Death of King William

1214 December 10; Arbroath Abbey
Funeral of King William, and burial before the high altar of the abbey church. Lawrie, *Annals*, 398–400

LIST OF SOURCES

(*a*) ORIGINALS *including purported originals*

ABERDEEN
Royal Burgh of Aberdeen, Muniments **153, 429**

AUCHMAR, DRYMEN
Duke of Montrose's Muniments **125, 136, 486**

AYR
Royal Burgh of Ayr, Muniments **462**

BLAIR CASTLE, BLAIR ATHOLL
Duke of Atholl's Muniments **206, 524**

DALKEITH HOUSE, DALKEITH
Duke of Buccleuch and Queensberry's Muniments (Buccleuch) **145**

DARNAWAY CASTLE, MORAYSHIRE
Earl of Moray's Muniments **10, 154, 279, 414**

DRUMLANRIG CASTLE
Duke of Buccleuch and Queensberry's Muniments (Douglas) **62**

DUMFRIES HOUSE, AYRSHIRE
Marquis of Bute's Muniments (Loudoun Charters) **309**

DUNROBIN CASTLE, SUTHERLAND
Countess of Sutherland's Muniments **520**

DURHAM
Dean and Chapter Muniments (Miscellaneous Charters) **44, 46, 47, 66, 67, 73, 101A, 105, 113, 178, 181, 294, 313, 368, 369, 380, 444–446, 460, 461, 514, 521**

EDINBURGH
City and Royal Burgh of Edinburgh (Royal Charters) **39**
Messrs Dundas and Wilson, WS (Muniments of the Earl of Strathmore and Kinghorne) **343**
Edinburgh University Library (Laing Charters) **471**
National Library of Scotland **133, 167, 171, 201, 358, 489**
Scottish Record Office
Drummond Castle (Earl of Ancaster's Muniments, Lundin Charters) **42, 463**
GD 1 **75, 479**
GD 4 **350, 428**
GD 26 **45, 59, 266–269, 320, 451**
GD 28 **48, 85, 410, 459**
GD 40 **252, 340**
GD 45 **40, 199, 292, 302, 303, 314, 401, 405, 434, 435, 485, 517**

GD 48 **135**
GD 55 **79, 81–83, 86, 195, 214, 236, 264, 301, 342, 364, 365, 386, 483**
GD 90 **28, 40, 235, 292, 338, 367, 470, 496, 516**
GD 124 **323**
GD 147 **137**
GD 198 **375**
GD 203 **286, 402**
GD 248 **474**
RH 6 **25–27, 165, 293, 508**

GLASGOW
City of Glasgow Archives Office
(Stirling-Maxwell of Pollok Muniments) **422**

INVERNESS
Royal Burgh of Inverness, Muniments **176**
Mr William Mackay, junior, 19 Union Street **14**

KIMMERGHAME, BERWICKSHIRE
Brig. Alan Swinton of Kimmerghame **484**

LINCOLN
Dean and Chapter Muniments **41**

LONDON
British Museum
Campbell Charters **146, 469**
Cotton Charters **175, 253, 263, 265, 398, 493**
BM Loans 29 **114, 152**
Lincoln's Inn Library (MS. Hale XII) **119**
Public Record Office **80, 144, 505**

NORTHUMBERLAND COUNTY RECORD OFFICE
County Archivist, Melton Park, Gosforth, Northumberland **143, 424**

OLD SLAINS, ABERDEENSHIRE
Countess of Erroll's Muniments (Erroll Charters) **204, 211, 322, 341, 383**

PERTH
City and Royal Burgh of Perth, Charters **467**
Messrs Condie, Mackenzie, and Co., WS (Kinnoull Trustees' Muniments) **377, 403, 427, 432, 439, 464, 504**

WHITFIELD HALL, NORTHUMBERLAND
Mr J. C. Blackett-Ord's Muniments **79**

YESTER HOUSE, EAST LOTHIAN
Marquis of Tweeddale's Muniments **418**

(*b*) FACSIMILES AND OTHER FULL TEXTS PRINTED FROM ORIGINALS NOT NOW KNOWN TO BE EXTANT

ANDERSON, *Diplomata*, Plate xxvi. (Purported original *penes* Robert Harley earl of Oxford, 1711–24) **287**

APS, i, facsimile to face p.88. (Original among Inverness Burgh Muniments, 1844) **213**

Family of Seton, i, 68 (= *Fraser Facsimiles*, no.10). (Original *penes* the earl of Winton, 1896) **200**

Holyrood Liber, nos.31, 48, 51, 56. (Originals *penes* Lord Panmure, 1840–50) **141, 238, 297, 492**

Newbattle Registrum, Appendix, *Carte Originales*, nos.III, IV. (Originals *penes* W.E.Aytoun, 1849) **174, 510**

SCOTTISH RECORD OFFICE, J.Maitland Thomson's Photographs of Charters. (Original *penes* J.F.Mackay, WS, 1911) **43**

(*c*) MANUSCRIPT COPIES

BRECHIN CASTLE, ANGUS

Earl of Dalhousie. Transcript of the Registrum Vetus of Glasgow. [Cf. Davis, no.1150] **210, 216, 261**

CAPRINGTON CASTLE, AYRSHIRE

Capt. R. Fergusson-Cuninghame of Caprington. Cartulary of Lindores Abbey. [Davis, no.1164] **205, 363**

CARLISLE

Dean and Chapter Muniments. Cartulary of Holm Cultram. [Davis, no.492] **87, 256**

CASTLE HOWARD, YORKSHIRE

Mr George Howard. Cartulary of Newminster Abbey. [Davis, no.691] **4**

DURHAM

Dean and Chapter Muniments. Cartulary IV. [Davis, no.331] **313**

EDINBURGH

Blairs Archives (formerly at St Mary's College, Blairs, Kincardineshire), 16 Drummond Place. MS. Registrum Vetus of Glasgow. [Davis, no.1150] **106, 179, 189, 190, 192, 210, 215–217, 249, 260, 261, 283, 308, 315, 316, 325, 374, 430, 442, 507**

Edinburgh University Library. Laing MSS., La II–512 (loose paper sheet, xvii cent.) **131**

National Library of Scotland

Advocates MSS.:

16. 1. 10. (Cartulary of Aberdeen bishopric). [Davis, no.1111] **193, 251, 295, 348, 399**

29. 4. 2. (MS. Collections of General Hutton. xviii–xix cent.) **197, 390, 463**

31. 2. 4. (Transcript by Alexander Brown. xviii cent.) **133**

33. 2. 9. (Abridgement by Sir James Balfour of Denmilne of Coupar Angus Abbey cartulary. xvii cent.). [cf. Davis, no.1132] **10–12, 69, 148, 154, 155, 222, 274, 275, 298, 322, 384, 397, 414, 420, 509**

34. 1. 2. (Cambuskenneth Abbey cartulary). [Davis, no.1126] **36, 60, 99, 126, 160–162, 208, 278, 324, 371–373, 431, 433**

34. 1. 3a. (Dunfermline Abbey cartulary). [Davis, no.1139] **22, 30, 31, 34, 35, 38, 107, 108, 130, 156, 163, 164, 166, 242, 304, 305, 321, 337, 396, 409, 463, 495, 500, 502**

34. 2. 1B. (Transcripts by the earl of Haddington of rolls of great seal charters, etc. xvii cent. Cf. *RMS*, i, p.xii; Robertson, *Index*, pp.xlviff.) **311**

34. 3. 25. (Collections of Walter Macfarlane of Macfarlane. xviii cent.) **463**

34. 3. 28. (Scone Abbey cartulary. xvi cent.). [Davis, no.1180] **15–18, 20, 111, 118, 124, 138, 259, 270, 276, 326, 331, 336, 353, 398, 415, 523**

34. 4. 1. (Cartulary of Soutra hospital). [Davis, no.1182] **400**

34.4.2. (Arbroath Abbey cartulary, 'Registrum Vetus'). [Davis, no.1118] **117, 186, 198, 203, 209, 223–234, 277, 280, 282, 284, 285, 300, 318, 327, 328, 332, 339, 354–357, 408, 413, 416, 417, 419, 436–438, 452–458, 466, 477, 487, 494, 498, 499, 503, 506, 511–513, 515, 522**

34. 4. 3. (Arbroath Abbey cartulary, 'Registrum Nigrum'). [Davis, no.1120] **351**

34. 4. 4. (Cartulary of Aberdeen bishopric and cathedral). [Davis, no.1114] **193, 251**

34. 4. 7. (Dryburgh Abbey cartulary). [Davis, no.1138] **65, 89, 121, 122, 187, 262, 290, 291**

34. 4. 10. (Composite register or cartulary of cathedral church and bishopric of Moray, mainly xiii cent.). [Davis, no.1171] **132, 139, 142, 212, 272, 273, 281, 312, 259–362, 393–395, 421, 465, 476, 478**

34. 4. 11. (Fragment of Melrose Abbey cartulary). [Davis, no.1167] **104, 236, 287, 382, 440, 441, 449**

34. 4. 13. (Newbattle Abbey cartulary). [Davis, no.1173] **61, 70, 90, 91, 191, 241, 243, 256, 296**

34. 4. 14. (Paisley Abbey cartulary). [Davis, no.1174] **184, 218–221, 310, 378, 518**

34. 5. 1. (Kelso Abbey cartulary). [Davis, no.1162] **63, 64, 68, 74, 95, 96, 101, 120, 180, 183, 188, 239, 239A, 245, 246, 248, 254, 289, 299, 306, 317, 319, 349, 367, 379, 381, 387, 440, 448, 480, 481, 493**

34. 5. 3. (Balmerino Abbey cartulary. xiv cent.). [Davis, no.1124] **147**

34. 6. 24. (Transcripts and notes of charters, etc., by Father Richard Hay. xvii cent.) **102, 250, 497**

34. 7. 1. (Lindores Abbey cartulary. xvi cent.). [Davis, no.1165] **366**

35. 3. 13. (Transcripts of Walter Macfarlane of Macfarlane. xviii cent.) **159**

MS. Charters 74, vol. 1. (Collections of Sir Archibald Lawrie. xix–xx cent.) **196**

Minto Papers (Charters, Box 30/212). (Copy, xvi cent., of notarial transumpt of 1395) **330, 347, 411, 412**

Scottish Record Office
Acta Dominorum Concilii
Vol. XXI **473**
Vol. XXXI **335**
Drummond Castle (Earl of Ancaster's Muniments, Stobhall titles, uncatalogued) **334**
GD 45/13 **115**
GD 45/27/8 (St Andrews Priory cartulary. xiii cent.). [Davis, no. 1175] **13, 23, 24, 28, 29, 32, 33, 37, 71, 76, 77, 110, 112, 127–129, 134, 149–151, 168–170, 173, 247, 271, 329, 333, 352, 490, 491**
GD 49/1 **404**
GD 103 (Society of Antiquaries of Scotland Papers). Transcript (xix cent.) of MS. entitled 'Cartae Variae' (xviii cent.) **116**
GD 137/2/6 **140**
Earl of Northesk's Muniments, uncatalogued. 'Ethie MS.' (Cartulary of Arbroath Abbey, fragmentary. xiii cent.). [Davis, no.1117] **203, 223, 224, 226, 228, 231–234, 280, 282, 284, 285, 318, 327, 328, 332, 355–357, 408, 417, 436–438, 458, 494, 499, 511, 513**
Registrum Magni Sigilli Regum Scotorum
Liber I **182**
Liber V **235**
Liber XXVII **202, 370, 385**
RH 1/2/1 **5**
RH 9/11/16 **102, 250**
Transcripts of Royal Charters **194, 390, 407**
Messrs Strathern and Blair, WS (Earl of Home's Muniments. Douglas Charters, no.280) **140**

GLASGOW
Glasgow University Library. MS. BE 8, d 6 (Transcripts of cartularies and original charters of Glasgow cathedral and bishopric. xviii cent.) **426**

KIRKINTILLOCH
Kirkintilloch Burgh Muniments **501**

LINCOLN
Dean and Chapter Muniments. MS. 'Registrum'. [Davis, no.584] **41**

LONDON
British Museum
Additional MSS.
18, 111 **467**
24, 276 **497**
33,245 (Cartulary of Arbroath Abbey). [Davis, no.1119] **344–346, 413, 423**
Cotton MSS.
Cleopatra C iv **157**
Faustina A iv. (Cartulary of St. Neot's Priory). [Davis, no.859] **53, 54**

Faustina B ii. (Cartulary of Clerkenwell Priory). [Davis, no.263] **57, 146**

Faustina C i. (Cartulary of Huntingdon Priory). [Davis, no.499] **51**

Vespasian E xvii. (Cartulary of St Andrew's Priory, Northampton). [Davis, no.700] **49, 50, 55**

Vespasian E xix. (Cartulary of Nostell Priory). [Davis, no.721] **1**

Egerton MS. 3031. (Cartulary of Reading Abbey). [Davis, no.801] **6–8, 92, 93, 109**

Harleian MSS.

3688. (Cartulary of Missenden Abbey). [Davis, no.670) **19**

3891. (Cartulary of Holm Cultram Abbey). [Davis, no.494] **88, 256**

3911. (Cartulary of Holm Cultram Abbey). [Davis, no.493] **87**

3960. (Cartulary of Melrose Abbey). [Davis, no.1168] **21, 72, 97, 98, 104, 177, 240, 288, 307, 382, 406, 425, 441, 447, 449, 482**

4693. (Notebook of Sir James Balfour of Denmilne. xvii cent.) **472, 496**

Lansdowne MS. 391 (Abstract cartulary of Harrold Priory). [Davis, no.471] **56**

Royal MS. 11 B ix. (Cartulary of St Andrew's Priory, Northampton). [Davis, no.699] **49, 50**

Stowe MS. 926. (Cartulary of Brinkburn Priory). [Davis, no.76] **2**

Public Record Office

C 47/22/4 **103, 255**

C 53/93 **8, 93, 94, 103, 158, 207, 255, 376, 443**

C 66/76 **519**

E 13/56 **55**

E 36/274 **488**

E 164/2 **157**

J.I. 1/143 **84, 468**

Westminster Abbey

Dean and Chapter Muniments. MS. 'Domesday'. [Davis, no.1013] **52**

MELLERSTAIN HOUSE, BERWICKSHIRE

Earl of Haddington. MS. Notebook of Sir John Skene, Lord Clerk Register (xvii cent.) **472**

OXFORD

Bodleian Library

MS. Dodsworth 7 **450**

MS. Dodsworth 74 **3**

MS. Rawlinson B 142 (Transcript by Sir Richard St George of a cartulary of Sawtry Abbey. xvi–xvii cent.) **58, 263**

PERTH

Messrs Condie, Mackenzie and Co., WS (Kinnoull Trustees' Muniments). Cartulary of Inchaffray Abbey. [Davis, no.1156] **258, 427, 432, 464**

RUTHERGLEN
Royal Burgh of Rutherglen, Muniments **244**

(*d*) PRINTED TEXTS

APS, i, 89 **388, 475**

Arbroath Liber, ii, Appendix, no.1 **197**

Boarstall Cartulary, ed. H. E. Salter (Oxford Historical Society, 1930), no.302. [Cf. Davis, no.1310] **19**

Dugdale, *Mon. Angl.*, ii, 202–3 (also New edn, vi, Pt.1, 330–1) **56**

J. Gordon, *Description of both towns of Aberdeen* (Spalding Club, 1842) **237**

A. W. Haddan and W. Stubbs, *Councils and Ecclesiastical Documents relating to Great Britain and Ireland*, ii, Pt. 1 **157**

D. Haignère, ed., *Les Chartes de Saint-Bertin*, i (1886) **391**

Kinloss Recs., no.3 **392**

May Recs. (for titles only) **8, 93, 94, 158, 207, 376, 443**

W. Ross, *Lectures on the practice of the law of Scotland* (Edinburgh, 1792), ii, 126 **185**

Spalding Miscellany, v, 242 **9**

(W. B. D. D. Turnbull), *Fragmenta Scoto-Monastica* (1842) **407**

METHODS OF DATING

The methods of dating used for this collection are essentially the same as those explained in *R R S*, i. William I succeeded his brother as king at the end of the year 1165, being inaugurated on 24 December. He died on 4 December, 1214. Within these outer limits, the documents whose dates are not explained by special chronological notes have been assigned approximate dates within periods as short as possible, according to ordinary chronological criteria such as the known dates of appointment, promotion, consecration, resignation, death, etc., of witnesses, recipients or other individuals referred to in the documents. It would require too much space to give a full list here of the most commonly used of these basic criteria; reference should be made to Lawrie, *Annals*, Anderson, *Early Sources*, Anderson, *Scottish Annals*, Dowden, *Bishops*, *The Bibliotheck*, vol.ii, no.1, Dunbar, *Scot. Kings* and the *Handbook of British Chronology* (2nd edn). The following is a short list of datable events which have a special and recurring importance for determining the dates of William I's acts:

1171, Nicholas the chancellor dies.

1172, Matthew archdeacon of St Andrews consecrated bishop of Aberdeen.

1175, Jocelin consecrated bishop of Glasgow.

1177, Walter son of Alan, the Steward, dies.

1178, Walter de Bidun, chancellor, bishop-elect of Dunkeld, Richard bishop of St Andrews, and Geoffrey abbot of Dunfermline, die.

1183, John (the Scot) given the see of Dunkeld.

1184, Andrew bishop of Caithness dies.

1187, Richard consecrated bishop of Moray.

1188, Hugh bishop of St Andrews dies.

1189, Hugh of Roxburgh appointed chancellor.

1189 or 1190, Richard de Moreville, the Constable, dies.

1196, William de Moreville, the Constable, dies.

1198, Roger consecrated bishop of St Andrews. Archibald abbot of Dunfermline dies. Alexander son of William I born.

1199, Jocelin bishop of Glasgow, Hugh of Roxburgh, chancellor, bishop-elect of Glasgow, and Matthew bishop of Aberdeen die. William Malvoisin appointed chancellor and elected bishop of Glasgow.

1200, Roland son of Uhtred dies. William Malvoisin consecrated bishop of Glasgow.

1202, Roger bishop of St Andrews dies. William Malvoisin translated to St Andrews; Florence of Holland elected bishop of Glasgow.

1203, John (the Scot) bishop of Dunkeld and Richard bishop of Moray die.

1204, Alan son of Walter, the Steward, and Duncan earl of Fife die.

1207, Florence of Holland resigns see of Glasgow; Walter (of St Albans) elected in his place.

1208, Walter consecrated bishop of Glasgow.

1210, Richard (de Prebenda) bishop of Dunkeld dies.

1211 (28 June), William del Bois appointed chancellor.

1212, Alexander the king's son knighted.

1214, John (of Leicester) bishop of Dunkeld dies; Hugh (de Sigillo) elected in his place.

In attempting to group the acts chronologically within periods, weight has been given to the place-date in conjunction with the subject-matter and the witnesses. Thus, nos.81–3, written in the same hand and having almost identical witnesses, were all given at Lanark, and it has been assumed first, that they were issued on the same occasion, secondly, that because it seems likely that one witness, Imer the clerk, was the 'Master Imer' slain on 23 September, 1168 (*Chron. Holyrood*, 150–151), the occasion of the issue of these three acts fell between 24 December, 1165, and 23 September, 1168. Even greater weight has been given to the place-date as a factor in determining the date of issue in the period after April, 1195, when the acts begin regularly to bear the time-date by the day of the month. In the last two decades of the reign it begins to be possible to form an approximate idea of the king's itinerary. By taking into consideration all the possible factors, the place-date, the day-of-the-month date on the act, the witnesses and the subject-matter and general context, as well as what may be known of the king's movements from any other source, Mr Scott has been able to construct a convincing hypothesis of the sequence of surviving royal acts. While neither he nor his fellow-editor would claim complete accuracy in this matter, for there is obviously still room for doubt in a number of cases, it is hoped that this collection will present King William's acts, especially those of the later years of the reign, in an order which is chronologically more accurate than anything previously attempted.

METHODS OF EDITING

In general, the methods of editing remain the same for this volume as for *RRS*, i, but a few modifications have been introduced. The acts are given in approximately chronological order, with the proviso that the vast majority of acts have been assigned not to precise dates but to periods within the reign, and it does not follow that within any given period the acts will be arranged in true chronological order. A few acts have unfortunately been wrongly placed, the error being discovered too late for them to be put in a better chronological context. These misplacements have been noted. All acts treated separately have been numbered serially in Arabic numerals, nos.1 to 5 being acts given by William of Scotland before his accession as king, nos.6 to 524 (including nos.101A and 239A) being acts of William as king. Nos.525 to 589 are 'lost acts', and no.590, constituting an appendix, is an important unpublished agreement which throws light on royal government in Angus in the period 1189–95.

Each act is preceded by a summary of the main contents. For most of the long charters of confirmation, the summaries are no more than headings, but in one or two cases, where the charter has no earlier counterpart in *RRS*, i, the summary has been made much fuller. After the *apparatus criticus* for each act there has been added, in many cases, a new section under the heading *Comment*, in which information is provided or problems discussed which would otherwise have had to be dealt with in scattered footnotes. As many cross-references have been provided as seemed helpful or necessary.

The texts of the majority of cartulary and other copies have been presented with editorial punctuation, modernized use of capitals, and extension of abbreviated forms. But the MS. usage of a handful of early cartularies of good quality has been adhered to, and, as with the acts of Malcolm IV, an effort has been made to reproduce faithfully the spelling and punctuation of originals. The much more elaborate analysis of the handwriting of originals has removed the need for any description in the notes below the text; under the heading *Hand* there is merely a note of the Scribe, and the student should refer to the section of the Introduction which deals with Handwriting. Ultimately, he will be able to use this section in conjunction with the proposed volume of facsimiles.

A large number of printed versions have been noted, but it must be stressed that the listing of printed editions is not exhaustive; most of the versions cited are either of reasonably reliable quality or easily accessible or both. Where no printed version is noted, it may be assumed that none is known to the editor.

5. ADDITIONS AND CORRECTIONS

to *Regesta Regum Scottorum*, volume I

(i) INTRODUCTION

p.3, l.35 *For* August *read* September.
p.5, l.34 *For* July *read* June.
p.50, l.5 *For* 1165 × 1171 *read* 1175 × 1178.
p.55, l.35 *For* 298 *read* 300.
p.94, n.1 *Add:* Mrs M. O. Anderson proposes *sail orc*, 'heel of the Orcs (or of the pigs)' (*per litt.*, 24/12/1960).
p.111, ll.16–24 *Delete passage:* It may, however . . . conjecture. *Substitute:* At this point we may note the agreement of 23 March, 1131 (or 1132?), between the prior of Durham and Dolfin, Uhtred's son, regarding Staindropshire (Co. Durham).[1] In becoming the prior's liege man, Dolfin saved his allegiance to the king of England *and to the king of Scotland.* Dolfin, ancestor of the Nevilles of Raby,[2] was the son of Uhtred son of Meldred; the family had probably long been settled in Saint Cuthbert's Land. Dolfin's connexions with King David are unknown.
Add to footnote 1: Cf. H. S. Offler, *Durham Episcopal Charters* (Surtees Society, vol.179, 1968), 76–7, 109.
p.113, at foot *Add*: 1130, May Canterbury (dedication of cathedral) *The Historical works of Gervase of Canterbury* (ed. W. Stubbs, Rolls Ser., 1879–80), i, 96.
p.116 EDINBURGH, National Library of Scotland. *Add* MS. Acc. 4059 (original charter acquired 1966, formerly at Saltoun Hall) **195**.
p.117, ll.6–8 *Delete* Fraser, *Facsimiles* . . . **195**.

(ii) TEXTS AND LOST ACTS

p.138, n.1, l.3 from foot The more likely date of the Kirton-in-Lindsey charter is 1146 (*RRAN*, iii, no.494).
p.142, n.6 *Add*: For Eudo of Wadworth, deceased by 1165, see *Pipe Roll*, 11 *Henry II*, 49.
p.166 *Add the following lost act*: 64A. KING DAVID I grants to the monks of Melrose Abbey and all monks of the Cistercian Order freedom from toll and other customs on transactions carried out for their own use, anywhere in the king's land.*
Melrose Liber, no.17 (= no.177 below).
p.167, no.70 *Delete*: 10d. *Substitute*: the tenth penny of their revenues.
p.172 *Add the following lost act*: 104A. KING DAVID I grants to the

brethren of St Lazarus of Jerusalem the church (of St Giles) of Edinburgh, together with the lands of Spitalton and St Giles' Grange.

BM, MS Cott. Nero C xii, fo.99[r]; *Chron. Bower*, ii, 161. This appears to be the earliest reference to the church of St Giles, Edinburgh.

p.178, n.2 *Add after* Pathhead: via Ford. Cousland appears as Coukesland before 1236 (*Dunfermline Reg.*, no.142), possibly referring to Gocelin the cook; but cf. no.125 below.

p.190, no.127, notes *Delete*: Unruled: Hand, 'Chancery'. *Substitute*: *Hand*: 'Chancery', evidently identical with those of nos.149, 155. Unruled.

p.193, l.1 *For* TVEDE *read* TVEDĘ.

p.199, no.139, note on printed versions *Add after* pp.19–20: *The cartulary of Missenden Abbey*, ed. J.G. Jenkins, Part III (Hist. MSS. Comm., JP I, 1962), 181, no.808 (from BM, MS. Harl. 3688, fo.160[v]; without notice of *RRS*, i).

p.200, no.141, Summary, l.3 *Add after Kershope*: (in Bewcastle, Cumberland).

p.204, no.149, notes on *Hand* *Delete*: closely similar . . . no.155. *Substitute*: evidently identical with those of nos.149, 155.

p.208, no.155, notes on *Hand* *Delete*: possibly . . . no.149. *Substitute*: evidently identical with those of nos.127, 149.

p.213, no.164, Summary *For* Kirknewton *read* Newton[1]. *Add footnote*: 1. For the identification of Neutun see I.B. Cowan, *The Parishes of Medieval Scotland* (Scottish Record Society, vol.93, 1967), 156–7.

pp.231–2, no.195 *The following readings taken from the original, recently rediscovered, are to be substituted for the printed text (line numbers refer to text)*:

l.2 posteaquam arma suscepi.

l.8 PethefriN.

l.12 de [. . . . . . .][a] decimam molendini. *Emend note [a] to read*: Tear in parchment, 0·6″ across, space for seven or eight letters. Supply, probably, Anegus . &.

l.14 Kyneber . & To [tam deci][b] mam. *Emend note [b] to read*: Parchment torn.

l.21 unum Toft in Pert.

Ibid. StriueliN.

l.22 in Edenesb'.

Ibid. unum Toft in Forfar.

l.23 pertinentibus ad R [. . . . . .][d]. *Emend note [d] to read*: Parchment torn; supply (R)ostinoth.

l.26 [. . .] is[f] 7 concessi. *Emend note [f] to read*: Parchment torn; perhaps supply Dedi ill (is).

l.33 [. . . . .] s[g]. *Emend note [g] to read*: Parchment torn; supply Munro(s).

l.42 Glasg*uensi*.

l.48 Ric*ardo* Cumin. Phil*ippo* de Coleu*illa*.

For the notes on Endorsement and Description substitute:
ENDORSED: The charter is firmly pasted on to Bristol Board, making it impossible to see the dorse.
DESCRIPTION: 1′ (30·5 cm.), Top and bottom × 7·6″ (19·3 cm.), L, 7·9″ (20 cm.), R. Foot folded to a depth of 0·9″ at left, 0·7″ at right. Slit for tag, part of which, 1·8″ (4·5 cm.) long, remains in place, shewing traces of seal in red wax.
Add to note on Hand: Ruled in pencil or drypoint.
Emend note on Source to read: Original, NLS, MS. Acc. 4059 (formerly at Saltoun Hall, East Lothian, deposited in the National Library in 1966).
Add to note on printed editions: Fraser, *Facsimiles*, no.5.

p.259, note on printed edition of no.237 *For* 4 *read* 7–8.

p.260, no.239, l.10 of text *After* terra *delete* de.

p.271, no.256, l.19 of text *Add footnote number* 1 *after* Eggremunt *and add footnote*: 1 William 'de Agremont' witnessed an act issued probably at Woodstock in July, 1163, when King Malcolm was present (W. Farrer, *Lancashire Pipe Rolls and early charters*, 311).

p.274, no.260, l.16 *For* [Restenot] *read* [Oxenef'], *and add footnote number* 1.
Emend note [d] *to read*: MS. reads Oxenes', for which read Oxenef'.
Add footnote: 1. This witness was evidently Robert of Cricklade, prior of St Frideswide's, who witnessed nos.223 and 228.

p.275, no.263, note on printed versions *Add*: *The cartulary of Missenden Abbey*, ed. J. G. Jenkins, Part III (Hist. MSS. Comm., JP I, 1962), 81–2, no.665 (from *H*, without notice of *RRS*, i).

p.276, no.264, note on printed versions *Add*: *The cartulary of Missenden Abbey*, ed. J. G. Jenkins, Part III (Hist. MSS. Comm., JP I, 1962), 81, no.664 (from *H*, without notice of *RRS*, i).

p.278, no.266 *Add to reference*: For the Massett burn in 1676, cf. *Retours*, Elgin, no.187.

p.279 *Add the following lost act*: 275A. Grants to the brethren of the hospital of St John at Northampton thirty cartloads of wood yearly from the wood of Yardley Hastings.*
Castle Ashby, Marquess of Northampton's Muniments, F.D.247 (survey of Yardley Hastings manor, 2 September, 1565).

p.280 *Add the following lost act*: 278A. Confirms to Jedburgh Abbey William de Vieuxpont's grant of one ploughgate in his demesne of Carriden, West Lothian.*
SRO, RH 1/2/1 (*RRS*, ii, no.5).

p.281 *Add the following lost act*: 283A. Makes an agreement with Herbert bishop of Glasgow anent the churches of the burgh of Roxburgh and their parishes. (1153 × 1162)*
Kelso Liber, no.415. (The date may be that of no.114 above, or thereabouts.)

p.282, l.23 *For* ? ed. J. Gracie, 1828 *read* ed. J. Maidment, 1828–9.

p.283, no.295, reference *For* no.156 *read* nos.23, 216.

p.285, n.1, l.2 *For* Ginel *read* Gamel.

(iii) INDEXES

p.293 *Between* Agden *and* Aigneus *insert*: Agremont, William de. *See* Egremont.

p.300 At Cousland *add after* Midlothian: Coukesland. *Add page number*: 178n.

Ibid. *Between* Cro *and* Crefbarri *insert*: Cricklade, Robert of. *See* Robert prior of Oxford.

p.301 *At* Dolfin, son of Uhtred *add*: (son of Meldred).

p.303 *At* Egremont, William of, *add after* 79 *page number*: 271n.

Ibid. *At* Elstow, *for* 241 *read* 242.

p.304 *For* Florence I *read* Florence III.

p.309 *At* Huntingdon, priory of, *add page number*: 153.

p.311 *At* Keith, E. Lothian, *alias* Humbie, *add* church of, 194, 226–7. *At* Keith Marischal *delete page numbers* 194, 226–7.

Ibid. *At* Kershope *delete*: [in Castleton], Roxburghshire. *Substitute*: [in Bewcastle], Cumberland.

p.312 *Delete entry* Kirknewton.

p.317 *Add entry* Newton, Midlothian, Neutun, church of, 213.

p.318 *At* Northampton *add*: hospital of St John at, 279.

Ibid. *Delete entry* Orenestet. *See* Restenneth.

p.319 *At* Paxton, Little, *add page number*: 242.

p.320 *At* Proportuna (corrupt) *add*: 139. *See* Potton.

p.322 *Between* Robert *and* prior of Oxford *add* (of Cricklade). *Add page number*: 274 *after* 252.

p.326 *At* Thomas, brother of Henry, *for* Whitson *read* Whiston.

p.332 *At* clauini *delete* (?sacks). *After* 264 *add*: (For cleuin' as a measure of grain, fifty of which equalled 15 chalders 10 bolls, see *Exchequer Rolls*, i, 21).

p.335 *At* measures (3) *delete* (?sacks).

p.337 *At* rent, money rents (4) *delete*: 10d. *Substitute*: tenth penny.

p.338 *At* theft *for* fortum *read* furtum.

Ibid. *At* toll *for* 236–7 *read* 236 *and add*: 247.

ACTS OF WILLIAM I

Full Texts, numbers 1–524

Calendar of Lost Acts, numbers 525–589

Appendix 590

FULL TEXTS

1 William de Warenne son of Henry earl of the Northumbrians informs Henry (Murdac) archbishop of York, and the whole chapter of York, and all sons of God's Holy Church that for his own soul and for the souls of his father and mother and William the elder earl Warenne and the Countess Isabel he has confirmed the grant made by Elias de Bosville to Nostell Priory, viz. the mill of Harlington, one bovate of land with a toft in Barnborough which belonged to William the miller, six acres of land and one toft in the same vill which belonged to Huscarl, and also William the miller with his wife and children. (1148 × June, 1152)

Uenerabili[a] Dei gr*ati*a H*enrico* Eboracensi archiepiscopo totique capitulo Eboracensi omnibusque sancte Dei ecclesie filiis uniuersisque heredibus et successoribus suis, Willelmus de Warennia fil*ius* Henr*ici* Comitis Northanhimbrorum salutem. Notum sit caritati uestre me pro salute anime mee et pro salute animarum patris mei Henr*ici* comitis et matris mee Ade comitisse et pro anima Willelmi comitis senis de Warennia et comitisse Isabel et omnium parentum meorum concessisse et per presentem cartam confirmasse donationem quam dedit Helias de Bosauilla canonicis ecclesie Sancti Oswaldi de Nostlat et concessit, uidelicet molendinum de Herlatona et unam bouatam terre cum tofta in Barneburg' que fuit Willelmi molendinarii, et sex acres terre et unam toftam que fuit Huscarl in eadem uilla, Willelmum etiam molendinarium cum uxore sua et liberis suis in perpetuam elemosinam, liberam et quietam ab omni seruitio et consuetudine sicut unquam melius et quietius aliqua elemosina sancte ecclesie data est. T*estibus*.

RUBRIC. Hic incipiunt carte[b] de Barneburg'. Carta Willelmi de Warenna (top in red, hand of text). Herlington et Bernburgh[c] (black, top right, xiii–xiv cent.). Herlingto et Barneburgh' (black, right margin, xiv cent.).
SOURCE. BM, MS. Cott. Vesp. E xix, fo.57^r.
PRINTED. J. Hunter, *South Yorkshire*, i, 376; C.T. Clay, *EYC*, viii, 150–1 (no.101).
NOTES. [a] Initial blue flourished red. [b] cartae. with a expunged. [c] thorp after Bern expunged.
COMMENT. In view of the granter's style and the use of the phrases *pro salute anime* (*animarum*) and *pro anima* it is probable that this charter was issued before Earl Henry's death in June, 1152. If so, this is the earliest surviving written act of William, afterwards King William I. The interest in Harlington and Barnborough (Yorkshire, W.R.) was evidently a Warenne interest.

2 William de Warenne earl of Northumberland confirms to Brinkburn Priory the grant made by his father Earl Henry of one saltpan at Warkworth, and also the grant made by Roger Bertram of the place called Brinkburn with its appurtenances. (1152 × 1157)

Willelmus[a] de Gwarenne Comes Northumbr' Justicie sue, et baronibus, vicecomitibus et ministris et omnibus probis hominibus tam laicis quam clericis tocius Northumberland salutem. Sciatis me dedisse et concessisse Deo et Sancte Marie et ecclesie Sancti Petri de B[rinkburne][b] et canonicis ibidem Deo seruientibus et seruituris, pro anima Henrici comitis dilectissimi patris mei necnon eciam et pro anima mea et animabus antecessorum meorum eandem salinam quam pater meus Henricus comes apud Werkewurth' in tempore uite sue eis in elemosinam dedit et concessit.[c] Concedo eciam et confirmo predictis fratribus totam donacionem Rogeri Bertram, scilicet locum qui dicitur Brinkburne cum omnibus pertinenciis suis.[c] Volo eciam quatinus predicti canonici de Brinkburne predictam salinam et omnia sua habeant et teneant ita libere et quiete sicut[d] ipsi aliquam elemosinam liberius et quiecius in terra mea habent, et nullus uestrum super plenarium forisfactum meum eis iniuriam uel contumeliam inde conferat,[e] nec fieri permittat. Valete[f]. Hiis testibus, Gilberto de Umfrauilla, Willelmo de Vescy, Rogero de Merlay et aliis.

RUBRIC. donacio et confirmacio saline in Werkewurgh et de loco nostro cum pertinenciis . xvii[g].

SOURCE. BM, MS. Stowe 926, fo.72v (old ink foliation, 65v).

PRINTED. Dugdale, *Mon. Angl.*, ii (1661), 203–4 (reprinted, new edn, vi, I, 332, no.II); *Brinkburn Chartulary*, 142, no.176; Lawrie, *Charters*, no.271.

NOTES. [a] Written Villmus, with blue initial flourished red; Page and Lawrie print Malcolm. [b] B., MS. [c] Paragraph sign, MS. [d] ipsam deleted before ipsi, MS. [e] Punctus elevatus, MS. [f] Valete omitted by Page and Lawrie; Dugdale has volente. [g] In red, text hand, at foot of fo.72r.

COMMENT. In the Surtees Society edition of the Brinkburn cartulary, and in Lawrie, *Charters*, no.271, which is taken from the Surtees edition, the name of the donor is wrongly given as Malcolm. Lawrie's date, 1153, is based on this misreading.

3 William earl of Northumberland grants to William de Vesci the right to have a market at St Waleric's, which is called 'Neubiginge' (Alnmouth, Northumberland), with all the rights which most freely belong to any market in Northumberland. Edinburgh. (1152 × 1157, probably 1152 × *c.*1155)

Willelmus Comes Northumb' justiciis[a] suis, constabul*ariis* suis, vicecomitibus suis, ministris suis omnibus necnon omnibus hominibus suis Francis et Anglicis Northumb' qui sunt et qui venturi sunt, salutem. Notum vobis facio quatinus do et concedo Willelmo de Vescy ut habeat forum suum apud Sanctum Walericium qui vocatur Neubiginge, cum omnibus rebus et rectitudinibus omnibus que melius et liberius pertineant ulli foro totius Northumbr*ie*, ita libere, quiete et honorifice sicut aliquis in tota Northumbr*ia* habet et tenet forum suum liberius et honorabilius. Volo et iubeo quod idem Willelmus de Vescy teneat predictum forum et habeat. Testantibus hiis, Osberto priore de Jeddeworth', A*da* comitissa matre ejus, Gilleberto constabulario, Odenel Denframvilla, Edmundo Camerario, Hug*one* Giffard, Willelmo Masculo, Rodberto de Bailliol, Magistro Ricardo de Deuel'[b] Waltero de Peletot, Magistro Godfr*ido*, apud Edenburgh.

SOURCE. Bodleian Library, MS. Dodsworth 74, fo.29r (evidently from the Percy cartulary, for which cf. Davis, no.1306).
PRINTED. *Northumberland County History*, ii, 469n.; *Percy Chartulary* (ed. M.T. Martin, Surtees Soc., 1911), 349, no.833 (both from the Percy cartulary).
NOTES. [a] Source has Illustris. [b] Sic; printed versions have Deneb', Denel respectively; probably for Deuelston, i.e. Dilston.
COMMENT. Osbert prior of Jedburgh seems to have become abbot *c.*1155; he was abbot by the date of issue of *RRS*, i, no.114, before 7 April, 1156. For the identification of Neubiginge with Alnmouth, cf. *Northumberland County History* ii, 468–9.

4 William earl of Northumberland confirms to Newminster Abbey the land of Forum (in Ulgham, Northumberland), as Robert Bertram and Robert of Winchester granted it in fee-farm for six shillings a year. (1152 × 1157)

Will*elmus* Com*es* Northumbr*ie* justic*iis*, baronibus, vic*ecomitibus*, ministris et omnibus fidelibus suis hominibus Francis et Anglis, clericis [et laicis][a], tocius terre sue, tam futuris quam presentibus, salutem. Sciatis me concessisse et hac mea carta confirmasse monachis abbacie Novi Monasterii terram de Forum in bosco et plano, pratis et pascuis, et in omnibus aliis, desicut Robertus Bertram et Robertus de Wyncestre eis dimiserunt in feudofirma, pro sex solidis unoquoque anno[b]. Volo itaque et firmiter precipio ut quod de ista terra prenominata inter monachos et illos prelocutum est firmum existat et stabile imperpetuum maneat. Testibus etc.

RUBRIC. iij[a] (at left). Forum (top of folio).
SOURCE. Mr George Howard, Castle Howard, MS. Cartulary of Newminster Abbey, fo.121v (modern pencil foliation), 125v (older ink foliation).
PRINTED. *Newminster Chartularium*, 220.
NOTES. [a] MS. omits. [b] Last two words obscure.
COMMENT. The name Forum is lost, but evidence that it lay where the modern farm of Farneybeds or Ferneybeds is situated, near Widdrington, is given in J. Hodgson, *Hist. of Northumberland*, Part II, vol. ii, 177, 246.

5 William brother of the king of Scotland confirms to Jedburgh Abbey the ploughgate of land granted by William de Vieuxpont in his demesne of Carriden (West Lothian), as his charter and that of King Malcolm IV bear witness. Jedburgh. (1157 × 1165)

Willelmus frater regis Scotie omnibus amicis et hominibus suis clericis et laicis . Salutem. Nouerint tam posteri quam presentes . me concessisse . et hac mea carta confirmasse Deo . et ecclesie Sancte Marie de Jeddewrde . et canonicis ibidem Deo seruientibus . illam carrucatam terre quam Willelmus de Veteri Ponte dedit eis de dominio suo in Careden ;' tam liberam et quietam . ut carta donacionis eiusdem Willelmi de Veteri Ponte . et carta confirmacionis *Malcolmi* fratris mei ;' eis contestantur . determinant . et confirmant. Testibus . Hugone Ridel . Roberto de Quinci . Jordano Ridel . Roberto de capella . Godefrido camerario . Hugone Giffard . Galfrido de Coniburc . Willelmo Giffard . Bernardo filio Brieni. Apud Jeddword.

SOURCE. SRO, Transcripts of Miscellaneous Charters (R.H. 1/2/1) (transcript of original formerly *penes* Andrew P. Melville, W.S.). Whereabouts of original unknown.

COMMENT. See below, no.62. William lost the earldom of Northumberland in 1157; it is not known how he came to have the superiority of Carriden, unless it formed part of the compensation which King Malcolm IV may have given him in Scotland after the loss of the earldom. As lord of the Liberty of Tynedale, he was lord of William de Vieuxpont for the lands of Alston, Kirkhaugh and Elrington.

6 King William I commands his sheriffs and other officers that wherever the prior of May or his brethren or his dependents may come with property of their house they are to be free of cain and toll throughout his land, and are to have liberty to sell their own property and buy necessaries for their house, as the charter of King David I bears witness. Perth. (1165 × 1171)

Willelmus[a] Rex Scot' Vicec*omitibus* Prepositis ⁊ ministris & omnibus hominibus tocius terre sue, salutem. Precipio ubicumque prior de Mai aut aliquis suorum fratrum aut clientum domus de Mai uenerint cum rebus domus sue quatinus sint quieti a cano & theloneo per totam terram meam , & ut licentiam habeant uendendi proprias res suas & emendi[b] necessarias domus sue, sicut carta regis Dauid aui mei testatur & confirmat. Et prohibeo firmiter ne quis eis aut eorum possessionibus iniuriam aliquam faciat super meum forisfactum. T*estibus* Nich*olao* cancell*ario* . Ricardo de Moruill' . & multis aliis apud Pert.

RUBRIC. Carta eiusdem de quietancia.
SOURCE. BM, MS. Egerton 3031, fo.62^{r}.
PRINTED. *Proc. Soc. Antiq. Scot.*, xc, 72, no.48.
NOTES. [a] Vuillelmus, MS., with large red initial. [b] MS. repeats & emendi.
COMMENT. Cf. Lawrie, *Charters*, no.201.

7 Confirms to May Priory common easements in the wood of Clackmannan, as the charter of King David I bears witness. Perth. (1165 × 1171)

Willelmus[a] Rex Scot' omnibus probis hominibus tocius terre sue, salutem. Sciatis me concessisse priori de Mai & fratribus ibidem Deo seruientibus in elemosinam communionem nemoris de Clacmanet sicut carta regis Dauid aui mei testatur & confirmat. Quare prohibeo ne quis eos aut eorum homines in nemore disturbet. T*estibus* Nicholao cancellario, Ric*ardo* de Moruill' const*abulario*, Waltero filio Alani, et multis aliis. Apud Pert.

TITLE. Carta Regis Willelmi de communione nemoris de Klacmanan.[b]
RUBRIC. Carta eiusdem de communitate nemoris de Clacmanet.[c]
SOURCE. BM, MS. Egerton 3031, fo.62^{r} = *E. May Recs.*, p.cxiii = *M* (Title only).
PRINTED. *Proc. Soc. Antiq. Scot.*, xc, 73, no.49.
NOTES. [a] Uuillelmus, *E*, with large red initial. [b] Title from *M* only. [c] Rubric in *E* only.
COMMENT. Cf. Lawrie, *Charters*, no.156.

8 Confirms to May Priory the grants made to it by King David I and King Malcolm IV, and also a lodging with toft in Dunbar and a berth for one ship to carry necessaries for the priory, granted by Earl Cospatric (III) and confirmed by King Malcolm; as the charters of the two kings bear witness; so that there shall always be a convent of thirteen

monks on the island, following the Cluniac Order, and that the prior of May shall not be removed save for open wrongdoing, previously reported to the king and the bishop of St Andrews. Perth. (1166 × 1171)

Will'[a] Rex Scot' Episcopis, Abbatibus, Comitibus, Baronibus, Justiciis, Vic*ecomitibus* et omnibus probis hominibus tocius terre sue, clericis et laicis, salutem. Sciant presentes et futuri me concessisse et hac carta mea confirmasse Deo et ecclesie omnium sanctorum de Mai et Willelmo[b] priori et fratribus ibidem Deo seruientibus et ordinem Cluniacensem ibidem tenentibus in liberam et perpetuam elemosinam donaciones quas rex Dauid auus meus pie memorie et predecessor meus rex Malc*olmus* frater meus eis dederunt et concesserunt. Scilicet ex Regis Dauid donacione Petneweme[c] et Inuerrin[d] que fuit Auerin per rectas utriusque uille diuisas, et dimidium de Balegallin, quia reliquam partem eiusdem uille dedi ex donacione mea eis per rectas utriusque partis illius uille diuisas. Concedo etiam eis communem pasturam in schira de Kellyn[e] et in schira de Karal[f], ita plenarie[g] sicut carta Regis D*aui*d testatur, et unum plenarium toftum in Burgo meo de Berewych[h]. Ex donacione uero Regis Malc*olmi* .v. marcas singulis annis de Cano meo de nauibus uenientibus apud Pert, sicut carta Regis M*alcolmi* fratris mei testatur et confirmat. Precipio etiam ut omnes qui piscantur circa insulam de Mai rectas decimas suas Deo et predicte ecclesie sine occasione soluant. Prohibeo etiam firmiter[i] ne quis decimas suas eis iniuste detineat, sicut habuerunt in tempore Reg*is* D*aui*d super meum forisfactum et[i] ne quis in aquis eorum piscari presumat nec edificia construere in insula de Mai, nec terram de Mai fodere, nec in ea herbam capere, nisi per eorum licenciam. Preterea etiam concedo eis et confirmo unam mansuram cum tofto in Dunbar, et applicacionem unius nauis ad necessaria domus sue transportanda, sicut Comes Gospatricius eis dedit et concessit, et rex M*alcolmus* frater meus eis carta sua confirmauit. Quare uolo et firmiter precipio ut predicti monachi prenominatas terras et tenuras teneant et habeant, ita plenarie, quiete, libere et honorifice, sicut carte antecessorum meorum regis D*aui*d et regis M*alcolmi*[j] eis testantur et confirmant, et sicut aliqua Abbatia in toto regno meo elemosinas suas liberius, quietius et honorificentius tenet et possidet. Ita tamen quod semper habeatur ibi conuentus xiii. monachorum de ordine Cluniac*ensi*, et quod prior eiusdem loci scilicet de Mai non ammoueatur nisi pro manifesta ipsius[k] culpa que prius cognita fuerit michi et episcopo Sancti Andr*ee*. T*estibus* D*aui*d fratre meo, Nich*olao* cancell*ario*,[l] Math*eo* Archid*iacono* Sancti Andree, Com*ite* Wald*euo*, Com*ite* Dunec*ano*, Ric*ardo* de Morevilla Constabul*ario*, Waltero filio Alani Dapifero, D*auid* Olif*ard*, Nesio filio Willelmi Hug*one* Ridel, Galfrido de Malevilla. Aput Pert.

TITLE. Confirmacio Regis Willelmi de donacione Regum David et Malcolmi[m].

SOURCE. PRO, C.53/93, rot. 14 (Charter Roll, 35 Edward I) = *C*. BM, MS. Egerton 3031, fos.61v–62r = *E*. *May Recs.*, p.cxii = *M* (Title only). Printed here from *C*, with variant readings of *E* noted.

PRINTED. *May Recs.*, no.12 (from *C*).

NOTES. [a] Uuillelmus, *E*, with large red initial. [b] *E* omits Willelmo. [c] Petnew', *E*. [d] Inuerin, *E*. [e] scira de Kellin, *E*. [f] scira de Kerel, *E*. [g] *C* omits ita plenarie, supplied from *E*. [h] Berewic, *E*. [i–i] *E* omits this passage. [j] *E* puts carte here instead of after sicut. [k] eius, *E*. [l] *E* concludes here with & multis aliis apud Pert. [m] Title from *M* only.

COMMENT. See no.109, which should perhaps have been placed before this act.

9 Confirms to Ralph Frebern Rosyth, Fife, and the land which belonged to Master Robert the ironsmith beside Newbattle (Masterton), as fully as he held it on the day King Malcolm IV granted it to Ralph; to be held as King Malcolm's charter bears witness, for the service of one knight. Perth. (1166 × 1171)

Willelmus[a] Rex Scottorum episcopis, abbatibus, comitibus, baronibus, justiciariis, vicecomitibus, prepositis, ministris, omnibus probis hominibus tocius terre sue, clericis et laicis, modernis et posteris, salutem. Sciant presentes et futuri me concessisse et hac carta mea confirmasse Radulfo Frebern Rossiue, per rectas diuisas suas, sicut aliquis eam melius et plenius tenuit tempore Regis D*aui*d aui mei, et terram que fuerat Magistri Roberti Ferronis juxta Neubottle, ita plenarie ut eam tenebat die illa quum[b] frater meus Rex Malcolmus eam dedit ipsi Radulfo. Tenend'[c] ita libere et honorifice sicut alii Barones mei terras suas de me liberius et honorificentius tenent et sicut carta Regis Malcolmi fratris mei testatur et confirmat, per servitium unius militis. Testibus D*aui*d fratre meo, Nicholao cancellario, Ricardo de Morevill constabulario, Galfrido abbate de Dunferm*e*lin, Comite Waldeve, Comite Dunecano, Waltero filio Alani dapifero, Willelmo Carpentario, Galfrido Malevin[d], Jordano Ridel. Apud Pert.

SOURCE. *Spalding Misc.*, v., 242, no.2, printed from a transcript of Harry Maule of Kellie, titular earl of Panmure, made from the original in the possession of Mr David Freburn, some time minister of the gospel at Dunning (afterwards bishop of Edinburgh). Cf. *RRS*, i, no.256. Whereabouts of original now unknown.

PRINTED. *Spalding Misc.*, v, 242, no.2.

NOTES. [a] Punctuation editorial. [b] Source places quum after Malcolmus. [c] Source prints, etc., here, suggesting that clauses similar to those in *RRS*, i, no.256, lines 10–13, have been omitted by the transcriber. [d] Sic; supply de before Malevin.

COMMENT. Cf. *RRS*, i, no.256. Robert Frembert was a Scottish hostage at the submission of Falaise in 1174 (Stones, *Documents*, 4), but whether he was related to Ralph Frebern is not clear. Roger Frebern, presumably Ralph's son, was granted land near Rosyth by Robert of London King William's son (*Spalding Misc.*, v, 243).

10 Grants to Coupar Angus Abbey the land of Aberbothrie (in Bendochy), Perthshire, to be held as freely as the monks of Melrose hold land belonging to their church. Perth. (1166 × 1171)

W' Rex Scott' . Omnibus probis hominibus totius terre sue clericis 7 laicis . Salutem. Sciant presentes 7 futuri me dedisse 7 concessisse . 7 hac carta mea confirmasse Deo 7 ecclesie de Cupre 7 Monachis ibidem Deo seruientibus Aberbotherin per rectas diuisas suas in liberam 7 perpetuam Elemosinam ita libere 7 quiete sicut alias tenueras suas de me liberius 7 quietius tenent. Volo itaque 7 firmiter precipio . ut Monachi predicti prefatam Aberbotherin in bona pace teneant 7 possideant ita liberam 7 quietam ab omni seculari exactione ⁏ sicut Monachi de Melros . aliqua ecclesie sue beneficia liberius 7 quietius 7 pacificentius 7 honorabilius tenent 7 possident in terra mea. Test*ibus* D*aui*d fratre meo .

Nichol*ao* cancellario . Wald*eu*o Comite . Dun*ecano* Comite . Ric*ardo* de Moreuilla constabulario . Waltero fil*io* Alani dapifero . D*aui*d Olif*ard*. Seih*er*io de Quinci . Roberto de Quinci Apud Pert.

ENDORSED. C' de Ab*er*both*er*in (xii cent., hand contemporary with and perhaps identical with that of text). De Aberbothin (xiii cent.). Abirbothrin . ab omni seculari exaccione (earlier xiv cent.). . m. (earlier xiv cent.). dupplicatur (xv cent.). 2. (xix cent.).
DESCRIPTION. 7·7″ (19·6 cm.), Top and bottom × 5·3″ (13·5 cm.), L, R. Foot folded to depth of 0·7″ (1·8 cm.). The seal tag has been cut through, but the remaining part measures 1·7″ long and 0·7″ wide. No seal remains.
HAND. Scribe Ac. Ruled in ink.
SOURCE. Original, Earl of Moray, Darnaway Castle, Moray Muniments, Box. 32, Div. IV, Bdle, 1, no.2 = *A*. Nat. Lib., MS. Adv. 33.2.9, pencilled fo.27r = *B* (brief abstract).
PRINTED. *Coupar Angus Chrs.*, 1, no.1 (from *A*). *Coupar Angus Rental*, i, 321, no.4 (from *B*).
COMMENT. For the grange of Aberbothrie cf. *Coupar Angus Chrs.*, i, pp.xxxiii–xxxiv. For the witness Saer de Quinci, an elder brother of Robert de Quinci, see *RRS*, i, no.204; Dr G. G. Simpson's unpublished Edinburgh University, Ph.D., thesis on 'Roger de Quincy earl of Winchester', pp.10–11; and *Red Book of the Exchequer* (ed. H. Hall, Rolls Series), i, 334.

11 Grants that the monks of Coupar Angus Abbey shall be free from all secular exactions. Perth. (1165 × 1169)

Carta R*egis* Willielmi eisdem monachis ut liberi sint ab omnibus exactionibus secularibus. Testibus: Andrea Episcopo Catanensi, Gregorio Episcopo Dunkeldensi, Nicolao Cancellario, D*aui*d Olifard. Apud Perth.

SOURCE. NLS, MS. Adv. 33.2.9, fo.28r.
PRINTED. *Coupar Angus Rental*, i, 323–4, no.9.

12 Brieve in favour of the monks of Coupar Angus Abbey anent searching for goods stolen from them. Perth. (1165 × 1166)

Carta Regis Willielmi eisdem monachis de querendo furta ab iis derepta. Testibus: Andrea Episcopo de Catneis, Gregorio Episcopo de Dunkeld, Nicolao Cancellario, Gospatricio Comite, Waltero filio Allani dapifero, Willielmo de Moreveill. Apud Perth.

SOURCE. NLS, MS. Adv. 33.2.9, fo.28r.
PRINTED. *Coupar Angus Rental*, i, 324, no.11.
COMMENT. The attestation of Earl Cospatric III of Dunbar provides a *terminus ante quem* of 1166; *William* de Moreville may be in error for *Richard*, but not necessarily, since William de Moreville witnesses Lawrie, *Charters*, no.196, *c*.1152. On the other hand, this might be a brieve of King Malcolm IV, wrongly attributed.

13 Confirms to St Andrews Cathedral Priory the land which belonged to Malsnauch, near St Andrews, granted by Richard bishop of St Andrews, with its toft in Kilrymont, as the bishop's charter bears witness. Perth. (1165 × 1172)

Willelmus[a] rex Scotorum . episcopis . abbatibus comitibus . baronibus . iusticiis . vicec*omitibus* et omnibus probis hominibus tocius terre sue salutem . Sciant presentes et futuri me concessisse et hac carta mea confirmasse canonicis in ecclesia Sancti Andree apostoli Deo seruientibus et seruituris terram Malsnauch iuxta Sanctum Andream quam Ricardus episcopus Sancti Andree eis dedit . Scilicet . Lethin . Poclin . Pethnathrene . Dowrehdin . Reschooch . Pethmolin . Balentagart . Pethwwenethe . Cremacharrin . Glasanagastch cum rectis diuisis suis in moris . in pratis . in pascuis et ceteris asiamentis suis et cum tofto in Kilrimund pertinente eidem terre . Tenend*am* ita libere et quiete sicut alias elemosinas . liberius . et quiecius . tenent . et sicut carta . Ricardi episcopi Sancti Andree testatur et confirmat. Testibus . Eng*elramo* episcopo de Glascu . Andrea episcopo de Katenes . Matheo archidiacono de Sancto Andrea . Com*ite* Dunecano . Com*ite* G. de Anegus . Waltero filio Alani dapifero . Nes filio Willelmi . Alexandro de Sancto Martino . Adam filio Thom*e* . apud Perth.

RUBRIC. De terra Malsnacht' (top in red).
SOURCE. SRO, GD 45/27/8 (St Andrews priory cartulary), fo.ci^{v}.
PRINTED. *St Andrews Liber*, 217.
NOTE. [a] Red initial U.
COMMENT. Bishop Richard's charter is given in *St Andrews Liber*, 179–80.

14 Grants (confirms?) to Orm son of Hugh (son of Gillemichel earl of Fife) Glenduckie and Balmeadie (in Dunbog), Fife, as Earl Duncan (of Fife) has quitclaimed them to Orm in exchange for Balbirnie (in Markinch). Perth. (1165 × 1171)

Will' Rex Scottorum omnibus probis hominibus totius terre sue Salutem. Sciant tam presentes quam futuri me concessisse 7 dedisse . 7 hac karta mea confirmasse . Orm filio Hug*onis* Glenduogin 7 Balemadethin per rectas diuisas sibi 7 heredibus suis tenend*um* de me 7 heredibus meis libere 7 quiete 7 honorifice ab omni seruitio . saluo mihi meo seruitio quod ad illam terram pertinet . sicut Com*es* Dunecanus illam quietam clamauit in excambio de Balebrenin. His t*estibus* . And*rea* episcopo de Catt' . Nich*olao* Cancell*ario* . Math*eo* Arch*idiacono* . Ric*ardo*[a] de Moru*illa* constab*ulario* . D*aui*d Olif*ard* Justic*ia* . W*altero* fil*io* Alani dapifero. Ap*ud* Pert.

ENDORSED. Carta de Glenduky et balmady (xvi cent.). James IV has a charter . . . (remainder obscure, but contains name of grantee. xvi cent.). Charter be King Williame To Orme sone to Heugo of the Landes of Glendougine and Bellemadthine. I R ~~10~~ 11 (xvii cent.).
DESCRIPTION. 5·8″ (14·5 cm.), Top and bottom × 2·1″ (5·3 cm.), L, 2·3″ (6 cm.), R. Foot folded with slits for seal tag, which remains in position. The seal is missing, but its traces remain on the tag.
HAND. Scribe Ak. Unruled.
SOURCE. Original, *penes* Mr William Mackay, junior, 19 Union Street, Inverness, 1954, and temporarily loaned to the Inverness Burgh Museum.
NOTES. [a] Parchment torn, but Ric' is readable.
COMMENT. Cf. *BIHR*, xxix, 24. The exchange was evidently made to allow Earl Duncan more complete possession of Strathleven. See no.559.

15 Frees Nar, a man of the abbot of Scone, from the charge which he had brought against him of coming into Moray; the abbot of Scone may have Nar and his heirs free and quit of claims by the king. Perth. (1165 × 1171)

Willelmus[a] Rex Scottorum omnibus probis hominibus tocius terre sue salutem. Sciatis me quietum clamasse Nar, hominem Abbatis de Scone, de calumpnia quam habui versus eum veniendi in Morauiam. Quare volo et precipio ut ecclesia de Scone et Abbas eiusdem ecclesie predictum Nar et heredes suos liberos et solutos a me et ab heredibus meis in perpetuum habeant. Test*ibus* Andr*ea* episcopo de Catenes, Nichol*ao* cancellario, Matheo archidiac*ono* Sanctiandr*ee*, Ric*ardo* de Moreuill' constabulario, D*aui*d Olif*ard* Justic*ia* Waltero filio Alani Dapifero, Nessio filio Willelmi, Ormio[b] de Abernithi, Gillecrist[c] mac inien Samuel. Apud Perth.

SOURCE. NLS, MS. Adv. 34.3.28, fo.10^{v}.
PRINTED. *Scone Liber*, no.34.
NOTES. [a] Initial omitted, MS. [b] Ornuo, MS. [c] de, MS.
COMMENT. Nar seems to have been a fugitive neyf originally claimed as the king's, and proved to be a tenant of the abbot of Scone. His journey to Moray is unexplained. Thomas son of Nar witnessed *Scone Liber*, no.106.

16 Commands Archibald and Hugh, sons of Swain of Forgan, to render to Scone Abbey every year eight chalders of wheat, being the teind of the king's wheat of Longforgan. (1165 × 1174)

Willelmus[a] Rex Scottorum Arkenb*aldo* et Hugoni filiis Suani de Forgrunde salutem. Precipio vobis quatenus singulis annis reddatis abbati de Scon octo celdras frumenti pro decima frumenti mei de Forgrunde, et nemini nisi ei inde respondeatis. Testibus.

SOURCE. NLS, MS. Adv. 34.3.28, fo.9^{r}.
PRINTED. *Scone Liber*, no.28.
NOTE. [a] Initial omitted, MS.
COMMENT. See *RRS*, i, 42 and n.

17 Confirms to Scone Abbey the teind of the whole parish of Scone in grain, cheese and catches of fish. Forteviot. (1165 × 1171)

Willelmus[a] Rex Scottorum episcopis, abbatibus, comitibus, baronibus, justiciis, vicecomitibus, prepositis, ministris cunctisque aliis probis hominibus tocius terre sue, salutem. Sciatis me concessisse et hac carta mea confirmasse Deo et ecclesie Sancte Trinitatis de Scon et abbati et canonicis ibidem Deo servientibus decimam tocius parrochie de Scon' in annona, in caseis, in capcionibus piscium et in omnibus aliis unde decima dari debet. Prohibeo itaque ne quisquam eiis aliquid predicte decime iniuste auferre siue detinere presumat, super forisfactum meum. Test*ibus* Andr*ea* episcopo de Caten*es*, Nichol*ao* cancellario, Waltero filio Alani dapifero, Matheo Archidiac*ono*. Apud Fetherteuiet.

SOURCE. NLS, MS. Adv. 34.3.28, fo.8^{v}.
PRINTED. *Scone Liber*, no.26.
NOTE. [a] Initial omitted, MS.
COMMENT. Cf. *RRS*, i, no.57 and p.264.

18 Confirms to Scone Abbey certain household revenues benorth Lammermuir. (1165 × 1174)

Willelmus[a] Rex Scottorum omnibus probis hominibus tocius terre sue salutem. Sciatis me concessisse et hac carta mea confirmasse Deo et ecclesie Sancte Trinitatis de Scon et abbati et canonicis ibidem Deo servientibus decimam tocius panis domus mee ex aquilonali parte de Lambremor, et omnes pelles agnorum et ouium ad coquinam meam pertinencium, excepta unaquaque sexta pelle; et dimidium tocius sepi et sanguinis[b] et uncti que ad partem meam de coquina mea spectant; et extra quadragesimam omni die dominica excepta qualibet sexta dominica unum corium uacce siue bouis; et omnia ista tantum ex aquilonali parte de Lambremor; et medietatem coriorum de occisionibus ad opus meum factis, et dimidium sepi et uncti earundem occisionum, scilicet ex aquilone fluminis de Tei. Prohibeo itaque ne aliquis eis quicquam inde iniuste detineat, super defensionem meam. Testibus etc.

SOURCE. NLS, MS. Adv. 34.3.28, fo.11v.
PRINTED. *Scone Liber*, no.38.
NOTES. [a] Initial omitted, MS. [b] Sic, for sagiminis.
COMMENT. See *RRS*, i, no.244.

19 Confirms to Missenden Abbey the hermitage of Muswell (in Piddington, Oxon), with the chapel and all appurtenances, with the whole tithe of the demesne of Piddington and the tithe of the pannage, to be held as freely as in the time of King David I and King Malcolm IV. Dunfermline (1165 × 1171, perhaps December, 1165)

Willelmus rex Scocie[a] omnibus[b] hominibus tocius terre sue, clericis et laicis, futuris et presentibus, salutem. Sciant presentes et futuri me concessisse et hac carta mea in perpetuam elimosinam confirmasse Deo et ecclesie Sancte Marie de Missendene[c] et canonicis ibidem Deo seruientibus, pro salute mea et antecessorum[d] meorum, hermitorium de Musewella[e] perpetuo possidendam, libere et quiete, cum capella et omnibus pertinenciis suis in bosco et plano, in aquis et pratis et cum tota decima de dominio de Pedyngton[f] in omnibus rebus que decimari[g] debent et decima de padlnagio.[h] Quare volo et precipio ut predicti canonici ecclesie de Missendena[i] habeant et teneant hec omnia in liberam elemosinam bene et in pace, sicut umquam melius et plenius ea habuerunt in tempore David[j] regis aui mei et regis Malcolmi fratris mei. Testibus Nicholao cancellario, Waltero[k] filio Alani dapifero, Dauid Olif*ard*,[l] Gilberto de Umfranville, Ricardo Cumin, Hugone Ridel,[m] Nessio filio Willelmi, Roberto de Quinci, Jordano Ridel. Apud Dunfermelyn.

SOURCE. *The Boarstall Cartulary*, ed. H.E. Salter (Oxford Historical Society, 1930), 104–5, no.302 = *B* (from a MS. cartulary *penes* Maj. Sir H.L. Aubrey-Fletcher, Bt., 1958 [Davis, no.1310], fo.31). BM, MS. Harl. 3688, fo.128v = *H*. Printed here from *B*, with more important variants of *H* noted.
PRINTED. (From *B*): as above, and Kennet, *Parochial Antiquities*, i, 172; (from *H*): *The cartulary of Missenden Abbey*, ed. J.G. Jenkins, Part III (Hist. MSS. Comm., JP I, 1962), 65–6, no.637.
NOTES. [a] Scottie, *H*. [b] *H* adds probis. [c] Messend', *H*. [d] *H* adds et successorum. [e] heremitorium de Musewelle, *H*. [f] Pidintune, *H*. [g] addecimari, *H*. [h] pasnagio, *H*. [i] Messendene, *H*. [j] Henr', *H*. [k] Willelmo, *H*. [l] *H* omits. [m] *H* ends here with et aliis.
COMMENT. Perhaps this was issued in December, 1165, soon after King Malcolm's funeral, since King Malcolm's similar charter, which this confirms, was issued at Jedburgh shortly before his death (*RRS*, i, no.263) and the emissaries from Missenden who obtained that charter may have waited to secure a confirmation from the next king.

20 Confirms to Scone Abbey the churches of 'Louchferuer' (Borthwick) and Carrington, Midlothian. Dunfermline. (1165 × 1171)

Willelmus[a] Rex Scottorum omnibus probis hominibus tocius terre sue salutem. Sciatis me concessisse et hac mea carta confirmasse Deo et ecclesie Sancte Trinitatis de Scon et abbati et canonicis ibidem Deo seruientibus ecclesiam de Louchferuer et ecclesiam de Kerinton', cum terris et decimis et rectitudinibus omnibus ad utramque illarum pertinentibus. Volo itaque et precipio ut canonici prefati predictas ecclesias ita libere et quiete cum omnibus ad eas pertinentibus teneant et possideant sicut alique ecclesie in terra mea liberius et quiecius tenentur et possidentur. Test*ibus* Andr*ea* episcopo de Caten*es*, Nichol*ao* cancellario, Waltero filio Alani dapifero, Matheo archidiac*ono*. Apud Dunfermelin.

SOURCE. NLS, MS. Adv. 34.3.28, fo.8r.
PRINTED. *Scone Liber*, no.23.
NOTE. [a] Initial omitted, MS.
COMMENT. See *RRS*, i, nos.57, 243.

21 Confirms to Melrose Abbey the twenty acres of arable with one toft in Berwick which King Malcolm IV had granted to Walter son of Alan the steward. (1165 × 1174)

U.[a] rex Scot' omnibus probis hominibus tocius terre sue, clericis et laicis, modernis et posteris, salutem. Sciant presentes et futuri me concessisse et hac mea carta confirmasse Deo et ecclesie Sancte Marie de Melros et monachis ibidem Deo seruientibus illas . xx^ti . acras terre cum tofto de Berwic, quas rex Malcolmus frater meus Waltero filio Alani dapifero dedit, tenend*as* in liberam et perpetuam elemosinam, ita libere et quiete et honorifice sicut alias teneuras suas liberius, quiecius et honorificencius tenent. Test*ibus*.

RUBRIC. Confirmacio reg*is* W. de xx. acris de Berwic etc.
SOURCE. BM, MS. Harl. 3960, fo.86v.
PRINTED. *Melrose Liber*, no.20.
NOTE. [a] Initial red.
COMMENT. Cf. *RRS*, i, no.308.

22 Grants to Dunfermline Abbey one full toft in his burgh of Kinghorn. Dunfermline. (1165 × 1172, perhaps *c*.1165–6)

Will'[a] Rex Scott' omnibus probis hominibus tocius terre sue clericis ⁊ laicis salutem. Sciant presentes ⁊ futuri me dedisse ⁊ concessisse ⁊ hac carta mea confirmasse Deo ⁊ ecclesie Sancte Trinitatis de Dunfer*melin* et monachis ibidem Deo seruientibus unum plenarium toftum in burgo meo de Kingorn'. Quare uolo et firmiter precipio ut predicti monachi prenominatum toftum teneant in liberam elemosinam . ita libere et quiete et honorifice . sic*ut* alias elemosinas suas tenent in regno meo. T*estibus* Matheo Archid*iacono* S*ancti* Andr*ee* . Walt*ero* fil*io* Al*ani* Dapifero . Ness*io* fil*io* Willelmi . Ric*ardo* clerico . Walt*ero* de Berkel'. Apud Dunfermel*in*.

RUBRIC. De tofto de Kinghorn' (red with red initial).
SOURCE. NLS, MS. Adv. 34.1.3a, fo.xiir.
PRINTED. *Dunfermline Registrum*, no.55.
NOTE. [a] Initial blue.

COMMENT. Possibly this grant was made on the occasion of King Malcolm's funeral.

23 Confirms to St Andrews Cathedral Priory the church of Inchture, Perthshire, with the chapel of Kinnaird. Dunfermline. (1165 × 1170)

Willelmus[a] rex Scotorum . Omnibus probis hominibus tocius terre sue clericis et laicis salutem . Sciatis me dedisse et concessisse et hac mea carta confirmasse Deo et ecclesie Sancti Andree et canonicis ibidem Deo seruientibus in liberam et perpetuam elemosinam ecclesiam de Inchethore cum capella de Kinnard' et cum omnibus eidem ecclesie iuste pertinentibus . Quare uolo et firmiter precipio ut predicti canonici prenominatam ecclesiam teneant et habeant ita libere et quiete et honorifice sicut alias elemosinas suas liberius et quiecius tenent in regno meo . Testibus . Ricardo episcopo Sancti Andree . Andrea episcopo de Kate*n*' . Galfrido abbate de Dunf*ermelin* . Nicholao cancellario . Matheo archidiacono Ricardo cap*ellano* . Comite Dunecano . Waltero filio Alani Dapifero . Dauid Olifard . Nesio filio Willelmi . Ricardo Comin Hug*one* Ridel . Gauf*rido* de Maleuile apud Dunfermelin .

RUBRIC. De ecclesia de Inchethor (top in red).
SOURCE. SRO, GD 45/27/8 (St Andrews priory cartulary), fo.cii^{r}.
PRINTED. *St Andrews Liber*, 218–19.
NOTE. [a] Blue initial V.
COMMENT. In the form of a fresh grant, but cf. *RRS*, i, no.240, a confirmation of Bishop Richard's grant of the *chapel* of Inchture, whose status had by the date of this act been raised to that of a parish church.

24 Takes the brethren of the Hospital of St Andrews into his firm peace and forbids anyone to injure them or their property unjustly. Debts are to be paid to them promptly, and bequests are not to be withheld. Dunfermline. (1165 × 1171)

Willelmus[a] rex Scotorum . Omnibus probis hominibus tocius terre sue salutem . Sciatis me fratribus hos[b]pitalis Sancti Andree ubicunque in totam terram meam uenerint meam firmam pacem iuste dedisse . Ea propter prohibeo ne quis eis aut rebus suis iniuste forisfaciat . et si quis eis aliquod debitum debet ;' minime detineat . set scicius iuste soluat . firmiter precipio . et qui bonum aliquod pro amore Dei et[c] sue anime salute ad sustamentum pauperum peregrinorum eis impenderit ;' a Deo remuneraciones . et magnas grates a me recipie[t] . preterea modis omnibus[d] prohibeo quod diuisum uel assignatum hospitali predicto fuerit ne quis super meum forisfactum iniuste detineat uel disturbet. Testibus Nicholao cancellario . Waltero filio Alani . D*aui*d Olifard . Gill*berto* de Unframuill' . Ricardo Cumin . apud Dunfermelin .

RUBRIC. De hospitali (top in red).
SOURCE. SRO, GD 45/27/8 (St Andrews priory cartulary), fos.xcviii^{v}–xcix^{r}.
PRINTED. *St Andrews Liber*, 211–12.
NOTES. [a] Blue initial V. [b] Fo.xcix^{r}. [c] Written &. [d] precipio expunged.
COMMENT. Cf. *RRS*, i, no.170.

25 Commands that wherever the abbot of Scone or his sergeand may discover *cumlawes* and *cumherbes* belonging to the lands of Scone Abbey they are to have them justly without delay, and no one is to detain

them unjustly contrary to the king's firm prohibition. Dunfermline. (1165 × 1171)

W. Rex Scott'. Omnibus probis hominibus totius Scocie . sal*utem*. Mando 7 firmiter precipio . ut in cuiuscunque uestrum terra aut potestate Abbas de Scon aut eius seruiens inuenire poterit Cumlawes 7 Cumherbes ad terras abbacie de Scon pertinentes .·/ eos iuste absque dilatione habeat. Nullus itaque quemquam ex illis ei iniuste detineat super firmam defensionem meam 7 forisfacturam meam. T*estibus* Andr*ea* episcopo de Caten' . Nicol*ao* cancell*ario* . Waltero fil*io* Alani Dapifero . Matheo Archidiac*ono*. Apud Dunfermelin;

ENDORSED. Will*elm*us de Cumherbis (xii cent.). Also modern endorsements.
DESCRIPTION. 5·1″ (13 cm.), Top and bottom × 3·2″ (8 cm.), L, 2·2″ (5·5 cm.), R, Tie and tongue cut 1·4″ (3·7 cm.) from left-hand edge, both now torn away. No seal remains.
HAND. Scribe Ah. Ruled in drypoint. This is the same hand as that of *RRS*, i, no.166.
SOURCE. Original, SRO, RH 6/3.
PRINTED. *Scone Liber*, no.36.
COMMENT. Cf. *RRS*, i, 62–4; and no.31 below.

26 Confirms to Scone Abbey the cain and customs of one ship, and commands that all merchants residing outwith the realm of Scotland who may wish to bring a ship to Scotland with their merchandise shall have his and God's peace going and returning, and shall answer to no one but the abbot for the customs of that ship. Dunfermline. (1165 × 1171)

.W. Dei gr*ati*a Rex Scotorum . Omnibus mercatoribus Anglie sal*utem*. Sciatis me concessisse & dedisse in elemosina ecclesie Sancte Trinitatis de Scon' . 7[a] abbati fratribusque ibidem Deo seruientibus . Can . 7 consuetudines unius nauis 7 ideo uolo & firmiter precipio . ut omnes mercatores extra regionem Scotie manentes qui nauem illam cum mercibus suis ascendere atque in Scotiam uenire uoluerint .·/ pacem Dei 7 meam eundo 7 redeundo pacemque tenendo habeant 7 nulli nisi abbati . 7 fratribus predicte ecclesie de consuetudinibus predicte nauis respondeant. T*estibus* Andr*ea* episcopo de Catern'[b] Nicol*ao* cancell*ario* . Waltero filio Alani. Dapifero Matheo archidiac*ono*. Apud DunfermeliN.

ENDORSED. Willelmus Rex de Cano Nauis (xii cent.).
DESCRIPTION. 7·9″ (20 cm.), Top and bottom × 4·1″ (10·4 cm.), L, R. Foot folded to a depth of 0·5″ (1·2 cm.). Single slits, but no tag or seal remains.
HAND. Scribe Ag. Upright charter hand with thick strokes, practised but somewhat clumsy in appearance. The triangular tails of the g's in gratia and Anglie are striking; note also use of ampersand twice and unusually sloping form of tironian et, with a short cross-stroke.
SOURCE. Original, SRO, RH 6/5.
PRINTED. *Scone Liber*, no.29.
NOTES. [a] Here and throughout, the tironian sign has a very slight cross-stroke. [b] Parchment slightly damaged.
COMMENT. This confirms an act of King Alexander I, *RRS*, i, no.4. The *dei gratia* in the style is no doubt due to drafting and writing by the beneficiary's own scribe.

27 Confirms to Scone Abbey the liberty of holding its court with judicial combat, and ordeals of iron and water, as King Malcolm IV's charter bears witness. Dunfermline. (1165 × 1171)

W. Rex Scott' . Episcopis . Abbatibus . Comitibus . Baronibus . Justiciis . Vice*comitibus* . Prepositis . Ministris . Cunctisque aliis probis hominibus totius terre sue . Francis 7 Anglis . Scottis . 7 Galwelensibus . Clericis 7 Laicis . Sal*utem*. Sciatis me concessisse 7 hac mea karta confirmasse Deo 7 ecclesie Sancte Trinitatis de Scon . 7 abbati 7 canonicis ibidem Deo seruientibus .' omnes libertates suas sicut carta regis Malcolmi fratris mei testatur . scil*icet* curiam suam plenarie habendam . in duello . in ferro . in aqua . Cum omnibus libertatibus ad curiam pertinentibus . Cum libertate nulli respondendi extra curiam suam propriam. Nullus itaque fidelium meorum hanc eorum libertatem cassare attemptet . super forisfactum meum. T*estibus* Andr*ea* episcopo de Caten' . Nichol*ao* cancellario . Com*ite* Dunec*ano* . Waltero filio Alani . D*aui*d Olif*ar*d . Gill*eberto* de Hunfr*amuilla* . Ric*ardo* Cumin . Hugo Ridel . Robberto de Quinci . Bern*ardo* fil*io* Brien. Apud DunfermeliN.

ENDORSED. Willelmus Rex. De Libertatibus (xii cent.). et carta propria cum libertate nemini respondendi. Also modern endorsements.
DESCRIPTION. 6·6″ (16·6 cm.), Top, 6·8″ (17·4 cm.), Bottom × 4″ (10·3 cm.), L, 3·8″ (9·7 cm.), R. Foot formerly folded, with tie cut from left-hand edge. No tag or seal remains.
HAND. Scribe Ah. This is the same hand as that of *RRS*, i, no.166.
SOURCE. Original, SRO, RH 6/4.
PRINTED. *Scone Liber*, no.31.
COMMENT. This confirms *RRS*, i, no.247.

28 Confirms the property and privileges of St Andrews Cathedral Priory. Dunfermline. (1165 × 1169)

Will*elmus*[a] Dei gr*ati*a Rex Scotorum . Omnibus episcopis . Abbatibus . Comitibus . Vicecomitibus . Justiciis . Baronibus . Ministris . 7 omnibus fidelibus suis tam presentibus quam futuris . Sal*utem*. Ad hoc nos diuina prouidentia in populo suo principes uoluit esse .' ut debeamus 7 uelimus Ipsi tanquam Domino 7 Creatori omnium subesse 7 subditis nostris non tam preesse quam prodesse . Mala penitus extirpare . bonum non solum ipsi facere . uerum etiam benefacientes adiuuare . Proinde illustris regis D*aui*d aui mei . necnon 7 patris mei comitis Henrici . simul 7 dilecti fratris mei Malcolmi . necnon 7 regis Alexandri . ceterorumque sancte ecclesie fundatorum circa ecclesie Dei diligentiam uestigia sequens .' quecunque dona . quascunque possessiones . uel redditus ipsi Deo inspirante . uel pie memorie Robertus episcopus . 7 successores sui . uel quelibet alia ecclesiastica secularisue persona ipsis concedentibus Deo 7 ecclesie S*ancti* Andree apostoli 7 canonicis ibidem Deo seruientibus 7 seruituris . dederunt 7 concesserunt .' ego quoque do . 7 concedo . 7 pro salute anime mee 7 predecessorum . 7 successorum meorum regia auctoritate confirmo . 7 hec quidem propriis duxi exprimenda uocabulis. Videlicet ex dono Regis D*aui*d .' ecclesiam de Forgr*unt*[b] cum tofta . ubi eorum sunt edificia . 7 cum decimis 7 rectitudinibus ecclesie pertinentibus de tota schyra de Forgr*unt*.[b] Unam aquam in Berewic . cum tofta que est iuxta ecclesiam . 7 alteram toftam in eadem uilla iuxta Twede. Unam toftam in Hadegtona.[c] Unam toftam in Clacmanan[d]. 7 boschum in Clacmanan[d] tam ipsis quam hominibus suis prout eis fuerit necessarium. Transfretationem ad portum maris ad nauem regine ipsis 7 propriis hominibus suis . 7 omnibus rebus suis sine naulo.[e] Decimam molendini de Lilledcu.[f] Tractum unius retis in aqua de Perth . cum propriis retibus meis. Tres marchas de meo can[d] :' de nauibus de Perth :' singulis annis ad uestitum canonicorum.[g] Unam marcham de firma de Perth :' ad pascha ad luminare ecclesie. Curiam quoque suam cum libertatibus immunitatibus 7 quietudinibus placitorum 7 querelarum a predecessoribus meis constitutis . 7 concessis . sicut liberius 7 honorificentius habet aliqua ecclesia uel elemosina in toto regno meo . & libertatem quam dedit predictus auus meus canonicis ne aliquis namum capiat super illos uel in terra sua pro alicuius forisfacto uel debito :' nisi pro illorum proprio super plenarium forisfactum meum. Ex dono Regis Malcolmi fratris mei dimidiam carrucatam terre de qua ecclesia de Forgr*un*t dotata est . secundum diuisas perambulatas . 7 tractum unius retis in aqua de Perth cum propriis retibus meis. Unam toftam in burgo de Inuerketh.[h] Unam carrucatam terre de Adnacht :' nomine Melgrethre[i]. cum rectis diuisis suis. Unam toftam in burgo de Perth . que fuit Baldewini lorem*ar*ii cum botha una in uico de North apud castellum. Ex dono uero pie memorie domini Roberti episcopi . ecclesiam de Lilledcu[f] cum terris 7 domibus infra burgum 7 extra . 7 decimis 7 redditibus capellis 7 omnibus rebus 7 rectitudinibus eidem ecclesie pertinentibus. Terras autem[j] istas . Barrim*un*th[k]. Struuithin . Gastduuenold . Drunkarakin . Ledokin . Stradkines . 7 aliam Stradkines pro commutatione Kinines . 7 Lethin . quas keledei habent . Balehucca . Rodmanan . Petultin . Balegoua cum salina . Kinastare . Kinamone . Drumsach . Balemacduuegin . Eglesnemin . Balloden . Sconin . Kinnimoniht . cum tota schyra . & cum una tofta in Kilrimund. Tres toftas in burgo Sancti Andree. Molendinum de Kilrimund. Molendinum de Putakin . Molendinum de Nidin. Liberam uero prioris sui electionem . ut quemcunque capitulum totum uel eius sanior pars elegerit :' ipse in eorum regimen sullimatus . subiectorum recipiat professionem. Hospitale etiam S*ancti* Andree in susceptione hospitum . pauperum . peregrinorum . cum terris 7 possessionibus . 7 redditibus eidem hospitali pertinentibus . Videlicet medietatem decime carrucarum episcopi . 7 uaccariarum & bercariarum . 7 porcariarum . 7 equariarum . de parochia Sancte Trinitatis . 7 medietatem de Can[a] episcopi eiusdem parochie . 7 totam decimam de can episcopi de Bladebolgschira[l]. 7 de aliis prouinciis . 7 locis undecunque fuerit allatum uel adductum ad Sanctum Andream. Carrucatam etiam terre quam Simon filius Micael*is* . 7 heredes sui predicto hospitali dederunt 7 concesserunt . per easdem diuisas quas prefatus Simon cum propriis hominibus suis perambulauerunt. Terram etiam de Kenlekin quam auus meus rex D*aui*d predicto hospitali dedit 7 concessit pro salute anime sue in perpetuam elemosinam. Et sicut per cartam Regis D*aui*d prohibitum est quod predicto hospitali ab aliquo diuisum fuerit :' super forisfactum meum nullus detineat. Communitatem etiam in paschuis de Fif pecoribus hospital*is*. Firmam etiam pacem meam procuratoribus hospitali deputatis ne quis eis forisfacere presumat in tota terra mea . uel debitum qualemcunque iniuste detineat. Ceteras etiam possessiones quas prefatum hospitale iuste tenet ⁊ possidet. Ex donatione autem uenerabilis Ærnaldi episcopi ecclesiam de Derueisin . cum terris ⁊ decimis ⁊ oblationibus eidem pertinentibus . ⁊ unam carrucatam terre. Capellam etiam de Foules cum omnibus pertinenciis suis. Ecclesiam de Porthmoach[m] cum terra ⁊ cum omnibus eidem pertinentibus. Decimam de omnibus placitis suis tam secularibus quam ecclesiasticis . ⁊ de omnibus releuiis suis. Totam oblationem altaris cui deseruiunt integram illibatamque ⁊ sine omni partium distributione quietam ⁊ liberamque.[n] Terram etiam totam de Kilrimund que est a uico qui est inter burgum ⁊ nouum hospitale . usque ad pontem Stermolin[o]. ⁊ inde sicut fluuius Kines cadit in mare . ⁊ per uiam qua itur a burgo ad ecclesiam iterum in mare. Ex donatione autem domini Ricardi episcopi ecclesiam S*ancte* Trinitatis in Kilrimund parrochialem cum terra Kindargog . de qua prefata ecclesia dotata est cum capell*is* in tota schyra de Kilrimund cum tofta in burgo ⁊ domibus in ea edificatis . sicut Matheus archidiaconus melius ⁊ liberius eas tenuit . cum decimis ⁊ oblationibus ⁊ omnibus rectitudinibus prefate ecclesie iuste pertinentibus tam de Scotis quam de Franccis[n]. de Anglicis ⁊ Flandrensibus infra burgum ⁊ extra. Terram etiam extra burgum in uico de North apud furcas . ⁊ apud Turdafche.[p] Capellam etiam de Hynchethore[q] cum omnibus eidem capelle iuste pertinentibus. Ex donatione Mathei archidiaconi de Sancto Andrea Rossinclerach cum rectis diuisis suis ⁊ ecclesiam eiusdem uille cum omnibus eidem ecclesie iuste pertinentibus . ⁊ ea que nobis inde debeantur. Ex donatione autem cuiusdam militis nomine EGU . filii Hug*onis* filii Gillemihel comitis de Fif . ecclesiam de Markinke[r] . cum una tofta ex orientali parte ecclesie . ⁊ cum decimis . ⁊ omnibus rectitudinibus eidem ecclesie iuste pertinentibus. Ista igitur ⁊ quecunque postmodum predicte ecclesie Beati Andree apostoli ⁊ canonicis ibidem Deo seruientibus ⁊ seruituris collata fuerint ;· libera ⁊ quieta esse ab omni exactione decernimus. Hanc igitur donationem ⁊ concessionem pie memorie Roberti episcopi . ⁊ piissimi Regis D*aui*d aui mei . ⁊ uenerabilis patris mei comitis Henrici . necnon ⁊ dilecti fratris mei Regis Malcolmi . ⁊ aliorum fidelium ;· Ego Will*elmu*s dei gr*ati*a Rex Scotorum regia auctoritate confirmo . ⁊ sigilli mei impressione consigno. T*estibus* Ricardo episcopo de S*ancto* Andrea . Andrea episcopo de Katen' . Galfrido abbate de DunfermeliN . Roberto priore de Mai . Nicholao cancellario . Matheo archid*iacono* . Ricardo capell*ano* . Dunecano comite de Fif . Gillebrido comite de Anegus . Malcolmo comite de Ethotle[s]. Waltero filio Alani . Roberto de Quinci . D*auid* Olifard . Gilleberto de Umfrauilla . Patricio filio comitis . Nies[t]filio Willelmi . Ricardo Comin[u] . Hugone Ridel . Alexandro de S*ancto* Martino . Hug*one* Gifard . Michaele clerico de Berewic . Willelmo clerico de Kingor . Magistro Hereberto . Stephano clerico . Ricardo clerico de prebenda . Magistro Turpino . Hugone clerico de Carel[v]. Halano de Lasceles[w]. Orm[x] filio Hugonis . Gillecrist de Ferteuieth . Galfrido de Maleuin[y]. Gillemur uenatore[z]. Gilleberto de Kinros . Gillebride uicecomite de Dunfermelin . Alano filio Simundi[aa]; Apud DuNfeRMeliN;

ENDORSED. *A*: Carta Will*elm*i regis (xii cent.). King William's Charter. Ratifying all former Gifts and Grants made by the kings his predecessors and others. To the see (Priorie) of St Andrews.
Without a date but it must have been granted before 1174 (xvii cent.).
B: Confirmacio communis (rubric at top, red).
DESCRIPTION. *A*: 16·4″ (41·7 cm.), Top, 15·8″ (40 cm.), Bottom × 1′ (30·5 cm.), L, 1′ 0·3″ (31 cm.), R. Foot folded to a depth of 1·4″ (3·5 cm.). Double slits with tag 2·9″ (7·3 cm.) long, 0·5″ (1·3 cm.) wide. No seal remains.
HAND. Scribe Ae. A large, angular unattractive charter hand, on parchment producing a blotted effect. Ruled in pencil. Among the scribe's peculiarities are a tendency to make a terminal 'an' a monogram, and the use of an elaborate sign for 'est'. He has made several mistakes.
SOURCE. Original, SRO, GD 90/5 =*A*. SRO, GD 45/27/8 (St Andrews Priory Cartulary) fos.xcix[v] – ci[v]=*B*. *B* cannot be a copy of *A*. Printed here from *A*, with principal variants of *B* noted.
PRINTED. *St Andrews Liber*, 213–16 (from *B*).
NOTES. [a] Vill*elmu*s *B*, with large blue initial. [b] Forgrund, *B*. [c] Hadintuna, *B*. [d] Last two letters monogram in *A*. [e] *B* adds Decimam de coriis meis de Fif. [f] Linlithcu, *B*. [g] canoninorum, *A*. [h] Inuerkethin, *B*. [i] Melcrether, *B*. [j] eciam, *B*. [k] *B*'s variants of the names are as follows: Barrimonitht, Drumkarackin, Ledochin, Strathkines, Kininnis, Balhucca, Petulthin, Kinnamone, Drumsachc, Balemacdunegin, Eglesnamin, Balelothen, Kinninemoneth, Kilrimoneth (once), Puthekin. [l] Bladebobgschira, *A*; Bladebolg syra, *B*. [m] Portmoachc, *B*. [n] Sic, *A*. [o] Stermulin, *B*. [p] Turdapsche, *B*. [q] Inchethore, *B*. [r] Marchinche, *B*. [s] Ethouchle, *B*. [t] Sic, *A*; Nes, *B*. [u] Sic, *A*, *B*. [v] Karal, *B*. [w] Alano de Laceles, *B*. [x] Ohrm, *B*. [y] Malleuille, *B*. [z] uenanore, *A*. [aa] Simonis, *B*.
COMMENT. Probably issued soon after the king's inauguration.

29 Confirms to St Andrews Cathedral Priory the grants made to it by his mother the Countess Ada of one silver merk annually from Pitmilly in Crailshire for the work of the new church, and afterwards for lighting, and of one full toft in the burgh of Crail. Dunfermline. (1165 × 1172)

Willelmus[a] rex Scotorum Omnibus probis hominibus tocius terre sue clericis et laicis salutem . sciant presentes et futuri me concessisse et hac mea carta confirmasse Deo et ecclesie Sancti Andree apostoli in Scocia et canonicis ibidem Deo seruientibus donacionem quam Ada comitissa mater mea fecit eis de una marcha argenti singulis annis in perpetuam elemosinam in schira de Karel de Petmulin[b] ad operacionem noue ecclesie . et cum ecclesia perfecta fuerit ad luminare eiusdem ecclesie. Concedo eciam et confirmo eidem ecclesie et fratribus donacionem de uno tofto plenario in burgo de Karel .˙ quam mater mea fecit \eis/ pro anima patris mei comitis Henrici et pro animabus antecessorum nostrorum et successorum. Volo itaque et firmiter precipio ut predicti canonici prenominatas elemosinas teneant ita libere et quiete sicut carte matris mee testantur et confirmant et sicut alias elemosinas suas liberius et quiecius tenent in regno meo. Testibus Matheo archidiacono Sancti Andree . Comite Dunecano . Waltero filio Alani dapifero Nesio filio Willelmi . Waltero de Berkelei apud Dunfermelin .

RUBRIC. De marca (top in red).
SOURCE. SRO, GD 45/27/8 (St Andrews priory cartulary), fo.cv[r].
PRINTED. *St Andrews Liber*, 226.
NOTES. [a] Blue initial V. [b] Petmulin added in different ink, perhaps by a different hand.

COMMENT. The countess's charter of the toft in Crail is given in *St Andrews Liber*, 208. Her charter of the annual rent in Pitmilly, ibid., 209, seems to antedate her grant of land there (ibid., 208–9), and stipulates that the tenant, Malise of Pitmilly, shall pay the rent, and his successor in the estate after him.

30 Confirms the property and privileges of Dunfermline Abbey, adding to the gifts of previous kings 100s. from the *firma burgi* of Edinburgh, given on the day of King Malcolm IV's funeral, and 20 acres of arable and one toft in Dunfermline. St Andrews. (1165 × 23 September, 1168, probably *c*.1166)

In[a] nomine Sancte Trinitatis ego Willelmus[b] Dei gr*ati*a Rex Scottorum. auctoritate regia ac potestate . episcoporum . Comitum baronumque regni mei consensu atque testimonio . clero etiam adquiescente 7 populo . ecclesie Sancte Trinitatis Dunfermel' . predecessorum meorum pietatis studio 7 largitionis iniciate : omnia subscripta concedo . 7 pace perpetua confirmo. Attaui itaque mei Regis Malcolmi 7 Regine eiusdem bone memorie Margarite dona subsequencia propono . Hec scilicet . Pardusin . Pethnaurcha . Petbachlin . Pethcorthin . Lauer . Bolgin . Schyram de Kircalethin . Inueresc minorem. Dona[b] Duncani Regis : duas uillas nomine Luskar. De[c] dono Edgari Regis . Schyram de Gellald. De[b] dono Ethelredi . Hales. De[c] dono Alexandri Regis . Primros . Schyram de Gatemilc . Petconmarchin . Balekerin . Drumbernin . Keth. De[b] dono Sibille regine : Bééth. Hec[c] predicta predecessorum meorum dona concedo liberaliter prefate ecclesie cum omnibus apendiciis suis 7 rectis diuisis. De[b] dono aui mei excellentissimi Regis Dauid[c]:. Dunfermelin citra aquam . in qua eadem ecclesia sita est . Kingor*en* : cum suis apendiciis que propinquior est Dunfer*melin* . Foet . Inuiresch maiorem[d]. 7 molendinum 7 piscinam . 7 Smithebi . 7 Crebarrin . 7 ecclesiam de Inuiresc[d] . 7 Wymet . cum suis rectis diuisis . 7 Fotheros iuxta Sanctum Andream cum suis rectis diuisis . 7 Pethenach . cum suis rectis diuisis . 7 unam carucatam terre Petioker . 7 Nithbren cum suis apendiciis . 7 Balcristine cum suis rectis diuisis . in pratis 7 pascuis . excepta rectitudine quam keledei inde habere debent . cum omnibus rebus iuste ad eas pertinentibus . sicut date fuerunt predicte ecclesie in dotem ab auo meo rege Dauid : die qua dedicata fuit. Et preterea : unam mansuram in Berwich' . aliam in Rokesburg' . aliam in Hadingtun' . aliam in Edenburg . aliam in Linlithcu . aliam in Striuelin . 7 in eadem uilla duas ecclesias . 7 unam carucatam terre que adiacet ipsi ecclesie . 7 omnem decimam meorum dominiorum in frugibus 7 in animalibus . 7 in piscibus de propriis retibus 7 etiam in denariis . 7 decimam mei Can tocius castrensis prouincie . 7 mansiones Rogerii presbiteri . ita plene sicut ipse sanus 7 incolumis tenuit . 7 unum rete 7 dimidium . 7 unam mansionem in Burgo Dunfermel' . liberam et quietam . 7 omnem decimationem firme Burgi . 7 decimationem molendini 7 de omnibus dominiis meis de Dunfer*melin* . 7 unam mansionem in burgo de Perth . 7 ecclesiam eiusdem uille . 7 capellam de castello cum omnibus apendiciis utriusque . Et unam mansionem que pertinet ipsi ecclesie . 7 omnem decimam de dominio meo. Et omnem octauam partem de omnibus placitis 7 lucris meis de Fiif 7 de Fotherif . 7 omnem decimam de auro quod michi eueniet de Fif 7 de Fotherif . 7

omnem decimam tocius mei Can 7 brasei de Fif 7 de Foth*erif* . exceptis rectitudinibus que abbacie Dunkeld*ensi* pertinent. Et decimam omnium uenacionum que capiuntur inter Lambermor 7 Tay. Et medietatem omnium coriorum 7 seporum 7 sagiminis omnium bestiarum que occidentur ad festiuitates tenendas in Striuelin 7 inter Forth 7 Tay. Et ut habeant in nemoribus meis omnia necessaria ad ignem 7 ad edificia sua [sicut][e] ego ipse . 7 homines eorum sicut 7 [f] mei. Et ut omnes oblaciones que ad maius altare eiusdem ecclesie offerentur ·/ sine calumpnia liberaliter habeant. Et de Selichis que ad Kingorn' capientur postquam decimati fuerint ·/ omnes septimos Selichis habeant. Salis quoque 7 ferri que ad opus meum apud Dunfer*melin* allata fuerint ·/ omnem decimam concedo. Et parochiam totam Fothrif.[g] Et in Berewich tractum de Aldestelle . 7 omne quod ei iuste pertinet. Prohibeo etiam ne aliquod náám capiatur super terram uel super homines Sancte Trinitatis pro forisfacto alicuius ·/ nisi pro proprio forisfacto illorum. Concedo etiam quod iuste reddantur ecclesie Sancte Trinitatis ·/ omnes serui sui ·/ quos attauus meus 7 auus meus Dauid . 7 fratres sui ·/ ei dederunt . 7 omnes sui Cumerlaches a tempore Edgari Regis usque nunc . cum tota pecunia sua ubicumque inueniantur . 7 prohibeo super meum forisfactum ·/ ne iniuste retineantur . 7 ut habeant omnes homines cum omni pecunia eorum in cuiuscunque[h] terra fuerint . qui fuerunt in terris die qua fuerunt oblate 7 date ecclesie [Sancte][i] Trinitatis. Et decimam de omnibus meis siluestribus equabus de Fif 7 de Fothr*if*. Et ut habeant per totam terram meam theloneum quietum de cunctis rebus quas mercati fuerint ad propria eorum necessaria. Et passagium 7 nauem de Inuirket' . sicut habui in dominio meo . tali condicione quod peregrinantes 7 nuncii ad me uenientes 7 a me redeuntes . 7 homines curie mee transeant in eadem naui sine precio. Et si contingat aliquem istorum sine precio transire non posse . 7 abbas inde clamorem audierit 7 illud non emendauerit ·/ ego ipse illud emendabo sine abbatis 7 fratrum ecclesie molestia. Et abbas 7 monachi ecclesie Sancte Trinitatis non respondeant alicui calumpnianti de hominibus qui fuerunt in terris die qua oblate 7 date fuerunt ecclesie Sancte Trinitatis. Concedo etiam eidem ecclesie decimam tocius mei Can de Clacm*anan*. Et ut citra Lambermor in tota regia potestate singulis sabbatis in curia habeant unum corium . 7 in Sexto sabbato duo coria. Et duas partes de sepo . 7 Sextam pellem arietum 7 agnorum . 7 dimidiam partem decimi mei de Ærgaithel 7 Kentir. Et quandam piscaturam apud Perth . ita libere 7 quiete ·/ sicut meas ibi habeo. De[c] dono Regis Malcolmi fratris mei ·/ Ledmacduuegil cum suis rectis diuisis . sicut magister Ælricus cementarius illam tenuit . quam in die sepulture predicti aui mei eidem ecclesie obtulit . 7 .xx^{ti}iii^{a} . iugera terre . 7 quoddam pratum prope Dunfer*melin* . que prius in dominio suo habuit. Et quodcumque cete ex parte Scocie applicuerit . siue captum fuerit ·/ totum capud preter linguam eidem ecclesie remaneat . 7 dimidietatem tocius sagiminis mei omnium cetuum que capiuntur inter Forth 7 Thay ad luminaria coram altaribus ecclesie. Et omnes homines eorum sint liberi ab omni operacione poncium 7 castellorum . 7 omnium aliorum operum. Et ecclesiam Sancte Trinitatis de Dunkeld' ·/ cum terris ad illam pertinentibus . 7 cum omnibus aliis rectis pertinenciis suis . optinendam in perpetuam elemosinam post decessum Andréé episcopi Katinens*is* . pro salute anime méé . 7 omnium predecessorum meorum . cum omni libertate 7 rectitudine cum quibus idem episcopus eam unquam melius tenuit .' et[j] dono Regis D*aui*d .' possedit. Et unum Toft*um* in Edenburg' . quod Rob*ertus* de Londoniis habuit. Et unum plenarium toft*um* cum croft*o* in villa de Clacman*an*. Et ecclesiam de Kellin . et capellam de Abercrumbi . cum omnibus ad eas iuste pertinentibus. Ex[b] dono uero meo proprio .' Redditum Centum solidorum de firma burgi de Edenburg' . quos dedi in die exequiarum fratris mei Regis Malcolmi. Et .xx. acras terre. Et unum toft*um* in Dunfer*melin* . quas Walterus dapifer meus concessione mea dedit eidem ecclesie .' die sepulture Regis predicti. Omnia autem sicut prenotata sunt . que a bonis antecessoribus meis scilicet Rege Malcolmo . 7 Regina eiusdem bone memorie Margarita . Duncano Rege . Ædgaro rege . Æthelredo fratre eius . Alexandro Rege . Sibilla regina eiusdem . Dauid Rege excellentissimo . Malcolmo Rege . ecclesie Trinitatis de Dunfer*melin* data . concessa sunt 7 confirmata . sicut in autenticis eorum scriptis continetur . cum omni illa plenitudine 7 integritate regia auctoritate . consilio proborum hominum meorum . predicte ecclesie 7 fratribus ibidem Deo seruientibus .' concedo . 7 in perpetuum integra 7 illibata conseruanda confirmo. Testibus hiis D*aui*d fratre Regis . Nich*olao* cancell*ario* . Duncano comite . Dauid Olif*ard* . Philippo de Vallon*iis* . Ric*ardo* de Warewich[k] . Willelmo de la Haya . Nesio fil*io* Will*elmi* . Rob*erto* de Quinci . Jordano Ridel . Radulpho de Cler . Rad*ulpho* Malchael . Gillecrist mac Samuel . Galfrido de Maleuill' . Waltero de Berkelai. Apud Sanctum Andream.

RUBRIC. Confirmacio Willelmi Regis (red with blue initial).
SOURCE. NLS, MS. Adv. 34.1.3a, fo.xiiii^{r-v}.
PRINTED. *Dunfermline Registrum*, no.50.
NOTES. [a] Large blue initial. [b] Red initial. [c] Blue initial. [d] Muskilburg written above in hand of text. [e] Sicut wrongly placed after homines eorum sicut 7. [f] MS. has a superfluous 7. [g] In margin in xiii cent. hand supra parochiam de Fother'. [h] Fo.xiiii^{v}. [i] MS. omits. [j] Altered from ex. [k] Apparently a miscopying of Morewill'.
COMMENT. Probably issued soon after the king's accession.

31 Commands that wherever the monks of Dunfermline Abbey or their sergeands may find their *cumerbae* and *cumerlachi* they are to have them justly; no one is to detain them or their cattle unjustly, on pain of the king's full forfeiture. St Andrews. (1165 × 1171)

Will'[a] Rex Scott' omnibus probis hominibus tocius terre sue salutem. Precipio firmiter ut ubicunque monachi de Dunfer*melin* aut seruientes eorum cumerbas 7 cumerlachos suos inuenire poterint .' eos iuste habeant . 7 prohibeo firmiter ne quis eis quemquam de illis aut pecuniam eorum iniuste detineat .' super meum plenarium forisfactum. T*estibus* Nich*olao* cancell*ario* . Galfrido de Malauill'. Apud Sanctum Andream.

RUBRIC. De fugitiuis qui uocantur cumerlaches (red with blue initial).
SOURCE. NLS, MS. Adv. 34.1.3a, fo.xiii^{r}.
PRINTED. *Dunfermline Registrum*, no.68.
NOTE. [a] Initial red.
COMMENT. Cp. *RRS*, i, no.118; and see ibid., pp.62–4.

32 Confirms to St Andrews Cathedral Priory one full toft in his burgh of Berwick, as the charter of King David I bears witness. St Andrews. (1165 × 1171)

Willelmus[a] rex Scotorum . Omnibus probis hominibus tocius terre sue salutem . Sciatis me concessisse et hac carta mea confirmasse Deo et ecclesie Sancti Andree et canonicis ibidem Deo seruientibus in liberam et perpetuam elemosinam unum plenarium toftum in burgo meo de Berewic tenendum ita libere et quiete et honorifice ab omni seruicio et consuetudine sicut aliqua elemosina in tota terra . liberior et quiecior est. Volo eciam ut homines qui in illo tofto manserint iuste meam firmam pacem habeant et quieti sint ab omni exaccione et consuetudine et teloneo et omnibus aliis rebus sicut alii burgenses sunt de aliis meis elemosinis et sicut carta . Regis Dauid testatur aui mei et confirmat . prohibeo eciam[b] ne quis eis iniuriam[c] aliquam faciat super meam defensionem Testibus . Nicholao cancellario . Ricardo de Moreuill' const*abulario* . Matheo archidiacono Sancti Andree . Waltero filio Alani dapifero . D*aui*d Olifard . Justic' . Nessio filio Willelmi apud Sanctum Andream.

RUBRIC. De tofto in B[erewic][d] (top in red).
SOURCE. SRO, GD 45/27/8 (St Andrews priory cartulary), fo.ciii^r.
PRINTED. *St Andrews Liber*, 221.
NOTES. [a] Red initial U. [b] q expunged. [c] fiaciat expunged. [d] MS. has only B'.
COMMENT. King David's charter is given in Lawrie, *Charters*, no.226; see also *RRS*, i, no.174.

33 Confirms to St Andrews Cathedral Priory the abbey of Loch Leven, as the charter of Richard bishop of St Andrews bears witness. St Andrews. (1165 × 1171)

Willelmus[a] rex Scotorum . Omnibus probis hominibus tocius terre sue clericis et laicis salutem . Sciant presentes et futuri me concessisse et hac carta mea confirmasse Deo et ecclesie Sancti Andree et canonicis ibidem Deo seruientibus abbaciam de Louleuen cum terris et redditibus et cum omnibus ad eam iuste pertinentibus tenendam ita libere et quiete et plenarie sicut carta Ricardi episcopi Sancti Andree testatur et confirmat . Testibus . Nicholao cancellario . Comite Dunecano . D*aui*d Olifard . Filippo de Valonis . Willelmo de Haia apud Sanctum Andream .

RUBRIC. De Lochl*euen* (top in red).
SOURCE. SRO, GD 45/27/8 (St Andrews priory cartulary), fo.cii^v.
PRINTED. *St Andrews Liber*, 219–20.
NOTE. [a] Blue initial V.
COMMENT. Bishop Richard's charter does not seem to have survived, but the grant by Bishop Robert (1152 × 1159) is given in *St Andrews Liber*, 43.

34 Confirms to Dunfermline Abbey the bequest made by his brother King Malcolm IV, viz. 100s. a year from the *firma burgi* of Edinburgh until the king can provide this revenue from elsewhere; and also grants and confirms for his brother's soul 20 acres of arable and one toft in Dunfermline, granted by Walter son of Alan the steward on the day when King Malcolm was buried at Dunfermline Abbey. Kinghorn. (1165 × 1172, probably 1165 or early 1166)

Will'[a] Rex Scott' . episcopis . abbatibus . Comitibus . Baronibus Justic*iis* . vicecomitibus . prepositis . ministris . ceterisque probis hominibus suis uniuersis salutem. Sciant clerici 7 laici presentes 7 posteri me in liberam elemosinam concessisse 7 confirmasse Deo 7 ecclesie Sancte Trinitatis de Dunfer*melin* 7 monachis ibidem Deo seruientibus diuisam illam quam Rex Malcolmus frater meus eidem ecclesie fecit . *scilicet* redditum .C. solidorum habendum sibi singulis annis de firma burgi mei de Edenburg' . quousque eundem redditum prefate ecclesie aliunde reddendum constituam. Preterea concedo eidem ecclesie pro anima fratris mei .xx. acras terre . 7 unum toft*um* in Dunfer*melin* liberas 7 quietas sicuti ceteras possessiones suas liberius 7 quiecius tenet . quas Walterus fil*ius* Alani dapifer meus prefate ecclesie dedit ea die qua Rex Malcolmus frater meus ibidem sepultus fuit. T*estibus* Andr*ea* episcopo Kat' . Matheo archidiac*ono* . Ric*ardo* cappellano[b]. Waltero fil*io* Alani . D*aui*d Olifard . Philippo de Vallon*iis* . Bern*ardo* filio Briani . Walt*ero* de Berkelai . 7 Rob*erto* de Berkelai . Rob*erto* filio Saul*fi*. Apud Kingorn'.

RUBRIC. De .c. sol*idis* de Edenburg' (red).
SOURCE. NLS, MS. Adv. 34.1.3a, fo.xii[r].
PRINTED. *Dunfermline Registrum*, no.52.
NOTES. [a] Initial red. [b] Sic.
COMMENT. The contents, and the statement in no.30, suggest an early date. The toft granted by Walter the Steward was no doubt one of those given to him by King Malcolm (*RRS*, i, no.184).

35 Announces the settlement in his presence of a dispute between Dunfermline Abbey and the canons of St Andrews Cathedral Priory anent the land of Balchristie (in Newburn, Fife), to which the canons put forward a claim from King David I's time, as representing the *célidé* (of Loch Leven). The abbey is to have the land, saving the revenue which the *célidé* used to have from that land under David I, which is to be paid by the abbey to St Andrews Priory. Kinghorn. (1165 × 1171)

Will'[a] Rex Scott' omnibus probis hominibus tocius terre sue salutem. Sciatis quod controuersia que uersabatur inter monachos de Dunfer*melin* 7 Canonicos de Sancto Andrea super terra de Balcristin in qua canonici de Sancto Andrea ius clamabant per keledeos de tempore Regis D*aui*d aui mei in presencia mea terminata est . ita quod monachi terram illam habeant . salua elemosina ipsis canonicis ab ipsis monachis de Dunfer*melin* quam keledei habuerunt de terra illa tempore Regis D*aui*d. T*estibus* Nich*olao* cancell*ario* . Ric*ardo* de Moreuill' constabul*ario* . Walt*ero* fil*io* Alani dapifero . D*aui*d Olifard' just*icia* . Hug*one* Ridel . Matheo archid*iacono* . Nesio fil*io* Will*elmi* . Rob*erto* de Berkel' . Galfrido de Maleuill'. Apud King*orn*.

RUBRIC. De controuersia de Balcristin (red with blue initial).
SOURCE. NLS, MS. Adv. 34.1.3a, fo.xii[v].
PRINTED. *Dunfermline Registrum*, no.59.
NOTE. [a] Initial red.
COMMENT. Newburn and Balchristie, 'saving the revenue which the *célidé* ought to have there', had been granted to Dunfermline by David I (Lawrie,

Charters, no.209; cp. ibid., nos.8 and 263, the latter shewing that the revenue which the *célidé* had from Balchristie was twenty measures of barley).

36 Confirms to Cambuskenneth Abbey the church of St Ninians, Stirlingshire, to be held as the charter of Richard bishop of St Andrews grants and confirms it; and the toun of St Ninians likewise. Kinghorn. (1165 × 1171)

Wilelmus[a] rex Scotorum omnibus probis hominibus tocius regni sui salutem. Sciatis me concessisse et hac carta mea confirmasse Deo et ecclesie Sancte Marie de Striueling et canonicis ibidem Deo seruientibus ecclesiam de Egglis tam in capellis et decimis quam in ceteris ecclesiasticis beneficiis in perpetuam elemosinam; tenendam adeo libere et quiete et honorifice sicut carta Richardi episcopi Sanctiandree eis donat et concedit;[b] et villam de Egglis cum suis rectis diuisis, in bosco et plano et pascuis et omnibus iustis pertinenciis, sicut carta episcopi eis donat et concedit.[b] Testibus, Richardo[c] cancellario, Dauid Olifardo, Philippo de Valoniis camerario, Roberto de Quinci, apud Kingorne.

RUBRIC. Donatio ecclesie de Kirketoun (at top). concordat cum principali Jacobus Foulis (at end).
SOURCE. NLS, MS. Adv. 34.1.2, fo.72v.
PRINTED. *Cambuskenneth Registrum*, no.113.
NOTES. [a] Large blue initial U. [b] MS. concedat. [c] Sic, for Nicholao.
COMMENT. Bishop Richard's charter is given in *Cambuskenneth Registrum*, no.112. The original grant of St Ninians had been made to William, first abbot of Cambuskenneth, by Bishop Robert (d. 1159), or by him in conjunction with one of the kings, David I or Malcolm IV (ibid., no.109 and pp.40, 44). The name Egglis and its variants for St Ninians (Primitive Cumbric, *eglēs?) suggests a very early date for the foundation of this important mother church, whose *parochia* at one time embraced Stirling itself as well as Dunipace and Larbert. This suggestion is strengthened by the use during the medieval period of the name Kirkton for the parish, as though it were the 'kirkton' *par excellence*.

37 Confirms to St Andrews Cathedral Priory the grant made by Richard bishop of St Andrews of the offerings of Whitsun processions throughout the diocese. Edinburgh. (1166 × 1168)

Willelmus[a] rex Scotorum . episcopis . abbatibus . Comitibus . baronibus . Justiciis . et omnibus probis hominibus tocius terre sue clericis et laicis salutem . Sciant presentes et futuri me concessisse et hac carta mea confirmasse Deo et ecclesie Sancti Andree et canonicis ibidem Deo seruientibus donacionem quam Ricardus episcopus Sancti Andree eis[b] fecit de oblacione processionum pentechostalium tocius dyocesis sue tenend*am* in perpetuam elemosinam ita libere et quiete sicut carta ipsius episcopi testatur et confirmat . Testibus . Ricardo episcopo Sancti Andree . Eng*elramo* episcopo de Glasgu . Nicholao cancellario . W*illelmo* abbate de Sancta Cruce . Comite Wald*ef* . Comite Dunecano . D*auid* Olif*ard* Justic' . Waltero filio Alani dapifero Nes filio Willelmi . Radul*fo* Malcheel . Alano filio Simonis apud Castellum Puellarum .

RUBRIC. De process' pent' (margin, in later hand).
SOURCE. SRO, GD 45/27/8 (St Andrews priory cartulary), fo.civ.
PRINTED. *St Andrews Liber*, 217–18.
NOTES. [a] Bluc initial V. [b] dedit expunged.
COMMENT. Bishop Richard's charter is given in *St Andrews Liber*, 133. Ralph

Malchael was killed 'through the treachery of the Scots' on 23 September, 1168 (*Chron. Holyrood*, 150–1). A Ralph Malcael figures on the Norman exchequer roll for 1180 (Stapleton, *Rot. Scacc. Norm.*, i, 35); a family bearing this name were established at Crackenthorpe, Westmorland, in the first half of the twelfth century, one of whom, Humphrey Malchael, was among those punished for surrendering Appleby Castle to William I in 1174 (*Pipe Roll*, 22 *Henry I*, 119; see also Dugdale, *Mon. Angl.* (New), vi, 144, and E. Bellais, 'The Machells of Crackenthorpe', in *CWAAS Trans.*, viii, 416ff.).

38 Commands that Dunfermline Abbey shall have all its lands by the marches by which it held them in the time of King David I, unless it has sold, granted away or exchanged them. Edinburgh. (1165 × 1171)

Will'[a] Rex Scott' . Comiti Duncan*o* 7 Justiciis 7 vicecomitibus suis de Fif 7 Fotherif salutem. Precipio firmiter ut ecclesia Sancte Trinitatis de Dunfer*melin* 7 abbas 7 monachi eiusdem loci habeant omnes terras suas per easdem diuisas . per quas tenuerunt temporibus Regis D*aui*d aui mei . nisi forte eas uel uendiderint uel donauerint uel commutauerint. Et prohibeo firmiter ne quis eis de terris suis aliquid iniuste recindat super meum forisfactum. T*estibus* Nichol*ao* cancell*ario* . Matheo Archid*iacono* . Walt*ero* fil*io* Alani dapifero . Ric*ardo* Cumin. Apud Edenburg'.

RUBRIC. De proteccione (red with red initial).
SOURCE. NLS, MS. Adv. 34.1.3a, fo.xii^{v}.
PRINTED. *Dunfermline Registrum*, no.56.
NOTE. [a] Initial blue.

39 Confirms the privileges and possessions of Holyrood Abbey; in particular, by the gift of King David I: the church of Edinburgh castle, with Saughton; the church of St Cuthbert; Broughton; Inverleith nearer the harbour; the land on which the abbey is built with that part of Arthur's Seat belonging to it; 40s. a year and a full toft in the burgh of Edinburgh; the right to build a burgh between Edinburgh and the abbey; one toft in Stirling and the draught of one net there; the church of Airth, with land in Airth perambulated and handed over to Abbot Alwin by Gilbert sheriff of Stirlingshire; one saltpan in Airth with 27 acres of land; the right to take wood for their needs in the king's own wood of Airth; the right to pasture their swine without payment of pannage; one toft in Linlithgow; one toft in Renfrew with salmon fishing; Pittendriech (in Lasswade, Midlothian); Whitekirk (East Lothian), and Ford, and the church of Whitekirk; one toft in Berwick and the draught of two nets in 'Scypwel'; half the tallow and grease and hides of all the beasts slaughtered for the king at Edinburgh; the tenth of all the king's judicial revenues (*placita*) between the River Avon and Cockburnspath; half the tenth part of the cain of Kintyre and of Argyll and the same fraction of the king's judicial revenues from those districts; all the skins of rams, ewes and lambs which die in the royal demesne of Edinburgh and Linlithgow; one of the king's mills of Dean and the teind of his mills of Dean and Liberton; eight chalders of malt and eight chalders of meal from the royal demesne of Liberton, and thirty cartloads of brushwood; the privilege that no one may take anything from any man of the abbot travelling on the highway on account of any injury or

claim save for theft and bloodshed, until he has first complained to the abbot, whereupon the abbot shall do justice upon his man on behalf of the pursuer, and if the abbot fails in this the king's sheriff and justice shall do justice (upon the wrongdoer); and the privilege that no one shall take poinds from the land of Holyrood unless the abbot has denied him right; and that the abbey shall be free from toll on its own goods throughout the realm; and no one is to detain unjustly neyfs or fugitives of the church. By the gift of King Malcolm IV: the churches of Tranent (E. Lothian), Bathgate, Livingston, Kinneil, Carriden (W. Lothian), Great Paxton (Huntingdonshire), and Crawford (Lanarkshire). By the gift of Fergus lord of Galloway Dunrod with its church, and the Isle of Trail (St Mary's Isle) with the land of 'Galtweied' (later Galtway, in Kirkcudbright). By the gift of Uchtred lord of Galloway the church of Kirkcudbright (St Cuthbert of Desnesmor) and the church of Tongland. One toft in Inverkeithing and one toft in Haddington. By the gift of Philip de Vermelles one ploughgate of land and pasture for 1,000 sheep in Romanno (Peeblesshire). Edinburgh. (1165 × 1170, probably 1165 or 1166)

Will*elmus* Dei gr*ati*a rex Scottorum . Episcopis . Abbatibus . Comitibus . Justiciis . Uicecomitibus . Ministris . 7 omnibus probis hominibus tocius regni sui . Francis . Anglis . Scottis . Galuuens*ibus* . tam futuris quam presentibus . Salutem. Ex officio suscepte a Deo regni administrationis ;' incumbit nobis non solum ecclesias 7 ecclesiasticas personas diligere . 7 honorare ;' uerumetiam elemosinas 7 beneficia ad eorum sustentationem impendere . 7 ea que ab antecessoribus nostris 7 ab aliis Dei fidelibus eis collata sunt tueri . concedere 7 confirmare. Unde 7 dignum duxi . omnia sicut subscripta sunt . que ab omnibus antecessoribus meis scilicet rege Dauid . 7 dilecto fratre meo rege Malcolmo . 7 ab aliis Dei fidelibus ecclesie Sancte Crucis de Edenesburch . 7 canonicis eiusdem loci data sunt concessa . aut confirmata . sicut in autenticis eorum scriptis cum omni illa plenitudine 7 integritate continetur ;' regia auctoritate consilio proborum hominum meorum predicte ecclesie 7 fratribus concedere 7 confirmare. In primis ;' de dono regis D*aui*d aui mei . Ecclesiam castelli cum Salectuna per rectas diuisas suas . 7 cum ceteris appenticiis eidem ecclesie pertinentibus. Et ecclesiam Sancti Cutberti cum parrochia 7 omnibus que eidem ecclesie pertinent . 7 Broctunam cum suis rectis diuisis . 7 Inverleth . illam uidelicet que propinquior est portui cum suis rectis diuisis . 7 medietatem piscationis . 7 terram illam in qua abbatia sita est . cum parte Cragge que ad eam pertinet. Et quadraginta solidos de burgo meo . de Edenesburch . et unum plenarium toftum in eodem burgo. Et inter burgum 7 abbatiam herbergare quoddam burgum . concedendo burgensibus eiusdem burgi meliores custumas quas habet aliqua ecclesia in terra mea. Et unum toftum in Striuelin . 7 unius retis tractum ad piscandum. Et ecclesiam de Heret cum parrochia 7 omnibus que eidem ecclesie pertinent . 7 terram in eadem Heret eisdem diuisis quibus Gillebertus uicecomes 7 alii ministri de Striuelinschire perambulauerunt 7 tradiderunt Alwino abbati . 7 in eadem uilla unam salinam cum uiginti septem acris. Et in bosco dominico meo ibi eis necessaria sumere concedo . ubi ad mea propria negotia necessaria sumuntur. Et porcos dominicos eiusdem ecclesie concedo ibi esse quietos de padnagio. Et unum toftum in Linlitcu. Et unum toftum in Rinfriu quinque perticarum . 7 piscationem de salmonibus[a]. Et Pethendreiam cum suis rectis diuisis. Et Hameram 7 Fordam cum suis rectis diuisis . Et ecclesiam eiusdem uille . cum omnibus que ad eam pertinent . sicut karta Rodberti episcopi de Sancto ANDReA testatur. Et unum toftum in Berewic . 7 tractum duorum retium in Scypwel. Et medietatem sepi 7 uncti 7 coriorum de occisione de Edenesburch. Et decimam omnium placitorum meorum ab Auin flumine . usque Colbrandespeth. Et medietatem decime de Cano de Chentyr . 7 de Erregail. Et medietatem decime de eisdem locis placitorum meorum . 7 omnes pelles arietinas . 7 ouinas . 7 agninas . de Castello Puellarum . 7 de Linlitcu que moriuntur de meo dominio. Et unum de meis molendinis de Dene . 7 decimam de meis molendinis de Dene . 7 de Libertuna . 7 octo celdras de brasio . 7 octo farine . de dominio de Libertuna . & triginta caretas de busche. Et quod nullus capiat aliquem de hominibus abbatis eiusdem ecclesie errantem per uiam pro aliquo forisfacto . uel pro aliqua calumpnia . excepto Latrocinio . 7 effusione sanguinis . antequam cum abbate prius inde loquatur . 7 requirat . 7 abbas faciat plenum rectum calumpnianti de homine suo . 7 si abbas ei a recto deficiat . tunc uicecomes 7 Justicia faciant ei rectum secundum quod calumpnians hominem abbatis iuste calumpniauerit. Et ne quis capiat pandum super terram Sancte Crucis . nisi abbas rectum 7 ius facere recusauerit. Et ut quieti sint de theloneo . 7 de omni consuetudine . de propriis catellis[b] per totam terram meam. Et ut nullus retineat natiuos aut fugitiuos eiusdem ecclesie super meam plenariam forisfacturam. De dono 7 concessione 7 confirmatione fratris mei regis Malcolmi ecclesiam de Trauernent ad indumenta canonicorum . cum terris & decimis . & omnibus appenticiis 7 rectitudinibus suis . sicut unquam Walerannus meliu\s/ eam 7 plenius tenuit . tempore regis D*aui*d aui mei. Et ecclesiam de Batchet cum terra illa quam Galfridus de MaleuiN . 7 Uctred uicecomes de Linlitcu perambulauerunt. Et ecclesiam de uilla Leuing cum dimidia carrucata terre . & ceteris que ad eam pertinent. Et ecclesiam de Kinel cum carrucata terre . 7 omnibus eius pertinentiis . sicut Herbertus camerarius eam dedit . concedentibus filiis suis . Stephano . 7 Willelmo. Et ecclesiam de Kerreden . cum terris 7 libertatibus ad eandem ecclesiam pertinentibus. Et ecclesiam de Paxstuna . cum omnibus pertinentiis 7 libertatibus que ecclesie predicte iuste pertinent. Et ecclesiam de Crauford cum duabus carrucatis terre . 7 omnibus rectitudinibus suis. Et de dono Fergus . Dunroden . cum ecclesia 7 omnibus appenticiis suis . 7 insulam Trail . cum terra de Galtweied per rectas diuisas. Et de dono Uctredi ecclesiam Sancti Cutberti de Desenesmor . Et ecclesiam de Tungeland . cum decimis 7 piscationibus . 7 omnibus rectitudinibus eisdem ecclesiis iuste pertinentibus. Et unum toftum in InverchethiN. Et unum in HadigtuN. Et de dono Philippi de Euermele unam carrucatam terre . 7 pasturam mille ouium in Rumanach. Uolo autem ut omnia prescripta ita liberaliter & quiete teneat . sicut aliqua ecclesia uel abbatia in toto regno meo liberius & quietius res suas possidet. His testibus . Nicholao cancellario . Matheo archidiacono . Osberto abbate de Jedeuurde . Ricardo capellano regis . Ada comitissa . Waltero filio Alani . Ricardo de Moreuila . Roberto de Quinci . Philippo de Valuines . Ricardo CumiN . Bernardo filio BrieN . Willelmo Carpentario . Gilleberto de Umframuill*a* . Willelmo de Aldri . Galfrido de MaleuiN . Serlone de Edenesburch . Rodberto Janitore castelli . Rodberto 7 Waltero de Berchelai. Apud EdeNesbVRch.[c]

ENDORSED. Confirmacio Regis Will*elmi* super prima fundacione (xiii–xiv cent.). 2 (medieval?). Also modern endorsements, including lengthy abstract of contents (xvii–xviii cent.).
DESCRIPTION. 1′ 0·5″ (31 cm.), Top, 1′ 0·3″ (31 cm.), Bottom × 1′ (30·5 cm.), L, R. Foot folded to a depth of 1·2″ (3 cm.). Single slit with tag 1′ (30·5 cm.) long, 0·9″ (2·3 cm.) wide, made from parchment twice as wide and folded vertically. Seal complete in green wax, fair impression.
HAND. Scribe Ad. This is the same hand as that of BM, Harley Charters 111. B 14, a charter for Holyrood by Richard bishop of St Andrews whose date is given in the charter as Berwick, A.D. 1166 (cf. *Holyrood Liber*, Appendix II, no.4). Ruled in ink.
SOURCE. Original, Edinburgh City Archives, Royal Charters no.2.
PRINTED. *Holyrood Liber*, no.27.
NOTES. [a] Written salmonis, but cp. onis for omnibus in line 3 of original. [b] Sic. [c] Name extended almost to complete the line, with a mixture of minuscule and rustic capital forms.
COMMENT. For 'Cragge' meaning Arthur's Seat, cf. *Book of the Old Edinburgh Club*, XXX (1959), 1–9. Hamera or Hamere was the older name of Whitekirk in East Lothian, and Ford was evidently the name of land in this parish. For Holyrood Abbey's possession of Great Paxton, cf. *RRS*, i, no.197. The tofts in Haddington and Inverkeithing should have been listed as the gifts of the Countess Ada and King Malcolm IV respectively: cf. ibid., nos.231–2. King David I's great charter of confirmation to Holyrood is printed in Lawrie, *Charters*, no.153.

40 Confirms to Holyrood Abbey the church of Tranent (East Lothian), granted by King Malcolm IV to provide clothing for the canons. No place-date. (1165 × 1170, probably 1165 or 1166)

Will*elmu*s Dei gr*ati*a Rex Scott' . Episcopis . Abbatibus . Comitibus . Baronibus . Just*iciis* . Vicecomitibus . 7 omnibus suis probis hominibus tam futuris quam presentibus salutem. Sciatis me concessisse 7 hac mea carta confirmasse ecclesie Sancte CRVcis que est iuxta Edenesburch 7 fratribus ibidem Deo seruientibus . Ecclesiam de Treuernent . quam eis Malcolmus Rex frater meus ad indumenta eorum dedit in perpetuam elemosinam . 7 carta sua confirmauit . cum omnibus pertinentiis 7 libertatibus que predicte ecclesie iuste pertinent[a]. terris uidelicet 7 aquis . pascuis 7 pratis . bosco 7 plano . ita liberam 7 quietam ut aliqua elemosina in tota terra mea liberius 7 quietius possidetur . 7 sicut Walerannus capellanus D*aui*d Regis eam melius unquam 7 liberius tenuit. His testibus . Nicholao cancellario . Ricardo capellano Regis . Waltero dapifero . Ricardo de Moreuila . D*aui*d Olifiard[b].

ENDORSED. Confirmatio regis Willelmi de Trauernent (xii cent.). Rex (xv cent.?).
DESCRIPTION. 7·3″ (18·6 cm.), Top, 7·4″ (18·7 cm.), Bottom × 4·2″ (10·6 cm.), L, R. Foot folded to a depth of 0·5″ (1·3 cm.). Single slits, with tag 5·3″ (13·3 cm.) long, 0·4″ (1 cm.) wide. No seal, but traces of pink wax remain on tag.
HAND. *A*: Scribe Ah. Ruled in drypoint. *B*: A clever but not very exact copy of *A*, the hand sloping slightly forward and failing to space adequately.

SOURCE. Original, SRO, GD 45/13/240=*A*. Modern copy, SRO, GD 90/3=*B*. Printed here from *A*.
PRINTED. *Holyrood Liber*, no.35 (from *A*).
NOTES. [a] For last five words *B* has ei ecclesie iuste pertinentibus. [b] Scribe of *A* started to write Oliu, his correction producing an ill-written Olifiard. *B* has Olifiard written deliberately, pointing to the work of a slavish imitator.
COMMENT. For date, see note to no.41.

41 Confirms to Holyrood Abbey the church of Great Paxton (Huntingdonshire) granted by King Malcolm IV. No place-date. (1165 × 1166)

. Will*elmus*[a] rex Scott'. Episcopo Lincolniensi 7 uniuersis sancte matris ecclesie filiis . clericis 7 laicis tam futuris quam presentibus totius comitatus de Huntedunia :' salutem. Sciatis me concessise[b] 7 hac mea carta confirmasse ecclesie Sancte Crucis que est iuxta Edenesburc . 7 fratribus ibidem Deo seruientibus . Ecclesiam de Pacstonia quam eis Malcolmus Rex frater meus dedit in perpetuam elemosinam . cum omnibus pertinentiis 7 libertatibus que ecclesie predicte iuste pertinent . terris uidelicet 7 aquis . pascuis 7 pratis . bosco 7 plano . ita liberam 7 quietam ut aliqua elemosina in tota terra mea liberius 7 quietius possidetur. His testibus . Nicholao cancellario . Ricardo capellano regis . Waltero dapifero . Ricardo de Moreuil' . Dauid Olifard.

ENDORSED. De Paxtunia (xii cent.). Secunda (xiv cent.). Willelmus Rex Scotorum Paxton (xviii cent.). Also modern endorsements.
DESCRIPTION. 7·1″ (18 cm.), Top and bottom × 4·3″ (10·9 cm.), L, R. Torn and fragile along folds, and the whole document has been backed with a very thin vellum. Foot folded, slits for seal tag, 0·6″ wide. No seal or tag remains.
HAND. Scribe Ah. This is the same hand as that of D. & C. Lincoln, D ij 90/3/19, facsimile in *RAL*, iii, facing p.156, printed ibid. no.805.
SOURCE. Original, Lincoln, D. & C. Muniments, D ij 90/3/23=*A*. Lincoln, D. & C. Muniments, MS. 'Registrum', no.283=*B*. Printed here from *A*.
PRINTED. *RAL*, iii, no.809, with facsimile facing, Pl.III.
NOTES. [a] Written Wills, with mark of suspension through ll. [b] Sic.
COMMENT. This charter was issued on the same occasion as no.40 (*Holyrood Liber*, no.35). It is in the same hand, has the same witnesses in the same order, and is written on a piece of parchment almost the same size as no.40. Bishop Robert de Chesney of Lincoln died 27 December, 1166, the see being then vacant until 1173.

42 Re-grants to Walter, son of the chamberlain Philip, Lundin in Fife, to be held in feu and heritage, for the service of one knight, as freely as the king's other knights hold their feus in the kingdom of Scotland, and as the charter of King Malcolm IV bears witness. Edinburgh. (1166 × 1171)

W'. Rex Scott' Episcopis . abbatibus . Comitibus . Baronibus . Justic*iis* . Vice*comitibus* 7 Omnibus probis hominibus tocius terre sue salutem. Sciant presentes 7 posteri me dedisse 7 concessisse 7 hac carta mea confirmasse Waltero filio Philippi camerarii Lundin in Fif cum omnibus iustis pertinenciis suis per rectas diuisas suas . Tenend*um* sibi 7 heredibus suis de me 7 heredibus meis in feudo 7 hereditate libere 7 quiete plenarie 7 honorifice cum cum[a] omnibus libertatibus 7 rectitudinibus ad idem feudum pertinentibus in bosco 7 plano in pratis 7 pascuis in terris 7 aquis in campis 7 moris 7 in omnibus aliis rectis pertinenciis suis per seruicium unius militis. Quare uolo 7 firmiter precipio ut predictus Walterus 7 heredes sui predictum feudum teneant de me 7 heredibus meis ita libere 7 quiete sicut alii milites mei liberius 7 quiecius feuda sua de me tenent in regno Scocie . sicut carta Reg*is* M. fratris mei testatur 7 confirmat. Test*ibus* Eng*elramo* episcopo de Glasgu . Nic*holao* cancell*ario* . Com*ite* Wald*euo* . Com*ite* Dunec*ano* . Ric*ardo* de Moruill' constabulario . Waltero filio Alani dapifero . Roberto Auenel . Willelmo de Mortem*er* . Rad*ulfo* de Clere . Waltero de Berkelai . Ric*ardo* clerico. Apud Castellum puellarum.

ENDORSED. Charter gevin be King William to Walter sone to Philip chalmerlane of the lands of Lundin in Fyff not Datit (xvi–xvii cent.). Also a modern endorsement.
DESCRIPTION. 5″ (12·6 cm.), Top 5·6″ (14·3 cm.), Bottom × 4·1″ (10·5 cm.), L, 4·8″ (12 cm.), R. Foot has been folded, with slits for seal-tag. Parchment thin and of poor quality, possibly kept in unsatisfactory conditions and now very soft and worn. No tag or seal remains.
HAND. Scribe Aj (Richard of Lincoln). Unruled.
SOURCE. Original, SRO, Drummond Castle Muniments (Lundin Charters) = *A*. NLS, MS. Adv. 29.4.2, vol.vi, fo.11, copy by Mr Dillon from original then in possession of Lord Perth = *B*. Printed here from *A*.
PRINTED. SHS, *Miscellany*, iv, 306–7, no.2, from a transcript of Sir William Fraser.
NOTE. [a] Sic, the second cum commencing a new line.
COMMENT. King Malcolm's charter to Philip, Walter's father, is *RRS*, i, no.255.

43 Grants to Henry, son of Gregory the clerk, Rossie (Angus), in feu and heritage, as the king's other knights hold their feus, for the service of one knight. Edinburgh. (1165 × 1174)

W'. Rex Scott' Omnibus probis hominibus tocius terre sue salutem. Sciant presentes 7 futuri me dedisse 7 concessisse 7 hac carta mea confirmasse Henrico filio Gregorii clerici Rossin per suas rectas diuisas Tenend*um* sibi 7 heredibus suis de me 7 heredibus meis in feudo 7 hereditate ita libere 7 quiete 7 honorifice in bosco 7 plano in pratis 7 pascuis 7 aquis 7 in omnibus iustis pertinenciis suis sicut alii milites mei feuda sua de me tenent per seruicium unius militis. Test*ibus* Andr*ea* episcopo de Catenes . S*amsone* episcopo de Brechin . Ric*ardo* de Moruill' constabulario . Waltero filio Alani dapifero . Ricardo [Cu][a] min . Liolfo filio Macus . Bald*ewino* vicecomite de Lanarc. Apud Edeneb'.

ENDORSED. Unknown.
DESCRIPTION[1]. 4·6″ (11·6 cm.), Top, bottom × 1·9″ (5 cm.), L, 2·5″ (6·3 cm.), R. Tongue and, probably, tie torn away from left-hand bottom corner. The charter was evidently in poor condition when photographed.
HAND. Scribe Aj (Richard of Lincoln). Unruled.
SOURCE. Photograph of original, SRO, J.M. Thomson photographs. The present whereabouts of the original is not known; when seen and photographed by J.M. Thomson in 1911 it was in the possession of J.F. Mackay, W.S.
NOTES. [a] Parchment torn, supplied conjecturally. [1] The dimensions are those of the photograph, which according to J.M. Thomson's covering letter to Sir Archibald Lawrie (3 July, 1911) accompanying a print, was 'life size'.
COMMENT. The identification of Rossin with Rossie in Angus, though not certain, seems supported by the subsequent emergence of Rossie in Angus as a barony and by the use of Henry as a personal name in the family of Rossy of that ilk (cf. *Arbroath Liber*, i, 337–8).

44 Commands that wherever outwith the royal demesne the prior of Coldingham or his sergeands may discover fugitives and neyfs of the lands of Coldingham and Coldinghamshire, they are to have them justly and no one is to detain them. Berwick-upon-Tweed. (1165 × 1174)

W'. Rex Scott'. Justiciis Vice*comitibus* . 7 Omnibus probis hominibus tocius terre sue salutem. Mando 7 firmiter precipio ut ubicunque extra mea dominia prior de Coldincham aut seruientes sui inuenerint fugitiuos 7 natiuos homines de terris suis de Coldinch*am* 7 Coldinchameschire .·/ eos iuste habeant . 7 prohibeo firmiter ne quis eis quemquam ex hominibus illis iniuste detineat super meum forisfactum. Test*ibus* Ric*ardo* Cumi*n* . Roberto de Costenti*n* . Johanne de Vallibus . Hug*one* clerico . Ric*ardo* clerico . apud Berewic'.

ENDORSED. C W Reg*is* de fugitiuis et natiuis Prioris de Cold' quod possid[a] eos licite capere (xv cent.). Q iij[a] vj[te] (xv cent.).
DESCRIPTION. 5·8″ (14·7 cm.) Top, 5·6″ (14·2 cm.), Bottom × 2·8″ (7·3 cm.), L, 2·7″ (6·8 cm.), R. Tie torn off. Tag 6·6″ long, 0·7″ wide; seal rather rubbed but complete, in natural wax, diameter 3·2″ from lug to lug.
HAND. Scribe Aj (Richard of Lincoln). Unruled.
SOURCE. Original, Durham, D. & C. Muniments, Misc. Chr. no.587.
PRINTED. Raine, *North Durham*, no.34.
NOTE. [a] Sic.

45 Grants to Gregory de Melville Granton (Midlothian), in exchange for two ploughgates of land which King Malcolm IV granted him in Ednam; to be held free of multure for his own household, in feu and heritage, for the service of one archer with a horse in the army. Berwick-upon-Tweed. (1166 × 1171)

W'. Rex Scott'. Omnibus probis hominibus tocius terre sue . Clericis . 7 lai [cis sa][a] lut*em*. Sciant presentes . 7 futuri me dedisse . 7 concessisse . 7 hac [c][a]arta mea confirmasse . Gregori[o d][a]e MaleuiN . GrenduN . per rectas diuisas suas . in excambium d[ua][a]rum carrucatarum terre . quas Rex [.M'.] [a] frater meus ei dederat . in Edenham . tenendum sibi . 7 [h][a]eredibus meis . cum quietancia multure dominice domus sue . in feudo . 7 hereditate . plenarie . 7 honorifice . libere . 7 quiete .·/ per seruicium unius arcarii cum equo in exercitu. T*estibus* D*aui*d fratre meo . Nichol*ao* Cancellario . Comite Waldeuo . D*aui*d Olif*ard* Justic*ia* . Philippo de Valoniis Camerario . Gileberto fil*io* Richerii . Roberto de Quinci . Willelmo de Haia . Willelmo de Lindesi . Roberto filio Ursi . Waltero de Berkelai. Apud Berewic.

ENDORSED. Carta regis W. de Grendun' (xv cent.). Grendune (xvi cent.). Also modern endorsements.
DESCRIPTION. 6·6″ (16·6 cm.), Top, bottom × 3·2″ (8 cm.), L, R. Foot folded to a depth of 0·6″ (1·7 cm.). Single slits, no tag or seal remains.
HAND. Scribe Ai. Unruled.
SOURCE. Original, SRO, GD 26, 1/4/2.
PRINTED. Fraser, *Melville*, iii, 2, no.2 (with facsimile); also *Fraser Facsimiles*, no.7.
NOTE. [a] Tear in parchment; supplied conjecturally.

46 Commands that the woods of the monks of Coldingham, viz. Greenwood, the whole wood of Reston, Brockholeswood, Aikieside Wood, 'Kirchedeneswde', 'Harewde', 'Denewde', Swinewood and

Houndwood shall be under the defence and custody of the prior and monks of Coldingham, and forbids anyone to take anything there, neither wood nor wild animals, without the prior's leave on pain of £10 forfeiture, save for the king's necessary materials for his castle of Berwick. The monks may have the right of warren in their woods and throughout their land as it stretches by the ancient marches, viz. from the marches between Berwick and Lamberton as far as Billie (in Bunkle and Preston) and as far as 'Drieforde' and so by the 'Mereburne' as far as 'Crachoctre' and as far as 'Eieforde' and as far as the burn which flows into the sea by Oldcambus peth (i.e. Pease Burn). Berwick-upon-Tweed. (1165 × 1171)

.W'.[a] Rex Scott' Episcopis . Abbatibus . Prioribus . Comitibus . Justiciis . Baronibus . Vicecom*itibus* . Prepositis . Ministris . 7 Omnibus hominibus Francis 7 Anglis 7 Scottis tam presentıbus quam futuris tocius terre sue salutem. Sciatis quod uolo 7 firmiter precipio . quod nemora monachorum de Collingaham . uidelicet Grenewde . 7 totum nemus de Ristuna . 7 Broccheholewde[b] . 7 Akesside . 7 Kirchedeneswde[c] . 7 Harewde . 7 Denewde . 7 Swinewde . 7 Hundewde . 7 Omnia nemora 7 Gwastina[d] sua sint sub defensione prioris 7 custodia . necnon 7 monachorum[e] de Collingaham . ne aliquis super .x. libras forisfacture quicquam in predictis nemoribus uel Gwastinis capiat . nisi per ipsum priorem . uel per monachos prenominati loci :' si ipse presens non fuerit. Exceptis tantummodo necessariis de Castello meo de Berewich . que mihimet ipsi solummodo conueniunt. Et si clientes mei pro necessariis meis ad opus Castelli mei de Berewich ad nemora predicta uenerint :' per priorem uel per clientes suos que opus fuerint mihi 7 ubi ipse uel clientes sui monstrauerint accipiant. Insuper addo 7 illis concedo quod predictus prior 7 monachi habeant Gwarennam in predictis nemoribus . 7 per totam terram suam . sicut extenduntur recte 7 antique[e] diuise . Uidelicet a diuisis inter Berewich 7 Lambertunam usque ad Bilie . 7 usque ad DRieforde[f]. 7 ita per Mereburne usque ad Crachochtre 7 usque ad Eieforde . 7 usque ad Riuulum qui manat in mare per Aldechambuspethe . ita quod nullus ibi aliquid capiat . nec ligna . nec aliquam bestiam siluestrem nisi per ipsos. Quod si aliquis in predictis nemoribus uel Gwastinis capiatur uenando uel ligna secando . uel aliquid inde accipiendo . preter licentiam prioris 7 monachorum . habeant prior 7 monachi quod super illum & cum illo inuenerint . 7 ego forisfacturam prenominatam. Testibus his[g] . Ricardo episcopo S*ancti* Andree . Ingelr*amo* episcopo de Glescu[h] . Nich*olao* Cancellario . Abbate de Jeddewrth' . D*aui*d Olifart Justic*ia* . Dolfin' capellano . Hug*one* clerico reg*is* . Waltero de Windleshore . Roberto Frebern. Apud Berewich.

ENDORSED. *A*: Carta Willelmi Reg*is* Scocie concess*a* priori et monach*is* Dunelm' manentibus apud Cold' in nemoribus suis vel gwastinis sub pena xli. (xv cent.). A tercia vj (xv[te] cent.). *B*: W. de nemoribus; 7 Gwastinis (xii–xiii cent.). Cart' regis (xv cent. insertions). D tercia sexte (xv cent.).

DESCRIPTION. *A*: 1′ 0. 1″ (30·5 cm.), Top, 11·6″ (29·8 cm.), Bottom × 7″ (17·6 cm.), L, 6·8″ (17·3 cm.), R. Foot folded 1·1″. Double slits. Tag 7·1″ long, 1″ wide. Seal almost entire, natural wax, fair impression. *B* : 7·9″ (22·5 cm.), Top, 7·4″ (21·3 cm.), bottom × 6·3″ (16 cm.), L, 6·5″ (16·1 cm.), R. Foot folded

0·9″. Single slit. Tag 5·6″ long, 0·9″ wide. Seal entire, in natural wax, fair condition.
HAND. *A*: Scribe Af. Tailed e used twice, in antiquę, Andreę. Ruled in ink on thick parchment. *B*: Scribe Bb. Unruled.
SOURCE. Originals, Durham, D. & C. Muniments, Misc. Chr. no.602 = *A*; Ibid., Misc. Chr. no.594 = *B*.
PRINTED. Raine, *North Durham*, no.46 (*A*), no.45 (*B*). Printed here from *A*, with major variants of *B* noted.
NOTES. [a] Large roman capital, surmounted by a broad mark of contraction, *A*. Diagonal stroke through left-hand side of letter, *B*. [b] Brocheholewde, *B*. [c] Richedeneswde, *B*. [d] Gwastinia, *B*. [e] Capital initial, *B*. [f] *B* omits next eleven words. [g] Test*ibus*, *B*. [h] Glesgu, *B*.
COMMENT. The identifiable woods named are or were all in Coldingham parish, except Aikieside Wood which is in Cockburnspath. Swinewood, now lost, evidently lay south of the Eye Water (Raine, *North Durham*, no.389), but Swinewood mill (disused) is north of the river, between W. and E. Reston. For the marches named, see the comment on no.181.

47 Grants to Durham Cathedral Priory freedom from toll on its own chattels and merchandise throughout his land. Mitford (Northumberland). (1166 × 1174, probably 1166)

W'. Rex Scott' Omnibus probis hominibus tocius terre sue salutem. Sciatis me concessisse Deo . 7 Sancto Cudberto de Dunelmo . 7 monachis ibidem Deo seruientibus .' ut ipsi 7 eorum seruientes per totam terram meam liberi sint 7 quieti ab omni teloneo de propriis catallis 7 mercaturis eorum .' sicut carta Reg*is* M'.[a] Fratris mei testatur 7 confirmat. Et prohibeo . ne aliquis contra hanc libertatem eis infra terram meam iniuriam faciat .' super meam forisfacturam. T*estibus* Ric*ardo* de Moreu*illa* constabulario . Philippo de Valon*iis* camerario . Alano fil*io* dapiferi. Apud MitFORD.

ENDORSED. Carta Willelmi Reg*is* Scotie de Teloneo quiet' (xiii cent.). Concess' monachis Dunelm' (xiv–xv cent.). D iij vj[te] (xv cent.).
DESCRIPTION. 5·6″ (14 cm.), Top and bottom × 2·8″ (7·3 cm.), L, 2·1″ (5·3 cm.), R. Tie remains entire; tongue torn, 0·7″ wide. Seal detached, almost entire, natural wax, in fair condition.
HAND. Scribe Ai. Unruled.
SOURCE. Original, Durham, D. & C. Muniments, Misc. Chr. no.613.
PRINTED. Raine, *North Durham*, no.48.
NOTE. [a] Diagonal stroke through letter.

48 Confirms to Hugh Giffard the lands and tenements which he holds by the grant of King Malcolm IV, the Countess Ada, and Herbert the chamberlain, viz. Yester, that part of Lethington which Edolf son of Gamel held, and the land of the muir of Haddington (all East Lothian); one full toft in Linlithgow which Toke held; Borrowstoun (West Lothian) which Herbert the chamberlain granted to Hugh with his daughter in marriage; four librates of land in Potton (Bedfordshire) perambulated by Walter of Lindsay and Ingram the clerk; and Auldcathie (in Kirkliston), West Lothian; to be held in feu and heritage as the donors' charters bear witness. Durham. (1166 × 1171, probably 1166)

W'. Rex Scott' . Omnibus probis hominibus tocius terre sue . Clericis . 7 laicis . Francis . 7 Anglis . Scottis . 7 Galweiensibus salutem. Sciant presentes . 7 futuri . me concessisse . 7 hac carta mea confirmasse Hugoni

Giffard . 7 heredibus suis . in fewdo 7 hereditate . omnes terras 7 teneuras quas idem Hugo habet ex donacione Reg*is* .M'. fratris mei . 7 .A. Comitisse matris mee . 7 Herberti Camerarii . scilicet Jhestrith per Rectas diuisas suas . 7 illam partem de Lafditune . quam Edolf filius Gamel[a] tenuit . 7 terram more de Hadingtun per diuisas per quas ei perambulata fuit . 7 unum plenarium toftum in Linlidqu . scilicet toftum quod Toke tenuit. Et Berewaldestune per Rectas diuisas suas . quam Herbertus Camerarius cum filia sua ei dedit. Et quatuor libratas terre in Pottun sicut Walterus de Lindesi . 7 Engelramus clericus illas ei perambulauerunt . 7 Aldekathi*n* per rectas diuisas suas. Volo itaque 7 precipio ut idem Hug*o* . 7 heredes sui . terras . 7 teneuras prenominatas hereditarie teneant 7 habeant . ita libere . 7 quiete . 7 honorifice .· sicut Carte Reg*is* .M'. fratris mei . 7 A Comitisse matris mee 7 .H'. Camerarii . testantur . 7 confirmant. T*estibus* Nicol*ao* Cancellario . R*icardo* de Moreuill' constabulario . D*aui*d Olif*ard* . Willelmo de Vesci . Philippo de Valon*iis* Camerar*io* . W*illelmo* de Veteri Ponte . Bern*ardo* fil*io* Brien Gileb*erto* fil*io* Richerii . Rob*erto* de Costenti*n*. Apud Dunelm'.

ENDORSED. ye chart off ȝest' and Lethynton' be Kyng Wylȝam (xv–xvi cent.). Giff' (?).
DESCRIPTION. 6·4″ (16·4 cm.), Top and bottom × 6·4″ (16·4 cm.), L, 5·8″ (14·6 cm.), R. Tongue, 1″ wide, cut 2″ from left edge of foot, with tie cut below tongue. Small central portion of seal remains on tongue.
HAND. Scribe Ai. Unruled.
SOURCE. Original, SRO, GD 28/1.
PRINTED. *Yester Writs*, no.1; *East Lothian Trans.*, viii (1960), 2 (with facsimile and translation).
NOTE. [a] This is almost certainly the preferable reading, since there is a mark of suspension above the minims.
COMMENT. It is not certain how much of the East Lothian property was granted to Hugh Giffard by King Malcolm and how much by the countess Ada. Possibly (contrary to the statement in *RRS*, i, no.303) King Malcolm's grant was limited to the toft in Linlithgow. Auldcathie is in Kirkliston, but has an ancient association with the barony of Kinneil, held by Herbert the chamberlain, to which 'Berewaldestune' (Borrowstoun) belonged. This seems to be the earliest recorded mention of Borrowstoun. Walter of Lindsay was steward of the Honour of Huntingdon under Malcolm IV (*RRS*, i, 204–5, and see ibid., 204 for Ingram the clerk).

49

Commands that the monks of St Andrew's Priory, Northampton, shall hold the church of Brafield-on-the-Green, Northants, with its yardland of arable, and that they may have two carts in the wood of Yardley Hastings to collect dead wood. (1165 × 1173)

W Rex Scottorum[a] dapifero suo et omnibus baronibus et ministris suis tocius Anglie salutem. Precipio quod monachi de Norh't[b] teneant ecclesiam de Bragefeld[c] cum uirgata terre que ad eam pertinet liberam et quietam ab omni seruicio mihi pertinenti. Concedo eciam eis ut habeant[d] duas carectas in nemore de Gerdele ad capiendum mortuum boscum. Teste Dauid Olifard . et Gaufr*ido* Ridel et Hugone Ridel[e] dap*ifero*[f].

RUBRIC. Confirmacio Willelmi Regis Scott' de ecclesia de Brawfield cum una virgata terre . et de duabus carect*is* de Yerdele in nemore (red, contemporary with text[g]).

SOURCE. BM, MS. Royal 11 B ix, fo.13v=*R*. BM, MS. Cott. Vesp. E xvii, fo.13v =*V1*. BM, MS. Cott. Vesp. E xvii, fo.63r=*V2*. Printed here from *R* with minor variants of *V1* and *V2* not noted.
NOTES. [a] D Rex Scott', *V2*. [b] North', *V1*, *V2*. [c] Bragefyld, *V1*, Bragfeld, *V2*. [d] ut habeant repeated, *V1*. [e] Rydel, *V1*. [f] This word invisible in *R*, supplied from *V1*. [g] *V1* only.
COMMENT. Cf. *RRS*, i, no.151.

50 Confirms to St Andrew's Priory, Northampton, all that it had in the time of King David I in churches, tithes, lands and revenues; and orders his steward (of the Honour of Huntingdon) to maintain the priory and its property. (1165 × 1173)

[W.][a] Rex Scotie Dapifero suo et omnibus baronibus suis et ministris[b] tocius Anglie salutem. Sciatis me concessisse et confirmasse ecclesie Sancti Andree de Norh't[c] et monachis ibidem Deo seruientibus omnia que ipsi tenuerunt in tempore Dauid reg*is* aui mei, in ecclesiis, in decimis, in terris, et redditibus et quibuslibet aliis; et uolo ut ea omnia libere et quiete teneant in elemosinam. Quare precipio uobis quod eos iuste manuteneatis et omnes res eorum, sicut meas proprias res, et siquis de meis tenentibus eis iniuriam facere presumpserit plenarium rectum eis habere fac*iatis*. Teste Dauid Olifard, Gaufr*ido* Ridell'[d] et Hugon*e* Ridell'[d].

RUBRIC. Confirmacio generalis Henrici Regis Scocie de omnibus possessionibus (red, contemporary with text[e]).
SOURCE. BM, MS. Royal 11 B ix, fo.14r=*R*. BM, MS. Cott. Vesp. E xvii, fo.13v =*V*. Printed here from *R*, with editorial punctuation.
NOTES. [a] *R* and *V* have H. [b] suis, struck through, *V*. [c] North', *V*. [d] Rydell', *V*. [e] *V* only.
COMMENT. Cf. *RRS*, i, no.144.

51 Confirms to Huntingdon Priory the grant made by his father Earl Henry of the tenth penny of his revenues from Huntingdon in exchange for lands and meadows throughout the enclosed and built-up part of the town which had been taken away from the canons. Huntingdon. (1165 × 1171)

W. Rex Scott' Senesc*allo* suo et omnibus baronibus et probis hominibus suis tocius Comitatus de Huntend*un* salutem. Sciatis me concessisse et hac carta mea confirmasse in perpetuam elemosinam Deo et canonicis ecclesie Sancte Marie de Hunted*un* donacionem quam Comes Henricus pater meus eis fecit de decimo denario redditus mei de Huntedon' in excambium pro terris et pratis eorum per uillam clausam et firmatam sibi ablatis et subtractis. Quare volo et precipio firmiter dapifero meo et ministris meis ut predictum decimum denarium redditus mei singulis annis predictis canonicis secundum terminos meos capiendi redditus sine disturbatione reddant sicut carta Comitis Henrici patris mei testatur et confirmat. Testibus, Dauid fratre Reg*is*, Nich*olao* cancellario, Ricardo de Moreuil' constabulario, Dauid Olifard, Hug*one* Ridel. Apud Huntendon'.

SOURCE. BM, MS. Cott. Faustina C i, fo.2r.
COMMENT. See *RRS*, i, no.70, where '10d.' is no doubt an error for 'tenth penny'.

52 Confirms to Westminster Abbey the land in Tottenham held by Aldwin (Queen Maud's) chamberlain and by his son Adam after him. (1165 × 1173)

Willelmus Dei gr*ati*a Rex Scotorum Dapifero suo et baronibus et ministris et omnibus fidelibus suis Franc*is* et Angl' tam futuris quam presentibus salutem. Sciatis me dedisse et concessisse ecclesie Sancti Petri de Westmonasterio et monach*is* ibidem Deo seruientibus in perpetuam elemosinam terram illam quam Aldewinus camerarius tenuit in Toteham et quam Adam filius suus post eum tenuit. Hanc uero elemosinam do et concedo predicte ecclesie pro anima Matild*is* Regine sororis aui mei ad faciendum anniuersarium annuatim pro anima sua et animabus patris et matris mee et antecessorum et successorum meorum. Ita quod predictus Adam et heres suus hanc terram teneant de eadem ecclesia, reddendo per annum .xxx. solid*os* .viii. dies ante festum apostolorum Philippi et Jacobi pro omni seruicio. Et si Adam aut heres suus ab hoc seruicio defecerint .' predicta ecclesia et fratres eiusdem ecclesie recognoscant ad predictam terram placitum suum et uoluntatem suam sicut de sua propria terra inde faciendum. Presentibus testibus, Ricardo de Moreuilla, Hugone Ridel, Willelmo de Veteri Ponte, Roberto de Quinci, Hugone Giffard, Waltero de Windelesor'.

RUBRIC. Carta Willelmi Regis Scocie de Tote*n*ham (top in red).
SOURCE. Westminster Abbey Muniments, MS. 'Domesday', fo.157^v^.
COMMENT. See *RRS*, i, nos.6, 13 and 154. The style may be due to the Westminster copyist or to the drafting of this act by the beneficiary.

53 Confirms to St Neots Priory the grant made by Lancelin of Hardwicke, and grants that all lands held by the monks of St Neots within the Honour of Huntingdon are to be free of secular services. (1165 × 1173)

.W.[a] Rex Scott'. Senescall*o* suo et omnibus probis hominibus suis honoris Huntend' . salutem. Sciatis me concessisse et hac carta mea confirmasse monachis ap*ud* Sanctum Neotum Deo seruientibus donationem illam . quam Lancelinus ho*mo* meus de Herdewic eis fecit . tenendum ita libere et quiete . sic*ut* Carta Reg*is* .M. fratris mei testatur . et confirmat. Preterea precipio quod predicti monachi . et omnes terras et tenuras quas tenent in honore meo de Huntendon' . bene et in pace . libere et quiete . teneant ab omnibus secularibus seruiciis . et prohibeo firmiter . ne quis eos aut res eorum aliquatenus iniuste disturbet. T'.

RUBRIC. Herdewik (in right margin, black, xv cent.?), xxix (red).
SOURCE. BM, MS. Cott. Faustina A iv, fo.48^r^.
NOTE. [a] Initial black with slight red flourish.
COMMENT. See *RRS*, i, no.209.

54 Informs his steward and all his barons and responsible men of the Honour of Huntingdon, that he has confirmed to St Neots Priory the revenue of 40s. a year in the mills of Little Paxton (Hunts.) granted by his father and brother. (1165 × 1173)

W. Rex Scott'. Senescalo suo et omnibus Baronibus et probis hominibus suis honoris Huntendon' salutem. Sciatis me concessisse et hac carta mea confirmasse . Deo et Ecclesie Sancti Neoti et monachis[a]. ibidem Deo seruientibus . xl sol*idos* per annum in molendinis meis de Parua Paxtona quos[b] pater meus . et frater meus . in elemosinam eis dederunt . tenendum in perpetuam elemosinam . libere et quiete . sicut carta Reg*is*. M. fratris me testatur . et confirmat. T'.

RUBRIC. relax' xl s nuper Simonis Comitis de mol' parue Paxton' (in left margin, black, contemporary with text), xxvi[a] (red).
SOURCE. BM, MS. Cott. Faustina A iv, fos.47v–48r.
NOTES. [a] Fo.48r. [b] s rubbed out.
COMMENT. See *RRS*, i, no.210.

55 Confirms to Elstow Abbey the grants made to it by King David I, Queen Maud and Earl Henry, and also the grant of the third penny of Bedford made by King Malcolm IV. Kempston. (1165 × 1171, probably *c.*1166)

.W. Rex Scoc' Omnibus Baronibus et ministris suis et omnibus sancte matris ecclesie filiis presentibus et futuris :' Sciatis me concessisse et hac carta mea confirmasse ecclesie Sancte Marie de Alnestowe[a] et monialibus ibidem Deo seruientibus omnes possessiones et libertates quas Rex Dauid auus meus et Comes H*enricus* pater meus et Regina Matild*is* auia[b] mea eis dederunt et concesserunt . scilicet terram Willelmi medici que reddit .xx. s*olidos* de censu et .iiij. virgatas terre in Kemestun . et in eadem villa unum molendinum quod reddit .c. s*olidos* per annum . et molendinum de Box cum terra et prato eidem pertinente. Et preterea totum redditum de tercio denario de Bedeford'[c] :' quem Rex M*alcolmus* frater meus eis concessit et carta sua confirmauit. Et libertatem quam Rex Dauid auus meus eis dedit[d] in curia et extra curiam et quoque anno unam summam vini de redditibus de Toteham. Quare volo et precipio ut predicte moniales prenominatas libertates et possessiones et omnes alias elemosinas quas prefati antecessores mei eis dederunt et concesserunt in perpetuam elemosinam teneant ita libere et quiete et honorifice sicut carte eorum testantur et confirmant. T*estibus* Ada Comit*issa* matre mea .[e] Nicholao Cancellar*io* . Ricardo de Moreu*illa* constab*ular*io . Hugone Giffard . Alano fil*io* Dapif*eri* . Simone de Essebi apud Kemestonam.

SOURCE. PRO, E 13/56, m.22 (Exchequer Plea Roll, 2–3 Edward III) = *E*. BM, MS. Cott. Vesp. E xvii, fo.230r = *V*. Printed here from *E*, with more important variants of *V* noted.
NOTES. [a] Elnestowe, *V*. [b] auua, *V*. [c] Bedford, *V*. [d] dedit, *E* only. [e] *V* omits Nicholao . . . Essebi and has et aliis etc.
COMMENT. See *RRS*, i, nos.148, 204.

56 Confirms to the nuns and brethren of Harrold Priory the grants made to them by Sampson Fortis and Robert, son of Pain de Briouze. (1165 × 1170)

Willielmus rex Scotiae episcopis,[a] abbatibus, comitibus, baronibus et omnibus aliis probis suis hominibus totius terrae suae, tam clericis quam laicis, tam Francis quam Anglis, salutem. Sciant tam presentes quam futuri me concessisse et hac carta mea confirmasse, pro salute mea et pro salute omnium parentum meorum et antecessorum, Deo et ecclesiae

Beati Petri de Harewolde et monialibus ibidem Deo seruientibus et fratribus easdem moniales secundum institutiones ecclesiae Sancti Nicholai de Arrowasia tuentibus, omnes donationes quas Sanson Fortis et Robertus filius Pagani de Breuse illis donaverunt et cartis suis confirmaverunt, in ecclesiis, in decimis, in terris, in aquis, in pratis, in pascuis, in piscatione, in bosco et in pasnagio, et in omnibus aliis rebus quas illis in elemosinam contulerunt, ut eas habeant et possideant in perpetuam elemosinam, liberas et quietas et ab omni seculari servitio et exactione absolutas, sicut cartae eorum testantur, et sicut carta Malculmi fratris mei testatur. Hiis testibus, Nicholao cancellario, Ricardo capellano, Comite Simone, Galfrido Ridello, Roberto Foliot, Roberto de Costentin, Roberto Wilibi, Helia Foliot, Simone de Essebie, Thoma Barton.

SOURCE. Dugdale, *Mon. Angl.*, ii, 202–3 (reprinted, New edition, vi, 1, 330–1, no.IV). Taken by Dugdale from 'an ancient parchment in the Cotton Library', presumably destroyed in the fire of 1731. An abridged version is given in BM, MS. Lansdowne 391, fo.5^{r}, no.iiij.
PRINTED. G.H. Fowler, *Records of Harrold Priory* (BHRS, vol. xvii, 1935), p.18, no.5. Dugdale, *Mon. Angl.*, as above.
NOTE. [a] Punctuation editorial.
COMMENT. See *RRS*, i, no.180. This is the only Scottish royal charter witnessed by Elias Foliot, for whom see ibid., no.320, *EYC*, ii, 438 and *Cartularium abbathiae de Rievalle*, ed. J.C. Atkinson (Surtees Soc., 1889), 48 and 115–16.

57 Confirms to Robert son of Sewin of Northampton 140 acres of land in the hanger of Tottenham which Uhtred of London held, for a rent of one mark of silver each Michaelmas, as the charter of King Malcolm IV bears witness. (1165 × 1171)

Villelmus[a] Rex Scott' Senescall*o* suo de Hunted' et omnibus probis hominibus suis de honore Huntedon' salutem. Sciatis me concessisse et hac carta mea confirmasse Roberto filio Sewini de Norhamton' illas septies xx^{ti}. acras terre in hangre de Toteham quas Whctredus de London' tenuit et dimidium holmum quem Engelramus prius eo tenuerat et quatuor trunchos ad ignem suum de bosco meo de Totenham et x. porcos quietos a pasnagio. Tenend*um* sibi et heredibus suis de me et de heredibus meis in feudo et hereditate ita libere et quiete et cum eadem conditione .' qua carta regis Malcolmi fratris mei testatur et confirmat. Reddendo inde mihi singulis annis unam marcam argenti ad festum Sancti Mich*aelis*. T*estibus* Nicholao cancellario . Ricardo de Morewill' constabulario . D*aui*d Olif*ard* . Philippo de Walon*iis*.

RUBRIC. De confirmatione Willelmi Reg*is* Scocie (top in red). [hang] re de conf[irmatione Willelmi] R*egis* Scocie (at left in brown ink).
SOURCE. BM, MS. Cott. Faustina B ii, fo.11^{v} (pencil).
PRINTED. *Cartulary of St Mary Clerkenwell*, ed. W.O. Hassall (Royal Historical Society, Camden Series, 1949), 15, no.14.
NOTE. [a] Initial blue.
COMMENT. See *RRS*, i, no.206, and no.146 below.

58 Confirms to Sawtry Abbey the mills of Paxton in fee-farm, for 50s. 8d. a year. (1165 × 1173)

Will' rex Scotie senescallo suo et omnibus probis hominibus suis totius honoris Huntendun salutem.[a] Sciatis me concessisse et presenti charta confirmasse abbati et monachis de Saltreia molendina[b] de Paxton in feodali firma tenenda, cum omnibus iustis pertinentiis, reddendo mihi annuatim[c] plenariam firmam quam predicta molendina reddiderunt[d] anno quo rex Malcolmus[e] frater meus fuit vivus et mortuus, scilicet quinquaginta[f] solidos et octo denarios. Test*ibus*.

SOURCE. Bodleian Library, MS. Rawlinson B 142, fo.19v.
NOTES. [a] Punctuation editorial, [b] MS. mollendina. [c] MS. anuatim. [d] MS. rediderunt. [e] MS. Malcolinus. [f] MS. quinquaginti.
COMMENT. Cf. *RRS*, i, no.259.

59 Confirms to Geoffrey de Melville and his heir Gregory the land which Malbeth held in Liberton (Midlothian) by the same marches as those by which Malbeth held it, and the land of Leadburn (in Penicuik), Midlothian, on the same terms and by the same service as those testified in King Malcolm IV's charter. Linlithgow. (1166 × 1170)

W'. Rex Scott' Omnibus probis hominibus tocius terre sue clericis 7 laicis futuris 7 presentibus salutem. Sciatis me concessisse 7 hac carta mea confirmasse Galfrido de Mala uilla[a] 7 Gregorio heredi suo terram illam quam Malbeth tenuit in Libertona . per [illas][b] diuisas per quas idem Malbeth eam tenuit . 7 terram de Lecbernard per suas rectas diuisas . tenendas sibi 7 heredibus suis de me 7 heredibus meis ita libere 7 quiete 7 eadem condicione . 7 eodem seruicio quo carta Reg*is* .M'. fratris mei eis testatur 7 confirmat. Test*ibus* Nichol*ao* can[ce][b]ll*ario* . Comite Waldeuo . D*aui*d Olifard . Philippo de Valon*iis* Camerario . Ric*ardo* capellano . Ricardo Cum*in* . fratre Willelmo Dolepene . Jordano de Ord. APUD LINLIDQ[U][b].

ENDORSED. Confirmacio de Lecbernard et de Stanhus (xiii cent.). Also modern endorsements.
DESCRIPTION. 6″ (15·2 cm.), Top, 5·8″ (14·9 cm.), Bottom × 2·4″ (6·1 cm.) L, R. Tongue probably cut away from foot. No seal remains.
HAND. Scribe Aj (Richard of Lincoln). Unruled.
SOURCE. Original, SRO, GD 26, 1/4/1.
PRINTED. Fraser, *Melville*, iii, 1, no.1 (with facsimile); also *Fraser Facsimiles*, no.8.
NOTES. [a] Mala uilla written as two words. [b] Tear in parchment; supplied conjecturally.
COMMENT. It is clear from *ESC*, no.153, *Newbattle Registrum*, no.195, *RRS*, i, no.302 and nos.268, 269 below, that the Malbeth of this act is to be identified with Macbeth Bere, lord of Liberton in the time of David I, and donor of certain rights in 'Legbernard' (Leadburn) to the church of St Cuthbert in Edinburgh.

60 Confirms the property and privileges of Cambuskenneth Abbey, granted by King David I and King Malcolm IV. (1166 × 1171)

Wilelmus[a] Dei gracia Rex Scotorum episcopis, abbatibus, comitibus, justiciis, baronibus, vicecomitibus, ministris et omnibus probis hominibus suis, clericis et laicis totius regni sui, tam presentibus quam futuris, salutem. Sciatis me concessisse, et hac mea carta confirmasse, Deo et ecclesie Sancte Marie de Strivueling, et canonicis ibidem Deo seruientibus, donaciones quas antecessores mei eis in elemosinam dederunt, *scilicet*, ex donatione Regis Dauid aui mei[b] terram de Cambuskynneth, et piscaturam inter eandem terram et[c] Pollemase, et unum rethe in aqua; terram quoque de Colling, cum nemore suo ad eandem terram pertinente, cum suis rectis diuisis; terram eciam de Tulibyen' que est inter aquam ejusdem terre et terram de Login; quadraginta quoque solidos de redditu meo de Strimeling; et canum unius nauis; et unam salinam, et tantum terre quantum habet una de salinis meis; et decimam firme de dominiis meis de Striueling; et oblaciones que in predicta ecclesia oblate fuerint; et insulam que est inter Pollemase et Tulliboyen'; viginti cudermis de caseis redditus mei de Striueling et Katelistun' cum suis rectis diuisis; et ecclesiam de Clacmanan[d] cum quadraginta acris terre; et toftum sacerdotis in eadem villa, et asiamenta in bosco et plano; et decimas placitorum et lucrorum meorum de Striueling et de Striuelingschire et de Calentyr; et ut eorum dominii[e] homines sint quieti de toloneo et de omnibus rectitudinibus et consuetudinibus, et ut habeant meam firmam pacem juste ubicunque venerint in tota terra mea; et ex donatione regis Malcolmi fratris mei totum molendinum de Clacmanan preter multuram dominice mense mee quotiens ad opus meum molitur contra aduentum meum in eandem villam, et preter multuram proprie mense prepositi mei ejusdem ville, multuram eciam et sectam prouincie de Clacmanan,[f] cum aliis rectitudinibus suis sicut melius et plenarius habebat cum idem molendinum in manu mea tenebam; et unum toftum plenarium in burgo meo de Innerkethin, et sexaginta solidos de cano meo de Perth singulis annis habendos; et pecuniis abbacie sue communionem pascue ubicunque habuerunt tempore regis Dauid aui mei melius et plenarius. Volo itaque et firmiter precipio quatenus predicta ecclesia omnes possessiones prenominatas ita libere et quiete possideat sicut aliqua ecclesia in toto regno meo aliquam elemosinam vel possessionem quietius et liberius possidet, et ut carte regis Dauid aui mei et Malcolmi regis fratris mei testantur et confirmant. Testibus, Nicholao cancellario, Johanne abbate de Kelcho, Walleuo Comite, Richard*o* de Moreuille, Waltero filio Alani, Dauid Olifer, Philippo de Valing, Roberto Auenell, fratre Willelmo de Olepen'.

RUBRIC. Cambuskynneth terrarum et piscarie confirmatio per Regem Wilelmum (at top). Concordat cum principali Jacobus Foulis (at end).

SOURCE. NLS, MS. Adv. 34.1.2, fos.36v–37r.

PRINTED. *Cambuskenneth Registrum*, no.52.

NOTES. [a] Large red initial U. [b] Fo.37r. [c] MS., de. [d] MS., Clacmanam. [e] Sic. [f] With mark of contraction.

COMMENT. Brother William de Olepen', a knight-hospitaller, witnesses no.59, and also *Kelso Liber*, no.214, a charter of Bernard son of Brien (1165 × 1171). He served as one of the king's envoys in 1173 (*Chron. Fantosme* (Michel), p.16). For his status, cf. *St Andrews Liber*, 319 (1172 × 1178).

61 Confirms the property and privileges of Newbattle Abbey. (1165 × 1173)

Will*elmus* Rex Scottorum Episcopis, Abbatibus, Comitibus, Baronibus,

Justic*iis*, Vic*ecomitibus*, prepositis, ministris et omnibus probis hominibus tocius terre sue, Francis Angl*icis* et Scott*is*, clericis et laicis, modernis et posteris, salutem. Sciant presentes et futuri me concessisse et hac mea carta confirmasse Deo et ecclesie de Neu*botle* et fratribus ibidem Deo seruientibus Neubotle, Ruchalc', Montleuen et terram quam Robertus ferrarius eis dedit et concessit, et unam salinam de Blanckelande cum aysiamentis suis[a] et pasnagium per totum forestum meum, et materiem ad edificia sua construenda sicud ad meum dominicum, sicud Rex Dauid auus meus et comes Henr*icus* pater meus predictas terras et redditus eis donauerunt et cartis suis confirmauerunt. Similiter uero concedo eis et confirmo ex dono Malcolmi fratris mei terram Jocelini Coci cum diuisis suis, et Dunpeldre per rectas diuisas suas, cum Metherauch et omnibus aliis pertinenciis suis iustis, sicud Gylpatrik Mackeruy eam antea tenuit. Et terram[b] illam que iacet secus Clud nomine Kermyl, quam idem Rex Malcolmus eis concessione et consensu Hereberti Episcopi et capituli Gla[s]guensis dedit et confirmauit, cum aquis et piscariis ad terram illam pertinentibus, sicud Baldewinus vicecomes de Lanark' et Galfridus de Maleu*illa*, Fergus filius Ferchert et Douenal filius Ewini cum quibusdam aliis probis hominibus ipsam illis perambulauerunt et saisiauerunt. Et preterea terram que fuit Roberti filii Galfridi in Hadyngtonscire, scilicet Bereford per rectas diuisas suas, et unam carucatam terre super Pefre prout carta matris mee eis testatur. Et[c] terram quamdam infra portam australem burgi de Eden*burg* proximam ipsi porte ex occidentali parte introitus, quam Willelmus gener Forni eis dedit. Preterea terram de Montlothien atque unum toftum in Leth, quod Edwardus filius Petri de Lastalrik' eis dedit sicud carta ipsius testatur. Preterea ex dono Randulphi de Soulis unam carucatam terre in Gilmuriston' sicud ipsius carta testatur. Et unam mansuram in Muxelburg' ex dono abbatis de Dunfermelyn, ita liberam et quietam sicud carta ipsius testatur. Preterea concedo eis et confirmo omnes libertates et consuetudines quas antecessores mei eis dederunt et concesserunt, sicud in cartis eorum continetur. Volo itaque et firmiter precipio ut monachi predictas terras et tenuras prefatas cum omnibus eorum iustis pertinenciis teneant et possideant eadem pace, quietudine et libertate qua aliqua elemosina liberius et quiecius tenetur, sicud carte antecessorum meorum et aliorum donatorum suorum eis testantur. Et prohibeo firmiter ne quis infra diuisas predictarum suarum [terrarum] in aliquo forisfaciat super meum plenarium forisfactum. T*estibus* Ada comitissa matre mea et multis al*iis*.

RUBRIC. Confirmacio Reg*is* Willelmi generalis.
SOURCE. NLS, MS. Adv. 34.4.13, fo.46^{r-v}.
PRINTED. *Newbattle Registrum*, no.156.
NOTES. [a] fo.46^{v}. [b] In margin Nota Kermyl. [c] In margin Nota burgagium.
COMMENT. This is fairly close in substance to Alexander III's bull of 1174 (*Newbattle Registrum*, Appendix, no.XXVIII), which, however, adds certain property not included here. Properties mentioned here for which separate royal confirmations do not survive are Carmyle, Lanarkshire (*RRS*, i, no.271), land within the South Port of Edinburgh, granted by William son-in-law of Forn, the land of Mountlothian and a toft in Leith, granted by Edward son of Peter of Restalrig, and a lodging in Musselburgh granted by the abbot of Dunfermline.

Mountlothian was exchanged for Holyrood Abbey's land in Romanno in 1223 (*Newbattle Registrum*, no.127). Blanckelande has not been located.

62 Confirms the property and privileges of Jedburgh Abbey. (The name of the benefactor is given first, followed by the benefaction). King David I: the monastery of Jedburgh; the chapel (of Old Jedward?) founded in a clearing of the wood opposite Mervinslaw (?); the teind of the king's venison in Teviotdale; Ulston (in Jedburgh), 'Alnecliue' (lost) beside Ancrum; 'Crumesethe' (lost); Raperlaw (in Lilliesleaf); one burgage dwelling in Roxburgh; two burgage dwellings in Berwick, one with its toft around it; a fishing opposite the island called 'Tonsmidhop' (lost, but perhaps in the River Tweed at Norham); Long Edwardly (in Jedburgh); pasture for the canons' animals wherever the king's animals have theirs; likewise timber and wood wherever the king has his, save in 'Quikeheg' (lost); multure for all the canons' tenants in Jedburgh 'where the castle is'; one salt-pan by Stirling; Abbotrule (in Southdean), granted in exchange for 10 librates of land in Hardingstone (Northants). King Malcolm IV: the churches of Earls Barton and Grendon (Northants); one toft and 7 acres in the burgh of Jedburgh; freedom in their houses in Berwick to receive tonnels of wine brought thither by merchants and emptied there without the king's officers demanding anything therefrom; the fishing in the Tweed above (Berwick) bridge, surrendered to King David I by William of Lamberton. Cospatric the sheriff (of Roxburgh): 1½ ploughgates, 3 acres and 2 tofts in Crailing. Berenger Engaine: 1 silver merk in Crailing mill, 2 oxgangs with one neyf (*villanus*) and one toft, and (to supply food for the chaplain serving the chapel of Crailing) other 2 oxgangs with a toft, and one further toft beside the church. David Olifard: the teind of Crailing mill. Orm son of Eilaf: 1 ploughgate in the 'other Crailing' (Crailinghall). Richard Inglis: 2 oxgangs in Scraesburgh (*alias* Hunthill) and 2 oxgangs in Lanton. Gamel the clerk, with the consent of his sons Osulf and Uchtred: Cavers. Margaret, wife of Thomas of London, with the consent of Thomas and of Henry Lovel, Margaret's son: Outerside (in Roberton). Christian, wife of Gervase Ridel: the third part of the toun of Mervinslaw (?). Geoffrey de Percy: the church of Oxnam, with 2 ploughgates and 2 oxgangs lying by the church, and common pasture and fuel in the toun; Newbigging (in Oxnam) with common pasture and fuel, which land was granted by Henry de Percy to be given to the canons before King Malcolm IV, after Henry's brother Geoffrey died. Ralph son of Dunegal and his wife Bethoc: 1 ploughgate in Ruecastle (in Bedrule) with common pasture of the toun. Turgis of Rosedale: the religious house of Liddel (Canonbie priory) with adjacent land; the church of Kirkandrews on Esk (Cumberland). Guy of Rosedale, with the consent of his son Ralph: 42 acres between Esk and Liddel at their confluence; free fishing from the ditch of Liddel to the church of Liddel. Ranulf de Sules: the church of Liddesdale (Castleton); the church of Great Doddington by Earls Barton (Northants); half a ploughgate in 'Nasebith' (Nisbet in Crailing?). Gervase Ridel, who afterwards became a canon of Jedburgh, and his brother Ralph: the church of

Abbotsley (Huntingdonshire). William de Vieuxpont: 1 ploughgate of his demesne of Carriden (West Lothian). Peebles. (1165 × 1170)

Will*elmus*[a] Dei gr*ati*a Rex Scott'. Episcopis . Abbatibus . Prioribus . Comitibus . Baronibus . Justiciis . Vicecomitibus . Ceterisque hominibus totius terre sue . Francis . Anglis 7 Scottis . Cunctisque Sancte Dei Ecclesie filiis :' Sal*utem*. Ex suscepto regimine Regni incumbit nobis Ecclesiam 7 Ecclesiasticas diligere personas . Et non solum de nostris eis benefacere :' sed & Beneficia ab aliis Dei fidelibus eis collata ~ auctoritate Regia confirmare . 7 cum sua eis integritate conseruare. Inde est[b] quod nos consilio proborum hominum nostrorum ~ Possessiones 7 bona que a Predecessoribus nostris . 7 ab aliis Regni nostri principibus 7 fidelibus . Deo 7 Ecclesie Sancte MARIE de Jeddew' . 7 Canonicis ibidem Deo seruientibus collata sunt :' presenti eis Priuilegio confirmamus. Videlicet Ex dono Reg*is* D*aui*d Monasterium Jeddew' cum omnibus ad illud pertinentibus. Capellam quoque que fundata est in Saltu nemoris contra Xernwingeslawe. Decimam Tocius venationis Reg*is* in Theuietedal'. Uluestonam. Alnecliue iuxta Alnecrumb. Crumesethe. Rapeslawe ~ cum rectis diuisis ad easdem pertinentibus in Bosco 7 plano . pratis . pascuis 7 culturis. Unam maisuram in Burgo Rochb'. Unam maisuram in Berew'. Terciam quoque Maisuram in eadem Berew' super Tuedam cum Tofto suo circumiacente. Unam Aquam que est contra insulam que uocatur Tonsmidhop. Eadwardesle. Pascua animalium :' proprie ubi 7 Reg*is*. Ligna nemorum . 7 materiem ad suas necessitates :' ubi 7 ipse ~ preter in Quikeheg. Molturam molendini de omnibus hominibus Jeddew' ubi castellum est. Unam Salinam iuxta Streuel*in*. Rulam Hereuei ~ per suas rectas diuisas . in nemore 7 plano . pratis 7 pascuis . 7 aquis . 7 in omnibus rebus ad eandem villam iuste pertinentibus . datam in Escambio .x. Libratarum terre quas prefati canonici habuerant in HardinghestorN. Ex Dono Dilecti fratris mei Reg*is* M :' Ecclesiam de Bartona . 7 Ecclesiam de Grendona. Et in Burgo meo de Jeddew' unum toft . 7 .vii. acras. Et in domibus suis quas habent in Burgo meo de Berew' :' talem libertatem ~ scilicet ut nullus ministrorum Reg*is* Tunella vini a mercatoribus illuc allata . 7 ibi euacuata :' exigere presumat. Et unam Piscariam in Tuede . illam scilicet que est supra Pontem . quam Willelmus de Lambertona Auo meo liberam 7 quietam reddidit. Ex dono Gospatrici vicecomitis . in Craaling unam Carrucatam terre 7 dimidiam . & tres acras cum .ij. maisuris. Ex dono Bereng*arii* Eng*aine* :' unam marcam argenti in molendino eiusdem Craal*ing* . 7 .ij. Bouatis terre cum uno villano . 7 uno Tofto . 7 ad sustentamentum uictus capellani capelle eiusdem ville seruituri :' alias .ij. bouatas terre cum alio Tofto . 7 unum aliud toftum iuxta ecclesiam. Ex dono D*aui*d Olif*ard* :' Decimam molendini eiusdem Craal*ing*. Ex dono Oromi fil*ii* Eilaui :' unam carrucatam terre in altera Craal*ing*. Ex dono Ric*ardi* Angli :' duas bouatas terre in Scrauesb' . 7 duas Bouat*as* terre in Langt'. Ex dono Gameli clerici :' Cauerum . Osulfo 7 Ughtr*edo* fil*iis* eius concedentibus illius donationem. Ex dono Margar*ete* uxoris Thome de London*iis* . concedentibus eodem Thoma ~ 7 Henr*ico* Louel fil*io* eiusdem Margar*ete* :' Ughtredesxaghe ~ cum suis rectis diuisis. Ex dono

Christiane[c] uxoris Ger*uasii* Ridel .' terciam partem ville de Xernwingeslawe. Ex Dono Gaufr*idi* de Perci .' Ecclesiam de Oxenham ~ cum .ij. carrucatis terre . 7 .ij. Bouatis eidem Ecclesie adiacentibus . 7 communem Pasturam 7 communem foaliam[d] eiusdem Oxenham. Et Niwebigginghe 7 communem pasturam 7 communem foaliam[d] cum ceteris hominibus eiusdem ville Oxenham quam ~ scilicet Niwebigg*ing*— Henricus de Perci post mortem predicti .G. fratris sui ~ ante dilectum fratrem meum Regem M. concessit canonicis datam. Ex dono Rad*ulfi* fil*ii* Duneg*al* . 7 uxoris eius Bethoc .' unam carrucatam terre in Rughechestre . 7 communem eiusdem ville pasturam. Ex Dono Turg*isii* de Rossedal' .' Domum Religionis de Lidel . cum tota terra ei adiacente . Ecclesiam quoque de Kirchandr*es* cum omnibus ad illam pertinentibus. Ex dono Guid*onis* de Rossed*al* ~ assensu 7 consensu Rad*ulfi* fil*ii* sui .' xlii. acras inter Esch 7 Lidel ~ ubi Esch 7 Lidel conueniunt. Et libertatem aque a fossa de Lidel usque ad ecclesiam de Lidel. Ex dono Ran*ulfi* de Sol*is* .' Ecclesiam de Valle Lidel . 7 Ecclesiam de Dodint*ona* iuxta Bertonam 7 dimidiam carrucatam terre in Nasebith. Ex dono Geruasii Ridel ~ qui post factus est canonicus Jeddew' . 7 Rad*ulfi* fratris sui .' Ecclesiam de Alboldesle—cum omnibus pertinentiis 7 rectitudinibus suis. Ex dono Willelmi de Veteri Ponte .' unam Carrucatam terre de dominio suo in Caredene . cum communi aisiamento ville. Hec[e] autem omnia ita integre 7 plenarie ~ Deo 7 Beate Marie ~ 7 supradictis canonicis concedo 7 confirmo .' sicut in autenticis predecessorum meorum 7 aliorum proborum uirorum qui bona predicta eis contulerunt .' scriptis continetuR. Volo[e] itaque ac firmiter precipio . ut omnia quecumque modo possident . uel deinceps iuste possessuri sunt .' ita libere 7 pure—omni remota exactione . suprafati Canonici mei pace perpetua cum omnibus monasterii sui libertatibus ~ liberisque consuetudinibus confirmatione 7 auctoritate mea possideant .' sicut aliqui Canonici Possessiones . Libertates . liberasque consuetudines sui monasterii siue quelibet ecclesiastica iura . liberius . quietius . atque honestius possident. Huius[e] autem concessionis 7 confirmationis mee Testes hi sunt. Ric*ardus*[e] Episcopus de S*ancto* Andr*ea* . Engelramus Episcopus de Glasg*u* . Joh*annes* Abb*as* de Calceo . Euer*ardus* Abb*as* de Holcultr' . Nich*olaus* Cancellar*ius* . Math*eus* Archidi*aconus* de Sancto Andr*ea* . Ric*ardus* capellanus . Walt*erus* fil*ius* Al*ani* . Ric*ardus* de Moreuill' . Phil*ippus* de Valoniis . Rob*ertus* Auenel . Bernardus fil*ius* Brien . Gilleb*ertus* fil*ius* Richerii . Dauid Ouieth. Ap*ud* Pebles.

ENDORSED. [Generalis ?] confirma[cio] Willelmi Reg*is* (xii–xiii cent.). Confirmacio Willelmi Regis ? (xiv–xv cent.). Ewisdal[e ?] (xvi cent.). The kirk off Liddell (xvi–xvii cent.). Also other illegible endorsements, apparently of the xvi or xvii cents., including one beginning Duas bouatas de.

DESCRIPTION. 12·8″ (32·5 cm.), Top and bottom × 12·9″ (32·9 cm.), L, R. There is a single slit at the foot for a seal tag, but no tag or seal remains. The document is considerably stained by damp, and having formerly been folded has apparently at a later date been framed.

HAND. Scribe Af. Note the uncial form for capital E in the phrase *Ex dono*. Unruled, but expertly set out on the large parchment.

SOURCE. Original, Duke of Buccleuch and Queensberry, Drumlanrig Castle.

PRINTED. Fraser, *Buccleuch*, ii, 1–3, no.1 (with facsimile); *Nat. MSS. Scot.*, i, Pl.xxxviii.

NOTES. [a] Large roman W. [b] ÷ is used for est throughout. [c] Written Xpīane. [d] Sic. [e] Capital emphasized by thickened strokes.

COMMENT. With Tonsmidhop compare the place called Midhop by Norham mentioned by Reginald of Durham, *Libellus de admirandis beati Cuthberti virtutibus* (Surtees Soc., 1835), p.115. For the identification of 'Eadwardesle' and 'Xernwingeslawe', cf. George Watson in *Hawick Trans.* (1923), 46–7; it may be added that *Exchequer Rolls*, i, 43 refers to the lands of 'Serlinglaw' in 1288, in the bailiary of Jedburgh. For the identification of 'Ughtredesxaghe', cf. *OPS*, i, 326, Uchterseatmylne, and *Hawick Trans.* (1963), 14, Utterside (1690). Evidently this land formed part of the lordship of Hawick held by the Lovels, presumably through the marriage of Ralph Lovel II to Margaret, whose parentage has not been established. Outerside is four miles west of Branxholm, where land was granted to St Andrews Cathedral Priory by Henry Lovel before 30 March, 1183, by an undated charter (*St Andrews Liber*, 60, 261). The family of de Soules seem to have held Old Roxburgh from an early period, but there does not seem to be any evidence of their holding in adjacent Nisbet.

63 Confirms the property and privileges of Kelso Abbey as confirmed in the charter of King Malcolm IV. (Probably *c.*1165 or 1166)

Will*elmus*[a] Dei gr*ati*a Rex Scott' Episcopis, abbatibus, comitibus, baronibus, justic*iis*, vicecom*itibus*, prepositis, ministris et omnibus probis hominibus tocius terre sue, clericis et laicis, salutem. Nouerint omnes tam presentes quam futuri pie memorie D*aui*d Regem Scottorum auum meum dum comes fuit fundasse quandam abbathiam apud Selekirke in honore Sancte Dei genetricis uirginis Marie, et Sancti Johannis Ewangeliste, pro salute anime sue et patris et matris sue, fratrumque et sororum suarum, omniumque antecessorum successorumque suorum. Set postquam, diuina clemencia, post obitum fratris suis Alexandri ei successit in regnum, consilio et ammonicione uenerabilis memorie Johannis tunc Glasguensis episcopi et procerum suorum Deum timencium, predictam abbaciam apud Rokesburg', quia locus erat congruencior, transtulit, in ecclesiam Beate Marie uirginis que sita [est][b] super ripam fluminis Twede in loco qui dicitur Kalch*o*. Quam ecclesiam Rob*ertus* episcopus Sancti Andree in cuius erat episcopatu pro Dei amore et suo ab omni episcopali subieccione liberam esse concessit, ita scilicet ut abbas et monachi supradicte ecclesie a quocunque episcopo uoluerint in Scocia uel in Cumbria crisma suum et oleum et ordinacionem ipsorum abbatum et monachorum et cetera sancte ecclesie sacramenta accipiant. Hanc libertatem cum aliis libertatibus et possessionibus quas ex liberalitate aui mei regis D*aui*d, patris mei comitis Henrici, Regis Malcolmi fratris mei siue mea possident, eis quantum ad me pertinet inperpetuum concedo et potestate regali in perpetuam elemosinam confirmo. Videlicet, uillam de Kalch*o* cum suis rectis diuisis in terris et in aquis solutam et quietam et ab omni exaccione liberam; et quandam terram quam Geroldus dedit iuxta diuisas ipsius uille, que terra descendit in uiam qua itur ad Neythanesthirn; et quocienscunque in ipsa ecclesia in solempnitatibus uel aliis diebus seruicium Dei audiero,[c] omnes offerendas meas et omnium qui mecum erunt ipsi ecclesie confirmo. Et in Hedenham de molendino xii[cim] celdras de brasio unoquoque anno; et de mora de Hedenham ad fodiendum petas, a quodam fossato quod descendit de quadam alia mora, transeundo recto tramite illam moram, usque ad tres magnos lapides ex altera parte existentes; et in territorio eiusdem uille ex dono Pagani de Bosseuilla unam bouatam terre. Et in burgo de Rokesburg' quadraginta solidos de censu unoquoque anno; et unam toftam iuxta ecclesiam Sancti Jacobi et alteram in nouo burgo; et terram que fuit Gauteri cimentarii; et ecclesias ipsius burgi cum terra sua, sicut unquam Acellinus archidiaconus eas melius et liberius habuit; et dimidiam toftam que fuit Aculfi; et in molendinis xx[ti] celdras inter farinam et frumentum; et partem septimam piscature. Et in Sproustona unam carucatam terre et x. acras et maisuras carucate pertinentes, et tres acras de prato; et ecclesiam eiusdem uille, et terram ecclesie pertinentem, et iuxta Prestesbrige duas bouatas terre quas dedi eis in escambio duarum bouatarum quam mihi accomodauerunt monachi de terra ecclesie Sancti Laurencii de Berewic'. Et uillam de Reueden in terris et in aquis; et pasturas de Sproustona et moras ad fodiend*um* turuas communes hominibus de Reuedenna sicut hominibus de Sproustona; et unam carucatam terre de Haudena, cum crofta et tofta in eadem uilla, ex donacione Waldeui. Et in Berewic' unam carucatam terre et unam maisuram carucate pertinentem, iuxta ecclesiam Sancti Laurencii, et alteram maisuram in burgo; et xl. sol*idos* de censu eiusdem burgi unoquoque anno; et dimidiam partem unius piscature que uocatur Berewic'streme; et septimam partem molendinorum; et terram Dodini in eadem uilla; et terram Walclini filii Ernebaldi. Et uillam de Middilham et de Bothelden' cum suis rectis diuisis in terris et in aquis, in bosco et in plano; et xxx[ta] acras terre de territorio Lillisclef, inter Alnam et riuulum qui diuidit terram de Medilham et de Lillescliue, et decimam molendini ipsius uille, scilicet Lillescliue. Et Whytelau et Whytemere cum suis rectis diuisis. Et terram de Selekirc' cum suis rectis diuisis in terris, in aquis et in bosco et in plano; et aquas meas circa Selekirc' communes ad piscandum suis propriis piscatoribus ut meis; et boscos meos domibus suis faciend*is*, et ad ardendum ut mihi; et ecclesiam alterius Selekirche cum dimidia carucata terre. Et ecclesiam et terram de Lesmahag*u* cum suis rectis diuisis. Et Trauerlen cum suis rectis diuisis, sicut Uuieth eam melius et plenius tenuit et habuit, cum omnibus aisiamentis uicini strodre[d] quod Cameri dicitur; et Craggham eiusdem uille sicut Dompnus Abbas Alfwynus Sancte Crucis et Ernaldus tunc abbas de Kalchou se adinuicem concordauerunt de quadam calumpnia que fuit inter eos de ipsa cragga coram hiis testibus: Rad*ulfo* Abbate de Neubotil, Willelmo abbate de Striuelyn, Osberto priore de Jeddeword, Ricardo clerico, Machebet. Hanc autem Trauerlen dedit auus meus predicte ecclesie de Kalch*o* in excambium x. librarum terre quam habuerunt in Hardengasthorn iuxta Norhamtoun. Et in Renfru unam toftam et unam navim, et piscaturam unius retis solutam et quietam et ab omni consuetudine liberam. Et in Edinburg' unam toftam; et in Hadington' unam toftam; et in Jedd' unam toftam; et in Pebl*es* unam toftam; et in Lanarc' unam toftam. Et ecclesiam de Keth. Et dimidium segimen craspesiorum qui in Ford applicuerint. Et decimam animalium et porcorum et caseorum de can. Et de quatuor cadred de Galweia quam uiuente Rege Alexandro auus meus habuit per unumquemque annum. Et decimam caseorum de Tweddale singulis annis similiter; et dimidietatem coriorum coquine mee et omnium occisionum meorum, ita ut ubicunque ego uel aliquis successorum meorum unum corium habuerit, habeant et monachi alterum; et similiter de unctis et de sepis sicut de coriis; et omnes pelles arietum et agnorum, et decimam coriorum ceruorum et ceruarum quos ueltrarii mei capient. Hos autem redditus coquine mee et occisionum mearum habebunt monachi per illam terram tantum quam uiuente Rege Alexandro auus meus habuit. Et in Kars unam salinam. Preterea quantum ad me spectat concedo et confirmo ecclesie prenominate: ex donacione Comitis Patricii[e] ecclesiam de Home cum duabus carucatis terre et cum prato uno in territorio eiusdem uille; et ecclesiam de Foggou cum una carucata terre; et ecclesiam de Grenelaue cum terra ad eandem pertinentem et capella de Lambedena. Ex donacione Herberti de Maccuswel ecclesiam de Maccuswel. Ex donacione Hie et Petri filii eius ecclesiam de Sympring'. Ex donacione Rogeri de Ou ecclesiam de Langetune cum omnibus ad eam pertinentibus. Ex donacione Rogerii fil*ii* Willelmi ecclesiam Sancti Laurencii de Berewyc'. Ex donacione Walteri Corbet ecclesiam de Malcaruiston' cum una carucata terre. Ex donacione Uctredi de Molla ecclesiam de Molla cum terra ad eam pertinente. Ex donacione Wische ecclesiam uille sue. Ex donacione Willelmi Finemund ecclesiam de Kambusnaythan. Ex donacione Ricardi Cumyn ecclesiam de Lyntonrotherick. Prenominatas igitur terras et possessiones omnes ego ecclesie Beate Marie virginis de Kalch*o* et monachis ibidem Deo seruientibus iure perpetuo possidendas concedo, et hac carta mea in perpetuam elemosinam confirmo, ut ita libere, quiete et honorifice teneant et possideant[f] omnes terras suas et possessiones et uniuersa tenementa sua sicut aliqua ecclesia liberius et quiecius et honorabilius elemosinas suas tenet et possidet; ita ut nemo de hac nominata ecclesia de Kalch*o*, neque de possessionibus eius neque de ulla re que ad eam pertinet, aliquid presumat exigere, nisi solas oraciones ad anime salutem. Hiis testibus.

RUBRIC. Carta Regis Willelmi super fundacione.[g] Idem per omnia dicit Malcolmus frater eius qui fuit Rex ante ipsum . nichil omnino addens aut subtrahens.[h]

SOURCE. NLS, MS. Adv. 34.5.1., fos.11^{v}–13^{r}.

PRINTED. *Kelso Liber*, no.12.

NOTES. [a] Initial red. [b] MS. omits. [c] Fo.12^{r}. [d] Scoodre, MS. Fo.12^{v}. [e] Com inserted before Patricii, for Cos. [f] Fo.13^{r}. [g] Fo.11^{v}, red. [h] Fo.13^{r}, added immediately after Testibus in text hand.

COMMENT. Probably this was issued very early in the reign and confirms only grants which had been made down to the time of Malcolm IV's death. Property confirmed here which does not appear in King Malcolm's charter of 1159 (*RRS*, i, no.131) comprises one ploughgate in Hadden by the gift of one Waltheof (see no.101); one oxgang — 14 acres — in Ednam by the gift of Pain de Bosville (see no.317); the church of Greenlaw with the chapel of Lambden; the church of Langton; and a toft in Jedburgh.

64 Grants to Kelso Abbey that its men dwelling at Kelso may have licence on every day of the week except the day appointed for the king's market of Roxburgh to buy within their own toun fuel, timber and grain, and those travelling to sell these commodities may likewise have licence. The abbey's men may sell bread, ale and flesh in their shops. If they bring fish in their own carts or on their horses, and wish to sell it,

they may do so in their shops. Carts coming from elsewhere and travelling through must not unload or have their loads sold except at the king's market. On the day appointed for the king's market, the abbey's men shall not buy anything in their toun, but come to the market and buy what they want with the king's other burgesses, in accordance with their rightful customs. Peebles. (1165 × 1171)

.W. Rex Scott' . Justicie sue . 7 vicecom*iti* suo . 7 prepositis suis de Rokesburg' . salutem. Sciatis me concessisse Deo 7 Ecclesie Sancte Marie de Kelch' . 7 monachis ibidem Deo seruientibus pro anima Comitis H*enrici* patris mei . 7 pro animabus antecessorum meorum . 7 pro salute anime mee . ut homines sui qui in Kelchou sunt manentes . omnibus diebus septimane . excepto die statuto fori mei de Rokesburg' . licenciam habeant emendi in uilla sua focale . 7 materiem . 7 annonam . 7 transeuntes licenciam habeant eis ista uendendi. Habeant etiam homines sui licenciam uendendi in fenestris suis panem 7 ceruisiam . 7 carnem. Si autem piscem in propriis suis quadrigis uel equis attulerint :' 7 inde uendere uoluerint :' in fenestris suis liceat eis uendere. Quadrige autem aliunde uenientes 7 perinde transeuntes neque ibi exhonerent neque ibi uendant :' set ad forum meum ueniant. Die autem fori mei statuti de Rokesburg non liceat eis quicquam emere in uilla sua :' set ad forum meum ueniant . 7 ibi cum aliis burgensibus meis que uoluerint emant :' per rectas consuetudines suas. T*estibus* Enge*lramo* Episcopo de Glas*gu*. Nic*olao* Cancell*ario*. Willelmo de Haia. Rob*erto* de Chartres. Apud Pebbles;

RUBRIC. Carta super quasdam libertates ville de Kelch' (top in red).
SOURCE. NLS, MS. Adv. 34.5.1, fo.145^{v}.
PRINTED. *Kelso Liber*, no.387.
COMMENT. This brieve marks one of the earliest recorded stages of the development of Kelso as an urban community.

65 Confirms the property and privileges of Dryburgh Abbey. (Probably early, *c.*1165–1171)

Willelmus Rex Scotie episcopis, abbatibus, comitibus, baronibus, justiciariis vicecomitibus prepositis ministris et omnibus probis hominibus totius terre sue salutem. Sciant tam posteri quam presentes me concessisse et hac mea carta[a] confirmasse Deo et ecclesie Sancte Marie de Driburgh et canonicis ibidem Deo servientibus omnes donationes et possessiones et libertates que eis temporibus Dauid regis aui mei et Malcolmi regis fratris mei concesse sunt et confirmate. In primis ex dono Dauid regis aui mei ecclesiam de Lanerk cum terra ad eandem pertinente et capellam de Paduynnan et in eadem villa terram illam quam Nycholaus clericus meus tempore Dauid regis aui mei tenuit hiisdem terminis et divisis; et landam totam que vocatur Caddisleya sicut nemore accingitur, cum pascuis infra forestam meam circumquaque, et licenciam accipiendi in nemoribus meis ea que necessaria fuerint usibus suis et edificiis; et quietanciam de teloneo quantum ad propria catalla sua per totam terram meam. Confirmo etiam eis illud toftum quod fuit Johannis sacerdotis in Rogesburgh; ex dono M*alcolmi* regis duas marcas in Edinham singulis annis et dimidiam carucatam terre in eadem villa et terram illam que vicina est muro juxta portam occidentalem de Rogesburgh; ex dono Hugonis de Morevilla ecclesiam de Mertoun et ecclesiam de Childinchirch et piscationes de Berwic et decimam molendinorum de Lauder et de Saultoun; ex dono Beatricis de Bello campo ecclesiam de Bosyet et terram in Rogesburgh quam emit de Rogero janitore et decimam molendini de Nathanth*irn*; ex dono Ricardi de Morevill*a* ecclesiam de Saultoun; ex dono R*ogeri*[b] Bartram decimam molendini de Newthoun; ex dono Dauid Olifard unam plenariam carucatam terre in Smalham; ex dono G*alfridi* de Percy duas bovatas terre in Hetoun. Volo itaque et firmiter precipio ut predicti canonici tenuras predictas et libertates ita libere et quiete et honorifice perpetuo teneant et possideant sicut aliqua [domus][c] relig*iosa* in tota terra mea liberius et quietius et honorificentius tenet et possidet. Testibus etc.

RUBRIC. Confirmatio generalis et super licencia accipiendi in nemoribus regis que necessaria sunt et super quietancia telonei ubique. cclv.
SOURCE. NLS, MS. Adv. 34.4.7, fo.72^{r-v}.
PRINTED. *Dryburgh Liber*, no.241.
NOTES. [a] Fo.72^{v}. [b] Ric', MS. [c] MS. omits.
COMMENT. This confirmation adds nothing to what Dryburgh Abbey already held by *c*.1165.

66

Confirms to Durham Cathedral Priory Nisbet (in Edrom) and Edrom with the church of that toun and all its chapels (all Berwickshire). Roxburgh. (1165 × 1171)

Will'.[a] Rex Scott' . Omnibus probis hominibus tocius terre sue . Clericis 7 laicis salut*em*. Sciant presentes 7 futuri me concessisse 7 hac carta mea confirmasse Deo 7 Sancto Cuthberto[b]. 7 Monachis eius de Dunelmo donationem[c] Gospatrici comitis . 7 successorum eius . scilicet[d] Nesebite . 7 uillam de Ederham[e] 7 ecclesiam eiusdem uille . cum omnibus capell*is* 7[f] pertinentiis suis . in liberam 7 perpetuam elemosinam tenendas[g] ita libere . 7 quiete plenarie 7 honorifice ;' sicut carte comitis Gospatr*ici* 7 successorum eius testantur . 7 confirmant. T*estibus* Ric*ardo* Episcopo Sancti Andr*ee* . Nichol*ao* Cancellario . Ric*ardo* capell*ano* . Ric*ardo* de Moreuill' constabulario . W*altero* fil*io* Alani dapifero . D*auid* Olif*ard* . Dolfino capell*ano* . Johanne filio Ormn[h]. uicecomite de Rokesburgo apud RokesburGVM.

ENDORSED. *A*: Willelmi reg*is* de Eaderham (crude hand of xii–xiii cent.). et Nesebit (xiii cent.). Carta (xv cent. insertion). N. tercia vj^{te} (xv cent.). Illegible word in xiii cent. hand at foot of dorse. *B*: Willelmi Reg*is* Scottorum de Nesebit. Æderam 7 ecclesia eiusdem uille (xii cent.). Carta W. Regis Scottorum de Nesbytt Ederham et ecclesia eiusdem uille. 2^{a} pyxide (xv cent.).
DESCRIPTION. *A*: 7·5″ (19 cm.), Top, 7·7″ (19·5 cm.), Bottom × 3·2″ (8·2 cm.), L, R. Foot folded, 0·9″. Double slits. Tag 7·5″ long, 0·5″ wide. Seal natural wax stained brown, rubbed on obverse, otherwise excellent condition with clear impression; attached back to front. *B*: 6·5″ (16·6 cm.), Top, 6·3″ (16·2 cm.), bottom × 3·6″ (9 cm.), L, 2·7″ (6·6 cm.), R. Tie almost entire. Tongue 5·2″ long, 0·7″ wide. Seal, natural wax, stained brown, in excellent condition, attached back to front.
HAND. *A*: Scribe Af. Ruled in drypoint or pencil. *B*: Scribe Ai. Unruled.
SOURCE. Duplicate originals. Durham, D. & C. Muniments, Misc. Chr. no.596 = *A*. Ibid., Misc. Chr. no.601 = *B*. Printed here from *A*, with major variants of *B* noted.
PRINTED. Raine, *North Durham*, no.42 (*A*), no.43 (*B*).

NOTES. [a] W', *B.* [b] Cudberto, *B.* [c] donacionem, *B.* [d] scilic 7, *A* and *B.* [e] Ederam, *B.* [f] *B* adds iustis. [g] tenendum, *B.* [h] Ormij, *B,* with horizontal stroke joining the verticals.
COMMENT. See no.105.

67 Prohibits his sergeands of the sheriffdom of Berwick from having customs or making demands in Coldingham and its shire in respect of pleas and lawsuits touching them which are different from those enjoyed by his sergeands in eleemosynary land in his other sheriffdoms. Roxburgh. (1165 × 1171)

W'.[a] Rex Scott' . Justiciis suis . 7 Vicecomiti suo de Berewic . salutem. Prohibeo firmiter ne seruientes mei uicecomitatus de Berewic . alias habeant consuetudines . aut alias faciant exacciones[b] . in elemosina mea de Goldingham[c] . 7 Goldinghamshire[c]. de placitis . 7 querelis quas ipsi mouent .' quam seruientes mei aliorum uicecomitatuum meorum habent in aliis elemosinis meis in terra mea. T*estibus* Eng*elramo*[d] Episcopo de Glasg*u* . Nich*olao* Cancellario . Dauid Olif*ard*[e] . Justic*ia* . Hug*one* Rid*el*[e] . Rob*erto* Auenel. Apud Rokesburg'.

ENDORSED. *A*: Carta W. Reg*is* contra balliuos de Berewyk ne alias habeant consuetudines aut exacciones fac in Coldingham aut Coldynghamshire quam seruientes aliorum vicecomit*atuum* habent aut fac' in aliis elemosinis suis in terra Scocie. (xv cent.). E. iij[a] vj[te] (xv cent.). *B*: Carta Willelmi reg*is* de liberis consuetudinibus (xiii cent.) in Cold' et Coldynghamshire (xv cent.). m. carta Willelmi R' de liberis consuet' in Coldynghamshyr (xv cent.). M. M. iij[a] vj[te] (xv cent.).
DESCRIPTION. *A*: 6·5″ (16·5 cm.), Top, 6·3″ (16 cm.), Bottom × 2·2″ (5·7 cm.), L, R. Foot folded 0·6″. Single slit. Tag 5·7″ long, 0·7″ wide. Seal in natural wax, chipped at right; attached back to front and upside down. *B*: 6·5″ (16·5 cm.), Top, 6·7″ (17 cm.), bottom × 3″ (7·5 cm.), L, R. Foot folded 0·9″. Single slit. Tag 5·2″ long, 0·7″ wide. Seal in natural wax, entire, good impression.
HAND. *A*: Scribe Ai. Unruled. *B*: Scribe Db. Unruled.
SOURCE. Originals, Durham, D. & C. Muniments, Misc. Chr. no.610 = *A*. Ibid., Misc. Chr. no.607 = *B*. Printed here from *A*, with major variants of *B* noted.
PRINTED. Raine, *North Durham*, no.37 (*A*), no.38 (*B*).
NOTES. [a] Diagonal stroke through left-hand side of letter, *A*; *B* reads, with similar but curled stroke, W. Dei gr*ati*a. [b] exactiones, *B.* [c] Initial C in *B.* [d] Engalram', *B.* [e] Name in full, *B.*
COMMENT. The sergeands referred to here may have been the Lothian counterpart of the northern English serjeants of the peace, for whom see R. Stewart-Brown, *The Serjeants of the Peace in Medieval England and Wales* (1936).

68 Forbids the officers of the church of Wedale (Stow, Midlothian) and those who guard the peace there to detain the men of the abbot of Kelso who come to Wedale with their cattle to seek sanctuary, provided that the abbot offers to do them right and justice; on pain of the king's forfeiture. Roxburgh. (1165 × 1171)

W. Dei gr*ati*a Rex Scott' . Ministris ecclesie de Wedale . 7 illis qui pacem ibidem custodiunt .' salutem. Prohibeo uobis firmiter ne detineatis homines Abbatis de Kelch' qui ueniunt ad uos ad pacem uel catalla eorum . desicut ipse Abbas offert . eis 7 pro eis omnem rationem 7 iusticiam . super meam forisfacturam . Test*ibus* . Nich*olao* Cancell*ario* meo . D*aui*d Olifard' . apud Rokesburc' .

RUBRIC. Carta super homines 7 catalla Abbatis de Kelch' (Top, in red).
SOURCE. NLS, MS. Adv. 34.5.1, fo.150[v].
PRINTED. *Kelso Liber*, no.410.
COMMENT. On the girth, or sanctuary, of St Mary of Wedale see *RRS* i, 24; cf. also *Northern History*, i (1966), 35–6, 41. The *dei gratia* may be due to the copyist.

69 Confirms generally the property and privileges of Coupar Angus Abbey. Roxburgh. (1165 × 1171)

Confirmatio regis Willielmi de omnibus donationibus Malcolmi regis fratris sui Deo Sanctæ Mariæ et monachis de Cupro. Apud Roxbrughe. Testibus: Richardo Episcopo Sancti Andreæ, Engelramo Episcopo Glasguensi, Nicolao Cancellario, Waltero filio Alani dapifero, Richardo de Moreweill constabulario, Philipo de Wallon camerario, Willielmo de Haya pincerna, Heugone Redell, Villelmo Juuene de Veteri Ponte, Bernardo filio Briani.[a]

SOURCE. NLS, MS. Adv. 33.2.9, fo.27[r].
PRINTED. *Coupar Angus Rental*, i, 320, no.3.
NOTE. [a] Bani, MS.

70 Commands his sheriffs and other officers that they are to treat the lawsuits of Newbattle Abbey as if they were his own, and that they shall justly maintain the monks and lay-brothers of Newbattle. Traquair. (1165 × 1171)

Will*elmus* Rex Scott' Justiciis Vicecomitibus Ministris et omnibus probis hominibus tocius terre sue salutem. Mando et firmiter[a] precipio ut ubicunque monachi siue fratres de Neu*botle* ad placita mea inter vos venerint . placita eorum sicut mea placitetis et iuste manuteneatis. Prohibeo etiam firmiter ne quis infra diuisas terrarum suarum umquam forisfaciat super meum plenarium forisfactum. T*estibus* Nich*olao* cancell*ario* . W*altero* filio Alani dapifero.[b] Apud Trauerquer.

TITLE. Carta Reg*is* Willelmi de fugitiuis [c].
SOURCE. NLS, MS. Adv. 34.4.13, fo.57[r].
PRINTED. *Newbattle Registrum*, no.210.
NOTES. [a] MS. has pro here, not deleted. [b] MS. dapiferi. [c] Table of contents, fo.3[v].

71 Commands the sheriffs and officers in whose bailiaries the canons of St Andrews Cathedral Priory hold churches to cause the canons to have the teinds due to them from their parishioners, as in the time of King Malcolm IV; in the case of refusal, they are to compel payment and take the penalty from defaulters as was enacted in Scotland north of Forth by King David I. Traquair. (1165 × 1171)

Willelmus[a] rex Scotorum omnibus vicecomitibus et ministris tocius terre sue in quorum potestatibus canonici Deo et Sancto Andree apostolo seruientes ecclesias tenent salutem. Mando uobis et firmiter precipio quatinus predictis canonicis decimas suas et omnes rectitudines catholice ecclesie pertinentes de parochianis suis habere faciatis et parochias suas ita integras sicut in tempore Malcolmi regis fratris mei plenius et melius fuerunt. Quod si noluerint .˙ precipio uobis quod cogatis illos facere et plenarium forisfactum ab eis accipiatis sicut a rege Dauid auo meo statutum est in Scocia. Testibus Nicholao cancellario . Dauid Olifard . apud Trauerqueir .

RUBRIC. nota bene (note at top in later hand).
SOURCE. GD, SRO 45/27/8 (St Andrews priory cartulary), fo.ciiii[v].
PRINTED. *St Andrews Liber*, 225.
NOTE. [a] Blue initial V.
COMMENT. See *RRS*, i, no.233, and cf. ibid., 65–6.

72 Confirms to Melrose Abbey the whole land which John son of Orm granted it in the territory of 'Hunedun' (Hownam Grange, in Hownam, Roxburghshire), as the charter of John bears witness. Selkirk. (1166 × 1170)

U.[a] Dei gr*ati*a Rex Scot', omnibus probis hominibus tocius terre sue, presentibus et futuris, salutem. Sciatis me concessisse et hac mea carta confirmasse Deo et ecclesie Sancte Marie de Melros et monachis ibidem [Deo][b] seruientibus in perpetuam elemosinam totam terram quam Johannes filius Orm' eis dedit et carta sua confirmauit in territorio de Hunedun, per ipsas diuisas que continentur in carta predicti Johannis quam habent de eo de eadem terra, ita ut quicquid fuerit infra ipsas diuisas habeant et possideant inperpetuum ita libere, quiete, plenarie et honorifice sicut aliqua elemosina possidetur liberius, quiecius, [plenius et][c] honorificencius in regno meo, et sicut carta ipsius Johannis testatur melius[d] et confirmat, saluo seruicio meo. Test*ibus* Dauid fratre meo, Com*ite* Walleuo, D*aui*d Olifer, Roberto Auenil, Ric*ardo* capell*ano*, W*illelmo*[e] capell*ano*, Hug*one* clerico meo, Alex*andr*o de Sancto Martino, Ric*ardo* de Sancto Albano, Ric*ardo* clerico cancell*arii*, Magistro Johanne de Rokisburgh'. Apud Seleskirk.

RUBRIC. Confirmacio regis Willelmi de Hunedune.
SOURCE. BM, MS. Harl. 3960, fo.11[v].
PRINTED. *Melrose Liber*, no.128.
NOTES. [a] Initial red. [b] MS. omits Deo. [c] MS. omits plenius et. [d] Sic. [e] Full name supplied from *Melrose Liber*, no.127.
COMMENT. John son of Orm (whose charter is given in *Melrose Liber*, no.127) was lord of Hownam, in succession to his father Orm son of Eilaf, for whom see *RRS*, i and Lawrie, *Charters*, references in indices. See also no.314. Hunedun is obsolete, but was evidently the old name of Hownam Law (cf. *Melrose Liber*, no.137), while the land itself, referred to in 1454 as 'grangea de Hunedoune' (ibid., no.571), is represented by Hownam Grange.

The witnesses shew that this confirmation was issued on the same occasion, or almost the same occasion, as the donor's charter which dates 1165 × 1174. Richard the chaplain may therefore be identified with Richard bishop of Dunkeld. Richard here called clerk of the chancellor (Nicholas) was probably Richard of Lincoln. John's charter was witnessed by two royal clerks called Hugh: the senior doubtless Hugh of Roxburgh, the junior perhaps Hugh *de sigillo*.

73 Confirms to Coldingham Priory Fishwick (in Hutton) and half of Prenderguest (in Ayton) and the land which Swein the priest of Fishwick had in Coldingham and Lumsdaine (all Berwickshire), which lands Swein the priest of Fishwick restored to the monks of Coldingham in the presence of Earl Henry the king's father. Selkirk. (1165 × 1174)

W'. Rex Scott'. Omnibus probis hominibus tocius terre sue salutem. Sciant presentes 7 futuri me Concessisse 7 hac carta mea Confirmasse

Monachis de Goldincham Fiswich cum omnibus ad illam iuste pertinentibus in terris 7 aquis . 7 dimidiam Prendergest . 7 terram quam Swein presbiter de Fiswic habuit in Goldincham . 7 Lummesdene . quas terras Swein presbiter de Fiswic in presencia Comitis Henrici patris mei reddidit illis 7 quietas clammauit[a]. Quare uolo ut predicti monachi prenominatas terras teneant ita libere 7 quiete plenarie 7 honorifice . sicut carta Comitis Henrici patris mei testatur 7 Confirmat. Test*ibus* Eng*elramo* episcopo de Glasgu . Ric*ardo* Cumi*n* . Dolph*in* capellano . Roberto de Sancto Mich*aele* . Waltero de Berkel' . Hug*one* clerico meo . Ric*ardo* clerico . apud Selesch'.

ENDORSED. Confirm*atio* reg*is* Willelmi de quieta Clama*tione* terrarum quas Swanus presbiter tenuit (xiii cent.). s. ffyswyk et dimidia Prendergest etc. (xv cent.). Z. iij[a] vj[te] (xv cent.).
DESCRIPTION. 6·8″ (17·2 cm.), Top and bottom × 3·3″ (8·3 cm.), L, 2·5″ (6·3 cm.), R. Tie torn off. Tongue 4·7″ long. Seal almost entire, in natural wax, rather rubbed.
HAND. Scribe Aj (Richard of Lincoln). Unruled.
SOURCE. Original, Durham, D. & C. Muniments, Misc. Chr. no.597.
PRINTED. Raine, *North Durham*, no.44.
NOTE. [a] Sic.
COMMENT. Earl Henry's notification of Swein's quitclaim is Raine, *North Durham*, no.106 (= Lawrie, *Charters*, no.236).

74 Confirms to Kelso Abbey the toun of Traverlen (Duddingston, Midlothian), together with the land which belonged to Dodin in Berwick; and gives warrandice against all men. Roxburgh. (1165 × 1174)

.W. Rex Scott'. Episcopis . Abbatibus . Comit*ibus* . Baronibus . Justiciis . 7 Omnibus probis hominibus tocius terre sue . Francis 7 Anglis . clericis 7 laicis . salutem. Sciant omnes tam posteri quam presentes . me concessisse 7 hac presenti carta confirmasse . Ecclesie Sancte Marie de Kelcho 7 monachis ibidem Deo seruientibus uillam de Trauerlen cum suis rectis diuisis . 7 cum omnibus ad eam iuste pertinentibus . 7 illam terram que fuit Dodini in Berwic' ;· in liberam 7 perpetuam elemosinam . ita plenarie de me 7 de heredibus meis tenendam 7 habendam ;· sicut predictus Dodinus eam unquam melius 7 plenius tenuit 7 habuit ;· 7 ita liberam 7 quietam ;· sicut aliquam aliam elemosinam . liberius 7 quiecius tenent . 7 ita quod ego 7 heredes mei contra omnes homines . eis predictas terras warantizabimus. Hiis test*ibus* . Eng*elramo* Glasguensi episcopo . Ric*ardo* de Moreuill' constabulario . Waltero dapif*ero* . Rob*erto* Auenel . Sim*one* Arch*idiacono* . Waldeuo fil*io* Baldwini . Rogero de Munetoth . Sim*one* fratre eius. Apud Rochesburg'.;

RUBRIC. Confirmacio super villam de Trauerlen . 7 terram Dodini in Berewyc' (top in red).
SOURCE. NLS, MS. Adv. 34.5.1, fo.146[r].
PRINTED. *Kelso Liber*, no.389.
COMMENT. For the identification of 'Traverlen' with Duddingston see *Book of the Old Edinburgh Club*, xxx (1959), 1–9.

75 Confirms to Manuel Priory (Cistercian nunnery) the land in Manuel, Stirlingshire, granted by King Malcolm IV and perambulated for the nuns by G(eoffrey) de Melville and Thor son of

Swain; the teind of the mill of Yetholm, Roxburghshire, granted by Walter Corbet; and one toft in Roxburgh granted by Rawenild of Yetholm, as her chirograph bears witness. Yarrow Meres (St Mary's Loch). (1166 × 1171)

W'. Rex Scott'. Episcopis. Abbatibus. Comitibus. Baronibus. Justic*iis* . Vicecomitibus . Ministris prepositis . 7 Omnibus probis hominibus tocius terre sue . clericis . 7 laicis . Francis . 7 Anglis ·/ Scottis . 7 Galweiensibus ·/ salutem. Sciant presentes . 7 posteri . me concessisse . 7 hac carta mea confirmasse . Deo . 7 Monialibus . apud Manuel manentibus . 7 Deo seruientibus . in liberam 7 perpetuam elemosinam . terram illam in Manuel . quam Rex .M. frater meus eis dedit . cum omnibus iustis pertinenciis suis . 7 per rectas diuisas suas . sicut G. de Maleu*illa* 7 Thore filius Swani . 7 alii probi homines mei illam eis perambulauerunt. Cum communi pastura . 7 cum aisiamentis nemoris . de Materie . 7 Claustura . 7 focali . quantum ad proprios usus suos . eis opus fuerit. Et ex dono Walteri Corbet decimam molendini de Jhetham sicut Carta eius testatur. Et ex dono Rawenild de Jetham unam Maisuram in Rokesburgo sicut Cirografum eius testatur. Volo itaque . 7 precipio firmiter . ut predicte Moniales . terras . 7 teneuras prenominatas . habeant . 7 teneant . ita libere . 7 quiete . plenarie . 7 honorifice ·/ sicut aliqua elemosina in tota terra mea . liberius 7 quietius . plenius . melius . 7 honorificencius tenetur. Et prohibeo firmiter ne quis eis . aut alicui suorum . infra diuisas terrarum suarum in aliquo forisfaciat ·/ super meam plenariam forisfacturam. T*estibus* A*da* Comitissa . matre mea . Nichol*ao* Cancellario . Ric*ardo* de Moreu*illa* constabulario . Waltero filio Alani dapifero . D*aui*d Olif*ard* . Philippo de Valon*iis* Camerario . G. de Maleu*illa* . Alexandro de Sancto Mart*ino*. Apud JarwemeRes.

ENDORSED. Carta Reg*is* (xii cent.). Confirmatio Reg*is* W de terra de Manuel (xiii cent.).

DESCRIPTION. 10·1″ (25·7 cm.), Top, 9·8″ (25 cm.), Bottom × 5·7″ (14·6 cm.), L, R. Foot folded to a depth of 0·8″ (2 cm.) with tag folded double vertically, 5″ (13 cm.) long, 0·6″ (1·5 cm.). No seal, but traces of red wax.

HAND. Scribe Ai. Unruled.

SOURCE. Original, SRO, GD 1/88/1.

PRINTED. SHS *Misc.*, iv, 305–6.

COMMENT. Ralph of Yetholm and his wife Raganild granted land and houses in Roxburgh, in free burgage, to Brinkburn Priory in the time of Aldred the dean (of Teviotdale), probably *c.*1150–60 (*Brinkburn Chartulary*, 129).

76

Grants his firm peace to the Hospital of St Andrews and confirms to it the land of Kenly, Fife. Yarrow Meres (St Mary's Loch). (1165 × 1171)

W. Rex Scot'. Omnibus probis hominibus tocius terre sue salutem. Sciatis me concessisse . 7 dedisse . hospitali de Sancto Andrea . 7 omnibus rebus ad idem hospitale iuste pertinentibus meam firmam pacem. Quare uolo . 7 precipio firmiter . ut ipsi habeant . 7 possideant . terram de Kenlekin[a] perpetualiter quam auus meus rex Dauid predicto hospitali pro salute anime sue concessit . 7 dedit. Eapropter prohibeo ne aliquis huic predicto hospitali . uel terris suis aud[b] rebus suis ad illud iuste pertinentibus in aliquo forisfaciat super meum plenarium forisfactum. Test*ibus* Nicholao Cancell*ario* . D*aui*d Olif*ard*. Apud Jarumeres.

ENDORSED. De Kenlachin (xii cent.).
DESCRIPTION. 5·2″ (13·3 cm.) Top, bottom × 2·2″ (5·7 cm.), L, 1·2″ (3·2 cm.), R. Tie and tongue cut from left foot of document, both now torn away. No seal remains.
HAND. Scribe Aa. Unruled.
SOURCE. Original, SRO, GD 90/4 = *A*. SRO, GD 45/27/8 (St Andrews Priory cartulary), fo.xcviii[v] = *B*. Printed here from *A*, with one reading from *B* noted.
PRINTED. *St Andrews Liber*, 211 (from *B*).
NOTES. [a] Kenlakin, *B*. [b] Sic, *A*.
COMMENT. Cf. *RRS*, i, no.125.

77 Informs his responsible men of Fife that the beasts of the Hospital of St Andrews may have common pasture with their beasts and those of their tenants. Yarrow Meres (St Mary's Loch). (1165 × 1171)

Willelmus[a] rex Scot' . Omnibus probis hominibus suis de Fif . tam clericis quam laicis salutem . Sciatis me concessisse pro Dei amore et salute antecessorum meorum et mea quatinus peccora hospitalis de Sancto Andrea habeant communitatem in pascuis uobiscum et cum hominibus uestris. Quare firmiter prohibeo ne aliquis huic mee concessioni aliquod impedimentum faciat. Testibus Nicholao cancellario . D*aui*d Olifard apud Jarumeres.

RUBRIC. De hospitali (top in red).
SOURCE. SRO, GD 45/27/8 (St Andrews priory cartulary), fo.xcviii[v].
PRINTED. *St Andrews Liber*, 210–11.
NOTES. [a] Blue initial V.
COMMENT. Cf. *RRS*, i, no.124.

78 Confirms to Melrose Abbey the grant made to it by Walter son of Alan of the land of Mauchline, Ayrshire and of pasture in his forest and one ploughgate of arable towards the land of Douglas and of a fishery at the mouth of the River Ayr, as the charters of Walter and his son Alan bear witness. Jedburgh. (1165 × 1174, probably 1165 × 1173)

W. Rex Scott' . Omnibus probis hominibus totius terre sue Francis . & Anglicis . 7 Scottis . Salutem. Sciant tam posteri quam presentes me concessisse 7 hac mea carta confirmasse . ecclesie Sancte Marie de Meylros . 7 monachis ibidem Deo seruientibus donationem quam Walterus filius Alani fecit eidem ecclesie & monachis de terra de Machelin 7 de pastura in foresta eius . & de una carucata terre uersus terram de Duueglas . & de piscatura in hostio fluminis . Ar . in omnibus ita libere 7 quiete in perpetuam elemosina sicut liberius 7 quietius uel honorificentius carta ipsius Walteri . 7 carta Alani filii eius eis testantur. Saluo seruicio meo quod Walterus mihi debet de ipso Waltero 7 heredibus eius. Testibus his . Enge*lramo* episcopo Glasguensi . Osberto Abbate de Jedd' . Ric*ardo* Cumin . Odenel de Umframuill' . Hugone Giffard . Alex*andro* de Sancto Martino . Roberto de Sancto Michaele . Gregorio filio Gauf*ridi* . Hug*one* clerico Reg*is* . Dolfino capellano Reg*is* . Ric*ardo* clerico Reg*is* . Rogero de Merebotle . Willelmo de Huntedun. Apud Jeddewurd';

ENDORSED. Confirmacio Reg*is* W. de carta Walteri fil*ii* Alani (xiii cent.). O (red, xv cent.?). J. Scott (xvi cent.).
DESCRIPTION. 7·2″ (18·1 cm.), Top, 7·4″ (18·8 cm.), Bottom × 4·6″ (11·8 cm.) L, R. Foot folded to a depth of 0·6″ (1·5 cm.). Tag 6″ (15·5 cm.) long, 0·7″ (1·8 cm.) wide. Most of seal remains, in green wax, rev. to front, exceptionally sharp impression.
HAND. Scribe Bc. Unruled.
SOURCE. Original, SRO, GD 55/68.
PRINTED. *Melrose Liber*, no.68.
COMMENT. Odinel de Umfraville can hardly have witnessed any acts of William I after the outbreak of war in August, 1173. The attestation of the chaplain Dolfin also suggests a date relatively early in the reign. The charters of Walter son of Alan and his son Alan are given in *Melrose Liber*, nos.66, 67. Between 1189 and 1194, Alan granted an annual rent of 4s., payable out of the rent owed by Melrose Abbey for its land at Mauchline, to Warden Abbey, which like Melrose was a daughter house of Rievaulx (*Wardon Cartulary*, BHRS (1931), 235–6).

Gregory son of Geoffrey may have been Gregory de Melville, or the same as Gregory 'son of Geoffrey the sheriff', who witnesses *Holyrood Liber*, Appendix II, no.2 (p.208).

79 Confirms to Hexham Priory the whole of Whitfield (Northumberland), with the mill and all adjacent to the manor, except for those lands held of the king's mother by Robert son of William and Joel of Corbridge; to be held of his mother in fee farm and in perpetuity, free of all service, custom, aids and geld, by the same marches as those by which the king's mother held it of her husband Earl Henry, the king's father, and afterwards of the king himself, and as land from Earl Henry's own waste land which the king's mother and Robert (her) chaplain through her cultivated and provided with inhabitants. For an annual rent of six pounds of pepper at Michaelmas, as the king's mother's charter bears witness. Hunting lodges of Donkley Haugh (in Thorneyburn, Northumberland). (1166 × 1178, probably 1166)

W'. Rex Scott' Omnibus probis hominibus tocius terre sue salut*em*. Sciant presentes 7 futuri me concessisse 7 hac carta mea confirmasse Deo 7 ecclesie Sancti Andr*ee* Hagustald*ensi* 7 canonicis ibidem Deo seruientibus in perpetuum . totam Witefeld cum bosco 7 plano cum prato 7 pastura cum molendino . 7 cum omnibus eidem uille de Witefeld adiacentibus . preter illas terras quas Rob*ertus* fil*ius* Willelmi 7 Johel de Corebrig de matre mea tenent in uilla illa. Tenend*am* de Matre mea 7 heredibus eius in feodo firmo[a] 7 in perpetuum . libere 7 quiete ab omni seruicio 7 consuetudine . 7 omnibus auxiliis . 7 ab omni Geld per easdem diuisas per quas Mater mea tenuit illam de Henrico Comite patre meo 7 postea de me . 7 per illas diuisas per quas Robertus capell*anus* matris mee tenuit . 7 sicut illam quam Mater mea 7 Rob*ertus* capell*anus* per eam de dominio[b] guast H*enrici* comitis patris mei coluerunt 7 inhabitauerunt. Reddendo inde annuatim Matri mee 7 heredibus suis .VI. libras piperis ad festum Sancti Michael*is* sicut carta Comitisse Matris mee testatur 7 confirmat. Test*ibus* D*aui*d fratre meo . Com*ite* Wald*euo* . Hug*one* Ridel . Ric*ardo* Cumin . Rogero de Coigneres . Waltero de Windlesoure . Hug*one* Giffard . Liolfo filio Maccus . Gileb*erto* fil*io* Rich*erii* . Gileberto de Umframuill' . Willelmo de Haia . Willelmo de Mortem*er*. Apud Logias De Dunclliueshalch.

ENDORSED. Willelmi Reg*is* Scotie de Whitefeld (xii cent.). ne videatur quia nihil prodest (xv cent.). Let this deed be inrolled for the preservation thereof May 20th 1639 Humfrey Davenport (xvii cent.). 1 (red ink, uncertain date). xxj^mo^ die Junii 1634 In testem Tho. Brinley Auditor (on front of folded foot, xvii cent.).

DESCRIPTION. 8·6″ (21·9 cm.), Top, 8·4″ (21·2 cm.), Bottom × 4·8″ (12·3 cm.), L, R. Foot folded, with holes for silk cords. Seal attached by a length of woven silk cord doubled and passed through the holes in such a way that the cords cross at the back and at the front. Two doubled lengths of cord pass through the seal, and between the seal and the document the cords are brought together loosely by a small parchment tie. Silk now a pale yellow, perhaps originally white or green.

Large part of seal remains on cords, white wax with a marked pinkish tinge. Obv. to front, at about 45° to the right of vertical. Max. diameter, 2·7″. Legend fragmentary (obv.): OTTORV, (rev.): ELM.

HAND. Scribe Aj (Richard of Lincoln). Unruled.

SOURCE. Original, J.C. Blackett-Ord Esq., Whitfield Hall, Northumberland, Whitfield Box no.1, bundle of 'ancient documents'.

PRINTED. J. Hodgson, *History of Northumberland*, Pt. II, vol. iii (1840) p.18b (with errors); J. Raine, *Priory of Hexham* (Surtees Soc., 1865), ii, 86–7, no.V.

NOTES. [a] Sic. [b] Written dn̄io, evidently an adjective.

COMMENT. The wording of this charter follows closely the wording of a charter by the Countess Ada of which there is a copy in a vellum-bound paper cartulary and rent book of 1630, preserved at Whitfield in the same deed box as the above, p. 1 (printed Hodgson, *Hist. of Northumberland*, II, iii, 17). Probably both these charters date soon after William's accession. Donkley Haugh would refer to the stretch of flat ground by the North Tyne below Donkley Wood (in Thorneyburn); the name appears as Duncliffe in 1279 (*Proc. Archaeological Institute of Newcastle*, 1852, ii, Appendix, p.lv) and Doncliwod in 1315 (*Cal. Inq. post mortem*, vi, 426). This charter has what appears to be the earliest recorded form of the name. I have to thank Mr W. Percy Hedley for these references and for proposing this identification of the place-date, which was obscured by Hodgson's and Raine's misreading.

The fifth witness, Roger Conyers II, was a leading baron of the bishopric of Durham under Bishop William de Ste Barbe and Bishop Hugh du Puiset.

80

Re-grants and confirms to Robert de Brus all the land which his father and he held in Annandale, by the same marches as those by which they held it, to be held in feu and heritage, as freely as his father or he himself held it in the time of King David I and King Malcolm IV, for the service of ten knights, exempt from ward of the king's castles; saving also to the king the *regalia* pertaining to his regality, viz. treasure trove, murder, premeditated assault, rape of women, arson and plunder, which causes the king has reserved to himself. But the king grants that prosecutions for these causes shall be made by a man of the fief of Robert de Brus chosen by the king, and dealt with and impleaded before the king's justices within the sheriffdom (*comitatus*) of (Roxburgh?). Robert de Brus may take such toll and such customs from the men of the kingdom of Scotland as are taken at Roxburgh, saving the fixed render (*asisa*) of his barony. Lochmaben. (1165 × 1173, probably × 1172)

W'. Rex Scott'. Episcopis . Abbatibus . Comitibus . Baronibus . Justiciis . Vicecomitibus . Ceterisque probis hominibus tocius terre sue Francis 7 Anglis . Scottis 7 Galwahensibus clericis 7 Laicis salutem. Sciant presentes 7 futuri me reddidisse 7 Concessisse 7 hac carta mea Confirmasse Roberto de Brvs . 7 heredibus suis totam terram quam pater suus 7 ipse tenuerunt in Valle de Anand per easdem diuisas per quas pater suus eam tenuit . 7 ipse post patrem suum. Tenend*am* sibi 7 heredibus suis de me 7 heredibus meis In feudo 7 hereditate . In bosco 7 plano . In pratis 7 pascuis . In Moris 7 Mareisis . In aquis 7 stagnis 7 Molendinis . In forestis 7 tristriis . In saltubus 7 portubus . In Viis 7 semitis . In piscariis . 7 Omnibus aliis iustis pertinenciis suis . Ita libere 7 quiete plenarie 7 honorifice sicut pater suus uel ipse eam tempore Reg*is* D*aui*d aui mei . uel Reg*is* M' . fratris mei . liberius . 7 quiecius . plenius 7 honorificencius tenuit . Exceptis regalibus que ad regalitatem meam spectant. Scilicet Causa de Inuentione thesauri . Causa de murdra . Causa de assaltu premedit [ato][a] . Causa de femina efforciata . Causa de arsione . [Causa][a] de Rapina . quas causas mihi reseruaui. Concedo etiam ei ut hęę cause [sint][a] atacheate per unum hominem de feudo suo quem elegero . 7 tractate 7 placitate per ante Justicias meas infra Comitatum de [ ][b] [7 tale teloneum][a] 7 tales consuetudines capiet de hominibus Regni mei quales capiuntur apud Rokesbur[c][c] . excepta asisa baronie sue. Volo itaque [ut][a] predictus [Robertus 7 heredes sui prenominatum feudum][a] de me 7 heredibus meis [teneant 7 habeant ita][a] libere sicut superius diuisum est[d] . per seruicium .x. militum excepta custodia castellorum meorum unde ipsum quietum clamaui. Test*ibus* Eng*elramo* episcopo de Glasgu . Christiano[e] episcopo de Withern . Ricardo de Moreuil[f] const*abulario* . Waltero fil*io* Alani dapifero . Odenello de Umfr*am*uill' . Henrico Luuel . Huctr*edo* fil*io* Fergus . Gileberto fil*io* Fergus . Roberto fil*io* Truite . Waltero de Windlesou*er* . Waltero Corbet . Gileb*erto* fil*io* Rich*erii* . Rollando fil*io* Huctr*edi* . Willelmo de Haia . Willelmo de Mortem*er* . Rogero de Munethou . Simone Locard . Hug*one* clerico meo . Roberto de Chartres . Ricardo clerico. Apud LocmabaN.

ENDORSED. Carta W. Regis Scottorum facta Roberto de Brus de Valle de Anand (xviii cent.).

DESCRIPTION. 11·3″ (28·5 cm.), Top, 11·4″ (28·8 cm.), Bottom × 7·5″ (19 cm.), L, 7″ (17·9 cm.), R. Foot folded 0·9″ (2·4 cm.). Single slit, through which passes a handsome seal ribbon of woven silk, in a rectangular chequer pattern of green and white, the entire ribbon being some 22″ (56 cm.) long. Seal remains almost entire, in natural wax, with a fair impression, obv. to front. Legend visible: WILLELMVS DE[ ]ECTORE [ ] SCOTTO[ ] (obv.); WILLELMVS [ ] REX SCOTTORUM (rev.).

HAND. Scribe Aj (Richard of Lincoln). Unruled. This is a particularly fine example of his work, and before it suffered injury has been a very handsome charter.

SOURCE. Original, PRO, DL 27/37 (Duchy of Lancaster charters) = *A*. *Nat. MSS. Scot.*, i, Plate xxxix (facsimile of *A*) = *B*.

PRINTED. J. Ayloffe, *Calendars of the ancient charters, etc.* (1774), 348–9; *Nat. MSS. Scot.*, i, Plate xxxix (facsimile with text); Fraser, *Annandale*, i, 130, no.103; *Cal. Docs. Scot.*, i, no.105 (summary in translation); *ESC*, 308 (part only, from Ayloffe).

NOTES. [a] Obscure or illegible through injury. [b] This word is illegible, but two letters which partly survive are probably to be read as bu, and the whole name as Rokesburc. Ayloffe prints Ka...... [c] c, now illegible, supplied from *B*. [d] Written ÷. [e] Written xpiano. [f] Perhaps Moreuill'.

81 Confirms to Melrose Abbey the land of 'Edmundestun' granted by Walter son of Alan. Lanark. (1165 × 23 September, 1168)

.W. Rex Scott'. Omnibus probis hominibus totius terre sue . Francis 7 Anglis . 7 Scottis :' salutem. Sciant tam posteri quam presentes me concessisse 7 hac mea carta confirmasse ecclesie Sancte Marie de Maylros 7 monachis ibidem Deo seruientibus donationem quam Walterus filius Alani fecit eidem ecclesie 7 monachis de terra Edmundestun' . in omnibus ita libere 7 quiete in elemosina perpetua :' sicut liberius 7 quietius Carta ipsius Walteri eis testatur. Teste Ric*ardo* episcopo Sancti Andree . Engelramo Episcopo Glasguensi . Johanne Abbate de Kelchou . Osberto Abbate de Gedewrde . Nicholao Cancellario . Ric*ardo* Capellano . Ric*ardo* de Morauilla . Waltero filio Alani . Philippo de Valunnes . Roberto Auenel . Waltero Corbet . Gilleb*erto* filio Richerii . Willelmo de Haia . Willelmo de Mortemer . Radulfo Namo . Imero Clerico . Waltero de Berchelai. Apud Lannarc.

ENDORSED. Confirmatio reg*is* W.' de Edmundeston' (xii cent.). J. Scott (xvi cent.).
DESCRIPTION. 6·4″ (16·3 cm.), Top, 6·6″ (17 cm.), Bottom × 2·8″ (7·1 cm.), L, R. Foot not folded; single slit, with tag, 5·7″ (12 cm.) long, 0·7″ (1·7 cm.) wide. Seal complete, obv. in red wax, rev. in green wax, diameter 3·2″ (8 cm.). Fair impression.
HAND. Scribe Ab. Unruled.
SOURCE. Original, SRO, GD 55/47.
PRINTED. *Melrose Liber*, no.47.
COMMENT. For the date see no.82. 'Edmundestun', now lost, consisted of four ploughgates in Stenton parish, East Lothian: cf. *RRS*, i, no.307.

82 Confirms to Melrose Abbey the land of Ringwood (in Teviothead, Roxburghshire) granted by Osulf son of Uhtred and his son Uhtred. Lanark. (1165 × 23 September, 1168)

.W. rex Scott' . Omnibus probis hominibus[a] terre sue . Clericis 7 laicis . Francis . Angl*is*[b] . 7 Scottis . salutem. Sciant tam posteri quam presentes . me concessisse 7 hac mea carta confirmasse ecclesie Sancte Marie de Mailros 7 monachis ibidem Deo seruientibus donationem quam Osulfus filius Uctredi 7 Uctredus filius eius contulerunt eidem Ecclesie de terra Ringwde . in omnibus ita libere 7 quiete . in elemosina perpetua :' sicut liberius 7 quietius cartæ[c] eorum eis testantur :' 7 carta regis Malcolmi fratris mei concedit 7 affirmat. Teste [Ric*ardo*][d] episcopo Sancti Andree . Engelramo episcopo Glasguensi . Johanne Abbate de Kelchou . Osberto Abbate de Gedewrde . Nicholao Cancellario . Matheo Archidiacono . Ric*ardo* Capellano . Ricardo de Morauilla . Waltero filio Alani . Philippo de Valunnes . Valtero[e] Corbet . Roberto Auenel . Gilleberto filio Richerii . Bernardo filio Breani . Roberto filio Guidonis . Willelmo de Haia . Willelmo de Mortemer . Radulfo Namo . Imero clerico . Waltero de Berchelai. Apud Lannarc.

ENDORSED. Confirmatio regis W. de Ringuud' (xii cent.). J. Scott (xvi cent.).
DESCRIPTION. 8·5″ (21·5 cm.), Top, 8·3″ (21 cm.), Bottom × 3·1″ (7·8 cm.), L, R. Single slit in foot. Neither tag nor seal survives.
HAND. Scribe Ab. Unruled.
SOURCE. Original, SRO, GD 55/151.
PRINTED. *Melrose Liber*, no.151.

NOTES. [a] totius omitted. [b] 7 added awkwardly before Anglis. [c] Written carta, with final letter subsequently made into a diphthong. [d] Supplied from no.81. [e] Sic.

COMMENT. The date depends on identifying Imer the clerk with Master Imer who was killed by the Scots 'treacherously' on 23 September, 1168 (*Chron. Holyrood*, 150–1). For the land granted, cf. *RRS*, i, no.105.

83 Confirms to Melrose Abbey the land of Hartside and Spott and a certain saltpan granted by Cospatric III earl of Dunbar. Lanark. (1165 × 23 September, 1168)

.W. Rex Scott'. Omnibus probis hominibus[a] terre sue . Clericis 7 Laicis . Francis . Angl*is* . 7 Scottis . salutem. Sciant tam posteri quam presentes me concessisse 7 hac mea carta confirmasse Ecclesie Sancte Marie de Maylros 7 monachis ibidem Deo seruientibus dona[tionem][b] quam Gospatricus comes fecit eidem ecclesie 7 monachis consensu 7 concessu heredis sui de terra Hertesheued 7 Spot[c] [7 de quadam salina][b] pro salute anime sue 7 animarum predecessorum suorum . in omnibus ita libere 7 quiete in elemosina perpetua ⁏ sicut liberius 7 quietius Carta [ipsius Gospa][b] trici eis testatur ⁏ 7 carta regis Malcolmi fratris mei concedit 7 confirmat. Teste Ricardo episcopo Sancti Andree . Engelramo [Episcopo][d] Glasguensi . Johanne Abbate de Kelchou . Osberto Abbate de Geddewrde . Nicholao Cancellario . Matheo Archidiacono S*ancti* Andree . Ric*ardo* de Morauilla . Waltero filio Alani . Waltero Corbet . Roberto Auenel . Gilleberto filio Richerii . Philippo de Valu[nnes][d] . Bernardo[e] filio[e] Breani . Roberto filio Guidonis . Radulfo de Cler . Willelmo de Mortemer . Ricardo Capellano . Imero [Cleri]co[d] . Willelmo de Haia . Radulfo Namo . Waltero de Berchelai. Apud Lannarc.

ENDORSED. Confirmatio regis W. de Herteshefd (xii cent.). X (xv cent.?). J. Scott (xvi cent.).

DESCRIPTION. 8·5″ (21·7 cm.), Top, bottom × 3·8″ (9·5 cm.), L, 3·4″ (8·8 cm.), R. Single slit in foot for tag. Tag 7·2″ (18·5 cm.) long, 0·7″ (1·8 cm.) wide; three-quarters of seal remain in greenish-brown wax, repaired, diameter 2·3″ (6 cm.). The right-hand part of the document is repaired.

HAND. Scribe Ab. Unruled.

SOURCE. Original, SRO, GD 55/53.

PRINTED. *Melrose Liber*, no.53.

NOTES. [a] totius omitted. [b] Parchment perished; reading supplied from *RRS*, i, no.133. [c] Partly obscure; form supplied from *RRS*, i, no.133. [d] Supplied from no.82. [e] Written Bernard*us* fili*us*, with o added after former word.

COMMENT. For the date see no.82. For King Malcolm's confirmation of this grant see *RRS*, i, no.133.

84 Grants, and by the judgement of his court regrants, to William de Vieuxpont Hardingstone (Northamptonshire), Carriden (West Lothian), Horndean (Berwickshire), Elrington (in Haydon, Northumberland), Kirkhaugh (in Slaggyford, Northumberland) and Alston (Cumberland), by their right marches, to be held in feu and heritage with toll and team, soke and sake and infangthief, for the service of four knights. Lanark. (1165 × 1170)

W.[a] Rex Scottorum, Episcopis, Abbatibus, Comitibus, Baronibus, justici*is*, vicecomitibus et omnibus probis hominibus tocius terre sue salutem. Sciant presentes et futuri me judicio curie mee reddidisse et dedisse et concessisse et hac carta mea confirmasse Willelmo de Veteri ponte Ardinchesthorp' et Karhedenen, Hornerhedenen, Alrinton', Kircheale et Aldeneby per suas rectas divisas, cum omnibus justis pertinenciis suis in bosco et plano, in pratis et pascuis et aquis; tenend' sibi et heredibus suis de me et heredibus meis in feodo et hereditate libere et quiete per servitium quatuor militum. Quare volo et firmiter precipio ut predictus Willelmus et heredes sui prenominatas terras et tenuras teneant et habeant ita libere et quiete, plenarie et honorifice, cum tol et theam et socca[b] et sacca et infanganthef, sicut pater suus eas melius, liberius, quiecius et honorificencius et plenius tenuit. Testibus David fratre meo, Nicho*lao* Cancell*ario*, Waltero fil*io* Alani Dapifero, David Olifard, Ricardo capellano, Willelmo de Haya pincerna, Waltero de Windelesouere, Gilberto fil*io* Ric*heri*, Rogero de Valon*iis*, Roberto de Berkeley, Waltero de Berkeley, apud Lanarc.

SOURCE. PRO, J.I. 1/143 (Assize Roll).
PRINTED. F.W.Ragg, 'Mauld's Meaburn, the Alston Mines, and a branch of the Veteriponts', in *CWAAS*, New Ser., xi (1911), 270–1 (inaccurate and abridged).
NOTES. [a] Punctuation editorial. [b] Source has scoca.
COMMENT. See no.468. According to a narrative history of the honour of Huntingdon written in French, *c*.1237, of which a copy survives in the hand of Sir William Dugdale (Bodleian Library, MS. Dugdale 18, fos.27ff.), King Malcolm IV disseised the nuns of Delapré of the land of (east) Hardingstone granted to them by the founder of their house, Earl Simon II de Senlis, and gave it to William de Vieuxpont, who held it a long time until Earl Simon III recovered the honour of Huntingdon (i.e., 1174). This act suggests that the land of Hardingstone had belonged to William de Vieuxpont's father, and the court judgement referred to may have been the result of litigation between the recipient of this charter and Delapré Abbey (N.Denholm-Young, 'An early thirteenth-century Anglo-Norman MS.', *Bodleian Quarterly Record*, vi (1931), 225–30, esp. p.230). I owe this reference to Mr Keith Stringer. No.146, given at Northampton probably in 1174, is witnessed by William de Vieuxpont as 'William son of Emma'.

85

Grants to Hugh Giffard that part of Yester (East Lothian) which Gamel formerly held, by the same marches as those by which Gamel held it, in feu and heritage, for the service of the fifth part of one knight. The grant has been made at the request of Hugh (*alias* Eggu), son of Hugh (son of Gillemichel earl of Fife), who resigned the land to the king in his court before his good men, and to whom the king has quitclaimed the annualrent of 21s. 4d. which he paid the king for the land. Lanark. (1166 × 1170)

W'.[a] Rex Scott'. Omnibus probis hominibus tocius terre sue . clericis . 7 laicis :' salutem. Sciant presentes . 7 futuri . Hugonem[b] filium Hugonis peticione sua coram probis hominibus meis in curia mea reddidisse mihi Ghiestrith[c] quam Gamel tenuerat . 7 eiusdem Hugonis[d] peticione me terram illam dedisse . 7 concessisse . 7 hac carta mea confirmasse Hugoni Giffard per easdem diuisas per quas Gamel illam tenuerat . tenendum sibi . 7 heredibus suis . de me . 7 de heredibus meis . in feudo . 7 hereditate . in bosco . 7 plano . in pratis . 7 pascuis . 7 aquis . 7 omnibus iustis pertinenciis suis . libere . 7 quiete . 7 honorifice :' faciendo inde mihi . 7 heredibus meis :· quintam partem seruicii unius militis. Et ego Hugonem[b] filium Hugonis. 7 heredes suos . de me . 7 de heredibus meis . quietos clamaui . de .xxj.[e] solidis . 7 iiij. denariis . quos ipsi annuatim de terra illa mihi . 7 heredibus meis . persoluere debebant. T*estibus* Comite Wald*euo*[f] . Ric*ardo* capellano . Willelmo de Lindesi . Willelmo de Veteri Ponte . Willelmo de Haia . Patricio filio comitis . Gileberto de Unframuill' . Willelmo de Mortem*er*[g] . Walkelino de Mortem*er*[g]. Apud LanaRC.[h]

ENDORSED. *A*: Conf of certain lands to Hew Giffert quhilk perteinit to Gamell (xvi cent.). Undated. m (on foot of fold, xiii cent.?). *B*: Ane auld charter of Shirifsyd[i] be King Willm (xvii cent.).
DESCRIPTION. *A*: 6·6″ (16·7 cm.), Top, 6·3″ (16·1 cm.), Bottom × 4″ (10·3 cm.), L, R. Foot folded to a depth of 0·6″ (1·7 cm.). Tie cut from left-hand edge of fold. Tag through single slits 6″ (15 cm.) long, 0·6″ (1·7 cm.) wide. No seal remains. *B*: 7·3″ (18·5 cm.), Top and bottom × 4·3″ (10·8 cm.), L, R. Foot folded to a depth of 0·9″ (2·3 cm.). Tie torn away from left-hand edge of fold. Double slits with tag 6·6″ (17 cm.) long, 0·5″ (1·3 cm.) wide. No seal remains.
HAND. *A*: Scribe Ab. Unruled. *B*: Scribe Dc. Unruled.
SOURCE. Originals, SRO, GD 28/2=*A*; GD 28/3=*B* (a 'renovation' of *A*).
PRINTED. *Yester Writs*, nos.2 and 3; *East Lothian Trans.*, viii (1960), 6, no.11 (with facsimile of *B* and translation).
NOTES. [a] *B* adds Dei gr*ati*a; in both *A* and *B* there is a diagonal stroke through the left-hand side of W, in *B* with a curl at the top. [b] Eggu, *B*. [c] Jhestrid, *B*. [d] Eggu, *B*. [e] viginti . et .j., *B*. [f] Waldew', *B*. [g] Mortuo mari, *B*. [h] Lanarc', *B*. Punctuation and use of capitals differ somewhat in *B*, for an example of whose usage cf. no.403. *B* was written at a considerably later date than *A*. [i] Yester deleted before this name.
COMMENT. For Hugh or Eggu, son of Hugh son of Gillemichel, cf. *St Andrews Liber*, 216. The apparent equation of an annualrent of 21s. 4d. with the service of one-fifth of a knight suggests a valuation for the knight's fee of eight merks. The endorsement on *B* shews that the estate granted was Sheriffside, in Yester.

86 Confirms to Melrose Abbey the half ploughgate in Lessudden (St Boswells) granted by Richard of London, as Richard's charter bears witness. Selkirk. (1165 × 1171)

W'. Rex Scott'. Omnibus probis hominibus tocius terre sue . Clericis . 7 laicis :· salutem. Sciant presentes 7 futuri . me concessisse . 7 hac carta mea confirmasse . Deo . 7 ecclesie Sancte Marie de Mailros . 7 Monachis ibidem Deo seruientibus . dimidiam carucatam terre quam Ric*ardus* de London*iis* eis dedit in Lessedwin tenendam in liberam . 7 perpetuam elemosinam . ita libere . 7 plenarie . quiete . 7 honorifice :· sicut carta ipsius Ricardi eis testatur. T*estibus* D*aui*d fratre meo . Nichol*ao* cancellario . Alano filio dapiferi . Willelmo de Haia . Hugone de Exart*is* . Willelmo de Mortem*er* . Rob*erto* filio Jordani. ApUD Seleschirche.

ENDORSED. Confirmatio Wil'e'*mi* Reg*is* de terra de Lesedwin (xii cent.). E (red, xv cent.?). J. Scott (xvi cent.).
DESCRIPTION. 8·6″ (21·8 cm.) Top, bottom × 2·5″ (6·2 cm.) L, R. Foot folded to an average depth of 0·6″ (1·5 cm.). Single slits, with tag 5″ (12·5 cm.) long, 0·5″ (1·3 cm.) wide. Seal almost complete in natural wax stained brown, fair impression.
HAND. Scribe Ai. Unruled.
SOURCE. Original, SRO, GD 55/89.
PRINTED. *Melrose Liber*, no.89.
COMMENT. Richard's charter has apparently not survived, but it was confirmed

with additional grants of land by his son Robert of London (*Melrose Liber*, no.88). Hugh des Essarts witnessed sixteen surviving charters of King Stephen, chiefly of the later years of his reign (*RRAN*, iii, references in the index, s.v. Essartis), and also witnessed *Kelso Liber*, no.214, a charter of Bernard son of Brien dating 1165 × 1171.

87 Grants his firm peace to the monks and lay brothers of Holm Cultram Abbey, and their cattle, and permission to carry their wool and merchandise for sale in burghs in the kingdom of Scotland wherever they wish. No one is to disturb them on pain of the king's forfeiture. (1165 × 1174)

W[a] Rex Scottorum , Justiciis, vicecomitibus, prepositis, Ministris, et omnibus probis hominibus tocius terre sue, salutem. Sciatis me firmam meam pacem dedisse monachis et fratribus de Holm' et eorum catall*is* per totam terram meam et licenciam deferendi lanam suam et mercaturas suas quas venales habuerint in terram meam ad venden*dum* in Burgis meis ubicumque eis placuerit. Quare prohibeo firmiter ne quis eos in eundo aut redeundo disturbet, aut aliquam eis iniuriam inferat, super meam forisfacturam. T*estibus* etc.

RUBRIC. Carta .W. Reg*is* Scocie de p\roteccione super forisfacturam (top right red).[b] Carta W regis Scocie (foot of fo.114v, red, much rubbed).[c]
SOURCE. Carlisle, Dean and Chapter Muniments, MS. Cartulary of Holm Cultram, p.112 = *C*. BM, MS. Harl. 3911, fo.115 (mod. pencil), 109 (older ink), numbered in red xxxij = *H*. Printed here from a collation of *C* and *H*.
PRINTED. Dugdale, *Mon. Angl.* (New), v, 605, no.XLVI; *Holm Cultram Recs.*, 54 (translation).
NOTES. [a] blue initial, *H*; *C* has V in red. Punctuation is editorial. [b] *C*. [c] *H*.

88 Confirms to Holm Cultram Abbey the land called Kirkgunzeon which it holds of Uhtred son of Fergus; and one saltpan in Colvend, with all easements of wood and in the port of Urr as far as 'Polstursheuid', as the charter of Uhtred and the chirograph (bear witness). (1165 × 1174)

W[a] Rex Scocie Episcopis Abbatibus . Com*itibus* . baronibus Justic*iis* vic*ecomitibus* et omnibus probis hominibus tocius terre sue . presentibus et futuris . s*alutem*. Sciatis me concessisse et hac carta mea confirmasse . ecclesie Sancte Marie de Holm' et monachis ibidem Deo seruientibus terram que dicitur Kirkewinin cum omnibus iustis pertin*enciis* suis et rectis diuisis quam terram tenent de Huctredo fil*io* Fergus. Et unam salinam in Culwene et omnia aisiamenta nemoris et portus[b] . Hur . usque ad Polstursheuid . tenend*as* ita libere et quiete etc sicut carta ipsius . Huctredi filii Fergus et cirograff' etc testatur.[c] Concedo eciam eis habere easdem vias et semitas et eorundem[c] portus quos Huctredus filius [Fergus][d] eis concessit sicut carta ipsius Huctredi testatur et confirmat. T' etc.

RUBRIC. Too badly rubbed to be readily legible.
SOURCE. BM, MS. Harl. 3891, fo.98r.
PRINTED. *Holm Cultram Recs.*, 54 (brief abstract).
NOTES. [a] red initial. [b] MS. portu. [c] Sic. [d] MS. omits.
COMMENT. Probably issued early within the limit-dates stated, since Uhtred later deprived Holm of the land of Kirkgunzeon and gave it to Walter of Berkeley,

whereupon, after a complaint to the king, Uhtred himself was ordered to enquire into the matter with Roger of Minto. See no.256 below.

89 Confirms to Dryburgh Abbey the grants made by his mother the Countess Ada of the church of Kilrenny, Fife, half a ploughgate in Pitcorthie (in Kilrenny), and one full toft in the burgh of Crail, as the countess's charter bears witness. (1165 × 1174)

Villelmus rex Scotorum omnibus probis hominibus totius terre sue, clericis et laicis, salutem. Sciant presentes et futuri me concessisse et hac carta mea confirmasse Deo et ecclesie Sancte[a] Marie de Dryburgh et canonicis ibidem Deo servientibus donacionem quam Ada comitissa mater mea eis fecit de ecclesia de Kilreny et de dimidia carucata terre in Petchorthin, cum communi pastura, et unum plenum toftum in burgo meo de Karele, ita libere et quiete sicut carta ipsius eis testatur et confirmat. Testibus etc.

RUBRIC. Confirmacio regis super Kylrethny Petcorthy et Carele. xvij.
SOURCE. NLS, MS. Adv. 34.4.7, fo.4^{r-v}.
PRINTED. *Dryburgh Liber*, no.17.
NOTE. [a] Fo.4^{v}.
COMMENT. The countess's charter (1165 × 1178) is given in *Dryburgh Liber*, no.16.

90 Confirms to Newbattle Abbey the ploughgate of arable in Gilmerton, Midlothian, granted by Randulf de Soules, as his charter bears witness. (1165 × 1170)

W. Rex Scot' omnibus probis hominibus tocius terre sue salutem. Sciant presentes et futuri me concessisse . et hac carta mea confirmasse . ecclesie Sancte Marie de Neu*botle* et monachis ibidem Deo seruientibus . illam carucatam terre quam Rand*ulfus* de Sules eis dedit in Gillemoreston' . tenendam in liberam et perpetuam elemosinam . ita libere et quiete et honorifice . sicud carta ipsius Rand*ulfi* eis testatur et confirmat. Test*ibus* Ricardo Episcopo Sancti Andr*ee* . Nich*olao* Cancellario . Dauid Olyfard.

Confirmacio Reg*is* Willelmi.[a]
SOURCE. NLS, MS. Adv. 34.4.13, fo.17^{r}.
PRINTED. *Newbattle Registrum*, no.40.
NOTE. [a] Table of contents, fo.1^{v}.
COMMENT. Randulf's charter is given in *Newbattle Registrum*, no.37 (× 22 April, 1170); the donor styles himself *pincerna regis Scottorum*, and states that the ploughgate, from his demesne of Gilmerton, has been measured by Geoffrey de Melville and other responsible men.

91 Confirms to Newbattle the grant made by his mother the Countess Ada of Bearford (in Haddington), East Lothian, and one ploughgate of arable on the Peffer Burn called Prora, to be held as Robert son of Geoffrey held it, with warrandice by the countess, as her charter bears witness. (1165 × 1174)

W. Rex Scott' episcopis, abbatibus, comitibus, baronibus, justiciis, vicecomitibus, prepositis, ministris, cunctisque probis hominibus tocius terre sue salutem. Sciant presentes et futuri me concessisse et hac mea carta confirmasse in liberam et quietam et perpetuam elemosinam Deo et ecclesie Sancte Marie de N*eubotle* et monachis ibidem Deo seruientibus donaciones quas Ada comitissa mater mea fecit eis de Bereford, et carucata terre super Pefre que dicitur Por Hoy. Quare volo et firmiter precipio ut predicti monachi prenominatas terras teneant de matre mea et heredibus suis, ita plenarie sicud Robertus filius Galfridi eas plenius et melius tenuit et ita libere et quiete ab omni seculari exaccione et consuetudine sicud alias elemosinas suas tenent et possident. Mater autem mea et heredes sui contra omnes calumpniantes predictis monachis terras illas debent warantizare, sicut carta ipsius matris mee testatur et confirmat. Teste D*aui*d fratre meo.

Confirmacio Reg*is* Willelmi.[a]
SOURCE. NLS, MS. Adv. 34.4.13, fo.24v.
PRINTED. *Newbattle Registrum*, no.72.
NOTE. [a] Table of contents, fo.1v.
COMMENT. Cf. *RRS*, i, no.136. The countess's charter is printed in *Newbattle Registrum*, no.69.

92 Commands that the monks of May Priory shall hold their lands in Scotland (north of Forth) free of all services, and especially that they shall be free of aids and labour service during the time that Prior William has charge of the house of May. Edinburgh. (1165 × 1171)

Willelmus[a] Rex Scot' omnibus probis hominibus tocius Scotie, salutem. Mando & firmiter precipio ut monachi de Mai teneant tenuras suas quas habent in Scotia libere & quiete ab omnibus seruitiis , & nominatim quieti sint ab auxiliis & operationibus tempore W*illelmi* prioris quamdiu ipse de domo de Mai curam capiet. T*estibus* Eng*elramo* episcopo de Glascu , Nic*holao* cancellario , et multis aliis. Apud Eneburg.

RUBRIC. Carta eiusdem ut monachi quieti sint ab auxiliis & oeprationibus.
SOURCE. BM, MS. Egerton 3031, fo.62r–v.
PRINTED. *PSAS*, xc, 73, no.50.
NOTE. [a] Vuillelmus, MS., with large blue initial.

93 Commands the fishermen who fish around the Isle of May to pay their teinds and render their customs to May Priory as under King Malcolm IV and as before the time of Prior William, in all things great and small. Edinburgh. (1165 × 1171)

W.[a] Rex Scott'[b] omnibus piscatoribus qui piscem capiunt circa Mai, salutem. Mando et firmiter precipio quatinus plenarie et integre reddatis Priori de Mai et monachis ibidem Deo seruientibus decimas suas et consuetudines et rectitudines quas habuerunt tempore Regis M*alcolmi* fratris mei sicut carta sua quam inde habent testatur & confirmat[c] et sicut habuerunt ante tempus Prioris Willelmi de omnimodis redditibus et de rectitudinibus et de modico et de magno, et prohibeo ne quis eis inde quicquam detineat, super meam forisfacturam, quia eis iuste meam firmam pacem concessi. Test*ibus* Nic*olao*[d] Cancell*ario*, Ric*ardo* de Moruill' constabulario, Waltero filio Alani[e] Dapifero. Apud Edeneb'.[f]

TITLE. Scriptum Regis Willelmi de decima piscarie circa Insulam de May.[g]
SOURCE. PRO, C.53/93, rot. 13 (Charter Roll, 35 Edward I) = *C*. BM, MS. Egerton 3031, fo.62r = *E*. *May Recs.*, p.cxiii = *M* (Title only).

PRINTED. *May Recs.*, no.18 (from *C*).
NOTES. [a] Vuillelmus, *E*, with large blue initial. [b] Scot', *E*. [c] & confirmat supplied from *E*. [d] Nich', *E*. [e] *E* omits filio Alani. [f] Eneburg', *E*; Edeneburgum, *May Recs.*, no.18. [g] *M* only.
COMMENT. Cf. *RRS*, i, no.162.

94 Grants to May Priory liberty to sell and buy wherever necessary in his land; the monks of May and their servants are to be free of toll. Men who come to the priory's lands to fish are to be free of toll on the sale and purchase of fish, save for what is due to the prior and monks. Edinburgh. (1165 × 1171)

W.[a] Rex Scot'[b] Vicecomitibus, prepositis, ministris et omnibus probis hominibus totius terre sue, salutem. Sciatis me dedisse et sigillo meo confirmasse priori de Mai et monachis ibidem seruientibus Deo licenciam et liberam potestatem vendendi et emendi quo opus habent per totam terram meam. Quare volo et firmiter precipio ut ipsi et seruientes eorum et homines sint liberi et quieti a Cano et theloneo et ab omni alia consuetudine ubicumque pro tali negocio venerint. Precipio etiam ut homines qui causa piscandi in terra ipsorum applicuerint liberi et quieti sint a cano et theloneo et alia consuetudine pro vendicione piscium et emcione, preter ea que Priori et monachis debentur. Testibus Nicol*ao* Cancell*ario*, Walt*ero* Dapifero, Ric*ardo* de Moru*illa*. Apud Edeneb'[c].

TITLE. Carta Regis Willelmi de acquietacione Cani et tolnei.[d]
SOURCE. PRO, C.53/93, rot.13 (Charter Roll, 35 Edward I) = *C*. *May Recs.*, p.cxiii = *M* (Title only).
PRINTED. *May Recs.*, no.17 (from *C*).
NOTES. [a] Willelmus, *May Recs.*, no.17. [b] Scotie, ibid. [c] Edeneburgum, ibid. [d] *M* only.
COMMENT. See no.207, which amplifies and amends this brieve.

95 Forbids anyone to take poinds against the abbot of Kelso, within or outwith the lands of his church, until the abbot or his officers have first been required to do justice and have failed to do it. Edinburgh. (1165 × 1171)

Will*elmus*[a] Dei gr*aci*a Rex Scott' . Justic' . vice*comitibus* . et omnibus probis hominibus tocius terre sue salutem. Mando et firmiter precipio . ne quis unquam namum capiat super Abbatem de Kelch' neque infra neque extra terras eiusdem ecclesie . priusquam ipse abbas uel ministri sui requirantur de rectitudine facienda . et ipsi a rectitudine facienda defecerint. Si quis autem balliuorum uel aliorum hominum meorum huic precepto meo contraire presumpserit .˙ in plenam misericordiam meam uel successorum meorum se nouerit incidisse. Test*ibus* hiis . Nicholao cancellario. Ricardo de Moruill' const*abulario*. Hugone Ridel apud Edinburg'.

RUBRIC. Carta Regis Willelmi . ne quis unquam namum capiat super Abbatem neque infra neque extra (red, at top).
SOURCE. NLS, MS. Adv. 34.5.1, fo.10^r.
PRINTED. *Kelso Liber*, no.5.
NOTE. [a] Initial red.
COMMENT. The *dei gracia* may be due to the copyist.

96 Confirms to John abbot of Kelso the toft of Dodin in Berwick granted to Abbot Arnold by the king's father Earl Henry; as Earl Henry's charter bears witness. (1165 × 1174)

Will*elmus*[a] Rex Scott' . Episcopis . Abbatibus . Com*itibus* . Baronibus . Justic*iis* . et omnibus probis hominibus tocius terre sue Francis . et Anglis . clericis et laicis salutem. Sciant presentes et futuri me concessisse et hac carta mea confirmasse Johanni abbati de Kelchou illam Toft Dodini de Berewyc' que est super Twedam ad tenend*um* de me in feudo . quam etiam Toft comes .H. pater meus dedit Ernaldo abbati. Volo itaque et firmiter precipio quatinus illam prenominatam Toft teneat et habeat ita plenarie sicut predictus Dodin illam unquam plenius tenuit et habuit . et ita libere et quiete istam Toft de me teneat in feudo sicut possessiones ecclesie sue liberius et quiecius tenet in elemosinam sicut carta Comitis Henr*ici* patris mei testatur et confirmat. Test*ibus*.

RUBRIC. Carta Willelmi Reg*is* . super toft*am* Dodini in villa Berwyci (top in red).
SOURCE. NLS, MS. Adv. 34.5.1, fo.18v.
PRINTED. *Kelso Liber*, no.32.
NOTE. [a] Initial red.
COMMENT. Earl Henry's charter is given in Lawrie, *Charters*, no.193.

97 Informs his sheriff, provosts, officers and burgesses of Berwick that he has granted to Melrose Abbey the house and land of William Lunnok in the corner of the Briggate in Berwick, as it stretches lengthwise from Briggate to the River Tweed on the south, and in breadth from the land of Aernald Hanyn on the west to the land of Walter son of Alan the steward on the east; William Lunnok having surrendered his house, land and service to the king. (1165 × 1174)

U.[a] rex Scotorum vicecomiti de Berwic et prepositis et ministris et omnibus burgen*sibus* de Berwic, salutem. Sciant tam posteri quam presentes me pro salute anime mee et antecessorum et successorum meorum concessisse et dedisse ecclesie de Melros' et fratribus monachis ibidem Deo seruientibus et eorum successoribus inperpetuum domum et terram Willelmi Lunnok in cornerio de Briggat in Berwic, sicut se extendit in longitudine de Briggate usque in aquam de Twede uersus austrum, et in latitudine de terra Aernaldi Hanyn uersus occidentem usque in terram Walteri filii Alani sinescalli mei uersus orientem; quam idem Willelmus mihi sursum reddidit, et seruicium eiusdem [ ][b] et heredum suorum de omnibus aliis terris suis in Berwic. Quare volo et precipio quod dicti abbas et conuentus habeant dictas domum, terram et seruicia in liberam et puram elemosinam inperpetuum, nichil inde facientes temporibus pacis uel guerrarum preter orationes et elemosinas infra monasterium suum. Et quod ipse Willelmus sit quitus[c] de omnibus consuetudinibus et seruiciis que ad me et ad villam pertinent, seruiendo abbati et monachis predictis ipse et heredes sui, sicut mihi fecerunt. Test*ibus* etc.

RUBRIC. Carta domorum de Briggate.
SOURCE. BM, MS. Harl. 3960, fo.86r. PRINTED. *Melrose Liber*, no.23.
NOTES. [a] Initial red. [b] Blank in MS.; supply Willelmi? [c] Sic.
COMMENT. See no.98.

98 Informs his sheriff, provosts, officers and burgesses of Berwick that he has granted to Melrose Abbey the service of William Lunnoc with his house and land in Berwick, so that he may serve the abbey as he previously served the king. (1165 × 1174)

U.[a] Rex Scot' vicecomiti de Berwic et prepositis et ministris et omnibus burgen*sibus* de Berwic, salutem. Sciant tam posteri quam presentes me pro salute anime mee et antecessorum et successorum meorum concessisse et dedisse ecclesie Sancte Marie de Melros et fratribus monachis ibidem Deo seruien*tibus* seruicium Willelmi Lunnoc, et terram et domum eius de Berwic, in perpetuam elemosinam. Quare volo et firmiter precipio quod ipse Willelmus sit quietus de omnibus consuetudinibus et omnibus seruiciis que ad me pertinent, seruiendo abbati et monachis eiusdem loci, sicut michi deberet. Test*ibus*.

RUBRIC. Item carta eiusdem.
SOURCE. BM, MS. Harl. 3960, fo.86r.
PRINTED. *Melrose Liber*, no.24.
NOTE. [a] Initial red.
COMMENT. William Lunnoc and his father Jocelin evidently farmed certain of the Berwick fisheries (*Melrose Liber*, nos.21, 22). See no.97.

99 Confirms to Cambuskenneth Abbey one full toft in the burgh of Crail and half a ploughgate of arable in Pitcorthie (in Kilrenny, Fife), granted by his mother the Countess Ada, as her charter bears witness. Edinburgh. (1165 × 1171)

Villelmus[a] rex Scotorum omnibus probis hominibus totius terre sue salutem. Sciatis me concessisse et hac carta mea confirmasse Deo et ecclesie Sancte Marie de Striueling et canonicis ibidem Deo seruientibus unum plenum toftum in burgo de Karell quod A*da* Comit*issa* mater mea eiis dedit cum dimedia carrucata terre in Petcorthim[b] cum communi pastura. Tenendum ita libere et quiete in liberam et perpetuam ele-[c]mosinam sicut carta A*de* Comit*isse* matris mee testatur et confirmat.[d] Testibus Engenio[e] episcopo Glasgw*ensi*, Nic*olao* cancell*ario*, Matheo archidiacono Sanctiandree, Waltero filio Alani dapifero,[f] Alexandro de Sancto Martino, Gilberto filio Rich*eri*, apud Castellum Puellarum.

RUBRIC. Confirmatio de Karell (at top). Concordat cum principali Jacobus Foulis (at end).
SOURCE. NLS, MS. Adv. 34.1.2, fo.128r–v.
PRINTED. *Cambuskenneth Registrum*, no.175.
NOTES. [a] Large blue initial V. [b] Sic, for Petcorthin. [c] Fo.128v. [d] MS. confirmatur. [e] Or Engemo; for Engelramo. [f] MS. dapu̅o.
COMMENT. The countess's charter is given in *Cambuskenneth Registrum*, no.192.

100 Confirms to Robert, chaplain of his mother the Countess Ada, the land of Whitfield (Northumberland), to be held of the canons of Hexham Priory in fee and inheritance, as the canons' charter bears witness. Haddington. (1165 × 1171)

Will*el*mus[a] Rex Scocie omnibus probis hominibus totius terre sue salutem. Sciatis me concessisse et hac Charta mea confirmasse Roberto Capellano Ade Comitisse matris mee terram de Witefeld tenendum sibi et heredibus suis de Canonicis[b] de Hextold' in feodo et hereditate, ita libere et quiete et plenarie sicut carta predictorum Canonicorum testatur et confirmat. Quare uolo et precipio ut predictus Robertus et heredes sui terram predictam teneant et habeant. Teste Ada Comitissa, Dauidi[c] fratre meo, Nicholl' Cancell*ario*, Hugone Giffard', Alexandro de Sancto Martino. Apud Haddington'.

SOURCE. J. C. Blackett-Ord Esq., Whitfield Hall, Northumberland, Whitfield Box no.1, vellum-bound paper cartulary and rent book of 1630, p.2, collated with a copy of the same transcript in a paper volume preserved in the same box, dated 1732, made when the earlier book had not suffered quite so much wear as it has now.
PRINTED. J. Hodgson, *History of Northumberland*, Pt.II, vol.iii, 19a (incomplete).
NOTES. [a] Punctuation editorial. [b] MS. Canonibus. [c] Sic.
COMMENT. The Countess Ada's two charters to Robert her chaplain preserved in the same source (pp.1–2) except the land held by William or his son Robert (of Dilston) and by Johel (of Corbridge). Cf. J. Hodgson, *History of Northumberland*, Pt. II, iii, 17.

101 Confirms to Kelso Abbey one ploughgate of arable in the toun of Hadden (in Sprouston, Roxburghshire) by the same marches as it had it before Bernard son of Brian acquired Hadden; confirms also one toft in the toun of Hadden, their tenant settled in the toft to be free of all service and custom, as the charter of Bernard bears witness. Stirling. (1165 × 1171)

W. Rex Scott'. Episcopis. Abbatibus. Comit*ibus*. Baron*ibus*. Justic*iis*. Vice*comitibus*. prepositis. Ministris cunctisque aliis probis hominibus terre sue clericis et laicis. salutem. Nouerint omnes tam posteri quam presentes ∴ me concessisse 7 presenti carta mea confirmasse Ecclesie Sancte Marie de Kelch' 7 monachis ibidem Deo seruientibus unam carrucatam terre in uilla de Hawedene. per easdem diuisas per quas eas[a] habuerunt antequam Bernardus fil*ius* Briani habuisset predictam Hauden'. cum omnibus aisiamentis infra diuisas ipsius carrucate terre. ita libere 7 quiete tenendam ∴ sicut aliqua elemosina liberius 7 quiecius tenetur. in regno meo. Concedo etiam eis 7 hac mea carta confirmo ∴ unam toftam in predicta uilla de Hawedene liberam 7 quietam ab omni seruicio. 7 hominem eorum qui super toftam illam sedebit. liberum 7 quietum ab omni seruicio 7 alia consuetudine sicut carta predicti Bernardi testatur. T*estibus* Engelr*amo* episcopo Glasg*uensi*. Nich*olao* cancell*ario*. Rob*erto* Auenel. Ric*ardo* Cumyn'. Apud Striuelyn.

RUBRIC. Confirmacio super unam carrucatam terre in uilla de Haweden (top in red).
SOURCE. NLS, MS. Adv. 34.5.1, fo.150[r].
PRINTED. *Kelso Liber*, no.408.
NOTE. [a] Sic. Read eam.
COMMENT. According to no.63 Kelso Abbey acquired its ploughgate in Hadden by the gift of Waldeuus (Waltheof); it was stated at the end of the thirteenth century to have been always in the hands of the monks of Kelso (*Kelso Liber*, p.456). Bernard son of Brien, evidently one of the numerous continental military vassals whom William I drew to his service, seems to have been given Hadden, doubtless as a military fief, early in the reign, and confirmed the abbey's possession by a charter dating 1165 × 1171 (ibid., no.214), by which he also granted the toft confirmed above. He was succeeded by his nephew Bernard, ancestor of the Haddens of that ilk.

101A Grants to Coldingham Priory, its monks and their servants throughout the whole of his land freedom from toll on their own chattels and merchandise. Stirling. (1165 × 1171)

W'. Rex Scott' Justic*iis* Vice*comitibus* prepositis. Ministris. Cuntisque[a] aliis probis hominibus tocius terre sue salutem. Sciatis me concessisse Deo 7 Sancto Cuthberto de Goldincham[b] 7 monachis ibidem Deo seruientibus. ut ipsi 7 eorum seruientes per totam terram meam sint liberi 7 quieti ab omni theloneo de propriis catallis 7 mercaturis eorum. Prohibeo itaque ut nemo contra hanc libertatem eis infra terram meam uim aut iniuriam faciat super meam forisfacturam. sicut[c] carta Reg*is* M'. fratris mei testatur 7 confirmat. T' Eng*elramo* episcopo de Glasgu. Nic*olao* cancell*ario*. Waltero filio Alani dapifero. Apud Striuelin.

ENDORSED. W. Reg*is* de teloneo (xii–xiii cent.). quieto (xiii–xiv cent.). Carta (xv cent. insertion). L iij[a] vj[te] (xv cent.). Early endorsement on tongue, now illegible.
DESCRIPTION. 7·8″ (19·7 cm.), Top, 7·6″ (19·4 cm.), Bottom × 2·6″ (6·5 cm.), L, 1·5″ (4·2 cm.), R. Tie torn. Tongue 5·7″ long, 0·6″ wide. Central portion of seal remains on tongue, in natural wax, fair impression, diameter 2·9″.
HAND. Scribe Aj (Richard of Lincoln). Unruled.
SOURCE. Original, Durham, D. & C. Muniments, Misc. Chr. no.608.
PRINTED. Raine, *North Durham*, no.47.
NOTES. [a] Sic. [b] Tail of G present but not joined to rest of letter; Raine prints C. [c] Scribe has written T (este?) and erased.

102 Confirms to his provosts and other burgesses of Inverkeithing, for the common benefit of the burgh, the land on the south side of the burgh called 'Croc', by its right marches; paying therefor on the king's behalf half a merk of silver a year to whoever shall hold the demesne land of Inverkeithing, Clackmannan. (1165 × 1172)

W.[a] Rex Scott'. uniuersis probis hominibus tocius terre sue sal*utem*. Sciatis me concessisse 7 hac carta mea confirmasse permanenter Prepositis 7 ceteris burgensibus meis de Inuerkethin[b] ad aisiamentum burgi communiter terram illam ex australi parte burgi que appellatur Croc[c]. per rectas diuisas illius terre. Volo itaque 7 precipio ut ipsi terram illam teneant 7 habeant ad commune aisiamentum Burgi illius permanenter libere 7 quiete sicut terram ad ipsum burgum appendentem. Soluendo singulis annis ex parte mea dimidiam marcam argenti homini illi quicunque tenuerit terram dominii de Inuerkethin.[b] T*estibus* Ada Comitissa. Matheo archidiac*ono*. Waltero filio Alani Dapifero. Ricardo constabulario. Philippo de Valoniis. Serlone de Edeneburg. Apud Clacmannac.[d]

ENDORSED. No endorsement is known.
SOURCE. SRO, RH 9/11/16/2 (transcript of the original, July, 1812, said then to have been in the possession of Sir John Henderson of Fordell, Bt.). The original has not been traced, and no description of it is provided with the transcript.
NLS, MS. Adv. 34.6.24, p.164 (brief note only, mentioning William I's charter to Inverkeithing 'of the Cruiks besouth the toun').
PRINTED. *Municipal Corporations Report* (1836), Appendix to General Report, Cl. 11, p. 8, no.[2] = *M* (evidently not taken direct from the original).
NOTES. [a] *M* adds Dei gracia. [b] Inuyrkethin, *M*. [c] Cruke, *M*. [d] Clacmanan, *M*.
COMMENT. See no.250.

103 Confirms to the Hospital of St Peter, York, one ploughgate of land and one toft in Troqueer (Kirkcudbright) granted by Uhtred son of Fergus; an annualrent of five shillings in Legerwood (Berwickshire) granted by Walter son of Alan, the king's steward; and commands that the brethren of the hospital shall have his firm peace throughout all his land. Clackmannan. (1165 × 1170)

W.[a] Rex Scott'. Omnibus probis hominibus tocius terre sue salutem. Sciatis me concessisse et hac carta mea confirmasse Deo et fratribus hospit*alis* Beati Petri de Ebor' unam carrucatam terre et unum toftum in Creuequer[b] que H*utredus* fil*ius* Fergus eis in liberam elemosinam dedit, tenend' ita libere et quiete sicut carta ipsius H*utredi* testatur et confirmat. Postea[c] etiam concedo eis et confirmo redditus quinque solid*orum* per annum in Leggardeswod' quos Walterus filius Alani Dapifer meus eis in liberam elemosinam dedit sicut carta ipsius W*alteri* testatur et confirmat. Quare volo et firmiter precipio ut predicti fratres iuste meam firmam pacem habeant per totam terram meam et ita libere et quiete prenominatas tenuras teneant et habeant sicut elemosine hospitalium regni mei liberius et quiecius tenentur. Test*ibus* Nicholao Cancellario, Matheo Archid*iacono* Sancti Andr*ee*, R.[d] capellano, Ricardo de Moruill' const*abulario*, D*aui*d Oliuer,[e] Willelmo de Haya pincerna, apud Clacman*an*.

SOURCE. PRO, C. 47/22/4=*A*; PRO, C. 53/93, m.8=*B*; Printed from *A*, with variants of *B* noted.
PRINTED. *Cal. Chart.* iii, 92 (from *B*).
NOTES. [a] Punctuation editorial. [b] Sic; for Treuequer. [c] Sic; for preterea? [d] Ric*ardo*, *B*. [e] Olif', *B*.

104 Confirms to Melrose Abbey the land of Eskdale, viz. Tomleuchar and Watcarrick (in Eskdalemuir, Dumfriesshire), as the charter of Robert Avenel bears witness. (1165 × 1171?)

Will*elmus*[a] Dei gr*atia* rex Scott'[b] omnibus probis hominibus totius regni sui, salutem. Sciatis me concessisse et hac mea carta confirmasse Deo et Sancte Marie de Melros et monachis ibidem Deo seruientibus, in perpetuam elemosinam, terram de Eschedale,[c] id est Thumerloch[d] et Weitkerroc,[e] cum omnibus pertinenciis suis, ita libere et quiete et integre, sicut carta Roberti Auenil eis testatur et confirmat. Test*ibus* etc.

RUBRIC. Confirmacio Reg*is* Willelmi de Eschedale (red).
SOURCE. NLS, MS. Adv. 34.4.11, fo.xlii^{v}=*A*. BM, MS. Harl. 3960, fo.55^{v}=*H*. Printed here from *A*, with variants of *H* noted.
PRINTED. *Melrose Liber*, no.38.
NOTES. [a] Initial red. [b] Scot', *H*. [c] Eskedal, *H*. [d] Sic, probably for Thumlocher. *H* has Tumloher. [e] Weidkerroc, *H*.
COMMENT. See no.264. Despite the *dei gratia* this may belong to 1165 × 1171; the phrase *totius regni sui* belongs to early acts.

105 Announces that the dispute between the church of Durham and the church of Crowland anent the toun and church of Edrom (Berwickshire) has been settled in his court in the presence of himself and of his bishops and responsible men; in such a way that the church of Edrom shall be in the possession of the church of Durham in perpetuity. Perth. (1167 × 1170)

W'.[a] Rex Scott'. Omnibus probis hominibus tocius terre sue clericis 7 laicis salutem. Sciatis quod controuersia que fuit inter ecclesiam Dunhelmensem[b] 7 ecclesiam Croilandensem de uilla de Ederham[c] 7 ecclesia eiusdem uille[d] in presencia mea 7 episcoporum 7 proborum hominum meorum in curia mea[e] terminata est . ita quod ecclesia de Ederham[c] cum omnibus suis appenticiis[f] ecclesie Dunhelmensi[g] cessit[h] in perpetuum. Test*ibus* Ric*ardo* episcopo Sancti Andr*ee* . Eng*elramo* episcopo de Glasgu . Nichol*ao* cancell*ario* . Johanne abbate de Kelchou[i] . Comite Wald*euo* . Ric*ardo* de Moruill'[j] constabulario . W*altero* filio Alani Dapifero . Dauid Olifard . A*pud* Pert.

ENDORSED. *A*: Willelmi Regis Scot' de controuersia (xii cent.). C (xv cent. insertion). inter priorem Dunelm' et ecclesiam Crowlandie de villa de Ederham et ecclesia eiusdem (xv cent. insertion). T. iij. vj[te] (xv cent.). *B*: de Ederam 7 ecclesia eiusdem uille (xii–xiii cent.). Testimonium Reg*is* W. de controuersia terminata inter Ecclesiam Dunel*mensem* et Ecclesiam Crowlandie (xiii–xiv cent. insertion). de uilla added before de Ederam in a different hand of xiv cent. G. iij[a] vj[te].

DESCRIPTION. *A*: 5·8″ (14·7 cm.), Top, 5·7″ (14·5 cm.), Bottom × 3·1″ (7·9 cm.), L, 3″ (7·5 cm.), R. Foot folded, 0·8″. Tie remains entire, cut from top left of fold. Seal in natural wax stained brown, fair impression. *B*: 7·8″ (19·7 cm.), Top, 7·5″ (19·2 cm.), bottom × 3·1″ (8 cm.), L, 3·2″ (8·1 cm.), R. Foot folded 1·1″. Tag 8·7″ long, 0·5″ wide. Double slits. Seal in natural wax, in excellent condition, clear impression; attached back to front.

HAND. *A*: Scribe Aj (Richard of Lincoln). Unruled. *B*: Scribe Af. Ruled in pencil or drypoint?

SOURCE. Original, Durham, D. & C. Muniments, Misc. Chr. no.612=*A*. Ibid., Misc. Chr. no.609=*B*. Printed here from *A* with major variants of *B* noted.

PRINTED. Raine, *North Durham*, no.40 (*A*). Ibid., no.41 (*B*).

NOTES. [a] Will's, *B*. [b] Dunelmensem, *B*. [c] Hederham, *B*. [d] *B* adds 7 omnibus pertinentiis suis. [e] in curia mea omitted, *B*. [f] *B* has cum omnibus capellis 7 pertinentiis suis. [g] Dunelmensi, *B*. [h] cesserit, *B*. [i] *B* omits this witness. [j] Moræuilla, *B*. *B* makes occasional use of tailed e; punctuates with ? before salutem and after terminata est; and has more extended forms of some witnesses' names.

COMMENT. The dispute was heard and settled in a session of the *curia regis* at Stirling in 1167. Besides the king there were present Bishop Richard of St Andrews, Bishop Ingram of Glasgow, Abbot Geoffrey of Dunfermline, Abbot William of Melrose, Earl Waltheof, Nicholas the chancellor, Richard the chaplain, David Olifard and other responsible clergy and laymen. After faith was pledged by both parties, it was decided that the abbot and convent of Crowland had renounced their right in the church and toun of Edrom, which passed in perpetuity, without subsequent challenge, into possession of the church of Durham. In return, the prior and convent of Durham undertook to pay annually to Crowland, at the church of St Leonard, Stamford, the sum of nine marks of silver, in pence, 60s. on 5 February and 60s. on 5 August (Raine, *North Durham*, no.642). There seems to be no record either of this dispute or of how Crowland acquired a claim to Edrom in the unpublished MS. cartulary of Crowland abbey, *penes* the Spalding Gentlemen's Society (I have to thank Mr S. W. Woodward, Hon. Secretary of the society and Mr Short, of Maples Ltd, solicitors, Spalding, for letting me have access to this MS.). The cartulary contains a number of *acta* of Waltheof, brother of Cospatric II earl of Dunbar, in his capacity of abbot of Crowland (1124–38), and it may be that Edrom, which was on the demesne of the earls of Dunbar, was granted to Crowland by Waltheof while he was still a layman, by his father, Earl Cospatric I, or by his brother Cospatric II, perhaps after 1112, in which year miracles began to be worked at Crowland at the tomb of Earl Waltheof of Northumbria (*Ecclesiastical History of Orderic Vitalis*, ed. M. Chibnall, ii (1969), 349). Waltheof of Crowland witnessed the important declaration anent Archbishop Thurstan's consecration of Robert bishop of St Andrews in 1128 (Lawrie, *Charters*, nos.75, 76). For grants and confirmations of Edrom and Nisbet to Durham by successive earls of Dunbar from Cospatric II onwards, see Raine, *North Durham*, nos.111–14, 116, 135.

106 Confirms, with the consent of his brother David, to the bishopric of Glasgow Kinclaith (Glasgow Green), Cadder and 'Badermonoc' granted by King Malcolm IV. Stirling. (1166 × 1170)

W'. Rex Scott'. uniuersis episcopis Abbatibus . Comitibus . Baronibus . Justitiis . vicecomitibus . prepositis . ministris Cunctisque aliis probis hominibus totius terre sue . Francis et Anglis . Scotis et Galweinsibus[a] Salutem. Sciant Clerici et laici . presentes et posteri . me dedisse et hac carta mea confirmasse Deo et Sancto Kentegerno et Episcopatui Glasg*uensi* . Conclud et Cader . et Badermonoc cum uniuersis earundem terrarum pertinentiis et diuisis . pro salute anime mee et pro animabus antecessorum meorum omnium et successorum et nominatim pro animabus reg*is* D*aui*d aui mei . et comitis Henr*ici* patris mei . et reg*is* Malcolm fratris mei . qui easdem terras prenominato episcopatui dedit et concessit in elemosinam perpetuam . liberas et quietas et solutas ab omni seruitio et consuetudine et seculari exaccione . et omnium hominum calumpnia . sicut aliqua elemosina in regno meo liberius et quietius possidetur . D*aui*d fratre meo idem ex parte sua plenarie concedente et hoc coram me confitente. Testibus hiis . Johanne abbate de Kelcho . Osberto abbate de Jedd' . Comite Wald*euo* . Comite Dunc*ano* . Ricardo de Moruill' constabulario . Ric*ardo* capellano . Philippo camer*ario* . D*aui*d Olifard . Willelmo de Veteri Ponte . Philippo de Coleuill' . Gilleb*erto* fil*io* Rich*erii* . Willelmo de Haia pincerna . Gilleb*erto* de Umframuill'. Apud Striuel*in*.

RUBRIC. De Conclud . Cader et Badermonoch (in margin in different hand).
SOURCE. Blairs Archives, 16 Drummond Place, Edinburgh, MS. Registrum Vetus of Glasgow, fo.iiij[r].
PRINTED. *Glasgow Registrum*, no.29.
NOTE. [a] Sic.
COMMENT. Cf. *RRS*, i, nos.265, 291. Badermonoc has been identified with Monkland, but whereas the former (presumably Cumbric) means 'the monk's habitation', the latter (middle Scots) means 'the land of the monks' and undoubtedly refers to the possession of Drumpellier by the Cistercians of Newbattle (ibid., no.198). The precise locality of Badermonoc, no longer recorded as a church after 1186 (*Glasgow Registrum*, no.62) remains uncertain.

107 Confirms to Dunfermline Abbey the whole teind of his revenues from Kinghorn and Kellie, Fife, in wheat, malt and oats. Stirling. (1165 × 1171)

Will'[a] Rex Scott' omnibus probis hominibus tocius terre sue salutem. Sciatis me concessisse 7 hac carta mea confirmasse Deo 7 ecclesie Sancte Trinitatis de Dunfer*melin* 7 monachis ibidem Deo seruientibus in perpetuam elemosinam totam decimam redditus mei de frumento 7 braseo 7 prebenda de Kingorn' 7 de Kellin . tenend*am* 7 habend*am* ita libere 7 plenarie sicut alias elemosinas suas plenius 7 liberius tenent. T*estibus*

D*aui*d fratre meo . Nich*olao* cancell*ario* . R*icardo* de Moreuill' constabul*ario* . M*atheo* archidi*acono* S*ancti* Andr*ee* . Walt*ero* fil*io* Al*ani* Dapifero . D*aui*d Olif*ard* iustic*ia* . Nessio fil*io* Will*elmi* . Walt*ero* Olif*ard* Will*elmo* de Mortimer. Apud Striuelin.

RUBRIC. De decimis de Kingorn' ⁊ de Kellin (red with blue initial) nota (in margin, xv–xvi cent.).
SOURCE. NLS, MS. Adv. 34.1.3a, fo.xii^{v}.
PRINTED. *Dunfermline Registrum*, no.61.
NOTE. [a] Initial red.

108

Commands that Dunfermline Abbey shall have fully the teind of eels which Donald of Forthar renders to the king yearly, as it had of cheese when the king received cheese from Forthar; however the food-render may be altered, the abbey is always to enjoy the teind. Dunfermline. (1165 × 1171)

Will'[a] Rex Scott' omnibus probis hominibus tocius terre sue salutem. Mando ⁊ firmiter precipio ut monachi de Dunfer*melin* plenarie habeant decimam anguillarum quas Douenaldus de Forether reddit mihi per annum sicut habuerunt de caseo quamdiu inde caseum habui. Et si forte redditum aliter mutari contigerit ·/ uolo ut semper decima redditus salua sit monachis. T*estibus* Nic*holao* cancell*ario* . Walt*ero* fil*io* Alani dapifero . D*aui*d Olif*ard* iustic*ia*. Apud Dunfer*melin*.

RUBRIC. De decimis anguillarum (red with red initial).
SOURCE. NLS, MS. Adv. 34.1.3a, fo.xiii^{r}.
PRINTED. *Dunfermline Registrum*, no.63.
NOTE. [a] Initial blue.
COMMENT. Donald was possibly the thane of Forthar. East and West Forthar are in Kettle, Kirkforthar is in Markinch, Fife. This area may have been specially rich in eels, since Robert de Quinci granted Inchcolm Priory 1000 eels in Strathenry (*Inchcolm Chrs.*, no.2, p.3).

109

Grants to May Priory 'Balegallin' (Boglily, in Kinghorn, Fife?). St Andrews. (1166 × 1171)

Willelmus[a] Rex Scott' Episcopis , Abbatibus , Comitibus , Baronibus , Justic*iis* , Vicec*omitibus* , ministris & omnibus probis hominibus tocius terre sue,[b] salutem. Sciant presentes & futuri me dedisse & concessisse & hac carta mea confirmasse Deo & ecclesie omnium sanctorum de Mai , & priori eiusdem loci & successoribus eius & fratribus ibidem Deo seruientibus, in liberam & quietam & perpetuam elemosinam, Balegallin per suas rectas diuisas,[c] ita tamen quod prior iste de Mai non debeat aliquo tempore remoueri nisi pro manifesta culpa que prius cognita fuerit coram me uel successoribus meis & coram episcopo Sancti Andree . & quod amodo erit ibi conuentus xiii. monachorum ex ordine Cluniacensi.[c] Quare uolo & firmiter precipio ut predicti monachi prenominatam terram de Balegallin cum omnibus tenuris suis quas rex Dauid auus meus & rex M*alcolmus* frater meus eis dederunt & concesserunt ita libere & quiete & honorifice teneant sicut aliqua abbatia liberius & quietius & honorificentius elemosinas suas tenet & possidet in regno meo. T*estibus* Dauid fratre meo , Nich*olao* canc*ellario* , Com*ite* Wald*euo* , Com*ite* Dunec*ano* , et multis aliis. Apud Sanctum Andream.

RUBRIC. Carta eiusdem de donatione Balegallin & conuentu monachorum.
SOURCE. BM, MS. Egerton 3031, fo.62r.
PRINTED. *PSAS*, xc, 72, no.47.
NOTES. [a] Uuillelmus, MS., with large blue initial. [b] MS. repeats terre sue. [c–c] Sic, perhaps misplaced and attributable to a different act.
COMMENT. The identification of Balegallin with Boglily (Baglillie, xvii cent., *Retours*, Fife) is tentative. Abbot G(eoffrey) of Dunfermline conceded the teinds of Balgally to the prior of May × 1178 (*St Andrews Liber*, 392–3), which points to Boglily as being in Dunfermline's *parochia* of Fothrif; alternatively, the place might be Ballingall, associated with Ramornie (in Kettle), xvii cent. (*Retours*, Fife). Cf. Lawrie, *Charters*, no.207 for King David I's grant of half of Ballegallin, where its association with common pasture in the shires of Crail and Kellie may suggest that it was neither of the two places mentioned, but a now lost locality in Carnbee or Crail.

110

Confirms to St Andrews Cathedral Priory the church of Longforgan, Perthshire, with the half-ploughgate with which it is endowed, the toft on which the canons' buildings are erected, and teinds and other revenues from the whole shire of Longforgan. Alyth. (1165 × 1170)

Willelmus[a] Dei gracia rex Scotorum . Omnibus probis hominibus tocius terre sue salutem . Sciatis me concessisse et hac carta mea confirmasse Deo et ecclesie Sancti Andree et canonicis ibidem Deo seruientibus donacionem quam rex Dauid auus meus . et rex .M. frater meus eis fecerunt de ecclesia de Foregrund et dimidia carucata terre de qua illa ecclesia dotata est secundum diuisas perambulatas . et cum tofto in quo eorum edificia fundata sunt et cum decimis et rectitudinibus ecclesie illi pertinentibus de tota syra de Foregrund tenend*am* ita libere et plenarie . sicut ecclesiasticum beneficium liberius[b] plenius teneri debet. T. Andrea episcopo de Katenes . Nicholao cancellario . Matheo Archidiacono Sancti Andree . Fulc*one* abbate de Cupir . Nesio filio Willelmi . Ricardo de Sancto Albano clerico regis . Magistro Turpino apud Alitht .

RUBRIC. De ecclesia de Forgrund (top in red).
SOURCE. SRO, GD 45/27/8 (St Andrews priory cartulary), fo.ciiiv.
PRINTED. *St Andrews Liber*, 222–3.
NOTES. [a] Red initial U. [b] MS. omits et.
COMMENT. See Lawrie, *Charters*, no.225 and *RRS*, i, nos.122, 123. The *dei gracia* in the king's style may be due to the copyist.

111

Grants to Scone Abbey one full toft in Scone with 20 acres of arable. Forfar. (1165 × 1171)

Willelmus[a] Rex Scotorum omnibus probis hominibus tocius terre sue salutem. Sciant clerici et laici, presentes et futuri, me dedisse et concessisse et hac mea carta confirmasse Deo et ecclesie Sancte Trinitatis de Scon et canonicis ibidem Deo seruientibus unum plenarium tofftum in Scon cum viginti acris terre; tenendum et habendum in liberam et perpetuam elimosinam, ita libere et quiete et honorifice sicut alias elimosinas suas liberius, quiecius et honorificencius tenent. Test*ibus* Andr*ea* episcopo de Caten*es*, Nichol*ao* canc*ellario*, Dauid Olifard, Philippo de Valon*iis* camerario, Ric*ardo* Cumyn. Apud Forfare.

SOURCE. NLS, MS. Adv. 34.3.28, fo.7v. PRINTED. *Scone Liber*, no.19.
NOTE. [a] Initial omitted, MS.

112 Confirms to St Andrews Cathedral Priory the disposition of the church of the isle (of Loch Leven) and of the form of religious life observed within it, as the charter of King David I bears witness. Forfar. (1165 × 1171)

Willelmus[a] rex Scotorum . episcopis . abbatibus . Comitibus . baronibus et omnibus probis hominibus tocius terre sue clericis et laicis salutem . Sciant presentes et futuri me concessisse et confirmasse priori Sancti Andree disposicionem ecclesie de insula et religionis secundum ordinacionem ipsius prioris[b] sicut carta regis D*aui*d aui mei testatur et confirmat . Testibus Nicholao cancellario . Matheo archidiacono Sancti Andree . Waltero[c] filio Alani . apud Forfare .

RUBRIC. de ecclesia de Insula (margin in later hand).
SOURCE. SRO, GD 45/27/8 (St Andrews priory cartulary), fo.cii^{r-v}.
PRINTED. *St Andrews Liber*, 219.
NOTES. [a] Red initial U. [b] Fo.cii^{v}. [c] MS., Willelmo.
COMMENT. King David I's charter is given in Lawrie, *Charters*, no.232. This act refers to the suppression of the *célidé* of Loch Leven and their supersession by Augustinian canons.

113 Commands that wherever the sergeand of the monks of Coldingham may discover fugitives and neyfs of Coldinghamshire or of the other lands of Coldingham Priory, he is to have them justly and no one is to detain them. Forfar. (1165 × 1171)

W' Rex Scott'. Justiciis . Vicecomitibus . 7 Omnibus probis hominibus tocius terre sue :' salutem. Precipio firmiter ut ubicunque seruiens Monachorum de Goldingham inuenire poterit fugitiuos . 7 natiuos eorum . de Goldinghamshire . siue aliarum terrarum suarum :' eos iuste habeat cum omnibus rebus . 7 catallis eorum . 7 prohibeo . ne quis illos iniuste detineat :' super meam forisfacturam. T*estibus* Nicholao Cancellario . Math*eo* archid*iacono*. Apud Forfare.

ENDORSED. de fugitiuis (xii cent.). Carta W. Regis de (xv cent. insertion). prioris de Coldingham (xv cent. insertion). Q. tercia sexte (xv cent.).
DESCRIPTION. 6·9″ (17·6 cm.), Top, 6·8″ (17·3 cm.), Bottom × 2·2″ (5·5 cm.), L, 1·4″ (3·5 cm.), R. Tie remains, 1·5″ long, 0·2″ wide. Tongue 4·6″ long, 0·7″ wide. Lower half of seal only remains, somewhat rubbed, natural wax.
HAND. Scribe Ai. Unruled.
SOURCE. Original, Durham, D. & C. Muniments, Misc. Chr. no.591.
PRINTED. Raine, *North Durham*, no.39.

114 Grants to Orm son of Hugh (son of Gillemichel earl of Fife) Inverarity (Angus), in feu and heritage, and commands that Orm may have his neyfs and fugitives wherever he may find them and no one is to detain them unjustly against the king's prohibition. Forfar. (1166 × 1171)

W'. Rex Scott' Omnibus probis hominibus tocius terre sue presentibus 7 futuris salutem. Sciatis me dedisse 7 concessisse Orm fil*io* Hug*onis* Inueraricthin per suas rectas diuisas Tenend*um* sibi 7 heredibus suis de me 7 heredibus meis in feudo 7 hereditate libere 7 quiete saluo mihi seruicio meo quod ad terram illam pertinet. Precipio etiam firmiter ut ubicumque inuenerit natiuos homines 7 fugitiuos ad terram illam pertinentes eos iuste habeat. 7 prohibeo firmiter ne quis ei quenquam ex illis iniuste detineat super meam defensionem. Test*ibus* Nic*olao* cancel*lario* . Com*ite* Wald*euo* . Waltero fil*io* Alani dapifero . Nesso fil*io* Will*elmi* . Ric*ardo* Cumin . Gilberto fil*io* Rich*erii* . Willelmo de Haia . Waltero de Berkelai. Apud Forfar.

ENDORSED. Carta de Inueraryti (xiv cent.). Carta Orm de Inueraridy (xv cent.). Charter be kyng Willame the Lyone of the lands of Inner yn (xvi cent., faded). Charter be king Williame To Orme the sone of Hew of the lands of Innerarichthine At Forfar but ane Dait (xvii cent.).
DESCRIPTION. 7·8″ (19·8 cm.), Top, 7·4″ (18·8 cm.), Bottom × 3·5″ (9 cm.), L, 3·2″ (8 cm.) R, including depth of tongue and tie. Tongue and tie cut from foot. Remains of seal (natural wax?) on tongue.
HAND. Scribe Aj (Richard of Lincoln). Unruled.
SOURCE. Original, BM, MS. Loans 29/242, no.1.
PRINTED. *HMC Portland*, ii, 1 (abstract).

115 Confirms to the bishop and *célidé* of Brechin the grant made to them by King David I of a market in the town of Brechin every Sunday, as freely as the bishop of St Andrews has his market. Brechin. (1165 × 1171)

Willelmus Rex Scotie omnibus probis hominibus totius Scotie salutem. Sciatis me concessisse et carta mea confirmasse episcopis et keldeis[a] de ecclesia de Brechine donationem illam quam dedit eis[b] Rex Dauid auus meus per cartam suam de foro imperpetuum habituro in villa per dies dominicos, adeo libere sicut episcopus Sanctiandree forum habet. Testibus Andrea episcopo de Cathenes[c], Nicholao[d] cancellario, apud Brechine.

RUBRIC. Carta Willelmi regis confirmationis Dauid regis Scotorum de foro Brechinen*si* (top).
SOURCE. SRO, GD 45/13/301 (Register of the bishopric of Brechin), fo.v^v = *A*. Ibid., fo.cxxiiij^v = B^1. Ibid., fos.cxxiiij^v–cxxv^r = B^2. Ibid., fo.cxxvij^v = C^1. Ibid., fo.cxxxiij^r = C^2. Printed here from *A*, with one reading of C^1 preferred.
PRINTED. *Brechin Registrum*, i, no.1 and no.69 (p.139).
NOTES. [a] Caldeis, C^2. [b] illis, B^1. [c] Cateness, B^1, Catenes, B^2. [d] Nichilominus, *A*; Nostro, B^1; Nicholaio, C^2.
COMMENT. The burgh market of St Andrews, of which this is the earliest mention, is said in a charter of Bishop Roger (1189 × 1198) to have been established on the land of Lambin in the time of Bishops Richard and Hugh (SRO, 'Black Book' of St Andrews, fo.35).

116 Grants to William son of Freskin Strathbrock (Uphall), West Lothian, and Roseisle, Inchkeil and Duffus (in Duffus), Moray, and Kintrae (in Spynie), Moray, and 'Machar' (unidentified, probably in Duffus, Spynie or Drainie); i.e., the land which William's father Freskin held in the time of his grandfather King David I; to be held in feu and heritage with soke and sake, toll team and infangthief, and all liberties which the king's other barons have, for the service of two knights. Elgin. (1166 × 1171)

W. Rex Scotie, Episcopis, Abbatibus, Comitibus, Justiciis, Vicecomitibus, Ministris, Prepositis cunctisque aliis probis hominibus totius terre sue, Francis, Anglis, Scotis, Clericis et Laicis, salutem. Sciant presentes et futuri me dedisse et concessisse et hac carta mea confirmasse Willelmo filio Freskin Stratbroc per suas rectas diuisas, et Rossile et Inchekell et Duffus et Machar et Kintray[a] per suas rectas diuisas, scilicet terram[b] quam Freskin pater suus tenuit tempore Regis Dauid aui mei. Tenend*um* sibi et heredibus suis de me et heredibus meis in feodo et hereditate, libere et quiete, plenarie et honorifice, in bosco et plano, in pratis et pascuis, in aquis et in omnibus aliis justis pertinentiis, cum socco et sacca, tol et them et infanganthef, et cum omnibus libertatibus quas[c] alii Barones mei habent. Quare uolo et firmiter precipio ut predictus Willelmus et heredes sui prenominatas terras et tenuras teneant[d] de me et heredibus meis libere et quiete plenarie et honorifice, per servitium duorum militum. Test*ibus* Dauid fratre meo, Andrea Episcopo Catenes, Felici Episcopo Morauiensi, Matheo Archidiacono Sancti Andree, Comite W[aldeuo], Comite Dunec*ano*, Ric*ardo* de Moruil Constabulario, Nessio filio Willelmi, Ric*ardo* Cumin, Gileberto filio Rich*erii*, Willelmo de Veteri[e] Ponte, Willelmo de Lyndesaya, Henrico Luuel, Johanne de Vallibus, Willelmo de Haya, Waltero de Berkelai, Ricardo Clerico. Apud Elgin.

RUBRIC. 'The Originall in the hands of Dame Katherine Stewart Lady Dowager of Cardross.'
SOURCE. SRO, Society of Antiquaries of Scotland, MS. Cartae Variae, fo.299 (xix-cent. transcript of a collection of Harry Maule of Kellie, titular earl of Panmure).
NOTES. [a] Kinerdy, MS. [b] terra, MS. [c] quam, MS. [d] teneat, MS. [e] Vetere, MS.
COMMENT. The land of 'Machar' is not mentioned in Shaw's *History of Moray*, nor does it figure in *Moray Registrum*. The name suggests the links in the west of Duffus parish, but might refer to land by the edge of the Loch of Spynie, which stretched from Kintrae to the River Lossie.

117

Grants to the (parish) church of Saint Mary of Inverness and to Thomas the priest, parson of that church, one ploughgate of arable. Elgin. (1165 × 1171)

W.[a] Dei gr*ati*a Rex Scott' omnibus probis hominibus tocius terre sue salutem. Sciatis me dedisse et concessisse Deo et ecclesie Sancte Marie de Inuernys et Thome sacerdoti . eiusdem ecclesie persone Unam Carucatam terre in perpetuam elemosinam. Quare volo ut predictus Thomas predictam terram teneat adeo libere et quiete . sicut aliqua elemosina in terra mea liberius et quiecius tenetur. Test*ibus* Nicholao Cancellario Matheo arch*idiacono* Sancti Andr*ee* . D*aui*d Olifard' , Ric*ardo* Cumyn . apud Elgyn.

RUBRIC. De terra pertinente ad dictam ecclesiam (red). . xxxij . (in margin).
SOURCE. NLS, MS. Adv. 34.4.2, fo.xlix[r].
PRINTED. *Arbroath Liber*, i, no.32.
NOTE. [a] Initial red.
COMMENT. King William's endowment of the church of Inverness before the period in which he was engaged in military activity in Moray is further evidence that the burgh of Inverness antedates his reign (cf. G. S. Pryde, *Burghs of Scotland*, no.20). *Dei gratia* in the style may be due to the copyist.

118

Confirms to Scone Abbey certain revenues for the lighting of the church. (1165 × 1174)

Willelmus[a] Rex Scottorum omnibus probis hominibus tocius terre sue salutem. Sciatis me concessisse et hac carta mea confirmasse Deo et ecclesie de Scon et abbati et canonicis ibidem Deo seruientibus ad lumen prefate ecclesie viginti solidos de firma mea de Perth et ad idem negocium decem solidos de firma duorum molendinorum meorum de Perth que sunt super amnem de Amund, et decimam eorundem molendinorum pariter. Prohibeo itaque ut nullus eis quicquam iniuste auferre vel detinere presumat, super forisfactum meum. Test*ibus*.

SOURCE. NLS, MS. Adv. 34.3.28, fo.12^{r}.
PRINTED. *Scone Liber*, no.43.
NOTE. [a] Initial omitted, MS.
COMMENT. See *RRS*, i, no.250.

119 Recounts that Morgund, son of Gillocheri formerly earl of Mar, came into the king's presence at Hyndhope Burn mouth, in the king's 'new forest', on 23 May A.D.1171, to seek his right to the whole earldom of Mar, before the common council and army of the kingdom of Scotland there assembled. The king ordered the matter to be investigated by many trustworthy thanes and barons, and after they had found Morgund to be the lawful heir of Gillocheri the king restored to him the whole earldom of Mar as his heritage, to be held of the king as freely as any earl in the kingdom of Scotland holds his earldom, for the forinsec service, i.e. Scottish service, wont to be performed by his predecessors. The king promises to do right to Morgund in respect of a similar claim anent the earldom of Moray, as soon as he can bring his war with the English to a conclusion and subdue the men of Moray; and he has given Morgund his letters-patent to this effect. Hyndhope Burn mouth (in Kirkhope), Selkirkshire. (1171) (Spurious)

Willelmus Rex Scottorum universis episcopis, comitibus, abbatibus, prioribus, baronibus, militibus, thanis et prepositis, et omnibus aliis probis hominibus tocius terre sue, tam clericis quam laicis, salutem eternam in Domino. Sciatis presentes et futuri Morgund' filium Gillocheri quondam comitis de Marr' in mea presencia venisse apud Hindhop burnemuthe in mea noua foresta decimo kalend*arum* Junii anno gr*acie* .m^{o}. centesimo septuagesimo primo, petendo ius suum de toto comitatu de Marr' coram communi consilio et exercitu regni Scocie ibidem congregato. Ego vero, cupiens eidem Morgundo et omnibus aliis iura facere secundum peticionem suam ius suum inquesiui per multos viros fidedignos, videlicet per baronias et thanos regni mei, per quam inquisicionem inveni dictum Morgundum filium et heredem legitimum dicti Gillocheri Comitis de Marr' per quod concessi et reddidi eidem Morgundo totum comitatum de Marr' tanquam ius suum hereditarium, sicut predictus Gillocheri[a] pater suus obiit vestitus et saisitus. Tenendam et habendam eidem Morgundo et herdibus suis de me et heredibus meis in feodo et hereditate cum omnibus pertinenciis, libertatibus et rectitudinibus suis, adeo libere, quiete, plenarie et honorifice, sicut aliquis comes in regno Scotie liberius, quiecius, plenarius et honorificencius tenet vel possidet, faciendo inde ipse et heredes sui mihi et heredibus meis forinsecum seruicium videlicet seruicium Scoticanum sicut antecessores sui mihi et antecessoribus meis facere consueuerunt. Eodem vero die et loco, post homagium suum mihi factum coram communi consilio regni mei, predictus Morgundus petiit sibi ius fieri de toto comitatu Morauie, de quo predictus Gillocheri[a] pater suus obiit vestitus et saisitus, super qua peticione sua per quam plures viros fidedignos barones, milites, et thanos regni mei inquisicionem facere feci, et per illam inquisicionem inveni dictum Morgund' verum et legitimum heredem de comitatu Morauie, et quod eodem tempore propter gerram[b] inter me et Anglicos graviter fuissem occupatus et Morauienses pro voluntate mea non potuissem iustificare dicto Morgundo nullum ius facere potui. Sed cum gerram[b] inter me et aduersarios meos compleuero et rebelles Morauienses superare potero, dicto Morgundo sibi et heredibus suis promitto pro me et heredibus meis fideliter et plenarie ius facere de toto comitatu Morauie. Et ut hoc factum meum aliis certificaretur predicto Morgundo has litteras meas dedi patentes, teste me ipso eodem anno, die et loco supradicto.

ENDORSED. No early endorsement.
DESCRIPTION. 10·9″ (27·2 cm.), Top, 11″ (27·4 cm.), Bottom × 3·25″ (8·3 cm.), L and R. Very thin transparent parchment, yellowish in colour. Foot cut straight across; no sign of sealing.
HAND. Scribe UDf. Court or chancery hand of the fourth quarter of the xiii cent., similar in general character to the hand of PRO, E. 39/89, the 'Appeal of the Seven Earls', Palgrave, *Docs. Hist. Scot.*, 14–21. Unruled, with almost no margins.
SOURCE. 'Copy' of original, or purported original, Lincoln's Inn, MS. Hale XII (Collectanea Seldeni), item 78 (numbered in pencil H 56).
PRINTED. J. Selden, *Titles of Honor* (1631), 700–1; *APS*, i, 19–20n.; W. F. Skene, *Celtic Scotland*, iii, 446–7 (also, *PSAS*, xii (1878), 603–9).
NOTES. [a] Sic; Skene's text has Gillocherus. [b] Sic.
COMMENT. This document is evidently the 'writing' (or copy thereof) said to have been in the possession of Earl Donald of Mar *c.*1290–1; cf. the memorandum associated with the 'Appeal of the Seven Earls', Palgrave, *Docs. Hist. Scot.*, 21. This 'writing' contained that King William restored the earldom of Mar to Morgund M: Gyloclery (alternative and better reading: M[c]Gylochery). The handwriting of this document is similar in general character to the handwriting of the Appeal and the accompanying memoranda; it is an English chancery hand of *c.*1290. It seems possible that this forgery and the Appeal were concocted at about the same time, principally in the interests of Earl Donald of Mar but incidentally in the interests of Robert Bruce the Competitor. It seems that only the memorandum accompanying the Appeal and this document give the name of Earl Morgund's father as Gillocheri (Gylochery); this may have been his name, but there does not seem to be any twelfth-century evidence for it. Earl Morgund died probably in 1182 or 1183. The army of Scotland assembled at Caddonlee, Selkirkshire, for the invasion of northern England in 1173, but in 1171 King William was at peace with the English and the men of Moray were not, so far as is known, in rebellion.

120 Confirms to Kelso Abbey the churches of Campsie and Antermony in Lennox, granted by his brother David, as his charter bears witness. Traquair. (1165 × 1174)

.W. Rex Scott'. Episcopis. Abbatibus. Com*itibus*. Baronibus. Justiciis. Vice*comitibus*. 7 omnibus probis hominibus tocius terre sue. salutem. Sciatis me concessisse 7 hac carta mea confirmasse Deo 7 ecclesie Sancte Marie de Kelch' 7 monachis ibidem Deo seruientibus[a] in liberam 7 perpetuam elemosinam . Ecclesiam de Chamsy . 7 Ecclesiam de Altermunin in Leuenach' . quas D*au*id frater meus eis dedit . 7 carta sua confirmauit. Quare uolo ut predicti monachi prenominatas ecclesias . ita libere 7 quiete . plenarie 7 honorifice teneant . sicut tenent alias ecclesias suas in regno meo . 7 sicut carta D*au*id fratris mei testatur 7 confirmat. Test*ibus* . Ric*ardo* de Morewill' const*abulario* . Ric*ardo* Cumyn . Gilb*erto* fil*io* Rich*eri* . Waltero de Berkel' . Willelmo capellano . Hug*one* clerico . Ric*ardo* clerico apud Traverqueir;

RUBRIC. Confirmacio super Ecclesias de Chamsy . 7 Altermunin (top in red).
SOURCE. NLS, MS. Adv. 34.5.1, fo.145^{r-v}.
PRINTED. *Kelso Liber*, no.386.
NOTE. [a] Fo.145^{v}.
COMMENT. This may have been issued on the same occasion as no.145. Campsie and Antermony are both in Stirlingshire, the former a parish, the latter now in Campsie parish. David's charter is given in *Kelso Liber*, no.226, with the place-date Roxburgh. The churches were granted to Kelso 'after the decease of the son of Ralph de Camera' who presumably then held them. For this important chamber official and his family, see above, pp.33–34.

121

Confirms to Dryburgh Abbey the church of Lessudden (St Boswells), Roxburghshire, granted by Robert of London, as his charter bears witness. (1165 × 1174)

W. rex Scotorum omnibus probis hominibus totius terre sue salutem. Sciatis me dedisse, concessisse et hac carta mea confirmasse ecclesie Sancte Marie de Driburgh et canonicis ibidem Deo servientibus in liberam et perpetuam elemosinam ecclesiam de Lessedewyn, cum omnibus justis pertinentiis suis, quam Robertus de Londonia eis dedit pro animabus antecessorum suorum, tenendam ita libere, quiete, plenarie et honorifice sicut alias elemosinas suas tenent et sicut carta ipsius Roberti de Londonia testatur et confirmat. Testibus etc.

RUBRIC. Confirmacio regis super ecclesia de Lassedevyn.
SOURCE. NLS, MS. Adv. 34.4.7, fo.20^{r}.
PRINTED. *Dryburgh Liber*, no.55.
COMMENT. The charter of Robert of London (to be distinguished from King William's bastard son of that name) is given in *Dryburgh Liber*, no.53. An examination of ibid., nos.56 and 57 shews that Robert's grant and the royal confirmation were themselves confirmed by Bishop Ingram of Glasgow, hence the limit-dates suggested above, supported by the style.

122

Confirms to Dryburgh Abbey 'Langelaw' (lost, in Haddington, East Lothian), granted by Alexander of St Martin for the soul of Malcolm de Moreville; as the charters of Alexander and of the Countess Ada bear witness. Confirms also one toft in the toun of Aberlady, East Lothian, granted by Richard bishop of Dunkeld, as his charter bears witness. (1170 × 1174)

Willelmus rex Scotie abbatibus, comitibus, baronibus, justiciariis, vicecomitibus et omnibus probis hominibus totius terre sue salutem. Sciant presentes et futuri me concessisse et hac mea carta confirmasse Deo et Sancte Marie et canonicis de Driburgh donacionem quam Alexander de Sancto Martino fecit eis pro anima Malcolmi de Moreuilla, scilicet Langelaw per suas rectas diuisas. Volo itaque et firmiter precipio ut[a] prefati canonici prenominatam Langelaw cum omnibus justis pertinentiis suis teneant et possideant in liberam et perpetuam elemosinam ita libere, quiete et honorifice sicut aliquas alias elemosinas suas liberius et quietius tenent in regno me et sicut carta Alexandri de Sancto Martino et carta Ade comitisse matris mee testantur et confirmant. Confirmo et eis hac carta mea unum toftum in villa de Abirleuedi quod Ricardus episcopus Dunkeldensis eis in liberam elemosinam et perpetuam dedit. Quare volo et precipio ut prenominatum toftum ita libere et quiete teneant sicut carta Ricardi episcopi Dunkeldensis testatur et confirmat. Testibus etc.

RUBRIC. Confirmacio regis Willelmi super Langelaw. [c]vj.[b]
SOURCE. NLS, MS. Adv. 34.4.7, fos.30^{v}–31^{r}.
PRINTED. *Dryburgh Liber*, no.96.
NOTES. [a] Fo.31^{r}. [b] Fo.30^{v}.
COMMENT. Alexander of St Martin, a prominent tenant and vassal of the Countess Ada, and presumably related to the family of St Martin connected with the Warennes, granted 'Langelau' to Dryburgh in reconciliation with the family of de Moreville because his brother Adulph had accidentally killed Malcolm de Moreville while hunting (*Dryburgh Liber*, no.94). Countess Ada's charter follows, ibid., no.95, and Richard de Moreville's is ibid., no.97. Ibid., no.98 shews that the lost land of Langelaw lay in Haddington parish. Bishop Richard's charter of Aberlady is not preserved.

123 Commands his provosts of Berwick to pay Kelso Abbey the 40s. owed to it annually from the *firma burgi* of Berwick. (1165 × 1174)

Will*elmus*[a] Rex Scott' . prepositis suis de Berewyc' salutem. Precipio vobis quatinus faciatis Abbatem ⁊ monachos de Kelchou habere .xl. sol*idos* quos debent annuatim habere de firma mea de Berewic' sicut carta eorum quam inde habent testatur . ⁊ ad terminos statutos. Testibus.

RUBRIC. Carta Regis Willelmi de .xl. s. in Berwico (top in red).
SOURCE. NLS, MS. Adv. 34.5.1, fo.37^{v}.
PRINTED. *Kelso Liber*, no.101.
NOTE. [a] Initial red.
COMMENT. See Lawrie, *Charters*, no.35, and cp. no.289, below.

124 Commands his men who dwell or who are about to dwell on the muirland within the territory of 'Leuchoruer' (Borthwick, Midlothian) to render fully (to the parish church) the teinds and all other obligations with which they ought to shew reverence in Christian fashion to their mother church, as they or any others before them have been accustomed to do in the time of King David I, as King Malcolm IV's brieve commands and confirms. The king wills that whatever King David I justly enacted in his days, especially with regard to the church, shall be justly maintained. (1165 × 1174)

Willelmus[a] Rex Scottorum omnibus probis hominibus qui manent aut mansuri sunt in moris infra territorium de Leuchoruer' salutem. Mando vobis et firmiter precipio ut de decimis et de omnibus aliis rectitudinibus quibus vestram matrem ecclesiam more Christianorum venerari debetis sitis plenarie spectantes ad ecclesiam de Louchoruer' sicut uos[b] aut aliqui alii ante uos[b] in eodem territorio manentes melius erant respicientes ad eandem ecclesiam tempore regis D*aui*d aui mei, sicut carta regis

M*alcolmi* fratris mei precipit et confirmat. Volo quod ut ea que Rex Dauid auus meus in diebus suis iuste statuit, et maxime in ecclesia, per me iuste manuteneantur. Quare super meam plenariam forisfacturam vobis prohibeo[c] ut de uobis sinatis ulterius pro penuria recti pro predictis rectitudinibus clamorem audire. Test*ibus* etc.

RUBRIC. Carta Willelmi Regis de decimis et rectitudinibus ecclesie de Louchoruer.

SOURCE. NLS, MS. Adv. 34.3.28, fo.12v.

PRINTED. *Scone Liber*, no.44.

NOTES. [a] Initial omitted, MS. [b] *Scone Liber* prints nos. [c] *Scone Liber* has a blank after prohibeo, followed by de nobis.

COMMENT. Malcolm IV's brieve has not survived. The men dwelling in the muirland of Borthwick may have been opening up new cultivation, and it may have been especially difficult to extract teind from them.

125

Confirms (re-grants?) to Ralph of Graham Cousland, Pentland and Gogar (Midlothian), in feu and heritage, with sake and soke, toll, team and infangthief, as the king's other knights hold their feus, for the service of one and a half knights. Grants also that (the marriage of) Ralph's mother may be in Ralph's gift. Linlithgow. (1165 × 1174)

W'. Rex Scott'. Episcopis. abbatibus. Comitibus. Baronibus. Justiciis · Vicec*omitibus* . 7 Omnibus probis hominibus tocius terre sue salutem· Sciatis me Concessisse 7 hac carta mea Confirmasse Rad*ulfo* de Graham . Cousland 7 Pentland 7 Gogger per suas rectas diuisas . Cum omnibus justis pertinenciis suis. Tenend*a* sibi 7 heredibus suis de me 7 de heredibus meis . in feudo 7 hereditate ita libere 7 quiete 7 honorifice Cum Socca 7 Sacca . Cum tol 7 them 7 infangenthef sicut alii milites mei liberius 7 quietius 7 honorificencius feuda sua de me tenent per seruicium unius militis 7 dimidii. Concedo etiam ut mater eiusdem Rad*ulfi* sit in eius donatione. Test*ibus* Ric*ardo* Cumi*n* . Roberto Auenel . Alano filio Walteri filii Alani . Waltero de Berkel' . Roberto fratre suo . Osberto Olif*ard* . S*imone* hostiario . Henrico de Mundeuill' . Ric*ardo* clerico. Ap*ud* Linlitqu.

ENDORSED. Carta de Couysland. (xiv cent.) Charta Confir. granted be King William to Ld. Graham of Cousland of the lands of Pentland and Midel [ ] (xvii cent.). P R 9 (xvii cent.). Ch: D Sh: I Bun: 3 no.1 (xviii cent.).

DESCRIPTION. 6·95″ (17·6 cm.), Top and bottom × 4·8″ (12·2 cm.), L, R. Foot folded to a depth of 1·1″ (2·7 cm.). Tie 6·4″ long and 0·15″ wide, cut from fold, and has been much knotted. Blue and green silk cords pass through single slits in the fold and foot, the ends of the cord projecting below the seal. Seal remains, almost at right angles to the document, in green wax with a slight brown stain here and there. The seal is almost entire, diameter 3·2″ (8 cm.). Legend: (obv.)+WILLELMVS . . D . . RE . . REX SCOTTORVM; (rev.)+WILLELMV . . DEO RECTORE . . SCOTTORVM.

HAND. Scribe Aj (Richard of Lincoln). Unruled.

SOURCE. Original, Duke of Montrose, Montrose Muniments, Auchmar, Drymen, D.1.3.1.

PRINTED. *HMC, 2nd Report*, Appendix, p.166, no.3.

COMMENT. The origin of the Scottish Grahams remains to be established; the first two or three pages of the article 'Graham duke of Montrose' in *SP*, vi, are worthless. The earliest member of the family known to Scottish record was William of Graham, for whom see *ESC, passim*. Peter of Graham granted to Newbattle

Abbey Balnebucth (later Bellyboucht, now lost, in Dalkeith) in the middle years of William I's reign (*Newbattle Registrum*, no.7), but the relationship between Peter and William has not been established with certainty. *SP*, vi, 193–4, 198–9, makes Ralph of Graham the youngest son of Peter, but the available evidence makes it at least as likely that Ralph was Peter's brother. Peter had sons named William and Henry, who witness *Newbattle Registrum*, no.69, which must date ×1178; it is not the charter confirmed by ibid. no.71 (=*RRS*, i, no.136) but evidently a later charter confirmed by no.91 (=*Newbattle Registrum*, no.72).

126 Confirms to Cambuskenneth Abbey an annualrent of one merk of silver from the *firma burgi* of Crail, granted by his mother the Countess Ada for the lighting of the abbey church. Linlithgow. (1171×1174)

Wilelmus[a] Rex Scotorum episcopis, abbatibus, comitibus, baronibus, justiciis, ministris et omnibus probis hominibus tocius terre sue, clericis et laicis, salutem. Sciant presentes et futuri me concessisse et hac carta mea confirmasse Deo et ecclesie Sancte Marie de Cambuskynneth et canonicis ibidem Deo servientibus in liberam et perpetuam elemosinam unam marcam argenti in burgo de Carel de firma ipsius burgi quam A*da* Comitissa mater mea eis dedit ad luminare ipsius ecclesie; tenendam ita libere et quiete et honorifice sicut carta matris mee testatur et confirmat[b]. Testibus, W*altero* de Bid*un* cancellario, Hugone capellano meo, Philippo de Coleuill', Thoma de Muschamp', apud Linlidqw.

RUBRIC. Marca annui redditus de Carel (at top). Concordat cum principali Jacobus Foulis (at end).
SOURCE. NLS, MS. Adv. 34.1.2, fo.44ʳ.
PRINTED. *Cambuskenneth Registrum*, no.66.
NOTES. [a] Large blue initial U. [b] MS. confirmatur.
COMMENT. See also no.160; the countess's charter has not survived.

127 Takes the canons of St Andrews Cathedral Priory and their lay brothers into his firm peace and protection, wherever they stay to cultivate their lands or collect their revenues. St Andrews. (1170–1171)

Willelmus[a] rex Scotorum episcopis . abbatibus . Comitibus . Baronibus . Justiciis . vicecomitibus . ministris . et omnibus probis hominibus suis tocius regni sui salutem . Sciatis canonicos ecclesie Sancti Andree apostoli et fratres suos esse in mea firma pace et proteccione ubicunque manserint ad excolendas terras suas uel elemosinas colligendas. Quare prohibeo ne aliquis illis iniuriam uel aliquam exaccionem faciat super[b] plenariam forisfacturam. Testibus Andrea episcopo Chat' . Ricardo episcopo Dunekeld*ensi* . Nicholao cancellario Matheo archidiacono . Comite Dunecano Roberto Auenel . Nesio filio Willelmi apud Sanctum Andream .

RUBRIC. De proteccione (top in red).
SOURCE. SRO, GD 45/27/8 (St Andrews priory cartulary), fos.ciiiiᵛ–cvʳ.
PRINTED. *St Andrews Liber*, 225–6.
NOTES. [a] Red initial U. [b] Fo.cvʳ.

128 Commands his foresters of Banchory to allow the canons of St Andrews Cathedral Priory and their men to have timber from the king's forest of Banchory, Mearns, for the purpose of completing the church of St Andrews and the canons' buildings. They are not to be obstructed, on pain of the king's penalty of £10. Crail. (1171 × 1174)

Willelmus[a] rex Scotorum forestariis suis de Benchorin salutem . precipio uobis firmiter quatinus faciatis canonicis de Sancto Andrea et eorum hominibus habere materiem ad ecclesiam[b] Sancti Andree perficiendam et ad eorum edificia in foresto meo de Benchorin . ita ne ipsi disturbentur super meam forisfacturam .x. librarum Testibus . Com*ite*[c] Gilleberto de Stradthern . Nesio filio Willelmi . Hugone clerico meo apud Karel .

RUBRIC. De Materie (top in red).
SOURCE. SRO, GD 45/27/8 (St Andrews priory cartulary), fo.cv^{r-v}.
PRINTED. *St Andrews Liber*, 227.
NOTES. [a] Blue initial V. [b] Fo.cv^{v}. [c] Cam', MS.
COMMENT. The date suggested for this brieve depends on the royal style and Earl Gilbert's succession. Hugh the clerk may be Hugh of Roxburgh.

129 Confirms to St Andrews Cathedral Priory the church of Tarland, Aberdeenshire, with a ploughgate of arable and a mill, granted by Morgun (Morgrund) earl of Mar. Kinghorn. (1170 × 1171)

Willelmus[a] rex Scotorum .' omnibus probis hominibus tocius[b] terre sue salutem . Sciatis me concessisse et hac carta mea confirmasse Deo et ecclesie Sancti Andree et canonicis ibidem Deo seruientibus donacionem quam Comes Morgun eis fecit pro salute anime sue et antecessorum suorum de ecclesia de Tharflund cum omnibus iustis pertinenciis suis et cum una carucata terre per rectas diuisas suas . saluo michi seruicio meo de terra et cum molendino in eadem terra fundato . et cum decima de omnibus redditibus suis tenend*am* eis ita libere et quiete plenarie et honorifice sicut alias suas elemosinas tenent et sicut carta ipsius comitis testatur et confirmat. Testibus . Ricardo episcopo Dunkeld*ensi* . Nicholao cancellario . Matheo archidiacono Sancti Andree . Comite Dunecano de Fif . Roberto Auenel Justic' . Hugone Giffard Willelmo de Mortemer . apud Kingor .

SOURCE. SRO, GD 45/27/8 (St Andrews priory cartulary), fos.cii^{v}–ciii^{r}.
PRINTED. *St Andrews Liber*, 220–1.
NOTES. [a] Blue initial V. [b] Fo.ciii^{r}.
COMMENT. Earl Morgrund's charter is given in *St Andrews Liber*, 246–7 (1165 × 1172), giving the name of the ploughgate as Hachadgonan (read Hachadgouan, 'smith's field'), now lost.

130 Grants to Dunfermline Abbey and the chapel of Stirling Castle, in exchange for the abbey's land which the king enclosed when he first enclosed his Park at Stirling (the King's Park), the land which is between the land which the abbey has outwith the Park and the marches of St Ninian's, and, on the other side, the land between Cambusbarron belonging to Peter of Stirling and the land of Roger son of Odo, as the high road goes to 'Cuiltedouenald'; as perambulated by Richard de Moreville the constable, Robert Avenel the justiciar, Ralph the sheriff and Peter of Stirling. Stirling. (1165 × 1174)

Willelmus[a] Rex Scott' omnibus probis hominibus tocius terre sue clericis 7 laicis salutem. Sciatis me concessisse 7 dedisse 7 hac Carta mea confirmasse Deo 7 ecclesie Sancte Trinitatis de Dunfer*melin* 7 monachis ibidem Deo seruientibus 7 capelle castelli mei de Striuel*in* in escambium terre sue quam primum clausi in parco meo quando parcum meum primum clausi . terram que est inter terram suam quam habent extra parcum 7 diuisas terre de Kirketun 7 ex alia parte terram que est inter Cambusbarun terram Petri de Striuelin 7 terram Rogeri filii Odonis . sicut magna strata uadit ad Cuiltedouenald . sicut Ric*ardus* de Moreuill' constabular*ius* . 7 Rob*ertus* Auenel justic*ia* . 7 Rad*ulfus* vic*ecomes* . 7 Petrus de Striuel*in* perambulauerunt. Tenend*am* in perpetuam elemosinam . ita libere 7 quiete .' sicut alias elemosinas suas tenent. T*estibus* Ric*ardo* de Moruill' const*abulario* . Rob*erto* Auenel justic*ia* . Alano fil*io* Dapiferi . Adam fil*io* Thom*e* . Rog*ero* de Valon*iis* . Rad*ulfo* vic*ecomite* de Striuel*in* . Petro de Striuel*in* . Walt*ero* de Berkelai . Ric*ardo* clerico apud Striuel*in*.

RUBRIC. De escambio terre de Striuelin (red with red initial).
SOURCE. NLS, MS. Adv. 34.1.3a, fo.xiii^v.
PRINTED. *Dunfermline Registrum*, no.72.
NOTE. [a] Initial red.
COMMENT. This is the earliest reference in record to the King's Park.

131

Confirms to Robert of Newham the whole of Cambo (in Kingsbarns), Fife, with one full toft in free burgage in Crail and common pasture, to be held of the Countess Ada in feu and heritage, as her charter bears witness, for the service of one man on foot in the king's army, and performing forinsec service for half a Scottish ploughgate of land. Stirling. (*c.*1171 × 1174)

Wilielmus Rex Scottorum Justiciis Vicecomitibus ministris et omnibus probis hominibus tocius terre sue clericis et laicis Salutem. Sciant presentes et futuri me concessisse et hac carta mea confirmasse Roberto de Newham totam Camboc per rectas diuisas suas et unum plenarium toftum in libero burgagio in Karel et communem pasturam. Tenendum sibi et heredibus suis de A*da* Comitissa matre mea et heredibus suis in feodo et hereditate ita libere et quiete et honorifice, sicut carta matris mee testatur et confirmat, per seruicium unius hominis pedalis[a] in exercitu meo et defendendo totum predictum Kamboc pro dimidia carrucata terre Scotica in forinseco seruicio meo. Testibus Wilielmo[b] de Berkele camerario, Alexandro de Sancto Martino. Apud Striuelin.

HEADING. Cambow charter copied by me the 2^d of Aprile 1652.
SOURCE. Edinburgh University Library, MS. Laing La. II, 512. (Loose sheet of transcripts in a seventeenth-century hand, perhaps of Father Richard Hay) = *A*. Macfarlane, *Genealogical Collections*, i, 46, first item in section headed 'Morton of Cambo his old writs' (abstract with witnesses) = *B*. Printed here from *A*.
PRINTED. (*B* only) Macfarlane, *Genealogical Collections*, i, 46.
NOTES. [a] The edge of the paper is crumpled here. The word appears to be pedl, with down-stroke familiarly used for terminal -is or -es; but peditis might be intended. [b] Sic, for Waltero.
COMMENT. Robert of Newham was a Northumbrian landowner, taking his name from Newham (West, Mid and East Newham), in Belsay, Northumberland. I am grateful to Mr W. Percy Hedley for information concerning him. A 'Scottish ploughgate' (davoch ?) is mentioned in no.469; and cf. nos.286, 402.

132 Commands his sheriffs and officers of Moray to pay to God and to their churches and their parsons the rightful teinds and dues as required by Holy Church. If anyone withholds his teinds, the sheriff in whose jurisdiction he lives shall compel him to pay, in the same manner as teinds are paid in the diocese of St Andrews and he shall take the same forfeiture as is taken in that diocese. Stirling. (23 January × 2 April, 1172)

Will'. Dei gratia Rex Scott' vicecom*itibus* suis et ministris suis Morau*ie* ceterisque probis hominibus tocius Morau*ie* salutem. Mando et firmiter precipio quatinus persoluatis Deo et ecclesiis et personis ecclesiarum uestrarum rectas decimas uestras de quibus sancta ecclesia exigit decimas dari . et alias rectitudines ecclesiasticas . Et prohibeo firmiter ne quis decimas suas uel alias rectitudines ecclesiasticas iniuste detineat super meum plenarium forisfactum. Si quis autem decimas suas et rectitudines ecclesiasticas detinere presumpserit precipio ut vicecom*es* in cuius potestate ille manserit eum distringat ad reddendum rectas decimas . secundum quod decime redduntur in episcopatu Sancti Andr*ee* . et tale forisfactum capiat quale capitur in episcopatu Sancti Andr*ee* de illis qui decimas suas detinent. Test*ibus* Engel*ramo* episcopo de Glascu . Matheo electo de Aberdon' . Ric*ardo* de Moreuill' const*abulario* . Waltero filio Alani dapif*ero* . Ric*ardo* Cumin . Hug*one* clerico meo . Ric*ardo* clerico. Apud Striuelin.

MARGINAL NOTE. ista non scribitur in libro decani.
SOURCE. NLS, MS. Adv. 34.4.10, fo.xxxvii^{v}.
PRINTED. *Moray Registrum*, no.1.
COMMENT. Richard the clerk is no doubt Richard of Lincoln, a witness to no.133. Simon de Toeni was consecrated bishop of Moray on 23 January, 1172, and this brieve was no doubt issued at his behest. *Dei gratia* in the style may be due to the copyist.

133 Confirms to Gilbert nephew of (Andrew) bishop of Caithness the lands of Monorgan (in Longforgan), Perthshire, to be held in feu and heritage of the king's brother David, for a reddendo of one two-year-old hawk. Stirling. (1172 × 2 April)

W'. Rex Scott'. Episcopis . abbatibus . Com*itibus* . Bar*onibus* . Justic*iis* . Vic*ecomitibus* . 7 Omnibus probis hominibus tocius terre sue :' salut*em*. Sciatis me concessisse 7 hac carta mea confirmasse . Gileberto nepoti episcopi de Catenes Andr*ee*[a] :' Monorgrun . per suas rectas diuisas Tenend*am* sibi 7 heredibus suis de D*aui*d fratre meo 7 heredibus suis . In feudo 7 hereditate . In bosco 7 plano In pratis 7 pascuis 7 aquis . In moris 7 Mareisis . 7 Omnibus aliis iustis pertinenciis suis libere 7 quiete. Reddendo fr[atri m][b]eo D*aui*d 7 heredibus suis [unum][c] hosturum sorum . sicut carta D*aui*d fratris mei testatur 7 confirmat. Test*ibus* M*atheo* electo de Aberdeon . Comite Dunec*ano* . [Ricardo][d] Cumin . Waltero de Berkel' . Willelmo de Haia . Roberto de Quenci[e] Hug*one*[f] clerico meo . Ric*ardo* clerico meo de Lincoln'. Apud StrivelIN.

ENDORSED. Backed by vellum at a later date, and no endorsements are visible.
DESCRIPTION. 4·6″ (11·8 cm.), Top, 4·15″ (10·5 cm.), Bottom × 2·9″ (7·4 cm.), L, 2·8″ (7·2 cm.), R. Foot folded (0·7″, 1·8 cm.), with slit for seal tag. Tag and seal missing. The document is considerably injured.

HAND. Scribe Aj (Richard of Lincoln). Unruled.
SOURCE. Original, NLS, Ch. 7711 (acquired at sale of Phillipps MSS., Sotheby and Co., 26 June, 1967) = *A*. NLS, MS. Adv. 31.2.4, p.11 (transcript by Alexander Brown from original then *penes* Henry Crawfurd of Monorgan, Collector of Customs in Dundee, 1785) = *B*. Printed here from *A*.
NOTES. [a] terras de, *B*. [b] Obscure through injury. [c] Illegible; supplied from NLS, Ch. 7710. [d] Supplied conjecturally; *B* omits this and the next name. [e] Apparently altered to Graham by a later pen; *B* reads Grem. [f] *B* omits.
COMMENT. Cf. *RRS*, i, 42 and n. Earl David's charter is now NLS, Ch. 7710.

134 Grants to St Andrews Cathedral Priory the church of St Cyrus, Mearns, after the death of Richard, the king's clerk of the liverance, parson of the church. Kinghorn. (1172 × 1173)

Willelmus[a] rex Scotorum . episcopis . abbatibus . Comitibus . Baronibus . iusti[b]ciis Ministris et omnibus probis hominibus tocius terre sue clericis et laicis salutem . Sciant presentes et futuri me pro salute anime mee et antecessorum meorum dedisse et concessisse et hac carta mea confirmasse Deo et ecclesie Sancti Andree et canonicis ibidem Deo seruientibus et seruituris ecclesiam Sancti Cirici de Eglesgirg post decessum Ricardi clerici mei de liberacione eiusdem ecclesie persone in liberam et perpetuam elemosinam tenendam . cum capellis . decimis . et terris . et omnibus eidem ecclesie iuste pertinentibus et adiacentibus ita libere . et quiete . plenarie et honorifice . sicut alias elemosinas suas liberius . quiecius plenius et honorificencius tenent . Testibus . Matheo episcopo de Haberden . Waltero de Bid*un* cancellario . Comite Dunecano . Justic' . Willelmo capellano meo . Hugone capellano meo . Waltero de Berkel' camerario . Nes filio Willelmi . Hugone clerico meo . Ricardo clerico meo apud Kingor .

RUBRIC. De ecclesia de Eglisgirg (top in red). Alia melior inferius (note at foot in later hand).
SOURCE. SRO, GD 45/27/8 (St Andrews priory cartulary), fos.ci^{v}–cii^{r}.
PRINTED. *St Andrews Liber*, 218.
NOTES. [a] Red initial U. [b] Fo.cii^{r}.
COMMENT. See also no.352. This is the earliest appearance of a royal clerk of the liverance or livery (*RRS*, i, 33). This Richard never appears again under this description. It may be that he was none other than King William's kinsman Richard clerk of the *prebenda* or provend, who first appears a little earlier than this, became bishop of Dunkeld in 1203, and died in 1210. This is suggested by the report that a seventeenth-century laird of Lauriston in St Cyrus possessed a charter of King William granted to 'his kinsman' (cf. no.581). For King Girg and St Cyric, and the Celtic ecclesiastical foundation at St Cyrus or Eglesgirg, containing their names, see J. M. Mackinlay, *Ancient Church Dedications in Scotland, Non-scriptural*, 455–6 and Watson, *CPNS*, 324.

135 Grants to Ralph Ruffus Kinnaird (Perthshire), except Pitmiddle belonging to Richard the king's clerk, in feu and heritage, with sake and soke, toll, team and infangthief, for the service of one knight. Perth. (1172 × 1174)

W. Rex Scott'. Episcopis . Abbatibus . Comitibus . Baronibus . Justiciis . Ministris . 7 Omnibus probis hominibus tocius terre sue . Clericis . 7 laicis .' salutem. Sciant presentes . 7 futuri . me dedisse 7 concessisse . 7 hac carta mea confirmasse . Radulfo Ruffo . Kinard per rectas diuisas suas . excepta Petmeodhel Ricardi clerici mei. Tenend*um* sibi . 7 heredibus suis de me . 7 de heredibus meis in feudo . 7 hereditate . in boscho . 7 plano . in terris 7 aquis . in pratis . 7 pascuis . 7 Omnibus iustis pertinenciis suis . Cum Sacca . 7 Socca . Cum tol . 7 tem . 7 infangenthef . libere . 7 quiete . plenarie . 7 honorifice :' per seruicium unius militis. Test*ibus* M*atheo* Episcopo de Aberdo*n* . Andr*ea* Episcopo de Caten*es* . W*altero* de Bid*un* Cancellario . Comite Dunec*ano* Justic*ia* . W*altero* de Berkel' Camerario . Philippo de Coleuill' . Toma de Muschamp' . Henrico fil*io* Jord*ani* . Ric*ardo* Malluu*el*. Apud Pert.

ENDORSED. .I. (medieval ?). No other early endorsement visible.
DESCRIPTION. 7·3″ (18·6 cm.), Top, bottom × 3·1″ (8 cm.), L, R. Foot folded to a depth of 0·6″ (1·5 cm.). Single slits, through which pass four tightly woven silk cords, green, blue and white (?). Fragment of seal, diameter 1·7″ (4 cm.).
HAND. Scribe Ai. Unruled.
SOURCE. Original, SRO, GD 48 / 1.
PRINTED. Macfarlane, *Genealogical Coll.*, i, 52.
COMMENT. Henry son of Jordan witnessed a grant by Robert of London to Walter of Berkeley his kinsman of land in Lessudden (St Boswells) and Plenmeller (Northumberland) (BM, Loans 29 / 355).

136

Confirms to Malise, son of Ferteth earl of Strathearn, Muthill, 'Tuliedel', Ogilvie, Bardrill, Kincardine, Auchtermachany and Rossie (in Comrie, Muthill, Blackford and Dunning), Perthshire; to be held of Earl Gilbert of Strathearn, his brother, in feu and heritage, with sake and soke, toll, team and infangthief, with pit and gallows, for the service of one knight. Perth. (1172 × 1173)

W. Rex Scott'. Episcopis . Abbatibus . Comitibus . Baronibus . Justiciis . Vicecomitibus . Ministris . 7 Omnibus probis hominibus tocius terre sue . Clericis 7 laicis :' salut*em*. Sciant presentes 7 futuri . me concessisse . 7 hac carta mea confirmasse . Malisio filio Fertet[a] comitis de Stradhern . Mothel . 7 Tuliedel . 7 Oggoueli . 7 Barderal . 7 Kinkarden . 7 Ouctermafen . 7 Rossi . per earundem terrarum rectas diuisas. Tenend*um* sibi 7 heredibus suis . de Comite Gileberto fratre suo 7 heredibus suis in feudo 7 hereditate . in boscho 7 plano . in terris . 7 aquis . in pratis 7 pascuis . in Molendinis 7 stagnis . in forestis . 7 tristriis . in Moris . 7 Scalingis . 7 Omnibus aliis iustis pertinenciis suis . Cum Sacca . 7 Socca Cum tol . 7 tem . 7 infangenthef . Cum furca 7 fossa . ita libere 7 quiete . plenarie . 7 honorifice :' sicut Carta prefati Comitis Gileberti fratris sui :' testatur 7 confirmat :' per seruicium unius militis. [Testibus Matheo][b] episcopo de AberdoN . W*altero* de Bid*un* Cancellario . Comite Dunec*ano* Justic*ia* . Comite Malcol*mo* Ethol' . [Comite Gilebride][b] de Anegus . W*altero* de Berkel' Camerario . Hugone Giff*ard* . Roberto de Boseuill'. Apud Pert.

ENDORSED. Muthill (xiv cent. ?). The chartour of King Allex[r] [c] Wam of the lands of the barony of Kincardin giffin to the erle of Strathern' broth [c] sone Malisius (xvi–xvii cent.). Ch: A. Sh: 1. B. 3 No.1 (xviii cent.). (2) (xix cent.).
DESCRIPTION. 6·9″ (17·4 cm.), Top and bottom × 3·3″ (8·5 cm.). Foot torn away, probably including seal tongue; no seal remains.
HAND. Scribe Ai. Unruled.
SOURCE. Original, Duke of Montrose, Auchmar, Drymen, Montrose Muniments, A. 1.3.1.

PRINTED. *Inchaffray Chrs.*, Appendix, no.1, p.153. Cf. *HMC*, 2nd report, Appendix, p.166.
NOTES. [a] Tironian 7 used for last two letters. [b] Parchment torn away; words in brackets supplied on authority of *Inchaffray Chrs.*, p.153. [c] Last word struck through.
COMMENT. Auchtermachany is now Strathallan, in Blackford. For Tuliedel, cf. *Inchaffray Liber*, 114, shewing that if, as is most probable, Tuliedel = Tulliechettill, it was more or less equivalent to Glen Artney.

137 Grants to Merleswain Ardross, Fife, in feu and heritage, with soke, sake, toll, team and infangthief, as freely as the king's other knights hold their feus of the king, for the service of one knight. Perth. (1172 × 1174, probably 1172 or 1173)

W'. Rex Scott'. Episcopis. Abbatibus. Comitibus. Baron*ibus*. Justiciis. Vicec*omitibus*. 7 Omnibus probis hominibus tocius terre sue salutem. Sciant presentes 7 posteri me dedisse 7 Concessisse 7 hac carta mea Confirmasse. Merleswano 7 heredibus suis Ardros per rectas diuisas cum omnibus iustis pertinenciis suis in terris 7 aquis Stagnis 7 piscariis. pratis 7 pascuis Moris 7 Mareisis[a]. ceterisque omnibus iustis pertinenciis suis. Tenend*um* sibi 7 heredibus suis de me 7 de heredibus meis in feudo 7 hereditate ita libere 7 quiete. plenarie 7 honorifice. Cum Socca 7 Sacca cum thol 7 them 7 Infangenthef. sic*ut* alii milites mei liberius 7 quietius feuda sua de me tenent .˙ per seruicium unius militis. Test*ibus* Matheo episcopo de Aberdeon. Andr*ea* episcopo de Catenes. Com*ite* Dunec*ano*. M*alcolmo* comite de Ethotle. Comite Gileb*erto* de Strathern. Comite G*illebrid* de Anegus. Ricardo Cumi*n*. Nesso fil*io* Willelmi. Willelmo de Morteme*r*. Waltero Olif*ard*. Waltero de Berkel'. Wald*ef* fil*io* Gospatric. Alano de Laceles. Rad*ulfo* de Clere. Roberto de Berkel'. Hug*one* clerico. Ric*ardo* clerico de prebenda. Ricardo clerico de Lincoln'. Gillecristo maciniene Samuel. Gillecolm maresc*allo*. Gillemich*el* mac Dunec*an*. Apud Pert.

ENDORSED. Carta terrarum de Ardros, per Willelmum Regem (xvii or xviii cent. ?).
DESCRIPTION. 9·6″ (24·4 cm.), Top, 9·4″ (24 cm.), Bottom, × 3·4″ (8·7 cm.), L, 3·3″ (8·3 cm.), R. Foot folded to depth of approximately ·9″ (2·2 cm.). Some three-quarters of the seal remains on tag, in natural wax stained brown; obv. to front, king's head 45° to right of vertical; traces of lug above king's head visible. A small amount of the legend is visible on the rev. only.

The seal tag has been cut from parchment previously written on, with the following mid-twelfth-century lettering still legible: lluuel pera, haiae 7 . ex, .xii. s', 7 .i.pipere, s'. The document has one horizontal and three vertical folds.
HAND. Scribe Aj (Richard of Lincoln). Unruled.
SOURCE. Original, SRO, GD 147/1.
PRINTED. *Inchcolm Chrs*, 126–7.
NOTE. [a] Sic.
COMMENT. Merleswain son of Colban, lord of Kennoway, was probably a descendant of Merleswain, a prominent English nobleman, who seems to have fled Northumbria after 1070 (Anderson, *Scottish Annals*, 88, 91).

138 Confirms to Scone Abbey the church of Invergowrie, with the land on the west of the church named Dargie. Perth. (1172 × 1174)

Willelmus[a] Rex Scottorum episcopis, abbatibus, comitibus, baronibus, justiciis, vicecomitibus et omnibus probis hominibus tocius terre sue salutem. Sciatis me concessisse et hac mea carta confirmasse Deo et ecclesie Sancte Trinitatis de Scon et abbati et canonicis ibidem Deo seruientibus ecclesiam de Invergorin, cum terra que jacet in occidentali parte ecclesie prenominate, nomine Dargoch, et cum omnibus pertinenciis ad eandem ecclesiam vel terram pertinentibus in liberam et perpetuam elimosinam. Quare firmiter prohibeo ne quis inde quicquam iniuste auferre uel diminuere presumat. Test*ibus* Matheo episcopo de Aberdon, Andr*ea* episcopo de Caten*es*, Comite Gilleberto, Ric*ardo* Cumyn. Apud Pert.

SOURCE. NLS, MS. Adv. 34.3.28, fo.10r.
PRINTED. *Scone Liber*, no.32.
NOTE. [a] Name omitted, MS.
COMMENT. See *RRS*, i, no.251.

139 Grants to the church of the Holy Trinity of the bishopric of Moray, and to Bishop Simon (de Toeni) and his successors, the teind of his revenues in Moray and of his pleas throughout the diocese of Moray, and of the king's cain in cows, pigs, wheat, malt and oats, and in cheese and butter, such as has not already been assigned to other churches by his predecessors. Montrose. (1172 × 1174)

.W. Rex Scott'[a] episcopis . abbatibus . comitibus . baronibus . justic*iis* . vicecom*itibus* . et omnibus probis hominibus tocius terre sue salutem. Sciant presentes et futuri me dedisse et concessisse et hac[b] carta mea confirmasse Deo et ecclesie Sancte Trinitatis de episcopatu Morau*iensi* et domino Sim*oni*[c] episcopo Moraule et successoribus suis in liberam et perpetuam elemosinam . pro animabus antecessorum meorum et pro salute anime mee . decimam meam de redditibus meis in Moravia et de placitis meis per totum episcopatum Morau*iensem* . de redditibus meis scilicet de cano meo . de uaccis et porcis . de frumento et braseo . et prebenda . et de caseo et butiro . quod antecessores mei non dederunt nec assignauerunt ad ecclesias alias. Quare precipio firmiter ballivis meis de Moreuia . ut ipsi sine disturbatione faciant domino Sim*oni*[d] episcopo et successoribus suis singulis annis plenarie et integre habere predictam decimam . sicut superius in carta ista determinatum est. Test*ibus* Matheo episcopo de Abberdon . Andr*ea* episcopo de Katenes . Samsone episcopo de Brechin . Com*ite* Dunec*ano* . Ric*ardo* Cumin . Roberto de Lundon' . Radulff*o* Veir .[e] Willelmo de Lindes*ei* . Waltero de Berchel*ai* . Hug*one* clerico . Ric*ardo* clerico. Apud Munros.

MARGINAL NOTE. ista non scribitur in libro decani.
SOURCE. NLS, MS. Adv. 34.4.10, fos.xxxviv–xxxviir = *A*. Ibid., fo.xiiiv = *B*. Printed here from *A*, with some variants of *B* noted.
PRINTED. *Moray Registrum*, no.2 (from *A*).
NOTES. [a] W dei gracia Rex Scoc', *B*. [b] *B* adds presenti. [c] Ricardo, *B*. [d] Symoni, *B*; fo.xxxviir, *A*. [e] de Ver', *B*.
COMMENT. It is not clear whether the king's pleas were thought of as distinct from his cain. King David I had granted cain revenues from western Moray to Urquhart priory (Lawrie, *Charters*, no.255).

140 Grants to Gilbert son of the earl of Angus Pourie (in Murroes), and Ogilvie and Kilmundie (in Glamis), Angus, to be held in feu and heritage for the service of one knight, as freely as any knights hold their lands of the king in the realm of Scotland. Montrose. (1166 × 1171 or 1172 × 1174)

Wilelmus rex Scotorum Episcopis Abbatibus comitibus baronibus iusticiariis vicecomitibus ministris prepositis cunctisque aliis probis hominibus totius terre sue Francis Anglis et Scotis salutem. Sciatis me dedisse et concessisse et hac charta mea confirmasse Gilberto filio comitis de Anguis[a] Purin et Ogguluin et Kynminethen per suas rectas diuisas cum omnibus iustis pertinentiis suis in bosco et plano in pratis et pascuis in moris et maresiis Tenend*um* sibi et heredibus suis de me et heredibus meis in feodo et hereditate libere et quiete plenarie et honorifice per seruitium unius militis. Quare uolo ut predictus Gilbertus et heredes sui prenominatas terras teneant et habeant per prenominatum seruitium ita libere et quiete plenarie et honorifice ut aliqui milites liberius et quietius plenius et honorificentius terras suas de me tenent in regno Scotie. Testibus Episcopo de Abirdonen'[b], Dauid[c] fratre meo, Comite Valdev, Comite Dunec*ano*, Richardo de[d] Morvill constabulario[e], Valtero filio Alani dapifero[f], Nesso filio Wilelmi[g], Willelmo de Lindsay, Valtero Oliepheir, Patricio filio Comitis, Valtero de Barkell, Abraham milite et Simone fratre suo, Valtero Giffer, Rodolpho Ruffo, Richardo clerico. Apud Montroiss.

SOURCE. Earl of Home's Muniments, Douglas Charter no.280 (extract from Liber Actorum made by Alexander Hay of Eister Kennet, clerk of rolls, register and council, containing a transumpt, made by order of the Lords of Council, of the original charter produced before them by Gilbert Ogilvy of that ilk, 'quhilk charter is verray auld, worne and consumit, and skantlie may be weill red', and was 'vantand ane seill' 14 February, 1577) = *A*.

SRO, GD 137 (Scrymgeour-Wedderburne Muniments, Dudhope), Box 2, Bdle. 6, no.1 (copy of *A* made by Sir John Hamilton of Magdalens, clerk of rolls, register and council, 26 July, 1631) = *B*. *A* and *B* collated here.

PRINTED. (From *A*) Fraser, *Douglas*, iii, 349, no.280.

NOTES. [a] Angus, *B*. [b] Sic, *A*; *B* has Aberdon'. [c] Dauid omitted, *A*, *B*. [d] domino, *A*, *B*. [e] confratre, *A*, *B*. [f] dapon, *A*, *B*. [g] Wilelmi omitted, *B*.

COMMENT. The style points to an early date, × 1174. If the unnamed bishop of Aberdeen was Edward, the date is × 1171; if Matthew, after his consecration on 2 April, 1172, but before the steward's death in 1177. Abraham the knight was probably Abraham of Lour (in Forfar, Angus), whose son Adam appears in *Coupar Angus Chrs.*, no.10. The absence of a clause granting rights of justice is noteworthy.

141

Grants to Holyrood Abbey the churches and chapels in Galloway in which Iona Abbey has proprietary right, viz. the churches of Kirkcormack (in Kelton), St Andrew (Balmaghie), Barncrosh (in Tongland), and Kelton, Kirkcudbrightshire. Forfar. (1172 × 1174)

W. Rex Scott'. Episcopis Abbatibus . Comitibus . Baronibus . Justiciis . Uicecomitibus . Ministris . 7[a] Omnibus probis hominibus totius terre sue Clericis . 7 Laicis .' salutem. Sciant presentes 7 futuri me dedisse 7 concessisse 7 hac carta mea confirmasse . Deo 7 ecclesie Sancte Crucis de Edenesburch 7 canonicis in eadem ecclesia Deo seruientibus . in liberam 7 perpetuam elemosinam . ecclesias siue capellas in Galweia . que ad ius abbatie de Hij Columchille pertinent cum omnibus decimis

7 aliis beneficiis ecclesiasticis Scilicet ecclesiam que dicitur Kirchecormach . 7 ecclesiam Sancti Andree . 7 illam de Balencros . 7 illam de Cheletun. Uolo itaque ut predicti canonici predictas ecclesias siue capellas cum terris 7 omnibus rectitudinibus 7 libertatibus suis . in bosco . 7 plano . in pascuis 7 Pratis . in aquis 7 piscationibus . 7 in omnibus predictarum ecclesiarum iustis pertinentiis teneant 7 possideant . ita libere 7 quiete . plenarie 7 honorifice .' sicut alias elemosinas suas liberius . quietius . plenius 7 honorificentius tenent. His testibus . Matheo episcopo de Aberdon . Andrea episcopo de Caten' . Waltero Cancell*ario* . Johanne abbate de Chelcho . H*erberto* priore de Cold' . Comit*e* Dunec*ano* . Nesio fil*io* Willelmi . Hug*one* clerico regis . Hug*one* capell*ano* . Hug*one* clerico cancellarii . Johanne clerico cancell*arii*. Apud ForfaR.

ENDORSED. Ecclesiarum de Iikolumkil (date of hand unknown).
SOURCE. *Holyrood Liber*, no.51, printed from the original then (1840) *penes* Lord Panmure, present whereabouts unknown. It was not among the Holyrood charters recently deposited in the SRO by Messrs Dundas and Wilson, W.S., on behalf of the Earl of Dalhousie.
PRINTED. *Holyrood Liber*, no.51.
NOTE. [a] It is not clear from the printed version whether the scribe used the tironian sign for et with or without a horizontal cross stroke.
COMMENT. It appears from *Holyrood Liber*, no.49 (1200 × 1206; confirmed by no.485 below) that these four churches or chapels had been granted to Holyrood Abbey by Uhtred son of Fergus (therefore × 22 September, 1174). If so, their grant to Holyrood cannot have been a consequence of the death of Dugald son of Somerled, who was still alive on 24 August, 1175 (Lawrie, *Annals*, 204). The wording of the king's charter is that of a fresh grant, and suggests a definite act of deprivation, possibly connected with the reform of Iona under the impetus of the family of Somerled and of Flaithbertach Ua Brolchain, abbot of Derry, whose kinsman Donald Ua Brolchain died, probably as prior of Iona, in 1203 (Anderson, *Early Sources*, ii, 253–4, 361; W. Reeves, *Life of Saint Columba* (Historians of Scotland edn, 1874), 343; P. J. Dunning in *Father John Colgan, O.F.M. Tercentenary Commemoration Essays* (Dublin, 1959), 54–7).

142 Confirms to John the hermit the grant made to him at the king's request by Simon (de Toeni) bishop of Moray (1172–1184) of the island which is in the loch of Lunnin (Loch Moy, Inverness-shire?), on the east side, and of the half-ploughgate of land in Duldauach (now Culdoich, in Croy and Dalcross, Inverness-shire); John to hold these during his life without disturbance, as the bishop's charter bears witness. Inverness. (1172 × 1174)

Will' Rex Scott' episcopis . abbatibus . comitibus . baronibus . justic*iis* . vicecom*itibus* . et omnibus probis hominibus tocius terre sue salutem. Sciatis me concessisse et hac carta mea confirmasse Joh*anni* heremite donationem quam Simo episcopus Moraviensis ei rogatu meo fecit . scilicet insulam que est in lacu de Lunnin ex parte orientali . et dim*idiam* carucatam terre in Duldauach. Quare volo et firmiter precipio ut predictus Johannes quam diu uixerit . ita libere et quiete et sine vexatione teneat predictam terram sicut carta ipsius episcopi testatur et confirmat. Test*ibus* Matheo episcopo de Aberdon' . Andr*ea* episcopo de Katenes . Greg*orio* episcopo de Ros . Com*ite* Waldeuo . Com*ite* Dunc*ano* . Ric*ardo* de Moreuill' constab*ulario* . Will*elmo* filio Fress*ekin* . Walt*ero* de Berchel*ai* . Ric*ardo* clerico. Apud Inuernis.

MARGINAL NOTES. ista non scribitur in libro decani. Nota de Duldawych.
SOURCE. NLS, MS. Adv. 34.4.10, fo.xxxvi^{v}.
PRINTED. *Moray Registrum*, no.3.
COMMENT. Bishop Simon's charter has not survived. Duldauach may be identified with Duldawacht, Duldaich, etc., and as 'Daldouhaugh or Culdoich' appears as late as 1794 (Inverness Sasines Index, 23 October, 1794). On Timothy Pont's draft Map of Murray (early xvii cent.) the name appears as Douldaiech (NLS, Pont Maps, no.8); on Blaeu's map (1654) based on Pont, it is Couldaiech. I am much indebted to Mrs R.W. Munro for elucidating this identification satisfactorily. Croy, Lunnin (which both had churches) and Duldauach are associated in thirteenth-century record (*Moray Registrum*, nos.31, 46, 47). Lunnin church formed part of a prebend established in his cathedral church by Bishop Brice (ibid., no.46). In 1226 the churches of Croy and Lunyn were united to form one prebend in Elgin cathedral by Bishop Andrew (ibid., no.68), and they appear so united in record of the papal taxation of 1274 (SHS *Misc.*, vi, 45). Thereafter no mention has been found of Lunnin or Lunyn, but by the mid-sixteenth century Croy and Moy are found, forming a prebend in Elgin cathedral (*Thirds of Benefices* (ed. G. Donaldson, SHS, 1949), 214), distinct from Moy now with Dyke, Moray. Moreover, in James II's charter establishing the barony of Spynie for the bishop of Moray in 1451, Croy, Moy and Duldawauch are together in the list of estates (*Moray Registrum*, no.193, p.233). An identification of Lunnin with Moy with its loch and island (admittedly hardly on the *east* side!) seems preferable to the suggestion of Dr I.B. Cowan that Lunnin was absorbed into Croy, while Moy had Croy united to it 'about the Reformation period' (*Parishes of Medieval Scotland*, SRS, 1967, 153). Dr Cowan does not distinguish between Moy, now with Dyke (to which it was united in 1618), which had been a church at least since 1223 and was erected *de novo* into a prebend by Bishop Andrew in 1226 (*Moray Registrum*, nos.55, 69), and Moy in Inverness-shire, to which there seems to exist no recorded reference before the fifteenth century. The lands, among others, of Croy, Duldavy, Moymore, Moybeg, with the island called Ellane-a-moy were recovered by the bishop of Moray, John Winchester, at a general council at Edinburgh in August-September, 1458 (*Cawdor Bk.*, 29).

143 Grants (confirms?) to Reginald Prath of Tynedale, his esquire, the third part of the whole vill of Haughton (in Humshaugh), Northumberland, granted to Reginald by Ranulf son of Uchtred with his daughter in frank marriage. Grants also that Reginald may hold the land free of the drengage service which Ranulf used to render to the king for it. Grants also that Reginald may have four shielings within 'Le Hunteland' wherever he may wish in winter and summer. To be held as freely as other free men hold within the kingdom of England, for an annual *reddendo* to the king of one two-year-old sparrowhawk or 6d. at Wark on Tyne. Edinburgh. 4 October, 1177 (1173?). (Inflated)

Will*elmus* Dei gr*ati*a Rex Scottorum. Omnibus probis hominibus tocius terre sue clericis et laicis salutem. Sciant presentes et futuri me dedisse concessisse et hac carta mea confirmasse. Reginaldo Prath de Tindale armigero meo tertiam partem tocius ville de Haluton. cum omnibus pertinenciis. in boscis in planis in pratis et pasturis in moris et mariscis. in aquis et stagnis. in molendinis. in piscariis. in viuariis et in omnibus aliis pertinenciis libertatibus et aisiamentis tam non nominatis quam nominatis. quam terciam partem cum pertinenciis :' Ranulfus filius Huttred' concessit predicto Reginaldo cum filia sua in liberum maritagium. Concedoecciam quod ipse Reginaldus et heredes sui teneant et habeant dictam terciam partem predicte ville cum pertinenciis quiete imperpetuum ab omni seruicio Drengagii . quod predictus Ranulfus mihi inde facere solebat. Concedo ecciam predicto Reginaldo ut ipse habeat quatuor scalengas infra le Hunteland ubicunque uoluerit . tam in yeme quam in estate tam in pratis et pasturis quam in terris arrabilibus . et in omnibus aliis aisiamentis et commoditatibus quibus sibi et heredibus suis melius prodesse et valere poterunt. Habend*um* et tenend*um* predicto Reginaldo et heredibus suis de me et heredibus meis in feodo et hereditate cum omnibus pertenenciis pro bono et laudabili servicio quod ipse Reginaldus mihi fecit . libere . quiete . de sectis omnimodarum curiarum . maritagiis . ward*is* . et releviis . et de cornagiis . scuttagiis . et auxiliis . excercitibus . Geldis . Wapentagiis . Vigiliis . tolnagiis . et de omnibus aliis serviciis consuetudinibus . exaccionibus . seu vexacionibus et demandis tam non nominatis quam nominatis. Et adeo libere in omnibus et per omnia sicuti alii liberi homines terras suas tenent et possident liberius vel quiescius infra regnum Anglie. Et sciend*um* est quod prenominatus Ranulphus et heredes sui facient de suis duabus partibus predicte ville omnia forinseca et intrinseca servicia . pro prenominato Reginaldo et heredibus suis que ad predictam partem tertiam pertinent vel pertinere poterunt in posterum excepto predicto servicio Drengagii eiusdem tertie partis quod relaxavi et quietum clamavi predicto Reginaldo et heredibus suis in perpetuum . pro bono servicio quod ipse mihi fecit. Reddend*o* inde annuatim mihi et heredibus meis ipse et heredes sui unum essperuarium sorum vel sex denarios apud Werc in Tyndal' . pro omnibus serviciis in mundo. Et dictus Ranulphus et heredes sui prenominatam terciam partem predicte ville de Haluton cum pertinenciis predicto Reginaldo et heredibus suis contra omnes in mundo adeo libere et quiete in omnibus sicut predictum est . Warantizabunt . acquietabunt . et defendent in perpetuum. Test*ibus* . Engen'[a] episcopo Glasg*uensi* . Matheo episcopo Abirdenens*i* . Comite Duncano . Odenell' de Umfravill' . Ric*ardo* Cum*in* . Hugon*e* Ridele . Gileb*erto* fil*io* Rich*erii* . Willelmo de Haya . Waltero de Berkeley . Ric*ardo* de Moruill' constabelario . Rob*erto* Auenell' . Philippo de Valones . Roberto de Quency . Ranulfo de Sules . Willelmo de Munford . Herberto de Camer*a* . Ric*ardo* clerico meo de Lincoln' . Symon*e* fil*io* Huttred' . Ad*am* fratre suo. Apud Castrum puellarum . iiij[to] . die Octobr*is* . anno regni mei . xii°. In Cujus rei testimon*ium* huic carte magnum sigillum meum apponere feci . dicto die et loco.

ENDORSED. Grant from Kinge Wylliam of Scotland unto Ra[ ][b] Prath of the third partt of Haughton painge a sp[ ][b] hawk or vj d. to be payd in Wark in Com. de [ ][b]. The said king doth also grant iiij. Shealeing places in all grounde in his huntelande. This king W. rainged about Ao Dni 1178. Alexander 1 raygned 1105 Ale: 2 raigned 1204 Ale: 3 raigned 1250 (xvi cent.). Also modern endorsement.

DESCRIPTION. 7·25″ (18·4 cm.), Top, 7·4″ (18·8 cm.), Bottom × 4·8″ (12·2 cm.), L, 5″ (13·0 cm.), R. Foot folded, slits for seal-tag. Tag remains, 0·9″ (2·2 cm.) wide, with traces of seal in green wax.

HAND. Scribe UDc. Written in a business hand of the middle of the xiii cent., with very close spacing and not very wide margins.

SOURCE. Non-authentic 'original', Northumberland County Record Office, Gosforth, Swinburne of Capheaton Muniments, vol. 1 (ZSW/1), no.1.

PRINTED. J. Hodgson, *History of Northumberland*, Part III, vol. i (vol. v) (1820), pp.2–3.
NOTES. [a] Sic, for Engel*ramo*. [b] Wording illegible.
COMMENT. See no.424. The eschatocol and much of the internal phraseology are anachronistic, belonging to the thirteenth century. The time-date is inconsistent with one of the witnesses, since Bishop Ingram died in 1174; but possibly the clerk responsible for this version miscopied the name Jocelin from a genuine original. Almost certainly this inflated charter is based on a genuine original in favour of Reginald Prat, for whom cf. no.320. To judge from the style and witnesses, the date-limits would be 1173 × 1174, but since Odenel de Umfraville would not be likely to witness an act of King William after the outbreak of war in 1173, the date is probably 1173. The name 'Hunteland' is now obsolete, but the area included Middleburn (in Wark), and comprised the upland district of Wark parish about the higher reaches of the Wark Burn and its tributaries (cf. Northumberland Record Office, ZSW/1/40). Simon son of Uhtred is probably the Simon of Halton, a witness to no.320.

144 Grants his firm peace to Furness Abbey. Carlisle. (1173 or 1174)

W. Rex Scott'. Episcopis . abbatibus . Comitibus . Baronibus Justiciis . Vicecom*itibus* . 7 Omnibus probis hominibus tocius terre sue Francis 7 Anglis . Scottis . 7 Galwahensibus salutem. Sciatis me concessisse meam firmam pacem ecclesie Sancte Marie de Furneis 7 Monachis 7 fratribus ibidem Deo seruientibus . 7 omnibus rebus suis 7 terris 7 hominibus 7 possessionibus. Prohibeo itaque firmiter ne quis hominum meorum uel hominum terre mee . predictis monachis uel eorum rebus aut possessionibus iniuriam uel contumeliam aliquam faciat super meam defensionem. Test*ibus* Com*ite* Dunec*ano* . Com*ite* Wald*euo* . Ric*ardo* de Moruill' const*abulario* . Philippo de Coleuill' . apud Karleolum.

ENDORSED. Willelmus Rex Scotie (xii cent.). xxxviij (xiv–xv cent.?). Also modern endorsements.
DESCRIPTION. 5·75″ (16·6 cm.), Top, 5·9″ (17·1 cm.), Bottom, × 2·2″ (5·5 cm.), L, 1·8″ (4·6 cm.), R. Sealed on tongue, now missing; possibly tie also.
HAND. Scribe Aj (Richard of Lincoln). Unruled.
SOURCE. Original, PRO, DL 25/79 (Ancient Deeds, L 79).
PRINTED. Farrer, *Lancashire Pipe Rolls and early charters*, 314; *Cal. Docs. Scot.*, i, no.165 (calendared).
COMMENT. This protection was no doubt issued on the occasion of one of the Scottish sieges of Carlisle, either in August or September, 1173 (cf. *Chron. Holyrood*, 153–4), or in the spring or early summer of 1174 (Anderson, *Scottish Annals*, 249–50). The absence of *dei gratia* in the royal style suggests 1173, and this is confirmed by Jordan Fantôme's statement, referring to the Scottish invasion of 1173, that King William ordered peace to be kept with holy church and severely punished those who disobeyed his order (*Chron. Fantosme* (Michel), 32, lines 682–4).

145 Grants to Andrew son of Uviet Whitslaid (in Ashkirk), Selkirkshire, by its right marches, viz. from Langhope Burn to the slope on the south side of the Ale Water, as the high road climbs, and from the same side (i.e., north?) of the Harden Burn to the nearest watercourse on the west side of 'Wivenesae' (Hangingshaw Hill?); and on the north side of the Ale Water, from the standing stone between Whitslaid and Alemoor Loch as far as the source of 'Blakeden' and from that source to the watercourse (Todrig Burn?) which rises in the neigh-

bourhood and flows into Langhope Burn, and then as the Langhope Burn falls to the marches of Orm of Ashkirk. To be held heritably with freedom of the mill, for an annualrent of 20s. Traquair. (Probably 1173 or 1174)

W. Dei gr*ati*a rex Scocie Omnibus probis hominibus tocius terre sue tam clericis quam laicis salutem. Sciant presentes 7 futuri me dedisse[a] 7 concessisse 7 hac mea carta confirmasse . Andree filio Uuiet . Witslade per rectas diuisas . scilicet de riuulo de Longhope usque ad condosum ex australi parte Alne . sicut magna uia graditur . 7 ex eadem parte de riuulo de Haruude usque ad proximum wacellum ab occidentali parte de Wiuenesae . 7 ex parte aquilonari Alne a petra stante que est inter Witeslade 7 Aunemer usque ad ortum de Blakeden . 7 ab eodem ortu usque ad wacellum qui in proximo oritur uersus aquilonem . 7 descendit in riuulum de Longhope . 7 riuulum de Longhope descendendo usque ad diuisas Orm de Askechirche. Tenendo[b] de me 7 heredibus meis sibi 7 heredibus suis . libere . 7 quiete 7 honorifice ab omni seruicio . 7 consuetudine . in bosco 7 plano . in pratis 7 pascuis 7 aquis . cum libertate molendini. Reddendo mihi inde singulis annis .xx. sol*idis*. T*estibus* Episcopo Yngelram de Glascu . Johanne abbate de Kelchou . Ric*ardo* de Morev*illa* . Ric*ardo* Cumin . Rob*erto* Auenel. Apud TreuequeR.

ENDORSED. Dorse has been repaired with paper, and the only words of endorsement legible are: et diuisio marchiarum eiusdem (xv cent.).

DESCRIPTION. 7″ (17·8 cm.), Top and bottom × 3·2″ (8·2 cm.), L, R. Foot folded to a depth of 0·8″ (2·1 cm.). Tag for seal remains, through single slits, 2″ (5·1 cm.) long, 0·8″ (2·1 cm.) wide. Seal missing.

HAND. Scribe Ak.

SOURCE. Original, Duke of Buccleuch and Queensberry, Dalkeith House, Buccleuch Muniments (Fraser), vol. i, no.2.

PRINTED. Fraser, *Buccleuch*, ii, 3, no.2 (with facsimile). Also *Fraser Facsimiles*, no.9.

NOTES. [a] A short word before dedisse is given in Fraser's facsimile as me (i.e., a repetition); this may be correct, since the first me completes a line. But conceivably the beginning of the next line, which is now obscure, should read reddidisse. [b] Sic.

COMMENT. It seems possible that Andrew son of Uviet was identical with Andrew of Synton whom King William made sheriff of Selkirk, and whose descendants held the sheriffdom heritably as late as the fourteenth century. Cf. nos.581A, 582 below. The marches indicated appear to follow the road running from Ashkirk to Harden, as far as Harden Cottage, and then roughly to follow the parish boundary of Ashkirk as far as the Langhope Burn. The last section coincides with the last section of the marches in no.215.

146 Confirms to Clerkenwell Priory 140 acres of arable in the Hanger of Tottenham, Middlesex, granted by Robert son of Sewin of Northampton, and the half holm which Ingram had held, and four tree trunks for their fire from the king's wood of Tottenham, and ten swine free of pasture dues, also granted by Robert, to be held as freely as the charters of King Malcolm IV and himself confirm them to Robert, and as Robert's charter grants them to Clerkenwell Priory. Northampton. (1174?)

W'.[a] Dei gr*ati*a Rex Scott' . Episcopis . Abbatibus . Comitibus . Baronibus . Justic*iis* . Ministris . 7 Omnibus probis hominibus tocius terre sue .

Clericis . 7 laicis .·' salutem. Sciant presentes 7 futuri . me concessisse . 7 hac carta mea confirmasse Deo atque ecclesie Sancte Marie de Fonte clericorum . 7 Monialibus ibidem Deo seruientibus . illas .vij. xx.[b] acras terre in Hangre de Toteham . quas Robertus filius Sewin[c] de Norhamton' eis dedit . 7 de dono eiusdem dimidium holmum quem Engelramus tenuerat . 7 .iiij^or. truncos ad ignem suum de bosco meo de Toteham . 7 decem porcos quietos a pasnagio . Tenendum in perpetuam elemosinam . ita libere . 7 quiete . plenarie . 7 honorifice .·' sicut Carta Regis Malcol*mi* fratris mei 7 mea[d] tenuras illas predicto Roberto filio Sewini confirmant . 7 Carta eiusdem Roberti . eis liberius . quiecius . plenius . 7 honorificencius . testatur . 7 confirmat .·' saluo seruicio meo. Test*ibus* Ricardo de Moreu' constabulario[e] . Ricardo Cumin . Philippo de Valon*iis* . Hugone Ridel . Waltero de Berkel' . Waltero de Windesour' . Roberto de Berkel' . Willelmo filio Emme . Johanne de Hasting'. Apud Norha*m*ton'.

ENDORSED. N (?) confirmatione W. rex Scot' (xii–xiii cent.). de terra apud Hangre (xiii–xiv cent.). De Hanger (xv cent.). iiij (xiv or xv cent.). Long passage in xvii cent. hand discussing the date of the document. Also modern numeral and other endorsements.

DESCRIPTION. 6·9″ (17·6 cm.), Top, 7·0″ (17·9 cm.), Bottom × 4·5″ (11·5 cm.), L, 4·3″ (10·9 cm.), R. Foot folded, slits in centre of fold for tag, no remains of seal or tag. For a sketch and brief description of the seal, cf. BM. MS. Add. 5937, fo.160: obv. the king in majesty, rev. equestrian; green wax; legend, WILLELMUS DEO RECTORE REX SCOTTORVM. Cf. Hassall, *Clerkenwell Cartulary*, 17. The document has two primary horizontal folds and three secondary vertical folds.

HAND. Scribe Ai. Unruled.

SOURCE. Original, BM, Campbell Charter xxx, 2 = *A*. BM, MS. Cott. Faustina B ii, fo.12^r = *B*. Printed here from *A*, with some variants in *B* noted.

PRINTED. Hassall, *Clerkenwell Cartulary*, 16–17, no.16 (from *A*, with some misreadings).

NOTES. [a] Villelmus, *B*. [b] xx^ti, *B*. [c] Sewini, *B*. [d] meas, *B*. [e] *B* ends here. In *B* are the rubrics, De confirmatione Regis Willelmi de Scot (at top in red), and hangre de confirmacione Willelmi de (at right in brown ink).

COMMENT. Cf. *RRS*, i, no.206, and no.57 above. The handwriting and the attestation of Richard Cumin make it improbable that this confirmation was issued as late as 1185, when the Honour of Huntingdon was restored to King William. On the other hand, the use of *dei gratia* by a known royal scribe points to a date in or after 1173. King William could not have been in Northampton after the outbreak of war in 1173, and seems unlikely to have issued any charters when brought there as a captive to King Henry II in July, 1174. The most likely date, therefore, would appear to be about December, 1174, when William was returning from captivity in Normandy but before he had been formally deprived of the Honour of Huntingdon. Henry II's confirmation of Robert's grant was issued in 1175 or 1176, and makes no reference to King William's confirmation (*Clerkenwell Cartulary*, no.8).

William 'son of Emma' was William II de Vieuxpont, son of Emma de St.-Hilaire; cf. no.84.

147 Grants to Henry Revel Coultra (Fife), in feu and heritage, with sake and soke, toll, team and infangthief, for the service of half a knight. Clunie in Stormont. (1173 × 1178)

Will*elm*us[a] Dei gracia Rex Scoc' episcopis . abbatibus . comitibus . baronibus . justiciis . vic*ecomitibus* . prepositis . ministris . et omnibus probis hominibus tocius terre sue clericis et laicis salutem. Sciant presentes et futuri me dedisse et concessisse et hac carta mea confirmasse Henrico Reuel Cultrach per rectas diuisas suas. Tenend*um* sibi et heredibus suis de me et heredibus meis in feudo et hereditate . in bosco et plano . in terris et aquis . in pratis et pascuis . in molendinis et stagnis . et omnibus justis pertinenciis suis . cum saca[b] et socca . cum tol et tehm[c] . et infangene thef . libere et quiete . plenarie et honorifice . per servicium dimidii militis. Testibus Waltero de Bidun cancellario . Comite Duncano . Thoma[d] de Muschamp . Ricardo Cumin . Patricio filio Com*itis* Cospatric . Malisio filio Com*itis* Ferteth . Willelmo de Mortemer . Willelmo de Lindesei . Willelmo de Haia . Rogero de Valloniis . Johanne de Lond*oniis*. Apud Clonin.

RUBRIC. Donacio regis Henrico Riuel de Cultra (top in red).
SOURCE. NLS, MS. Adv. 34.5.3, fo.1^v.
PRINTED. *Balmerino Liber*, pp.4–5, no.2.
NOTES. [a] red initial. [b] sara, MS. [c] Sic, MS. [d] h added in red above line.
COMMENT. Coultra evidently formed part of the lands of the ancient abbey of Abernethy, which had become partly secularized by the twelfth century and was in the hands of a branch of the family to which the earls of Fife belonged. Coultra formed the tocher or *maritagium* granted to Henry Revel in marriage with Margaret, daughter of Orm, the lay abbot of Abernethy. Cf. no.152 and *Balmerino Liber*, nos.2, 4, 5, 6; *Arbroath Liber*, i, nos.34 and 35.

148 Grants (confirms?) to Coupar Angus Abbey the land of Keithick (in Coupar Angus) by the marches which they (it?) had in King David I's time. Perth. (1171 × 1178)

Carta Regis Villielmi terram de Kethet per rectas diuisas suas quas plenius et melius habuerunt tempore regis Dauid aui mei, &c., ita libere sicut aliqua abacia Cisterciensis in toto regno Scotiæ, &c. Testibus: Matheo Episcopo Aberdonense, Andrea Episcopo Katenens*i*, Villielmo de Ridel[a] Cancellario, Comite Duncano Justiciario, Vil*lelmo* de Berklei Camerario, Thoma Muschampe, Nesso filio Villielmi, Samuel, Maloch mack-Gillesp'. Apud Perth.

SOURCE. NLS, MS. Adv. 33.2.9, fo.27^v.
PRINTED. *Coupar Angus Rental*, i, 321–2, no.5.
NOTES. [a] Sic, for Waltero de Bidun.
COMMENT. The reference to David I's time is obscure, since Coupar was not founded till the end of Malcolm IV's reign; probably the reference is to the marches which Keithick had before 1153. Maloch mack-Gillesp' is perhaps Malcolm mac Gillise, a witness to no.149, at Perth, and to *RRS*, i, no.243. On the other hand, the uncommon name Samuel suggests the name of Gillecrist mac inien Samuel, and if Gillecrist were written Gillexpo Balfour might easily have read this as Gillesp'.

149 Confirms to St Andrews Cathedral Priory the half of 'Hadgillin' in Dundeeshire, and an annualrent of 10s. from the other half, granted by Hugh Giffard, as his charter bears witness. Perth. (1173 × 1178)

Willelmus[a] Dei gracia rex Scotorum . Episcopis abbatibus . Comitibus . Baronibus . Justiciis uicecomitibus et omnibus probis hominibus tocius terre sue salutem . Sciant presentes et futuri me concessisse et hac mea carta confirmasse canonicis in ecclesia Sancti Andree apostoli Deo seruientibus et seruituris elemosinam illam quam Hugo Giffard eis dedit perpetualiter sibi tenendam scilicet medietatem de Hadgillin in Dunde syra et de altera medietate decem solidos annuatim. Quare uolo et firmiter precipio ut predicti canonici prescriptam elemosinam ita libere et quiete teneant perpetuo et possideant sicut liberius et quiecius ceteras elemosinas suas in regno meo tenent et possident et sicut carta Hugonis Giffard eis testatur saluo seruicio meo. Testibus . Andrea episcopo de Katen' Waltero de Bidun cancellario . Comite Dunecano . Malcolmo comite de Athewethle Gilleberto comite de Stradherin . Malisio fratre comitis . Nesio filio Willelmi . Willelmo de Mortemer . Willelmo de Haia . Ricardo de prebenda clerico regis Hugone clerico Malcolmo Machgilish apud Pertht .

SOURCE. SRO, GD. 45/27/8 (St Andrews priory cartulary), fo.ciiii^{v}.
PRINTED. *St Andrews Liber*, 224–5.
NOTE. [a] No initial. The whole text has been struck out line by line in red ink.
COMMENT. Hugh Giffard's charter has not survived, and this grant may have been of no effect. The name 'Hadgillin' is obsolete, but its second element may be preserved in Balgillo, formerly in Monifieth. The first element is presumably *àth*, 'ford'. This charter may contain the earliest recorded reference to Dundee.

150 Confirms to St Andrews Cathedral Priory the church of Lathrisk, Fife, granted by Ness son of William. Perth. (1173 × 1178)

Willelmus[a] Dei gracia rex Scotorum . episcopis . abbatibus . Comitibus . baronibus . iusticiis . vicecomitibus et omnibus probis hominibus tocius terre sue salutem . Sciant presentes et futuri me concessisse et hac carta mea confirmasse canonicis in ecclesia Sancti Andree apostoli Deo seruientibus et seruituris ecclesiam de Loseresch quam Nes filius Willelmi eis dedit in elemosinam perpetuo cum capell*is*[b] terris decimis et cum omnibus iustis pertinenciis suis. Quare uolo et firmiter precipio ut predicti canonici predictam ecclesiam perpetualiter teneant et possideant ita libere et quiete sicut alias ecclesias in regno meo sibi in elemosinam datas liberius et quiecius tenent et possident . testibus Andrea episcopo de Katenes . Waltero cancellario regis . Dunecano comite de Fif . Gilleberto comite de Straderen . Malcolom comite de Athwethle . Gillebride comite de Anegus . Ricardo de prebenda clerico regis . Willelmo de Haia . Willelmo de Mortemer. apud Perth .

RUBRIC. De ecclesia de Loseres (top in red). de ecclesia [de Los] resch (margin in later hand).
SOURCE. SRO, GD 45/27/8 (St Andrews priory cartulary), fo.ciiii^{r}.
PRINTED. *St Andrews Liber*, 224.
NOTES. [a] Red initial U. [b] Justified by *St Andrews Liber*, 254.
COMMENT. The joint charter of Ness and his daughter and heir Orabilis is given in *St Andrews Liber*, 254–5; witnessed by, among others, Henry the *judex*, who was not included in the list published in *SHR*, xlv, 21–4.

151 Confirms to St Andrews Cathedral Priory the church of Scoonie and the church of Markinch with the chapel of Kettle, Fife, granted by Duncan earl of Fife, as his charters bear witness. Perth. (1173 × 1178)

Willelmus[a] Dei gracia rex Scotorum . episcopis abbatibus . Comitibus . Baronibus . Justiciis . vicecomitibus . ministris et omnibus probis hominibus tocius terre sue clericis et laicis salutem . Sciant presentes et futuri me concessisse et hac mea carta confirmasse Deo et ecclesie Sancti Andree apostoli et canonicis ibidem Deo seruientibus et seruituris elemosinas illas quas Dunecanus comes de Fif eis perpetualiter tenendas dedit concessit et confirmauit . videlicet ecclesiam de Sconin et terram eidem ecclesie pertinentem .' cum decimis et ceteris pertinenciis suis . ecclesiam de Markinge cum terra eidem pertinente cum decimis et cum omnibus rectitudinibus suis . et capellam de Katel cum omnibus eidem iuste pertinentibus. Quapropter uolo et firmiter precipio ut predicti canonici elemosinas prescriptas teneant et possideant ita libere et quiete . sicut ceteras elemosinas suas in regno meo liberius et quiecius . tenent et possident . et sicut carte comitis Dunec*ani* eis testantur. Testibus . Andrea episcopo de Katenes . Waltero cancellario . Gilleberto comite de Stradtherin . Malcolmo comite de Athewethle . Nesio filio Willelmi . Willelmo de Morthemer . Hugone Giffar*d* . Willelmo de Haia . Willelmo Mathle . Adam filio Iuette apud Perth .

RUBRIC. De Scon' (top in red).
SOURCE. SRO, GD 45/27/8 (St Andrews priory cartulary), fo.cii^{v}.
PRINTED. *St Andrews Liber*, 220.
NOTE. [a] Red initial U.
COMMENT. Earl Duncan's charters are given in *St Andrews Liber*, 241 and 242–3, and a further charter granting the church of Markinch, issued by Hugh (alias Eggu) son of Hugh son of Gillemichel earl of Fife, probably Earl Duncan's first cousin, is given ibid., p.xxi. St Andrews priory had a claim to the churches of Markinch and Scoonie derived from the *célidé* of Loch Leven, to whom they had been given in the eleventh century (ibid., 116 = Lawrie, *Charters*, nos.6, 7).

152 Confirms (re-grants ?) to Orm son of Hugh (son of Gillemichel earl of Fife) the abbey of Abernethy (Perthshire), as it was in the year and on the day when King David I died (24 May, 1153), save for ten pounds' worth of land granted by the king to Henry Revel in marriage with Orm's daughter (Margaret). To be held in feu and heritage, freely save for common aid, common army service and common labour service, with soke and sake, toll, team and infangthief, with pit and gallows in two places only, viz. at Abernethy for his vassals of Fife and Gowrie, and at Inverarity for the vassals of his other lands; for an annual rent of £20, half to be paid on St John Baptist's day (24 June), half on St Bride's day (1 February). Perth. (1173 × 1178)

W'. Dei gr*atia* Rex Scott' Episcopis . abbatibus . Comit*ibus* . Baronibus . Justic*iis* . Vicec*omitibus* prepositis Ministris . Ceterisque probis hominibus tocius terre sue salutem. Sciant presentes 7 futuri me concessisse 7 hac carta mea confirmasse Orm fil*io* Hugonis 7 heredibus suis abbaciam de Abernithi cum omnibus iustis pertinentiis suis 7 rectitudinibus eidem abbacie iuste pertinentibus sicut fuit anno 7 die quo Rex D*aui*d auus meus fuit uiuus 7 mortuus in bosco 7 plano in pratis 7 pascuis Moris 7 aquis . Viis 7 Semitis . Stagnis 7 molendinis . exceptis .x. libratis terre quas dedi Henrico Reuel cum filia predicti Orm. Tenend*am* sibi 7 heredibus suis de me 7 de heredibus meis in feudo 7 hereditate libere 7 quiete ab omnibus seruiciis . 7 consuetudinibus excepto comuni[a] auxilio . Comuni[a] exercitu . Comuni[a] operatione . Cum Socca 7 Sacca .

Cum tol 7 them 7 infangenthef . ita tamen quod non habeat furcam neque fossam nisi in duobus locis . scilicet apud Abernithi . 7 apud Inuerarecthin. Reddendo mihi inde 7 heredibus meis singulis annis .xx. libras argenti. Scilicet .x. libras ad festum Sancti Johannis baptiste . 7 x. libras ad festum Sancte Brigide. Volo etiam ut homines sui de Fif 7 de Gouer*in* ueniant ad fossam de Abernithi. De aliis uero terris suis ueniant ad fossam de Inuerarecthin. Test*ibus* Matheo episcopo de Aberdeon . Andr*ea* episcopo de Caten' . Hug*one* capellano meo . Com*ite* Dunec*ano* . Com*ite* Gileb*erto* . Hug*one* Giff*ard* . Nesso fil*io* Willelmi . Galfr*ido* de Maleuill' . Waltero de Berkel' . Willelmo de Mortem*er* . Willelmo de Lindesia. Apud Pert.

ENDORSED. Carta regis Willelmi de abbacia de Abirnythin (xiii cent.).
DESCRIPTION. 5·5″ (14 cm.), Top and bottom × 5·5″ (14 cm.), L, 5·8″ (14·4 cm.), R with foot unextended. Foot folded, depth 0·8″ (1·9 cm.), with slits for a double tag, which remains with traces of seal in pink wax.
HAND. Scribe Aj (Richard of Lincoln). Unruled.
SOURCE. Original, BM, Loans 29/242, unnumbered charter with no.1.
NOTE. [a] Sic.
COMMENT. This charter is in the form of a confirmation, no doubt in recognition of Orm's hereditary claim to the abbey. St Bride or Bridget was the patron saint of Abernethy. The *maritagium* or tocher granted to Henry Revel was Coultra (Fife), for which see no.147. For his wife's name see *St Andrews Liber*, p.xxxviii, no.44.

153 Confirms to his burgesses of Aberdeen and to all his burgesses of Moray and benorth the Mounth their free 'hanse' (guild), to be held wherever and whenever they wish, as their predecessors held their guild in the time of King David I. No one is to interfere with them on this account on pain of the king's full forfeiture. Perth. (1173 × 1184, probably × *c.*1180)

W'. Dei gr*ati*a Rex Scott' . Omnibus probis hominibus totius terre sue salutem. Sciant presentes 7 futuri me Concessisse . 7 hac Carta mea Confirmasse Burgensibus meis de Aberdoen . 7 Omnibus Burgensibus de Morauia . 7 Omnibus Burgensibus meis ex aquilonali parte de Muneh manentibus liberum ansum suum Tenendum ubi uoluerint ·/ 7 quando uoluerint . Ita libere 7 quiete . plenarie 7 honorifice ·/ sicut antecessores eorum tempore Reg*is* D*aui*d aui mei Ansum suum liberius 7 honorificentius habuerunt. Quare prohibeo firmiter Ne quis eos inde vexet aut Disturbet super meam plenariam forisfacturam. Test*ibus* Andr*ea* Episcopo de Katenes . Comit*e* Dunec*ano* . Justic*ia* . Gilleberto Comit*e* de Stradhern . Comite G*illebride* de Anegus . Ricardo de Moreuill' . Constab*ulario* . Waltero de Berkel' . Cam*erario* . G*alfrido* de Maleuill' . Hugone Giffard . Malisio fratre Comitis de Strah*ern*. Apud PeRT

ENDORSED. Infeodacio Hansi (xiii cent.). K Wm protectioun to the toun of Abn (xvi cent.). Wm the Lyon's Protection dated at Perth (xviii cent.).
DESCRIPTION. 8·4″ (21·3 cm.), Top, 8·9″ (22·5 cm.), Bottom × 3·4″ (8·7 cm.), L, 2·9″ (7·5 cm.), R. Foot folded to a depth of approximately 0·5″ (1·4 cm.). Slits in fold and foot for seal tag, but neither tag nor seal remains.
HAND. Scribe Ba. Unruled.
SOURCE. Original, Aberdeen Burgh Records, A[1] 1.
PRINTED. *Municipal Corporations Report* (1835), Local Report, p.46; ibid. (1836), Appendix, II, p.6; *Aberdeen Burgh Chrs.*, 3, no.1.

COMMENT. For a discussion of this confirmation and the meaning of 'hanse', there defined as the fee for admission as a burgess or the communal burgess membership symbolized by the fee, cf. *Aberdeen Burgh Recs.*, pp.xci–xciii.

154 Grants to Coupar Angus Abbey a half-ploughgate of land for the site of the abbey, and also Campsie (in Cargill), Perthshire, i.e. the king's chase and the waste land belonging to it. The monks are to hold Campsie in free forest, and no one is to fell timber or hunt there without the monks' leave on pain of the king's full forfeiture of £10. The monks are to be free of the annual revenue formerly due to the king from that land by way of waiting. Charleton (in Montrose). (1173 × 1178)

.W. Dei gr*aci*a Rex Scot' omnibus probis hominibus tocius terre sue clericis et laicis salutem. Sciant presentes et futuri . me dedisse concessisse . et hac carta mea confirmasse Deo et Beate Marie de Cupr' . et monachis ibidem Deo seruientibus et seruituris dimidiam carrucatam terre ad situm abbacie sue faciend*um* . et Kamsy . scilicet chaciam meam cum tota Wastina mea que ad illam pertinet . Tenend*am* et habend*am* eis in puram et perpetuam elemosinam . ita libere . et quiete . plenarie et honorifice . sicut aliqua elemosina tocius terre mee . liberius et quiecius . plenius et honorificencius . tenetur et possidetur. Volo itaque et precipio ut predicti monachi predictam terram . et chaciam . et Wastinam habeant et teneant . in liberum forestum . ita ut nullus infra eandem terram sine predictorum monachorum licencia secet aut uenetur . super meam plenariam forisfacturam Decem libr*arum*. Preterea concedo eis ut quieti sint in perpetuum de illo annuo redditu qui in singulis annis de eadem terra soluebatur . ad Waitingam meam faciend*am* . quantum ad eandem terram pertinebat die qua eis predictam terram in puram et perpetuam elemosinam donaui. Test*ibus* Hugon*e* capellano meo . Hugon*e* Ridel . Philippo de Valon*iis* . Waltero de Berkel' camerario . Roberto de Berkel' . Gilberto de Umfranu*i*ll'[a] . Osberto Olifard . Roberto de Laundel' . Herberto de Camera. Apud Cherleton'.

ENDORSED. Carta .W. reg*is* de Kamsy (xiii cent.). in lib*erum* forestum (xiv cent.). Carta Regis Willelmi de Kamsy in lib*erum* forestum (xiv cent.). 4. (xix cent.).

DESCRIPTION. 9·2″ (23·4 cm.), Top and bottom × 4·4″ (11·2 cm.), L, R. Foot folded to a depth of 0·9″ (2·3 cm.). Single slits for seal tag, but neither tag nor seal exists.

HAND. Scribe UDb. Practised and pleasing business hand of the earlier or middle thirteenth century.

SOURCE. Engrossment of mid-thirteenth century in the form of an original, Earl of Moray, Darnaway Castle, Moray Muniments, Box 32, Division IV, Bdle. 1, no.4 = *A*. Nat. Lib., MS. Adv. 33.2.9, fo.28r (brief inaccurate abstract) = *B*.

PRINTED. *Coupar Angus Chrs.*, i, no.11 (from *A*). *Coupar Angus Rental*, i, 324, no.12 (from *B*).

NOTE. [a] four minims between a and ll.

COMMENT. There seems no reason to doubt the authenticity of this act in substance, or even in the whole of its wording, but the hand in which it is written belongs to a generation or so after William I's death, and some sixty years later than the date of its issue, if it was in fact issued. The 'waiting' referred to would doubtless be equivalent to the 'conveth' due to the canons of Scone from their lands referred to in *RRS*, i, no.243 (p.264).

155 Grants that no one may take poinds from the monks of Coupar Angus Abbey for the debt or injury of anyone (save his own?). Charleton. (1173 × 1178)

Carta Willielmi regis eisdem monachis ut nullus eos namare possit pro alicuius debito vel forisfacto. Testibus: Waltero de Barcley camerario, Gilberto de Wmphraveill, Osberto Oliphard, Ro*berto* de Laundell, Herberto de Camera. Apud Cherleton.

SOURCE. NLS, MS. Adv. 33.2.9, fo.28[r].
PRINTED. *Coupar Angus Rental*, i, 323, no.8.
COMMENT. Same date as no.154. Osbert Olifard seems to have gone on crusade in the time of Bishop Richard of St Andrews (× 1178), and is not known to have returned to Scotland (cf. *Spalding Misc.*, v, 210–1).

156 Takes into his protection and firm peace the abbey of Dunfermline with its possessions and tenants, while the abbot goes to England with the king. Perth. (Probably 1175 or 1176)

Will'[a] Dei gr*ati*a Rex Scott' . Justic*iis* . Vicecomitibus . 7 omnibus ministris suis salutem. Sciatis me in proteccione mea 7 in firma pace iuste cepisse abbaciam de Dunfer*melin* . cum omnibus possessionibus 7 hominibus suis dum abbas mecum proficiscitur in Angliam. Et prohibeo firmiter ne quis predictam abbaciam aut homines aut possessiones[b] illius interim iniuste vexare presumat . super meam plenariam forisfacturam. T*estibus* Ric*ardo* Cumin . Bernardo filio Briani apud Pert.

RUBRIC. De proteccione 7 firma pace (red with blue initial).
SOURCE. NLS, MS. Adv. 34.1.3a, fo.xiii[r–v].
PRINTED. *Dunfermline Registrum*, no.70.
NOTES. [a] Initial red. [b] Fo.xiii[v]. [c] The text of this brieve on fo.xiii[r] has been crossed out.
COMMENT. This probably refers either to the king's attendance at York for the formal promulgation of the treaty of Falaise, 10 August, 1175, or to his attendance at the council at Northampton, 25 January, 1176 (Lawrie, *Annals*, 201, 206).

157 Informs Pope Alexander III that he has learned from authentic writings and the statements of old and truthful men that the church of York lost its rightful claim to the subjection of the Scottish church because of the enmity and power of his own predecessors, kings of Scotland. Now peace has been made between him and the king of England, his lord, he humbly requests the pope to command that York's possession of authority over the Scottish church and the latter's subjection to York be restored and made entire. (1176) (Spurious).

Reuerentissimo[a] domino et patri A*lexandro* Dei gr*ati*a summo pontifici et Sancte Romane ecclesie cardinalibus, W. eadem gr*ati*a Rex Scocie salutem et deuotam reuerenciam. Nouerit excellencia uestra quod de subieccione ecclesie Scocie quam Ebor*acensis* ecclesia antiquo iure sibi uendicat, tam ex scriptis autenticis que inspexi quam ex relacione et testimonio uirorum antiquorum[b] et ueredicorum diligenter veritatem inuestigando conperi quod ab antiquis temporibus ad Ebor*acensem* ecclesiam de iure pertineat,[c] quod possessionem eius hostilitate et potencia regum predecessorum meorum amiserit. Set iam per Dei graciam inter dominum meum regem Angl' et me pace imperpetuum reformata, suppliciter postulo quatinus domino meo Regi et regno suo et Ebor*acensi* ecclesie predictam possessionem et subieccionem uestra auctoritate, omni occasione et appellacione remota, restitui et redintegrari precipiatis, nec sine maximo dampno meo et terre mee detrimento pretermitti posset[d] quin ita fiat; quoniam in pace reformata ita inter dominum meum regem et me conuenit, et illud idem iuramento firmaui. Scio enim quod in maximum periculum animarum nostrarum redundaret, si id quod pro certo scimus debere conpetere[e] effectui non manciparetur. Valeat semper sanctitas vestra.

RUBRIC. Nota pro domino . . Ebor' Archiepiscopo contra episcopos Scotie (in margin at left).

SOURCE. PRO, E 164/2 (Red Book of the Exchequer), fo.176=*E*. BM, MS. Cott. Cleopatra C iv, fo.20=*C*. Haddan and Stubbs, *Councils and Ecclesiastical Documents*, ii, Pt.I (1873), 244–5=*H*. Printed here from *E*, with only the more important variants of *H* noted. *H* is apparently printed from *C*, which has not been consulted for this edition.

PRINTED. D. Wilkins, *Concilia*, i, 481–2; W. Nicolson, *The Scottish Historical Library* (1726), 108 (from *C*); Dugdale, *Mon. Angl.* (New), vi, 1186, no.XLIII (from the York Registers); Haddan and Stubbs (as above); Bain, *Cal. Docs. Scot.*, i, no.147 (from *E*, abstract only, in translation, with errors).

NOTES. [a] Punctuation editorial. [b] *H* adds auctenticorum. [c] *H* adds et. [d] potest, *H*. [e] competere debere, *H*.

COMMENT. In *C*, this letter is contained in a letter from Pope Alexander III to Archbishop Roger of York, dated Anagni, 13 May (1176). If the papal letter be accepted as genuine the above letter must have been forged in a particularly barefaced manner on behalf of York either in 1175 or in 1176. Lord Hailes (Hailes, *Annals*, i, 141) considered both letters forgeries. Haddan and Stubbs apparently judged them genuine, but supposed the above letter to have been extorted from King William under duress. Certainly, the above letter appears to be incompatible with the genuine letter of Pope Alexander to the bishops of Scotland, dated Anagni, 30 July, 1176 (*Glasgow Registrum*, i, no.38) which declares that Henry II ought not to have compelled them to swear obedience to the English church, and promises to forbid the archbishop of York to exercise his metropolitical authority over them; nor is it easily compatible with Pope Alexander's writing to King William at the end of his pontificate that he had laboured to give freedom to the kingdom of Scotland (*Chron. Howden*, ii, 212). Finally, as Lord Hailes saw, the terms of the above letter are inconceivable in a genuine letter from a king whose recent Treaty of Falaise with Henry II, undoubtedly made under duress, offered no more than that 'the church of Scotland shall henceforward owe such subjection to the church of England as it should do' (Stones, *Documents*, 2).

158 Grants to May Priory that its lands and tenants shall be free from army and expedition service. Reading (or Haddington?). (1173 × 1178)

W.[a] Dei gratia Rex Scott'[b] Episcopis, Abbatibus, Com*itibus*, Baronibus, Justiciis[c], Vic*ecomitibus*, Ministris et ceteris probis hominibus tocius terre sue, clericis et laicis, salutem. Sciant presentes et posteri me concessisse et hac carta mea confirmasse Deo et Priori de Mai et monachis ibidem Deo seruientibus quod omnes terre eorum et omnes homines eorum in terris ipsorum manentes sint liberi et quieti de exercitu et expedicione. Test*ibus* D*aui*d fratre meo, Comite Dunecano, Waltero de Bydun Cancellario, Waltero de Wyndleshor', Philippo de Valoniis, Rogero de Valoniis, Roberto de Berchel', Waltero de Berchel' Camerario, Willelmo de Haia. Apud Rad*ing*.[d]

TITLE. Carta Regis Willelmi de acquietacione excercitus et omni expedicione[e].
SOURCE. PRO, C.53/93, rot.13 (Charter Roll, 35 Edward I) = *C*. *May Recs.*, p.cxiii = *M* (Title only).
PRINTED. *May Recs.*, no.16 (from *C*).
NOTES. [a] Willelmus, *May Recs.*, no.16. [b] Scotie, ibid. [c] Justiciariis, ibid. [d] Radḡ, *C*, perhaps by mistake for Hadḡt, i.e. Haddington. [e] Title from *M* only. One would expect omnis expedicionis.
COMMENT. Cf. *RRS*, i, no.280. If this act was issued at Reading, the date would probably be 1176 or 1177 (see Itinerary), and in any case could not be 1173 or 1174. This privilege, as granted by Malcolm IV, was confirmed by Earl Duncan of Fife (*PSAS*, xc, 74).

159 Grants to Kinloss Abbey the whole land of Burgie, to the north of the king's highway leading from Forres to Elgin; from the 'West' burn at the exit from the wood, along the highway as far as the great wood of Kilbuiack (in Alves) and thence across country to the marches of Kinloss. Elgin. (1173 × 1177, probably 1176)

W.[a] Dei gratia Rex Scottorum, episcopis, abbatibus, comitibus, baronibus, justiciis, vicecomitibus, ministris et omnibus probis hominibus totius terre sue, clericis et laicis, salutem. Sciant presentes et futuri me pro salute anime mee et animarum predecessorum et heredum meorum dedisse et concessisse et hac carta mea confirmasse Deo et ecclesie de Kinlos et monachis ibidem Deo servientibus totam terram illam de Burgin que est ex aquilonali parte vie mee regie que vadit de Fores versus Elgin, scilicet a riuulo de West qui est in exitu nemoris sicut via predicta vadit de Fores usque ad Elgin usque ad magnam silvam de Kelbuthac, et abinde de transverso usque ad divisas terre de Kinlos. Tenendam et possidendam in liberam et perpetuam elemosinam, ita bene et plenarie et honorifice, et ita libere et quiete ab omni servicio et exactione seculari, sicut alias tenandrias et possessiones suas ad eandem ecclesiam perpetualiter pertinentes liberius, quietius, plenius et honorificencius tenent. Testibus Matheo Episcopo de Abred*on*, Andr*ea* Episcopo de Catenes, David fratre meo, Waltero de Bidun Cancellario, Comite Dunecano, Comite Gilberto, Comite Malcolmo, Ricardo de Morevil Constabulario, W*altero* filio Alani Dapifero, W*altero* de Berkel', W*illelmo* filio Fresekin, Petro de Polloc. Apud Elgin.

RUBRIC. Carta donacionis Willelmi Regis tocius terre de Burgin ex autographo pergameno penes suprascriptum[b].
SOURCE. NLS, MS. Adv. 35.3.13, fo.240^{v} (old pagination, p.66) (a transcript made by Walter Macfarlane).
PRINTED. *Moray Registrum*, 454 (Carte Originales, no.2); *Kinloss Recs.*, 108–9, no.2.
NOTES. [a] Punctuation editorial. [b] Blank left in MS.
COMMENT. In 1173 and 1174 the king was occupied with war against Henry II, and he was a prisoner from July until December, 1174.

160 Confirms to Cambuskenneth Abbey an annualrent of one merk of silver granted by his mother the Countess Ada in the burgh of Crail. Stirling. (1173 × 1177)

Wilelmus[a] Dei gracia Rex Scotorum iusticiis, vicecomitibus, ministris et omnibus probis hominibus totius terre sue, clericis et laicis, salutem. Sciant presentes et futuri me concessisse et hac carta mea confirmasse

Deo et ecclesie Sancte Marie de Cambuskynneth[b] et canonicis ibidem Deo seruientibus unam marcam argenti annuatim ad luminare, quam A*da* Comitissa mater mea eiis dedit in burgo de Karell. Tenendam et habendam in liberam et perpetuam elemosinam ita libere et quiete et honorifice sicut carta matris mee testatur et confirmat. Teste Willelmo Lud'[c] cancellario, Hugone capellano meo, Waltero filio Alani dapifero, Roberto Auen*el*, Willelmo filio Thoraldi, Roberto Costent*in*, apud Striueling.

RUBRIC. Confirmatio Willelmi Regis de marca Kerrall (at top). Concordat cum principali Jacobus Foulis (at end).
SOURCE. NLS, MS. Adv. 34.1.2, fo.128r.
PRINTED. *Cambuskenneth Registrum*, no.174.
NOTES. [a] Large undecorated red initial U. [b] MS. Cambuskyynneth. [c] Sic, for Waltero de Bid*un*.
COMMENT. See also no.126.

161 Grants to Cambuskenneth Abbey the church of Forteviot, Perthshire, after the death of Richard the priest, in exchange for the tenth of the king's pleas and profits of Stirling, Stirlingshire and Callendar. Stirling. (1173 × 1177)

Willelmus[a] Dei gracia rex Scotorum, episcopis, abbatibus, comitibus, baronibus, iusticiariis, vicecomitibus, prepositis, ministris, et omnibus probis hominibus suis, clericis et laicis, salutem. Sciant presentes et posteri me concessisse et dedisse et hac mea carta confirmasse Deo et ecclesie Sancte Marie de Striueling et canonicis ibidem Deo seruientibus in liberam et perpetuam elemosinam, ecclesiam de Forteuiet, post obitum Ricardi sacerdotis, cum omnibus iustis pertinenciis suis, cum capellis et terris et decimis, cum omnibus asiamentis ad eandem ecclesiam iuste pertinentibus, in excambium decimarum placitorum et lucrorum meorum de Striueling et de Striueling schiria et de Calathir, pro anima regis Dauid aui mei, et Henrici patris mei et M*alcolmi* fratris mei, et ceterorum antecessorum et successorum meorum, ita libere et quiete, plenarie et honorifice, sicut ceteras elemosinas suas liberius et quietius, plenius et honorificentius tenent et possident. Testibus Willelmo[b] de Bid*un* cancellario, Waltero fil*io* Alani dapifero, Roberto Auenell, Willelmo filio Thoroldi, Petro de Striuiling, Radulfo de Camera, Ric*ardo* fil*io* Hug*onis*, Magistro Johanne de Houeden, Rogero clerico, Waltero clerico, Richardo clerico, Magistro Turpino, Symone de Liberatione, apud Strіueling.

RUBRIC. Donatio ecclesie de Forteuieth (at top). Concordat cum principali Jacobus Foulis (at end).
SOURCE. NLS, MS. Adv. 34.1.2, fo.66v.
PRINTED. *Cambuskenneth Registrum*, no.100.
NOTES. [a] Large blue initial U. [b] Sic, for Waltero.
COMMENT. Cf. *RRS*, i, no.257, probably a grant of this church to Richard of Stirling his chaplain by King Malcolm IV rather than King William. This cannot have been the chaplain named Richard who was made bishop of Dunkeld in 1170.

162 Confirms to Cambuskenneth Abbey the church of Alva, Clackmannanshire. Stirling. (1173 × 1190, probably 1173 × 1178)

Wilelmus[a] Dei gracia Rex Scotorum˙ episcopis, abbatibus, comitibus baronibus, justiciis, ministris et omnibus probis hominibus tocius terre sue, clericis et laicis, salutem. Sciant presentes et futuri me concessisse et hac carta mea confirmasse Deo et ecclesie Sancte Marie de Striuelyn' et canonicis ibidem Deo seruientibus ecclesiam de Alweth, cum decimis omnimodis et omnibus eiusdem ecclesie iustis pertinentiis; tenendam et habendam ita libere et quiete, plenarie et honorifice, in liberam et perpetuam elemosinam, sicut alias suas ecclesias liberius, quiecius, plenius et honorificencius tenent. Testibus, Richardo de Moreuill[b] constabulario, Waltero Olikis[c] justiciario, Waltero de Barkillie camerario, Roberto de Berkyl', apud Striuelyn.

RUBRIC. Donatio Willelmi regis Scocie ecclesie de Alueth (at top). Concordat cum principali Jacobus Foulis (at end).
SOURCE. NLS, MS. Adv. 34.1.2, fo.13^{r-v}.
PRINTED. *Cambuskenneth Registrum*, no.16.
NOTES. [a] Large blue initial U. [b] Fo.13^{v}. [c] Sic, for Olifard.
COMMENT. The original grant was evidently that of Richard bishop of Dunkeld (*Cambuskenneth Registrum*, no.12). On the other hand, Walter Olifard was justiciar in the decade after *c.*1178.

163 Commands that wherever the abbot of Dunfermline or his sergeands may find fugitive (neyfs) from the land of Dunfermline Abbey, they are to have them with their dependents; no one is to detain them unjustly, outwith the king's demesne, on pain of the king's full forfeiture. Stirling. (1173 × 1177)

Will'[a] Dei gr*ati*a Rex Scott' omnibus probis hominibus tocius terre sue salutem. Mando 7 firmiter precipio quatinus ubicunque abbas de Dunfer*melin* aut eius seruientes inuenerint fugitiuos de terra Sancte Trinitatis de Dunfer*melin* :' eos cum secta sua iuste habeant . 7 prohibeo firmiter ne quis eis quemquam ex illis iniuste detineat super meam plenariam forisfacturam :' si extra dominia mea inuenti fuerint. T*estibus* Waltero de Bid*un* cancell*ario* . W*altero* fil*io* Alani dapifero. Apud Striuelin.

RUBRIC. De fugitiuis (red with red initial).
SOURCE. NLS, MS. Adv. 34.1.3a, fo.xiii^{r}.
PRINTED. *Dunfermline Registrum*, no.67.
NOTE. [a] Initial blue.

164 Grants to Dunfermline Abbey Gillandreas mac Suthen and his offspring, and quitclaims them to the abbey in perpetuity. Stirling. (1173 × 1177)

Will'[a] Dei gr*ati*a Rex . Scot' . omnibus probis hominibus tocius terre sue clericis 7 laicis salutem. Sciant presentes 7 futuri me dedisse . 7 concessisse 7 hac carta mea confirmasse Deo 7 ecclesie Sancte Trinitatis de Dunfer*melin* 7 abbati 7 monachis ibidem Deo seruientibus in liberam 7 perpetuam elemosinam Gillandream mac Suthen 7 eius liberos 7 illos eis quietos clamasse de me 7 heredibus meis in perpetuum. T*estibus* Walt*ero* de Bid*un* cancell*ario* . W*altero* fil*io* Al*ani* dapifero . Ro*berto* Auen*el* . Gillecristo Rennerio . Willelmo Thorald'. Apud Striuel*in*.

RUBRIC. De seruis (red with blue initial).
SOURCE. NLS, MS. Adv. 34.1.3a, fo.xiii^{r}.
PRINTED. *Dunfermline Registrum*, no.64. NOTE. [a] Initial red.

COMMENT. This is the last royal act to be witnessed by a *rannaire*, for whose office in the household cf. *RRS*, i, 32–3.

165 Announces that after the charter of the canons of Scone had been read in his presence by his bishops and responsible men, it was judged that the canons should have fully the teind of catches of fish from all the king's fishings in the River Tay opposite the territory of Scone, Kinnoull Hill and Kinfauns. Stirling. (1173 × 1178)

W. Dei Gr*ati*a Rex Scott' . Omnibus Probis Hominibus Totius Terre sue .·' salutem. Sciatis quod uisa 7 lecta Carta Canonicorum de Scone in Presentia mea ab Episcopis 7 probis Hominibus meis .·' consideratum fuit quod plenarie debent habere Decimam Capture Piscium de Omnibus Piscationibus meis que sunt Super Thei contra territorium Scon' 7 Cragh 7 Kinfathenes . tam de Piscationibus Insularum quam firme terre adiacentibus. Quare firmiter Prohibeo . ut nullus quicquam predictarum decimarum auferre minuere uel detinere Presumat super Plenarium forisfactum meum. Test*ibus* . Andr*ea* Episcopo Katen' . Waltero de Bidun Cancellario. Apud StriueliN.

ENDORSED. WillelmusRex De decimis piscium parrochie de Scon. (xii cent.), et de insulis (xiii cent.). De consensu Episcoporum (xiii cent.). istam cartam sigillatam sigillo regis uiderunt Abbas et conuentus de Scone (xiii cent.). Also modern endorsements.

DESCRIPTION. 7·8″ (19·9 cm.), Top, bottom × 2·6″ (6·8 cm.), L, R. Foot folded to a depth of 0·6″ (1·5 cm.). Single slits with tag 6·2″ (16 cm.) long, 0·6″ (1·5 cm.) wide. No seal remains.

HAND. Scribe Ba. Unruled.

SOURCE. Original SRO, RH 6/8.

PRINTED. *Scone Liber*, no.20.

COMMENT. King Malcolm IV's great charter to Scone (*RRS*, i, no.243, p.264) gives as one of King David I's grants to the abbey the teind of the whole parish of Scone in, *inter alia*, catches of fish.

166 Grants to Dunfermline Abbey an annualrent of 23s. 4d. out of his ferme of Fettykil (Leslie, Fife), representing the teind of his revenue from that land in malt and oats. Kinghorn. (1173 × 1178)

Will'[a] Dei gr*ati*a Rex Scot' . episcopis abbatibus . Comitibus . baronibus . Justic*iis* . vicecomitibus . ministris . 7 omnibus probis hominibus tocius terre sue clericis 7 laicis salutem. Sciant presentes 7 futuri me dedisse 7 concessisse 7 hac carta mea confirmasse Deo 7 ecclesie Sancte Trinitatis de Dunfer*melin* 7 monachis ibidem Deo seruientibus de firma mea de Fithkil singulis annis .xxiii. sol*idos* . 7 iiij. d*enarios* pro decima brasei 7 prebende quam de eadem terra habere solebant. Volo autem 7 precipio ut predictos denar*ios* in liberam 7 perpetuam elemosinam habeant 7 possideant . 7 prohibeo firmiter ne quis eos inde disturbet. T*estibus* D*aui*d fratre meo . M*atheo* episcopo de Aberdon . Andr*ea* episcopo de Katen' . Ric*ardo* de Moreuill' const*abulario* . Hug*one* capellano . Waltero de Berkel' . Galfrido de Maluil'. Apud Kingor'.

RUBRIC. De xxiij. solid*is* 7 iiii d*enariis* de Fitkil . pro decima brasei 7 prebende (red, with red initial, fo.xii^v^).

SOURCE. NLS, MS. Adv. 34.1.3a, fo.xiii^r^.

PRINTED. *Dunfermline Registrum*, no.62. NOTE. [a] Initial red.

COMMENT. Hugh the chaplain was made bishop of St Andrews in 1178 or 1179. The original name of Barthol Chapel in Tarves, Aberdeenshire, Futhcul, seems to be identical with the name Fithkil (*Arbroath Liber*, i, no.197). It may be inferred from this act that the royal revenue from Fettykil in malt and oats was valued at $17\frac{1}{2}$ merks *per annum*.

167 Confirms to St Andrews Cathedral Priory the land of 'Adhebrecces' granted by Walter son of Philip, as Walter's charter bears witness. Kinghorn. (1173 × 1178)

W'. Dei gr*ati*a Rex Scott'. Episcopis. Abbatibus. Comitibus. Baronibus Justiciis. Vicecomitibus. Ministris. 7 Omnibus probis hominibus tocius terre sue. Clericis 7 Laicis 7[a] Salutem. Sciant presentes 7 futuri me concessisse. 7 hac Carta mea confirmasse Deo. 7 Ecclesie Sancti Andree Apostoli 7 Canonicis ibidem seruientibus Deo 7 inperpetuum seruituris terram de Adhebrecces. quam Walterus filius Philippi eis in perpetuam elemosinam dedit concessit. 7 Confirmauit. Cum communi pastura. Tenend' perpetualiter ita libere 7 quiete. ab omni seruicio 7 consuetudine 7 exaccione. sicut fratres de hospitali 7 de templo ubique tenent. 7 sicud[a] Carta predicti Walteri filii Philippi testatur 7 confirmat. Test*ibus* Ric*ardo* Episcopo de Dunkeld'. Waltero de Bid*un* Cancellario. Com*ite* Dunec*ano*. Ricardo de Moreuill' constabulario. Waltero de Winles'. Galfrido de Maleuilla apud Kingor.

ENDORSED. confirm*atio* regis \Will*elm*i/ de terra adhe brecches de Lundin (xii–xiii cent.).
DESCRIPTION. 6·7″ (16·9 cm.), Top and bottom × 3·5″ (9 cm.), L, 4″ (10 cm.), R. Foot formerly folded, with single slits for tag. No tag or seal remains.
HAND. Scribe Bb. Unruled.
SOURCE. Original, NLS, MS. Adv. 15.1.18, no.2 = *A*. SRO, GD 45/27/8 (St Andrews Priory Cartulary), fo.cv[v] = *B*. Printed here from *A*.
PRINTED. *St Andrews Liber*, 227–8 (from *B*).
NOTE. [a] Sic.
COMMENT. Walter's charter is given in *St Andrews Liber*, 264. 'Adhebrecces' is obsolete, but presumably lay in Lundin (in Largo), Fife, of which Walter son of Philip was lord. The first element looks like *àth*, 'ford'.

168 Confirms to St Andrews Cathedral Priory the following grants made by Duncan earl of Fife: the churches of Cupar and Strathmiglo; the teind of the mills of Cupar and Strathmiglo; and permission for the canons to make their mill dam of Nydie on the earl's land on the north bank of the River Eden, with freedom to repair it when broken or weakened by floods, as Earl Duncan's charter bears witness. Kinghorn. (1173 × 1178)

Willelmus[a] Dei gracia rex Scotorum. episcopis. abbatibus. Comitibus. Baronibus. Justiciis uicecomitibus. Ministris et omnibus probis hominibus tocius terre sue clericis et laicis salutem. Sciant presentes et futuri me concessisse et hac carta mea confirmasse Deo et ecclesie Sancti Andree apostoli et canonicis ibidem Deo seruientibus et imperpetuum seruituris :' elemosinas quas Dunecanus comes de Fif eis perpetualiter tenendas dedit. concessit. et confirmauit. Silicet[b] ecclesiam de Cupre cum terris et decimis. et oblacionibus et cum omnibus eiusdem ecclesie[c] iustis pertinenciis et ecclesiam de Stradmigeloch cum terris et decimis et oblacionibus et cum omnibus eiusdem ecclesie iustis pertinenciis . Et decimam molendini de Cupre et de Stradmigeloc plenarie . Et preterea ut idem canonici fundent stagnum molendini sui de Nidin super terram comitis ex aquilonali parte fluuii Hedene perpetualiter ita quod si stagnum illud occasione aliqua dirutum uel quassatum fuerit uel aque inundacione debilitatum liceat predictis canonicis sine omni calumpnia et exaccione libere et quiete illud reparare. Volo autem et firmiter precipio . ut canonici predicti elemosinas prescriptas perpetualiter teneant et possideant ita libere et quiete plenarie et honorifice sicut alias elemosinas suas liberius Quiecius plenius et honorificencius tenent . et sicut carta Comiti[s] Dunecani testatur et confirmat. T' Ricardo episcopo de Dunekeld' . Waltero de Bid*un* cancellario . Comite Dunecano . Ricardo de Moreuill' const*abulario* . Waltero de Winles' . Galfrido de Maleuill' apud Kingor .

RUBRIC. De ecclesia de Cuper (top in red).
SOURCE. SRO, GD 45/27/8 (St Andrews priory cartulary), fos.ciii^{v}–ciiii^{r}.
PRINTED. *St Andrews Liber*, 223.
NOTES. [a] Blue initial *V*. [b] Fo.ciiii^{r}. [c] pertinentibus expunged.
COMMENT. Earl Duncan's charter of Cupar is given in *St Andrews Liber*, 241, and his agreement anent the mill of Nydie, ibid. 243–4; his charter of Strathmiglo does not seem to survive.

169 Confirms to the Hospital of St Andrews the ploughgate of arable in Kedlock (in Logie, Fife), granted by Simon son of Michael and confirmed by his son Alan, as Alan's charter bears witness. Kinghorn. (1173 × 1178)

Willelmus[a] Dei gratia rex Scotorum episcopis abbatibus . Comitibus baronibus iusticiis . vicecomitibus ministris . et omnibus probis hominibus tocius terre sue clericis et laycis salutem . Sciant presentes et futuri me concessisse et hac carta mea confirmasse Deo et hospitali Sancti Andree apostoli illam carucatam terre in Chathelach quam Simon filius Michael*is* eis in perpetuam elemosinam dedit et Alanus filius suus concessit et confirmauit per eiusdem terre rectas diuisas . In pratis . et moris et cum communi pastura xx^{ti} iiii animalium et lxxx . Bidentum liberam et quietam ab omni seruicio exaccione seculari et ab omni consuetudine ad predictum Simonem et heredes suos pertinente . Ita quod idem Simon et heredes sui terram illam adquietabunt de exercitibus et operacionibus et de omnibus secularibus exaccionibus excepto quod idem hospitale adquietabit illam carucatam terre de Geldo regio quod communiter capietur de terris et de elemosinis per regnum Scocie. Quare uolo et precipio ut hospitale predictum elemosinam prenominatam tam libere et quiete plenarie et honorifice teneat et possideat sicut alias elemosinas suas liberius quiecius plenius et honorificencius tenet et possidet et sicut carta Alani filius Simonis testatur et confirmat. T*estibus* Ricardo episcopo de Dunkeld' . Waltero de Bid*un*[b] cancellario . Com*ite* Dunecano . Ricardo de Moreuill' const*abulario* . Waltero de Winles' . Galfrido de Malleuill' . apud Kingor .

RUBRIC. De hospitali (top in red)[c].
SOURCE. SRO, GD 45/27/8 (St Andrews priory cartulary), fo.xcix^{r-v}.
PRINTED. *St Andrews Liber*, 212.

NOTES. [a] Red initial U. [b] Fo.xcix^v. [c] The whole text of this document on fo.xcix^r (as far as de Bid*un*) has been struck out line by line in red ink.
COMMENT. Cf. *RRS*, i, no.138. This grant may have been ineffective. The donors' charters do not seem to have survived, but Walter prior of St Andrews feued Kedlock, said to have been granted to the priory by Alan's father, to Alan himself, 1172 × 1195 (*St Andrews Liber*, 306–7). The donors were ancestors of the family of Kinnear of that ilk. For a later grant to St Andrews priory of land in Kedlock, cf. ibid., 292.

170 Confirms to St Andrews Cathedral Priory and their hospital the grants made by the Countess Ada: the land of Pitmilly which Malise held, as perambulated by Hugh Giffard and other responsible men, with common pasture on the [king's] muir; the land in Crail where Ralph of Aluerbas dwelt, by the marches specified and having the breadth of one full toft; as the charters of the countess bear witness. Kinghorn. (1173 × 1178)

Willelmus[a] dei gratia rex Scotorum . episcopis . abbatibus . comitibus . baronibus . iusticiis . uicecomitibus ministris et omnibus probis hominibus tocius terre sue clericis et laicis salutem . Sciant presentes et futuri me concessisse et hac mea carta confirmasse Deo et ecclesie Sancti Andree apostoli et canonicis ibidem Deo seruientibus et seruituris imperpetuum ·/ et hospitali eorum ·/ elemosinas quas Ada . comitissa mater mea eis specialiter tenendas dedit concessit et confirmauit . Silicet totam terram de Pethmulin quam Malisius tenuit Sicut Hugo Giff*ard* et ceteri probi homines sui eandem terram perambulauerunt . et preterea communem pasturam in mhora et preterea terram illam in Karel quam Radulfus de Aluerbas inhabitauit . desuper uiam infra aliam uiam que est iuxta[b] toftum abbatis de Dunfermelin et infra ueterem fossam et riuulum et illam terram subtus uiam a toffto Radulfi de Morpat usque in mare per latitudinem unius plenarii tofti ex transuerso. Uolo autem et firmiter precipio ut canonici predicti elemosinas predictas teneant . et possideant ita libere et quiete . plenarie et honorifice ab omni exaccione . et seruicio seculari sicut alias elemosinas suas . liberius . quiecius . plenius . et honorificencius tenent . Et sicut carte Ade comitisse matris mee testantur et confirmant. Testibus Ricardo episcopo Dunkeldensi . Waltero de Bidun cancellario . Dunec*ano* comite. Ricardo de Moreuill' constabulario . Waltero de Windessor' Galfrido de Maleuill' . Johanne de London' . Willelmo de Mortemer. Apud Kingorn.

RUBRIC. De hospitali (top, red).
SOURCE. SRO, GD 45/27/8 (St Andrews priory cartulary), fo.xcviii^r–v.
PRINTED. *St Andrews Liber*, 210.
NOTES. [a] Red initial V. [b] Fo.xcviii^v.
COMMENT. The Countess Ada's charters are given in *St Andrews Liber*, 208–9. Ralph of Aluerbas seems to have been one of the countess's dependents in the Liberty of Tynedale, taking his name from Allerwash, in Newbrough, Northumberland.

171 Grants to Walter of Berkeley his chamberlain Neutun (Longnewton (in Ancrum), Roxburghshire, or Newton in Forgandenny, Perthshire?) in feu and heritage, with sake and soke, toll, team and infangthief, for the service of half a knight. Kinghorn. (1173 × 1182)

W'. Dei Gr*ati*a Rex Scott'. Episcopis . Abbatibus . Comitibus . Baronibus . Justiciis . Vicecomitibus . Ministris 7 Omnibus Probis Hominibus totius Terre sue . Clericis 7 Laicis Salutem. Sciant presentes 7 futuri me Dedisse . 7 Concessisse . 7 hac Carta mea Confirmasse Waltero de Berk' Camerario meo Neutun' per Rectas Diuisas suas. Tenend' sibi 7 heredibus suis de me 7 heredibus meis in feudo 7 hereditate in Bosco 7 plano . in Terris 7 Aquis . in Pratis 7 Pascuis . in Molendinis 7 Stagnis . in Moris 7 Maresiis . 7 omnibus eiusdem Terre iustis pertinentiis . cum Sacca . 7 Socca . cum Tol 7 Tem . 7 Infangehethef . libere 7 quiete . Plenarie 7 Honorifice .' per Seruitium dimidii Militis. Test*ibus* Com*ite* Wald*euo* . Com*ite* Dunec*ano* . Com*ite* Gilleb*erto* . Ric*ardo* de Moreuill' Consta*bulario* . Waltero Olif*ard* . Philipp*o* de Vallon*iis* . Waltero de Windesoue[a] . Willelmo de Lindesi . Rogero de Wallon*iis* . Willelmo de Haia . Radulfo de Clere. Apud Kingor;

ENDORSED. Carta de Newtona (xiv–xv cent.). King William charter to Walter of Barclay of Newtoun (xvi–xvii cent.). W' (xii–xiii cent., written inside fold at foot).
DESCRIPTION. 7·2″ (18·3 cm.), Top, 6·8″ (17·2 cm.), Bottom × 4·5″ (11·3 cm.), L, 4·3″ (11 cm.), R. Foot folded to a depth of 0·5″ (1·3 cm.). Single slits, with tag 5·4″ (13·6 cm.) long, 0·6″ (1·5 cm.) wide. Large fragment of seal remains on tag, in green wax; clear impression.
HAND. Scribe Ba. Unruled.
SOURCE. Original, NLS, Charters B 1353.
PRINTED. Anderson, *Oliphants*, Documents, no.1, p.1 (with facsimile); *Arbroath Liber*, i, Appendix, *Cartae Originales*, no.1 (abridged).
NOTE. [a] Sic, with a superscript.
COMMENT. This charter was in the Gask charter chest in the later eighteenth century, when it was transcribed, with mistakes, by Charles Steuart of Dalguise, Gask's brother-in-law; cf. SRO, Dalguise Muniments, Box 2, No. 1. For Newton of Forgandenny, cf. Anderson, *Oliphants*, 216, 351. An identification with Longnewton, formerly in St Boswells, seems more attractive, since Robert of London granted to his kinsman Walter of Berkeley one ploughgate in Lessudden (St Boswells) in the reign of William I (BM Loans 29/355). Cf. comment on no.86.

172 Confirms to Matthew son of his chaplain Robert the grant made to him by the prior and convent of Hexham of the land of Whitfield (Northumberland), and grants that Matthew may build upon and bring inhabitants into this land as fully and well as this was done before the time of war. Crail (1175 × 1178)

Will*el*mus[a] Dei gracia Rex Scocie omnibus probis hominibus totius terre sue Clericis et Laicis salutem. Sciant presentes et posteri me concessisse et hac Charta mea confirmasse donacionem quam Prior de Extoldeham et conuentus eiusdem Domus fecerunt Matheo filio Rodberti Capellani mei et heredibus suis de terra de Whitfeld. Quare uolo et precipio quod prenominatus Matheus et heredes sui predictam terram teneant et possideant libere et quiete, plenarie et honorifice, sicut Charta Canonicorum testatur et confirmat, saluo eorum seruicio. Concedo etiam eidem Matheo et heredibus suis edificare et hospitari predictam terram in bosco, plano, in pratis et pasturis, in Scalingis et Ridingis et in omnibus ita plenarie sicut aliquo tempore ante[b] warram[c] melius edificata et hospitata fuit. Teste Ada Comitissa matre mea, Roberto de Quinci, Alexandro de Sancto Martino, Willelmo de Mortimer, Barnardo[d] filio Birani[e]. Apud Carell.

SOURCE. J.C.Blackett-Ord Esq., Whitfield Hall, Northumberland, Whitfield Box no.1, vellum-bound paper cartulary and rent book of 1630, p.2, collated with a copy of the same transcript in a paper volume preserved in the same box, dated 1732, made when the earlier book had not suffered quite so much wear as it has now.
PRINTED. J.Hodgson, *History of Northumberland*, Part II, vol.iii, 19a (incomplete).
NOTES. [a] Punctuation editorial. [b] MS., ann (in copy of 1732, anni, wrongly).
[c] Sic; in the corresponding charter of the Countess Ada (ibid., p.1), guarram.
[d] Sic. [e] Sic, for Briani.
COMMENT. This follows closely the terms of Countess Ada's charter in the same source, p.1, and was probably given at about same time, and before Countess Ada's death in 1178. The reference to the war (1173–4) places it in or after 1175.

173

Confirms to St Andrews Cathedral Priory the (parish) church of Haddington with the land of Clerkington, saving the tenure of the nuns of Haddington, as the charter of the bishop of St Andrews and the chirograph made between the canons of St Andrews and the nuns of Haddington bear witness. Haddington. (1175 × 1178)

Willelmus[a] Dei gracia . rex Scotorum . episcopis abbatibus . Comitibus . baronibus iusticiis . uicecomitibus . prepositis ministris . omnibus probis hominibus tocius terre sue clericis et laicis salutem . Sciant presentes et posteri me concessisse et hac mea carta[b] confirmasse Deo et ecclesie Sancti Andree in Scocia et canonicis ibidem Deo seruientibus et seruituris ecclesiam de Hadintun cum terra de Clerkenetun . et cum omnibus aliis eiusdem ecclesie iustis pertinenciis tam in decimis quam in aliis rectitudinibus et libertatibus . Tenend*am* in liberam et perpetuam elemosinam ita libere et quiete plenarie et honorifice sicut alias elemosinas suas liberius et quiecius . plenius et honorificencius tenent Salua tenura monialium de Hadintun' sicut carta episcopi Sancti Andree et cyrograffum inter predictos canonicos et easdem moniales factum testantur et confirmant. Testibus . Jocel*ino* episcopo Glesg*uensi* . Andrea episcopo Katen*ensi* . Johanne abbate de Kelco . Ricardo abbate de Jedd'. Laurenc*io* abbate de Melr*os* . Comite Wald*ef* . Comite Dunecano[c] . Hugone Giffard . apud Hadintun .

RUBRIC. De ecclesia de Hadint*un* (top in red).
SOURCE. SRO, GD 45/27/8 (St Andrews priory cartulary), fo.ciii^{r-v} = *A*. NLS, MS. Adv. 15.1.18, no.9 (3) (transumpt of original?) = *B*.
Printed here from *A*.
PRINTED. *St Andrews Liber*, 222.
NOTES. [a] Blue initial V. [b] Fo.ciii^{v}. [c] Comite omitted, *A*, supplied from *B*.
COMMENT. See Lawrie, *Charters*, no.234, for King David's grant of the land of Clerkington to Haddington parish church; which was then granted to St Andrews priory by Bishop Richard (*St Andrews Liber*, 135). The chirograph between St Andrews priory and the nuns of Haddington, dating 1175 × 1178 and witnessed by the king himself, is given ibid. 334, and refers to a grant made to the nuns by Bishop Richard on the day when he blessed their cemetery. Probably the chirograph and this act are contemporary.

174

Grants to Ailif his baker the whole land which Reginald, janitor of Edinburgh castle, held of the king in Inverleith, to be held heritably for personal service. Edinburgh. (1173 × 1178)

W'. Dei g*ratia* Rex Scott' . Episcopis . abbatibus . Comitibus . Baronibus

. Justiciis . Vicecomitibus . Ministris . Et ceteris probis hominibus tocius terre sue . clericis 7 laicis . Salutem. Sciant presentes 7 posteri me concessisse et dedisse 7 hac carta mea confirmasse Ailifo pistori meo totam terram quam Reginaldus ianitor castelli de Edenburg' de me tenuit in Inuerleth cum omnibus iustis pertinentiis suis . tenend*am* sibi 7 heredibus suis de me 7 heredibus meis per seruicium sui corporis. T*estibus* Waltero de Bid*un* Cancellario . Ricardo Cumin justiciar*io* . Waltero Olifardo Roberto de Cost*entin*. Apud Castellum puellarum.

ENDORSED. Carta de Inuerleth[a].
SOURCE. *Newbattle Registrum*, Appendix, Carte Originales, no.111 (printed from the original, *penes* W.E. Aytoun, 1849). The present whereabouts of the original is unknown. In 1849 a fragment of the seal survived attached by silk cords.
PRINTED. As above.
NOTE. [a] Heading probably represents early endorsement.
COMMENT. See no.510.

175 Confirms the earliest endowments of Melrose Abbey: the land of Melrose, Eildon and Darnick; easements of wood, timber and pannage throughout the king's forest of Selkirk and Traquair; pasture rights on the east bank of the Gala Water and thence by the marches of Richard de Moreville's land as far as the Leader Water; fishing within the abbey's marches on both banks of the Tweed; Gattonside by marches specified; a site in the lower part of Colmslie to build a byre for 100 cows and a fold; the fishing of Selkirk and one net out of the two the king has in 'Berewichstrem'. Roxburgh. (1173 × 1177)

W[a] Dei gr*ati*a Rex Scott' . Episcopis . Abbatibus . Com*itibus* . Baronibus . Justiciis . Ministris . 7 Omnibus probis hominibus totius terre sue . Clericis 7 Laicis . Salutem. Sciatis me pro anima mea 7 pro animabus patris 7 matris mee 7 Aui mei regis D*aui*d . 7 fratrum 7 sororum . 7 Antecessorum . 7 Successorum meorum . concessisse 7 dedisse Deo 7 ecclesie Sancte Marie de Melr*os* 7 monachis ibidem Deo seruientibus . de Rieualle . in perpetuam 7 liberam[b] elemosinam terram de Melros . 7 terram de Eldune[c] . 7 terram de Dernewich[d] . libere 7 honorifice perpetuo tenore possidere. Insuper sciatis me dedisse 7 Concessisse eis per totum Forestum meum de Seleschirche 7 de Treuequair Aisiamenta sua . Scilicet ligna . materiem 7 pasnagium . ad suos proprios usus ubicunque sibi melius 7 utilius poterunt inuenire. Insuper do eis 7 confirmo totam pasturam per fluuium Galche[e] uersus eos scilicet ab orientali parte . sicut idem fluuius currit . usque ad terminos de Wedale . 7 inde per rectas diuisas terre Ric*ardi* de Moreuilla scilicet de Galche[e] usque ad Leddre[f] . 7 totum usagium nemoris infra prenominatas Diuisas ad suos proprios usus sicut opus eis fuerit. Preterea 7 in aquis de Tweda infra terminos eorum piscaturam tam ex mea parte fluminis quam ex eorum parte ubique. Et preter supradicta dedi 7 concessi eis ad incrementum Galtuneside[g] per has Diuisas scilicet sicut Ledder[h] fluuius cadit in Thweda . 7 ita sursum usque ad Burnam de Fachope[i] que cadit in Leddre.[f] Et ita sursum per eandem Burnam . 7 sicut per transuersum moram[j] usque ad Raburne que cadit in Aloent . 7 sic per eundem fluuium de[k] Aloent usque in Thwedam. Preter omnia prenominata dedi 7 concessi eis in inferiori parte de Cumbesleia locum ad edificandam unam uaccariam centum uaccarum . 7 unam Faldam. Dedi 7 concessi eis piscaturam de Seleschirche . 7 unum rete in Berewichstrem[l]. de duobus retibus meis que habui in Berewichstrem[l] . ita libere 7 quiete sicut ipse melius tenui ad opus meum. Hec autem omnia predictis monachis de Melr*os* do 7 concedo 7 Hac Carta mea confirmo . in perpetuam 7 liberam elemosinam . 7 uolo 7 precipio ut omnia supradicta ita libere 7 quiete . plenarie 7 honorifice teneant . sicut carta Reg*is* Malcolmi fratris mei testatur 7 confirmat. His testibus . Waltero Bidun Cancell*ario* . Comite Dunecano . Ric*ardo* de Moreuill' constabulario . Ricardo Cumin Justicia . Roberto Auenel . Waltero de Berchelaie Cam*erario* . Willelmo de Sumeruill' . Waltero Ridale[m] . Hug*one* clerico regis . Willelmo capel-l*ano* . Roberto Capell*ano* . Hug*one* clerico Cancell*arii* . Magistro Johanne . Com*ite* Waltheuo . Waltero filio Alani Dapifero . Alano filio eius . Thoma de Muscamp . Willelmo de la Haie . Radulfo Ruffo. APUD Rokesburch.[n]

ENDORSED. *A*: confirmacio Willelmi Reg*is* de abbacia (xii cent.). J. Scott (xvi cent.). *B*: confirmacio Regis Will*elmi* (xiii cent.). carta Will*elm*i Reg*is* super fundatione abbatie (xiv cent.).
DESCRIPTION. *A*: 10″ (25·3 cm.) Top and bottom × 10·3″ (26·1 cm.), L, R. Foot folded to a depth of 1·1″ (2·8 cm.). Double slits for seal-tag, but instead of a tag, cords of green or yellow silk are passed through two holes, the length of cord between document and seal being 3·2″. The seal, in red wax, diameter 3·4″, has been built up and is almost complete, with all lugs clearly shewing and a good impression of the design. *B*: 9·8″ (25 cm.), Top and bottom × 6·3″ (16 cm.), L, R. Foot folded to a depth of 1″ (2·5 cm.). Foot torn away, no slits, tag, or seal remains.
HAND. *A*: Scribe Ab. Ruled in ink. *B*: Scribe Ab. Ruled.
SOURCE. Original, BM, Cotton Chr. xviii, 13 = *A*. Original, BM, Cotton Chr. xviii, 14 = *B*. Printed here from *A* with most variants of *B* noted.
PRINTED. *Melrose Liber*, no.13 (from *A*).
NOTES. [a] .W., *B*. [b] liberam 7 perpetuam, *B*. [c] Heldune, *B*. [d] Dernewic, *B*. [e] Galghe, *B*. [f] Ledre, *B*. [g] Two words, Galtune side, *B*. [h] Leder, *B*. [i] Fauchope, *B*. [j] more, *B*. [k] *B* omits de. [l] Berewicstrem, *B*.[m] de Rid', *B*. [n] Rokesburc, *B*.
COMMENT. Compare *RRS*, i, nos.41, 235, and Lawrie, *Charters*, no.141.

176

Grants to his burgesses of Moray the privilege that no one may take poinds from them save for his own debt. Bunkle. (1173 × 1196, probably × *c*.1180)

W'. Dei gr*ati*a Rex Scott'. Omnibus vicecomitibus 7 Bailliis totius terre sue salut*em*. Sciatis me hanc libertatem dedisse burgensibus meis de Morauia ut nullus scilicet in terra mea eorum namum capiat pro alicuius debito nisi pro eorum debito proprio. Quare prohibeo firmiter ne quis in terra mea eorum namum aliter capiat super meam plenariam defen-sionem. Test*ibus* Willelmo de Haia . Philippo de Vallon*iis* . Ricardo clerico meo de prebenda. Apud Bonekil.

ENDORSED. There are faint traces of an early endorsement, illegible to the naked eye.
DESCRIPTION. 5·9″ (15 cm.), Top, 5·8″ (14·75 cm.), Bottom × 2·1″ (5·3 cm.), L, R. Foot folded to a depth of 0·4″ (1 cm.). Seal tag remains, 4·4″ (11 cm.) long, 0·6″ (1·5 cm.) wide, passing through single slits in the fold and foot. Seal missing.
HAND. Scribe Al. Unruled.
SOURCE. Original, Inverness Burgh Muniments.
PRINTED. *APS*, i, 88a.

COMMENT. This brieve is the only original act of William I surviving among the Inverness Burgh Muniments, although the *Municipal Corporations Report* (1836) mentions the existence of four charters of William I at Inverness, and *APS*, i, 88–89, prints four charters, one with facsimile.

177 Confirms that the monks of Melrose Abbey and all monks of the Cistercian Order shall be free of toll and all other customs on all transactions which they carry out for their own use, wherever they may be in the king's land, as King David I's brieve bears witness. Selkirk. (1173 × 1177)

Uill*el*m*us*[a] Dei gr*ati*a Rex Scottorum, Justiciariis, vicecomitibus, prepositis et omnibus probis hominibus tocius terre sue salutem. Precipio quod fratres mei de Melros et omnes fratres eiusdem ordinis sint quieti de theloneo et omnibus aliis consuetudinibus et rectitudinibus de omnibus mercatis que ad suos proprios usus fecerint ubicumque in tota terra mea uenerint, sicut carta regis Dauid testatur et confirmat. Test*ibus* Ricard*o* Cumyn' . Roberto Auenell . Alano filio dapiferi. Apud Selecherche' etc[b].

RUBRIC. Carta Regis Willelmi de Theoleneo.
SOURCE. BM, MS. Harl. 3960, fo.108v.
PRINTED. *Melrose Liber*, no.17.
NOTES. [a] Initial red. [b] Sic.
COMMENT. David I's brieve has not survived, and his grant should have been included among the Lost Acts in *RRS*, i, 162–72.

178 Quitclaims Coldingham Priory of the two shillings which used to be demanded by the king's sergeands of Berwick in respect of any pleas and lawsuits they might discover. Selkirk. (1173 × 1178)

.W'. Dei gratia Rex Scott'. Justiciis . Vicecomitibus . Ministris . 7 Omnibus probis hominibus tocius terre sue Salutem. Sciatis me quietam clammasse[a] Ecclesiam de Coldingham . 7 Domnum priorem . 7 Omnes Monacos eiusdem Ecclesie . Et Omnes homines terre illorum de Coldingham Sirre . de duobus Solidis quos Seruientes mei de Berewic ab illis exigere solebant de placitis 7 querelis quas inuenire possent. Quare uolo 7 firmiter precipio ut Omnes homines de Coldingham Sirre de predicta exactione quieti sint in perpetuum . pro anima Reg*is* D*aui*d aui mei . 7 Comitis H. patris mei . 7 mea . 7 Omnium Antecessorum meorum. Test*ibus* D*aui*d fratre meo. Waltero de Bid*un* Cancellario . Ric*ardo* de Moreuill' constabulario . Roberto de Quinci . Waltero de Berkel' Camerario . Philippo de Vall*oniis* . Roberto de Berkel' . Johanne de Londoniis . Bernardo filio BriaNi . Roberto de Beoseuill' . Apud Selescherche —

ENDORSED. Carta W. Reg*is* de quieta clam' ij solidorum quos seruientes sui de Berewic solebant exigere de Priore de Cold' et hominibus de Baron*ia* (xv cent.). Y. iij[a]. vj[te] (xv cent.).
DESCRIPTION. 7·4″ (18·7 cm.), Top and bottom × 5·3″ (13·5 cm.), L, 5·1″ (13 cm.), R. Foot folded 1·1″. Single slits for leather thongs. Seal remains on thongs, entire, fair impression, natural wax.
HAND. Scribe Bb. Unruled.
SOURCE. Original, Durham, D. & C. Muniments, Misc. Chr. no.593.
PRINTED. Raine, *North Durham*, no.35.
NOTE. [a] Sic.

179 Commands those dwelling in the diocese of Glasgow to render teinds and other ecclesiastical dues to their churches fully and without repugnance, just as the king has ordered teinds to be paid most fully throughout the other bishoprics of his realm, namely in corn, flax, wool, cheese, butter, lambs, calves, piglets, horses and foals and all else from which Christian law requires that teind should be paid. Jedburgh. (1173 × *c*.1191)

Will*elmu*s Dei gratia Rex Scottorum Justic*iis* Baronibus Vice-comitibus ministris Francis et Anglicis Scottis et Galwiensibus et Walensibus et omnibus ecclesie Sancti Kentegerni de Glasg*u* et eiusdem episcopi parrochianis salutem. Quoniam diuina prouidencia nos in Regno nostro clero et populo preesse uoluit ;' utriusque excessus emendare et saluti potestate tradita prouidere . nobis necesse est ;' unde dominica institucione et sancte Romane ecclesie matris nostre . et domini pape hortatu ac precepto commoniti ;' omnibus vobis Regia auctoritate mandamus . hortamur et precipimus in Domino . quatinus episcopo vestro . et Archidiacono eorumque ministris debitam obediencie reuerenciam exibeatis . Decimasque vestras et cetera iura ecclesiastica ecclesiis vestris in omnibus plenarie et sine repugnancia persoluatis . sicut per alios episcopatus Regni mei Decimas plenarius et melius ;'[a] dari precepi . Scilicet de Blado . de Lino et Lana . de Caseo . de Butiro . de Agnis . de vitulis . de porcellis . et de capellis . de pullis . Necnon et de ceteris omnibus non nominatis de quibus Lex Christiana decimam dari postulat. Si uero aliquis vestrum quicquam recte decime sue temere detinere presumpserit ;' vicecomes meus de eo capiat forisfactum meum . scilicet duodecim vaccas. Si uero vicecomes illi consenserit ;' aut propriam decimam detinuerit ;' Justicia mea de ipso vic*ecomite* forisfactum meum capiat . Decimasque detentas ecclesiis plenarie solui faciat ne pro defectu iusticie querela ad me perueniat. Test*ibus* Roberto de Brus . Roberto de Quinci . Hugone Rid*el* . Waltero de Windesour' . Johanne de Vall*ibus*. Apud Jedewurth.

RUBRIC. De Decimis persoluendis et obediencia obseruanda (in margin).
SOURCE. Blairs Archives, 16 Drummond Place, Edinburgh, MS. Registrum Vetus of Glasgow, fos.lij^{v}–liij^{r}.
PRINTED. *Glasgow Registrum*, no.70.
NOTE. [a] Fo.liij^{r}.
COMMENT. Cf. *RRS*, i, no.258, which this repeats; and see no.507.

180 Confirms to Kelso Abbey the 10 acres of arable in the territory of Hadden (in Sprouston, Roxburghshire) assigned to them by Bernard son of Brian, as his charter bears witness. Jedburgh. (1173 × 1178)

W.Dei gr*ati*a Rex Scott' . Episcopis . Abbatibus . Comitibus . Baronibus . Justiciis . Ministris . 7 omnibus probis hominibus totius terre sue ;' salutem. Sciant presentes 7 futuri me concessisse 7 hac carta mea confirmasse Deo 7 Ecclesie Sancte Marie de Kelkou . 7 monachis eiusdem loci .x^{cem}. acras terre in territorio[a] de Haweden . ubi Bernardus filius Briani illas eis assignauit . Tenendas in liberam 7 perpetuam elemosinam . ita libere 7[b] quiete . plenarie . 7 honorifice ;' sicut aliquam elemosinam .

liberius . quiecius . 7 honorificencius tenent . 7 sicut carta Bernardi fil*ii* Briani testatur 7 confirmat . saluo seruicio meo. Test*ibus* . W*altero* de Bid*un* Cancellario . Rob*erto* de Quinci Justic' . Hug*one* Ridel . Willelmo de Veteri Ponte . Galfrido Ridel . apud Jeddewrdh'.;

RUBRIC. Confirmacio super .x. acras terre in territorio de Hawden (top in red).
SOURCE. NLS, MS. Adv. 34.5.1, fos.145v–146r.
PRINTED. *Kelso Liber*, no.388.
NOTES. [a] MS. has meo here, struck through. [b] Fo.146r.
COMMENT. Bernard's charter is given in *Kelso Liber*, no.217. It speaks of 10 acres to the west of the toun 'ubi . . assignaui' (this phrase suggests that the acres were scattered), and also of land on the other side of the toun on either side of the road to Carham. It is not clear whether the 10 acres included this or not.

181 Confirms the marches between Coldinghamshire and Bunkleshire as the charter of King David I bears witness. Jedburgh. (1173 × 1178)

W'. Dei gr*atia* Rex Scott' . Episcopis . Abbatibus . Com*itibus* . Baronibus . Justiciis . Vicecom*itibus* . Ministris 7 Omnibus probis hominibus tocius terre sue . salutem. Sciant presentes 7 futuri me concessisse 7 hac Carta mea confirmasse . Diuisas inter Coldinghamsire . 7 Bonekillesire . Tenend*as* ita libere 7 quiete plenarie 7 honorifice . Sicut Carta Reg*is* D*aui*d aui mei testatur 7 Confirmat . scilicet a Midlesdene heued per Mereburnes heued . uersus Occidentem usque ad Crhachoctrestrete . 7 inde per eandem stratam usque ad Eiford. Testibus his . Waltero de Bid*un* Cancellario . Com*ite* Waldeuo . Ric*ardo* de Moreuill' constabulario . Roberto de Quinci . Waltero de Winlesor' . Waltero Cam*erario* . Philippo de Valloniis . Willelmo de Veteri Ponte . Johanne de Lond' apud Jeddewurch'

ENDORSED. C W. reg*is* de diuisis inter Coldinghamscyre et Bonekilleschyre. (xiii cent.) P. iij[a] vj[te] (xv cent.).
DESCRIPTION. 7·2″ (18·2 cm.), Top, 6·7″ (17·1 cm.), Bottom × 3·6″ (9·2 cm.), L, 3·7″ (9·3 cm.), R. Foot folded, 0·8″. Doubled tag, 7·6″ long, 0·7″ wide. Seal entire, in natural wax, good impression.
HAND. Scribe Bb. Unruled.
SOURCE. Original, Durham, D. & C. Muniments, Misc. Chr. no.595.
PRINTED. Raine, *North Durham*, Appendix, no.36.
COMMENT. These marches correspond closely to the present marches between the parishes of Coldingham and Bunkle with Preston. They were confirmed by Ranulf of Bunkle in the twelfth century (Raine, *North Durham*, no.168). The ford over the Eye Water referred to is no doubt that shewn on the 1″ Ordnance Survey a quarter of a mile north of the point at which the marches of Abbey St Bathans, Bunkle and Coldingham meet (Grid ref. 799638), and this was perhaps the ford known as 'Halyford' in 1431 (ibid., no.639). For King David I's charter, see *ESC*, no.90. 'Crhachoctrestrete' seems to have been the name of an old road running from Gallows Law in Bunkle north westward to Oldhamstocks. 'Mereburne' is probably represented today by Mire Burn and its continuation Billiemire Burn.

182 Confirms to William de Vieuxpont the whole land of Bolton (East Lothian), Carriden (West Lothian) and Langton (Berwickshire) in feu and heritage, to be held with rights of warren. No one may hunt there without William's licence on pain of the king's full forfeiture. Jedburgh. (1173 × 1178)

Willelmus Dei gracia rex Scocie justiciariis,[a] vicecomitibus, ministris et omnibus probis hominibus tocius terre sue salutem. Sciant presentes et futuri me concessisse et hac carta mea confirmasse Willelmo de Veteri ponte et heredibus suis totam terram suam de Boulton et de Caredyn et de Langtone in warrennam, in feodo et hereditate. Quare prohibeo firmiter ne quis in predictis terris venetur absque ejus licencia, super meam plenariam forisfacturam. Testibus David fratre meo, W*altero* de Bidun cancellario, Roberto de Quincy justiciario, Hugone Ridel[b], Johanne de London',[c] Bernardo filio Briant.[d] Apud Jedworthe.

SOURCE. SRO, Registrum Magni Sigilli Regum Scotorum, Liber I, no.137 (charter of inspection of David II, 16 April, 1366).
PRINTED. *RMS*, i, 76, no.233.
NOTES. [a] Punctuation editorial. [b] MS. Ridelle. [c] MS. Loudone. [d] Sic.

183 Confirms to Kelso Abbey the church of Morton in Nithsdale (Dumfriesshire) granted, in the king's presence, by Hugh Sansmanche (*Sine Manicis*), together with one ploughgate of land. Jedburgh. (1173 × 1177)

W. Dei gr*ati*a Rex Scott'. uniuersis sancte matris ecclesie filiis . salutem. Sciant tam presentes quam posteri me concessisse . ⁊ hac carta mea confirmasse ecclesie Sancte Marie de Kelch' . ⁊ monachis ibidem Deo seruientibus in liberam ⁊ perpetuam elemosinam donacionem ecclesie de Mortune in Strahnith . quam Hugo sine manicis in presencia mea eis fecit . cum una carrucata terre . ⁊ cum omnibus iustis pertinenciis suis. Volo itaque ut predicti monachi prenominatam ecclesiam habeant ⁊ possideant . ita libere . quiete . ⁊ plenarie . sicut aliquam ecclesiam liberius . quiecius ⁊ plenarius possident. Test*ibus* W*altero* de Bidun Cancell*ario* . Walt*ero* filio Alani dapifero . Henr*ico* Luuel . Patricio fil*io* Com*itis* Cospatr*ici* . apud Jedd'.

RUBRIC. Carta super donacionem ecclesie de Mortun' in Strahnith (top in red).
SOURCE. NLS, MS. Adv. 34.5.1, fo.149[r].
PRINTED. *Kelso Liber*, no.404.
COMMENT. Hugh *sine manica* and his brother Geoffrey witnessed a charter of Alexander Musard and his heir in favour of Easby Abbey, *c*.1152 × 1162 (*EYC*, v (Richmond, Pt.II), no.179). Hugh was apparently a tenant on the Honour of Richmond in Count Conan's time and later, and must have been taken prisoner while fighting for the king of Scots in the war of 1173–4, for in 1175 land in the Honour paid £5 towards his ransom, and £5 was also paid for his forfeited chattels (*Pipe Roll* 21 *Henry II*, 6). Roger Sine Manicis (Senzmanz, etc.), evidently a member of the same family, witnessed Honour of Richmond charters towards the end of the twelfth century, and held land on the Honour at Wendy, Cambs. (*EYC*, v, 171 and nos.276, 370). It would seem that Hugh Sansmanche acquired his interest in Morton before 1173, but it is not known how; perhaps he married a daughter of Ralph son of Dunegal, and Morton formed her marriage portion. The odd name *sine manicis* suggests the sleeveless undershirt in which a penitent was required to parade publicly.

184 Confirms to Paisley Priory (afterwards Abbey) one ploughgate of arable in Mow (in Morebattle, Roxburghshire), by the marches measured and perambulated, with pasture for 500 sheep and for as many animals as are allowed with one ploughgate in that toun, granted by his steward Walter son of Alan and his wife Eschina, as their charters bear witness. Lanark. (1173 × 1177)

Uilelmus Dei gratia rex Scotorum episcopis, abbatibus, comitibus, baronibus, justiciariis, vicecomitibus,[a] ministris et omnibus probis hominibus totius terre sue, clericis et laicis, salutem. Sciant presentes et futuri me concessisse et hac carta mea confirmasse Deo et Sancte Marie Virgini[b] et ecclesie beati apostoli Jacobi, Sancti Mirini et Sancte Milburge de Passelet, et priori et monachis ibidem Deo servientibus, in liberam et perpetuam elemosinam, unam carucatam terre in Molla, per easdem divisas per quas eis mensurata fuit et perambulata, et pasturam quingentis ovibus, et aisiamenta pasture ceteris animalibus quantum[c] pertinet ad unam carucatam terre in eadem villa, cum omnibus aliis aisiamentis, ita plenarie et honorifice et ita libere et quiete ab omnibus consuetudinibus et exactionibus et omni servicio seculari, sicut carte Walteri filii Alani dapiferi mei et Eschine uxoris sue eis testantur et confirmant.[d] Testibus Roberto de Quinci justiciario, Waltero de Berkel' camerario, Wilelmo de Veteri Ponte, Gilleberto filio Richerii, Philippo de Valon*iis*, Johanne de Londoniis, Roberto de Berkelei, Simone Loccard, apud Lanarcum.

RUBRIC. Confirmatio Wilelmi regis Scotorum de Molla (at top).
SOURCE. NLS, MS. Adv. 34.4.14, fo.xliiii^{r-v}.
PRINTED. *Paisley Registrum*, 76.
NOTES. [a] MS., vicecomitatibus. [b] MS., virginis. [c] Fo.xliiii^{v}. [d] MS., confirmantur.
COMMENT. Two charters of Eschina of Mow are given in *Paisley Registrum*, 74, 75, the first in her husband's lifetime, the second apparently after his death in 1177.

185 Grants to his chamberlain, Walter of Berkeley, Inverkeilor by its right marches, in feu and heritage, with sake and soke, toll, team and infangthief, and pit and gallows, for the service of one knight. (1173 × *c*.1194, probably × 1180)

Willielmus[a] Dei gratia Rex Scotorum Episcopis, Abbatibus, Comitibus, Baronibus, Justiciariis, Vicecomitibus et Ministris et omnibus probis hominibus totius terre sue, clericis et laicis, salutem. Sciant presentes et futuri me dedisse, concessisse et hac carta mea confirmasse Waltero de Berkelay Camerario meo Inverkileder, per rectas divisas suas, tenend*um* sibi et heredibus suis de me et heredibus meis, in feudo et hereditate, in bosco et plano, in terris et aquis, in pratis et pascuis, in molendinis et stagnis, in moris et stalangis,[b] in viis et semitis, et omnibus aliis justis pertinentiis suis, cum sacka et socka, cum tol[c] et theme et infangenethief, cum furca et fossa, libere et quiete, plenarie et honorifice, per servitium unius militis. Testibus, &c.

SOURCE. Walter Ross, *Lectures on the Practice of the Law of Scotland* (2 vols., Edinburgh, 1792), ii, 126 (n.† referring to p.125). Whereabouts of original, and provenance of Ross's text, unknown.
PRINTED. W. Ross, as above.
NOTES. [a] Punctuation editorial. [b] Sic; for scalingis. [c] Source prints tel.
COMMENT. This grant probably antedated the foundation of Arbroath Abbey in 1178.

186 Confirms to the (parish) church of Inverkeilor, Angus, and to Master Henry, parson of the same church, and the king's clerk, the remission, granted by Walter of Berkeley, of *grescan* (pasture tribute?) and every other service which the land of the church of Inverkeilor and the men dwelling on that land used to render to the thanes of Inverkeilor and afterwards to Walter of Berkeley. Lanark. (1173×c.1178)

W.[a] Dei gr*ati*a Rex Scott'. Episcopis. Abbatibus. Comitibus. baronibus. Just*iciis*. Vi*cecomitibus*. Ministris et omnibus probis hominibus tocius terre sue clericis et laicis salutem. Sciant presentes et futuri me concessisse et hac carta mea confirmasse Deo et ecclesie Sancti Macconoc de Inuerkileder et Magistro Henr*ico* eiusdem ecclesie persone clerico meo. in perpetuum remissionem quam Walterus de Berk' eis fecit de grescano et omni seruicio quod terra ecclesie et homines super terram manentes solebant facere thainis de Inuerkileder et postmodum eidem Waltero. Quare volo et precipio ut idem Henr*icus* et omnes homines super terram illam manentes quieti sint in perpetuum a grescano et ab omni Cano et redditu ad eundem[b] Walterum siue ad aliquam laicam personam pertinente. et habeant communem pasturam per totum territorium de Inuerkileder. sicut carta predicti Walteri testatur et confirmat. Test*ibus* Dauid fratre meo. Rob*erto* de Berkel'. Rogero de Valon*iis*. Hug*one* clerico de sigillo. Alardo clerico. Roberto de Bosseuill'. Symone Marescall*o*. Apud Lanark'.

RUBRIC. Confirmacio W. Reg*is* de grescano (red).. Lvij. (in margin).
SOURCE. NLS, MS. Adv. 34.4.2, fos.lv^{v}–lvi^{r}.
PRINTED. *Arbroath Liber*, i, no.57.
NOTES. [a] Initial red. [b] Fo.lvi^{r}.
COMMENT. Walter of Berkeley's charter is given in *Arbroath Liber*, i, no.56, issued on the same occasion as this confirmation. This must be compared with the agreement preserved in BM, MS. Add. 33245, fo.128^{r}, a similar remission to the same Henry, also parson of Inverlunan, of the thane's rights over the parish church and its land (see Appendix, no.590). For Mo-Chonóc, the saint of Inverkeilor, see Watson, *CPNS*, 282; J.M.Mackinlay, *Ancient Church Dedications in Scotland*, Non-Scriptural, 499.

187 Grants to the parish church of Lanark the whole parish of Nemphlar and Cartland (in Lanark) with certain teinds. (1173×1214)

Willelmus Dei gr*aci*a Rex Scotorum episcopis, abbatibus, comitibus, baronibus, justiciariis, vicecomitibus, prepositis, ministris et omnibus probis hominibus tocius terre sue, clericis et laicis, salutem. Sciant presentes et futuri me dedisse et concessisse et hac carta mea confirmasse Deo et ecclesie de Lanark totam parochiam de Nenflare et de Carteland et decimam uniuersam de omnibus averiis et vicariis[a] meis que in predictis villis posita sunt aut ponentur, in liberam et quietam[b] et perpetuam elemosinam. Quare volo et firmiter precipio ut omnes homines in predictis villis aut eciam infra divisas predictarum villarum manentes omnes decimas suas tam de vivis quam de mortuis et de omnibus aliis de quibus sancta ecclesia decimas dari exigit prefate ecclesie de Lanark inperpetuum persolvant et eidem in omnibus intendant sicut matrici ecclesie sue intendere debent. Testibus etc.

RUBRIC. Super decimis de Nemflare et Cartland. xlvj.
SOURCE. NLS, MS. Adv. 34.4.7, fo.17^{r-v}.
PRINTED. *Dryburgh Liber*, no.46. NOTES. [a] Sic. [b] Fo.17^{v}.
COMMENT. See Lawrie, *Charters*, no.218, for David I's grant of Lanark church (presumably the patronage only) to Dryburgh.

188 Grants to Kelso Abbey the mill of Ednam with its whole sphere of operations in (temporary) exchange for revenues formerly derived from Roxburgh, viz. 40s. from the *firma burgi*, 20 chalders of wheat and flour from the mills of the burgh of Roxburgh, and also in exchange for 12 chalders of malt from Ednam mill. No one but the monks of Kelso may build a mill in Ednam, and they may move it wherever they wish or build another one. The king's men of Ednam who were accustomed or who ought of right to build a new mill or repair the old and lead water and carry mill-stones to it are to serve the monks in everything as they would normally serve the king, and the king's officers shall compel them to do this. In addition, the king grants that ploughgate of arable which Hereward and his nephew Randulf held; the land held by Roger the clerk and David son of Thrust; the half ploughgate held by Edward son of Auti; and four oxgangs held at ferme by Elzi and Alfred. Kelso Abbey is to hold this property until the king can restore fully the revenues from Roxburgh, and when he can the abbey is to give back the mill of Ednam and the lands, saving its right to 12 chalders of malt from Ednam mill as before. Lanark. (1175 × 1178)

W. Dei gratia Rex Scott'. Episcopis. Abbatibus. Comitibus. Baronibus. Justiciis. Vicecomitibus Ministris. et omnibus probis hominibus tocius terre sue Clericis 7 Laicis. salutem. Nouerint presentes 7 futuri quod bone memorie. Rex D*aui*d auus meus dedit in liberam 7 perpetuam elemosinam 7 Carta sua confirmauit Ecclesie Sancte Marie de Kalchou. 7 monachis ibidem Deo seruientibus. xl. solidos de censu burgi de Rokesburg' singulis annis[a]. 7. xx^ti. cheldras inter frumentum 7 farinam singulis annis de molendinis burgi de Rokesburg'. Et preterea de molendino de Hedenham singulis annis. xii^cim. celdras brasei. Pro hiis elemosinis. 7 redditibus adquietandis dedi. 7 concessi. 7 hac carta mea confirmaui in liberam elemosinam predicte ecclesie de Kalch'. 7 monachis ibidem Deo seruientibus molendinum de Edinham cum integritate parochie sue. sicut ego illud unquam melius in manu mea habui. Ita scilicet. ut nulli liceat nisi predictis monachis in territorio de Edenham aliud molendinum facere. Liceat autem ipsis monachis quo uoluerint infra ipsum territorium illud transferre. uel aliud facere. Homines autem predicte uille qui solebant uel de iure debebant molendinum illud nouum facere uel uetus reformare. 7 aquam ad molendinum attornare. 7 molas asportare ;' volo ut monachis in hoc per omnia seruiant ;' sicut mihi seruire debent[b]. si illud in manu mea haberem. 7 ministri mei hoc eos facere compellant. Preterea dedi eis 7 presenti carta confirmaui in predicta uilla illam carucatam terre quam Herewardus. 7 Randulfus nepos eius tenuerunt ea die qua hanc donacionem eis feci cum homagiis. 7 seruiciis suis. 7 illam terram quam Rogerus clericus. 7 D*aui*d filius Thrust' eadem die tenuerunt intra uillam. uel extra uillam. cum homagiis 7 seruiciis suis. 7 illam dimidiam carucatam terre quam Edwardus filius Auti tenuit in predicta uilla. cum homagio 7 seruicio suo. 7 .iiij^or. bouatas terre quas ad firmam tenuerunt. Elzi. 7 Alfredus in predicta uilla. Volo igitur 7 firmiter precipio ;' ut predicti monachi predictum molendinum de Hedenham. 7 predictas terras in uilla 7 extra uillam cum omnibus aysiamentis uille ad predictas terras pertinentibus . in pratis . 7 pastura 7 petaria . Ita libere 7 quiete teneant 7 possideant . sicut aliquam elemosinam liberius 7 quiecius in regno meo tenent 7 possident . quousque ego redditus prenominatos eis ex integro restituam in burgo 7 molendinis de Rokesburg'. Et cum hoc eis fecero .· reddent mihi molendinum de Eden' . 7 terras prenominatas . 7 homines meos sicut prius habui . Saluis tamen sibi .xij. celdras brasei quas prius habuerunt in molendino de Edenham. Prohibeo etiam super meam plenariam forisfacturam .· ut nullus ministrorum meorum aliquam inde eis iniustam uexacionem faciat . uel ab aliis fieri permittat. T'. J*ocelino* Episcopo de Glesg*u* . W*altero* de Bid*un* Cancellario . Com*ite* Dunec*ano* . Com*ite* Gilb*erto* . Sim*one* Arch*idiacono* . Ric*ardo* de Moreuill' consta*bulario* . Rob*erto* de Quinci . J*ohanne* de Wall*ibus* . Ric*ardo* Cumin. Apud Lanarck';

RUBRIC. Carta super molendinum de Hedenham 7 unam carucatam terre cum alii libertatibus (top in red).
SOURCE. NLS, MS. Adv. 34.5.1, fos.143^{v}–144^{r}.
PRINTED. *Kelso Liber*, no.383.
NOTES. [a] Fo.144^{r}. [b] debent precedes seruire and is marked for transposition by two pairs of diagonal strokes.
COMMENT. This exchange was one of the transactions forced on King William by the English occupation of Roxburgh and other Scottish castles after the submission of Falaise, 1174. See nos.199, 288, 317. In 1177, £40 was charged to the farm of Westmorland for provisioning Roxburgh castle (*Cal. Docs. Scot.*, i, no. 150).

189 Commands his justices and other officers to render to Bishop Jocelin of Glasgow all his dues, whether in teinds, cain, pleas and profits or any other dues, as they were accustomed to render them to the previous bishops. Dumfries. (1175 × 1177)

Will*elmu*s Dei gr*ati*a Rex Scottorum Justic*iis* vicecomitibus et omnibus ministris et Balliuis suis salutem. Mando vobis atque firmiter precipio . quatinus ita bene et plenarie et sine disturbacione soluatis Domino Jocel*ino* Episcopo Glasg*uensi* omnes rectitudines suas . de Decimis et canis et placitis et lucris et omnes alias rectitudines suas sicut unquam melius aut plenius . Johanni aut Herberto . aut Engelramo . Episcopis aut alicui Episcopo ante eum soluere solebatis . ne pro defectu vestri inde clamorem audiam super meam forisfacturam. Test*ibus* Ric*ard*o de Moreu*illa* constabulario . Waltero filio Alani dapifero . Waltero Olif*ard* . Roberto de Quinci . Willelmo de Veteri Ponte. Apud DunfreZ.

RUBRIC. De Decimis et omnibus iuribus ecclesie Glasguensis (in margin).
SOURCE. Blairs Archives, 16 Drummond Place, Edinburgh, MS. Registrum Vetus of Glasgow, fo.liij^{r}.
PRINTED. *Glasgow Registrum*, no.71.
COMMENT. This would have been issued soon after Bishop Jocelin's succession, and probably belongs to the period when the king was trying to suppress unrest in Galloway, in 1175 or 1176 (Lawrie, *Annals*, 205–6, 217).

190 Grants that Jocelin bishop of Glasgow and his successors may have a burgh at Glasgow with a market every Thursday and with all the liberties and customs best enjoyed by any burgh within the king's land. Traquair. (1175 × 1178)

W' Dei gr*ati*a Rex Scott'. Episcopis. Abbatibus. Comitibus. Baronibus. Justic*iis* . vicecomit*ibus* . ministris . et Omnibus probis hominibus totius terre sue clericis et laicis modernis et posteris Salutem. Sciant presentes et futuri me concessisse et hac Carta mea confirmasse Deo et Sancto Kentegerno et Jocelino episcopo Glasguen*si* . et singulis eius successoribus in perpetuum :' ut Burgum habeant apud Glasgu . cum foro diei Jouis . bene et honorifice quiete et Plenarie cum omnibus libertatibus et consuetudinibus :' quas aliquis Burgorum meorum in tota terra mea melius plenius quietius et honorificentius habet. Quare uolo et firmiter precipio ut omnes Burgenses qui in predicto Burgo manentes erunt :' meam firmam pacem iuste habeant per totam terram meam . in eundo et redeundo . Et prohibeo firmiter ne quis eos aut eorum catalla iniuste disturbet . aut uexet . aut aliquam eis iniuriam aut contumeliam inferat . super meam plenariam forisfacturam. Test*ibus* Comite D*aui*d fratre meo . Waltero Bid*un* Cancell*ario* meo . Comit*e* Dunec*ano* . Com*ite* Gilleb*erto* . Com*ite* Gillecrist de Meneth' . Ric*ardo* de Moruill Const*abulario* . Rob*erto* de Quinci . Ric*ardo* Cum*in* . Walt*ero* de Berkel' Camer*ario* . W*illelmo* de Veteri Ponte . Philippo de Vall*oniis* . Rob*erto* de Berkel' . Ad*am* de Stanford. Apud TraueqeR.

RUBRIC. De Burgo de Glasg*u* (in margin in different hand).
SOURCE. Blairs Archives, 16 Drummond Place, Edinburgh, MS. Registrum Vetus of Glasgow, fo.v[r].
PRINTED. *Glasgow Registrum*, no.40; *Glasgow City Chrs.*, Part II, 4.
COMMENT. If the title of earl given to David the king's brother is not a copyist's anachronism, it may be explained as a courtesy title bestowed because David held the earldom of Lennox (see no.205 and comment), though the charter granting the earldom must be rather later than this act.

191

Confirms to Newbattle Abbey the peatary of Loquhariot (in Borthwick, Midlothian), called 'Wulvestrother', with facilities for drying peats, granted by David son of Robert, as David's charter bears witness. (1175 × *c*.1185)

W. Dei gr*ati*a Rex Scott' Omnibus probis hominibus tocius terre sue salutem. Sciant presentes et posteri me concessisse et hac mea carta confirmasse Deo et ecclesie Sancte Marie de Neu*botle* et monachis ibidem Deo seruientibus in perpetuam elemosinam illam peteram de Lochqwerwerd, que vocatur Wuluestrother, quam etiam Dauid filius Roberti eis dedit et carta sua confirmauit. Concedo etiam eis eadem aysiamenta in terra eiusdem Dauid ad focalia sua siccanda, que predictus Dauid eis dedit, et liberum ingressum in terram eiusdem Dauid et egressum ad ea carianda, tenend*am* sibi ita libere, quiete et honorifice sicud carta prescripti Dauid eis testatur et confirmat, saluo seruicio meo. Test*ibus* D*aui*d fratre meo, Matheo episcopo Aberdonen*si*, Comite Duncano, Roberto de Quency, Phylippo de Wallon*iis* et aliis.

Confirmacio Reg*is* Willelmi [a].
SOURCE. NLS, MS. Adv. 34.4.13, fo.12[r].
PRINTED. *Newbattle Registrum*, no.15.
NOTE. [a] Table of contents, fo.1[r].
COMMENT. The charter of David of Lyne, son of Robert, is given in *Newbattle Registrum*, no.13 (1175 × 1199).

192 Grants to Glasgow Cathedral Church and Bishop Jocelin, in recompense for the excesses perpetrated by himself and his officers against the church since the death of Bishop Ingram, Bedlay (in Cadder, Lanarkshire). Linlithgow. (1175 × 1178)

Will*elmus* Dei gr*ati*a Rex Scotorum Episcopis . Abbatibus . Comitibus . Baronibus . Justiciis . vicecomitibus . ministris . et Omnibus probis hominibus totius terre sue Clericis et laicis Salutem. Sciant presentes et futuri me pro excessibus a me et a meis pro me Sancto Kentegerno . et ecclesie Glasguensi . post decessum Engelrami Episcopi illatis :[a] dedisse et concessisse et hac carta mea confirmasse Deo et Sancto Kentegerno et ecclesie Glasguen*si* et Jocelino Glasguen*si* episcopo . et uniuersis episcopis eiusdem J*ocelini* successoribus ad incrementum episcopatus de Glasgu . BalaiN . per rectas diuisas suas tenendam in liberam et perpetuam elemosinam . in bosco et plano . in terris et aquis . in pratis et pascuis . et Omnibus iustis pertinentiis suis . ita libere et quiete . plenarie et honorifice : sicut alias tenuras eiusdem episcopatus liberius . quietius . plenius et honorificentius tenent. T*este* et concedente D*auid* fratre meo . Waltero de Bidu*n* Cancell*ario* . Joh*anne* abbate de Kelcho . Ric*ardo* de Moruill' constabul*ario* . Rob*erto* de Brus . Willelmo de Veteri Ponte . Galfrido de Maleuill' Justitia . Willelmo de Lindeseia . Philippo de Valuins . Rob*erto* fil*io* Wernebald' . Herb*erto* de Macuswell' . Eadwad[b] Delstalrich' . Rob*erto* de Berchelei . Roberto de Boseuill' . Adam de Stanford . Iuone de Crossib' . Apud Linlidqu.

RUBRIC. De Badlayn (in margin, in different hand).
SOURCE. Blairs Archives, 16 Drummond Place, Edinburgh, MS. Registrum Vetus of Glasgow, fos.iii^{v}–iiij^{r}.
PRINTED. *Glasgow Registrum*, no.39.
NOTES. [a] Fo.iiij^{r}. [b] Sic.
COMMENT. Cadder had already been granted to Glasgow by Malcolm IV (cf. *RRS*, i, no.291). 'Baidlae' is mentioned in 1644 in Macfarlane, *Geographical Coll.*, ii, 579.

193 Commands Alan the doorward, his justiciar benorth (Forth), to render to Bishop Matthew of Aberdeen the second teinds of all his revenues within the sheriffdoms of Aberdeen and Banff. Edinburgh. 1175 (Spurious).

Will*elmus* Dei gratia Rex Scottorum Alano Hostiar*io* Justiciar*io* suo ex parte boreali salutem. Cum frater[a] meus concesserit domino Matheo episcopo Aberdonensi secundas decimas de omnibus redditibus firmis escaetis suis infra vicecomitatus de Aberden et de Banff, tibi precipio quod de dictis decimis dicto domino Episcopo et suis successoribus responderi facias.[b] Datum apud Edynburgh Anno Regni nostri decimo.[c]

RUBRIC. Carta Regis Willelmi de solutione secundarum decimarum omnium reddituum in vicecomitatibus de Aberden et Banff (in margin, *M*).
SOURCE. NLS, MS. Adv. 16.1.10, fo.49^{r-v} = *M*. NLS. MS. Adv. 34.4.4, fo.40^{r} = *A*. Printed here from *M*.
PRINTED. *Aberdeen Registrum*, i, 9.
NOTES. [a] pater struck through, frater added, MS. [b] Fo.49^{r}. [c] Anno Domini 1175 added in hand of xvi cent.
COMMENT. There seems no reason to think that this spurious brieve has any basis in an authentic act of King William.

194 Confirms to Holyrood Abbey the grant made to it by Richard Cumin (with the consent of his wife Hextilda of Tynedale) of the land of Slipperfield (in West Linton), Peeblesshire, within the following marches: from King Seat Burn as it falls to Lyne Water, and as Lyne Water falls to 'Bigerfuird', and thence by the high road to the first burn beside the cross and as that burn falls into the West Water, and as the West Water falls into the White Moss and through the White Moss as far as Allary Burn and as Allary Burn rises to the west of Mendick Hill, and so to the clefts of the Garvald Burn and so to the Catstone and so to the head of the West Water and so to the head of the King Seat Burn. Jedburgh. (1173 × 1178, perhaps 1178)

Williame[a] be the grace of God King of Scotes to all bishopes, abites, earles, barrones, justiceearies, shireffes, proveistes, ministeres and all good men of his land Greeting. Witt ȝe ws be thir presentes to have grantit and be this present chairtoure to have confirmed to the house[b] and kirk of Hellirudhouse of Edinburgh and to the cannones serveing God thair the landes quhich[c] Richard Cuming gave in elimosinam[d], to witt, all the land from the heid of Kingsydburne as it deschendes to the Lin and as the Lin deschendes even to Bigerfuird and so throw the great way even to the first burne besyd the croce and as the burne deschendes in Pollintarfe and as Pollintarfe deschendes to the great mose and swa throw the great mose even to Alrie burne and as Alrie burne aschendes to the wast Mendick and sua to the cliftes of the Garrill and so[c] to the Cake[c] staine and sua to the heid of Pollintarfe and sua to Kingsyd burne. To be holdin in frie and perpetuall elimosionarie[c] als friely, qwyetly, fullie and honorabillie as any uthir his elimosionaries more friely, qwyetlie, fullie and honorabillie holdes, and as the chairtoure of Richard Cumin witnessed and confirmed. Saifand my service be the said Richard and his aires. Witness Walter Boyd[e] chancellar etc. Sahled[f], earle Walter[g], Richart Morvell constable, Walter Cliffe[h], Walter of Berkelaie, Robert of Berkell, John of Loundoun, Robert of Bosuell. Apud Jedburght.

SOURCE. SRO, Transcripts of Royal Charters (1165–1214), 'from a copy on paper in a hand of the middle of the seventeenth century, the property of the representatives of the late Dr Kennedy, communicated by Mr Thomas Thomson, W.S., Thistle Street, 19 April, 1862'.

PRINTED. *Notes and Queries*, 3rd ser., ix (1866), p.8 (abstract with witnesses).

NOTES. [a] Punctuation editorial. [b] Sic, misrendering of Deo, to God. [c] Sic. [d] Source has elimoseonarie. [e] Sic, for de Bid*un*. [f] Sic, perhaps for electo Dunkeldensi? [g] Sic, for Waldeuo, Waltheof. [h] Sic, for Oli*fard*.

COMMENT. Walter de Bidun the chancellor was elected bishop of Dunkeld in 1178 but died the same year. The original of Richard Cumin's charter survived in 1862 and a copy from this is in SRO, Transcripts of Miscellaneous Charters (R.H. 1/2/1); a version from a Macfarlane transcript is printed in *Holyrood Liber*, 210–211. With the help of this text, the charter of King William may be hypothetically restored thus:

'Willelmus Dei gracia rex Scottorum episcopis, abbatibus, comitibus, baronibus, justiciis, vicecomitibus, prepositis, ministris et omnibus probis hominibus totius terre sue, salutem. Sciant presentes et futuri me concessisse et hac presenti carta mea confirmasse Deo et ecclesie Sancte Crucis de Edeneburg et canonicis ibidem Deo seruientibus terram quam Ricardus Cumin dedit eis in elemosinam, scilicet totam terram a capite Kingeseteburne sicut descendit ad Linam, et sicut Lina descendit usque ad Biggeresford et sic per magnam uiam usque ad proximum torrentem iuxta crucem et sicut torrens descendit in Pollentarf et sicut Pollentarf descendit ad magnum mos et sic per magnum mos usque Alreburne, et sicut Alreburne ascendit ad occidentem Menedicte et ita ad loca ueterum scalingarum et ita ad lapidem Catti et ita ad caput Pollentarf et ita ad Kingeseteburne. Tenend*am* in liberam et perpetuam elemosinam ita libere, quiete, plenarie et honorifice sicut aliqua alia elemosina liberius, quiecius, plenius et honorificencius tenetur, sicut carta Ricardi Cumin testatur et confirmat, saluo seruicio meo a predicto Ricardo et heredibus suis. Testibus, Waltero de Bidun cancellario [electo Dunkeldensi], Comite Waldeuo, Ricardo de Moreuilla constabulario, Waltero Olifard, Waltero de Berkelaie, Robert de Berkel', Johanne de Londoniis, Roberto de Bosuille. Apud Jedewrth.'

The 'cliftes of the Garrill (Garvald)' do not appear in Richard Cumin's charter, and may be a misrendering of the phrase *loca ueterum scalingarum*, 'steads of the old shielings'.

195 Grants to Melrose Abbey the land which it has of Patrick of Ryedale in the territory of Whitton (in Morebattle, Roxburghshire). Lanark. (1175 × 1185, perhaps 1177 × 1185)

.W. Dei gr*ati*a Rex Scott' Episcopis . Abbatibus . Comitibus . Baronibus . Justic*iis* . Vicecomitibus . Ministris . & Omnibus probis hominibus tocius terre sue Clericis & laicis Salutem. Sciant presentes & posteri me concessisse & dedisse & hac Carta mea confirmasse Deo & Ecclesie Sancte Marie de Melros . & monachis ibidem Deo seruientibus terram illam quam habent de Patricio de Ridale in territorio de Wittun .' per ipsas diuisas que continentur in carta Patricii de Ridale quam habent de eo de eadem terra . ita ut quicquid infra easdem diuisas fuerit . habeant & possideant imperpetuum . ita libere & quiete . honorifice & pacifice . sicut aliqua elemosina liberius & quietius & honorificentius in regno meo possidetur. Dedi enim eis & confirmaui terram illam liberam ab omnibus auxiliis placitis . Geldis . & ab omni seruicio & consuetudine & exactione seculari . ita quod ego & heredes mei manutenebimus & warantizabimus eam illis contra omnes homines in perpetuum . saluo seruicio meo de Patricio & heredibus suis. Test*e* Jocelino episcopo Glasguensi . Dauid fratre meo . Walt*ero* Olifard Justic*ia* . Alano filio Walteri . Hug*one* clerico de sigillo . Hug*one* Ridel . Waltero de Windeshoure . Waltero de Berkel' camerario . Willelmo de Mortimer . Roberto de Berkel' . Johanne de London*iis* . Apud LANARch.

ENDORSED. Confirmatio regis Willelmi de Wittun (xii cent.), C (Red, xv cent.?). J. Scott (xvi cent.).
DESCRIPTION. 10·3″ (26 cm.), Top, 10·6″ (27 cm.), Bottom × 5·2″ (13·3 cm.), L, R. Foot folded to a depth of 1·3″ (3·1 cm.). Neither tag nor seal survives.
HAND. Scribe Cc. Ruled in drypoint.
SOURCE. Original, SRO, GD 55/170.
PRINTED. *Melrose Liber*, no.170.
COMMENT. Patrick of Ryedale was the youngest son, and eventual heir, of Ansketil of Ryedale, brother and heir of Walter of Ryedale. Patrick's elder son Walter was ancestor of the family of Riddell of that ilk. See *EYC*, ii, 116; and cf. *RRS*, i, nos.42 and 312.

196 Grants to Winemer and his heirs Wormistone (in Crail), Fife, within the marches specified, with common pasture in the common of Crail, sufficient turf and peats, and free ish and entry into the common; in feu and heritage, for an annualrent of 2d. at Whitsun if requested by way of blench ferme. (1178 × 1185) (Inflated, but probably based on a genuine grant).

Willelmus[a] Dei gracia Rex Scotorum omnibus probis hominibus suis[b] salutem. Sciatis me dedisse, concessisse et hac presenti carta confirmasse [Winemero][c] et heredibus suis totam terram que jacet inter propinquiorem fontem de Balcolmy et portam sanctimonialium[d] de Hadingtoun versus occidentem et aquilonem per suas diuisas, sic*ut* extend*unt* usque ad upcast arrati terrarum de Tornakitfeild et sic*ut* extend*unt* ad terras arrabiles de Pittowie ex occidentali, et sic descendendo inter dictas terras de Pittowie et orientalem partem de Gidecald usque ad maresium jacens inter Pittowie et finem de Torbrekis et sic extendendo ab illo maresio usque ad orientalem partem de Stewartflat, que dicitur Dow Grein, et sic extendendo inter dictas terras de lie Stewartflat et predictas terras de Balcolmy usque ad predictum fontem propinquiorem de Balcolme juxta mare, cum communi pastura in communi de Carraill, cum turbariis et petariis sufficien*tibus*, cum libero introitu et exitu ad predictum comune de Carraill, sibi et heredibus suis de me et heredibus meis, in feodo et hereditate, bene et in pace, libere et quiete, solute et honorifice et sine consuetudine et exactione, in campis, in pratis et pasturis, in aquis et omnibus asiamentis que pertinent ad eandem terram. Reddendo inde mihi annuatim et heredibus meis duos denarios nomine albe firme ad Pentecosten, si petatur, pro omni alio seruitio seculari et exactione seu demanda. Testibus Dauid[e] fratre meo, Philippo etc. etc. etc.

ENDORSED. Copie of the chartour grantit be King William of the landis of Wilmerstoun.

SOURCE. NLS, MS. Charters 74 (Lawrie's Collections), vol.I.

PRINTED. *HMC*, *5th Report*, Appendix, p.623.

NOTES. [a] Punctuation editorial. [b] Sic. [c] Source has Venero. [d] Source has castri monialium. [e] Source has dominis.

COMMENT. This was probably issued after the Countess Ada's death in 1178. For Winemer cf. no.469, and Hodgson, *Hist. of Northumberland*, Pt.II, vol.iii, 17; *St Andrews Liber*, 208. Wormistone was previously Wolmerstoun, probably from *Winemerestun. J. Ainslie's *Map of Fife and Kinross* (1775) gives Gathercold between Nakedfield and Pittowie, and also Greenend (cp. Dow Grein above), between Pittowie and Hollowflat. Stewartflet appears in *Retours* (Fife), no.1482, associated with Balcomie. For Torbrekis cp. *St Andrews Liber*, 384–6, Turbrech or Turbrek in Fife in litigation between May priory and John and Henry of Denmuir, 1260–1286. Tornakitfeild may be a partial translation involving Gael. *tornocht*, 'stark naked'. It appears in *Retours* (Fife), *passim*, as Tornakatay, Tornakiters, etc.

197 Announces that he has founded (an abbey) church at Arbroath in honour of God and of Saint Thomas, archbishop and martyr; and lists its initial endowments, including Arbroath with its whole shire and church, with freedom to found a burgh and have a harbour, and to hold a market every Saturday; Ethie with its church; 'Adinaglas' (lost, in Arbroath and St Vigeans); Dunnichen with its whole shire and church; Kingoldrum with its whole shire and church; the church of Maryton of Old Montrose, with its land called in Gaelic *abthen*; the churches of Newtyle, Banchory-Ternan, Glamis, Haltwhistle in Tynedale; one full toft in all the various burghs and lodgings which the king has or shall have; freedom to take whatever the abbey needs in the king's forests; one net in the king's water at Perth called 'Sthoc'; one full net on the water of North Esk beside Montrose; one saltpan beside the king's saltpans in the Carse of Stirling; and with the liberties of its own court, with sake, soke, toll, team, infangthief, ordeal of iron, trial by battle, pit and gallows, and with freedom of abbatial election; saving the defence of the realm and royal justice, should the abbot fail to give justice in his own court. No place-date. (Probably 1178)

W. Dei gr*ati*a Rex Scott'. Episcopis. Abbatibus. Comitibus. Baronibus. Justic*iis*. vicecomitibus. & Omnibus probis hominibus tocius terre sue. Clericis & laicis salutem. Sciant presentes & futuri. me pro amore Dei & pro salute anime mee & animarum antecessorum & successorum meorum dedisse. & concessisse & hac carta mea confirmasse. Deo & Ecclesie quam fundaui in honore Dei & Sancti Thome archipresulis & Martiris Apud Aberbrutoh. & Monachis ibidem Deo & Sancto Thome seruientibus. In liberam & perpetuam elemosinam. Aberbrotoht cum tota schira sua per rectas diuisas suas. in bosco. & plano. in terris & aquis. in pratis & pascuis. & cum omnibus iustis pertinentiis suis. & ecclesiam eiusdem uuille. Scilic& Aberbrethot cum plenariis decimis suis & cum omnibus aliis iustis pertinentiis suis. Dedi etiam & concessi eis licentiam & libertatem faciendi Burgum. & habendi portum. & habendi forum :' unaquaque die Sabbati in eadem terra. Concessi etiam eis in perpetuum hanc in eorum burgo predicto libertatem :' ut omnes eorum burgenses. qui in eodem burgo. terram uel domum. habuerint :' & in eo manentes fuerint. & burgenses eorum qui in toftis eorum manent in burgis meis :' quieti & liberi sint a teloneo & consuetudine per totam terram meam & per omnes portus terre mee de omnibus & omnimodis mercibus & mercaturis suis propriis quas emerint uel vendiderint. Dedi etiam eis & concessi. [A]thin per rectas diuisas suas. & cum omnibus iustis pertinentiis suis. & ecclesiam eiusdem uille cum plenariis decimis suis. & cum aliis iustis pertinentiis suis. Dedi etiam eis Adinaglas per rectas diuisas suas. & cum omnibus iustis pertinentiis suis. & Duneicht' cum tota schira sua per rectas diuisas suas. & cum omnibus aliis iustis pertinentiis suis. & ecclesiam eiusdem uille cum omnibus ad eam iuste pertinentibus. Et Kingoueldrum cum tota schira sua per rectas diuisas suas. & ecclesiam eiusdem uille. cum omnibus ad eam iuste pertinentibus. Et ecclesiam Sancte Marie de ueteri Munros. cum terra eiusdem ecclesie. que Scottice abthen uocatur. per rectas diuisas suas. & cum decimis plenariis. & cum omnibus aliis iustis pertinentiis suis. Et ecclesiam de Neutile cum omnibus iustis pertinentiis suis. Et ecclesiam de Benchorin :' cum omnibus iustis pertinentiis suis. Et ecclesiam de Glamenes cum omnibus iustis pertinentiis suis. Et ecclesiam de Hakatwisel in Tindalia. cum omnibus pertinentiis suis. In capellis. In terris. In decimis. In elemosinis. & in omnibus aliis ecclesiasticis Rectitudinibus. consuetudinibus. & beneficiis. Cum communi etiam pastura. Omnibusque aliis aisiamentis earundem parochiarum. Et unum plenarium toftum in singulis burgis meis & Gistis que habeo & habiturus sum. Et licentiam capiendi in forestis meis quecunque eis necessaria fuerint ad edificia sua & ad usus proprios. Et unum Rete super aquam meam de Pert que uocatur Sthoc . & unum plenarium Rete super aquam de Nor Esech . iuxta Munros . Et unam salinam iuxta salinas meas in Kars apud Striuelin . cum .v. acris terre . cum pastura & focali . ad predictam salinam sufficientibus. Concedo etiam eis in terra sua liberam curiam suam . Cum Sacca & socca . & cum Tol & Them & infangentheN . & ferrum . & Duellum . fossam . & furcas & liberam electionem abbatis . & firmam pacem intra diuisas de Aberbrothot. Omnia autem dona predicta ita liberaliter & quiete prefate ecclesie concedo .' sicut ego terras meas proprias possideo . defensione regni mei excepta & Regali iusticia .' si abbas in curia sua aliqua negligentia de iusticia deciderit. Quare uolo & firmiter precipio quod ipsa ecclesia Sancti Thome de Aberbrothot & ipsius ecclesie abbas & conuentus habeant & teneant imperpetuum omnia predicta tenementa . & libertates sicut superius determinatum est .' cum terris & cum omnibus possessionibus . & cum omnibus tenementis ecclesiasticis & secularibus que ego & fideles mei eis contulimus & collaturi sumus . Bene & in pace . libere & quiete . integre . & plenarie . & honorifice . In bosco & plano . In pratis & pasturis . In aquis & molendinis . In uiuariis & stagnis . In piscariis & Mariscis . In Wastis & Scalinggis . In viis & semitis . & in omnibus aliis locis . & aliis rebus ad eas pertinentibus . & cum omnibus libertatibus & liberis consuetudinibus suis . sicut eidem ecclesie concessi . & hac carta mea confirmaui . Nec aliquis successorum meorum aliquam aliam secularem exactionem ab eadem ecclesia Sancti Thome exigat. Teste Jocel*ino* episcopo Glasg*uensi* . Andr*ea* episcopo Caten*ensi* . A*rkenbaldo* abbate de Dunfermel*in* . Rob*erto* abbate de Scone . Comite Dunec*ano* . Com*ite* Gilleberto . Com*ite* Wald' . Gillebride com*ite* de Anegus . M*alcolmo* com*ite* Ethal' . Com*ite* Colbano . Ric*ardo* de Moruill' constab*ulario* . Waltero Olif*ard* Justic*ia* . Waltero de Berkel' camerario . Willelmo de Mortemer . Willelmo de Lindes' . Willelmo de Haia . Alano fil*io* Walteri . Waltero de Windesouer . Roberto de Berkel' . Willelmo fil*io* Toraldi . Rogero de Vallan' . Johanne de Lundon'.

HEADING. Carta compendiosa regis Willelmi.[a]
SOURCE. *Arbroath Liber*, ii, Appendix, no.I (printed from a transcript in General Hutton's Collections, which are NLS, MS. Adv. 29.4.2). The original has not been traced; the Hutton transcript is said to have been made 'ex archivis de Panmure'.
PRINTED. As above.
NOTE. [a] This probably represents the endorsement of the original.
COMMENT. Arbroath Abbey was founded in 1178, during the vacancy in the see of St Andrews (*Arbroath Liber*, no.2). This charter would no doubt have been issued more or less simultaneously with the act of foundation, or soon after. Richard bishop of St Andrews died in the summer of 1178; the subsequent election of John the Scot without the king's leave probably caused a breach between the king and Bishop Matthew of Aberdeen, John's uncle, who witnesses no.223 below. Possibly no.223 was issued before the date of this act.

198 Grants to Arbroath Abbey the church of Glamis, Angus. Dunfermline. (1178 × 17 September, 1184)

W.[a] Dei gr*ati*a Rex Scott' , Episcopis , Abbatibus , Comitibus , Baronibus , Justic*iis* . Vicec*omitibus* , ministris et omnibus probis hominibus tocius terre sue , clericis et laicis, salutem. Sciant presentes et futuri me dedisse et concessisse et hac carta mea confirmasse Deo et ecclesie Sancti Thome archiepiscopi de Aberbroth*oc* et monachis ibidem Deo seruientibus Ecclesiam de Glampnes, cum capellis et terris et decimis omnimodis et cum omnibus ad ean[b]dem ecclesiam iuste pertinentibus . Tenend*am* in liberam et perpetuam elemosinam, ita libere et quiete ab omni seculari exactione et seruicio et ita plenarie et honorifice sicut aliquam elemosinam liberius, quiecius, plenius et honorificencius tenent. Test*ibus* M*atheo* episcopo Abirdon*ensi*, A*ndrea* episcopo Katen*ensi*, Symon*e* episcopo Morau*iensi*, Symon*e* episcopo Dunblan*ensi*, Comite Dunecan*o*, Comite Gilb*erto*. Apud Dunfermelyn.

RUBRIC. Carta domini W. regis de ecclesia de Glampnes (red, *E*). Carta .W. Reg*is* de ecclesia de Glampnes (red, *A*) . xvij . (in margin, *A*, *E*).
SOURCE. NLS, MS. Adv. 34.4.2, fos.xliv^v–xlv^r = *A*. SRO, Northesk Muniments (uncatalogued), Ethie MS., fo.3^v = *E*. Printed here from *A*.
PRINTED. *Arbroath Liber*, i, no.17 (from *E*).
NOTES. [a] Initial red. [b] Fo.xlv^r.
COMMENT. Bishop Matthew was in exile for much of the years 1180 and 1181.

199 Grants to Holyrood Abbey, in exchange for the alms which it has lost through the agency of the (English) garrison in (Edinburgh) castle, 4 merks from the king's mill of Cramond, 33s. from the mill of Liberton, 20s. from the ferme of Merchiston, 8s. from the land of the furbisher, and 5s. 8d. from the ferme of Clerenbaud (Clermiston); to be held until the king can warrant the alms which the abbey has lost or shall assign it an income of 9 merks elsewhere. Haddington. (1178 × 1186)

.W. Dei gr*ati*a Rex Scott' . Omnibus probis hominibus totius terre sue salutem. Sciant presentes 7 posteri me dedisse . 7 concessisse . 7 hac mea carta confirmasse . Deo 7 ecclesie Sancte Crucis de Edenburc . 7 canonicis ibidem Deo seruientibus . in exscambio[a] elemosinarum quas per castellanos amiserunt .' iiij. marc*as* de molendino meo de Karramunt . 7 .xxxiij. sol*idos* de molendino de Libertun' . 7 de firma de Merihennest*un* .xx. sol*idos* . 7 de terra furbarii . viij. sol*idos* . 7 de firma Clerenbaud .v. sol*idos* . 7 .viij. d*enarios*. Tenendu*m* sibi in liberam 7 quietam elemosinam ita libere 7 quiete . sicut alias elemosinas suas liberius 7 quietius tenent 7 possident . donec predictas elemosinas quas per castellanos de Edenburc amiserunt .' eis warrantizare potero . uel alibi redditum .ix. marc*arum* assignauero. Test*ibus* Hug*one* Episcopo Sancti Andr*ee* . Waltero Olifart Justic*ia* . Hug*one* Giffart . Waltero de Berchelei . Willelmo de Haia . Roberto de Berchelei. Apud Adingtun'.

ENDORSED. De exscambio[a] (xiii cent.).
de xx s. in molendino de Craumond.
xxxiij s. in molendino de liberton.
de firma clerembaud v s. viij d.
de firmis de Merchamston' xx s. de terra fourbarij
viij s. (xv cent.). J. Scott (xvi cent.).
DESCRIPTION. 7·1″ (18·1 cm.), Top, bottom × 3·7″ (9·5 cm.), L, R. Foot folded to a depth of 0·5″ (1·3 cm.). Single slits with tag 5·7″ (14·5 cm.) long, 0·7″ (1·8 cm.) wide. Fragment of seal remains in natural wax stained brown, diameter 2·5″ (6·5 cm.), poor impression.
HAND. Scribe Bc. Unruled. SOURCE. Original, SRO, GD 45/13/237.
PRINTED. *Holyrood Liber*, no.29. NOTE. [a] Sic.

COMMENT. The *castellani* were the English garrison put into Edinburgh castle by the terms of the Treaty of Falaise, 1174–5 and withdrawn after the king's marriage, 5 September, 1186 (Stones, *Docs.*, 3; D. Hunter Marshall, in *SHR*, xxv, 20ff.). This charter is one of the earliest pieces of evidence for the keeping of royal demesne accounts. The accounts of the sheriffdom of Edinburgh in 1290 refer to the loss of revenue (*decidentia*) from the 'terra de Clerribaldi' (*Exch. Rolls*, i, 41). The land is represented by Clermiston in Corstorphine (cf. *Dunfermline Registrum*, nos.171, 324).

200 Confirms to Philip of Seton the land which belonged to his father, viz. Seton (in Tranent) and Winton (in Pencaitland), East Lothian, and Winchburgh (in Kirkliston), West Lothian, in feu and heritage, with sake and soke, toll, team and infangthief, with pit and gallows, for the service of one knight. Stirling. (1177 × 1185)

W'. Dei Gr*atia* Rex Scott'. Episcopis. Abbatibus. Comitibus Baronibus. Justiciis. Vicecomitibus. Ministris. 7 Omnibus probis Hominibus totius terre sue Clericis 7 Laicis salutem. Sciant presentes 7 futuri me Concessisse. 7 Hac Carta mea Confirmasse Philippo de Setune ;' terram que fuit patris sui. scilicet Setune. 7 Wintune. 7 Wincelburh. Tenend' sibi. 7 heredibus suis de me. 7 heredibus meis in feudo. 7 hereditate. in Bosco. 7 Plano. in terris. 7 aquis. in pratis. 7 pascuis. 7 in omnibus earundem terrarum Justis pertinentiis. Cum Sacca. 7 Socca. 7 Tol. 7 Tem. 7 Infanghenethef'. Cum furca. 7 fossa ;' Libere 7 quiete. plenarie 7 honorifice ;' per Seruicium unius Militis. Test*ibus* D*aui*d fratre meo. Comit*e* Dunec*ano* Justic*ia*. Ricardo de Moreuill' Constab*ulario*. Waltero Olif*ard* Justic*ia*. Alano Dapifero. Waltero de Berk' Cam*erario*. Willelmo de Lind'. Ricardo de Munf'. Johanne de London'. Apud Striuelin,

ENDORSED. No endorsement known.
DESCRIPTION[1]. 7·2″ (18·2 cm.), Top, 7·35″ (18·7 cm.), Bottom × 3·3″ (8·3 cm.), L, 3·1″ (7·8 cm.), R. Foot folded to a depth of 0·4″ (1·2 cm.). Seal-tag shewn in facsimile passing through single slits in foot and fold, with large fragment of seal in green wax shewn still adhering to tag, reverse to front.
HAND. Scribe Ba. Unruled.
SOURCE. G. Seton, *History of the family of Seton* (1898), i, 68, with facsimile; see also *Fraser Facsimiles*, no.10. The original from which this facsimile was made seems now to be lost.
PRINTED. G. Seton, as above; and also vol.ii, 842; R. Maitland, *Genealogy of the House of Setoun* (1830), 14–15; Mackenzie, *Writers*, iii, 208–9.

[1] Dimensions given are those of the facsimile, which appears to be actual size or nearly so.

COMMENT. Alexander (de) Setone, presumed to have been Philip of Seton's father, witnessed *RRS*, i, no.42. See also no.390 below.

201 Confirms to St Andrews Cathedral Priory the church of Meigle (Perthshire), with the chapel adjacent to the church, granted by Simon of Meigle. Crail. (1178 × 1185)

W'. Dei gr*ati*a Rex Scott'. Episcopis. Abbatibus. Comitibus. Baronibus. Justic*iis*. Vicec*omitibus*. Ministris. 7 Omnibus Probis Hominibus totius Terre sue ;' Clericis 7 Laicis salutem,[a] Sciant Presentes 7 futuri me Concessisse. 7 hac karta mea Confirmasse Canonicis in Ecclesia Sancti Andr*ee* Apostoli Deo seruientibus 7 seruituris Ecclesiam de Micghel quam Sim*on* de Micghel eis dedit in perpetuam Elemosinam cum Capella eidem Ecclesie adiacente . cum Terris . Decimis . 7 cum omnibus justis Pertinentiis suis .· sicut Carta Sim*onis* testatur. Quare uolo 7 firmiter Precipio .· ut Predicti Canonici predictam Ecclesiam ita libere 7 quiete teneant 7 possideant .· sicut alias Ecclesias in Regno meo sibi in Elemosinam datas liberius 7 quietius tenent 7 possident.[a] Test*ibus* Hug*one* Episcopo Sancti Andr*ee* . D*aui*d fratre meo . Comite Dunec*ano* . Philippo de Vallon*iis* . Thoma de Muscampo . Waltero de Berk' Cam*e*-*rario* . Roberto Capellano meo . Hug*one* de Sigillo Clerico meo . Hug*one* Giffard. Apud Karal,[a]

ENDORSED. Confirmatio Reg*is* Will*elm*; de Ecclesia de Migel (xii–xiii cent.).
DESCRIPTION. 7·2″ (18·2 cm.), Top, 6·9″ (17·5 cm.), Bottom × 4·4″ (11·2 cm.), L, 4·3″ (10·9 cm.), R. Foot formerly folded, with single slits for seal-tag. No tag or seal survives.
HAND. Scribe Ba. Unruled.
SOURCE. Original, NLS, MS. Adv. 15.1.18, no.3.
NOTE. [a] Comma.
COMMENT. Simon of Meigle appears as Simon son of Euard in *Coupar Angus Rental*, i, 343; the form of the father's name cannot be trusted. See also *Coupar Angus Chrs.*, i, no.16.

202 Confirms to the lepers of St Nicholas's Hospital, St Andrews, the two oxgangs of land in Powgavie (in Inchture), Perthshire, granted to them by Hugh Giffard, with pasture for 20 beasts and six horses. Crail. (1178 × 1185)

Willelmus[a] Dei gr*ati*a rex Scotorum omnibus probis hominibus tocius terre sue salutem. Sciatis me concessisse et hac carta mea confirmasse infirmis leprosis de Sancto Andrea illas duas bouatas terre in Polgawin quas Hugo Giffert in perpetuam elemosinam eis dedit cum pastura viginti animalium et sex equorum; tenendas ita libere et quiete, sicut carta ipsius Hugonis testatur et confirmant, saluo jure meo. Testibus Henrico[b] episcopo Sanctiandree, Dauid fratre meo, Phillippo de Valon*iis*, Thoma de Muscampo, Waltero de Berkell camerario. Apud Karell.

SOURCE. SRO, Registrum Magni Sigilli Regum Scotorum, Liber XXVII, no.222.
PRINTED. *RMS*, 1513–1546, no.2132 (3).
NOTES. [a] Punctuation editorial. [b] Sic; for Hugone.
COMMENT. Same date as preceding.

203 Grants to his clerk Hugh of Roxburgh the land of the *abthen* (*abbacia*) of (Old) Montrose, to be held of Arbroath Abbey for the term of Hugh's life, for a *reddendo* of three stones of wax yearly payable on 29 December. Clunie in Stormont. (1178)

W.[a] Dei gr*ati*a Rex Scotorum[b] . Episcopis . Abbatibus . Comitibus . Baron*ibus* . Justic*iis* . Vicec*omitibus* . et omnibus probis hominibus tocius terre sue salutem. Sciant presentes et futuri . me dedisse . & concessisse . et hac carta mea confirmasse . Hugoni de Rokisburg[c] clerico meo terram abbacie de Monros[d] . cum omnibus iustis pertinenciis suis . in terris . et aquis . pratis . et pascuis . moris . et ceteris omnibus . ad illam iuste adiacentibus . per rectas diuisas suas . ad tenend*um* de Deo . et de Sancto Thoma archipresule . et martire de Abirbr*othoc* . in liberam . et quietam elemosinam. Quare uolo ut prefatus Hugo . prenominatam terram . per rectas diuisas suas . ita libere . et quiete . et hono[e]rifice . omnibus diebus uite sue teneat & possideat . sicut ecclesia Sancti Thome . de Abirbrothoc . terram illam de me uel alias terras et tenuras suas . de me . et heredibus meis . liberius . & quiecius . in liberam et perpetuam elemosinam . tenent et possident. Reddendo inde singulis annis . ecclesie Sancti Thome de Abirbrothoc . ad festum Sancti Thome martyris .iii. petras cere. Test*ibus* Dauid fratre meo . M*atheo* episcopo[f] Aberdon*ensi* , Andr*ea* episcopo de Katen' . Comite Dunec*ano* . Com*ite* Gilleb*erto* . Ric*ardo* de Moreuill' constab*ulario* . Waltero de Berkel' Cam*erario* . Hugon*e* et Will*elmo* Capellanis meis . Hugone Giffard' . Ric*ardo* clerico. Apud Klonin'.

RUBRIC. Carta Willelmi Regis de terra Abbacie de Munros (red, *E*). Carta Reg*is* W. de terra abbacye de Munros' (red, *A*). .xcv. (in margin, *A*, *E*).
SOURCE. NLS, MS. Adv. 34.4.2, fo.lxviii^{r-v}=*A*. SRO, Northesk Muniments (uncatalogued), Ethie MS., fo.6^{r-v}=*E*. Printed here from *A*.
PRINTED. *Arbroath Liber*, i, no.95 (from *E*).
NOTES. [a] Initial red. [b] Scoltorum, *E*. [c] Rokesburc', *E*. [d] Munros, *E*. [e] Fo.lxviii^{v}, *A*. [f] de, *E*.
COMMENT. Hugh of Roxburgh was made chancellor of King William in 1189. 29 December was the anniversary of St. Thomas's martyrdom. Hugh the king's chaplain was made bishop of St Andrews in 1178; but there was another chaplain named Hugh officiating in the period 1178–88. Seen nos.225, 227.

204 Grants to William de la Hay Errol (Perthshire), in feu and heritage, with sake and soke, toll, team and infangthief, as freely as the king's other barons hold their fiefs, for the service of two knights. Clunie in Stormont. (1178 × 1182)

W'. Dei gratia Rex Scott' . Episcopis . Abbatibus . Comitibus . Baronibus . Justiciis . Vicecom*itibus* 7 Omnibus probis hominibus tocius terre sue clericis 7 laicis salutem. Sciant presentes 7 futuri me dedisse 7 Concessisse 7 hac carta mea confirmasse . Willelmo de Haia Herol per suas rectas diuisas cum omnibus iustis pertinentiis suis in bosco 7 plano pratis 7 pascuis moris 7 mareisis aquis 7 piscariis stagnis 7 molendinis . 7 ceteris aliis iustis pertinentiis. Tenend*um* sibi 7 heredibus suis de me 7 de heredibus meis in feudo 7 hereditate libere 7 quiete plenarie 7 honorifice . Cum sacca 7 Socca Cum thol 7 them 7 infangenthef per seruicium duorum militum. Quare uolo 7 firmiter precipio ut predictus Willelmus 7 heredes sui prenominatam terram teneant 7 possideant de me 7 de heredibus meis ita libere 7 quiete 7 honorifice 7 plenarie sicut alii barones mei liberius 7 quietius 7 honorificentius feuda sua de me tenent. Test*e* D*aui*d fratre meo 7 hoc idem concedente. Test*ibus* Hugon*e* episcopo Sancti Andre*e* . Com*ite* Wald*euo* . Com*ite* Dunec*ano* . Com*ite* Gileberto . Com*ite* Malc*olmo* . Ric*ardo* de Moruill' const*abulario* . Alano dapifero . Waltero Olif*ard* . Roberto de Quenci . Johanne de Vallibus . Waltero de Berkel' . Roberto de Berkel' . Rad*ulfo* de Ver . Ric*ardo* de Munfichet . Rob*erto* de Landeles . Hugone Ridel . Philippo de Valon*iis* . Roberto de Boseuill' . Apud CloNiN.

ENDORSED. . de Erol . (xiii cent.). Chartour of Erroll be William King of Scotts (xvi cent., faint). (Also modern endorsements, xviii and xix cent.).

DESCRIPTION. 9·3″ (23·7 cm.), Top and bottom × 4″ (10·2 cm.), L, R. Foot folded to a depth of 0·9″ (2·3 cm.). A tie has been cut off at top left-hand edge of fold; a seal-tag remains, 6·3″ (16 cm.) long, 0·8″ (2 cm.) wide, passing through single slits in foot and fold. No seal remains, but traces of green wax adhere to tag.
HAND. Scribe Aj (Richard of Lincoln). Unruled.
SOURCE. Original, Countess of Erroll, Erroll Charters, no.1.
PRINTED. *Spalding Misc.*, ii, 303, no.1.

205 Grants to his brother David the earldom of Lennox, and in addition, Lindores (Fife), Dundee, Longforgan, Pitmiddle (in Kinnaird, Perthshire), Newtyle (Angus), Morton beside Edinburgh, and, in Aberdeenshire, the lands of Garioch with the following places: Fintray, 'Rothiod', Inverurie, Monkeigie, Bourtie, Durno (in Chapel of Garioch), Oyne, Ardoyne; to be held in feu and heritage, with sake, soke, toll, team and infangthief, for the service of ten knights. Perth. (1178 × 1182, probably 1178)

W Dei gracia Rex Scott' Episcopis, Abbatibus, Com*itibus*, Baron*ibus*, Justiciar*iis*, vicecom*itibus*, prepositis, ministris et omnibus probis hominibus tocius terre sue, clericis et laicis, salutem. Sciant presentes et futuri me dedisse et concessisse et hac carta mea confirmasse Dauid fratri meo comitatum de Leuenaus, cum omnibus pertinenciis suis, et Lundors et Dunde et Forgrund et Petmothel et Neutyle et Fintrith et Rothiod et Inuerurin et Munkegyn et Boverdyn et Durnach et Uuen et Arduuen et Garuiach, et Mertonam que est in Laudon*ia* iuxta Castellum Puellarum. Volo itaque et precipio ut predictus Dauid frater meus et heredes sui de me et heredibus meis in feudo et hereditate teneant et possideant omnes terras istas prenominatas per rectas diuisas suas quas habuerunt quando illas ei dedi, et cum omnibus iustis pertinenciis suis, in bosco et plano, in terris et aquis, in pratis et pascuis, in molendinis et stangnis, in moris et maresiis, in viis et semitis, et omnibus aliis iustis pertinenciis suis tam non nominatis quam nominatis; cum sacca et socca, cum tol et tem, et infangenthef', bene et plenarie et honorifice, et ita libere et quiete in omnibus sicut ego ipse unquam terras illas tenui et possedi, faciendo inde mihi et heredibus meis seruicium decem militum. Test*ibus* H*ugone* Episcopo Sancti Andr*ee*, Jocel*ino* episcopo Glasg*uensi*, M*atheo* episcopo de Aberden, S*imone* episcopo Morau*iensi*, A*ndrea* episcopo Catenensi, Com*ite* Duncano, Com*ite* Gileberto, Com*ite* Waldevo, Malcolmo Com*ite* Ethol, G*illebrid* comite de Anegus, Com*ite* Colbano, Ricardo de Moreu*ille* Constabulario, Roberto de Quincy, Waltero Olif*ard*, Alano filio Walteri Senesc*allo*, Willelmo de Haya, Rad*ulfo* de Ver', Ric*ardo* de Munfichet, Willelmo de Lindesey, Malcolmo filio Com*itis* Dunc*ani*, Patricio filio Com*itis* Waldevi, Willelmo filio Ric*ardi* de Moreu*ille*, Rand*ulfo* de Sol*is*, apud Perth.

RUBRIC. Carta Comitis Dauid de Rege Willelmo (top right red).
SOURCE. Capt. R. F. Cuninghame of Caprington, Caprington Castle, Ayrshire, Cartulary of Lindores Abbey, fo.29^{r-v}.
PRINTED. *Lindores Chartulary*, no.1.
COMMENT. Earl David's tenure of Lennox was only temporary, probably during the minority of Earl Alwin who had an hereditary claim to the earldom. According to Jordan Fantôme, David was granted the earldom of Lennox in May, 1174, 'in the sight of the baronage' (i.e. at a great council), probably at Perth on the

occasion of Bishop Jocelin's election to the see of Glasgow (*Chron. Stephen*, iii, 296). Despite the fact that this charter seems to be at least four years later than the grant, Jordan's statement is too circumstantial to be dismissed as a slip. 'Rothiod', now lost, seems to have been the ancient mother-church of both Inverurie and Monkeigie, and is represented now by Polnar Chapel (St Apollinaris's Chapel) a mile and a half west of Inverurie.

206 Grants to Gilbert earl of Strathearn Kinveachy (in Duthil and Rothiemurchus), Inverness-shire, to be held heritably as freely as the earl holds the earldom of Strathearn. Perth. (1178 × 1185)

W'. Dei gr*atia* Rex Scott'. Episcopis. Abbatibus. Comitibus. baronibus. Justiciis. Vicecomitibus. Ministris. 7 Omnibus probis hominibus tocius terre sue salutem. Sciant presentes 7 futuri me dedisse 7 concessisse. 7 hac carta mea confirmasse Comit*i* Gileb*erto* de Stradhern. Kinbethach. per suas rectas diuisas. 7 cum omnibus iustis pertinenciis suis. Tendendu*m* sibi 7 heredibus suis. de me. 7 heredibus meis. ita libere. 7 quiete. sicut tenet[a] comitatum de Stradhern. Test*ibus* Hug*one* episcopo Sancti Andr*ee*. D*auid* fratre meo. Comit*e* Dunec*ano*. Comit*e* .G. de Anegus. Waltero de Berkel' Camerario. Johanne de Lundoniis. Rob*erto* de Berkel'. Malcolm' mac Gillis. Gillecristo mac inien Saműel. Gillemich*el* mac Dunec*an*. Gillecolm' Marescald*o*. Apud P[ert[b]]

ENDORSED. Carta de Kynbethach (xiv cent.). Lands of Kenbethach (xvii–xviii cent.). Kinbechach to Earl Gilbert of Strathearn (xviii cent.). Charter by K. William the Lyon of the Lands of Tullibardine[c] (xix cent.).
DESCRIPTION. 5·5″ (14 cm.), Top, 5·4″ (13·75 cm.), Bottom × 3·9″ (10 cm.), L, R. Foot folded, with single slit in centre for seal tag. A tag 0·6″ wide, remains, but has been cut away, probably with the seal on it, to leave only the two upper lengths, 2·2″ long. No seal is known to survive.
HAND. Scribe Al. Unruled.
SOURCE. Original, Duke of Atholl, Blair Castle, Athole Charters, vol.1, no.1.
PRINTED. Fraser, *Grant*, iii, 1, no.1 (with facsimile); see also *Fraser Facsimiles*, no.15; *Inchaffray Liber*, p.xxiii.
NOTES. [a] The scribe has apparently begun to write uice [comitatum], then erased ui and altered e to o. [b] Letters in brackets supplied conjecturally. The whole place-date has been carefully erased, and what appears to read Eustachio de Tayla rok filio uoeun Wa, evidently meaningless and in faded ink, has been added, at an indeterminate but scarcely modern date. [c] Last five words crossed out.
COMMENT. See no.474.

207 Grants to the monks of May Priory the liberty and free power of selling and buying whatever they have need to sell and buy for their own use throughout his land. They and their servants shall be free of cain, toll and all other custom on their own goods whenever they sell them or on goods for their own use whenever they buy them. Grants further 4d. from four nets of the fishing-boats which may put in at their ports of Pittenweem and Anstruther for the purpose of fishing or of selling fish, and likewise from boats fitted with rudders. The king reserves the cain from these ports, and commands that the teind of it shall be paid to the monks by his officers who collect it. Perth. (1178 × 1188)

W.[a] Dei gratia Rex Scott'[b] Justiciis[c], Vicecomitibus, Baronibus, Ministris et omnibus probis hominibus totius terre sue, salutem. Sciatis me dedisse et concessisse et hac carta mea confirmasse Priori de Mai et monachis ibidem Deo seruientibus licenciam et liberam potestatem vendendi et emendi quodcunque opus habent ad proprios usus suos per totam terram meam. Quare uolo et firmiter precipio ut ipsi et seruientes proprii domus sue de dominicis[d] catallis predictorum monachorum que vendiderint, et de omnibus que ad eorundem proprios usus emerint, sint liberi et quieti a Cano et theloneo et ab omni alia consuetudine ubicumque pro tali negocio venerint. Precipio etiam ut homines eorum alii in terra ipsorum manentes sint liberi et quieti a Cano et theloneo et omni alia consuetudine tantum in portibus terre ipsorum monachorum de vendicione et empcione. Concedo etiam ut quatuor d*enarios* habeant de quatuor retinaculis singularum nauium que in portibus suis de Pednewem et de Ainestroder causa piscandi vel piscem vendendi applicuerint, et de batell*is* similiter qui annexa habuerint gubernacula. Canum uero tantum de eisdem portibus ad opus meum retineo, et de Cano illo per manus ministrorum meorum ibidem canum suscipientium quemque decimum d*enarium* predictis monachis dari precipio. T*estibus* H*ugone* Episcopo Sancti Andr*ee*, Com*ite* Dunec*ano*, Com*ite* Gileb*erto*, W*altero* de Berkel' Camerar*io*, Willelmo de Mortem*er*, Galfrido de Maleu'[e]. Apud Pert.

TITLE. Carta Regis Willelmi de libertate tolnei et consuetudinis.[f] Carta Regis Willelmi de licencia emendi et vendendi[f].
SOURCE. PRO, C.53/93, rot.14 (Charter Roll, 35 Edward I) = *C. May Recs.*, pp.cxii–cxiii = *M* (Titles only).
PRINTED. *May Recs.*, no.14 (from *C*, with wrong heading: De acquietacione Cani et Tolnei).
NOTES. [a] Willelmus, *May Recs.*, no.14. [b] Scotie, ibid. [c] Justiciariis, ibid. [d] dominiis, ibid. [e] Malever, ibid. [f] Titles from *M* only, nos.8 and 42.
COMMENT. See no.94.

208 Grants to Cambuskenneth Abbey four acres of arable in Forteviot and one toft and croft for the abbey's buildings. Perth. (1178 × 1188)

Wilelmus[a] Dei gracia Rex Scotorum episcopis, abbatibus, comitibus, baronibus, justic*iis*, vicecomitibus, prepositis, ministris et omnibus probis hominibus totius terre sue, clericis et laicis, salutem. Sciant presentes et futuri me dedisse et concessisse et hac carta mea confirmasse Deo et ecclesie Sancte Marie de Striueling et canonicis ibidem Deo seruientibus quatuor acras terre in Fortheuiet, et unum toftum et croftum ad edificia sua facienda; tenendas eis in liberam et perpetuam elemosinam ita libere et quiete, plenarie et honorifice, sicut alias elemosinas suas liberius, quietius, plenius et honorificentius tenent. Testibus, Hugone episcopo Sanctiandree, Comite[b] Dunecano iustic*ia*, G*ilberto* comite de Strathern', Alano dapifero, Geruasio Auenell, Waltero de Werk[c] camerario, Rannulfo de Sol', W. de Lascelis, Roberto de Wilt*un*, apud Perth.

RUBRIC. Donatio quatuor acrarum terre in Forteuiet per regem Willelmum (at foot of fo.66^{v}). Concordat cum principali Jacobus Foulis (at end).
SOURCE. NLS, MS. Adv. 34.1.2, fo.67^{r}.
PRINTED. *Cambuskenneth Registrum*, no.101.
NOTES. [a] Large red initial U. [b] MS. inserts de. [c] Sic, for Berk[eley].

COMMENT. W. de Lascelis was probably Walter de Lascelles, father of Alan (II) de Lascelles whose charter granting St Andrews priory two acres of arable in Naughton is given in *St Andrews Liber*, 274–5.

209 Confirms to Walkelin his brewer the land of Inverpeffer (in Panbride), Angus, to be held of Arbroath Abbey in feu and heritage as the charter of that land bears witness. Perth. (1178 × 1195)

W.[a] Dei gracia Rex Scotorum Omnibus probis hominibus tocius terre sue clericis et laicis salutem. Sciant presentes et futuri me concessisse et hac carta mea confirmasse Walkelyno braciatori meo et heredibus suis terram de Inuerpefir per rectas diuisas suas , cum omnibus iustis pertinenciis suis in bosco et plano , in pratis et pascuis in aquis et in omnibus aliis rectis pertinenciis suis. Tenendam sibi et heredibus suis de monachis ecclesie Sancti Thome martiris de Abirbr*othoc* in feodo et hereditate ita libere et quiete, plenarie et honorifice, sicut carta de terra illa eidem data testatur et confirmat, saluo seruicio meo. Test*ibus* Comite Dunecan*o*, Com*ite* Gilberto, Roberto de Quensy , W. de Lyndes' , Roberto de Lundon*iis* fil*io* Regis , Willelmo de Haya ,[b] Ranulpho de Sulis , Willelmo Gyfard' , Waltero Murdac , Eustachio Papedy , Rogerio de Wyltona. Apud Perth'.[c]

RUBRIC. Carta de Inuerpefir' (red).
SOURCE. NLS, MS. Adv. 34.4.2, fos.xi^{v}–xii^{r}.
PRINTED. *Arbroath Liber*, i, no.[233].
NOTES. [a] Red initial. Punctuation editorial. [b] Fo.xii^{r}. [c] letters spaced widely evidently to simulate original.
COMMENT. The 'Laws of Malcolm Mackenneth' include a brewer among the household officers along with a baker, master cook and lardiner (*APS*, i, 710).

210 Grants to Bishop Jocelin and his successors one full toft in his burgh of Montrose, viz. that held by his predecessor Ingram. Montrose. (1175 × *c.*1180, probably *c.*1178)

W'. Dei gr*ati*a Rex Scott'[a] . omnibus probis hominibus totius terre sue clericis et laicis .' Salutem. Sciant[b] presentes et posteri me dedisse et concessisse et hac carta mea confirmasse Jocel*ino*[c] episcopo Glasguen*si*[d] et successoribus suis unum plenarium toftum in burgo meo de Munros . scilicet illud .' quod Eng*elramus*[c] antecessor suus tenuit . tenendum sibi et successoribus suis in liberam et perpetuam elemosinam ita libere et quiete .' sicut alias elemosinas suas liberius et quietius tenet et possidet. Test*ibus* Andrea episcopo Katen*ensi*[e] . T*urpino* Electo de BrechiN . Com*ite* Dunecan . Com*ite* Gilleberto . Waltero Olif*ard* . Waltero de Berchel'[f] . Willelmo de Lindesei[g]. Apud Munros.

RUBRIC. C. Willelmi R.[h] De uno tofto in burgo de Munros (in margin, *A*, in later hand). Ex autograph et fo.4^{a} Vet. Cart. Gl.[i]
DESCRIPTION. Original not described in *B*, which, however, gives this note of the seal: 'Huic Carte appensum est Sigillum magnum eiusdem Regis fere integrum, exhibens ex una parte Regem W. Equestrem, ex altera sedente in solio, inscriptum utrinque *Willelmus Deo Rectore Rex Scottorum.*'
SOURCE. Blairs Archives, 16 Drummond Place, Edinburgh, MS. Registrum Vetus of Glasgow, fo.iiij^{r-v}=*A*. Earl of Dalhousie, Brechin Castle, MS. copy of Glasgow Registrum Vetus and certain original charters, collated, p.14=*B*. Printed here from *A*, with more important variants of *B* noted.
PRINTED. *Glasgow Registrum*, no.33 (from *A*).

NOTES. [a] Scot', *B*. [b] Fo.iiij[v], *A*. [c] Name in full, *B*. [d] Glasg$_{ns}$, *B*. [e] Katten', *B*, with Katen written over. [f] k substituted for ch, *B*, with Berkel written over. [g] i substituted for ei, *B*. [h] Only in *B*. [i] In margin, *B* only.

211 Confirms to James of Perth Rossie (in Inchture), Perthshire, granted to him in feu and heritage by Walter the prior and the convent of St Andrews Cathedral Priory, together with the patronage of the church, and with the mill, as the charter of the prior and convent bears witness. Forfar. (1178 × 1188)

.W. Dei gr*ati*a Rex Scott' Omnibus hominibus tocius terre sue Clericis 7 laicis sal*utem*. Sciant presentes 7 posteri me concessisse 7 hac mea Carta confirmasse Jacobo de Pert . 7 heredibus suis Rosin Clerac cum omnibus pertinentiis 7 libertatibus suis ad eandem uillam pertinentibus . 7 cum donacione Ecclesie cum molendino cum pratis 7 pascuis 7 omnibus aisiamentis que ibidem haberi possunt tenend*um* sibi 7 heredibus suis de priore .W. 7 conuentu Sancti Andr*ee* in feudo 7 hereditate ita libere 7 quiete ex omni seruitio 7 consuetudine sicut Carta prioris .W. 7 conuentus Sancti Andr*ee* ei testatur 7 confirmat. T*estibus* Hug*one* episcopo . Dunek*ano* Comite . Walt*ero* de Berkel' . Adam de Syreis . [ ][a] apud Forfar.

ENDORSED. de Rossiclerach' (xiii cent.).
DESCRIPTION. 5·7″ (14·5 cm.), Top and bottom × 2″ (5·1 cm.), L, R. Tongue and tie both cut off at their roots, but separately preserved, measuring 4·4″ (11·2 cm.) long and, respectively, 0·5″ (1·3 cm.) and 0·2″ (0·5 cm.) wide. Seal preserved on tongue, natural, varnished brown; only a small central fragment remains, 1·5″ (5·8 cm.) in diameter.
HAND. Scribe Cd. Unruled.
SOURCE. Original, Countess of Erroll, Erroll Charters no.3.
PRINTED. *Spalding Misc.*, ii, 318, no.XXIV.
NOTE. [a] Name obscured by staining.
COMMENT. Prior Walter's charter is printed *Spalding Misc.*, ii, 318, no.XXIII. It was evidently copied into the lost Great Register of St Andrews (cf. *St Andrews Liber*, p.xxx, no.72). For James son of Simon of Perth, one of the king's provosts of Perth, cf. no.415, and for James's heir Duncan cf. *Spalding Misc.*, ii, 317; *Cal. Papal Letters*, i, 74.

212 Quitclaims to Simon (de Toeni), bishop of Moray, Aulon Macbele. Aberdeen. (1173 × 1184)

.Will'. Dei gratia Rex Scott' omnibus probis hominibus tocius terre salutem. Sciatis me quietum clamasse Simoni episcopo Morau*iensi* et successoribus suis Aulon Macbele de me et heredibus meis. Test*ibus* Rob*erto* de Quinci . Philippo de Valon*iis*. Apud Aberdon'.

RUBRIC. Ista non scribitur in libro decani (top, in later hand). Ista non scribitur (margin).
SOURCE. NLS, MS. Adv. 34.4.10, fo.xxxviii[r].
PRINTED. *Moray Registrum*, no.4.
COMMENT. The king made northern expeditions in 1179 and (?) 1181.

213 Grants that his burgesses of Inverness shall be free for all time of toll and customs throughout his land, and forbids anyone, on pain of his full forfeiture, to demand toll or custom on the burgesses' own chattels. Forbids anyone to buy or sell within that burgh or to trade within that sheriffdom outwith the burgh unless he be a burgess or stall-holder of that burgh or do it by permission of the burgesses. Grants also to the burgesses for the support of the burgh the land outwith the burgh called the Burgh Haugh, between the hill and the River Ness, so that no one is to cultivate that land or use it for pasture without the burgesses' leave. The burgesses have made agreement with the king that when he has made a ditch round the burgh they will enclose the whole burgh by a stout palisade upon the ditch and, once this is made, will maintain it and always keep it strong and complete. Auldearn. (1173 × 1190, perhaps 1179)

W. Dei gr*ati*a Rex Scott'. Omnibus Probis Hominibus totius Terre sue . Clericis 7 Laicis salutem. Sciant Presentes 7 futuri me omnes Burgenses meos de Inuernis quietos Clamasse omni Tempore a Tolneio 7 omni Consuetudine per totam Terram meam. Quare Prohibeo firmiter Ne quis ab eis de eorum dominicis Catallis Tolneium aut aliquam Consuetudinem exigat . super meam Plenariam forisfacturam. Prohibeo etiam Ne quis emat aut vendat in Burgo illo . aut in vicecomitatu illo extra Burgum aliquam Mercaturam exerceat .ʼ nisi fuerit Burgensis aut Stalagarius eiusdem Burgi . aut per grantum Burgensium hoc fecerit. Dedi etiam 7 Concessi predictis Burgensibus ad sustentamentum Burgi Terram illam que est extra Burgum . que vocatur Burchhaleu scilicet que est inter Montem 7 Aquam . Ita quod nullus in ea Wannagium faciat . aut pasturam habeat .ʼ nisi per eorum Licentiam. Burgenses uero uniuersi mihi conuentionauerunt quod cum circa predictum Burgum fossatum fecero .ʼ ipsi super fossatum totum Burgum claudent bono palitio . 7 exquo clausum fuerit .ʼ palitium illud sustentabunt . 7 semper bonum 7 integrum conseruabunt. Test*ibus* M*atheo* Episcopo Aberdoenn' Comite Dunec*ano* Justic*ia* . Ric*ardo* de Moreuill' . Const*abulario* . Waltero Olif*ard* . Philippo de Vallon*iis* . Hugone Giff*ard* . Rogero de Vallon*iis* . Roberto de Berk' . Apud EREN.

ENDORSED. No endorsement known.
DESCRIPTION[1]. 7·3″ (18·7 cm.), Top, 7″ (17·8 cm.), Bottom × 5·6″ (14 cm.), L, R. Foot folded to a depth of 0·8″ (2 cm.); seal-tag, 0·6″ (1·5 cm.), wide, passes through single slits in foot and fold. Fragment of seal shewn in facsimile.
HAND. Scribe Ba. Unruled.
SOURCE. *APS*, i, facsimile facing p.88. When this facsimile was made, the original was evidently still in the Inverness Burgh Muniments.
PRINTED. *APS*, i, 88b, with facsimile facing.
[1] The dimensions given are those of the facsimile, which is probably actual size, or nearly so.
COMMENT. This act is to be connected with King William's military activity in Moray and Ross, 1179–1187. Bishop Matthew was in exile for part of the years 1180–1181.

214

Confirms to Melrose Abbey the land in the territory of Clifton (in Morebattle, Roxburghshire) granted by Walter of Windsor. Perth. (1173 × 1185)

W'. Dei gr*ati*a Rex Scott' . Episcopis . Abbatibus . Comitibus . Baronibus . Justiciis . Vicecomit*ibus* . Prepositis . Ministris . 7 omnibus probis hominibus totius terre sue . Salutem. Sciant presentes 7 posteri me dedisse . 7 hac mea carta confirmasse Deo 7 Ęcclesie Sancte Marie de

Melros 7 Monachis ibidem Deo seruientibus illam terram quam tenent in territorio de Cliftuna per ipsas diuisas que continentur in Carta Walteri de Windlesoure . quam habent de eo de Eadem terra . ita ut quicquid infra easdem diuisas fuerit . habeant 7 possideant in perpetuum . ita 7[a] libere 7 quiete . honorifice 7 pacifice .' sicut aliqua elemosina liberius . quietius . 7 honorificentius in regno meo possidetur. Dedi enim eis 7 confirmaui eam liberam ab omnibus auxiliis . Placitis . Geldis . Scutagiis . Cornagiis . 7 ab omni seruitio 7 Consuetudine 7 Exactione seculari . ita quod ego 7 heredes mei manutenebimus 7 Warantizabimus eam illis Contra omnes homines in perpetuum . saluo seruitio meo. de Waltero 7 heredibus suis. Teste D*aui*d fratre meo . Comite Dunecano . Com*ite* Gilberto . Willelmo de Lindesaie . Rogero 7 Philippo de Valoniis . Waltero de Berchel' . Johanne de Londoniis. APUD PERT

ENDORSED. Confirmatio Will*elm*i Reg*is* de terra de Clift' (xii cent.). D (red, xv cent. ?). J. Scott (xvi cent.).
DESCRIPTION. 8·4″ (21·3 cm.), Top, 8·1″ (20·5 cm.), Bottom × 6·7″ (17 cm.), L, 6·3″ (16 cm.), R. Foot folded to a depth of 1·2″ (3 cm.). Double slits with tag 6·5″ (16 cm.) long, 0·9″ (2·2 cm.) wide. Seal almost complete in red wax; moderately clear impression.
HAND. Scribe Ab. Ruled in ink.
SOURCE. Original, SRO, GD 55/117.
PRINTED. *Melrose Liber*, no. 117.
NOTE. [a] sic.
COMMENT. For Walter of Windsor cf. W. Percy Hedley, 'The sons of Halden, lord of Catterlen', in *CWAAS Transactions*, New Series, lxiv.

215 Grants to Glasgow Cathedral Church and to (its tenants) Orm of Ashkirk and his heirs that Orm, his heirs, and their men of Ashkirk, Selkirkshire, may have pasture rights in the direction of the king's forest and within the forest, as King Malcolm IV caused it to be perambulated for them and as King William caused it to be recited by his constable Richard de Moreville and other responsible men who were present at the first perambulation. The marches are as follows: from 'Staniford' (at Synton Mill?) to the cross, from the cross to the big alder tree beside the peat-moss, thence to 'Illieslade', thence to the little burn to the east of Huntly, and from that burn up as far as the burn of Akermoor (Blindhaugh Burn), thence up to the hunting-station of Richard Cumin, thence up to the sike next below Todrig, thence to the sike which flows into the Langhope Burn, thence as the march runs to the west of Leap Hill to the Ale Water, between Ashkirk and Whitslaid. Grants also that they may plough, sow and cultivate everywhere within the fence which was erected on the day this charter was made, Sunday next before the feast of SS. Simon and Jude next after the king of France first came to England to visit the shrine of Saint Thomas (of Canterbury); no one is to offer them injury or violence in their pasture or tillage. Selkirk. (21 October, 1179)

Will*elmu*s Dei gr*ati*a Rex Scottorum Episcopis Abbatibus Com*itibus* Baron*ibus* Justic*iis* . vicecom*itibus* prepositis ministris et omnibus probis hominibus[a] tocius terre sue clericis et laicis salutem. Sciant presentes et futuri me concessisse et hac carta mea confirmasse Deo et ecclesie

Glasg*uensi* et Ormo de Askirke et heredibus suis de me et heredibus meis in feodo et hereditate ut predictus Ormus et heredes sui et eorum homines de Askirke habeant pasturam suam uersus forestam meam . et in foresta ita bene et plenarie sicut M*alcolmus* Rex frater meus illam eis perambulare fecit . et sicut ego per Ricardum de Moreuill' constabularium meum et alios probos homines meos qui predicte perambulationi interfuerunt illam perambulacionem eis feci recitare[b] . scilicet a Staniford usque ad Crucem et a Cruce usque ad magnam aln*um*[c] iuxta Turberam et inde usque ad Illieslade . et inde usque ad paruum Riuulum in orientali parte de Huntleie . et de illo Riuulo sursum usque in Riuulum de Akermere . et de sic sursum usque ad Wenelaciam Ricardi Cumin et sic deinde sursum ad sicum quod est propinquius sub Todholerig' . et sic ab illo sico usque ad sicum quod vadit in Riuulum de Langhope et deinde sicut diuisa vadit in occidentali parte de Lepes inter Askirke et Whiteslade in Alne. Concedo etiam eis ut ubique infra sepem que facta fuit circa eorum Wainagia die qua hec carta facta fuit scilicet Dominica proxima ante festum Simonis et Jude proximum postquam Rex Francorum primo venit in Angliam ad Sanctum Thomam . liceat eis arare et seminare et Waynagia facere . et prohibeo firmiter ne quis eis de predicta pastura siue waynagio iniuriam aut aliquam violenciam inferat. Test*ibus* D*aui*d fratre meo . Com*ite* Wald*euo* . Ricardo de Moreuill' const*abulario* . Roberto de Quinci . Waltero de Berk' Camerario . Alano Dapifero . Waltero Olif*ard* . Hug*one* Ridel' . Rob*erto* de Berk' . Willelmo de Haia . apud Selsch'.

RUBRIC. Pro Pastura de Askirk' uersus forestam (in margin fo.liiij^{r}).
SOURCE. Blairs Archives, 16 Drummond Place, Edinburgh, MS. Registrum Vetus of Glasgow, fo.liiij^{r-v}.
PRINTED. *Glasgow Registrum*, no.30.
NOTES. [a] Fo.liiij^{v}. [b] reiustare, MS. [c] The context clearly distinguishes this word from the river-name Alne.
COMMENT. King Louis VII visited Canterbury from 22 to 26 August, 1179. The marches here described seem to follow the modern boundary of Ashkirk parish as far as Langhope. The final section is identical with the final section of the marches in no.145 above, witnessed by Richard Cumin at Traquair. The reference to Richard Cumin's hunting station is interesting; it suggests that he may have held the office of keeper of the royal forest, to which a descendant, William son of John Cumin, was appointed in 1292 by Edward I of England (*Rotuli Scotiae*, i, 5, 7).

216 Grants to Glasgow Cathedral Church and Bishop Jocelin that toft at Dumfries which is between the ancient fortification and the (parish) church, i.e. from the fortification as far as the churchyard. Selkirk. (1179 × 1185, probably 1179)

W'. Dei gr*ati*a Rex Scott' . Episcopis\Abbatibus/Comitibus . Baronibus . Justiciis . vicecomitibus . ministris et omnibus probis hominibus totius terre sue clericis et laicis Salutem. Sciant presentes et futuri me dedisse et concessisse et hac carta mea confirmasse Deo et ecclesie Glasgue*nsi* et Jocelino episcopo et eius successoribus . toftum illud apud Dunfres que est inter uetus castellarium et ecclesiam . scilicet a castellario usque ad cimiterium ecclesie plenarie tenend*um* in liberam et perpetuam elemosinam . ita libere et quiete plenarie et honorifice . sicut alias tenuras suas liberius quietius plenius et honorificentius tenet[a] . Test*ibus* D*aui*d fratre meo . Abbate E*rnaldo* de Malr*os* . Ric*ardo* de Moruill' Constab*ulario* . Waltero de Berkel' Camerar*io* . Philippo de Valu*n*[b] . Apud Seleschirch'.

RUBRIC. C. Willelmi R.[c] De uno tofto apud Dunfres[d] (in margin, *A*, in later hand). Ex autographo et f 4[b] Vet. Car.[e]
DESCRIPTION. Original not described in *B*, which, however, has a note on the seal: 'Sigillum ex cera viridi ut supra,' referring to the note to no.210.
SOURCE. Blairs Archives, 16 Drummond Place, Edinburgh, MS. Registrum Vetus of Glasgow, fo.iiij[v] = *A*. Earl of Dalhousie, Brechin Castle, MS. copy of Glasgow Registrum Vetus together with certain original charters, collated, pp.15–16 = *B*.
PRINTED. *Glasgow Registrum*, no.50.
NOTES. [a] tenent, *B*. [b] Valon, *B*. [c] *B* only. [d] Instead of apud, *B* has in burgo de. [e] In margin, *B* only.
COMMENT. For the date cf. no.215.

217 Quitclaims to Glasgow Cathedral Church and Bishop Jocelin and his successors Gillemachoi of Kinclaith with his children and all his dependents. Selkirk. (1175 × 1190)

Will*elmus* Dei gratia Rex Scottorum omnibus probis hominibus tocius terre sue salutem. Sciatis me concessisse et quietum clamasse de me et de heredibus meis Deo et ecclesie Sancti Kentegerni de Glasg*u* et episcopo Jocel*ino* suisque successoribus inperpetuum . Gillemachoi de Conglud . cum liberis suis et tota eius secta . que de ratione eum sequi debuerint. Quare prohibeo firmiter ne quis Balliuorum meorum inpediat quin eos libere habere possint. Test*ibus* Ricardo de Moruille const*abulario* . Roberto de Quenci . Waltero Olif*ard* . apud Selekirke.

RUBRIC. Concessio de Gillemakoy et[a] Conclud (in margin).
SOURCE. Blairs Archives, 16 Drummond Place, Edinburgh, MS. Registrum Vetus of Glasgow, fo.liij[v].
PRINTED. Glasgow Registrum, no.34.
NOTE. [a] Sic.
COMMENT. Gillemachoi ('devotee of Saint Mungo') was evidently a neyf dwelling at Kinclaith or Glasgow Green; it is not clear what claim the king had on him, since the land had been granted to Glasgow Cathedral church by Malcolm IV (*RRS*, i, no.265). For the linguistic aspects of the name, cf. K. Jackson in *Studies in the early British church* (ed. N. Chadwick, 1958), 298–303, esp. 302.

218 Confirms generally the lands, churches and other property granted to Paisley Priory (afterwards Abbey) by Walter son of Alan I, the steward, as his charter bears witness. Selkirk. (1179 × 1190)

Wilelmus Dei gratia rex Scotorum episcopis, abbatibus, comitibus, baronibus, justiciariis, vicecomitibus,[a] prepositis, ministris et omnibus probis hominibus tocius terre sue, clericis et laicis, Francis et Angliis, Scotis, Galwidiensibus, salutem. Sciant presentes et futuri me in liberam et perpetuam elemosinam concessisse et hac carta mea confirmasse Deo et ecclesie de Passelet et priori et monachis ibidem Deo servientibus et in posterum servituris omnes terras illas et ecclesias, ceterasque possessiones et rectitudines et libertates quas Walterus filius Alani dapifer meus eisdem monachis imperpetuam[b] elemosinam dedit et concessit et carta sua confirmavit: tenendas ita libere et quiete et pacifice sicut eis testatur carta predicti Walteri, et sicut alique elemosine in terra mea liberius, quietius, melius et pacificencius tenentur et possidentur; excepta illa carrucata terre quam Ricardus capellanus tenuit in Hastenesd*en*, quam ipsi ubique remiserunt et imperpetuum quietam clamaverunt, quando ego unam carrucatam terre eis in eadem villa dedi, quam scilicet Ernaldus[c] abbas Melross et Philippus de Valoniis[d] et Walterus Corb*et* vicecomes[e] meus precepto meo eis thradiderunt.[b] Testibus Ricardo de Morevill constabulario, Alano dapifero, Wilelmo de Morevill, Waltero de Berk' camerario, Waltero Corb*et*, Bernardo filio Brieni, Adam de Stanford', Herberto de Macceswell', Wilelmo Passelew, apud Selesch'.

RUBRIC. Confirmatio Wilelmi regis Scotie de toto (at top).
SOURCE. NLS, MS. Adv. 34.4.14, fo.lii^{v}.
PRINTED. *Paisley Registrum*, 89.
NOTES. [a] MS., vicecomitatibus. [b] Sic. [c] MS., Eraddus. [d] MS., Wallais. [e] MS., vicarius.

219 Grants to Paisley Priory (afterwards Abbey) one ploughgate of arable in Hassendean (Huntlaw, in Minto, Roxburghshire), of which it was given sasine at the king's command by Abbot Arnold of Melrose, Philip de Valognes and Walter Corbet the king's sheriff; with a dwelling house free of multure at the king's mill; in exchange for another ploughgate in the same *manerium* which was held by Richard the chaplain, granted by Walter son of Alan when he held Hassendean. Selkirk. (1179 × 1189)

Wilelmus Dei gratia rex Scottorum episcopis, abbatibus, comitibus, baronibus,[a] justiciariis, vicecomitibus,[b] prepositis, ministris et omnibus probis hominibus tocius terre sue, clericis et laicis, salutem. Sciant presentes et futuri me dedisse et concessisse et hac carta mea confirmasse Deo et ecclesie de Passelet et monachis ibidem Deo servientibus unam carrucatam terre in Hastenesden', illam scilicet quam Ernaldus[c] abbas Melrosensis et Philippus de Valon*iis* et Walterus Corbet vicecomes meus eis precepto meo tradiderunt, cum communi pastura in eadem villa quantum ad unam carrucatam terre pertinet; tenendam in liberam et perpetuam elemosinam ita libere, quiete, plenarie et honorifice sicut alias terras et tenuras suas liberius, quiecius, plenius et honorificencius tenent. Concessi eciam eis [ut][d] dominicam domum suam quietam habeant de multura ad molendinum meum. Et quando terram istam eis dedi, remiserunt et quietam clamaverunt imperpetuum illam carrucatam terre que fuit Ricardi capellani, quam Walterus filius Alani in eodem manerio eis dederat quamdiu in manu sua fuit. Testibus Ricardo de Morvill constabilario, Alano filio Walteri dapifero, Waltero Corbet, Wilelmo de Morvill, Waltero de Berk' camerario, Adam de Standfort, Herberto de Maxwell, apud Selschirch.

RUBRIC. Confirmatio Wilelmi regis de terra Hestennesden (at top).
SOURCE. NLS, MS. Adv. 34.4.14, fo.clv^{v}.
PRINTED. *Paisley Registrum*, 254–5.
NOTES. [a] MS., baronis. [b] MS., vicecomitatibus. [c] MS., Edwardus. [d] MS. omits. *Paisley Registrum* prints quoniam.
COMMENT. Walter son of Alan I had held Hassendean since 1161 (*RRS*, i, no.184); it seems to have returned to the Crown after his death. The ploughgate then given in exchange was called Huntlaw (for 'Hunreberie' in *Paisley Registrum*, 411, read 'Hunteleie'; cf. *OPS*, i, 320).

220 Confirms to Paisley Priory (afterwards Abbey) the churches of Cathcart (Glasgow, formerly Renfrewshire) and Carmunnock (Lanarkshire). Traquair. (1177 × 1185)

Wilelmus Dei gratia rex Scotorum episcopis, abbatibus, comitibus, baronibus, justiciariis, vicecomitibus, prepositis, ministris et omnibus probis hominibus tocius terre sue, clericis et laicis, salutem. Sciant presentes et futuri me concessisse et hac carta mea confirmasse Deo et ecclesie Sancti Mirini de Passelet et monachis ibidem Deo servientibus ecclesiam de Catkert et ecclesiam de Cormannoc, cum terris et decimis et omnimodis oblationibus, et cum omnibus aliis ad predictas ecclesias juste pertinentibus; tenendam[a] in liberam et perpetuam elemosinam, ita libere et quiete, plenarie et honorifice, sicut alias elemosinas suas liberius, quiecius, plenius et honorificencius tenent. Testibus David fratre meo, Ricardo de Morevill constabulario, Roberto de Quinci, Alano dapifero meo, Waltero Oliphart, Philippo de Vallon*ii*s, Rogerio de Vallon*ii*s, Roberto de Berk', Bernardo filio Brien', apud Trauequair.

RUBRIC. Confirmatio de Catkert et Cormannoc per Wilelmum regem Scotorum (at top).
SOURCE. NLS, MS. Adv. 34.4.14, fo.lxiii[v].
PRINTED. *Paisley Registrum*, 106.
NOTE. [a] Sic.
COMMENT. The church of Cathcart was granted by Walter son of Alan I, that of Carmunnock by Henry son of Anselm, otherwise Henry of Carmunnock (cf. *Paisley Registrum*, 5, 105–6).

221 Grants to Paisley Priory (afterward Abbey) the church of Rutherglen. Traquair. (1177 × 1185)

Wilelmus Dei gratia rex Scotorum episcopis, abbatibus, comitibus, baronibus, justiciariis, vicecomitibus, prepositis, ministris et omnibus probis hominibus tocius terre sue, clericis et laicis, salutem. Sciant presentes et futuri me dedisse et concessisse et hac carta mea confirmasse Deo et ecclesie Sancti Mirini de Passelet et monachis ibidem Deo servientibus ecclesiam de Ruthglen, cum terris et decimis et omnimodis oblationibus, et cum omnibus aliis ad predictam ecclesiam juste pertinentibus; tenen[a]dam in liberam et perpetuam elemosinam, ita libere et quiete, plenarie et honorifice, sicut alias elemosinas suas liberius, quietius, plenius et honorificencius tenent. Testibus David fratre meo, Ricardo de Morvill constabulario, Roberto de Quinci, Alano dapifero meo, Waltero Oliphart, Philippo de Valon*ii*s, Rogerio de Valon*ii*s, Roberto de Berk', Bernardo filio Brien', Simone filio Melbech, apud Trauequair.

RUBRIC. Donatio et concessio ecclesie de Ruthglen per Wilelmum regem Scotorum (at top).
SOURCE. NLS, MS. Adv. 34.4.14, fos.lxiii[v]–lxiiii[r].
PRINTED. *Paisley Registrum*, 106–7. NOTE. [a] Fo.lxiiii[r].

222 Grants to Coupar Angus Abbey two measured ploughgates of arable in the territory of Rattray, Perthshire, adjacent to the monks' land, measured by Earl Duncan the justiciar and other responsible men, by the king's command. Kinross. (1177 × 1204, probably × 1180)

Carta predicti regis Willielmi de duabus carrucatis[a] terræ mensuratis[b] in territorio de Rettrefe iuxta terram ipsorum monachorum de Cupro quas Comes Duncanus justicia mea ceterique probi homines mei precepto[c] eis mensurauerunt, &c. Testibus: Comite Duncano justiciario, Alano Dapifero, Heugone Giffard, Radulpho Veir, Gervasio Anveill[d], Valtero Bercklay Camerario, Philipo marischallo, Radulpho Nano. Apud Kinros.

SOURCE. NLS, MS. Adv. 33.2.9, fo.28r.
PRINTED. *Coupar Angus Rental*, i, 324–5, no.13.
NOTES. [a] duas carrucatas, MS. [b] mensuratas, MS. [c] Supply meo. [d] Sic; read Auenel.

223 Grants to Arbroath Abbey, after the death of Andrew bishop of Caithness, 'Achinglas', Dunnichen and Kingoldrum, Angus. Stirling. (1178 × 1180)

W.[a] Dei gr*ati*a Rex Scott' , omnibus probis hominibus tocius terre sue, clericis & laicis , salutem. Sciant presentes & posteri me dedisse , concessisse et hac carta mea confirmasse Deo & ecclesie Sancti Thome de Aberbroth' . & monachis ibidem Deo seruientibus , post decessum Andr*ee* episcopi Katenensis , Achinglas et Dunechtyn[b] et Kyngoldrum[c], per earundem terrarum rectas diuisas, in bosco et plano , in terris et aquis , in pratis et pascuis , in moris et mar[d]resiis , in stagnis et molendinis et omnibus aliis iustis pertinenciis suis . Tenend*as* in liberam et perpetuam elemosinam , ita libere et quiete , plenarie et honorifice , sicut alias elemosinas suas liberius , quiecius , plenius et honorificencius tenent. Test*ibus* *M*at*heo* episcopo Abirdon*ensi* , Comit*e* Gilberto , J*ohanne* abbate de Kalcou, Waltero Archidiacono de Sancto Andrea , Waltero Olif*ard* , Nessyo fil*io* Willelmi , Waltero de Berkelay Camerario , Willelmo de Lindes' , Roberto de Berkel' . Apud Striuelyn.

RUBRIC. Carta .W. Regis de Achinglas et Dunectin et Kingold' (red, *E*). Carta Reg*is* .W. de Achineglas et Dunechtyn et Kingold*rum* (red, *A*). iiij (in margin, *A*, *E*).
SOURCE. NLS, MS. Adv. 34.4.2, fo.xliir–v = *A*. SRO, Northesk Muniments (uncatalogued), Ethie MS., fo.2r = *E*. Printed here from *A*.
PRINTED. *Arbroath Liber*, i, no.4 (from *E*).
NOTES. [a] Red initial. Punctuation editorial. [b] Dunectin, *E*. [c] Kingoudrum, *E*. [d] Fo.xliiv, *A*.
COMMENT. These three shires were evidently part of the extensive property of Bishop Andrew, who died in 1184. 'Achinglas', now lost, was in Arbroath and St Vigeans parish, and seems to be the Achnaglis mentioned in *Retours* (Forfar), no.154. It marched with Kinblethmont, one point on the boundary being Magungie (*Arbroath Liber*, i, no.228). This act may be of earlier date than the Arbroath 'foundation charter', no.197 above, q.v.

224 Grants to Arbroath Abbey one net on the king's water at Perth called 'Stok'. Montrose. (1178 × 1184)

W.[a] Dei gr*ati*a Rex Scott' , Episcopis , Abbatibus , comitibus , Baronibus , Justiciar*iis* , Vicecomitibus , ministris et omnibus probis hominibus tocius terre sue , clericis et laicis , salutem. Sciant presentes et futuri me dedisse, concessisse et hac carta mea confirmasse Deo et ecclesie Sancti Thome de Aberbruthoch' et monachis ibidem Deo seruientibus . unum rethe super aquam meam de Pert que uocatur Stok',[b] tenend*um* in perpetuam elemosinam ita libere et quiete , plenarie et honorifice , sicut alias elemosinas suas liberius , quiecius , plenius et honorificencius te[c]nent et possident. Test*ibus* A*ndrea* episcopo Katen*ensi* , Comite Dunecano Justic*ia* , Ricardo de Moreuill' Constabulario , Philippo de Vallon*iis* , Rog*ero* de Vallon*iis* , Waltero de Berkel' Camer*ario* , Rob*erto* de Costent*in*[d]. Apud Munros.

RUBRIC. Carta domini regis de aqua de Pert (red, *E*). De aqua de Perth que uocatur Stok' (Red, *A*) .vj. (in margin, *A*, *E*).
SOURCE. NLS, MS. Adv. 34.4.2, fos.xlii^v–xliii^r = *A*. SRO, Northesk Muniments (uncatalogued), Ethie MS., fo.2^v = *E*. Printed here from *A*.
PRINTED. *Arbroath Liber*, i, no.6 (from *E*).
NOTES. [a] Initial red. Punctuation editorial. [b] Stoc, *E*. [c] Fo.xliii^r, *A*. [d] Const', *A*; Costent*in*, *E*.
COMMENT. Cf. *Retours* (Perth), no.443. The name 'Stok' suggests the old ford which carried the main road across the River Tay at Perth before a bridge was built, on the line of High Street.

225 Confirms to Arbroath Abbey the half ploughgate of arable in the territory of Mondynes (in Fordoun), Mearns, granted by Richard de Frivill. Kinghorn. (1178 × 1188, perhaps 1178)

W.[a] Dei gr*ati*a Rex Scott' omnibus probis hominibus tocius terre sue clericis et laicis salutem. Sciant presentes et posteri me concessisse et hac carta mea confirmasse Deo et ecclesie Sancti Thome martiris de Abirbroth*oc* et monachis ibidem Deo seruientibus in liberam et perpetuam elemosinam illam dimidiam carucatam terre in territorio de Monethen quam Ricardus de Friuill' eis dedit . Tenend*am* sibi ita libere et quiete plenarie et honorifice :' sicut carta eiusdem Ricardi testatur et confirmat . saluo seruicio meo. Test*ibus* Rob*erto* de Quincy . Philipp*o* de Valon*iis* . Hug*one* et Rob*erto* et Will*elmo* capellanis meis . Rob*erto* de Bosseuill' . Ric*ardo* de prebenda clerico meo . Waltero clerico meo. Apud Kyngor*n*.

RUBRIC. Confirmacio Regis W. de terra de Monethen (red)[b].
SOURCE. NLS, MS. Adv. 34.4.2, fo.lxvi^v.
PRINTED. *Arbroath Liber*, i, no.91 (*bis*).
NOTES. [a] Initial red. [b] No marginated numeral; entered between xci and xcij.
COMMENT. Richard de Frivill's charter (*Arbroath Liber*, i, no.91) and this were cancelled by no.277, below, dating 1183 × 1188, probably 1183 × 1186. The family to which he belonged was probably the family of de Freville (de Frieuill', etc.) attached to the house of Warenne (*EYC*, viii, references in index s.v. FREVILLE). It may be noted that one Ralph de Freville witnessed Warenne charters of 1159 × 1196 (ibid., nos.70, 111). Hugh the chaplain became bishop of St Andrews in 1178, but there was another royal chaplain of the same name.

226 Grants to Arbroath Abbey one saltpan in the Carse of Stirling with five acres of land; the tenant to have common pasture and fuel along with the tenants of the king's saltpans. Stirling. (1178 × 1184)

W.[a] Dei gr*ati*a Rex Scott' , Omnibus probis hominibus tocius terre sue , clericis et laicis, salutem. Sciant presentes et futuri me dedisse , concessisse et hac carta mea confirmasse Deo et ecclesie Sancti Thome[b] de Aberbruth' et monachis ibidem Deo seruientibus unam salinam in Kars iuxta salinas meas cum quinque acris terre . Tenend*am* et habend*am* sibi in liberam et perpetuam elemosinam , ita libere et quiete sicut aliquas elemosinas suas[c] liberius, quiecius et honorificentius tenent. Precipio etiam ut homo illorum qui salinam illam de eis tenebit communem pasturam et focale habeat cum hominibus meis qui salinas meas in eodem Kars tenent. Test*ibus* Andr*ea* episcopo Katen*ensi*, Arkenb*aldo* Abbate de Dunfermel*in*, Rogero de Valon*iis*, Waltero de Berkel' Cam*erario*. Willelmo filio Thorald', Radulfo de Cam*era*, Johanne de Lond*oniis*, Ricardo de Lincoln' Clerico meo, Roberto de Boseuill'. Apud Striuelyn.

RUBRIC. Carta domini Regis de salina in Kars (red, *E*). De salina in le Kars (red, *A*). .vij. (in margin, *A*, *E*).
SOURCE. NLS, MS. Adv. 34.4.2, fo.xliii^r = *A*. SRO, Northesk Muniments (uncatalogued), Ethie MS., fo.2^v = *E*. Printed here from *A*.
PRINTED. *Arbroath Liber*, i, no.7 (from *E*).
NOTES. [a] Initial red. Punctuation editorial. [b] Sancti Thome repeated, *A*. [c] *E* adds alias.

227 Grants to Arbroath Abbey the church of Haltwhistle in Tynedale, Northumberland. Arbroath. (1178 × 1187)

W.[a] Dei gr*at*ia Rex Scott' Episcopis Abbatibus Comit*ibus*. Baron*ibus*. Just*iciis*. Vic*ecomitibus*. prepositis. Ministris et omnibus probis hominibus tocius terre sue clericis et laicis salutem. Sciant presentes et futuri me dedisse concessisse et hac carta mea confirmasse Deo et ecclesie Sancti Thome archipresulis et martiris de Abirbr*othoc* et monachis ibidem Deo seruientibus in liberam et perpetuam elemosinam ecclesiam de Hautwysill' in Tyndal' cum omnibus pertinenciis suis in[b] Capellis. in terris. in decimis. in elemosinis. et in omnibus aliis ecclesiasticis rectitudinibus. consuetudinibus et beneficiis. cum communi etiam pastura. omnibusque aliis aisiamentis eiusdem parochie. Tenend*am* ita plenarie sicut aliqua persona eamdem ecclesiam unquam plenius tenuit. et ita libere et quiete bene et in pace et honorifice. sicut aliqua elemosina in tota terra mea liberius et quiecius melius et honorificencius ab aliqua ecclesia possidetur. Test*ibus* Matheo episcopo Abird*onensi*. Rob*erto* de Quency. Philippo de Valon*iis*. Rogero fratre eius. Hug*one* et Rob*erto*. et Will*elmo* capellanis meis. Hug*one* Gifard'. Willelmo de Moreuill'. Ric*ardo* de Friuill'. Hug*one* de sigillo et Ric*ardo* de preb*enda* et Ric*ardo* de Abirbr*othoc* et Waltero de Hayroun clericis meis apud Aberbr*othoc*.

RUBRIC. Confirmacio Reg*is* W. de ecclesia de Hautwysill (red). .xxxvj. (in margin).
SOURCE. NLS, MS. Adv. 34.4.2, fo.l^{r-v}.
PRINTED. *Arbroath Liber*, i, no.36.
NOTES. [a] Initial red. [b] Fo.l^v.
COMMENT. This grant was made before Haltwhistle was given to Robert de Brus, afterwards to Robert de Ros (cf. *Arbroath Liber*, i, nos.37, 38; below, nos.513, 574). Hugh the chaplain became bishop of St Andrews in 1178, but there was another royal chaplain of the same name. Bishop Hugh was a witness to Robert de Brus's charter of this church.

228 Grants to Arbroath Abbey his ferry-boat of Montrose with the land belonging to it, which the king's clerk Elias had held. Forfar. (1178 × 1187, perhaps 1178)

W.[a] Dei gr*at*ia Rex Scott', Episcopis, Abbatibus, comitibus, Baronibus, Justic*iis*, vicecom*itibus*, prepositis, ministris et omnibus probis hominibus tocius terre sue , clericis et laicis , salutem. Sciant presentes et futuri me dedisse, concessisse et hac carta mea confirmasse[b] Deo et ecclesie Sancti Thome martiris de Aberbruth*oc* et monachis ibidem Deo seruientibus Batellum passagii mei de Munros , cum terra ad predictum Batellum pertinente, et cum omnibus rectitudinibus ad batellum et ad terram illam pertinentibus, quam scilicet terram Helias clericus meus de Munros tenuerat. Tenend*um* in liberam et quietam et perpetuam elemosinam, libere et quiete ab exercitu et expedicione et operacione et auxilio et ab omnibus consuetudinibus et omni seruicio et exactione. Test*ibus* M*atheo* episcopo Abirdon*ensi* , A*rkenbaldo* Abbate de Dunfermel*in* , Willelmo Priore de Rostynot'[c], Rob*erto* et Willelmo capellanis meis , Hug*one* de sigillo et Ricardo de prebenda et Ricardo de Scocia clericis meis , Alano dapifero , Willelmo de Moruill' , Willelmo Comyn[d], Waltero de Berkel' Camerar*io* , Geruasio Auenel , Rann*ulfo* de Sol*is* . Apud Forf*ar*.

RUBRIC. De Batello de Munros (Red, *E*). De Batella[e] de Munros (red, *A*). .ix. (in margin, *A*, *E*).
SOURCE. NLS, MS. Adv. 34.4.2, fo.xliii^{r-v} = *A*. SRO, Northesk Muniments (uncatalogued), Ethie MS., fos.2^{v}–3^{r} = *E*. Printed here from *A*.
PRINTED. *Arbroath Liber*, i, no.9 (from *E*).
NOTES. [a] Initial red. [b] Fo.xliii^{v}, *A*. [c] Rostinoth', *E*. [d] Cumin, *E*. [e] Sic.
COMMENT. Hugh of Benholm, brother of Elias the clerk, was granted the ferry to be held of Arbroath Abbey heritably for 1 merk (1179 × *c*.1194; BM, MS. Add. 33245, fo.138^{v}).

229 Confirms to Arbroath Abbey the grant made by Turpin bishop of Brechin of one toft and croft in the toun of Stracathro, Angus, and two acres of arable in the field belonging to that toun; and in addition the teind of that net in the River North Esk which the king gave to the monks of Arbroath to be held of Bishop Turpin and his successors; as the bishop's charter bears witness. Montrose. (1178 × *c*.1190)

W.[a] Dei gr*ati*a Rex Scotorum . episcopis abbatibus comitibus Baronibus . Justic*iis* . Vicec*omitibus* . prepositis ministris et omnibus probis hominibus tocius terre sue clericis et laicis salutem. Sciant presentes et futuri me concessisse et hac carta mea confirmasse Deo et ecclesie Sancti Thome martiris de Abirbroth*oc* et monachis ibidem Deo seruientibus donacionem illam quam Turpinus episcopus de Brech*in* eis fecit . scilicet unum toftum et croftum in villa de Strukatherach' et duas acras terre in campo pertinente ad eamdem villam . et preterea decimam illius plenarii Retis . quod ego eisdem monachis dedi super aquam de Northesk' tenend*am* in liberam et perpetuam elemosinam de predicto Turpino episcopo de Brech*in* et eius successoribus ita libere et quiete plenarie et honorifice . sicut carta sua testatur et confirmat. Test*ibus* Matheo episcopo de Abirden . Comite Dunecano Justic*ia* . Malcolmo comite Atholie . G*illebride* comite de Anegus . G*illecrist*[b] comite de Mar' . Rob*erto* de Berkel' . Willelmo Cumyn . Hugon*e* de Kaledou*er* . Willelmo de Mountfort . Willelmo de Ram'. Apud Munros.

RUBRIC. Confirmacio Reg*is* W. super eadem terra (red). .lxxvj. (in margin).
SOURCE. NLS, MS. Adv. 34.4.2, fo.lxi^{r-v}.
PRINTED. *Arbroath Liber*, i, no.76. NOTES. [a] Initial red. [b] Fo.lxi^{v}.

COMMENT. Bishop Turpin's charter is given in *Arbroath Liber*, i, no.75, with confirmations by successors Ralph, Hugh and Gregory, ibid., nos.77–79.

230 Confirms to Arbroath Abbey the church of Inverkeilor, Angus, as the charter of Walter of Berkeley (the donor) bears witness. Forfar. (1178 × 1187)

W.[a] Dei gr*ati*a Rex Scott' omnibus probis hominibus tocius terre sue clericis et laicis salutem. Sciant presentes et posteri me concessisse et hac carta mea confirmasse Deo et ecclesie Sancti Thome de Abirbr*othoc* et monachis ibidem Deo seruientibus ecclesiam de Inuerkileder , cum omnibus iustis pertinenciis suis , in capellis et terris et omnimodis decimacionibus et in omnibus aliis rectitudinibus et libertatibus eidem ecclesie iuste pertinentibus. Tenend*am* sibi in liberam et perpetuam elemosinam ita libere et quiete[b] plenarie et honorifice sicut alias elemosinas suas liberius et quiecius plenius et honorificencius tenent . sicut carta Walteri de Berkel' eis testatur et confirmat. Test*ibus* Will*elmo* de Lindes', Johanne de Londin*iis*, Ric*ardo* de preb*enda*, Ric*ardo* de Lincoln' clericis. Apud Forfar.

RUBRIC. Confirmacio Reg*is* W. super eadem (red). .Lv. (in margin).
SOURCE. NLS, MS. Adv. 34.4.2, fo.lv^{r-v}.
PRINTED. *Arbroath Liber*, i, no.55.
NOTES. [a] Initial red. [b] Fo.lv^{v}.
COMMENT. The thanage of Inverkeilor had been granted to Walter of Berkeley while he held the chamberlain's office (above, no.185). His charter granting the church is in *Arbroath Liber*, i, no.54.

231 Grants to Arbroath Abbey the church of Newtyle, Angus. Forfar. (1178 × 1187)

W.[a] Dei gr*ati*a Rex Scott' , Omnibus probis hominibus tocius terre sue, clericis et laicis, salutem. Sciant presentes et posteri me dedisse et concessisse et hac carta mea confirmasse Deo et Ecclesie Sancti Thome de Aberbr*othoc* et monachis ibidem Deo seruientibus ecclesiam de Neutyl, cum omnibus iustis pertinenciis suis, in capellis et terris et omnimodis decimacionibus et in omnibus aliis rectitudinibus et libertatibus eidem ecclesie iuste pertinentibus. Tenendam sibi in liberam et perpetuam elemosinam , ita libere et Quiete , plenarie et honorifice , sicut alias elemosinas suas liberius quiecius , plenius et honorificentius tenent. Test*ibus* Will*elmo* de Lyndes' , Johanne de London*iis* , Rogero de Valon*iis* , Ric*ardo* de prebenda , Ric*ardo* de Lyncoln[b], clericis meis. Apud Forfare.

RUBRIC. De Ecclesia de Neutil' (red, *E*). Carta Reg*is* .W. de ecclesia de Neutyl (red, *A*). .xviij. (in margin, *A*, *E*).
SOURCE. NLS, MS. Adv. 34.4.2, fo.xlv^{r} = *A*. SRO, Northesk Muniments (uncatalogued), Ethie MS., fo.3^{v} = *E*. Printed here from *A*.
PRINTED. *Arbroath Liber*, i, no.18 (from *E*).
NOTES. [a] Initial red. [b] Lincoln', *E*.
COMMENT. If Newtyle church was granted to Arbroath before Newtyle was granted to Earl David, a date of *c*.1178 seems probable for this act.

232 Grants to Arbroath Abbey the churches of Banchory-Ternan and Catterline, Kincardineshire. Forfar. (1178 × 1187, probably *c*.1178)

W.[a] Dei gr*ati*a Rex Scott' . omnibus probis hominibus . tocius terre sue ∴ clericis et laicis ∴ salutem. Sciant presentes et futuri . me dedisse . et concessisse & hac carta mea confirmasse . Deo et ecclesie . Sancti Thome Martiris de Aberbr*othoc* . et monachis ibidem Deo seruientibus . et seruituris . ecclesiam de Bencoryn . et ecclesiam de Katerin[b] . cum omnibus ad predictas ecclesias iuste pertinentibus . in terris . et aquis . in pratis . et pascuis et omnimodis decimacionibus . et cum omnibus iustis pertinenciis predictarum ecclesiarum . Tenend*as* in liberam . et puram . et perpetuam elemosinam . ita libere . et quiete . plenarie . & honorifice ∴ sicut alias elemosinas suas . liberius . et quiecius . plenius . et honorificencius ∴ tenent. Test*ibus* Will*elmo* de Lindes' . Johanne de Lond*oniis* . Rogero de Valon*iis* . Ric*ardo* de prebenda . Ric*ardo* de Lincoln' clericis meis . apud Forfar.

RUBRIC. De ecclesia de Bencor' . et de ecclesia de Kat' (red, *E*). De ecclesiis de Banchry et Kateryn (red, *A*). .xxx. (in margin, *A*, *E*).
SOURCE. NLS, MS. Adv. 34.4.2, fo.xlviii[v] = *A*. SRO, Northesk Muniments (uncatalogued), Ethie MS., fo.5[v] = *E*. Printed here from *A*.
PRINTED. *Arbroath Liber*, i, no.30 (from *E*).
NOTES. [a] Initial red. [b] Caterin, *E*.

233 Grants to Arbroath Abbey one full toft outwith his burgh of Perth, perambulated for it between the two ports; its tenants of this toft to enjoy full rights with the king's burgesses. Forfar. (1178 × 1187)

W.[a] Dei gr*ati*a Rex Scott', Omnibus probis hominibus tocius terre sue, clericis et laicis, salutem. Sciant presentes et futuri me dedisse, concessisse et hac carta mea confirmasse Deo et Ecclesie Sancti Thome de Aberbruth*oc* et monachis ibidem Deo seruientibus in liberam et perpetuam elemosinam unum plenarium toftum extra Burgum de Perth,[b] sicut eis perambulatum fuit inter duas portas. Tenend*um* ita libere et quiete, plenarie et honorifice, sicut alias elemosinas suas liberius, quiecius, plenius et honorificencius tenent. Concessi etiam eis ut homines eorum qui super terram illam manentes erunt communionem habeant in burgo meo de Pert cum burgensibus meis vendendi et emendi et alias rectitudines habendi. Test*ibus* Waltero Olif*ard* Justic*ia*, Nesso fil*io* Willelmi, Willelmo de Lyndes', Waltero de Berkel', Ricardo de Munfichet'[c], Johanne de Lund*oniis*. Apud Forf*ar*.

RUBRIC. De tofto de Pert (red, *E*). De tofto de Perth (red, *A*). .x. (in margin, *A*, *E*).
SOURCE. NLS, MS. Adv. 34.4.2, fo.xliii[v] = *A*. SRO, Northesk Muniments (uncatalogued), Ethie MS., fo.3[r] = *E*. Printed here from *A*.
PRINTED. *Arbroath Liber*, i, no.10 (from *E*).
NOTES. [a] Initial red. [b] Pert, *E*. [c] Muficheth', *E*.
COMMENT. This suggests that Perth had already outgrown the boundaries it had presumably had since David I's time, but that King William's 'new burgh' of Perth had not yet been founded. See no.278.

234 Commands all his foresters throughout Scotland (north of Forth) to allow the men of the abbot of Arbroath to take whatever they need for the abbey's buildings in the king's forests. Forfar. (1178 × 1193, probably × 1189)

W.[a] Dei Gr*ati*a Rex Scott' , Omnibus forestariis suis tocius Scocie salutem. Mando vobis atque precipio quatinus permittatis homines Abbatis de Aberbr*othoc* capere in forestis meis per Ballias vestras quecunque eis necessaria fuerint ad edificia sua et ad usus proprios , et prohibeo vobis firmiter ne sustineatis ut quisquam de vestris eos super hoc uexet uel contumeliam aliquam inferat. Test*ibus* Waltero de Berkel' , Johanne de Lond*oniis* . apud Forfar.

RUBRIC. De forestis (red, *A*, *E*). .xv. (in margin, *A*, *E*).
SOURCE. NLS, MS. Adv. 34.4.2, fo.xliv^{v}=*A*. SRO, Northesk Muniments (uncatalogued), Ethie MS., fo.3^{v}=*E*. Printed here from *A*.
PRINTED. *Arbroath Liber*, i, no.15 (from *E*).
NOTE. [a] Initial red.

235 Confirms to the church of SS Mary and Michael, Haddington, the land between the house of Pain and the king's garden and the cemetery, granted to the church by his mother Countess Ada. Haddington. (1178 × 1188)

W'. Dei gr*ati*a Rex Scott'. Omnibus probis hominibus totius terre sue salutem. Sciant presentes 7 posteri me Concessisse 7 hac mea carta Confirmasse Deo 7 ecclesie Sancte Marie 7 Sancti Michael*is* de HadintuN terram illam inter domum Pagani 7 ortum meum 7 Cimiterium .· quam Ada Comitissa mater mea eidem ecclesie in liberam 7 perpetuam elemosinam dedit. Tenend*am* sibi ita bene 7 in pace . 7 ita libere 7 quiete .· sicut carta Ade Comitisse Matris mee testatur 7 Confirmat. Test*ibus* Hug*one* episcopo Sancti Andr*ee* . Ylberto priore de HadintuN . Waltero archidiacono Sancti Andr*ee* . Hug*one* . Rob*erto* . 7 Willelmo .· capellanis Reg*is* . Rob*erto* de Quenci . Willelmo de Veteri ponte . Hug*one* Ridel . Alexandro de Sancto Martino . Rob*erto* de Boeseuill'. APUD HADINTUN.·

ENDORSED. Confirmacio (xii cent., faded). Carta Will*elm*i regis de una terra ecclesie de Hadigtun' (xiii cent.).
DESCRIPTION. 5·6″ (14·2 cm.), Top, 5·5″ (14 cm.), Bottom × 4″ (10·2 cm.), L, 3·8″ (9·7 cm.), R. Foot folded to a depth of 0·6 (1·5 cm.). Double slits with tag 7″ (17·5 cm.) long, 0·6″ (1·5 cm.) wide. Tie cut from top left of fold, now torn away. About half the seal remains in natural wax stained brown, rev. to front, diameter 2·8″ (7 cm.). Fair impression.
HAND. Scribe Ce. Unruled.
SOURCE. Original, SRO, GD 90/7=*A*. SRO, Registrum Magni Sigilli Regum Scotorum, Liber V, no.4 (abridgement only)=*B*. Printed here from *A*.
PRINTED. *RMS*, ii, no.610 (from *B*).

236 Settles the dispute between the monks of Melrose Abbey and Richard de Moreville and his heirs anent the forest between the Gala and Leader Waters. Richard and his heir William have quitclaimed to Melrose Abbey the forest within the marches specified, save for the wood called Threepwood without pasture rights. The monks are to hold the forest within the marches specified freely for whatever purpose they wish, with all the pasture as well of Threepwood as the rest, and a site in Colmslie for making a byre for 100 cows, a fold, and as much building in Buckholm as was there before the date of this chirograph, provided this is not increased. Richard and his heirs are not to build a house or shieling or lodges or a fence nor to carry out any manual work in Threepwood. Within the area outlined Richard and his heirs are to have only the wild animals and birds, and each party may have a forester to guard their rights. If anyone is convicted of injuring the monks' rights in the forest, the monks shall have the penalty called *trigild*, and Richard the forfeiture. If Richard should accuse any of the monks' servants of a forest offence, the monks shall do justice to Richard at the gate of the abbey. If any of the monks' servants should be taken and convicted of an offence against Richard's forest rights, the monks shall pay Richard the servant's wage for half a year and shall dismiss the servant and not hire him again save with Richard's consent. The king himself has perambulated the marches in question with his brother and the bishop of Glasgow and earls and responsible men, and the agreement has been made in his presence in his court. The king has set his seal to both parts of the agreement, and the bishop of Glasgow and the king's brother have done likewise. The abbot of Melrose has set his seal to Richard's part and Richard de Moreville has set his seal to the abbey's part. For the quitclaim, the monks have paid Richard 100 merks of silver. (Haddington, 30 March, 1180)

CYROGRAPHUM.[a]

W. Dei gr*ati*a rex Scott'. Episcopis. Abbatibus. Com*itibus*. Baron*ibus*. Justi*ciis*. Vicecom*itibus*. 7 Omnibus probis hominibus totius terre sue. Clericis 7 Laicis. Salutem. Sciatis me fecisse pacem inter monachos de Melr*os* 7 R*icardum* de Moreuill' 7 heredes eius super controuersia que erat inter monachos de Melr*os* 7 R*icardum* de Moreuill' de foresta inter Galhe 7 Leder per has diuisas. scilicet per fluuium Galhe uersus monachos ab orientali parte eiusdem fluminis sursum usque ad terminos de Wedale. 7 item per rectas diuisas terre Ricardi de Moreuill' scilicet de sicut Mereburne cadit in Leder. usque ad sursam eiusdem Mereburne. 7 inde per Sicum qui exit deM ereb*urne* usque ubi sicus ille cadit in Riuulum de Standene. 7 inde usque ad pot. 7 de pot usque ad standande stan. 7 sic deinceps usque ad uiam regiam. ubi illa intrat nemus 7 diuidit nemus de Standene 7 de Threpwude. 7 sic per eandem Regiam uiam usque ad Faireforde. 7 postea per illam uiam que uadit in dextrum usque ad predictos terminos de Wedale. 7 sic per rectos terminos de Wedale usque in Galhe. Ric*ardus* de Moreuill' 7 W*illelmus* heres eius clamauerunt quietum de se 7 heredibus suis Deo 7 Sancte Marie de Melr*os* 7 monachis ibidem Deo seruientibus quicquid iuris 7 Calumpnie habuerunt de Bosco 7 Pastura infra prenominatas diuisas uersus austrum ab illa uia que diuidit Threpwude 7 nemus de Standene excepto quod Ricardus de Moreu*illa* 7 heredes illius habebunt illud nemus quod uocatur Threpwude sine pastura. quod eis monachi quietum clamauerunt per has diuisas. scilicet de Fairforde deorsum per Aloent usque ad mussam que est inter Threpwude 7 Cumbesleie cnol. 7 sic per eandem mussam usque ad predictum pot. Monachi autem de Melros habebunt totum Reliquum nemus inter Galhe 7 Leder. per predictas diuisas libere. quiete. 7 plenarie. 7 utentur eo ad suos proprios usus sicut eis placuerit 7 utilius fuerit sine dare 7 uendere. Habebunt etiam monachi de Melr*os* infra diuisas prescriptas totam pasturam infra boscum 7 extra tam de Threpwude quam de reliquo nemore ad sua propria aueria quietam 7 solutam ac perpetuo tenore possidendam 7 tenendam 7 utendam sicut eis utilius fuerit . 7 locum in Cumbesleie ad edificandum unam vaccariam centum uaccarum . 7 unam faldam . 7 tantum edificii in Bucchehelm quantum ibi fuit die quo Cyrographum istud factum erat . 7 in loco ubi tunc fuit . ita quod tantum edificii 7 non magis ibi habeant quam tunc fuit . 7 non liceat eis alibi in foresto edificia facere nisi per licentiam Ric*ardi* de Moreuill' aut heredum suorum. Ric*ardus* uero 7 heredes eius non facient nec habebunt domum . nec scalingas . nec logias . nec sepem . nec ullum omnimodo opus manuale[b] . in Threpwude . nec alibi infra prenominatas diuisas . scilicet inter Galhe 7 Led*er*. Nec monachi calumpniabuntur ultra prenominatas diuisas uersus Louweder. Monachi uero de Threpwude [ ][c] nichil capient nisi pasturam :' 7 Ric*ardus* 7 heredes eius de pastura eiusdem Threpwude 7 de tota alia pastura . 7 de toto Reliquo nemore infra predictas diuisas inter Galhe 7 Leder nichil habebunt preter saluaginam bestiarum 7 auium. Ricardus habebit suum forestarium ad custodiendam suam saluaginam . 7 monachi habebunt suum forestarium ad custodiendum nemus suum 7 pasturam. Ric*ardus* habebit omnia forisfacta de foresta. Et si forestarius Ric*ardi* uel forestarius monachorum inuenerit aliquem facientem monachis dampnum uel iniuriam de Bosco suo uel pastura . aut de pecoribus suis :' monachi habebunt emendationem scilicet Trigild . 7 Ric*ardus* forisfactum. Et si Ric*ardus* aliquem ex seruientibus monachorum calumpniatus fuerit de predicta foresta :' monachi facient rectum Ric*ardo* de seruiente suo ad portam de Melr*os*. Et si aliquis ex seruientibus monachorum super saluaginam Ric*ardi* fuerit captus . aut de defensione sua ad portam de Melr*os* defecerit . 7 sit conuictus :' monachi dabunt Ricardo mercedem seruientis de dimidio anno . 7 postea ipsum seruientem amouebunt a se 7 ab abbatia 7 ulterius illum non retinebunt . nisi per uoluntatem Ric*ardi*. Suprascriptas uero diuisas inter monachos 7 predictum Ric*ardum* ego cum Episcopo de Glasg*u* 7 fratre meo . 7 Comitibus 7 probis hominibus meis perambulaui. Ista compositio inter monachos 7 R*icardum* . 7 heredes eius in mea presentia 7 curia est facta . 7 pax ista me concedente 7 confirmante inter eos est firmata. Quare uolo 7 precipio . ut ista pax 7 compositio quam in utraque parte scilicet monachorum 7 Ric*ardi* meo sigillo confirmo stabilis 7 firma atque illesa ab eis perpetualiter teneatur. Quod si aliquis illorum siue successorum aut[d] heredum suorum a prescripta compositione aliquo tempore resilire uoluerit :' ego 7 heredes mei ab eis 7 eorum successoribus . 7 heredibus illam firmiter teneri faciemus. Ad testificandam uero perpetuam unitatem 7 firmitatem huius compositionis . cum sigillo meo . Jocelinus Glasg*uensis* episcopus . 7 D*aui*d frater meus in utraque parte cyrographi sua sigilla apposuerunt . 7 Abbas pro se 7 pro conuentu de Melr*os* in parte Ric*ardi* suum sigillum posuit :' 7 Ric*ardus* pro se 7 pro suis heredibus in parte monachorum suum sigillum posuit. Et quia Ric*ardus* 7 W*illelmus* heres eius clamauerunt quietum de se 7 heredibus suis quicquid iuris 7 calumpnie habuerunt de prenominato Bosco [7][e] pastura infra prescriptas diuisas inter Galhe

7 Leder ·/ monachi dederunt Ric*ardo* centum marcas argenti. His testibus . Siluano Abbate Rieu*allensi* . Hug*one* Abbate de Neubothl' . Abbate Rad*ulfo* de Cubro . Will*elmo* Abbate de Dundrein*an* . Comite Dunecano . Walth*euo* Comite . Gilberto Comite . Nich*olao* de Treilin . Petro de Ros . Waltero Olifard . Willelmo de Lindeseie de Luffenac . Stephano Camerario . Rollando filio H*uctredi* . Philippo de Valuin' . Alano filio Walteri[f] . Willelmo de Mortem*er* . Rogero de Valuin'.

ENDORSED. Confirmatio reg*is* de compositione facta inter nos et Ric*ardum* de Moreuill' (xiii cent.). T (red, xv cent.?). perambulacio de Alwentschaws (xvi cent.). J. Scott (xvi cent.).
DESCRIPTION. 1′ 6″ (45·5 cm.), Top and bottom × 11″ (28 cm.), L, R. Foot folded to a depth of 1·3″ (2·4 cm.). Double slits at four places in foot and fold. Stumps of tags remain in first three, complete tag remains in fourth slit, with seal of Richard de Morville in red wax (equestrian). The document has been repaired vertically in centre.
HAND. Scribe Ab. Ruled in drypoint.
SOURCE. Original, SRO, GD 55/111 = *M*. NLS, MS. Adv. 34.4.11, fo.lviii^{r-v} = *A*.
PRINTED. *Melrose Liber*, no.111.
NOTES. [a] Cut through letters. [b] Tear in parchment; manuale supplied from *A*. [c] Tear, but no word missing; *A* has de Threpuud nichil capient. [d] *A* ends here. [e] 7 supplied conjecturally. [f] Written Waltero.
COMMENT. The place and date of the settlement of the dispute are given in *Chron. Melrose*, 43. The marches of the forest between Gala and Leader within which Melrose Abbey was allowed pasture rights seem to have corresponded closely to the present northern boundary of Melrose parish from Caitha Hill to Blainslie. Threepwood, representing the 'Threpwude' of the twelfth century, means 'wood involved in a dispute'.

237 Grants to Kinloss Abbey five full tofts, one each in Inverness, Auldearn, Forres, Elgin and Aberdeen. Melrose. (1179 × 1182)

Willelmus Dei gracia rex Scocie episcopis, abbatibus, comitibus, baronibus, justiciis, vicecomitibus, ministris et omnibus probis hominibus tocius terre sue, clericis et laicis, salutem. Sciant presentes et futuri me dedisse et concessisse et hac carta mea confirmasse Deo et Sancte Marie de Kynlos et monachis ibidem Deo seruientibus quinque plenaria tofta in liberam et puram et perpetuam elemosinam, scilicet unum toftum in burgo meo de Inuernys et unum in Eren et unum in Foreys et unum in Elgyn et unum in Abyrden, tenenda et possidenda ita libere et quiete, plenarie et honorifice sicut aliqua elemosina liberius, quiecius, plenarius et honorificencius teneri vel possideri potest. Concessi eciam eis et dedi et hac carta mea confirmaui ut homines eorum super tofta predicta manentes liberi sint et quieti ab omnibus auxiliis et seruiciis et consuetudinibus et ab omni exactione seculari ad me pertinentibus per redditum et seruicium quod prenominatis monachis facient vel facere debent. Testibus Jocelino Episcopo de Glesgo, Abbate Ernaldo de Melros, Hugone Abbate de Neubotil, Dauid fratre meo, Comite Walleuo, Ricardo de Moreuill Constabulario, Waltero Olifer Justiciario, Alano filio Walteri dapifero, Willelmo de Lauder,[a] Waltero de Berchelai Camerario, Ranulfo de Sules. Apud Melros.

SOURCE. Aberdeen burgh muniments, transumpt of 29 August, 1355, under the seal of John bishop of Moray. (Not inspected for this edition.)

PRINTED. James Gordon, *Description of both towns of Aberdeen* (Spalding Club, 1842), p.44; *Kinloss Recs.*, 124.
NOTE. [a] Sic, probably for Lindes'.
COMMENT. The witness William 'de Lauder' was probably William de Lindsay.

238 Confirms to Holyrood Abbey the church of Bolton, East Lothian, saving the right of Ralph of St Martin in that church during his lifetime. Montrose. (1173 × 1195, probably × *c*.1180)

.W. Dei gr*atia* Rex Scott'. Episcopis. Abbatibus. Comitibus. Baronibus. Justiciis. vicecomitibus. Ministris. 7[a] Omnibus probis hominibus tocius terre sue. salutem. Sciant presentes 7 futuri me concessisse 7 hac carta mea confirmasse. Abbatie Sancte Crucis de Edeneburg 7 Canonicis ibidem Deo seruientibus .' in perpetuam elemosinam ecclesiam de BoweltuN. cum terris 7 decimis. 7 Omnibus aliis iustis pertinenciis suis. Tenend*am* ita libere 7 quiete. plenarie 7 honorifice sicut alias elemosinas suas liberius 7 quiecius. plenius 7 honorificencius possident. Saluo .' Radulfo de Sancto Martino Jure suo in eadem Ecclesia in uita sua. Test*ibus* Matheo Episcopo de AbredeoN. Waltero de Berkel' cam*erario*. Philippo de Vall*oniis*. Waltero Olif*ard*. Johanne de Vall*ibus*. Willelmo de Lindesei apud Munros.

ENDORSED. De Ecclesia de Boteltune (date of hand unknown).
SOURCE. *Holyrood Liber*, no.31, printed from the original then (1840) *penes* Lord Panmure, present whereabouts unknown. It was not among the Holyrood charters recently deposited in the SRO by Messrs Dundas and Wilson, W.S., on behalf of the Earl of Dalhousie.
PRINTED. *Holyrood Liber*, no.31.
NOTE. [a] It is not clear from the printed version whether the scribe used the tironian sign for et with or without a horizontal cross stroke.
COMMENT. *Holyrood Liber*, no.33 shews that Bolton church had been granted by the elder William de Vieuxpont (husband of Emma de Saint-Hilaire), and this was confirmed by Richard bishop of St Andrews, 1172 × 1178 (ibid., no.32). Bishop Matthew was in exile for part of the years 1180–81.

239 Takes into his firm peace and protection the land, vassals and possessions of the abbot of Kelso, until he shall return from conducting the king's business. Haddington. (1173 × 1189, probably 1182)

W. Dei gratia Rex Scottorum. Omnibus probis hominibus tocius terre sue salutem. Sciatis me terram Abbatis de Kelch'. 7 eius homines. 7 catalla sua uniuersa in firma pace 7 proteccione mea juste suscepisse .' 7 in custodia mea. quousque de negocio meo redeat. Quare[a] prohibeo firmiter. ne quis ei aut alicui suorum[b] iniuriam. violenciam. aut aliquam contumeliam interim inferat. super meam plenariam forisfacturam. Test*ibus*. Ric*ardo* de Moreuill' Constab*ulario*. Phillipp*o* de Vallon*ïis*. apud Hadint'.

RUBRIC. Protectio super terram Abbatis de Kelch' 7 homines 7 catalla (top in red).
SOURCE. NLS, MS. Adv. 34.5.1, fo.146^{r-v}.
PRINTED. *Kelso Liber*, no.391.
NOTES. [a] Fo.146^{v}. [b] eorum underlined for deletion, suorum written above the line.
COMMENT. The king's business was probably the successful mission to the papal *curia* in 1182, consisting of Bishop Jocelin of Glasgow, Abbot Osbert of Kelso,

Abbot Arnold of Melrose and Walter prior of Inchcolm, which brought about a reconciliation between the Scottish king and the papacy and brought back the Golden Rose for King William as the gift of Pope Lucius III (cf. Lawrie, *Annals*, 243–5). Note Pope Lucius's bull for Kelso mentioned in the comment on no.239A.

239A

Confirms to Kelso Abbey the church of Keith (i.e. Humbie, East Lothian), granted by Simon Fraser, as his charter bears witness. (Probably *c.*1182 × 1195)

Will*elmus*[a] Dei gr*ati*a Rex[b] Scocie Omnibus probis hominibus tocius terre sue clericis et laicis salutem. Sciant presentes 7 futuri me concessisse 7 hac carta mea confirmasse Deo 7 ecclesie Sancte Marie de Kelchou 7 monachis ibidem Deo seruientibus Ecclesiam de Keth . cum terris 7 decimis 7 omnibus iustis pertinenciis suis . tenendam in liberam 7 perpetuam elemosinam . ita libere 7 quiete plenarie 7 honorifice sicut [carta] [c] Symonis Fraser testatur 7 confirmat . saluo seruicio meo. Hiis test*ibus*.

RUBRIC. Confirmacio Regis Willelmi super eadem ecclesia de Keth 7 pertin*enciis* (top in red).
SOURCE. NLS, MS. Adv. 34.5.1, fo.35^r.
PRINTED. *Kelso Liber*, no.91.
NOTES. [a] Initial red. [b] Rex follows Willelmus and is marked for transposition by two pairs of diagonal strokes. [c] MS. omits.
COMMENT. In *RRS*, i, index s.v. Keith Marischal, the Keith whose church was granted to Kelso Abbey by Simon Fraser was wrongly identified with Keith Marischal, instead of Keith Hundeby, i.e. Humbie. Simon Fraser's charter granting Humbie church to Kelso is in *Kelso Liber*, no.85. The date-limits seem determined by the fact that Lucius III's solemn privilege for Kelso, 25 March, 1182 (SRO, Papal Bulls, no.3) confirms the gift of Keith church without reference to Simon Fraser, while no.367, × 1195, confirms the gift with reference to this act.

240

Confirms to Melrose Abbey the half ploughgate of arable and meadow in the feu of Mow (in Morebattle, Roxburghshire) granted by Anselm of Whitton, as in the charter of Anselm. Haddington. (1175 × 1190)

U[a] Dei gracia Rex Scot' episcopis, abbatibus, comitibus, baronibus, iustic*iis*, vicecomitibus, prepositis, ministris et omnibus probis hominibus tocius terre sue, salutem. Sciant presentes et posteri me concessisse et hac mea carta confirmasse Deo et ecclesie Sancte Marie de Melros et monachis ibidem Deo seruientibus illam dimidiam carrucatam terre in terra et prato quam Anselmus de Withetun eis dedit de feudo suo de Molle, per easdem diuisas sicut continetur in carta ipsius Anselmi, quam ipsi monachi habent de eo. Tenend*am* sibi ita quiete, plenarie et honorifice in liberam et perpetuam elemosinam et ita libere ab omni exactione seculari, sicut alias elemosinas suas liberius, quiecius, plenius et honorificencius tenent, saluo seruicio meo de prefato Anselmo et de heredibus suis. Test*ibus* Jocel*ino* episcopo Glasguen*si*, Ric*ardo* de Moreuill' const*abulario*, Roberto de Quency, Walt*ero* Olifer, Rogero de Wallon*iis*, Walt*ero* de Berkel' camerario. Apud Hadintun.

RUBRIC. Confirmacio Regis Willelmi de Molle.
SOURCE. BM, MS. Harl. 3960, fo.7^r.
PRINTED. *Melrose Liber*, no.138.
NOTE. [a] Initial red.

COMMENT. The charter of Anselm of Whitton (alias 'of Mow') is given in *Melrose Liber*, no.137, with the marches in detail.

241 Confirms to Newbattle Abbey the grant made by Robert de Quinci and confirmed by his son Saer de Quinci of Prestongrange, East Lothian, as their charters bear witness. Haddington. (1179×1189)

W. Dei gr*ati*a Rex Scott' Episcopis, abbatibus, comitibus, baronibus, justiciis, vicecomitibus, ministris et omnibus hominibus tocius terre sue, clericis et laicis, salutem. Sciant presentes et futuri me concessisse et hac mea carta confirmasse Deo et ecclesie Sancte Marie de Neu*botle* et monachis ibidem Deo seruientibus donacionem grangie de Preston', quam Robertus de Quency et Seyr de Quency filius eius eis dederunt et cartis suis confirmauerunt in perpetuam elemosinam, et hoc ita libere et quiete, plenarie et honorifice, sicut aliquam elemosinam liberius et quiecius tenent et possident, et sicut eorum carte in omnibus testantur et confirmant, saluo seruicio meo. Test*ibus* Jocelino Glas*guensi* Episcopo, Ern*aldo* Abbate de Melr*os*, Ricardo de Morewyll' constabular*io*, Waltero Olifard apud Hadington.

Confirmacio Reg*is* W*illelmi*[a].
SOURCE. NLS, MS. Adv. 34.4.13, fo.24r.
PRINTED. *Newbattle Registrum*, no.67.
NOTE. [a] Table of contents, fo.1v.
COMMENT. On this cf. *SHR*, xxx, 41–49: the grange of Preston had at first been leased to Newbattle (1170) by Robert de Quinci for twenty years, in return for which the abbey was to pay off Robert's debt of £80 to a certain Jew named Abraham. Robert's charter of Prestongrange does not survive, but two charters of Saer (in the former of which he is anachronistically styled earl of Winchester) are given in *Newbattle Registrum*, nos.64, 65.

242 Grants to Dunfermline Abbey the church of Strathardle (Kirkmichael), Perthshire. Haddington. (probably 1183×1195)

Will'[a] Dei gr*ati*a R*ex* Scot' . omnibus probis hominibus tocius terre sue . clericis 7 laicis salutem. Sciant presentes 7 futuri me dedisse . 7 concessisse . 7 hac carta mea confirmasse Deo 7 ecclesie Sancte Trinitatis de Dunfer*melin* 7 monachis ibidem Deo seruientibus ecclesiam de Strathardolf cum terris 7 decimis 7 elemosinis 7 oblacionibus omnimodis 7 cum omnibus aliis rectitudinibus 7 iustis pertinenciis suis. Tenendam in liberam 7 perpetuam elemosinam . ita libere 7 quiete . plenarie 7 honorif*ice* ∴ sicut alias ecclesias suas . liberius . quietius . melius[b] 7 honorificencius tenent. T*estibus* Comite Duncano Justic*ia* . Gilleb*erto* Comite de Stratheren' . Rob*erto* de Quinci . Ph*ilippo* de Vallon*iis* . Walt*ero* Olifard' . Hug*one* Giffard' . Alex*andro* de Sancto Martino . Ph*ilippo* de Setun. Apud Hadingtun'.

RUBRIC. De ecclesia de Strathardolf (red with red initial).
SOURCE. NLS, MS. Adv. 34.1.3a, fo.xiiiv (in a hand different from the remaining William I charters in this MS.); also ibid., fo.xiiiiv (in same hand as remainder of William I's charters).
PRINTED. *Dunfermline Registrum*, no.73.
NOTES. [a] Initial red, fo.xiii, blue, fo.xiiii. [b] Only fo.xiiiiv; apparently erased on fo.xiiiv.

COMMENT. For the date, cf. *Dunfermline Registrum*, no.127: Bishop John (the Scot) was the first bishop of Dunkeld to give episcopal authority to this grant, which is likely to have been sought contemporaneously with the royal grant itself. Strathardle was one of the four royal 'manors' (i.e. thanages) of Gowrie from which Scone Abbey drew cain revenues (*RRS*, i, no.243). By an agreement of *c*.1279 with Sir John of Inchmartin, Dunfermline Abbey surrendered its right to the *abthen* of Kirkmichael (*alias* Kylmichel) in return for an annualrent of three merks (*Dunfermline Registrum*, no.227).

243 Confirms to Newbattle Abbey the grant made by Philip dc Vermelles of the land in Romanno (in Newlands), Peeblesshire, formerly held of Philip and of his father by Hugh of Pettinain and his son Reginald, in exchange for land and pasture which the abbey previously held in Romanno; as the charter of Philip bears witness. (1179 × *c*.1189)

Willelmus Dei gratia Rex Scott' episcopis, abbatibus, comitibus, baronibus, justiciis, ministris et omnibus probis hominibus tocius terre sue, clericis et laicis, salutem. Sciant presentes et futuri me concessisse et hac mea carta confirmasse Deo et ecclesie Sancte Marie de Neu*botle* et monachis ibidem Deo seruientibus terram illam quam Philippus de Euermel' eis dedit in Rumanoch, in excambium terre illius et pasture quam prius in eadem Rumanoch habuerunt, scilicet terram illam quam Hugo de Paduynan et Reginaldus filius eius de patre eiusdem Philippi et de ipso Philippo tenuerunt, tenend*am* predictis monachis in liberam et perpetuam elemosinam, ita libere et quiete, plenarie et honorifice sicud carta predicti Philippi de Euermel' testatur et confirmat, et per easdem diuisas, saluo seruicio meo de eodem Philippo et heredibus suis, quod ipsi pro monachis michi perficient. T*estibus* Philippo de Valon*iis*, Willelmo de Mortimer, Alexandro de Sancto Martino et aliis.

Confirmacio Willelmi Reg*is*.[a]
SOURCE. NLS, MS. Adv. 34.4.13, fo.35^{v}.
PRINTED. *Newbattle Registrum*, no.126.
NOTE. [a] Table of contents, fo.2^{v}.
COMMENT. The charter of Philip de Vermelles *secundus* is given in *Newbattle Registrum*, no.125 (1179 × 1189), stating that he and his father had granted Newbattle the land now given up in exchange for the present grant, and giving the marches of the newly granted land in detail. The first or second Philip de Vermelles had granted land in Romanno to Holyrood Abbey before 1165 (*RRS*, i, no.261); by an agreement of 1223, Holyrood surrendered this land to Newbattle (*Newbattle Registrum*, no.127), in exchange for Newbattle's land of Mountlothian (in Temple), Midlothian.

244 Confirms to his burgh and burgesses of Rutherglen all the customs and dues which they had in the time of King David I, and the marches which he granted to them, viz. from Nethan to Polmadie, from Garrion Burn to Kelvin, from Loudoun to 'Prenteneth', and from 'Karnebuth' to 'Karun'. Wherever the provost of the burgh or his sergeand may find toll withheld the lord of the land where it is discovered shall help them recover it, or else incur the king's forfeiture of £10. No one is to expose anything for sale within these marches unless it has first been to the burgh of Rutherglen. Jedburgh. (1179 × 1189, perhaps 1180 × 1185)

Willelmus Dei gr*aci*a Rex Scott' Episcopis Abbatibus Comitibus Baronibus Justic*iis* Vicecom*itibus* prepositis ministris et omnibus probis hominibus tocius terre sue Clericis et Laicis :' Salutem. Sciant presentes et futuri me concessisse et dedisse et hac carta mea confirmasse Burgo meo de Ruth*er*glen et burgensibus meis eiusdem ville omnes consuetudines et rectitudines quas habuerunt tempore Reg*is* Dauid aui mei et illas diuisas quas eis concessit . Scilicet de Neithan usque Polmacde . et de Garin usque Keluin . et de Loudun usque Prenteneth . et de Karnebuth ad Karun. Et quicunque detulerit Tholneum uel alia iura que predicte ville tempore Regis Dauid pertinuerunt . ubicunque prepositus prefate ville vel seruiens eius illum attingere possit :' in cuiuscunque terra attingatur dominus terre illius inueniat preposito de Ruth*er*glen uel seruienti suo auxilium ut disturbetur donec habeant iura regis. Et nisi dominus ville hoc fecerit :' volo ut ipse sit in forisfacto meo de decem libris. Et prohibeo firmiter ne aliquis educat aliquid ad vendendum infra istas diuisas prenominatas :' nisi prius fuerit ad burgum de Ruth*er*glen. Test*ibus* Ern*aldo* Abbate de Melros . Jocelino Arch*idiacono* de Dunkeldin' . Roberto de London' . Waltero Corbet . Willelmo Comyn . Waltero de Berclai Camerario . Johanne de Lond' . Apud Jeddevurth'.

SOURCE. Rutherglen Burgh Charter Chest, original charter of confirmation of Robert I, 20 April, 1323.

PRINTED. *Municipal Corporations Report* (1836), Appendix, II, p.9; *SHR*, xxiii (1926), 42–3.

COMMENT. The Garrion Burn partly forms the march between Carluke and Cambusnethan parishes. 'Prenteneth', unidentified, may be represented in the name Tinny Bank, a hill close to the county boundary between Lanark and Dumfries near Beattock Summit. 'Karnebuth' is probably to be identified with Cairn in Mearns, Renfrewshire. 'Karun' may be somewhere on the extreme western boundary of Renfrewshire and Ayrshire (compare Crawhin Hill in Inverkip?). Loudoun and 'Karnebuth' clearly correspond to the Ayr burgh boundaries listed in no.462.

245 Confirms to Kelso Abbey the lands, possessions, pastures, liberties and rights which it has in the territory of Mow (in Morebattle, Roxburghshire) by right of the church of Mow, as the charters of the donors bear witness. Jedburgh. (1173 × 1189, probably 1180 × 1185)

W. Dei gratia Rex Scott' . Episcopis . Abbatibus . Comit*ibus* . Baron*ibus* . Justic*iis* . Vicecom*itibus* . Ministris . 7 Omnibus probis hominibus tocius terre sue clericis 7 laicis salutem. Sciatis me concessisse 7 hac mea carta confirmasse Ecclesie Sancte Marie de Kalkou 7 monachis ibidem Deo seruientibus omnes terras 7 . possessiones . pasturas . libertates . 7 iura que tenent . tam nomine ecclesie de Molle :' quam in aliis rebus . quas habent in territorio de Molle in uilla 7 extra uillam . Tenenda 7 possidenda in liberam 7 perpetuam elemosinam per diuisas nominatas in cartis donatorum ita libere 7 quiete plenarie 7 honorifice sicut carte donatorum testantur 7 confirmant . 7 sicut aliquam aliam elemosinam in toto regno meo . liberius 7 quiecius tenent 7 possident. Test*ibus* Ric*ardo* de Moruill' Constab*ulario* . Waltero Olifard . Philipp*o* de Valon*iis* . Willelmo de Haia . Waltero de Berkelaie Camerar*io* . Apud Geddeworde.

RUBRIC. Confirmacio super terras 7 libertates ecclesie 7 ville de Molle (top in red).
SOURCE. NLS, MS. Adv. 34.5.1, fo.149^{v}.
PRINTED. *Kelso Liber*, no.406.
COMMENT. In the index to *RRS*, i, Mow is wrongly stated to be in Hownam parish. Now largely depopulated, Mow has been part of Morebattle parish since the seventeenth century. In the twelfth and thirteenth centuries, Mow was an intensively populated and cultivated parish, in which the abbeys of Kelso and Melrose both held considerable property. The original grant of Mow church to Kelso was made by Uhtred son of Liulf in the reign of David I (Lawrie, *Charters*, no.196; cp. *RRS*, i, no.131, p.194). Mow was granted to Walter son of Alan the steward by Malcolm IV, *c*.1161 (ibid., no.183), apparently because Walter had married Eschina, surnamed 'de Londoniis', heiress of Mow. In view of her surname, Eschina can hardly have been Uhtred's daughter, but was perhaps his granddaughter, i.e. daughter of his daughter by a husband who belonged to the family 'de Londoniis' established in the Roxburgh area since David I's time. Eschina 'of London' confirmed the grant of Mow church by a charter dated 31 January, 1186 (*Kelso Liber*, no.146), and by two further charters (the former later than 1198) she and her second husband, Henry 'of Mow', repeated the confirmation (ibid., nos.147, 178). It may be noted that Adam son of Uhtred, presumably the Adam of Mow who witnessed Walter the Steward's charter of land at Mow for Kelso Abbey (*Kelso Liber*, i, nó.170), was a landowner at Dearham and Gilcrux, Cumberland, and had a nephew called William son of Liulf of Mow (*St Bees Register*, Illustrative Docs., no.xxxiii, p.551).

246 Confirms to Kelso Abbey the church of Makerstoun, Roxburghshire, granted by Walter Corbet, as his charter bears witness. Jedburgh. (1179 × 1189, probably 1180 × 1185)

W. Dei gratia Rex Scott' . Episcopis . Abbatibus . Comit*ibus* . Baron*ibus* . Justic*iis* . Vicecom*itibus* . prepositis . ministris . 7 omnibus probis hominibus tocius terre sue[a] clericis 7 laicis salutem. Sciant presentes 7 futuri me concessisse 7 hac carta mea confirmasse Deo 7 Ecclesie Sancte Marie de Kelch' . 7 monachis ibidem Deo seruientibus . donacionem quam Walterus Corbet eis fecit de Ecclesia de Malkarweston' . 7 de omnibus eiusdem ecclesie iustis pertinenciis . 7 omnibus terris . 7 possessionibus 7 libertatibus quas predictus Walterus Corbeth prenominatis[b] monachis de Kelcho donauit. Tenend' 7 habend' in liberam 7 perpetuam elemosinam ita libere 7 quiete plenarie 7 honorifice sicut carta predicti Walteri Corbeth testatur . saluo seruicio meo. Test*ibus* Ern*aldo* Abbate de Melros . Ric*ardo* Abbate de Jedde' . Rob*erto* de Quinci . Philipp*o* de Valon*iis* . Waltero de Windesour' apud Jedde' .

RUBRIC. Carta super Ecclesiam de Malcarwest' (top in red).
SOURCE. NLS, MS. Adv. 34.5.1, fo.149^{r-v}.
PRINTED. *Kelso Liber*, no.405.
NOTES. [a] MS. has salutem here as well as after laicis. [b] Fo.149^{v}.
COMMENT. Walter's charter is given in *Kelso Liber*, no.235.

247 Confirms to St Andrews cathedral Priory the two ploughgates of arable in Garioch (Seggieden, in Kennethmont, Aberdeenshire) granted by his brother (Earl) David, as his charter bears witness. Jedburgh. (1178 × 1185, probably 1180 × 1185)

Willelmus[a] Dei gracia rex Scotorum . Omnibus probis hominibus tocius terre sue clericis et laicis salutem . Sciant presentes et futuri me concessisse et hac carta mea confirmasse Deo et ecclesie Sancti Andree de

Scocia et canonicis ibidem Deo seruientibus illas duas carucatas terre quas Dauid frater meus eis dedit in Garuiach tenendum in liberam elemosinam ita libere et quiete plenarie et honorifice sicut carta ipsius \D*aui*d / testatur et confirmat quousque in reditu ecclesie excambium ad ualenciam terre illius eis donet in perpetuam elemosinam tenend*um*. Testibus . Ricardo de Moreu*ille* const*abulario* . Walltero de Berkel' . Roberto de Landel' apud Jedewrdh .

RUBRIC. De terra in Garuiach (in margin in later hand).
SOURCE. SRO, GD 45/27/8 (St Andrews priory cartulary), fo.cv[r].
PRINTED. *St Andrews Liber*, 226–7.
NOTE. [a] Red initial U.
COMMENT. Earl David's charter is given in *St Andrews Liber*, 239, dating 1172 × 1199 (probably 1178), and the rubric identifies the land with Seggieden.

248 Grants to Kelso Abbey and Abbot Osbert the same liberties and customs which Abbot Arnold and Abbot John had before, in the time of King David I and King Malcolm IV. Wherever they may find their fugitive (neyfs) they are to have them justly and without delay, and no one is to detain them unjustly on pain of the king's forfeiture of 100s. Jedburgh. (1180 × 1188, probably 1180 × 1185)

W. Dei gr*ati*a Rex Scott'. Episcopis . Abbatibus . Comit*ibus* . Baron*ibus* . Justic*iis* . Vicec*omitibus* . 7 omnibus aliis probis hominibus tocius terre sue clericis 7 laicis . salutem. Sciatis me concessisse Ecclesie Sancte Marie de Kelch' . 7 O*sberto* abbati eiusdem loci omnes easdem libertates 7 consuetudines quas Ernabaldus abbas . 7 Joh*annes* abbas ante ipsum habuerunt 7 tenuerunt tempore Regis D*aui*d aui mei . 7 Malcol*mi* fratris mei . ita bene 7 libere 7 quiete sicut alii abbates eas unquam melius 7 liberius habuerunt . 7 tenuerunt. Et ubicunque in tota terra mea fugitiuos suos[a] inuenerint . iuste 7 sine dilatione illos habeant. Unde prohibeo firmiter 7 super forisfactura .c. sol*idorum* ut nemo illos uel catalla sua sibi iniuste detineat nec ipsum uel ministros eius propter hoc iniuste uexet. Test*ibus* Hug*one* Episcopo Sancti Andr*ee* . Ric*ardo* de Morewill' Const*abulario* . Walt*ero* Olif*ard* . Just*icia* . Will*elmo* de Haia . Walt*ero* de Berk' . Camerario . Rob*erto* de Landel*es* apud Jeddewrth.

RUBRIC. Confirmacio super omnes libertates de Kelch' (top in red).
SOURCE. NLS, MS. Adv. 34.5.1, fo.148[v].
PRINTED. *Kelso Liber*, no.401.
NOTE. [a] meos underlined for deletion, suos written above the line.
COMMENT. Probably this was issued soon after Osbert succeeded as abbot of Kelso, in 1180; Bishop Hugh visited the papal *curia* in 1180 and 1183.

249 Announces that the patronage of the church of East Kilbride, Lanarkshire, had been acknowledged and proved in his presence and in his full court at Lanark, by responsible older men and lawful witnesses to belong to the bishop of Glasgow from olden time; and that John bishop of Glasgow (*c*.1115–1147) and his successors had freely bestowed the church. In consequence, Roger de Valognes in the king's presence has renounced his claim to the patronage, which, together with one ploughgate of arable, is to remain with Bishop Jocelin and his successors in perpetuity. Traquair. (1182 × 1190)

W'. Dei gratia Rex Scott'. Episcopis Abbatibus. Com*itibus*. Bar*onibus*. Just*iciis*. vicec*omitibus*. prepositis. ministris et Omnibus probis Hominibus totius terre sue clericis et laicis Salutem. Sciant presentes et futuri quod recognitum fuit et probatum in presentia et plena curia mea apud Lanarc per probos et antiquos homines patrie et legitimos testes quod Donatio ecclesie de Kellebride antiquitus pertinuit ad ecclesiam et ad episcopum Glasg*uensem* et pertinere debet. et quod Joh*annes* episcopus Glasguen*sis* et sui successores libere et quiete et sine aliqua contradictione uel reclamacione ipsam dederunt. Et ideo Rogerus de Vall*oniis* in presentia mea renuntiauit calumpnie et juri quod dicebat se habere in predicta ecclesia. Quare concedo et presenti carta mea confirmo donacionem prenominate ecclesie de Kellebride liberam et quietam cum una carrucata terre et omnibus aliis justis pertinentiis suis Ecclesie et Jocel*ino* episcopo Glasguen*si* et suis successoribus in perpetuum. Test*ibus* Rob*erto* Capellano meo. Hug*one* de sigillo clerico meo. Com*ite* Patricio. Ric*ardo* de Moruill constab*ulario*. Alano dapifero. Philipp*o* de Vall*oniis*. Walt*ero* de Berkel' Camer*ario*. Joh*anne* de London*iis*. Ada fil*io* Gileb*erti*. Apud Trauequeir.

RUBRIC. Item de Ecclesia de Kylbride (in margin in later hand).

SOURCE. Blairs Archives, 16 Drummond Place, Edinburgh, MS. Registrum Vetus of Glasgow, fo.vj[r].

PRINTED. *Glasgow Registrum*, no.56.

COMMENT. The agreement between Bishop Jocelin and Roger de Valognes, witnessed by the king, is given in *Glasgow Registrum*, no.55; it provides that Roger may have his own chapel and chaplain at his castle of Kilbride, supported independently of the parish church, which, however, is to receive all teinds due from Roger's land within the parish.

250 Grants to his burgesses of Inverkeithing that they may levy toll and customs and all dues pertaining to their burgh between the rivers Leven (Fife) and Devon, by water and land and from boats and ships. No one may take toll or carry on trade within these marches without the licence of the burgesses. Kinghorn. (*c.*1173 × 1189)

Willelmus Dei gracia Rex Scottorum,[a] Justiciariis, Vicecomitibus, Prepositis, Ministris et omnibus probis hominibus tocius terre sue salutem. Sciatis me concessisse burgensibus meis de Inuyrkethin ut capiant tolneum[b] et consuetudines et omnes rectitudines ad burgum pertinentes inter aquam de Leuene[c] et aquam de Douane,[d] et in aquis et in terris, tam de batellis quam de nauibus; et prohibeo firmiter ne quis tolneum[b] aut aliquam consuetudinem ad predictum burgum pertinentem, aut in aquis aut in terris, infra predictas divisas, absque eorum licencia[e] capiat, aut aliquam mercaturam extra burgum exerceat, super meam[f] plenariam forisfacturam. Test*ibus* Comite Dunec*ano* Just*iciario*, Ricardo de Moreuill' Constabulario, Hugone Giffart, Waltero de Berk' Camerario. Apud Kyngorne.

SOURCE. SRO, RH 9/11/16/6 (transcript, made February, 1812, of an original charter of inspection of Robert III, 24 April, 1399, then in the possession of Sir John Henderson of Fordell Bt. This original has not been traced) = *A*. NLS, MS. Adv. 34.6.24, p.164 (brief abstract of charter, commencing 'K. Wm. gives that brugh power' and reproducing with errors the passage from 'ut capiant' to 'forisfacturam') = *B*.

PRINTED. *Municipal Corporations Report* (1836), Appendix to the General Report, Cl. II, p.8, no.[1].
NOTES. [a] Punctuation editorial. [b] toloneum, *B*. [c] Levin, *B*. [d] Douan, *B*. [e] valencia, *B*. [f] nostram, *B*.
COMMENT. See no.102.

251 Confirms to the cathedral church of Aberdeen the properties granted by King David I and King Malcolm IV, and adds by his own gift the lands of Birse, with the forest of Birse, with all neyfs, saving only the king's thanes. Kinghorn. '1170'. (1180 × 1184?) (Doubtful).

Will*elmus*[a] Dei gratia Rex Scottorum omnibus probis hominibus tocius terre sue, clericis et laicis, salutem. Sciant presentes et futuri me dedisse, concessisse et hac carta mea confirmasse Deo et Beate Marie et Beato Machorio et Matheo Episcopo Aberdonensi omnes illas donaciones et libertates, terras et ecclesias, decimas reddituum meorum inter duas aquas que Dee et Spee dicuntur, decimam escaetarum me contingencium infra vicecomitat*us* de Aberden et de Banff quas Nectanus et Edwardus predecessores sui Episcopi Aberdonenses habuerunt ex donacione Regis Dauid aui mei et Regis Malcolmi fratris mei, cum omnibus iustis pertinenciis suis. Tenend*as* sibi et successoribus suis in puram et perpetuam elimosinam ita libere et quiete, plenarie et honorifice, sicud predicti Reges Dauid avus meus et Malcolmus frater meus predecessoribus suis predictis episcopis dederunt et concesserunt, et ita libere sicut aliqua elimosina in Regno meo possidetur seu tenetur. Preterea dedi et concessi et hac carta mea confirmaui de incremento predicto Episcopo Matheo et successoribus suis Episcopis pro salute anime mee et antecessorum meorum totas terras meas de Brass, videlicet Ouchtirbrass , Drummenathy , villam ecclesie Kynmonedy , Balfoure , Tulysnacht , Erbentuly , Ardensoule , Innercat , Parci , Migstrath , Clone, Balneboth', Enachy , Ballynfady , Tulyschrosk'[b] , Tulycarman , et forestam meam de Brass cum omnibus natiuis dictarum terrarum , thaynys meis tantum exclusis , cum aliis iustis pertinenciis et rectitudinibus in puram, liberam et perpetuam elimosinam, ita libere, quiete, plenarie et honorifice sicut aliqua elimosina in Regno meo liberius, quiecius, plenius et honori[c]ficencius tenetur seu possidetur. Testibus Jocelino episcopo Glasguen*si* , Hugone Dunkelden*si*, Episcopo Ricardo Moravie , Turpino Episcopo Brechinen*si* , Andrea Episcopo Catanen*si* , David fratre meo , A.[d] de Kalchuch , H*enrico* abbate de Abirbrothoch' , W*illelmo* abbate Sancte Crucis , Roberto abbate de Schona , Ricardo abbate de Cupro , Hugone abbate de Newbottyl , Reynerio abbate de Kynloss' , Comite Duncano Justiciar*io* , Comite Patricio , Comite Gilberto de Strathern , Gilbrid Comite de Angus , G. comite de Marr' , Willelmo Cumyne , Roberto , W*illelmo*, capellanis meis , Hugone de sigillo clerico meo , Willelmo de Haya , Galfrido de Maleuile , Willelmo de Morauyle . Apud Kyngorn anno Regni mei quinto.[e]

RUBRIC. Confirmacio Regis Willelmi super premissis una cum dominio et terris de Brass cum natiuis et libera foresta earundem (red, *A* only).
SOURCE. NLS, MS. Adv. 16.1.10, fos.49v–50r = *M*. NLS, MS. Adv. 34.4.4, fos. 40r–41r = *A*. Printed here from *M*.

PRINTED. (From *M*) *Aberdeen Registrum*, i, 12–13.
NOTES. [a] Initial red. [b] Tulyquhorske, *A*. [c] Fo.50r. [d] Sic, for J. or O. Abbate. [e] Anno domini 1170 added in hand of xvi cent.
COMMENT. This must be inflated or tampered with to say the least, but it may be based on an authentic act of King William. The witnesses will fit the dates suggested above, if we ignore Hugh bishop of Dunkeld, Richard bishop of Moray, Richard abbot of Coupar, and read 'O' for 'A' as the initial of the abbot of Kelso (Osbert).

252 Announces that by his command on 14 September, 1184, the marches of Moorfoot (Midlothian) between the monks of Newbattle and David Uviat were perambulated and sworn to in the presence of Alexander, the king's sheriff of Haddington, and Simon son of Malbet, sheriff of Traquair, and many other responsible men sent there by the king for this purpose. In consequence of this perambulation, the king now confirms to the monks of Newbattle the following marches, as the charter of King David I bears witness: as the Black Burn descends from the hills and falls into Gladhouse, and as 'Pardavanesburne' comes from the hills and falls into (South) Esk, and as two burns descend from the moss behind Toxside and fall respectively into Gladhouse and Esk. The monks are to hold the land of Moorfoot by these marches as the charter of King David bears witness. Haddington. 1184

W'. Dei gr*ati*a Rex Scott'. Episcopis. Abbatibus. Comitibus. Baronibus. Justic*iis*. Vicecom*itibus*. Ministris. 7 Omnibus probis hominibus totius Terre sue Clericis 7 Laicis salutem. Sciant presentes 7 futuri quod anno ab incarnatione domini .M°.C°.lxxx.iiij° die exaltationis sancte crucis precepto meo fuerunt iurate. 7 perambulate diuise de Mordwheit inter Monacos de Neubott*el*. 7 D*aui*d Uuiat presentibus Alex*andro* vicecom*ite* meo de Hadintun'. 7 Simone fil*io* Malbet vicecom*ite* de Trauequeir. 7 aliis quamplurimis probis hominibus meis. quos cum eis ad hoc ipsum miseram. quas sicut tunc perambulate fuerunt. 7 sicut carta Regis D*aui*d aui mei testatur.' predictis Monachis confirmo. 7 firmiter teneri precipio. scilicet sicut Blakeburne descendit de montibus. 7 cadit in Gledewis. 7 sicut Pardauanesburne uenit de montibus 7 cadit in Esch. 7 sicut duo riuuli descendunt de mussa. que est retro Tockesheued. 7 cadit hinc 7 inde in Gledewis. 7 Esch. Volo itaque 7 precipio ut predicti Monachi predictam Modwehit infra predictas diuisas adeo. libere 7 quiete. plenarie 7 honorifice in perpetuam elemosinam teneant sicut aliquam liberius 7 quietius. plenarius. 7 honorificentius tenent. 7 possident. 7 sicut carta Regis D*aui*d aui mei testatur. Test*ibus* Æ*rnaldo* abbate de Melros. Ric*ardo* de Moreuill' const*abulario*. Roberto de Quenci. Waltero Olif*ard*. Philippo de Vallon*iis*. Alex*andro* de Sancto Martino Vicecom*ite* de Hadingtun'. Simone fil*io* Melbet. Vicecom*ite* de Trauequeir. Simone Fraser. Apud Hadingtuniam.

ENDORSED. De perambulacione W.℞ Morthweit (xii–xiii cent.). Also modern endorsements.
DESCRIPTION. 7·2″ (19·4 cm.), Top, bottom × 3·8″ (9·6 cm.), L, 3·7″ (9·4 cm.) R. Foot folded to a depth of 0·7″ (1·9 cm.). Single slits, with tag 5·7″ (14 cm.)

long, 0·7″ (1·9 cm.) wide. Large fragment of seal remains, in dark green wax, rev. to front, diameter 3·2″ (8 cm.). Fair impression.
HAND. Scribe Ca. Unruled.
SOURCE. Original, SRO, GD 40/1/7.
PRINTED. *Newbattle Registrum*, no.20 (with facsimile).
COMMENT. For King David I's charter see Lawrie, *Charters*, no.145. 'Pardavanesburne', whose name may be preserved in Parduvine in Carrington, was perhaps the burn now called Tweeddale Burn, Fullarton Water and Redside Burn.

253 Announces that on 18 October [1184], in the presence of himself and the bishops, barons and other men of his kingdom, a perambulation and definitive demarcation of marches was carried out between Melrose Abbey and the men of Wedale (Stow, Midlothian). Faithful witnesses took oath in the presence of the king and responsible men that the forest in which Melrose Abbey has pasture rights stretches as far as the road which runs on the west side of Stow church and as far as the burn called 'Fasseburne'. (Spurious)

Willelmus Dei gratia Rex Scottorum . omnibus probis hominibus tocius terre sue salutem. Sciatis quod me presente . et presentibus episcopis . baronibus . et pluribus aliis hominibus Regni mei die Sancti Luce Euuangeliste . inter monachos de Meylros et homines de Wedal' super pastura foreste mee quam antecessores mei et ego dictis monachis de Meylros in puram et perpetuam elemosinam dedimus . per iuramenta fidelium uirorum facta fuit perambulacio et certa finium limitacio jurauerunt siquidem coram me et probis hominibus meis predicti fideles . quod foresta mea que est pastura dictorum monachorum de Meylros . tendit usque ad uiam que uadit ad occidentem partem ecclesie de Wedal' . et usque ad riuulum qui uocatur Fasseburne. Quare uolo . concedo et precipio . quod dicti monachi totam prefatam pasturam cum omnibus aisiamentis et libertatibus suis . pacifice teneant et possideant . usque ad prefatas diuisas . in puram . liberam et perpetuam elemosinam . proprie sibi et suis successoribus. Ita quod nulli communiam habeant inter ipsos aut cum ipsis infra prefatas diuisas predicte pasture . saluis mihi et heredibus meis . feris et auibus et uenacione infra dictam forestam. Test*ibus* Ricardo Episcopo Sancti Andr*ee* . Jocelino Episcopo Glasg*uensi* . Johanne Abbate de Kalchou . Osberto Abbate de Jedword' . Comite D*aui*d . Ricardo de Moruyll' constabulario . et multis aliis.

ENDORSED. Perambulacio Reg*is* Will*elm*i de terminis de Wytley. (xiii cent.(?), same hand as text). T (xiv–xv cent.?). J. Scott. (xvi–xvii cent.). Also modern endorsements.
DESCRIPTION. 6·9″ (17·5 cm.), Top and bottom × 3·6″ (9·3 cm.) L, 3·9″ (9·9 cm.), R. Foot folded to a depth of 0·8″ (1·9 cm.). A seal-tag, 6·2″ (15·2 cm.) long, 0·7″ (1·7 cm.) wide, passes through double slits in foot and fold. No seal remains.
HAND. Scribe UDe. Unruled. This hand is almost certainly of the second half of the thirteenth century. It is closely similar to, but not identical with, the hand of the older of the two surviving Melrose cartularies, NLS, MS. Adv. 34.4.11 (*tempore* Alexander III?).
SOURCE. Purported original, BM, Cotton Chr. no.xviii, 18.
PRINTED. *Melrose Liber*, no.112.
COMMENT. This document is not an authentic original act of William I, although it obviously purports to be. Nor can it, as it stands, represent a genuine original, since Osbert abbot of Jedburgh died in 1174 while Jocelin was not consecrated

bishop of Glasgow until 1175 (*Chron. Melrose*, 41). On the other hand there is no reason to doubt the statement in the Melrose chronicle (ibid., 44) that on 18 October, 1184, the dispute between Melrose and the men of Stow was settled at Crosslee (on the boundary between the parish of Stow and county of Midlothian and the parish of Melrose and county of Roxburgh) by Richard de Moreville and other twelve faithful men, in the presence of the king, his brother David and bishops, earls and barons. In the chronicle account, the limits of the king's forest (in which Melrose enjoyed pasture rights) were 'as far as the road which runs on the west side of the church of the Blessed Mary of Wedale, and it is pasture of the church of Melrose as far as the marches of Wedale and as far as the burn which is called "Fasseburne", by the gift of three kings, viz. David Malcolm and William'.

254 Grants to Kelso Abbey for the use and building work of the abbey the church of Dumfries with its land, teinds and offerings, and with the chapel of St Thomas in the burgh of Dumfries, with its toft, and with five acres of arable which the king has given to Dumfries church in free alms with which he has caused Philip de Valognes to invest the church. Dumfries. (1183 × 1188)

W. Dei gr*ati*a Rex Scott'. Episcopis. Abbatibus. Comit*ibus*. Baron*ibus*. Justic*iis* . Vicecom*itibus* . prepositis . ministris . 7 omnibus probis hominibus suis clericis 7 laicis. salutem. Sciant presentes 7 posteri[a]. me dedisse. 7 concessisse. 7 hac [carta][b] mea confirmasse Deo 7 Ecclesie Sancte Marie de Kelcho. 7 monachis ibidem Deo seruientibus ad usus 7 operacionem ipsius Ecclesie . Ecclesiam de Dunfres . cum terris 7 decimis. 7 omnimodis oblacionibus. 7 Capella Sancti Thome in ipso burgo. 7 Tofta ad ipsam capellam pertinentem. 7 cum quinque acris terre. quas eidem Ecclesie 7 capelle in liberam elemosinam dedi. 7 per Philippum de Valoniis eis tradi feci. 7 cum omnibus aliis eiusdem ecclesie iustis pertinenciis . ita ne liceat alicui illam ecclesiam uel capellam. aut earum redditus. siue beneficia ab operacione ecclesie de Kelcho. 7 usibus fratrum quoquomodo alienare. Quare uolo 7 firmiter precipio ∴ ut iam dicti monachi ecclesiam supradictam de Dunfres. cum capella . terris . decimis . 7 omnibus earum iustis pertinenciis infra burgum 7 extra in liberam 7 perpetuam elemosinam teneant 7 possideant . ita libere 7 plenarie 7 honorifice ∴ sicut aliquas elemosinas liberius 7 quiecius tenent. Test*ibus* J*ocelino* Glasguensi Episcopo . H*ugone* Sancti Andree . 7 J*ohanne* Dunkeld*ensi* . 7 M*atheo* Aberd*onensi* episcopis . H*enrico* Abbate Sancti Thome. Comite Dunec*ano*. Philippo de Valoniis . Willelmo de Lindesia. apud Dunfres.

RUBRIC. Carta super Ecclesiam de Dunfres 7 Capellam Sancti Thome (foot of fo.150^{v}, in red).

SOURCE. NLS, MS. Adv. 34.5.1, fo.151^{r}. PRINTED. *Kelso Liber*, no.411.

NOTES. [a] futuri struck through, posteri added, MS. [b] MS. omits.

COMMENT. The king seems to have gained possession of Dumfries *c.*1185 (cf. *Dumfriesshire Trans.*, 3rd ser., ii, 166–170), and the beginning of the royal burgh may be assigned to this period. The reference to Philip de Valognes suggests that he was acting as chamberlain, with the responsibility for royal burghs which certainly belonged to that office by the thirteenth century. The somewhat unusual attestation of the abbot of Arbroath in the south-west of Scotland may go to confirm the suggestion that St Thomas's chapel in Dumfries was dedicated to Thomas of Canterbury (cf. J. M. Mackinlay, *Ancient Church Dedications in Scotland, Non-scriptural* (1914), 284).

This act belongs to the period when John the Scot had accepted the see of Dunkeld (by the award of Pope Lucius III in 1183) and when he and Bishop Matthew had been received into the King's peace.

255 Grants to the Hospital of St Peter, York, two and a half ploughgates of land in the territory of Dumfries and Conheath (in Caerlaverock). All men of the hospital dwelling on this land are to be free of toll, unless any of them are merchants carrying on trade. Gretna. (1175 × 1190, probably *c.*1185)

W. Dei gr*aci*a Rex Scott'. Omnibus probis hominibus tocius terre sue, clericis et laicis, salutem. Sciant presentes et posteri me dedisse et concessisse et hac mea carta confirmasse Deo et hospitali Sancti Petri in Ebor' et fratribus ibidem Deo seruientibus duas carrucatas terre et dimidiam in territorio de Drunfres et de Kulenath[a], tenendam[b] sibi in liberam et perpetuam elemosinam cum communi pastura et cum omnibus libertatibus ad eandem terram iuste pertinentibus, ita libere et quiete, plenarie et honorifice sicut aliqua elemosina in regno meo liberius et quiecius, plenius et honorificencius tenetur et possidetur. Concessi etiam eis et precipio ut omnes homines sui super terram illam manentes quieti sint a theelon' et omni consuetudine per totam terram meam, nisi fuerint aliqui eorum qui mercaturam exercuerint sicut mercatores. Test*ibus* Jocel*ino* Episcopo Glasg*uensi*, Ricardo de Moruill' const*abulario*, Roberto Capellano, Roberto de Quinci, Hugone de Sigillo et Ricardo de prebenda clericis meis, Roberto de Bruys,[c] Alano fil*io* Walteri, Roll*ando* filio Utredi,[d] Waltero de Berkel' Camerario, Willelmo de Lyndesee,[e] apud Gretenho.

MARGINAL NOTE. Dunfres et Kulenath[f].
SOURCE. PRO, C.47/22/4, no.8 = *A*. PRO, C.53/93, m.8 = *B*. Printed from *A*, with variants of *B* noted.
PRINTED. *Cal. Chart.*, iii, 90–91.
NOTES. [a] Kulenhath, *B*. [b] Sic. [c] Brus, *B*. [d] Uctredi, *B*. [e] Lindesi, *B*. [f] *A* only.
COMMENT. This grant probably belongs to the period after *c.*1185 when the king gained control of Dumfries. See above, p.14. Robert de Brus died in 1191.

256 Confirms to Holm Cultram Abbey the land in Galloway granted by Walter of Berkeley the king's chamberlain, and confirmed by his charter. (1173 × 1193, probably *c.*1180–1190)

W[a] Dei gr*ati*a Rex Scottorum[b], Episcopis, Abbatibus, Comit*ibus*, Baronibus, Justic*iis*, vicecom*itibus*, prepositis, ministris et omnibus probis hominibus totius terre sue, clericis et laicis, salutem. Sciant presentes et futuri me concessisse et hac presenti[c] carta mea confirmasse Deo et ecclesie Sancte Marie de Holm' et monachis ibidem Deo seruientibus[d] terram illam in Galweia quam Walterus de Berkelay camerarius meus eis dedit et carta sua confirmauit. Tenendam in liberam et perpetuam elemosinam per diuisas nominatas in carta predicti Walteri[e] ita libere et[f] quiete, plenarie et honorifice[d] sicut aliqui monachi ordinis Cist*erciensis* elemosinas suas in tota terra mea liberius, quiecius, plenius et honorificencius[d] tenent, et sicut carta prefati Walteri[g] testatur, saluo seruicio meo etc.

RUBRIC. Confirmacio Will' Reg*is* Scottorum (top right, red, somewhat rubbed).[h] Confirmacio W. Regis Scottorum (top right, red, much rubbed).[i]

SOURCE. Carlisle, Dean and Chapter Muniments, MS. Cartulary of Holm Cultram, p.103r = *C*. BM, MS. Harl. 3891, fo.86v = *H*. Printed here from a collation of *C* and *H*, with *C*'s readings generally preferred.
PRINTED. Dugdale, *Mon. Angl.* (New), v, 597, no.XVIII; *Holm Cultram Recs.*, 51 (brief abstract).
NOTES. [a] Blue initial, *C*, red, much rubbed, *H*. Punctuation is editorial. [b] Scocie, *C*. [c] *H* omits presenti. [d] For last three words *H* has etc. [e] *C* has in predicta carta Walteri. [f] *H* omits et. [g] *C* omits Walteri. [h] *C*. [i] *H*.
COMMENT. The land of Kirkgunzeon was granted to Holm Cultram by Uhtred son of Fergus (1162 × 1175). The grant was in feu ferme, with the option of giving up the land if Holm Cultram was not satisfied with it. It was alleged that afterwards Uhtred rescinded the grant and granted the land to Walter of Berkeley, whereupon the king was requested to hold an inquest and appointed Uhtred son of Fergus and Roger of Minto to find out the truth of the matter with the help of the older men of the neighbourhood. The letter in which Bishop Christian of Galloway narrates the foregoing (× October, 1186) concludes by saying that Walter of Berkeley still retains the land unjustly. Probably Walter's charter and this royal confirmation belong to *c.*1180–1190 (BM, MS. Harl. 3891, fos.85 and 87–88).

257 Confirms to Newbattle Abbey the grant made by William of Lindsay of a certain part of his land of Crawford, Lanarkshire, which William holds of Swain son of Thor, to be held as William's charter bears witness. (Probably *c.*1185 × *c.*1190)

Willelmus Dei gr*ati*a Rex Scott' omnibus probis hominibus tocius terre sue, clericis et laicis, salutem. Sciant presentes et futuri me concessisse et hac carta mea confirmasse donacionem illam quam Willelmus de Lyndd' dedit Deo et ecclesie Sancte Marie de Neu*botle* et monachis ibidem Deo seruientibus de quadam parte terre sue de Cracheford, quam scilicet Cracheford ipse Willelmus tenet de Swano filio Thore, tenend*am* sibi in liberam et perpetuam elemosinam, ita libere et quiete, plenarie et honorifice, sicud carta ipsius Willelmi testatur et confirmat, saluo seruicio meo. T*estibus* Comite Dauid fratre meo, Roberto de Quency et al*iis*.

Carta Reg*is* Willelmi.[a]
SOURCE. NLS, MS. Adv. 34.4.13, fo.37v.
PRINTED. *Newbattle Registrum*, no.137.
NOTE. [a] Table of contents, fo.2v.
COMMENT. The charter of William of Lindsay and its confirmation by his son and heir David of Lindsay given in *Newbattle Registrum*, nos.135, 136 are unfortunately very hard to date. They speak of Swain son of Thor (a witness to no.258) as still living, and if he is the same as the witness to *RRS*, i, no.239 (1163–4), a date later than the decade *c.*1180–1190 seems unlikely. On the other hand, William's charter and this confirmation are witnessed by the king's brother as earl. William's charter, which has marginal notes 'Fynglen et Glengeth' (Fingland and Glengeith), gives the marches of the land granted as from the source of 'Brothiralewyn' (Elvan Water) to the Clyde, and as 'Polnetrinoth' (Potrenick Burn) falls from the mountains into 'Deiher' (Potrail Water) and thence downstream to Elvanfoot. The church of Crawford had been granted to Holyrood Abbey before 1164 (*Holyrood Liber*, p.169), and Newbattle gained remission of teinds from its land in the parish by an agreement of 1223 (*Newbattle Registrum*, no.127).

258 Grants to Gilbert earl of Strathearn Madderty (Perthshire) in feu and heritage, with sake and soke, toll, team and infangthief, for the service of one knight; in such manner that neither he nor his heirs shall be required at any time to be challenged with regard to this land by Gillecolm the marischal or his heirs or any of his kin, should they wish to pursue him for possession of the land, since Gillecolm has lost the land on account of his felony, inasmuch as he yielded the king's castle of 'Heryn' (Auldearn?) treacherously and then went over to the king's enemies as a wicked traitor and stood with them against the king to do him as much harm as he could. Linlithgow. (1185 × *c.*1190, probably 1187 × 1189)

Will*elmus*[a] Dei gr*ati*a [Rex[b]] Scottorum episcopis, abbatibus, comitibus, baronibus, justiciariis, vicecomitibus, ministrisque omnibus probis hominibus tocius terre sue, clericis et laicis, salutem. Sciant presentes et futuri me dedisse, concessisse et hac presenti carta mea confirmasse comiti Gilberto de Stratheryn Maddyrnin per rectas diuisas suas et cum omnibus iustis pertinenciis in bosco et plano, in terris et aquis, in pratis et pascuis, in moris et marresiis, in molendinis et stagnis et omnibus aliis justis pertinenciis suis, cum sacca et socca, cum tholl et theame et infangandthefe. Tenend*am* sibi et heredibus suis de me et heredibus meis in feodo et hereditate, libere et quiete, plenarie et honorifice per seruicium unius militis. Ita eciam quod nec ipse nec heredes sui aliquo tempore respondeant de terra Gillecolme Marescallo aut heredibus suis aut alicui de parentela sua, siquando querelam inde erga eos mouere uoluerint, quoniam predictus Gillecolm pro felonia quam[c] erga me fecit terram prenominatam amisit, sicut ille qui in felonia reddidit castellum meum de Heryn et postea sicut iniquus[d] et proditor iuit ad inimicos meos mortales et cum eis stetit contra me ad forisfaciendum pro posse suo. Test*ibus*, Comite D*aui*d fratre meo, Ric*ardo* de Moruile Constabulario,[e] Philipp*o* de Valon*iis*, Alano dapifero, Waltero Olif*ard*, Willelmo de Lyndesay, Waltero Corb*et*, Willelmo Cumyn, Rann*ulfo* de[f] Sules,[g] Swano filio Thore, Willelmo filio Thore. Apud Lillidqw.

RUBRIC. Carta Regis Willelmi super terris de Maddyrnyn.[h]

SOURCE. Kinnoull Trustees Muniments, MS. Cartulary of Inchaffray Abbey, in custody of Messrs Condie, Mackenzie and Co. Ltd., Perth, fos.2^{v}–3^{r}.

PRINTED. *Inchaffray Liber*, p.6, no.2. *Inchaffray Chrs.*, Appendix, no.2, pp.153–4.

NOTES. [a] Punctuation editorial. [b] MS. omits. [c] MS. quem. [d] MS. iniqus. [e] MS. Constan. [f] Fo.3^{r}. [g] MS. Sal'. [h] Fo.2^{v}, top.

COMMENT. The events referred to in this charter relate to the king's efforts to suppress the rebellions of Donald Macwilliam in the north, and to bring Moray and Ross firmly under royal control. Castles were built in 1179 at Eþerdouer (Redcastle on the Black Isle, in Killearnan, Ross-shire) and 'Dunscath' (Dunskeath, in Nigg, Ross-shire), and in 1187 a major royal campaign against Macwilliam in Moray and Ross resulted in Macwilliam's defeat and death at the hands of Roland, Uhtred's son (*Chron. Melrose*, 42, 46; *Gesta Henrici*, ii, 7–9). After a vacancy of two and a half years, the see of Moray was filled by the election of the king's clerk Richard (1 March, 1187). It is probably significant that the last known references to Auldearn as a royal burgh belong to the 1180s and the earliest known references to Nairn as a royal burgh suggest that its foundation dates *c.*1190 (G.S. Pryde, *Burghs of Scotland*, 12–13). Moreover, it is known that King William took land at Nairn from the bishop of Moray in order to build his castle and burgh of Nairn, and this may have been at the time of the appointment of Richard as bishop (*Moray Registrum*, no.25). It seems probable that the castle of 'Heryn' mentioned in this charter was Auldearn, and that its betrayal was an incident in the Macwilliam rebellion of 1179–87. Gillecolm, the royal marischal, who held Madderty prior to his forfeiture, is known to have been active in the area of Perth from other acts in this collection (cf. nos.137, 206). It is most improbable that he was the same Gillecolm who was slain by Roland, Uhtred's son, in Galloway in 1185; that Gillecolm seems rather to have been one of Roland's numerous Gallovidian enemies (*Inchaffray Chrs.*, 304; *Chron. Fordun*, 269).

259 Commands those who ought to make annual payments to Scone Abbey, from the king's teinds and grants, to pay promptly at the appointed terms. Should any such payment be withheld, the king's sheriff or bailie in whose jurisdiction the debtor lives is to take poinds from him until he has paid. (1173 × 1214)

Willelmus[a] Dei gracia Rex Scottorum justiciis, vicecomitibus, prepositis, burgensibus et omnibus ministris tocius terre sue salutem. Mando et firmiter precipio ut quicunque aliquid de decima vel de elemosina mea Deo et abbati de Scon annuatim soluere debuerit illud ad terminos michi statutos plenarie eis persoluat. Et prohibeo ne quis quicquam ecclesie de Scon siue canonicis de predicta decima siue elemosina supra predictos terminos detineat, super meam plenariam forisfacturam. Si quis uero super hoc eis aliquid detinere presumpserit, precipio ut vicecomes siue balliuus meus in cuius potestate debitor fuerit eum distringat donec eis debitum suum plenarie persoluerit. Testibus etc.

SOURCE. NLS, MS. Adv. 34.3.28, fos.11^{v}–12^{r}.
PRINTED. *Scone Liber*, no.39.
NOTE. [a] Initial omitted, MS.
COMMENT. Possibly issued on the occasion of the election of a new abbot: either Robert II, in or after 1186, or Reinbald, in 1198.

260 Confirms the agreement made between Ingram bishop of Glasgow and Robert de Brus, with faith pledged by both parties, and afterwards concluded and confirmed between Robert de Brus and Jocelin bishop of Glasgow, anent the churches of Moffat, Kirkpatrick Juxta, Dryfesdale, Hoddam and Castlemilk (St Mungo), Dumfriesshire, as the chirograph between the parties bears witness. Lanark. (1187 × 1189)

W'. Dei gr*ati*a Rex Scott'. Episcopis abbatibus . Com*itibus* . Baron*ibus* . Vicecom*itibus* . Justic*iis* . Ministris et Omnibus probis hominibus tocius terre sue .' Clericis et laicis Salutem. Sciant Presentes et Futuri me concessisse et hac carta mea confirmasse Conuencionem que facta fuit inter Eng*elramum* Glasgue*nsem* Episcopum. et Rob*ertum* de Brus utriusque partis fide interposita . et inter Joceli*num* Episcopum Glasguen*sem* finita et confirmata .' de Ecclesia de Moffet et Ecclesia de Kirkepatric et Ecclesia de Driuesdal' et Ecclesia de Hodelm . et Ecclesia de Castelmilc .' cum omnibus earundem ecclesiarum iustis pertinentiis .' et libertatibus. Tenend*am* ita libere et quiete plenarie et honorifice .' sicut cirographum inter eos factum testatur. Test*ibus* Ric*ardo* episcopo de Morauia . Ern*aldo* abbate de Melros . Ric*ardo* de Moreuill' Constab*ulario* . Roll*ando* filio Uchtredi . Rob*erto* de Quinci . Al*ano* Dapifero . Willelmo de Moruill' . Willelmo Cumin . Roberto fil*io* Rob*erti* filio[a] Weremb*aldi* . Simone Locard . Thoma Thancard . Thoma de Colbainestu*n* . Adam de Aschechirche . apud Lannarc.

RUBRIC. Item de Ecclesiis de Moffet . de Kirkepatrik . de Driuesdale . de Hodelm . et de Castelmilc (in margin in different hand).
SOURCE. Blairs Archives, 16 Drummond Place, Edinburgh, MS. Registrum Vetus of Glasgow, fo.vj^v = *A*. Ibid., fo.liij^{r-v} = *B*. Printed here from *A*.
PRINTED. *Glasgow Registrum*, no.73. *Guisborough Cartularium*, ii, 345–6, no.1183.
NOTE. [a] Sic; perhaps suppress last two words, or add Roberto after Roberti.
COMMENT. The chirograph referred to is given in *Glasgow Registrum*, no.72; the agreement involved homage to the bishops of Glasgow by Robert de Brus and his heirs, supporting the belief that these lands in Annandale had been granted to the first Robert de Brus by David I in spite of the fact that they belonged to the church of Saint Kentigern.

261 Grants to Glasgow Cathedral Church 40s. annually from the *firma burgi* of his burgh of Rutherglen for the lighting of the church, payable half at Martinmas and half at Whitsun. Rutherglen. (1182 × 1190)

W. Dei gr*atia* Rex Scott'. Episcopis . Abbatibus . Comitibus . baronibus . Just*iciis* . vicecom*itibus* . prepositis . ministris[a] et omnibus probis hominibus tocius terre sue . Salutem. Sciant presentes et futuri me dedisse et concessisse . et hac carta mea confirmasse Deo et Sancto Kentegerno et ecclesie Glasguen*si* in perpetuam elemosinam[a] .xl. sol*idos* de firma burgi mei de Rutherglen . ad luminare predicte ecclesie. Quare precipio firmiter balliuis meis de Rutherglen ut prenominate ecclesie de Glasgu singulis annis illos .xl[a] . solidos de firma prefati[b] burgi absque omni[c] disturbacione habere faciant scilicet .xx^{ti}. sol*idos* ad festum Sancti Martini et xx^{ti}. sol*idos* ad Pentecosten. Test*ibus* Comite Dunec*ano* . Just*icia* . Comite Patricio . Com*ite* Gilberto . Ricardo de Moreuill' Constab*ulario* . Waltero Olifard . Alano dapifero . Seierio de Quinci . Willelmo de Moreuill '. Willelmo de Haia . Ricardo Mareschall*o* . Simone Loggart . apud Ruthergle*n*.

RUBRIC. Carta .W. reg*is* de .xl^a. sol*idis* de Rutherglen ad luminare.[d] Ex autographo in Archiv. Glasg. apud [ ] in arcula ligne*a* sub littera A.[e]
DESCRIPTION. Original not described in *B*, which however has this note of the seal: 'Sigillo magno Scotie ex cera alba integro (vel parum fracto) (vel pene attrito) appenso exhiben*te* ex uno latere imaginem regis equestrem dextra strictum gladium, leva vexillum (ut videtur) tenent*is* et in circ*ulo* circa oram sig*illi* Will. Deo Rectore Rex Scottor'. Ex altero vero latere etc.'
SOURCE. Blairs Archives, 16 Drummond Place, Edinburgh, MS. Liber Rubeus of Glasgow, fo.18^r = *A*. Earl of Dalhousie, Brechin Castle, MS. copy of Glasgow Registrum Vetus together with certain original charters (in this case apparently only a copy of the original, not collated with the Registrum), p.317 = *B*. Printed here from *A*, with more important variants of *B* noted.
PRINTED. *Glasgow Registrum*, no.31.
NOTES. [a] elemosynam, *B*. [b] predicti, *B*. [c] ulla, *B*, with omni written over. [d] In margin, *A* only. [e] In margin, *B* only.

262 Confirms to Dryburgh Abbey the land in Pettinain, Lanarkshire, which Robert son of Werenbald, his sheriff of Lanark, perambulated for the abbey and gave it sasine, by the king's command, viz. the land which the canons of Dryburgh held in the time of King Malcolm IV and King David I. Confirms also the toft and croft belonging to the chapel of Pettinain. (1173 × 1214)

Willelmus Dei gr*aci*a rex Scotorum episcopis, abbatibus, comitibus, baronibus, justiciariis, ministris et omnibus probis hominibus tocius terre sue, clericis et laicis, salutem. Sciant presentes et futuri me dedisse et concessisse et hac carta mae confirmasse Deo et ecclesie Sancte Marie de Dryburgh et canonicis ibidem Deo servientibus in liberam et perpetuam elemosinam terram illam in Padenan'[a] quam Robertus filius Werenberti vicecomes meus de Lanark ad opus meum perambulavit et syesivit precepto meo; illam scilicet terram quam canonici predicti tenuerant tempore regis David aui mei et regis Malcolmi fratris mei et meo. Concedo eciam eis toftum et croftum ad capellam de Paduenan' et communem pasturam ejusdem ville quantum ad personam ipsius capelle pertinet. Volo itaque et firmiter precipio ut elemosinam predictam ita libere et quiete et honorifice habeant et teneant sicut alias elemosinas suas liberius, quiecius et honorificencius tenent. Test*ibus* etc.

RUBRIC. Super grangia de Ingbuston' et super tofto et crofto pertinentibus et communi pastura ejusdem ville. xlvij.
SOURCE. NLS, MS. Adv. 34.4.7, fo.17ᵛ.
PRINTED. *Dryburgh Liber*, no.47.
NOTE. [a] Or Padeuan'.
COMMENT. This begins in the form of a fresh grant, but is apparently a confirmation. The rubric locates the land at Inglisberry Grange, now Grangehall (*OPS*, i, 138–9).

263 Confirms to Sawtry Abbey the whole of Sawtry as granted by King Malcolm IV. Kingscliffe, Northamptonshire. (1185)

W' Dei Gr*ati*a Rex Scott' . Episcopis . Abbatibus . Comitibus . Baronibus . Justiciis . Vicecomitibus . prepositis . Ministris . ⁊ Omnibus probis hominibus Tocius Terre sue clericis ⁊ laicis Salutem. Sciant tam posteri quam presentes me Concessisse ⁊ hac carta mea Confirmasse Deo ⁊ Sancte Marie ⁊ Monachis de Saltereia ordinis Cistercii . In perpetuam elemosinam pro salute anime mee ⁊ antecessorum meorum ⁊ successorum meorum .˒ Totam Saltereiam cum omnibus Justis pertinenciis suis . In Bosco . ⁊ in plano . In Terris ⁊ Aquis . In pratis ⁊ pasturis . ⁊[a] Marescis . ⁊ in Omnibus aliis Rebus . Sicut Rex Scociæ Malcolmus bone memorie frater meus eis eam dedit . ⁊ Carta sua Confirmauit. Quare uolo ⁊ firmiter precipio ut predicti Monachi eam habeant ⁊ teneant de me ⁊ heredibus meis In perpetuam Elemosinam bene ⁊ In pace . honorifice . ⁊ quiete libere ab omni exaccione Temporali ⁊ seruicio . sicut Carta Malcolmi Regis Scocie bone memorie eis testatur. Test*ibus* Roberto capellano meo[b] . Ricardo de Morevill' Const*abulario* . Alano Dapifero . Willelmo de Morevill' . Rann*ulfo* de Sol' . Geruasio Auenel . Bernardo filio Brien' . Waltero de Windesh' . Thoma de Colev' . APD' Cliue.

ENDORSED. No early endorsement visible.
DESCRIPTION. 9·2″ (23·5 cm.), Top, 8·9″ (22·5 cm.), Bottom × 5·7″ (14·5 cm.), L, 5·3″ (13·3 cm.), R. Foot formerly folded, now flat. Slits for tag, but nothing remains of tag or seal. The document has been damaged by fire.
HAND. Scribe Ba. Unruled, save for one line in (?) drypoint at foot.
SOURCE. Original, BM, Cotton Charter xii, 79 = *A*. Bodleian, MS. Rawlinson B 142, fo.16ᵛ = *B*. Printed here from *A*.
NOTES. [a] Everywhere else the Tironian et has a cross stroke. [b] *B* stops here.
COMMENT. The attestation of Alan the Steward indicates a date after 1177, when his father Walter died. But in 1185 King William handed over the Honour of Huntingdon to his younger brother David. This act must be dated between the

restoration of the honour to William and the transfer to David, which may have been carried out at the *caput* of the Honour, perhaps at Fotheringay, a few miles from Kingscliffe.

264 Confirms to Melrose Abbey the whole land of Eskdale granted by Robert Avenel and his son and heir Gervase (i.e., Tomleuchar and Watcarrick, in Eskdalemuir parish, Dumfriesshire). (1180 × 1193, probably 1185)

Will*elmu*s Dei gr*ati*a rex Scot' . Episcopis . Abbatibus . Comit*ibus* . Baron*ibus* . Justic*iis* . Vicecom*itibus* . prepositis . ministris . 7 omnibus probis hominibus totius terre sue salutem. Sciant presentes 7 posteri me concessisse 7 hac mea carta confirmasse Deo 7 ecclesie Sancte Marie de Meylr*os* . 7 monachis ibidem Deo seruientibus totam illam terram de Eschedale . per easdem diuisas que nominantur 7 continentur in cartis Domini Roberti Auenel 7 Geruasii heredis ipsius . quas habent de eis de eadem terra. Ita ut quicquid infra easdem diuisas fuerit . habeant 7 possideant imperpetuum . ita libere 7 quiete . integre 7 pacifice . sicut aliqua elemosina liberius 7 quietius in regno meo possidetur. Confirmaui enim 7 concessi eis eandem terram imperpetuum liberam . 7 solutam ab omnibus auxiliis . 7 ab omni seruitio 7 consuetudine 7 exactione seculari . saluo seruitio meo de Geruasio 7 heredibus eius. His testibus . Osberto Abbate de Kelcho . Hug*one* Abbate de Neubotle . Willelmo Malueisin . Ricardo de la prouende . Hug*one* del séél . Dauid comite fratre Regis . Roberto de Quinci . Hug*one* Ridel . Ricardo de Munfichet . Philippo de Valuines . Rogero de Valuines . Waldeuo filio Baldewini . Alexandro de Seint Martin . Herueio le Marescal . Ricard*o* le Marescal . Roberto de Seint Michel . Adam de Stanford.

ENDORSED. Comfirmatio[a] regis Will*elm*i de Eskedale (xii–xiii cent.). Confirmacio reg*is* W. de Eskedale (faded, xiv cent.?) L (red, xv cent.?). J. Scott (xvi cent.).
DESCRIPTION. 9·3″ (23·5 cm.), Top, 9·5″ (24·2 cm.), Bottom × 6·7″ (17 cm.), L 7·1″ (18 cm.), R. Foot folded to a depth of 1·3″ (3·2 cm.). Woven silk cords pass through four holes in foot and fold; a detached length of cord remains with seal almost complete, in natural wax stained brown, diameter 3·3″ (8 cm.). Fair impression.
HAND. Scribe Cb. Ruled in drypoint.
SOURCE. Original, SRO, GD 55–42.
PRINTED. *Melrose Liber*, no.42.
NOTE. [a] Sic.
COMMENT. For the charters of Robert and Gervase Avenel, see *Melrose Liber*, nos.39, 41. Robert Avenel died on 8 March, 1185, having entered the monastery of Melrose as a novice and 'familiaris' (*Chron. Melrose*, 45). But King William's brother David was given the earldom of Huntingdon at the Council of Windsor, about the middle of March, 1185. He is already styled 'earl' in Robert Avenel's charter. The probability seems to be that the Avenels' charters and King William's confirmation of them were issued in 1185, the former shortly before Robert's death, the latter shortly afterwards. The writer of no.264, who also wrote no.265, shews a tendency to render personal names in a French vernacular form.

265 Grants to Melrose Abbey the part of Blainslie formerly granted by King David I to his foresters and subsequently granted by King William to William son of Oein, viz. the toft and croft (*masagium*) held by William; the monks of Melrose may build there as they wish, and cultivate all and only that land previously broken up and ploughed;

together with all liberties of the forest between Gala and Leader. The king will give warrandice against all men. (1180 × 1193, probably 1185)

Will*elmus* Dei gr*ati*a Rex Scottorum . Episcopis . Abbatibus . Comitibus . Baron*ibus* . Justiciis . Ministris . 7 Omnibus probis hominibus totius terre sue . Clericis 7 laicis salutem. Sciatis me dedisse 7 hac mea carta confirmasse Deo 7 Sancte Marie . 7 ecclesie de Mailr*os* . 7 Monachis ibidem Deo seruientibus pro anima Reg*is* D*aui*d aui mei . 7 pro anima Henrici comitis patris mei . 7 matris mee . 7 pro anima Malcolmi Regis . 7 pro salute mea . 7 omnium antecessorum 7 successorum meorum . illam partem terre de Bleineslei . quam Rex D*aui*d olim concesserat forestariis suis . 7 Ego postea Willelmo filio Oein[a] concesseram. Scilicet illum toftum 7 masagium quod predictus Willelmus tenuit 7 possedit . ut edificent illud . sicut eis utilius uisum fuerit pro libitu suo . 7 liceat eis arare 7 colere totam terram illam tantum . que ante fracta fuerat 7 arata . cum omnibus libertatibus foreste inter Galeghe 7 Ledre . sicut continetur in cartis Antecessorum meorum . 7 meis. Hanc ergo terram concedo eis . 7 presenti Carta confirmo in perpetuam Elemosinam . ut eam habeant . 7 possideant predicti monachi . Libere 7 quiete . plenarie 7 honorifice . sicut aliqua Elemosina quietius 7 liberius teneri potest. Solutam ab omni terreno seruicio . 7 seculari exactione. Ita quod Ego 7 heredes mei Warantizabimus eis hanc terram . contra omnes homines. His testibus . Osberto Abbate de Kelcho . Hug*one* Abbate de Neubotle . Willelmo Malueisin . Ricardo de la prouende . Hug*one* del seel . Dauid comit*e* fratre Reg*is* . Roberto de Quinci . Hug*one* Ridel . Ricardo de Munfichet . Philippo de Valuin' . Rogero de Valuin' . Waldeuo filio Baldewin . Alexandro de Sent[b] Martin . Herueio le Mareschal . Ricardo de[b] Marescal . Roberto de Seint Michel . Alano filio Hug*onis* senescallo com*itis* D*aui*d . Ricardo filio Eissun[c] . Adam de Stanford.

ENDORSED. Carta regis Willelmi de Bleineslei (xii cent.). Confirmatio regis Willelmi de b de (xii cent., erased?). Also illegible early endorsement, including the word libertatibus (?). Also modern endorsements.

DESCRIPTION. 10″ (25·3 cm.), Top and bottom × 5·6″ (14·2 cm.), L, 5·4″ (13·7 cm.) R. Foot torn and repaired; no slit, tag or seal remains.

HAND. Scribe Cb. Ruled in drypoint (or pencil?).

SOURCE. Original, BM, Cotton Chr. xviii, 15.

PRINTED. *Melrose Liber*, no.93 = *M*.

NOTES. [a] Oem, *M*. [b] Sic. [c] *M* prints Lissun, wrongly.

COMMENT. Issued on the same occasion as no.264, which see for date. William son of Oein was perhaps the William brother of Roger son of Audoenus who witnessed a charter of Edward son of Peter of Restalrig for Newbattle Abbey (*c*.1170–80?), *Newbattle Registrum*, p.287.

266

Confirms to Geoffrey de Melville, uncle of Richard de Melville and son of Maud Malherbe, the whole land of Granton (Midlothian), and the whole land of Stenhouse (Stirlingshire), by those marches by which Richard's father Gregory held it; and the land held by Richard Hangdevil; all granted to him by Richard de Melville. Kinghorn. (1185 × 1189)

W'. Dei gr*ati*a Rex Scott' . Omnibus probis Hominibus Totius terre Sue . Clericis 7 Laicis . Salutem. Sciant presentes 7 futuri . me Concessisse 7 Hac carta mea confirmasse . Donationem illam quam Ri*cardus* de Maleuill' . fecit Galfr*ido* de Maleu*i*ll' Auunculo Suo . filio Matild*is* Malherbe . Scilicet Totam terram de Grendun . per rectas Diuisas suas. Et totam terram de Stanhus . per illas diuisas . per quas Gregorius[a] pater prefati Ric*ardi* eas tenuit. Et terram illam quam Ric*ardus* Hangdeuil per suas rectas diuisas tenet. Tenendas sibi . 7 heredibus suis de prefato Ric*ardo* . 7 heredibus suis . in feudo 7 hereditate . Cum omnibus libertatibus 7 justis pertinentiis suis . ita libere 7 quiete plenarie 7 honorifice .' sicut carta ipsius Ricardi testatur 7 confirmat . Saluo seruitio meo. Test*ibus* Com*ite* D*aui*d . Com*ite* Dunec*ano* . Waltero Olifard' . Willelmo de Lindes' . Alexandr*o* de Sancto Mart*ino* . Hug*one* Giffard' . Roberto de Lond*oniis* . Roberto de Berk' . Waltero de Berk' Camerario . Malcolm*o* fili*o* Comitis Dunec*ani* Apud Kingor[b] .

ENDORSED. Kg William Confirmatioun of Grendoun (xvi–xvii cent. ?). No early endorsement legible.
DESCRIPTION. 9·2″ (21·5 cm.), Top, bottom × 5·1″ (13 cm.), L, R. Foot folded to a depth of 1″ (2·5 cm.). Double slits with tag 8″ (21 cm.) long, 0·4″ (1 cm.) wide. Small central fragment of seal remains in natural wax, stained brown.
HAND. Scribe Bb. Unruled.
SOURCE. Original, SRO, GD 26, 1/4/5.
PRINTED. Fraser, *Melville*, iii, 3, no.5 (with facsimile); also *Fraser Facsimiles*, no.13.
NOTES. [a] Written GG with marks of suspension. [b] r extended in a horizontal stroke for 3½″, but n has not been added at the end.
COMMENT. The beneficiary was presumably Geoffrey II de Melville, son of Geoffrey I and brother of Gregory. But the witness to no.78, 'Gregory son of Geoffrey' was not necessarily Gregory de Melville, since *Holyrood Liber*, 208 (no.2) is a charter of Geoffrey de Melville, witnessed by Gregory 'son of Geoffrey the sheriff', and also by Richard Hangdevil.

267 Confirms to Richard son of Gregory de Melville Granton (Midlothian) in exchange for two ploughgates previously granted to him in Ednam (Roxburghshire) by King Malcolm IV. Kinghorn. (1185 × 1189)

W'. Dei gratia Rex Scot'. Omnibus probis hominibus Totius terre sue . clericis 7 Laicis . Salutem. Sciant presentes 7 futuri . me concessisse . 7 hac carta mea confirmasse . Ricardo filio Gregorii[a] de Maleuill' GRENDUN' per rectas diuisas suas . in excambium duarum karrucatarum terre quas Rex M'. frater meus patri suo dederat in Edenam. Tenend*um* sibi 7 heredibus suis de me 7 heredibus meis . in feudo 7 hereditate . ita libere 7 quiete plenarie 7 honorifice . sicut Carta mea data super hoc Gregorio[a] testatur 7 confirmat . Saluo seruitio meo. Test*ibus* Comite D*aui*d fratre meo . Waltero Olifard' . Willelmo de Lindes' . Roberto de Lond*oniis* . Willelmo de Haia . Willelmo Giffard' Malcolmo filio Comitis Dunec*ani*. Apud KINGOR[b].

ENDORSED. Confirmacio de Grendune (xiv cent. ?). Also modern endorsements.
DESCRIPTION. 7·9″ (20 cm.), Top, 7·3″ (18·5 cm.), Bottom × 5·2″ (13·3 cm.), L, R. Foot folded to a depth of 1·5″ (3·5 cm.), but most of the fold has been cut away. Double slits with tag 4·8″ (12 cm.) long, 0·4 (1·1 cm.) wide. About half the seal remains, natural wax stained brown.
HAND. Scribe Bb. Unruled. SOURCE. Original, SRO, GD 26, 1/4/3.
PRINTED. Fraser, *Melville*, iii, 2, no.3 (with facsimile); also *Fraser Facsimiles*, no.14.
NOTES. [a] Written GG with marks of suspension over. [b] r extended by a horizontal stroke of 1·6″.

268 Confirms to Richard son of Gregory de Melville, in feu and heritage, the land in Liberton held by Malbeth, and the land of Leadburn (Midlothian). Kinghorn. (1185 × 1189)

.W'. Dei gr*ati*a Rex Scot'. Omnibus probis Hominibus totius Terre sue Salutem. Sciant Presentes 7 futuri me concessisse . et[a] hac carta mea confirmasse . Ric*ardo* de Maleuin . filio Gregor*ii* in feudo 7 Hereditate terram illam quam Malbet tenuit in Libertun' . per easdem diuisas per quas idem Malbet eam tenuit. et terram de Lecbernard' per suas rectas diuisas. Tenendas sibi 7 Heredibus suis de me et Heredibus meis ita libere et quiete 7 eadem condicione 7 eodem seruicio quo carta Reg*is* Malcolm*i* fratris mei super hoc data Galfrid*o* 7 Gregor*io* de Maleuin testatur et confirmat. Test*ibus* Comite Dauid fratre meo . Roberto de London*iis* . Waltero Olif*ard* . Willelmo de Lindes' . Willelmo de Haia . Roberto Capellano meo . Ricardo de prebend*a* . 7 Willelmo Maluesin . Clericis meis. Apud KingorN.

ENDORSED. Confirmacio de Lecbernard (xiii cent.). Also modern endorsements.
DESCRIPTION. 7″ (7·8 cm.), Top, bottom × 3·8″ (9·6 cm.), L, R. Foot folded to a depth of 1″ (2·6 cm.). Double slits with tag 5″ (12 cm.) long, 0·4″ (1 cm.) wide. Large fragment of seal remains in natural wax stained brown, diameter 2·8″ (7·3 cm.), fair impression.
HAND. Scribe Ca. Unruled.
SOURCE. Original, SRO, GD 26, 1/4/7.
PRINTED. Fraser, *Melville*, iii, 4, no.7 (with facsimile); also *Fraser Facsimiles*, no.17.
NOTE. [a] Here and throughout et indicates a crossed tironian sign.

269 Confirms to Richard son of Gregory de Melville the land beside the house which belonged to Malbeth Bere in Liberton (Midlothian), previously granted to Geoffrey de Melville by King Malcolm IV. Kinghorn. (1185 × 1189)

.W'. Dei gr*ati*a Rex Scot' Omnibus probis hominibus totius terre sue Clericis et[a] laicis Salutem. Sciant presentes et futuri me concessisse . et Hac carta mea confirmasse . Ric*ardo* filio Gregorii[b] de Maleuill' Terram illam que est iuxta domum que fuit Malbet Bere in Libertun' . quam Galfridus de Maleuill' tenuit Tempore Reg*is* M'. fratris mei de dono suo. Tenend*am* sibi et heredibus suis de me et heredibus meis in feudo et hereditate ita libere et quiete . Sicut Carta Reg*is* .M'. fratris mei data Galfr*ido* de Maleuill' super hoc testatur et confirmat. Saluo seruicio meo. Test*ibus* Com*ite* Dau*id* fratre meo . Waltero Olifard' . Willelmo de Lindes' . Roberto de London*iis* . Willelmo de Haia . M*alcolmo* filio Comitis Dunec*ani*. Apud KINgor[c].

ENDORSED. Confirmacio terre iuxta liberton (xiii–xiv cent.). Also modern endorsements.
DESCRIPTION. 6·3″ (16 cm.), Top, bottom × 4″ (10·2 cm.), L, 3·7″ (9·5 cm.), R. Foot folded to a depth of 1″ (2·5 cm.). Tie cut 1″ from left-hand edge of fold. Double slits; no tag or seal remains.
HAND. Scribe Ca. Unruled. SOURCE. Original, SRO, GD 26, 1/4/6.
PRINTED. Fraser, *Melville*, iii, 3, no.6 (with facsimile); also *Fraser Facsimiles*, no.21.
NOTES. [a] Crossed tironian sign used throughout. [b] Written GG. [c] r extended by a horizontal stroke (with three intervals made by triple diagonal strokes) for 3·4″ to complete the line.

270 Grants to Scone Abbey the revenues in the queen's household which it already has in the king's, in the spence and the kitchen, whenever the queen keeps her household separately. Crail. (1 × 15 March, 1187)

Willelmus[a] Dei gracia Rex Scotorum omnibus probis hominibus totius terre sue salutem. Sciatis me concessisse Deo et ecclesie de Scon et abbati et canonicis ibidem Deo seruientibus ut habeant in domo regine omnes rectitudines quas habent in domo mea, scilicet in expensa et coquina, quando ipsa curiam suam per se tenuerit. Quare precipio ballivis et seruientibus suis[b] ut eis absque disturbatione habere faciant. Test*ibus* Ricardo electo Morauien*si*, Roberto et Willelmo capellanis meis, Hugone de sigillo clerico meo, Roberto de Quinci, Willelmo de Moreuill', Willelmo de Haia, Hug*one* Giffarde. Apud Carale.

SOURCE. NLS, MS. Adv. 34.3.28, fo.10^{r-v}.
PRINTED. *Scone Liber*, no.33.
NOTES. [a] Name omitted, MS. [b] Fo.10^{v}.
COMMENT. This grant was a consequence of the king's marriage in September, 1186. It may be inferred from it that Richard (of Lincoln?) the king's clerk, elected to the see of Moray on 1 March, 1187, and consecrated at St Andrews on 15 March, was elected at Crail, in the royal chapel.

271 Confirms to St Andrews Cathedral Priory the church of Leuchars, Fife (granted by Ness son of William), as the charter of Ness bears witness. Crail. (1175 × 1190)

[Willelmus][a] Dei gracia Rex Scot'. Omnibus probis hominibus tocius terre sue clericis et laicis . salutem . Sciant presentes . et futuri . me concessisse et hac carta mea confirmasse . Deo et ecclesie Sancti Andree apostoli in S[cocia][a] . et canonicis ibidem Deo seruientibus et seruituris . ecclesiam de Lochres . cum omnibus iustis pertinenciis suis tenendam in liberam et perpetuam elemosinam ita libere et quiete . plenarie et honorifice ⁏ sicut carta Nesii testatur. Test*ibus* Jocel*ino* episcopo Glasc*uensi* . Matheo episcopo Aberdon*ensi* . Com*ite* Dunc*ano* . Com*ite* Gileberto . Malc*olmo* Com*ite* Etholie . Ricardo de Moreuill' . Waltero Olifardo . Willelmo de Haia . Ric*ardo* Maresc*allo* . Apud Karel .

SOURCE. SRO, GD 45/27/8 (St Andrews priory cartulary), fo.cxxx^{v}.
PRINTED. *St Andrews Liber*, 289.
NOTE. [a] MS. blank.
COMMENT. Ness's charter is given in *St Andrews Liber*, 287, elaborately supported by charters of his daughter and two witnesses, ibid. 287–9.

272 Confirms to Richard bishop of Moray the bishopric of Moray, to be held as freely as any of the bishops in his realm hold their bishoprics or as any of his predecessors held this bishopric; and grants in augmentation the (parish) church of Elgin after the death of his clerk Richard *de prebenda* and of Richard's clerk Walter, with the chapel of St Andrew and the chapel of Manbeen; and the church of Auldearn, likewise after the death of Richard *de prebenda*, with the chapels of Invernairn (Nairn), Rait (in Nairn) and Moyness (in Auldearn). Kinghorn. (15 March, 1187 × 23 March, 1189, perhaps 1187)

Will' Dei gratia Rex Scott' episcopis, abbatibus, comitibus, baronibus, justic*iis*, vicecomitibus, prepositis, ministris et omnibus probis hominibus tocius terre sue, clericis et laicis, salutem. Sciant presentes et futuri me concessisse et hac carta mea confirmasse Ric*ardo* Dei gratia episcopo Morau*ie* episcopatum Morau*ie* cum omnibus justis pertinenciis suis, tenendum sibi ita libere et quiete et honorifice sicut aliquis episcoporum in regno meo episcopatum liberius et quiecius et honorificencius tenet et possidet, et ita plenarie sicut aliquis antecessorum suorum episcoporum episcopatum illum plenius tenuit. Preterea concessi et dedi de incremento episcopatui Moraure, et predicto Ricardo episcopo Morau*ie* et successoribus suis episcopis, pro salute anime mee et antecessorum meorum, ecclesiam de Elgin, post decessum Ric*ardi* de Prebenda clerici mei et Walteri clerici ejusdem Ricardi, cum capella Sancti Andree et cum capella de Munben, cum omnibus aliis pertinentiis suis, in capellis et terris et omnibus decimis et elemosinis et rectitudinibus ecclesiasticis, et ecclesiam de Eren, post decessum Ricardi de Prebenda clerici mei similiter, cum capella de Inuernaren et cum capella de Rathe et cum capella de Maichas[a] cum omnibus justis pertinentiis suis, tenendas in liberam et perpetuam elemosinam, ita libere et quiete, plenarie et honorifice, sicut alios redditus episcopatus liberius, quiecius, plenius et honorificencius tenet. Testibus Jocelino[b] episcopo Glasguensi[c], Mattheo episcopo Aberdonensi, Turpino episcopo Brechinensi, Æ*rkenbaldo* abbate de Dunf*ermelin*, O*sberto* abbate de Kelch*o*, H*enrico* abbate de Aberbruthoc, W*illelmo* abbate de Sancta Cruce, Rob*erto* abbate de Scona, Rad*ulfo* abbate de Cupre, Hug*one* abbate de Neuboth*il*, Reinero abbate de Kynlos, comite Duncano justic*ia*, Gill*eberto* comite de Stradherin, Gillebride com*ite* de Henegus, Rob*erto* et Will*elmo* capellanis meis, Hugone de Sigillo meo clerico, Will*elmo* de Haya, Galfrido de Maleuile, Willelmo de Moreuilla. Apud Kyngor'.

RUBRIC. Confirmatio Regis Ricardo episcopo de episcopatu Moravie.[d] Confirmatio Ricardi episcopi de episcopatu Moraviensi.[e]
SOURCE. NLS, MS. Adv. 34.4.10, fo.xxxv^{r} = *A*. Ibid., fo.xiij^{r-v} = *B*. Printed here from *A*, with some variants of *B* noted.
PRINTED. *Moray Registrum*, no.6 (from *A*?).
NOTES. [a] Moythas, *B*, Marchus, *Moray Registrum*, no.6. [b] Johelino, *B*. [c] Glascuensi, *B*. [d] In margin, fo.xxxv^{r}. [e] In margin, fo.xiij.
COMMENT. Date determined by the consecration of Bishop Richard and election of Abbot Reiner of Kinloss as abbot of Melrose.

273 Grants to the church of the Holy Trinity of the bishopric of Moray and to Bishop Richard and his successors the teind of his revenues of Moray and of his pleas throughout the diocese of Moray and of his cain, not already assigned to other churches, in cows, pigs, wheat, malt, oats, cheese and butter. Perth. (15 March, 1187 × 1190, perhaps 1187)

Will' Dei gratia Rex Scott' episcopis, abbatibus , com*itibus* , baron*ibus* , justiciis , vicecom*itibus* , prepositis , ministris et omnibus probis hominibus tocius terre sue clericis et laicis salutem. Sciant presentes et futuri me dedisse et concessisse et hac carta mea confirmasse Deo et ecclesie Sancte Trinitatis de episcopatu Morau*ie* et domino Ric*ardo* episcopo Moraule et successoribus suis in liberam et perpetuam elemosinam , pro animabus antecessorum meorum et pro salute anime mee , decimam meam de redditibus meis de Morau*ia* et de placitis meis per totum episcopatum Morau*iensem* de redditibus meis , scilicet de cano meo , de vaccis et porcis , de frumento , braseo et prebenda , et de caseo et de butiro , quod antecessores mei non dederunt nec assignaverunt ad alias ecclesias. Quare precipio firmiter ballivis meis de Morau*ia* ut ipsi sine disturbatione faciant domino Ric*ardo* episcopo et successoribus suis singulis annis plenarie et integre habere predictam decimam , sicut superius in carta nostra determinatum est. Test*ibus* Jocel*ino* episcopo Glascuen*si* , Matheo episcopo Aberdon*ensi* , Com*ite* Dunec*ano* justic*ia* , Com*ite* Gille*berto* de Stratheren , M*alcolmo* Com*ite* Ethol' , Jocel*ino* archideac*ono* Dunkelden*si* , Ric*ardo* de Morauill' constab*ulario* , Walt*ero* Olif*ard* , Ric*ardo* de Munfichet , Seier[a] de Quinci , Malis fil*io* com*itis* Ferteth , Ric*ardo* et Philippo Marscaldo. Apud Pert.

RUBRIC. [Carta Re]*gis* Willelmi de [decima red]dituum suorum (margin).
SOURCE. NLS, MS. Adv. 34.4.10, fo.xxxvii^r.
PRINTED. *Moray Registrum*, no.7.
NOTE. [a] Serer, MS.
COMMENT. See no.139 above, of which this is a repetition in favour of Bishop Simon's successor; and cp. nos.281, 421.

274 Confirms to Coupar Angus Abbey the lands of 'Letcassy' (in Blairgowrie), Perthshire, granted by Stephen of Blair. Perth. (1183 × 1195)

This Donatione is confirmed be K*ing* William, saluo seruitio nostro. Apud Perth. Testibus: Jo*hanne* Episcopo de Dunkelden, Com*ite* Gilleberto, Comite Malcolmo Etholiæ, Philippo de Valloune, Henrico filio Jordani.

SOURCE. NLS, MS. Adv. 33.2.9, fo.32^r.
PRINTED. *Coupar Angus Rental*, i, 334, no.36.
COMMENT. Stephen (son of Waltheof) of Blair's grant is in *Coupar Angus Rental*, i, 333. Letcassy, apparently obsolete, was on the Lunan Burn and in Blair parish (*Coupar Angus Chrs.*, 143, 253).

275 Confirms to Coupar Angus Abbey a piece of land in Dunkeld, granted by William 'de Ougilby', servant (of the treasurer?) of Dunkeld, and confirmed by Bishop Richard. Perth. (1177 × 1190)

This former donatione of the piece land in Dunkelden givin Deo Sanctæ Marriæ et monachis de Cupro be Villielmus de Ougilby, seruiens tesaurariun[a] de Dunkelden, and confirmed by Bischope Richard, is also confirmed be K*ing* Villiam, under hes grate seall. Dat*um* apud Perth. Testibus: Comite Duncano Justitiario Scotiæ, Roberto[b] de Morueill Constabulario, Villielmus[c] Olifard, Alanus Senescallus,[d] Villielmus[d] de Lindess, Vil*lielmo* de Haye, Ro*berto* de Bercklai, Jo*hanne* de Hastinge.

SOURCE. NLS, MS. Adv. 33.2.9, fo.32^v.
PRINTED. *Coupar Angus Rental*, i, 335, no.41.
NOTES. [a] Sic, read tesaurarii? [b] Sic, for Ricardo. [c] Sic, probably for Waltero. [d] Sic.
COMMENT. The charter of the donor, whose name may be corrupt, is given in abstract in *Coupar Angus Rental*, i, 334, no.39.

276 Confirms to Scone Abbey the grant made to it by Richard bishop of St Andrews of the church and land of 'Logydunde' (Lochee, in Dundee, Angus), as the charters of Bishop Richard and Bishop Hugh bear witness. (1178 × 1214, probably × 1188)

Willelmus[a] Dei gracia Rex Scott' episcopis, abbatibus, comitibus, baronibus, justiciis, vicecomitibus, ministris et omnibus probis hominibus tocius terre salutem. Sciant presentes et futuri me concessisse et hac carta mea confirmasse Deo et ecclesie de Scon et abbati et canonicis ibidem Deo seruientibus donacionem quam Ric*ardus* Episcopus Sanctiandr*ee* eis fecit de ecclesia et terra de Logydunde, scilicet de omni jure quod Episcopi Sancti Andr*ee* habere debent in predicta ecclesia et terra; tenend*am* in liberam et perpetuam elemosinam ita libere, quiete, plenarie et honorifice cum omnibus earum iustis pertinenciis, sicut carte Ric*ardi* et Hug*onis* Episcoporum Sancti Andr*ee* testantur et confirmant,[b] saluo servicio meo. Test*ibus* etc.

SOURCE. NLS, MS. Adv. 34.3.28, fo.12r.
PRINTED. *Scone Liber*, no.42.
NOTES. [a] Initial omitted, MS. [b] confirmantur, MS.
COMMENT. Probably issued before the death of Bishop Hugh. The bishops' charters are given in *Scone Liber*, nos.40, 41.

277 Grants to Arbroath Abbey one ploughgate of arable in Mondynes (in Fordoun), Mearns, on the Bervie Water, measured at his command by William de Montfort, Humphrey of Berkeley, Walter Scott and Alan son of Simon; this ploughgate to acquit from the abbey the one and a half ploughgates (in Mondynes) previously given it by Richard de Frivill, so that none of Richard's heirs may bring any lawsuit against the abbey in respect of the 1½ ploughgates if they should recover them. Perth. (1183 × 1188)

W.[a] Dei gr*ati*a Rex Scott' Episcopis Abbatibus Comit*ibus* Justic*iis* Vicec*omitibus* Ministris et omnibus probis hominibus tocius terre sue clericis et laicis salutem. Sciant presentes et futuri me dedisse et concessisse et hac carta mea confirmasse Deo et [Sancto][b] Thome et ecclesie de Abirbr*othoc* et monachis ibidem Deo seruientibus unam carucatam terre in Munethene super aquam de Beruyn quam Willelmus de Montfort et Umfridus de Berkel' et Walterus Scotus et Alanus filius Symonis et alii probi homines mei eis precepto meo mensurauerunt . in liberam et perpetuam elemosinam cum communi pastura et cum omnibus aisiamentis ad terram illam pertinentibus . ita plenarie et honorifice . libere et quiete ab operacione[c] et ab omni seculari exaccione .' sicut aliquam elemosinam liberius quiecius plenius et honorificencius tenent in regno meo. Uolo quidem ad omnium noticiam peruenire . quod per hanc carucatam terre quam eis dedi . adquietaui ab eis unam carucatam terre et dimidiam quas ex dono Ricardi Friuill' habuerunt . et de quibus cartas suas eis dederat. Unde non liceat alicui heredum predicti Ric*ardi* . si qui eorum terram illam recuperauerint .' super predicta terra erga eos aliquam questionem mouere. Test*ibus* H*ugone* episcopo Sancti Andr*ee* . J*ohanne* episcopo Dunk*eldensi* . Rob*erto* Abbate de Scona . Comite Dunec*ano* Justic*ia* . Ric*ardo* de Moreuill' const*abu*-

lario . Waltero Olifard' . Philippo de Valon*iis* . Rog*ero*[d] de Berkeley . Waltero de Berkel' Camerar*io*. Apud Perth.

RUBRIC. Carta Regis W. de una carucata terre in Monethen (red). .xcij. (in margin).
SOURCE. NLS, MS. Adv. 34.4.2, fos.lxvi^{v}–lxvii^{r}.
PRINTED. *Arbroath Liber*, i, no.92.
NOTES. [a] Initial red. [b] MS. omits. [c] Fo.lxvii^{r}. [d] Read Rob*erto*?
COMMENT. It appears that Richard de Frivill's title to Mondynes was challenged, and the king was moved to compensate Arbroath for the loss of 1½ ploughgates by granting it a different ploughgate, perhaps in warrandice of Richard's original grant; cf. no.225.

278 Grants to Cambuskenneth Abbey one full toft in his new burgh of Perth. Perth. (1178 × 1195)

Wilelmus[a] Dei gracia rex Scotorum omnibus probis hominibus totius terre sue clericis et laicis, salutem. Sciant presentes et futuri me dedisse et concessisse et hac carta mea confirmasse Deo et ecclesie Sancte Marie de Striueling et canonicis ibidem Deo seruientibus unum plenarium toftum in nouo burgo meo de Perth; tenendum eis in liberam et perpetuam elemosinam ita libere, quiete, plenarie et honorifice sicut alie abbacie mee toftum aliquod in aliquo burgorum meorum liberius, quietius, plenius et honorificentius tenent.[b] Testibus, Com*ite* Dunec*ano*, Com*ite* Gileb*erto*, *Malcolmo* com*ite* Ethol, Galfr*ido* de Maluill, Hugone Giffert, Geruasio Auenell, Radulfo de Ver, Roberto de Berk*eley*, Johanne de Hastingg', Geruasio Riddell, apud Perth.

RUBRIC. Confirmatio Wilelmi regis de crofta de Perth (at top). Concordat cum principali Jacobus Foulis (at end).
SOURCE. NLS, MS. Adv. 34.1.2, fo.144^{r}.
PRINTED. *Cambuskenneth Registrum*, no.193.
NOTES. [a] Large blue initial U. [b] MS. tenentur.
COMMENT. King William seems to have founded the 'new burgh' of Perth, evidently as an addition to the burgh which had been in existence since David I's reign, some time after the foundation of Arbroath Abbey, which was granted a full toft outwith the burgh, but with full burghal rights, before *c.*1189 (no.233). No.467 was presumably issued in favour of the 'new burgh'.

279 Confirms by inspection a charter of Thomas of Galloway earl of Atholl granting the land of Tulach (in Blair Atholl), Perthshire, to Coupar Angus Abbey, and recites the earl's charter. Perth. (1178 × 1189?) (Spurious)

Will*elmus* Dei gr*aci*a Rex Scottorum Omnibus probis hominibus tocius terre sue clericis et laicis salutem. Sciatis me inspecsisse[a] ac veraciter intellexisse Quamdam Cartam Thome de Galweia Comitis Atholie factam religiosis viris abbati et conuentui de Cupre non rasam non abolitam non cancellatam nec in aliqua sui parte viciatam in hec verba. Sciant omnes tam presentes quam futuri quod ego Thomas de Galweia Comes Atholie dedi concessi et hac mea carta confirmaui Deo et Ecclesie Beate Marie de Cupre et monachis ibidem Deo seruientibus pro salute anime mee antecessorum et successorum meorum Totam terram illam que uocatur Tholaw per suas rectas diuisas cum omnibus pertinenciis libertatibus . et aisiamentis suis Tenend' de me et heredibus meis in puram et perpetuam Elemosinam . ita libere et quiete . plenarie et honorifice sicut aliqui viri religiosi per regnum Scocie aliquam terram de dono alicuius Comitis . Militis . uel Baronis in elemosinam concessam . liberius . quiecius . plenius et honorificencius tenent vel possident. Hiis test*ibus* Willelmo Olifart . Alexandro de Seth' . Reginaldo Const*abulario* . Rob*erto* de Crowel' . Johanne le Loreng . Alano Clerico Com*itis* et multis aliis. Quam quidem Donacionem et concessionem in eadem contentas in omnibus et singulis punctis . condicionibus et modis suis forma pariter et effectu approbo . ratifico et presenti carta et confirmacione mea pro me et successoribus meis in perpetuum confirmo. In cuius rei testimonium presenti carte mee sigillum meum apponi feci. Test*ibus* Joh*anne* Episcopo Glascuen*si* . M. Episcopo Ross*ensi* . Alano Abbate de Dunf*ermelin* . Ricardo de Morwill' Const*abulario* . Waltero Olifert . Alano Scenscal*lo*[a] . Willelmo de Lindesei. Apud Pert.

ENDORSEMENT. W^us Rex de Tulaw (xiv cent.). Confirmacio de Tolaw (xiv cent.). Confirmacio de Tolaw (xiv cent.), with reg*is* Willelmi (xv cent.) placed for insertion before de. Confirmacio Regis Vilȝelmi de Tholaw (xvi cent.).
DESCRIPTION. 8″ (20·4 cm.), Top and bottom × 5″ (12·7 cm.), L, R. Foot folded to a depth of 0·6″ (1·5 cm.). Seal-tag passes through double slits in foot and fold, 1·1″ (2·9 cm.) long, 0·6″ (1·5 cm.) wide. There is no seal.
HAND. Scribe UDh. Apparently a hand of xiv cent. simulating a charter hand of twelfth or thirteenth-century date. Unruled.
SOURCE. Spurious 'original', probably fourteenth-century, Earl of Moray, Darnaway Castle, Moray Muniments, Box 32, Division IV, Bdle. 1, no.3.
PRINTED. *Coupar-Angus Chrs.*, i, no.23.
NOTE. [a] Sic.
COMMENT. This charter is a manifest forgery, but may have been based on (a) a genuine charter of Earl Thomas granting Tulach to Coupar (*Coupar Angus Chrs.*, no.22, 1211 × 1231) and/or (b) a genuine charter of King William, in favour of another beneficiary, given at Perth, witnessed by Jocelin bishop of Glasgow, Matthew bishop of Aberdeen, Archibald abbot of Dunfermline, Richard de Morville the constable, Walter Olifard, Alan the steward, and William de Lindsay (1178 × 1189).

280 Confirms to Arbroath Abbey the full toft which Andrew bishop of Caithness held in his burgh of Forfar, granted by the bishop. Forfar. (1178 × 1195, perhaps 1184 ×)

W.[a] Dei gr*ati*a Rex Scott' , Omnibus probis hominibus tocius terre sue salutem. Sciatis me dedisse , concessisse et hac car[b]ta mea confirmasse Deo et Sancto Thome de Aberbroth*oc* et monachis ibidem Deo seruientibus unum plenarium toftum quod A*ndreas* episcopus Katen*ensis* tenuit in Burgo meo de Forfar' , et quod eis dedit et concessit. Tenend*um* in liberam et perpetuam elemosinam ita libere et quiete sicut alias elemosinas suas liberius et quiecius tenent et possident. Test*ibus* Com*ite* Dunec*ano* Justic*ia* , Rad*ulfo* de Ver , Bern*ardo* fil*io*[c] Bryen , Rob*erto* de Boseuill' . Apud Forfar.

RUBRIC. De tofto de Forfar (red, *A*, *E*). .xi. (in margin, *A*, *E*).
SOURCE. NLS, MS. Adv. 34.4.2, fos.xliii^v–xliv^r = *A*. SRO, Northesk Muniments (uncatalogued), Ethie MS., fo.3^r = *E*. Printed here from *A*.
PRINTED. *Arbroath Liber*, i, no.11 (from *E*).
NOTES. [a] Initial red. [b] Fo.xliv^r, *A*. [c] *A* has de instead of filio.
COMMENT. The wording suggests that Bishop Andrew was already dead before this confirmation was issued.

281 Commands all his responsible and faithful men of Moray to pay to their churches, and to the parsons and officers of those churches, all ecclesiastical dues and all teinds of corn, wool, flax, foals, calves, piglets and lambs, butter and cheese, and fisheries, and of everything else which by God's grace has annual increase and from which Holy Church requires teind to be paid. If anyone withholds his teind, he is to be compelled to pay it along with the forfeiture according to the assize of King David I and as was the custom in his day and still is in the diocese of St Andrews; i.e., if a neyf refuses to pay his teind, the thane in whose jurisdiction he lives, or his lord if he has a lord, shall compel him to pay and take the forfeiture from him, viz. one cow and one sheep; if the thane himself, or the lord, will not compel him, or withholds his own teind, the sheriff in whose jurisdiction he lives shall compel the detainer to pay and make him pay a forfeiture to the king, viz. eight cows; if the sheriff himself should be negligent in executing this command or withhold his own teind, the king's justiciar shall compel the detainer to pay the teind, and make the transgressor of King David's assize, whether he be sheriff, thane or lord, pay a forfeiture to the king of eight cows. Elgin. (1185 × 1189, probably 1187 × 1189)

Will' Dei gratia Rex Scott' omnibus probis hominibus suis Morau*ie* et fidelibus salutem. Mando vobis et firmiter precipio quatinus persoluatis sine omni occasione et contradictione Deo et ecclesiis vestris et[a] ecclesiarum rectoribus et ministris omnes rectitudines ecclesiasticas et omnes decimas vestras de blado et lana et lino, de pull*is* et vitulis, de purcellis[b] et agnis, de butiro et caseo, de piscariis et de omnibus aliis rebus que Dei operante gr*ati*a vobis per[c] annum fuerint innouata, et de omnibus aliis rebus[d] de quibus sancta ecclesia exigit decimas dari. Prohibeo eciam firmiter ne quis decimas suas siue alias rectitudines ecclesiasticas eis iniuste detineat, super meam plenariam forisfacturam. Si quis autem decimas vel rectitudinem ecclesiasticam[e] detinere presumpserit, precipio ut compellatur decimam vel rectitudinem illam simul cum forisfacto reddere secundum quod asisa fuit[f] Regis Dauid aui mei, et sicut mos fuit in eius tempore et adhuc est consuetudo in episcopatu Sancti Andr*ee*. Scilicet ut si villanus fuerit qui decimam suam vel aliam rectitudinem ecclesiasticam dare noluerit, Theynus sub quo rusticus est[g] vel dominus eius si dominum habuerit, distringat illum decimam illam siue aliam rectitudinem ecclesiasticam ecclesie reddere, et suum ab eo[h] forisfactum accipiat, scilicet unam vaccam et unam ovem. Si vero Theynus sub quo rusticus iste fuerit vel dominus eius si dominum habeat illum ad hoc non distrinserit, vel si propriam decimam vel aliam rectitudinem ecclesie detinuerit, Vicecomes in cuius balliua hoc fuerit compellat detentorem decimam vel[i] rectitudinem suam ecclesie soluere, et contemptorem asise Regis D*aui*d et mandati mei, siue Theynus siue dominus rustici fuerit, mihi forisfactum suum reddere, scilicet .viii^{to}. vaccas. Si autem Vicecom*es* huius mandati negligens executor fuerit, vel propriam decimam vel aliam rectitudinem ecclesiasticam detinere presumpserit, Justic*ia* mea compellat detentorem quicunque fuerit ecclesie decimam suam vel aliam rectitudinem ecclesiasticam reddere, et transgressorem asise Regis D*aui*d et precepti mei quicunque fuerit, siue Vicecomes, siue Theynus, siue dominus rustici, mihi forisfactum reddere, scilicet .viii. vaccas. Ut nos ita qui filii sancte matris ecclesie esse debemus ei amore et timore divino iura sua integra conseruemus et illibata, ut qui ei rebelles fuerint non impune ferant, nec per proteruitatem suam et obstinationem iura et rectitudines sancte matris ecclesie vel diminuant vel auferant. Test*ibus* Matheo episcopo Aberd*onensi*, Johanne episcopo de Katenes, Rob*erto* et Willelmo[j] capellanis meis, Hug*one* clerico meo, Comite Patricio, Comite Gill*eberto*, Will*elmo* fil*io* Fresk*in*, Will*elmo* de Lindes', Rob*erto* de Lund*oniis*, Will*elmo* de Haia, Ranulf*o* de Sulis, Petro de Polloc, Philippo Marscaldo, He*rueio*[k] Marscaldo. Apud Elgin.

RUBRIC. De decimis soluendis (top, in later hand).
SOURCE. NLS, MS. Adv. 34.4.10, fo.xxxvii^{r-v} = *A*. Ibid., fos.xv^{v}–xvi^{r} = *B*. Printed here from *A*, with three readings of *B* preferred and certain other variants of *B* noted.
PRINTED. *Moray Registrum*, no.5.
NOTES. [a] Fo.xxxvii^{v}. [b] Sic. [c] pro, *A*; per from *B*. [d] *A* omits aliis rebus. [e] rectitudines ecclesiasticas, *B*. [f] asysa fuerit, *B*. [g] ille sit, *B*. [h] episcopo, *A*; eo from *B*. [i] *B* adds aliam. [j] W, *A*. [k] Henrico, *B*.
COMMENT. The date depends on identifying Hugh the king's clerk with Hugh of Roxburgh, made chancellor in 1189, and on the probability that this act came after the consecration of Richard bishop of Moray following a three years' vacancy. The forfeiture of eight cows corresponds with that allowed to the justiciar benorth Forth in the 'Laws of Malcolm Mackenneth', c.8 (*APS*, i, 711).

282

Commands that all the burgesses of Arbroath Abbey, whether dwelling in the burgh of Arbroath or in the abbey's tofts in other burghs, shall be free of toll and custom throughout the king's land. Forfar. (1187 × 1195)

W.[a] Dei Gr*ati*a Rex Scott', Omnibus probis hominibus tocius terre sue, clericis et laicis, salutem. Mando et firmiter precipio quatinus omnes burgenses Abbatis de Aberbroth*oc* . qui in burgo illo vel qui in eorum toftis in aliis burgis meis manserint, quieti sint ab omni consuetudine et teloneyo[b] per totam terram meam. Test*ibus* Jocel*ino* episcopo Glasg*uensi*, Matheo episcopo Abird*onensi*, Ric*ardo* episcopo, Morau*iensi*, Comite Gillebryd'[c] de Anegus, Comite Gillebryd'[d] de Strathern', Waltero Olif*ard*. Apud Forfar.

RUBRIC. De libertate toftorum (red, *A*, *E*). .xij. (in margin, *A*, *E*).
SOURCE. NLS, MS. Adv. 34.4.2, fo.xliv^{r} = *A*. SRO, Northesk Muniments (uncatalogued), Ethie MS., fo.3^{r} = *E*. Printed here from *A*.
PRINTED. *Arbroath Liber*, i, no.12 (from *E*).
NOTES. [a] Initial red. [b] tolneyo, *E*. [c] Gillebrid', *E*. [d] Gilleb', *E*.

283

Grants to Glasgow Cathedral Church and Bishop Jocelin one full toft in his burgh of Forfar. Perth. (1187 × 1190)

W'. Dei gr*ati*a Rex Scott'. Omnibus probis hominibus totius terre sue clericis et laicis Salutem. Sciant presentes et futuri me dedisse et concessisse et hac carta mea confirmasse Deo et ecclesie Sancti Kentegerni de Glasgu . et Jocel*ino* eiusdem loci episcopo et successoribus suis episcopis unum plenarium toftum in burgo meo de Forfar' . tendendu*m* in liberam et perpetuam elemosinam ita libere et quiete plenarie et honorifice sicut alii episcopi aut prelati terre mee tofta aliqua in aliis burgis meis liberius quietius plenius et honorificentius tenent. Test*ibus* Matheo episcopo Abberdon*ensi*. Ric*ardo* episcopo Morauien*si*. Com*ite* Dunec*ano* Just*icia*. Com*ite* Gileberto. Ric*ardo* de Moruill' Constabul*ario*. Waltero Olif*ard*. Apud Pert.

RUBRIC. De uno tofto in Burgo de Forfar' (in margin in later hand).
SOURCE. Blairs Archives, 16 Drummond Place, Edinburgh, MS. Registrum Vetus of Glasgow, fo.iiij^{v}.
PRINTED. *Glasgow Registrum*, no.74.

284 Grants to Arbroath Abbey the church of Foethmuref (Barry), Angus. Perth. (1183 × 1 August, 1189, probably April, 1189)

W.[a] Dei gr*ati*a Rex Scott'. Omnibus probis hominibus tocius terre sue clericis et laicis :' salutem. Sciant presentes et futuri. me dedisse. et concessisse. et hac carta mea confirmasse Deo et ecclesie Sancti Thome[b] de Aberbr*othoc*. et monachis ibidem Deo seruientibus. in perpetuam elemosinam ecclesiam de Foethmuref'. cum capellis. et terris. et omnimodis decimis. et oblacionibus. et cum omnibus aisiamentis et libertatibus. ad predictam ecclesiam pertinentibus. et cum omnibus aliis iustis pertinentiis suis. Tenend*am* sibi inperpetuum. ita libere[c]. et quiete. plenarie. et honorifice. sicut alias elemosinas meas eis datas liberius. et quiecius plenius et honorificencius :' tenent et possident. Test*ibus* Johanne Dunk*eldensi*. Math*eo* Aberdon*ensi*. Gocell*ino* Glasg*uensi* episcopis. Archenb*aldo* de Dunfermel*in*. Osb*erto* de Kalc'. Willelmo de Sancta Cruce. Rad*ulfo* de Cupro. Hug*one* de Neubotyl. Rob*erto* de Scon'. Abbatibus. Waltero de Sancto Andr*ea*. Waltero de Insula Sancti Columbe :' Prioribus. Rogero cancell*ario*. Com*ite* Dunec*ano*. Com*ite* Gilb*erto*. Com*ite* Patric*io*. Com*ite* Adam de Anegus. Com*ite* Gillecrist de Marre. Rob*erto* de Quincy[d]. Will*elmo* de Lindes'. Philippo de Valon*iis*. Willelmo de Haya[e]. Waltero de Berkal'[f] Came*rario* Regis. apud Perth[g]

RUBRIC. De ecclesia de Foethmuref' (red, *E*). De ecclesia de Fethmuref (red, *A*). .xxj. (in margin, *A*, *E*).
SOURCE. NLS, MS. Adv. 34.4.2, fos.xlv^{v}–xlvi^{r} = *A*. SRO, Northesk Muniments (uncatalogued), Ethie MS., fo.4^{r} = *E*. Printed here from *A*.
PRINTED. *Arbroath Liber*, i, no.21 (from *E*).
NOTES. [a] Initial red. [b] *E* adds martiris. [c] Fo.xlvi^{r}. [d] Quinci, *E*. [e] Haia, *E*. [f] Berkel', *E*. [g] Pert, *E*.
COMMENT. Probably issued about the time of the election of Roger 'de Beaumont', then chancellor, to the see of St Andrews (13 April, 1189, at Perth). This is the only surviving act to be witnessed by Roger as chancellor, suggesting that his term of office was brief.

285 Commands that the tenant of Arbroath Abbey's saltpan in the Carse of Stirling shall be free of toll on his salt wherever he may transport it within the king's land. Stirling. (1189 × 1190)

W.[a] Dei gr*ati*a Rex Scottorum, Omnibus probis hominibus tocius terre sue salutem. Mando et firmiter precipio ut ubicunque homines Abbatis de Aberbrothoch', qui salinam suam tenent in Kars quam eis in elemosinam dedi, in terram meam uenerint cum sale quod de salina illa attulerint, quieti sint inde de theloneyo[b] et consuetudine. Test*ibus*

Hug*one* Cancell*ario* meo, Ricardo de Moreuill' Constab*ulario*, Philippo de Valon*iis*, Willelmo de Haya. Apud Striuelyn.

RUBRIC. De libertate saline (red, *A*, *E*). .viij. (in margin *A*, *E*).
SOURCE. NLS, MS. Adv. 34.4.2, fo.xliii^{r} = *A*. SRO, Northesk Muniments (uncatalogued), Ethie MS., fo.2^{v} = *E*. Printed here from *A*.
PRINTED. *Arbroath Liber*, i, no.8 (from *E*).
NOTES. [a] Initial red. Punctuation editorial. [b] tolneyo, *E*.

286 Grants to Robert, son of Henry the butler, Cassingray (in Carnbee), Fife, by the right marches perambulated for him by Abbot Archibald of Dunfermline and the king's good men at the king's command; in feu and heritage, with common pasture on the muir of Kellie, performing the forinsec service due from a half-ploughgate (half-davoch?) of land in Kellie-shire. Robert is to be free of multure for his own household at the king's mill of Kellie, but his men are to pay multure. Kinghorn. (1189 × 1195)

.W'. Dei gr*at*ia Rex Scott'. Omnibus probis Nominibus totius terre sue clericis 7 laicis .·. Salutem. Sciant presentes 7 futuri me dedisse . 7 concessisse . 7 hac carta mea confirmasse . Rob*erto* fil*io* Henr*ici* Pincerne . Gasgingrei . per easdem diuisas per quas Ærchenb*aldus* Abbas de Dunfermel*in* cum probis hominibus meis 7 per preceptum meum terram illam ei perambulauit. Tenend*am* sibi 7 heredibus suis de me 7 heredibus meis in feudo 7 hereditate . in terris 7 pratis 7 pascuis . 7 cum communi pastura de mora de Kellin . libere 7 quiete .·. faciendo inde forinsecum seruicium . tantum scilicet quantum pertinet ad dimid*iam* Carucatam terre in Kellin Shire. Concessi etiam predicto Rob*erto* 7 heredibus suis ut quieti sint de multura de domo sua propria ad molendin*um* meum de Kellin . Set volo quod homines sui dent multuram. Test*ibus* Hug*one* Cancell*ario* meo Henr*ico* Abbate de Aberbrothoc Rob*erto* de London*iis* Johanne de Hasting '. Bernard*o* de Hauden' . Dunec*ano* de Lascel*es* . Herb*erto* Maresc*allo* . Herb*erto* de Camera . Apud KingoR[a].

ENDORSED. kasyngray (xiv cent.).
DESCRIPTION. 7·2″ (18·2 cm.), Top, 7·3″ (18·5 cm.), Bottom × 4″ (10 cm.), L, 4·2″ (10·6 cm.), R. Foot folded to a depth of 0·6″ (1·5 cm.). Double slits, with tag 5·1″ (13 cm.) long, 0·7″ (2 cm.) wide. No seal remains.
HAND. Scribe Da. Unruled.
SOURCE. Original, SRO, GD 203, Section 2, no.1.
PRINTED. *HMC 5th Report*, Appendix, p.623.
NOTE. [a] R extended with five strokes to fill up the line.
COMMENT. *Carucata* may be used here for davoch; cf. *Scottish Studies*, vi, 138–9. Kellie shire seems to have been identical with the later parish of Carnbee. See nos.131, 402, 469.

287 Declares that whereas it was necessary for him on the accession of King Richard I to pay a sum of money to redeem himself and his kingdom from the servitude by which they had been bound to Henry II king of England, and to restore himself and his kingdom to their former freedom, and whereas it is well known that the Cistercian Order should be free from exactions of all kinds, and yet in this great necessity has come to the aid of the king, this spontaneous act, never done before and not, God willing, to be done again, shall not prejudice the Order

for the future. Restalrig. (1189) (Spurious, but possibly based on an authentic original)

Will*elmus* Dei gr*ati*a Rex Scottorum . Omnibus fidelibus sancte matris Ecclesie filiis . maxime autem suis Episcopis . Comitibus . Baronibus Justic*iis* . Vicecomitibus . et[a] omnibus probis hominibus suis salutem. Notum sit uobis quod ego ipse et totum Regnum meum cum seruituti Henrico quondam Regi[b] Anglie esset addictum . succedenti in regnum Ricardo filio suo .' oportuit me tam pro me ipso et capcione mea redimenda quam pro toto regno meo pristine libertati restituendo pecuniam persoluere. Et quoniam ordo Cisterciensis tam in regno meo quam ubique ab omni exaccione merito liber esse dinoscitur ita ut nemini liceat seruitutis exaccionem imponere Volo ut sciatis quod eiusdem ordinis domus in regno meo constitute . in illa mea tanta necessitate spontanea voluntate sua obnixe mihi succurrerunt. Et quidem vobis presentibus literis significo .' ne quod in tali euentu semel factum est . qui nec prius euenit . nec in posterum Deo miserante futurus est . eis ullo modo in consuetudine uel seruitute conuertatur .' ut videlicet per[c] quod ipsi pro redimenda regni libertate gratis fecerunt .' seruitus eis imponatur. Test*ibus*[d] Hugone Cancellario meo . Comite Dunecano . Ricardo de Moreuill' constab*ulario* . Ricardo Cumin Just*icia* . Will*elmo*[e] de Ber[ke]-lai[f] Camerar*io* . Willelmo de Lindes'. Willelmo de Haia . apud Lastalr'.

ENDORSED. No endorsement known.[g]
DESCRIPTION. If the facsimile is actual size, the approximate dimensions of the writing block would have been 9·6″ (24·4 cm.), Top and bottom × 3·3″ (8·5 cm.). According to the facsimile, a seal of William I in perfect condition was attached on a tag, but the facsimile is hardly reliable on this point.
HAND. It is impossible to tell from the facsimile whether it is a poor representation of an authentic late twelfth- or early thirteenth-century hand, or a later forgery.
SOURCE. Anderson, *Diplomata*, Pl.XXVI (from the 'original' *penes* the earl of Oxford, apparently not among the Harley Charters in the BM) = *A*. NLS, MS. Adv. 34.4.11, fo.xxv^{v} = *B*.
PRINTED. Anderson, *Diplomata*, Pl.XXVI (*A*); *Melrose Liber*, no.16 (*B*). Printed here from *A*, with some variants of *B* noted.
NOTES. [a] *A* uses crossed tironian sign for et throughout. [b] H. quondam reg', *B*. [c] *B* adds hoc, correctly. [d] *B* ends here with etc. apud Lastalr'. [e] Sic; for Waltero. [f] *A* has Berlai. [g] *B* has rubric: Carta Regis Willelmi super indempnitate ordinis conseruanda.
COMMENT. This act raises several problems, and its study has not been helped by the poor version given in *Melrose Liber*, no.16 (later xiii cent.), in which *regis* after *H. quondam* should read *regi*. If this act were genuine, it would have been issued at the end of 1189, when, as William of Newburgh reports, the Scottish king came home from Richard I's court and 'scraped together' the sum of 10,000 merks to pay for the cancellation of the obnoxious treaty of Falaise (*Chron. Stephen*, i, 304). The raising of this sum seems to have been agreed upon at Musselburgh (*RRS*, i, 54 and nn.); if King William did issue an indemnity for the Cistercians on this occasion, its place of issue might well have been Restalrig. But the document as it stands cannot be accepted as authentic. Richard de Moreville's death is placed in 1189 by the Melrose chronicle, but so is Frederick Barbarossa's, which actually took place on 10 June, 1190 (*Chron. Melrose*, 47); possibly Richard de Moreville died early in 1190, and if so his attestation here could be accepted. It is a different matter with Richard Cumin the justiciar and William de Berkeley the chamberlain. The scribe of an authentic act would never write William by mistake for Walter; and Richard Cumin the elder does not

witness King William's acts after *c.*1178, and the latest mention of him as (apparently) still alive may be in no.215, above (1179). He can hardly be the Richard Cumin referred to in 1203–4 (*Cal. Docs. Scot.*, i, no.341), since his position as a justiciar implies that at the date of this act he was well-known and that he cannot have left only one trace on contemporary record. Moreover, making every allowance for the deficiencies of an early eighteenth-century facsimile engraving, the hand-writing as it appears on Anderson's plate bears no resemblance to any hand familiar at the time, although it might have been written in the thirteenth century, perhaps by a scribe trying to imitate a twelfth-century hand.

We should note a slight echo of the wording of this act in the nearly contemporary passage of the Melrose chronicle (*Chron. Melrose*, 47): 'sic, Deo suffragante, eius dominationis et seruitutis iugum graue a regno Scottorum digne et honorifice submouit.' It is unfortunate that nothing seems now to be known of the whereabouts of this document, which was in the possession of the Earl of Oxford when Anderson had his facsimile made and might have been expected to be among the Harley charters. The probability seems to be that this act was concocted in the thirteenth century at Melrose Abbey; but it seems possible that King William did issue an indemnity to the Cistercians at Restalrig at the end of 1189.

288 Grants to Melrose Abbey that part of their building and toft in Berwick which was taken into the king's hand because the abbey erected a building there during the time when Geoffrey de Neville had the keeping of the king's castle of Berwick. (1189 × 1214, probably soon after 1189)

U.[a] Dei gratia rex Scot' omnibus probis hominibus tocius terre sue, clericis et laicis, salutem. Sciant presentes et futuri me dedisse et concessisse et hac carta mea confirmasse Deo et ecclesie Sancte Marie de Melros et monachis ibidem Deo seruientibus illam partem domus sue et tofti sui de Berwic que saisita fuit in manu mea quia domum illam fecerunt tempore quo Gaufridus de Neeuill' habuit custodiam castelli mei de Berwic. Tenend*am* in liberam et puram et perpetuam elemosinam, ita libere et quiete, plenarie et honorifice, sicut alias elemosinas suas liberius, quiecius, plenius et honorificencius tenent et possident. Test*ibus*.

RUBRIC. Carta reg*is* Willelmi.
SOURCE. BM, MS. Harl. 3960, fo.92[r].
PRINTED. *Melrose Liber*, no.25.
NOTE. [a] Initial red.
COMMENT. The castle of Berwick was placed in the custody of Geoffrey de Neville by Henry II in 1177, as part of the English occupation of Berwick, Roxburgh and Edinburgh under the terms of the submission of Falaise (*Chron. Howden*, ii, 133). Presumably the action of Melrose abbey in erecting a building at Berwick during the English occupation, and therefore without leave of the king of Scots, was regarded as an offence against royal authority, and the property had been confiscated. But in view of the king's indebtedness to the Cistercians in the matter of the payment to Richard I, the confiscation is not likely to have been prolonged.

289 Commands his provosts of Berwick to pay annually to Kelso Abbey or its messengers 40s. out of the *firma burgi* of Berwick, 20s. on 20 March and 20s. on 4 September, as King David I's charter bears witness. (1173 × 1214, probably *c.*1189)

Willelmus[a] Dei gr*ati*a Rex Scottorum . prepositis suis de Berewyc' salutem. Precipio vobis firmiter quatinus annuatim habere faciatis monachos de Kalchou aut eorum nunciis[b] .xl. sol*idos* de firma burgi mei de Berewyc' scilicet .xx. sol*idos* ad festum Sancti Cuthberti in quadragesima et xx. sol*idos* ad festum Sancti Cuthberti in autumpno . sicut carta Regis Dauid aui mei testatur. T*estibus*.

RUBRIC. Carta Regis Willelmi de .xl[a]. s. in Berwico (top in red).
SOURCE. NLS, MS. Adv. 34.5.1, fo.17[v].
PRINTED. *Kelso Liber*, no.30.
NOTES. [a] Initial red. [b] Sic.
COMMENT. See no.123, above. This rent was one of King David's original endowments for the monks of Kelso when they were still at Selkirk (Lawrie, *Charters*, no.35). The payments may have ceased during the English occupation of Berwick castle, 1175–89. It is not easy to explain why Lucius III's solemn privilege to Kelso of 1182 (SRO, Papal Bulls, no.3) mentions a rent from Berwick of only 20 shillings.

290 Grants to Dryburgh Abbey an annualrent of 20s. from the *firma burgi* of Roxburgh, for lighting the church, 10s. at Martinmas and 10s. at Whitsun. (1173 × 1214, possibly 1189 × 1214)

Willelmus Dei gratia Rex Scotorum omnibus probis hominibus totius terre sue, clericis et laycis, salutem. Sciant presentes et futuri me dedisse et concessisse et hac carta mea confirmasse Deo et ecclesie Beate Marie de Driburgh et canonicis ibidem Deo servientibus pro salute anime mee et Malcolmi filii[a] mei et antecessorum et heredum meorum vigenti[b] sollidos singulis annis percipiendos de firma burgi mei de Rogesburgh in liberam et perpetuam elemosinam ad luminare prefate ecclesie de Driburgh. Quare precipio prepositis meis de Rogysburgh ut prescriptos vigenti[b] sollidos prenominatis canonicis annuatim sine contradictione et molestia persolvant, scilicet decem sollidos ad festum Sancti Martini et decem sollidos ad Pentecost*en*. Test*ibus* etc.

RUBRIC. Super vigenti solidis de firma burgi de Rogesburgh annuatim percipiendis. [c]lij.
SOURCE. NLS, MS. Adv. 34.4.7, fo.44[v].
PRINTED. *Dryburgh Liber*, no.142.
NOTES. [a] Sic, for fratris. [b] Sic.
COMMENT. The command to the provosts of Roxburgh probably would not be made between 1174 and 1189.

291 Grants to Dryburgh Abbey the half-ploughgate in Ednam, Roxburghshire, perambulated by Archibald abbot of Dunfermline and other responsible men by command of the king, of which they gave sasine to the abbey, in exchange for the half-ploughgate which King David I had given in the same toun to his clerk Nicholas. (1178 × 1214, probably × 1198)

Willelmus Dei gratia rex Scotorum omnibus probis hominibus totius terre sue, clericis et laycis, salutem. Sciant presentes et futuri me dedisse et concessisse et hac carta mea confirmasse Deo et ecclesie Beate Marie de Driburgh et canonicis ibidem Deo seruientibus illam dimidiam carucatam terre in Edinham quam Erchibaldus abbas de Dunfermelyne et alii probi homines mei precepto meo eis tradiderunt et perambulaverunt, in excambium illius dimidie carucate terre quam rex David auus meus Nicholayo clerico in eadem villa dederat, cum toftis et croftis que Godewynus homo Nicholayi predicti tenuit ad predictam carucatam terre. Quare volo et precipio ut predicti canonici prefatam dimidiam carucatam terre habeant et teneant in liberam et perpetuam elemosinam ita libere et quiete, plenarie et honorifice sicut alias elemosinas suas liberius, quietius, plenius et honorificentius tenent et possident. Testibus etc.

RUBRIC. Super dimidia carucata terre in Hedinham danda in excambium. clxx.
SOURCE. NLS, MS. Adv. 34.4.7, fo.48r.
PRINTED. *Dryburgh Liber*, no.160.
COMMENT. See *RRS*, i, no.129 and Lawrie, *Charters*, no.198. This was probably issued before Abbot Archibald's death. Cf. no.317.

292 Confirms to Holyrood Abbey one ploughgate in Kinnaird (in Larbert), Stirlingshire, granted by Gilbert de Umfraville, with freedom from multure for the canons and their tenants dwelling on that land. Edinburgh. (1189 × 1193)

.W'. Dei gratia Rex Scott'. Omnibus probis hominibus Tocius terre sue Clericis 7 Laicis Salutem. Sciant presentes et[a] futuri me concessisse . 7 hac Carta mea confirmasse Deo 7 Ecclesie Sancte Crucis de Edeneburg . 7 Canonicis ibidem Deo seruientibus . donationem illam quam Gilebertus de Umframvilla eis fecit de una Carukata terre in Kinard' . sicud eis per probos homines patrie perambulata fuit . cum communi pastura sicut in Carta predicti G*ileberti* continetur. Et cum libertate multure sue et hominum suorum super terram illam sedentium ;' sicut in Carta predicti G*ileberti* continetur. Tenend*am* in liberam et quietam 7 perpetuam elemoysinam . ita libere . 7 quiete . plenarie . 7 honorifice . sicut alias terras 7 tenuras suas tenent et possident . et sicut Carta predicti G*ileberti* testatur saluo seruicio meo. Test*ibus* Hug*one* Cancellario meo . Roberto Capellano meo . Joc*elino* archid*iacono* Dunk*eldensi* . Ric*ardo* de prebenda clericis meis . Philippo de Valon*iis* . Waltero de Berch' Cam*erario* . Ricard*o* fil*io* Hugonis . Willelmo de Rameseia . Adam de Sireis. Apud Edeneburg.

ENDORSED. Confirmacio de Kinard (xii cent.). s(cilicet) de Scaythmor (?) (xiii–xiv cent. ?). J. Scott (xvi cent.).
DESCRIPTION. 6·9″ (17·9 cm.), Top, 7·1″ (18 cm.), Bottom × 4·2″ (10·8 cm.), L, 4·3″ (11 cm.), R. Foot folded to a depth of 0·7″ (1·8 cm.). Double slits with tag 6·2″ (15·3 cm.) long, 0·5″ (1·2 cm.) wide. No seal remains, but its location is visible.
HAND. *A*: Scribe Dc. Unruled. *B*: Painfully exact copy of *A*, by a modern hand. Unruled.
SOURCE. Original, SRO, GD 45/13/244=*A*. Modern copy, SRO, GD 90/10=*B*. Printed here from *A*.
PRINTED. *Holyrood Liber*, no.42 (from *A*).
NOTE. [a] et in full indicates crossed Tironian sign.

293 Confirms to the church of (St Mary) of the Isle of Trail (St Mary's Isle, in Kirkcudbright) the church of Eggerness (Kirkmadrine, in Sorbie, Wigtownshire), and two ploughgates of land in Eggerness, granted by Roland son of Uchtred; and the teind of all the consumption of food, drink, wax and tallow in Roland's household at Kirkcudbright. Edinburgh. (1189 × *c.*1193)

Will' Dei gr*ati*a Rex Scocie . Omnibus probis [ ][a] clericis 7 laicis Salutem. Sciant presentes 7 futuri me concessisse 7 hac carta mea confirmasse Deo 7 [ ][b] de Trellesholm 7 canonicis ibidem Deo seruientibus [ ][c] Egernesse cum terris 7 decimis 7 oblationibus omnimodis 7 omnibus aliis ad predictam ecclesiam iuste pertinentibus quam Rollandus filius Uctredi eis dedit . 7 preterea ex donatione eiusdem[d] duas carrucatas terre in predicta uilla de Egernesse cum communi pastura 7 aliis aisiamentis sicut in carta predicti Rolland*i* continetur. Saluo tamen de predictis duabus carrucatis terre seruicio meo. Et preterea totam decimam tocius expense que fit in domo prefati Rolland*i* in cibo 7 potu in cera 7 sepio . 7 omnibus aliis rebus ad mensam eius pertinentibus ap*ud* Kirkecutdbrid. Tenend' in liberam 7 puram 7 perpetuam Elemosinam . ita libere 7 quiete plenarie 7 honorifice sicut carta prefati Rolland*i* testatur 7 confirmat. Test*ibus* Hug*one* Cancellario meo . Archenbaldo abbate de Dunfermel*in* . Sim*one* archid*iacono* Glasg*uensi* . Ric*ardo* de prebenda clerico meo . Comite Dunecht' . Willelmo de Lindes' . Willelmo de Moreuill' . Philippo de Valon*iis* . Randol*fo* de Sol*is* . Walltero Corbet . Walltero de Berchel' Camerario . Willelmo de Vallibus . Willelmo de Cuninchesb'. Apud Castell*um* Puellarum.

ENDORSED. de ecclesia de Egernesse (xiii–xiv cent.). Also modern endorsements.
DESCRIPTION. 9·4″ (25·8 cm.), Top, 9·2″ (25·5 cm.), Bottom × 3·2″ (8 cm.), L, R. Foot folded to a depth of 0·7″ (1·8 cm.). Double slits with tag 10″ (27·8 cm.) long, 0·5″ (1·3 cm.) wide. Seal almost complete, in natural wax stained dark brown, diameter 2·8″ (7 cm.).
HAND. Scribe Cc.
SOURCE. Original, SRO, RH 6/14.
NOTES. [a] Large tear in parchment. Supply hominibus tocius terre sue? [b] Supply ecclesie Sancte Marie? [c] Supply ecclesiam de. [d] Last two words obscured through injury.
COMMENT. The parish of Kirkmadrine was united with Cruggleton and Sorbie in 1635. It does not figure in the record of the papal tenth of 1275, presumably because it was included among the property of the *Insula de Thrahil* (Isle of Trail); cf. SHS, *Miscellany*, vi, 74. For another example of the grant of the teind of *expensa* and of all victuals brought to a particular residence, in this instance belonging to the bishop of Dunkeld, see *Inchcolm Chrs.*, no.1.

294 Forbids any of his justices, sheriffs, officers or men to maintain any of the tenants of the prior of Coldingham in opposition to the priory and in refusal to perform what they reasonably ought to perform. Edinburgh. (1189 × 1195)

W'. Dei gr*ati*a Rex Scott'. Justiciis Uicecomitibus . Ministris et Omnibus probis hominibus totius terre sue . Salutem.[a] Mando et firmiter precipio . Ne quis uestrum aliquem de hominibus prioris de Coldingham contra ipsum priorem siue contra domum suam iniuste manuteneat ·/ quin quod de ratione facere debeat ei faciat. Test*ibus* Com*ite* D*aui*d fratre meo . Hug*one* Cancellario meo . Comite Dunec*ano* Apud Castellum puellarum.

ENDORSED. W. Reg*is*[b] ne quis manuteneat homines prioris contra priorem (xii–xiii cent.). Mandatum W regis (xv cent.). de Cold (xv cent. insertion). R iij[a] vj[te] (xv cent.).
DESCRIPTION. 9″ (22·8 cm.), Top and bottom × 3·6″ (9·4 cm.), L, 2·4″ (6·2 cm.), R. Tongue 6″ long, 1″ wide. Seal in natural wax, excellent condition.
HAND. Scribe Bb. Unruled.
SOURCE. Original, Durham, D. & C. Muniments, Misc. Chr. no.604.
PRINTED. Raine, *North Durham*, no.33.

NOTES. [a] Mando has been written at the end of a line, and then erased; possibly after a false start with Sciant. Mando has then been written again at the beginning of a new line. [b] Struck through.

295 Confirms to his brother Earl David the quittance of all teinds and customs which the church of Saint Mary of Aberdeen and the bishops of Aberdeen used to have in the time of King David I and King Malcolm IV and in King William's own time in Garioch, Durno, Rothkes, Monkeigie, Fintray and Bourtie; this quittance has been granted by Bishop Matthew in exchange for the two measured plough-gates of land in Kennethmont, Aberdeenshire, near to the land which the church of Aberdeen has in that neighbourhood. Edinburgh. (March, 1189 × 1190)

Will*elmus*[a] Dei gr*aci*a Rex Scottorum omnibus probis hominibus totius terre sue, clericis et laicis, salutem. Sciant presentes et futuri me concessisse et hac carta mea confirmasse Comiti Dauid fratri meo quietanciam decimarum et consuetudinum omnium quas ecclesie Sancte Marie et episcopi de Aberdon habere solebant tempore Regis Dauid aui mei et regis Malcolmi fratris mei et tempore meo in Garwyach' et in Durnach' et in Rothkes et Munkegyn et Fyntrach' et Bourdyn, quam scilicet quietanciam Matheus episcopus ei fecit de se et de successoribus suis imperpetuum pro duabus carucatis terre mensuratis in Kelalcmund' propinquioribus terre sue illius vicine. Quare volo et precipio ut prefatus Comes Dauid frater meus et heredes sui habeant hanc prefatam quietanciam decimarum et consuetudinum de terris prenominatis de ecclesia et de Matheo episcopo Aberdon*ensi* et de successoribus[b] suis episcopis imperpetuum, ita libere et quiete, plenarie et honorifice, sicut carta prefati episcopi testatur. Test*ibus* J*ocelino* episcopo Glasg*uensi*, E*rnaldo*[c] abbate Rieuall', R*einerio* abbate de Melr*os*, H*ugone* abbate de Newbotyl, Comite Duncan*o*, Comite Gilberto, Ricardo de prebenda clerico meo, W. de Lyndesay, A*lano* dapifero meo, Willelmo de Moreuill', Malcolmo filio Comitis Duncan*i*, Waltero de Berk' camerario. Apud Edynburh'.

RUBRIC. Nota Kynalmond (margin in later hand).
SOURCE. NLS, MS. Adv. 16.1.10, fo.80r–v (old foliation, fo.lxxxir–v).
PRINTED. *Aberdeen Registrum*, i, 9–10.
NOTES. [a] Red initial; punctuation editorial. [b] Fo.80v. [c] *Aberdeen Registrum* prints G.
COMMENT. See no.348. Rothkes, obsolete, is represented by Polnar Chapel in Inverurie, the old mother church of Inverurie. Monkeigie or Monkegie is now Keithhall. This quittance was obtained so that Earl David could grant these churches unencumbered to his foundation at Lindores: see no.363.

The charters by which Richard de Moreville the constable and his wife Avice of Lancaster and their son and heir William granted Selside (Yorkshire, West Riding) to Furness Abbey, witnessed by Bishop Jocelin of Glasgow and Abbot Reiner of Melrose, seem to belong to the same period as this act (*Coucher Book of Furness Abbey*, ed. J. Brownbill (Chetham Society, II, pt.ii (1916), 334–8).

296 Confirms to Newbattle Abbey the land of 'Kressewelle' (Monkrigg, in Haddington), East Lothian, granted by Hugh and William Giffard, as their charters bear witness. Edinburgh. (1189 × 1195)

Willelmus Dei gratia Rex Scott' episcopis, abbatibus, comitibus, baronibus, justiciis, vice*comitibus*, ministris et omnibus probis hominibus tocius terre sue, clericis et laicis, salutem. Sciant presentes et futuri me concessisse et hac carta mea confirmasse Deo et ecclesie Sancte Marie de Neu*botle* et monachis ibidem Deo seruientibus donacionem terre de Kressewelle quam Hugo Gyffard et Willelmus filius eius et heres eis dederunt, tenend*am* in liberam et perpetuam elemosinam, ita libere et quiete, plenarie et honorifice, sicut aliquam elemosinam liberius, quiecius, plenius et honorificencius tenent et possident et sicud carte eorundem testantur, saluo seruicio meo. Test*ibus* A*rnaldo* Abbate de Ryeualle, Willelmo de Morewill', Henrico de Graham vicecomite meo. Apud Castrum Puellarum.

Confirmacio Reg*is* Willelmi.[a]

SOURCE. NLS, MS. Adv. 34.4.13, fo.27^r.

PRINTED. *Newbattle Registrum*, no.85.

NOTE. [a] Table of contents, fo.2^r.

COMMENT. The charters of Hugh and William Giffard are given in *Newbattle Registrum*, nos.81, 82, the former stating that the land had been perambulated by Alexander (of St Martin) sheriff (of Haddington) 'from the road leading from Lethington to Bearford as far as the marches of Morham and Coalstoun'. The name 'Kressewelle' or 'Cressewelle' seems to be obsolete.

297 Confirms to Holyrood Abbey the church of Melginch (St Martins), Perthshire, with the land called in Gaelic *abthen*, and the land called Petfrethin (Pitreddie?), lying on the west side of the church; as the charter of John bishop of Dunkeld bears witness. Edinburgh. (1189 × 1195)

.W'. Dei gratia Rex Scott' . Omnibus probis hominibus tocius terre sue clericis 7[a] laicis ·/ Salutem. Sciant presentes et futuri me concessisse . 7 hac carta mea confirmasse Deo 7 ecclesie Sancte Crucis de Edeneb' . 7 canonicis ibidem Deo seruientibus ecclesiam de Melginche cum omnibus iustis pertinenciis suis 7 cum terra que scotice uocatur Abthen . 7 cum terra que uocatur Petfrethin que iacet ex occidentali parte ecclesie de Melginche 7 cum decimis 7 oblationibus 7 omnibus aliis rectitudinibus ecclesiasticis 7 cum omnibus ad eandem ecclesiam iuste pertinentibus. Tenend*am* in liberam 7 perpetuam elemosinam . ita libere . Quiete . Plenarie 7 honorifice . Sicut carta Johannis Dunkeld*ensis* Episcopi testatur. Test*ibus* Hug*one* Cancellario meo . Ric*ardo* de prebenda clerico meo . Henr*ico* de Graham . Willelmo de Rameshei . Ric*ardo* filio Hug*onis* . Philipp*o* Maresc*allo* . Herb*erto* Maresc*allo*. Apud Edeneburg'.

ENDORSED. Melginch (date of hand unknown).

SOURCE. *Holyrood Liber*, no.48, printed from the original then (1840) *penes* Lord Panmure, present whereabouts unknown. It was not among the Holyrood charters recently deposited in the SRO by Messrs Dundas and Wilson, W.S. on behalf of the Earl of Dalhousie.

PRINTED. *Holyrood Liber*, no.48.

NOTE. [a] It is not clear from the printed version whether the scribe used a tironian sign for et with or without a horizontal cross stroke.

COMMENT. The barony of Pitreddie, comprising lands in Melginch parish, appears in *Retours* (Perth), no.744. The charter of Bishop John of Dunkeld (1183–1203), in whose diocese Melginch lay, does not appear to have survived.

298 Commands that debts are to be paid promptly to Coupar Angus Abbey, on pain of his full forfeiture. Edinburgh. (1189 × 1199, probably × 1195)

Carta Regis Willielmi eisdem monachis ut quisquis debuerit eis debitum immediate eiis soluat sine ulla dilatione supra regis plenariam forisfacturam. Testibus: Comite D*aui*d fratre meo, Heugone Cancellario meo, Comite Duncano. Apud Edinburg.

SOURCE. NLS, MS. Adv. 33.2.9, fo.28^{r}.
PRINTED. *Coupar Angus Rental*, i, 324, no.10.

299 Confirms to Kelso Abbey the church of Pencaitland, East Lothian, granted by Everard of Pencaitland, as his charter bears witness. Edinburgh. (1189 × 1195)

W. Dei gr*ati*a Rex Scott' . Omnibus probis hominibus tocius terre sue clericis 7 laicis salutem. Sciant presentes 7 futuri me concessisse 7 hac carta mea confirmasse Ecclesie Sancte Marie de Kelchou . 7 monachis ibidem Deo seruientibus donacionem illam quam Euerardus de Pencatlan eis fecit de ecclesia de Pencatlan . Tenend*am* in liberam 7 perpetuam elemosinam . cum terris 7 decimis . 7 oblacionibus omnimodis . ita libere 7 quiete 7 honorifice . sicut carta predicti Euerardi testatur 7 confirmat. Hiis test*ibus* . Joc*elino* episcopo Glasg*uensi* . Hug*one* cancellario meo . Comit*e* Dunec*ano* . Rodland' fil*io* Ucdr*edi* . Willelmo de Lyndes' apud Edenburg'.[a]

RUBRIC. Confirmacio super Ecclesiam de Pencateland (top in red).
SOURCE. NLS, MS. Adv. 34.5.1, fo.146^{r}.
PRINTED. *Kelso Liber*, no.390.
NOTE. [a] g apparently altered from h.
COMMENT. Everard's charter is given in *Kelso Liber*, no.370, dating 1165 × 1189; his son Walter's confirmation is ibid., no.369. Note the attestation of Earl Duncan, Roland son of Uhtred and William of Lindsay, probably justiciars of Scotia, Galloway and Lothian respectively.

300 Confirms to Arbroath Abbey the grant made by Fergus earl of Buchan of an annualrent of one merk of silver. Edinburgh. (1193 × 1195)

W.[a] Dei gr*ati*a Rex Scott' . omnibus probis hominibus tocius terre sue clericis[b] et laicis salutem. Sciant presentes et futuri me concessisse et hac carta mea confirmasse Deo et ecclesie Sancti Thome[c] de Abirbroth*oc* et monachis ibidem Deo seruientibus et seruituris donacionem illam quam comes Fergus eis fecit in perpetuam elemosinam de una marca argenti annuatim. Quare volo ut prefati monachi prefatam marcam argenti de predicto Fergus Comite de Buchan et heredibus eius annuatim in liberam et puram et perpetuam elemosinam percipiant et habeant ita libere et quiete plenarie et honorifice . sicut aliqua domus religiosa in regno meo . aliquam elemosinam liberius et quiecius plenius et honorificencius recipit et possidet. Test*ibus* Arch*enbaldo* Abbate de Dunfermel*in* . Willelmo Abbate de Sancte Cruce . Hug*one* Cancell*ario* meo . Philippo de Valon*iis* Camerar*io* meo . Roberto de Quency . Willelmo de Vall*ibus* . Will*elmo* de Mountfort . Will*elmo* Giffard' . Ph*ilippo* Marescallo . Apud Edinburg'.

RUBRIC. Confirmacio Regis W. super dicta marca (red)[d].
SOURCE. NLS, MS. Adv. 34.4.2, fos.lxiii^{v}–lxiv^{r}.
PRINTED. *Arbroath Liber*, i, no.85 (*bis*).
NOTES. [a] Initial red. [b] Fo.lxiv^{r}. [c] Sancti Thome repeated and expunged, MS. [d] No marginated numeral; entered between lxxxv and lxxxvj.
COMMENT. Earl Fergus's charter, providing for the merk to be paid yearly at Whitsun, is given in *Arbroath Liber*, i, no.85, witnessed by the king and his brother David and dating 1173 × 1195. This act should have been placed between nos.368 and 369.

301

Confirms to Melrose Abbey the whole clearing (*landa*) of Blainslie by the marches named in the charter of Richard de Moreville, to be ploughed and cultivated without making an assart, and with permission to erect buildings wherever they wish on the burn between Blainslie and 'Milcheside'. Confirms also the whole land of 'Milcheside' granted by Richard de Moreville and his heir; the chapel of Park (Chapel on Leader); and the buildings of Colmslie, Buckholm and Whitelee as they were at Michaelmas next after the first coronation of Richard son of Henry king of England (29 September, 1189), provided they are not increased without the king's permission. None of the king's foresters is to grant away or sell wood within the marches specified in the king's charter. Traquair. (29 September, 1189 × 1190)

.W'. Dei gr*ati*a Rex Scott . Episcopis . Abbatibus . Comitibus . baronibus . Justiciis . Vicecomitibus . prepositis . 7 Omnibus probis hominibus tocius terre sue . clericis 7 laicis salutem. Sciant presentes 7 futuri me dedisse 7 hac presenti carta mea confirmasse Deo 7 ecclesie Sancte Marie de Meilros . 7 monachis de Rieualle ibidem Deo seruientibus pro animabus patris mei 7 matris mee . 7 Reg*is* D*aui*d aui mei . 7 pro salute anime mee . 7 omnium fratrum 7 sororum 7 antecessorum 7 successorum meorum in liberam 7 puram 7 perpetuam elemosinam totam landam de Bleineslei per diuisas nominatas in carta Ric*ardi* de Moreuilla . ad arandam[a] 7 colendam sicut eis melius 7 utilius uisum fuerit . sine sarto faciendo . 7 licentiam faciendi edificia sua ubi uoluerint super riuulum qui est inter Blaineslei 7 Milcheside . 7 totam terram de Milcheside quam Ricardus de Moreuill' 7 heres eius eis dederunt 7 cartis suis confirmauerunt per easdem diuisas que in cartis eorum continentur . 7 capellam de Parco sicut in cartis eisdem continetur . 7 edificia de Cumbesleia 7 de Buchelm 7 de Witheleia sicut fuerunt ad festum Sancti Michaelis proximum post primam coronationem Ric*ardi* filii Henrici Reg*is* Anglie . ita quod non ampliora aut plura edificia ibi faciant quam tunc temporis ibi fuerunt nisi per licentiam meam ∴ Et ut nullus forestariorum meorum det uel uendat [boscum][b] infra diuisas eorum que in mea carta continentur. Hec autem omnia do 7 concedo eis perpetuo tenore possidere . 7 hac carta mea confirmo in liberam 7 perpetuam elemosinam . 7 uolo 7 precipio ut omnia supradicta habeant 7 possideant ita libere 7 quiete plenarie 7 honorifice sicut ulla elemosina liberius 7 quietius . plenius 7 honorificentius haberi potest 7 possideri a monachis ordinis Cisterciensis. Testibus Jocel*ino* episcopo Glasguen*si* . Ærnaldo Abbate de Rieu*alle* . Hug*one*[c] cancellario meo . Roberto capellano meo . Phillippo de Vallon*iis* . Rob*erto* de Lond*oniis* . Willelmo de Lindesei .

Malcolm*o* filio Com*itis* Dunec*ani* . Willelmo Cumin . Geruasio Auenel . Willelmo de Haia . Adam filio Gill*eberti* . Adam de Sireis . Adam de Stanfort . Herberto Marecallo[d] apud TrauerqueR.

ENDORSED. Will*elm*us Rex de foresta (xiii–xiv cent.). S (red, xv cent.?). J. Scott (xvi cent.).

DESCRIPTION. 9·9″ (25 cm.), Top, bottom × 7·1″ (18 cm.), L, 6·8″ (17 cm.), R. Foot folded to a depth of 0·7″ (1·8 cm.). Double slits, with tag 5·5″ (14 cm.) long, 0·4″ (1 cm.) wide. Seal almost complete, in brown wax, fair impression.

HAND. Scribe Cc. Ruled in drypoint or pencil.

SOURCE. Original, SRO, GD 55/96.

PRINTED. *Melrose Liber*, no.96 = *M*.

NOTES. [a] edificandam, *M*. The dam is not in doubt, but there seem to have been attempts to write before it aran and edifican. [b] Reading obscure and supplied conjecturally. *M* has d' bos. [c] Source has Hog'. [d] Sic.

COMMENT. The identified places are all in Melrose parish, Roxburghshire. 'Milcheside,' now obsolete, lay adjacent to Blainslie (*Melrose Liber*, no.108), and seems to appear in 1550 as Milseyburn (*Laing Chrs.*, no.569). The wording of this confirmation suggests that Richard de Moreville was still alive at the time it was issued, and he probably died early in 1190.

302

Grants to Roger de Mortemer Fowlis Easter (Angus), which belonged to William Maule and was held by Archibald of Forgan (Longforgan) with William Maule's daughter; to be held in feu and heritage, with soke and sake, toll, team and infangthief, with pit and gallows, for the service of one knight; and also the two tofts given by King Malcolm IV to William Maule, viz. one in Selkirk and one in Clackmannan. Haddington. (1189 × 1194)

W'. Dei gr*ati*a Rex Scott'. Episcopis . Abbatibus . Comitibus . Baronibus . Justiciis . Vicecomitibus . Prepositis . Ministris . et[a] omnibus probis hominibus totius terre sue Clericis et Laicis . Salutem. Sciant presentes et futuri me dedisse . 7 concessisse . et hac carta mea confirmasse . Rogero de Mortuo Mari . Foweles . que fuit Willelmi Masculi . quam Arkebald' de Forgrund' tenuit :' cum filia ipsius Willelmi Masculi . per rectas diuisas suas . et Cum omnibus iustis pertinentiis suis. Tenend*um* sibi 7 heredibus suis de me 7 heredibus meis in feudo 7 hereditate . in Bosco 7 plano . in Terris 7 Aquis . in pratis 7 pascuis . in molendinis et stagnis . in piscariis et viuariis . in mosis[b] et Maresiis . et in omnibus aliis ad predictam terram iuste pertinentibus. Cum Socca . et Sacca . Cum furca . et fossa . Cum Tol . et Them . et Infangenethef . libere et quiete plenarie 7 honorifice per seruitium unius militis. Preterea dedi eidem Rogero 7 heredibus suis illa duo tofta que Rex Malcolm*us* frater meus Willelmo Masculo dedit et carta sua confirmauit . scilicet unum toftum in Selesch' . et unum toftum in Clacm*anan*. Tenend*a* sibi 7 heredibus suis . de me 7 heredibus meis ita libere 7 quiete plenarie 7 honorifice . sicut alii Barones mei tofta sua in Regno meo liberius 7 quietius tenent 7 possident. Test*ibus* Hug*one* Cancellario meo . Com*ite* Dunec*ano* . Com*ite* Gilberto . Rob*erto* Capellano meo . Ric*ardo* de prebend*a* clerico meo . Willelmo CumiN . Malcolm*o* fil*io* Com*itis* Dunec*ani* . Willelmo de Lacel*es* . Roberto de Berk' . Waltero de Lindeseia . D*aui*d de Haia . D*aui*d de Lindesia[c] . Apud HadiNtuNe.[d]

ENDORSED. karta de Foules (xii cent.). Rogero de Mortuo mari (xiv cent.). Valde libera (xv cent.). Also modern endorsements.

DESCRIPTION. 7·9″ (20 cm.), Top, 8·7″ (22 cm.), Bottom × 7·5″ (19 cm.), L, 7·9″ (20 cm.), R. Foot folded to a depth of 1·2″ (3 cm.). Double slits, but no tag or seal remains.
HAND. Scribe Bb. Unruled.
SOURCE. Original, SRO, GD 45/27/92.
PRINTED. *Panmure Registrum*, ii, 80–81 (with facsimile).
NOTES. [a] In full. Scribe Bb employs both et and uncrossed tironian sign. [b] Sic. [c] Mark of contraction over second i. [d] Letters extended to fill the line.
COMMENT. For Archibald and Hugh, sons of Swain of Longforgan (perhaps the king's thane of Longforgan), see *RRS*, i, 42 and n., and see also no.16 and no.338.

303 Concedes to Holyrood Abbey that no one may take poinds from the canons or from their men, save for their own debts, and forbids anyone, whether in Scotland benorth Forth or on the Isle of May when the abbot of Holyrood's men should come there to fish, to take poinds from the canons or from their men, on pain of the king's forfeiture. Haddington. (1189 × 1195)

.W'. Dei gratia Rex Scott'. Omnibus probis hominibus tocius terre sue Salutem. Sciatis me concessisse Abbati 7 Conuentui de Sancta Cruce ut nullus super eos aut super homines suos namum capiat nisi pro dominicis debitis suis aut pro debitis hominum suorum. Quare prohibeo firmiter ne quis uel in Scotia . uel apud Insulam de May . cum homines predicti Abbatis illuc ad piscand*um* uenerint .' super canonicos de Sancta Cruce aut super eorum homines namum capiat nisi sit pro dominicis debitis suis . aut pro debitis hominum suorum . Super meam forisfacturam. Test*ibus* Hug*one* Cancellario meo . Ric*ardo* de Prebenda clerico meo. Apud Hadint'.

ENDORSED. De namo non capiendo (xii–xiii cent.). J. Scott (xvi cent.).
DESCRIPTION. 6·4″ (16 cm.), Top, 6·2″ (15·6 cm.), Bottom × 3·2″ (8 cm.), L 2·3″ (6 cm.), R. Tie and tongue cut from foot, 1·5″ (4 cm.) from left-hand edge, both 3·4″ (8·6 cm.) long. No seal remains.
HAND. Scribe Da. Unruled.
SOURCE. Original, SRO, GD 45/13/236.
PRINTED. *Holyrood Liber*, no.28.

304 Grants to Dunfermline Abbey, for the lighting of its church, an annualrent of three merks from the *firma burgi* of Haddington, payable 20s. at Martinmas and 20s. at Whitsun. Selkirk. (1189 × 1194)

Willelmus[a] Dei gr*ati*a Rex Scott' . episcopis . abbatibus . Comit*ibus* . Baron*ibus* . Justic*iis* . Vicec*omitibus* . Prepositis . ministris . 7 omnibus probis hominibus tocius terre sue clericis 7 laicis salutem. Sciant presentes 7 futuri me dedisse 7 concessisse 7 hac carta mea confirmasse Deo 7 ecclesie Sancte Trinitatis de Dunfer*melin* 7 monachis ibidem Deo seruientibus Tres marcas de firma burgi mei de Hadington' ad luminare prefate ecclesie in perpetuum. Quare volo 7 firmiter precipio ut predicti monachi illas .iii. marcas singulis annis de firma prenominati burgi de Hadigtun' habeant 7 teneant in liberam 7 quietam 7 perpetuam elemosinam . ita libere 7 quiete . plenarie 7 honorifice .' sicut alias elemosinas suas liberius . quiecius plenius 7 honorificencius tenent 7 possident . scilicet .xx. sol*idos* ad festum Sancti Martini . 7 .xx. sol*idos* ad Pentecosten. Testibus Hugone cancellario meo . Symone Archidiacono de Teuidal' . Roberto 7 Radulfo capellanis meis . Alano dapifero meo . Malcolmo filio Comitis Duncani . Geruasio Auenel . Willelmo Cumin . Waltero Corbet . Willelmo de Haya . Ricardo de prebenda clerico meo . Adam de Syreis . Eustachio Papedi . Philippo Marescallo. Apud Seleschirche.

RUBRIC. De tribus marcis de Hadigtun' (red with blue initial).
SOURCE. NLS, MS. Adv. 34.1.3a, fo.xii^r.
PRINTED. *Dunfermline Registrum*, no.51.
NOTE. Large red initial U or monogram W, flourished in blue.

305 Commands his sheriff and provosts of Haddington to let Archibald abbot of Dunfermline have yearly from the *firma burgi* of Haddington three merks for lighting his abbey church, half at Martinmas and half at Whitsun. Selkirk. (1189 × 1194)

Will'[a] Dei gratia Rex Scot' . Vicecomiti 7 prepositis suis de Hadigt' salutem. Precipio uobis quatinus de firma burgi de Hadigtun' faciatis habere annuatim Ærchebaldo abbati de Dunfermelin .iij. marcas ad luminare ecclesie Christi[b] de Dunfermelin . scilicet .xx. solidos ad festum Sancti Martini . 7 xx. solidos ad Pentecosten . sicut carta mea testatur. Testibus Hugone cancellario meo . Roberto capellano meo Apud Selesk'.

RUBRIC. De Hadingtun ad luminare (red with red initial).
SOURCE. NLS, MS. Adv. 34.1.3a, fo.xiii^r.
PRINTED. *Dunfermline Registrum*, no.65.
NOTES. [a] Initial blue. [b] Written x^i.
COMMENT. See no.304 above.

306 Confirms to Kelso Abbey the oxgang of arable in Sprouston, Roxburghshire, granted by Ralph de Veir, as his charter bears witness. Traquair. (1189 × 1195)

W. Dei gratia Rex Scott' . Omnibus probis hominibus suis Tocius terre sue clericis 7 laicis salutem. Sciant presentes . 7 futuri me concessisse . 7 hac carta mea[a] confirmasse Deo . 7 Ecclesie Sancte Marie de Kelchou . 7 monachis ibidem Deo seruientibus illam bouatam terre . in Sproweston . quam Radulfus de Wer in liberam elemosinam predictis monachis de Kelch' dedit 7 carta sua confirmauit . Tenendam in quietam 7 perpetuam elemosinam . ita libere 7 quiete plenarie 7 honorifice sicut carta predicti Radulfi testatur . saluo seruicio meo. Testibus . Hugone Cancellario meo . Roberto capellano meo . Alano filio Walteri dapiferi . Malcolmo filio Comitis Dunecani . Petro de Polloc' . Rogero de Wiltun' . Symone filio Melbet . Adam de Hasketh. Apud Trauequeir.

RUBRIC. Confirmacio super unam bouatam terre in territorio de Sproweston' (top in red).
SOURCE. NLS, MS. Adv. 34.5.1, fo.145^r.
PRINTED. *Kelso Liber*, no.385.
NOTE. [a] mea precedes carta and is marked for transposition by two pairs of diagonal strokes.
COMMENT. Ralph de Veir's charter is given in *Kelso Liber*, no.215. It is hard to date precisely, but belongs to the reign of King William. Adam de Hasketh is presumably Adam de Hasteng.

307 Confirms to Melrose Abbey the land which William de Moreville granted in augmentation of the land of 'Milcheside' previously granted by Richard de Moreville, as the charter of William bears witness. (1189 × 1196)

Uill*elmus*[a] Dei gr*ati*a rex Scot' omnibus probis hominibus tocius terre sue, clericis et laicis, salutem. Sciant presentes et futuri me concessisse et hac carta mea confirmasse Deo et ecclesie Sancte Marie de Melros et monachis ibidem Deo seruientibus totam terram quam Willelmus de Moreuill' constab*ularius* eis dedit in augmentum terre de Milcheside, quam Ric*ardus* de Moreuill' eis dederat, per diuisas nominatas in carta predicti Willelmi, tenend*am* in liberam et puram et perpetuam elemosinam, ita libere et quiete, plenarie et honorifice, sicut carta prefati Willelmi testatur, saluo seruicio meo. Test*ibus* etc.

RUBRIC. Confirmacio Reg*is* Willelmi super terram quam W. de Moreuill' addidit terre de Blanesl'.
SOURCE. BM, MS. 3960, fo.36[r].
PRINTED. *Melrose Liber*, no.100.
NOTE. [a] Initial red.
COMMENT. Probably before the death of William de Moreville in 1196. His charter is given in *Melrose Liber*, no.99. The name 'Milcheside', now apparently obsolete, seems to be preserved as Milseyburn in a document of 1550 (*Laing Chrs.*, no.569).

308 Grants that Glasgow Cathedral Church and Bishop Jocelin and his successors may have a fair at Glasgow to be held for eight days, one week after 29 June; with firm and full peace, and with all the liberties granted to any fairs within the king's whole land as freely as any fairs in any of the king's burghs. Edinburgh. (1189 × 1195)

W'. Dei gratia Rex Scott' . Episcopis Abbatibus . Com*itibus* . Baron*ibus* . Justic*iis* . vicec*omitibus* prepositis . ministris . et Omnibus probis hominibus totius terre sue clericis et laicis Salutem. Sciant presentes et futuri me dedisse et concessisse et hac carta mea confirmasse Deo et Sancto Kentegerno et Ecclesie de Glasg*u* et Joc*elino* eiusdem loci episcopo Omnibusque successoribus eius inperpetuum . Nundinas apud Glasgu habendas et singulis annis tenendas . ab Octab*is* apostolorum Petri et Pauli . Plenarie per octo dies . Cum firma et plenaria pace .[a] et Cum omnibus libertatibus aliquibus Nundinis in tota terra mea concessis . et Cum omnibus rectitudinibus ad Nundinas pertinentibus . ita libere Quiete . Plenarie et honorifice .' sicut alique Nundine in aliquo Burgorum meorum liberius quietius plenius et honorificentius tenentur aut teneri debent. Test*ibus* Joh*anne* Dunkelden*si* episcopo. Hug*one* cancell*ario* meo . Arch*embaldo* abbate de Dunfermeli*n* . O*sberto* abbate de Kelcho . Comit*e* Dunecan . Roll*ando* fil*io* Ucdr*edi* . Willelmo de Lindese' . Walt*ero* Corbet . Willelmo Cumi*n* . Rob*erto* filio Werneburc[b] . Alexandro vicecom*ite* de Striueli*n* . Henr*ico* de Graham . Henr*ico* de Cormanoc. Apud Edenburc.

RUBRIC. De Nundinis apud Glasg*u* (in margin, fo.v[r], in different hand).
SOURCE. Blairs Archives, 16 Drummond Place, Edinburgh, MS. Registrum Vetus of Glasgow, fo.v[r–v].
PRINTED. *Glasgow Registrum*, no.42. NOTES. [a] Fo.v[v]. [b] Sic.

COMMENT. This act marks the foundation of Glasgow Fair. For a comment on the witness list, see p.45.

309 Confirms to James (son of Lambin) of Loudoun the land of Loudoun (Ayrshire) by the marches named in the charter of William de Moreville; to be held of William in feu and heritage as William's charter bears witness. Lanark. (1189 × 1195)

W' Dei gr*ati*a Rex Scott'. Omnibus probis hominibus tocius terre sue clericis 7 laicis :' Salutem. Sciant presentes 7 futuri me concessisse . 7 hac carta mea confirmasse Jacobo de Laudun terram de Laudun per diuisas in carta Will*elmi* de Moreuill' Constab*ularii* nominatas . 7 cum omnibus justis pertinenciis suis. Tenend*am* sibi 7 heredibus suis de predicto Willelmo de Moruill' . 7 heredibus suis . in feudo 7 hereditate . in monasterio . in bosco 7 plano . in pratis 7 pascuis . in molendin*o* . 7 cum omnibus aliis ad predictam terram iuste pertinentibus . ita libere . Quiete . Plenarie 7 Honorifice :' Sicut carta prefati Willelmi de Moreuill' testatur . Saluo seruicio meo. Test*ibus* Roll*ando* fil*io* Ucdr*edi* Justic*ia* . Alan*o* fil*io* Walt*eri* Dapifero . Ric*ardo* de prebenda clerico meo . D*aui*d de Lindes' . Rob*erto* fil*io* Warneb*aldi* . Henr*ico* de Corman*oc* . Will*elmo* Mansell' . Will*elmo* Passelew' . D*aui*d Uuied' . Apud Lann'.

ENDORSED. Loudoun confirmatioun of King Wilȝe*m* (xvi–xvii cent.). Also modern numeral endorsements.
DESCRIPTION. 6·5″ (16·5 cm.), Top, 6·3″ (16 cm.), Bottom × 3·6″ (9·2 cm.), L, R. Foot folded to a depth of 0·6″ (1·5 cm.). Tie torn off at top left-hand edge of fold. Seal-tag passes through double slits in foot and fold, 7·5″ (19·1 cm.) long, 0·6″ (1·5 cm.) wide. No seal remains.
HAND. Scribe Da. Unruled.
SOURCE. Original, Marquess of Bute, Dumfries House, Loudoun Charters, no.2.
PRINTED. Cf. *SP*, v, 488.
COMMENT. Richard de Moreville's charter to James son of Lambin survives (Marquess of Bute, Dumfries House, Loudoun Charters, no.1) and gives the marches as 'from the burn called Polbahuf (i.e., the Polbaith Burn, the march between the parishes of Loudoun and Kilmarnock) to the marches of Strathaven, and from the river called Irvine to the marches of Eaglesham'. Richard's charter names the land 'Kelnnhel (Kelmihel?) and Cobale and Loudun'. The first two names are obsolete, but since Loudoun must originally have applied to Loudoun Hill at the east end of the parish, the two lost names may refer to the west end, where the castle of Loudoun was built.

310 Confirms to Paisley Priory (afterwards Abbey) the church of Mearns, Renfrewshire, granted by Elias of Partick with the consent of his brother Peter of Pollok. Lanark. (1189 × 1195)

Wilelmus Dei gratia rex Scotorum omnibus probis hominibus tocius terre sue, clericis et laicis, salutem. Sciant presentes et futuri me concessisse et hac carta mea confirmasse Deo et ecclesie Sancti Mirini de Passelet et monachis ibidem Deo servientibus donationem illam quam Helias de Pertheic eis fecit per concessionem Petri de Polloc fratris sui, de ecclesia de Mernes'; tenend*a* in liberam et perpetuam elemosinam ita libere, quiete, plenarie et honorifice sicut alias ecclesias suas liberius, quiecius, plenius et honorificencius tenent, et sicut carta predicti Helye testatur. Testibus hiis, Arkenbaldo[a] abbate de Dunfermelyn, Hugone cancellario meo, Rollando filio Ucdred, comite Patricio, Wilelmo de

Lyndsay, Philippo de Valoniis,[b] Roberto de Londoniis,[c] Henrico de Cormannoc, apud Lanryk.

RUBRIC. Confirmatio Wilelmi regis Scocie ecclesie de Mernes' (at top).
SOURCE. NLS, MS. Adv. 34.4.14, fo.lx[r].
PRINTED. *Paisley Registrum*, 100–1.
NOTES. [a] MS., Alano. [b] MS., Walons'. [c] MS., Londe.
COMMENT. The charters of Elias of Partick and his brother Peter of Pollok are given in *Paisley Registrum*, 98, 100. Elias of Partick was a canon of Glasgow. Cf. *The Stewarts*, x, no.2 (1956), 166–7.

311

Grants to Jordan son of William son of Nigel, in exchange for the land which King Malcolm IV granted William in Ednam (Roxburghshire), the whole land which Uchtred Presun held of the king beside Lanark, in feu and heritage, for a reddendo of half a stone of wax on St James's day (25 July). Lanark. (1189 × 1195)

Willelmus[a] Dei gratia rex Scotorum omnibus probis hominibus totius terre sue, clericis et laicis, salutem. Sciant presentes et futuri me dedisse, concessisse et hac carta mea confirmasse Jordano filio Willelmi filii Nigelli, in excambium terre illius quam Malcolmus frater meus rex Scotie dederat predicto Willelmo in Edenham, totam terram illam quam Ucdredus Presun de me tenuit juxta Lanark, cum omnibus justis pertinentiis suis. Tenendam sibi et heredibus suis de me et heredibus meis in feodo et hereditate, libere et quiete absque omni servitio et exactione et absque omnibus auxiliis et geldys, et ita plenarie sicut predictus Ucdredus predictam terram aliquo tempore plenius tenuit. Reddendo inde annuatim dimidiam petram cere ad festum Sancti Jacobi. Concessi etiam predicto Jurdano et heredibus suis ut ipsi et homines eorum qui in predicta terra manserint quieti sint de operatione molendini, et ut quieti sint de multura de blado terre illius ad molendinum meum de Lanark. Test*ibus* Jocelino[b] Glaskuensi Episcopo, A*rkenbaldo* abbate de Dumfermelyne, Hugone cancellario meo, Comite Dunecano, Ricardo de Prebenda clerico meo, Willelmo de Moruil constabulario, Philippo de Valoun, Rannu*lfo* de Sulys, Roberto filio Wernebaldi[c], Henrico de Cormanok. Apud Lanyn[d].

HEADING. Ex Rotulo XV.[e] [Carta Jordani filii Willelmi][e]. Carta Jurdani filii Willielmi filii Nigelli de terris juxta Lanerk.[f] Carta Jurdano filio Willielmi filii Nigelli, in excambioun, the land quhilk King Malcolm his brother, king of Scots, gave to the said William in Edinhame, and the lands quhilks . . . had near Lanerk. William de Moruill constable is witness. *Wil. R.* 20.[g]
SOURCE. NLS, MS. Adv. 34.2.1 B, fo.116.
PRINTED. *RMS*, i, App. I, no.97; cf. also ibid. p.550.
NOTES. [a] Punctuation editorial. [b] Source has Jacobo. [c] Source has Bernebaldi. [d] Sic, probably for Lanark. [e] *RMS*, i, 476. [f] Index A, *RMS*, i, 550. [g] Index B, *RMS*, i, 550.
COMMENT. It has been suggested that Presun might be corrupt for *persona*, parson, but it seems more likely to stand for *prestes sune*, 'priest's son'.

312

Commands his sheriffs and baillies of Moray to cause those excommunicated by the bishop of Moray for some offence or for their contumacy in refusing to compear in a church court to be shunned until they obey the law and return to the church as Christians;

whenever royal authority is needed to supplement the sanction of the church. Melrose. (1189 × 1195)

Will' Dei gratia Rex Scott' omnibus vicecomitibus et balliuis suis de Morau*ia* salutem. Mando et firmiter precipio quatinus homines illos quos episcopus Morau*iensis* ad curiam Christianam rationabiliter citauerit et qui in curia Christiana iuri debent parere et hoc facere noluerint, et qui postea propter suam contumaciam aut propter aliud delictum iuste fuerint excommunicati, nec excommunicationi deferre uoluerint, sicut excommunicatos donec iuri paruerint euitari faciatis, et ut sicut Christiani ad ecclesiam redeant et iudicio stent[a] ecclesie, ubi districtio ecclesie non sufficit per auctoritatem regiam compellatis.[b] Hug*one* cancellario meo, A*rkenbaldo* abbate de Dunfermelin. Apud Melros.

MARGINAL NOTE. Ista non scribitur in libro decani.
SOURCE. NLS, MS. Adv. 34.4.10, fo.xxxviii^{r}.
PRINTED. *Moray Registrum*, no.10.
NOTES. [a] stetit, MS. [b] MS. omits Testibus.

313 Takes into his firm peace and protection the church of St Cuthbert of Holy Island and its monks and their men; they are to be free of toll throughout his land for their own goods; they are to have their fugitive neyfs restored wherever found outwith the king's demesne; no one is to offer them injury or violence, demand toll or detain their neyfs unjustly, on pain of the king's full forfeiture. Roxburgh. (1189 × 1195)

.W'. Dei gr*ati*a Rex Scott'. Omnibus probis Hominibus tocius terre sue Clericis 7 Laicis :' Salutem. Sciatis me Ecclesiam Sancti Chutberti de Halieland' . 7 Monachos ibidem Deo seruientes . 7 eorum homines . 7 eorum possessiones uniuersas . in mea firma pace 7 protectione juste recepisse. Concessi etiam eis ut ubique per totam terram meam liberi sint 7 quieti ab omni tolneio de dominicis catallis suis . Et precipio ut ubicunque fugitiuos terre sue extra dominia mea inuenire poterunt :' illos juste habeant. Quare prohibeo firmiter Nequis prefatis monachis . aut eorum hominibus iniuriam uel uiolentiam aliquam inferre presumat . aut ab eis tolneium exigat de dominicis catallis suis . aut fugitiuos terre sue eis iniuste detineat :' super meam plenariam forisfacturam . Sicut Carta Reg*is* D*aui*d aui mei . Et Carta Reg*is* Malcolm*i* fratris mei . testantur. Test*ibus* Hugone Cancellario meo . *Ærkenbaldo* Abbate de Dunfermel*in* . Willelmo de Lindes' . Rob*erto* de London*iis* fil*io* meo . Geru*asio* Auenel . D*aui*d de Lindes'. Apud Rokesb'.

ENDORSED. C. Willelmi Regis de protexione ecclesie Sci Cuthberti de Halieland' concedo eciam eis quod ubique per terram suam liberi sint et quieti ab omni theoloneo de catell*is* suis dominicis et ubicunque fugitiuos suos extra dominia sua inuenire poterunt illos iuste habeant (xv cent.). C. iij vj^{te} (xv cent.).
DESCRIPTION. 6·1″ (15·5 cm.), Top and bottom × 4″ (10·1 cm.), L, 3·8″ (9·6 cm.), R. Foot folded, 0·6″. Double slits. Tie cut from top of fold, complete. Tag 5·4″ long. Central portion of seal only, natural wax, rather rubbed.
HAND. Scribe Da. Unruled.
SOURCE. Original, Durham, D. & C. Muniments, Misc. Chr. no.598 = *A*. Durham, D. & C. Muniments, Cartulary IV, fo.1 = *B*. Printed here from *A*.
PRINTED. Raine, *North Durham*, no.51 (from *B*).

314 Grants to William son of John (son of Orm son of Eilaf) that he may hold his land of Hownam (Roxburghshire), and his wood of Hownam in forest; no one may hunt or cut wood therein save by William's permission, on pain of the king's forfeiture of £10. Roxburgh. (1189 × 1195)

.W'. Dei gr*ati*a Rex Scott'. Omnibus probis Hominibus tocius terre sue clericis 7 laicis Salutem. Sciant presentes 7 futuri me concessisse et[a] Hac carta mea confirmasse Willelmo filio Johannis totam terram suam de Hunum 7 boscum suum de Hunum in forestum. Quare prohibeo firmiter Nequis[b] in predicto bosco aut infra Diuisas Suas de Hunum uenetur aut secet nisi per eius licenciam :' super meam forisfacturam de .x.[cem] libr*is*. Test*ibus* Hug*one* Cancellario meo . Com*ite* Dunec*ano* . Willelmo de Lindes' . Geruasio Auenel const*abulario* suo de Rokesb' . Walt*ero* Corb*et*. Ap*ud* Rokesburg.

ENDORSED. Carta reg*is* Will*elm*i facta de terra de Hunum in forest' (xiv cent.).
DESCRIPTION. 7·1″ (18 cm.), Top, 7·2″ (18·3 cm.), Bottom × 3·6″ (9·1 cm.) L, 3·2″ (8·4 cm.), R. Foot folded to a depth of 0·8″ (2 cm.). Tie torn away from top edge of fold. Double slits with tag 3·5″ (9·2 cm.) long, 0·4″ (1 cm.) wide. No seal remains.
HAND. Scribe Db. Unruled.
SOURCE. Original, SRO, GD 45/27/93.
PRINTED. *HMC*, *12th Report*, Appendix viii, p.185 (falsified text).
NOTES. [a] Crossed tironian sign. [b] Written as one word.
COMMENT. The descent of William from Eilaf, whose son Orm was a contemporary of David I, may be traced in *Melrose Liber*, i, nos.127, 130–1 and *RRS*, i, no.114. See also no.72.

315 Confirms to the church of St John of Roxburgh Castle that ploughgate of arable in the demesne of Roxburgh granted to it by King David I; together with one full toft and one lodging within the castle; and all the offerings of those staying in the castle, and a (fourth?) part of the king's offerings whenever he or his household stays in the castle, as one of the king's chaplains has; and the whole teind of his orchard (?), and of the tallow from the slaughter of the king's animals in Teviotdale; all as the charter of King David bears witness. Roxburgh. (1189 × 1195)

Will*elmu*s Dei gr*ati*a Rex Scott' omnibus probis hominibus totius terre sue clericis et laicis salutem. Sciant presentes et futuri me concessisse et hac carta mea confirmasse Deo et ecclesie Sancti Johannis de Castello de Rokesburg' illam carucatam terre de Dominico de Rokesburg' quam Rex D*aui*d auus meus eidem ecclesie dedit et unum plenarium toftum et unam meisuram in Castello et totam oblacionem illorum qui manent uel residentes sunt in castello et[a] partem oblacionis mee quando fuero in Castello uel familia mea sicut unus de Capellanis meis habebit . et totam Decimam virgulti mei . et totam Decimam sepi occisionis mee que fit in Teuietesdale. Quare uolo et precipio ut predicta ecclesia omnia prescripta teneat et habeat . ita libere et quiete plenarie et honorifice sicut carta Reg*is* D*aui*d Aui mei testatur. Test*ibus* Ricardo episcopo Morau*iensi* . Johanne episcopo Dunkelden*si* . Hug*one* cancell*ario* meo . Com*ite* Dunkan*o* . Com*ite* Patricio . Willelmo de Lindeseya . Philipp*o* de Valon*iis* . Waltero Corbet . Geruas*io* Auenel . Herb*erto* de Macuswell' . Henrico medico. Apud Rokesburg'.

RUBRIC. Confirmacio Reg*is* W. super donacione unius carucate terre ecclesie Sancti Johannis de Rokesburg' per D*auid* Regem de dominico suo (in margin).
SOURCE. Blairs Archives, 16 Drummond Place, Edinburgh, MS. Registrum Vetus of Glasgow, fo.lviij^{v}.
NOTE. [a] quartam occurs in this context only in Earl Henry's charter (ibid.), not in King David's charter, fo.lviij^{r}.
COMMENT. King David I's charter is given in Lawrie, *Charters*, no.83, and Earl Henry's confirmation ibid., no.195; only the latter specifies the fourth part of the granter's own offerings. It is surprising to find this somewhat old-fashioned grant confirmed so late.

316 Confirms by royal authority to the brotherhood established by Jocelin bishop of Glasgow to help in the re-building of the cathedral church of Glasgow recently destroyed by fire; and grants his firm peace and protection to those who on behalf of the brotherhood collect funds for the re-building. Roxburgh. (1189 × 1195)

Will*elmu*s Dei gratia Rex Scottorum . omnibus probis hominibus tocius terre sue clericis et Laicis salutem. Necessitati Glasguens*is* ecclesie pietate debita compacientes et eam Summi Regis et sanctissimi Kentegerni confessoris intuitu deuocione non modica diligentes ·/ desolacioni ipsius curam uolumus consolacionis adhibere et eam quoad possumus regie protectionis munimine confouere. Quoniam autem mater multarum gentium exilis antehac et angusta ad honorem Dei ampliari desiderat ·/ et preterea in hiis diebus nostris igne consumpta ad sui reparacionem amplissimis expensis indigens et nostrum et plurium proborum hominum subsidium expostulat ·/ fraternitatem quam ad eius constructionem venerabilis Joc*elinus* eiusdem ecclesie episcopus de consilio abbatum priorum et alterius cleri episcopatus sui constituit ·/ Deuote recipimus . et regie concessionis munimine usque ad ipsius ecclesie perfectionem confirmamus et omnes eiusdem fraternitatis collectores[a] et ad eius fabricam auctoritate Episcopi et capituli ipsius ecclesie auxilium postulantes ·/ in nostra firma pace et protectione suscipimus, omnibus Balliuis nostris et ministris firmiter precipientes ·/ ut eos ubique in Regno nostro protegant et manuteneant et destricte prohibentes ·/ ne quis eis iniuriam violenciam aut contumeliam aliquam inferat super nostram plenariam forisfacturam. Test*ibus* Hugone cancellar*io* nostro . Archenb*aldo* Abbate de Dunfermel*in* . Willelmo de Lindes'[b] iustic*ia* . Philippo de Valonia. Apud Rokesburg'.

RUBRIC. De proteccione benefactorum ecclesie Glasg*uensis* (in margin).
SOURCE. Blairs Archives, 16 Drummond Place, Edinburgh, MS. Registrum Vetus of Glasgow, fos.liij^{v}–liiij^{r}.
PRINTED. *Glasgow Registrum*, no.76.
NOTES. [a] Fo.liiij^{r}. [b] MS., Lundes'.
COMMENT. Bishop Jocelin dedicated his cathedral church, which he had built anew, on Sunday, 6 July, 1197 (*Chron. Melrose*, 49); presumably this refers to the first part of the new church begun after the fire. For the architectural history, see C.R. Radford and E.L.G. Stones, 'The remains of the cathedral of Bishop Jocelin at Glasgow (*c.*1197)', in *Antiquaries Journal*, xliv (1964), 220–232. Bishop Jocelin's enlargement of his cathedral which had been 'quite small at his accession' is noted in Bishop Ralph of Down's eulogy (*Lives of S. Ninian and S. Kentigern*, ed. A.P. Forbes, Edinburgh, 1874, 311).

317 Grants to Kelso Abbey three ploughgates of arable in the territory of Ednam, Roxburghshire, as Archibald abbot of Dunfermline gave the abbey sasine by command of the king; viz. two and a half ploughgates adjacent to the marches of Kelso to the north of the peatary of Ednam, by the marches specified, with pasture on a certain piece of land between the marches of Kelso and the peatary, provided that the king's men of Ednam may spread their peats on it; and a half ploughgate to the east of the monks' quarry; and the fishing in Tweed from the marches of Kelso to the marches of Birgham. The king makes this grant in exchange for certain revenues which the monks of Kelso had received since the time of King David I, viz. 20 chalders of wheat and flour at the king's mill of Roxburgh, 3 merks out of the *firma burgi* of Roxburgh, and 12 chalders of malt at the king's mill of Ednam. Grants further that if the monks' mill of Kelso cannot be worked because of floods, frost or breakdown, the monks may grind their corn at the mill of Ednam for their own sustenance free of multure and next after the corn already in the hopper, unless there is king's corn waiting; but the monks must not grind for more than three or four days in succession, to save inconvenience for the men of Ednam. Roxburgh. (1189 × 1195)

W. Dei gr*ati*a Rex Scott'. Episcopis. Abbatibus. Comit*ibus*. Baron*ibus*· Just*iciis*. Vicecom*itibus*. Prepositis. Ministris. 7 Omnibus probis hominibus Tocius terre sue Clericis 7 Laicis. salutem. Sciant presentes 7 futuri me dedisse. 7 concessisse. 7 hac carta confirmasse Deo 7 Ecclesie Sancte Marie de Kelch'[a]. 7 monachis ibidem Deo seruientibus 7 seruituris in liberam 7 puram 7 perpetuam elemosinam tres carrucatas terre in territorio de[b] Edenham sicut Ærk*enbaldus*[c] Abbas de Dunfermel*in*[d] eis per preceptum meum tradidit. Duas scilicet 7 dimidiam ∴ propinquiores diuisis terre sue de Kelch' ab aquilonari parte petharie de Edenham[e]. que terra tendit a petharia proximo loco iuxta diuisas eorundem monachorum usque ad diuisas de Neutun[f]. 7 sic per diuisas australes de Neutun. usque in Edene. 7 sic per Edene usque ad pontem vadi ∴ ab occidentali parte de Edeneham. 7 inde ∴ in uiam que ducit uersus hospitale ∴ usque ad furchaturam uie que uenit ab aquilonari parte petharie. 7 sic per eandem uiam usque ad primum locum prenominate diuise. Et pasturam cuiusdam particule terre ∴ que est inter diuisas de Kelchou. 7 predictam petariam. ita ut monachi habeant pasturam eiusdem terre. et homines mei de Edenham habeant aisiamentum ipsius terre ad expandendum ibi pethas suas. Et dimidiam carucatam terre ab orientali parte Quarrerie ipsorum monachorum. inter quatuordecim acras terre quas habent ex dono Pagani de Bosewill'[g]. 7 terram infirmorum ∴ 7 inter pethariam ∴ 7 viam que tendit uersus vadum de Sprowest'.[h] Et piscaturam in Tweda que pertinebat ad Edenham a diuisis de Kelch' usque ad diuisas de Brigham. Predictas autem tres carrucatas terre 7 piscaturam ∴ dedi eis in excambium viginti celdrarum frumenti 7 farine de illa mensura que fuit tempore Regis D*aui*d aui mei. quas predicti monachi habere solebant in molendino meo de Rokesburg'. et in escambium trium marcarum quas habere solebant de firma burgi mei de Rokesburg'. et in escambium duodecim celdrarum brasei quas habere solebant de molendino meo de Edenham . ex dono Regis D*aui*d aui mei. Quare volo 7 firmiter precipio ·/ ut prefati monachi prefatas tres carrucatas terre cum predictis diuisis ·/ 7 predictam piscaturam habeant 7 teneant in liberam 7 puram 7 perpetuam elemosinam . ita libere . quiete . plenarie . 7 honori[i]fice ·/ sicut alias elemosinas in Regno meo . liberius . quiecius . plenius . 7 honorificencius tenent 7 possident. Concessi etiam prefatis monachis quod si molendinum eorum de Kelch' . aut per inundaciones aquarum aut propter gelu molere non possit ·/ uel aliquo casu fractum sit ·/ ut molant ad molendinum meum de Edenham bladum quod creuerit super terram prenominatam de Edenham ad eorum victum . libere absque multura proximius ad illud quod fuerit super Trameyl[j] . nisi fuerit dominicum bladum meum . ita tamen ut ad uitandum grauamen hominum meorum de Edenham . non nisi per tres aut quatuor dies ·/ idem monachi insimul molant. Concessi autem eis ut liceat ipsis libere 7 absque multura bladum quod super terram predictam creuerit ·/ quo uoluerint asportare. T*estibus*[k] Hug*one* Cancell*ario* meo Ærkenb*aldo* Abbate de Dunferm*elin* . Henrico Abbate de Aberbrothoc . Guid*one* Abbate de Lundores . Ricardo de prebenda . Hug*one* capellano Clerico meo . Willelmo de Lind' Justic*ia* . Waltero Corbet . Philipp*o* de Valon*iis* . Geruasio Auenel . Willelmo de Sumervill' . Willelmo de Wallibus . Herberto de Machuswell' . Willelmo Pasleu ·/ apud Rokesburg'.

RUBRIC. Carta super tres carucatas terre in territorio de Edenham[l] (at top, in red).
SOURCE. NLS, MS. Adv. 34.5.1, fos.144^{v}–145^{r}=*A*. Ibid., fos.14^{v}–15^{r}=*B*. Printed here from *A*, with more important variants of *B* noted.
PRINTED. *Kelso Liber*, no.384 (=*A*), no.14 (=*B*).
NOTES. [a] Kalch' *B* here and throughout. [b] Letter erased, perhaps H, *A*. [c] Erkenbaldus *B*. [d] Dunfirmelyn *B*. [e] Hedenham *B*. [f] Neuton *B*. [g] Besewill', *A*; Boseuill', *B*. [h] Sprouist' B. [i] Fo.145^{r}. [j] tremyl *B*. [k] *B* has Hiis test' and no more. [l] Edinham *B*.
COMMENT. This land in Ednam was perhaps the land given up by William son of Nigel according to no.311; and cf. no.291.

318 Grants to Arbroath Abbey the churches of Gamrie, Banffshire, and Tarves, Aberdeenshire. Roxburgh. (1189 × 1195)

W.[a] Dei gr*atia* Rex Scott' . omnibus probis hominibus tocius terre sue clericis . et laicis ·/ salutem. Sciant presentes & futuri me dedisse . et concessisse . et hac carta mea confirmasse . Deo . et ecclesie Sancti Thome martiris de Aberbrothoc . et monachis ibidem Deo seruientibus . et seruituris . ecclesiam de Gameryn[b] . et ecclesiam de Tarueys[c] . cum omnibus ad predictas ecclesias iuste pertinentibus . Tenend*as* in liberam . et puram et perpetuam elemosinam . ita libere et quiete . plenarie et honorifice ·/ sicut alias ecclesias suas . liberius . quiecius . plenius . et honorificencius ·/ tenent[d] et possident. Test*ibus* Hugon*e* Cancellario meo . A*rkenbaldo* Abbate de Dunferm*elin* . Willelmo Abbate de Edinburg'[e] . Wyd*one* Abbate de Lundors . Comite Patric*io* . Willelmo de Lindes' . Philippo de Valon*iis* . Geruasio Auenel' . Will*elmo* de Somirvill'[f] . apud Rokisburg'.[g]

RUBRIC. De ecclesiis . de Gamerin . et de Tharueis (red, *E*). De ecclesiis de Gameryn et de Taruays (red, *A*). .xxvij. (in margin, *A*, *E*).

SOURCE. NLS, MS. Adv. 34.4.2, fos.xlvii^v–xlviii^r = *A*. SRO, Northesk Muniments (uncatalogued), Ethie MS., fo.5^r = *E*. Printed here from *A*.
PRINTED. *Arbroath Liber*, i, no.27 (from *E*).
NOTES. [a] Initial red. [b] Gamerin, *E*. [c] Tharueis, *E*. [d] Fo.xlviii^r. [e] Edenburg', *E*. [f] Sumirvill', *E*. [g] Rokesburg', *E*.

319 Confirms the agreement (for a tack) made between Kelso Abbey on the one hand and, on the other, Robert of Kent, Robert Hunaud, Roland son-in-law of Nicholas de Côtentin anent arable, pasture and wood in the territory of Innerwick, East Lothian, as contained in the chirograph made between them; to be in force from Martinmas next after King Richard of England and King Philip of France set off towards Jerusalem until the term of 33 years has elapsed; and as confirmed by Alan son of Walter, the king's steward. (*c*.1190)

Will*elmus* Dei gr*ati*a Rex Scott' . Omnibus probis hominibus tocius terre sue clericis 7 laicis Salutem. Sciant presentes 7 futuri me dedisse 7 hac carta mea confirmasse conuencionem factam inter Abbatem 7 Conuentum de Kelchou . 7 Robertum de Kent 7 Robertum Hunaud . 7 Roland*um* generum Nichol*ai* de Costentin . *scilicet* de terra . 7 pastura . 7 bosco in territorio de Inuerwic' per easdem diuisas sicut in Cyrographo inter eos facto continetur . 7 cum omnibus eisdem iustis pertinenciis . Tenend*am* a festo Sancti Martini proximo postquam Ricardus rex Anglie . 7 Philippus Rex Francie profecti sunt uersus Ierosolimam . usque ad terminum triginta trium annorum peractum . ita libere 7 quiete . plenarie 7 honorifice sicut Cyrographum inter eos factum testatur 7 sicut confirmacio Alani fil*ii* Walteri dapiferi Regis[a] confirmat . saluo seruicio meo. Test*ibus* Roberto capellano meo . Philippo de Valon*iis* . Malc*olmo* fil*io* Com*itis* Dunekan*i* . Willelmo Comyn.

RUBRIC. Item Confirmacio super eandem conuencionem factam inter Abbatem 7 Conuentum de Kelch' 7 R. de Kent . 7 alios (top in red).
SOURCE. NLS, MS. Adv. 34.5.1, fo.105^v.
PRINTED. *Kelso Liber*, no.261.
NOTE. [a] Regis struck through.
COMMENT. The chirograph is given in *Kelso Liber*, no.256, probably dating 1190, and the confirmation by Alan son of Walter is given ibid., no.260. No doubt the king's confirmation would be obtained as soon as possible after the agreement had been made. Robert of Kent, Robert Hunaud and Roland were all knights of the steward, Alan son of Walter, and his tenants in Innerwick (cf. *The Stewarts*, x, no.2, (1956), 171–2).

320 Confirms to Richard de Melville the land of Muiravonside (West Lothian), granted to him in free marriage by Reginald Prat, with his daughter Margaret; to be held as freely as any marriage portion is held in the whole kingdom. Linlithgow. (1189 × 1195)

.W'. Dei gr*ati*a Rex [Scot][a]t. Omnibus probis Hominibus tocius terre sue clericis 7 laicis Salutem. Sciant presentes 7 futuri me concessisse 7 hac [car][a]ta mea confirmasse Donacionem illam quam Regin*aldus* Prat fecit Ricardo de Maleuin . de terra de Murganesete quam Regin*aldus* predicto Ric*ardo* cum Margareta filia eius in liberum maritagium dedit. Tenend*am* sibi 7 heredibus suis de predicto Reginaldo 7 heredibus suis per rectas Diuisas suas 7 Cum omnibus justis pertinentiis suis . ita libere 7 quiete plenarie 7 honorifice sicut aliquod maritagium in toto

Regno meo liberius 7 quietius plenius 7 honorificen[ti][a]us tenetur 7 teneri debet 7 sicut carta predicti Reginald*i* testatur saluo seruicio meo. Test*ibus* Hug*one* Cancellario meo . Willelmo Cumi*n* . Malc*olmo* fil*io* Com*itis* Duneca*ni* . Will*elmo* de Haia . Geruasio Auenel . Henr*ico* medico . Hug*one* de Kaledouer[b] . Sim*one* de Haheltu*n* . D*aui*d de Graham Ap*ud* Lillidq'.

ENDORSED. Confirmacio de Morwenseit (xiii–xiv cent.). Also modern endorsements.
DESCRIPTION. 7·9″ (19·9 cm.), Top, 8·2″ (20·8 cm.), Bottom × 3·4″ (8·7 cm.). L, R. Foot folded to a depth of 1″ (2·4 cm.). Tie cut from left-hand edge of fold. No tag or seal remains.
HAND. Scribe Db. Unruled.
SOURCE. Original, SRO, GD 26, 1/4/9.
PRINTED. Fraser, *Melville*, iii, 5, no.9 (with facsimile); also *Fraser Facsimiles*, no.20.
NOTES. [a] Letters in brackets missing through injury to parchment. [b] Written Kaledour, with sign for er above r.
COMMENT. The original charter of the donor, who calls himself Reginald Prat 'de Tindal', is SRO, GD 26, 1/4/8, printed in Fraser, *Melvilles*, iii, no.8. It is witnessed by, among others, Simon of Halton, William of Halton, David of Graham and Malcolm thane of Callendar. Cf. no.143.

321 Confirms to Dunfermline Abbey the church of Moulin, Perthshire, granted by Malcolm earl of Atholl, together with three ploughgates of land, namely 'Petduuedi', 'Petmalduith', 'Balecunene' and 'Petmacduuegile', as the earl's charter bears witness. Stirling. (1189 × 1195)

Will'[a] Dei gra*ti*a Rex Scott' omnibus probis hominibus tocius terre sue clericis 7 laicis salutem. Sciant tam presentes quam futuri me concessisse 7 hac carta mea confirmasse donationem illam quam Comes M*alcolmus* Etholie me presente dedit ecclesie Christi[b] de Dunfer*melin* 7 monachis ibidem Deo seruientibus in liberam 7 perpetuam elemosinam . Ecclesiam scilicet de Molin cum omnibus pertinenciis suis . 7 tres carucatas terre . Petduuedi . Petmalduith . Balecunene . Petmacduuegile . tenendas adeo libere 7 quiete 7 honorifice .ⸯ sicuti donaciones predecessorum meorum 7 meas tenent 7 possident . 7 sicut carta predicti Comitis testatur 7 confirmat. T*estibus* Jocelino Glasg*uensi* episcopo . J*ohanne* Dunk*eldensi* [episcopo][c] . H*ugone* cancell*ario* meo . Comite Duncan*o* . Gilb*erto* Comite de Stratheren . Willelmo de Lindes' . Alex*andro* filio W*illelmi* filii Thoraldi . Hugone de Caledoure. Apud Striuelin.

RUBRIC. De ecclesia de Molin cum pertinenciis (red with red initial).
SOURCE. NLS, MS. Adv. 34.1.3a, fo.xii^{v}.
PRINTED. *Dunfermline Registrum*, no.58.
NOTES. [a] Initial blue. [b] Written x^{i}. [c] MS. omits.
COMMENT. Earl Malcolm's charter is given in *Dunfermline Registrum*, no.147; and record of a lawsuit between David (of Strathbogie) earl of Atholl and the abbey anent these lands (whose names seem now to be lost) is given, ibid., no.365 (25 July, 1323). See no.337.

322 Confirms to Coupar Angus Abbey the grant made to it by William de la Hay of the land of 'Ederpolles' (Grange, in Errol), Perthshire, as William's charter bears witness. Stirling. (1187 × 1195)

Will*elmus* Dei gr*ati*a Rex Scott'. Omnibus probis hominibus tocius terre sue Clericis 7 laicis salutem. Sciant presentes et[a] futuri me concessisse et hac carta mea confirmasse Deo et ecclesie Sancte Marie de Cupre et monachis ibidem Deo seruientibus et seruituris . donationem quam Will*elmu*s de Haya fecit prenominatis monachis de Cupre de terra de Ederpolles tenendam in liberam et perpetuam elemosinam . ita libere et quiete . plenarie et honorifice ;' sicut carta predicti[b] Willelmi testatur . Saluo seruicio[c] meo. Test*ibus* Jocel*ino* Glasguen*si* episcopo . Ricardo Morauien*si* episcopo . Comit*e* Dunec*ano* Just*icia* . Comit*e* Gileberto de Strahern' . Philippo de Valon*iis* . Alano fil*io* Walt*er*i Dapifero . Willelmo de Moruill' Bernardo filio Briani . Willelmo filio Thore. Apud StrivelyN.[d]

ENDORSED. Ederpolles (xii–xiii cent.). Conf*irmacio* (?) Reg*is* W. de Ederpollis (?) de Cupro (xiii cent., barely legible). Confirmacio regis Willelmi super donacione Willelmi de Haya de Edirpoll' duplicatur (xv cent.).
DESCRIPTION. 7·8″ (19·8 cm.), Top and bottom × 4″ (10·2 cm.), L, R. Foot folded to a depth of 1·2″ (3·1 cm.). Seal-tag passes through double slits in foot and fold, 5·7″ (14·5 cm.) long, 0·9″ (2·3 cm.) wide. No seal remains.
HAND. Scribe Cf. No ruling visible.
SOURCE. Original, Countess of Erroll, Erroll Charters no.4 = *A*. NLS, MS. Adv. 33.2.9, fo.33ᵛ (brief abstract) = *B*. Printed here from *A*.
PRINTED. *Spalding Misc.*, ii, 304, no.111 (from *A*). *Coupar Angus Rental*, i, 337, no.47 (from *B*).
NOTES. [a] 7 used throughout after this. [b] sign resembling small o written above ct. [c] scarcely legible. [d] Spaced out to fill last line, Stri, ve, Ly N, and terminated by a point above a semi-colon.
COMMENT. This has been placed too late, since Alexander son of William son of Thor had succeeded his father as sheriff of Stirling by the date of no.308. An abstract of William de la Hay's charter is given in *Coupar Angus Rental*, i, 336–7. The name 'Ederpolles' means 'between the pows', where pow has the sense of a sluggish stream in carseland. The lands of Grange lie between the Powgavie Burn and the burn coming down from Rait and Fingask. For Coupar Abbey's grange in the Carse of Gowrie, cf. *Coupar Angus Chrs.*, xxxiv and 84; but Dr Easson does not seem to have realised that this was the land of 'Ederpolles'.

323 Grants to Cambuskenneth Abbey the church of Kinclaven, Perthshire. Stirling. (1189 × 1194)

W. Dei gratia Rex Scotorum omnibus probis hominibus totius terre sue clericis et laicis Salutem. Sciant presentes et futuri me dedisse et concessisse et hac mea carta confirmasse Deo et Ecclesie Sancte Marie de Kambeskinnel et canonicis ibidem Deo seruientibus ecclesiam de Kinclechvene cum terris et decimis et oblationibus omnimodis et omnibus aliis terris[a] pertinentiis suis. Tenen*dam* in liberam et perpetuam elimosinam ita libere, quiete, plenarie, honorifice sicut alias ecclesias liberius, quietius et plenius tenent ;' T*estibus* H*ugone* cancellario, A*rkenbaldo* abbate de Dumfermlin, Comite Gilberto, Rob*erto* capellano meo, Willelmo de Moreu*illa* constabulario, Willelmo de Lindese, A*lexandro* vicecom*ite* de Striveling, Waltero Corb*et*. Apud Striveling.

ENDORSED. Copie of the charter of mortificatioun gevin be King Williame to the abbacie of Cambuskennell of the Kirk of Kinclevin with the Landis, teindis oblatiounes anno 1190 (xvii cent.).
SOURCE. SRO, GD 124/MM2 (loose sheet).
PRINTED. *Cambuskenneth Registrum*, p.xxxii (translation only).
NOTE. [a] Sic, for rectis or iustis?

324 Grants to Cambuskenneth Abbey the church of Tillicoultry, Clackmannanshire. Stirling. (1189 × 1194)

Wilelmus[a] Dei gracia rex Scotorum omnibus probis hominibus totius terre sue, clericis et laicis, salutem. Sciant presentes et futuri me dedisse et concessisse et hac carta mea confirmasse Deo et ecclesie Sancte Marie de Cambuskynneth et canonicis ibidem Deo seruientibus ecclesiam de Tullicultre cum terris et decimis et oblationibus omnimodis et omnibus iustis pertinentiis suis; tenendam in liberam et perpetuam elemosinam ita libere, quiete, plenarie et honorifice sicut alias ecclesias suas liberius, quietius, plenius et honorificentius tenent et possident. Testibus, Hugone cancellario nostro,[b] A*rkenbaldo* abbate de Dunfermeling, Roberto capellano meo, Com*ite* Gilberto,[c] Willelmo de Moruill' constabulario nostro,[b] Wilelmo de Lindesay, Alexandro vic*ecomite* de Strivueling, apud Strivueling.

RUBRIC. Donatio Wilelmi regis de ecclesia Tulicultre (at top).
SOURCE. NLS, MS. Adv. 34.1.2, fo.164r.
PRINTED. *Cambuskenneth Registrum*, no.220.
NOTES. [a] Large handsomely illuminated initial U in blue, gold, red and green. [b] Sic, for meo. [c] MS. Culbert'.

325 Grants to Jocelin bishop of Glasgow and his successors one full toft in his burgh of Stirling. Stirling. (1189 × 1195)

W'. Dei gr*ati*a Rex Scott' . Omnibus probis hominibus tocius terre sue Clericis et laicis :· Salutem. Sciant presentes et futuri me dedisse et concessisse et hac carta mea confirmasse Deo et Sancto Kentegerno et Joc*elino* Episcopo Glasg*uensi* Omnibusque eius successoribus unum plenarium toftum in Burgo meo[a] de Striuel*in*. Tenend*um* in liberam et quietam et perpetuam elemosinam ita libere . Quiete Plenarie et honorifice :· sicut aliquis Episcopus in toto regno meo Aliquod toftum in aliquo Burgorum meorum . liberius . Quietius . Plenarius et honorificentius :· tenet et possidet. Test*ibus* Com*ite* D*aui*d fratre meo . Hugo[b] Cancell*ario* meo . Willelmo de Lindeseie . Alex*andro* vicecom*ite* de Striuelin . D*aui*d de Lindes' . Rob*erto* fil*io* Weneb*aldi*[c] . Henr*ico* de Cormanoc . Ric*ardo* fil*io* Hug*onis* . Henr*ico* de Brade marescall*o*. Apud Striuel*in*.

RUBRIC. De uno tofto in Burgo de Striuelin (in margin, fo.iiijv, in different hand).
SOURCE. Blairs Archives, 16 Drummond Place, Edinburgh, MS. Registrum Vetus of Glasgow, fos.iiijv–vr.
PRINTED. *Glasgow Registrum*, no.77.
NOTES. [a] Fo.vr. [b] Sic. [c] Sic, for Wernebaldi.

326 Commands that wherever the abbot of Scone or his sergeand may discover men who have left their land on account of the aid, after the aid was decided upon and assessed at Musselburgh, these men are to return and stay on the abbot's land until the aid has been uplifted. Forfar. (1189 × 1195, probably *c*.1190)

Willelmus[a] Dei gracia Rex Scottorum omnibus probis hominibus tocius terre sue salutem. Mando et firmiter precipio ut ubicumque abbas de Scone aut seruiens eius invenire poterint homines qui pro auxilio a terra sua fugerint, postquam auxilium assisum fuerit apud Muxelbur,[b] ad eum et ad terram suam redeant, et cum eo sint quousque auxilium reddatur. Et prohibeo firmiter ne eos ei iniuste aliquis detineat, super meam plenariam forisfacturam, ita tamen quod si aliquis aliquod ius in eis clamauerit, post solucionem auxilii ei rectum inde teneatur. Test*ibus* Hug*one* cancell*ario* meo, M*alcolmo* filio comit*is* Dunec*ani*. Apud Forfar.

SOURCE. NLS, MS. Adv. 34.3.28, fos.10^v–11^r.
PRINTED. *Scone Liber*, no.35.
NOTES. [a] Name omitted, MS. [b] Sic, for Muxelburg. *Scone Liber*, no.35, prints Murelb.
COMMENT. This aid was no doubt the sum of 10,000 merks (of gold and silver) raised by King William at the end of 1189 or early in 1190 to pay for the cancellation of the 'treaty' of Falaise (*Chron. Melrose*, 47; *Chron. Stephen*, i, 304).

327 Grants to Arbroath Abbey the church of Panbride, Angus Forfar. (1189 × 1194)

W.[a] Dei gr*ati*a Rex Scottorum . episcopis . Abbatibus . Comit*ibus* . Baron*ibus* . Just*iciis* . Vic*ecomitibus* . prepositis . Ministris . et omnibus probis hominibus . tocius terre sue clericis . et laicis . salutem. Sciant presentes et[b] futuri me dedisse . et concessisse . et hac carta mea confirmasse Deo et ecclesie Sancti Thome de Aberbroth*oc* . et monachis ibidem Deo seruientibus ecclesiam de Pannebryd[c] . cum terris . et decimis . et oblacionibus omnimodis . et omnibus aliis . ad predictam iuste pertinentibus ecclesiam . Tenend*am* . in liberam et quietam . in puram et perpetuam elemosinam . ita libere et quiete . plenarie . et honorifice . sicut aliqua elemosina . in toto regno meo . liberius . et quiecius . plenius . et honorificencius :' tenetur et possidetur. Test*ibus* Hug*one* cancell*ario* meo . Jocel*ino* archid*iacono* Dunk*eldensi* . Rob*erto* capellano meo . Ric*ardo* de prebenda et Will*elmo* Maluesyn[d] clericis meis . Com*ite* Dunec*ano* . Com*ite* Gilb*erto* . Rob*erto* de Lond*oniis* . Malcolmo filio comitis Dunec*ani* . Will*elmo* Cumyn[e] . Geruas*io* Auenel'. Willelmo de Lyndes' . Adam de Syreys . Willelmo de Haya . Herb*erto*[f] Marescallo . Apud Forfar.

RUBRIC. De ecclesia de Pannebrid' (red, *E*). De ecclesia de Panbryd' (red, *A*). .xxiij. (in margin, *A*, *E*).
SOURCE. NLS, MS. Adv. 34.4.2, fo.xlvi^{r-v} = *A*. SRO, Northesk Muniments (uncatalogued), Ethie MS., fo.4^v = *E*. Printed here from *A*.
PRINTED. *Arbroath Liber*, i, no.23 (from *E*).
NOTES. [a] Initial red. [b] Fo.xlvi^v. [c] Pannebrid', *E*. [d] Malueisin, *E*. [e] Cumin, *E*. [f] Hereberto, *E*.

328 Grants to Arbroath Abbey the church of Monikie, Angus. Forfar. (1189 × 1194)

W.[a] Dei gr*ati*a Rex Scottorum . Episcopis . Abbatibus . Com*itibus* . Baronibus . Just*iciis* . Vicecom*itibus* . prepositis . ministris . et omnibus probis hominibus . tocius terre sue clericis et laicis :' salutem. Sciant presentes et futuri me dedisse . et concessisse . et hac carta mea confirmasse Deo . et Ecclesie Sancti Thome de Aberbroth*oc* . et monachis ibidem Deo seruientibus . Ecclesiam de Muniekу[b] . cum terris et decimis . et oblacionibus omnimodis . et cum communi pastura tocius parochie de Munieky[b] . et cum omnibus aliis . ad predictam ecclesiam iuste pertinentibus . Tenend*am* in liberam et quietam . et perpetuam elemosinam . ita libere . et quiete . plenarie & honorifice . sicut aliqua alia elemosina . in toto regno meo . liberius . et quiecius . plenius . et honorificencius .' tenetur et possidetur. Test*ibus* Hug*one* cancell*ario* meo . Jocell*ino* archidi*acono* Dunk*eldensi*. Willelmo priore de Rostynoth[c] . Rad*ulfo*[d] capellano meo . Ric*ardo* de prebenda clerico meo . com*ite* Dunec*ano* . com*ite* Gilb*erto* . Willelmo de Lyndes'[e] . Rob*erto* de Lond*oniis* . Malc*olmo* fil*io* com*itis* Dunec*ani* . Johanne de Hasting' . Will*elmo* Cumyn' . Will*elmo* de Haya . Geruas*io* Auenel' . Thoma de Colleuil'[f] . apud Forfar'.

RUBRIC. De ecclesia de Muniekkin' (red, *E*). De ecclesia de Monieky (red, *A*). .xxij. (in margin, *A*, *E*).
SOURCE. NLS, MS. Adv. 34.4.2, fo.xlvi^{r} = *A*. SRO, Northesk Muniments (uncatalogued), Ethie MS., fo.4^{r-v} = *E*. Printed here from *A*.
PRINTED. *Arbroath Liber*, i, no.22 (from *E*).
NOTES. [a] Initial red. [b] Muniekky, *E*. [c] Rostinot, *E*. [d] Sic, *A*; Rob*erto*, *E*. [e] Lindes', *E*. [f] Coleuill', *E*.

329 Grants to St Andrews Cathedral Priory 40s. yearly, for the lighting of the church, payable from the revenue of his burgh of Crail, 20s. at Martinmas and 20s. at Whitsun, until he shall have assigned it the equivalent in land or from some other revenues. St Andrews. (1189 × 1194)

Willelmus[a] Dei gracia rex Scotorum . Omnibus probis hominibus tocius terre sue clericis et laicis salutem . Sciant presentes et futuri me dedisse et concessisse et hac carta mea confirmasse Deo et ecclesie Sancti Andree apostoli et canonicis ibidem Deo seruientibus perpetuo ad luminare ecclesie sue xl. solidos singulis annis . et eos de redditu burgi mei de Karel annuatim recipiend*os* assignaui Scilicet .xx. solidos ad festum Sancti Martini et xx. solidos ad pentecosten . quousque eis redditum .xl. solidorum aut in terra aut in alia redditu assignauero . et uolo ut reditum assignatum inperpetuum habeant et teneant ita libere et quiete . plenarie . et honorifice sicut alias elemosinas suas liberius et quiecius plenius et honorificencius tenent et possident. Testibus . Hugone cancellario meo . Roberto capellano meo . Comite Dunecano . Malc*olmo* fil*io* eius . Adam de Syreis . Henrico Reuel' . Rogero de Willtun . Hugone clerici cancellarii.[b] Ladowico clerico . Adam de Aschechirche . apud Sanctum Andream.

RUBRIC. De .xl. solidis (top in red).
SOURCE. SRO, GD 45/27/8 (St Andrews priory cartulary), fos.cv^{v}–cvi^{r}.
PRINTED. *St Andrews Liber*, 228.
NOTES. [a] Blue initial V. [b] Fo.cvi^{r}.
COMMENT. This grant suggests that some progress had been made with the building of the new cathedral church at St Andrews, begun by Bishop Arnold *c*.1162.

330 Confirms to Odo, brother of Bishop Matthew of Aberdeen, Kinninmonth, with the whole shire of Kinninmonth, and the toft in the burgh of St Andrews, as contained in the charter of the prior and convent of St Andrews, for an annualrent of two merks. St Andrews. (1189 × 1194)

Wilielmus[a] Dei gratia Rex Scotorum, episcopis, abbatibus,[b] baronibus justic*iis*, vic*ecomitibus*, prepositis, ministris et omnibus probis [hominibus][c] totius terre sue, clericis et laicis, salutem. Sciant presentes et futuri me concessisse et hac carta mea confirmasse Odoni fratri Mathei episcopi de Aberdoen' Kynninmon' per rectas diuisas suas et cum omnibus iustis pertinentiis suis, et cum tota syra de Kynninmonth, et cum tofto in burgo Sancti Andree sicut in carta prioris et conuentus ecclesie Sanctiandree apostoli continetur. Tenend' sibi et heredibus suis in feodo et hereditate de priore et canonicis et domo Sanctiandree. Reddendo inde singulis annis duas marcas pro omni seruitio ad predictam domum pertinen*ti* ita libere et quiete, plenarie et honorifice, sicut carta inde confecta testatur, saluo seruitio meo. Testibus Hugone cancellario meo, Roberto [capellano][d], Comite Duncano, Malcolmo filio eius, Adam de Syres, Henrico Reuel, Alano filio suo, Henrico medico, Hugone clerico. Apud Sanctum Andream.

HEADING. Confirmatio.
SOURCE. NLS, Minto Papers, Charters, Box 30, no.212/2. (Copy in hand of xvi cent., on paper roll, of notarial transumpt made 20 October, 1395).
PRINTED. Macfarlane, *Genealogical Coll.*, ii, 533 (brief abstract only).
NOTES. [a] Punctuation editorial. [b] MS. omits comitibus. [c] MS. omits. [d] MS. seems to read de Aula, with alteration; capellano is suggested by the witness-lists of nos.329, 331.
COMMENT. Same date as no.329. The prior and convent's charter also grants heritably the stewardship of the convent's household; Odo was already steward before July, 1186 (NLS, Minto Papers, Charters, Box 30, no.212/2; *Chron. Howden*, ii, 312).

331 Confirms to Scone Abbey the land of 'Ahenepobbel' (lost, in Tibbermore, Perthshire) by the marches by which Robert the chaplain held it; one toft in Tibbermore; and the meadow on the Lochty Burn; all granted by Swain son of Thor, as his charter bears witness. Clunie in Stormont. (1189 × 1194)

Willelmus[a] Dei gratia Rex Scotorum omnibus probis hominibus tocius terre sue, clericis et laicis, salutem. Sciant presentes et futuri me concessisse et hac carta mea confirmasse Deo et ecclesie Sancti Michaelis[b] de Scon et canonicis ibidem Deo seruientibus donationem illam quam Suanus filius Thori eis fecit de terra de Ahenepobbel, per easdem diuisas per quas Robertus capellanus illam tenuit, et unum toftum in Tubermure, et pratum quod est super Lochethin, cum communi pastura et aliis asiamentis sicut in carta eiusdem Suani continetur; tenend*am* in liberam et perpetuam elimosinam ita libere, quiete, plenarie et honorifice sicut carta predicti Suani testatur, saluo servicio meo. Test*ibus* Hugone cancellario meo, Com*ite* Dunc*ano*, Roberto capellano meo, Ric*ardo* de prebenda clerico meo, Roberto Berkelai, Willelmo Uviet[c]. Apud Clunin.

RUBRIC. Confirmatio Willelmi Regis de terra de Ahenepobbel.
SOURCE. NLS, MS. Adv. 34.3.28, fos.7v–8r.
PRINTED. *Scone Liber*, no.22.
NOTES. [a] Initial omitted, MS. [b] Fo.8r. [c] Uniec, MS.
COMMENT. The original of Swain son of Thor's charter is BM, Add. Chrs. 66568 (printed, from the cartulary text, in *Scone Liber*, no.21). It names the land

Ahednepobbel ('tent field'), and identifies the toft in Tibbermore as that held by the goldsmith. Swain's gift was specifically for the soul of Earl Henry, and his charter dates 1183 × 1199.

332 Grants to Arbroath Abbey the church of Nigg, Kincardineshire. Perth. (1189 × 1194)

W.[a] Dei gr*ati*a Rex Scott' . Omnibus probis hominibus . tocius terre sue Clericis . et laicis ∴ salutem. Sciant presentes et futuri me dedisse . et concessisse . et hac carta mea confirmasse Deo et ecclesie Sancti Thome de Aberbroth*oc* . et monachis ibidem Deo seruientibus . ecclesiam de Nyg[b] . in terris . et decimis . et cum aliis omnibus ad ecclesiam illam iuste pertinentibus . et cum communi pastura . tenend*am* in liberam et perpetuam elemosinam . ita libere . et quiete . plenarie et honorifice . sicut alias elemosinas suas in terra mea . liberius . quiecius . plenius & honorificencius ∴ tenent et possident. Testibus M*atheo* episcopo Ab*erdonensi* . J*ohanne* episcopo Kat*enensi* . Hug*one* cancell*ario* . A*rkenbaldo* Abbate de Dunferm*elin* . Jocell*ino* archid*iacono* Dunk*eldensi* . Waltero priore de Insula . Rob*erto* capellano . Rob*erto* de Quinci . Willelmo de Lyndes'[c] . Willelmo de Haya . apud Perth[d].

RUBRIC. De ecclesia de Nig (red, *A*, *E*). .xx. (in margin, *A*, *E*).
SOURCE. NLS, MS. Adv. 34.4.2, fo.xlv^{v} = *A*. SRO, Northesk Muniments (uncatalogued), Ethie MS., fo.4^{r} = *E*. Printed here from *A*.
PRINTED. *Arbroath Liber*, i, no.20 (from *E*).
NOTES. [a] Initial red. [b] Nig, *E*. [c] Lindes', *E*. [d] Pert, *E*.

333 Confirms to St Andrews Cathedral Priory churches and other property, chiefly granted by private subjects as their charters bear witness, including the church of Dull, Perthshire, granted by Malcolm earl of Atholl; the church of Conveth (Laurencekirk), Mearns, granted by Humphrey of Berkeley; the church of Tannadyce, Angus, granted by Richard Maluuel; 20 acres of arable on the north side of the loch of Lundin, Fife, with one toft which Gillemur held, from the smith's house to the high road, granted by Walter of Lundin; the church of Kennoway, Fife, with the lands which Simeon the priest held with the church, viz. 'Chenoch' and the valley from the den of 'Mandrethin' to the western limit of the valley, and 'Pettenduem' and 'Petthaschen' with which Merleswain endowed the church, and a fourth part of 'Drumchatin' (Drumcaldie?) and of 'Fanclarathin', and a certain land called Kilmux, all granted by Merleswain. Perth. (1189 × 1195)

Willelmus[a] Dei gracia rex Scotorum . Episcopis abbatibus . Comitibus . Baronibus Justiciis vicecomitibus . prepositis ministris . et omnibus probis hominibus tocius terre sue clericis et laicis salutem . Sciant presentes et futuri me dedisse et concessisse et hac carta mea confirmasse Deo et ecclesie Sancti Andree et canonicis ibidem Deo seruientibus et seruituris in liberam et perpetuam elemosinam . pro salute anime mee et predecessorum et heredum meorum ecclesiam de Eglesgirg cum terra abbacie et cum omnibus eidem ecclesie iuste pertinentibus et cum capella Sancti Reguli et dimidia carucata eidem capelle pertinente . Et ecclesiam de Inchethore cum omnibus iustis pertinenciis suis . Concedo eciam eisdem canonicis . et hac carta mea confirmo ex donacione Comitis Dunecani . ecclesiam de Sconin cum terra eidem ecclesie pertinente et cum omnibus iustis pertinenciis suis . Et ecclesiam de Marchinche cum capella de Katel . et cum terra ad eandem capellam iuste pertinente et cum omnibus iustis pertinenciis suis . Et ecclesiam de Cupre cum terris et decimis . et cum omnibus aliis iustis pertinenciis suis . Ex donacione Malcolmi comitis de Atthol' :' ecclesiam de Dul . cum capell*is* et terris et omnibus aliis iustis pertinenciis suis . preterea ex donacione Comitis Morgunt :' ecclesiam de Tharflond cum omnibus iustis pertinenciis suis . et cum una carucata terre saluo inde seruicio meo et cum molendino in eadem terra fundato :' et cum decima de omnibus redditibus suis . Ex donacione Neisi filii Willelmi . ecclesiam de Louchres cum capellis terris decimis et omnibus iustis pertinenciis suis . Ex donacione Umfredi de[b] Berkelei ecclesiam de Coneued cum terris et decimis . et omnibus aliis iustis pertinenciis suis . Et ex donacione Ricardi Maluuel . ecclesiam de Thanetheis cum omnibus iustis pertinenciis suis . Et ex donacione Walteri de Lundin :' viginti acras terre iuxta lacum suum de Lundin a parte aquilonali cum una tofta quam Gillemur tenuit scilicet a domo fabri usque ad uiam et cum communi pastura . Et ex donacione Merleswani ecclesiam de Kennakin cum decimis et omnibus aliis iustis pertinenciis suis . et cum terris quas Simeon presbyter cum ecclesia tenuit . Scilicet Chenoch[c] et uallem a speluncca Mandrethin usque ad metam occidentalem ipsius uallis et Pettenduem et Petthaschen[d] :' quam Merleswanus eidem ecclesie optulit . et quartam partem Drumchatin . et quartam partem Fanclarathin . et quandam terram que dicitur Chenmochaueth per rectas diuisas suas . in pratis . in moris et cum communi pastura et cum omnibus ad eandem terram iuste pertinentibus. Quare uolo et precipio ut prenominati canonici omnia prescripta ita libere quiete . plenarie . et honorifice teneant . et possideant . sicut alias elemosinas suas liberius quiecius . plenius et honorificencius . tenent et possident . et sicut carte donatorum testantur . Saluo seruicio de terris hac inscriptis :' de quibus seruicium habere[e] debeo Testibus . Matheo Aberdenen*si* episcopo . Johanne episcopo de Dunkeldin . Hugone[f] cancellario meo . *Ærkenbaldo* abbate de Dunfermelin . Comite Dunecano . Comite Gilleberto . Willelmo de Lindeseya . Willelmo de Moreuill' . const*abulario* . Roberto de Lund*oniis* . Malcolmo filio Comitis Dunec*ani* . Willelmo Cumin' . Willelmo de Haya . Dauid de Lindes' . Philippo Maresc*allo*. apud Perth .

RUBRIC. Confirm*acio* commu*nis* (top in red).

SOURCE. SRO, GD 45/27/8 (St Andrews priory cartulary), fos.cvi^v–cvii^r.

PRINTED. *St Andrews Liber*, 230–1.

NOTES. [a] Red initial U. [b] Fo.cvii^r. [c] Chlenoth, Chlenohc, *St Andrews Liber*, 258, 259. [d] Pethchaschen, *St Andrews Liber*, 259. [e] debere expunged. [f] Hougone, MS. with first o expunged.

COMMENT. Earl Malcolm of Atholl's charter of Dull is given in *St Andrews Liber*, 245; the donors' charters of Conveth and Tannadyce do not survive; Walter of Lundin's charter is given, ibid., 263–4; Merleswain son of Colban's charter, confirming in part the grants of an earlier Merleswain, is ibid., 258–9. For Kilmux in the possession of the church of St Andrews, cf. G. Martine, *Reliquiae Divi Andreae*, 180. The other place-names, presumably in Kennoway parish, seem to be obsolete, unless Drumchatin is Drumcaldie, in Markinch. The den of Mandrethin may be Meggie Den, in Kennoway and Scoonie.

334 Grants to Richard de Montfiquet (Muschet) Cargill, Perthshire, as fully as when the king held it in his own hands on the day he granted it; and in addition Kincardine in Menteith, Perthshire; to be held in feu and heritage, with soke and sake, pit and gallows, toll, team and infangthief, for the service of one knight. Richard may hold Cargill in forest, and no one may hunt or cut down wood there without his permission, on the king's forfeiture of £10. Perth. (1189 × 1195)

Will*elmus*[a] Dei gracia Rex Scotorum, episcopis, abbatibus, comitibus, baronibus, justiciariis, vicecomitibus, prepositis, ministris et omnibus probis hominibus tocius terre sue, clericis et laicis, salutem. Sciant presentes et futuri me dedisse, concessisse et hac carta mea confirmasse Richardo de Mountfich*et*[b] Kergille ita plenarie sicut ego in manu mea tenui die qua predictam terram ei dedi per illas rectas diuisas que ad terram illam pertinuerunt quando eam ei dedi, in bosco et plano, in terris et quis, in pratis et pascuis, in viis et semitis, in moris et marresiis, in vivariis et piscariis, in stagnis et molendinis. Et preterea Kincardin iuxta Striuelin per rectas diuisas suas et cum omnibus iustis pertinenciis suis, in bosco et plano, in terris et aquis, in pratis et pascuis, in viis et semitis, in moris et marresiis, in vivariis et piscariis, in stagnis et molendinis et in[c] omnibus aliis ad predictam terram iuste pertinentibus. Quare volo ut prefatus Richardus et heredes sui prefatas terras habeant et teneant de me et heredibus meis in feodo et hereditate cum socca et sacca, cum furca et fossa, cum toll et them et infangtheif, per seruicium unius militis, ita libere, quiete, plenarie et honorifice, sicut aliquis baronum meorum feudum suum liberius, quiecius, plenius et honorificencius tenet et possidet. Concessi eciam prefato Ricardo[c] et heredibus suis ut habeant prefatam terram de Kergille in forest*o*, et prohibeo firmiter ne quis in ea venetur vel secet sine licencia eorum, super meam forisfacturam decem librarum. Test*ibus* Hugone cancellario meo, Comite Dunec*ano* Justiciario, Ricardo de prebenda, Comite Gilb*erto*, Willelmo de Moreuilla Constabulario, Alano filio Walteri dapifero, Willelmo de Haya, Adam de Syreis, Hugone de Caled[ouer][d], Rogero de Mortimare, Dunec*ano* de Sereis, Harberto Marescall*o*. Apud Pert.

AT FOOT. Notarial note signed by Gavin Dunbar, beginning Tenet hoc transumptum cum carta originali, and bearing that the original having been read, etc. in the presence of the Lords of Council it was ordered to be transumed, on account of its age and fragility, by Master Gavin Dunbar, clerk of rolls, register and council.

SOURCE. SRO, Drummond Castle Muniments (Earl of Ancaster), uncatalogued, notarial transumpt of xvi cent.

NOTES. [a] Written Willm. Punctuation editorial. [b] Written Mountficht', with mark of suspension. [c] Sic. [d] Supplied editorially.

COMMENT. For the Muschets of Burnbank in Kincardine, 'chief of that name now (xviii cent.) extinct', cf. *Macfarlane's Geographical Collections* (Scot. Hist. Soc.), i, 339. The lands of Richard de Montfiquet descended to Sir William de Montfiquet (Muschet) living in the fourteenth century, and seem to have been resigned to the Crown *c.*1345 by one of his daughters and co-heiresses Mary and regranted to John Drummond of Concraig, whose wife Mary may have been; cf. *SP*, vii, 35–6.

335 Grants to William de Montfort Kinneff (Mearns), in feu and heritage, with sake and soke, toll, team and infangthief, with pit and gallows, for the service of one knight. Grants also that William may have four greyhounds and hunt with them in the feu of Kinneff, except for 'Ferthes'. (Unrecorded place-date). (1189 × 1199)

Willelmus[a] Dei gracia Rex Scottorum episcopis, abbatibus, comitibus, baronibus, justiciariis, vicecomitibus, prepositis, ministris et omnibus probis hominibus tocius terre sue, clericis et laicis, salutem. Sciant presentes et futuri me dedisse et concessisse et hac carta mea confirmasse Willelmo[b] de Munfort Kynef per rectas diuisas suas et cum omnibus justis pertinentiis suis, in bosco et plano, in terris et aquis, in pratis et pascuis, in stagnis et molendinis et omnibus aliis libertatibus. Tenendam sibi et heredibus suis de me et heredibus meis in feudo et hereditate, cum sakcha et sokcho, cum thole et them et infangenethef et cum furca et fossa, libere et quiete, plenarie et honorifice, per seruicium unius militis. Concedo eciam eidem Willelmo ut habeat quatuor leporarios et cum eis venetur in feudo de Kynnef, excepto Ferthes. Testibus M*atheo* episcopo de Abirden, Johanne episcopo de Kat', Comite Dauid fratre meo, Hugone cancellario meo, Comite Dunecano, Gilberto comite de Strathern, G*illecrist* comite de Menteth, [M][c]alisio filio comitis Ferth', Willelmo[b] Giffard. Apud etc.[d]

SOURCE. SRO, transumpt in *ADC*, xxxi, fo.66–7 (of date 6 July, 1518).
NOTES. [a] Punctuation editorial. [b] Written W°. [c] Source omits. [d] Sic.
COMMENT. 'Ferthes', unidentified, may be an error of transcription for 'Fothes', i.e. Fiddes, part of which is in Kinneff and Catterline parish, at the north-western extremity; it is Fotheis, *c.*1200 (*Arbroath Liber*, i, nos.93, 94).

336 Confirms to Scone Abbey the grant made by Malcolm earl of Atholl of the church of 'Login Mahedd' (Logierait, Perthshire), with the chapel of Killiehangie and with the chapels of Dunfallandy, Killiechassie (in Weem), and 'Kelmichel' of Tulliemet, as the earl's charter bears witness. Perth. (1189 × 1195)

Willelmus[a] Dei gratia Rex Scottorum omnibus probis hominibus tocius terre sue, clericis et laicis, salutem. Sciatis me concessisse et hac carta mea confirmasse Deo et ecclesie Sancti Michaelis de Scon et canonicis ibidem Deo seruientibus donacionem illam quam Malcolmus Comes Atholie eiis fecit de ecclesia de Login Mahedd', cum capellis ad eam juste pertinentibus, scilicet cum capella Kilchemi, et Dunfolenthi, et Kelkassin, et Kelmichel de Tulimath, et cum omnibus aliis iustis pertinenciis suis; tenend*am* in liberam et perpetuam elemosinam ita libere et quiete, plenarie et honorifice, sicut alias elimosinas suas liberius, quiecius, plenius et honorificencius tenent et possident, et sicut carta ipsius comitis testatur. Test*ibus* Hug*one* cancell*ario* meo, Com*ite* Dune*cano* Justic*ia*, Comite Gilleb*erto*, Willelmo de Haia, Roberto de Berkel'. Apud Pert.

SOURCE. NLS, MS. Adv. 34.3.28, fos.8v–9r.
PRINTED. *Scone Liber*, no.27.
NOTE. [a] Initial omitted, MS.
COMMENT. Earl Malcolm's charter does not survive, but there are early confirmations by the bishops of Dunkeld John and Richard (*Scone Liber*, nos.55,

109, the former dating 1183 × 1203). Earl Malcolm died *c.*1197, and the king's confirmation probably dates 1189 × 1192. Bishop John's confirmation shews that the church of Logierait – dedicated to Saint Coeddi, hence *Mahedd*, 'of my Coeddi' – was the principal church of the earldom of Atholl, entitled to the teind from Rait, 'the caput of the earldom', from the whole thanage of 'Dulmonych' (probably Dalmarnock, in Little Dunkeld), and from the whole thanage of Findowie in Strathbraan. On Killiehangie see Watson, *CPNS*, 314; for Killiechassie, see J. M. Mackinlay, *Ancient Church Dedications of Scotland, Non-scriptural*, 195, where it may be the Kilhassie, 'Saint Asaph's chapel', said to be near Loch Rannoch.

337 Confirms to Dunfermline Abbey the church of Moulin, Perthshire, granted by Malcolm earl of Atholl, together with three ploughgates of land, viz. 'Petduuedi', 'Petmalduit', 'Balconene' and 'Petmacduuegile'; as the earl's charter bears witness. Perth. (1187 × 1195)

Will'[a] Dei gr*ati*a Rex Scot' omnibus probis hominibus tocius terre sue clericis . 7 laicis salutem. Sciant presentes . 7 futuri me concessisse . 7 hac carta mea confirmasse . ecclesie S*ancte* Trinitatis de Dunfer*melin* 7 monachis ibidem Deo seruientibus donacionem illam quam M*alcolmus* Comes de Atholia eis fecit de ecclesia de Molin cum omnibus iustis pertinenciis suis 7 cum tribus carucatis terre . s*cilicet* Petduuedi . Petmalduit . Balconene[b] . Petmacduuegile . in liberam 7 perpetuam elemosinam . tenend*am* eis de prefato comite M*alcolmo* 7 heredibus suis . ita libere 7 quiete plenarie 7 honorifice sicut carta ipsius comitis testatur 7 confirmat. T*estibus* J*ohanne* episcopo Dunkeld*ensi* . R*icardo* episcopo Morau*iensi* . R. abbate de Scon' . Comite G*ilberto* iusticia . Com*ite* Dunc*ano* . Comite Mauricio de Meneteth' . Willelmo de Lyndes' . Willelmo de Haia. Apud Pert.

RUBRIC. Item confirmacio de ecclesia de Molin (red with red initial).
SOURCE. NLS, MS. Adv. 34.1.3a, fo.xii^{v}.
PRINTED. *Dunfermline Registrum*, no.60.
NOTES. [a] Initial blue. [b] Altered from Balcunene.
COMMENT. A variant of no.321 above issued on a different occasion. This may be later in date, since it uses the more usual title of Dunfermline, 'church of the Holy Trinity', instead of 'Christ Church' as in no.321, and stipulates that the abbey shall hold 'of the earl' which no.321 does not. The notification of no.321 is also somewhat unusual.

338 Grants to Roger de Mortemer the land which belonged to William Maule, viz. Fowlis Easter (Angus), together with Cristina, William's daughter; the land is to be held in feu and heritage, with pit and gallows, with soke and sake, toll, team and infangthief for the service of one knight; if Cristina should die, the king will warrant the land to Roger as that which he has granted him in return for his service; should Roger die, the land will remain to Cristina without conditions. Perth. (1189 × 1195)

W' Dei gr*ati*a Rex Scott'. Episcopis . Abbatibus . Com*itibus* . Baronibus . Justic*iis* . Uicecom*itibus* . prepositis . Ministris . et[a] omnibus probis hominibus totius terre sue clericis et laicis . Salutem. Sciant presentes et futuri . me dedisse . et concessisse . et hac carta mea confirmasse . Rogero de Mortem*er* terram illam que fuit Willelmi Masculi, cum

Cristina[b] que fuit filia eiusdem Willelmi . scilicet Fuhles . per Rectas diuisas suas . et Cum omnibus iustis pertinentiis suis. Tenend*am* sibi et heredibus suis de me 7 heredibus meis in feudo 7 hereditate . in Bosco 7 plano . in pratis 7 Aquis in terris . 7 Pascuis . in moris et maresiis . in Stagnis et molendinis . et in omnibus aliis ad predictam terram iuste pertinentibus . Cum furca et fossa . Cum Socca . et Sacca . Cum thol . et Them . et Infangenethef . libere . et quiete . plenarie 7 honorifice . per seruitium unius militis. Concessi etiam predicto Rogero . quod si aliquid humanitus de Cristina[c] uxore illius filia predicti Willelmi contigerit ./ ego et heredes mei . predicto Rogero et heredibus suis predictam terram sicut eam quam ei dedi pro seruitio suo warentizabimus. Et si aliquid humanitus de ipso Rogero contigerit ./ predicta terra prefate Cristine[d] quieta remaneat. Test*ibus* Matheo Episcopo de Aberdo*n* . Hug*one* Cancellario meo . Com*ite* Dunec*ano* Just*icia* . Com*ite* Gilberto . Will*elmo* de Moreuill' Constabulario . Willelmo Cumi*n* . Willelmo de Haia . Johanne de Hasting' . Malisio fratre Com*itis* Gilb*erti* . Rad*ulfo* Ruffo. Apud PERT.

ENDORSED. Mortymer' (xiv cent.). Also modern endorsements.
DESCRIPTION. 7·4″ (18·8 cm.), Top, 7·5″ (19 cm.), Bottom × 5·1″ (13 cm.) L, R. Foot folded to a depth of 0·7″ (2 cm.), with double slits for tag. No tag or seal remains.
HAND. Scribe Bb. Unruled.
SOURCE. Original, SRO, GD 90/9.
PRINTED. *Panmure Registrum*, ii, 84.
NOTES. [a] In full. Scribe Bb employs both et and uncrossed tironian sign. [b] Written xp̄ina. [c] Written in full. [d] Written xp̄ine.
COMMENT. See no.302.

339

Grants to Arbroath Abbey the church of Abernethy, Perthshire, with the chapel of Dron, the chapel of Dunbog (Fife), the chapel of (Abdie?) and the lands of Ballo (in Abernethy) and Pitlour (in Strathmiglo, Fife). Half the teinds from the abbot of Abernethy's own (animals and crops?) are to belong to Arbroath Abbey, the remaining half to the *célidé* of Abernethy. Arbroath Abbey shall have all the teinds from the territory of Abernethy, saving the teinds belonging to the churches of Flisk and Coultra (in Balmerino), Fife, and saving the teinds from the abbot of Abernethy's demesne which the *célidé* of Abernethy used to have, viz. from Mugdrum, Carpow, 'Balehirewell', 'Balcolly' and Innernethy to the east of the burn. Perth. (1189 × 1195)

W.[a] Dei gr*ati*a Rex Scott' . Episcopis abbatibus . Comit*ibus* . Baron*ibus* . . Just*iciis*[b] . Vic*ecomitibus* . prepositis . Ministris . et omnibus probis hominibus tocius terre sue clericis et laicis salutem. Sciant presentes et futuri me dedisse concessisse et hac carta mea confirmasse Deo et ecclesie Sancti Thome de Aberbr*othoc* . et monachis ibidem Deo seruientibus in liberam et puram et perpetuam elemosinam . ecclesiam de Abirnythyn cum istis pertinenciis . scilicet cum capella de Dron . et cum capella de Dunbulc' et cum capella de Erolyn . et cum terra de Belach' et de Petinlouer . et cum medietate omnium decimarum proueniencium ex propria[c] Abbatis de Abirnythyn quarum alteram medietatem habebunt keledei de Abirnythyn . et cum omnibus decimis territorii de Abirnythyn

. et cum omnibus iustis pertinenciis eiusdem ecclesie . preter illas decimas que spectant ad ecclesiam de Flisk et ad ecclesiam de Cultram . et preter decimas de dominio ipsius Abbatis quas keledei de Abirnythi habere solebant . scilicet de Mukedrum de Kerpul et de Balehirewell' et de Balcolly . et de Inuernythy ex orientali parte riuuli. Quare volo ut prenominati monachi de Aberbrothoc prefatam ecclesiam de Abernythy cum omnibus prescriptis pertinenciis suis habeant et teneant in liberam et puram et perpetuam elemosinam . ita libere et quiete plenarie et honorifice . sicut alias elemosinas suas liberius . quiecius plenius et honorificencius tenent et possident. Test*ibus* Hug*one* Cancellario meo . A*rkenbaldo* abbate de Dunfermelyn . Comite Dunec*ano* Just*icia* . Comite Gilb*erto* . Ric*ardo* de prebenda clerico meo . Rad*ulfo* et Walt*ero* Capellanis meis . W*illelmo* Cumyn . W*illelmo* de Haya . Rad*ulfo* Rufo . Rob*erto* de Berkel' . Rogero de Mortim*er* . Merleswain', Herberto Marescallo meo. Apud Perth'.

RUBRIC. Carta domini Reg*is* de ecclesia de Abernythyn (red). .xxxiiij. (in margin).
SOURCE. NLS, MS. Adv. 34.4.2, fo.xlix^{r-v}.
PRINTED. *Arbroath Liber*, i, no.34.
NOTES. [a] Initial red. [b] Fo.xliv^{v}. [c] *Arbroath Liber*, i, no.34 suggests supplying pecunia.
COMMENT. Erolyn appears to be a scribal error for Ebdyn, that is Abdie, whose church, very soon after the date of this act, seems to have been given to his new foundation of Lindores by Earl David, the king's brother (*Lindores Chartulary*, nos.2, 107). The abbot of Abernethy at this period was a layman, Orm son of Hugh (see nos.114, 152), whose death may have been the occasion of this grant. Pitlour, formerly in Abernethy, was transferred to Strathmiglo in 1889.

340 Grants to William Giffard Strachan (Mearns) in feu and heritage, with pit and gallows, soke and sake, toll, team and infangthief, for an annual rent of nine merks, 60s. at Whitsun and 60s. at Martinmas. William is to hold Strachan in forest, and no one is to cut timber or hunt there without his licence, on pain of the king's forfeiture of £10. Forfar. (1189 × 1195)

.W'. Dei gr*ati*a Rex Scott'. Episcopis . Abbatibus . Com*itibus* . Baron*ibus* . Justic*iis* . Vic*ecomitibus* . Prepositis . Ministris . 7 omnibus probis hominibus tocius terre sue clericis 7 laicis :' salutem. Sciant presentes 7 futuri me dedisse . 7 concessisse . 7 hac carta mea confirmasse . Willelmo Giffard' . Stradhehhan per rectas diuisas suas 7 cum omnibus iustis pertinentiis suis . tenend*am* sibi 7 heredibus suis de me 7 heredibus meis . in feudo 7 hereditate . in bosco 7 plano . in terris 7 aquis . in pratis 7 pascuis . in moris 7 maresiis . in uiis 7 semitis . in stagnis 7 molendinis . in uenacionibus 7 piscariis . 7 in omnibus aliis ad terram predictam iuste pertinentibus . Cum furca 7 fossa . Cum socca 7 sacca[a] . Cum tol 7 them 7 infangenthef' . libere . Quiete . Plenarie 7 honorifice :' reddendo inde annuatim nouem marc*as* . scil*icet* sexaginta solid*os* ad Pentecost*en* . 7 sexaginta solid*os* ad festum Sancti Martini. Preterea concessi predicto Willelmo 7 heredibus suis predictam terram de Stradehhan in forestam. Quare prohibeo firmiter ne quis in terra illa secet aut uenetur sine licencia prefati Willelmi aut heredum suorum super meam forisfacturam de decem libris. Test*ibus* Matheo Abberdon*ensi* Episcopo . Hug*one* Cancellario meo . *Ærkenbaldo* Abbate de Dunfermel*in* . Com*ite* Dunec*ano* . Justic*ia* . G*illecrist* Com*ite* de Mar . Ric*ardo* de Munfichet . Willelmo Cumin . Willelmo de Haia . Merleswann' . Willelmo de Muntfort . Umfrid*o* de Berkel' . Rogero de Mortim*er*. Apud Forfar'.

ENDORSED. donatio terrarum de Strathauen (xv–xvi cent.). Also modern endorsements.
DESCRIPTION. 8·5″ (21·5 cm.), Top, 8·1″ (20·5 cm.), Bottom × 4·9″ (12·5 cm.), L, 4·8″ (12·2 cm.), R. Foot folded to a depth of 0·8″ (2 cm.). Tag 5·5″ (14 cm.) long passes through double slits in foot and fold; only the mark of the seal remains.
HAND. Scribe Da. Unruled.
SOURCE. Original, SRO, GD 40/1/8.
PRINTED. *Newbattle Registrum*, Appendix, Carte Originales, no.11 (=*N*).
NOTE. [a] *N* omits last four words.

341 Grants to William de la Hay one full toft in his burgh of Forfar. Forfar. (1189 × 1195)

.W'. Dei gr*ati*a Rex Scott' . Omnibus probis hominibus tocius terre sue clericis 7 laicis .' Salutem. Sciant presentes 7 futuri me dedisse . 7 concessisse 7 hac carta mea confirmasse Willelmo de Haia unum plenarium thoftum in burgo meo de Forfar'. Tenendum sibi 7 heredibus suis de me 7 heredibus meis in feudo 7 hereditate . ita libere Quiete . Plenarie . 7 honorifice .' Sicut aliquis baronum meorum aliquod Thoftum in aliquo burgorum meorum . liberius . Quietius . Plenius . 7 honorificentius tenet 7 possidet. Test*ibus* Hugone Cancellario meo . *Ærkenbaldo* Abbate de Dunfermel*in* Willelmo de Veteri Ponte . Will*elmo* Cumin . Will*elmo* Giffard' . Hug*one* de Caledou*er* . Her*berto* Maresc*allo* meo . Apud Forfar'.[a]

ENDORSED. Carta W. regis de tofto in Forfar (xiv–xv cent.). Also two distinct modern endorsements.
DESCRIPTION. 5·9″ (15 cm.), Top and bottom × 3·2″ (8·2 cm.), L, 3·1″ (7·9 cm.), R. Foot folded to a depth of 0·8″ (2 cm.). Seal-tag passes through double slits in foot and fold, approximately 5·5″ (14 cm.) long, 0·75″ (1·9 cm.) wide. Central fragment of seal remains on tag, diameter 1·9″ (4·8 cm.).
HAND. Scribe Da. Unruled.
SOURCE. Original, Countess of Erroll, Erroll Charters, no.5.
PRINTED. *Spalding Misc.*, ii, 303–4, no.11.
NOTE. [a] Short wavy horizontal stroke completes line.

342 Confirms to Melrose Abbey the ploughgate in Maxton, Roxburghshire, granted by Robert of Berkeley and his wife Cecily, daughter of Liulf (son of Maccus), by the marches perambulated for the monks by Robert and contained in the charter of himself and his wife; with common easements of pasture and fuel in Maxton and stone from the quarry of 'Alwerdene' sufficient for building the buildings of the monastery of Melrose; saving the teinds of Maxton church. Forfar. (1189 × *c*.1193)

.W'. Dei gr*ati*a Rex Scott'. Episcopis . Abbatibus . Com*itibus* . Baron*ibus* . Just*iciis* . Vicecom*itibus* . prepositis . Ministris . 7 Omnibus Probis Hominibus tocius sue terre clericis 7[a] laicis Salutem. Sciant presentes 7 futuri . me concessisse 7 hac carta mea confirmasse Deo 7 Ecclesie Sancte

Marie de Melros 7 monachis ibidem Deo seruientibus donacionem quam Robertus de Berkel' 7 Cecilia filia Liulfi Sponsa eius eisdem monachis fecerunt .' de illa carrucata terre in territorio de Mackestun' quam predictus Robertus prefatis monachis perambulauit . 7 per easdem diuisas que continentur in carta prenominati Rob*erti* 7 Cecilie Sponse sue . 7 cum communibus aisiamentis eiusdem uille tam in pasturis quam in aisiamentis fochalium . 7 petram quadrarii de Alwerdene ad sufficienciam ad edificia domus de Melr*os* edificanda . Sicut in carta predictorum continetur. Quare uolo 7 firmiter precipio ut predicti monachi prefatam terram cum omnibus suprascriptis aisiamentis habeant 7 possideant in liberam 7 puram 7 perpetuam elemosinam ita libere 7 quiete plenarie 7 honorifice .' sicut aliqua alia elemosina in toto Regno meo liberius 7 quiecius plenius 7 honorificencius tenetur 7 possidetur . 7 sicut carta predicti Roberti de Berk' 7 Cecilie sponse sue testatur 7 confirmat . saluo seruicio meo . 7 saluis decimis ecclesie de Mackestun'. Test*ibus* Hug*one* Cancellario meo . Roberto 7 Rad*ulfo* capellanis meis . Ric*ardo* de prebenda clerico meo . Roberto de London' . Willelmo de Lindes' . Malcolm*o* fil*io* Com*itis* Dunec*ani* . Willelmo Cumi*n* . Willelmo de Haia . Will*elmo* Giffard' . Waltero de Berkel' Camerar*io* Herberto de Camera. APUD FORFARE.[b]

ENDORSED. [ ] reg*is* Will*elmi* de terra [ ] dono Rob' de Berkeley (xv cent.?). J. Scott (xvi cent.).

DESCRIPTION. 8·6″ (21·8 cm.), Top, 7·7″ (19·5 cm.), Bottom × 6·7″ (17 cm.), L, R. Foot folded to an average depth of 1″ (2·7 cm.). Double slits in foot and fold, with stump of tag. No seal.

HAND. Scribe Db. Unruled.

SOURCE. Original, SRO, GD 55/91.

PRINTED. *Melrose Liber*, no.91.

NOTES. [a] Scribe Db employs variously the crossed and uncrossed tironian et.
[b] Chiefly minuscule forms written very large, but not to complete the line.

COMMENT. The land was known as 'la Morhus', represented by Muirhouse (law) in Maxton. For the marches, cf. *Melrose Liber*, no.90 and *OPS*, i, 299.

343

Grants to Restenneth Priory Ardfork (now Cossans, in Glamis), Angus, in exchange for Foffarty (in Kinnettles), Angus, by the same marches as those by which Joheri held Ardfork. Forfar. (1189 × 1195)

.W. Dei gr*ati*a Rex Scott'. Omnibus probis hominibus tocius terre sue clericis 7 laicis .' Salutem. Sciant presentes 7 futuri me dedisse . 7 concessisse 7 hac carta mea confirmasse .' Deo 7 ecclesie Sancti Petri de Rostinot 7 Canonicis ibidem Deo seruientibus . Ardnequerc . in excambium de FofferiN per easdem diuisas per quas Joheri . predictam Ardnequerc tenuit. Tenend' in liberam 7 perpetuam elemosinam in bosco 7 plano . in terris . 7 aquis in pratis 7 pascuis . in moris 7 maresiis . ita libere . quiete . 7 honorifice .' sicut alias elemosinas suas liberius . Quietius 7 honorificentius tenent. Test*ibus* Hug*one* Cancellario meo . Æ*rkenbaldo* Abbate de Dunferm*elin* . Joc*elino* Archid*iacono* . Dunkelden*si* . Ric*ardo* de Prebenda . Malcolm*o* fil*io* Com*itis* Dunec*ani* . Rob*erto*[a] de Mortim*er* . Willelmo de Haia . Briccio Judice. Apud Forfar'.

ENDORSED. Ardequer (xiv cent.). Carta ~~Alexandri~~ Willielmi R (xvii cent.). Also modern numeral endorsements.

DESCRIPTION. 6·1″ (15·5 cm.), Top and bottom × 4·1″ (10·4 cm.), L, R. Foot folded to a depth of 0·7″ (1·8 cm.). Seal-tag torn away, originally 0·7″ (1·8 cm.) wide.
HAND. Scribe Da. Unruled.
SOURCE. Original, Earl of Strathmore and Kinghorne, Strathmore Charters, in custody of Messrs Dundas and Wilson, W.S., Edinburgh.
PRINTED. *HMC, 14th Report*, Appendix iii, p.189.
NOTE. [a] Sic; for *Rog*ero?
COMMENT. The exchange may have been necessary because the king could not give Restenneth warrandice for Foffarty, which may have been claimed by Orm of Abernethy or his son Laurence, or by Duncan of Foffarty or his son Alwin. An unprinted charter of the early thirteenth century (BM, Loans 29/355, unnumbered charter wrapped in paper) was given by Alwin son of Duncan of Foffarty, and refers to land in the neighbourhood in dispute between him and Laurence son of Orm. No other mention of Joheri has been found. For the identification of Ardfork with Cossans, cf. *HMC, 14th Report*, App. iii, 189.

344 Grants to Agatha wife of Humphrey son of Theobald the four ploughgates of arable in Conveth (Laurencekirk), Mearns, as in no.345; in exchange for the land in Ardoyne, Aberdeenshire, which the king has taken from her. Forfar. (1189 × *c*.1193)

Uillelmus[a] Dei gracia Rex Scotorum Episcopis Abbatibus et Comitibus Baronibus Just*iciis* Vicecomitibus prepositis ministris et omnibus probis hominibus tocius terre sue clericis et laicis, salutem. Sciant presentes et futuri me dedisse et concessisse et hac carta mea confirmasse Agacie uxori Umfrid*i* filii Teodbald*i* illas quatuor carrucatas terre in Coneued uersus orientem, quas Galfridus de Maleuill' et Gillecrist mac inien Samuel et alii probi homines mei ei per preceptum meum perambulauerunt, quas eidem Agacie dedi in excambium terre de Arduuen quam ab ea cepi. Et preterea omne jus quod Thainus habere solebat in terra ecclesie de Cuneued et jus aduocacionis eiusdem ecclesie tenend' sibi et heredibus suis de me et heredibus meis in feodo et hereditate, in bosco et plano, in pratis et pascuis, cum jure aduocacionis predicte ecclesie et cum rectitudinibus que de terra ecclesie ad theinum pertinebat et cum omnibus aliis ad prefatas quatuor carrucatas terre juste pertinentibus, cum socca et sacca, cum tol et them et infangenthef, libere et quiete, plenarie et honorifice, per seruicium dimidii Militis. Test*ibus* Hugone Cancell*ario* meo, Henrico Abbate de Aberbr*othoc* , Ricardo de prebenda , Comite Dunecan*o* Just*icia* , Com*ite* Gilb*erto* , Gillecrist comite de Mar , Fergus Comite de Buchan , Rann*ulfo* de Sull'[b] , Willelmo Cumyn , Willelmo de Haya , Willelmo de Muntf*ord* . Apud Forfar.

RUBRIC. Wilelmi regis Carta concessionis . Agacie sponse Umfridi de Berklay de ipsis quatuor carrucatis terre in Conueth uersus orientem (red).
SOURCE. BM, MS. Add. 33245, fo.144^{v} (old foliation, fo.cxxv^{v}).
NOTES. [a] Initial blue, flourished red. [b] MS., full'.
COMMENT. It appears that Agatha was the heir of Walter of Berkeley the chamberlain, and that her husband Humphrey son of Theobald (de Addeville) took the surname of Berkeley on marrying her. The origin of her claim to Ardoyne is not known. The family of Barclay of Mathers, and the numerous families of Barclay descended from them, were the descendants of John son of Theobald, brother of Humphrey of Berkeley (BM, MS. Add. 33245, fo.152^{r}).

345 Grants to Humphrey son of Theobald the four ploughgates of arable in Conveth (Laurencekirk), Mearns, towards the east, which Geoffrey de Melville and Gilchrist Mac Inien Samuel and other responsible men perambulated for him by the king's command; and in addition all the right which the thane used to have in the kirkton of Conveth, the patronage of the church, and the right to multure from the whole parish of Conveth; to be held in feu and heritage, with sake, soke, toll, team and infangthief for the service of half a knight. Forfar. (1189 × *c.*1193)

Villelmus[a] Dei gracia Rex Scotorum Episcopis Abbatibus Comitibus Baronibus Justiciariis Vicecomitibus prepositis Ministris et omnibus probis hominibus tocius terre sue clericis et laicis Salutem. Sciant presentes et futuri me dedisse et concessisse et hac carta mea confirmasse Umfrido filio Theobaldi illas quatuor carrucatas terre in Cuneued uersus orientem quas Galfridus de Maleuil' et Gillecrist mac inien Samuel et alii probi homines ei per preceptum meum perambulauerunt. Et preterea omne jus quod Thainus habere solebat in terra ecclesie de Cuneued et jus aduocacionis eiusdem ecclesie Et preterea totam multuram tocius parochie de Cuneued. Quare uolo et firmiter precipio ut predictus Umfridus heredes sui terras predictas cum aduocacione ecclesie et cum rectitudinibus de terra ecclesie ad Thainum pertinen*tibus* et cum multura predicta de me et heredibus meis teneant et possideant in feodo et hereditate, in bosco et plano, in terris et aquis, in pratis et pascuis et omnibus aliis justis pertinen*tiis*, cum Sacha et Socha, cum tol et them' et infangtheif, libere et quiete[b], plenarie et honorifice, per seruicium dimidii Militis. Test*ibus* Com*ite* Dunecan*o* Just*icia* , Gilleb*erto* Com*ite* de Stradherth , Com*ite* Patricio , Gilleb*ride* Com*ite* de Anegus , Alano dapifero , Willelmo de Moreuill' constab*ulario* , Waltero de Berk' Camerario , Geruasio Auenel , Waltero de Windesh' , Radulfo de Ver , Henrico de Graham , Johanne de Hasting, Philippo marescall*o*. Apud Forfar.

RUBRIC. Wilelmi regis carta concessionis Umfrido Berklay filio Theobaldi de quatuor terre carrucatis in parochia de Conueth' uersus orientem (red).
SOURCE. BM, MS. Add 33245, fo.144^{r-v} (old foliation, fo.cxxv^{r-v}).
NOTES. [a] Initial red, flourished blue. [b] Fo.144^{v}.
COMMENT. The land granted evidently included 'Halton' and Scotston (*Arbroath Liber*, i, no.272).

346 Grants that Humphrey son of Theobald and his heirs may hold *in forestam* the seven davochs which he has given to Humphrey, viz. the two Tippertys, Glenfarquhar, Kinkell, Newlands and Monboddo (in Fordoun), Mearns; no one may cut wood or hunt there without Humphrey's permission, on pain of the king's full forfeiture. Forfar. (1189 × 1195)

Villelmus[a] Dei gracia Rex Scotorum omnibus probis hominibus tocius terre sue salutem. Sciant presentes et futuri me concessisse et hac carta mea confirmasse Umfrido filio Teodbald*i* et heredibus suis illas septem dauahs in forestam quas predicto Umfrido et heredibus suis dedi, scilicet duas Tuberthas et Glenferkaryn' et Kenkelle et Culbac et

Monebodathin. Quare prohibeo firmiter ne quis in predictis terris secet aut uenetur sine licencia predicti Umfridi aut heredum suorum super meam plenariam forisfacturam. Test*ibus* Hugone Cancell*ario* meo, Archenb*aldo* Abbate de Dunfermelyn, Comite Dunecan*o* Just*icia*, Com*ite* Gilb*erto* , Gilleb'[b] Comite de Mar, Willelmo de Muntfort, Galfrido de Maleu'.[c] Apud Forfar.

RUBRIC. Wilelmi regis concessionis Carta Umfrido de Barklay de septem dawathis in forestam . videlicet duas Tuberthais . Glenfarquharyn' . Kynkell' . Cowbak et Monbodathyn' (red).
SOURCE. BM, MS. Add. 33245, fos.144v–145r (old foliation, fos.cxxvv–cxxvir).
NOTES. [a] Initial red, flourished blue. [b] Sic. [c] MS., Malen'.
COMMENT. This upland area of Humphrey of Berkeley's feu of Kinkell was where he afterwards granted summer shieling pasture to Arbroath Abbey (no.413 below). 'Culbac' is identified with Newlands in BM, MS. Add. 33245, fos.8v, 156r.

347 Confirms to Adam, son of the Odo the steward, the grant made to his father Odo by Gilchrist the abbot and the convent of the *célidé* of St Andrews of Kinkell, 'Petkynninn' (Peekie?) and 'Petsprochyn', to be held of the *célidé* as their charter bears witness, saving the king's service. Forfar. (1189 × 1195)

Wilielmus[a] Dei gratia Rex Scotorum, episcopis, abbatibus, comitibus, baronibus, justic*iis*, vic*ecomitibus*, prepositis, ministris et omnibus probis hominibus totius terre sue, clericis et laicis, salutem. Sciant presentes et futuri me concessisse et hac carta mea confirmasse Ade filio Odonis Senescald*i* donationem illam quam Gilchrist' abbas et conuentus kyldeorum de Sancto Andrea [fecit][b] nostro predilecto Odoni dapifero nostro[c] de Kynkel et Petsprochyn et Petkynninn. Tenen*dum* sibi et heredibus suis de predictis kyldeis et ecclesia eorum per rectas diuisas suas et cum omnibus ad predictas terras juste pertinentibus, in feodo et hereditate, ita libere et quiete, plenarie et honorifice, sicut carta prefati abbatis et conuentus kyldeorum testatur, saluo seruitio meo. Testibus Comite Duncano Justic*ia*, Ricardo de prebenda clerico meo, Philippo de Valon*iis* camerario, Malcolmo filio Comitis Duncani, Wilielmo Cumyn, Wilelmo de Haya, Umfrido de Berk', Dauid de Haya, Philippo de Lundyn, Adam de Lundin, Rogero de la Kernel. Apud Forfar.

HEADING. Alia confirmatio.
SOURCE. NLS, Minto Papers, Charters, Box 30, no.212/2.
PRINTED. Macfarlane, *Genealogical Coll.*, ii, 533 (brief abstract only).
NOTES. [a] Punctuation editorial. [b] Blank in MS., fecit supplied conjecturally. [c] The text is clearly corrupt here; one might expect predicto Odoni dapifero patri suo or some such.
COMMENT. The charter of Abbot Gilchrist is given in the same source, and is the only twelfth-century charter issued by the *célidé* of St Andrews known to have survived. It dates from the time of Prior Walter of St Andrews (a witness), i.e. 1160 × *c.*1195. The rent stipulated in the charter was 32 *melas* of cheese, 32 *melas* of barley and one year-old pig. Kinkell is in St Andrews and St Leonards parish, and it appears from the agreement between the priory of St Andrews and the *célidé*, printed *St Andrews Liber*, 318, that the other two places, there called 'Petkennin' and 'Petsporgin', were close by. The identification of 'Petkynninn' with Peekie, in the same parish and on the Kenly Water, is supported by documents of a later period (*ex inf.* R.G.Cant).

348 Confirms to William de Tattenell two ploughgates of land (Ardlair, in Kennethmont, Aberdeenshire) which Earl David the king's brother granted to the church of Aberdeen and to Bishop Matthew, and which the bishop has granted to William. (1189 × *c.*1193)

Willelmus[a] Dei gratia Scottorum rex omnibus probis hominibus tocius terre sue, clericis et laicis, salutem. Sciant presentes et futuri me concessisse et hac presenti carta mea confirmasse Willelmo de Tattenell donacionem illam quam Matheus episcopus Aberdonensis fecit de duabus carrucatis terre quas comes Dauid frater meus ecclesie Aberdonensi et Matheo eiusdem loci episcopo et successoribus suis dedit. Tenendas[b] sibi et heredibus suis de predicto episcopo et successoribus suis in feodo et hereditate ita libere et quiete, plenarie et honorifice, sicut carta prefati episcopi testatur, saluo seruicio meo. Testibus [Hugone][c] cancellario nostro[d], Ade[e] abbate de Dunfermelyne, Comite Duncano justiciar*io*, Malicio filio Comy*tis* Ferteth, Willelmo Comyn, Willelmo de Haya, Willelmo de Mofforde[f], Waltero de Berclay camerario.

SOURCE. NLS, MS. Adv. 16.1.10, fos.68ᵛ–69ʳ.
PRINTED. *Aberdeen Registrum*, i, 13–14.
NOTES. [a] Punctuation editorial. [b] Sic; fo.69ʳ. [c] MS. has Hijs. [d] Sic. [e] Sic, for Arkenbaldo. [f] Sic, for Munfort.
COMMENT. See no.295. The land is identifiable with Ardlair by means of documents in *Aberdeen Registrum*, especially ibid., i, 218. Tattenell is presumably for Tattenhall, Cheshire. Bishop Matthew's charter is ibid., 13.

349 Grants to Kelso Abbey the church of Peterculter, Aberdeenshire. (1173 × 1199)

Will*elmus*[a] Dei gr*ati*a rex Scott'. Omnibus probis hominibus tocius terre sue salutem. Sciant presentes et futuri me dedisse et concessisse . et hac presenti carta confirmasse Deo et ecclesie Sancte Marie de Kalch' . et monachis ibidem Deo seruientibus ecclesiam de Kultre iuxta Abirdene . tenendam in liberam et perpetuam elemosinam . cum decimis et oblacionibus omnimodis . et cum omnibus aliis ad ipsam ecclesiam iuste pertinentibus . ita libere . quiete . plenarie . et honorifice sicut alias ecclesias et elemosinas suas . liberius . quiecius . plenius . et honorificentius . tenent et possident. Hiis Testibus.

RUBRIC. Super Ecclesia de Cultre (top, red).
SOURCE. NLS, MS. Adv. 34.5.1, fo.16ᵛ.
PRINTED. *Kelso Liber*, no.22.
NOTE. [a] Initial red.
COMMENT. This is probably close in date to the earlier of the two confirmations of the grant by Matthew bishop of Aberdeen, 1189 × 1199 (*Kelso Liber*, no.449).

350 Grants to Hugh, brother of Elias the clerk, Benholm (Mearns), in feu and heritage, with pit and gallows, with soke and sake, toll, team and infangthief, for the service of half a knight. Montrose. (1189 × 1195)

.W'. Dei gr*ati*a Rex Scott'. Omnibus probis hominibus tocius terre sue clericis 7 laicis :' Salutem. Sciant presentes 7 futuri me dedisse 7 concessisse . 7 hac carta mea confirmasse . Hug*oni* fratri Helie clerici . Benne . per rectas diuisas suas . 7 Cum omnibus justis pertinenciis suis.

Tenend*um* sibi 7 heredibus suis . de me 7 heredibus meis . in feudo . 7 hereditate . in bosco 7 plano . in terris 7 aquis . in pratis 7 pascuis . in moris 7 maresiis in stagnis 7 molendinis . et cum omnibus aliis ad predictam terram juste pertinentibus . Cum furca 7 fossa. Cum socca . 7 sacca. Cum Tol 7 Them . et infanginthef' libere . Quiete . Plenarie . 7 honorifice.' Faciendo inde mihi 7 heredibus meis seruicium dimid*ii* militis. Test*ibus* Com*ite* D*aui*d fratre meo . Hug*one* Cancell*ario* meo . Com*ite* Dunec*ano* . Com*ite* Gilb*erto* . Willelmo de Moruill' Const*abulario* . Malcolm*o* fil*io* Com*itis* Dunec*ani* . Ric*ardo* de Prebenda clerico meo . Johanne de Hasting' . Willelmo de Haia . Umfrid*o* de Berk' . Willelmo de Muntfort . Rogero de Mortem*er* . Ada*m* de Syreis Apud MUNROS.

ENDORSED. Chartour of the landis of Benholme grantit be king Wm (xvii cent.). Ane chartour gewein be king Villiame.
DESCRIPTION. 7·3″ (18·6 cm.), Top and bottom × 5·9″ (15 cm.), L, R. Foot folded to a depth of 0·8″ (2 cm.). Double slits in foot and fold for seal-tag. Detached portion of tag remains, 0·5″ (1·4 cm.) wide, with fragment of seal in poor condition, natural wax, diameter 2″ (5·2 cm.).
HAND. Scribe Da. Unruled.
SOURCE. Original, SRO, GD 4/1.
COMMENT. See no.428.

351 Grants to his son Robert of London one full toft in his burgh of Montrose, viz. the toft between that belonging to Alexander sheriff of Stirling and that belonging to the king's doorward Jocelin; to be held in free burgage, as any of the king's barons hold their tofts in his burghs. Montrose. (1189 × 1195)

Willelmus[a] Dei gracia Rex Scotorum omnibus probis hominibus tocius terre sue, clericis et laicis, salutem. Sciant presentes et futuri me dedisse et concessisse et hac carta mea confirmasse Roberto de London*iis* filio meo unum plenarium toftum in burgo meo de Munros, scilicet illud toftum quod est inter toftum Allexandri vicecomitis de Striuelyn et toftum Jocelini hostiarii mei. Tenendum in liberum burgagium de me et heredibus meis in feodo et hereditate ita libere et quiete, plenarie et honorifice, sicut aliquis baronum meorum aliquod toftum in aliquo burgorum meorum quiecius, plenius et honorificencius tenet. Testibus H*ugone* cancellario meo, Comite Dauid fratre meo, Willelmo de Morauill constabulario, Alano filio Walteri dapiferi, Adam Syreis, Rogero[b] de Mortimar. Apud Munros.

RUBRIC. Montros tofti . Carta Roberti de London*iis* (at top).
SOURCE. NLS, MS. Adv. 34.4.3 (Reg. Nigrum of Arbroath).
PRINTED. *Arbroath Liber*, i, 260, no.[304].
NOTES. [a] Punctuation editorial. [b] Georgio, MS.

352 Confirms to St Andrews Cathedral Priory the church of St Cyrus, Mearns, with the chapel of St Regulus and its half-ploughgate; and with the land of the *abthen* of Ecclesgreig with common pasture for the canons and their tenants dwelling with the king's thane and tenants throughout the parish of Ecclesgreig. Montrose. (1189 × 1195)

Willelmus[a] Dei gracia Rex Scotorum omnibus probis hominibus tocius terre sue clericis et laicis salutem . Sciant presentes et futuri me dedisse . concessisse et hac carta mea confirmasse Deo et ecclesie Sancti Andree apostoli et canonicis ibidem Deo seruientibus et seruituris ecclesiam de Eglesgirg cum omnibus iustis pertinenciis suis in liberam et perpetuam elemosinam cum capella Sancti Reguli . et cum dimidia carucata terre in qua eadem capella sita est per rectas et antiquas diuisas suas et cum terra abbacie de Eglesgirg per antiquas et rectas diuisas suas et cum communi pastura eisdem canonicis et hominibus eorum in predictis terris manentibus cum theyno meo et cum hominibus meis per totam parochiam de Eglesgirg. Quare uolo et firmiter precipio ut predicti canonici prefatam ecclesiam cum capella Sancti Reguli et cum terra eidem capelle pertinente et cum terra abbacie et cum communi pastura supradicta et cum omnibus aliis eidem ecclesie iuste pertinentibus in terris in aquis habeant et teneant . ita libere . quiete . plenarie . et honorifice . sicut[b] alias elemosinas suas a me uel a predecessoribus meis eis datas . liberius . quiecius et honorificencius tenent et possident in regno meo Testibus . Matheo Aberdenensi episcopo . Æ*rkenbaldo* abbate de Dunfermelin . Henrico abbate de Aberbrothoc . Hugone cancellario meo . Hugone Giffard . Ricardo de Munfic' . Willelmo de Haya . Willelmo Cumin . Willelmo de Mumfort[c] . Roberto de Berkelay Unfrido de Berk' . Rogero de Mortimer apud Munros .

RUBRIC. De Eglisgirg (top in red).
SOURCE. SRO, GD 45/27/8 (St Andrews priory cartulary), fo. cvi^{r-v}.
PRINTED. *St Andrews Liber*, 229–230.
NOTES. [a] Blue initial V. [b] Fo.cvi^{v}. [c] Sic.
COMMENT. See also no.134. The chapel of St Regulus, known in 1471 as Eglisreul (*RMS*, ii, no.1039), is said to have been situated in the lands of Morphie (J.M. Mackinlay, *Ancient Church Dedications in Scotland, Non-scriptural*, 475).

353

Quitclaims to Scone Abbey Ronald Mac Malmur Goueran and Malmur Mac Hercar, whom Archibald abbot of Dunfermline had claimed against Scone Abbey on the king's behalf, but who have been adjudged to belong to Scone Abbey in the king's full court at Montrose. Montrose. (1189 × 1195)

Willelmus[a] Dei gracia Rex Scottorum omnibus probis hominibus tocius terre sue, clericis et laicis, salutem. Sciant presentes et futuri me quietos clamasse de me et heredibus meis in perpetuum R*oberto* abbati de Scon et canonicis eiusdem loci Ronaldum mac Malmur Goueran et Malmur mac Hercar, quos A*rkenbaldus* abbas de Dunfermelin calumpniabatur erga eum ad opus meum. Quare uolo ut predictos homines quietos habeant de me et heredibus meis in perpetuum sicut illos qui adiudicati fuerunt predicto abbati de Scon in plena curia mea apud Munros. Test*ibus* Hug*one* canc*ellario* meo, Arkebaldo abbate de Dunfermelin. Apud Munros.[b]

SOURCE. NLS, MS. Adv. 34.3.28, fo.11^{r}.
PRINTED. *Scone Liber*, no.37.
NOTES. [a] Initial omitted, MS. [b] Name spread out, MS.
COMMENT. Cp. no.15. 'Goueran' is presumably adjectival, 'of Gowrie'; 'Mac Hercar' means 'son of Farquhar'.

354 Commands that reasonable bequests which have been made towards the building operations of the monks of Arbroath Abbey, or for their other purposes, shall be handed over without delay. If anyone, contrary to this brieve, should presume to detain such bequests, or delay handing over bequests already detained, the king's sheriff in whose bailiary the bequests were made shall compel them to be handed over. Montrose. (1189 × 1194).

W.[a] Dei gr*ati*a Rex Scotorum[b] . Justic*iis* . Vicecom*itibus* . prepositis . ministris . et omnibus probis hominibus tocius terre sue clericis et laicis :' salutem. Mando et firmiter precipio . ut diuise racionabiles que fuerint ad edificacionem monachorum . Sancti Thome de Abirbrothoc . aut ad alios eorumdem usus . ubicunque per terram meam . eis facte fuerint :' eis sine dilacione reddantur. Et prohibeo firmiter ne quis diuisas eis racionabiliter factas eis detineat . super meam plenariam forisfacturam. Si quis uero super hoc diuisas racionabiliter factas . detinere presumpserit :' aut detentas sine dila[c]cione non reddiderit :' precipio ut uicecomes meus . in cuius Ballia . diuise eis facte fuerint :' detentores diuisarum . ad diuisas eis reddendas sine dilacione . et disturbacione . iuste distringat. Test*ibus* Hug*one* Cancell*ario* meo . Will*elmo* de Lindesay[d], Rob*erto* capellano meo . Ric*ardo* de prebenda . clerico meo . Geruasio Auenell'[e] . Apud Monros.[f]

RUBRIC. Carta domini Regis de diuisis (red, *E*). Carta Reg*is* de diuisis (red, *A*). .xcvij. (in margin, *A*, *E*).
SOURCE. NLS, MS. Adv. 34.4.2, fos.lxviii^v–lxix^r = *A*. SRO, Northesk Muniments (uncatalogued), Ethie MS., fo.6^v = *E*. Printed here from *A*.
PRINTED. *Arbroath Liber*, i, no.97.
NOTES. [a] Initial red. [b] Scottorum, *E*. [c] Fo.lxix^r. [d] Lindes', *E*. [e] Auenel', *E*. [f] Munros, *E*.
COMMENT. An example of a bequest to Arbroath Abbey, *tempore* William I, made *viva voce* on the death-bed by William de Malherbe of 2s. from the land of Balneaves (in Kinnell) which William had granted to his son Ewin, and its confirmation by William's other son Thomas, is in *Arbroath Liber*, i, no.98.

355 Grants to Arbroath Abbey the church of Inverlunan, Angus. Montrose. (1189 × 1194)

W.[a] Dei gr*ati*a Rex Scott', Episcopis, Abbatibus, Com*itibus*, Baron*ibus*, Justic*iis* , Vicecom*itibus* , prepositis , Ministris et omnibus probis hominibus tocius terre sue , clericis et laicis, salutem. Sciant presentes et futuri me dedisse et concessisse et hac carta mea confirmasse Deo et Ecclesie Sancti Thome de Aberbr*othoc* et monachis ibidem deo seruientibus Ecclesiam de Inuirlunan , cum terris et decimis et oblacionibus omnimodis et cum communi pastura et aliis aisiamentis et omnibus aliis ad predictam ecclesiam iuste pertinentibus . Tenend*am* in liberam et quietam et perpetuam elemosinam , ita libere et quiete , plenarie et honorifice , sicut[b] aliqua alia elemosina in toto regno meo liberius et quiecius , plenius et honorificencius tenetur et possidetur. Test*ibus* M*atheo* episcopo Aberdon*ensi* , Ric*ardo* episcopo Morau*iensi* , Hug*one* Cancellario meo , Rob*erto* et Rad*ulfo* Capellanis meis , Com*ite* Dunec*ano* , Com*ite* Gilleb*erto* , Rob*erto* de Lond*oniis* , Willelmo de Morau*illa* Constabulario , Alano filio Walteri dapiferi , Malcolmo fil*io* comit*is*

Dunec*ani* , Willelmo Cumyn , Willelmo de Haya , Rob*erto* de Berkal' , Rad*ulfo* Ruffo , Adam de Syreis , Hereb*erto* Marescallo , H*enrico* med*ico* . Apud Munros.

RUBRIC. De ecclesia de Inuirlunan (red, *E*). Carta Reg*is* .W. de ecclesia de Inuerlunan (red, *A*). .xix. (in margin, *A*, *E*).
SOURCE. NLS, MS. Adv. 34.4.2, fo.xlv^{r-v} = *A*. SRO, Northesk Muniments (uncatalogued), Ethie MS., fos.3^{v}–4^{r} = *E*. Printed here from *A*.
PRINTED. *Arbroath Liber*, i, no.19 (from *E*).
NOTES. [a] Initial red. [b] Fo.xlv^{v}.
COMMENT. This must be studied in conjunction with the agreement of 1189 × 1195 (probably earlier than this act) whereby Nigel Mac Ywar resigned to Henry the physician, clerk of the king and parson of Inverlunan, the *abthen* (MS., Athan, read Abthan) of Inverlunan and all cain and conveth and other services and exactions pertaining to a lay person, in return for an annualrent of eight merks (BM, MS. Add. 33245, fo.128^{r}). Nigel was probably thane of Inverlunan. See Appendix, no.590.

356 Grants to Arbroath Abbey the church of Fyvie, Aberdeenshire. Montrose. (1189 × 1194)

W.[a] Dei gr*atia* Rex Scott' . Episcopis . Abbatibus . Com*itibus* . Baron*ibus* . Justic*iis* . Vic*ecomitibus* . Prepositis . ministris . et omnibus probis hominibus tocius terre sue . clericis et laicis .' salutem. Sciant presentes et futuri . me dedisse . et concessisse . et hac carta mea confirmasse . Deo et ecclesie Sancti Thome de Aberbr*othoc* . et monachis ibidem Deo seruientibus ecclesiam de Fyvyn[b] . cum capellis . terris . et decimis . et oblacionibus omnimodis . et cum communi pastura . et aliis aisiamentis . & omnibus aliis . ad predictam ecclesiam iuste pertinentibus . Tenend*am* in liberam . et quietam . et perpetuam elemosinam . ita libere . et quiete . et plenarie et honorifice .' sicut aliqua alia elemosina . in toto Regno meo . liberius . quiecius . plenius et honorificencius .' tenetur et possidetur. Test*ibus* Matheo episcopo Abirdon*ensi* . Ricardo episcopo Morau*iensi* . Hug*one* Cancell*ario* meo . Rob*erto* et Rad*ulfo* capellanis meis . Com*ite* Dunec*ano* . Com*ite* Gilleb*erto* . Rob*erto* de London*iis* . Will*elmo* de Moreuill' const*abulario* . Alano fil*io* Walteri dapiferi . Malcolmo fil*io* com*itis* Dunec*ani* . Willelmo Cumyn . Will*elmo* de Haya . Rob*erto* de Berkel'[c] . Rad*ulfo* Rufo[d] . Adam de Syreis[e], Hereb*erto* Marescallo . apud Munros.

RUBRIC. De ecclesia de Fiuin (red, *E*). De ecclesia de Fyvyn (red, *A*). .xxviij. (in margin, *A*, *E*).
SOURCE. NLS, MS. Adv. 34.4.2, fo.xlviii^{r} = *A*. SRO, Northesk Muniments (uncatalogued), Ethie MS., fo.5^{r-v} = *E*. Printed here from *A*.
PRINTED. *Arbroath Liber*, i, no.28 (from *E*).
NOTES. [a] Initial red. [b] Fifin, *E*. [c] Berhkel', *E*. [d] Ruffo, *E*. [e] Sireys, *E*.

357 Grants to Arbroath Abbey the church of Inverness. Montrose. (1189 × 1194)

W.[a] Dei gr*atia* Rex Scott' . Episcopis . Abbatibus . Comitibus . Baron*ibus* . Justic*iis* . vic*ecomitibus* . prepositis . ministris . et omnibus probis hominibus . tocius terre sue clericis . et laicis .' salutem. Sciant presentes . et futuri . me dedisse . et concessisse . et hac carta mea confirmasse . Deo . et ecclesie Sancti Thome de Aberbr*othoc* . et monachis ibidem . Deo seruientibus . ecclesiam de Inuernys[b] . cum capellis . terris . et decimis.

et oblacionibus omnimodis . et cum communi pastura . et aliis aisiamentis . et omnibus aliis . ad predictam ecclesiam iuste pertinentibus . Tenend*am* in liberam . et quietam . et perpetuam elemosinam . ita libere et quiete . plenarie . et honorifice . sicut aliqua elemosina in toto regno meo . liberius & quiecius ; plenius . et honorificencius ; tenetur . et possidetur. Test*ibus* M*atheo* episcopo Aberd*onensi*[c] . Ric*ardo* episcopo Morau*iensi* . Hugon*e* Can[d]cellario meo . Rob*erto* et Rad*ulfo* Capellanis meis . Comite Dunec*ano* . Comite Gilb*erto* . Rob*erto* de Lond*oniis* . Willelmo de Morau*illa* Constab*ulario* . Alano fil*io* W*alteri* . dapiferi . Malcolmo filio Comitis Dunec*ani* . Willelmo Cumyn . W*illelmo* de Haya . Roberto de Berkel' . Rob*erto*[e] Rufo . Adam de Syreis . Herberto Marescall*o* apud Munros.

RUBRIC. De ecclesia de Inuirnis (red, *E*). De ecclesia de Inuernys (red, *A*). .xxxj. (in margin, *A*, *E*). Inuernys (in margin, *E*, contemporary with text). End of first fragment of Ethie MS. which begins in no.1 (marginal note in pencil, first half of xix cent.).
SOURCE. NLS, MS. Adv. 34.4.2, fo.xlviij^v–xlix^r = *A*. SRO, Northesk Muniments (uncatalogued), Ethie MS., fo.5^v = *E*. Printed here from *A*.
PRINTED. *Arbroath Liber*, i, no.31 (from *E*).
NOTES. [a] Initial red. [b] Inuirnis', *E*. [c] *E* ends here. [d] Fo.xlix^r. [e] Sic, for Radulfo?
COMMENT. See no.117 above. Apparently the gift included the chapel (of St Columba) of Petty (*Arbroath Liber*, i, p.155), afterwards a church of parochial status.

358

Confirms to St Andrews Cathedral Priory the church of Tealing (Angus) with the priest's toft and the toft of the *deòradh* (relic or relic-keeper), granted to it by Hugh Giffard and his son William, saving the ploughgate which belongs to that church. Kincardine. (1189 × 95)

W. Dei gr*atia* Rex Scott' Omnibus probis Hominibus tocius terre sue clericis 7 laicis Salutem. Sciant presentes 7 futuri me concessisse 7 Hac Carta mea confirmasse Deo 7 ecclesie Sancti Andr*ee* Apostoli in Scocia . 7 canonicis ibidem Deo seruientibus donacionem illam quam eis fecerunt Hugo Giffard . 7 Willelmus filius eius de ecclesia de TheliN cum Tofto sacerdotis 7 Tofto dereti . cum omnibus rectitudinibus suis . excepta illa Carrucata terre que ad eandem ecclesiam pertinet. Tenend*am* Sibi in liberam 7 perpetuam elemosinam . ita libere 7 Quiete sicut Carte predicti Hug*onis* Giffard . 7 Willelmi filii eius testantur . 7 confirmant. Test*ibus* Hug*one* Cancell*ario* meo . Henrico Abbate de Aberbrohth' . Com*ite* Dunec*ano* Just*icia* . Will*elmo* Cumin . Will*elmo* de Veteri Ponte . Will*elmo* de Haia . Rad*ulfo* Ruffo . Rog*ero* de Mortemer . Alano fil*io* Sim*onis* . Herberto Marescallo. Apud Kinkard'.

ENDORSED. Conf*irmatio* R*egis* W. de e*cclesia* de Telin (xii–xiii cent.). de ecclesia de Telyn (xv cent.).
DESCRIPTION. 6″ (15·2 cm.), Top, bottom × 4·3″ (11 cm.), L, 4·2″ (10·6 cm.), R. Foot formerly folded, with tie cut from top left of fold, now torn away. Double slits for seal-tag. No tag or seal survives.
HAND. Scribe De (William de Boscho?).
SOURCE. Original, NLS, MS. Adv. 15.1.18, no.1.
COMMENT. For the office of 'dewar' or *deòradh* cf. *Dunfermline Registrum*, no.234; and see W.C. Dickinson, 'The *Toschederach*', *Juridical Review*, liii (1941), 85–111. Examples of lands attached to the dewar's office are cited ibid., 108n.

359 Grants to Richard bishop of Moray one toft each in Banff, Cullen, Elgin, Forres, Auldearn and Inverness. Elgin. (1189 × 1195)

Will' Dei gratia Rex Scott' omnibus probis hominibus tocius terre sue clericis et laicis salutem. Sciatis me dedisse et concessisse et hac carta mea confirmasse Ricardo episcopo Morau*ie* et successoribus ejus in liberam et perpetuam elemosinam . unum toftum in Banef[a] . unum in Inuerculan[b] . unum in Elgin . unum in Foreys . unum in Eren . unum in Inuernis . tenenda ita libere quiete plenarie et honorifice . sicut alii episcopi in terra mea tofta sua in burgis meis liberius . quiecius . plenius et honorificencius tenent. Test*ibus* Hug*one* cancell*ario* meo . A*rkenbaldo* abbate de Dunf*ermelin* . Com*ite* Dunc*ano* . Com*ite* Gille*berto* . Ric*ardo* de Prebenda clerico meo . Will*elmo* fil*io* Fresk*ini* . Petro de Polloc . Will*elmo* de Laceles.[c] Apud Elgin.

RUBRIC. De toftis episcopi in Banef . et in Inverculan.
SOURCE. NLS, MS. Adv. 34.4.10, fo.xxxviii^r = *A*. Ibid., fos.xii^r–xiij^v = *B*. Printed here from *A* with some variants of *B* noted.
PRINTED. *Moray Registrum*, no.14.
NOTES. [a] Banf, *B*. [b] Inuercolan, *B*. [c] Lascell', *B*.

360 Grants to Richard bishop of Moray £10 annually out of the *firma burgi* of his burgh of Elgin, until the churches of Forres and Dyke shall fall vacant. Grants these churches, when vacant, on condition that if the income from them should not amount to £10 the king will make up the difference from elsewhere, according to the estimate of responsible men. If one of the churches falls vacant before the other, there will be a *pro rata* reduction in the annualrent of £10. Meanwhile, the money will be payable half at Easter and half at Michaelmas. Elgin. (1189 × 1195)

Will' Dei gratia Rex Scotorum omnibus probis hominibus tocius terre sue clericis et laicis salutem. Sciant presentes et futuri me dedisse et concessisse et hac carta mea confirmasse Ric*ardo* episcopo de Moravia decem libras de firma burgi mei de Elgin singulis annis percipiendas . donec ecclesiam de Foreys et ecclesiam de Dich vacare contigerit. Quas cum vacaverint dedi et concessi predicto Ric*ardo* episcopo et successoribus ejus in perpetuum in liberam et puram et perpetuam elemosinam . ita quidem quod si redditus predictarum ecclesiarum cum vacaverint ∴ summam decem librarum non contineant ∴ quod deerit in ecclesiis istis de decem libris perficiam ei alibi secundum estimacionem legittimam proborum hominum. Et si forte unam predictarum ecclesiarum priusquam aliam vacare contigerit de predictis decem libris episcopo tantum decidet ∴ quantum redditus illius ecclesie cum vacuerit ∴ secundum legittimam proborum hominum estimacionem valebit. Quare firmiter precipio ballivis meis de Elgin . ut prefato Episcopo predictas decem libras singulis annis de firma prenominati burgi mei de Elgin sine aliqua molestia vel vexatione persolvant . v^{que} . ad pascha . et v^{que} . libras ad festum Sancti Michaelis. Test*ibus* comite David fratre meo . Æ*rkenbaldo* abbate de Dunfermelyn . Hug*one* cancell*ario* meo . com*ite* Dunc*ano* . comite Patricio . comite Gille*berto* . Roberto de Lund*oniis* . Ric*ardo* de

Prebenda clerico meo . Will*elmo* fil*io* Fresek*ini* . Will*elmo* de Lacel*es* . Petro de Polloc. Apud Elgin.

RUBRIC. De ecclesiis de Foreys et Dyk.
SOURCE. NLS, MS. Adv. 34.4.10, fo.xxxv[r].
PRINTED. *Moray Registrum*, no.11.
COMMENT. Payment at Easter and Michaelmas was unusual.

361 Grants to Richard bishop of Moray the churches of Forres and Dyke. Elgin. (1189 × 1195)

Will' Dei gratia Rex Scott'[a] episcopis . abbatibus . comitibus . baronibus . justic*iis* . vicecomitibis . prepositis . ministris et omnibus probis hominibus tocius terre sue clericis et laicis salutem. Sciant presentes et futuri me dedisse concessisse et hac carta mea confirmasse Ric*ardo* episcopo Moraviensi et successoribus suis imperpetuum . ecclesiam de Foreys[b] et ecclesiam de Dich[c]. in terris et decimis et ceteris obventionibus ecclesiasticis et cum omnibus earum justis pertinentiis . tenendas in liberam et perpetuam elemosinam . ita libere et quiete . plenarie et honorifice . sicut aliquis episcopus in tota terra mea aliquam ecclesiam liberius . quiecius . plenius et honorificencius tenet et possidet. Test*ibus* Comite D*avi*d fratre meo . *Ærkenbaldo* abbate de Dunfermelyn . Hug*one* cancell*ario* meo . Comite Dunec*ano* . Comite Patricio . Comite Gilleb*erto* . G*illecrist* com*ite* de Mar[d] . Roberto de Lund*on* . Willelmo Cumin . Willelmo fil*io* Freskyn . Hugone filio suo.[e] Apud Elgin.

RUBRIC. Carta de ecclesiis de Dike et de Foreys.[f] De eisdem ecclesiis.[g]
SOURCE. NLS, MS. Adv. 34.4.10, fo.xxxv[r] = A^1. Ibid., fo.xxxv[v] (another copy in same hand) = A^2. Ibid., fo.xvij[r–v] = *B*. Printed here from A^1.
PRINTED. *Moray Registrum*, no.12.
NOTES. [a] Scoc', *B*. [b] Forays, *B*. [c] Dyc', *B*. [d] Marr, *B*. [e] *B* omits this witness. [f] A^1 only. [g] *B* only.

362 Grants to Richard bishop of Moray leave to build a mill above the cruives on the River Lossie below the castle of Elgin; and grants that the bishop and his successors that they and their men may have timber and fuel from the woods they have in Moray in the king's forests around Elgin, Forres and Inverness, saving the easements of the king's burgesses of these three burghs, as they used to have (these easements) in the time of King David I or in the time of King Malcolm IV or in his own time. Forres. (1189 × 1195)

Will' Dei gratia Rex Scott' episcopis, abbatibus, comitibus, baronibus, justic*iis*, vicecomitibus, prepositis, ministris et omnibus probis hominibus tocius terre sue clericis et laicis salutem. Sciant presentes et futuri me dedisse, concessisse et hac[a] carta mea confirmasse Ric*ardo* episcopo Morauien*si* ut firmet molendinum suum super terram meam desupra crohas que sunt super Lossin[b] subtus castellum de Elgin. Concessi etiam et hac carta mea confirmaui eidem Ric*ardo* episcopo et successoribus ejus imperpetuum ut de toto bosco suo in Morauia quod habet in foresto meo circa Elgyn et Foris[c] et Inuernis ipsi et homines eorum habeant alimentum[d] de materie et focali sine aliqua vexatione vel molestia ad proprios usus suos, ita quod nulli vicinorum suorum liceat aliquid inde capere nisi cum licentia eorum, nec etiam liceat alicui forestariorum meorum de predicto bosco aliquid dare vel vendere, sine eorum voluntate, salvo tamen alimento[d] burgensium meorum de Elgin et de Foreys et de Inuernis, sicut habere solebant tempore Regis D*aui*d aui mei, aut tempore Reg*is* Malcolmi fratris mei, aut meo tempore. Preterea concessi predicto Ric*ardo* episcopo ut ipse in prefato bosco suo pannagium suum sibi quietum habeat, et ut ipse habeat pannagium hominum suorum. Concessi etiam eidem R*icardo* episcopo et successoribus ejus imperpetuum ut habeant sibi et hominibus suis pasturam in predicto bosco suo ita libere et plenarie sicut antecessores sui habuerunt liberius et plenius tempore Regis D*aui*d aui mei, aut tempore Malcolmi Reg*is* fratris mei, aut meo tempore. Quare prohibeo firmiter ne quis forestariorum meorum nec aliquis alius prenominato R*icardo* episcopo uel successoribus ejus super aliquo prescriptorum que eis concessi et hac carta mea confirmaui injuriam, molestiam aut vexationem aliquam inferat, super meam plenariam forisfacturam. Test*ibus* Com*ite* D*aui*d fratre meo, Hug*one* cancell*ario* meo, *Ærkenbaldo* abbate de Dunf*ermelin*, Jod*elino* archideacono[e] de Dunkeld', Com*ite* Dunc*ano*, Com*ite* Patricio, Com*ite* Gill*eberto*, Gillecrist[f] comite de Mar, Ric*ardo* de Prebenda, Alano fil*io* Walt*eri* dapifero, Roberto de Lund*oniis*, Will*elmo* Cumyn, Will*elmo* filio Freskyn, Hug*one* fil*io* suo, Will*elmo* de Lacel*es*, Petro de Polloc. Apud Foreys.

RUBRIC. De bosco episcopi et confirmacio molendini desuper crohos Reg*is*.[g] Carta molendini de Elgin.[h]

SOURCE. NLS, MS. Adv. 34.4.10, fo.xxxv^{v} = *A*. Ibid., fo.xvij^{v} = *B*. Printed here from *A* with chief variants of *B* noted.

PRINTED. *Moray Registrum*, no.13 (from *B*).

NOTES. [a] *B* adds presenti. [b] Loscyn, *B*. [c] Forays, *B*. [d] aisiamentum, aysiamento, *B*. [e] Sic. [f] *A* omits; supplied from *B*. [g] *A* only. [h] *B* only.

COMMENT. The mill presumably first built by Bishop Richard became known as Bishopmill.

363

Confirms the property and privileges of Lindores Abbey, founded by his brother Earl David. Unrecorded place-date. (1190 × 1195, probably *c*.1190–1191)

Will*elmus* Dei gracia Rex Scott' . episcopis, abbatibus, comitibus, baronibus, just*iciis*, vicecomitibus, prepositis, ministris et omnibus probis hominibus tocius terre sue, clericis et laicis, salutem. Sciant presentes et futuri me concessisse et hac carta mea confirmasse Deo et ecclesie Sancte Marie et Sancti Andree de Lundors et abbacie quam comes Dauid frater meus ibi fundavit et monachis ibidem Deo servientibus et servituris, in liberam et puram et perpetuam elemosinam, ecclesiam de Lundors, cum omnibus justis pertinenciis suis, et terram ad predictam ecclesiam pertinentem, per rectas divisas suas in bosco et plano, et totam terram ab occidentali parte rivuli descendentis de magno lacu usque in They, preter insulam que vocatur Redinche. Et preterea unam piscariam in They juxta predictam insulam et aisiamenta ipsius insule, scilicet Redinche, ita eis communia ad proprios usus eorum sicut prefato comiti aut heredibus suis, et molendinum de Lundors, scilicet molendinum ipsius ville de Lundors, cum omni secta sua et molitura, ita quod homines com*itis* facient omnia que pertinent ad molendinum sicut facere solebant tempore quo comes illud in manu sua habuit.

Si autem molendinum comitis non possit molere, ipse bladum suum proprium molere faciet ad molendinum monachorum sine moltura. Et si molendinum monachorum molere non possit, ipsi molent ad molendinum com*itis* bladum suum proprium, similiter sine moltura. Concedo eciam eisdem monachis ecclesiam de Dunde cum omnibus pertinenciis suis, et unum thoftum in burgo de Dunde, liberum et quietum ab omni servicio et exaccione. Et ultra Moneth Fyntre per rectas diuisas suas et cum omnibus iustis pertinenciis suis et ecclesiam eiusdem ville de Fyntre cum omnibus pertinenciis suis; et in Garviach Letgavel et Malinth per rectas divisas suas, et cum omnibus pertinenciis suis. Concedo eciam eis ecclesiam de Inverury cum capella de Munethekin, et cum omnibus aliis iustis pertinenciis suis, et ecclesiam de Durnach, et ecclesiam de Prame, et ecclesiam de Radmuriel, et ecclesiam de Inchemabanin, et ecclesiam de Kursamuel, et ecclesiam de Kelabemunt[a], cum capellis earundem ecclesiarum, et terris et decimis et oblacionibus omnimodis et omnibus iustis pertinenciis suis, ad proprios usus et sustentaciones eorundem monachorum, et unum toftum in burgo de Inverury, liberum et quietum ab omni servicio et exaccione. Concedo eciam eis decimam omnium lucrorum et placitorum infra terram comitis et extra, ultra Moneth, quam habuit tempore quo fecit donacionem istam, et decimam omnium lucrorum que ei proveniunt de lucris meis in toto regno meo, et decimam omnium rerum comitis et heredum suorum ultra Moneth, scilicet decimacionem bladi et farine, butiri et casei, carnis et venacionis, cibi et potus, et coriorum ferarum cum mota canum captarum, cere et salis, uncti et sepi, et omnium aliarum rerum que decimari possunt, et que dabuntur vel vendentur vel ad firmam ponentur de maneriis comitis ultra Moneth, vel eciam que in eis expendentur, preter assisos redditus denariorum quos comes habuit tempore quo fecit hanc donacionem. Ita ut prenominati monachi omnia supradicta et in terris et in ecclesiis et in omnibus aliis ad proprios usus et sustentaciones suas habeant et teneant. Concedo eciam eis curiam suam omnino liberam, et dignitatem pacis, et omnes alias libertates quas abbacia habere debet. Quare volo et precipio ut monachi prefate abbacie de Lundors habeant et possideant omnes predictas terras, tenementa et possessiones et ecclesias, cum capellis et terris et decimis et omnibus aliis iustis pertinenciis suis, in bosco et plano, in pratis et pascuis, in aquis et molendinis, in stagnis et viuariis, in piscariis, in viis et semitis, cum omnibus libertatibus et liberis consuetudinibus, sine omni servicio et consuetudine et auxilio et seculari exaccione, in liberam et puram et perpetuam elemosinam, ita bene et in pace, libere, quiete, plenarie, integre et honorifice sicut aliqua abbacia uel domus religionis in toto regno meo melius et liberius, quiecius, plenius et honorificencius aliquam elemosinam tenet et possidet. Ita ut nullus heredum prefati comitis fratris mei a predictis monachis quicquam, nisi solas oraciones ad anime salutem, exigere presumat; ita libere, quiete et plenarie et honorifice sicut carta eiusdem comitis fratris mei testatur et confirmat. Test*ibus*, et cetera.

RUBRIC. Carta Willelmi regis Scocie (at top, red).
SOURCE. Capt. R. F. Cuninghame of Caprington, Caprington Castle, Lindores Abbey Cartulary, fos. 12^r–13^r.

PRINTED. *Lindores Chartulary*, no.138 (pp.181–2).
NOTE. [a] Sic, for Kelalcmunt.
COMMENT. Pope Celestine III's solemn privilege of 8 March, 1195 (*Lindores Chartulary*, no.93), recites the grants included here, and adds *inter alia* King William's grant of burgh tofts (no.366). The probability is that Earl David's 'great charter' for Lindores (*Lindores Chartulary*, no.2) and Abbot Osbert of Kelso's quitclaim to Abbot Guy of Lindores (ibid., 284–5) were contemporaneous, and that *Rogero episcopo* in the former is a copyist's error for *Rogero electo*. The king, who witnessed both these documents, probably issued his confirmation at about the same time.

364 Confirms to Melrose Abbey the quitclaim granted to it by Alan son of Walter, the king's steward, in the king's presence and in his full court, of all the claim and right which Alan and his heirs might have in the pasture on the west bank of the Leader Water; as Alan's charter bears witness. Edinburgh. (1189 × 1193).

Will*elmus* Dei gr*ati*a Rex Scott' . episcopis Abbatibus Com*itibus* Baron*ibus* Just*iciis* Vice*comitibus* prepositis ministris & omnibus probis hominibus tocius terre sue clericis & laicis Salutem. Sciant presentes & futuri me concessisse & hac carta mea confirmasse Deo & ecclesie Sancte Marie de Melr*os* & monachis ibidem Deo seruientibus illam quietam clamationem quam Alanus filius Walteri dapifer meus eisdem monachis in presentia & plena curia mea fecit de tota calumpnia & omni iure quod predictus Alanus aut heredes sui habuerunt uel unquam habere poterunt de pastura ex occidentali parte de Led*er*. Quare uolo & precipio ut prefati monachi de Melros prenominatam pasturam teneant inperpetuum & habeant liberam & quietam de omni calumpnia de prefato Alano & heredibus [suis][a] ita libere & quiete plenarie & honorifice sicut carta predicti Alani fil*ii* Walteri dapiferi testatur. Test*ibus* Joc*elino* episcopo Glasg*uensi* . Johanne episcopo Dunkeld*ensi* . Com*ite* Da*ui*d fratre meo . Com*ite* Dunec*ano* . Com*ite* Gilb*erto* . Will*elmo* de Moru*illa* const*abulario* . Willelmo de Lindes' . Malc*olmo* fil*io* Com*itis* Dunec*ani* . Walt*ero* de Berk' . Rob*erto* de Berk' . Henrico de Graham. Apud Edenburg.

ENDORSED. Confirmacio Regis W[b] de [ ] (xii–xiii cent.), de terra quam Alanus dapifer contulit (xiii cent.). S (red, xv cent.?). J. Scott (xvi cent.).
DESCRIPTION. 6·3″ (16 cm.), Top, 6″ (15·3 cm.), Bottom × 4·3″ (11 cm.), L, R. Foot folded to a depth of 1·2″ (3 cm.). Double slits, with tag 5·8″ (14·5 cm.) long, 0·7″ (1·8 cm.) wide. Seal complete in greenish brown wax, fair impression.
HAND. Scribe Cc. Ruled probably in drypoint.
SOURCE. Original, SRO, GD 55/98.
PRINTED. *Melrose Liber*, no.98.
NOTES. [a] Illegible in source. [b] W (xiii cent.) inserted afterwards.
COMMENT. Alan's charter (*Melrose Liber*, no.97) shews that the pasture in question was part of Blainslie.

365 Confirms to Melrose Abbey the church of Hassendean, for the reception and maintenance of poor people and pilgrims coming to Melrose. The church has been granted to the abbey for this purpose by Jocelin bishop of Glasgow, on the king's advice, following a dispute between the king and the bishop over the patronage of the church. Melrose Abbey is to hold the church as freely as any religious house holds a parish church anywhere in the kingdom, saving an annual pension of 20s. payable to the church of Glasgow. To prevent any future dispute over pasture, it has been adjudged that the monks of Melrose ought to have pasture in Hassendean for 200 ewes, 16 oxen and 4 cows. Melrose. (1193 × 1195, perhaps 1193)

Willelmus Dei gr*ati*a Rex Scott'. Episcopis . Abbatibus . Comitibus . Baronibus . Just*iciis* . Uicecomitibus . Prepositis . Ministris . et Omnibus probis Hominibus tocius terre sue clericis 7 laicis :· Salutem. Sciant presentes 7 futuri nos concessisse 7 hac carta mea confirmasse Deo 7 Sancte Marie 7 ecclesie de Melros 7 monachis ibidem Deo seruientibus in liberam 7 quietam 7 perpetuam elemosinam . ecclesiam de Hatstanesden' . cum terris 7 decimis 7 omnibus ad ipsam ecclesiam pertinentibus . ad susceptionem 7 sustentationem pauperum 7 peregrinorum ad domum de Melros uenientium :· a Joc*elino* Glasguensi episcopo per consilium nostrum assignatam. De qua ecclesia cum esset inter nos 7 eundem episcopum controuersia . ad quem nostrum donatio ipsius ecclesie pertineret :· ius nostrum quod in ea habuimus . uel habere potuimus :· eidem episcopo concessimus . ad ipsam ecclesiam secundum Deum ordinandam. Et ipse episcopus ut prouentus ipsius ecclesie in caritatis operibus expendantur :· 7 in bonos usus perpetuo conuertanttur :· ipsam ecclesiam cum omnibus pertinenciis suis pro animabus omnium predecessorum nostrorum 7 suorum . 7 salute 7 anima nostra 7 sua . 7 omnium heredum nostrorum . 7 successorum suorum . per consilium 7 concessionem nostram ad perpetuos usus pauperum 7 peregrinorum . ecclesie 7 conuentui de Melros pia consideratione contulit 7 confirmauit. Ut autem hoc pium factum 7 rationabile perpetuam 7 illibatam habeat firmitatem :· predictam ecclesiam de Hatstanesden' cum omnibus pertinenciis suis . Deo 7 Sancte Marie 7 ecclesie de Melros . in liberam 7 perpetuam elemosinam ad sanctos usus prenominatos concedimus 7 hac carta nostra confirmamus. Tenendam in perpetuum ita libere . Quiete plenarie 7 honorifice :· Sicut aliqua parrochialis ecclesia in regno nostro liberius . Quietius . Plenius . 7 Honorificentius . ab aliqua conuentuali ecclesia tenetur 7 possidetur. Salua pensione viginti solidorum ecclesie Glasguen*si* de ipsa ecclesia de Hatstanesd' ab ipsis monachis singulis annis persoluenda . Sicut carta eiusdem Joc*elini* Glasguen*sis* episcopi testatur. Et ne inter nos uel heredes nostros uel ipsos qui de nobis manerium predictum tenuerint . 7 ipsos monachos aliqua in posterum super pastura predicte uille possit esse controuersia :· per preceptum nostrum 7 per considerationem proborum Hominum nostrorum prouisum est . quantum predicti monachi in pastura predicte uille habere debeant. Scilicet ducentas matrices oues . 7 sexdecim boues . 7 quatuor uaccas . quo illis in pastura illa perpetuo habend*um* :· concessimus . 7 hac carta nostra confirmauimus. Firmiter prohibentes nequis eis super hoc :· iniuriam aut uexationem aliquam inferat . Super nostram plenariam forisfacturam. Test*ibus* Joc*elino* Glasg*uensi* episcopo . Ricardo Episcopo Morauiensi . *Ærkenbaldo*[a] Abbate de Dunferm*elin* . Com*ite* Dauid fratre nostro . Hug*one* Cancellario nostro . Willelmo de Lind' Just*icia* . Phil*ippo* de Valon*iis* Dauid de Lindes' . Hugone de Normanuill'

. Waltero de Berkel' camerario nostro . Herberto de Camera. Apud MelROS.[b]

ENDORSED. Confirmatio Reg*is* W. De Ecclesia de Hast'. (xii cent.). I (red, xv cent?). J. Scott (xvi cent.).
DESCRIPTION. 10·3″ (26·2 cm.), Top, 10·6″ (26·9 cm.), Bottom × 8·1″ (20·7 cm.), L, R. Foot folded to a depth of 1″ (2·4 cm.). Double slits with tag 5·9″ (15·3 cm.) long, 0·9″ (2·3 cm.) wide. Seal complete, in red wax, clear impression.
HAND. Scribe Da. Unruled. In this document Scribe Da has made a deliberate effort to imitate the layout and letter-forms of a papal privilege, making exaggeratedly tall capitals in the top line and bunching his minuscule letters very close throughout the document. He uses the *titulus* as a mark of abbreviation eight times in the top line and once for Test*ibus*.
SOURCE. Original, SRO, GD 55/123=A.
PRINTED. *Melrose Liber*, no.123.
NOTES. [a] *Melrose Liber*, no.123, prints R., wrongly. [b] Wavy horizontal lines join Apud to Camera and Melros so as to complete the bottom line.
COMMENT. The exceptional use of the plural is noteworthy. According to *Chron. Melrose*, 48, Bishop Jocelin made his grant of Hassendean church in 1193. His charter survives (printed, *Melrose Liber*, no.121), witnessed by, among many others, Roger of Howden, the English royal servant and chronicler, who made considerable use of the Melrose chronicle in his own historical work. Bishop Jocelin's grant was confirmed by Pope Celestine III on 10 March 1195 (*Melrose Liber*, no.124) which probably gives us a *terminus ante quem* for the king's confirmation also. But it must be noted that the confirmation of the grant issued by the dean and chapter of Glasgow (*Melrose Liber*, no.122) cannot be earlier than 10 September, 1195, because witnessed by Reginald bishop of Ross; and this confirmation was also witnessed by Roger of Howden. Two visits by Howden to Scotland about this time are certainly not impossible, and the visit in 1193 may have been in connexion with King William's freewill contribution of 2,000 merks towards the ransom of King Richard I of England.

366 Grants to Lindores Abbey one full toft each in the burghs of Berwick, Stirling, Crail, Perth, Forfar, Montrose and Aberdeen. Selkirk. (1189 × 1195)

Will*el*m*us* Dei gr*aci*a Rex Scotorum omnibus probis hominibus tocius terre sue, clericis et laicis, salutem. Sciant presentes et futuri me dedisse et concessisse et hac carta mea confirmasse Deo et abbati de Lundor*is* et monachis ibidem Deo seruientibus unum plenarium thoftum in burgo meo de Bereuic, et unum plenarium thoftum in burgo meo de Striuelin, et unum plenarium thoftum in burgo meo de Karel, et unum plenarium thoftum in burgo meo de Pertht, et unum plenarium thoftum in burgo meo de Forfare, et unum plenarium thoftum in burgo meo de Munros', et unum plenarium thoftum in burgo meo de Aberdene. Tenend*a* in liberam et quietam et perpetuam elemosinam, ita libere, quiete, plenarie, honorifice, sicut alia elemosinarum suarum liberius, quiecius, plenius et honorificencius tenent et possident. Test*ibus* Comite[a] Dauid fratre meo, Hug*one* cancellario meo, Willelmo de Lindiss', Roberto de London filio meo, Willelmo de Haya, Willelmo de Sumervill, Henrico de Brade marescallo Ricardo filio Hugonis. Apud Selechirche.

RUBRIC. Rex super toftis burgorum.
SOURCE. NLS, MS. Adv. 34.7.1, fo.7[v].
PRINTED. *Lindores Liber*, no.6. NOTE.[a] MS., comes.
COMMENT. This grant is included in Pope Celestine III's solemn privilege of 8 March, 1195 (*Lindores Chartulary*, no.93).

367 Confirms the property and privileges of Kelso Abbey, including property not included in the king's first comprehensive confirmation (no.63). Roxburgh. (1189 × 1195, possibly 1193)

WILLELMVS[a] Dei gr*ati*a Rex Scott'. Episcopis . Abbatibus . Comitibus . Baronibus . Justiciis . Vicecomit*ibus* . Prepositis . Ministris . 7 Omnibus probis hominibus Totius terre sue Clericis 7 laicis .' Salutem. Nouerint omnes tam posteri quam presentes me concessisse 7 presenti Carta mea confirmasse pro salute anime Regis D*aui*d aui mei . 7 Comitis Henr*ici* patris mei . 7 pro salute anime mee 7 Omnium antecessorum 7 successorum meorum .' Deo et Ecclesie Sancte Marie de Kelchou 7 monachis ibidem Deo seruientibus . in liberam 7 perpetuam elemosinam .' Omnes terras 7 ceteras possessiones suas quas habuerunt 7 tenuerunt in tempore Regis D*aui*d aui mei . 7 in tempore Regis Malcholmi fratris mei . Tenendas per easdem libertates 7 Rectitudines .' per quas ipsi eas umquam melius 7 plenius . liberius 7 quietius .' tenuerunt 7 possederunt. Concedo etiam predicte Ecclesie Sancte Marie de Kelchou 7 eiusdem loci monachis . ut homines sui qui in Kelchou sunt manentes omnibus diebus septimane excepto die statuto fori mei de Rokesburg' licentiam habeant uendendi in uilla sua focale . 7 materiem . 7 annonam. Et transeuntes licentiam habeant eis ista uendendi. Habeant etiam ipsi homines sui licentiam uendendi in fenestris suis Panem . 7 Ceruisiam . 7 carnem. Si autem piscem in propriis suis quadrigis uel equis attulerint 7 inde uendere uoluerint .' in fenestris suis liceat eis uendere. Quadrige autem aliunde uenientes 7 per inde transeuntes .' neque ibi exhonerent neque ibi uendant .' set ad forum meum ueniant. Die autem fori mei statuti de Rokesburg non liceat eis quicquam emere in villa sua . set ad forum meum ueniant 7 ibi cum aliis burgensibus meis quod uoluerint emant per Rectas consuetudines suas. Dedi etiam 7 concessi prenominatis monachis ad usus 7 operationem ipsius ecclesie de Kelchou .' Ecclesiam de Dunfres cum Terris 7 decimis . 7 omnimodis oblationibus . 7 cum Capella Sancti Thome in ipso burgo . 7 cum Tofta ad ipsam capellam pertinentem . 7 cum quinque acris terre . quas eidem Ecclesie 7 capelle in liberam elemosinam .' dedi 7 per Philippum de Valoniis eis tradi feci. 7 cum omnibus aliis eiusdem Ecclesie justis pertinentiis. Ita ne liceat alicui Ecclesiam illam uel capellam aut earum redditus siue beneficia . ab operatione Ecclesie de Kelchou 7 propriis usibus monachorum .' quoquomodo alienare. Et capellam castelli de Pebles . cum carrucata terre ad ipsam pertinentem . 7 cum redditu decem solidorum de firma burgi de Pebles . que Rex D*aui*d auus meus eidem capelle assignauit ad diuinum officium in ea perpetuo celebrandum .' pro anima Comitis HENR*ICI* patris mei . ita etiam quod prefati monachi ibidem ydoneam 7 pulcram capellam facient . 7 inuenient ibi honesta hornamenta ecclesiastica 7 capellanum qui in ea pro anima Comitis HENR*ICI* patris mei perpetuo ministret. Et Ecclesiam de Kultre juxta Aberdoen cum omnibus ad ipsam ecclesiam juste pertinentibus. Et unum toftum in Hadintona . 7 terram illam que est iuxta toftum illum uersus forum .' de qua solebam habere singulis annis quatuor denarios. Concedo etiam eis 7 confirmo decimam animalium 7 porcorum 7 caseorum de cano meo de quatuor

Kadred de Galweia . 7 decimam caseorum similiter de Twededale per unumquemque annum . 7 dimidietatem coriorum coquine mee . 7 de omnibus occisionibus meis 7 Regine mee 7 omnium successorum meorum . ita ut ubicunque unum corium habuero :· habeant monachi aliud . 7 similiter de unctis . 7 de sepis :· sicut de coriis . 7 omnes pelles arietum 7 agnorum . 7 decimam coriorum ceruorum 7 ceruarum quos veltrarii mei capient 7 Sicut Carta Regis D*aui*d aui mei testatur 7 confirmat. Et annuatim tredecim vaccas 7 totidem porcos de cano meo de terra quam filii Duuenaldi tenent . pro excambio redditus quem predicti monachi solebant habere de cano de terra quam Radulfus filius Dunegal 7 Duuen*aldus* frater suus tenuerunt 7 de terra quam Gillepatric frater eorum tenuit in Glencharn. Et ut loca Wasti mei de Selechirche ad que transtuli homines meos de Elrehope sint de parochia ville mee de Selechirche . 7 omnes in illis locis habitantes cum uniuersis possessionibus suis sint intendentes ad ecclesiam de Selechirche tanquam ad matricem ecclesiam suam. Et si forte contigerit quod in eisdem locis matrix ecclesia aut capella fundata fuerit :· eam cum omnibus justis pertinentiis suis Do 7 concedo Deo 7 prefate ecclesie Kalchoensi 7 eiusdem ecclesie monachis :· in liberam 7 perpetuam elemosinam. Et ex donacione pie memorie Regis Malcholmi fratris mei :· Ecclesiam de InuerlethaN . Et ex donacione Comitis D*aui*d fratris mei Ecclesiam de Chamsi . 7 Ecclesiam de AltermuniN . in Leuenachs. Et ex donacione Willelmi Finemund :· Ecclesiam de KambusneythaN. Et ex donacione Ricardi Cumin :· Ecclesiam de LintunRutheri. Et ex donacione Wice :· Ecclesiam de villa Wice cum capellis suis. Et ex donacione Fergus Macbard :· Ecclesiam de Dunsier . cum capellis . 7 terris 7 decimis 7 omnibus aliis predictarum ecclesiarum justis pertinentiis Ita libere quiete . plenarie 7 honorifice :· sicut carte donatorum 7 aduocatorum eis donant 7 confirmant 7 sicut carta Jocel*ini* Glasguensis episcopi :· eis confirmat. Et ex donacione Hugonis Ridel :· Ecclesiam de Crennestun . cum terra ad eam pertinente 7 cum omnibus aliis justis pertinentiis suis. Et ex donacione Euerardi de Penchathlen :· Ecclesiam de Penchathlen cum omnibus justis pertinentiis suis. Et ex donacione Walcheri de Karnoto :· Ecclesiam de Trauerflet . 7 Ecclesiam de DungRey :· cum omnibus earum justis pertinentiis. Et ex donacione Radulfi de Clere :· Ecclesiam de Kaledoure que fuit eiusdem Radulfi de Clere :· cum omnibus justis pertinentiis suis. Et ex donacione Hugonis sine manicis :· Ecclesiam de MortuN in Strahnith . cum una carrucata terre 7 cum omnibus aliis justis pertinentiis suis. Et ex donacione Willelmi de Kuningburg :· Ecclesiam de StapelgortuN . cum capellis 7 terris 7 decimis . 7 omnibus aliis justis pertinentiis. Concedo etiam eis 7 confirmo unam carrucatam terre in villa de Haudene . per easdem diuisas per quas eam habuerunt antequam Bernardus filius Briani habuisset predictam Haudene . Cum omnibus aisiamentis infra diuisas ipsius carrucate terre. Et unam toftam in predicta villa de Haudene liberam 7 quietam ab omni seruitio . 7 hominem eorum qui super toftam illam sedebit :· liberum 7 quietum ab omni seruitio 7 alia consuetudine sicut Carta Bernardi testatur. Et duas bouatas terre in territorio de Molle . quas Eschina de Londoniis eis dedit . 7 pasturam 7 alia aisiamenta in villa de

Molle sicut carta eiusdem Eschine testatur. Et sex bouatas terre in territorio de Brochesmuthe . quas Willelmus de Morevill' 7 Robertus de Landeles . 7 MuRiel uxor eiusdem Roberti eisdem monachis dederunt 7 confirmauerunt. Et donacionem scalingarum illarum quas Willelmus de Veteri Ponte eis dedit 7 carta sua confirmauit. Et scalingas de Bothkil per rectas diuisas suas . ita plenarie 7 libere 7 quiete :' sicut Cospatricius Comes illas eis dedit . 7 carta sua confirmauit. Et ex donacione Pie memorie Regis Malcholmi fratris mei :' unum Toftum in RutherglеN. Et donacionem quam Walterus Corbet fecit eis de Ecclesia de Malkaruestun . 7 de omnibus eiusdem ecclesie justis pertinentiis . 7 omnibus terris 7 possessionibus 7 libertatibus :' quas idem Walterus Corb*et* prenominatis monachis de Kelch' donauit . sicut carta eius testatur . saluo seruitio meo. Et unam bouatam terre in SprowestuN . quam Radulfus de Ver' eis dedit :' sicut carta eius testatur . saluo seruitio meo. Et in territorio de Molle Totam terram 7 pratum 7 nemus . Et totum Hulocheshou in bosco 7 plano . 7 pastura . excepta una acra terre que Anselmus dedit .W. cementario . Que :' predictus Anselmus de Molle dedit predicte ecclesie Kelchoensi 7 que Ricardus de Linc*olnia* 7 Mathild' filia 7 heres legitima eiusdem Anselmi eidem ecclesie concesserunt 7 carta sua confirmauerunt . Tenend*am* per diuisas nominatas in cartis predictorum Anselmi . Ricardi de Linc*olnia* . 7 Mathild' filie Anselmi sicut Carte eorum testantur . saluo seruitio meo. Et in territorio de Lesmahaggu :' donacionem illam quam Willelmus Cumin fecit eis de terra illa de qua controuersia fuit inter eundem W*illelmum* CumiN :' 7 abbatem de Kelchou . Tenend*am* per easdem diuisas que continentur in carta eiusdem W*illelmi* CumiN . sicut carta eius testatur . saluo seruitio meo. Et ex donacione Symonis Fraser :' Ecclesiam de Keth que fuit eiusdem Symonis . cum terra ad eandem ecclesiam pertinente per diuisas nominatas in carta predicti Symonis Fraser . 7 cum omnibus eiusdem ecclesie justis pertinentiis . sicut carta iamdicti Symonis testatur. saluo seruitio meo. Preterea concedo 7 firmiter precipio . ut abbas de Kelchou 7 eiusdem loci monachi teneant 7 habeant in perpetuum terram de qua controuersia fuit inter eos 7 monachos de MaylRos per easdem diuisas per quas illam tenuerunt anno 7 die quo Rex D*aui*d auus meus fuit uiuus 7 mortuus . ita ut nec erga eos . nec erga aliquem alium in posterum intrent in Placitum de Diuisis illis :' neque de terra siue de boscho que infra diuisas illas sunt. Prohibeo etiam firmiter ne quis eis in posterum iniuriam inde faciat :' super meam plenariam defensionem. Prenominatas igitur terras omnes . 7 Ecclesias 7 earum capellas . 7 omnes earum obuentiones . cum terris . decimis . 7 omnibus earum justis pertinentiis 7 Rectitudinibus :' prenominate ecclesie Sancte MaRie de Kelchou . 7 propriis usibus 7 sustentionibus monachorum ibidem Deo seruientium :' in liberam 7 perpetuam elemosinam concedo 7 presenti Carta mea confirmo. Ut omnes predictas terras . 7 ecclesias 7 Tenementa . cum omnibus justis pertinentiis suis ita libere . quiete Plenarie . 7 honorifice habeant 7 in liberam 7 perpetuam elemosinam possideant :' sicut aliquas alias elemosinas IN Regno Scott*orum* liberius . quietius . plenius . 7 honorificentius habent 7 possident . Et sicut Carte donatorum 7 aduocatorum predictarum terrarum siue Ecclesiarum :'

eisdem monachis donant 7 confirmant . saluo seruitio meo de Illis ·/ de quibus seruitium de Jure habere debeo. Testibus Jocelino Episcopo Glasguensi. Comite D*aui*d fratre meo. Ærkambaldo abbate de Dunfermelin. Hugone Cancellario meo. Symone archidiacono Glasguen*si*. Willelmo de Morevill' Constabulario. meo. Roberto de Londoniis. Roland' fil*io* Uchtred'. Willelmo de Lindes'. Malcholmo fil*io* [Comitis Dunecani][b]. Philippo de Valoniis. Alano fil*io* Walteri. Geruasio Auenel constabulario de Rokesburg'. Waltero Corbet. Ranulfo de Sules. Herberto de Machuswell'. Thoma de Colevill. Roberto [ ].[c] Philippo de Setune. Herberto Maresch*allo*. Bernardo de HaudeNe. Apud ROKESBURG.

ENDORSED. Will*elmus* Rex (xii cent.). YOδqH (in pale ink inside fold, Greek letters?).
DESCRIPTION. 1′ 6″ (45·7 cm.), Top, 1′ 5·7″ (45 cm.), Bottom × 1′ 9·3″ (54 cm.), L, 1′ 9·4″ (54·2 cm.), R. Foot folded to a depth of 2″. There is a double slit in the centre of the fold for a seal-tag, but tag and seal are missing.
HAND. Scribe Ca. A bold, elaborate charter hand, on thick parchment ruled in drypoint or very faint pen.
SOURCE. Original, SRO, GD 90/8 = *A*. NLS, MS. Adv. 34.5.1, fos. 13r–14v = *B*. Printed here from *A*.
PRINTED. *Kelso Liber*, no.13 (from *B*).
NOTES. [a] Large roman letters flourished in red: WIL'EMVS. [b] Obscured by staining. [c] Illegible through staining.

368 Confirms the agreement made between the church of St Andrews and Roger, bishop-elect of St Andrews, on the one hand, and the church of Durham and Prior Bertram and the convent of Durham on the other, whereby the bishop-elect has granted to the church of Durham that the church of Coldingham with its chapels shall be free in perpetuity of cain, conveth, procurations, hospitality, sinodals, aids and all other exactions demanded by the bishop-elect or by his successors or diocesan officials. All other parish churches in the diocese of St Andrews belonging to the convent of Durham shall be free in perpetuity of cain, conveth, procurations and hospitality, unless offered freely. Officials of the diocese of St Andrews are to demand no more of these churches than they demand in the parish churches belonging to the abbot of Kelso or any abbot who holds most freely within the diocese. When a common aid is levied throughout St Andrews diocese, the convent of Durham shall answer for their parish churches as those abbots and priors who hold most freely within the diocese answer for theirs. The prior and convent of Durham shall have such power, dignity and freedom of disposition with respect to their parish churches as are enjoyed by the abbeys which hold most freely within the diocese. In exchange for these liberties, Prior Bertram and his convent, with the counsel and consent of Hugh (du Puiset) bishop of Durham, have granted to the church of St Andrews the chapel of Nenthorn, Berwickshire, free of the mother church of Ednam. Edinburgh. (on or about 2 February, 1194)

.W'. Dei gr*ati*a Rex Scott'. Episcopis . Abbatibus . Com*itibus* . Baron*ibus* . Justic*iis* . Vicecom*itibus* . Prepositis . Ministris . et[a] Omnibus probis

Hominibus totius terre sue Clericis et Laicis Salutem. Sciant presentes ⁊ futuri me concessisse . ⁊ hac carta mea confirmasse conuentionem factam inter Ecclesiam Sancti Andr*ee* . ⁊ Ecclesiam Sancti Cudberti de Dunelmo . ⁊ inter Rogerium Electum Sancti Andr*ee* . et Bertramum priorem . ⁊ conuentum ecclesie Sancti Cudberti de Dunelmo. Scilicet quod prefatus Electus concessit Deo et Sancto Cudberto et prenominato priori ⁊ conuentui Dunelm*ensis* ecclesie quod Ecclesia de Coldigham cum capellis ad eam pertinentibus libera sit ⁊ quieta sit in perpetuum a Cano ⁊ Coneuetho . et procurationibus ⁊ hospiciis . et Omnibus aliis exactionibus . et sinodalibus et auxiliis . ⁊ omnibus aliis tam ab ipso Electo quam a successoribus suis . et ab omnibus officialibus Episcopatus Sancti Andr*ee* Salua tamen ipsi Electo ⁊ successoribus suis canonica iusticia et obedientia. Et quod omnes alie parrochiales ecclesie quas prefatus conuentus Dunelm*ensis* ecclesie in Episcopatu Sancti Andr*ee* possidet :' libere sint et quiete in perpetuum a cano ⁊ Coneuetho . ⁊ procurationibus et hospiciis tam a predicto Electo quam a successoribus suis nisi gratis :' huiusmodi facere uoluerint. Nec aliquid in predictis ecclesiis parrochialibus magis exigetur ab officialibus episcopatus Sancti Andr*ee* quam in Ecclesiis parrochialibus Abbatis Kalcoen*sis* uel alicuius Abbatis qui liberius et melius tenet in Episcopatu Sancti Andr*ee*. Et quando commune auxilium ponetur per totum Episcopatum Sancti Andr*ee* :' prior et predictus conuentus ecclesie Dunelm*ensis* de prescriptis ecclesiis suis parrochialibus predicto Electo et successoribus suis respondebunt :' Sicut Abbates uel Priores qui liberius tenent in Episcopatu Sancti Andr*ee* :' faciunt de suis. Prior itaque ⁊ antedictus conuentus Dunelm*ensis* ecclesie habebunt in perpetuum tantam potestatem . dignitatem et dispositionem in omnibus ecclesiis suis parrochialibus :' quantamcunque alique abbacie habent in ecclesiis suis que liberius et melius tenent in Episcopatu Sancti Andr*ee*. Et propter predictas quietantias et libertates . et pro bono pacis predictus Bertramus prior . ⁊ conuentus ecclesie Dunelm*ensis* de consilio ⁊ Assensu Hug*onis* Dunelm*ensis* Episcopi et totius Capituli sui dederunt et concesserunt Deo et ecclesie Sancti Andr*ee* ⁊ predicto Electo . ⁊ successoribus eius capellam de Naithanesthurn' tenendam et cui uoluerint concedendam in perpetuum liberam et quietam et absolutam tam ab eis quam a matrice ecclesia de Edenham. Quare uolo ut ista conuentio prescripta :' inter prenominatas ecclesias firmiter ⁊ inuiolabiliter obseruetur :' sicut scriptum autenticum inter predictum Electum Sancti Andr*ee* . et prefatum B*ertramum* priorem et conuentum Dunelm*ensis* ecclesie factum :' testatur. Test*ibus* Hug*one* Cancellario meo . Ærkenbald*o* Abbate de Dunfermel*in* . Willelmo Abbate de Sancta Cruce . Sim*one* Archid*iacono* Glasg*uensi* . Willelmo Maleuicino Archid*iacono* Laod*onie* . Roll*ando* fil*io* Uchtred*i* . Com*ite* Dunec*ano* . Willelmo de Lindesia . Robert*o* de Lond*oniis* . Rannulf*o* de Sol*is* . Willelmo de Ramesh' . Henr*ico* de Graham . Willelmo de Cuninghesburg'. Apud EdeNebuR

ENDORSED. Confirmatio Reg*is* Scotie Willelmi de pace facta inter nos ⁊ Electum Sancti Andree . Rogerum super Can ⁊ Coneveth (early xiii cent.). S. iij^{a} vj^{te} (xv cent.).

DESCRIPTION. 10·2″ (25·7 cm.), Top, 10″ (25·4 cm.), Bottom × 7·3″ (18·5 cm.),

L, R. Foot folded 1″. Double slits. Tag 6·8″ long, 0·8″ wide. Seal in natural wax, somewhat chipped, fair impression.
HAND. Scribe Ca. Unruled.
SOURCE. Original, Durham, D. & C. Muniments Misc. Chr. no.589.
PRINTED. Raine, *North Durham*, no.52.
NOTE. [a] Here and throughout, et represents a crossed tironian sign, employed by Scribe Ca variously with a simple tironian sign.
COMMENT. The agreement referred to is printed in Raine, *North Durham*, no.462 (dated 2 February, 1194), and commented on in F. Barlow, *Durham Jurisdictional Peculiars* (1950), 131–8. A copy was evidently entered into the Great Register of St Andrews, now lost (*St Andrews Liber*, p.xxvii, no.28). See no.460. No.300 should probably have followed this act.

369 Grants to Coldingham Priory one full toft in his burgh of Haddington. Selkirk. (1189 × 1195, probably 1193 × 1195)

.W. Dei gr*ati*a Rex Scott'. Omnibus Probis Hominibus tocius terre sue Clericis 7 Laicis Salutem. Sciant presentes 7 futuri me dedisse 7 concessisse 7 hac carta mea confirmasse Deo 7 Ecclesie de Coldingham et[a] monachis ibidem Deo seruientibus unum plenarium toftum in burgo meo de Hadingt'. Tenend*um* in liberam puram 7 perpetuam Elemosinam ita libere 7 Quiete plenarie 7 honorifice sicut alie domus relligiose tofta sua in aliis burgis meis liberius quiecius plenius 7 honorificencius tenent 7 possident. Test*ibus* H*ugone* Cancellario meo . Ric*ardo* de prebenda clerico meo . Walt*ero* capellano meo . Henric*o* de Graham . Adam Hasteng' . Bern*ardo* de Hauden' . Rob*erto* le Bastard'. Apud Seleschirc'.

ENDORSED. C. W. Reg*is* de j tofto in Hathyngton concess*o* monach*is* apud Cold' comorantibus (xv cent.). H. iij[a] . vj[te] (xv cent.).
DESCRIPTION. 6·9″ (17·6 cm.), Top, 7·0″ (17·8 cm.), Bottom × 3″ (7·6 cm.), L, 3·2″ (8·1 cm.), R. Foot folded 1·6″. Tie torn off. Double slits. Tag 7″ long, 0·5″ wide. Seal entire in natural wax, fair impression.
HAND. Scribe Db. Unruled.
SOURCE. Original, Durham, D. & C. Muniments, Misc. Chr. no.606.
PRINTED. Raine, *North Durham*, no.50.
NOTE. [a] Crossed tironian sign.
COMMENT. This toft was the subject of a lawsuit, prior and convent of Coldingham *versus* Robert Buring, to settle which a final concord was made before W. master of the nuns of Haddington (deputed by the abbot of Dunfermline) and David vicar of Haddington (deputed by the abbot of Holyrood), judges-delegate of the pope (Durham, D. & C. Muniments, Misc. Chr. no.1017). No.300 should probably have preceded this act.

370 Gives permission to the sick brethren (lepers) of St Nicholas's Hospital, St Andrews (Fife), to have one cart going to the King's Muir of Crail to fetch heath, whins etc. for the use of their house, in perpetuity. Forbids any of his bailies or sergeands of Crail to interfere with them in this matter. Crail. (1189 × 1195, perhaps *c.*1195)

Willelmus[a] Dei gr*aci*a rex Scotorum omnibus probis hominibus tocius terre sue, clericis et laicis, salutem. Sciant presentes et futuri me dedisse, concessisse et hac carta mea confirmasse Deo et infirmis fratribus hospitalis Sancti Nicholaii[b] de Sancto Andrea in liberam et puram et perpetuam elimosinam ut habeant unam quadrigam errantem ad bruariam in mora mea de Carell ad proprios usus domus sue imperpetuum, ita libere et quiete, plenarie et honorifice sicut alias elimosinas suas liberius, quiecius, plenius et honorificencius tenent et possident. Quare prohibeo firmiter ne quis balliuorum aut seruiencium meorum de Karell eos inde disturbare presumat. Testibus Hugone cancellario meo, Richardo de prebenda clerico meo, Radulph*o* [et][c] Waltero capellanis meis, Willelmo de Moreu*illa* const*abulario*, Malcolmo filio Comitis Dunec*ani*, Roberto de Berkell, Phillippo[b] de Lundye, Phillippo[b] Mariscallo. Apud Karell.

SOURCE. SRO, Registrum Magni Sigilli Regum Scotorum, Liber xxvii, no.222.
PRINTED. *RMS*, 1513–1546, no.2132 (1).
NOTES. [a] Punctuation editorial. [b] Sic. [c] Source omits.

371 Grants to Cambuskenneth Abbey the church of Kincardine in Menteith, Perthshire. Stirling. (1189 × 1195, probably 1193 × 1195)

Willelmus[a] Dei gracia rex Scotorum omnibus probis hominibus totius terre sue, clericis et laicis, salutem. Sciant presentes et futuri me dedisse et concessisse et hac carta mea confirmasse Deo et ecclesie Sancte Marie de Cambuskynneth et canonicis ibidem Deo seruientibus ecclesiam de Kyncardyn, cum capellis et terris, decimis et oblationibus omnimodis, et omnibus aliis iustis pertinenciis suis; tenendam in liberam et perpetuam elemosinam ita libere et quiete, plenarie et honorifice sicut alias ecclesias suas liberius et quietius, plenius et honorificentius tenent et possident. Testibus, Hugone cancellario meo, Com*ite* Patricio, Roll*ando* filio Uctred*i*, W.[b] de Lindesay, Ric*ardo* de Prebenda clerico meo, Rad*ulfo* et Waltero capellanis meis, Herberto marescallo, W*illelmo* de Passel*ew*, Ric*ardo* de Camera, apud Strivueling.

RUBRIC. Donatio ecclesie de Kincardin (at foot of fo.79v). Concordat cum principali Jacobus Foulis (at end).
SOURCE. NLS, MS. Adv. 34.1.2, fo.80r.
PRINTED. *Cambuskenneth Registrum*, no.121.
NOTES. [a] Large undecorated red initial U. [b] Read probably Willelmo.
COMMENT. See no.334, the king's infeftment of Richard de Montfiquet (Muschet) in Kincardine in Menteith, probably close in date to this act.

372 Grants to Cambuskenneth Abbey the church of Kincardine in Menteith, Perthshire, thirteen acres of arable, a brewer's toft with a garden, a toft for Saint Lolan's Bell with a garden, a toft for Saint Lolan's Staff with a garden, and the whole land between the well of 'Faylayat' on the east to the burn falling from 'Garthow' on the west, with meadow on each side as far as the muir of 'Lanpurry' and grazing for 13 cows in the Borland. (1189 × 1195) (Inflated)

Wilelmus[a] Dei gracia rex Scotorum omnibus probis hominibus totius terre sue clericis et laicis salutem. Sciant presentes et futuri me dedisse et concessisse et hac carta mea confirmasse Deo et ecclesie Sancte Marie de Cambuskynneth et canonicis ibidem Deo seruientibus et seruituris ecclesiam de Kincardin cum capellis et decimis et oblationibus omnimodis et tresdecim acras terre arabilis et unum toftum brasiatoris cum uno orto, et unum toftum ad campanam Sancti Lolani cum uno orto, et unum toftum ad baculum Sancti Lolani cum uno orto, et totam terram iacentem inter fontem Faylayat ex parte orientali ad riuulum descendentem de Garthow ex parte occidentali, cum prato ex utraque parte usque ad moram de Lanpurry, et herbagium ad tresdecem vaccas in[b] terra nostra de Borland et cum omnibus aliis iustis pertinenciis suis; tenendam et habendam in liberam et perpetuam elemosinam ita libere et quiete, plenarie et honorifice sicut alias ecclesias et terras suas liberius et quietius, plenius et honorificentius tenent et possident. Testibus, Hugone cancellario nostro, comes[c] etc.

RUBRIC. Donatio Wilelmi regis ecclesie Kyncardyn et terrarum (at top). Concordat cum principali Jacobus Foulis (at end).
SOURCE. NLS, MS. Adv. 34.1.2, fo.83^{r-v}.
PRINTED. *Cambuskenneth Registrum*, no.127.
NOTES. [a] Large undecorated red initial U. [b] Fo.83^{v}. [c] Sic.
COMMENT. This is almost certainly an inflated version of no.371, the phrase *terra nostra de Borland* being a particularly clumsy slip.

373 Confirms to Cambuskenneth Abbey the grant made by Walter son of Philip of Lundin of four oxgangs of arable and one full toft in the toun of Balcormo (in Largo), Fife, with common pasture for 500 sheep, 20 cows, one plough-team of oxen and for horses, and free of multure on the abbey's own land, as the charter of Walter bears witness. Stirling. (1189 × 1195)

Wilelmus[a] Dei gracia Rex Scotorum[b] omnibus probis hominibus tocius terre sue, clericis et laicis, salutem. Sciant presentes et futuri me concessisse et hac carta mea confirmasse Deo et ecclesie Sancte Marie de Striueling et canonicis ibidem Deo seruientibus donationem illam quam Walterus filius Philippi de Lundin eis fecit de quatuor bouatis terre cum uno plenario tofto in villa de Balcormac, cum communi pastura totius terre sue, ita quod ubicunque propria animalia ipsius Walteri siue hominum suorum pascunt habebunt predicti canonici pasturam, nominatim ad quingentas oues et ad viginti vaccas et ad unam carucatam boum et ad equos et ad cetera que ad hec pertinent; tenendam sibi de predicto Waltero et heredibus suis in liberam et quietam et perpetuam elemosinam cum propria multura dominii sui libera et quieta, ita libere et quiete, plenarie et honorifice sicut carta predicti Walteri testatur, saluo seruicio meo. Testibus, Comitibus[c] Gilleberto, Ricardo de Prebenda clerico meo, Roberto de Quenci, Philippo de Valoniis camerario meo, Alexandro vicecomite meo de Striueling, Philippo de Lundin, Rad*ulfo* de Camera, Ric*ardo* filio Hug*onis*, apud Striueling.

RUBRIC. Confirmatio Willelmi regis super predicta terra de Balcormok (at top). Concordat cum principali Jacobus Foulis (at end).
SOURCE. NLS, MS. Adv. 34.1.2, fos.28^{v}–29^{r}.
PRINTED. *Cambuskenneth Registrum*, no.38.
NOTES. [a] Blue initial U. [b] Fo.29^{r}. [c] Sic, for comite.
COMMENT. Walter of Lundin's charter is given in *Cambuskenneth Registrum*, no.36 (1178–9).

374 Informs his sheriffs and bailies of Galloway, Carrick and Lennox that he has heard the charters of King David I and King Malcolm IV anent the liberties granted to the bishops of Glasgow in dues and teinds belonging to them throughout the diocese of Glasgow; namely, that the bishops' sergeands ought to receive teinds and dues

granted by the king's predecessors just as the king's sergeands receive royal dues for the king's use. Commands them to allow the episcopal officers to receive these dues without obstruction. Stirling. (*c*.1193 × 1195)

Will*elmus* Dei gr*ati*a Rex Scott'. vicecom*itibus* et Balliuis suis de Galweia et Carrik. et Leuen' salutem. Sciatis quod audiui cartas Reg*is* Dauid aui mei et Cartas Reg*is* Malcolmi fratris mei super libertatibus concessis Episcopis Glasg*uensibus* de rectitudinibus et de decimis que ipsos contingent per episcopatum Glasguensem scilicet quod seruientes ipsorum debent recipere decimas et rectitudines ad prefatum episcopatum ex dono predictorum antecessorum meorum pertinentes per se sicut seruientes mei cana et rectitudines meas ad opus meum recipiunt. Quare precipio vobis firmiter quatinus eos ita recipere permittatis et eos inde non disturbetis super meam forisfacturam. Test*ibus* Roberto de Quinci. Philippo de Valon*iis* camerario. Alex*andro* vic*ecomite* de Striuelin. Willelmo de Munfort. Willelmo Cumin. Willelmo Giffard. apud Striuelin.

RUBRIC. De Decim*is* de cane per totum episcopatum Glasg*uensem* (in margin).
SOURCE. Blairs Archives, 16 Drummond Place, Edinburgh, MS. Registrum Vetus of Glasgow, fo.liiij[r].
PRINTED. *Glasgow Registrum*, no.25.
COMMENT. The date is after Philip de Valognes had succeeded Walter de Berkeley as chamberlain but before the day-of-the-month date had been introduced.

375 Grants to Roger de Mortemer the whole land of Fowlis Easter (Perthshire), in feu and heritage, with soke and sake, toll, team and infangthief, with pit and gallows, for the service of one knight. The king will warrant the land to Roger as that which he has granted him in return for his service. Clackmannan. (1195?)

.W. Dei gr*ati*a Rex Scott'. Episcopis. Abbatibus. Com*itibus*. Baronibus. Justic*iis*. Vicecomitibus. prepositis. ministris. et[a] Omnibus probis Hominibus totius terre sue clericis et laicis .˙. salutem. Sciant presentes et futuri me dedisse. et concessisse. et hac carta mea confirmasse. Rogero de Mortem*er*[b]. totam terram de F[uhles][c] in [Gouerin][d] per rectas diuisas suas. et cum omnibus iustis pertinentiis suis. Tenend*am* sibi. et heredibus suis. de me et heredibus meis. in feudo. et hereditate. in boscho et plano. in terris et aquis. in pratis et pascuis. in moris et maresiis. in stagnis et molendinis. et omnibus aliis ad predictam terram iuste pertinentibus. Cum socca. et sacca. cum furca. et fossa. cum tol. et them. et infangenethef'. libere. et quiete .˙. plenarie. et honorifice per seruicium unius militis. Ego autem et heredes mei. predictam terram predicto Roger*o*. et heredibus suis warentizabimus. sicut eam quam ei dedi pro seruicio suo. Test*ibus* Matheo Episcopo Aberdonen*se*. Com*ite* Dunecan*o*. Com*ite* Gilleb*erto*. Ricardo de prebenda. Philipp*o* de Valoniis Camerario meo. Willelmo Cumin. Johanne de Hasting'. Malisio fratre Com*itis* Gilleb*erti*. Malcolm*o* filio Com*itis* Dunecan*i*. Willelmo de Valon*iis*. D*aui*d de Haia. Alexand*ro* filio Thor'. apud Clacman*an*.

ENDORSED. Karta de Foules per W. Reg*em* (xiii cent.). King Williams charter of Frandie to Roger de Halden 1175 (xvii–xviii cent.).
DESCRIPTION. 7·7″ (19·5 cm.), Top, 7·4″ (18·9 cm.), Bottom × 3·3″ (8·5 cm.), L, 3·2″ (8·2 cm.), R. Foot folded to a depth of 0·5″ (1·3 cm.). Single slits with tag 5·5″ (14 cm.) long, 0·4″ (1·1 cm.) wide, split for seal. No seal, but traces of pink wax.
HAND. Scribe Dd. Unruled.
SOURCE. Original, SRO, GD 198/1.
PRINTED. J.A.L. Haldane, *The Haldanes of Gleneagles* (1929), 341–2 (with facsimile).
NOTES. [a] Scribe D employs crossed tironian sign throughout. [b] Originally written so; partly erased, with haden substituted in a later hand. [c] Supplied conjecturally by analogy with no.338. Letters have been erased and Frande substituted in a later hand. [d] Blackened and illegible; apparently Glendevin has been substituted for an original Gouerin.
COMMENT. This charter is discussed in J.A.L. Haldane, *The Haldanes of Gleneagles* (1929), 341–4, where there is an explanation of how it may have come to be tampered with to provide an ancestor for the family of Haldane of Gleneagles in the quite distinct and different family which took its name from Hadden in Roxburghshire.

376 Grants to May Priory Pitottar (in Anstruther Wester), Fife. Clackmannan. (17 April, 1195 × 1199, probably 1195)

W.[a] Dei gratia Rex Scott'[b] Episcopis, Abbatibus, Comitibus, Baronibus, Justic*iis*[c], Vicecomitibus, prepositis, ministris et omnibus probis hominibus totius terre sue, clericis et laicis, salutem. Sciant presentes et futuri me dedisse et concessisse et hac carta mea confirmasse Deo et ecclesie Sanctorum de Mai et monachis ibidem Deo seruientibus Petother per rectas diuisas suas cum omnibus justis pertinenciis suis. Tenend*um* in liberam et puram et perpetuam elemosinam, in terris et aquis, in pratis et pascuis, in moris et maresiis, et in omnibus aliis ad predictam terram iuste pertinentibus, ita libere, quiete, plenarie et honorifice sicut alias terras et elemosinas suas liberius, quiecius, plenius et honorificencius in regno meo tenent et possident. Test*ibus* Hug*one* Cancellario meo, Ricardo de Prebenda clerico meo, Rad*ulfo* et Waltero Capellanis meis, Phil*ippo* de Valon*iis* Camerario meo, Magistro Henr*ico* clerico meo, Willelmo de Haia, Alexandro Vic*ecomite* de Striuel*in*, Ric*ardo* fil*io* Hug*onis*, Willelmo Flandr*ensi*, Herberto de Camera. Apud Cla[c]m*anan*[d] .xvij. die April*is*.

TITLE. Carta Willelmi Regis de terra de Pethtoter.[e]
SOURCE. PRO, C. 53/93, rot. 13 (Charter Roll 35 Edward I) = *C*. *May Recs.*, p.cxiv = *M* (Title only).
PRINTED. *May Recs.*, no.15 (from *C*).
NOTES. [a] Willelmus, *May Recs.*, no.15. [b] Scotie, ibid. [c] Justiciariis, ibid. [d] Clam', *C*. [e] Title from *M* only.
COMMENT. King William fell ill at Clackmannan in 1195 (*Chron. Howden*, iii, 298).

377 Confirms to William son of Alexander the grant made to him by Richard de Montfiquet (Muschet) of a half-ploughgate in Whitefield (in Cargill), Perthshire, with one oxgang perambulated for him and one toft beside Layston between the burn and the moor as the burn falls, and one toft and croft between the castle and the church of

Cargill; to be held of Richard in feu and heritage, as Richard's charter bears witness, saving the king's service. Stirling. (5 May, 1195 × 1199, probably 1195)

W. Dei gr*ati*a Rex Scott'. Omnibus probis Hominibus totius terre sue clericis et laicis :' Salutem. Sciant presentes et futuri me concessisse et hac carta mea confirmasse Willelmo filio Alexand*ri* illam dimidiam carrucatam terre in Withefeld' . cum communi pastura que ad terram illam pertinet . quam Ric*ardus* de Munfiched' ei pro seruicio suo dedit . cum una bouata terre ei perambulata . 7 cum uno masuagio iuxta Lesingestune . inter riuulum et moram . sicut riuulus descendit . 7 cum uno tofto et Crofto . inter castellum 7 ecclesiam de Kergille. Tenend*um* sibi 7 heredibus suis de predicto Ricardo et heredibus suis in feudo et hereditate . ita libere [et][a] quiete . plenarie . et honorifice :' sicut Carta prenominati Ricardi testatur . saluo seruicio meo. T[estibus Hug*one*][a] Cancellario meo . Rob*erto* de Quinci . Philippo de Valon*iis* . Camerario meo . Rob*erto* de London*iis* filio meo . Rogero de Mortem*er* . Alex*andro* vicecomite meo de Striueli*n*. apud Striueli*n* .v. die Maij

ENDORSED. Confirmacio de [ ] lstun (xvi cent., barely legible).
DESCRIPTION. 6·5″ (16·5 cm.), Top, 6·6″ (16·7 cm.), Bottom × 3·2″ (8·1 cm.), L, 3·0″ (7·6 cm.), R. Foot folded, slits for seal-tag. Tag, 0·5″ wide, remains, with large fragment of seal in natural wax with a slightly pink tinge, obv. to front, 30° to right of vertical, maximum diameter 2·9″. No legend visible.
HAND. Scribe De (William de Boscho?). Unruled.
SOURCE. Original, Kinnoull Trustees Muniments, Dupplin Charters, no.119.
NOTE. [a]Parchment torn; supplied conjecturally.
COMMENT. Richard de Montfiquet's charter survives (Dupplin Charters no.121) with a fine equestrian seal in green wax; witnessed by, *inter alios*, Richard de Montfiquet the granter's nephew and Thomas de Montfiquet. It stipulates for the service of the tenth part of half a knight. Layston is in Cargill. The half plough granted may be represented by Hatton, between Layston and Mains of Cargill. See no.334.

378 Confirms to Paisley Priory (afterwards Abbey) the land of Moniabrock in Strathgryfe (in Lochwinnoch, Renfrewshire), granted by Alan son of Walter, with the marches specified in Alan's charter; along with half a fishery at the mouth of Lochwinnoch, with liberty to fish in the loch as often as Alan himself does; as his charter bears witness. Clackmannan. (25 May, 1195 × 1199, probably 1195)

Wilelmus Dei gratia rex Scottorum omnibus probis hominibus tocius terre sue, clericis et laicis, salutem. Sciant presentes et futuri me concessisse et hac carta mea confirmasse Deo et ecclesie Sancte Marie et Sanctorum Jacobi et Mirini de Passelet, et monachis ibidem Deo servientibus, terram de Moniabrok in Stragriff, quam Alanus filius Walteri eis dedit, per easdem rectas divisas que scripte sunt et nominate in carta predicti Alani; tenendam in liberam et perpetuam elemosinam, cum dimidia piscatura in exitu lacus[a] de Loucwynhok, et cum libertate piscandi in ipso lacu de Loucwynhok quociens ipse Alanus ibi piscari faciet[b], et cum omnibus aisiamentis prescripte terre ita libere, quiete, plenarie et honorifice sicut alias elemosinas suas liberius, quiecius, plenius et honorificencius tenent et possident, et sicut carta predicti Alani testatur, salvo servicio meo. Testibus Hugone cancellario meo,

Philippo de Valon*iis* camerario, Roberto de Londoniis[c] filio meo, Wilelmo de Haia, Wilelmo Gyffard, Alexandro vicecomite de Streuleyn, Wilelmo Flandre*nsi*, Henrico de Graham, Henrico de Cormannok, Philippo de Lundin,[d] apud Clacmannan, vicesimo quinto die Maii.

RUBRIC. Confirmatio Wilelmi regis Scocie de Moniabrok et de piscatura Loucwynhok (at top).
SOURCE. NLS, MS. Adv. 34.4.14, fo.cliii^{v}.
PRINTED. *Paisley Registrum*, 253.
NOTES. [a] MS., laci. [b] MS., facie. [c] MS., Londe. [d] MS., Lundun.
COMMENT. Alan the steward's charter is given in *Paisley Registrum*, 13–14. The loch here called Lochwinnoch is now called Castle Semple Loch.

379 Confirms to Kelso Abbey the gift and concession made by Jocelin bishop of Glasgow of the churches which the abbey has within the diocese of Glasgow by the reasonable grant of their patrons, viz. the churches and schools of the burgh of Roxburgh, granted by Herbert bishop of Glasgow; the church of Maxwell with the chapel of Harlaw, according to the agreement between the monks of Kelso and the lepers of Harlaw; the following churches: Sprouston, Mow, Bowden, Selkirk and 'the other Selkirk', Dumfries, Lesmahagow, Kilmaurs, West Linton, Innerleithen, Wiston with its two chapels, viz. Roberton and Crawford John, Thankerton, Symington, Cambusnethan, Dunsyre, Campsie, Antermony, Staplegorton, Drumgrey, Traillflat and Morton, with all their chapels and other rightful pertinents. These are confirmed to Kelso abbey with their rectorial rights for the monks' own use and for their support, as the charter of Bishop Jocelin and the charters of the patrons bear witness. Jedburgh. (4 July, 1195)

W. Dei gr*ati*a Rex Scott'[a] . Episcopis . Abbatibus . Com*itibus* . Baronibus . Justic*iis* . Vicecom*itibus* . Prepositis . Ministris . 7 Omnibus probis hominibus tocius terre sue clericis 7 laicis . salutem. Sciant presentes 7 futuri me concessisse 7 hac carta mea confirmasse . Deo 7 Ecclesie Sancte Marie de Kelch' . 7 monachis ibidem Deo seruientibus in liberam 7 perpetuam elemosinam donacionem 7 concessionem . quam Joc*elinus* Glasguensis episcopus eis fecit de Ecclesiis quas habent in episcopatu Glasg*uensi* . que eis racionabiliter date sunt 7 concesse ab aduocatis ecclesiarum illarum . ut idem monachi habeant . Ecclesias illas . videlicet . Ecclesias 7 Scolas burgi de Rok' . liberas 7 quietas ab omni consuetudine . s*cilicet* ab omni redditu Sinodi . 7 ab omnibus auxiliis . hospiciis . 7 corrediis . sicut bone memorie Herb*ertus* Glasguensis Episcopus eisdem[b] monachis carta sua confirmauit. Et preterea Ecclesiam de Maccuswell' . 7 capellam de Harelawe . sicut inter ipsos monachos . 7 leprosos predicti loci de ipsa capella conuenit. Ecclesiam de Sproueston'. Ecclesiam de Molle. Ecclesiam de Botheldene. Ecclesiam de Selechirc'. Ecclesiam de alia Selechir'. Ecclesiam de Dunfres. Ecclesiam de Lesmahag'. Ecclesiam de Kilmaurum. Ecclesiam de Lintunrotheri. Ecclesiam de Inuerlethan. Ecclesiam de uilla Wice cum duabus capellis suis . scilicet uille Roberti fratris Lambini . 7 uille Johannis priuigni Baldwini. Ecclesiam de Wdekirke. Ecclesiam de uilla Symonis Loccard. Ecclesiam de Cambusneithan. Ecclesiam de Dunsier. Ecclesiam de Camsy. Ecclesiam de Altermunin. Ecclesiam de Stapilgortun'. Ecclesiam de Dungrey.

Ecclesiam de Trauerflat' . 7 Ecclesiam de Mortun' . cum omnibus predictarum ecclesiarum capellis 7 aliis iustis pertinenciis suis. Prenominatas autem Ecclesias 7 capellas . 7 omnes earum obuenciones cum terris 7 decimis . 7 omnibus earum iustis pertinenciis 7 rectitudinibus . 7 personatum earundem Ecclesiarum prelibate Ecclesie de Kelch' . 7 propriis usibus . 7 sustentacionibus monachorum ibidem Deo seruiencium concedo . 7 presenti carta confirmo. Quare 7 precipio ∴ ut predicti monachi habeant . teneant . 7 pacifice possideant predictas ecclesias 7 earum capellas cum omnibus iustis pertinenciis suis . in liberam 7 perpetuam elemosinam . ita libere . quiete . plenarie . 7 honorifice sicut carta predicti Joc*elini* Glasg*uensis* Episcopi eis concedit . 7 sicut carte aduocatorum prescriptarum ecclesiarum testantur. T*estibus* Hug*one* cancell*ario* meo . Regin*aldo* Electo Rosen*si* . Rob*erto* de Quinci . Rob*erto* de Lond*oniis* fil*io* meo . Seihero de Quinci . Willelmo de Haia. Apud Jedd' .iiij. die Julii.

RUBRIC. Confirmacio super Ecclesias nostras in Episcopatu Glasguensi (top in red).
SOURCE. NLS, MS. Adv. 34.5.1, fo.150^{r-v}.
PRINTED. *Kelso Liber*, no.409.
NOTES. [a] Rex Scott' follows W. immediately and is marked for transposition by two pairs of diagonal strokes. [b] Fo.150^{v}.
COMMENT. Most of these churches are dealt with in *OPS*, i. The church of 'the other Selkirk' was evidently the church of what later came to be known as Selkirk Regis; but there was only one parish church of Selkirk by the end of the medieval period. Kilmaurs is in Cunningham, and was granted to Kelso by Robert son of Werenbald (*Kelso Liber*, no.283). Drumgrey was a parish in Annandale, now suppressed, adjacent to Garvald (represented by Dumgree in Kirkpatrick); Trailflat, also suppressed, is in Tinwald parish. These were granted by Walcher de Chartres (ibid., no.344). Morton in Nithsdale was granted by Hugh Sansmanche (*sine manicis*). The date is fixed by the attestation of Reginald as bishop-elect of Ross.

380

Informs his sheriff of Berwick and men of Lothian and the Merse that he has permitted the prior of Coldingham to move his tenants of Coldinghamshire into the toun of Coldingham to increase its population. Selkirk. 17 July (1195?)

.W'. Dei gr*ati*a Rex Scott' Vic*ecomiti* suo de Berewic 7 omnibus probis Hominibus suis de Laodonia 7 de Merskes . Salutem. Sciatis me concessisse . .[a] Priori de Coldigham quod remoueat homines suos de Coldighamsciria ad uillam de Coldingh*am* hospitandam quos de iure remouere poterit. Quare prohibeo firmiter nequis predictum priorem iniuste disturbet omnes illos remouere ad prefatam uillam hospitandam ∴ quos de iure remouere poterit 7 debebit. T*estibus* Hug*one* Cancellario meo . Ricardo de prebenda clerico meo Apud Selechirch'. xvij. die Julii[b].

ENDORSED. C.W.Reg*is* de libera ammotione hominum de Coldinghamschyre (xiii cent.). ad villam de Coldyngh' hospitand*am* (xiv–xv cent.). X. iij^{a} vj^{te} (xv cent.).
DESCRIPTION. 6·5″ (16·4 cm.), Top and bottom × 3·3″ (8·4 cm.), L, 2·5″ (6·4 cm.), R. Tie complete, cut from foot. Tongue torn off. Seal detached on piece of tongue 0·5″ wide; in natural wax, three-quarters complete, rather rubbed; formerly attached back to front. HAND. Scribe Da. Unruled.

SOURCE. Original, Durham, D. & C. Muniments, Misc. Chr. no.588.
PRINTED. Raine, *North Durham*, no.49.
NOTES. [a] Space left between full points in substitution for initial. [b] Julii written at end of line, with a wavy horizontal line connecting it to die.

381 Confirms to Kelso Abbey the church of Langton, Berwickshire, granted by William de Vieuxpont, as William's charter bears witness. Selkirk. (29 July, 1195)

Will*elmu*s Dei gr*ati*a Rex Scott' . Omnibus probis hominibus tocius terre sue clericis 7 laicis salutem. Sciant presentes 7 futuri me concessisse 7 hac carta mea confirmasse Deo 7 Ecclesie Sancte Marie de Kelchou 7 monachis ibidem Deo seruientibus donacionem illam quam Willelmus de Veteri Ponte eis fecit de Ecclesia de Langtune . Tenendam sibi in liberam 7 puram 7 perpetuam elemosinam cum terris 7 decimis 7 omnibus aliis ad predictam ecclesiam iuste pertinentibus ita libere 7 quiete . plenarie 7 honorifice . sicut alias ecclesias suas liberius . quiecius plenius 7 honorificencius tenent 7 possident 7 sicut carta prefati Willelmi testatur . per diuisas terre quam predictus Willelmus eidem ecclesie dedit nominatas in carta ipsius . saluo seruicio meo si quod seruicium me contingere debet de terris ab eodem Willelmo datis prefate ecclesie. Test*ibus* Hug*one* Cancell*ario* meo . Com*ite* Patric*io* Justic*ia* . Roberto de Quinci . Roberto de London*iis* fil*io* meo . Alano fil*io* Walteri . Willelmo de Haia . Ric*ardo* fil*io* Hug*onis* . Willelmo Flandr*ensi*. Apud Selechirch' .xxix. die . Julii.

RUBRIC. Confirmacio super Ecclesiam de Langtune (top in red).
SOURCE. NLS, MS. Adv. 34.5.1, fo.56^{r}.
PRINTED. *Kelso Liber*, no.144.
COMMENT. The church of Langton was first granted to Kelso, apparently before 1152, by Roger de Eu (*Kelso Liber*, no.138), and was again granted, without any mention of the earlier grant, by William de Vieuxpont, *c.*1190 (ibid., no.142). It is this second grant which King William confirms above.

382 Confirms to Melrose Abbey the land (of Raeshaw) granted by William son of John within the feu of Hownam, Roxburghshire, as the charter of the donor bears witness. Selkirk. (31 August, 1195 × 1198)

Will*el*mus[a] Dei gr*ati*a rex Scott'[b] episcopis, abbatibus, comitibus, baronibus, just*iciis*, vicecomitibus, prepositis, ministris[c] et omnibus probis hominibus tocius terre sue, clericis et laicis, salutem. Sciant presentes et futuri me concessisse et hac mea carta confirmasse donacionem illam quam Willelmus filius Johannis fecit Deo et ecclesie Sancte Marie de Melros et monachis ibidem Deo seruientibus de tota terra illa infra feudum de Hunum, a riuulo de Cuidenop[d] sursum per totam semitam illam usque ad fossatum inter Raschahe[e] et Cudbrihteshope[f], et ab inde per easdem rectas diuisas que continentur in carta predicti Willelmi filii Johannis, et cum omnibus iustis suis pertinenciis. Tenend*am* in liberam et perpetuam elemosinam, in bosco et plano, in pratis et pascuis, in aquis et omnibus aliis asiamentis, ita libere, quiete, plenarie et honorifice sicut carta prenominati Willelmi filii Johannis testatur, saluo seruicio meo. Teste Jocelino episcopo Glasg*uensi*, Com*ite* Patricio, Philip*po* de Val*oniis* camerario meo, Rob*erto* de Quinci,

Willelmo de Lindes', Geruasio Auenil, Johanne de Hasting', Willelmo Cumin, Thom*a* de Coleuill', Henr*ico* Biset, Alexandro de Sintun, Willelmo de Heriz[g], Philippo de Lundin. Apud Selechirche[h], ultimo die Augusti.

RUBRIC. Confirmacio Regis Willelmi de Rasawe. xxxij.
SOURCE. NLS, MS. Adv. 34.4.11, fos.viii^v–ix^r = *A*. BM, MS. Harl. 3960, fo.13^r = *H*. Printed here from *A* with variants of *H* noted.
PRINTED. *Melrose Liber*, no.132.
NOTES. [a] Initial green, A; red U, *H*. [b] Scot', *H*. [c] Fo.ix^r, *A*. [d] Apparently Cnidenop, *H*, but Cuidenop, Cuithenop elsewhere in same MS., fos.12, 13. [e] Raschaw', *H*. [f] Cudbrihteshop', *H*. [g] Herise, *H*. [h] Selekirke, *H*.
COMMENT. The charter of William son of John (grandson of Orm son of Eilaf, and lord of Hownam) is given in *Melrose Liber*, no.131, dating 1185 × 1199. It makes mention of William's wife Dunantia de Clerefei, presumably a relative of William de Clerfai well-known in south Yorkshire in the twelfth century (Dugdale, *Mon. Angl.* (New), v, 486; J. Hunter, *South Yorkshire*, i (1828), 333; John of Hexham in *Priory of Hexham* (Surtees Soc.), i, 134–5). One Clerfai was 'at Leicester with the king's enemies', perhaps with David of Scotland, in 1174 (*Pipe Roll* 20 *Henry II*, 104). The name Raeshaw is now represented by Raeshaw or Rushy Fell, on the southern edge of Hownam parish and on the Anglo-Scottish Border. 'Cuidenop' seems to be obsolete, but may have been the name of either the Capehope Burn or the Yett Burn. Cuthberthope (Rig) survives, and the marches of Raeshaw coincided with the Border from about Raeshaw Fell to Dere Street, and with Dere Street northward to the lands of Chatto.

383

Confirms to David de la Hay, son of William de la Hay, Errol, Perthshire by its right marches, to be held with sake and soke, pit and gallows, toll, team and infangthief, for the service of two knights. Jedburgh. (17 September, 1195 or 1196, probably 1195)

W'. Dei gr*atia* Rex Scott' . Episcopis . Abbatibus . Com*itibus* . Baron*ibus* . Just*iciis* . Vicecom*itibus* . Prepositis . Ministris . 7 Omnibus probis hominibus tocius terre sue Clericis 7 laicis Salutem. Sciant presentes 7 futuri me concessisse 7 hac Carta mea confirmasse . D*aui*d de Haia fil*io* Willelmi de Haia Herol . per rectas diuisas suas . 7 cum omnibus iustis pertinenciis suis. Tenend*am* sibi 7 heredibus suis de me 7 heredibus meis in feudo 7 hereditate in Boscho 7 plano . in terris 7 aquis . in pratis 7 pascuis . in moris 7 maresiis . in stangnis 7 molendinis . in viuariis 7 Piscariis . 7 omnibus aliis ad predictam terram iuste pertinentibus. Cum socco 7 sacca . cum furca 7 fossa . cum Tol . 7 Them . 7 infangenthef . libere 7 Quiete plenarie . 7 Honorifice per seruicium duorum militum. Quare uolo 7 firmiter precipio . ut prefatus D*aui*d 7 heredes sui prenominatam terram de Herol . teneant . 7 possideant de me 7 heredibus meis ita libere 7 Quiete . plenarie . 7 honorifice ∴ sicut alii Barones mei feuda sua liberius . Quiecius . plenius . 7 honorificencius tenent . 7 sicut Carta mea patri suo facta testatur. Test*ibus* Jocelino Glasg*uensi* episcopo . Hug*one* Cancellario meo . Radulfo .[a] Waltero Capellanis meis . Com*ite* Patric*io* . Com*ite* Dunec*ano* . Will*elmo* de Moreuill' Const*abulario* . Rob*erto* de Quinci . Philipp*o* de Valon*iis* Camerario . Alano fil*io* Walt*eri* Dapifero . D*aui*d de Valon*iis* . Henr*ico* de Grah*am* . Rob*erto* de Landel' . Thom*a* Tancard' . Ada*m* fil*io* Gilleb*erti* . Will*elmo* Flandr*ensi* . Thom*a* de uilla Colban*i* . Rog*ero* de la Kerneil' . Herbert*o* Marescall*o*. Apud Jedde'. xvij. die . Septembr*is*.

ENDORSED. De Erol' (xiii–xiv cent.). Chartour be W[m] King of Scotland To David Hay of Eroll of the lands of Erroll (xvi–xvii cent.). Also three distinct modern endorsements.
DESCRIPTION. 9·4″ (23·9 cm.), Top, 8·8″ (22·4 cm.), Bottom × 5·8″ (14·5 cm.), L, 5·4″ (12·75 cm.), R. Foot folded to a depth of 0·7″ (1·9 cm.). Double slits for seal-tag. The remains of the seal are affixed not to a parchment tag but to a handsome ribbon of woven silk, 0·7″ (1·9 cm.) wide; for a description of this, see above p.93. Only the central fragment of the seal remains, badly defaced, diameter 2″.
HAND. Scribe De (William de Boscho?). Unruled.
SOURCE. Original, Countess of Erroll, Erroll Charters no.6.
PRINTED. *Spalding Misc.*, ii, 304–5, no.IV.
NOTE. [a] Sic.
COMMENT. This grant was evidently made while David de la Hay's father was still alive; but there is no surviving record of William de la Hay's resigning Errol.

384 Confirms to Coupar Angus Abbey the land of Carsegrange (in Errol), Perthshire, granted by William de la Hay and confirmed by his son David. Kinghorn. 4 January (1195 × 1214, possibly 1196)

This Confirmation of Dauid del Hayes of the lands of Ederpolls monachis de Cupro is confirmed be K*ing* William. Apud Kingorn, iiii Januarii.

SOURCE. NLS, MS. Adv. 33.2.9, fo.33[v].
PRINTED. *Coupar Angus Rental*, i, 338, no.49.
COMMENT. See no.322. This may belong to a later year.

385 Confirms to the sick brethren (lepers) of St Nicholas's Hospital, St Andrews, the land of 'Putekin' (Buddo(?) in St Andrews and St Leonards), Fife, granted to them by Roger bishop-elect of St Andrews. Kinghorn. (16 February, 1195 or 1196)

Willelmus[a] Dei gr*ati*a Rex Scotorum omnibus probis hominibus tocius terre sue, clericis et laicis, salutem. Sciant presentes et futuri me concessisse et hac presenti carta mea confirmasse infirmis fratribus hospitalis Sancti Nicholai apud Sanctumandream totam terram de Putekin, quam Rogerus electus Sanctiandree eisdem infirmis fratribus dedit per rectas diuisas suas; tenend*am* in liberam et puram et perpetuam elemosinam, in moris et mossis et marresiis, in aquis et molendinis, et in omnibus aliis asiamentis et iustis pertinenciis suis, ita libere, quiete, plenarie et honorifice sicut carta predicti electi testatur, saluo seruicio meo. Testibus comite Dauid fratre meo, Hugone cancellario meo, Phillippo[b] de Valon*iis* camerario meo, Willelmo de Haia, Willelmo Giffart, Dunecano de Syreis, Dunecano de Lassallas[b], Herberto mariscallo. Apud Kinghorn', decimo sexto die Februarii.

SOURCE. SRO, Registrum Magni Sigilli Regum Scotorum, Liber xxvii, no.222.
PRINTED. *RMS*, 1513–1546, no.2132 (2).
NOTES. [a] Punctuation editorial. [b] Sic.
COMMENT. Peekie appears as Pukie in the map of Fife in Blaeu's Atlas (1654). Putekin was no doubt the Puttechin of *RRS*, i, no.174, which was identified in the index as Buddo. Probably this identification is correct, and the place is to be distinguished from Peekie, formerly Petkinnin. Cf. no.347.

386 Confirms to Melrose Abbey Hartside and Spott, granted and confirmed by the earls of Dunbar Cospatric III, Waltheof and Patrick I, by the right marches between the monks' land and Stenton; with common pasture of the moor for three flocks of wethers with 500 in each flock. Confirms also those five acres on the south side of 'Mosiburnerig' added by Earl Patrick so that the monks may enclose them with a ditch to make a sheep fold for the flocks. Confirms also whatever right Earl Patrick or his heirs or vassals might have had in the meadowland which the monks of Melrose hold of the knights of Alan son of Walter in the feu of Innerwick below 'Brunrig'. Berwick. (16 April, 1195 or 1196, probably 1196)

W'. Dei gr*ati*a Rex Scott'. Omnibus probis hominibus Tocius terre sue clericis 7 laicis Salutem. Sciant presentes 7 futuri me concessisse . 7 hac Carta mea confirmasse Deo 7 ecclesie Sancte Marie . de Melros . 7 monachis ibidem Deo seruientibus donacionem illam quam Auus 7 pater Comitis Patric*ii* 7 Comes Patricius eis fecerunt . de Hertesheued' . 7 de Spot .' per rectas diuisas predictarum terrarum . inter predictos monachos 7 SteintuN . quas habuerunt temporibus aui 7 patris predicti Comit*is* Patr*icii* . 7 que nominantur in confirmacione prefati Com*itis* Patric*ii* . in Boscho . 7 Plano . in pratis . 7 pascuis . 7 omnibus aliis ad predictas terras iuste pertinentibus. Et preterea cum communi pastura de mora . ad tres greges arietum . ita ut unusquisque Grex contineat . Quingentos arietes . cum aisiamentis eiusdem more. Preterea . concedo 7 hac Carta mea confirmo . prefatis monachis illas Quinque Acras terre . quas prefatus Com*es* Patric*ius* eis dedit in incrementum in Australi parte de Mosiburnerig . ut includant eas fossato ad faciend*am* Berkariam ad prefatos tres greges arietum . 7 illis Quinque acris terre utentur sicut melius eis uisum fuerit . ita tamen ut eas non colant. Et preterea . quicquid iuris prefatus Com*es* Patric*ius* uel heredes sui uel homines sui habebant uel habere poterant de communi in prato illo quod prefati monachi tenent . de militibus Alani filii Walteri in feudo de Inuerwic' subtus Brunrig que prefatus Comes Patric*ius* prefatis monachis concessit . 7 carta sua confirmauit. Tenend' in liberam 7 puram 7 perpetuam elemosinam ita libere . 7 quiete . plenarie 7 honorifice . sicut Carta prefati Comit*is* Patr*icii* Testatur . Saluo seruicio meo. Test*ibus* Hug*one* Cancell*ario* meo . Willelmo de Moruill' const*abulario* . Philipp*o* de Valon*iis* Cam*erario* . Willelmo CumiN . Johanne de Hasting' . Ric*ardo* Marescall*o* . Rob*erto* de Burneuill' . D*aui*d de Haia . Rob*erto* de Moruill'. Apud Berewic' .xvi. die April*is*.

ENDORSED. [ ][a] Will' Regis de Hert [ ][a] et Spot secundum cartam Comitis Patricii (xii–xiii cent.). Lammermure (xv cent.). Confirmacio Regis Wilelmi super terris de Spot et Ha[ ][a] cum pastura de Lammermure (xvi cent.). J. Scott (xvi cent.).

DESCRIPTION. 9·3″ (23·7 cm.), Top, 9″ (23 cm.), Bottom × 6·3″ (15·8 cm.), L, 6″ (15·2 cm.), R. Foot folded to a depth of 0·9″ (2·4 cm.). Double slits in foot and fold, with tag 6·7″ (17 cm.) long, 0·6″ (1·5 cm.) wide. Seal almost complete, in natural wax, diameter 3·2″ (8 cm.).

HAND. Scribe De (William de Boscho?). Unruled.

SOURCE. Original, SRO, GD 55/57.

PRINTED. *Melrose Liber*, no.57. NOTE. [a] Illegible.

COMMENT. 'Mosiburnerig' was presumably above the Mossy Burn, partly in Spott and partly in Stenton parishes, East Lothian. For King Malcolm IV's confirmations, see *RRS*, i, nos.132, 133. The word *aries* used in this charter and in Earl Patrick's own grant (*Melrose Liber*, no.56), presumably means 'wether' rather than 'ram'.

387 Commands that wherever the prior of Lesmahagow or his sergeand bearing this brieve may find neyfs and fugitives of Lesmahagow, outwith the king's demesnes, he is to have them justly, and no one is to detain them unjustly on pain of the king's full forfeiture. Restalrig. (6 May, 1195 × 1207)

W. Dei gr*ati*a Rex Scott' . Omnibus probis hominibus tocius terre clericis 7 laicis . salutem. Mando 7 firmiter precipio . quatinus ubicunque Prior de Lesmahag*u* uel eius seruiens presentis lator . Natiuos homines suos 7 fugitiuos de Lesmahag*u* extra dominia mea inuenerit :' eos iuste habeat. Et prohibeo firmiter ne quis aliquem eorum ei iniuste detineat . super meam plenariam forisfacturam. Test*ibus* Rob*erto* de Quenci . Waltero de Sancto Albano capellano meo. Apud Lastalric' . vj°. die Maii.

RUBRIC. Carta super Natiuos Homines 7 fugitiuos de Lesmahag*u* (top in red).
SOURCE. NLS, MS. Adv. 34.5.1, fo.148^{v}.
PRINTED. *Kelso Liber*, no.402.
COMMENT. This brieve gives us a surname for the king's chaplain Walter, who became bishop of Glasgow in 1208. It may be noted that Bishop Walter had clerks named Master Robert of St Albans and Robert of Hertford, parson of Castleton (*Glasgow Registrum*, i, 97, 100, 106, 123, 129–30).

388 Grants to Geoffrey *Blundus* his burgess of Inverness and his heirs, and to all his burgesses of Inverness and their heirs, the liberty in perpetuity of never engaging in trial by combat among themselves. No burgess from elsewhere, nor any man in the whole realm, may compel any of the king's burgesses of Moray to undergo trial by combat but only to undergo trial by oath (compurgation). The king's burgesses of Moray are to offer only half the oath [i.e., an oath sworn by only half the number of compurgators?] and to incur only half the penalty offered and incurred by the other burgesses of the realm. They are to be free from toll throughout the realm in perpetuity. Elgin. (2 May, 1196 or 1197)

Willelmus Dei gratia Rex Scottorum omnibus probis hominibus tocius terre sue clericis et laicis salutem. Sciatis nos dedisse concessisse et hac presenti carta mea confirmasse Gaufrido Blundo burgensi nostro de Inuernys et heredibus suis et omnibus burgensibus nostris de Inuernys et heredibus eorum perpetuam libertatem quod nunquam inter eos bellum habebunt nec aliquis alius burgensis nec aliquis alius homo de toto regno nostro super eosdem burgenses nostros de Moravia nec super heredes eorum bellum habebunt nisi tantum juramentum. Preterea concessi eisdem burgensibus meis de Moravia et heredibus eorum ut dimidium juramentum et dimidiam forisfacturam faciant quod ceteri burgenses mei faciunt in toto regno meo et quieti erunt de tolleneto per totum regnum meum in perpetuum. Teste David comite fratre meo . [Duncano] Comite de Fife justiciario Scotie . Gilberto Comite de Stradhern . Hugone Cancellario . Joanne de Asting . Philippo de Valloniis . Willelmo Cumyn . Petro de Pollok . Willelmo filio Freskin . Hugone filio suo et Willelmo filio eius. Apud Elgin die secundo Maii.

SOURCE. *APS*, i, 89. No trace of this has been found in the Inverness burgh muniments. PRINTED. As above.
COMMENT. The plural style is used in the first dispositive clause, the singular

in the second. This is curious, but hardly enough to cast doubt on the authenticity of the act. Count Baldwin VII of Flanders freed the burgesses of Ypres from trial by combat in 1116, substituting compurgation (*juramentum*) with four oath-helpers. In 1127 Count William of Flanders, in a grant of privileges to the burgesses of St Omer, ordained that if anyone brought a charge against them in any market of Flanders they should submit themselves to the judgement of the *èchevins* without combat, from which they were to be completely free. See F. Vercauteren, *Actes des comtes de Flandre*, 1071–1128 (Commission royale d'histoire, Brussels, 1938), nos.79, 127. The Moray liberty seems to resemble these Flemish exemptions rather more closely than the English exemptions, which may be studied in A. Ballard, *British Borough Charters*, 133–4.

Earl David was in Normandy on 1 September, 1197.

Geoffrey Blundus was the name of a citizen of London in the household of William Longchamp, chancellor of Richard I, in 1190 (J.H. Round, *Commune of London* (1899), 253–4).

389 Grants to Melrose Abbey one full toft in his burgh of Lanark. Perth. (1 June, 1196 × 1199)

W'. Dei gr*ati*a Rex Scott'. Omnibus probis Hominibus Totius terre sue Clericis et Laicis Salutem. Sciant presentes et futuri me dedisse et concessisse et Hac carta mea confirmasse Deo et Ecclesie Sancte Marie de Melros . et monachis ibidem Deo seruientibus unum plenarium Toftum in Burgo meo de Lanarc. Tenend*um* in liberam et puram et perpetuam Elemosinam . ita libere Quiete Plenarie et Honorifice ;' Sicut alias Elemosinas suas ;' liberius . Quietius . Plenius et Honorificentius ;' tenent . et possident. Test*ibus* Hug*one* Cancell*ario* meo . Philippo de Valoin' Camerario . Ric*ardo* de prebenda . Willelmo de Haia . Willelmo Giffard' . Dunec*ano* de Laceles. Apud Pert Primo die Junii.

ENDORSED. De Tofto in Lann' [W'][a] R*egis* (xii–xiii cent.). Lanarch (xv cent.). J. Scott (xvi–xvii cent.). O (Large capital, indeterminate date prior to xvi cent.). Also modern endorsements.

DESCRIPTION. 5·5″ (14·2 cm.), Top and bottom × 2·6″ (6·6 cm.), L, R. Foot-folded to a depth of 0·8″ (1·9 cm.). Double slits in foot and fold, but neither tag nor seal remains.

HAND. Scribe Df. Unruled.

SOURCE. Original, BM, Cotton Chr. xviii, 16.

PRINTED. *Melrose Liber*, no.78.

NOTE. [a] Illegible, supplied conjecturally.

390 Confirms to Alexander son of Philip of Seton the land which belonged to his father Philip, viz. Seton, Winton (East Lothian) and Winchburgh (West Lothian), to be held in feu and heritage, with sake and soke, toll, team and infangthief, pit and gallows, for the service of one knight. Forfar. (16 June, 1196)

W'. Dei gr*ati*a Rex Scott' Episcopis Abbatibus Com*itibus* Baron*ibus* Justic*iis* vicecom*itibus* prepositis ministris 7 omnibus probis hominibus terre sue Clericis et Laicis Salutem. Sciant[a] presentes 7 futuri me concessisse 7 hac carta mea confirmasse Alexandro filio Philippi de Setune terram que fuit Philippi patris sui scilicet Setune 7 Wintune 7 Wincelburg' Tenend*am* sibi 7 heredibus suis de me 7 heredibus meis in feudo 7 hereditate in Boscho 7 plano in terris 7 aquis in pratis 7 pascuis in moris 7 maresiis in stagnis et molendinis per rectas diuisas[b] predictarum terrarum 7[c] cum omnibus aliis ad prefatas terras juste pertinentibus cum socca 7 sacca cum tol 7 them 7 infangenthef cum furca 7 ffossa[d] libere 7 quiete plenarie et honorifice per seruicium unius militis sicut carta mea patri suo inde facta testatur. Test*ibus* Hug*one* Cancellario meo Willelmo de Moreu*ille* Const*abulario* Rob*erto* de Quinci Alano fil*io* Walt*eri* Dapif*ero* Philippo de [Va]llon*iis*[e] Camerario Henr*ico*[f] de Quinci Willelmo de Haia Johanne de Hasting Rob*erto* de Berkel' Dauid de Haia Willelmo Flandr*ensi* Herb*erto* Marescallo. Apud Forfar xvi die[g] Junii

SOURCE. SRO, Transcripts of Royal Charters (loose sheet evidently in the handwriting of James Anderson, editor of *Diplomata*) = *A*. NLS, MS. Adv. 29.4.2 (Hutton's Collections), vol.xii, no page or folio number = *B*. R. Maitland, *History of the house of Seytoun* (Maitland Club, 1829), p.91 = *C*. Printed here from *A*, which seems to be the holograph copy made by James Anderson, and bears the note, which refers to this charter and no.200 above: '24 Sept 1701 I copied these two Charters from the Originalls, at Seton by the noble courtesy of the Earl of Winton.' Both *B* and *C* give this note, and *C* is evidently an inferior copy of *B* and not taken directly from *A*.

PRINTED. R. Maitland, *History of the house of Seytoun* (as above). G. Seton, *History of the family of Seton* (1896), ii, 842 (abstract only); Mackenzie, *Writers*, iii, 209.

NOTES. [a] Sciatis, *C*. [b] uniuersas, *B* and *C*; the reading of *A* is Unusas, no doubt for an original diuisas with an unusual or illegible d. [c] *B*, *C* omit from 7 to pertinentibus. [d] Sic, *A*. [e] Mou' or Mon', *A*; Mon', *B*; Philippo [Valoines ?], *C*. [f] Sic, *A*, for Seherio? [g] *B*, *C* omit.

COMMENT. See no.200.

391 Grants to Kinloss Abbey Strathisla (Banffshire). Elgin. (31 July, 1196)

Willelmus Dei gratia Scottorum rex, episcopis, abbatibus, comitibus, baronibus, justiciis, vicecomitibus, prepositis, ministris et omnibus probis hominibus tocius terre sue, clericis et laicis, salutem. Sciant presentes et futuri me dedisse et concessisse et hac carta mea confirmasse Deo et ecclesie Sancte Marie de Kinlos et monachis ibidem Deo servientibus Stradhilif'[a] per rectas divisas suas, et cum omnibus justis pertinentiis suis, tenendum in liberam et perpetuam elemosinam, in boscho et plano etc. Testibus, R*icardo* episcopo de Morau'[b], J*ohanne* episcopo de Caten', R*eginaldo* episcopo Rosens*i*, H*ugone* cancellario meo, Ric*ardo* de Prebenda clerico meo, Comite Patric*io*, Comite Dunec*ano*, Comite Gilleberto, Willelmo de Morvill', cons*tabulario*, Roberto de Quinci, Philippo de Valon*iis*, camerario, Willelmo fil*io* Fresek*in*, Willelmo Cumin, Willelmo de Haia, Johanne de Hasting, Hugone et Willelmo filiis Willelmi de Fresek*in*, D*aui*d de Haia, Rog*ero* de Mortem*er*, Philippo de Lundin,[c] Waltero Murdac, Herberto marescallo. Apud Elgin[d] ultimo die Julii.

SOURCE. D. Haignère, *Les chartes de Saint-Bertin, d'après le Grand Cartulaire de Dom Charles-Joseph de Witte, dernier archiviste de ce monastère* (4 vols., St Omer, 1886–90), vol.i (1886), 189–190, no.436. MS. source not seen for this edition.

A footnote reads: 'NB. Cette pièce est copiée d'une manière peu satisfaisante. Elle est datée du 31 juillet et scellée du grand sceau royal, rond, 77mm., à deux faces. 1°, le roi assis, couronné, tenant le sceptre et la boule du monde: WILLELMVS . DEO . RECTORE . REX . SCOTTORVM; 2°, type équestre, même légende.'

PRINTED. As above; also J.H.Round, *Calendar of Documents preserved in France* (1899), no.1351 (abstract).
NOTES. [a] Source, Stradhilifus. [b] Source, Marau'. [c] Source, Lundino. [d] Source, Vergin (!).
COMMENT. The estate here granted became known as the Grange of Strathisla, now Grange.

392 Grants to Kinloss Abbey Strathisla (Banffshire), by the marches specified. Elgin. (31 July, 1196) (Inflated)

Willelmus[a] Dei gracia Rex Scotorum episcopis, abbatibus, comitibus, baronibus, justiciariis, vicecomitibus, prepositis, ministris et omnibus probis hominibus tocius terre sue, clericis et laicis, salutem. Sciant presentes et futuri me, diuine caritatis intuitu, pro salute anime mee et animarum omnium predecessorum et successorum meorum regum Scocie et animarum omnium fidelium defunctorum, dedisse, concessisse et hac presenti carta mea confirmasse Deo et Beate Marie et omnibus sanctis et abbati ac monachis de Kynlos ibidem Deo seruientibus et imperpetuum seruituris totam terram de Strathylaf, cum omnibus suis justis pertinentiis ad eandem terram iuste spectantibus, seu quoquomodo spectare valentibus in futurum, per rectas suas metas et diuisas quas eisdem fecimus per meliores et antiquiores patrie perambulari; videlicet, a loco ubi Lagyn' descendit in Hylaf ascendendo per altum sicum in rubeo musso usque ad summitatem orientalis Belach' et per summitatem utriusque Belach' usque eque[b] ultra fontem qui vocatur Lesking Ewin; et ab eodem fonte sicut riuolus ipsius fontis descendit per Gradokis in Hylef; et sic ascendendo per Hylef usque Geth' ubi Forgyn descendit in Hylef; et inde ascendendo per Forgyn usque Algars ; et sic usque Aldrochin et ab inde usque Algargadin et ita usque Fertheken'[c] et usque Telinire et Badnagir et sic per ascensum aque usque Hachindaling et ita usque Polenterf et inde usque Clargynloy et sic[c] usque Tubirnaneam et usque Clochindiston' et ab inde descendendo per Lagyn in Hylef. Tenendam et habendam eisdem monachis et eorum successoribus inperpetuum in liberam, puram et perpetuam elimosinam in bosco et plano. in terris et aquis, in pratis et pascuis, in moris et maresiis, in siluis et venacionibus, in aucupacionibus et piscationibus, in stagnis et molendinis et omnibus aliis ad predictam terram juste pertinentibus, ita libere et quiete, plenarie et honorifice, sicut prefati monachi vel alii viri religiosi Cistertiensis ordinis aut cuiuscunque alterius religionis elemosinas suas in regno meo liberius, quiecius, plenius et honorificencius tenent et possident. Testibus R*icardo* episcopo Morauiensi, J*ohanne* episcopo de Cathenesia, R*eginaldo* episcopo Rossensi, Hugone cancellario meo, R*icardo* de Prebenda clerico meo, Comite Patricio, Comite Duncano, Comite Gilberto, Willelmo de Moruil constabulario, Roberto de Quinci, Philippo de Valoniis camerario, Willelmo filio Fresk*in*, Willelmo Cuming, Willelmo de Haya, Rogero de Mortimer, Phylippo de Lundin, Waltero Murdach, Harbarto Marescallo. Apud Elgyn' . ultimo die Julii.

HEADING. Carta Willelmi Regis de terra de Strathylaf data Monasterio de Kynlos.
SOURCE. *Kinloss Recs.*, no.3 (printed from earlier printed versions). No MS. source has been traced for this edition.

PRINTED. L. Shaw, *History of the province of Moray* (Edinburgh, 1775), 406 (Appendix, no.XXVII, provenance of text not given; version considerably reduced, but includes Hugh son of Freskin among witnesses, as in no.391); Ferrerius, *Historia*, 89; *Aberdeen-Banff Illustrations*, ii, 230; *Kinloss Recs.*, no.3.
NOTES. [a] Punctuation editorial. [b] Sic. [c] Placed within square brackets by source, but not by Shaw.
COMMENT. This is an obviously inflated version of no.391, which see for date. The inflation may have been composed as late as the fourteenth or fifteenth centuries. The marches correspond closely with the modern marches of Grange parish and of the northern part of Keith parish, running from the confluence of the Shiel Burn ('Lagyn') with the Isla, up to the top of Little Balloch Hill, thence to the top of the Meikle Balloch, thence down to the Isla, following up the river to its confluence with the Forgie Burn, then up the Forgie to 'Algars', thence to 'Aldrochin', thence to 'Algargadin' (probably represented by the modern name Garral, standing for *garbh allt*, otherwise *allt garbh*), thence to Fernking, thence to 'Telinire' and 'Badnagir', and so up the burn to 'Hachindaling' (cp. Inverkindling, in Fordyce), thence to 'Polenterf' and 'Clargynloy' and so to Ternemny and Clovenstone (both in Rothiemay), thence down the Shiel Burn to the Isla. The eastern section of this march is referred to as 'diuisas monachorum de Kynlos subtus le Chnoc' in a charter of Alexander II, 8 April, 1242 (*Aberdeen-Banff Illustrations*, ii, 109).

393 Grants to Richard bishop of Moray one full toft in his burgh of Kintore. Aberdeen. (25 September, 1189 × 1198, probably 1196 or 1197)

Will' Dei gratia Rex Scott' omnibus probis hominibus tocius terre sue clericis et laicis salutem. Sciant presentes et futuri me dedisse concessisse et hac[a] carta mea confirmasse Ric*ardo* episcopo Morauen*si* unum plenarium toftum in burgo meo de Kintor[b] . tenendum sibi et successoribus suis de me et heredibus meis in perpetuam elemosinam . ita libere . quiete . plenarie et honorifice sicut aliquis episcopus aliquod toftum in aliquo burgo meo liberius . quiecius . plenius et honorificencius tenet et possidet. Test*ibus* Matheo episcopo de Aberdon' . Com*ite* Dunc*ano* justic*ia* . Roberto de Quincy . Malis fil*io* comiti[s] Ferthet . Malc*olmo* fil*io* com*itis* Dunc*ani* . Philippo de Mubrai . Will*elmo* Cumin . Willelmo de Haia. Apud Aberdon'[c] . xxv. die Septembris.

RUBRIC. de tofto [ ] (at right, cut or worn away). De tofto de Kyntor (top, in later hand)[d].
SOURCE. NLS, MS. Adv. 34.4.10, fo.xxxviii^{r} = *A*. Ibid., fo.xvi^{v} = *B*. Printed here from *A* with some readings of *B* noted.
PRINTED. *Moray Registrum*, no.15 (from *B*).
NOTES. [a] *B* adds presenti. [b] Kynthor, *B*. [c] Aberden, *B*. [d] *B* has Carta Tofti de Kyntor'.

394 Commands his baillies of Moray to see that Richard bishop of Moray and his clergy have all their rightful teinds from their parishioners and from everything from which Holy Church commands that teind should be paid; they are to forbid parishioners to withhold teind, on pain of the king's full forfeiture, so that the bishop and his clergy do not have to complain to the king of their default. Elgin. (10 October, 1196 or 1197)

Will' Dei gratia Rex Scott' omnibus balliuis suis de Morauia salutem. Mando uobis et firmiter precipio quatinus faciatis Ric*ardum* episcopum

Morau*ie* . et clericos suos habere omnes rectas decimas de parochianis suis . et de omnibus unde sancta ecclesia decimas debet percipere sicut carta mea quam habent testatur . et prohibeatis predictis parochianis suis ne illi decimas suas detineant . super meam plenariam forisfacturam et tantum predicto episcopo et clericis suis faciatis ne oporteat eos inde inde conqueri pro defectu uestri. Test*ibus* Hug*one* cancell*ario* meo . Dunec*ano* com*ite* justic*ia* . Com*ite* Gilleb*erto.* Apud Elgin . x . die Octobris.

MARGINAL NOTE. Ista non s[cribitur in libro decani].
SOURCE. NLS, MS. Adv. 34.4.10, fo.xxxvii^r.
PRINTED. *Moray Registrum*, no.8.
COMMENT. See nos.189, 281 above.

395 Commands all who hold lands of the bishopric of Moray to pay to Bishop Richard and his successors all the dues, cain and conveth which were received by the bishop's predecessors in the time of King David I, King Malcolm IV or by Bishop Richard most fully in King William's own time. Elgin. (11 October, 1196 or 1197)

Will' Dei gratia Rex Scott' omnibus probis hominibus suis Morau*ie* salutem. Mando et firmiter precipio quatinus omnes homines qui terram tenent de episcopatu Morau*ie* reddant Ric*ardo* episcopo et successoribus suis omnes rectitudines . et cana et coneueta sicut antecessores sui episcopi tempore Regis D*aui*d aui mei . et tempore Malc*olmi* fratris mei rectitudines et cana et coneueta plenius perceperunt . aut sicut predictus Ric*ardus* episcopus ea tempore meo plenius percepit. Quare prohibeo firmiter ne quis ea eidem Episcopo detinere presumat super plenariam meam forisfacturam. Test*ibus* Hug*one* cancell*ario* meo . Philippo de Valon*iis* camerario . Will*elmo* fil*io* Fresk*ini*. Apud Elgin .xi.[a] die Octobris.

RUBRIC. Carta de coneuethis.
SOURCE. NLS, MS. Adv. 34.4.10, fo.xxxviii^r.
PRINTED. *Moray Registrum*, no.9.
NOTE. [a] A variant on fo.xvij^v gives x die.

396 Confirms to Dunfermline Abbey that part of the land of Beath (Fife) which Waldef held, granted by Saer de Quinci, as Saer's charter bears witness. Perth. (20 August, 1196 × 1203, perhaps 1197)

Will'[a] Dei gratia Rex Scot' . omnibus probis hominibus . tocius terre sue clericis 7 laicis salutem. Sciant presentes 7 futuri me concessisse 7 hac Carta mea confirmasse Deo 7 ecclesie Sancte Trinitatis de Dunfer*melin* 7 monachis ibi Deo seruientibus totam terram de Béé th quam Seierius de Quinci eis dedit in perpetuam elemosinam . *scilicet* terram illam de Bééth quam Waldeuus tenuit . tenendam in liberam 7 perpetuam elemosinam ita libere 7 quiete . plenarie 7 honorifice ·/ sicut carta prefati Seierij testatur . saluo seruicio meo. T*estibus* Ric*ardo* de prebenda clerico meo . Comite Dunc*ano* justic*ia* . Roberto de Quinci . Willelmo Cumin . Will*elmo* de Veteri Ponte . Will*elmo* de Vallibus D*aui*d de Haya. Ap*ud* Pert .xx. die Augusti.

RUBRIC. De Beeth quam Seierius de Quinci dedit (red with blue initial).
SOURCE. NLS, MS. Adv. 34.1.3a, fo.xiii[r].
PRINTED. *Dunfermline Registrum*, no.66.
NOTE. [a] Initial red.
COMMENT. Saer de Quinci's charter of 'Beeth Waldef' (in Beath or Dunfermline, Fife), is in *Dunfermline Registrum*, no.154. An agreement concerning it (1278) appears, ibid., nos.86, 87. It does not seem possible to say which part of Beath this was, except that it was not Wester Beath.

397 Grants to Coupar Angus Abbey the lands of Persey (in Kirkmichael), Perthshire, and that part of Cally (Monks Cally?) which Mack-holffe held, reserving for the king's use that part of Cally lying to the south of the River Ardle, towards Clunie. Edinburgh. (19 September, 1195 × 1206)

Carta Donationis regis Willielmi eisdem monachis de terris de Parthesin per suas rectas diuisas, et illam Kalathin quam Mack-holffe tenuit per suas rectas diuisas, excepta illa parte terræ de Kalathyn que est ex australi parte aquæ de Ferdil versus Clonyn quam ad opus meum reseruaui, &c. Testibus: Philippo de Valloun Camerario meo, Roberto de London, Syero de Quinci, Philippo de Mubray, Villielmo Cumyn. Apud Edinburg, xix Septembris

SOURCE. NLS, MS. Adv. 33.2.9, fo.27[v].
PRINTED. *Coupar Angus Rental*, i, 322, no.6.

398 Grants that on the death of an abbot of Scone the canons of Scone may freely elect one of their convent to be abbot, with the counsel and consent of the king, provided that a suitable person may be found within the house of Scone. Forfar. (29 May, 1198)

Willelmus[a] Dei gracia Rex Scottorum omnibus probis hominibus tocius terre sue, clericis et laicis, salutem. Sciant presentes et futuri me concessisse et hac carta mea confirmasse canonicis de Scon ut obeunte abbate suo liceat eis, assensu et consilio meo, unum de conuentu suo in abbatem libere eligere, si ydonea persona ad hoc in domo de Scone inveniri possit. Test*ibus* [Rogero][b] episcopo Sanctiandr*ee*, Arnaldo abbate de Cuper, Henrico abbate de Aberbruthoc, Hug*one* de Mortuo Mari priore de Maii, Comite Dunec*ano* Justic*ia*, Roberto de Quinci, Willelmo Cumin, Willelmo de Haia, Johanne de Hasting'. Apud Forfar, xxix die Maii.

SOURCE. NLS, MS. Adv. 34.3.28, fo.9[v].
PRINTED. *Scone Liber*, no.30.
NOTES. [a] Name omitted, MS. [b] Ric', MS.
COMMENT. This brieve was doubtless issued on the occasion of the election at Forfar in 1198 under royal pressure (*sicut placuit curialibus*) of Reinbald, cellarer of Holyrood, as abbot of Scone, following the resignation of Abbot Robert who had been abbot of Scone since 1162 (*Chron. Bower*, i, 513). It follows that the statement in *Chron. Howden*, iv, 91 that *William*, prior of May, took part in an embassy to King John about May, 1199, must be an error for *Hugh* (de Mortemer).

399 Confirms to the cathedral church of Aberdeen and to Matthew bishop of Aberdeen the whole toun of Old Aberdeen; half the water of Don; Sclattie and other lands in the neighbourhood of Aberdeen; the shires of Clatt, Tullynessle, Rayne and Daviot; a tenth of the cain of ships coming to Aberdeen and of corn there, and a tenth of his revenues of Aberdeen, and a tenth of thanages, revenues and escheats belonging to the king in the sheriffdoms of Aberdeen and Banff. Forfar. (30 August) (Spurious).

Will*elmus* Dei gratia Rex Scottorum omnibus probis hominibus tocius terre sue, clericis et laicis, salutem. Sciant presentes et futuri me dedisse, concessisse et hac carta mea confirmasse Deo et Beate Marie et Beato Machorio et Matheo Episcopo Aberdonensi totam villam de veteri Aberdon, dimidiam aquam de North, Slaty, Goule, Murcroft, Kynmonedy, Malmeulach, Schiram de Clat, Schiram de Tulynestyn, Schiram de Rane, Schiram de Dauyot cum pertinentiis et ecclesiis, decimam canum[a] nauium que veniunt apud Aberden, decimam annone in eodem loco, decimam meam de redditibus de Aberden, decimam thanagiorum, reddituum et escaetarum me contingencium infra vic*ecomitatus* de Aberden et de Banff. Tenendas et habendas dicto episcopo et eius successoribus in puram et liberam elimosinam adeo libere et quiete sicut aliqua elemosina liberius et quiecius tenetur et possidetur. Testibus Alano Hostiario, Willelmo Comyne, Johanne Camerario, apud Forfar tricesimo die mensis Augusti.

RUBRIC. Carta Regis Willelmi confirmantis donationes predicti Dauid Regis.
SOURCE. NLS, MS. Adv. 16.1.10, fo.49r.
PRINTED. *Aberdeen Registrum*, i, 8–9.
NOTE. [a] Sic.
COMMENT. Cf. *RRS*, i, nos.116, 237. It seems futile to try to assign a date to this act.

400 Confirms the property and privileges of the Hospital of Soutra. Haddington. (5 August 1195 × 1199, perhaps 1198) (Inflated)

Will*elmus* Dei gr*aci*a Rex Scottorum episcopis, abbatibus, comitibus, baronibus, iusticiariis, vicecomitibus, prepositis, ministris et omnibus probis hominibus tocius terre sue salutem. Sciant presentes et futuri me dedisse et concessisse et hac presenti carta mea confirmasse Deo et hospitali Sancte Trinitatis de Soltre omnes donaciones terrarum et hominum et elimosinarum que eis racionabiliter date sunt in omnibus rebus et possessionibus mundanis in terra mea. Quare volo et firmiter precipio ut predictum hospitale et fratres ibidem Deo seruientes omnes possessiones et elimosinas suas habeant et teneant cum socca et sacca, cum tolle et them et infangenthef et cum omnibus aliis libertatibus et liberis consuetudinibus et quietanciis suis in bosco et plano, in pratis et pascuis, in aquis et molendinis, in viis et semitis, in moris et marresiis, in stagnis et viuariis, in grangiis et virgultis, infra burgum et extra, et in omnibus rebus liberas et quietas de placitis et querelis et scutagio, auxilio, asisis, et de operacione castellorum et poncium, et de blodwyte et de fehtwyte, et quietas de omni tolloneo et passagio et pontagio et lestagio et estalagio et de omni seculari seruicio et opere seruili et exactione et de omnibus aliis consuetudinibus secularibus excepta sola iusticia mortis et membrorum, et exceptis quatuor querelis que ad coronam meam pertinent, scilicet de roberia, de murdir, de combustione, de femina efforciata. Quare volo et firmiter precipio ut fratres antedicti omnia prescripta habeant et teneant in liberam et perpetuam elimosinam pro amore Dei et pro anima regis Dauid aui mei et regis Malcolmi fratris mei et pro anima comitis Henrici patris mei et omnium antecessorum et heredum meorum. Test*ibus* Hugone cancellar*io* meo, Ricardo de prebenda clerico meo, Ricardo et Waltero capellanis meis, Rolando filio Utredi iustic*ia*, Waltero[a] de Lyndissay iusticiar*io*, Willelmo Cumin,[b] Willelmo de[c] Someruilla, Thoma de Coleuile, Philippo[d] Marescallo. Datum quinto die Augusti apud Hadyngton'.

RUBRIC. Confirmacio in large scr*ipta*[e].
SOURCE. NLS, MS. Adv. 34.4.1, fo.3^{r-v}.
PRINTED. *Midlothian Chrs., Soutra Registrum*, no.7.
NOTES. [a] Sic, for Willelmo. [b] Comite, MS. [c] Fo.3^{v}. [d] Pho, MS. *Soutra Reg.* prints Johanne wrongly. [e] Last three words in a later hand of xvi or xvii cent.
COMMENT. It seems probable that the whole passage from the first *quare volo* to *femina efforciata* has been inserted anachronistically; but there is no reason to doubt the existence of an authentic confirmation by King William with protocol and eschatocol approximately as given here. If 'Richard', king's chaplain, in the testing clause, is an error for 'Ralph', the latest possible year would be 1198.

401 Confirms to Holyrood Abbey the ploughgate and ten acres of land in the territory of Tranent (East Lothian) towards Falside, granted by Robert de Quinci in exchange for the ploughgate in Preston (East Lothian) which the canons of Holyrood claimed from Robert and the monks of Newbattle. Haddington. (19 August, 1195 × 1203, perhaps 1198)

.W. Dei gr*ati*a Rex Scott'. Omnibus probis hominibus totius terre sue Clericis et laicis :' salutem. Sciant presentes 7 futuri me concessisse . et hac carta mea confirmasse Deo 7 ecclesie Sancte Crucis de Edenburg . et canonicis ibidem Deo seruientibus illam carrucatam terre . et decem acras in territorio de Trauernent . uersus Phauheside . quam Robertus de Quinci eis dedit pro excambio illius Carrucate terre de Prestune quam idem canonici uersus eundem Rob*ertum* . 7 monachos de Neubothle calumpniauerunt. Tenend*am* sibi in liberam . et puram et perpetuam elemosinam cum libero exitu . et communi pastura de Trauernent . quantum ad tantum terre pertinet . ita libere . et quiete . plenarie . et honorifice :' sicut Carta predicti Rob*erti* testatur :' saluo seruicio meo. Test*ibus* Ric*ardo* de prebend*a* . clerico meo . Rob*erto* de Quinci . Philipp*o* de Mubrahi . Willelmo de Lindes' . Willelmo de Vallibus . Herb*erto* de Camer*a* . Philipp*o* de Londin . Waltero Murdach'. Apud Hadingtun .xix. die Augusti[a].

ENDORSED. De terra de Trauernent. (xiii cent.). J. Scott (xvi cent.). Also modern endorsements.
DESCRIPTION. 6·1″ (15·5 cm.), Top, 6·4″ (16·1 cm.), Bottom × 4″ (10 cm.), L, 4·2″ (10·5 cm.), R. Foot folded to a depth of 0·8″ (2 cm.). Double slits with tag 6·1″ (15·5 cm.) long, 0·6″ (1·5 cm.) wide. Small central fragment of seal remains in natural wax, stained brown.
HAND. Scribe Dd. Unruled. SOURCE. Original, SRO, GD 45/13/242.
PRINTED. *Holyrood Liber*, no.39.
NOTE. [a] The scribe has started to form a minuscule t and then extended the letter to complete the line by a long horizontal stroke ending with an uncial form of t followed by i.
COMMENT. Falside Hill is in Tranent. The ploughgate in Preston was presumably

part of the land which Robert de Quinci had leased to Newbattle Abbey for twenty years from 11 November, 1170, and subsequently granted to Newbattle outright, *c.*1189 (*SHR*, xxx (1951), 42–4; *Newbattle Registrum*, no.64). The king's son Alexander was born at Haddington on 24 August, 1198.

402 Confirms to William son of Robert, son of Henry the butler, Cassingray (in Carnbee), Fife, by the marches perambulated for his father by Abbot Archibald of Dunfermline and the king's good men, in feu and heritage, with common pasture on the muir of Kellie; performing the forinsec service due from a half-ploughgate in Kellieshire. William is to be free of multure for his own household at the king's mill of Kellie, but his men are to pay multure. Stirling. (28 August, 1195 × 1198, perhaps 1198)

.W'. Dei gr*ati*a Rex Scott' Omnibus probis Hominibus Tocius terre sue Clericis et laicis Salutem. Sciant presentes et futuri me dedisse et concessisse et hac Carta mea confirmasse Willelmo filio Roberti filii Henrici pincerne Glasgingrei per easdem diuisas per quas Ærkenbaldus abbas de Dunfermelin cum probis hominibus meis et per preceptum meum terram illam Roberto patri suo perambulauit. Tenend*um* sibi et heredibus suis de me et heredibus meis . in feudo et hereditate in terris et pratis . ⁊ pascuis . ⁊ cum communi pastura de mora de Kellin . libere et quiete . faciendo inde forinsecum seruicium tantum scilicet quantum pertinet ad dimidiam Carucatam terre in Kellinshire. Concessi etiam predicto Willelmo et heredibus suis ut quieti sint de multura de domo sua propria ad molendinum meum de Kellin . Set uolo quod homines sui dent multuram . Et ut predictus Willelmus predictam terram adeo libere et quiete . plenarie et honorifice teneat et possideat .' sicut Carta patris sui testatur. Test*ibus* Hugone cancellar*io* meo . Roberto de London*iis* . Rob*erto* de Quinci . Willelmo de Lindesia . Willelmo de Haia . Henrico Biset . Willelmo Giffard' . Waltero Murdahc apud Strivelin xxviii. die Augusti.

ENDORSED. kasingray (xiv cent.).
DESCRIPTION. 5·2″ (13·2 cm.), Top, bottom × 3·9″ (9·8 cm.), L, 4″ (10·2 cm.), R. Foot folded to a depth of 0·7″ (2 cm.). Double slits with tag 4·8″ (12 cm.) long, 0·5″ (1·3 cm.) wide. No seal remains.
HAND. Scribe Dc. Unruled.
SOURCE. Original, SRO, GD 203, Section 2, no.2.
COMMENT. See no.286. The shire of Kellie, royal demesne in the twelfth century, seems to have been identical with the later parish of Carnbee.

403 Confirms to the brethren of Inchaffray (Inchaffray Abbey) the grant made to them by Earl Gilbert of Strathearn of the church of St Cathan of Aberuthven (in Auchterarder), Perthshire. Scone. (5 September, 1198 × 1203, probably 1198)

.W'. Dei gr*ati*a Rex Scott'. Omnibus probis Hominibus tocius terre sue Clericis et Laicis Salutem. Sciant presentes et futuri me concessisse et Hac Carta mea confirmasse Deo et ecclesie Sancti Johannis apostoli et ewangeliste de Inche Affrenne in Foules . et fratribus ibidem Deo seruientibus . Ecclesiam Sancti Cathani de Aberrotheven in Stardhern' . quam Comes Gilebertus eidem loco dedit. Tenend*am* in liberam puram et perpetuam elemosynam . cum omnibus libertatibus ad eandem ecclesiam iuste pertinentibus . adeo libere et quiete . plenarie et honorifice .· sicut Carta predicti Com*itis* Gileberti testatur. Test*ibus* Ricardo de prebenda clerico meo . Com*ite* Dunecan*o* Just*icia* . Henr*ico* Com*ite* Athol' . Roberto de London*iis* . Malisio filio Ferthet . Malcolm*o* filio Com*itis* Dunec*ani* . Johanne de Hasting' . Adam de Syreis . Henr*ico* de Graham . Henr*ico* Revel . apud Scone .v. die Septembris.

ENDORSED. De ecclesia de Aberrotheuen (xiii cent.).
DESCRIPTION. 6·8″ (17·3 cm.), Top, 6·75″ (17·2 cm.), Bottom × 4·3″ (11 cm.), L, 4·65″ (11·9 cm.), R. Foot folded. Slits with tag, 0·7″ (1·7 cm.) wide. Fragment of seal remains in natural wax stained brown. Diameter 2·9″.
HAND. Scribe Dc. Unruled.
SOURCE. Original, Kinnoull Trustees (Dupplin Charter Chest), Chrs. no.23. *Inchaffray Chrs.*, Facsimile no.2.
PRINTED. *Inchaffray Chrs.*, no.6 (and Facsimile no.2).
COMMENT. The group of persons mentioned in this act compares closely with those mentioned in a charter of Earl Gilbert of 1194 × 1198 given probably at or near Scone (*P S A S*, lxxxvii, 60–1) and with those mentioned in an agreement between Bishop Roger of St Andrews and Arbroath Abbey of 1198 (after 24 August) (*Arbroath Liber*, i, no.148).

404 Grants to Walter, son of Walter Scott, Allardyce (Mearns), in feu and heritage, for the service of one archer with horse and haubergel and the performance of the common aid due from thirteen oxgangs of land. Stirling. (16 October, 1198)

W[a]. Dei gratia Rex Scott' Episcopis, Abbatibus, Comitibus, Baronibus, Justiciis, Vicecomitibus, prepositis, ministris et[b] omnibus probis hominibus totius terre sue, Clericis et Laicis, Salutem. Sciant presentes et futuri me dedisse et concessisse et hac carta mea confirmasse Waltero filio Walteri Scotti Alreches per rectas diuisas suas et cum omnibus justis pertinentiis suis, tenen*dum* sibi et heredibus suis de me et heredibus meis in feudo et hereditate, in boscho et plano, in pratis et pascuis, in moris et maresiis, in stagnis et molendinis, et cum omnibus aliis ad predictam terram iuste pertinen*tibus*, libere et quiete, plenarie et honorifice, per servitium unius Archarii cum equo et halburgello et faciendo commune auxilium quantum ad tresdecim bovatas terre pertinet[c], sicut carta patris sui testatur. Teste Hug*one* Cancellario meo, H[enrico] abbate de Aberbrothock, Com*ite* Dunec*ano* Justic*ia*, Rob*erto* de Quinci, Rob*erto* de London, Philippo de Mubray, Willelmo de Haia, Johanne de Hastinges, Ric*ardo* filio Hugon*is*, Alex*andro* vic*ecomite* de Striuel*in*, Philippo de Lundin, Roberto de Upsetlingt*un*, Yuone de Veteri ponte, Walt*ero* Murdac, Rog*ero* de Lakern', Thom*a* fil*io* Tancard. Apud Striuelin xvi die Octobris.

DESCRIPTION. There is no account of the document itself, but there is a note of the seal as follows: 'The seall & Counterseall on a tag intire in the effigies but the words about the seall worne away.'
HAND. The source contains two copies, one written out in full, the other reproducing the punctuation and abbreviations, and even simulating the hand, of the original. From this it seems almost certain that the hand was that of Scribe De (William del Bois).
SOURCE. SRO, GD 49/1 (transumpt by order of the Lords of Council and Session, 20 August, 1703, of original charter produced for George Alderdyce of that ilk; extracted by James Dalrymple. Two copies).

PRINTED. *HMC 5th Report*, Appendix, 629.
NOTES. [a] Punctuation editorial. [b] Tironian et evidently used throughout in original. [c] Both copies have pertinen'.
COMMENT. Presumably granted after the death of Walter Scott the elder (of Allardyce), who was interviewed on his death-bed in the winter of 1197–8 by Master Isaac, clerk of Roger bishop-elect of St Andrews, while on his way north to invite the bishops of Moray, Ross and Caithness to attend Roger's consecration, which took place on 15 February, 1198 (*Spalding Misc.*, v, 211).

405 Re-grants to William de Valognes, son of Philip de Valognes, those lands in Scotland benorth Forth which the king granted to his father Philip; viz., Benvie and Panmure (Angus), in feu and heritage, with sake and soke, toll, team and infangthief, with pit and gallows, for the service of half a knight. Stirling. (1198 × 1200)

.W'. Dei gr*ati*a Rex Scott'. Episcopis . Abbatibus . Comitibus . Baronibus . Justic*iis* . Vicecomitibus . Prepositis . Ministris . et[a] Omnibus probis Hominibus totius terre sue Clericis et Laicis ·/ salutem. Sciant presentes et futuri me reddidisse . et concessisse . et hac carta mea confirmasse . Willelmo de Valoniis filio Philipp*i* de Valon*iis* . terras illas in Scotia . quas eidem Philipp*o* patri eius dedi . scilicet Baneuin per rectas diuisas suas . et cum omnibus iustis pertinentiis suis . Et Pannemor[b] per rectas diuisas suas . et cum omnibus justis pertinentiis suis. Tenend*as* sibi et heredibus suis . de me et heredibus meis . in feudo et hereditate . in bosco . et plano . in terris . et aquis . in pratis . et pascuis . et moris . et mossis . et maresiis . in stangnis et molendinis . in viuariis . et piscariis . in viis . et semitis . in sabulis . et salinis . in portubus . et cum omnibus aliis ad predictas terras iuste pertinentibus . Cum socca . et sacca . cum furca . et fossa . cum thol . et them . et infangenthef . libere . et quiete . plenarie . et honorifice ·/ per seruicium dimidii Militis . sicut carta predicti Philipp*i* de Valon*iis* patris sui testatur. Test*ibus* R*ogero* Episcopo Sancti Andr*ee* . Johan*ne* Episcopo Dunkeld*ensi* . Ric*ardo* Episcopo Morauie . Com*ite* Patricio . Com*ite* Dunecan*o* de Fif . Com*ite* Gilleberto de Stradheren . Rolland*o* fil*io* Uchtred*i* Constabulario . Willelmo de Lindes' . Rob*erto* de Quinci . Willelmo CumiN . Willelmo de Bruis . Willelmo de Haia . Johanne de Hasting' . Willelmo Giffard' . Rogero de Mortem*er* . Alexand*ro* Vicecomite de StriueliN . Ric*ardo* filio Hugonis. Philippo de LundiN. Apud StriueliN[c].

ENDORSED. Confirmatio (xiii cent.).
DESCRIPTION. 8·4″ (21·4 cm.), Top, 8·2″ (21 cm.), Bottom × 3·6″ (9·3 cm.), L, 4″ (10 cm.), R. Foot folded to a depth of 1·1″ (2·8 cm.). Tie, 6″ long, cut from top left of fold. Double slits with tag 7·1″ (18 cm.) long, 0·6″ (1·5 cm.) wide. No seal remains, but traces are visible.
HAND. Scribe Dd. Unruled.
SOURCE. Original, SRO, GD 45/27/28.
PRINTED. *Panmure Registrum*, ii, 132–3 (with facsimile); Anderson, *Diplomata*, Pl.XXVII; *APS*, i, 94–5.
NOTES. [a] Scribe Dd employs et in full and crossed tironian sign variously. [b] Sic. *Dipl. Scot.* and *APS*, i, loc. cit., have Pannomor. [c] Final N extended to complete bottom line.
COMMENT. No charter recording King William's grant to Philip de Valognes has survived. Cf. *BIHR*, xxix, 7. The omission of the day of the month is remarkable.

406 Commands his responsible men of Galloway that wherever the monks of Melrose dwelling in Galloway shall enter their land while following the track of thieves, the lord whose land they have entered shall give help to the monks to make their pursuit, according to the king's assize of Galloway. Forbids anyone to obstruct the monks while making such pursuit, on pain of his full forfeiture. Selkirk. (11 December, 1195 × 1198)

Uill*el*m*us*[a] Dei gr*ati*a Rex Scottorum omnibus probis hominibus de Galweia salutem. Mando et firmiter precipio quatinus, ubicunque fratres de Melros in Galweia manentes uenerint in terram uestram sequendo uestigia latrocinii sui, Dominus terre illius in quam predicti fratres uestigia latrocinii sui secuti fuerint ipsis fratribus auxilium habere faciat ad uestigia latrocinii sui prosequenda, secundum assisam meam de Galweia. Et prohibeo firmiter ne quis predictos fratres uestigia latrocinii sui sequi iniuste disturbet, super meam plenariam forisfacturam. Test*ibus* Hug*one* Cancellario meo, Roll*ando* fil*io* Ucdr*edi* Justiciario, Willelmo de Lynd' Justic*ia*. Apud Selech' undecimo die Decembr*is*.

RUBRIC. De latrocinio prosequendo.
SOURCE. BM, MS. Harl. 3960, fo.107r.
PRINTED. *Melrose Liber*, no.18.
NOTE. [a] Initial red.
COMMENT. The king's assize of Galloway has not survived; this brieve recalls the provision anent sleuth hounds made by chapter VII of the Statutes of Robert I (*APS*, i, 468).

407 Grants to Manuel Priory the whole teind of his revenues from the sheriffdom of Linlithgow and of the ferme of the burgh of Linlithgow, and of fermes outwith the burgh, and in mills, monies, wheat, flour, malt and *prebenda* and everything from which the king receives revenues. Commands his sheriff and bailies of Linlithgow to pay the nuns of Manuel these teinds annually without obstruction. Linlithgow. (31 December, 1196 × 1198)

Wilelmus[a] Dei gratia Rex Scotorum omnibus probis hominibus totius terre sue, clericis et laicis, salutem. Sciant presentes et futuri me dedisse et concessisse et hac carta mea confirmasse Deo et ecclesie Beate Marie de Manwel et monialibus ibidem Deo seruientibus totam decimam omnium reddituum meorum de vicecomitatu de Lillidgw et de firma burgi de Lillidgw et de firmis extra burgum, et de molendinis, et in denariis, et in frumento, et in farina, et in brasio, et in prebenda, et in omnibus aliis de quibus redditus habeo vel habere me continget. Tenendam in libera et pura et perpetua elimosina ita libere, quiete, plenarie et honorifice sicut ille vel aliqui viri religiosi elemosinas suas liberius, quiecius, plenius et honorificencius tenent et possident. Quare precipio vicecomiti et balliuis meis de Lillidgw predictis monialibus predictas decimas de omnibus prescriptis absque omni disturbatione singulis annis integre persoluant. Testibus Joselino episcopo Glascuensi, Reginaldo[b] episcopo de Ross, Hugone cancellario meo, Ricardo de Prebenda clerico meo, Radulfo et Waltero capellanis meis, Alano filio Walteri dapifero meo, Wilelmo de Lyndesei, Malcolmo filio comitis

Duncani, Geruasio Auenel, Alexandro vicecomite de Striuelin, Wilelmo de Lyndesei[c], Ricardo de Maleuill, Ricardo filio Hugonis, Wilelmo Flendrense[c], Iuone de Veteri Ponte. Apud Lillidgw, ultimo die Decembris.

SOURCE. *Fragmenta Scoto-Monastica* (*etc*), by a Delver in Antiquity (W.B.D.D. Turnbull) (Edinburgh: Thomas G. Stevenson, 1842), Appendix, p.xl, no.x. Taken from the 'original MS.' *penes* J.A. Maconochie Esq., possibly a roll of transcripts of charters, formerly at Auchinleck, Ayrshire, of which there is a partial transcript in SRO, Transcripts of Royal Charters (1214–1249).
PRINTED. As above.
NOTES. [a] Punctuation editorial. [b] Source has Rogirio, no doubt a wrong extension of Reginaldo. [c] Sic, for Waltero?
COMMENT. Reginald bishop of Ross, elected 27 February, 1195, was consecrated 10 September, 1195. He consecrated altars at Christ Church, Twyneham, Hampshire, on 29 December, 1195 (*VCH*, Hants, ii, 153), so that 1196 is the earliest possible year for this act.

408 Grants to Arbroath Abbey the church of Guthrie, Angus. Montrose. (12 January, 1196 × 1199)

W.[a] Dei gr*ati*a Rex Scotorum[b] . omnibus probis hominibus tocius terre sue clericis et laicis :' salutem. Sciant presentes et futuri . me dedisse . et concessisse . et hac carta mea confirmasse . Deo et ecclesie . Sancti Thome de Aberbroth*oc* . et monachis ibidem Deo seruientibus ecclesiam . de Gutheryn[c] . cum capellis . et terris . et decimis . et oblacionibus . et omnibus aliis iustis pertinenciis suis . Tenend*am* . in liberam . et puram et perpetuam elemosinam . ita libere . et quiete . plenarie et honorifice :' sicut alias elemosinas suas . liberius . quiecius . plenius . et honorificencius :' tenent . et possident. Test*ibus* Hug*one* Cancellario meo . Ric*ardo* de prebenda . clerico meo . Rad*ulfo* . et Walt*ero* . capellanis meis . Philippo de Valon*iis* . Cam*erario* . Rob*erto* de Quincy[d] . Will*elmo* Cumyn[e] . Will*elmo* de Haya . Will*elmo* Flandr*ensi* . Apud Monros[f] . .xii°. die Jan*uarii*.

RUBRIC. Carta domini Regis W. de ecclesia de Gutherin (red, *E*). Carta Reg*is* Willelmi de ecclesia de Gutheryn (red, *A*). .xcvj. (in margin, *A*, *E*).
SOURCE. NLS, MS. Adv. 34.4.2, fo.lxviii^v = *A*. SRO, Northesk Muniments (uncatalogued), Ethie MS., fo.6^v = *E*. Printed here from *A*.
PRINTED. *Arbroath Liber*, i, no.96.
NOTES. [a] Initial red. [b] Scottorum, *E*. [c] Gutherin, *E*. [d] Quinci, *E*. [e] Cumin, *E*. [f] Munros, *E*.
COMMENT. This was evidently a grant, not a confirmation, but it seems likely that the king had granted the barony of Guthrie to Roger de la Carneille before *c*.1195. See no.473.

409 Grants to Dunfermline Abbey one full toft in his burgh of Montrose. Montrose. (13 January, 1195 × 1199)

Will'[a] Dei gr*ati*a Rex Scott' omnibus probis hominibus tocius terre sue clericis 7 laicis salutem. Sciant presentes 7 futuri me dedisse 7 concessisse 7 hac carta mea confirmasse Deo 7 ecclesie S*ancte* Trinitatis de Dunfer*melin* 7 monachis ibidem Deo seruientibus :' unum plenarium toftum in burgo meo de Munros. Tenend*um* in liberam 7 puram 7 perpetuam elemosinam . ita libere . quiete . plenarie . 7 honorif*ice* :' sicut alias elemosinas suas . liberius . quietius . plenarius . 7 honorificencius tenent.

Test*ibus* Hug*one* cancell*ario* meo . Philippo de Vallon*iis*: camerario meo . Willelmo de Haia . Willelmo Cumin . Will*elmo* Giffard' . Eustach*io* Papedi. Ap*ud* Munros .xiij. die Januar*ii*.

RUBRIC. De toft*o* de Munros (red with red initial).
SOURCE. NLS, MS. Adv. 34.1.3a, fo.xiii[r].
PRINTED. *Dunfermline Registrum*, no.69.
NOTE. [a] Initial blue.

410 Grants to William Giffard one full toft in his burgh of Forres, and also one in each of the following places: Cullen, Banff, Kintore, Cowie, Kincardine (Mearns), Alyth castle, Clunie (in Stormont), of which the king's sheriffs put him in sasine by the king's command; to be held in feu and heritage as any other of the king's barons hold their tofts in the king's burghs. Alyth. (2 March, 1196 × 1199)

W'. Dei gr*ati*a Rex Scott' Omnibus probis Hominibus Tocius terre sue clericis ⁊ Laicis Salutem. Sciant presentes ⁊ futuri me dedisse ⁊ concessisse ⁊ hac carta mea confirmasse Willelmo Giffard' unum plenarium toftum in burgo meo de Foreis . ⁊ unum plenarium toftum apud Inuerculan . ⁊ unum plenarium toftum apud Banef . et[a] unum plenarium toftum apud Kintor . ⁊ unum plenarium toftum apud Inuercollin[b] . ⁊ unum plenarium toftum apud Kincarden[c] . ⁊ unum plenarium toftum apud castellum de Alith . ⁊ unum plenarium toftum apud Clunin. Scilicet tofta illa de quibus vicecomites mei ipsum precepto meo saisierunt. Tenend*a* sibi ⁊ heredibus suis de me ⁊ heredibus meis in feudo et[a] hereditate ita libere ⁊ quiete plenarie ⁊ honorifice sicut alii Barones mei tofta sua in illis et[a] aliis burgis meis liberius quietius plenius ⁊ honorificencius tenent. Test*ibus* H*ugone* Cancellario meo . Philipp*o* de Valon*iis* Camerario . Willelmo de Haia . Johanne de Hasting' . Rogero de Mortuomari . Umfr*ido* de Berk' . Apud Alith' secundo die Marcii.

ENDORSED. Carta de tofftis man' to Williame Giffert be king William (xvi cent.).
DESCRIPTION. 8·9″ (22·5 cm.), Top and bottom × 3·3″ (8·5 cm.), L, R. Foot folded to a depth of 0·8″ (2·2 cm.). Double slits, with tag 6·8″ (17·5 cm.) long, 0·7″ (1·8 cm.) wide. Seal repaired with obverse in natural wax stained brown, reverse in green wax.
HAND. Scribe Db. Unruled.
SOURCE. Original, SRO, GD 28/5.
PRINTED. *Yester Writs*, no.5.
NOTES. [a] Crossed tironian sign. [b] Sic. *Yester Writs*, loc. cit., prints Inuertollin. [c] Sic. *Yester Writs*, loc. cit., prints Kincardin.
COMMENT. This is an early mention of Cowie (Invercollin), for which as a royal residence cf. *Exch. Rolls*, i, 12. See also *Coupar Angus Chrs.*, no.48, in which the Collin not located by the editor is certainly Cowie.

411 Confirms to Adam, son of Odo the steward, the grant made to his father and to him by the prior and convent of St Andrews Cathedral Priory of the whole land of Kinninmonth with the three Magasks, 'Inchcalc', Ladeddie, 'Incherech', and Baldinnie, and of the full toft in the burgh of St Andrews, for an annualrent of two merks, as the charter of the prior and canons bears witness. Forfar. (10 March, 1196 × *c.*1201)

Wilielmus[a] Dei gratia Rex Scotorum, episcopis, abbatibus,[b] baronibus, justic*iis*, vice*comitibus*, prepositis, ministris et omnibus probis hominibus totius terre sue, clericis et laicis, salutem. Sciant presentes et futuri me concessisse et hac carta mea confirmasse Ade filio Odonis Senescalli donationem illam quam ei fecerunt de tota terra de Kynninmond cum tribus Malgaskis et Inchcalc et Ledethyn et Incherech, Ballechodyn per rectas diuisas suas et cum omnibus iustis pertinent*iis* suis, et de uno integro tofto in burgo Sanctiandree, tenend' sibi et heredibus suis in feodo et hereditate de predicto priore et canonicis et domo Sanctiandree. Reddendo inde iis singulis annis duas marcas pro omni seruitio ad ipsam domum pertinente, ita libere et quiete, plenarie et honorifice, sicut carta predicta prioris et canonicorum testatur, saluo seruitio meo. Testibus Comite Duncano, Philippo de Valon*iis* camerario meo, Malcolmo filio comitis, Wilielmo de Haia, Wilielmo Cumyn, Philippo de Lundin, Rogero de la Kernel. Apud Forfar, decimo die Martij.

HEADING. Alia confirmatio.
SOURCE. NLS, Minto Papers, Charters, Box 30, no.212/2.
PRINTED. Macfarlane, *Genealogical Coll.*, ii, 534 (abstract).
NOTES. [a] Punctuation editorial. [b] MS. omits comitibus.
COMMENT. The places identified with certainty are in Ceres parish; doubtless all the places together comprised the 'shire' of Kinninmonth. In a poor transcript (xvii–xviii cent.) of a lost terrier of lands belonging to the church of St Andrews, *c.*1230, which gives the names in a corrupt form, Adam son of Odo is said to hold of the prior and convent 'Kinninmonth where the hall is, Malgasc Madeth, Malgasc amerren and Leodhethin' (BM, MS. Harl. 4628, fos.240ff.). It is clear from the documents given or cited in George Martine's *Reliquiae Divi Andreae* (1797), 114–15, 181, beginning with the 'Golden Charter' of 4 October, 1479, that the shire of Kinninmonth included Over and Nether Magask, Baldinnie with its mill and Ladeddie.

412

Confirms to Adam, son of Odo the steward, the grant made to him by Malcolm son of Malpatric of the land of Denork (in Cameron), Fife. Forfar. (13 March, 1196 × 1199)

Wilelmus[a] Dei gratia Rex Scotorum, episcopis, abbatibus, comitibus, baronibus, justic*iis*, vice*comitibus*, prepositis, ministris et omnibus probis hominibus totius terre sue, clericis et laicis, salutem. Sciant presentes et futuri me concessisse to hac carta mea[b] confirmasse Ade filio Odonis senescald*i* donationem illam quam Malcolmus filius Malpat*ri*k[c] ei fecit de terra de Dunork et Torlkelly[d] per rectas diuisas suas, cum omnibus aliis justis pertinent*iis* suis, tenend' sibi et heredibus suis de predicto Malcolmo et heredibus suis in feodo et hereditate, ita libere, quiete, plenarie et honorifice sicut carta predicti Malcolmi testatur, saluo seruitio meo. Testibus Comite Duncano, Ricardo de prebenda, Philippo de Valon*iis* camerario meo[e], Willelmo de Haya, Malcolmo filio [Comitis Duncani][f], [ ][g] fratre episcopi [Mathei,][h] clerico. Apud Forfar, decimo tertio die Martij.

HEADING. Carta confirmationis de Dunork et Cortkelly.
SOURCE. NLS, Minto Papers, Charters, Box 30, no.212/2.
PRINTED. Macfarlane, *Genealogical Coll.*, ii, 534 (brief abstract only).
NOTES. [a] Punctuation editorial. [b] nostra, MS. [c] Malpatk, MS., with mark of contraction. [d] So in MS., but heading reads Cortkelly. [e] nostro, MS. [f] MS. omits. [g] name omitted in MS. [h] MS. reads fratre episcopi Matheo clerico, possibly corrupt.

COMMENT. Malcolm son of Malpatric, who witnessed the important agreement of *c.*1198–9 anent the *célidé* of St Andrews (*St Andrews Liber*, 318–19), was no doubt the son of Master Malpatric, who was evidently master of the poor scholars of St Andrews (perhaps in virtue of being *ferleighinn*?) in the third quarter of the twelfth century. Prior Walter of St Andrews bought land from Master Malpatric which he subsequently granted to Hugh the butler (St Andrews University Library MS. 30276) and Master Malpatric witnessed charters of Bishop Richard of St Andrews (1165–1178) and of Merleswein of Kennoway and his son (*St Andrews Liber*, 133, 137, 259–60). Ibid., 317, shews that in the time of Prior Simon (*c.*1212–1225) the scholars of St Andrews, then under a Master Patrick, had a claim to cain from 'the other Denork' held by Adam son of Odo. I have not identified 'Cortkelly' *alias* 'Torlkelly', but the terrier of *c.*1230 cited in the comment on no.411 mentions 'Dunorg macorgelsin' (?) held by the bishop or his tenant.

413 Confirms to Arbroath Abbey the grant made by Humphrey of Berkeley of the whole land of Balfeith (in Fordoun), Mearns, with common pasture and all easements of Kinkell and Conveth, as Humphrey of Berkeley's charter bears witness. Forfar. (16 March, 1199 × 1205, probably 1199)

W.[a] Dei gr*ati*a Rex Scott' omnibus probis hominibus tocius terre sue clericis et laicis salutem. Sciant presentes et futuri me concessisse et hac carta mea confirmasse Deo et ecclesie Sancti Thome[b] martiris de Aberbrothoc[c] et monachis ibidem Deo seruientibus totam terram illam de Balfeuth' quam Umfridus de Berkelay[d] eis dedit et[e] per easdem rectas diuisas per quas eam eis dedit[e]. Tenend*am* in liberam et puram et perpetuam elemosinam cum communi pastura et aliis aisiamentis[f] de Kinkelle[g] et de Cuneueth in carta ipsius Umfridi contentis . ita libere et quiete plenarie et honorifice sicut carta predicti Umfridi iuste testatur . saluo seruicio meo. Test*ibus* Waltero et Will*elmo* Capellanis meis . Willelmo Cumyn . Philippo de Mubray . Rob*erto* de London*iis* . Will*elmo* Giffard . Rob*erto* de Berkelay[d] . Philippo de Lundin[h] . Rogero de Lakerneill'[i] . Rogero de Wiltun'[j] Apud Forfar decimosexto[k] die Marcii.

RUBRIC. Confirmacio Regis W. super premissa carta (red, *A*). Willelmi regis carta concessionis terrarum de Balfeith' . quas quondam Wmfridus de Barklay monasterio contulit . cum communi pastura et aisiamentis de Kynkell' et Conueth' . saluo commune seruicio regis (red, *B*).

SOURCE. NLS, MS. Adv. 34.4.2, fos.lxv^{v}–lxvi^{r} = *A*. BM, MS. Add. 33245, fo.155^{v} = *B*. Printed here from *B*.

PRINTED. *Arbroath Liber*, i, no.89 *bis* (from *A*).

NOTES. *a* Initial blue, flourished red, *B*; red, *A*. [b] Sancti Thome repeated, *A*. [c] Abirbroth', *A*. [d] Berkel', *A*. [e–e] *A* omits. [f] Fo.lxvi^{r}, *A*. [g] Kyngel, *A*. [h] London', *A*. [i] de la Kernal, *A*. [j] Wilton, *A*. [k] xxvj^{o}, *A*.

COMMENT. Humphrey of Berkeley's long and detailed charter is given in *Arbroath Liber*, i, no.89 (24 August, 1198 × 20 August, 1199). It gives an account of the perambulation of Balfeith according to the assize of the realm (cf. *SHR*, xlv, 25–6), and states the marches as 'between the burn of Monboddo and the Bervie Water, and between Bervie Water on one side and 'Fewth' (a name now lost, but preserved in Balfeith itself) on the other side, flowing into Bervie'. Easements and pasture comprised peats and pasture for 100 beasts and their followers, as many pigs and horses as are required, and a shieling from Easter to All Saints for the rearing of the foregoing beasts in Tipperty, Corsebauld or Glenfarquhar; together with licence to build a mill on the land.

414 Confirms to Coupar Angus Abbey the grant made by Thomas son of Malcolm of Lundie of one merk of silver annually, to be taken from his land of 'Balmetiremahc', with common rights in the peatary beside Lochindores (in Lundie), Angus, with easements in the land by the peatary as Thomas's charter sets forth. Forfar. (3 April, 1196 × 1207, perhaps 1199)

.W. Dei gr*ati*a Rex Scott'. Omnibus probis hominibus tocius terre sue . Clericis 7 laicis Salutem. Sciatis me concessisse 7 hac carta mea confirmasse Deo 7 ecclesie Sancte Marie de Cupre . 7 monachis ibidem Deo seruientibus donacionem illam quam Thomas fil*ius* Malcolm*i* de Lundin eis fecit de una marca argenti annuatim in elemosina percipienda de terra eius de Balmetiremahc cum communione Petere eius iuxta Lokendor . 7 aisiamentis terre eius iuxta peteram illam secundum quod carta eius proportat. Quare uolo ut ipsi monachi in liberam 7 perpetuam elemosinam predictam marcam argenti de predicta terra de Bal*me*tiremahc[a] annuatim percipiant 7 habeant cum communione predicte petere 7 aisiamentis iuxta peteram . ita libere 7 quiete . Plenarie 7 honorifice . sicut carta predicti Thome testatur . saluo seruicio meo. Test*ibus* G. Com*ite* de Mar . Walt*ero* . 7 Will*elmo* Capellanis . A. vice*comite* de Striuelin . Malc*olmo* fil*io* G. Comitis de Mar . Alex*andro* fil*io* Thore . Dauid Marescall*o* . Philippo de Lundin. Apud Forfar . iii. die Aprilis.

ENDORSED. .T'. de Lundin. (xiii cent.). De marca Thom*e* Ostiarii (xiii cent.). confirmacio unius marce de Balmetiremahc et communis petere et aliorum asiamentorum de Lokyndor etc ., annui redditus (xv cent.). G (xiv–xv cent.).
DESCRIPTION. 7·1″ (18 cm.), Top and bottom × 4″ (10·1 cm.), L, R. Foot folded to a depth of 0·5″ (1·8 cm.). Single slits in foot and fold for seal-tag, but neither seal-tag nor seal remains.
HAND. Scribe Da. Unruled.
SOURCE. Original, Earl of Moray, Darnaway Castle, Moray Muniments, Box 32, Division IV, Bdle. 1, no.1 = *A*.
Nat. Lib., MS. Adv. 33.2.9, fo.35r (brief abstract) = *B*.
PRINTED. *Coupar Angus Chrs.*, i, no.XVII (from *A*). *Coupar Angus Rental*, i, 341, no.63 (from *B*).
NOTE. [a] Written Baltiremahc, with stroke through l.
COMMENT. Thomas of Lundie's charter is given in abstract only, *Coupar Angus Rental*, i, 341, no.62. This abstract says nothing of the peatary or easements, but stipulates that if Thomas die in the kingdom of Scotland his body is to be brought to Coupar for burial 'in the cloister before the church door'.

415 Grants to Henry Bald the land in the burgh of Perth with which James son of Simon and the king's other provosts of Perth invested him by the king's command; viz. that which is on the front of the street leading from the church of St John Baptist to the castle, on the west side, opposite the house of Andrew son of Simon. To be held in feu and heritage, for an annual render into the king's chamber of one pound of pepper at Michaelmas. Perth. (14 April, 1196 × 1199)

Willelmus[a] Dei gracia Rex Scottorum omnibus probis hominibus tocius terre sue, clericis et laicis, salutem. Sciant presentes et futuri me dedisse et concessisse et hac carta mea confirmasse Henrico Baldo terram illam in burgo meo de Pert quam Jacobus filius Simonis et alii prepositi mei de Pert ei per preceptum meum tradiderunt; illam scilicet que est in fronte vici illius qui tendit de ecclesia Sancti Johannis Baptiste usque ad castellum de Perth ex orientali parte, contra domum Andree filii Simonis; tenend*am* sibi et heredibus suis de me et heredibus meis in feodo et[b] hereditate libere et quiete, plenarie et honorifice, reddendo inde annuatim camere mee unam libram piperis ad festum Sancti Michaelis. Test*ibus* Hug*one* Canc*ellario* meo, Philippo de Valoniis[c] camerario meo, Malcolmo fil*io* comitis Duncani, Willelmo de Haia, Alexandro vicec*omite* meo de Striuelin, Rogero de Mortuo Mari, Philippo de Lundyn. Apud Pert, xiiii die April*is*.

SOURCE. NLS, MS. Adv. 34.3.28, fos.12^v–13^r.
PRINTED. *Scone Liber*, no.45.
NOTES. [a] Initial omitted, MS. [b] Fo.13^r. [c] Volone, MS.
COMMENT. See no.211 for James of Perth.

416 Confirms to Arbroath Abbey the grant made by his chancellor Hugh (of Roxburgh) of one toft in his burgh of Forfar, as Hugh's charter bears witness. Montrose. (20 April, 1196 × 1199)

W.[a] Dei gr*ati*a Rex Scotorum . omnibus probis hominibus tocius terre sue clericis et laicis salutem. Sciant presentes et futuri me concessisse et hac carta mea confirmasse Deo et ecclesie Sancti Thome de Abirbroth*oc* et monachis ibidem Deo seruientibus toftum illud in burgo meo de Forfar . quod Hugo Cancellarius meus eis dedit et carta sua confirmauit. Tenend*um* in liberam et puram et perpetuam elemosinam . ita libere et quiete plenarie et honorifice . sicut carta predicti Hug*onis* Cancell*arii* mei testatur. Test*ibus* Ric*ardo* de prebenda clerico meo . Waltero et Willelmo Capellanis meis . Philippo de Valon*iis* Camerar*io* meo . Roberto de London*iis* . Malcolmo filio comitis Dunecani . Rob*erto* de Berkel' . Philippo de London' . Apud Monros .xx°. die Aprilis.

RUBRIC. Confirmacio Regis W. super eadem carta (red)[b].
SOURCE. NLS, MS. Adv. 34.4.2, fo.lxii^r.
PRINTED. *Arbroath Liber*, i, no.80 (*bis*).
NOTES. [a] Initial red. [b] No marginated numeral; entered between lxxx and lxxxj.
COMMENT. Hugh's charter is given in *Arbroath Liber*, i, no.80, stating that the toft had been given to him by the king, by charter, and that it lay next to the toft of Walter of Berkeley on the west. Elected bishop of Glasgow after 17 March, 1199, Hugh of Roxburgh died on 10 July, 1199. Eulogistic verses composed in honour of Hugh the chancellor are printed in Surtees Soc., vol. lxx (1880), 86–8.

417 Grants to Arbroath Abbey the church of Coull in Mar, Aberdeenshire. Aberdeen. (7 June, 1198 or 1199)

W.[a] Dei gr*ati*a Rex Scott'[b] . omnibus probis hominibus . tocius terre sue clericis . et laicis .· salutem. Sciant presentes et futuri . me dedisse . et concessisse . et hac carta mea confirmasse . Deo et ecclesie Sancti Thome martiris de Aberbroth*oc* . et monachis ibidem Deo seruientibus Ecclesiam de Cul in Marr',[c] cum terris . et decimis . et oblacionibus et obuencionibus omnimodis et omnibus aliis iustis pertinenciis suis . Tenend*am* sibi in liberam . et puram . et perpetuam elemosinam . cum communi pastura . et omnibus aliis aisiamentis . ad predictam ecclesiam iuste pertinentibus . ita[d] libere . et quiete . plenarie . & honorifice :· sicut aliquam ecclesiam . liberius . & quiecius . plenius et honorificencius :· tenent et possident. Test*ibus* Rogero episcopo Sancti Andr*ee* . M*atheo* episcopo Abird*onensi* . Philippo de Valon*iis* . Cam*erario* meo . Rob*erto* de Quenci . W*illelmo*[e] de Haya . Johanne de Hasting' . Henr*ico* Reuel' . Waltero Murdach. Apud Abirden .vii°. die Junii.

RUBRIC. De ecclesia . de Cula . in Mar (Red, *E*). De ecclesia de Cule in Marr' (red, *A*). .xxix. (in margin, *A*, *E*).

SOURCE. NLS, MS. Adv. 34.4.2, fo.xlviii[r–v] = *A*. SRO, Northesk Muniments (uncatalogued), Ethie MS., fo.5[v] = *E*. Printed here from *A*.

PRINTED. *Arbroath Liber*, i, no.29 (from *E*).

NOTES. [a] Initial red. [b] Scoc', *E*. [c] Mar, *E*. [d] Fo.xlviii[v]. [e] Will*elmo*, *E*.

418

Grants to William Giffard, son of Hugh Giffard, Tealing (Angus) and Powgavie (in Inchture), Perthshire, by the marches by which Ferthnauh held that land, to be held in feu and heritage, with soke and sake, toll, team and infangthief, with pit and gallows, as other of the king's barons hold their lands and feus, for the service of one knight. Montrose. (1 September, 1196 × *c*.1201)

.W'. Dei gr*atia* Rex Scott'. Episcopis . Abbatibus . Com*itibus* . Baron*ibus* . Justic*iis* . Vicecom*itibus* . Prepositis . Ministris . 7 Omnibus probis hominibus tocius terre sue clericis 7 laicis Salutem. Sciant presentes 7 futuri me dedisse 7 concessisse et[a] hac carta mea confirmasse Willelmo Giffard' filio Hug*onis* Giffard' Thelin per rectas diuisas suas et[a] cum omnibus justis pertinenciis suis . et[a] Polgauethin per rectas diuisas suas per quas Ferthnauh terram illam tenuit 7 cum omnibus aliis ad predictam terram juste pertinentibus. Tenend*a* sibi 7 heredibus suis de me 7 heredibus meis in feudo 7 hereditate in bosco 7 plano in terris 7 aquis in pratis 7 pascuis in moris 7 maresiis . in piscariis 7 Scalingis in stagnis 7 molendinis . 7 omnibus aliis ad predictas terras juste pertinentibus cum furca 7 fossa Cum socca 7 sacca cum tol 7 them . 7 infangenthef ita libere 7 Quiete Plenarie 7 honorifice sicut alii Barones mei terras 7 feuda sua liberius quietius plenius 7 honorificentius de me tenent . faciendo de predictis terris seruicium unius militis. Test*ibus* Regin*aldo* Rosen*si* Episcopo. Com*ite* Dunec*ano* Justic*ia* . Roberto de Quinci . Philippo de Valon*iis* Camerar*io* . Willelmo Cumin . Johanne de Hasting' . Willelmo de Haia . Rann*ulfo* de Sol*is* . Umfrido de Berk' . Rog*ero* de Mortem*er* . Philippo de Lundin . Walt*ero* Murdac . Rogero de la Kerneil . Hugone clerico de Sigillo Ap*ud* Munros primo die Septem*bris*

ENDORSED. Telyn et Polgauy (xiv cent.). carta terrarum de Thelin et Polgauethin (xv–xvi cent.).

DESCRIPTION. 8″ (20·3 cm.), Top and bottom × 5·7″ (14·5 cm.), L, R. Foot folded to a depth of 1·2″ (3 cm.). Seal-tag passes through single slits in foot and fold, 6·5″ (16·4 cm.) long, 0·9″ (2·2 cm.) wide. No seal remains.

HAND. Scribe Db. Unruled.

SOURCE. Original, Marquis of Tweeddale, Yester House, Yester Writs, no.6.

PRINTED. Fraser, *Carlaverock*, ii, 403–4, no.2 (with facsimile); *Fraser Facsimiles*, no.25; *Yester Writs*, no.6.

NOTE. [a] Crossed tironian sign.

COMMENT. No other reference to Ferthnauh has been found; he may have been thane of Tealing.

419 Confirms to Arbroath Abbey the grant made by Malise son of Ferteth earl of Strathearn of half a merk of silver from the fishery of Meikleour, Perthshire, as the charter of Malise bears witness. Montrose. (*c.*1199)

W.[a] Dei gr*ati*a Rex Scott' . omnibus probis hominibus tocius terre sue clericis et laicis salutem. Sciant presentes et futuri me concessisse et hac carta mea confirmasse Deo et ecclesie Sancti Thome martiris de[b] Abirbroth*oc* et monachis ibidem Deo seruientibus donacionem illam quam Malisius filius Ferteth'[c] comitis de Strathern eis fecit de una dimidia marca argenti in piscaria sua de Vr . Tenendam sibi in liberam et puram et perpetuam elemosinam . ita libere et quiete plenarie et honorifice . sicut carta predicti Malisii testatur. Test*ibus* Philippo de Valon*iis* Camerario meo . Roberto de Quency . Willelmo Cumyn . Johanne de Hastyng' . Will*elmo* de Haya . Will*elmo* Giffard' . Waltero Murdach' . Dauid de Haya. Apud Monros.

RUBRIC. Confirmacio Regis W. de dicta dimidia marca (red)[d].
SOURCE. NLS, MS. Adv. 34.4.2, fo.lxiv^{r-v}.
PRINTED. *Arbroath Liber*, i, no.86 (*bis*).
NOTES. [a] Initial red. [b] Fo.lxiv^{v}. [c] Added in margin in text hand. [d] No marginated numeral; entered between lxxxvj and lxxxvij.
COMMENT. The day of the month may have been omitted by the copyist. Malise's charter is given in *Arbroath Liber*, i, no.86, evidently issued on the same occasion as the royal confirmation; providing for the half merk to be paid yearly at Whitsun. It is not clear whether the fishery was in the River Tay or the River Isla, or both.

420 Grants to Coupar Angus Abbey the whole marsh in the territory of Blairgowrie, Perthshire, belonging to the king's demesne of Blair on the day when he granted it, and when by his command Earl Duncan, Hugh of Calder, Roger de Mortemer, Macbeth judex of Gowrie, Duncan son of Donald and other responsible men put the abbey in sasine of it. Forfar. (1198 × 1202)

Carta regis Villielmi eisdem monachis facta de toto maresio meo in territorio de Blair[a], quod pertinebat ad dominium meum de Blar, die qua marescum illud iis dedi, et Comes Duncanus, et Heugo de Kaledone[b], et Rogerus de Mortuomari, et Mack-beth Judex de Goury, et Duncanus filius Douenaldi, et alii probi homines per preceptum meum eiis tradiderunt, &c. Testibus: Rogero Episcopo St Andreæ, Com*ite* Dauide fratre meo, Duncano justiciario, Com*ite* Gillebryd, Phil*i*ppo de Walloun camerario meo, Roberto de Quinci, Malcolmo filio Comitis Duncani, Villielmo[c] Cumyn, Johanne Hasting, Villielmo de Haya, &c. Apud Forfar.

SOURCE. NLS, MS. Adv. 33.2.9, fo.28^{v}.
PRINTED. *Coupar Angus Rental*, i, 325, no.14.
NOTES. [a] Probably altered to Blare. [b] For Kaledouer. [c] MS. adds de.
COMMENT. This act seems to refer to an area in the south of Blairgowrie parish, represented by Muirton of Ardblair and perhaps other lands. 'Gillebryd' among the witnesses may be an error for *Gilbert* earl of Strathearn.

421 Grants to the church of the Holy Trinity of the bishopric of Moray and to Bishop Richard and his successors the teind of his revenues of Moray and of his pleas throughout the diocese of Moray and of his cain, not already assigned to other churches, in cows, pigs, wheat, malt, oats, cheese and butter. Forfar. (26 December, 1199)

.W. Dei gratia Rex Scott' episcopis . abbatibus . comitibus . baronibus . justiciis . vicecom*itibus* . prepositis . ministris . et omnibus probis hominibus tocius terre sue clericis et laicis salutem. Sciant presentes et futuri me dedisse et concessisse et hac carta mea confirmasse Deo et ecclesie Sancte Trinitatis de episcopatu Morau*iensi* et Ric*ardo* episcopo et successoribus suis in liberam et perpetuam elemosinam . pro animabus antecessorum meorum et pro salute anime mee . decimam meam de redditibus meis de Moreu*ia* . et de placitis meis per totum episcopatum Morau*iensem* de redditibus meis . scilicet de cano meo . de vaccis et porcis . et de frumento et braseo . et prebenda . et de caseo et de butiro quod antecessores mei non dederunt nec assignaverunt ad alias ecclesias. Quare firmiter precipio ballivis meis de Morav*ia* . ut ipsi sine disturbatione faciant Ric*ardo* episcopo et successoribus suis singulis annis plenarie et integre habere predictam decimam de redditibus meis . siue redditus mei in denariis reddantur siue alio modo per quamcunque permutationem. Test*ibus* Will*elmo* electo Glasguen*si* cancell*ario* meo . Johanne electo de Aberdon . Henrico abbate de Aberbrodoch . Ric*ardo* de Prebenda clerico meo . Com*ite* Dunec*ano* justic*ia* . Com*ite* Gilleb*erto* . Philippo de Valon*iis* . Will*elmo* Cumin . Will*elmo* de Haia . Malc*olmo* fil*io* com*itis* Dunc*ani* . Alano filio Rollandi . Willelmo Gigfarth . Will*elmo* de Vallibus. Apud Forfar xxvi. die Decembris.

MARGINAL NOTE. [Ista non scribitur in li]bro decani.
SOURCE. NLS, MS. Adv. 34.4.10, fo.xxxvii^r.
PRINTED. *Moray Registrum*, no.17.
COMMENT. See no.273 above, from which it differs only in providing for the commutation of revenues in kind to money payments.

422 Grants to Robert son of Maccus one ploughgate of land in the territory of Lessudden (St Boswells), Roxburghshire, which Herbert of Maxwell his sheriff and Geoffrey the clerk handed over to him on the king's command; to be held in feu and heritage, for an annualrent of 20s., 10s. at Martinmas and 10s. at Whitsun, and for all the services belonging to the land save for ploughing and reaping. Forfar. (29 December, 1199)

W'. Dei gr*ati*a Rex Scott'. Omnibus probis hominibus tocius terre sue Clericis 7 Laicis .ʾ Salutem. Sciant presentes 7 futuri me dedisse 7 concessisse 7 hac carta mea confirmasse Rob*erto* fil*io* Maccus . unam carucatam terre in territorio de Lesedwin'. illam scilicet quam Herb*ertus* de Maccuswell' vic*ecomes* meus 7 Galfridus clericus per preceptum meum ei tradiderunt. Tenend*am* sibi 7 heredibus suis de me 7 heredibus meis in feudo 7 hereditate . Reddendo Inde annuatim . viginti sol*idos* . scilicet decem ad festum Sancti Martin*i* 7 decem solid*os* ad Pentecost*en* . Et faciendo omnia seruicia que ad terram illam pertinent . 7 que terra illa facere consueuit . preter arare 7 metere. Test*ibus* Willelmo Glasg*uensi*

Electo Cancell*ario* meo . Ric*ardo* de prebenda Clerico meo . Phil*ippo* de Valon*iis* Camerar*io* meo . Willelmo Cumi*n* . Alex*andro* de Sintun. Apud Forfar' xxviiij die Decembr*is*[a].

ENDORSED. E (xiv or xv cent.). 21. J. Scott (xvi–xvii cent.).
DESCRIPTION. 5·5″ (14 cm.), Top, 5·7″ (14·5 cm.), Bottom × 5″ (10·2 cm.), L, 3·5″ (8·9 cm.), R. Foot folded to a depth of 0·7″ (1·9 cm.). Seal-tag passes through double slits in foot and fold, approximately 6·75″ (17·2 cm.) long, 0·5″ (1·4 cm.) wide. Large fragment of seal remains on tag.
HAND. Scribe Da. Unruled.
SOURCE. Original, formerly Sir John Stirling-Maxwell of Pollok, Pollok House (uncatalogued), now Glasgow City Archives.
PRINTED. Fraser, *Pollok Cartulary*, 1, no.1 (with facsimile); Fraser, *Pollok*, *Fraser Facsimiles*, no.26.
NOTE. [a] Short wavy horizontal stroke completes line.

423 Confirms to Humphrey son of Theobald de Addeville the grant made to him by Humphrey son of Theobald of one davoch in Glenfarquhar (in Fordoun), Mearns, on the east side, to be held in feu and heritage as the charter of Humphrey bears witness. Kincardine. (29 December, 1195 × 1203)

Villelmus[a] Dei gracia Rex Scotorum omnibus probis hominibus tocius terre sue clericis et laicis salutem. Sciant presentes et futuri me concessisse et hac carta mea confirmasse Umfrido filio Teob*aldi* de Adeuile donacionem illam quam Umfridus filius Teobald*i* ei fecit de uno dauach in Glenfercharin uersus orientalem partem tenendam sibi et heredibus suis in feodo et hereditate, ita libere et quiete, plenarie et honorifice, sicut carta predicti Umfridi testatur, saluo seruicio meo. Test*ibus* Com*ite* Dunecan*o* Just*icia*, Rob*erto* Cumin, Rob*erto* de Lond', Willelmo de Haya, Johanne de Hasting, Willelmo Gilfard', Waltero Murdach, Thoma Thancard'. Apud Kinkard' .xxix. die Decembr*is*.

RUBRIC. Wilelmi regis carta confirmationis . Umfrido de Barklay . filio Theobaldi de Aduile . unius dauath' in Glenferquharyn uersus orientalem partem (red).
SOURCE. BM, MS. Add. 33245, fo.145[r] (old foliation, fo.cxxvi[r]).
NOTE. [a] Initial blue, flourished red.
COMMENT. Earl Duncan of Fife died in the year ending 24 December, 1204 (*Chron. Melrose*, 52). The grantee was evidently the 'young Humphrey' who witnessed *Arbroath Liber*, i, no.89.

424 Confirms to John son of Reginald Prat the whole third part of the vill of Haughton (in Humshaugh) which Ranulf son of Uchtred gave to his father Reginald with his daughter in frank marriage. Grants that John may be free of the drengage service which Ranulf used to render to the king for the land. To be held as freely as any free men hold in the kingdom of England, for an annual *reddendo* to the king of one two-year-old sparrowhawk at Wark on Tyne. Stirling. (5 February, 1200) (Inflated)

W. Dei gr*ati*a Rex Scot' Omnibus probis hominibus Tocius terre sue clericis et laycis salutem. Sciant presentes et futuri me concessisse et hac carta mea confirmasse Johanni fil*io* Reginaldi Prat totam illam terciam partem totius ville de Haluton' cum pertinenc*iis* quam Rand*ulfus* fil*ius* Huctred' concessit predicto Reginaldo patri eiusdem Johannis in liberum Maritagium cum filia sua . Tenend*um* et habend*um* dicto Johanni et heredibus suis de me et heredibus meis libere et quiete ab omni servicio seculari . exaccione et demand*a*. Concedo ecciam eisdem quod quieti sint ab omni servicio Drengagii . quod predictus Rand*ulfus* facere solebat pro predicta terra et quod quieti sint de sectis omnimodarum . curiarum . maritagiis . Wardis . et releuiis . et de omnibus seruiciis . consuetudinibus . consuetudinibus[a] . exaccionibus . et demand*is* . et adeo libere in omnibus sicuti aliqui liberi homines terras suas tenent et possident infra regnum Anglie . et adeo libere in omnibus sicut carta mea predicto Reginaldo patri suo confecta melius ac plenius testatur. Reddendo inde annuatim ipse et heredes sui mihi et heredibus meis unum Nisum Sorum apud Werc in Tyndal' . pro omnibus seruiciis in mundo tam non nominatis quam nominatis . pro bono seruicio quod predictus Reginaldus pater suus mihi fecit. Test*ibus* Willelmo Mauuaysin . Cancell*ario* meo . Com*ite* Duncano . Philippo de Valones . Camer*ario* meo Roberto de Quency . Willelmo de Lindesay . Willelmo de Haya . Ranulph*o* de Sules . Willelmo de Munford . Herberto de Camer*a*. Apud Striuelin . v Febr*uarii*.

ENDORSED. A confirmation from Wi: kinge of Scots to John Prat of all his lands in Haughton. Haughton (xvi–xvii cent.).

DESCRIPTION. 7·7″ (19·6 cm.), Top, 7·8″ (19·8 cm.), Bottom × 3·5″ (8·9 cm.), L, 3·4″ (8·7 cm.), R. Foot folded, slits for seal-tag. Tag remains, 0·6″ (1·5 cm.) wide, with central fragment of seal in natural wax, obv. to front, max. diam. 2·4″. This seal seems genuine, and the partial impression of the horse on the rev. is especially fine.

HAND. Scribe UDc. Apparently a hand of the mid- or later xiii cent. Cp. hand of ZSW/1/11 (*tempore* Nicholas de Vieuxpont steward of Tynedale) and ZSW/1/17.

SOURCE. Non-authentic 'original', Northumberland County Record Office, Gosforth, Swinburne of Capheaton charters (ZSW/1/2).

NOTE. [a] Sic.

COMMENT. See no.143, and no.578 for witnesses. Were it not for the handwriting and the presence of certain phrases, e.g. suits of every kind of court, and all services in the world named and unnamed, this could pass for an authentic act of William I. Almost certainly it is based on a genuine original, and the testing clause and place- and time-dates may be accepted as authentic, although the omission of William Malvoisin's title as bishop-elect of Glasgow is noteworthy. Note witnesses and date of no.578.

425

Confirms to Melrose Abbey the fishery near the church of Rainpatrick (i.e., Redkirk, in Gretna, Dumfriesshire), on the south side, together with one acre of arable and pasture for four cows and six oxen, and easements of the toun of Rainpatrick, granted by William de Brus, as his charter bears witness. (1194 × 1213)

Uill*elmus*[a] Dei gr*ati*a rex Scot' omnibus probis hominibus tocius terre sue, clericis et laicis, salutem. Sciant presentes et futuri me concessisse et hac carta mea confirmasse Deo et ecclesie Sancte Marie de Melros et monachis ibidem Deo seruientibus donacionem illam quam Willelmus de Bruse eis fecit de quadam piscaria iuxta ecclesiam de Renpatrik a parte australi, ubicumque eam facere aut firmare voluerint infra diuisas in carta predicti Willelmi scriptas, cum una acra terre et pastura quatuor vaccarum et sex boum, et cum omnibus aliis asiamentis ville de Renpatrik. Tenend*am* in liberam et quietam et perpetuam elemosinam, ita libere et quiete, plenarie et honorifice, sicut carta predicti Willelmi testatur, saluo seruicio meo[b] Test*ibus*.

RUBRIC. Confirmacio reg*is* Willelmi super piscatura de Ranpatrik.
SOURCE. BM, MS. Harl. 3960, fo.57^r.
PRINTED. *Melrose Liber*, no.171; *Holm Cultram Recs.*, 35 (brief note).
NOTE. [a] Initial red. [b] MS. omits meo.
COMMENT. William de Brus's charter, from the Holm Cultram cartulary, is given in *Melrose Liber*, ii, Appendix, no.3. It is undated, but since it appears to be earlier than ibid., no.4, which in turn must be earlier than ibid., no.5 which dates × 1200, its date limits may be taken to be *c*.1195 × 1200. Rainpatrick, afterwards called Reidkirk or Redkirk, is a suppressed parish now in Gretna; in the early eighteenth century the minister of Gretna wrote that 'about half a mile to the westward of the old house of Graitney upon Solloway Firth stands the remains of the church and churchyard of Reidkirk, in which churchyard the fountstone still continues althoe the half of the churchyard is wash'n away by Solloway Firth' (*Macfarlane's Geographical Collections*, SHS, i, 381–2).

426 Grants to Glasgow Cathedral Church and its deacons and subdeacons, in the episcopate of William (Malvoisin), three merks annually from the *firma burgi* of his burgh of Rutherglen to augment the three merks he has already given from the same source in the episcopate of Jocelin, to maintain the service of deacons and subdeacons in surplices and black copes. The six merks are to be paid punctually, three at Whitsun and three at Martinmas. Edinburgh. (1 or 10 April, 1201 or 1202)

W.[a] Dei gra*ti*a Rex Scott' episcopis, abbatibus, comitibus, baronibus, justiciis, vicecomitibus, prepositis, ministris et omnibus probis hominibus totius terre sue, clericis et laicis, salutem. Sciant presentes et futuri me ad incrementum trium marcarum quas dederam tempore Jocelini episcopi Glasg*uensis* ad sustentationem unius diaconi et unius subdiaconi in ecclesia de Glasgu, tempore Willelmi episcopi eiusdem loci dedisse et concessisse et hac carta mea confirmasse Deo et ecclesie B*eati* Kentegerni et predictis diaconis et subdiaconis in ecclesia de Glasg*u* servituris alias tres marcas de firma burgi mei de Rutherglen; ita ut ipsi secundum statuta ecclesie de Glasgu decenter et ordinate incedant cum superpelliciis et nigris cappis sicut alii vicarii incedunt, tenend*as* et habend*as* in liberam, puram et perpetuam elemosinam, ita libere, quiete et honorifice sicut aliqua elemosina liberius et quietius et honorificentius in toto regno meo tenetur et possidetur. Quare precipio prepositis meis de Rutherglen ut singulis annis predictas sex marcas eisdem clericis in ecclesia Beati Kentegerni pro me et Alexandro filio meo servientibus et servituris in omni distributione habere faciant ad duos anni terminos, scilicet tres marcas ad Pentecost*en* et tres marcas ad festum Sancti Martini, et prohibeo firmiter ne prefate sex marce ultra terminos suos prescriptos eis detineantur, super meam plenariam forisfacturam. Testibus Philippo de Valon*iis* camerario meo, Waltero et Willelmo capellanis meis, Willelmo Cumin, Gervasio Avenel', Willelmo Giffard', Thom*a* de Colevill', D*aui*d de Haia, Alexandro filio Thore, Philippo de Lundin, Thom*a* de Chart[r]es,[b] Rog*ero* de la Kerneille, Rogero de Wilton'. Apud Edeneburg. i°[c] die Aprilis.

TRANSCRIBER'S NOTES. Carta Willelmi R. qua dat sex marcas de burgo de Rutherglen Diaconis et Subdiaconis Ecclesie Glasg*uensis* (at top). Ex autog*rapho* in archiv*is* Eccl*esie* Glasg*uensis* apud in pyx*ide* ligne*a* sub litt*era* A (in margin). Huic cartæ appensus est sigillum magnum multum attritum ut supra (at foot).
SOURCE. Glasgow University Library, MS. BE 8, d 6, pp. 95–6.
PRINTED. *Glasgow Registrum*, no.92.
NOTES. [a] Punctuation editorial. [b] Written Chartes, but stroke through t may represent mark of suspension. [c] Written 10, either for primo or decimo in original.
COMMENT. Probably issued four days before or five days after no.427.

427 Confirms to Inchaffray Abbey the grant made to it by Earl Gilbert of Strathearn of the lands of Ardunie, Craig, and Dubheads (in Madderty), Perthshire, and also of that land of Madderty which was anciently called 'abbethen'; on condition that the earl and his heirs perform for the remainder of Madderty the whole service due to the king for the whole feu of Madderty. Stirling. (5 April, 1201 or 1202)

.W. Dei gr*ati*a Rex Scott'. Omnibus probis Hominibus totius terre sue clericis et laicis :' salutem. Sciant presentes et futuri me concessisse . et hac carta mea confirmasse Deo et ecclesie Sancti Johannis apostoli et ewangelist*e* de Inche affren . et Canonicis ibidem Deo seruientibus et seruituris . donationem illam quam Com*es* Gilleb*ertus* de Stradheren' eis rationabiliter fecit de tota terra de Ardehewni per rectas diuisas suas . et cum omnibus iustis pertinentiis . et de tota terra de Archadlongsih[a] . per rectas diuisas suas . et cum omnibus iustis pertinentiis suis . et de tota terra de Dufhinder . per rectas diuisas suas et cum omnibus iustis pertinentiis suis . et de terra illa de Madernin que antiquitus abbethen uocabatur per rectas diuisas suas . et cum omnibus iustis pertinentiis suis. Tenend*am* in liberam et puram . et perpetuam elemosinam . per rectas diuisas predictarum terrarum . et cum omnibus ad predictas terras iuste pertinentibus . ita libere . et Quiete . plenarie . et honorifice :' sicut carta predicti Com*itis* Gilleb*erti* iuste testatur . ita tamen quod predictus Com*es* et heredes sui facient michi et heredibus meis de residuo de Madernin totum seruicium . quod michi debetur de toto feudo de Madernin. Test*ibus* Willelmo Episcopo Glasguen*si* Cancell*ario* meo . Philipp*o* de Valon*iis* Camerario meo . Will*elmo* Cumin . Willelmo Giffard' . Thom*a* de Coleuill' . Alex*andro* vic*ecomite* de Striuelin . Rad*ulfo* de Camera . Herb*erto* de Camera . D*aui*d de Haia . Philipp*o* de Lundin . Thom*a* Hostiar*io*. Apud Striuelin . quinto die Aprilis.

ENDORSED. De abthein de Manerdin (altered to Maderdin) (xiii cent.). Confirmacio Regis Willelmi super terris de Ardeuny Achlonxich Duffindir Maddirdyn Rubrica .vj.[b]
DESCRIPTION. 8·2″ (21·4 cm.), Top, 7·3″ (18·1 cm.), Bottom × 3·7″ (9·5 cm.), L, 4·4″ (11·1 cm.), R. (Parchment cut away at bottom left-hand corner before document was written). Foot folded, four holes for silk cords. Woven silk cord remains, double, pale gold, with seal almost complete in green wax, diameter 3·1″. Clear impression.
HAND. Scribe Dd. Unruled.
SOURCE. Original, Kinnoull Trustees Muniments, in custody of Messrs Condie, Mackenzie and Co., W.S., Perth (Dupplin Charters, no.120) = *A*. Kinnoull Trustees Muniments (as above), MS. Cartulary of Inchaffray Abbey, fo.45^{r-v} = *B*. Printed here from *A*.

PRINTED. *Inchaffray Chrs.*, no.20 (from *A*), and facsimile no.7. *Inchaffray Liber*, 70–71, no.73 (from *B*).
NOTES. [a] Sic; for Acchadlongsih? *B* has Achlongsich. [b] *B* only. Numeral refers to section beginning on fo.43.
COMMENT. For the identification of the place-names, cf. *Inchaffray Chrs.*, 318–19 and accompanying map. The 'abbethen' (*apdaine*) of Madderty was so named because it had anciently been given to the abbot and church of Dunkeld; the bishops of Dunkeld, as successors to the abbots, granted and confirmed the abthen to Inchaffray Abbey (*Inchaffray Chrs.*, nos.7 and 23). Note witnesses and date of no.578.

428 Re-grants to Hugh, son of Hugh of Benholm, Benholm (Mearns) in feu and heritage, with pit and gallows, soke and sake, toll, team and infangthief, for the service of half a knight. Kincardine. (20 August, 1200 × 1203, probably 1201)

.W. Dei gr*ati*a Rex Scott'. Omnibus probis Hominibus totius terre sue Clericis et laicis :' salutem. Sciant presentes . et futuri . me reddidisse . et concessisse . et hac carta mea confirmasse . Hug*oni* filio Hug*onis* de Benne :' Benne per rectas diuisas suas . et cum Omnibus iustis pertinentiis suis. Tenend*um* sibi . et[a] heredibus suis . de Me et heredibus meis . in feudo . et hereditate . in bosco . et plano . in terris . et aquis . in pratis et pascuis . in Moris . et Maresiis . in stangnis et molendinis . et cum Omnibus aliis ad predictam terram iuste pertinentibus. Cum furca et fossa . cum socca . et sacca . cum thol . et them . et infangenethef. libere . et quiete . plenarie et honorifice :' faciendo inde mihi et heredibus meis . seruicium dimid*ii* militis :' sicut Carta predicti Hug*onis* patris sui testatur. Test*ibus* Reginald*o* Rossensi episcopo . Willelmo et Walt*ero* Capellanis meis . Comite Dunecan*o* de Fif . Philipp*o* de Valon*iis* Camer*ario* . Rob*erto* de Quinci . Alano fil*io* Rolland*i* constabul*ario* . Willelmo Cumi*n* . Johanne de Hasting' . Willelmo de Haia . Yuone de Veteri Ponte . Roger*o* de la Kerneill' . Malcolm*o* de Lacel*es*. Apud Kinkarden .xx^{mo}. die . Augusti[b].

ENDORSED. The kingis chartour of the landis of Bennem (xvii cent., barely legible). Chartour of the landis of Bennem grantit be k. Wm to Hew Bennem (xvii cent.).
DESCRIPTION. 8·2″ (21·3 cm.), Top and bottom × 4·4″ (11·2 cm.), L, R. Foot folded to a depth of 0·9″ (2·3 cm.), L increasing to 1·5″ (7·8 cm.), R. Seal-tag, 3·5″ (9 cm.) long, 0·6″ (1·5 cm.) wide passes through double slits in foot and fold. No seal remains.
HAND. Scribe Dd. Unruled.
SOURCE. Original, SRO, GD 4/2.
NOTES. [a] Hitherto et has been written in full; henceforward inclusive the alternation between crossed tironian sign and full form is as follows: 3, 1, 3, 1, 3, 1, 1, 2, 1. [b] cross stroke of t prolonged 7·2″ to fill bottom line.
COMMENT. See no.350.

429 Quitclaims his burgesses of Aberdeen, for the good service they have rendered him, of toll on their own goods throughout his realm; no one is to demand such toll from them on pain of the king's full forfeiture. Aberdeen. (28 August, 1200 × 1203, probably 1201)

.W. Dei gr*ati*a Rex Scott'. Episcopis . Abbatibus . Com*itibus* . Baron*ibus* . Justic*iis* . Vicecom*itibus* . prepositis . Ministris . 7 omnibus probis hominibus tocius[a] terre sue clericis 7 Laicis salutem. Sciant presentes 7 futuri me in perpetuum quietos clammasse[b] burgenses[c] meos de Aberdon a tolneio de propriis catallis suis per totum Regnum meum ⁝ pro bono seruicio quod idem burgenses mei mihi fecerunt. Et ideo uolo ut nullum per Regnum meum dent tolneium ⁝ de propriis catallis suis 7 firmiter precipio ut ubicunque in Regno meo uenerint ⁝ perpetuo a tolneio quieti sint de propriis catallis suis. Quare prohibeo firmiter Ne quis in Regno meo eos iniuste uexare presumpmat[d] in exigendo ab eis de propriis catallis eorum tolneium ⁝ super meam plenariam forisfacturam. Test*ibus* Ricardo Episcopo Morau'[e]. Com*ite* Dunec*ano* Just*icia*[f]. Gillecrist com*ite* de Mar. Willelmo 7 Waltero capellanis meis. Philippo de Valon*iis*. Alan*o* fil*io* Rolland*i*. constab*ulario*. Willelmo de Haia. Willelmo Giffart[g]. Umfr*ido* de Berk'[h]. Henr*ico* Reuel. Thoma Thancart[i]. Yuone de Veteri ponte. Waltero filio Sibald*i*. Apud Aberdon. xx.viii. die Augusti.

ENDORSED. *A*: Infeodacio tollonij de propriis catallis (xiii cent.). A chartour of the toll of . . all gudis (xvi cent.). 28 Au[gust] (xvi cent.?). *B*: Infeodacio de tolloniis de propriis catallis (xiii cent.). The chartour of the toll of cattel (xvi cent.).

DESCRIPTION. *A*: 8″ (20·4 cm.), Top and bottom × 3·5″ (9 cm.), L, R. Foot folded to a depth of 1″ (2·5 cm.). A tie may have been cut away from left-hand edge of fold. Seal-tag, 7·5″ (19 cm.) long and 0·6″ (1·6 cm.) wide, passes through double slits in foot and fold. Seal remains on tag, dark green wax, diameter 3″ (7·6 cm.), good impression. *B*: 7″ (19·8 cm.), Top and bottom × 4·1″ (10·4 cm.), L, R. Foot folded to a depth of 1·2″ (3 cm.). Tie cut from left-hand top corner of fold, 5·7″ (14·5 cm.) long, 0·3″ (0·7 cm.) wide. Seal-tag, 6·4″ (16·3 cm.) long and 0·6″ (1·5 cm.) wide, passes through double slits in foot and fold. Seal remains on tag, green wax, diameter 3·1″ (7·9 cm.), edges badly chipped and surface rubbed.

HAND. *A*: Scribe Db. Unruled. *B*: Scribe Dd. Unruled.

SOURCE. Duplicate originals, Aberdeen Burgh Records A¹2 = *A*, A¹3 = *B*. Printed here from *A*, with variants of *B* noted.

PRINTED. *Municipal Corporations Report* (1836), Appendix II, p.6; *Aberdeen Burgh Charters*, 4–5, no.II.

NOTES. [a] totius, *B*. [b] clamasse, *B*, with stroke of suspension over first a. [c] omnes burgenses, *B*. [d] presupmat, *B*. [e] Morauie, *B*. [f] Justic', *B*. [g] Giffard', *B*. [h] Berkal', *B*. [i] Thancard', *B*.

430 Announces that William Cumin in the king's presence and in his court [at Alyth] has quitclaimed to Glasgow Cathedral Church and to William (Malvoisin) bishop of Glasgow and his successors all the right which he believed himself to have in the land called Muckcroft (in Cadder, Lanarkshire), over which there was a lawsuit between him and the bishop, William Cumin affirming that the land belonged to Kirkintilloch, the bishop that it belonged to Bedlay. The king confirms William Cumin's quitclaim, as his charter bears witness. Roxburgh. (1 March, 1201 or 1202)

W'. Dei Gr*ati*a Rex Scott'. Omnibus probis hominibus totius terre sue clericis et laicis ⁝ Salutem. Sciant presentes et futuri Willelmum Cumi*n* in presentia mea. et in curia mea quietum clamasse pro se et heredibus suis inperpetuum Deo et Sancto Kentegerno. et Willelmo episcopo Glasguen*si* et successoribus suis inperpetuum totum ius quod idem Willelmus Cumi*n* dicebat et credebat se habere in terra illa que dicitur

Muncraht . unde loquela fuit inter predictum Willelmum Episcopum et predictum Willelmum Cumi*n* . quam terram idem Willelmus Cumi*n* dicebat esse de Kirkentulaht . et quam predictus episcopus dicebat esse de Ballain. Et quod ego adquietantiam illam ratam et firmam habeo et concedo . et hac carta mea confirmo. Quare uolo et firmiter precipio ut predictus Willelmus Episcopus et successores sui inperpetuum habeant . et teneant predictam terram de Muncrath cum iustis pertinentiis suis . liberam et quietam pro predicto Willelmo et heredibus suis inperpetuum ab omni iure quod idem Willelmus Cumi*n* dicebat uel credebat se habere in predicta terra sicut carta ipsius Willelmi Cumi*n* testatur. Test*ibus* O*sberto* abbate de Kelhou[a] . Com*ite* Patric*io* . Alan*o* fil*io* Roll*andi* Constab*ulario* meo . Roberto de Lund*oniis* . Willelmo de Lindes' . Geruasio Auenel . Thom*a* de Colleuill' . Hen*rico* de Cormanoc . Herbert*o* de Macuswell' . Bernardo de Hauden' . Waltero Murdach' . Philipp*o* Maresc*allo* . D*aui*d Maresc*allo*. Apud Rochesburc . primo die Marc*ii*.

RUBRIC. Item De terra de Muncrath iacente inter Badlayn . et Kirkentulaht (in margin in different hand).
SOURCE. Blairs Archives, 16 Drummond Place, Edinburgh, MS. Registrum Vetus of Glasgow, fo.vij[r].
PRINTED. *Glasgow Registrum*, no.91.
NOTE. [a] Or Kelkou.
COMMENT. See no.501. William Cumin's charter, which shews that the session of the *curia regis* referred to was at Alyth, is given in *Glasgow Registrum*, no.90. William Malvoisin, returning from his consecration on the continent, did not reach Dover until 1 February, 1201.

431 Confirms to Cambuskenneth Abbey the grant made by Saer de Quinci of his whole land of Abbots Deuglie (in Arngask), Perthshire, as the charter of Saer bears witness. Edinburgh. (7 July, 1196 × 1203)

Wilelmus[a] Dei gracia Rex Scotorum omnibus probis hominibus totius terre sue, clericis et laicis, salutem. Sciant presentes et futuri me concessisse et hac carta mea confirmasse Deo et ecclesie Sancte Marie de Cambuskynneth et canonicis ibidem Deo seruientibus donationem illam quam Seherus de Quinci eis fecit de tota terra sua de Duglyn; tenendam in liberam et puram et perpetuam elemosinam per rectas diuisas predicte terre et cum omnibus aliis ad eandem terram iuste pertinentibus ita libere et quiete, plenarie et honorifice sicut carta predicti[b] Seheri iuste testatur, saluo toto forinseco seruicio meo quod ad dictam terram illam pertinet. Testibus, Comite Patricio iustic*iario*, Willelmo capellano meo, Ric*ardo* de Prebenda clerico meo, Philippo marescallo meo, Dauid marescallo meo, Alexandro filio Thore, Rog*ero* de Wilt*un*, Herberto de Camera, apud Edinburgh, septimo die Julii.

RUBRIC. Douglie terrarum confirmatio (at top). Concordat cum principali Jacobus Foulis.
SOURCE. NLS, MS. Adv. 34.1.2, fo.46[r–v].
PRINTED. *Cambuskenneth Registrum*, no.72.
NOTES. [a] Large blue initial U. [b] MS. predicta.
COMMENT. Three charters of Saer de Quinci survive which relate to Deuglie. The earliest, confirmed here, is *Cambuskenneth Registrum*, no.71; the others were

issued after Saer became earl of Winchester in 1207 (ibid., nos.70, 73). They shew that Deuglie had belonged to Saer's maternal grandfather, Ness son of William, and that Ness's former chamberlain, Duncan son of Hamelin (*alias* Emlin, Hemli), had some claim on the land (cf. *St Andrews Liber*, pp.288, 290, 291).

432 Confirms to the religious of Inchaffray (Inchaffray Abbey) the grant made to them by Earl Gilbert of Strathearn of the churches of Madderty, St Bean of Kinkell (in Trinity Gask) and St Mahessoch (Kessog) of Auchterarder (Perthshire). Stirling. (13 August, 1201 × 1203)

.W Dei gr*ati*a Rex Scott' . Omnibus probis Hominibus totius terre sue clericis et laicis :' salutem. Sciant presentes et futuri me concessisse . et hac carta mea confirmasse Deo et ecclesie Sancti Johannis ewangeliste . de Inche afren . et uiris religiosis ibi Deo seruientibus et seruituris donationem illam quam Gillebertus Com*es* de Stradheren eis rationabiliter fecit de ecclesia de Madernin . cum omnibus iustis pertinentiis . et de ecclesia Sancti Beani de Kinkelle cum omnibus iustis pertinentiis suis . et de ecclesia Sancti Mahessoch de Uchterardouer' . cum omnibus iustis pertinentiis suis. Tenend*am* in liberam et puram et perpetuam elemosinam cum Omnibus ad predictas ecclesias iuste pertinentibus ita libere et quiete . plenarie . et honorifice sicut carta predicti Com*itis* Gilleb*erti* iuste testatur. Test*ibus* Ric*ardo* de prebenda clerico meo . Willelmo Capellano . Alan*o* fil*io* Rollandi constabul*ario* . Malcolm*o* fil*io* Com*itis* Dunecani . Malisio fil*io* Com*itis* Ferteth' Will*elmo* Giffard . Roberto Croch' . Alex*andro* vice*comite* de Striueli*n* . Rad*ulfo* de Camera . Heruico de Kinros . Ric*ardo* fil*io* Hug*onis* . Philipp*o* Marescall*o* . Will*elmo* de Morauia . Alexand*ro* fil*io* Thore. Apud Striuelin xiij. die Augusti.

ENDORSED. De Madredin. de ecclesia. (xiii cent.). Confirmacio Willelmi Regis super ecclesia de Maddirdyn rubrica .v.[a]
DESCRIPTION. 6·8″ (17·2 cm.), Top, 6·5″ (16·5 cm.), Bottom × 4″ (10·2 cm.), L, 4·1″ (10·5 cm.), R. Foot folded. Double slits with tag 0·8″ (2·1 cm.) wide. Well preserved seal remains in green wax. A tie has been cut from the seal-tag.
HAND. Scribe Dd. Unruled.
SOURCE. Original, Kinnoull Trustees Muniments (Dupplin Charters no.112) = *A*. Kinnoull Trustees Muniments, MS. Cartulary of Inchaffray Abbey, fos.44^{v}–45^{r} = *B*. Printed here from *A*.
PRINTED. *Inchaffray Chrs.*, no.18 (from *A*). *Inchaffray Liber*, 70, no.72 (from *B*).
NOTE. [a] *B* only. The numeral refers to the section beginning on fo.43.

433 Grants to Cambuskenneth Abbey one toft in his burgh upon (Ayr?). Stirling. (29 September, *c.*1197 × 1203, probably 1203)

Wilelmus[a] Dei gracia Rex Scotorum omnibus probis hominibus tocius terre sue, clericis et laicis, salutem. Sciant presentes et futuri me dedisse et concessisse et hac carta mea confirmasse Deo et ecclesie Sancte Marie de Striuelyn', et canonicis ibidem Deo seruientibus unum plenarium toftum in burgo meo super Harth; tenendum in liberam et puram et perpetuam elemosinam, ita libere et quiete, plenarie et honorifice sicut aliqua domus religiosa aliquod toftum in predicto burgo meo super

Harth liberius et quietius, plenius et honorificentius tenet et possidet. Testibus, Richardo de prebenda clerico meo, Geruasio Auenell, Johanne de Hasting[b], Alexandro vic*ecomite* meo de Striuelin, Radulfo de Camera, Ricardo filio Hugonis, Heruico de Kinross, Rogero de Wiltum[c], apud Striuelin, vicesimo nono die mensis Septembris.

RUBRIC. Donatio terre de Harth (at top). Concordat cum principali Jacobus Foulis (at end).
SOURCE. NLS, MS. Adv. 34.1.2, fo.14v.
PRINTED. *Cambuskenneth Registrum*, no.18.
NOTES. [a] Large blue initial U. [b] MS. Hastitig. [c] Sic.
COMMENT. Cf. G.S.Pryde, *Burghs of Scotland*, p.17: Professor Duncan's argument there that this act refers to Ayr, not Airth, and that this is the earliest reference to the burgh of Ayr, is accepted here.

434

Confirms to Holyrood Abbey the land of Ogilface (in Torphichen), West Lothian, granted by William de Vieuxpont. Forfar. (4 November, 1203)

W'. Dei gr*ati*a Rex Scott'. Omnibus probis hominibus Tocius Terre sue clericis 7 Laicis :' Salutem. Sciant presentes 7 futuri me concessisse 7 hac Carta mea confirmasse . donacionem quam Willelmus de Veteri Ponte fecit Deo 7 Sancte Cruci de Edeneb' . 7 Canonicis ibidem Deo seruientibus de terra de Okelfas' . per rectas diuisas suas 7 cum omnibus iustis pertinenciis suis. Tenend*am* sibi in liberam . et[a] puram et[a] perpetuam elemosinam . cum omnibus ad predictam Terram iuste pertinentibus . ita libere . 7 Quiete plenarie 7 honorifice :' Sicut Carta predicti Willelmi de Veteri Ponte eis inde facta Testatur . Saluo seruicio meo de terra illa . 7 in auxiliis 7 in aliis de heredibus prefati Willelmi. Teste Walt*ero* Capellano meo . Ph*ilippo* de Valon*iis* Cam*erario* meo . Willelmo Cum*in* . Will*elmo* de Bosch*o* . D*aui*d de Haia . Willelmo de Morau*ia* . Ric*ardo* Reuel' . Henric*o* Reuel. Apud Forfar .iiij. die Nouemb*ris*.
Datum per manum Willelmi de Bosch*o* tempore Flor*entii* Cancell*ar*ii . anno ab incarnacione Domini m.cciij.[ab]

ENDORSED. De Okelfas (xiii cent.). J. Scott (xvi cent.).
DESCRIPTION. 6·7″ (17 cm.), Top, 6·3″ (16 cm.), Bottom × 3·8″ (9·7 cm.), L, 3·9″ (9·9 cm.), R. Foot folded to a depth of 0·7″ (1·8 cm.). Double slits with tag 6·3″ (16 cm.) long, 0·7″ (1·6 cm.) wide. Large fragment of seal, natural wax stained brown, formerly detached; diameter 2·6″ (6·7 cm.), fair impression.
HAND. Scribe De (William de Bosco?). Unruled.
SOURCE. Original, SRO, GD 45/13/246.
PRINTED. *Holyrood Liber*, no.45.
NOTES. [a] Stroke through tironian sign. [b] This note is written on the face of the document at the foot, normally hidden by fold. It is in the same hand as the text.
COMMENT. The date of this act was that on which Dirck (Thierry) VII, count of Holland, brother of Florence, King William's chancellor, died. It is probable that Florence was not in Scotland at the date of this act, nor until 1205.

435

Confirms the settlement of the dispute between the canons of St Andrews Cathedral Priory and Eva, widow of William de la Hay, and his son David, anent the land (of Falside) in Pitmilly (in Kingsbarns), Fife, as the charter of Eva and David bears witness. No place-date. (*c*.1201 × 1205)

W.[a] Dei gr*aci*a Rex Scott' . omnibus probis hominibus tocius terre sue clericis et laicis .:' sal*utem*. Sciant presentes et futuri me concessisse . et hac carta mea confirmasse . conuencionem factam inter canonicos de Sancto Andrea et Euam que fuit uxor Willelmi de Haya et D*aui*d filium eiusdem Willelmi de loquela que mouebatur inter eos et predictos canonicos de terra de Petmulyn. Quare volo et firmiter precipio ut predicti canonici predictam terram de Petmulyn . de predicta Eua et predicto D*aui*d et heredibus eorum in liberam et perpetuam elemosinam habeant et possideant . ita libere et quiete sicut carta eiusdem Eue et eiusdem D*aui*d iuste testatur saluo seruicio meo. Test*ibus* Philippo de Valon' . camerario meo . Willelmo Cumyn . Umfrido de Berkelay . Rogero de Mortuo Mari . et aliis .

RUBRIC. De Fausid (top in red).
SOURCE. SRO, GD 45/27/8, fo.cxl^{v}.
PRINTED. *St Andrews Liber*, 314.
NOTE. [a] Black initial flourished in red.
COMMENT. The place-date and perhaps the time-date may have been omitted by the copyist, who was not the careful copyist responsible for the larger part of the cartulary. The land in question, one ploughgate in Pitmilly, is identified with Falside by the rubric. Originally part of the tocher of William de la Hay's wife Eva, it was leased to St Andrews priory and hospital by William for twenty years from 1172 at a rent of half a merk (*St Andrews Liber*, 313). William's widow Eva and their son David afterwards quitclaimed the land to St Andrews, retaining the annualrent of half a merk of silver (ibid., 313–14).

436

Commands his responsible men of the shires of Arbroath and Ethie that all dwelling in these shires who do not have their own mill, and their vassals, shall grind their corn at Arbroath mill. Alyth. (30 November, 1202 × 1213)

W.[a] Dei gr*ati*a Rex Scott' , Omnibus probis hominibus de schyra de Aberbroth*oc* et de Athyn[b] salutem. Mando et firmiter[c] precipio ut omnes in predictis schyris manentes qui suum proprium molendinum non habent et eorum homines ueniant molere ad molendinum de Aberbroth*oc* , nec alibi eant molere super meam defensionem. Test*ibus* Willelmo de Valon*iis* , Hereberto de Camera . Apud Alitht , ultimo die Nouembris.

RUBRIC. De libertate molendinorum (red, *A*, *E*). .xiiij. (in margin, *A*, *E*).
SOURCE. NLS, MS. Adv. 34.4.2, fo.xliv^{r-v}=*A*. SRO, Northesk Muniments (uncatalogued), Ethie MS., fo.3^{r-v}=*E*. Printed here from *A*.
PRINTED. *Arbroath Liber*, i, no.14 (from *E*).
NOTES. [a] Initial red. [b] Athin', *E*. [c] Fo.xliv^{v}, *A*.
COMMENT. For date, see no.437.

437

Commands all his responsible men of *Scotia* that the lands given to Arbroath Abbey, and their tenants, shall have common pasture with all neighbouring lands and tenants. Alyth. (30 November, 1202 × 1213)

W.[a] Dei gr*ati*a Rex Scott', Omnibus probis hominibus suis tocius Scocie salutem. Mando et firmiter precipio quatinus terre quas dedi Deo & Sancto Thome archiepiscopo in elemosinam et homines super terras illas manentes communem pasturam habeant cum omnibus uicinis suis , ita bene et plenarie sicut homines qui in terris illis manentes erant antequam illas dederam in elemosinam melius et plenius habere solebant tempore meo vel antecessorum meorum. Test*ibus* Rad*ulfo* Episcopo Brechynensi, Willelmo de Valon*iis*. Apud Alitht, ultimo die Nouembris.

RUBRIC. De communi pastura (red, *A*, *E*). .xvj. (in margin, *A*, *E*). communis pastura (in margin, xv cent., *A*).
SOURCE. NLS, MS. Adv. 34.4.2, fo.xliv^v = *A*. SRO, Northesk Muniments (uncatalogued), Ethie MS., fo.3^v = *E*. Printed here from *A*.
PRINTED. *Arbroath Liber*, i, no.16 (from *E*).
NOTE. [a] Initial red.

438 Grants that all the tofts which he has granted to Arbroath Abbey in his burghs and residences shall be free of aids and labour service. Linlithgow. (23 April, 1201 × 1207)

W.[a] Dei gr*ati*a Rex Scott', omnibus probis hominibus tocius terre sue salutem. Sciatis me concessisse et hac carta mea confirmasse Deo et Ecclesie Sancti Thome martiris de Aberbroth*oc* et monachis ibidem Deo seruientibus ut omnia tofta que eis dedi in burgis meis et maneriis omnibus per totam terram meam libera sint et quieta ab omnibus auxiliis et operacionibus ad me et ad heredes meos pertinentibus. Quare prohibeo firmiter ne quis de predictis toftis auxilia uel operaciones aliquas exigere presumat, super meam defensionem. Test*ibus* Waltero et Willelmo Capellanis meis, Philippo de Valon*iis* Camerario meo, Alano fil*io* Rolandi Constab*ulario* meo, Alex*andro* vicec*omite* de Striuelyn. Apud Linlithc*u* .xx^{o}iij. die Aprilis.

RUBRIC. Item de libertate toftorum (red, *A*, *E*). .xiij. (in margin, *A*, *E*).
SOURCE. NLS, MS. Adv. 34.4.2, fo.xliv^r = *A*. SRO, Northesk Muniments (uncatalogued), Ethie MS., fo.3^r = *E*. Printed here from *A*.
PRINTED. *Arbroath Liber*, i, no.13 (from *E*).
NOTE. [a] Initial red.

439 Confirms to Inchaffray Abbey the grant made to it by Earl Gilbert of Strathearn of the churches of Dunning and St Serf of Monzievaird (Perthshire). Haddington. (24 April, 1203 or 1204)

.W. Dei gr*ati*a Rex Scott'. Omnibus probis Hominibus totius terre sue clericis et laicis ; salutem. Sciant presentes. et futuri me concessisse et hac carta mea confirmasse Deo et ecclesie Sancti Johannis ewangeliste. de Incheaffren. et Canonicis ibidem Deo seruientibus et seruituris donationem illam quam Com*es* Gilleb*ertus* eis fecit de ecclesia de Dunin'. cum omnibus iustis pertinentiis suis. et de ecclesia Sancti Seruani de Moneward'. cum omnibus iustis pertinentiis suis. Tenend*am* in liberam et puram et perpetuam elemosinam ita libere. et quiete. plenarie. et honorifice ; sicut Carte predicti Com*itis* Gilleb*erti* inde facte iuste testantur. Test*ibus* Waltero Capellano meo. Willelmo Cumin. Willelmo de Boscho et Hug*one* clericis meis. Adam Hasteng' apud Hadingt' .xxiiij. die April*is*.

ENDORSED. De Dunin (xiii cent.). confirmacio regis Willelmi (xiv cent.). kirk Monyward (xvi cent.).
DESCRIPTION. 7·25″ (18·4 cm.), Top, 7·1″ (18·1 cm.), Bottom × 3·15″ (8 cm.), L, R. Foot folded. Slits with tag 0·5″ (1·2 cm.) wide. Fragment of seal in green

wax, reverse to front, diameter 2·5″. Tie cut from top left-hand 'corner' of fold.
HAND. Scribe Dd. Unruled.
SOURCE. Original, Kinnoull Trustees, Dupplin Charters, no.129.
PRINTED. *Inchaffray Chrs.*, no.22.
COMMENT. Dunning church was also dedicated to St Serf; *Inchaffray Chrs.*, no.39.

440 Announces that after receiving letters from Pope Celestine III (1191–98) and after being enjoined to act by the papal legate, John (of Salerno), he held a preliminary hearing of the dispute between Kelso and Melrose abbeys anent the marches of Melrose and Bowden, at Melrose, on 14 January, 1203, at which the respective abbots, Osbert and William, agreed that the king should cause an inquisition to be made by the older and more responsible men of the neighbourhood; after which, in the king's full court at Selkirk, on 9 May, 1204, the dispute was terminated by a judgement in favour of Kelso abbey; in return for which, Kelso abbey has granted to Melrose abbey two oxgangs of arable and two acres of meadow in Primside (in Morebattle, Roxburghshire) with pasture there for 400 sheep. Selkirk. (9 May, 1204)

Will*elmus*[a] Dei gr*ati*a rex Scottorum episcopis, abbatibus, comitibus, baronibus, justiciis, vicecom*itibus*, prepositis, ministris et omnibus probis hominibus tocius terre sue, clericis et laicis, salutem. Sciant presentes et futuri quod cum controuersia per multos annos durasset inter domos de Kelchou et de Melros de diuisis inter Melros et Bouldene[b] terram monachorum de Kelchou[c], tandem dominus papa Celestinus per litteras suas mihi significauit et in remissionem peccatorum mihi iniunxit ut, facta diligenti inquisicione de diuisis ill*is*, quod iustum esset inquirerem [et] partibus assignarem. Johannes etiam titulo Sancti Stephani in Celio Monte presbiter cardinalis, dum legacione fungeretur in terra mea, me instanter inde precatus est, et autoritate sua mihi iniunxit. Tandem veni aput Melros anno ab incarnacione Domini m°.cc°.ij°. in oct*abis* Epiphanie et, presentibus multis clericis et laicis, cum sermo fieret de diuisis illis, Willelmus qui tunc fuit abbas de Melros, habito tractatu et consilio per consensum conuentus sui, et Osbertus abbas de Kelchou[c] per consensum capituli sui, compromiserunt in me et affidauerunt quod starent dicto meo super diuisis illis, et quod illud quod ego secundum inquisicionem meam inde dicerem ex utraque parte firmiter et inuiolabiliter tenerent. Cumque postea diligentem inquisicionem per probos et antiquos homines patrie inde fecissem, pluries in presentiam meam partes conuenire feci. Tandem uenerunt ad me apud Selechirche[d], anno ab incarnacione Domini m°. cc°. iiij°, die dominica post clausum Pascha, et ibi in plena curia sentenciando pronunciaui, presentibus clericis et laicis, quod terra illa, unde controuersia fuit, fuit monachorum de Kelcho[c] et esse debuit de iure, per diuisas illas per quas monachi de Kelcho[c] asserebant terram illam suam esse, scilicet per nemus quod scissum fuit inter domos illas per Regem Dauid auum meum, et per superficiem montis in cuius summitate fecit fossas fieri; et hoc fuit uerum dictum meum quod inde dixi et de iure dicere debui, per testimonium proborum et antiquorum hominum patrie. Volui autem ut monachi de Kelcho[c] concederent monachis de Melros inperpetuum duas bouatas terre et duas acras prati et pasturam ad cccc^{tas}. oues que habebant idem monachi de Kelcho[c] in Prenwenesete[e], et hoc eis concesserunt predicti monachi de Kelcho[c], et hoc modo terminata fuit loquela illa die illo. Quare uolo et precipio quatinus diuise predicte sicut prefatum est firmiter et inuiolabiliter futuris temporibis teneantur, et ne contencio ulterius super diuisis illis inter predictas domos audiatur. Test'.[f]

RUBRIC. Carta conuentus de Kalchou de terra et pastura de Prenwinesete (red, fo.xxv^{v}).[g] De controuersia inter nos et ipsos de Melros per Willelmum Regem (red)[h].
SOURCE. NLS, MS. Adv. 34.4.11, fos.xxv^{v}–xxvi^{r} = *M*. NLS, MS. Adv. 34.5.1, fo.16^{r} = *K*. Printed here from a collation of *M* and *K*, with *M*'s text generally preferred. The variants are unimportant, but a number are noted.
PRINTED. *Melrose Liber*, no.146 (from *M*; contained in a notification by Richard abbot of Kelso, 24 August × 9 December, 1208). *Kelso Liber*, no.19 (from *K*).
NOTES. [a] Punctuation editorial. [b] Boulden', *K*; fo.xxvi^{r}, *M*. [c] Kalch, *K*. [d] Seleschirche, *K*. [e] Prenwenessete, *K*. [f] *M* omits Test'. [g] *M* only. [h] *K* only.
COMMENT. For David I's original grant of Bowden to Selkirk Abbey, the predecessor of Kelso, see Lawrie, *Charters*, no.35. The marches had already been the subject of dispute by the date of no.367.

441

Confirms to Melrose Abbey two oxgangs of arable and two acres of meadow with pasture for 400 sheep in Primside (in Morebattle, Roxburghshire), granted by the abbot and convent of Kelso for the sake of peace; to be held as the charter of the abbot and convent of Kelso, and also the charter of Geoffrey Ridel, bear witness. (1204)

Will*elmus*[a] gr*ati*a rex Scott' omnibus probis hominibus tocius sue [terre][b], clericis et laicis, salutem. Sciant presentes et futuri me concessisse et hac carta mea confirmasse monachis de Melros duas bouatas terre et duas acras prati cum pastura ad quadringentas oues in Prenwensete, que abbas et conuentus de Kelch*o*[c] eis dederunt nomine pacis inter eos facte; tenend*as* ita libere et quiete sicut [carta][d] abbatis et conuentus de Kelch*o*[c] et concessio et confirmacio Gaufr*idi* Ridel testantur et confirmant, saluo seruicio meo[e] Test*ibus* etc.

RUBRIC. Confirmacio Reg*is* W. de Prenwensete.
SOURCE. NLS, MS. Adv. 34.4.11, fo.xxvii^{v} = *A*. BM, MS. Harl. 3960, fo.42^{r} = *H*. Printed here from *A*, with variants of *H* noted.
PRINTED. *Melrose Liber*, no.148.
NOTES. [a] Initial red, *A*; U, red, *H*. [b] *A* omits terre: *H* also omits and leaves a blank. [c] Kelchou, *H*. [d] *A*, *H* omit carta. [e] etc., *H*.
COMMENT. See no.440. Geoffrey Ridel was lord of Primside; his charter is given in *Melrose Liber*, no.147.

442

Grants his firm peace to all who shall come to Glasgow Fair and to the burgh of Glasgow, in coming thither, remaining, and lawfully returning; provided they do what they ought to do according to the assize of his burghs. Edinburgh. (27 June, *c*.1195 × 1211, probably *c*.1202 × 1210)

Will*elmus* Dei gratia Rex Scottorum omnibus probis hominibus tocius terre sue Clericis et Laicis salutem. Sciatis me firmam pacem meam iuste dedisse omnibus qui venient ad Nundinas de Glasgu quas concessi Deo et Sancto Kentegerno . et Burgo de Glasgu ad veniendum illuc et ibi standum et inde iuste redeund*um* ita ut faciant quod iuste et secundum assisam Burgorum meorum et terre mee facere debebunt. Test*ibus* Willelmo de Bosch*o* clerico meo . Philippo de Mubray . apud Edeneburg' .xxvii. die Jun*ii*.

RUBRIC. De libero accessu ad nundinas de Glasg*u* (in margin).
SOURCE. Blairs Archives, 16 Drummond Place, Edinburgh, MS. Registrum Vetus of Glasgow, fo.liiij[r].
PRINTED. *Glasgow Registrum*, no.43.
COMMENT. The *terminus post quem* is suggested by the probability that this brieve was issued during a vacancy in the see of Glasgow.

443 Confirms to May Priory the full toft in his burgh of Berwick granted by King David I, as his charter bears witness. Berwick. (4 July, 1203 × 1205)

W.[a] Dei gratia Rex Scott'[b] omnibus probis hominibus totius terre sue, clericis et laicis, salutem. Sciant presentes et futuri me concessisse et hac carta mea confirmasse ecclesie de Mai et priori et monachis ibidem Deo seruientibus illud plenarium toftum in burgo meo de Berewic' quod Rex D*aui*d auus meus eis dedit. Quare uolo et precipio quatinus predicti monachi toftum illud teneant et habeant libere et quiete, in liberam et perpetuam elemosinam. Volo etiam ut homines qui in tofto illo manebunt liberi sint ab omni seruicio et exaccione sicut carta Regis D*aui*d aui mei testatur. Test*ibus* Willelmo Episcopo Sancti Andr*ee*, Philippo de Valon*iis* Camerario meo[c], Willelmo de Boscho, Willelmo Cumin. Apud Berewic'[d] iiij. die Julii.

TITLE. Confirmacio Regis Willelmi de Burgo de Berwike.[e]
SOURCE. PRO, C.53/93, rot.14 (Charter Roll, 35 Edward I) = *C. May Recs.*, p.cxiii = *M* (Title only).
PRINTED. *May Recs.*, no.13 (from *C*).
NOTES. [a] Willelmus, *May Recs.*, no.13. [b] Scotie, ibid. [c] nostro, ibid. [d] Berewicum, ibid. [e] Title from *M* only.
COMMENT. King David's charter is given in Lawrie, *Charters*, no.184.

444 Confirms the renunciation and abjuration made in the full court of the prior of Coldingham by William of Gullane, with his brothers Nicholas and John and his maternal aunt Emme, on behalf of themselves and of all their kindred, of the toun of greater Lumsdaine (in Coldingham), in exchange for one ploughgate of land in the territory of Swinton given to William and his heirs by the prior and convent of Durham. Haddington. (8 July, *c.*1203 × 1207, perhaps 1204)

.W. De gr*ati*a Rex Scott' . Omnibus probis Hominibus totius terre sue clericis . et laicis .·' salutem. Sciant presentes et futuri me concessisse . et hac carta mea confirmasse . renuntiationem . et abiurationem quam Willelmus de Golin cum Nicholao . et Johanne fratribus suis . et cum Emme matertera sua pro se et congnatione[a] sua in plena curia prioris de Coldingham fecit de villa maioris Lumesdene cum omnibus ad eam spectantibus . et de iure quod in eadem villa habuit . pro una Carucata terre quam prior Dunelm*ensis* predicto Willelmo et heredibus suis concessit in territorio de Swinton' . Quare uolo . et firmiter precipio quatinus predicta renuntiatio . et abiuratio ita firmiter . et inuiolabiliter obseruetur :' sicut Carta predicti Willelmi testatur saluo seruicio meo. Test*ibus* Walt*ero* . et Willelmo Capell*anis* meis . Ph*ilippo* de Valon*iis* Cam*erario* meo . Will*elmo* Cumi*n* . Willelmo de Bosch*o* et Hug*one* clericis meis. apud Hadingtun' .viij. die Julii.

ENDORSED. Confirm*acio* W. Reg*is* super renunciacione quam fecit W. de Golyne cum aliis de villa maioris Lumesden' cum omnibus ad eam spectantibus in escambium j^us^ carucate terre in territorio de Swynton' (xv cent.). J. iij^a^ vj^te^ (xv cent.).
DESCRIPTION. 7·8″ (19·8 cm.), Top, 7·7″ (19·7 cm.), Bottom × 2·3″ (5·8 cm.), L, R. Foot folded 0·5″. Tie cut from top of fold, complete. Single slits. Tag 4·8″ long, 0·5″ wide. Seal in natural wax, slightly chipped at right hand, rather rubbed and worn. Attached back to front at precisely the same angle as that attached to no.445.
HAND. Scribe Dd. Unruled.
SOURCE. Original, Durham, D. & C. Muniments, Misc. Chr. no.605.
PRINTED. Raine, *North Durham*, no.55.
NOTE. [a] Written cognatione, with mark of suspension over first o.
COMMENT. Cp. no.445; and see Raine, *North Durham*, no.426.

445 Confirms the agreement made between the prior (Bertram) and convent of Durham and Edward of Oldcambus and his sons anent their abjuration and quitclaim to the priory of the toun of Oldcambus and the mill (in Coldingham), in exchange for greater Lumsdaine (in Coldingham) and a sum of money. Haddington. (8 July, 1203 × 1207, perhaps 1204)

.W'. Dei gr*ati*a Rex Scott'. Omnibus probis Hominibus Tocius terre sue Clericis et laicis :' Salutem. Sciant presentes et futuri . me Concessisse . et hac Carta mea Confirmasse . Conuentionem factam inter Bertramum Priorem et Conuentum Dunelmen*sem* . et Ædwardum de Aldecambus et filios suos de abiuratione et Quieta Clamatione quam idem Edwardus et filii sui fecerunt predicto priori et monachis . de uilla de Aldecambus . et de molendino . et Omnibus aliis ad uillam de Aldecambus pertinentibus :' pro maiore Lummesden' quam predictus Prior et monachi eis in excambium dederunt . et pro pecunia quam predictus prior et monachi pro predicto Ædwardo erga me adquietauerunt. Quare uolo et precipio . ut predicta Conuentio de prefata abiuratione et Quieta clamatione firmiter teneatur . sicut Cyrographum inter eos inde factum et Carta predicti Ædwardi testantur . Saluo seruicio meo. Test*ibus* Willelmo et Waltero Capellanis meis . Philipp*o* de Valon*iis* Camer*ario* meo . Willelmo de Boscho et Gilleb*erto* clericis meis apud Hadint' .viij. die Julii.

ENDORSED. Confirmatio W. Reg*is* Scot' De quieta clamatione de Aldecambus (early xiii cent.). K iij^a^ vj^te^ (xv cent.).
DESCRIPTION. 7·1″ (18·1 cm.), Top and bottom × 3″ (7·7 cm.), L, 2·7″ (6·9 cm), R. Foot folded 0·6″. Single slits. Tag 4·4″ long, 0·5″ wide. Seal in natural wax, two-thirds complete, rather rubbed and worn; attached back to front at exactly the same angle as that attached to no.444.
HAND. Scribe Df. Unruled.
SOURCE. Original, Durham, D. & C. Muniments, Misc. Chr. no.599.
PRINTED. Raine, *North Durham*, no.56.
COMMENT. The agreement referred to is printed in Raine, *North Durham*, no.647, with the relevant charter of Edward of Oldcambus, ibid., no.177,

mentioning his sons William, Ralph, Stephen, Patrick and Edward, and providing evidence that the agreement dated before the period 8 June–29 September, 1198. The sum of money should have been 107 merks. It appears from ibid., no.648 that Edward of Oldcambus had been accused of taking away the goods of a ship wrecked on the coast and had been condemned to death for this offence in the king's court. The exchange was forced upon Edward to enable him to find enough money to buy the king's pardon. His grandson and heir David of Lumsdaine declared that his grandfather had been given much less than the fair price for Oldcambus by the priory of Durham, and obtained a letter from Pope Gregory IX (Viterbo, 5 December, 1235) to initiate litigation anent his complaint before the bishop and chanter of Glasgow acting as judge-delegates. The terms of their judgement are given, ibid.

446 Confirms to Richard, nephew of Simon formerly prior of Coldingham, the sale made to him by Ralph son of Elwald of a 20-acre toft in Coldingham. Jedburgh. (2 August, *c.*1203 × 1207, perhaps 1204)

.W. Dei gr*ati*a Rex Scott'. Omnibus probis Hominibus totius terre sue clericis et laicis .·. salutem. Sciant presentes et futuri . me concessisse . et hac carta mea confirmasse . Ricard*o* nepoti Simonis quondam prioris de Coldingh*am* uenditionem quam Radulfus filius Elwald*i* ei fecit . de uno tofto . in Coldingham . de xx[ti]. acris terre .Tenend*am* sibi et heredibus suis de predicto Radulf*o* et heredibus suis . ita libere . et quiete sicut Carta eiusdem Radulf*i* iuste testatur saluo seruicio meo. Test*ibus* Walt*ero* et Willelmo Capell*anis* meis . Philipp*o* de Valon*iis* Camer*ario* meo . Willelmo de Bosch*o* . Philipp*o* de Lundin . Ricard*o* Reuel. apud Jeddewrd' secundo die August*i*.

ENDORSED. Conf*irmatio* Regis W. super vendicione unius tofti in Cold*ingham* et .xx. acris terre (xiv cent.). F. iij[a] vj[te] (xv cent.).
DESCRIPTION. 7″ (17·8 cm.), Top, 7·1″ (18 cm.), Bottom × 2·4″ (6·1 cm.), L, 2·2″ (5·7 cm.), R. Foot folded 0·5″. Single slits. Tie cut from top of fold, now torn off. Tag 5·7″ long, 0·6″ wide. Seal in natural wax, almost entire, fair impression; attached back to front at same angle as those attached to nos.444, 445.
HAND. Scribe Dd. Unruled.
SOURCE. Original, Durham D. & C. Muniments, Misc. Chr. no.611.
PRINTED. Raine, *North Durham*, no.57.
COMMENT. Ralph son of Elwald's charter of sale to Richard, Prior Simon's nephew, is printed in Raine, *North Durham*, no.265.

447 Confirms to Melrose Abbey the grant made by Walter Corbet, son of Walter, of a certain part of his land of Clifton (in Morebattle, Roxburghshire), as Walter's charter bears witness. Selkirk. (22 September, 1201 × 1209)

U.[a] Dei gr*ati*a rex Scot' omnibus probis hominibus tocius terre sue, clericis et laicis, salutem. Sciant presentes et futuri me concessisse et hac carta mea confirmasse Deo et ecclesie Sancte Marie de Melros et monachis ibidem Deo seruientibus donacionem illam quam Walterus Corbet filius Walteri eis fecit de quadam parte terre sue in territorio de Cliftun, per diuisas que nominantur in carta prefati Walteri Corbet, tenend*am* in puram, liberam et perpetuam elemosinam, ita libere et quiete et honorifice sicut alias terras et elemosinas suas liberius, quiecius, plenius et honorificencius tenent et possident, et sicut carta Walteri Corbet iuste testatur, saluo seruicio meo. Test*ibus* Phil*ippo* de

Val*oniis* camer*ario*, Roberto de London*iis*, Alano fil*io* Roll*andi* constabul*ario*, Philipp*o* de Mubray, Willelmo de Vallon*iis*, Henr*ico* Biset, Thoma de Coluill', Adam fil*io* Herb*erti*, Ferg*us* fratre[b] Roll*andi*, Alexandro de Sinton'. Apud Selekirk, xxij die Septembris.

RUBRIC. Confirmacio regis Willelmi de terra de Cliftun secundum cartam Walteri Corbet.
SOURCE. BM, MS. Harl. 3960, fo.8^{v}.
PRINTED. *Melrose Liber*, no.115.
NOTES. [a] Initial red. [b] MS., frate.
COMMENT. This might belong to 1208 (cp. no.483), but 1204 seems more likely. The charter of the donor, in which he styles himself Walter Corbet son of the daughter of Gilbert de Umfraville, and which dates 1201 × 1205, is given in *Melrose Liber*, no.114. Alan son of Roland was with King John in Ireland in 1210.

448 Confirms to Kelso Abbey five ploughgates of arable in Oxton in Lauderdale (in Channelkirk, Berwickshire) granted by Alan son of Roland and his mother Helen in exchange for the revenue which the abbey used to have in Galloway in the time of their predecessors, as the charters of Alan and Helen bear witness. Selkirk. (25 September, 1201 or 1203 × 1205)

W. Dei gr*ati*a Rex Scott' . Omnibus probis hominibus tocius terre sue clericis 7 laicis . salutem. Sciant presentes 7 futuri me concessisse 7 hac carta mea confirmasse Deo 7 Ecclesie de Kelch' . 7 monachis ibidem Deo seruientibus . donacionem illam . quam Alanus fil*ius* Rolandi 7 Elena mater eius eis fecerunt . scilicet de quinque Carrucatis terre in Ulfkilest' . in Lawederdal' . pro Redditu quem[a] habere solebant de Galweia temporibus antecessorum suorum . Tenend*am* in liberam 7 puram . 7 perpetuam elemosinam per diuisas predictarum terrarum eis traditas . 7 cum libertatibus 7 aisiamentis . 7 omnibus aliis ad easdem terras iuste pertinentibus . ita libere 7 quiete . plenarie 7 honorifice . sicut carte predictorum Alani et Elene matris eius testantur . saluo ser[b]uicio meo. Test*ibus* . Rob*erto* Archid*iacono* Morau*iensi* . Will*elmo* capellano meo . Seiher*o* de Quinci . Radulf*o* Licrello . Will*elmo* de Boscho . Magistro Nich*olao* medico . apud Selkirc' . xxv. die Septembr*is*.

RUBRIC. Confirmacio super quinque acras terre in Ulfkylest' (top in red).
SOURCE. NLS, MS. Adv. 34.5.1, fos.149^{v}–150^{r}.
PRINTED. *Kelso Liber*, no.407.
NOTES. [a] MS. has habent underlined for deletion. [b] Fo.150^{r}.
COMMENT. Alan son of Roland of Galloway's charter is given in *Kelso Liber*, no.245 (19 December, 1200 × 1206). The revenues from Galloway had apparently been granted originally by Uhtred son of Fergus, lord of Galloway, and had got into arrears, no doubt because of the disturbed state of Galloway from 1174 to 1185. Saer de Quincy was in France in September 1202 and 1206.

449 Confirms to Melrose Abbey the whole part of the land in the territory of 'Killebeccokestun' confirmed by Alan son of Roland (of Galloway), in exchange for land in Cunningham bequeathed to Melrose by William de Moreville, as the charter of Alan bears witness. (1200 × 1214)

Will*el*m*us*[a] Dei gr*ati*a rex Scott' omnibus probis hominibus totius terre sue, clericis et laicis, salutem. Sciant presentes et futuri me concessisse et hac mea carta confirmasse Deo et ecclesie Sancte Marie de Melros et monachis ibidem Deo seruientibus totam illam partem terre in territorio de Killebeccokestun quam Alanus filius Rollandi eis dedit, per diuisas nominatas in carta ipsius Alani, in escambium terre quam Willelmus de Moreuill' eis diuisit in Cunigham[b]. Quare uolo et precipio ut predicti monachi predictam terram habeant et teneant in puram et perpetuam elemosinam per predictas rectas diuisas nominatas in carta predicti Alani, et cum communi pastura eiusdem uille ad certum numerum pecudum et aueriorum nominatorum in eadem carta, et libero egressu et aliis aisiamentis eiusdem uille, ita libere et quiete, plenarie et honorifice, sicut carta eiusdem Alani testatur, saluo seruicio meo. Test*ibus* etc.

RUBRIC. Confirmacio Reg*is* Willelmi de noua terra Karelri.[c]
SOURCE. NLS, MS. Adv. 34.4.11, fo.lvii = *A*. BM, MS. Harl. 3960, fo.73[v] = *H*. Printed here from *A*, with variants of *H* noted.
PRINTED. *Melrose Liber*, no.85.
NOTES. [a] Initial red, part of letter, with dei, cut away, *A*. [b] Cuningham, *H*. [c] Read Karelzi.
COMMENT. The transaction is explained by charters given in *Melrose Liber*, nos.82, 83, 84. William de Moreville had in his last will bequeathed to Melrose Abbey land in Cunningham held by Simon de Beaumont. In exchange for this (because of failure to give possession and need to give warrandice?), Helen de Moreville, William's sister and heir, and her husband Roland of Galloway, granted to Melrose the 'new land' of Harehope, in Eddleston, Peeblesshire, by the marches specified, which included Widehope Shank, the fort on Harehope Hill (*vetus castellarium*), Crailzie Burn, Harehope Burn and the Water of Lyne. The name Kilbeccokestun (al. Gillebeccokestun, Gillebecchistun) is obsolete; the man after whom it was named was himself named in honour of Saint Begha (Bechoc or Bee), whose cult was marked in Peeblesshire by the church of Kilbucho, on the Lanarkshire border. Cp. the name Coremac Gillebecoc, belonging perhaps to the resident priest of St Bees in Coupland at the time that church was given to St Mary's abbey, York (*St Bees Register*, no.1).

450 Confirms to Guisborough Priory the churches of Annan, Lochmaben, Kirkpatrick Fleming, Cummertrees, Redkirk (in Gretna) and Gretna, granted by Robert de Brus and his son William de Brus, as their charters bear witness. Selkirk. (Probably *c*.1204 × 1207)

W.[a] Dei gr*ati*a Rex Scottorum omnibus probis hominibus totius terre sue clericis et laicis salutem. Sciant presentes et futuri me concessisse et hac carta mea[b] confirmasse Deo et ecclesie Sancte Marie de Giseb' et canonicis ibidem Deo seruientibus donacionem illam quam Robertus de Bruis et Willelmus de Bruis filius eius fecerunt eis de ecclesia de Anant et de ecclesia de Lochmaban[c] et de ecclesia de Kirkepatric et de ecclesia de Cumbertres et de ecclesia de Reinpatric et de ecclesia de Gretenhou, cum omnibus pertinen*tiis* predictarum ecclesiarum. Tenend*am* in liberam et quietam et perpetuam elemosinam sicut carte predicti Roberti de Bruis et Willelmi de Bruis filii eius iuste testantur et confirmant. Test*ibus* Waltero capellano meo, Johanne de Huntingdun officiali Glasguen*si*, Willelmo de Bosco et Hugon*e* clericis meis, Henr*ico* filio Comitis Dauid, Ada de Carleol' clerico meo, Adam fil*io* Herberti, Alexand*ro* de Sinton. Apud Seleschr'.

SOURCE. Bodleian Library, MS. Dodsworth, VII, fo.46^{v} = *A*. Printed here from *A*, which is a copy said to be made from the original in St Mary's Tower, York. The copy is headed, as though from an endorsement, Carta W. Regis Scottorum, and below is a diagram of the seal, shewing the legend, obverse and reverse, WILLIELMVS[d] DEO RECTORE REX SCOTTORUM; and these notes (for the obverse): 'a man sitting in his right hand a sword in his left a' [drawing of orb and cross]; (for the reverse): 'on horsebacke on his left arme a sheild in the right a speare held before his face'.
PRINTED. Dugdale, *Mon Angl.*, ii (1661), 152, reprinted, new edn, vi, 269 (apparently, but not very accurately, from *A*) = *B*. *Cartularium Prioratus de Gyseburne*, ed. William Brown (Surtees Society, 1889, 1894), ii, 341, no.1177 (from *A*).
NOTES. [a] Punctuation is editorial. [b] h.c.m., *A*. [c] Locmaben, *B*. [d] Sic.
COMMENT. The charter of William de Brus is given in *Guisborough Cartularium*, no.1176, not easy to date narrowly. Master John of Huntingdon's earliest recorded appearance is otherwise in the episcopate of William Malvoisin, 1200–1202 (*Glasgow Registrum*, nos.95, 98). Henry son of Earl David probably did not witness King William's acts much before 1205.

451 Confirms to Geoffrey son of Richard of Kinglassie the land of Balwearie (in Kirkcaldy), Fife, granted to him by the abbot (Patrick) and convent of Dunfermline. Clackmannan. (1 March, 1202 × 1206, probably 1203 × 1205)

.W'. Dei gr*ati*a Rex Scott'. Omnibus probis Hominibus totius terre sue clericis et laicis .' salutem. Sciant presentes et futuri me concessisse . et hac carta mea confirmasse Galfrid*o* filio Ric*ardi* de Inuerkunnigglas donationem illam quam Patricius abbas de Dunf*ermelin* et eiusdem loci conuentus ei fecerunt de terra de Balwer'. Tenend*am* sibi et heredibus suis . in feudo et hereditate per rectas diuisas predicte terre . et cum omnibus aliis ad eam iuste pertinentibus . ita libere . et quiete . plenarie et honorifice .' sicut Carta predicti P*atricii* et conuentus testatur .' saluo seruicio meo. Test*ibus* Willelmo Capellano meo . Willelmo de Boschø . Magistro Nichol*ao* medico meo . Alexand*ro* fil*io* Thore . Herb*erto* de Camera . Adam fil*io* eius . Johanne de Striueli*n* . Ricard*o* Reuel. Apud Clacman*an* primo die Marcii.

ENDORSED. Confirmacio de terra de Balwery (xiv cent.). Also modern endorsements.
DESCRIPTION. 6·4″ (16·2 cm.), Top, 6·3″ (16 cm.), Bottom × 3·6″ (9·1 cm.), L, R. Foot folded to a depth of 0·7″ (1·9 cm.). Single slits; no tag or seal remains.
HAND. Scribe Dd. Unruled.
SOURCE. Original, SRO, GD 26, 1/4/10.
PRINTED. Fraser, *Melville*, iii, 5, no.10 (with facsimile); Fraser, *Buccleuch*, ii, 410–11, no.371; also *Fraser Facsimiles*, no.28.
COMMENT. Cf. nos.470, 471. Balwearie (Balekerin) was originally granted to the church of Dunfermline by King Alexander I (*ESC*, no.74).

452 Confirms to Arbroath Abbey the church of Kinnernie (in Cluny and Midmar), Aberdeenshire, granted by Thomas the doorward, as his charter bears witness. Clackmannan. (22 March, 1205 × 1207)

W.[a] Dei gr*ati*a Rex Scott' . Omnibus probis hominibus tocius terre sue clericis et laicis salutem. Sciant presentes et futuri me concessisse et hac Carta mea confirmasse Deo et Sancto [Thome][b] martiri de Aberbr*othoc* et monachis ibidem Deo seruientibus et seruituris . donacionem illam quam Thomas Hostiarius fecit eisdem de ecclesia de Kinernyn . Tenend*am* in liberam et puram et perpetuam elemosinam . cum omnibus iustis pertinenciis suis . ita libere et quiete plenarie et honorifice . sicut aliquam ecclesiam liberius et quiecius plenius et honorificencius tenent et possident . et sicut Carta predicti Thome testatur. Test*ibus* Rob*erto* de Lond*oniis* filio meo . Alexandro vic*ecomite* meo de Clacm*anan* . Henr*ico* fil*io* comit*is* D*aui*d fratris mei . Ric*ardo* de Camera . Hereberto de Camera . Adam fil*io* eius . Ric*ardo* Reuel'. Apud Clacmanan .xxij°. die Marcii.

RUBRIC. Confirmacio Reg*is* W. de ecclesia de Kinerny (red). .Lx. (in margin).
SOURCE. NLS, MS. Adv. 34.4.2, fo.lvi[v].
PRINTED. *Arbroath Liber*, i, no.60.
NOTES. [a] Initial red. [b] MS. omits.
COMMENT. Thomas (of Lundie) the doorward's charter, issued on the same occasion as this confirmation, is given in *Arbroath Liber*, i, no.59. His grant to Coupar Angus abbey is confirmed by no.414 above.

453 Confirms to Arbroath Abbey the churches of Strathectyn (Stradighty Comitis or Earl's Stradighty, now Mains) and Kirriemuir, Angus, granted by Gilchrist earl of Angus, as the earl's charter bears witness. Forfar. (2 January, 1201 × 1205, probably 1204 or 1205)

W.[a] Dei gr*ati*a Rex Scott' omnibus probis hominibus tocius terre sue clericis et laicis salutem. Sciant presentes et futuri me concessisse et hac Carta mea confirmasse[b] Deo et ecclesie Sancti Thome de Abirbr*othoc* et monachis ibidem Deo seruientibus donacionem illam quam Gillecrist Comes de Anegus eis fecit de ecclesiis de Strathectyn et de Kerimor'. Tenend*am* in liberam et quietam et perpetuam elemosinam . cum omnibus ad predictas ecclesias iuste pertinentibus . ita libere et quiete plenarie et honorifice . sicut carta predicti . G*illecrist* comitis de Anegus testatur. Test*ibus* Philippo de Valon*iis* Cam*erario* meo . Willelmo Cumyn . Philipp*o* de Mubray . Johanne de Hasting' . Johanne de Striuel*in* . D*aui*d Marescall*o* Philippo de Lundyn . Ric*ardo* Reuel' . apud Forfar secundo die Januar*ii*.

RUBRIC. Confirmacio Regis W. de ecclesiis de Stradechtyn et Kerimor (red). .xlv. (in margin).
SOURCE. NLS, MS. Adv. 34.4.2, fo.lii[r–v].
PRINTED. *Arbroath Liber*, i, no.45.
NOTES. [a] Initial red. [b] Fo.lii[v].
COMMENT. Earl Gilchrist's two charters are given in *Arbroath Liber*, i, nos.43, 44 (1201 × 1205). The short series of grants made by the earl to Arbroath, confirmed by this and nos.455, 456 and 457 suggests gifts made when the earl believed his death to be imminent.

454 Confirms to Arbroath Abbey the church of Ruthven, Angus, granted by his son Robert of London, as his charter bears witness. Forfar. (1 February, 1196 × 1214, probably 1204 or 1205)

W.[a] Dei gr*ati*a Rex Scott' . omnibus probis hominibus tocius terre sue[b] clericis et laicis salutem. Sciant presentes et futuri me concessisse et hac carta mea confirmasse Deo et ecclesie Sancti Thome de Abirbr*othoc* . et monachis ibidem Deo seruientibus donacionem illam quam Rob*ertus* de Lundris eis fecit de ecclesia de Rothuen cum omnibus iustis pertinenciis suis. Tenend*am* in liberam et puram et perpetuam elemosinam ita libere et quiete plenarie et honorifice. sicut Carta predicti Roberti iuste testatur. Test*ibus* Philippo de Valon*iis* Camerar*io* meo. Ric*ardo* Reuel'. Dauid de Haya. Rogero de Wiltona. Dauid Marescallo. Bricio Judice. Apud Forfar'. primo die Februar*ii*.

RUBRIC. Confirmacio Regis W. de ecclesia de Rothue*n* (red). .Lxij. (in margin).
SOURCE. NLS, MS. Adv. 34.4.2, fos.lvi^{v}–lvii^{r}.
PRINTED. *Arbroath Liber*, i, no.62.
NOTES. [a] Initial red. [b] Fo.lvii^{r}.
COMMENT. Robert's charter is given in *Arbroath Lil er*, i, no.61.

455 Confirms to Arbroath Abbey the church of Monifieth, Angus, granted by Gilchrist earl of Angus, as the earl's charter bears witness. Alyth. (26 March, 1201 × 1205, probably 1204 or 1205)

W.[a] Dei gr*ati*a Rex Scott'. omnibus probis hominibus tocius terre sue clericis et laicis salutem. Sciant presentes et futuri me concessisse et hac carta mea confirmasse Deo et monasterio Sancti Thome de Aberbr*othoc* et monachis ibidem Deo seruientibus donacionem illam quam Gillecrist Comes de Anegus eis fecit de ecclesia de Monifod' cum capellis terris et decimis et oblacionibus et obuencionibus omnimodis et omnibus aliis ad predictam ecclesiam iuste[b] pertinentibus. Tenend*am* in liberam et puram et quietam et perpetuam elemosinam. ita libere et quiete plenarie et honorifice. sicut [carta][c] predicti Comitis Gilcrist testatur. Test*ibus* Rob*erto* de Lond*oniis*. Willelmo Cumyn. Magistro Nicholao medico meo. Willelmo de Valon*iis* Philippo de Mubray. Alexandro fil*io* Thor'. Waltero Murdac'. D*aui*d Marscall*o*. Apud Alicht .xxvj^{o}. die Marcii.

RUBRIC. Confirmacio Reg*is* W. de ecclesia de Monifod (red). .xl. (in margin).
SOURCE. NLS, MS. Adv. 34.4.2, fo.li^{r-v}.
PRINTED. *Arbroath Liber*, i, no.40.
NOTES. [a] Initial red. [b] Fo.li^{v}. [c] MS. omits.
COMMENT. Earl Gilchrist's charter is given in *Arbroath Liber*, i, no.39 (1201 × 1205).

456 Confirms to Arbroath Abbey the land granted by Gilchrist earl of Angus, which had previously been given by Gilchrist's father (Earl Gillebride?) in order to establish a hospital (or inn) at Portincrag (in Monifieth, Angus), together with the fishery which extends from the craig as far as the earl's land continues westward. Alyth. (26 March, 1201 × 1205, probably 1204 or 1205)

W.[a] Dei gr*ati*a Rex Scott'. Omnibus probis hominibus tocius terre sue clericis et laicis salutem. Sciant presentes et futuri me concessisse et hac carta mea confirmasse Deo et monasterio Sancti Thome de Aberbr*othoc* et monachis ibidem Deo seruientibus donacionem illam quam Gillecrist comes de Anegus eis fecit de terra illa. quam pater ipsius Gillecrist dedit ad faciendum unum hospitale apud Portincrag cum piscaria illa que durat a Crag' quantum terra predicti comitis Gillecrist protenditur versus occidentem. Tenend*am* in liberam et puram et quietam et perpetuam elemosinam. per rectas diuisas predicte terre cum communi pastura et omnimodis aliis aisiamentis de Monifod'.

et omnibus aliis ad predictam terram et piscariam iuste pertinentibus . ita libere et quiete plenarie et honorifice sicut carta predicti comitis Gillecrist iuste testatur saluo seruicio meo. Test*ibus* Rob*erto* de Lond*oniis* . Nicholao medico meo . Hug*one* clerico meo . Willelmo de Valon*iis* Phill*ippo* de Mubray . Alexandro fil*io* Thori . Waltero Murdac' . Phil*ippo* de Colleuill' . Dauid Marescall*o* Apud Alicht .xxvj°. die Marcii.

RUBRIC. Confirmacio Regis W. de terra de Portincrag et de piscaria (red). .Lj. (in margin).
SOURCE. NLS, MS. Adv. 34.4.2, fo.liv[r].
PRINTED. *Arbroath Liber*, i, no.51.
NOTE. [a] Initial red.
COMMENT. Portincrag, now lost, was evidently at Broughty Ferry, the northern end of the earl of Angus's ferry over the Tay; although, curiously enough, the same name seems to have been preserved in the parish name of Ferryport-on-Craig, on the south side of the same ferry. Earl Gilchrist's charter is given in *Arbroath Liber*, i, no.50 (1201 × 1205).

457 Confirms to Arbroath Abbey the church of Murroes, Angus, granted by Gilchrist earl of Angus, as the earl's charter bears witness. Forfar. (11 April, 1201 × 1205, probably 1204 or 1205)

W.[a] Dei gr*ati*a Rex Scott' Omnibus probis hominibus tocius terre sue clericis et laicis salutem. Sciant presentes et futuri me concessisse et hac carta mea confirmasse Deo et monasterio Sancti Thome de Abirbr*othoc* et monachis ibidem Deo seruientibus donacionem illam quam Gillecrist Comes de Anegus eis fecit de ecclesia de Muraus . Tenend*am* in liberam et puram et quietam et perpetuam elemosinam cum capellis terris et decimis et oblacionibus omnimodis et omnibus ad predictam ecclesiam iuste pertinentibus . ita libere et quiete plenarie et honorifice . sicut carta predicti comitis Gillecrist testatur. Test*ibus* Waltero Capellano meo . Rob*erto* de Lond*oniis* . Nicholao medico . Will*elmo* de Valon*iis* . Will*elmo* de Bosco . apud Forfar . xj°. die Aprilis.

RUBRIC. Confirmacio Reg*is* W. de ecclesia de Muraus (red). .xlij. (in margin).
SOURCE. NLS, MS. Adv. 34.4.2, fo.li[v].
PRINTED. *Arbroath Liber*, i, no.42.
NOTE. [a] Initial red.
COMMENT. Earl Gilchrist's charter is given in *Arbroath Liber*, i, no.41 (1201 × 1205).

458 Confirms to Arbroath Abbey the land in Mondynes (Abbeyton, in Fordoun), Mearns, which Philip de Melville and his wife Eve granted, which Walter son of Sibbald had given to Philip as Eve's tocher, and confirmed to the abbey by his charter; to be held as the charter of Philip and Eve, and the confirmation of Walter, bear witness. Forfar. (17 April, 1201 × 1207, probably 1205)

W.[a] Dei gr*ati*a Rex Scott' . Omnibus probis hominibus tocius terre sue clericis et laicis salutem. Sciant presentes et futuri me concessisse et hac carta mea confirmasse Deo et ecclesie Sancti Thome martiris de Abirbr*othoc* . et monachis ibidem Deo seruientibus . terram illam de Monethen quam Philippus[b] de Maleuill' . et E*ua* sponsa sua . eis dederunt . et quam Walterus filius Sib*aldi* eidem Philippo dedit in maritagium . cum predicta E*ua* filia sua . et quam eisdem monachis confirmauit . per cartam suam . Tenend*am* sibi in liberam . puram . et perpetuam elemosinam . cum omnibus libertatibus . et rectitudinibus . eisdem monachis . cum predicta terra iuste concessis . ita libere . et quiete . sicut carta predicti Philippi et E*ue* sponse sue . et confirmacio predicti Walteri . iuste testantur . saluo seruicio meo. Test*ibus* Philippo de Valon*iis* Cam*erario* meo . Seyr de Quinci . Rob*erto* de Lond*oniis* . Dauid de Haya . Rog*ero* de Mortem*er* . Philippo de Lond*in*[c] . Rog*ero* de Wiltona[d]. Apud Forfar . xvii. die Aprilis.

RUBRIC. Confirmacio Reg*is* super predicta carta (red)[e].
SOURCE. NLS, MS. Adv. 34.4.2, fo.lxvii^v = *A*. SRO, Northesk Muniments (uncatalogued), Ethie MS., fo.6^r = *E*. Printed here from *A*.
PRINTED. *Arbroath Liber*, i, no.93 (*bis*).
NOTES. [a] Initial red. [b] Text in *E* begins here. [c] Lund*in*, *E*. [d] Wiltun, *E*. [e] No marginated numeral; entered between xciij and xciiij.
COMMENT. The charter of Philip and Eve de Melville and its confirmation by Eve's father Walter son of Sibbald, are given in *Arbroath Liber*, i, nos.93, 94 (1201 × 1207), stating that the land carried common pasture in Mondynes and Kair (in Arbuthnott). This confirmation is included in no.513. The land became known as Abbottystona (xiii cent.), now Abbeyton (NLS, MS. Adv. 34.4.2, fo.lxvii). For the family of Sibbald of Kair, cf. C. A. Mollyson, *The Parish of Fordoun* (Aberdeen, 1893), 243–4.

459 Grants and confirms to William son of Hugh Giffard Yester (East Lothian) by its right marches, as William's father Hugh held it in the time of the Countess Ada, the king's mother and in the king's time; the whole of Lethington by its right marches, viz. that part which Ralph de Boseville held and that part which William de Bellencombre held; the land beside the River Tyne bounded by the land of the church of Haddington, by Lethington, by the marches of the land received by Godfrey the marischal with his wife, and by the land of the nuns (of Haddington) as far as the road which comes from Berwick and reaches to the bridge; that part of Yester which Gamel held, which Eggu, who held it at ferme, quitclaimed to the king in his court before responsible men; one full toft in the burgh of Crail, which Aernald Kiglepeni first built as far as the sea, together with the buildings of Richard Frere and David the priest and Ulkil of Pittenweem; and one toft in Haddington. To be held with sake and soke, toll, team and infangthief, for the service of one knight. Traquair. (7 May, 1202 × 1207, probably 1205 × 1207)

.W'. Dei gr*atia* Rex Scott'. Episcopis . Abbatibus . Comitibus . Baron*ibus* . Justic*iis* . Vicecom*itibus* . Prepositis . Ministris . et Omnibus probis Hominibus Tocius terre sue . Clericis et Laicis .·/ Salutem. Sciant presentes et futuri . me dedisse et Concessisse et hac carta mea confirmasse . Willelmo filio Hugon*is* Giffard' . et heredibus suis . Jhestrid' . per Rectas diuisas suas . in Boscho et plano . in terris et aquis . in pratis et pascuis . in molendino . in [ui][a]is et semitis . et cum Omnibus ad predictam terram iuste pertinentibus .·/ [ ] riscum[b] meum [ ][c] idem Willelmus et heredes ipsius . et Homines [in][a] eadem Jhestrid' [manente][a]s .·/ habebunt sibi m[ ][d] eorum . et ad ignem eorum . et pasturam [ ][e] sicut Hugo [pater][a] eiusdem Willelmi eam tenuit tempore Ade . Comitisse matris mee . et tempore meo. Et totam Lefditonam plenarie per rectas diuisas suas . illam scilicet partem . quam

Rad*ulfus* de Boseuill' . tenuit . et illam partem :' quam Will*elmus* de Belencumbr' tenuit. Et terram illam secus Tinam . per diuisas terre Ecclesie de Hadint' . et per diuisas supradicte Lefditun' . et per diuisas terre Godefrid*i* marescall*i* quam accepit cum uxore sua et per diuisas terre monialium usque ad uiam que uenit de Berewic'. et tendit ad pontem. Et illam Jhestrid' :' quam[a] Gamell' tenuit . per easdem rectas diuisas per quas Gamell' eam tenuit . et cum Omnibus iustis pertinentiis suis. Quam Jhestrid' Eggu qui terram illam ad firmam tenuit :' mihi quietam clamauit coram probis hominibus meis in curia mea. Et preterea in burgo de Karel illud plenarium Toftum . quod Ærnaldus Kiglepeni[e] primitus edificauit usque ad mare . cum edificiis Ric*ardi* Fratris . et D*aui*d presbiteri . et Ulkil . de Petnewem' . et unum Toftum in Hadintun'. Quare uolo . ut predictus Willelmus et heredes sui has predictas terras et tenuras teneant de me et heredibus meis in feudo et hereditate . per Rectas diuisas predictarum terrarum et cum Omnibus ad predictas terras iuste pertinentibus . in boscho et plano . in terris et aquis . in pratis et pascuis . in moris et marresiis . in stagnis et molendinis . et cum socca et sacca . cum Tol et Them .[f] infangenethef . Libere et Quiete . Plenarie et honorifice :' per seruicium unius militis .Test*ibus* Flor*entio* Electo Glasguen*si* Cancellario meo . Eustac*io* de Vescy . Rob*erto* de Ros' . Rob*erto* de London*iis* filio meo . Philipp*o* de Valon*iis* Camer*ario* meo . Ric*ardo* Reuel . Sim*one* Fraser . Ad*am* Hasteng'. Apud Trauequer .vij. die Maii.

ENDORSED. Carta de Jester facta Willelmo Gyffart (xv cent.). Yester Giffartgat P[?] (xv–xvi cent.). Boundand charter off Jester (xvi–xvii cent.).
DESCRIPTION. 8·5″ (21·6 cm.), Top, 8·25″ (21 cm.), Bottom × 5·9″ (15 cm.), L, 6·1″ (15·5 cm.), R. Foot folded, with slit in centre for seal tag. Tag (0·5″ wide) and seal remain. Length of tag approximately 5·5″. Seal in pink wax, obverse to front, in poor condition, built up.
HAND. Scribe Df. Unruled.
SOURCE. Original, SRO, GD 28/8.
PRINTED. *Yester Writs*, no.8 (with several errors).
NOTES. [a] Parchment injured, letters supplied conjecturally. [b] Parchment injured; perhaps read et mariscum? [c] Illegible through injury. [d] Parchment injured; perhaps read materiem ad edificia. [e] Sic; *Yester Writs*, no.8 prints Riglepeni. [f] Sic.
COMMENT. The king was at Selkirk on 9 May, 1204, but Florence the chancellor was probably not in Scotland until 1205. William de Bellencombre witnessed a charter of the Countess Isabel de Warenne (Countess Ada's niece), *c.*1179 (*EYC*, viii, 101). Bellencombre (dép. Seine Inférieure) was the *caput* of the Warenne family estates in Normandy. For John Frere, a Scots merchant engaged in the Eastland trade in 1297, see William Wallace's letter to Lübeck and Hamburg, facsimile in *Wallace Docs.*, frontispiece, text on p.159.

460 Confirms the agreement made between William bishop of St Andrews on the one hand and the prior and convent of Durham and church of Coldingham on the other, anent cain, conveth, procurations and hospitality; and the custody of and institutions to churches in the diocese of St Andrews belonging to the prior and convent of Durham, as well as the (bishop's) visitation and tour of those churches. Wedale (Stow). (16 May, 1205 or 1206, probably 1205)

.W'. Dei gr*ati*a Rex Scott'. Episcopis . Abbatibus . Comit*ibus* . Baronibus . Justiciis . Vicecomitibus . Prepositis . Ministris . et[a] Omnibus probis Hominibus Totius terre sue Clericis et Laicis Salutem. Sciant presentes et[b] futuri me concessisse et Hac Carta mea confirmasse Amicabilem pacem et compositionem factam inter Will*elmum* Episcopum Sancti Andr*ee* . et Priorem et Conuentum Dunelmen*sem* . et Ecclesiam de Coldigham . Super Cano et Cuneueto . et[b] procurationibus et Hospitiis et Custodiis . et institutionibus Ecclesiarum ad Predictos Priorem et Conuentum Dunelmen*sem* in Episcopatu Sancti Andr*ee* pertinentium . et[b] processione et uisitatione Earumdem Ecclesiarum. Quare uolo et firmiter precipio ut prefata pax et Compositio inter eos facta super predictis .·' futuris perpetuo temporibus firmiter et inuiolabiliter obseruetur sicut Scriptum inter eos inde factum testatur. Test*ibus* Will*elmo* abbate de Melros . Comit*e* Patr*icio* Justic*ia* . Alano fil*io* Rolland*i* Constabul*ario* . Ph*ilippo* de Valon*iis* Camerar*io* meo . Rob*erto* de London*iis* filio meo . Will*elmo* Cumin . Will*elmo* Capellano meo . Will*elmo* de Bosco . Alex*andro* Vicecom*ite* de Striuel*in* . Magistro Nicholao . Magistro Martino . Medicis . Gilb*erto* de Striuel*in* . D*aui*d Marescall*o* . Walt*ero* Murdac . Will*elmo* Olifard'. Apud Wedale .xvi. Die Maii;

ENDORSED. C. Reg*is* Will*elmi* de pace facta inter nos 7 Willelmum Episcopum S*ancti* Andree super Can 7 Coneveth (early xiii cent.). Carta W. Reg*is* de pace facta inter nos et Willelmum episcopum Sancti Andr*ee* super cano et cuneueto (xiv–xv cent.). S. iij[a] vj[te].
DESCRIPTION. 8·9″ (22·6 cm.), Top, 8·8″ (22·5 cm.), Bottom × 4·2″ (10·6 cm.), L, 4″ (10·3 cm.), R. Tie has been cut from top of fold, now torn off. Foot folded 0·7″. Single slits. Tag 6·5″ long, 0·6″ wide. Seal in natural wax, almost entire, fair impression.
HAND. Scribe Df. Unruled.
SOURCE. Original, Durham, D. & C. Muniments, Misc. Chr. no.586.
PRINTED. Raine, *North Durham*, no.53.
NOTES. [a] Crossed tironian sign here and throughout save where noted otherwise. [b] et in full.
COMMENT. The agreement referred to is printed in Raine, *North Durham*, no.473, and commented on in F. Barlow, *Durham Jurisdictional Peculiars* (1950), 131–8. A copy was evidently written into the Great Register of St Andrews, now lost (*St Andrews Liber*, p.xxvii, no.26). See no.368.

461 Confirms the renunciation and abjuration made by William of Gullane, with his brothers Nicholas and John and his maternal aunt Emme, on behalf of themselves and of all their kindred, of the toun of greater Lumsdaine (in Coldingham), in exchange for one ploughgate of land in the territory of Swinton given them by the prior and convent of Durham. Wedale (Stow). (16 May, 1205 or 1206, probably 1205)

.W'. Dei gr*ati*a Rex Scott'. Omnibus probis Hominibus Totius terre sue Clericis et Laicis Salutem. Sciant presentes et futuri me concessisse et Hac Carta mea confirmasse renuntiationem et abiurationem quam Will*elmus* de Goli*n* cum Nich*olao* et Johanne fratribus suis et Emme matertera sua pro se et tota cognatione sua fecit de uilla maioris Lummesdene cum omnibus ad eam spectantibus . et de iure quod in eadem uilla habuit . pro una Carucata terre ei et Heredibus suis in territorio de Swintun a Priore et Conuentu Dunelmen*si* concessa. Quare uolo et firmiter precipio . ut renuntiatio et abiuratio illa facta firmiter in posterum obseruetur ∴ sicut Carta ipsius Willelmi testatur . saluo seruitio meo de predictis terris .Test*ibus* Will*elmo* Episcopo Sancti Andr*ee* . Ph*ilippo* de Valon*iis* Camerar*io* meo . Rob*erto* de London*iis* fil*io* meo . Will*elmo* Cumin . Alex*andro* Vicecom*ite* de Striuel*in* . apud Wedale .xvi. die Maii;

ENDORSED. Confirm*atio* Reg*is* Willelmi de abiuratione Willelmi de Golin de villa Lumeden' maioris (early xiii cent.). B tercia vj[te] (xv cent.).
DESCRIPTION. 6·8″ (17·2 cm.), Top, 6·7″ (17 cm.), Bottom × 3·5″ (8·9 cm.), L, R. Foot folded 0·6″. Tie has been cut from top of fold, now torn off. Single slits. Tag 5·3″ long, 0·7″ wide. Seal in greenish brown wax, almost entire, fair impression.
HAND. Scribe Df. Unruled.
SOURCE. Original, Durham, D. & C. Muniments, Misc. Chr. no.590.
PRINTED. Raine, *North Durham*, no.54.
COMMENT. See no.444; and cf. Raine, *North Durham*, no.426.

462 Announces that he has founded a burgh at his new castle upon Ayr, and grants that all his burgesses dwelling within the burgh shall have all the liberties and free customs that his other burghs and burgesses have elsewhere in his realm. Establishes a market day every Saturday. Grants that burgesses coming to dwell at Ayr shall be free of toll and other customs throughout his land on their own chattels. Grants to the burgesses five pennylands belonging to the toun of Ayr by the marches stated. Each burgess residing in Ayr shall have with a full toft six acres of land cleared from the woodland of the five pennylands, rendering to the king for each toft and six acres 12d. annually. Grants his firm peace to all merchants coming to buy and sell at the burgh of Ayr and commands that toll and custom due to the burgh shall be given and received at Maich, 'Karnebuth', Loudoun, Corsencon and Laicht (in Inch, Wigtownshire). No toll or custom belonging to the burgh is to be taken outwith these marches. Lanark. (21 May, 1203 × 1207, probably 1205)

.W'. Dei gr*at*ia Rex Scott'. Episcopis .Abbatibus . Comit*ibus* . Baron*ibus* . Justic*iis* . Vicecom*itibus* . Prepositis . ministris . et Omnibus probis Hominibus Tocius terre sue . Clericis et laicis ∴ Salutem. Sciant presentes et futuri . me ad nouum castellum meum super AR' Burgum fecisse . et eidem Burgo et Burgensibus meis in eo manentibus . omnes libertates) et omnes liberos consuetudines concessisse quas alii Burgi mei et mei Burgenses in eis manentes per regnum meum habent. Assedi etiam in eo quolibet die sabbati diem fori. Concessi etiam Burgensibus qui illuc uenient ad Burgum meum inhabitandum . et ibi sedentes et manentes erunt ∴ ut quieti sint de Tolneio et omni alia consuetudine per totam terram meam de dominicis catallis suis. Prohibeo itaque firmiter ∴ Ne quis in regno meo ab aliquo illorum Tolneium aut aliquam aliam consuetudinem de dominicis catallis suis exigat . super meam plenariam forisfacturam. Concessi etiam eidem Burgo meo . et Burgensibus meis qui in Burgo illo sedentes et manentes erunt Quinque nummatas terre que pertinent ad uillam de AR' . per diuisas inferius scriptas . Scilicet de Inuerdon . sursum usque in Inuerpolcurtecan . et de Inuerpolcurtecan ∴

sursum usque ad Crottun . et sic per Curtecan usque ad capud Curtecan' . et sic a capite Curtecan .' ascendendo per Boghesken' . usque ad Monedamdereg .' et sic a Monedamdereg .' per sicum usque in Monemethonac' . et a Monemethonac' .' per sicum usque in Pollecleuan . et sic per Pollecleuan .' usque in Lochfergus .' et a Lochfergus descendendo usque in Dufhat . et a Dufhat .' descendendo per sicum usque ad riuulum ex orientali parte Drumnesauel . et a riuulo Drumnesauel . descendendo usque in sicum ex occidentali parte riuuli illius . et sic per sicum illum usque in Polleclonecrangali et sic per Polleclonecrangali .' usque in Dufloch . et inde usque in Pollemulin' . et sic per Pollemulin .' descendendo usque in AR' . et sic per AR' .' descendendo usque in mare. Concessi etiam Burgensibus meis ibidem manentibus . ut cum quolibet plenario Tofto suo habeant sex acras terre . quas de Boscho extirpauerint infra predictas v[que]. nummatas terre . ad faciendum inde commodum suum. Reddendo annuatim mihi pro quolibet tofto et sex acris terre illi adiacentibus xii denarios. Mando itaque et firmiter precipio . ut omnes homines qui cum merchaturis suis ad uendendum et emendum ad illum predictum Burgum meum uenerint . firmam pacem meam habeant . et forum exerceant . et in bene et pace redeant. Precipio etiam firmiter ut apud Mach . et Karnebuth' . et Lowdun' . et Crosenecon . et Lachtalpin . Tolneium et alie consuetudines que Burgo debentur .' dentur et recipiantur. Prohibeo itaque firmiter . ne quis tolneium aut aliquam aliam consuetudinem quam predicto Burgo meo de Ratione facere debet .' ultra predictas diuisas asportare presumat . super meam plenariam forisfacturam. Si quis uero tolneium uel aliquam aliam consuetudinem predicti Burgi mei ultra predictas diuisas asportare presumpserit . precipio firmiter ut omnes homines infra predictas diuisas manentes .' sint auxiliantes seruientibus meis ad adquirendum ius meum . et ad capiendum et attachiandum illum qui tolneia aut aliquam aliam consuetudinem ad predictum Burgum meum pertinentem ultra predictas diuisas asportauerit . uel asportare contenderit. Test*ibus* . Flor*entio* electo Glasguen*si* . Cancellario meo . Waltero et Willelmo Capellanis meis . Philippo de Valon*iis* Camerario meo . Rob*erto* de London' fil*io* meo . Willelmo de Bosch*o* et Hugone Clericis meis . Willelmo de Valon*iis* . Thom*a* de Coleuill' . Regin*aldo* de Crauford'. Apud Lanarc' .xxi. die Maii.

ENDORSED. Traces of an early endorsement, now illegible (?). King William his charter to the toune concerning the landis of Alloway and privileges wanting date Inventarit and copeit (xvi–xvii cent.). Inventarit (1) (xvi–xvii cent.). Also modern endorsements: Pro Boswell, and T.C.S. produced with the reply. Pro George Ferguson.

DESCRIPTION. 7·3″ (18 cm.), Top and bottom × 8·8″ (22·4 cm.), L and R. Foot probably folded, with slits for a seal-tag; but the document is damaged at the foot, and has been repaired. No trace remains of seal-tag, seal or method of sealing.

HAND. Scribe Df. No ruling visible.

SOURCE. Original, Ayr Burgh Charter Chest.

PRINTED. *Nat. MSS. Scot.*, i, Pl.XL; *Charters of the Royal Burgh of Ayr* (1883), 1–2, with facs.; *The Royal Burgh of Ayr* (1953), 1–3; and elsewhere.

COMMENT. This charter has been often printed and much commented upon. See in particular *Charters of the Royal Burgh of Ayr* (Ayr and Wigton Archaeological

Association, 1883), 1–2 (with facsimile) and, for detailed comment on place-names, pp.xix–xxv; G. S. Pryde in *The Royal Burgh of Ayr*, ed. A. I. Dunlop (1953), 1–3 (text), 4–18 (comment); and in *SHR*, xxix, and also A. Ballard and J. Tait, *British Borough Charters.*

463 Grants to his son, Robert of London, and his heirs, that he may hold his forest of Outh (in Dunfermline), Fife, in forest, as the king held it in forest on the day he granted it to Robert; no one is to fell timber or hunt there without Robert's leave, on pain of the king's full forfeiture of ten pounds. Stirling. (8 July, 1195 × 1210)

.W'. Dei Gr*aci*a Rex Scott' Omnibus probis Hominibus Tocius Terre sue . Clericis et Laicis :' Salutem. Sciant presentes et futuri . me Concessisse . et Hac Carta mea confirmasse . Rob*erto* de London*iis* fil*io* meo et heredibus suis in forestum . forestum meum de Uueth' . sicut illud habui in forestum :' die qua illud ei dedi. Quare prohibeo firmiter . ne Quis in foresto illo sine eorum licentia secet aut uenetur . super meam plenariam forisfacturam decem . librarum. Test*ibus* Philippo de Valon*iis* Camerario meo . Willelmo de Bosch*o* Clerico meo . Alex*andro* Vice*comite* meo de Striuel*in* . Ric*ardo* fil*io* Hugon*is* . Herb*erto* de camera. Apud Striuel*in*. viij. die Jul*ii*.

ENDORSED. Cartha W. Reg*is* de Uuiet (xiii cent.). Cartha Rob*erti* Lo' de Uuiet (xiii–xiv cent.). Also modern endorsement.
DESCRIPTION. 6·2″ (15·7 cm.), Top, 6·1″ (15·5 cm.), Bottom × 2·8″ (7 cm.), L, R. Foot folded, slits for seal-tag. Tag, 5·2″ long and 0·6″ wide, remains, split to take seal, of which only small traces remain in white wax. The seal is described in *C*: 'sigillum appensum attritum, eques ab una et rex in solio ex altera parte'.
HAND. Scribe Df. Unruled.
SOURCE. Original, SRO, Drummond Cas. Muniments (Lundin Charters) = *A*. NLS, MS. Adv. 34.1.3a, fo.xii^v = *B*. NLS, MS. 29.4.2, vol.vi, unnumbered folio between 10 and 11 (copy by Mr Dillon from original) = *C*. NLS, MS. 34.3.25, pp.182–8 (from original *penes* Lord Lundin) = *D*. Printed here from *A*, with description of seal from *C*.
PRINTED. *Dunfermline Registrum*, no.57 (from *B*).
COMMENT. Robert of London granted Outh to Dunfermline Abbey (see no.495 and *Dunfermline Registrum*, no.167).

464 Confirms to Inchaffray Abbey the grant made to it by Earl Gilbert of Strathearn of the lands of Craig, Ardunie, Dubheads, Ardbennie and Williamstone (in Madderty), Perthshire. Stirling. (19 July, 1204 or 1205, probably 1205)

.W'. Dei gr*ati*a Rex Scott'. Omnibus probis Hominibus Tocius Terre sue . Clericis et laicis :' Salutem. Sciant presentes et futuri . me Concessisse . et Hac Carta mea confirmasse Deo et Ecclesie Sancti Johannis Euuangeliste de Incheaffren' . et Canonicis ibidem Deo seruientibus et seruituris . donationem illam quam Comes Gilleb*ertus* de Stradheren' . eis fecit de Ahchelunchi . et Ardeweni . et Duffindir . et Ardbanin' . et Baleful. Tenend*am* in liberam et puram et perpetuam Elemosinam . per Rectas diuisas suas . et cum Omnibus iustis pertinentiis suis . ita libere et Quiete . Plenarie et Honorifice :' sicut Carta predicti Comitis Gilleb*erti* de Stradher*n* . iuste testatur . Saluo seruicio meo. Test*ibus* Willelmo Episcopo Sancti Andr*ee* . Hugon*e* de Mortem*er* Priore de May . Comite Malcolm*o* de Fif . Philipp*o* de Valon*iis* Camerar*io* . Willelmo Cumin . Malis*io* fil*io* Com*itis* Ferteth . Walter*o* Olifard' . Willelmo de Valon*iis* . Alex*andro* vice*comite* de Striuel*in* . Willelmo Gifard' . Philipp*o* de Lundin'. Apud Striuel*in* .xix. die Julii.

ENDORSED. De terris nostris (xiii cent.).
Confirmacio Willelmi regis super terris de Achlunxi Ardewny Duffindir et Ardbanni et Baleful' Rubrica xj [a].
DESCRIPTION. 6·35″ (16·1 cm.), Top, bottom × 2·9″ (7·5 cm.), L, 2·7″ (7·2 cm.), R. Foot folded. Slits with tag 0·6″ (1·5 cm.) wide. Large fragment of seal remains in natural wax stained brown, diameter 2·4″.
HAND. Scribe Df. Unruled.
SOURCE. Original, Kinnoull Trustees' Muniments (Dupplin Charters, no.126) = *A*. Kinnoull Trustees' Muniments, MS. Cartulary of Inchaffray Abbey, fo.7^{r-v} = *B*. Printed here from *A*.
PRINTED. *Inchaffray Chrs.*, no.24 (from *A*). *Inchaffray Liber*, 14, no.11 (from *B*).
NOTE. [a] *B* only; numeral refers to section beginning on fo.1.
COMMENT. For the identification of the place-names cf. *Inchaffray Chrs.*, 318–19 and accompanying map.

465 Confirms to Brice bishop of Moray the bishopric of Moray, and grants in augmentation the church of Elgin, saving the life tenure of his chaplain Walter (of St Albans), and the church of Auldearn. Alyth. (24 August, 1203 × 1207, probably 1205)

.W. Dei gratia Rex Scott' episcopis . abbatibus . comitibus . baronibus . justiciariis[a] . vicecomitibus . prepositis . ministris . et omnibus probis hominibus tocius terre sue tam[b] clericis quam[b] laicis salutem. Sciant presentes et futuri me concessisse et hac presenti[c] carta mea confirmasse . B*ricio* episcopo Moravie episcopatum Moraviensem cum omnibus justis pertinentiis suis . tenendum sibi ita libere et quiete et honorifice sicut aliquis episcoporum meorum in regno meo episcopatum suum liberius et quiecius et honorificencius tenet et possidet . et ita plenarie sicut aliquis antecessorum suorum episcoporum Moravie episcopatum illum plenius tenuit. Preterea concessi de incremento episcopatui Moraviensi et predicto B*ricio* episcopo Moraviensi et successoribus suis episcopis . pro salute anime mee et antecessorum meorum . ecclesiam de Elgin cum capellis et terris et decimis et obventionibus et omnibus aliis justis pertinenciis suis . salva tenura Walteri[d] capellani mei in eadem ecclesia. Et preterea ecclesiam de Eren cum capellis et omnibus aliis justis pertinenciis suis . tenendas in liberam et perpetuam elemosinam ita libere et quiete . plenarie et honorifice . sicut alios redditus episcopatus liberius . quiecius . plenius et honorificencius tenet. Test*ibus* Udardo abbate de Cupre . Will*elmo* et .W. capellanis meis . Willelmo de Bosco . Will*elmo* Cumin just*icia* . Philippo de Mubrei . Add'[e] filio Gylberti . Waltero Murthac . Ric*ardo* Reuel. Apud Alith .xxiiij.[f] die Augusti.

RUBRIC. Confirmacio regis de episcopatu Morauie B. episcopo (*A*). Confirmacio domini regis de episcopatu Mor'. B. episcopo (*B*, at top).
SOURCE. NLS, MS. Adv. 34.4.10, fos.xxxv^{v}–xxxvi^{r} = *A*. Ibid., fo.xiv^{r} = *B*. Printed here from *A*, with some of *B*'s readings noted.
PRINTED. *Moray Registrum*, no.18 (from *B*).
NOTES. [a] *A* omits. [b] *A* omits tam . . . quam. [c] *A* omits presenti. [d] Fo.xxxvj^{r}, *A*. *B* has .W. [e] Ada, *B*. [f] xxxiij, *A*; *B* has Abyrcht xxiiij; *Moray Registrum*, no.18 prints Abyrbrocht, wrongly.
COMMENT. Udard abbot of Coupar died in 1207, and Walter of St Albans, the king's chaplain, was elected to the see of Glasgow on 9 December, 1207.

466 Confirms to Arbroath Abbey the grant made by Donald abbot of Brechin of the davoch called Balegillegrand (Bolshan, in Kinnell, Angus), as Donald's charter bears witness. Forfar. (7 September, 1203 × 1206, probably 1205)

W.[a] Dei gr*ati*a Rex Scotorum omnibus probis hominibus tocius terre sue clericis et laicis salutem. Sciant presentes et futuri me concessisse et hac carta mea confirmasse Deo et ecclesie Beati Thome martiris de Abirbr*othoc* et monachis ibidem Deo seruientibus . et seruituris . donacionem illam quam Douenaldus abbas de Brech*in* eis fecit de illo dauach' qui vocatur[b] Balegillegrand'. Tenend*am* in liberam et perpetuam elemosinam per rectas diuisas predicte terre . et cum omnibus aliis ad eamdem terram iuste pertinentibus . ita libere et quiete plenarie et honorifice . sicut carta predicti Douenaldi testatur saluo seruicio meo. Test*ibus* Flor*entio* electo Glasg*uensi* Cancell*ario* meo . Willelmo de Bosco clerico meo . Willelmo Cumyn . Willelmo de Lindes' . Waltero Murdach' . Dauid Marescall*o* . Waltero de Vchtirlys . Bricio judice meo. Apud Forfar .vij°. die Septembris.

RUBRIC. Confirmacio Regis super ipsa carta (red)[c].
SOURCE. NLS, MS. Adv. 34.4.2, fos.lx^{v}–lxi^{r}.
PRINTED. *Arbroath Liber*, i, no.74 (*ter*).
NOTES. [a] Initial red. [b] Fo.lxi^{r}. [c] No marginated numeral; entered between lxxiiij and lxxv.
COMMENT. Donald's charter is given in *Arbroath Liber*, i, no.74 (*bis*) (1202 × 1206). In it he mentions his father Samson, probably the Samson who was bishop of Brechin and died before *c*.1178. The davoch of Balegillegrand is identified with Bolshan in BM, MS. Add. 33245, fo.5^{r}.

467 Declares generally the privileges and regulations of the burgh of Perth. No foreign merchant is to trade within the sheriffdom of Perth outwith the burgh; and foreign merchants may expose (or cut?) their cloth for sale in Perth only between Ascension Day and 1 August, during which period they may trade in Perth as though they were the king's own merchants. No village in the sheriffdom of Perth may have a tavern unless its lord is a knight residing in that village, and then there may be only one tavern. The burgesses of Perth are to have their merchant guild, save for the fullers and weavers. No one dwelling in the sheriffdom of Perth outwith the burgh of Perth may make dyed cloth or motley except for the king's burgesses of Perth, save for those who have previously had a charter giving them this liberty. The sheriff of Perth is to seize the cloth of those caught with illegal dyed or shorn cloth and deal with the matter as was done in the time of King David I. The king grants his peace to those bringing wood and timber to Perth, and forbids anyone to disturb those who come to sell or buy these commodities once they have entered within the lined marches of the burgh. No-one from outwith the burgh of Perth shall buy or sell hides or wool save in the burgh. Stirling. (10 October, *c*.1205 × 1210, probably 1205)

Will*elmus*[a] Dei gr*aci*a Rex Scotorum[b], omnibus probis hominibus, tam clericis quam laicis, salutem. Prohibeo firmiter ne quis mercator extraneus infra vic*ecomitatum* de Perth extra burgum meum de Perth aliquid emat vel vendat super meam defencionem, sed mercator extraneus veniat cum mercandisis suis ad burgum meum de Perth et ibi eas vendat et denarios suos inplicet. Si quis vero mercator extraneus super hanc defencionem meam inventus fuerit in vic*ecomitatu* de Perth aliquid emens vel vendens, capiatur et deteneatur donec voluntatem meam de eo precepero. Prohibeo eciam firmiter ne quis mercator extraneus scitet[c] pannum suum ad vendendum in burgo meo de Perth nisi a die Ascensionis Domini usque ad Vincula Sancti Petri. Infra quos terminos [volo][d] ut ipsi scitent[c] pannum suum ad vendendum in burgo meo de Perth, in foro de Perth, et ibi emant et vendant pannos et alias mercaturas suas communiter cum burgensibus meis, sicut dominici burgenses mei, saluis rectitudinibus meis. Precipio eciam ut omnes qui manent in burgo meo de Perth et cum burgensibus meis communicare voluerint, ad forum communicent[e] cum illis ad auxilia mea reddenda, cuiuscunque homines sint. Prohibeo eciam ne quis[f] aliqua taberna habeatur in aliqua villa infra vic*ecomitatum* de Perth nisi ubi miles sit dominus ville et in eo valeat, et ibi non habeatur nisi una taberna sola. Concedo eciam burgensibus eisdem meis de Perth ut habeant Gildam suam mercatoribus,[g] exceptis fullonibus et telar*iis*. Prohibeo eciam firmiter ne quis manens extra burgum meum de Perth in vic*ecomitatu* de Perth faciat pannum tinctum vel mixtum infra vic*ecomitatum* de Perth, nec facere faciat, preter burgenses meos de Perth qui sint[h] in gild*a* mercator*um* et communicant ad auxilia mea cum burgens*ibus* solvend*a*. exceptis illis qui de hac libertate cartam suam ucusque habuerunt. Quare firmiter prohibeo ne quis in vic*ecomitatu* de Perth facere presumat pannum tinctum vel tonsum super plenariam meam forisfactur*am*. Si vero aliquis pannus tinctus vel tonsus inuentus fuerit factus super hanc defencionem, precipio vicecomiti meo de Perth quatenus capiat pannum et inde faciat secundum consuetudinem que fuit tempore D*aui*d Regis aui mei. Concedo eciam iuste meam firmam pacem omnibus illis qui ligna vel materiem attra[h]unt ad Perth. Quare precipio ne quis [eos][i] disturbet ad ea vendenda vel emenda, postquam infra [diuisas lineatas][j] prope Perth venerint. Has autem libertates [et][d] consuetudines illis [concedo][k] et hac carta mea confirmo. Prohibeo eciam firmiter ne quis extraneus extra burgum meum de Perth emat vel vendat corea vel lanam nisi in burgo meo de Perth. Test*ibus* Comite D*aui*d fratre meo, Philippo de Vallone Camerario nostro[l], Roberto de London*iis* filio meo, Willelmo Cumyn, Willelmo de Bosco et Hugone de sigillo clericis meis, Alexandro [vice]comite[m] de Striuelyn, Henrico filio Comitis D*aui*d, Rogero de Mortemer[n], Dauid Marscallo[o], Johanne de Striuelyn. Apud Striuelyn x[o][p] Octobris.

ENDORSED.[q] Confirmacio W. Reg*is* (xiv cent.). Charter be King William To the toun of Perth first foundatour thairof in anno j m ij c Ten (xvi cent.).

DESCRIPTION. 10·5″ (26·8 cm.), Top and bottom × 3·7″ (9·3 cm.), L, R. Foot folded to a depth of 0·6″ (1·5 cm.). Double slits in foot and fold for seal-tag, part of which remains without any seal.

HAND. Scribe UDg. Business hand of the early fourteenth century. Decoration of crudely drawn whorls at top left-hand corner of document.

SOURCE. City and Royal Burgh of Perth, Perth City Chambers, Charter no. 1. Copy in the form of an original, probably of the earlier part of the fourteenth century = *A*. BM, MS. Add. 18,111, fo. 136^{r-v} (old pagination, 261–2) (collection of the Laws of Scotland, xv cent.) = *B*. Printed here from *A*, with some variants of *B* noted and a few readings of *B* preferred.

PRINTED. *APS*, i, 86–87 = *C*. *C* is evidently an eclectic text drawn from *A* and 'a collation of several of the Law MSS., in which this charter is entered apparently as a style' (*APS*, i, 53, n.5).

NOTES. [a] Punctuation editorial. [b] After Scotorum *B* has Episcopis, Baronibus, Justic', vic*ecomitibus* et ceteris ministris suis ac. [c] Sic. Cf. *MLWL*, s.v. situs. But *B* and *C* have secet, secent, probably preferable since these are the readings of Alexander II's charter for Aberdeen. [d] *A* omits; supplied from *B*. [e] communicant, *A*. [f] quis apparently expunged, *A*. [g] Sic. *B* has mercatricem, probably preferable since this unusual word is found in Alexander II's charter. [h] sunt, *B*. [i] Supplied from *B*, which has turbet. [j] diuisas supplied conjecturally. *B* has unam leucatam terre; *C* prints unam leucatam. Alexander II's charter does not help, since it omits this clause. [k] Supplied from *B*. *A* has concessi et; *C* prints concessas. [l] meo, *B*. [m] comite, *A*, *B*. [n] Mortn', *A*; Mortim', *B*. [o] Thus *B*; *A* has de Marichal'. [p] *B* adds die. [q] *A* only.

COMMENT. The year of issue cannot be as late as 1211. Earl David, at Newark on Trent on 3 October, 1205 (*Rot. Chart.*, 159), is known to have been in Scotland in 1205 (Lawrie, *Annals*, 348–9). His son Henry was born after 1190, and is not found witnessing any charters before *c.* 1205.

It may be inferred from Alexander II's charter (*APS*, i, 87; *Aberdeen Burgh Chrs.*, no.5) that some wording is missing from surviving versions of this act, including the grant of a weekly Saturday market and of the king's peace to those attending it.

468 Confirms to Ivo de Vieuxpont the lands which his father William held in Tynedale, viz. Elrington (in Haydon, Northumberland), Alston (Cumberland) and Kirkhaugh (in Slaggyford, Northumberland), in feu and heritage, for the service of one knight, as freely as his father held. Stirling. (11 October, probably 1205)

W.[a] Dei gratia Rex Scottorum omnibus probis hominibus tocius terre sue, clericis et laicis, salutem. Sciant presentes etfuturi me concessisse et hac presenti carta mea confirmasse Ivoni de Veteri ponte terras illas quas Willelmus de Veteri ponte pater eius tenuit in Tynedale, scilicet Alrington' et Aldeneston' et Kirkehale, cum justis pertinenciis suis, tenendas sibi et heredibus suis de me et heredibus meis in feodo et hereditate, per servitium unius militis, ita libere et quiete sicut predictus Willelmus de Veteri ponte pater eius illas tenuit. T*estibus* Comite Patricio, Philippo de Valoniis Cancell*ario*[b] tunc[c] Roberto de Lundon*iis* filio meo, Willelmo de Bosco clerico meo, Engelramo de Balliolo, Hugone de Norman*uilla*. Apud Striuel*in*, xi die Octobr*is*.

SOURCE. PRO, J.I.1/143 (Assize Roll).

PRINTED. *Placita de Quo Warranto* (Record Commission, 1818), 197; F.W. Ragg, in *CWAAS*, New Ser., xi (1911), 271–2.

NOTES. [a] Punctuation editorial. [b] Sic; for Camerario. [c] Sic; for meo.

COMMENT. See no.84. Philip de Valognes should be described as 'chamberlain'; either this is simply an error, or Florence the chancellor's name has been omitted.

469 Grants to John Waleram for his homage and service the whole land which William Carpenter held in 'Ballebotl' (Babbet, in Kingsbarns?), Fife, viz. every fifth rig of the whole half of 'Ballebotlia'; and in the fields of 'Dreinin' (Drony, in Kingsbarns?) the land which was perambulated for Roger of the Chamber on the orders of the Countess Ada, the king's mother, by Hugh Giffard, Alexander de

St Martin, Godfrey the marischal, Winemer and other responsible men. Grants in addition all the land in Airdrie (in Crail) held by William de Beauver, viz. the land to the east of the burn flowing beside the land of Geoffrey the chaplain as far as the well which in Gaelic is called 'Tolari' (Toldrie, in Crail); and all the land perambulated for William Carpenter on all sides towards the muir (Kingsmuir, in Crail) and elsewhere by Geoffrey de Melville (and others named); and common pasture of Crail, and one toft in Crail, which the Countess Ada gave to William Carpenter. To be held in feu and heritage for the service of one sergeand on a horse with a haubergel, and the performance of as much forinsec service as pertains to half a Scottish ploughgate in Crail-shire. John Waleram is to be free of multure at the mill immediately after the corn already in the hopper, unless the king's own corn should be there or arrive in the meantime. Clackmannan. (13 October, probably 1205)

.W'. Dei gr*ati*a Rex Scott'. Episcopis. Abbatibus. Com*itibus*. Baronibus. Justic*iis* . Vicec*omitibus* . Prepositis . Ministris . et Omnibus probis hominibus Tocius Terre sue Clericis et Laicis . Salutem. Sciant presentes et futuri . me dedisse et concessisse . et hac carta mea confirmasse . Johanni Waler' . pro homagio et seruicio suo totam terram illam quam Willelmus Carpentarius tenuit in Ballebotl' . Scilicet Quintam Reiam tocius medietatis de Ballebotlia . Et in campis de Dreinin .' illam terram quam Hugo Giffard' et Alex*ander* de Sancto Martin*o* et Godefridus Maresc*allus* et Winemerus et alii probi homines precepto Ade Comitisse matris mee Roger*o* de Camera perambulauerunt. Et preterea totam terram in Ardarie quam Willelmus de Beauuer tenuit. Scilicet terram illam que est ex orientali parte Riuuli qui currit iuxta terram Galfridi Capellani usque ad fontem illum uersus Karel' . qui Scottice Tolari nuncupatur. Et totam terram illam per easdem diuisas quas Galfridus de Maleuill' et Hug*o* Giffard' et Godefr*idus* Maresc*allus* et Winemerus et alii probi homines predicto Willelmo ex omni parte uersus moram et alibi perambulauerunt. Et communem pasturam de Karel . et unum Toftum in Karel . illud Scilicet quod[a] A. Comitissa mater mea predicto Willelmo dedit. Quare uolo et firmiter precipio ut predictus Johannes et heredes sui . omnes prescriptas tenuras habeant et teneant de me et heredibus meis in feudo et hereditate . in pratis et pascuis . in moris et marresiis , et in omnibus aliis aisiamentis que ad predictas terras iuste pertinent . libere et quiete . plenarie et honorifice . per seruicium unius seruientis in equo cum halbergello . et faciendo in auxiliis et aliis forincesis[b] seruiciis pro tota terra quam habet in Ardarie . tantum seruicii .' quantum pertinet ad dimid*iam* Carrucatam terre scotticam in Karelis-schire. Concessi etiam predicto Johanni et heredibus suis . ut quieti sint de multura ad molendinum primo post Bladum qui in tremello fuerit . nisi Bladus meus ibi sit aut superueniat. Testibus . Philippo de Valon*iis* . Camerar*io* meo . Willelmo Capellan*o* meo . Willelmo Cumin . Hug*one* et Willelmo et Adam Clericis meis . Magistro Nichol*ao* et Magistro Martin*o* Clericis meis . Alex*andro* Vicecomite de Striuel*in* . Willelmo de Valon*iis* . Alex*andro* fil*io* Thore . Johanne de Striuel*in* . Roberto Quarrantel'. Apud Clacm*anan* .xiij. die Octobr*is*.

ENDORSED. Charter maid by Williame king of Scotland to Johne Walram of certane Landis in Carele schyre (xvi–xvi cent.). William the Lion King of Scotland (xviii cent.?). Also modern endorsements.
DESCRIPTION. 9·2″ (23·5 cm.), Top, 9″ (23 cm.), Bottom × 6·1″ (15·5 cm.), L, 5·8″ (14·8 cm.), R. Foot folded, though fold has now been laid flat; an area of restored parchment in the centre of the foot presumably indicates presence of a slit for a seal-tag. No tag or seal remains.
HAND. Scribe Df. Unruled.
SOURCE. Original, BM, Campbell Charter xxx, 5.
PRINTED. *Illustrations of Scottish History* (Maitland Club, 1834), no.XIII.
NOTES. [a] Word obscured by tear in parchment. [b] Sic, for forinsecis.
COMMENT. William Carpenter witnessed *RRS*, i, nos.193, 215, 256, and may have been a royal sergeand. John Waleram witnessed the grant to Cambuskenneth Abbey of Abbots Deuglie (in Arngask), Perthshire, by Saer de Quinci earl of Winchester (*Cambuskenneth Registrum*, no.70), confirmed by King William, above, no.431. The name Tolari, now Toldrie, represents Gaelic *toll righ*, 'king's well', *toll* ('hole') for well being not uncommon. A 'Scottish ploughgate' (*carrucata scottica*) was perhaps a davoch; cf. *Scottish Studies*, vi, pt. 2 (1962), 131, 138–9. The parishes of Kingsbarns, Crail and Carnbee seem to have been extensively settled by royal servants and minor officers in the twelfth and thirteenth centuries. For Robert (de) Quarrantel, evidently a dependent of Philip de Valognes, cf. *Annales de Normandie*, xve année, 513–14.

470 Confirms to Geoffrey, son of Richard steward of Kinghorn, the toft and houses in the toun of Kinnaird (Perthshire), which Richard of Kinnaird nephew of Ralph Ruffus granted to him and of which he gave him sasine before the king's responsible men, to be held of Richard in feu and heritage. Auchtermuchty. (8 January, 1205 × 1211, perhaps 1209?)

.W'. Dei gr*ati*a Rex Scott'. Omnibus probis Hominibus Tocius terre sue . Clericis et laicis :· Salutem. Sciant presentes et futuri . me Concessisse et Hac Carta mea confirmasse . Galfrid*o* fil*io* Ric*ardi* senescall*i* de Kingor totam illam mansionem et domos in uilla de Kinnard' :· quas Ricardus de Kinnard' . nepos Rad*ulfi* Ruffi . ei dedit . et tradidit coram probis hominibus meis. Tenend*as* sibi et heredibus suis . de predicto Ric*ardo* et heredibus suis . in feudo et hereditate . ita libere et Quiete . plenarie . et Honorifice :· sicut Carta predicti Ricard*i* testatur . saluo seruicio meo. Test*ibus* Comite Malc*olmo* de Fif . Philipp*o* de Mubray . Willelmo de Bosco Clerico meo . Ric*ardo* fil*io* Hug*onis* . Ricardo Reuel . Ad*am* filio Herberti :· Apud Uchtermukethin' .viij. die Januar*ii*.

ENDORSED. Confirmacio de mansione et domibus in uilla de Kinard (xiii cent.).
DESCRIPTION. 6·7″ (17 cm.), Top and bottom × 3·1″ (7·8 cm.), L, 2·8″ (7·2 cm.), R. Foot folded to a depth of 0·6″ (1·5 cm.). Double slits, with tag 4″ (10·2 cm.) long, 0·5″ (1·3 cm.) wide. Small central portion of seal remains, pink wax, much defaced.
HAND. Scribe Df. Unruled.
SOURCE. Original, SRO, GD 90/13.
COMMENT. Cf. nos.451, 471.

471 Confirms to Geoffrey, son of Richard steward of Kinghorn, the land in 'Kinbrichtor' and the hunting lodges of that land, granted to him by Richard of Kinnaird nephew of Ralph Ruffus. Auchtermuchty. (8 January, 1205 × 1211, perhaps 1209?)

.W'. dei Gr*ati*a Rex Scott' . Omnibus probis Hominibus Tocius Terre sue . Clericis et laicis :· Salutem. Sciant presentes et futuri . me Concessisse . et Hac Carta mea Confirmasse . Galfrid*o* fil*io* Ricard*i* senescalli de Kingor . donationem illam quam Ricardus de Kinnard' . nepos Rad*ulfi* Ruffi ei fecit de terra illa quam ei dedit in Kinbrichtor . per diuisas contentas in carta eiusdem Ricard*i*. Et preterea donationem illam quam ei fecit de logiis de Kinbrichtor . per suas rectas diuisas. Tenend*am* sibi et heredibus suis . de predicto Ricard*o* et heredibus suis . in feudo et hereditate . ita libere et Quiete . plenarie et Honorifice :· sicut Carta predicti Ricard*i* testatur . saluo seruicio meo. Test*ibus* Comite Malc*olmo* de Fif . Philipp*o* de Mubray . Will*elmo* de Bosc*o* Clerico meo . Ric*ardo* fil*io* Hug*onis* . Magistro Rob*erto* de Stichil . Magistro Martin*o* . medicis meis . Ad*am* fil*io* Herb*erti* . Ric*ardo* Reuel. Apud Uchtermukethin'. viij. die Januar*ii*.

ENDORSED. Confirmacio de Kinbrithor et de logiis de Kinbrithor (xiii cent.). per Villelmum R (xvi cent.). Also numeral endorsements.
DESCRIPTION. 7·2″ (18·5 cm.), Top, (18·2 cm.), Bottom × 3·6″ (9 cm.), L, 3·5″ (8·8 cm.), R. Foot folded to a depth of 0·8″ (2 cm.). Single slits, with tag 5″ (13 cm.) long, 0·6″ (1·5 cm.) wide. Tag split for seal; no seal remains. There are a number of holes in the parchment.
HAND. Scribe Df. Unruled.
SOURCE. Original, Edinburgh University Library, Laing Charters, no.17.
PRINTED. *Laing Chrs.*, I, no.3 (brief abstract, with note '17, Box I').
COMMENT. Cf. nos.451, 470. Although 'Kinbrichtor' remains unidentified, the name should be compared with 'Kinbrithmund', the earliest known form of the name Kilbrackmont (in Kilconquhar), Fife; cf. *Dunfermline Registrum*, no.216.

472 Confirms to Malcolm earl of Fife the grant which he made to his father Earl Duncan of Strathleven, Fife, and the grant which King David I made to the same Earl Duncan of West Calder, Midlothian, to be held for the service of knights, as the charters of himself and King David I bear witness. Clunie in Stormont. (22 March, 1206 × 1207)

W. Dei gr*atia* Rex Scott'. Episcopis . Abbatibus . Comitibus . Baronibus . Justiciis . Vicecomitibus . prepositis Ministris et omnibus probis hominibus totius terre sue clericis et laicis salutem. Sciant presentes . et futuri me concessisse . et hac carta mea confirmasse . Com*iti* Malcolmo . de Fif . donacionem illam quam feci Com*iti* Dunec*ano* patri ejus de Stradleuene . et donationem illam quam Rex Dauid auus meus eidem[a] Comiti[b] Dunecan*o* fecit de Kaldou*er*. Tenend' sibi et heredibus suis de me et heredibus meis in feudo et hereditate per rectas diuisas predictarum terrarum et cum omnibus aliis ad predictas terras iuste pertinentibus . ita libere et quiete, plenarie et honorifice . sicut carta Regis D*aui*d aui mei et mea testantur . per seruicium militum[c] . Testibus Flor*entio* Electo Glasguen*si* Cancell*ario* nostro[d]. Willelmo Cumin Justic*iario* . Waltero Olifard . Henr*ico* fil*io* Com*itis* D*aui*d fratris mei Roger*o* Mortem*er*. Apud Clonin' xxij die Mart*ii*.

SOURCE. Earl of Haddington, Mellerstain, MS. Notebook of Sir John Skene, Lord Clerk Register, p.6 = *A*. BM, MS. Harl. 4693, fos.46^{v}–47 = *B*. Printed here from *A*.
PRINTED. G.W.S.Barrow, *PSAS*, lxxxvii (1952–3), p.62.
NOTES. [a] Sic. [b] Comite, *A*. [c] propter servitium duorum militum, *B*. [d] Sic.

COMMENT. Neither King David's charter, which must have been in favour of Earl Malcolm's grandfather, Earl Duncan I, nor King William's own charter for Earl Duncan II, has survived. For a comment on the significance of this act, cf. *PSAS*, lxxxvii, 51–9.

473 Confirms (re-grants?) to Walter de la Carneille Guthrie (Angus), in feu and heritage, with soke and sake, toll, team and infangthief, with pit and gallows, for the service of half a knight, as the charter of Roger de la Carneille bears witness. (Unrecorded place-date.) ([?] March, 1205 × 1207)

Willelmus[a] Dei gracia Rex Scottorum omnibus probis hominibus totius terre sue, clericis et laicis, salutem. Sciant presentes et futuri me concessisse et hac carta mea confirmasse Waltero de la Kernelle terram de Gutherin per rectas diuisas suas, cum omnibus iustis pertinentiis suis. Tenendam sibi et heredibus suis de me et heredibus meis in feodo et hereditate imperpetuum, in terris et aquis, in pratis et pascuis, in moris et maresiis, in stagnis et molendinis et omnibus aliis suis iustis pertinenciis, cum soka [et][b] saka, cum furca [et][b] fossa, cum toll et theme et infangthef et outfangthef, bene et in pace atque honorifice, per seruicium dimidii militis, sicut carta [R][b]ogeri de la Kernelle [testatur][b]. Coram hiis testibus, Florencio electo Glasguensi cancellario nostro, Waltero capellano nostro, Willelmo de Boscho et Hugone clericis meis, [ ] Galfridi[c], Henrico filio Comitis Dauid fratris mei, Alexandro filio Thore[d], Johanne de Lundin, Johanne[e] de Coluile, Richardo Reuell. Apud [ ][f] die Marcii.

SOURCE. SRO, transumpt in *ADC*, xxi, fo.35 (of date 22 November, 1509).
NOTES. [a] Punctuation editorial. [b] Source omits. [c] Blank, perhaps read Waltero Olifard. [d] Thome, Source. [e] Sic, perhaps for Philippo or Thoma. [f] Blank in source.
COMMENT. The king's charter to Roger de la Carneille is not known to survive. For the family see *Annales de Normandie* (15[e] année, No.4, 1965), 513. See no.408.

474 Confirms to Gilchrist son of Earl Gilbert of Strathearn Kinveachy and Glencarnie (in Duthil and Rothiemurchus), Inverness-shire, granted to him by his father, to be held of Earl Gilbert in feu and heritage. Forfar. (16 April, 1205 × 1207, probably 1206)

.W'. Dei gr*ati*a Rex Scott' . Omnibus probis hominibus Tocius terre sue :' Clericis et laicis :' Salutem. Sciant presentes et futuri . me concessisse . et Hac Carta mea confirmasse . donationem illam quam Com*es* Gilleb*ertus* de Stradher*n* fecit Gillecrist filio suo de Kinnebethin . et de Glantarnin'[a] per Rectas diuisas suas . et cum omnibus iustis pertinentiis suis. Tenend*am* sibi et heredibus suis . de predicto Com*ite* Gilleb*erto* et heredibus suis . in feudo et hereditate . cum omnibus ad predictas terras iuste pertinentibus . ita libere . et Quiete . Plenarie . et Honorifice :' sicut Carta predicti Com*itis* Gilleb*erti* iuste testatur . Saluo seruicio meo. Test*ibus* Flor*entio* Electo Glasguen*si* Cancellario meo . Com*ite* Malc*olmo* de Fif . Ph*ilippo* de Valon*iis* cam*erario* meo . Willelmo Cumin . D*aui*d de Haia . Willelmo Giffard' . D*aui*d Marescall*o* . Ric*ardo* Reuel. Apud Forfar' :' xvi. die Aprilis.

ENDORSED. Confirmacio domini W. Reg*is* de terra domini G. de Glencarni (xiii cent. hand of English type). Confirmatioun be King William of the charter granted be the Earle of Strathern to his sone Gilbert[a] of Kinnebethin and Glencharnie Glencharnie[a] (xvii cent.).
DESCRIPTION. 7·1″ (18 cm.), Top, 7″ (17·7 cm.), Bottom × 2·5″ (6·5 cm.), L, 2·6″ (6·7 cm.), R. Foot folded to a depth of 0·6″ (1·5 cm.). Single slits, with tag in poor condition, 7″ (17·5 cm.) long, 0·5″ (1·3 cm.) wide, split for seal. No seal remains. Tie cut from fold. The document is in poor condition.
HAND. Scribe Df. Unruled.
SOURCE. Original, SRO, GD 248/4/2.
PRINTED. Fraser, *Grant*, iii, 1, no.2 (with facsimile); also *Fraser Facsimiles*, no.29.
NOTE. [a] Sic.
COMMENT. The name Glencarnie is now obsolete; cf. Lachlan Shaw, *History of Moray* (1775), 39n. for a mention of Glenchernich. See no.206.

475 Appoints a market day in his burgh of Inverness, viz. every Saturday, and grants his firm peace to all who shall come to his market of Inverness. Confirms to his burgesses of Inverness all the laws and rightful customs which the burgesses of his other burghs of Scotland enjoy. No one is to make dyed or shorn cloth contrary to the assizes of King David I and himself. No one is to buy or sell outwith his burgh anything contrary to King David's assize and his own. There are to be no taverns in landward villages outwith his burgh, save where the lord of the village is of knight's rank and resident there, and then there shall be a tavern in accordance with the assize of King David and of himself. Kintore. (18 August, 1205 × 1207)

Willelmus Dei gratia Rex Scottorum episcopis abbatibus comitibus baronibus justiciariis vicecomitibus prepositis ministris et omnibus probis hominibus totius terre sue clericis et laicis salutem. Sciant presentes et futuri me constituisse diem fori in burgo meo de Inuernis scilicet diem sabbati in qualibet ebdomada meamque firmam pacem juste dedisse omnibus qui ad forum meum de Inuernis venient. Et prohibeo firmiter ne quis hiis qui ad forum meum venient in veniendo vel in reddeundo injuriam vel molestiam vel gravamen aliquod injuste inferre presumat super meam plenariam forisfacturam. Concessi etiam burgensibus meis qui burgum meum de Inuernis inhabitabunt omnes leges et rectas consuetudines quas alii burgenses mei in aliis burgis meis de Scotia habitantes habent. Et ut nullus infra bailliam de Inuernis faciat extra burgum meum pannum tinctum vel tonsum contra assisam Regis David avi mei et meam. Et si quis pannus inventus fuerit tinctus vel tonsus factus contra hanc meam defensionem, precipio ut vicecomes meus de Inuernis pannum illum capiat et inde faciat sicut consuetudo et assisa fuit tempore Regis David avi mei, nisi forte alicui libertatem talem per cartam meam dederim. Prohibeo etiam firmiter ne quis emat vel vendat extra burgum meum aliquid quod sit contra assisam Regis David avi mei et meam. Prohibeo etiam firmiter ne aliqua taberna habeatur in aliqua villa campestri extra burgum meum, nisi in villa ubi miles dominus ville sit manens, et tunc habeatur ibi taberna secundum assisam Regis David avi mei et meam. Precipio itaque firmiter ballivis meis de Inuernis quatinus predictis burgensibus meis de Inuernis auxiliantes sint et eos juste manuteneant ad predictas rectas consuetudines burgi habendas. Et prohibeo ne quis predictos burgenses meos contra predictas rationabiles leges et consuetudines injuste vexare presumat super meam plenariam forisfacturam. Teste Waltero Capellano meo . Willelmo Cumin justiciario . Willelmo de Boscho et Hugone clericis meis . Ada persona de Kingorn . Herberto de Camera . Rogero de Mortuo mari . Ricardo filio Hugonis. Apud Kintor .xviii. die Augusti.

SOURCE. *APS*, i, 89. No trace of this has been found in the Inverness burgh muniments.
PRINTED. As above.

476 Confirms the gift which Brice bishop of Moray made to Gilbert of Cathcart of the church of Kingussie with the chapel of Banchor (Inverness-shire), as the bishop's charter bears witness. Elgin. (25 August, 1203 × 1210)

Will*elmus* Dei gracia Rex Scott' omnibus probis hominibus tocius terre sue clericis et laicis salutem. Sciatis me concessisse et hac carta mea confirmasse donationem illam quam Bricius Morau*iensis* episcopus fecit Gill' de Kathkerd de ecclesia de Kingussin cum capella de Benchorin . et cum omnibus aliis pertinenciis suis . tenend*am* ita libere et quiete, plenarie et honorifice sicut carta predicti Bricii episcopi testatur. Testibus Willelmo capellano meo, Willelmo de Bosco et Hugone de sigillo clericis meis, Hugone Freskyn et Willelmo fratre ejus, Apud Elgin .xxv. die Augusti.

RUBRIC. Confirmacio Reg*is* de donacione Bricii episcopi de ecclesia de [ ] (later hand). confirmacio [ ] episcopi de ecclesia [ ].
SOURCE. NLS, MS. Adv. 34.4.10, fo.xxxviij^r = *A*. Ibid., fo.xxxix = *B*. Ibid., fo.xv = *C*. Printed here from *A*.
PRINTED. *Moray Registrum*, no.19 (from *B*, with facsimiles of *B* and *C* and a later text).
COMMENT. Gilbert of Cathcart was presumably related to (Sir) Gilbert of Cathcart who appears in record *c*.1208–1221 (*Glasgow Registrum*, pp.87, 88, 101, 103, 117). The version printed in *Moray Registrum* erroneously implies that Gilbert 'de Kathern' granted Kingussie church *to* Bishop Brice.

477 Announces that the dispute which there had been between himself, Brice bishop of Moray and Gilchrist earl of Mar anent the patronage of the church of Aberchirder (Marnoch), Banffshire, has been settled amicably, with the surrender to Arbroath Abbey by the parties of all their rights of patronage. Kintore. (18 September, 1203 × 1207)

W.[a] Dei gr*ati*a Rex Scott' Omnibus probis hominibus tocius terre sue clericis et laicis salutem. Sciant presentes et futuri quod cum controuersia inter me . et B*ricium* episcopum Morauiensem et G*illecrist* comitem de Marr' esset . de iure patronatus ecclesie de Abirkerdor . ita amicabiliter conuenit inter nos . quod quilibet nostrum totum ius quod in eadem ecclesia habuit . dedit Deo et Sancto [Thome][b] martiri et monachis de Aberbr*othoc* . in perpetuam elemosinam. Unde sciant presentes et futuri me dedisse et concessisse et hac carta mea confirmasse Deo et Sancto Thome et monachis de Abirbr*othoc* quicquid iuris in predicta habui ecclesia . cum omnibus ad eam iuste pertinentibus . Tenend*um* in liberam et perpetuam elemosinam ita libere et quiete et honorifice . sicut aliquam ecclesiam liberius et quiecius habent. Test*ibus* Waltero Capellano meo . Hug*one* Fretheskyn . Willelmo de Bosco et Hug*one* clericis meis . Henr*ico* Reuel' . Heru*ico*[c] de Kynros . Walt*ero* de Wictirlys . Michaele de Ferendrach' . apud Kintor .xviij°. die Septembris.

RUBRIC. De ecclesia de Aberkerdou*er* (red). .xxxiij. (in margin).
SOURCE. NLS, MS. Adv. 34.4.2, fo.xlix^r.
PRINTED. *Arbroath Liber*, i, no.33.
NOTES. [a] Initial red. [b] MS. omits. [c] Henr', MS.
COMMENT. Instruments issued by Bishop Brice and Earl Gilchrist on this occasion are printed in *Arbroath Liber*, i, nos.205, 206. The witnesses to the earl's instrument are identical with those named in this act with the addition of Brice the *judex*.

478 Commands all his baillies of Moray to see that the bishop of Moray receives all the teinds and dues which he ought to have by law, as his charters bear witness; if anyone withholds any of these dues, the bishop may compel him to pay by means of ecclesiastical penalties. Aberdeen. (12 November, 1203 × 1207)

Will' Dei gratia Rex Scott' omnibus balliuis suis tocius Morau*ie* salutem. Precipio uobis firmiter quatinus omnes decimas et rectitudines quas episcopus Morau*iensis* de jure habere debet sicut carte eius testantur ei plenarie et sine disturbatione habere faciatis . et prohibeo ne quis decimas aut rectitudines ei iniuste detineat super meam plenariam forisfacturam. Si quis uero super hoc illas ei detinere presumpserit . concessi ei ut per ecclesiasticam iusticiam illos ei plenarie iura sua reddere iuste distringat. Test*ibus* Walt*ero* capellano meo . Will*elmo* de Bosco clerico meo. Apud Aberd*en* .xii. die Nouembris.

MARGINAL NOTE. Ista carta non scribitur in libro decani.
SOURCE. NLS, MS. Adv. 34.4.10, fo.xxxvii^v.
PRINTED. *Moray Registrum*, no.20.
COMMENT. Probably after the succession of Bishop Brice; and perhaps dating to 1206.

479 Confirms to Holyrood Abbey the quitclaim made by Saer de Quinci earl of Winchester of any right he might possess in the church of Tranent; one ploughgate and ten acres in Tranent granted by Earl Saer's father (Robert de Quinci); and the land in Longniddry (East Lothian) granted by Robert de Quinci and confirmed by Earl Saer, to support the service of the chapel of Longniddry. Forfar. (17 March, 1207 × 1210, probably 1208)

W'. Dei Gratia Rex Scott'. Omnibus probis Hominibus Tocius Terre Sue .·' Clericis et laicis .·' Salutem. Sciant presentes et futuri . me Concessisse . et Hac Carta mea confirmasse . quietam clamantiam quam Seiher' de Quinci . Comes Winton' . fecit pro se et Omnibus Heredibus suis abbati Ecclesie Sancte Crucis de Edenburg . et Conuentui eiusdem domus in perpetuum de iure quod Habere uidebatur in ecclesia de Trauernent . et eius pertinentiis. Confirmo etiam eis unam Carrucatam terre . et decem . acras . in territorio de Trauernent . apud Faweside .

cum libero exitu et communi pastura quam pater predicti Seiher'. eis dedit in liberam elemosinam et perpetuam . quam idem Seiher' . eis confirmauit. Confirmo etiam eis totam illam terram in Nodrif . quam pater predicti Sehier'[a] . eis dedit ad seruiendum capelle eiusdem uille . quam idem Seiher' . eis confirmauit. Tenend*am* in liberam et puram Elemosinam . sicut Carta et confirmatio predicti Seiher' . testatur . saluo seruicio meo. Test*ibus* Rob*erto* de London*iis* filio meo . Flor*entio* Cancellario meo . Will*elmo* Cumin . Will*elmo* et Oliuero Capellanis meis . Will*elmo* de Boscho et Hugon*e* Clericis meis . Roger*o* de Mortuo Mari . Herbert*o* de Camera. Apud ForfaR' .xvij. die Marc*ii*.

ENDORSED. De Trauernent (xiii cent.). Confirmacio Reg*is* Willelmi (xiii cent.). in Trauernent et in Fauside (xiv cent.). J. Scott (xvi cent.). Also modern endorsements.

DESCRIPTION. 6·6″ (16·8 cm.), Top, 6·8″ (17 cm.), Bottom × 5″ (12·5 cm.), L, 4·8″ (12·2 cm.), R. Foot folded to a depth of 0·5″ (1·3 cm.). Single slits with tag 4·1″ (10·5 cm.) long, 0·7″ (1·7 cm.) wide, split for seal. No seal but traces of pink wax.

HAND. Scribe Df. Unruled.

SOURCE. Original, SRO, GD 1/17/1.

PRINTED. *Holyrood Liber*, no.38.

NOTE. [a] Sic.

COMMENT. Saer de Quinci became earl of Winchester on 13 March, 1207.

480 Confirms to Lesmahagow Priory the grant made to it by William Cumin of the land which had been in dispute between William Cumin and the abbot of Kelso. (Probably 1208 × 1214)

Will*elmus*[a] Dei gratia Rex Scott' . Episcopis . Abbatibus . Comitibus . Baronibus . Justic*iis* . Vice*comitibus* . prepositis . Ministris . et omnibus probis hominibus tocius terre sue clericis et laicis . salutem. Sciant presentes et futuri me concessisse Deo et Sancte Marie de Kalch' . et Sancto Machuto de Lesmachug*u* et monachis ibidem seruientibus . donacionem quam Willelmus Comyn fecit eis de terra illa de qua controuersia fuit inter eundem Willelmum Cumyn . et abbatem de Kalch' . per easdem diuisas que continentur in carta eiusdem Willelmi Cumyn . Tenend*am* in liberam et perpetuam elemosinam in bosco et plano . in pratis et pascuis . et omnibus aliis aisiamentis . ad prefatam terram pertinentibus . ita libere et quiete. plenarie et honorifice sicut carta prenominati W. Cumyn testatur . saluo seruicio meo. Test*ibus*.

RUBRIC. Concessio Willelmi Regis de terra Willelmi Comyne.

SOURCE. NLS, MS. Adv. 34.5.1, fo.11^r.

PRINTED. *Kelso Liber*, no.9.

NOTE. [a] Initial red.

COMMENT. The land in dispute seems to have been the whole or part of Draffan, in Lesmahagow, and the abbot of Kelso with whom William Cumin made his settlement of the dispute was Henry, who succeeded in 1208 (*Kelso Liber*, no.103 and p.x).

481 Grants to Kelso Abbey and Abbot Henry the same liberties and customs which the abbots, his predecessors, had before him. Wherever, outwith the king's demesnes, he may find his fugitive (neyfs) he is to have them justly and without delay, and no one is to detain them or their chattels unjustly. Traquair. (6 July, 1208)

W. Dei gr*ati*a Rex Scott'. Episcopis. Abbatibus. Com*itibus*. Baron*ibus*. Justic*iis* . Vicec*omitibus* . prepositis .[a] ministris . 7 Omnibus probis hominibus tocius terre sue clericis 7 laicis. salutem. Sciatis me concessisse Ecclesie Sancte Marie de Kelch'. 7 Henrico abbati eiusdem loci. omnes libertates . 7 consuetudines . quas Abbates antecessores sui ante ipsum habuerunt 7 tenuerunt . ita bene . 7 libere .' sicut Abbates antecessores sui eas unquam melius 7 liberius habuerunt 7 tenuerunt. Et ubicunque extra dominia mea in tota terra mea fugitiuos suos inuenerit .' iuste 7 sine dilacione illos habeat. Et prohibeo firmiter super meam plenariam forisfacturam . ut nemo illos uel catalla sua sibi iniuste detineat . uel ipsum uel ministros eius super hoc iniuste vexet. Test*ibus* Com*ite* Patricio . Will*elmo* . 7 Oliuer*o* capellanis meis . D*aui*d de Lindes' . 7 Geruasio Auenel. Justic*iis*. Will*elmo* de Bosch*o*. apud Trauequer vj°. die Jul*ii*.

RUBRIC. Confirmacio super omnes libertates 7 consuetudines ecclesie de Kelch' (top in red).
SOURCE. NLS, MS. Adv. 34.5.1, fos.148^{v}–149^{r}.
PRINTED. *Kelso Liber*, no.403.
NOTE. [a] Fo.149^{r}.

482 Confirms to Melrose Abbey the whole arable land called Sorrowlessfield beyond Leader on the west bank, towards the grange of the monks of Melrose, as William Soroules held it and as granted by Earl Patrick of Dunbar, as his charter bears witness. (1208 × 1214)

Will*elmus*[a] Dei gr*ati*a rex Scot' omnibus probis hominibus tocius terre sue, clericis et laicis, salutem. Sciant presentes et futuri me concessisse et hac carta mea confirmasse Deo et Sancte Marie de Melros et monachis ibidem Deo seruientibus donacionem illam quam Comes Patricius de Dunbar eis fecit de tota terra arabili que vocatur Sorouuelesfeld ultra Ledir ex occidentali parte uersus grangiam predictorum monachorum, sicut Willelmus Soroules eam umquam plenius tenuit, tenend*am* in liberam et puram et perpetuam elemosinam, ita libere et quiete, plenarie et honorifice, sicut carta predicti Comitis Patricii de Dunbar testatur, saluo seruicio meo. Test*ibus* etc.

RUBRIC. Confirmacio regis Willelmi de Sorouuelesfelde.
SOURCE. BM, MS. Harl. 3960, fo.37^{v}.
PRINTED. *Melrose Liber*, no.105.
NOTE. [a] Initial red.
COMMENT. Earl Patrick's charter is given in *Melrose Liber*, no.133, dating 17 June, 1208 × 28 June, 1211; see also no.483. For William Soroules, or Sorweles, see *Melrose Liber*, no.12, a charter of William of Lindsay, probably of the time of David I or Malcolm IV, to which William Sorueles was apparently a witness, although the name is given as *Willelmo de . . . eles* in the printed text.

483 Confirms the settlement made at Selkirk (6 July, 1208) in his presence and in his full court of the dispute between Patrick earl of Dunbar and Melrose Abbey anent pasture on the west bank of the Leader Water. The settlement is made with the consent of Earl Patrick's son and heir, Patrick, and is to be maintained inviolably as the chirograph made between the parties bears witness. Selkirk. (6 November, 1208)

.W'. Dei Gr*ati*a Rex Scott'. Episcopis . Abbatibus . Comit*ibus* . Baron*ibus* . Justic*iis* . Vicecom*itibus* . Prepositis . ministris . et Omnibus probis Hominibus Tocius Terre sue . Clericis et laicis ⁏ Salutem. Sciant presentes et futuri . me Concessisse . et Hac Carta mea Confirmasse . amicabilem compositionem factam apud Seleschr' in presentia mea . et in plena curia mea . ex una parte inter Com*item* Patric*ium* de Dunbar' . consentiente Patric*io* fil*io* ⁊ herede eius . et domum de Melros . ex altera parte . super controuersia que uertebatur inter eos de pastura uersus occidentem a Ledre. Quare uolo et firmiter precipio . quatinus predicta compositio inter eos inde facta inuiolabiliter et inconcusse teneatur ⁏ sicut Cyrographum inter eos inde factum ⁏ testatur . saluo seruicio meo. Test*ibus* B*ricio* episcopo Morauien*si* . Rad*ulfo* episcopo de Duhn' . Willelmo et Oliuero Capellanis meis . Rob*erto* de London*iis* fil*io* meo . D*aui*d de Lindes'. et Geruas*io* Auenel Justic*iis* . Will*elmo* de Bosch*o* et Hugon*e* de sigillo Clericis meis . Roger*o* de Mortem*er* . Ad*am* de Kingor . Johanne de Maccuswel' . Alex*andro* de Sint*on*. Apud Selesch' .vi. die Nouembr*is*.

ENDORSED. [ ] regis W. de concordia inter [nos ⁊ ?] comitem Patricium de pastura iuxta Led*er* (xiii cent.). Large red capital letter (xv cent.?). J. Scott (xvi cent.).

DESCRIPTION. 7·5″ (19·2 cm.), Top and bottom × 5″ (12·5 cm.), L, R. Foot folded to a depth of 0·6″ (1·5 cm.). Single slits with tag 5·4″ (13·5 cm.) long, 0·6″ (1·5 cm.) wide. Seal almost complete in pale brown wax.

HAND. Scribe Df. Unruled.

SOURCE. Original, SRO, GD 55/103.

PRINTED. *Melrose Liber*, no.103.

COMMENT. The pasture in dispute was associated with Sorrowlessfield, where arable had been granted to Melrose by Earl Patrick (see no.482). The procedure for settling the dispute was narrated at length by Bishop Brice of Moray, in his capacity of judge-delegate appointed by Pope Innocent III (*Melrose Liber*, no.101), and the details of the agreement itself are given in the chirograph made between the parties (ibid., no.102). For the date, see *Melrose Liber*, no.101. Ralph, bishop of Down(patrick) since 1202, had been abbot of Melrose (*Chron. Melrose*, 51). On 22 March, 1203, Bishop Ralph celebrated ordinations in St Cuthbert's chapel of St Albans Abbey (F. Liebermann, *Ungedruckte Anglo-Normannische Geschichtsquellen* (1879), 167). He wrote, while still abbot of Melrose, an interesting eulogy of Jocelin bishop of Glasgow, printed by Bishop Forbes, *Lives of St Ninian and St Kentigern* (*Historians of Scotland*, v, 1874), 308–312.

484 Confirms to Alan, son of Alan, son of Cospatric of Swinton Colzie (probably Wester Colzie and North and South Colzie (in Abernethy), Perthshire) and the land of Abernethy (probably Easter Colzie (in Newburgh, formerly in Abernethy detached), Fife); granted to him by Walter Olifard son of Walter Olifard; to be held of the granter in feu and heritage. Edinburgh. (8 November, 1208 × 1210)

.W'. Dei Gr*ati*a Rex Scott' . Omnibus probis Hominibus Totius Terre sue . Clericis et laicis ⁏ Salutem. Sciant presentes et futuri . me Concessisse . et Hac Carta mea confirmasse . Alan*o* fil*io* Alan*i* fil*ii* Cospatric*i* de Swinton' . donationem illam quam Walterus Olifard' . filius Walter*i* Olifard' . ei fecit de Culesin . per Rectas diuisas suas . et de terra de

Abernithin. Tenend*am* sibi et heredibus suis . de predicto Walter*o* Olifard' . et heredibus suis . in feudo et hereditate . cum Omnibus ad predictas terras iuste pertinentibus . ita libere et Quiete . plenarie et honorifice :' sicut Carta predicti Walter*i* Olifard' . testatur . saluo seruitio meo. Test*ibus* Oliuer*o* Capellano meo . Philipp*o* de Valon*iis* . Camer*ario* meo . Will*elmo* de Bosch*o* et Hugon*e* de sigill*o* . Clericis meis . Henr*ico* fil*io* Com*itis* D*aui*d. Apud Edenb' .viij. die Nouembr*is*.

ENDORSED. Charta Villelmi Reg*is* super terris de Cullessi 2 (xv–xvi cent.)
DESCRIPTION. 6·1″ (15·5 cm.), Top and bottom × 3·4″ (9·1 cm.), L, 3·3″ (8·5 cm.), R. Foot folded, with slits for seal tag. Tag remains, 6·5″ (16·5 cm.), with mark of seal.
HAND. Scribe Df. Unruled.
SOURCE. Original, Brigadier Alan H. C. Swinton of Kimmerghame, Kimmerghame, Duns, Berwickshire.
PRINTED. G. S. C. Swinton, 'Six Early Charters', *SHR*, ii, 175, with facsimile facing p.176.
COMMENT. The charter of Walter Olifard, in the same ownership as this one, is printed *SHR*, ii, 174–5, with facsimile facing p.174. The Olifard lordship of Colzie is not known from any other source, but the Olifards seem to have become established as landowners in Dupplin and Forgandenny from the turn of the twelfth and thirteenth centuries, and William Olifard witnessed a charter of the early thirteenth century relating to Dron (Fraser, *Douglas*, iii, 349–50, no.281; *Inchaffray Chrs.*, 291). Wester Colzie seems always to have been in Abernethy parish and Perthshire; Easter Colzie was in a detached portion of Abernethy parish, but in Fife, down to the Local Government (Scotland) Act, 1889 (cf. John Ainslie's Map of Fife and Kinross (1775); *Retours* (Fife, Perth); *Reg. Mag. Sig.*, ii, no.3662; H. Shennan, *Boundaries of counties and parishes of Scotland* (Edinburgh, 1892), 256).

485 Confirms to Holyrood Abbey those churches in Galloway granted to it by Fergus (lord of Galloway) and his son Uchtred and David son of Terri, which Bishop John of Galloway has permitted the canons to convert to their own uses. Jedburgh. (18 April, 1209 × 1211, perhaps 1209)

.W'. Dei Gr*ati*a Rex Scott'. Omnibus probis Hominibus Tocius Terre Sue . Clericis et laicis :' Salutem. Sciant presentes et futuri . me Concessisse . et Hac Carta mea Confirmasse . Deo et Ecclesie Sancte Crucis de Edenburg' . et Canonicis ibidem Deo seruientibus et seruituris :' Ecclesias illas in Galweia . quas Fergus . et Uchtredus filius eius . et D*aui*d filius Terri . eis dederunt. Quas Ecclesias :' Johannes Candide Case Episcopus . eisdem Canonicis Carta sua Confirmauit . et in proprios usus Conuertend*as* concessit. Tenend*as* in liberam et puram et perpetuam Elemosinam . cum Omnibus iustis pertinentiis suis . ita libere et Quiete . plenarie et honorifice :' sicut Carta predicti Joh*annis* Episcopi testatur. Test*ibus* Waltero Episcopo Glasguen*si* . Hug*one* abbate de Jedd' . Oliuero Capellano meo . Philipp*o* de Valon*iis* Camerario meo . Willelmo Cumin Justic*ia* Scott' . Will*elmo* de Bosch*o* Clerico meo . Will*elmo* de Valon*iis* . Ric*ardo* Reuel. Apud Jeddewrth' .xviij. die Aprilis.

ENDORSED. De ecclesiis de Galeweia. (xiii cent.). per Regem Willelmum (xv cent.). J. Scott (xvi cent.). Also modern endorsements.
DESCRIPTION. 6·5″ (16·6 cm.), Top, bottom × 4·3″ (11 cm.), L, 4·5″ (11·5 cm.), R. Foot folded to a depth of 0·7″ (1·8 cm.). Single slits with tag 5·9″ (16 cm.)

long, 0·6″ (1·7 cm.) wide, split and twisted for seal, of which a small fragment (top) remains in pink wax, rev. to front, clear impression.
HAND. Scribe Df. Unruled.
SOURCE. Original, SRO, GD 45/13/250.
PRINTED. *Holyrood Liber*, no.50.
COMMENT. The churches granted by Fergus were 'Dunroden', later Dunrod, and 'Galtweith', later Galtway, both obsolete parishes, now in Kirkcudbright. Cp. Galtway (farm) and Galtway Hill in Kirkcudbright, beside the Dunrod Burn which forms the march with Rerrick parish. By his son Uchtred, Kirkcudbright (St Cuthbert of Desnesmor), Tongland, Twynholm, the 'church of St Andrew' now represented by Balmaghie (cf. *Holyrood Liber*, nos.83, 84, 120), Kelton and 'Kyrkecormac' (obsolete, now in Kelton) with the chapel of 'Balnecros' (now Barncrosh in Tongland); and by David son of Terri, Anwoth with the chapel of 'Culenes' (unidentified).

This is the earliest appearance as bishop of Glasgow of Walter (of St Albans), the king's chaplain, a witness to nos.475, 478. Walter was alleged to have offered 100 merks to the chamberlain, Philip de Valognes, and 'a far larger sum' to the queen, that he might be elected bishop of Glasgow (Theiner, *Monumenta*, no.29), but no more was heard of these charges. Walter was elected 9 December, 1207, and consecrated 2 November, 1208.

486 Confirms to William Noble the two ploughgates and two oxgangs in Kilpunt (in Kirkliston), West Lothian, granted to him by Henry de Bohun earl of Hereford, and also the whole land in Illieston (in Kirkliston) which Gerald held, granted to him by Earl Henry. Clackmannan. (28 May, 1208 × 1211)

.W'. Dei Gr*ati*a Rex Scott' . Omnibus probis Hominibus Tocius Terre sue . Clericis et Laicis :' Salutem. Sciant presentes et futuri me Concessisse . et Hac Carta mea Confirmasse . Willelmo Nobili illas duas Carrucatas terre . et duas Bouatas in Kenpunt :' quas Henr*icus* de Boho*n* Comes Hereford' . ei dedit . et preterea totam terram illam in Ileuestun' . quam Geroudus tenuit . quam predictus Henr*icus* de Boho*n* Com*es* Hereford' . dedit predicto Willelmo Nobili. Tenendas sibi et heredibus suis . de predicto Henr*ico* et heredibus suis . ita libere et Quiete . plenarie et Honorifice :' sicut Carta predicti Henr*ici* testatur . Saluo seruicio meo. Test*ibus* Oliuero Capellano meo . Willelmo de Bosch*o* Clerico meo . Thom*a* de Coleuill' . Alex*andro* Vic*ecomite* de Clac*manan* . Ric*ardo* fil*io* Hugon*is* . Herberto de Camer*a*. Apud Clacm*anan* .xxviij. die Maii.

ENDORSED. Charter be King Wm of Kynpont Willielmo Nobili (xvi cent.) an. dom. 1165 (xvii cent.). Ch:A.Sh:1 B. 1 no.4 (xviii cent.).
DESCRIPTION. 6·9″ (17·5 cm.), Top and bottom × 4·2″ (10·6 cm.), L, R. Foot folded to a depth of 0·8″ (2 cm.). A tie has probably been torn away from top left-hand corner of fold, about 6·5″ long. Single slits in foot and fold, seal-tag remains, 6·3″ (16 cm.) long, 0·5″ (1·2 cm.) wide, split and twisted to take the wax of the seal. No seal remains.
HAND. Scribe Df. Unruled.
SOURCE. Original, Duke of Montrose, Montrose Muniments, Auchmar, Drymen, A.1.1.4.
PRINTED. *HMC*, *5th Report*, Appendix, p.611; Fraser, *Menteith*, ii, 207, no.1; also *Fraser Facsimiles*, no.27.
COMMENT. These lands formed part of the estate of Ratho which in turn formed part of the tocher of £100 worth of land and 20 knights' feus provided by King William for his sister Margaret, widow of Conan duke of Brittany, on her second

marriage (Feb., 1171 × Easter, 1175) to Humphrey de Bohun, father of Henry de Bohun earl of Hereford here mentioned (*APS*, i, 116; *Complete Peerage*, s.v. Richmond).

487 Confirms to Arbroath Abbey the grant made by John the abbot, son of Malise, of licence to take charcoal in his wood of Edzell, Angus, wherever it may most easily be found, and as much as is needful for work on the abbey's buildings. Alyth. (5 July, 1209 or 1210)

W.[a] Dei gr*ati*a Rex Scotorum omnibus probis hominibus tocius terre sue clericis et laicis salutem. Sciant presentes et futuri me concessisse et hac carta mea confirmasse monachis de Abirbr*othoc* concessionem illam quam Johannes abbas filius Malisii ipsis fecit in liberam et perpetuam elemosinam . de carbonibus capiendis in nemore suo de Edale ubicunque ad maius aisiamentum inuenire poterunt . quantum sufficiens erit ad opera domus sue . cum aisiamentis hospicii et pasture in terra ipsius Johannis animalibus eorum . sicut carta eiusdem Johannis testatur. Test*ibus* Oliuero Capellano meo . Willelmo de Bosco clerico meo . Ricardo filio Hug*onis* . Herberto de Cam*era* . Ric*ardo* Reuell'. Apud Alicht .v[o]. die Julii.

RUBRIC. Confirmacio Regis W. super prescripta carta (red). .lxxiij. (in margin).
SOURCE. NLS, MS. Adv. 34.4.2, fo.lx[r].
PRINTED. *Arbroath Liber*, i, no.73.
NOTE. [a] Initial red.
COMMENT. John seems to have belonged to the family of lay abbots of an ecclesiastical foundation in the North Esk valley, perhaps represented by Lightnie (Lethnot) and Navar. His charter here confirmed is given in *Arbroath Liber*, i, no.72 (1198 × 1210), with the contemporaneous confirmation by his son Morgrund, ibid., no.74.

488 Binds himself to pay to King John of England, in four equal instalments of 3,750 merks each, the sum of 15,000 merks, at the following terms: (1) 30 November, 1209; (2) 6 June, 1210; (3) 30 November, 1210; and (4) 22 May, 1211. The payment is made to have King John's goodwill and in order to observe the agreements made between himself and King John as confirmed in charters issued by both parties. To ensure payment of the money at the terms stipulated, he grants to King John the keeping of the hostages he already has, named in the said charters, except for his two daughters whom he has now handed over to King John. Norham on Tweed. (7 August, 1209)

Uuill*elm*us[a] Dei gr*ati*a Rex Scoc' omnibus ad quos presens carta peruenerit salutem. Sciatis quod tenemur reddere domino nostro Johanni illustri Regi Angl*ie* quindecim milia marc*arum* ad terminos sibi scriptos, sc*ilicet* ad festum Sancti Andr*ee* apostoli anno regni [regis][b] Johannis undecimo, tria milia marcarum et septengentas et quinquaginta marc'; et ad Pentecosten proximam, scilicet anno regni eiusdem Regis Johannis duodecimo, tria milia marcarum et septingentas et quinquaginta marc'; et ad subsequens festum Sancti Andr*ee* apostoli anno eodem, tria milia marcarum et septingentas et quinquaginta marc'; et ad Pentecosten proximo sequenti, scilicet anno regni eiusdem Reg*is* Johannis tercio decimo, tria milia marc' et septingentas et quinquaginta marc', pro habenda beneuolencia eiusdem domini nostri Johannis Reg*is* Angl*ie* et pro conuencionibus tenendis que inter ipsum et nos facte et per cartas nostras hinc et inde sunt confirmate. Et pro hac pecunia ei ad predictos terminos reddenda, et pro eisdem terminis fideliter tenendis, dedimus ei in tenenciam obsides nostros quos habet et qui in predictis cartis nostris nominati sunt, exceptis duabus filiabus nostris, quas ei liberauimus. Et cum predictam pecuniam ad terminos prescriptos ei persoluerimus, ipse nobis hanc cartam nostram reddet quietam. Teste domino W*illelmo* Episcopo Sancti Andr*ee*, Philipp*o* de Valoniis, Roberto de Ros, Roberto de Veteri ponte. Apud Norham vij. die Augusti.

RUBRIC. De xv. mill' marc' soluend' R. Angl' per Regem Scocie.
SOURCE. PRO, E 36/274, fo.185 ('Liber A').
PRINTED. Rymer, *Foedera* (Orig.), i, 155; (Rec. Com.), I, i, 103; *Cal. Docs. Scot.*, i, no.453 (abstract only, in translation).
NOTES. [a] Punctuation editorial. [b] MS. omits.
COMMENT. This document formed part of the lost 'Treaty of Norham' of August 1209, discussed in Anderson, *Early Sources*, ii, 374–77 and in Stones, *Documents*, xlv–xlviii. Unfortunately the latter authority ignores the account of the treaty in the Melrose Chronicle (*Chron. Melrose*, 54), which says that the kings met at Norham *with their armies*, and that the king of Scots handed over his daughters to John to be married, together with 13,000 pounds, and received permission to demolish the castle (Tweedmouth) built opposite Berwick, which was done. In order to maintain peace King William gave to the English king as hostages the sons of the responsible men (*probi homines*) of his realm, and this was done against the will of the Scots. Later in this year, King William gave a hospitable reception in Scotland to the bishops of Salisbury and Rochester, who had left England because of the excommunication of King John in October.

The fact that the Scottish king had his army with him means that the making of a treaty cannot in itself have been secret, but the surprisingly small number of witnesses and the lack of standing in Scotland of two of them, Robert de Ros, lord of Wark and King William's son-in-law, and Robert de Vieuxpont, may mean that the terms of the treaty were thought likely to displease the majority of the Scottish magnates and were kept moderately secret. Diplomatically, this is an unsatisfactory document, with an address unknown elsewhere among the acts of King William, the uncommon and suspicious use of the plural, and the unfamiliar title of *dominus* for the bishop of St Andrews. But if this document was issued and sealed in a hurry and in some secrecy, it might well have suspicious features. A reliable version of this document must have been known to Fordun, since he correctly gives 15,000 merks in four instalments as the amount to be paid, as against the Melrose chronicler's £13,000. Fordun also mentions, but not as derived from the Melrose Chronicle, the demolition of Tweedmouth Castle (cf. *Chron. Fordun*, i, 277); for which see also *APS*, i, 118. On the whole, it seems likely that this is an authentic act of King William, possibly drafted and even written for him by English royal clerks.

Half the sum due seems to have been remitted by King John (*APS*, i, 118).

489

Confirms to the church of St Cuthbert of Kirkcudbright that part of Sypland (in Kirkcudbright) held by Kineth; and to the church of St Oswald the Martyr of Kelton 32 acres in the territory of Kelton; granted to these churches by Alan son of Roland, the constable. Stirling. (7 January, 1210)

.W'. Dei Gr*ati*a Rex Scott'. Omnibus probis Hominibus Tocius Terre sue . Clericis et laicis .' Salutem. Sciant presentes et futuri . me Concessisse . et Hac Carta mea confirmasse donationem illam quam

Alanus filius Rollandi Constabularius fecit Deo et Ecclesie Sancti Cudberti . de Kircudbriht . de illa parte de Sipland . quam Kineth . tenuit. Et donationem illam . quam idem Alanus filius Rollandi Constabularius fecit Deo et Ecclesie Sancti Oswaldi martiris de Kelletun' . de Triginta . et duabus Acris terre in territorio eiusdem uille. Tenendam in liberam et puram et perpetuam Elemosinam . ita libere et Quiete . plenarie et Honorifice .' sicut Carte predicti Alani filii Rollandi testantur . saluo seruicio meo. Testibus Thoma Comite de Ethol' . Philippo de Valoniis Camerario . Willelmo Cumin Justicia Scott' . Oliuero Capellano meo . Willelmo de Boscho Clerico meo . Thoma de Coleuill' . Ricardo filio Hugonis. Apud Striuelin .vij. die Januarii.

ENDORSED. Confirmacio regis W. (xiii cent.). Scotland confirms grant of FizRolland to St Cuthbert, Kirkcudbright. Wm the Lion *ob.* 1214. Thos. became E. of Athol *circa* 1210 (xix cent.). Phillipps MS. 28738 (xix cent.).
DESCRIPTION. 7·1″ (18·1 cm.), Top and bottom × 4·2″ (10·8 cm.), L, R. Foot folded to a depth of 0·7″ (1·8 cm.). Seal-tag, 7″ (18 cm.) long, 0·6″ (1·5 cm.) wide, passes through single slits in foot and fold. Seal remains, in green wax varnished brown, bottom right fragment only.
HAND. Scribe Df. Unruled.
SOURCE. Original, NLS, Charters no.36 (formerly *penes* C. S. Romanes, Edinburgh, bought at the sale of Mr Romanes's MSS. at London, July, 1923, by Dr Walter Seton; cf. *Glasgow Herald*, 15 September, 1923).
PRINTED. *Berwickshire Hist.*, xvi, Pt. III, 263 (with facsimile, Plate VII).
COMMENT. Thomas de Colville was arrested in May, 1210, charged with treason, and imprisoned in Edinburgh castle; he ransomed himself on 30 November (*Chron. Melrose*, 54). He was presumably Thomas de Colville, surnamed 'the Scot', lord of Carsphairn in Galloway, a dependent of Duncan of Carrick. It was in this year that Duncan betrayed Maud wife of William de Briouze and her two sons to King John, after they had fled from Ulster to Scotland. In the summer of 1210 Alan son of Roland was with King John in Ireland. In the winter of 1210–1211 King William was ill at Kintore, according to *Chron. Bower*, i, 529.

490

Grants to the Hospital of St Andrews for the maintenance of poor pilgrims who come to it one silver merk yearly from the *firma burgi* of Crail, in exchange for the annual merk which it used to receive from the land of Auchtermuchty, Fife, which the king has granted free of the burden of that rent to Malcolm earl of Fife; payable half at Whitsun and half at Martinmas. Crail. (14 January, 1209 × 1210)

Willelmus[a] Dei gracia Rex Scotorum Omnibus probis hominibus tocius terre sue clericis et laicis salutem . Sciant presentes et futuri me dedisse et concessisse et hac carta mea confirmasse Deo et hospitali Sancti Andree ad sustentacionem peregrinorum illuc ueniencium in liberam et puram elemosinam et perpetuam unam marcam argenti singulis annis percipiendam de firma burgi mei de Karel pro marca illa quam annuatim percipere consueuit de terra de Uctermukethin quam ego liberam dedi de marcha illa . Comiti Malcolmo de Fif. Quare precipio uicecomiti meo et balliuis meis qui meum burgum de Karel tenebunt .' quatinus predictam marcham predicto hospitali sine disturbacione habere faciant singulis annis de burgo meo de Karel medietatem ad penthecosten' .' et medietatem ad festum Sancti Martini. Testibus . Willelmo Cumin Justicia Willelmo de Bosco . et Hugone clericis meis .

Herberto de camera . Ricardo filio Hug*onis* . Ricardo Reuel apud Karel . xiiii Januar*ii*.

RUBRIC. De marca (top in red).
SOURCE. SRO, GD 45/27/8 (St Andrews priory cartulary), fo.cvi[r].
PRINTED. *St Andrews Liber*, 228–9.
NOTE. [a] Red initial U.
COMMENT. The king's grant of Auchtermuchty to Earl Malcolm is not otherwise known.

491 Announces the settlement of a dispute between St Andrews Cathedral Priory and Saer de Quinci anent the patronage of the church of Leuchars, Fife. Stirling. (20 May, 1209 × 1211, probably 1210)

W.[a] Dei gratia Rex Scott' omnibus probis hominibus tocius terre sue clericis et laicis salutem. Sciatis quod controuersia que fuit inter Thomam Priorem et conuentum Sancti Andree ex una parte et Sa[erum?] de Quenci ex altera parte super iure patronatus ecclesie de Lochris . . . predicte [collate?] per cartam Nesii filii Willelmi . . . sopita . . . testantur et confirmant . . . quieti fuerunt . . . in pristina . . . alique carte . . . habuerint. Test*ibus* Will*elmo* episcopo Sancti Andr*ee*, Walt*ero* episcopo Glasguensi, Comite Patricio, Alano filio Rollandi, Philippo de Valoniis, [Roberto?] de . . ., Roberto de Lond*oniis* filio [meo?], Willelmo Cumyn, Philippo de Mubray, Willelmo de Bosco clerico [capell'?] . Apud Striuelyn, xx^{o} die Maij.

RUBRIC. De ecclesia de Lochris [?] (at top in red).
SOURCE. SRO, GD 45/27/8 (St Andrews priory cartulary), fo.cxl[r].
PRINTED. This charter, which should have appeared on p.313 of *St Andrews Liber*, was omitted entirely from the Bannatyne Club edition, presumably because of its almost total obliteration.
NOTE. [a] The whole document, including the rubric, has been crossed out with vertical and diagonal lines, and the surface of the vellum has been scraped; the whole has then been painted over with an obliterating agent. A substantial number of words between 'filii Willelmi' and 'Testibus' have been regarded as illegible, but a proportion of them might be recovered after prolonged study.
COMMENT. It seems probable that this act refers to the serious dispute between St Andrews priory and Saer de Quinci, lord of Leuchars, dealt with in four letters of Pope Innocent III of 24 October, 1205, 7 June, 1206, 9 June, 1206 and 6 June, 1207 (*St Andrews Liber*, 350–2; cp. also the same pope's letter anent the teinds of Leuchars parish, 14 March, 1207, ibid. 85–6). The very thorough-going obliteration of the text may have been due to the canons' indignation that the matter had been brought into the *curia regis* 'contrary to the custom of the Scottish Church' (ibid., 351), and that the prior had been compelled 'by the king's terrifying threats', as he alleged, to accept the agreement reached there (ibid., 352). But in view of the date of this act, it must either represent a fresh decision of the *curia regis*, or reiterate the earlier decision contrary to the sense of the papal documents. The second possibility seems preferable since Saer de Quinci is not given the title earl of Winchester which he obtained 13 March, 1207.

492 Confirms to Holyrood Abbey one ploughgate of arable in the territory of Dalgarnock (in Closeburn, Dumfriesshire), with a fishery in the River Nith and with common pasture for twenty-four animals and 100 sheep, and liberty to build and keep a mill; granted by Edgar son of Donald, as his charter bears witness. Edinburgh. (23 May, 1209 × 1211, probably 1210)

W. Dei Gr*ati*a Rex Scott'. Omnibus probis hominibus Tocius Terre sue . clericis et[a] laicis :' Salutem. Sciant presentes et futuri me Concessisse . et hac Carta mea confirmasse . donationem illam quam Ædgarus . filius Douenald' fecit Deo et Ecclesie Sancte Crucis de Edenburg . et Canonicis ibidem Deo seruientibus et seruituris . de una Carrucata terre in territorio de Dalegernoc'. Tenend*am* in liberam et puram et perpetuam Elemosinam . cum piscaria super Nit' . et cum communi pastura ad viginti . quatuor . animalia . et ad Centum . Oues . et cum Omnibus aliis aisiamentis . et cum libertate faciendi et habendi molendinum . ita libere et Quiete et honorifice . sicut Carta predicti Ædgar*i* testatur . Saluo seruicio meo. Test*ibus* Comite Patric*io* . Philipp*o* de Valon*iis* Camer*ario* meo . Will*elmo* Cumin . Justic*ia* Scott' . Will*elmo* de Bosch*o* . et Hug*one* de sigill*o* clericis meis . Will*elmo* de Duuegl*as*[b] . Thom*a* Tancard' . Thom*a* de Lastalric' . Henr*ico* de Brade. Apud Edenburg .xxiij. die Maii.

ENDORSED. Confirmacio Reg*is* Willelmi de Carucata terre de Dalegernoc (date of hand unknown).

SOURCE. *Holyrood Liber*, no.56, printed from the original then (1840) *penes* Lord Panmure, present whereabouts unknown. It was not among the Holyrood charters recently deposited in the SRO by Messrs Dundas and Wilson, W.S., on behalf of the Earl of Dalhousie.

NOTES. [a] It is not clear from the printed version whether the scribe used the tironian sign for et with or without a horizontal cross stroke. The punctuation and use of capitals in this text suggest the work of Scribe Df, who did use the cross stroke. [b] Source prints Dunegl'.

COMMENT. The charter of Edgar son of Donald is given in *Holyrood Liber*, no.55. Edgar's father was one of the sons of Dunegal, lord of Nithsdale in David I's reign. Donald's kin, as 'Duuenaldi', seem to appear in no.367, which also refers to the land held by Ralph son of Dunegal and his brother Donald, and to land in Glencairn held by their brother Gillepatrick. Edgar's daughter Affrica granted land at Dunscore in Glencairn to Melrose Abbey (*Melrose Liber*, nos.199–201).

493 Confirms agreements made between Kelso and Melrose Abbeys anent the marches of Bowden, Eildon and Darnick and anent the land of Mow and Clifton, as the chirographs made between the parties bear witness. Stirling. (22 June, probably 1210)

.W'. Dei gr*ati*a Rex Scott'. Episcopis . Abbatibus . Com*itibus* . Baron*ibus* . Justic*iis* Vicecomitibus . prepositis . ministris . et Omnibus probis Hominibus Tocius terre sue . Clericis et Laicis :' Salutem. Sciant presentes et futuri nos concessisse . et Hac Carta nostra confirmasse . amicabilem pacem factam inter conuentum et Ecclesiam de Kelch*o* ex una parte . et Conuentum[a] et Ecclesiam de Melros ex altera parte . super diuisis terrarum de Bowlden'[b] . et de Eldun . et de Dernewic'. Quare uolumus et precipimus quatinus predicta pax inter Conuentus et predictas domos facta . firmiter et inuiolabiliter futuris temporibus in perpetuum teneatur :' sicut in Cyrographo inter Conuentus et predictas domos inde facto euidentius continetur. Concedimus etiam et Hac Carta nostra confirmamus amicabilem pacem factam inter predictos Conuentus et predictas domos super controuersia que uertebatur inter predictos Conuentus et domos prenominatas . de terra de Molle et de Cliftun' . sicut in predicto Cyrographo inter eos facto continetur. Test*ibus*

Alex*andro* fil*io* domini Reg*is* . Philipp*o* de Valon*iis* Camer*ario* . Rob*erto* de Londoni*is* fil*io* domini Reg*is* . Will*elmo* Cumin . D*auid* de Lindes' . Justic*iis*[c] . Oliuer*o* Capellano domini Reg*is* Will*elmo* de Bosch*o* Clerico domini Reg*is* . Philipp*o* de Mubray[d] . Walter*o* Olifard' . Henr*ico* fil*io* Com*itis* D*auid* . Philipp*o* de Lundin' . D*auid* Marescall*o* . Ric*ardo* fil*io* Hugon*is* . Herb*erto* de Camera . Joh*anne* de Striuelin . Ric*ardo* Reuel . Ad*am* Hasteng'. Apud Striuel*in*. xxij. die Jun*ii*.

ENDORSED. Confirmatio Reg*is* .W. pacis 7 concordie facte inter[e] domum de Melros 7 domum de Kelco (early xiii cent.). J. Scott 12 (xvi–xvii cent.). Also modern numeral endorsements.
DESCRIPTION. 7″ (17·8 cm.), Top, 6·6″ (16·7 cm.), Bottom × 5·2″ (13 cm.), L, 5″ (12·8 cm.), R. Foot folded with slit in centre for seal-tag. Tag (0·7″) and seal remain. The seal, in green wax, has been built up; it hangs obverse to the front. Legend visible (1969), +WILLEL . . (obv.); . . . ORVM (rev.).
HAND. Scribe Df. Unruled.
SOURCE. Original, BM, Cotton Chr. xviii, 17 = *A*. NLS, MS. Adv. 34.5.1, fo.151^{r-v} = *B*. Printed here from *A*.
PRINTED. *Kelso Liber*, no.412 (from *B*).
NOTES. [a] *B* omits et Conuentum. [b] Boulden', *B*. [c] Assuming that William Cumin was justiciar at this date. [d] *B* omits remaining witnesses and concludes with date of place and time. [e] facte inter written across back of seal-tag.
COMMENT. On these agreements and previous royal intervention, see nos.367, 440, and cf. *Innes Review*, xi (1960), 35–6.

494 Confirms to Arbroath Abbey the grant made by Thomas son of Thancard of the whole land between Auchter Water and South Calder Water (now Auchterheadmuir, partly in Cambusnethan, partly in Carluke and Carstairs), Lanarkshire, as the charter of Thomas bears witness. Kincardine. (7 December, 1208 × 1210)

W.[a] Dei gr*atia* Rex Scott'. Omnibus probis hominibus . tocius terre sue . clericis et laicis :' salutem. Sciant presentes et futuri . me concessisse . et hac carta mea confirmasse donacionem illam quam Thomas filius Tankard'[b] fecit Deo . et ecclesie Sancti Thome de Aberbr*othoc* et monachis ibidem Deo seruientibus et seruituris . de tota terra inter Ethkar'[c] . et Kaledouer[d] . quam Rex Malcolmus dedit Tankard' patri predicti Thom*e* . Tenend*am* . in liberam . et puram . et perpetuam elemosinam . per rectas diuisas suas . et cum omnibus iustis pertinenciis suis . ita libere . et quiete . plenarie . et honorifice :' sicut carta predicti Thom*e* Tankard' predictis monachis inde confecta :' testatur, saluo seruicio meo. Test*ibus* Oliuero Capellano meo . Philippo de Valon*iis* Camerario meo . Will*elmo* de Boscho . et Hug*one* de sigillo clericis meis . Henr*ico* filio comitis Dauid . Ricar*do* filio Hug*onis* . Ric*ardo* Reuel' . Apud Kinkardyn, vii° die Decembris.

RUBRIC. Confirmacio Regis de terra Thome fil*ii* Thancard' (red, *E*). Confirmacio Regis Willelmi de terra Thome filii Thancard (red, A).
SOURCE. NLS, MS. Adv. 34.4.2, fo.lxix^{v} = *A*. SRO, Northesk Muniments (uncatalogued), Ethie MS., fo.7^{r} = *E*. Printed here from *A*.
PRINTED. *Arbroath Liber*, i, no.99 (from *E*).
NOTES. [a] Initial red. [b] Thancard', *E*. [c] Etkar, *E*. [d] Caledouer, *E*. [e] No marginated numeral; entered between xcix and c.
COMMENT. Cf. *RRS*, i, no.304; Thomas's charter is given in *Arbroath Liber*, i, no.99.

495 Confirms to Dunfermline Abbey Outh (in Dunfermline), granted by his son Robert of London, as his charter bears witness. Forfar. (29 February, 1208 × 1211, probably 1211)

Will'[a] Dei gratia Rex Scott' episcopis . abbatibus . comitibus . baronibus . Justic*iis* . vicecomitibus prepositis . ministris . 7 omnibus probis hominibus tocius terre sue clericis 7 laicis salutem. Sciant presentes 7 futuri me concessisse 7 hac Carta mea confirmasse Deo 7 ecclesie Sancte Trinitatis de Dunfer*melin* 7 monachis ibidem Deo seruientibus donacionem illam quam Rob*ertus* de Londoniis filius meus eis fecit de Uueht. Tenend*am* in liberam 7 puram 7 perpetuam elemosinam per rectas diuisas per quas .' illam dedi predicto Rob*erto* . cum iustis pertinenciis suis 7 libertatibus 7 aisiamentis . ita libere 7 quiete plenarie 7 honorifice .' sicut Carta predicti Rob*erti* eis inde facta .' testatur saluo seruicio meo. T*estibus* Oliuero capellano meo . Willelmo de Bosch*o* clerico meo . Herberto de Camera . Ricardo Reuel' . Thom*a* de Haya . Magistro Martino medico . Will*elmo* filio Orm . D*aui*d de Hasting . Matheo clerico. Apud Forfar .xxix. die Febr*uarii*.

RUBRIC. De Uueth . Confirmacio (red with blue D and C).
SOURCE. NLS, MS. Adv. 34.1.3a, fo.xiii^{v}.
PRINTED. *Dunfermline Registrum*, no.71.
NOTE. [a] Initial blue.
COMMENT. Robert of London's charter is given in *Dunfermline Registrum*, no.167; see also no.463 above. According to *Chron. Bower*, i, 529, King William lay ill at Kintore in the winter of 1210–1211 'until the feast of Matthias the Apostle' (24 February; emending Matthaei in the printed edition), after which he went to Forfar.

496 Narrates that when in his full court and in his presence he re-granted the land of Bangour (in Ecclesmachan), West Lothian, to Uchtred of Bangour, as his right and heritage, Uchtred recognised that he had no nearer heir than Malcolm earl of Fife, and presented him to the king as his heir and put him in sasine of his heritage; wherefore the king now confirms this land to Earl Malcolm, in feu and heritage, for the rent belonging to it, viz. 4 chalders of oatmeal, 4 merks, 4 swine and 8 shillings. Kincardine (?). (6 May, 1208 × 1211, probably 1211)

.W'. Dei Gr*ati*a Rex Scott'. Omnibus probis Hominibus Tocius Terre sue Clericis et [Laicis ? [a]] Salutem. Sciant presentes et futuri . quod Uchtredus de Bingouer' . in presentia mea . et in plena curia mea cum reddidissem ei terram de Bingou*er* . sicut ius suum et hereditatem suam . recongnouit quod nullum alium habuit heredem propinquiorem quam Comitem Malcolm*um* . de Fif . et ipsum fecit heredem suum . in plena Curia mea . et eum mihi presentauit . et ipsum in hereditatem illam saisiuit. Quare sciant presentes et futuri . me Concessisse . et Hac Carta [mea Con[a]] firmasse . predicto Com*iti* Malcolm*o* . predictam terram de Bingouer' . per Rectas diuisas suas . et cum Omnibus Justis pertinentiis suis . Tenend' sibi et heredibus suis . de me et heredibus meis in feudo et hereditate . Quiete . Plenarie . et Honorifice .' Reddendo inde redditum qui ad [terram[a]] illam pertinet . scilicet quatuor . Celdr*as* farrine . Auene . et Quatuor . marc*as* . et Quatuor . p[orcos et[b]] Octo solidos .

et faciendo forinsecum seruicium quod ad terram illam pertinet. Test*ibus* Oliuero Capellano meo . Willelmo Cumin' . Engelramo de Baillol . Willelmo de Bosch*o* . et Hug*one* de sigill*o* clericis meis . Dune*cano* fil*io* Com*itis* Dunec*ani* . Henr*ico* Reuel . Philipp*o* de Coleuill'. Apud Kin[ ][c] .vi. die Maij.

ENDORSED. Carta de Bingouer' (xiii cent.). confirmacio regis Willelmi terrarum de Bingouer (xvii cent.).
DESCRIPTION. 6·2″ (15·5 cm.), Top, 5″ (13 cm.), Bottom × 5·1″ (13 cm.), L. Right-hand border torn away. Foot folded to depth of 0·6″ (1·5 cm.). Double slits, with tag 3·7″ (9·5 cm.) long, 0·8″ (2 cm.) wide. No seal remains.
HAND. Scribe Df. Unruled.
SOURCE. Original, SRO, GD 90/12=*A*. BM, MS. Harl. 4693, fo.44=*B*.
PRINTED. Printed here from *A* with one reading from *B*. *APS*, i, 390 (from *A*).
NOTES. [a] Parchment torn away, wording supplied conjecturally. [b] porcos et supplied from *B*. [c] *B* has Kintor. *APS*, i, 390 has King', but the MS. has no trace of the tail of a g, nor of the pronounced leftward down-stroke of an r made by Scribe Df.
COMMENT. If this act belongs to the same year as nos.497–9 the place of issue may have been Kincardine (written Kinkard'). The nature of the rent suggests that Bangour was a thanage.

497 Grants to Ranulf the falconer, eldest son of Walter of Loutorp, 'Kingower' in Gowrie, and in Mearns five davochs of land called Balmakewan (?) (in Marykirk), Auchinzeoch (in Fordoun), Balbegno, 'Lacherachgeigh Kenni' (Haulkerton?) and the davoch of 'Endolach', to be held in feu and heritage for personal service, or else the service of one archer in the army. Montrose. (2 June, 1209 × 1211, probably 1211)

William be the grace of God To all whom thir presents concernes Witt ye me to haue giwin and granted and be this my present charter confirmed To Ranolph falconar eldest sone of Walter of Loutorp Kingower in Gowerin et in le Merne fyve dauchs of Land callit Balemacoy and Ackwendothan and Balebeggin et Lacherachgeigh Kenni[a] and davoch of Endolach with the pertinents to him and his aires To be holdine of me and my aires in few and heretage frielie honorablie weill and in peace for the seruice of his owne body and if it sall happine that he cannot giue the seruice of awin bodie the seruice unius archarii in the armie before the witness' Arneass[b] my chaplaine William Cuming my Justiciar Walter[c] de Bosco and Hugh my clerks de Camera[d] Walter de Wechterlis Richard Reuell Bric' iudice meo at Monross the second day of Junii.

INTRODUCTORY NOTE. Production for the Lord Halkerton the – day of Appryll 1656. Forfar and Kincardin (in margin). The whilk day produced Mr of Hallkertoun ane charter quhair off the double followes.
SOURCE. BM, MS. Add. 24, 276, fo.53=*A*. NLS, MS. Adv. 34.6.24, p.204 (fragment) =*B*. Printed here from *A*.
NOTES. [a] Reading doubtful. [b] Sic, probably for Olivero. [c] Sic, for Willelmo. [d] A name (Herbert?) doubtless omitted before de Camera.
NOTE ON SOURCE *B*. In this collection of genealogical and other jottings and transcripts in the hand of Father Richard Hay there is a note of the above act on p.284: 'C. Willielmus Rex – Rannulpho Falconer filio Mō Falconer de Innergowry meo falconario – Dat Lacheraw (nunc Halkerston) – & Balbeigno, & blank – Reddendo – ut seruiat nobis in sua persona tempore belli, aut mittat unum

Archarium – Dat' apud Montrose', with the note 'Mr J. Falc. told me both thir' (i.e., this charter and one for Straiton of Lauriston).

COMMENT. This is regarded as the first of the writs of progress of title for the family of Falconer of Haulkerton, but the poor quality of the surviving version makes identification of the places uncertain. Part at least must be represented by Haulkerton (in Laurencekirk), Mearns. The davoch of Endolach may refer to Bogendollo (in Fettercairn). 'Kingower' has been thought to stand for Kingoodie, in Longforgan, on the strength of a grant of land there by a Falconer to Ralph of Dundee (*SP*, v, 242); if so, the form is corrupt; and it must be noted that Kingoodie was part of the endowment of the church of Longforgan in the mid-twelfth century (*RRS*, i, no.123). The father of Ranulf the king's falconer may have taken his name from Lowthorpe (Yorks., E.R.).

498 Confirms to Arbroath Abbey the grant made by Roger of St Michael of the land of Mundurno (in Old Machar), Aberdeenshire, as his charter bears witness. Forfar. (11 June, 1208 × 1211, probably 1211)

W.[a] Dei gr*ati*a Rex Scottorum omnibus probis hominibus tocius terre sue clericis et laicis salutem. Sciant presentes et futuri me concessisse et hac carta mea confirmasse Deo et Beato Thome martiri de Abirbroth*oc* et monachis ibidem Deo seruientibus donacionem quam Rogerus de Sancto Michaele eis fecit de terra de Mundurnach' . Tenend*am* in liberam et puram et perpetuam elemosinam . cum omnibus ad predictam terram iuste pertinentibus . ita libere et quiete plenarie et honorifice . sicut predicti Rogeri carta testatur , saluo seruicio meo. Test*ibus* Om*ero* Archid*iacono* Abird*onensi* . Rob*erto* decano Abirden' . Oliuero Capellano meo . Rob*erto* de Lond*oniis* fil*io* meo . Willelmo de Bosco . Ad*am* de Kyngor' clerico meo . D*aui*d Marescall*o* . Malcolmo Pincerna . Apud Forf*ar* .xj°. die Junii.

RUBRIC. Confirmacio Regis W. super eadem terra (red)[b].
SOURCE. NLS, MS. Adv. 34.4.2, fo.lxii^v.
PRINTED. *Arbroath Liber*, i, no.81 (*bis*).
NOTES. [a] Initial red. [b] No marginated numeral; entered between Lxxxj and Lxxxij.
COMMENT. Roger of St Michael's charter is given in *Arbroath Liber*, i, no.81, witnessed by the king. It is not known what if any relationship existed between Roger and William of St Michael, who acted as the trusted envoy of King William in 1173 (*Chron. Fantosme* (Michel), p.20, l.422) and to whom the king gave a toft in Montrose before 1195 (*Lindores Chartulary*, no.38 and p.104).

499 Grants to Arbroath Abbey custody of the *Bracbennoch* (the reliquary of Saint Columba), together with the land of Forglen, Banffshire, assigned for its support, on condition of performing the service in the army with the reliquary owed from that land. Aberdeen. (28 June, 1208 × 1211, probably 1211)

W.[a] Dei gr*ati*a Rex Scott', Omnibus probis hominibus tocius terre sue, clericis & laicis, salutem. Sciant presentes et futuri me concessisse et hac carta mea confirmasse monachis de Aberbroth*oc* custodiam de Bracbennoch'[b] , et eisdem monachis dedi et concessi et hac carta mea confirmaui cum predicta Bracbennoch'[c] terram de Forglint datam Deo et Sancto Columbe et le Bracbennach'[d] . Quare uolo et precipio quatinus predicti monachi predictam terram et custodiam de Bracbennoch'[b] habeant libere et quiete, faciendo inde seruicium quod michi in exercitu debetur de illa terra cum predicta Bracbennoch'[d]. Test*ibus* G*illecrist* comite de Marre[e], Oliuero Capellano meo, Willelmo de Bosco clerico meo, Herberd' de Camera. Apud Aberden. xx°viij°. die Junii.

RUBRIC. Carta domini Regis de Brachbennach' (red, *E*). Carta de Brecbennacht' (red, *A*). .v. (in margin, *A*, *E*).

SOURCE. NLS, MS. Adv. 34.4.2, fo.xlii^{v}=*A*. SRO, Northesk Muniments (uncatalogued), Ethie MS., fo.2^{r-v}=*E*. Printed here from *A*.

PRINTED. *Arbroath Liber*, i, no. 5 (from *E*).

NOTES. [a] Initial red. Punctuation editorial. [b] brachbennoch', *E*. [c] brechbennoch', *E*. [d] Brachbennach', *E*. [e] Mar, *E*.

COMMENT. Cf. F.C. Eeles, 'The Monymusk Reliquary or Brecbennoch of St Columba', in *PSAS*, lxviii, 433–8. William del Bois was appointed chancellor on 28 June, 1211, and it might seem odd that he should witness only as clerk on the very day of his promotion; but the place-date suggests 1211.

500 Announces that when he built his castles in Ross the vassals of Dunfermline Abbey at his request and of their own good will worked at the building along with the king's other responsible men; this act is not to become a precedent to force them to do otherwise than they did in former times. Nairn. (18 August, 1211 × 1213, probably 1211)

Willelmus[a] Dei gr*ati*a Rex Scot' . omnibus probis hominibus tocius terre sue salutem. Sciatis quod quando firmare feci castella mea in Ros ·/ homines abbatis 7 monachorum de Dunfer*melin* ad peticionem meam de bona uoluntate sua operati sunt cum aliis probis hominibus meis ad eadem castella firmanda. Quare uolo 7 precipio quatinus hoc quod illa uice ad peticionem meam inde fecerunt ·/ non trahatur in exemplum quare aliud in posterum in talibus facere debeant ·/ quam fecerunt tempore meo 7 temporibus antecessorum meorum. T*estibus* Willelmo de Bosch*o* cancell*ario* meo . Ph*ilippo* de Vallon*iis* camer*ario* meo. Apud Innarr'[b].

RUBRIC. Quieta clamacio operum (red with blue initial).

SOURCE. NLS, MS. Adv. 34.1.3a, fo.xii^{r}.

PRINTED. *Dunfermline Registrum*, no.54.

NOTES. [a] Initial red. [b] Sic, probably for Inuernarren.

COMMENT. Presumably this refers to castle building or repairing later than 1179, when the king built Dunskeath and Red Castle.

501 Grants to William Cumin and his heirs the right to have a burgh at Kirkintilloch, and a market every Thursday; as freely as any of the king's barons has a burgh by the king's gift. Forres. (2 October, 1211)

Willielmus Dei gratia Rex Scotorum omnibus probis hominibus totius terre sue clericis et laicis salutem. Sciant presentes et futuri me concessisse et hac presenti carta mea confirmasse Willelmo Cumyng et heredibus suis ut burgum habeant apud Kirkintullot[a] et forum per diem Jouis cum libertatibus et rectitudinibus ad burgum pertinent*ibus* ita libere et quiete et honorifice sicut aliquis baronum meorum burgum habet ex dono meo in terra mea. Testibus Alano filio Ronaldi[b] constabulario meo, Willielmo de Boscho cancellario meo, Philippo de

Valon*iis* camerario meo, Philippo de Mowbra, Alexandro vicecomite meo de Striveling, Herberto de Camera, Adam filio eius apud Foreis secundo die Octobris.

RUBRIC. Concessio libertatis burgi apud Kirkintullo*t*.[c]
NOTARIAL NOTES. Extractum de registro decani canonicorum et capituli ecclesie metropolitane Glasguensis per me Richardum Harbertsoun notarium publicum ac scribam dicti capituli pro tempore teste manu propria.[d] Ita est Richardus Harbertsoun notarius publicus ac scriba dicti capituli ut supra manu propria.[d] Ita est Robertus Blair notarius publicus et connotarius in coroboracionem subscriptionis notarii prescripti per eum requisitus teste manu propria.[d]
SOURCE. Kirkintilloch Burgh Charter Chest, notarial transumpt (1584).
PRINTED. G.S.Pryde, in *SHR*, xxix (1950), 67–8.
NOTES. [a] Sic. [b] Sic, for Rolandi. [c] Probably representing endorsement. [d] Monograph signature.
COMMENT. On this charter see G.S.Pryde, *SHR*, xxix. William Cumin had become earl of Buchan by August, 1212.

502 Confirms to Dunfermline Abbey the church of Abercrombie (St Monance), Fife, granted by Malcolm earl of Fife, as his charter bears witness. Fyvie. (9 October, 1211 × 1213, probably 1211)

Willelmus[a] Dei gr*ati*a Rex Scott' . omnibus probis hominibus tocius terre sue clericis et laicis salutem. Sciant presentes 7 futuri me concessisse 7 hac carta mea confirmasse donacionem illam quam Malcolmus comes de Fif fecit Deo 7 ecclesie Christi[b] de Dunfer*melin* 7 abbati 7 monachis ibidem Deo seruientibus de Ecclesia de Abercrombin' . tenendam cum terris 7 omnibus aliis iustis pertinenciis suis . in liberam 7 puram 7 perpetuam elemosinam . ita libere 7 quiete :' sicut carta predicti Malcolmi comit*is* de Fif :' testatur. Testibus Will*elmo* de Bosch*o* cancell*ario* meo . Ph*ilippo* de Vallon*iis* :' camerario meo . Rob*erto* de London*iis* filio meo . Willelmo Cumin Justic*ia* Scoc*ie* . Ric*ardo* filio Hug*onis* . Herberto de Camera . Ricardo Reuel. Apud Fiuen' .ix. die Octobris.

RUBRIC. Confirmacio ecclesie de Abircrumbi*n* (red with red initial).
SOURCE. NLS, MS. Adv. 34.1.3a, fo.xii[r].
PRINTED. *Dunfermline Registrum*, no.53.
NOTES. [a] Initial blue. [b] Written x[i].
COMMENT. The chapel of Abercrombie had already been granted to Dunfermline by Malcolm IV (*RRS*, i, no.157). Earl Malcolm's charter is given in *Dunfermline Registrum*, no.144.

503 Confirms to Arbroath Abbey the grant made by Hugh Malherbe, son of Hugh Malherbe, of two oxgangs of arable in the territory of Rossie (in Craig), Angus, as the charter of Hugh bears witness. Forfar. (15 October, 1211 or 1212, probably 1211)

W.[a] Dei gr*ati*a Rex Scott' omnibus probis hominibus tocius terre sue clericis et laicis salutem. Sciant presentes et futuri me concessisse donacionem illam quam Hugo Malherb*e* filius Hugonis Malherb*e* fecit Deo et monasterio Sancti Thome de Abirbr*othoc* et monachis ibidem Deo seruientibus et seruituris . de duabus bouatis terre in territorio de Rossyn . Tenend*am* in puram et perpetuam elemosinam per rectas diuisas suas . et cum omnibus aisiamentis et aliis ad predictam terram iuste pertinentibus . ita libere et quiete plenarie et honorifice . sicut carta predicti Hugonis Malherb*e* testatur . saluo seruicio meo. Test*ibus* W*illelmo* de Bosco Cancellario meo . Roberto de Lund' fil*io* meo . Willelmo Capellano meo . Henrico fil*io* Com*itis* Dauid . Waltero de Lindes' . Dauid de Haya Vic*ecomite* de Forfar . Heruic*o* de Kinros. Apud Forfar .xv°. die Octobris.

RUBRIC. Confirmacio Reg*is* W. super dictis bouatis (red). .Lxiiij. (in margin).
SOURCE. NLS, MS. Adv. 34.4.2, fo.lvii^v.
PRINTED. *Arbroath Liber*, i, no.64.
NOTE. [a] Initial red.
COMMENT. Hugh Malherbe's charter is given in *Arbroath Liber*, i, no.63.
(1211 × 1214).

504 Confirms to Inchaffray Abbey the grant made to it by Earl Gilbert of Strathearn of the church of St Bean of Fowlis Wester (Perthshire). 'Forgrund' (Forgandenny or Longforgan?). (3 December, 1211 or 1212, probably 1211)

.W'. Dei Gr*aci*a Rex Scott'. Omnibus probis Hominibus Tocius Terre sue Clericis et laicis ⁖ salutem. Sciant presentes et futuri . me Concessisse . et Hac Carta mea confirmasse . donationem illam quam .G. Comes de Stradheren' fecit Deo et Sancto Johanni Euuangeliste de Incheaffren . et Canonicis ibidem Deo seruientibus et seruituris de Ecclesia Sancti Beani de Foulis. Tenend*am* in puram et perpetuam Elemosinam . cum Omnibus ad predictam Ecclesiam iuste pertinentibus . ita libere et Quiete . plenarie et honorifice ⁖ sicut Carta predicti .G. Comitis de Stradheren . testatur. Test*ibus* . Will*elmo* de Bosch*o* Cancellario meo . Oliuero et Will*elmo* Capellanis meis . Will*elmo* de Valon*iis* . Alex*andro* vicecom*ite* meo de Striuelin. Apud Forgr*und* .iij. die Decemb*ris*.

ENDORSED. De foulis (xiii cent.).
DESCRIPTION. 6·1″ (15·4 cm.), Top, 6·15″ (15·6 cm.), Bottom × 3·4″ (8·6 cm.), L, R. Foot folded, slits for seal-tag. Tag, 0·7″ (1·7 cm.) wide, remains, with large fragment of seal in natural wax stained brown, reverse to front, maximum diameter 2·5″.
HAND. Scribe Df. Unruled.
SOURCE. Original, Kinnoull Trustees, Dupplin Charters, no.111.
PRINTED. *Inchaffray Chrs.*, no.29.

505 Concedes to his dearest lord John king of England that King John may arrange the marriage of King William's son Alexander, as the king of England's liege vassal, within six years from (8 February, 1212). Undertakes that whatever may befall King John, he and his son will hold faith with King John's son Henry, as their liege lord, against all mortal men, and will help him to stay in possession of his kingdom with all their power, saving their faith to King John. (No time- or place-date). (22 July, 1211 × May, 1212) (Spurious, but probably based on an authentic original?)

.W Dei gr*ati*a Rex Scott' Omnibus fidelibus has litteras uisuris uel audituris Salutem. Sciatis quod concessimus karissimo Domino nostro[a] Johanni Illustri Regi Angl' ut maritet Alex*andrum* filium nostrum sicut hominem suum ligium infra sex annos proximos sequentes post diem cinerum anni Regni eiusdem Domini Regis .J. tercii decimi ubi uoluerit ad fidem ipsius domini Regis ita quod non disparagetur. Concessimus eidem Domino nostro .J. Regi Angl' quod quicquid de ipso contingat, nos et Alexander filius noster Henrico filio eius tanquam ligio domino nostro contra omnes mortales fidem et fidelitatem tenebimus, et iuuabimus eum pro uiribus nostris ad tenendum ipsum in Regno suo, salua fide qua predicto domino nostro Regi .J. tenemur. Et hec[b] predicta firmiter et fideliter obseruanda nos et Alex*ander* filius noster tactis sacrosanctis iurauimus. Et ad maiorem huius rei securitatem nos et dominus W*illelmus* Episcopus Sancti Andr*ee* Dominus W*alterus* Episcopus Glasg*uensis*[c] et Dominus J*ohannes* electus Dunkeld*ensis* et Com*es* Patric*ius* et Alanus fil*ius* Roll*andi* Constabul*arius* et [Philip]pus[d] de Mubray et Walterus Oli[*fard*][d] huic scripto sigilla nostra apponi fecimus et Alex*ander* fil*ius* noster cum miles [ ][e] sigillum[f] suum apponet.

DESCRIPTION. 7·2″ (18·3 cm.), Top, bottom × 2·6″ (6·6 cm.), L, R. No trace of fold or tongue, or of any sealing.
HAND. Scribe UDd. English chancery hand of the second or third quarter of the thirteenth century.
SOURCE. PRO, SC1/2/24 (Ancient Correspondence), either a purported 'original' or an office copy.
PRINTED. Stones, *Documents*, no.4 (q.v. for other printed editions, including *Foedera*, I, i, 104).
NOTES. [a] Might be read meo. [b] Stones, op. cit., p.12, suggests that ad may have been included before hec in the 'original'. [c] Italicized letters cannot be read because of injury to parchment. [d] Missing through injury and supplied conjecturally. [e] Some words missing through injury, perhaps effectus sit? [f] First four letters of this word missing through injury.
COMMENT. If this letter is genuine, or if an authentic letter, naming the same individuals as those named here, has formed the basis of the present document, its most probable date would seem to be February or March, 1212. The address of the letter is not one used in the Scottish royal chapel. The use of the plural would at once arouse suspicion, were it not that in the period 1210–1212 one or two authentic acts have the plural (cf. nos.493, 507). The absence of a time- or place-date is very remarkable in an act of this period. On the other hand, the names of John bishop-elect of Dunkeld, Philip de Mubray and Walter Olifard could hardly have been correctly included by a fabricator of the mid-thirteenth century unless he were extraordinarily well-informed, although he might have had access to some contemporary but quite unrelated Scottish royal act in which these names occurred. In February, 1212, King John's son Henry was aged 4½. The passage casting doubt on Henry's ability to keep possession of England seems odd, but would seem less so if written by someone familiar with the events of 1215–1217. It seems likely that King William did write some such letter as the above early in 1212, but this text cannot be trusted to give a true version of the king's letter. Cf. Stones, *Documents*, no.4 and discussion on pp.xlvi–xlviii. The substance of this letter, dated to John's thirteenth year (May, 1211–May, 1212) is given in *Chron. Lanercost*, 146 (s.a. 1292) as evidence that the king of Scotland was feudally subject to the king of England.

506

Confirms to Arbroath Abbey the whole wood of Trustach (in Banchory-Ternan, Mearns) granted by Thomas [of Lundie] the doorward, by the marches contained in Thomas's charter, and common pasture in the abbey's lands of Banchory as far as 'Loucherkar' (outwith the king's forest). Stirling. (20 May, 1212 × 1213, probably 1212)

W.[a] Dei gr*ati*a Rex Scott' . omnibus probis hominibus tocius terre sue clericis et laicis salutem. Sciant presentes et futuri me concessisse et hac Carta mea confirmasse Deo et ecclesie Sancti Thome martiris de Abirbr*othoc* et monachis ibidem Deo seruientibus et seruituris . totum nemus de Trostach' . quod Thomas de Lundyn Ostiarius meus eis dedit . et quietum clamauit per rectas diuisas contentas in carta eiusdem Thome inde facta predictis monachis . et communionem pasture quam idem Thomas prefatis monachis et eorum hominibus in terris eorum de Benchoryn manentibus concessit in terra sua usque ad Loucherkar' . Tenend*um* in liberam et puram et perpetuam elemosinam . ita libere et quiete et honorifice . sicut Carta predicti Thome testatur . saluo seruicio meo. Test*ibus* W*illelmo* de Bosco Cancellario meo . Philippo de Valon*iis* camerario meo . Hug*one* de sigillo clerico meo . P*hilippo* de Mubray . Ricar*do* fil*io* Hug*onis*. Apud Striuelyn .xx°. die Maii.

RUBRIC. Confirmacio Reg*is* W. de nemore de Trostauch' (red). .lxvj. (in margin).
SOURCE. NLS, MS. Adv. 34.4.2, fo.lviii^r^.
PRINTED. *Arbroath Liber*, i, no.66.
NOTE. [a] Initial red.
COMMENT. Thomas's charter is given in *Arbroath Liber*, i, no.65 (1203 × 1214), describing the wood of Trustach as between Dee and Canny, bounded on the west by burns whose names seem now to be lost.

507 Commands those dwelling in the diocese of Glasgow to render teinds to their churches. Stirling. (6 July, 1211 × 1214, probably 1212)

W.[a] Dei gr*ati*a Rex Scottorum Justic*iis* . Baronibus . vicecomitibus, ministris Francis et Anglis Scottis et Galwiensibus et Walensibus et omnibus ecclesie Sancti Kentegerni de Glasgu et eiusdem episcopi parochianis salutem. Quoniam diuina prouidencia nos in regno nostro clero et populo preesse uoluit, utriusque excessus emendare, et saluti potestate tradita prouidere, nobis necesse est unde dominica institucione et sancte Romane ecclesie matris nostre et domini pape hortatu ac precepto[b] commoniti, omnibus uobis regia auctoritate mandamus, hortamur et precipimus in Domino, quatinus episcopo vestro et archidiacono, eorumque ministris debitam obediencie reuerenciam exibeatis, decimasque vestras et cetera iura ecclesiastica ecclesiis vestris in omnibus plenarie et sine repugnancia persoluatis, sicut per alios episcopatus regni nostri decimas plenius et melius dari precepimus, scilicet de blado, de lino et de lana, de caseo et de butiro, de agnis et de vitulis, de porcellis, de capellis et de pullis, necnon et de ceteris non nominatis de quibus lex christiana decimam dari postulat. Si uero aliquis vestrum quicquam recte decime sue temere detinere presumpserit, vicecomes noster de eo capiat forisfactum nostrum, scilicet duodecim vaccas. Si uero vicecomes illi consenserit, aut propriam decimam detinuerit, Justiciar*ius* noster de ipso vicecom*ite* forisfactum nostrum capiat, decimasque detentas ecclesiis plenarie solui faciat, ne pro defectu iusticie querela ad nos perueniat. Test*ibus* Willelmo de Bosch*o* cancellario nostro, Philippo de Valoniis camerario nostro, Hugone de sigillo clerico nostro, Alex*andro* vic*ecomite* de Strivelin, Ricardo fil*io* Hug*onis*, Roberto[c] de Camera, Ricardo Reuel'. Apud Striuelin .vj. die Julii.

RUBRIC. De decimis dandis et de prestanda pro retentis (margin fo.lij[r]).
SOURCE. Blairs Archives, 16 Drummond Place, Edinburgh, MS. Registrum Vetus of Glasgow, fo.lij[r–v].
PRINTED. *Glasgow Registrum*, no.107.
NOTES. [a] Punctuation editorial. [b] Fo.lij[v]. [c] Sic; for Herberto?
COMMENT. A re-issue of no.179.

508

Confirms to Scone Abbey the grant made to it by Hugh of Calder of 40 acres of cultivated land in Buttergask (in Cargill), Perthshire, with one toft and croft in the toun and common pasture and other easements of Buttergask, as Hugh's charter bears witness. Clackmannan. (9 July, 1211 × 1214, probably 1212)

.W'. Dei Gr*ati*a Rex Scott' . Omnibus probis Hominibus Tocius Terre sue . Clericis et[a] laicis :' Salutem. Sciant presentes et futuri . me concessisse . et Hac Carta mea confirmasse . donationem illam quam Hugo . de Kaledou*er* fecit Ecclesie Sancte Trinitatis de Scon' . et Canonicis ibidem Deo seruientibus et seruituris . de quadraginta acris terre culte in Buthirgasc' . cum uno Tofto et Crofto in eadem uilla . et cum Communi pastura . et aliis aisiamentis de Buthirgasc' . Tenend*um* . in liberam et perpetuam Elemosinam . ita libere et Quiete :' sicut Carta predicti Hug*onis* de Caledou*er* testatur . saluo seruicio meo. T*estibus* Willelmo de Bosch*o* . Cancellario meo . Oliuer*o* . Capellano meo . Rob*erto* de London' filio meo . Hug*one* de sigillo . Clerico meo . Alex*andro* vic*ecomite* de Striuel*in* . Ricardo Reuel. Apud Clacm*anan* .ix. die Jul*ii*.

ENDORSED. Willelmus Rex de xl acris in Buthergask (xiii cent.). Willelmus de [ ] xl acris in Buthergas (xiii cent.). Also modern endorsements.
DESCRIPTION. 5·9″ (15 cm.), Top, bottom × 4·3″ (11 cm.), L, R. Foot formerly folded, probably with slits for tag. No tag or seal remains.
HAND. Scribe Df. Unruled.
SOURCE. Original SRO, RH 6/18.
PRINTED. *Scone Liber*, no.25 (with facsimile facing).
NOTE. [a] Here and throughout, crossed tironian sign.
COMMENT. Hugh of Calder's charter is printed *Scone Liber*, no.24, and states that the toft and croft were near the marches between Buttergask and Peattie (in Kettins, Angus).

509

Confirms that Coupar Angus Abbey shall be free of toll throughout his kingdom. Jedburgh. (Late)

Concessio regis Willielmi dictis monachis ut liberi sunt ab omnibus tolnagiis, passagiis, et mercatibus, et omnibus aliis consuetudinibus, et liberam potestatem habeant vendendi et emendi per totum regnum meum, &c. Testibus: Engelramo Cancellario meo, Willielmo de Lindesai, Johane de Wallibus, Lyulpho filio Machus[a], Willielmo de Haya. Apud Jedworth.

SOURCE. NLS, MS. Adv. 33.2.9, fo.27[v].
PRINTED. *Coupar Angus Rental*, i, 323, no.7.
NOTE. [a] MS., Mathus.
COMMENT. For the full text of this act, really a renovation of one of Malcolm IV, reissued unaltered save for the king's initial, see *RRS*, i, no.222. The practised, slightly mannered hand in which it is written seems to be unique among the original acts of William I, but probably belongs to the first two decades of the thirteenth century.

510 Confirms to Nicholas, son of Ailif, his baker, the land which his father Ailif held of the king, viz. the whole land which Reginald, janitor of Edinburgh castle held of the king in Inverleith; to be held by him and his heirs of the king and his heirs, for personal service. Grants that Nicholas and his heirs may grind their corn at the king's mill without multure, but his tenants must pay multure. Traquair. (14 January, 1212 × 1214, probably 1213)

W'. Dei gr*ati*a Rex Scott' . Omnibus probis hominibus tocius terre sue . Clericis 7 Laicis :' Salutem. Sciant presentes 7 futuri . me concessisse 7 hac carta mea confirmasse Nichol*ao* filio Ailif :' Pistori meo terram illam quam idem Ailif :' pater eius de me tenuit :' Scilicet totam terram quam Reginaldus Janitor Castelli de Edenburg' . de me tenuit in Inuerleth . tenend*am* sibi 7 heredibus suis . de me 7 heredibus meis . cum omnibus iustis pertinentiis suis . per seruicium sui corporis. Concessi etiam eidem Nichol*ao* 7 heredibus suis . ut bladum suum de propria domo sua molant ad molendinum meum libere absque multura inde danda . Homines uero sui dent multuram. Test*ibus* Willelmo de Bosch*o* Cancellar*io* meo . Philippo de Valon*iis* . Camerar*io* meo . Waltero de Lindes' . Willelmo de Valon*iis* . Herberto de Camera . Magistro Martino medico. Apud Trauequer . xiiij die Januar*ii*.[a]

ENDORSED. Carta Reg*is* Will*elm*i super terra de Inuerleyth[b].
SOURCE. *Newbattle Registrum*, Appendix, Carte Originales, no.IV, from the original *penes* W.E.Aytoun Esq. (1849), present whereabouts unknown.
PRINTED. As above.
NOTES. [a] Punctuation and abbreviations suggest the work of Scribe Df. [b] Heading probably represents early endorsement.
COMMENT. See no.174.

511 Grants to Arbroath Abbey the churches of Inverboyndie (Boyndie), Banffshire, and of Banff. Traquair. (19 January, 1213)

W.[a] Dei gr*ati*a Rex Scott' . Episcopis . Abbatibus . Comitibus . Baron*ibus* . Justic*iis* . Vicecom*itibus* . prepositis . ministris . et omnibus probis hominibus tocius terre sue clericis . et laicis :' salutem. Sciant presentes et futuri . me dedisse . et concessisse et hac carta mea confirmasse Deo et ecclesie Sancti Thome martiris de Aberbr*othoc* et monachis ibidem Deo seruientibus et seruituris ecclesiam de Inuerbondyn[b] et ecclesiam de Banef cum terris et decimis et oblacionibus omnimodis et cum omnibus aliis ad predictam ecclesiam de Inuerbondyn[b] et ad ecclesiam de Banef iuste pertinentibus . Tenend*as* in liberam et puram et perpetuam elemosinam ita libere et quiete plenarie et honorifice :' sicut alia ecclesias suas aut aliquod ecclesiasticum beneficium liberius et quiecius plenius et honorificencius tenent et possident. Test*ibus* Willelmo de Bosch*o* Cancell*ario* meo . Philippo de Valon*iis* Cam*erario* meo . Philippo de Mubray . Walt*ero* de Lindes' . Willelmo de Valon*iis* . Johanne de Maccuswell . Jordan*o* Cumyn'. Walter*o* Cumyn' . Hereb*erto* de Camera . Magistro Martino et Magistro Rad*ulfo* medicis meis . apud Trauequeir[c] .xix°. die Januar*ii*.

RUBRIC. De ecclesiis de Inuirbondin et Banef (red, *E*). De ecclesiis de Inuerbondy et de Banef (red, *A*). .xxvj. (in margin, *A*, *E*).

SOURCE. NLS, MS. Adv. 34.4.2, fo.xlvii^{v} = *A*. SRO, Northesk Muniments (uncatalogued), Ethie MS., fo.5^{r} = *E*. Printed here from *A*.
PRINTED. *Arbroath Liber*, i, no.26 (from *E*).
NOTES. [a] Initial red. [b] Inuirbondin, *E*. [c] Trauequeyr, *E*.

512 Confirms to Arbroath Abbey the grant made by his brother Earl David of one measured ploughgate of arable in Kennethmont, Aberdeenshire, as the earl's charter bears witness. Selkirk. (23 February, 1212 × 1214, probably 1213)

W.[a] Dei gr*ati*a Rex Scottorum . omnibus probis hominibus tocius terre sue clericis et laicis salutem. Sciant presentes et futuri me concessisse et hac carta mea confirmasse . donacionem illam quam comes Dauid frater meus fecit Deo et ecclesie Sancti Thome martiris de Abirbr*othoc* et monachis[b] ibidem Deo seruientibus de una carrucata in Kelalchmund mensurata et arabili cum communi pastura . Tenenda in liberam et puram elemosinam . ita libere et quiete et honorifice .' sicut carta predicti comitis Dauid testatur , saluo seruicio meo. Test*ibus* Henr*ico* abbate de Kalkou . Will*elmo* de Bosco Cancellario meo . Philippo de Valon*iis* Camerar*io* meo . Johanne de Makuswell'. Apud Selekirk .xxiij°. die Februar*ii*.

RUBRIC. Confirmacio Reg*is* W. super eadem (red)[c].
SOURCE. NLS, MS. Adv. 34.4.2, fo.lxiii^{r-v}.
PRINTED. *Arbroath Liber*, i, no.83 (*bis*).
NOTES. [a] Initial red. [b] Fo.lxiii^{v}. [c] No marginated numeral; entered between lxxxiij and lxxxiv.
COMMENT. Earl David's charter is given in *Arbroath Liber*, i, no.83.

513 Confirms the property and privileges of Arbroath Abbey. Selkirk. (25 February, 1213)

W.[a] Dei gracia Rex Scottorum , Episcopis , Abbatibus , Comitibus , Baronibus , Justiciariis , Vicecomitibus , et omnibus probis hominibus tocius terre sue, clericis et laicis, salutem. Sciant presentes et futuri me pro amore Dei et pro salute anime mee . et pro salute animarum antecessorum et successorum meorum dedisse, concessisse et hac carta mea confirmasse Deo et ecclesie quam fundaui in honore Dei et Sancte Thome archipresulis et martiris apud Abirbrothoc' et monachis ibidem Deo et Sancto Thome seruientibus et seruituris, in liberam et puram et perpetuam elemosinam , Abirbrothoc' cum tota schyra sua per rectas diuisas suas, in bosco et plano, in terris et aquis , in pratis et pascuis , cum omnibus iustis pertinenciis suis , et ecclesiam eiusdem ville scilicet Abirbrothoc' cum plenariis decimis suis et cum omnibus aliis iustis pertinenciis suis. Dedi eciam et concessi eisdem licenciam et libertatem faciendi burgum et habendi portum et habendi forum unaquaque die sabbati in eadem terra. Concessi eciam eis in perpetuum hanc in eorum burgo predicto libertatem , ut omnes eorum burgenses qui in eodem burgo terram vel domum habuerint et in eo manentes fuerint , et burgenses eorum qui in toftis eorum manent in burgis meis quieti et liberi sint a theolonio et consuetudine per totam terram meam et per omnes portus terre mee de omnibus et omnimodis mercibus et mercaturis suis propriis quas emerint vel vendiderint. Dedi eciam eis et concessi

Athyn per rectas diuisas suas et cum omnibus iustis pertinenciis suis et ecclesiam eiusdem ville cum plenariis decimis suis et cum aliis iustis pertinenciis suis. Dedi eciam eis Achinglas per rectas diuisas suas et cum omnibus iustis pertinenciis suis, et Dunechtyn cum tota schyra sua per rectas diuisas suas et cum omnibus aliis iustis pertinenciis suis , et ecclesiam eiusdem ville cum omnibus ad eam iuste pertinentibus , et Kyngoldrum[b] cum tota schyra sua per rectas diuisas suas et ecclesiam eiusdem ville cum omnibus ad eam iuste pertinentibus. Et ecclesiam Sancte Marie de Veteri Munros cum terra eiusdem ecclesie que scotice Abthen vocatur per rectas diuisas suas et cum decimis plenariis et cum omnibus aliis iustis pertinenciis suis. Et ecclesiam de Neutyl cum omnibus iustis pertinenciis suis. Et ecclesiam de Benchorin ·.' cum omnibus iustis pertinenciis suis. Et ecclesiam de Glampnes cum omnibus iustis pertinenciis suis. Et ecclesiam de Hautwysill' in Tyndale cum omnibus pertinenciis suis in capellis et terris, in decimis, in elemosinis et in omnibus aliis ecclesiasticis rectitudinibus, consuetudinibus et beneficiis, cum communi pastura et omnibus aliis aysiamentis eiusdem parochie. Et unum plenarium toftum in singulis burgis meis et gistis meis que habeo et habiturus sum. Et licenciam capiendi in forestis meis quecunque eis necessaria fuerint, ad edificia sua et ad usus proprios. Et unum rete super aquam meam de Perth que vocatur Stok' . Et unum plenarium rete super aquam de Northesk' iuxta Munros'. Et unam salinam iuxta salinas meas in Kars apud Striuelyn, cum quinque acris terre et cum pastura et focali ad predictam salinam sufficientibus. Concedo eciam eis liberam curiam suam cum sacca et socco, cum toll' et teme et infangandethef' et ferrum et duellum, fossam et furcas, et liberam eleccionem abbatis, et firmam pacem intra diuisas de Abirbrothoc'. Preterea concessi eis et hac carta mea confirmaui ut omnia tofta que eis dedi in omnibus burgis et maneriis meis per totam terram meam libera sint et quieta ab omnibus auxiliis et operacionibus ad me et heredes meos pertinentibus. Quare prohibeo firmiter ne quis de predictis toftis auxilia vel operaciones aliquas exigere presumat, super meam defensionem. Concessi eciam eis ut nami hominum suorum in terris eorum manencium[c] non capiantur pro alicuius debito nisi pro debitis eorum propriis. Concessi eciam eisdem et confirmaui ut omnes terre quas eis dedi et homines super illas terras manentes communem pasturam habeant cum omnibus vicinis suis, ita libere et plenarie sicut homines, qui in terris illis manebant antequam illas dederam in elemosinam, melius et plenius habere solebant tempore meo vel antecessorum meorum. Precepi eciam ut omnes homines in schyris de Abirbrothoc' et de Athyn manentes qui proprium molendinum non habent, et eorum homines, veniant molere ad molendinum de Abirbroth*oc*, nec alibi eant molere super meam defensionem. Preterea dedi eis ecclesiam de Inuernys, cum una carucata terre quam dedi eidem ecclesie in honore Sancte Marie in perpetuam elemosinam, et cum omnibus aliis iustis pertinenciis suis. Dedi eciam eis ecclesiam de Abirkerdouer et ecclesiam de Inuerbondyn , Ecclesiam de Banef , Ecclesiam de Gameryn , et ecclesiam de Tarvays, et ecclesiam de Nug' , et ecclesiam de Fyvyn , et ecclesiam de Cula in Marr' , et ecclesiam de

Kateryn, et ecclesiam de Inuerlunane , et ecclesiam de Panbryd, et ecclesiam de Fethmuref , et illas tredecim acras terre iuxta eamdem ecclesiam quas Willelmus Cumyn vicecomes meus de Forfar eis per preceptum meum tradidit , et ecclesiam de Monieky et ecclesiam de Gutheryn , et ecclesiam de Abirnythy cum capellis , terris, decimis , et oblacionibus omnimodis , cum communi pastura et omnibus aliis aisiamentis , et cum omnibus aliis ad predictas ecclesias iuste pertinentibus. Tenendam in liberam et quietam et perpetuam elemosinam . ita libere et quiete, plenarie et honorifice, sicut aliqua elemosina in toto regno meo liberius et quiecius, plenius et honorificencius, tenent et possident. Dedi eciam eis et concessi batellum passagii mei de Munros, cum terra ad predictum batellum pertinente, cum omnibus rectitudinibus ad batellum et ad terram illam pertinentibus, quam scilicet terram Helias clericus meus de Munros tenuerat; tenend*um* sibi in liberam et quietam et perpetuam elemosinam, libere et quiete ab excercitu et[d] expedicione et operacione et auxilio et ab omnibus consuetudinibus et omni seruicio et exaccione. Dedi eciam eis et concessi custodiam de Brecbennoch' et terram de Forglint cum predicto Brecbennoch', faciendo inde seruicium quod mihi in excercitu debetur de terra illa et de predicto Brecbennoch'. Dedi eciam eis unam carucatam terre in Monethen super aquam de Bervyn, quam Willelmus de[e] Munfort et Umfridus de Berkelay[f] et Walterus Scotus et Alanus filius Symon*is* et alii probi homines mei per preceptum meum eis mensurauerunt; tenend*am* in liberam et perpetuam elemosinam, cum communi pastura et cum omnibus aisiamentis ad terram illam pertinentibus, ita libere, plenarie et honorifice, et quiete ab operacione et ab omni seculari exactione, sicut aliquam elemosinam suam liberius et quiecius, plenius et honorificencius tenent in regno meo. Volo quidem ad omnium noticiam peruenire quod per hanc carrucatam terre quam eis dedi adquietaui ab eis unam carrucatam terre et dimidiam quam[g] ex dono Ricard*i* de Friuill' habuerunt, et de qua[h] cartas suas eis dederat. Unde non liceat alicui heredum predicti Ricardi, si qui eorum predictam terram recuperauerint, super predicta terra erga eos aliquam questionem mouere. Concessi eciam eis et confirmaui ex donacione Mariorie[i] comitisse de Buchan, ecclesiam de Turfred'[j]. Ex donacione Radulphi[k] Naym, ecclesiam de Inuerugyn[l]. Ex donacione Thome Hostiarii, ecclesiam de Kynernyn[m]. Ex donacione Walteri de Berkelay[n], ecclesiam de Inuerkeleder[o]. Ex donacione Gillecristi comitis de Anegus, ecclesiam de Monifoth[p], ecclesiam de Muraus, et ecclesiam de Kerimor[q], et ecclesiam de Stradechtyn[r]. Ex donacione Rogerii episcopi Sancti Andree, ecclesiam de Abirelot'[s]. Ex donacione Roberti de Lodon*iis*, ecclesiam de Rothuen. Omnes autem predictas ecclesias predictis monachis concedo et hac carta mea confirmo, cum capellis, terris, decimis et oblacionibus omnibus, cum communi pastura et omnibus aisiamentis et omnibus aliis ad predictas ecclesias iuste pertinentibus[t]. Tenend*as* in liberam et quietam et perpetuam elemosinam, ita libere et quiete, plenarie et honorifice, sicut aliqua elemosina in toto regno meo liberius, quiecius, plenius et honorificencius tenetur et possidetur. Concessi eciam eis et confirmaui ex donacione Umfridi de Berkeley terram de Balphe[u] per rectas diuisas suas per quas eis eam dedit, saluo seruicio meo. Ex donacione Johannis de Munfort terram de Glaskeler[v], saluo seruicio meo. Et donacionem illam quam Willelmus filius Bernardi fecit eis de duabus bouatis terre que uocatur Rath' in[w] territorio de Katerin[x], saluo seruicio meo. Et donacionem illam quam Hugo Malherbe filius Hugonis Malherbe fecit eis de duabus bouatis terre in territorio de Rossyn[y], saluo seruicio meo. Et terram illam de Munethen quam Philippus de Maleuill' et Eua sponsa sua eis dederunt, et quam Walterus filius Sibaldi dedit predicto Philippo in maritagium cum predicta Eua filia sua, saluo seruicio meo. Et donacionem illam quam Gilcrist[z] comes de Anegus eis fecit de terra illa quam pater ipsius Gilcrist[z] dedit ad faciendum unum hospitale apud Portincrag[aa], cum piscaria illa que pertinet ad terram illam, saluo seruicio meo. Et donacionem illam quam Thomas Tankard'[bb] fecit eis de tota terra inter Ethkar et Kalledouer, saluo seruicio meo. Ex donacione Douenald' Abbatis de Brechin, terram de Ballegillegrunde[cc], saluo seruicio meo. Ex donacione Rogeri de Sancto Michahele, terram de Mundurnachyn, saluo seruicio meo. Concessi eciam eis et confirmaui donacionem illam quam Fergus Comes[dd] de Buchan eis fecit in perpetuam elemosinam de una marca argenti annuatim. Et donacionem illam quam Turpinus[ee] episcopus de Brechyn[ff] eis fecit, scilicet unum toftum et croftum in uilla de Strucathrach[gg] et duas acras terre in campo pertinente ad eandem uillam. Et preterea decimam illius plenarii retis[hh] quod ego eisdem monachis dedi super aquam de Northesk'[ii]. Ex donacione Thome Hostiarii mei totum nemus de Tro[illegible]ch[jj], quod eis[kk] dedit et quietum clamauit. Ex donacione Comi[illegible] Dauid fratris mei, unam carucatam terre in Kinalcmund mensuratam et arabilem, cum communi pastura. Confirmaui eciam eis concordiam illam que facta est de controuersia que erat inter me et Bricium episcopum Morauiensem et Gilcrist[z] comitem de Marr[ll] de iure patronatus ecclesie de Abirkerdouer[mm], scilicet quod quilibet nostrum totum ius quod in eadem ecclesia habuit Deo et Sancto Thome Martiri de Abirbrothoc et monachis eiusdem loci dedit cum omnibus iustis pertinenciis suis. Et concessionem illam quam Johannes filius Malys[nn] eis fecit de carbonibus capiendis in nemore suo de Edale, ubicumque ad maius aisiamentum inuenire poterunt, quantum sufficiens erit ad opera domus sue, cum aisiamentis hospicii et pasture in terra ipsius Johannis animalibus suis. Et toftum illud in burgo meo de Forfar' quod Hugo cancellarius meus eis dedit, et unum plenarium toftum quod Andreas episcopus Katenensis tenuit in burgo meo de Forfar'. Et ex donacione Malis filii Comitis Ferteth[oo] unam dimidiam marcam in piscaria de Ur[pp]. Omnia autem dona predicta ita liberaliter et quiete prefate ecclesie concedo, sicut ego terras meas proprias possideo, defensione regni mei excepta, et regali iusticia si abbas in curia sua aliqua negligencia de iusticia deciderit. Quare uolo et firmiter precipio ut ipsa Ecclesia Sancti Thome Martiris de Aberbr*othoc* et ipsius ecclesie Abbas et conuentus habeant et teneant inperpetuum omnia predicta tenementa et libertates sicut superius determinatum est, cum terris et omnibus possessionibus et cum omnibus tenementis ecclesiasticis et secularibus que ego et fideles mei eis contulimus et collaturi sumus, bene et in pace, libere et quiete et integre, plenarie et honorifice, in bosco et plano, in pratis et pascuis, in aquis et molendinis, in uiuariis et stagnis, in piscariis et marresiis, in vastis et scalingis, in uiis et semitis, et in omnibus aliis locis et aliis rebus ad eas pertinentibus, cum omnibus libertatibus et[qq] liberis consuetudinibus suis, sicut eidem ecclesie concessi et hac carta mea confirmaui. Nec aliquis successorum meorum aliquam aliam secularem exactionem ab eadem ecclesia Sancti Thome exigat. Test*ibus* Domino Alexandro filio domini Regis, Henrico Abbate de Kalkou, Willelmo de Bosco cancellario, Philippo de Valon*iis* camerario, Johanne de Maccuswell', Roberto capellano domini regis, Roberto de Sancto Germano et Gilberto de Striuelyn clericis domini regis, Magistro Martino, Magistro Radulpho[rr], medicis, Jordano Cumyn, Waltero Cumyn. Apud Selekyrc' .xx°v. die Februarii.

RUBRIC. Confirmacio Reg*is* W. de terris et ecclesiis monasterio de Aberbr*othoc* concessis (red). .I. (red, in margin).
SOURCE. NLS, MS. Adv. 34.4.2, fos.xxxviii^{v}–xli^{v} = *A*. SRO, Northesk Muniments (uncatalogued), Ethie MS., fo.1^{r-v} = *E*. Printed here from *A*, with most of *E*'s readings noted.
PRINTED. *Arbroath Liber*, i, no.1 (from *A* until *E*'s text becomes available, then from *E*).
NOTES. [a] Large red initial. Punctuation editorial. [b] Fo.xxxix^{r}, *A*. [c] Fo.xxxix^{v}, *A*. In margin at top of folio, a pointing hand and the words communis pastura (xv cent.). [d] Fo.xxxx^{r}, *A*. [e] Pencil note in margin (xix cent.): here Begins Ethie fragment. [f] Berkeley, *E*. [g] quas, *E*. [h] quibus, *E*. [i] Margerie, *E*. [j] Turfred' or perhaps Turfreð, *E*. [k] Radulfi, *E*. [l] Inuirugyn, *E*. [m] Kynnerne, *E*. [n] Berkel', *E*. [o] Inuirkileder, *E*. [p] Munifod', *E*. [q] Kerimur, *E*. [r] Strathectin, *E*. [s] Aberhelot, *E*. [t] Fo.xl^{v}, *A*. [u] Belphe, *E*. [v] Glasker', *E*. [w] de, *E*. [x] Katerim, *E*. [y] Rossin, *E*. [z] Gillecrist, *E*. [aa] Portyncrag', *E*. [bb] Thancard', *E*. [cc] Ballegillegrande, *E*. [dd] Comes Fergus, *E*. [ee] Name omitted in *A*, supplied from *E*. [ff] Brechin, *E*. [gg] Strucather', *E*. [hh] rethis, *E*. [ii] Northesc, *E*. [jj] Trostrauch, *E*. [kk] Fo.xli^{r}, *A*. [ll] Mar, *E*. [mm] Aberkerdouer, *E*. [nn] Malis, *E*. [oo] Fertheth, *E*. [pp] Pointing hand in margin, *E*, directed at these words. [qq] Fo.xli^{v}, *A*. [rr] Radulfo, *E*.
COMMENT. In general the contents repeat those of no.197, and confirm further properties granted by the king himself and by private subjects. Among these for which separate royal charters have not survived are: the church of Turriff, Aberdeenshire, granted by Marjorie countess of Buchan; the church of Inverugie (St Fergus), Aberdeenshire, granted by Ralph Naym (probably including the chapel of Fetterangus; cf. *Arbroath Liber*, i, no.199); and the church of Arbirlot, Angus, granted by Roger bishop of St Andrews.

It appears that the lands of Boysack (in Inverkeilor), formerly Baleisaac, may have been granted to Arbroath Abbey in William I's reign (*Arbroath Liber*, i, no.224, 13 May, 1220).

514 Grants to Robert de Aubein' 20 merks yearly, owed to the king by Coldingham Priory as 'waiting' for the lands of Coldingham, until he shall have granted to Robert 20 merks of land besouth Forth or between Forth and the Mounth; the money to be paid at Easter. Selkirk. (28 February, 1213)

.W'. Dei Gr*ati*a Rex Scott'. Omnibus probis Hominibus Tocius Terre sue . Clericis et laicis :' Salutem. Sciant presentes et futuri . me dedisse . et Concessisse . et Hac Carta mea Confirmasse . Robert*o* de Aubein' et heredibus suis . illas uiginti marcas . que mihi debentur annuatim de Waitinga quam Prior et Conuentus de Coldingham . mihi debent de terris suis de Coldingham . donec ego uel heredes mei eidem Roberto . uel heredibus suis dederimus . viginti . marcatas . terre . ex australi parte maris Scott' . uel inter le Muneth . et mare Scott'. Quare uolo ut predictus Rob*ertus* de Aubein' . et heredes sui illas viginti . marcas percipiant singulis annis ad pascha . et precipio priori de Coldingham . et Bailliuis eius . quatinus annuatim sine inpedimento illas viginti . marcas eis reddant ad pascha .' donec ego uel heredes mei eis dederimus predictas viginti . marcatas terre. Test*ibus* Alex*andro* filio meo . Will*elmo* de Boscho Cancell*ario* meo . Philippo de Valon*iis* Camer*ario* meo . Johanne de Maccuswel' . Magistro Martin*o* medico meo . Walter*o* Cumin' . Jordan*o* Cumin'. Apud Seleschr' .xxviij. die FebruaRii.

ENDORSED. Confirm*atio* .W. regis quam Rob*ertus* de Alben' habuit de Watinga (early xiii cent.). O. iij[a] v[te] (xv cent.). Also other endorsements now erased and illegible.

DESCRIPTION. 7·1″ (18 cm.), Top, 7·2″ (18·1 cm.), Bottom × 4·7″ (12 cm.), L, 4·5″ (11·9 cm.), R. Foot folded 0·8″. A tie 0·4″ wide is cut from top of fold. Tag 6·3″ long, 0·7″ wide. Seal in dark green wax, entire, fair impression.

HAND. Scribe Df. Unruled.

SOURCE. Original, Durham, D. & C. Muniments, Misc. Chr. no.600.

PRINTED. Raine, *North Durham*, no.58.

COMMENT. For 'waiting', see above, pp.52–53. Robert de Aubein' may have been related to the brothers Marchisius and Oliver de Aubeney, dependents of Roger bishop of St Andrews and brothers of Philip de Aubeney, governor of the Channel Islands for King John.

515

Confirms to Arbroath Abbey the grant made by John de Montfort of the whole land called 'Glaskeler', viz. between the land of Catterline (church) and the Catterline Burn, with liberty to build a mill there, as the charter of John de Montfort bears witness. Haddington. (13 March, 1212 × 1213, probably 1213)

W.[a] Dei gr*ati*a Rex Scotorum . Omnibus probis hominibus tocius terre sue clericis et laicis salutem. Sciant presentes et futuri me concessisse et hac carta mea confirmasse donacionem illam quam Johannes de Mountfort fecit Deo et ecclesie Beati Thome martiris de Abirbroth*oc* et monachis ibidem Deo seruientibus et seruituris de tota terra illa que vocatur Glaskeler scilicet de tota terra illa que iacet inter terram illam[b] de Kateryn et riuulum qui vocatur Kateryn . cum libertate faciendi et habendi molendinum in terra illa . Tenend*am* in liberam et puram et perpetuam elemosinam ita libere et quiete plenarie et honorifice . sicut carta predicti Johannis de Mountfort testatur . saluo seruicio meo . Test*ibus* Willelmo de Bosco Cancellar*io* meo . Willelmo Capellano meo . Willelmo de Valon*iis* . Hugon*e* de sigillo clerico meo . Johanne de Mackuswell' . Magistro Martino medico meo . Bernardo de Hauden vicecom*ite* de Rokisburg' . Ricardo filio Michaelis expensario. Apud Hadington*am* .xiij°. die Marcii.

RUBRIC. Confirmacio Reg*is* W. de terra J. de Monfort (red). .lxxj. (in margin).

SOURCE. NLS, MS. Adv. 34.4.2, fo.lix[v].

PRINTED. *Arbroath Liber*, i, no.71.

NOTE. [a] Initial red. [b] Sic, probably for ecclesie; see *Arbroath Liber*, i, no.70.

COMMENT. See no.335. John de Montfort's charter (early thirteenth century) is given in *Arbroath Liber*, i, no.70.

516 Confirms to North Berwick Priory the grant made to it by Earl Duncan (II) of Fife and his son Earl Malcolm, viz. the church of North Berwick, the land on which the nunnery is founded, the land of the hospital of North Berwick (all East Lothian); the land of the hospital of Ardross (in Elie and Earlsferry), the churches of Kilconquhar and Largo (all Fife); the church of Logie (Stirlingshire) with its land called Drumnath; Aithernie and Montrave (in Scoonie), Fife; and half the land of Breich (in Livingston, West Lothian, formerly in West Calder, Midlothian). Edinburgh. (21 April, 1212 × 1214, probably 1213)

.W'. Dei Gr*ati*a Rex Scott'. Omnibus probis Hominibus . Tocius terre sue . Clericis . et laicis .' Salutem. Sciant presentes et futuri . me concessisse . et hac Carta mea confirmasse . Deo et Beate Marie . 7 monialibus de Northberewic' . donationem illam quam Comes . Dunec*anus* . de Fif . et Com*es* . Malcolmus filius eius eis fecerunt . Scilicet . Ecclesiam de Northberewic' . cum terra eiusdem ecclesie . et cum omnibus aliis iustis pertinentiis suis . et terram in qua domus predictarum monialium fundata est . et terram hospitalis de Northberewic' . et terram hospitalis de Ardros . et ecclesiam de Kilconkath . cum terra eiusdem Ecclesie . et cum omnibus aliis iustis pertinentiis suis . et Ecclesiam de Largach . cum omnibus iustis pertinentiis suis . et Ecclesiam de Login . cum Drumnath . scilicet terra eiusdem Ecclesie . et cum omnibus aliis iustis pertinentiis suis . et Æthernin. et Mathriue . et medietatem terre de Brech . per Rectas diuisas suas. Tenend' in liberam et puram et perpetuam elemosinam . ita libere et quiete . plenarie . et honorifice .' sicut Carte predictorum Com*itis* Dunec*ani* . de Fif . et Com*itis* Malcolm*i* . filii eius testantur . et confirmant . saluo seruicio meo. Test*ibus* Walter*o* . Abbate de Edenb' . Alano Abbate de Neubothl*e* . Will*elmo* de Bosch*o* Cancell*ario* meo . Magistro Martin*o* medico meo . Gilleb*erto* de Striuel*in* Clerico meo . Ric*ardo* fil*io* Hugon*is* . Johanne Hose. Apud Edenb' .xxj. die Aprilis.

ENDORSED. Confirmacio Reg*is* Willelmi de ecclesiis et terris eiusdem (xv cent.).
DESCRIPTION. 8·2″ (20·7 cm.), Top and bottom × 3·8″ (9·6 cm.), L, R. Foot folded to a depth of 0·7″ (1·8 cm.). Single slits with tag 5·3″ (13·5 cm.) long, 0·7″ (1·8 cm.) wide. About half the seal remains, in green wax, built up; clear impression. The document is in exceptionally good condition.
HAND. Scribe Df. Unruled.
SOURCE. Original, SRO, GD 90/14.
PRINTED. *North Berwick Carte*, no.9 (with facsimile).
COMMENT. Two general charters of Earl Malcolm of Fife for North Berwick nunnery are known, printed *SHS*, *Miscellany*, iv, 308–9 and *North Berwick Carte*, no.7. Specifically, the above act is a confirmation of the latter charter, whose wording it follows closely. For the locality of Drumnath, now lost, to the north of the church of Logie, cf. *SHS*, *Miscellany*, iv, 335. West Calder was granted to Earl Duncan I of Fife by King David I (*RRS*, i, no.86). The part of Breich referred to above may have been Grange of Breich, still in West Calder parish.

517 Confirms to Holyrood Abbey the annualrent of half a merk from the ferme of Athelstaneford mill (East Lothian), granted by Ada daughter of Alexander of St Martin. Edinburgh. (22 April, 1212 × 1214, probably 1213)

W'. Dei gr*ati*a Rex Scott'. Omnibus probis Hominibus Tocius terre sue . Clericis et laicis .' Salutem. Sciant presentes et futuri . me Concessisse . et Hac Carta mea confirmasse . donacionem illam quam Ada filia Alex*andri* de Sancto Martin*o* fecit Deo et Ecclesie Sancte Crucis de Edenburg . et Canonicis ibidem Deo seruientibus et seruituris de Redditu dimidie marce annuatim percipiend' de firma molendini de Alstanesford' . Tenend*am* ita libere et Quiete . plenarie et honorifice .' sicut Carta predicte Ade testatur. Saluo seruicio meo. Test*ibus* Will*elmo* de Bosch*o* Canc*ellario* meo . Philippo de Mubray . Magistro Martino medico meo . Gilleb*erto* de Striuelin Clerico meo . Ric*ardo* fil*io* Hugon*is*. Apud Edenburg' .xxij. die Aprilis.

ENDORSED. Confirmacio Regis de redditu [de Alstanesford]. (xiii cent., last two words now scarcely legible). J. Scott (xvi cent.).
DESCRIPTION. 6·7″ (17 cm.), Top, bottom × 2·7″ (6·8 cm.), L, R. Foot folded to a depth of 0·6″ (1·5 cm.). Single slits with tag 3·7″ (9 cm.) long, 0·7″ (1·8 cm.) wide, split and twisted for seal, which no longer remains.
HAND. Scribe Df. Unruled.
SOURCE. Original, SRO, GD 45/13/238.
PRINTED. *Holyrood Liber*, no.30.

518 Confirms to Paisley Priory (afterwards Abbey) the whole land between the Old Patrick Water and the burn of Espedair (in Paisley); the disafforested land between the Maich Water and the River Calder (in Lochwinnoch); a part of the land on the east of Paisley Mill; the land in Renfrew granted in free burgage (all Renfrewshire); timber and fuel in the forest of Sanquhar (in St Quivox, Ayrshire); and the quitclaim of 'Clohhary' (Mickle Cloak, in Lochwinnoch?); all granted by Walter son of Alan (II), as his charter bears witness. Edinburgh. (10 August, 1211 × 1214, probably 1213)

Wilelmus Dei gratia rex Scotorum omnibus probis hominibus tocius terre sue, clericis et laicis, salutem. Sciant presentes et futuri me concessisse et carta mea confirmasse Deo et Sancto Jacobo et Sancto Mirino de Passelet et monachis ibidem Deo servientibus totam terram inter Aldpatrik et Espdayr quam Walterus filius Alani eis dedit, per rectas divisas contentas in carta sua eisdem monachis inde facta, et cum libertatibus et aisiamentis maremii et aliorum que continentur in eadem carta ipsius Walteri. Concessi eciam eis totam terram inter Mach et Caledouer deforestatam quam idem Walterus eis dedit, et unam partem terre ex orientali parte molendini de Passelet quam eis similiter dedit, per rectas divisas contentas in carta sua. Concessi eciam eis terram quam idem Walterus eis concessit apud Renfru in liberum burgagium, et maremium et focale eis et hominibus eorum in foresto ejus de Senecastre, sicut in carta ejus continetur; tenendas in liberam et puram et perpetuam elemosinam, cum quieta clamantia calumpnie quam idem Walterus habuit in Clohhary, et cum libertate faciendi piscaturam juxta oppidum de Renfru ex utraque parte aque, et cum omnibus aliis libertatibus et aisiamentis contentis in carta ipsius Walteri, ita libere et quiete, plenarie et honorifice sicut carta ejusdem Walteri inde facta predictis monachis testatur, salvo servicio meo. Testibus Willelmo de Boscho cancellario meo, Wilelmo de Valon*iis*, Ricardo filio Hugonis[a],

Heruico Marescallo, Herberto de Camera, Magistro Martino medico, apud Edinburg', decimo die Augusti.

RUBRIC. Confirmatio Wilelmi regis Scotie de omnibus terris infra Aldpatrik et Espdayr, et de terra prope molendinum de Pasleto, et de piscaria de Renfru (at top).
SOURCE. NLS, MS. Adv. 34.4.14, fo.liii[r].
PRINTED. *Paisley Registrum*, 89–90.
NOTE. [a] MS., Huguonis.
COMMENT. The charter of Walter son of Alan II, the steward, is given in *Paisley Registrum*, 17–18.

519 Confirms in favour of Maurice the younger of Menteith the agreement made between him and his brother Maurice the elder of Menteith in the king's full court anent the earldom of Menteith, in the terms of the chirograph made between them. Maurice the elder has resigned the earldom to the king, who has granted it to Maurice the younger as his right. Edinburgh. (7 December, 1213)

W. Dei gracia Rex Scoc' omnibus probis hominibus tocius terre sue, clericis et laicis, salutem. Sciant presentes et futuri me concessisse et hac carta mea confirmasse conuencionem factam apud Edenb' in plena curia mea inter Mauricium seniorem de Monent' et Maur*icium* juniorem fratrem eius de com*itatu* de Monent', quem Maur*icius* junior petebat sicut ius et hereditatem suam et quem Maur*icius* senior resignauit in manu mea et quem reddidi Maur*icio* juniori sicut ius suum. Quare volo et firmiter precipio quatenus predicta conuencio inter eos facta firmiter et inuiolabiliter teneatur, sicut facta fuit in plena curia mea, et sicut cyr*ographum* inter eos inde factum testatur, saluo seruicio meo. Testibus, Alexandro filio meo, Comite Malc*olmo* de Fif', Willelmo de Bosch*o* cancellario, Comite Gilberto de Stradt', Philippo de Mubray, Rogero de Mortem*er*, Alan,[a] vicecomite de Striuel*in*, Waltero de Lindes', Heruico de Kinros, Heruico de[b] Marescall*o*. Apud Edenb', septimo die Decembris.

SOURCE. PRO, C.66/76 (Patent Roll, 45 Henry III), m.4, *inspeximus* of 20 September 1261.
PRINTED. Fraser, *Menteith*, ii, 215, no.8; *Cal. Docs. Scot.*, i, no.2275 (abstract); *Cal. Pat. R.*, 1258–66, 175.
NOTES. [a] Sic, read Alexandro. [b] Sic.
COMMENT. The date is fixed by the date of Maurice the elder's resignation (Fraser, *Menteith*, ii, 215, no.7; *Cal. Docs. Scot.*, i, no.2276), 6 December, 1213. Maurice the elder (presumably a bastard son of the previous earl, Gilchrist), having resigned his right to the earldom, was to hold for life the lands of Malling ('Muylun') and Rednock ('Radenoche'), in Port of Menteith; and also the lands of 'Tum', 'Cacelyn', 'Brathuli' and 'Cambuswethe'. Moreover, Maurice the younger granted his brother, as tocher for his daughters, Saline (Fife) and Menstrie (Clackmannanshire), and 'Keneltone' and 'Stradlochline', all to be held of Maurice the younger.

520 Confirms to Master Gilbert archdeacon of Moray the whole land of Skelbo (in Dornoch), Sutherland, and 'Ferenbeuthlin' (in Creich) and the whole land of Sutherland towards the west lying between these lands and the marches of Ross, granted to him and to those of his kin to whom he may choose to grant them, in heritage, by Hugh Freskin. Selkirk. (29 April, 1212 × 1214, probably 1214)

.W'. Dei Gr*ati*a Rex Scott'. Omnibus probis Hominibus Tocius Terre sue . Clericis et laicis :' Salutem. Sciant presentes et futuri . me Concessisse . et Hac Carta mea Confirmasse . donationem illam quam Hug*o* Fresekin . fecit Magistro Gilleberto Archidiacono Morauie . de tota terra de Scelebol . in Sutherland' . et de Ferenbeuthlin' . et de tota terra de Sutherland' . uersus Occidentem . que iacet inter has terras prenominatas :' et diuisas de Ros. Tenend*am* sibi et illis heredibus de parentela sua . quibus ipse terras illas dare et Concedere uoluerit . de predicto Hugon*e* Fresekin' . et heredibus suis . hereditarie . per Rectas diuisas suas . et cum Omnibus iustis pertinentiis suis . ita libere et Quiete . plenarie . et honorifice :' sicut Carta predicti Hugon*is* Fresek*in* testatur . Saluo seruicio meo. Test*ibus* Willelmo de Bosch*o* Cancellario meo . Oliuer*o* et Will*elmo* Capellanis meis . Philipp*o* de Valon*iis* Camerario meo . Hugon*e* de sigillo Clerico meo. Apud SeleschR' .xxix. die Aprilis.

ENDORSED. Confirmacio carte de Scelbol per Willelmum Reg*em* (xiv cent.). To Mr Gilbert Archedeane of Moray of the landis of Skelboll (xvi–xvii cent.). Also modern numeral endorsements.

DESCRIPTION. 7·6″ (19·4 cm.), Top and bottom × 3·6″ (9·2 cm.), L, R. Foot folded to a depth of 0·7″ (1·8 cm.). A tie has probably been torn away from top left-hand corner of fold. A seal-tag, 5″ (12·7 cm.) long, 0·7″ (1·8 cm.) wide, passes through slits in foot and fold; no seal remains.

HAND. Scribe Df. Unruled.

SOURCE. Original, Countess of Sutherland, Dunrobin Castle, titles, bundle 1, no.4.

PRINTED. Fraser, *Sutherland*, iii, 2, no.2; *Moray Registrum*, Appendix to Preface, no.11 (both with facsimile); also *Fraser Facsimiles*, no.31.

COMMENT. 'Ferenbeuthlin' seems to have been an alternative name for Ferincoskry, the eastern part of the parish of Creich. Probably this grant embraced the whole of the parish of Creich, together with Skelbo. Cf. *OPS*, ii, Pt.ii, 685; Watson, *CPNS*, 117. Ferincoskry seems to be the 'Ferancestgrayges' granted by Donald lord of the isles to Angus Mackay of Strathnaver in 1415 (*Clan Donald*, 1896, i, 573), and elsewhere it is evident that it included the lands of Spinningdale (*OPS*, loc. cit., 686).

521

Confirms to the Hospital of Oldcambus (in Cockburnspath), Berwickshire, and the lepers dwelling there the half-ploughgate of land in Oldcambus held by the Ralph the tanner, granted to them by David of Quixwood. Jedburgh. (16 May, 1212 × 1214, probably 1214)

.W'. Dei Gr*ati*a Rex Scott'. Omnibus probis Hominibus Tocius Terre Sue :' Clericis et laicis :' Salutem. Sciant presentes et futuri . me Concessisse . et Hac Carta mea Confirmasse . donationem illam quam D*aui*d de Quicheswde . fecit Hospitali de Aldecambus . et leprosis ibi manentibus . de illa dimidia Carrucata terre in Aldecambus . quam Radulfus pelliparius tenuit. Tenend*am* in liberam et puram . et perpetuam Elemosinam . Cum Omnibus libertatibus . et aisiamentis ad predictam terram iuste pertinentibus . ita libere et Quiete :' sicut Carta predicti D*aui*d testatur . Saluo Seruitio meo. Test*ibus* Willelmo de Bosch*o* Cancell*ario* meo . Walter*o* de Lindes' . Johanne de Maccuswel' . Walter*o* Cumin' . D*aui*d de Hastings. Apud Jeddewrth' .xvi. die Maii.

ENDORSED. Conf*irmatio* Reg*is* W. de di*midia* carucata terre in Aldcambouse hospitali eiusdem et leprosis ibidem manentibus concessa (xiv cent.). V. iij[a] vjM (xv cent.).
DESCRIPTION. 7·2″ (18·3 cm.), Top, 7·3″ (18·6 cm.), Bottom × 3·1″ (7·8 cm.), L, 2·9″ (7·3 cm.), R. Foot folded 0·7″. Single slits. Tie cut from top of fold. Tag 7·5″ long, 0·7″ wide. Seal in natural wax, chipped and a good deal worn.
HAND. Scribe Df. Unruled, on coarse parchment.
SOURCE. Original, Durham, D. & C. Muniments, Misc. Chr. no.592.
PRINTED. Raine, *North Durham*, no.59.
COMMENT. David of Quixwood's charter is printed in Raine, *North Durham*, no.186. Quixwood is in Abbey St Bathans.

522 Confirms to Arbroath Abbey the grant made by William son of Bernard of two oxgangs of arable called 'Rath' in the territory of Catterline, Mearns, with the liberty to build a mill there, as the charter of William and the confirmation by his son Bernard bear witness. Elgin. (17 August, 1212 × 1214, probably 1214)

W.[a] Dei gr*atia* Rex Scottorum Omnibus probis hominibus tocius terre sue clericis et laicis salutem. Sciant presentes et futuri me concessisse et hac carta mea confirmasse donacionem illam quam Willelmus filius Bernardi fecit Deo et ecclesie Sancti Thome de Abirbroth*oc* . et monachis ibidem Deo seruientibus de duabus bouatis terre que vocantur Rath' de territorio de Kateryn . Tenend*am* in puram et perpetuam elemosinam per rectas diuisas suas et cum omnibus iustis pertinenciis suis . cum libertate faciendi et habendi molendinum in terra illa . ita libere et quiete plenarie et honorifice . sicut Carta predicti Willelmi et confirmacio Bernardi filii eius predictis monachis inde facte testantur , saluo seruicio meo. Test*ibus* Willelmo de Bosco Cancellario meo . Willelmo Cumyn Comite de Buch*an* Justic*ia* . Philippo de Valon*iis* Cam*erario* . Willelmo capellano meo . Ricar*do* Reuel'. Apud Elgyn .xvij°. die Augusti.

RUBRIC. Confirmacio Regis W. de terra Willelmi filii Bernardi (red). .lxix. (in margin).
SOURCE. NLS, MS. Adv. 34.4.2, fo.lix[r].
PRINTED. *Arbroath Liber*, i, no.69.
NOTE. [a] Initial red.
COMMENT. The charters of William son of Bernard, and his son Bernard, are given in *Arbroath Liber*, i, nos. 67, 68, of early thirteenth-century date. 'Rath' is now lost. William Cumin seems to have been made earl of Buchan after October, 1211 (see no.502).

523 Grants to William the helmet-maker a 'place' in the burgh of Perth, 26 ft. long by 20 ft. wide, with which Roger de Mortemer the king's sheriff of Perth invested him by the king's command; viz., that which lies between the land of Serlo the die-cutter and the land of James the tinkler; to be held in feu and heritage for an annual render of two iron helmets. Stirling. (8 September, 1212 × 1214, probably 1214)

Willelmus[a] Dei gracia Rex Scott' omnibus probis hominibus tocius terre sue, clericis et laicis, salutem. Sciant presentes et futuri me dedisse et concessisse et hac carta mea confirmasse Willelmo Galeatori platyam illam de xx et sex pedibus in longitudine et de viginti pedibus in latitudine in burgo meo de Pert, quam Rogerus de Mortemer vic*ecomes* meus de Pert ei tradidit per preceptum meum; illam scilicet que iacet inter terram Serlon*is* incisoris et terram Jacobi tinkler; tenend*am* sibi et heredibus suis de me et heredibus meis in feudo et hereditate, libere et quiete; reddendo inde singulis annis duos capellos ferri. Test*ibus* Willelmo de Bosco cancellario, Willelmo Cumin comite de Buchan justiciario Scott*orum*, Hug*one* de sigillo clerico meo, Rogero de Mortemer vic*ecomite* de Pert, Ric*ardo* Reuel[b]. Apud Strivueline, viii die Septembris.

RUBRIC. Carta Willelmi Regis Willelmo Galeatori confecta.
SOURCE. NLS, MS. Adv. 34.3.28, fo.13[r].
PRINTED. *Scone Liber*, no.46.
NOTES. [a] Initial omitted, MS. [b] Keuel, MS.

524 Confirms to Gilbert earl of Strathearn Meikleour and Lethendy (Perthshire), by the marches by which Ness son of William, Geoffrey de Melville and Gilchrist perambulated them for Malise, Earl Gilbert's brother; to be held in feu and heritage, with sake and soke, toll, team and infangthief, with pit and gallows, for the service of one knight. Stirling. (25 November, 1211 × 1214, probably 1214)

[.W'. Dei gr*ati*a Rex][a] Scott'. Omnibus probis Hominibus Tocius Terre sue . Clericis et laicis .·' Salutem. Sciant [presentes et futuri][a] me Concessisse . et Hac Carta mea confirmasse . Comiti Gilleb*erto* de Stradh*eren* Ure . per [rectas diuisas suas][a] et Lethendin . per illas diuisas .·' per quas Nessus . filius Willelmi et Galfridus de Maleuill' et Gillecrist [ ][b] eam perambulauerunt Malis*io* fratri ipsius Comitis Gilleb*erti*. Tenend*as* sibi et heredibus suis . de me et heredibus meis in feudo et hereditate . in Boscho et plano . in pratis et pascuis . in aquis et stagnis . in molendinis et moris . et cum Omnibus iustis pertinentiis suis . cum socca et sacca . Cum furca et fossa . Cum Tol et Them . et infangenethef . libere et Quiete . plenarie et honorifice .·' per seruicium unius militis . sicut Carta predicti Malis*ii* testatur. Test*ibus* Will*elmo* de Bosch*o* Cancell*ario* meo . Philipp*o* de Mubray . Fulcon*e* de Sules . Henr*ico* fil*io* Comit*is* D*aui*d . Alex*andro* Vic*ecomite* de Striuel*in* . Ric*ardo* Reuel . Joh*anne* de Morau*ia* . Joh*anne* de Haya. Apud Striuel*in* .xxv. die Nouembr*is*.

ENDORSED. Carta de Lethendy et de Ure (xiv cent.). Charter of Ure and Lethendine Maid be King William To Erle Gilbert of Stradh' (xvi–xvii cent.). Also modern endorsements.
DESCRIPTION. 7·4″ (18·8 cm.), Top, bottom × 3·6″ (9·1 cm.), L, 3·8″ (9·2 cm.) R. Foot folded, with slit in centre for seal-tag. Only the upper lengths of the tag remain, 0·6″ wide and about 1·75″ long, the remainder, presumably with the seal attached, having been cut away.
HAND. Scribe Df. Unruled.
SOURCE. Original, Duke of Atholl, Blair Castle, Athole Charters, vol.I, no.2.
PRINTED. *Inchaffray Liber*, p.xxv; *HMC 7th Report*, Appendix, 704 (abstract in English).
NOTES. [a] Top left-hand corner of parchment torn away; wording supplied conjecturally. [b] One or two words missing through injury.
COMMENT. King William died at Stirling on 4 December, 1214.

CALENDAR OF ACTS OF WILLIAM I CERTAINLY OR PROBABLY THE SUBJECT OF WRITTEN RECORD, THE RECORD OF WHICH HAS NOT SURVIVED IN FULL

I. Acts in favour of Ecclesiastical Institutions[1]

525 Grants (to an unrecorded recipient) the church of Aberlemno, Angus.*[2] (1202)

HMC, 14th Report, iii, 183-4; Fraser, *Facsimiles*, no.46. (The source refers to a written act of the king, whose validity was upheld in the court case which gave rise to the source itself, on the somewhat questionable grounds that since King William was a just and pious man (*vir justus et pius*) he could not have conferred anything to the injury of a church which was in his hands.)

526 Grants to Arbroath Abbey a full toft in Aberdeen, consisting of two perches towards the castle and two perches in the street on the east side of St Nicholas' Church.

Arbroath Liber, i, no.367.

527 Grants to Cambuskenneth Abbey the patronage of the church of Glenisla, with the lands and all rights belonging to the church. (1165 × 1195)

Cambuskenneth Registrum, 138; cp. ibid., 44.

528 Confirms to Cambuskenneth Abbey the grant made by Jocelin bishop of Glasgow and William son of Thorald of the church of Kirkintilloch, with a half-ploughgate of land.* (1175 × 1195)

Cambuskenneth Registrum, no.25 (p.44).

529 Confirms to Carlisle cathedral priory one carucate of land in Haltwhistle, Northumberland.

Dugdale, *Mon. Angl.* (New), vi, 144, no.111.

530 Confirms the agreement between the abbeys of Dryburgh and Jedburgh anent the lands of Lessudden (St Boswells) and Longnewton.* (1177)

Dryburgh Liber, no.63. (The king, along with his brother David and (Richard) bishop of St Andrews, confirmed by attaching their seals.)

531 Grants to the cathedral church of Dunkeld the land of Dalguise, Perthshire ('Dulgus'), together with the tenth of the king's cain of the *prebenda* of palaces of malt from royal demesnes and thanages (*maneriis*) pertaining to the abbey of Dunkeld.

A. Myln, *Vitae Dunkeldensis Ecclesiae Episcoporum* (Bannatyne Club, 1831) 6; but cf. *RRS*, i, no.65.

[1] Arranged alphabetically under principal beneficiary.

[2] The asterisk denotes the explicit mention of written record in the reference.

532 Writes to Pope Innocent III to inform him that he has given his consent to the election as bishop of Dunkeld of John (of Leicester), archdeacon of Lothian.* (22 July, 1211 × 13 June, 1212, probably 1211)

Lawrie, *Annals*, 373.

533 Grants or confirms the church of Harringworth, Northants, to Elstow Abbey. (Possibly not an act of William I.)

BM, Harl. Chr. 43 A. 17. (Letter of Urban III, Verona, 4 March, 1185–7, confirming Elstow's title, suggesting a challenge to the abbey's right after Earl David had gained possession of the Honour of Huntingdon in 1185; the donor is not named, but may have been William I or another Scottish or Senlis lord of the honour.)

534 Grants to the monk, and his successors, serving the chapel of Saint Cuthbert on Farne Island half a chalder of wheat annually, to be rendered from the ferme of the king's mill of Berwick on Tweed.*

Raine, *North Durham*, no.77.

535 Writes to Pope Alexander III anent the election of Jocelin to the see of Glasgow.* (1174, after 23 May)

Glasgow Registrum, no.36.

536 Confirms to Haddington Priory the church of Crail and other property in Crailshire given by King Malcolm IV.

See *RRS*, i, no.289.

537 Grants to Haddington Priory £3 sterling from the burgh ferme of Haddington.

RMS, 1424–1513, no.611.

538 Grants to Hexham Priory, in severalty, a certain moor called Carrawside (by Carraw, in Newbrough, Northumberland).

Priory of Hexham (Surtees Soc., 1865), ii, 113.

539 Grants to Hinchingbrooke Priory, Huntingdonshire, the site upon which is the church of St James, where the nuns dwell. (1165 × 1174)

BM, Add. Chrs. 33596.

540 Commands Uhtred son of Fergus and Roger of Minto to convene the older men of the district to make a sworn perambulation of the marches of Kirkgunzeon, Kirkcudbright, on behalf of Holm Cultram Abbey and Christian bishop of Galloway. (1165 × 1173)

BM., MS. Harl. 3891, fos.87^{v}–88^{r} (cf. *Holm Cultram Recs.*, 49).

541 Confirms to the knights of the Hospital at Northampton King Malcolm IV's gift of 30 cartloads of wood every year from Yardley Hastings.* (1165 × 1174)

Castle Ashby, Marquess of Northampton's muniments, F.D. 247 (survey of Yardley Hastings, 2 Sept., 1565, transcript of charter by John of Scotland earl of Huntingdon).

542 Confirms to Jedburgh Abbey the church of Hutton in Dryfesdale, granted by Adam son of Gilbert [son of Richer].*

Glasgow Registrum, no.79.

543 Grants to Kinloss Abbey the land of Invererne, perambulated by Matthew bishop of Aberdeen, Earl Duncan, Hugh the clerk and W[illiam] son of Freskin; the land of the grieveship of Invererne (Greeshop, in Forres), perambulated by W[illiam] son of Freskin and Peter of Pollok; and one toft each in Banff, Berwick, Montrose, Perth and Stirling.

Kinloss Recs., 111–12 and 115. (This assumes that King William did not grant Kinloss more than one toft each in Auldearn and Aberdeen, included in no.237 above.)

544 Grants to Lindores Abbey one land in the town of Perth in free burgage.

Lindores Chartulary, no.94 (p.109); cf. also *Lindores Liber*, Appendix, no.II.

545 Confirms or grants to Manuel Priory 1½ chalders of salt (annually?) from the teind of the royal saltpans held (at ferme?) by Ralph 'Baretus'.*

SHS Misc., iv, 313.

546 Confirms to Newbattle Abbey one saltpan, with easements, and all his arable in Callendar, Stirlingshire.*

Newbattle Registrum, no.163, note at foot saying that this was a word for word repetition of Malcolm IV's charter, *RRS*, i, no.109.

547 Issues a brieve of replegiation to the bishop of St Andrews in respect of his tenants in the Kirkton of Arbuthnott, Mearns, exempting them from the jurisdiction of the sheriff and forester of Mearns.* (1165 × 1178)

Spalding Misc., v, 210.

548 Makes a grant of the vill of Piddington, Oxon, having removed it from the possession of St Frideswide's Priory, Oxford (?). (1165 × 1174)

S.R.Wigram, *Cartulary of St Frideswide at Oxford* (Oxford Historical Society, 1896), ii, 94–5, no.791. (The source is a bull of Pope Alexander III which speaks of King William's taking away Piddington from St Frideswide's, presumably to give to some beneficiary. Cf. *RRS*, i, nos.224, 225.)

549 Grants to Sawtry Abbey the hermitage of Stanwell (in Fotheringay), Northants. (1165 × 1174)

Bodleian Library, MS. Rawlinson B 142, fo.20v. (Granted before 3 June, 1176, when confirmed by Pope Alexander III (BM, MS. Cott. Aug. ii, no.125); cf. also J. Bridges, *History of Northamptonshire*, ii, 451.)

549A Grants to Scone Abbey the cain of corn from the lands of Inchmartine (in Errol), Perthshire, to be delivered well sieved and riddled according to the king's measure*.

Scone Liber, no.221.

550 Confirms rights and privileges to the knights of the Temple in Scotland.*

See *RRS*, i, no.287.

551 Grants to the knights of the Temple at North Ferriby, Yorkshire (E.R.), the land of 'Karneglun' (Craigloun, by Knights Ward in Carnbee, Fife).

Cal. Pat. R., 1317–21, 315.

II. Acts in favour of Private Individuals [1]

552 Acknowledges, by ten separate bonds, a debt of £2,776 to Aaron the Jew of Lincoln.*

Cal. Docs. Scot., i, no.433.

553 Grants to Humphrey of Berkeley the mill of Conveth (in Laurencekirk), Angus.*

Arbroath Liber, i, no.271. (By no.345 Humphrey of Berkeley was granted the multure of the whole parish of Conveth, but this may refer to a separate infeftment of the mill.)

554 Grants to his sister Margaret, countess of Brittany 100 librates of land and twenty infeft knights, as tocher on her (second) marriage to Humphrey de Bohun.* (*c.*1175)

APS, i, 116.

555 Grants to Robert 'de Cambray' Baledgarno (in Inchture), Perthshire.* (Doubtful)

HMC 12th Report, Pt. viii, 185. (The authenticity of this seems very doubtful; 'de Cambray' should in any case be 'de Cambrun', but no one of this name is recorded otherwise from William I's reign; and the place-name form in the source, 'Baligarnoche', belongs to a period much later than 1214.)

556 Grants to a certain man called Crane, in feu and heritage, the land of 'Inianey' beside 'Falerikkum' (Friockheim?), free of army and other service, for the service of being porter in the royal castle of Montrose.

APS, i, 100.

[1] Arranged alphabetically under principal beneficiary.

557 Grants to William Cumin Lenzie ('Lenneth') for one knight's service.*

Fraser, *Carlaverock*, ii, 404, no.3.

558 Confirms to Duncan II earl of Fife the earldom of Fife, as held under King David I (by Earl Duncan I).* (Probably early in reign)

Nat. MSS. Scot., i, Plate L. (Cf. *PSAS*, lxxxvii, 54–5.)

559 Confirms to Duncan II earl of Fife West Calder, Midlothian, granted to Earl Duncan I by King David I; and grants Strathleven, Fife; the whole to be held for knight's service.* (Probably 1165 × 1171)

PSAS, lxxxvii, 62. (Cf. nos.14, 472.)

560 Grants to Michael 'Flerdius' (read *Flandrensis*), the king's clerk, the land which belonged to Gilbert Suffach (Gilberton, Midlothian), for the service of one sergeand with horse and haubergel.* (Linlithgow, 16 October)

APS, vii, 144. Michael Fleming (*Flandrensis*) was sheriff of Edinburgh at some date between 1198 and 1214 (*Holyrood Liber*, Appendix II, no.7, p.213). As son of Jordan the Fleming, Michael was granted land at Woolmet, in Newton, S.E. of Edinburgh, by Archibald abbot of Dunfermline (*Dunfermline Registrum*, no.384).

561 Grants to Adam de Hasteng part of Kingledoors ('Kengildurs'), in Drummelzier, Peeblesshire. (Probably second half of reign)

Arbroath Liber, i, no.122.

562 Confirms to David de la Hay the agreement made in the king's presence in his full court at Forfar between David and William (Malvoisin) bishop of St Andrews anent the land of 'Ecclesdouenauin' and the patronage of the church of Errol.* (1202 × 1214)

Spalding Misc., ii, 306, no.VI. ('Ecclesdouenauin', perhaps 'the church of St Devenic' may have been the original name of the church at Errol, whose medieval dedication does not seem to be known.)

563 Commands Geoffrey son of Richard, sheriff of Crail, and other responsible men, to hand over to Ivo, the king's cook, son of Nigel the cook, certain lands in the territory of Kellie, Fife.

Balcaskie House, Muniments of Sir R. Anstruther, Bart. Cf. *RRS*, i, no.101.

563A Writes to John king of England anent the northern counties, excluding Tynedale from negotiations touching his claim to them.*

Rot. Litt. Claus., 43.

564 Grants or confirms to Alexander of Lamberton Linlathen, Angus, in marriage with Eda, daughter of Henry of 'Kinpunde', for the service of a third of a knight. (Probably late in reign)

NLS, MS. Adv. 34.6.24, p.271. (There seems no reason to suspect the authenticity of this act, referred to in a confirmation to Alexander of Lamberton by Alexander II of 1235.)

565 Confirms to Laurence son of Orm (of Abernethy) the land of Dunlappie (in Dunlappie and Stracathro), Angus, in free forest.*

NLS, MS. Adv. 35.4.12a, no.3 (cf. *RRS*, i, no.311.)

565A Grants a certain land (in the burgh of Perth) by charter to Hugh Lorimer and his heirs.*

Scone Liber, no.95.

566 Grants to William of Lindsay one saltpan in the Carse (of Stirling).

Newbattle Registrum, no.167.

567 Confirms to David of Lochore one third of Pitfirran, Fife, granted by William son of Constantine of Lochore. (Unauthentic)

Pitfirrane Writs, no.18. (This act cannot be accepted as authentic; the parties mentioned, if they had any existence at all, must belong to the later thirteenth century.)

568 Grants to Malcolm earl of Fife Auchtermuchty free from an annualrent of one merk to St Andrews hospital. (1204 × 1211)

St Andrews Liber, 228–9; above, no.494.

568A Grants in free marriage to his daughter Marjorie (countess of Pembroke, 1235–44) the lands of Strathord (in Moneydie) and Strathbraan (in Little Dunkeld), Perthshire.

Balmerino Liber, no.10. (This seems to indicate an earlier marriage of Marjorie of Scotland of which there is no other record. Cf. Dunbar, *Scot. Kings*, 83. She was perhaps of relatively advanced age at the time of her (childless) marriage to Gilbert Marshal earl of Pembroke (*Chron. Melrose*, 85; *Annales Monastici* (ed. H.R. Luard, Rolls Series), iii, 143). According to the source, a charter of Alexander II, Strathbraan was acquired from the countess by Malcolm II earl of Fife, to whose grandfather Earl Duncan II it had been granted as part of his wife's tocher by Malcolm IV (*RRS*, i, no.190, if that charter is to be relied on).

569 Grants to Osbert Olifard for his service the land of Arbuthnott, Mearns, with its whole jurisdiction. (1165 × 1178)

Spalding Misc., v, 210.

570 Grants to Pagan the goldsmith of Edinburgh certain land on the north side of the church of St Giles of Edinburgh, next to the land of Adam of Lothian, which was handed over to Pagan by William Lindsay at the king's command. (Probably *c.*1189 × 1200)

Inchcolm Chrs., no.8. William of Lindsay first appears as justice *c.*1189 × 1195. Pagan granted the land to Inchcolm Abbey 'saving to the king's chamber one pound of cumin every Michaelmas'.

571 Grants to Robert de Quinci one toft in Haddington.

Dryburgh Liber, no.141.

572 Grants to Robert de Quinci a plot (*placia*) in the old castle of Forfar in lieu of a toft.

St Andrews Liber, 354.

573 Confirms to Richard Revel the land of Coultra, Fife, and adds 'Esterardint' (cp. Ardie Hill in Balmerino); the whole to be held for the service of one knight.

Balmerino Liber, no.3.

574 Grants to Robert de Ros, probably in marriage with his daughter Isabel, formerly wife of Robert de Brus, Haltwhistle in Tynedale. (Probably 1191)

Cal. Docs. Scot., iii, no.236; cf. *Chron. Melrose*, 47–8.

575 Grants to Hugh of Roxburgh one toft in Forfar.* (Probably ×1189)

Arbroath Liber, i, no.80.

576 Grants to William de Rypeley Dallas, Moray ('Dolaysmykel'), for the service of the quarter of a knight.

SRO, RH 6/58.

577 Grants to William of St Michael and his heirs one toft in Montrose.

Lindores Chartulary, no.38.

578 Confirms to Bertram, son of Alexander of Seton, the grant made to him by Patrick earl of Dunbar of 'Richelkellach' with an addition to the furthest way of 'Stevenstone' and 'Salowhild' (East Lothian).* (Stirling, 22 February, 1200–1202)[1]

Family of Seton, ii, 842. 'Richelkellach' is evidently represented by Ruchlaw, in Whittingehame, 'Salowhild' by the Sauchet Water which forms the march between Whittingehame and Stenton; and 'Stevenstone' is probably the Standing Stone immediately south of Traprain Law.

[1] The witnesses named are William bishop of Glasgow, chancellor, William de Hay, Philip de Landyne (read Lundyn), and Ranulph de Soullis. See nos.424, 427, the former witnessed by William Malvoisin simply as chancellor, the latter by William bishop of Glasgow, chancellor, and by Philip of Lundin. Perhaps the word 'elect' has been omitted here, and this belongs to 1200.

579 Confirms to Bertram son of Alexander of Seton certain tofts in Tranent, granted by Earl Patrick of Dunbar.* (Probably late in reign)

Family of Seton, ii, 842.

580 Restores from forfeiture a member of the family of Skene of Skene.* (Very doubtful)

Family of Skene, 7. (Based on a report of 1678 that Alexander Skene had known of a charter of King William in the terms indicated having once been in the charter chest of the House of Skene; authenticity seems doubtful in the extreme.)

581 Grants to his kinsman (*consanguineo meo*) a charter afterwards in the possession of the family of Straiton of Lauriston (xvii cent.).*

NLS, MS. Adv. 34.6.24, p.204. (Notes and copies of historical and genealogical documents by Father Richard Hay, including the information, supplied by 'Mr J. Falc'. (Falconer of Phesdo, or Falconer of Haulkerton?), that Straiton of Lauriston had a charter of King William 'wherein he is designed Consaguineo [sic] meo.' This may represent an original charter in favour of the king's kinsman Richard de Prebenda, if he is to be identified with the king's clerk of the Liverance, Richard, who between 1171 and 1174 was parson of Ecclesgirg, i.e. St Cyrus, in which parish, and close to whose church, Lauriston is situated.)

581A Grants (to Andrew of Synton?) the lands of Synton, Selkirkshire.*

SRO, GD 124, temp. no.ET 239. The reference, in an inventory, is to 'ane auld bounding charter of the foirnamit landis [i.e. Synton] with the pertinentis' issued by King William. This might be the charter which must have been the authority for no.582.

582 Grants to Andrew of Synton the sheriffdom of Selkirk, heritably, exempting him from the castle ward formerly rendered at Roxburgh castle by the barony of Synton (in Ashkirk, Selkirkshire).

Cal. Docs. Scot., ii, no.1681.

583 Grants to Thomas the physician and his heirs, in free tenure, the land of 'Camelyne' (in Clackmannan).*

SRO, GD 235/1, fo.16r. (The source, a cartulary of the family of Bruce of Clackmannan, seems a good one. The relevant passage refers to a lawsuit of 1330, in which John of Fithell or Fythel put in as evidence two charters and one confirmation, one of the charters being one of King William I in favour of Thomas *medicus*; the evidence was accepted by the court. Thomas the physician, not otherwise known as such, may have been identical with Thomas of Stirling, a well-known royal clerk who became archdeacon of Glasgow in 1224 and chancellor of the king in 1226, dying in the following year.)

584 Confirms to Walter the butler one ploughgate of land in Learmouth (in Carham, Northumberland), granted to him by Helcuinus the knight.* (Act of William as earl of Northumberland, before his accession to the Scottish throne in December, 1165.)

Bodleian Library, MS. Fairfax 7, fo.82v (note that an act of Earl Henry, 1141 × 1151, was witnessed by Heluin; *RRS*, i, no.32.)

585 Writes to John king of England asking him to restore to William, his burgess of Berwick on Tweed, chattels worth £29 taken from his ship at Bamburgh.*

Cal. Docs. Scot., i, no.599.

586 Confirms to William of Gullane (de Golyn), son of Archibald of Gullane (de Golyn) the ploughgate of land in Swinton granted to him by Bertram the prior and the convent of Durham in quittance of his claim to the toun of (Greater) Lumsdaine.*

Raine, *North Durham*, no.426. (This may be identical with no.444 or no.461 above.)

587 Grants part of Blainslie (in Melrose, Roxburghshire) to William son of Oein.

Melrose Liber, no.93.

588 Confirms to William son of Thurstan (son of Osulf) half a ploughgate of land in Ednam, possibly with two burgages in the King's Street of Roxburgh.*

Melrose Liber, i, no.239 (referring to charters by David I and William I to Thurstan son of Osulf and William son of Thurstan, presumably respectively.)

589 Grants to Yothre mac Gilhys Meft (in Urquhart), Moray and a house in Elgin castle and one net in the Spey, for the service of one sergeand and performing 'Scottish army'.

APS, i, 101. (Perhaps Yothre should be emended to Rothre.)

ADDENDA

540A Confirms to Holyrood Abbey in free alms the church of Kinghorn, Fife ('Estrikingorn'), granted by Richard bishop of St Andrews.* (1165 × 1178)

Cal. Papal Letters, xii, 731; *Calendar of Scottish Supplications to Rome* 1418–22, edd. E.R.Lindsay and A.I.Cameron (SHS, 1934) 92; cf. I.B.Cowan, *The Parishes of Medieval Scotland* (Scottish Record Society, 1967), 112.

541A Grants or confirms to Inchcolm Priory the church of Dalgety, Fife, with the chapel of Beath. (1165 × 1179)

Cal. Papal Letters, vii, 144; *Calendar of Scottish Supplications to Rome* 1418–22, edd. E.R.Lindsay and A.I.Cameron (SHS, 1934), 195.

541B Grants to Inchcolm Priory twelve shillings (yearly) from the royal demesne of Kinghorn, Fife. (Possibly an act of Malcolm IV)

Inchcolm Chrs., no.2 (p.3).

APPENDIX

590 Agreement between Henry the physician, clerk of the king of Scotland and parson of Inverlunan, and Neil MacYwar (thane of Inverlunan ?) anent the *abthen* lands of the kirk of Inverlunan. (1189 × 1195)

Hec est conuencio facta inter Henricum Medicum Clericum Regis Scocie et Nigellum Mac Ywar quod Nigellus remittit Henrico terram ecclesie de Inuerlunan, tenendam libere et quiete, scilicet terram de Abthan[a] per rectas diuisas suas, sicut dominicam[b] terram ecclesie, et remittit Deo et ecclesie de Inuerlunan' et predicto Henrico persone eiusdem ecclesie et eius successoribus imperpetuum omne Canum et Coneuetum[c] et omne seruicium et omnes exacciones ad laicam personam pertinent*es* et omne jus quod habebat in predictis in prenominata terra ecclesie. Et Henricus remittit predicto Nigello octo marcas argenti quas Nigellus ei debebat et dat ei singulis annis pro predicto cano et Coneueto et ceteris predictis exaccionibus decem solidos, scilicet quinque sol*idos* ad Pentecosten et quinque ad festum Sancti Martini. Et hanc conuencionem fideliter et sine dolo tenendam affidauit predictus Nigellus in manu Comitis Dunecani, et Henricus in manu Hugonis Cancellarii. Huic conuencioni facte inter eos interfuerunt isti, et eiusdem conuencionis sunt testes: Hug*o* Cancellarius Regis, Archenb*aldus* Abbas de Dunfermelin, Jocelinus Archid*iaconus* Dunkeld*ensis*, Comes Dunec*anus*, G[illecrist] Comes de Mar, Merlesuanus, Petrus Capellanus Cancellarii, Hugo Clericus de Sigillo, Robertus de Berkel', Magister Adam de Pert, Bricius[d] , Brokinus[e], Macbeth Judices Regis. Et ad maiorem securitatem et firmitatem huius conuencionis firmiter et fideliter tenende, apposita sunt hec sigilla, scilicet Hugonis Cancellarii et Comitis Duncani de Fyf.

RUBRIC. Conuencionis concordia inter Henricum medicum et Nigellum Makywar penes terram ecclesiasticam de Inuerlownan, vulgariter vocatam Abthan' (top in red).

SOURCE. BM, MS. Add. 33245, fo.128^{r}.

NOTES. [a] MS., Athan. [b] MS., dominiam. [c] MS., Canenetum. [d] MS., Brigus. [e] MS., Brokn*us*.

COMMENT. Cf. no.355 for subject matter; and nos.339 and 340 for acts which appear to belong to the same period as this agreement. This agreement was probably concluded in the court of the justiciar of Scotia.

INDEX OF PERSONS AND PLACES

Christian names are given in a conventional modern form where this exists. Patronymics are indexed under the Christian name of the son, medieval patronymics in Fitz and Mac being similarly treated. W before a number means that the person appears as a witness on that page, the number of occurrences, if more than one, being shewn in square brackets. References to grants, to charters or confirmations, and to grants accompanied by charters or confirmations, made or issued by persons listed in the index are indicated by the letters (g), (c) and (g+c) respectively. Places of less than parochial status are located by parish (in square brackets) and county; places of parochial status, unless county-towns, by county. The authority for location has normally been the Ordnance Survey 6-in., 2½-in. and 1-in. Seventh Series maps, some use having also been made of the 1-in. 'Popular Edition' map of Scotland. The spelling of place-names has normally followed the Ordnance Survey.

INDEX OF SUBJECTS

Titles of dignitaries and officers are not usually indexed where they occur in the addresses or witness-lists of acts.